National Coalition To
AbolishThe Death Penalty
920 Pennsylvania Ave. SE
Washington, D.C. 20003
www.ncadp.org

FEDERAL HABEAS CORPUS PRACTICE AND PROCEDURE

Third Edition

James S. Liebman
Professor of Law
Columbia University School of Law

Randy Hertz
Professor of Law
New York University School of Law

Volume 1

LEXIS® LAW PUBLISHING
CHARLOTTESVILLE, VIRGINIA

Copyright © 1998

BY

LEXIS® Law Publishing

A Division of Reed Elsevier Inc.

———

Copyright © 1988, 1994

BY

THE MICHIE COMPANY

———

Library of Congress Catalog Card No. 98-89331

ISBN

Set: 0-327-00661-7

Volume 1: 0-327-00662-5

Volume 2: 0-327-00663-3

———

6433112

To Janet, again.

JSL

*   *   *

To Gerda and Erich Leyens,
who have been parents to me
in every sense of the word.

RAH

FOREWORD

When Congress enacted the Antiterrorism and Effective Death Penalty Act of 1996 ("AEDPA"), it added several layers of complications to the already complicated rules governing federal habeas corpus proceedings.

First, AEDPA undertook to rewrite the rules extensively, and it did so in a text that is both elaborate and obscure. The statutory language teems with problems and non-obvious alternative interpretations that need to be identified and sorted out by reference to a tangled legislative history. The history includes not only Congress's consideration of AEDPA itself but congressional action (and inaction) in connection with previous habeas corpus bills; prior congressional and judicial uses of terms that are incorporated (sometimes *verbatim*, sometimes with significant modifications) in AEDPA; and (worse yet) a webwork of *concepts* and *ideology* derived from prior statutory and court-made law that informs much of AEDPA's phraseology. Moreover, it is not simply the phraseology of individual provisions that counts. The *structure* of the statute, the relationships among its parts, is also vital to its construction. This became apparent in *Lindh v. Murphy*, 117 S. Ct. 2059 (1997), one of the Supreme Court's first important rulings construing AEDPA, in which co-author Jim Liebman successfully used a structural analysis to persuade the Justices to read AEDPA's habeas-curbing provisions as inapplicable to cases filed in federal court before the statute's effective date.

Second, AEDPA supersedes prior federal habeas corpus law only in patches. It leaves many areas of prior law — including some that were unsettled or arcane — untouched. In other areas, it changes aspects of the old rules without addressing how these changes should affect connected aspects that are not explicitly changed. And (to thicken the stew), pre-AEDPA doctrine sometimes needs to be consulted in order to determine the very question of *how much* prior doctrine AEDPA should be read as aiming to change. Witness *Felker v. Turpin*, 518 U.S. 651 (1996), where AEDPA was read in the light of nineteenth century precedents about the negative implications of statutes limiting federal judicial jurisdiction; and *Stewart v. Martinez-Villareal*, 118 S. Ct. 1618 (1998), where AEDPA was read restrictively to avoid "implications for habeas practice" that the Court concluded "would be far-reaching and seemingly perverse" in the light of pre-AEDPA jurisprudence (*id.* at 1621).

Third, AEDPA interacts in complex ways with pre-AEDPA constitutional doctrine. Insofar as the statute purports to deny federal judges powers they have long exercised to adjudicate and rectify violations of basic federal law, AEDPA is susceptible to constitutional challenges that can invalidate some of its provisions or applications and influence the construction of others through the operation of the established rule that statutes should be interpreted so that "grave and doubtful constitutional questions ... are avoided."[1] Conversely, if AEDPA is construed and permitted to eliminate federal judicial remedies that have been assumed to exist as a backstop throughout the entire process of development of contemporary constitutional criminal procedure, that will have important consequences for the resolution of a set of questions that has brooded unanswered since the Supreme Court explicitly reserved them a third of a century ago in *Case v. Nebraska*, 381 U.S. 336 (1965) — questions about the extent to which the federal Constitution requires full and fair *state* postconviction procedures.[2]

The third edition of *Federal Habeas Corpus Practice and Procedure* will guide practitioners and set the standard for the academy in working through these subjects and the many other difficult problems left in AEDPA's wake. It continues the great tradition of the 1988 and 1994 editions, which successively became the indispensable deskbooks for postconviction lawyers of every level of experience and the obligatory reference works for every scholar in the field.

I say this without exaggeration. Time and again in the past decade, *FHCPP* has helped my co-counsel and me to find our way through the trickiest mazes of postconviction procedure. It has informed our strategy and instructed our brief-writing at all stages of federal habeas corpus cases, from the District Courts through the Supreme Court of the United States. It has proven equally invaluable in our planning of trial and appellate proceedings in the state-court phases of potential federal habeas cases.

Representing death-sentenced inmates as we do, we need quick, clear guidance in a hurry. We need to deal with emergencies and to anticipate the consequences of our immediate decisions for litigation many years ahead. We need ideas to guide our selection and our shaping of claims. We need citations to the key cases that will enable us to produce briefs and stay applications fast and efficiently. We need balanced, up-to-date analyses of the law in order to assess the risks and benefits of one course of action or another. We need accessible, thorough doctrinal summaries to bring volunteer lawyers — some of them handling their first capital case, or their first federal habeas case — up to speed to make difficult judgments and effective arguments. We invariably, and thankfully, find everything we need in this book.

The authors, Jim Liebman and Randy Hertz, are experienced and savvy litigators as well as acute scholars with an encyclopedic knowledge of federal

---

[1] *United States v. Delaware & Hudson Co.*, 213 U.S. 366, 408 (1909). *See, e.g., United States v. C.I.O.*, 335 U.S. 106, 120-121 & n. 20 (1948).

[2] The lineup of opinions in *Ohio Adult Parole Authority v. Woodard*, 118 S. Ct. 1244 (1998), should serve as a sharp reminder that the issues reserved in *Case* are very much alive, although they have lain dormant throughout years when there was little cause to stir them because of the availability of federal habeas corpus relief for constitutional failings in the state criminal process.

habeas corpus jurisprudence. They understand the practical problems of the field as well as its doctrinal complexities. Their book combines the best features of a solid academic treatise and a sophisticated but user-friendly practitioner's manual. Comprehensive in its coverage of the procedural complications that an applicant for federal habeas corpus may encounter, it analyzes the issues incisively, warns of pitfalls to be avoided, and suggests particularly creative ways to get around the worst of them.

Its two volumes will reward your reading through from start to finish, if you have the time. They contain some of the most trenchant systematic analysis of procedural issues in postconviction litigation you can find anywhere. But they are also written, structured, and indexed so that, if you have a particular problem and know what it is, you can find the best available answer to the problem quickly by going directly to the pertinent sections. Even more important, their excellent organization will help you to identify problems that you have but do not know about or do not know the doctrinal name for, and to avoid trouble instead of having to dig yourself out of trouble after you have unwittingly put your foot in it.

❏

A book as useful as this deserves a foreword that is more than decoration. I'll devote the rest of mine to suggesting ways in which petitioners' lawyers can improve their chances of obtaining habeas relief from federal judges ill-disposed to criminal convicts and their claims.

Judges of this stripe have dominated the federal bench since at least the middle of the Reagan Presidency. The temper of these judges can be described by various labels ("conservative," "authoritarian," "tough on crime") and explained by various conceptual models. The most idealistic model posits two poles of judicial thinking:

> (1)   a basic belief that the ordinary criminal procedures established by legislatures and by the habitual practices of prosecutors and state trial courts are a fitting norm for measuring the "process that is due" under the Due Process Clause of the federal Constitution; that Due Process is all a criminal defendant is entitled to;[3] and that the role of courts charged with enforcing federal constitutional rights is therefore merely to remedy isolated instances of egregious deviation from prevailing procedural norms; and

---

[3] *See, e.g., Strickland v. Washington,* 466 U.S. 668 (1984), incorporating the Fourteenth Amendment into the Sixth.

(2)   a basic belief that standards of criminal justice are not measured by
      the practices that legislatures, prosecutors, and state trial courts are
      prone to accept at any given time; that an important purpose of the
      Constitution's procedural guarantees in criminal cases was to curb
      the expectable propensity of all agencies of popular government to
      deal summarily and harshly with unpopular people, such as most
      criminal defendants are; and that the role of courts charged with
      enforcing constitutional rights will therefore often call for
      invalidating the accepted or "normal" procedures of the times.

Within the terms of this bipolar model, the federal judiciary for a generation now
has been — and for the next generation or two will doubtless be — populated
overwhelmingly by judges who are at or near the first pole and very far from the
second.

A more cynical model posits that judges are relentlessly result-oriented —
that the true polarity is between judges who want to make it easier to punish
criminally accused persons and those who want to make it harder. This
difference in aims may (although it needs not) reflect the judges' differing views
on whether crime or governmental oppression is the greater danger. In any case,
the federal judiciary is now preponderantly populated by judges of the *make-it-
easier-to-punish-criminals* school.

For practical purposes, one does not have to choose between the two
conceptual models, for the same reason that one does not have to choose
between a philosophy that posits a Morally Indifferent Cosmos and one that
posits Good, Evil and Sin. Both models explain the observed phenomenon — the
existence of human misery — equally well. However you look at it, the bald fact
is that federal habeas petitioners' lawyers today and in the foreseeable future are
facing a whole lot of judges who are powerfully motivated to avoid making
rulings that they see as paving the way to relief for any large number of convicts.
"Releasing criminals in droves" is, for these judges, the Big Bogey.[4]

---

[4] Supreme Court decisions throughout the 1990's demonstrate the point. The Court's
evisceration of *Cage v. Louisiana*, 498 U.S. 39 (1990) (*per curiam*), in *Victor v. Nebraska*, 511
U.S. 1 (1994), can be explained only as a drastic aversion reaction to the prospect that invalidating
several States' pattern jury instructions under *Cage* would upset vast numbers of criminal
convictions. And the Court's imaginative *reductio* of Eighth Amendment law in *Tuilaepa v.
California*, 512 U.S. 967 (1994), was manifestly driven by an unwillingness to cloud California's
almost-400 death sentences by a decision in Tuilaepa's favor. By contrast, the opinions reversing
convictions or death sentences in *Powell v. Nevada*, 511 U.S. 79 (1994); *Stansbury v. California*,
511 U.S. 318 (1994); *Lankford v. Idaho*, 500 U.S. 110 (1991); *Parker v. Dugger*, 498 U.S. 308
(1991); and *Richmond v. Lewis*, 511 U.S. 79 (1992), were manifestly written with excruciating care
to avoid announcing rules extensible beyond the case at bar. And compare *Riggins v. Nevada*, 504
U.S. 127 (1992), with *Medina v. California*, 505 U.S. 437 (1992).

Thus, winning a habeas case for the petitioner has become in no small part a matter of developing a bolt-hole theory of the case: a narrow argument through which your individual client can be slipped away to freedom, with a door somewhere in the passageway that can be slammed shut in the faces of all other prisoners seeking to follow.[5] With many judges, it is at least as important for the petitioner's counsel to construct the door solidly as to construct the passageway solidly.[6] Unless the judge is satisfied that s/he can give relief *in this case* with no (or very little) prospect that other accused or convicted persons will escape punishment, the judge will simply not rule your way.

This reality requires that petitioners' lawyers be especially meticulous and creative in thinking through the possible interactions between the various doctrines governing federal habeas corpus procedure — the subject of the present book — and the various possible formulations of their clients' substantive constitutional claims. Frequently, it is possible to use the interaction as a way of narrowing the bolt-hole and thereby increasing one's chances of pulling one's client through.

Two examples are suggestive:

In *Amadeo v. Zant*, 486 U.S. 214 (1988), a condemned inmate's attorneys discovered after trial that his grand and petit juries had been selected through procedures designed to minimize the number of African-Americans and women permitted to serve. Instructions as to how to do this had been clandestinely conveyed by the prosecutor to the jury commissioners, in such a manner as to permit the inference that the prosecutor and the commissioners had connived in a scheme not only to keep African-Americans and women off juries but to conceal factual information that would have enabled defendants to challenge the practice. On these facts, federal constitutional claims for postconviction relief could have been asserted on either or both of two theories. The prosecutor's concealment of information necessary to support an important defensive contention could have been attacked as a violation of due process under the *Napue/Giglio/Brady*

---

[5] This foreword is not the place for me to make my apologies to my fellow law-reform advocates of the 60's and 70's for my apparent recusancy, or to attempt the justifications that can be offered to younger lawyers and law students for following a career in litigation despite the fact that, for the most part, law reform through litigation is dead for quite some time to come. My present assignment calls for dealing with these important matters as briefly and unfairly as Samuel Johnson dealt with the philosopher who had written that he accepted the Universe. Said Johnson: "He'd better."

[6] Good construction on both fronts ordinarily begins in the state-court phases of a case. Done there, it can win tough cases on direct review, *see, e.g., Simmons v. South Carolina*, 512 U.S. 154 (1994), as well as in federal habeas, *see, e.g., Stewart v. Martinez-Villareal*, 118 S. Ct. 1618 (1998).

doctrine.[7] Alternatively, the substantive constitutional claim could have been couched as a violation of the defendant's Sixth and Fourteenth Amendment rights against the systematic exclusion of African-Americans and women from his juries, and the prosecutor's concealment could be treated as "cause" for entertaining the systematic-exclusion claim in federal habeas corpus despite the defendant's failure to challenge the jury before trial, under the *cause and prejudice* doctrine of *Wainwright v. Sykes* (section 26.3 herein). The latter formulation had the advantage of requiring virtually no extension of existing legal doctrines in defendants' favor, plus the benefit that judges most likely to resist such extensions are also likely to believe that systematic-exclusion practices are ancient history and that the enforcement of challenges to them has relatively little "let 'em loose in droves" potential nowadays.

Making *both* claims together had the added virtue, once the case reached an appellate court, that judges of this mind were more likely to vote for Amadeo on the systematic-exclusion claim if, by doing so, they could avoid reaching the prosecutorial-concealment claim and thus the risk that the particularly egregious prosecutorial behavior in *Amadeo* might persuade their colleagues to extend the *Napue* doctrine to give Amadeo relief. Amadeo's lawyers chose to make both claims, and the jury-exclusion claim prevailed in the Supreme Court.

Ford v. Wainwright, 477 U.S. 399 (1986), presented a powerful record that a condemned inmate had become insane following his conviction. The Governor of Florida proposed to execute him anyway, rejecting his lawyers' evidence of his insanity after executive proceedings that had none of the attributes of a fair hearing. Here too the constitutional claim might have been cast in either of two ways: (1) as an argument that due process required fair procedures for determining the sanity of a condemned inmate who asserted that he was mentally incompetent to be executed (even if the right not to be executed while mentally incompetent was purely a matter of state law); and (2) as an argument that there was a substantive Eighth and Fourteenth Amendment right not to be executed while insane; that a federal habeas corpus court was obliged by *Townsend v. Sain*, 372 U.S. 293 (1963), and 28 U.S.C. § 2254(d) (as it then read) to make an independent determination of sanity for this purpose unless the State employed full and fair procedures to determine the facts bearing upon a death-row inmate's mental competency (*see* section 20.3 herein); and that the Florida Governor's procedures in *Ford* were neither full nor fair.

Here, however, the decision whether to make both forms of argument was quite complicated. Among other concerns, there was a risk that the first

---

[7] *Napue v. Illinois*, 360 U.S. 264 (1959); *Giglio v. United States*, 405 U.S. 150 (1972); *Brady v. Maryland*, 373 U.S. 83 (1963). *Brady* has been amplified by *United States v. Agurs*, 427 U.S. 97 (1976); *United States v. Bagley*, 473 U.S. 667 (1985); and *Kyles v. Whitley*, 514 U.S. 419 (1995) (another tribute to the advocacy of Jim Liebman).

argument, while easier to win because of its limited implications for other cases, would commend itself to the courts as a compromise but leave Ford exposed to execution after a second Governor's hearing, employing improved procedures, produced the same predictable determination by partisan state officials that Ford was mentally sound as a bell. Ford's lawyers did eventually choose to make both arguments but refined them by emphasizing that a competency hearing conducted by partisan executive officials could meet neither due process requirements nor the *Townsend*-§ 2254 standards requiring federal habeas courts to defer to state factfindings made pursuant to "full and fair" hearing procedures. In this form, the second constitutional argument was probably narrower in its implications than the first, and it prevailed in the Supreme Court.

The necessity for presenting one's case so as to minimize the potential precedential effect of winning it calls for a positive attitude toward such doctrines as exhaustion (sections 5.1a, 11.1, 23.1 - 23.5 herein) and procedural default (sections 26.1 - 26.4 herein). Instead of viewing these doctrines solely as obstacles to be overcome, petitioners' counsel should also look at them as devices for persuading a judge that s/he can give counsel's client relief without much risk that other inmates will get it too. For example, in *Hankerson v. North Carolina*, 432 U.S. 233 (1977), the Supreme Court was willing to invalidate a long-settled state procedure in part because it was convinced, and could suggest in its opinion, that procedural-default rules and other relief-avoidance doctrines would enable the courts to deny most prisoners the benefit of the favorable ruling that Hankerson won. When counsel is representing a client with a constitutional claim that was unmistakably well preserved in the prior state-court proceedings, s/he will often do well to find out (by talking with public-defender attorneys and other knowledgeable criminal practitioners, as well as by reading the state reports) whether the same claim and indistinguishably similar claims have been made frequently or rarely by other criminal defendants, so as to be able to tell a federal habeas corpus judge who asks about the implications of counsel's contention: "So far as I have been able to find out, Your Honor, this is the only case [*or* only one of three cases] ever to raise the claim in the state courts, and of course it is not the sort of claim that would be available to inmates who had not raised it in the state courts." The point should be coupled, obviously, with the argument that counsel's case is as unique on its facts as counsel can honestly portray it as being, so that the precedential implications of a favorable decision on the merits would be very scant in any event.

Counsel should also consider the possibility of casting his or her constitutional argument in terms that build procedural bars into the substantive right which s/he is claiming. For example, in *Estelle v. Williams*, 425 U.S. 501 (1976), the Supreme Court held that a defendant who requests to be tried in civilian clothes rather than in jail garb is constitutionally entitled to have that request honored. Instead of treating the failure to make a request as a ground for procedural default, the Court treated a request as a precondition of attachment of the constitutional right. Couching a client's constitutional claims in such a form is particularly important where the doctrines of exhaustion, procedural default, and delay would *not* bar other criminal defendants from making the same or indistinguishable claims in federal habeas corpus despite their failure to preserve them in the state courts. The Liebman-Hertz analyses of the doctrines are essential reading for this purpose as well as for their more obvious utility in salvaging a client's ill-preserved claims.

❐

Admittedly, much of what I have written here is painfully redolent of the old military joke. The Lieutenant bangs into the Colonel's office shouting, "Colonel! Colonel! We have got a helluva problem on our hands." The Colonel snaps back, "In this army, Lieutenant, we do not have problems. We have only opportunities." The Lieutenant says, "Yes, Sir! And, oh boy, have we got one helluva magnificent opportunity right now."

The federal judiciary has increasingly come to offer habeas petitioners' counsel one helluva magnificent opportunity. With the brilliant guidance of Professors Liebman and Hertz, you will sometimes be able to seize it.

Anthony G. Amsterdam

November 8, 1998

AUTHORS' PREFACE TO THE THIRD EDITION

This edition of *Federal Habeas Corpus Practice and Procedure* differs substantially from the second edition, primarily because of the intervening enactment of the Antiterrorism and Effective Death Penalty Act of 1996 (AEDPA). Title I of the Act makes several significant changes in habeas corpus and section 2255 practice and procedure, which this edition describes and analyzes in detail.

The nature of AEDPA's changes in the law complicates the writing of a treatise like this. As is explained in § 3.4, a consequence of those changes is that there are now three different sets of rules that may potentially govern in a federal postconviction proceeding. Which set applies depends upon one or more of four factors — the date on which a case was filed, the date on which other events in the case took place, whether or not the petitioner is under sentence of death, and, if so, the quality of capital postconviction review procedures available in the State that sentenced the petitioner. In contrast to the second edition, which covered a body of law that was relatively uniform, this edition discusses numerous doctrinal variations that apply to some cases but not to others. We do so by presenting an overview of AEDPA's provisions in Chapter 3 (which includes, in § 3.5b, an outline of the rules that apply to different types of cases) and then by delineating in each subsequent chapter the specific changes that AEDPA makes and the types of cases to which the changes apply.

Also complicating this edition is the poor drafting of AEDPA's postconviction provisions.[1] The courts' widely differing interpretations of the statute's many ambiguous provisions have thrown habeas corpus and section 2255 practice into great flux. We delayed producing this edition in the hope that many or most of these questions of statutory construction and application would be quickly resolved. Although some have indeed been settled, many vexing questions remain. This edition canvasses the current state of the law and offers our thoughts about the most satisfactory way to resolve the interpretive controversies that remain. We caution our readers, however, to supplement our analyses and predictions with a careful study of recent legal developments in the district and circuit courts as well as the Supreme Court, a significant number of which will assuredly occur in the months following this edition's publication. As in the past, we will use annual paperbound updates to help keep readers abreast of new developments and to elaborate upon and, where appropriate, revise the analyses we present in this hardcover edition.

---

[1] See Lindh v. Murphy, 117 S. Ct. 2059, 2069 (1997) ("All we can say [about AEDPA's habeas corpus title] is that in a world of silk purses and pigs' ears, the Act is not a silk purse of the art of statutory drafting.").

AEDPA's adoption also has required us to alter our coverage of federal court of appeals and district court decisions. In the first and second editions of this book, we comprehensively discussed all recent United States Supreme Court decisions and tried to report at least the relevant outcomes of all recent court of appeals decisions, while discussing only a handful of federal district court decisions that were likely to have an important effect on federal postconviction practice. AEDPA substantially increases the number of court of appeals cases that require close attention to their analyses as well as their outcomes, and the number of district court cases that deserve coverage of some sort. These changes in coverage are required because more lower federal court decisions are having to tackle novel issues of law and because a much higher proportion of the leading decisions at this point are district court decisions. Expanding the number of court of appeals decisions that we analyze in detail, and expanding our coverage of district court cases, has prevented us from maintaining the breadth of coverage of routine court of appeals cases that we offered in the first and second editions. While continuing to provide comprehensive discussions of all relevant Supreme Court decisions, this edition only covers the recent federal circuit and district court decisions that seem to us to be the most significant.

Subject to these caveats, this edition of the book is current through Volume 118 of the Supreme Court Reporter, Volume 143 of the Federal Reporter, Third Series, and Volume 998 of the Federal Supplement.

James S. Liebman
Randy Hertz

ACKNOWLEDGMENTS

This book owes its existence to the arduous and dedicated work of a large number of people. In the 18 years in which the book has been in existence (in various incarnations), well over a hundred people have devoted months or more of concentrated time to its production — too many to mention by name in a sufficiently dignified manner to express our deep appreciation for their assistance and the pleasure that their comradeship has brought to the task. We especially would like to acknowledge the work of Mark Graber, who was with the project at the beginning and who kept it going in the mid-1980s.

For help, ideas, and guidance in the production of this third edition, we are grateful to Janice L. Bergmann, John H. Blume, Deborah Fins, Timothy K. Ford, Eric M. Freedman, Barry Friedman, Stephen P. Garvey, Joseph L. Hoffmann, George H. Kendall, Matthew C. Lawry, Henry P. Monaghan, Richard C. Neuhoff, Mark E. Olive, William F. Ryan, Larry W. Yackle, and Denise Young. This edition also has benefited from the assistance and advice of Columbia and N.Y.U. Law School students Maureen Alger, Alicia Amezcua, Julie Brain, Nick Bravin, Matthew Kadushin, John Lundin, Andy Morgan, and Robin Walker, and from the many hours that Honri Marcel devoted to its production. Bryan Kay, Julie Garmel, Jean Moffat, and Susan Hornbuckle of Lexis Law Publishing have been consistently supportive and have given unstintingly of their time in the preparation of this edition.

We also note our longstanding and ever accumulating debt to Anthony G. Amsterdam, who has been a mentor and an inspiration to us both and who — along with many other dedicated lawyers — has toiled mightily to use the writ, as it was intended to be used, *in favorem vitae*.

Finally, we acknowledge with respect and appreciation the incarcerated men and women for whom one or the other of us has served as counsel, whom we count as friends, and who, despite all they have suffered and the suffering some of them have caused, have taught us a lot about human dignity and the role of law in preserving it.

SUMMARY OF CONTENTS

Volume 1

FOREWORD by Anthony G. Amsterdam
AUTHORS' PREFACE TO THE THIRD EDITION
ACKNOWLEDGMENTS
TABLE OF CONTENTS

PART I: INTRODUCTION

Chapter 1.   Format
Chapter 2.   A General Description of Habeas Corpus
Chapter 3.   Overview of the Federal Habeas Corpus Process Under AEDPA
Chapter 4.   The Client

PART II: TIMING OF A FEDERAL HABEAS CORPUS PETITION; STATE REMEDIES

Chapter 5.   Order of Remedies and Timing
Chapter 6.   State Postconviction Remedies
Chapter 7.   State Remedies: Professional and Constitutional Issues

PART III: HABEAS CORPUS JURISDICTION

Chapter 8.   Subject-Matter Jurisdiction: Custody
Chapter 9.   Subject-Matter Jurisdiction: Cognizable Claims
Chapter 10. Personal Jurisdiction
Chapter 11. The Petition

PART IV: ANCILLARY AND SUMMARY PROCEEDINGS UPON FILING

Chapter 12. Indigents and Appointment of Counsel
Chapter 13. Stays of Execution
Chapter 14. Modification of Custody Status
Chapter 15. Summary Proceedings
Chapter 16. The State's Response
Chapter 17. Traverse, Amendment, and Petitioner-Initiated Summary Proceedings

PART V: MAGISTRATE JUDGE PRACTICE AND FACT-DEVELOPMENT PROCEDURES

Chapter 18. Magistrate Judge Practice
Chapter 19. Prehearing Fact-Development Procedures

Chapter 20. Right to a Hearing; Effect of State Court Factfindings
Chapter 21. Conduct of the Hearing

Volume 2

PART VI: PROCEDURAL DEFENSES

Chapter 22. Introduction to Procedural Defenses
Chapter 23. Exhaustion of State Remedies
Chapter 24. Prejudicial Delay
Chapter 25. Nonretroactivity
Chapter 26. Adequate and Independent State Grounds
Chapter 27. "Full and Fair Opportunity to Litigate" 4th Amendment Ex-
             clusionary Rule Claims
Chapter 28. Successive Petitions

PART VII: ADJUDICATION OF THE MERITS

Chapter 29. Briefing
Chapter 30. Standards of Review of State Court Rulings
Chapter 31. Burden of Proof
Chapter 32. Harmless Error
Chapter 33. Relief

PART VIII: POSTJUDGMENT PROCEEDINGS; APPEALS

Chapter 34. Postjudgment Proceedings
Chapter 35. Initiating the Appeal
Chapter 36. Ancillary Appellate Proceedings
Chapter 37. The Appeal
Chapter 38. Postjudgment, Pre-*Certiorari* Proceedings
Chapter 39. *Certiorari*
Chapter 40. Original Habeas Corpus Proceedings

PART IX: FEDERAL PRISONER PROCEEDINGS

Chapter 41. Section 2255 Proceedings

APPENDICES OF RELEVANT STATUTES, RULES, AND LEGISLATIVE
    MATERIALS
TABLE OF CASES AND AUTHORITIES
INDEX

TABLE OF CONTENTS
Volume 1

FOREWORD by Anthony G. Amsterdam v
AUTHORS' PREFACE TO THE THIRD EDITION xiii
ACKNOWLEDGMENTS xv
SUMMARY OF CONTENTS xvii

PART I: ....INTRODUCTION

Chapter 1. Format 1
Section 1.1.   Scope and organization of the book 1

Chapter 2. A General Description of Habeas Corpus 5
Section 2.1.   Introduction 5
Section 2.2.   A civil, appellate, collateral, equitable, common
                       law, and statutory procedure 7
Section 2.3.   The broad rhetoric and applications of the writ 17
Section 2.4.   A surrogate for Supreme Court review as of right 22
Subsection 2.4a.   Introduction 22
Subsection 2.4b.   Direct appeal/habeas corpus parity 23
Subsection 2.4c.   The two standard descriptions of the writ 34
Subsection 2.4d.   History and function of the writ: 1789-1998 40
    i.   Federal question review under the 1789 Judiciary Act 42
    ii.   The antebellum removal and habeas corpus acts 46
    iii. Reconstruction-era accretions to writ of error, removal,
          and habeas corpus jurisdiction 47
    iv.   Broad post-Reconstruction federal-prisoner habeas
          corpus review 49
    v.   Post-Reconstruction limits on state-prisoner removal
          and habeas corpus review 53
    vi.   Late 19th century adoption of federal-prisoner appeals
          and contraction of federal-prisoner habeas corpus 58
    vii. The impact on habeas corpus of expanded but "certiorarified"
          writ of error review — *Frank* and *Moore* 59
    viii. *Moore* to *Brown*: criminal procedure revolution; direct
          review devolution 65
    ix.   Congressional affirmation: the 1966 amendments 69
    x.   Temporary expansion and contraction — the mid-1960s
          to the mid-1990s 72
    xi.   Congressional revisions of 1996 79
Subsection 2.4e.   Conclusions: Federal review as of right, 1789-
                               1998; the logic of direct appeal/habeas corpus
                               parity 80
Section 2.5.   The relevance of innocence 85
Section 2.6.   The writ's role in capital cases 100

Chapter 3.   Overview of the Federal Habeas Corpus Process
             Under AEDPA 107
  Section 3.1.   Introduction 107
  Section 3.2.   Overview of AEDPA 107
  Section 3.3.   AEDPA's "opt-in" provisions.. 118
    Subsection 3.3a.   Introduction; qualifying States 118
    Subsection 3.3b.   Prerequisites for opting in 122
    Subsection 3.3c.   Procedures in qualifying opt-in States................. 130
  Section 3.4.   AEDPA's applicability to cases filed before and
                 after April 24, 1996 143
    Subsection 3.4a.   Chapter 153 cases filed on or before
                       April 24, 1996... 144
    Subsection 3.4b.   Chapter 153 cases filed after April 24, 1996....... 157
    Subsection 3.4c.   Chapter 154 cases filed before or after
                       April 24, 1996... 169
  Section 3.5.   Overview of the habeas corpus process in non-
                 AEDPA and AEDPA cases.. 173
    Subsection 3.5a.   Stages of the case prior to federal habeas
                       corpus review; implications for federal
                       habeas corpus... 173
      i.   Pretrial Proceedings 174
      ii.   Trial 175
      iii.   Postverdict proceedings 176
      iv.   Sentencing 176
      v.   Direct appeal 177
      vi.   State postconviction review 179
    Subsection 3.5b.   Outline of federal habeas corpus proceedings..... 180
      i.   Preparation and filing of petition 181
      ii.   Responsive pleadings and summary proceedings 188
      iii.   Fact-development procedures 189
      iv.   Procedural defenses 193
      v.   Adjudication of merits.. 202
      vi.   Postjudgment proceedings; appeals 204

Chapter 4.   The Client 207
  Section 4.1.   The client 207
  Section 4.2.   The capital client 209

PART II: TIMING OF A FEDERAL HABEAS CORPUS PETITION; STATE
           REMEDIES

Chapter 5.   Order of Remedies and Timing 213
  Section 5.1.   General ordering and timing rules 213

Subsection 5.1a.　Proceedings that ordinarily should precede
federal habeas corpus 213
Subsection 5.1b.　Statutes of limitations 218
　　i.　Applicability to cases filed on or before April 24, 1997 219
　　ii.　One-year statute of limitations for nonopt-in cases............................. 228
　　iii.　180-day statute of limitations for opt-in cases 244
Subsection 5.1c.　Exceptions to general ordering and timing rules　249
Section 5.2.　Pretrial petitions 249
Section 5.3.　Pre-exhaustion proceedings in capital cases 251

Chapter 6.　State Postconviction Remedies 253
Section 6.1.　Introduction 253
Section 6.2.　Claim selection 255
Section 6.3.　Stays of execution 259
Section 6.4.　*Certiorari* review 263
Subsection 6.4a.　Introduction 263
Subsection 6.4b.　Noncapital cases 263
Subsection 6.4c.　Capital cases 266
Subsection 6.4d.　*Certiorari*, not appeal 270

Chapter 7.　State Remedies: Professional and Constitutional Issues 273
Section 7.1.　"Full and fair" proceedings 273
Subsection 7.1a.　Counsel's responsibilities 273
Subsection 7.1b.　Constitutional considerations 280
Section 7.2.　The indigent's right to counsel and
financial assistance 292
Subsection 7.2a.　Introduction; Supreme Court views 292
Subsection 7.2b.　Procedural due process 301
Subsection 7.2c.　Meaningful access to the courts 305
Subsection 7.2d.　Suspension Clause 308
Subsection 7.2e.　Equal protection — claims available for first
time in state postconviction proceedings............. 314
Subsection 7.2f.　Capital cases 318

PART III: HABEAS CORPUS JURISDICTION

Chapter 8.　Subject-Matter Jurisdiction: Custody 321
Section 8.1.　Introduction to subject-matter jurisdiction 321
Section 8.2.　Definition of "custody" 321
Subsection 8.2a.　Custody in general 321
Subsection 8.2b.　Mootness 323
Subsection 8.2c.　Sentences not being served 329
Subsection 8.2d.　Custodial statuses 333

Subsection 8.2e.   Noncustodial statuses 342
Section 8.3.   Petitions in behalf of persons in custody 344
Subsection 8.3a.   Introduction 344
Subsection 8.3b.   The third-party petitioner 347
Subsection 8.3c.   The prisoner 352

Chapter 9.   Subject-Matter Jurisdiction: Cognizable Claims 363
Section 9.1.   Violation of the Constitution, laws, or treaties 363
Section 9.2.   *Stone v. Powell* — 4th Amendment exclusionary
                rule claims 404

Chapter 10. Personal Jurisdiction 411
Section 10.1.   The respondent 411
Section 10.2.   Personal jurisdiction, venue, transfer 416
Subsection 10.2a.   Introduction 416
Subsection 10.2b.   Personal jurisdiction 416
Subsection 10.2c.   Transfer, not dismissal 421
Subsection 10.2d.   Venue and convenient forum 421

Chapter 11. The Petition 427
Section 11.1.   Exhaustion (reprise): implications
                for timing and claim selection 427
Section 11.2.   Identifying potential claims 433
Subsection 11.2a.   Introduction 433
Subsection 11.2b.   Potential sources of factual information 437
Subsection 11.2c.   Examples of federal habeas corpus claims
                that have prevailed 452
Section 11.3.   Claim selection 486
Subsection 11.3a.   Assembling potential claims 486
Subsection 11.3b.   Claim selection; selection and pleading
                implications of procedural defenses 487
Subsection 11.3c.   Order of pleading 503
Section 11.4.   Joinder 504
Subsection 11.4a.   Joinder of claims 504
Subsection 11.4b.   Joinder of petitioners 505
Section 11.5.   Form 507
Section 11.6.   Fact pleading 509
Section 11.7.   Checklists of additional pleading requirements 514
Subsection 11.7a.   Other matters to plead 514
Subsection 11.7b.   Other formal requirements 514
Subsection 11.7c.   Accompanying documents 517

Subsection 11.7d. Additional documents that may be filed with
the petition, or later 517
Section 11.8. Prayer for relief 520
Section 11.9. Filing and service 522
Subsection 11.9a. Place of filing 522
Subsection 11.9b. Copies 522
Subsection 11.9c. Filing fee 523
Subsection 11.9d. Service 523

PART IV: ANCILLARY AND SUMMARY PROCEEDINGS UPON FILING

Chapter 12. Indigents and Appointment of Counsel 525
Section 12.1. *In forma pauperis* proceedings 525
Section 12.2. Appointment of counsel: introduction 536
Section 12.3. The statutory right to counsel 538
Subsection 12.3a. Procedure and timing 538
Subsection 12.3b. The statutory right 547
i.   Commencement of proceedings — capital cases 547
ii.   Commencement of proceedings — noncapital cases 550
iii.   Discovery ordered — noncapital cases 558
iv.   Hearing ordered — noncapital cases 559
Subsection 12.3c. Compensation 559
Section 12.4. The constitutional right to counsel 562
Section 12.5. Denial and interlocutory appeal 563

Chapter 13. Stays of Execution 571
Section 13.1. Stay practice 571
Section 13.2. Legal standards 582
Subsection 13.2a. Stays generally 582
Subsection 13.2b. Prefiling stays — first petition 588
Subsection 13.2c. Postfiling stays — first petition 592
Subsection 13.2d. Postfiling stays — successive petition 596
Subsection 13.2e. District court discretion in non-AEDPA, AEDPA
nonopt-in, and AEDPA opt-in cases.................. 598
Section 13.3. Pre-exhaustion stays 599
Subsection 13.3a. The stay/abeyance procedure 599
Subsection 13.3b. Legal authority 603
Subsection 13.3c. Total exhaustion and stay/abeyance 608
Section 13.4. The stay hearing 609
Section 13.5. Effectuating stays 611
Section 13.6. Proceedings following denial 611
Subsection 13.6a. Explicit or implicit denial — prepetition stays .. 611
Subsection 13.6b. Explicit denial — postpetition stays 612

Subsection 13.6c. Implicit denial — postpetition stays 615

Chapter 14. Modification of Custody Status 619
Section 14.1. Transfer 619
Section 14.2. Release on recognizance or surety 619

Chapter 15. Summary Proceedings 625
Section 15.1. Return of defective petitions 625
Section 15.2. Summary dismissal 628
Subsection 15.2a. When appropriate 628
Subsection 15.2b. Tactical considerations 633
Subsection 15.2c. Legal standards 635
   i.   In general 635
   ii.   *Pro se* cases 638
   iii.   Fact-bound cases 641
Subsection 15.2d. Post-dismissal tactical considerations 645
   i.   Other than nonexhaustion grounds 645
   ii.   Nonexhaustion grounds 645
   iii.   Total exhaustion grounds — generally 646
   iv.   Total exhaustion grounds — capital cases 646

Chapter 16. The State's Response 649
Section 16.1. Service and answer 649
Subsection 16.1a. Service generally 649
Subsection 16.1b. Answer generally 649
Subsection 16.1c. Motions to dismiss or for summary judgment 653
Subsection 16.1d. Service and answer — capital cases 654
Section 16.2. Tactical considerations following answer 655
Subsection 16.2a. Introduction 655
Subsection 16.2b. Factual disputes 657
Subsection 16.2c. Legal disputes 657
Subsection 16.2d. Defenses 658
Subsection 16.2e. Motions to dismiss 658

Chapter 17. Traverse, Amendment, and Petitioner-Initiated
Summary Proceedings 659
Section 17.1. Traverse 659
Section 17.2. Amendment 661
Section 17.3. Petitioner-initiated summary proceedings 667

PART V: MAGISTRATE JUDGE PRACTICE AND FACT-DEVELOPMENT
         PROCEDURES

Chapter 18. Magistrate Judge Practice 671
   Section 18.1. Matters referable 671
     Subsection 18.1a. Nondispositive matters 671
     Subsection 18.1b. Dispositive matters 672
     Subsection 18.1c. Distinguishing between dispositive and
                        nondispositive matters 675
     Subsection 18.1d. Procedure for referral 676
   Section 18.2. Objections and *de novo* determinations on
                  dispositive matters 677
     Subsection 18.2a. Objections 677
     Subsection 18.2b. *De novo* determination 685

Chapter 19. Prehearing Fact-Development Procedures 689
   Section 19.1. Counsel's responsibility 689
   Section 19.2. The state record 690
   Section 19.3. Financial assistance 695
   Section 19.4. Discovery 705
     Subsection 19.4a. In general 705
     Subsection 19.4b. Pre-Rules discovery 709
     Subsection 19.4c. Habeas Rule 6 711
     Subsection 19.4d. In lieu of a hearing 714
     Subsection 19.4e. Capital cases 715
     Subsection 19.4f. Timing 716
     Subsection 19.4g. The discovery motion 717
     Subsection 19.4h. Discovery by the state 719
   Section 19.5. Expansion of the record 720

Chapter 20. Right to a Hearing; Effect of State Factfindings 727
   Section 20.1. Introduction 727
     Subsection 20.1a. Importance of hearings 727
     Subsection 20.1b. Evolution of fact-development standards 729
     Subsection 20.1c. Hearings on defenses 734
     Subsection 20.1d. Capital cases 738
   Section 20.2. Overview of fact-development and fact-determination
                  procedures in AEDPA and non-AEDPA cases 739
     Subsection 20.2a. Introduction 739
     Subsection 20.2b. Right to a hearing in AEDPA and
                        non-AEDPA cases 739

Subsection 20.2c. Presumption of correctness in AEDPA
and non-AEDPA cases 747
Subsection 20.2d. Relationship between *Townsend* and the
presumption of correctness................................. 756
Section 20.3. Mandatory hearings... 758
Subsection 20.3a. Introduction 758
Subsection 20.3b. Absence of state record 759
Subsection 20.3c. Absence of state factfindings 762
Subsection 20.3d. Inadequate state factfindings 767
Subsection 20.3e. Absence or inadequacy of state hearing 794
Subsection 20.3f. Unsupported state factfindings 816
Subsection 20.3g. Nexus to mandatory hearing issues 820
Subsection 20.3h. Rebuttal of state factfindings 821
Section 20.4. Discretionary hearings 822

Chapter 21. Conduct of the Hearing 827
Section 21.1. Preparing for the hearing 827
Subsection 21.1a. Preparation 827
Subsection 21.1b. Continuances; speedy hearing 830
Subsection 21.1c. Subpoenas 832
Subsection 21.1d. Prehearing conference 835
Section 21.2. Rules of evidence 836
Section 21.3. The petitioner's presence 841

PART I
INTRODUCTION
Chapter 1
FORMAT

§ 1.1. Scope and organization of the book.

This two-volume book is an introduction to the procedures available to state and federal prisoners for securing federal habeas corpus and other forms of postconviction review of their convictions and sentences, both capital and noncapital.

The book is *introductory* in that it tries to raise and discuss fully — but does not always fully answer — the major legal and practical questions that arise in litigating and adjudicating federal habeas corpus and related types of postconviction cases. Such questions abound in habeas corpus practice because the remedy lies at the confluence of so many usually distinct legal disciplines and so many competing legal values. Habeas corpus uses the tools of federal civil procedure to litigate the constitutionality of state criminal procedures. It places federal trial courts in an essentially appellate relationship to state appellate courts, while often assigning factfinding as well as law and fact review functions to those essentially appellate federal forums. And it combines all these typically distinct legal contexts in a setting in which many important, and often competing, values and interests are at stake — the enforcement of local criminal laws and of national constitutional norms; the integrity of the state and also of the federal judicial systems; and the security of local communities and the liberty and lives of the criminally accused. Understanding and effectively implementing federal habeas corpus practice and procedure accordingly requires large doses of the jurist's, lawyer's, and student's judgment and imagination, and it is those qualities that the book is designed to stimulate.

The book emphasizes federal habeas corpus and related postconviction *procedures*, rather than the substantive federal constitutional, statutory, and other laws that those procedures are available to enforce through the termination of custody imposed in violation of those laws.

The book's major emphasis is on *state* prisoners: It pays particular attention to procedures under 28 U.S.C. §§ 2241 and 2254 for securing federal review of convictions and sentences imposed under authority of state as opposed to federal law. The book does, however, devote significant attention to federal prisoner proceedings under 28 U.S.C. § 2255 and other similar mechanisms for postconviction review of federal custody.[1]

---

§ **1.1.** [1] See especially *infra* Chapter 41.

The book is written from the procedural perspective of *prisoners*. It is organized according to the succession of steps that the petitioning party typically follows in litigating a federal habeas corpus or similar case. It begins with the appellate and state postconviction proceedings that generally precede the filing of a federal habeas corpus or related petition. It then addresses the legal issues and strategic considerations affecting the drafting and filing of a petition and ancillary motions (for example, applications for appointment of counsel and a stay of execution). The book thereafter discusses the various pleadings that may be filed, the proceedings that may be held, the defenses that may be encountered, the burdens of persuasion and other decision rules that may apply, and the relief that may be obtained in the federal district court once a petition has been filed. Next come the proceedings that generally follow a district court's grant or denial of a petition: postjudgment proceedings in the district court, appeal, and *certiorari*. The book concludes by more specifically addressing original habeas corpus proceedings and federal prisoner proceedings under sections 2241 and 2255. Although much of what is said in the preceding chapters applies to original habeas corpus and federal prisoner section 2241 and section 2255 proceedings, the final two chapters discuss the unique aspects of those two important types of federal postconviction review.

This format has obvious advantages for lawyers and judges involved in federal habeas corpus and related proceedings: It enables them easily to find the law they need at the relevant stage of the case; it also avoids the untoward consequences of learning what a rhinoceros looks like from behind only to encounter the beast for the first time head on. On the other hand, the format risks a degree of redundancy, because certain doctrines (exhaustion, procedural default, and successive petitions, for example) are relevant at more than one stage of a federal postconviction case. To minimize this problem, the book places the primary treatment of a particular issue or doctrine in the most logical location and refers back or forward to that primary treatment in other, more truncated discussions of the same topic that appear elsewhere in the book.

The book is about *federal* habeas corpus in that it analyzes procedures and remedies available to state prisoners seeking habeas corpus relief and federal prisoners seeking similar relief in the United States District Courts, Courts of Appeals, and the Supreme Court. Although it also discusses state remedies for state prisoners,[2] it does so principally to identify the steps (for example, exhaustion of state remedies) that must be taken in the state courts to ensure that

---

[2] State court review of federal convictions (but not quite so clearly state court review of *non*judicially sanctioned — *e.g.*, executive or administrative — forms of federal custody) is barred by Ableman v. Booth, 62 U.S. (21 How.) 506 (1859); *see* James S. Liebman & William F. Ryan, *"Some Effectual Power": The Quantity and Quality of Decisionmaking Required of Article III Courts*, 98 COLUM. L. REV. 696, 804-09 (1998).

the federal courts will entertain the habeas corpus petition and to identify other ways in which state proceedings affect the federal habeas corpus remedy.

The book principally discusses federal postconviction review of the legality under federal law of criminal *convictions* and *sentences*. Habeas corpus also may be used to review the legality under federal law of pretrial incarceration,[3] government-imposed restrictions in military, immigration, mental health, and domestic settings,[4] state and federal custody alleged to violate probation, parole, and other administrative regulations affecting the length of postconviction incarceration,[5] and even possibly the physical conditions of confinement in jails and prisons.[6] Although these uses of the writ of habeas corpus are briefly discussed in the referenced sections, and generally can partake of the same procedures as are available to individuals challenging the legality of their convictions or sentences, the book is organized and written from the vantage point of individuals challenging convictions and sentences.

The book analyzes the remedies available in both *capital* and *noncapital* cases. It discusses not only the numerous legal and practical issues common to both types of cases but also the issues that only arise, or that lead to different conclusions, in one context or the other.

Finally, the book tries at once to be several kinds of publications — with all the potential "master of none" dangers that such an endeavor implies. Because it attempts to canvass, organize, fill gaps in, and give some structure and coherence to the law of the Supreme Court and the twelve federal circuits, it fairly may be called a treatise. Because it attempts to provide a comprehensive yet relatively accessible reference for persons concerned with the law, language, and litigation of federal habeas corpus cases, it also serves as a textbook. Because it attempts to speak directly to the minute-by-minute concerns of the habeas corpus lawyer and judge in the heat of the litigation, it functions at times as a handbook and manual.[7] Insofar as the book takes the controversial but, we believe, valid position that federal habeas corpus provides a well-developed, historically validated, highly specialized, and relatively efficient system of federal appellate review of the judicial treatment that States and localities afford the federally protected liberties of their least favored citizens,[8] the book endeavors as well to provide some food for scholarly, as well as judicial and legislative, thought about an important and highly contested topic.

---

[3] *See infra* §§ 5.2, 8.2.

[4] *See infra* §§ 8.2, 9.1, 33.4.

[5] *See infra* §§ 9.1, 33.4, 41.2b.

[6] *See id.*

[7] For example, § 3.5 *infra* provides a quick reference in chronological order to the major procedural steps in state and federal postconviction litigation.

[8] *See infra* Chapter 2.

Chapter 2

A GENERAL DESCRIPTION OF HABEAS CORPUS

§ 2.1. Introduction.

Generally describing the history, purpose, and operation of habeas corpus in this country is a task that has occupied scholars for years.[1] That same task is

---

§ 2.1. [1] *See, e.g.*, PAUL M. BATOR, PAUL J. MISHKIN, DAVID L. SHAPIRO & HERBERT WECHSLER, HART AND WECHSLER'S THE FEDERAL COURTS AND THE FEDERAL SYSTEM ch. X (2d ed. 1973) and BATOR, DANIEL J. MELTZER, MISHKIN & SHAPIRO, *id.*, ch. XI (3d ed. 1988) and RICHARD H. FALLON, MELTZER & SHAPIRO, *id.* ch. XI (4th ed. 1996); 1 JAMES S. LIEBMAN, FEDERAL HABEAS CORPUS PRACTICE AND PROCEDURE § 2.2b (1st ed. 1988); Anthony G. Amsterdam, *Criminal Prosecutions Affecting Federally Guaranteed Civil Rights: Federal Removal and Habeas Corpus Jurisdiction to Abort State Court Trial*, 113 U. PA. L. REV. 793, 805-28 (1965); Marc M. Arkin, *The Ghost at the Banquet: Slavery, Federalism, and Habeas Corpus for State Prisoners*, 70 TUL. L. REV. 1 (1995); Paul M. Bator, *Finality in Criminal Law and Federal Habeas Corpus for State Prisoners*, 76 HARV. L. REV. 441 (1963); John H. Blume & David P. Voisin, *An Introduction to Federal Habeas Corpus Practice and Procedure*, 47 S.C. L. REV. 271 (1996); William J. Brennan, Jr., *Federal Habeas Corpus and State Prisoners: An Exercise in Federalism*, 7 UTAH L. REV. 423 (1961); Irwin Chemerinsky, *Thinking About Habeas Corpus*, 37 CASE W. RES. L. REV. 748 (1986-87); Alan Clarke, *Habeas Corpus: The Historical Debate*, 14 N.Y.L. SCH. J. HUM. RTS. 375 (1998); Alan W. Clarke, *Procedural Labyrinths and the Injustice of Death: A Critique of Death Penalty Habeas Corpus*, 29 U. RICH. L. REV. 1327 (1995) (Part One), 30 U. RICH. L. REV. 303 (1996) (Part Two); Robert Cover & Alexander Aleinikoff, *Dialectical Federalism: Habeas Corpus and the Court*, 86 YALE L.J. 1035 (1977); Victor E. Flango & Patricia McKenna, *Federal Habeas Corpus Review of State Court Convictions*, 31 CAL. W. L. REV. 237 (1995); Clark D. Forsythe, *The Historical Origins of Broad Federal Habeas Review Reconsidered*, 70 NOTRE DAME L. REV. 1079 (1995); Barry Friedman, *Failed Enterprise: The Supreme Court's Habeas Reform*, 83 CALIF. L. REV. 485 (1995); Barry Friedman, *Habeas and Hubris*, 45 VAND. L. REV. 797 (1992); Barry Friedman, *Pas de Deux: The Supreme Court and the Habeas Courts*, 66 SO. CAL. L. REV. 2467 (1993); Barry Friedman, *A Tale of Two Habeas*, 73 MINN. L. REV. 247 (1988); Henry J. Friendly, *Is Innocence Irrelevant? Collateral Attack on Criminal Judgments*, 38 U. CHI. L. REV. 142 (1970); Henry Hart, *Foreword: The Time Chart of the Justices*, 73 HARV. L. REV. 84 (1959); Patrick E. Higginbotham, *Reflections on Reform of § 2254 Habeas Petitions*, 18 HOFSTRA L. REV. 1005 (1990); Chris Hutton, *The "New" Federal Habeas: Implications for State Standards of Review*, 40 S.D. L. REV. 442 (1995); Melissa L. Koehn, *A Line in the Sand: The Supreme Court and the Writ of Habeas Corpus*, 32 TULSA L. REV. 389 (1997); Evan Tsen Lee, *The Theories of Federal Habeas Corpus*, 72 WASH. U. L.Q. 151 (1994); James S. Liebman, *Apocalypse Next Time?: The Anachronistic Attack on Habeas Corpus/Direct Review Parity*, 92 COLUM. L. REV. 1997 (1992); David McCord, *Visions of Habeas*, 1994 B.Y.U. L. REV. 735; Daniel J. Meltzer, *Habeas Corpus Jurisdiction: The Limits of Models*, 66 SO. CAL. L. REV. 2507 (1993); Paul J. Mishkin, *Foreword: The High Court, the Great Writ, and the Due Process of Time and Law*, 79 HARV. L. REV. 56 (1965); Gary Peller, *In Defense of Federal Habeas Corpus Relitigation*, 16 HARV. C.R.-C.L. L. REV. 579 (1982); Curtis R. Reitz, *Federal Habeas Corpus: Postconviction Remedy for State Prisoners*, 108 U. PA. L. REV. 461 (1960); Yale L. Rosenberg, *The Federal Habeas Corpus Custody Decisions: Liberal Oasis or Conservative Prop?*, 23 AM. J. CRIM. L. 99 (1995); Jordan Steiker, *Innocence and Federal Habeas*, 41 UCLA L. REV. 303 (1993); Ronald J. Tabak, *Habeas Corpus as a Crucial Protector of Constitutional Rights: A Tribute Which May Also Be a Eulogy*,

inspiring a whole new generation of writing in the wake of Congress's adoption in 1996 of the Antiterrorism and Effective Death Penalty Act (AEDPA).[2] In this chapter, we provide several layers of our own description. Section 2.2 lists some of the one- or two-word labels that the Supreme Court has applied to the writ over the years, noting the labels' strategic and adjudicative implications. Section 2.3 widens the inquiry slightly, collecting over three centuries' worth of seemingly broad descriptions, and four decades' worth of seemingly broad applications, of the writ. Section 2.4 widens the inquiry still further, reviewing the debate over the *most* appropriate description of the historical and contemporary uses of habeas corpus in the United States and providing our own description of the writ — as a means of assuring essentially appellate federal court review of the state courts' resolution of certain especially important national legal questions, including review of state decisions by lower federal courts when the Supreme Court cannot itself provide that review.[3] Section 2.5 considers Judge Henry Friendly's famous description of habeas corpus, which he

---

26 SETON HALL L. REV. 1477 (1996); Herbert Wechsler, *Habeas Corpus and the Supreme Court: Reconsidering the Reach of the Great Writ*, 59 U. COLO. L. REV. 167 (1988); Ann Woolhandler, *Demodeling Habeas*, 45 STAN. L. REV. 575 (1993); Charles E. Wyzanski, Jr., *The Writ of Habeas Corpus*, 243 ANNALS 101 (1946); Larry W. Yackle, *Explaining Habeas Corpus*, 60 N.Y.U. L. REV. 991 (1985); Larry W. Yackle, *Form and Function in the Administration of Justice: The Bill of Rights and Federal Habeas Corpus*, 23 U. MICH. J.L. REF. 685 (1990); *Developments in the Law: Federal Habeas Corpus*, 83 HARV. L. REV. 1038, 1042-62 (1970); Note, *Federal Habeas Corpus for State Prisoners: The Isolation Principle*, 39 N.Y.U. L. REV. 78 (1964) (by Abraham D. Sofaer).

[2] Pub. L. 104-132, 110 Stat. 1214 (1996). *See, e.g.*, Charles F. Baird, *The Habeas Corpus Revolution: A New Role for State Courts?*, 27 ST. MARY'S L. REV. 297 (1996); Stephen B. Bright, *Is Fairness Irrelevant?: The Evisceration of Federal Habeas Corpus Review and Limits on the Ability of State Courts to Protect Fundamental Rights*, 54 WASH. & LEE L. REV. 1 (1997); Richard H. Fallon, Jr., *Response: Applying the Suspension Clause to Immigration Cases*, 98 COLUM. L. REV. 1068 (1998); Marshall J. Hartman & Jeanette Nyden, *Habeas Corpus and the New Federalism After the Anti-Terrorism and Effective Death Penalty Act of 1996*, 30 J. MARSHALL L. REV. 389 (1997); Evan Tsen Lee, *Section 2254(d) of the New Habeas Statute: An (Opinionated) User's Manual*, 51 VAND. L. REV. 103 (1998); James S. Liebman & William F. Ryan, *"Some Effectual Power": The Quantity and Quality of Decisionmaking Required of Article III Courts*, 98 COLUM. L. REV. 696 (1998); Gerald L. Neuman, *Habeas Corpus, Executive Detention, and the Removal of Aliens*, 98 COLUM. L. REV. 961 (1998); Michael O'Neill, *On Reforming the Federal Writ of Habeas Corpus*, 26 SETON HALL L. REV. 1493 (1996); Kent S. Scheidegger, *Response: Habeas Corpus, Relitigation, and the Legislative Power*, 98 COLUM. L. REV. 888 (1998); Mark Tushnet & Larry Yackle, *Symbolic Statutes and Real Laws: The Pathologies of the Antiterrorism and Effective Death Penalty Act and the Prison Litigation Reform Act*, 47 DUKE L.J. 1 (1997); Larry W. Yackle, *A Primer on the New Habeas Corpus Statute*, 44 BUFF. L. REV. 381 (1996).

[3] For a more comprehensive discussion of this understanding of the writ, see Liebman, *supra* note 1. A similar approach that anticipates our understanding of the modern writ is elegantly presented in the articles by Professor Barry Friedman that are cited *supra* note 1. *See also* 1 LIEBMAN, *supra* note 1, §§ 2.2, 5.2, 27.1, 28.1, 35.1b; Higginbotham, *supra* note 1.

rhetorically introduced with the question, "Is Innocence Irrelevant?"[4] Section 2.6 considers the writ's role in capital cases.

This introduction to habeas corpus is rendered provisional by continuing uncertainty as of this writing about the proper interpretation of AEDPA's amended section 2254(d). As we discuss in detail in §§ 30.2c and 30.2d, courts and commentators are sharply divided over that interpretation, and the Supreme Court has yet to resolve the controversy. Hanging in the balance is the continuing capacity of federal judges on whom jurisdiction has been conferred (1) to make an independent determination of federal legal issues that state courts resolved against habeas corpus petitioners before their cases reached the federal courts, (2) to issue relief sufficient to effectuate the federal courts' independent legal judgments, and (3) to neutralize the effect of state court decisions that, in federal judges' independent estimation, are contrary to the supreme law of the land. Also hanging in the balance, therefore, is the continuing capacity of federal judges upon whom habeas corpus jurisdiction has been conferred to afford the kind of review and relief that this chapter concludes has been the norm since 1789. In our view, which we briefly outline in this chapter[5] and set out in detail in §§ 30.2c and 30.2d, the language and history of section 2254(d) do not reasonably permit an interpretation that deprives judges of these foundational and until now ever-present capacities, particularly because of the serious constitutional questions that any such undermining of "[t]he judicial Power" would present under Article III, the Supremacy Clause, and, possibly, the Suspension Clause of the United States Constitution.

§ 2.2. A civil, appellate, collateral, equitable, common law, and statutory procedure.

As noted in section 1.1 *supra*, habeas corpus is "unique" in its conjunction of distinct legal disciplines.[1] For this reason, perhaps, the Court has applied a range of controversial and sometimes inconsistent labels to the writ. For example, although the "custody" prerequisite for habeas corpus jurisdiction[2] usually limits review to the legality of criminal prosecutions and sentences, the Court typically describes the writ as a "civil" remedy[3] — one that, indeed, is partly governed by

---

[4] *See* Friendly, *supra* note 1.

[5] *See infra* §§ 2.4b, 2.4d nn.316-23 and accompanying text.

§ 2.2. [1] Browder v. Director, 434 U.S. 257, 269 (1978).

[2] *See infra* § 8.2.

[3] *See, e.g.*, O'Neal v. McAninch, 513 U.S. 432, 440 (1995) ("habeas corpus, technically speaking, is a civil proceeding"); Keeney v. Tamayo-Reyes, 504 U.S. 1 (1992) (O'Connor, J., dissenting); Murray v. Giarratano, 492 U.S. 1, 8 (1989) (quoting Pennsylvania v. Finley, 481 U.S. 551, 556 (1987)); Teague v. Lane, 489 U.S. 288, 308 (1989) (plurality opinion); Houston v. Lack, 487 U.S. 266, 272 (1988); Hilton v. Braunskill, 481 U.S. 770, 776 & n.5 (1987); *Browder v.*

the Federal Rules of *Civil* Procedure.[4] No less paradoxically, the Court has long said that habeas corpus is a "clearly appellate" procedure,[5] yet, evidently in

---

Director, supra, 434 U.S. at 269; Harris v. Nelson, 394 U.S. 286, 293-94 (1969); Heflin v. United States, 358 U.S. 415, 418 n.7 (1959); Eagles v. United States ex rel. Samuels, 329 U.S. 304, 315 (1946); Fisher v. Baker, 203 U.S. 174, 181 (1906); Cross v. Burke, 146 U.S. 82, 88 (1892); Farnsworth v. Montana, 129 U.S. 104, 113 (1889); Kurtz v. Moffitt, 115 U.S. 487, 494 (1885); Ex parte Tom Tong, 108 U.S. 556, 559 (1883).

[4] Rule 11 of the Rules Governing § 2254 Cases (when appropriate and consistent with Habeas Rules, Federal Rules of Civil Procedure apply in habeas corpus proceedings); Advisory Committee Note to Rule 11 of the Rules Governing § 2254 Cases. *See, e.g.,* Calderon v. Ashmus, 118 S. Ct. 1694, 1700 (1998) (Breyer, J., concurring) (**citing FHCPP**) ("Federal Rule of Civil Procedure 15's liberal standard for amendment applies to [most] habeas petitions ....."); McFarland v. Scott, 512 U.S. 849, 866 n.2 (1994) (Thomas, J., dissenting) ("The Federal Rules of Civil Procedure apply in the context of habeas suits to the extent that they are not inconsistent with the Habeas Corpus Rules."); Anderson v. Butler, 886 F.2d 111, 113-14 (5th Cir. 1989). *See also, e.g.,* Withrow v. Williams, 507 U.S. 680, 695-96 & n.7 (1993) (**citing FHCPP**) (accepting litigant's contention that FED. R. CIV. P. 15(b) (amendment of pleadings by implied consent of parties) applies in habeas corpus proceedings, but concluding that prerequisites for Civil Rule 15(b) were not met under circumstances); authority cited *infra* §§ 16.1c, 16.2b, 17.2, 17.3, 18.1, 19.4, 34.2, 34.3, 35.1. *But cf.* Bracy v. Gramley, 117 S. Ct. 1793, 1796-97 (1997) ("habeas petitioner, unlike the usual civil litigant in federal court, is not entitled to discovery as a matter of ordinary course," and "'broad discovery provisions' of the Federal Rules of Civil Procedure d[o] not apply in habeas proceedings"; "'discovery [is] available under the Federal Rules of Civil Procedure ... [only] for good cause shown'"; where Civil Rules do not apply or are insufficient, All Writs Act gives "federal courts the power to 'fashion appropriate modes of procedure' ... to dispose of habeas petitions 'as law and justice require'" (quoting *Harris v. Nelson, infra,* at 295, 299, 300; Rule 6(a) of the Rules Governing § 2254 Cases; Schlanger v. Seamans, 401 U.S. 487, 490 n.4 (1971) (nationwide service of process available in federal civil actions under 28 U.S.C. § 1391(e) is not available in habeas corpus actions); Harris v. Nelson, 394 U.S. 286 (1969) (civil discovery rules do not automatically apply in habeas corpus cases); Kincade v. Sparkman, 117 F.3d 949, 950 (6th Cir. 1997) ("Although courts have often separated habeas corpus petitions from criminal actions by characterizing habeas proceedings as civil in nature, 'postconviction relief and prisoner civil rights relief are analytically very different.'" (quoting Martin v. United States, 96 F.3d 853, 855 (7th Cir.1996))); Anderson v. Singletary, 111 F.3d 801, 804-05 (11th Cir. 1997) (classification of "habeas corpus actions as 'civil' is ... somewhat illusive, as habeas corpus actions are not purely (and thus not plainly) 'civil actions'" (**citing FHCPP**)); Ewing v. Rodgers, 826 F.2d 967, 971 (10th Cir. 1987) (habeas corpus suit is not "civil action" for purposes of award of attorneys fees under Equal Access to Justice Act, 28 U.S.C. § 2412(d)(1)(A)); Baudin v. Thomas, 732 F.2d 1107 (2d Cir. 1984) (similar); *infra* §§ 12.1 n.16, 35.1 (view that FED. R. CIV. P. 54(b) does not apply to habeas corpus proceedings); *infra* note 6.

    In *O'Neal v. McAninch, supra,* the Court recognized this criminal-civil paradox and the danger of withdrawing protections from habeas corpus petitioners because they are invoking a "merely" civil remedy. In deciding to adhere to the more protective rules governing the burden of persuasion of harmless error applicable when courts "review[ ] errors from a criminal proceeding," and not to apply the less protective rules that may apply when errors in civil cases are reviewed, Justice Breyer wrote for the Court:

recognition of the federalism-etched divide between the state and federal judicial systems that the writ controversially crosses, the Court has also said that "[t]he writ of *habeas corpus* is not a proceeding in the original criminal prosecution but

> One problem with th[e] argument [that, as a civil remedy, habeas corpus should automatically use civil, not criminal procedures] lies in its failure to take into account the stakes involved in a habeas proceeding. Unlike the civil cases cited by the State, the errors being considered by a habeas corpus court occurred in a *criminal* proceeding, and therefore, although habeas is a civil proceeding, someone's custody, rather than mere civil liability, is at stake.

O'Neal v. McAninch, supra, 513 U.S. at 440. *See id.* at 442 ("civil [harmless error] standard" inappropriate for "habeas proceedings" because "they review errors in state *criminal* trials").

[5] *See, e.g.*, Ex parte Siebold, 100 U.S. 371, 374 (1879); Ex parte Yerger, 75 U.S. (8 Wall.) 85, 97 (1868); Ex parte McCardle, 73 U.S. (6 Wall.) 318, 324 (1867); Ex parte Milligan, 71 U.S. (4 Wall.) 2, 118-19 (1866); In re Kaine, 55 U.S. (14 How.) 103, 119 (1853); *id.* at 130-36 (Nelson, J., dissenting); Ex parte Watkins, 32 U.S. (7 Pet.) 568, 572-73 (1833); Ex parte Burford, 7 U.S. (3 Cranch.) 448, 495 (1806) (Marshall, C.J.); Ex parte Bollman, 8 U.S. (4 Cranch.) 75, 100-01 (1807); United States v. Hamilton, 3 U.S. (3 Dallas) 17 (1795); *infra* §§ 2.4d n.71 and accompanying text, 2.4d nn.84-91 and accompanying text, 40.1. *See also O'Neal v. McAninch, supra*, 513 U.S. at 440-42 (federal court's function in habeas corpus proceedings is to "review errors in state criminal trials" (emphasis omitted)); Anderson v. Butler, 886 F.2d 111, 113 (5th Cir. 1989) (modern habeas corpus procedure has same function as ordinary appeal). *Compare* Reed v. Farley, 512 U.S. 339, 349 (1994) (plurality opinion) ("institutional constraints preclude [the] Supreme Court from overseeing adequately whether state courts have properly applied federal law," warranting habeas corpus review in lower federal courts to carry out that essentially appellate oversight task (citing Stone v. Powell, 428 U.S. 465, 526 (1976) (Brennan, J., dissenting))) *and id.* at 361 & n.3 (Blackmun, J. dissenting) (habeas corpus review of state court decisions is needed because, "[a]s a practical matter, this Court's direct review of state court decisions cannot adequately ensure uniformity") *and* decisions cited *infra* § 2.4b n.24 *with Reed v. Farley, supra* at 358 (Scalia, J., concurring in the judgment) (because "this Court's direct review of state and federal decisions will ... suffice for th[e] purpose [of achieving uniformity], as it does in most other contexts," plurality's (and dissent's) enlistment of federal habeas corpus judges for that purpose "alter[s] the fundamental disposition that this Court, and not individual federal district judges, has appellate jurisdiction, as to federal questions, over the supreme courts of the States"). Illustrating the similarity between direct review in the Supreme Court and habeas corpus review in the federal courts as a whole are the numerous decisions cited *infra* § 2.4b n.4 that rely on habeas corpus precedent to define the standard of review that applies to cases on direct review and rely on direct review decisions to define the standard of review that applies to habeas corpus cases. *See generally* Liebman, *supra* § 2.1 n.1, at 2041-94; Liebman & Ryan, *supra* § 2.1 n.2, at 882-84; *infra* § 2.4.

The Antiterrorism and Effective Death Penalty Act of 1996, Pub. L. 104-132, 110 Stat. 1214 (1996) (AEDPA), enhances the extent to which habeas corpus proceedings resemble federal appeals of state court determinations of federal claims by for the first time explicitly requiring federal courts in each case to review the state court "*decision*" (rather than considering de novo the claims addressed in that decision) to determine whether the decision fairly "adjudicated ... the merits" and, if so, whether the "decision ... was contrary to ... clearly established Federal law, as determined by the Supreme Court ...." 28 U.S.C.A. § 2254(d)(1) (West 1994 & Supp. 1998). *See infra* §§ 2.4b nn.8-12 and accompanying text, 30.2.

an independent civil suit"[6] that does not afford "direct" appellate, but only "collateral," review of the legality of criminal judgments.[7] Similarly, although

---

[6] Riddle v. Dyche, 262 U.S. 333, 335-36 (1923). *See, e.g., Keeney v. Tamayo-Reyes, supra,* 504 U.S. at 14 (O'Connor, J., dissenting) ("[O]ver the writ's long history, ... one thing has remained constant: Habeas corpus is not an appellate proceeding, but rather an original civil action in a federal court."); *Murray v. Giarratano, supra,* 492 U.S. at 8 (quoting *Pennsylvania v. Finley, supra,* 481 U.S. at 556); *Teague v. Lane, supra,* 489 U.S. at 308 (plurality opinion); *Browder v. Director, supra,* 434 U.S. at 269; Ex parte Tom Tong, 108 U.S. 556, 559-60 (1883).

The "original civil action" characterization is questionable for two reasons. First, as the Court has recognized since 1807, its statutory power to hear so-called "original" habeas corpus actions — ones filed directly in that Court without first having passed through a lower federal court, *see infra* Chapter 40 — cannot be squared with the strict limitations on the Court's original jurisdiction in Article III of the Constitution unless habeas corpus is an "appellate," not an "original," procedure. *See* Marbury v. Madison, 5 U.S. (1 Cranch.) 137, 175-76 (1803). And three years later, the Court, through Chief Justice Marshall, rejected an Article III challenge to its jurisdiction to hear habeas corpus actions originating in the Court, relying on the ground that habeas corpus is indeed "clearly appellate" because it involves one court's review of incarceration ordered by another court. *Ex parte Bollman, supra,* 8 U.S. (4 Cranch.) at 100-10; other authority cited *supra* note 5; *infra* §§ 2.4c n.71 and accompanying text, 2.4d nn.84-91 and accompanying text, 40.1. Absent this understanding of the writ, a whole series of statutes giving the Court jurisdiction over habeas corpus actions that originate with it — statutes that have been in place continuously from 1789 until today, *e.g.,* 28 U.S.C. §§ 2241, 2254(a) — would be unconstitutional. Second, the "original action" description arose in a case, *Ex parte Tom Tong, supra,* that was exceptional in a way that proves the rule that habeas corpus is appellate. Unlike most other habeas corpus cases that have been adjudicated in the Supreme Court, *Tom Tong* called upon the Court to review custody imposed exclusively by local administrative officials, acting in the absence of judicial warrant or judgment. *See Ex parte Tom Tong, supra* at 558-59. (The Court could hear *Tom Tong,* notwithstanding limitations on its "original" jurisdiction, because the action was first filed in a lower federal court, whose judgment denying the writ was subject to the Court's appellate jurisdiction. *See Ex parte Yerger, supra,* 75 U.S. at 103 (discussed *infra* § 40.2 nn.10-15).) In any event, *Tom Tong's* and later decisions' distancing of habeas corpus from the "criminal prosecution," and their characterization of habeas corpus as a "new" or "separate" action, is not inconsistent with understanding the *scope* of habeas corpus review as commensurate with "appellate" review. Indeed, as one partisan of the view that habeas corpus "is not an appellate proceeding, but rather an original civil action in a federal court" has recognized, numerous aspects of habeas corpus practice cannot be explained by an "original civil action" analogy — though, as is demonstrated below, they *can* be explained by an "appellate" understanding. *Keeney v. Tamayo-Reyes, supra,* 504 U.S. at 14-16 (O'Connor, J., dissenting). For example, habeas corpus' "peculiar set of hurdles" (specifically, the "exhaust[ion] ..., procedural default ... and retroactiv[ity]" doctrines and the presumption of correctness of state court factfindings) makes habeas corpus actions *more* dependent than the usual "original civil action" on related proceedings undertaken before the supposedly separate action was filed. *Id.* And the suspension of the usual *res judicata* bar on habeas corpus, but no other, original civil action makes habeas corpus proceedings considerably *less* bound by the outcome of prior related proceedings than are most other original civil proceedings. *See id.* at 15; *infra* § 2.4. As discussed *infra* §§ 2.4b, 2.4d nn.275-315, all these attributes of habeas corpus that distinguish it from ordinary original civil litigation are easily explained by — indeed, they are classic indicia of — an appellate relationship (in this case,

habeas corpus historically was "a legal, not an equitable, remedy,"[8] the Court recently has treated the writ as "governed by equitable principles."[9] Posing a

_____

between the state and federal habeas corpus courts). *See also* Liebman & Ryan, *supra* § 2.1 n.2, at 882-84 (discussing these and other attributes of habeas corpus, including its freedom from any Eleventh Amendment sovereign immunity bar, that do not characterize original civil proceedings but do characterize appellate proceedings).

[7] *See, e.g.*, *Reed v. Farley, supra,* 512 U.S. at 358 (Scalia, J., concurring in the judgment) (*"this Court*, and not individual federal district judges, has appellate jurisdiction, as to federal questions, over the supreme courts of the States"); Wright v. West, 505 U.S. 277, 292-94 (1992) (plurality opinion); *Withrow v. Williams, supra,* 507 U.S. at 697-98 (O'Connor, J., concurring in part and dissenting in part) (citing cases); Brecht v. Abrahamson, 507 U.S. 619, 622-23, 633-35 (1993) (citing cases) ("The principle that collateral review is different from direct review resounds throughout our habeas jurisprudence."); *Teague v. Lane, supra,* 489 U.S. at 306 (plurality opinion); Greer v. Miller, 483 U.S. 756, 758 (1987) (Stevens, J., concurring in the judgment); *Pennsylvania v. Finley, supra,* 481 U.S. at 555. As discussed *infra* § 2.4, the albeit common description of — or epithet for — habeas corpus as "collateral" is based on an erroneous understanding of the history of habeas corpus in this country and is an inaccurate description of the current scope of the writ. For these reasons, we use the term sparingly in this book. Notably, the Court itself has defined "collateral" remedies and "collateral" attacks on judgments in a manner that *excludes* habeas corpus. Thus, unlike collateral attacks as defined by the Court, habeas corpus has *no* "independent purpose other than to [review and, if warranted,] overturn the prior judgment." Parke v. Raley, 506 U.S. 20, 30 (1993) ("Respondent, by definition, collaterally attacked his previous convictions; he sought to deprive them of their normal force and effect in a proceeding that had an independent purpose other than to overturn the prior judgments." (citing BLACK'S LAW DICTIONARY 261 (6th ed. 1990); Lewis v. United States, 445 U.S. 55, 58, 65 (1980))). *Accord* Custis v. United States, 511 U.S. 485, 497 (1994). *Cf.* Heck v. Humphrey, 512 U.S. 477, 480-81, 484-87 (1994) (exemplifying true "collateral" attack, Court discusses plaintiff's attempted federal section 1983 suit for damages based on allegedly unconstitutional conviction, which, by virtue of collateral estoppel or other preclusion doctrines might later "'oblige [a court on postconviction review] to release him even if he hadn't sought that relief'" in his section 1983 suit in federal court). Recently, moreover, the Court recognized that the truism "'that the writ of habeas corpus will not be allowed to do service for an appeal'" simply restates a rule that applies in the Court's own, undoubtedly appellate review on *certiorari*, as well as on habeas corpus review: A litigant generally cannot bypass a fair opportunity to raise a claim on direct appeal in the state courts in hopes of later substituting review in a federal court; only after *first* raising a claim in a state appeal may it then be reviewed by a federal court. *See Reed v. Farley, supra,* 512 U.S. at 354 (quoting *Sunal v. Large,* 332 U.S. 174, 178 (1947)). Limiting review to claims previously raised "below" is, of course, a standard *appellate* practice. Likewise, the statement that "the Great Writ is an extraordinary remedy that should not be employed to 'relitigate state trials,'" McFarland v. Scott, 512 U.S. 849, 859 (1994) (quoting Barefoot v. Estelle, 463 U.S. 880, 887 (1983)), applies equally to appeals, which (like habeas corpus proceedings) are not proper forums for relitigating guilt or innocence, *see infra* § 2.5, and, instead, are generally confined to a limited set of properly preserved *legal* issues. *McFarland's* and like statements (*see, e.g.*, Ex parte Watkins, 28 U.S. (3 Pet.) 193, 203 (1833)) are particularly descriptive of federal appeals of state court judgments, which are even more severely limited to a small set of *federal* legal issues. *See infra* § 2.4d nn.75-79 and accompanying text.

[8] Hunter v. Thomas, 173 F.2d 810, 812 (10th Cir. 1949). *See, e.g., Withrow v. Williams, supra,* 507 U.S. at 697 (1993) (O'Connor, J., concurring in part and dissenting in part) ("'The Great Writ'

final paradox, Chief Justice Marshall declared that, in this country, the writ's existence and scope would be governed exclusively by Congress through statutory law, and not by judicial application of the common law of the writ as previously or subsequently developed in the courts of England, the colonies, or the States.[10] Yet, more recently, the Court has described habeas corpus as

can be traced through the common law to well before the founding of this Nation ...." (quoting *Fay v. Noia*, 372 U.S. 391, 400-01 (1963)); *Fay v. Noia, supra* at 403; 3 WILLIAM BLACKSTONE, COMMENTARIES *131-32 (Chitty rev. ed. 1832); 2 *id.* at 104-05).

[9] *Fay v. Noia, supra*, 372 U.S. at 438 (citing United States ex rel. Smith v. Baldi, 344 U.S. 561, 573 (1953) (Frankfurter, J., dissenting)). *See, e.g.,* Schlup v. Delo, 513 U.S. 298, 319 (1995) ("Court has adhered to the principle that habeas corpus is, at its core, an equitable remedy"); *Reed v. Farley, supra*, 512 U.S. at 356 (Scalia, J., concurring in the judgment); *id.* at 361 n.2 (Blackmun, J., dissenting); *Withrow v. Williams, supra*, 507 U.S. at 686-87; Herrera v. Collins, 506 U.S. 390, 403-04 (1993); Gomez v. United States Dist. Ct., 503 U.S. 653, 653-54 (1992) (*per curiam*); McCleskey v. Zant, 499 U.S. 467, 502 (1991); Dugger v. Adams, 489 U.S. 401, 410 (1989); Kuhlmann v. Wilson, 477 U.S. 436, 447 (1986); *Stone v. Powell, supra*, 428 U.S. at 492 n.31; Sanders v. United States, 373 U.S. 1, 17 (1963). *See also* 28 U.S.C. § 2243 (1994) (federal courts shall "dispose of [habeas corpus applications] as law *and* justice require" (emphasis added)). Recourse to equitable concerns can lead to conflicting conclusions. *Compare Withrow v. Williams, supra*, 507 U.S. at 699-700 (O'Connor, J., concurring in part and dissenting in part) ("[c]oncerns for equity ... resonate throughout our habeas jurisprudence" and, among other concerns, "warrant restraint ... when [the Court] is asked to exclude a substantive category of issues from relitigation on habeas") *with id.* at 716-18 (Scalia, J., concurring in part and dissenting in part) ("restraints that accompany the [habeas corpus court's] exercise of equitable discretion" require rule excluding most substantive categories of issues from relitigation on habeas corpus in most circumstances). In Lonchar v. Thomas, 517 U.S. 314 (1996), the Court acknowledged "the fact that the writ has been called an 'equitable' remedy" but made clear that this characterization "does not authorize a court to ignore th[e governing] body of statutes, rules, and precedents"; "'courts of equity must be governed by rules and precedents no less than the courts of law.'" *Id.* at 323 (quoting Missouri v. Jenkins, 515 U.S. 70, 127 (1995); other citation omitted). Although praising "equitable rules that guide lower courts, reduce uncertainty, avoid unfair surprise, minimize disparate treatment of similar cases, and thereby help all litigants, including the State, whose interests in 'finality' such rules often further," the Court in *Lonchar* strongly resisted "*ad hoc* departure from settled rules ... particularly ... when dismissal of a first petition is at issue," *id.* at 324, and efforts "to try to devise some sensible way of supplementing first federal habeas rules with *ad hoc* equitable devices," *id.* at 330. "[G]iven the importance of a first federal habeas petition, it is particularly important that any rule that would deprive inmates of all access to the writ should be both clear and fair." *Id.*

[10] *Ex parte Bollman, supra*, 8 U.S. (4 Cranch.) at 93. *Accord, e.g.,* Brown v. Allen, 344 U.S. 443, 499, 500, 501 (1953) (opinion for the Court of Frankfurter, J.). *See, e.g., Lonchar v. Thomas, supra*, 517 U.S. at 324, 328 (discussed *supra* note 9) (noting "inappropriateness of amending [habeas corpus statutes and rules], in effect, through an *ad hoc* judicial exception, rather than through congressional legislation or through the formal rulemaking process"; Court's precedents have not "authorized *ad hoc* departures from the Habeas Corpus Rules"); *Schlup v. Delo, supra*, 513 U.S. at 350 (Scalia, J., dissenting) (quoted *infra* § 2.4d n.86). Congress's broad effort to regulate habeas corpus practice and procedure via Title I of the Antiterrorism and Effective Death Penalty Act of 1996, Pub. L. 104-132, 110 Stat. 1214 (1996), which is described *infra* § 3.2, seemingly underscores the writ's statutory nature. In the brief time that AEDPA has been in effect,

governed less by "statutory developments" than by "a complex and evolving body of equitable principles informed and controlled by historical usage ... and judicial decisions."[11] In the latter vein, the Court repeatedly has pronounced itself "willing[] to overturn or modify its earlier views of the scope of the writ, even where the statutory language authorizing judicial action has remained unchanged."[12] And it has freely "filled the gaps of the habeas corpus statute" with procedures and doctrines of a breadth and complexity that generally are thought to be the province of the legislature — even, recently, in contexts over which, and during periods when, Congress has arguably sought to reassign control over the writ to itself.[13]

---

however, the Court's interpretations have been at least as attentive to the Court's own precedents and sense of fairness as to the statute's plain terms, particularly when that more open-ended approach has avoided undue restrictions upon the availability of federal habeas corpus review. *See infra* note 13 and accompanying text; *infra* § 3.2 nn.38-43 and accompanying text.

[11] *McCleskey v. Zant, supra*, 499 U.S. at 489. *See* Jones v. Cunningham, 371 U.S. 236, 243 (1963) (habeas corpus "is not now and has never been a static, narrow, formalistic remedy; its scope has grown to achieve its grand purpose — the protection of individuals against erosion of their right to be free from wrongful restraints upon their liberty"). *See also infra* notes 21-25 and accompanying text. Discussing "Habeas as Federal Common Law" is Steiker, *supra* § 2.1 n.1, at 322-42. An example of the limited relevance of the habeas corpus statute is *Reed v. Farley, supra*. There, five members of the Court read a statute establishing habeas corpus jurisdiction over *all* "custody in violation of the Constitution *or laws* or treaties of the United States," 28 U.S.C. § 2254(a) (emphasis added), to withhold jurisdiction over *some* custody in violation of some laws of the United States. *Reed v. Farley, supra*, 512 U.S. at 348-49 (plurality opinion); *id.* at 356-58 (Scalia, J., concurring). *But see id.* at 369 (Blackmun, J., dissenting) ("the prerogative writ of habeas corpus should be exercised in accord with an express legislative command").

[12] Wainwright v. Sykes, 433 U.S. 72, 81 (1977).

[13] Brecht v. Abrahamson, 507 U.S. 619, 631-32, 632-33 (1993). *Accord* O'Neal v. McAninch, 513 U.S. 432, 445 (1995) ("When faced with ... gaps in the habeas statute, we have 'look[ed] first to the considerations underlying our habeas jurisprudence, and then determine[d] whether the proposed rule would advance or inhibit these considerations by weighing the marginal costs and benefits of its application on collateral review.'" (quoting *Brecht v. Abrahamson, supra*, 507 U.S. at 633)); Schlup v. Delo, 513 U.S. 298, 319 n.35 (1995) ("This Court has repeatedly noted the interplay between statutory language and judicially managed equitable considerations in the development of habeas corpus jurisprudence" (collecting quotations and citations)).

The first great example of the Court's peculiarly capacious notion of its authority to expand or contract the *statutory* remedy of habeas corpus is the Court's creation of the "exhaustion of state remedies" prerequisite to habeas corpus relief in Ex parte Royall, 117 U.S. 241 (1886), which the Court applied for 62 years before Congress codified it in 1948 in 28 U.S.C. § 2254(b). *See* Amsterdam, *supra* § 2.1 n.1, at 884-908 (criticizing Court's apparently cavalier adoption of exhaustion requirement). *Cf.* Darby v. Cisneros, 509 U.S. 137, 144-45 (1993) ("'of "paramount importance" to any exhaustion inquiry is congressional intent.'" (quoting McCarthy v. Madigan, 503 U.S. 140, 144 (1992); Patsy v. Board of Regents, 457 U.S. 496, 501 (1982))).

Also evidencing the Court's belief in its broad power unilaterally to supplement the statute, but exercising that power to expand rather than contract the writ, the Court in 1963 simultaneously (1) expanded substantially its interpretation of the statutory "custody" prerequisite for habeas corpus relief, *Jones v. Cunningham, supra,* 371 U.S. at 243; (2) widened the availability of habeas corpus to petitioners who defaulted their federal claims in the state courts, *Fay v. Noia, supra,* 372 U.S. at 426, 438-39; (3) expanded the availability of evidentiary hearings in habeas corpus cases, Townsend v. Sain, 372 U.S. 293 (1963); (4) admonished the lower federal courts to exercise caution before dismissing petitions, especially ones prepared without legal assistance, that instead might be amended to state valid grounds for relief, *Sanders v. United States, supra,* 373 U.S. at 19; and (5) took a broad view of the propriety of second or "successive" petitions, *id.* at 6-15. *See also* Linkletter v. Walker, 381 U.S. 618 (1965) (adopting broad approach to retroactivity of new constitutional rules in habeas corpus proceedings).

Although Congress acted fairly quickly to confirm some of these expansions of the writ, *see* 28 U.S.C. §§ 2244, 2254(d) (revised or adopted in 1966; affecting successive petitions and evidentiary hearings) and Rules 4, 6, 8, 9(b), and 11 of the Rules Governing § 2254 Cases (adopted in 1976; affecting summary dismissal, evidentiary hearings, successive petitions, and amendment of petitions), the Court since 1977 has repeatedly harked back to its 1963 cases to support dramatic re-revisions and contractions of its doctrine governing the availability of habeas corpus in cases involving (a) claims defaulted in the state courts, *see* Coleman v. Thompson, 501 U.S. 722, 744-752 (1991) (overruling *Fay v. Noia, supra,* and acknowledging broad shifts in Court's treatment of procedural defaults from Brown v. Allen, 344 U.S. 443 (1953) to *Fay* to *Wainwright v. Sykes, supra,* and thereafter); Murray v. Carrier, 477 U.S. 478, 496-97 (1986); *Wainwright v. Sykes, supra,* 433 U.S. at 81, (b) second or successive petitions, *Schlup v. Delo, supra* at 319 & n.35; *McCleskey v. Zant, supra,* 499 U.S. at 489 ("Because of historical changes and the complexity of the subject, the Court has not 'always followed an unwavering line in its conclusions as to the availability of the Great Writ.'" (quoting *Fay v. Noia, supra,* 372 U.S. at 411-12)); *Kuhlmann v. Wilson, supra,* 477 U.S. at 452-54 (plurality opinion of Powell, J.), (c) the requested retroactive application of new rules of law, *see* Teague v. Lane, 489 U.S. 288, 305-10 (1989) (plurality opinion), and (d) violations that are not obviously prejudicial or prejudicial as a matter of law, *see Brecht v. Abrahamson, supra,* 507 U.S. at 631-32, 632-33. *See also Stone v. Powell, supra,* 428 U.S. at 478 n.11. *But cf. Brecht v. Abrahamson, supra,* 507 U.S. at 650 (O'Connor, J., dissenting) (decisions cutting back on "the Great Writ 'warrant restraint,' ... for we ought not take lightly alteration of that "'fundamental safeguard against unlawful custody.'"" (quoting *Withrow v. Williams, supra,* 507 U.S. at 700 (O'Connor, J., concurring in part and dissenting in part); *Fay v. Noia, supra,* 372 U.S. at 449 (Harlan, J., dissenting))). *But see Lonchar v. Thomas, supra,* 517 U.S. at 324, 328 (quoted *supra* note 10).

Even in interpreting Congress's relatively detailed and comprehensive modifications of the habeas corpus statute in the Antiterrorism and Effective Death Penalty Act (AEDPA), Pub. L. 104-132, 110 Stat. 1214 (1996), the Court thus far has paid rather closer attention to its own precedents and its own notions of a fair and functional federal postconviction remedy than to the plain terms of the new statute. *See, e.g.,* Hohn v. United States, 118 S. Ct. 1969 (1998) (discussed *infra* § 3.2 nn.39-42 and accompanying text); Stewart v. Martinez-Villareal, 118 S. Ct. 1618 (1998) (discussed *infra* § 3.2 nn.38, 40-42 and accompanying text). *See also* Calderon v. Thompson, 118 S. Ct. 1489, 1500, 1502-03 (1998) (in post-AEDPA case, Court relies on its own pre-AEDPA precedent to devise restriction on use of *sua sponte* recalls of the mandate to frustrate limitations on successive habeas corpus litigation, even though standard adopted admittedly is "more lenient" than AEDPA's restrictions on successive habeas corpus litigation).

As we note *infra* § 2.4d nn.271-315 and accompanying text, it is important not to overstate the impact of the Court's exercise of a broad judicial power to interpret — and in the process to "amend" — the habeas corpus statute. Apart from the Court's creation of the exhaustion doctrine (which, we show, occurred at the behest of Congress, *see infra* § 2.4d nn.154-83 and

The Court's description of the writ as a prisoner-initiated civil remedy informed by equitable principles, and as a statutory procedure over which the courts, or at least the Court, exercises broad regulatory power, has several strategic, tactical, and adjudicative implications that may not be obvious. First, unlike in criminal proceedings, the litigative initiative in habeas corpus belongs to the individual whose liberty is being restrained.[14] It thus falls to the petitioner, at least in the first instance, to: select among the various procedures available to the parties (*e.g.*, pretrial motions, discovery, hearings, and briefing[15]); determine to the limited extent possible the timing and order of those procedures and to suggest an appropriate schedule for procedures controlled by the court; define the determinative factual and legal issues; and generally shape the form and

---

accompanying text) and its broadening of the definition of "custody" (which the Court may now be in the process of narrowing, *see* Spencer v. Kemna, 118 S. Ct. 978 (1998) (discussed *infra* §§ 8.2b nn.10-12, 8.2d n.33)), most of the Court's quasi-legislative actions in regard to the writ have occurred in the last 35 years and have largely canceled each other out via a series of narrowing decisions in the 1970s-1990s that undid the effect of a set of broadening decisions in the mid-1960s — leaving the writ about where it had been for the remainder of the nation's history. Indeed, the Court's moderating interpretations of AEDPA seem calculated to preserve the balance of fairness, functionality, and finality that the Court's habeas corpus decisions have so painstakingly stricken in the last two decades. See *supra* next preceding paragraph; *infra* §§ 2.4d n.315 and accompanying text, 3.2 nn.38-42 and accompanying text.

Justice Scalia has insisted that the Court hew more closely to the habeas corpus statute and disclaim any authority to substitute for "what the statute says" some view of "what is the fairest standard to apply." *Schlup v. Delo*, *supra* at 342-43 (Scalia, J., dissenting) ("[a] federal statute ... specifically addresses the problem of second and subsequent petitions for the writ of habeas corpus," but "[r]ather than asking what the statute says, or even what we have said the statute says, the Court asks only what is the fairest standard to apply, and answers that question by looking to the various semi-consistent standards articulated in our most recent decisions — minutely parsing phrases, and seeking shades of meaning in the interstices of sentences and words, as though a discursive judicial opinion were a statute"; Court should "proceed differently" because "[w]ithin the very broad limits set by the Suspension Clause, U.S. Const., Art. I, § 9, cl. 2, the federal writ of habeas corpus is governed by statute," and it should "control[ ]" as long as "disposition [statute] announces is plain enough, and our decisions contain nothing that would justify departure from that plain meaning"); *id.* at 350 (flexible "process of statutory interpretation that shades easily into a sort of federal common law" may be appropriate when statute has "gaps and ambiguities" that need to be "filled or clarified" but violates Article III constraints on judicial power when used to settle the "many legal questions on which the habeas corpus statute is neither silent nor ambiguous"). *See also Hohn v. United States*, *supra*, 118 S. Ct. at 1979, 1984 (Scalia, J., dissenting) (discussed *infra* § 3.2 nn.40, 42); *Stewart v. Martinez-Villareal*, *supra*, 118 S. Ct. at 1623 (Scalia, J., dissenting) (discussed *infra* § 3.2 nn.40, 42).

[14]*See O'Neal v. McAninch*, *supra*, 513 U.S. at 446 (Thomas, J., dissenting) ("The habeas petitioner comes to federal court as a plaintiff ... [who] 'seeks to change the present state of affairs....'" (citation omitted)).

[15] *See infra* Chapters 12-14, 17-20, 29.

substance of the litigation through devices that plaintiffs in civil litigation typically have at their disposal.

Second, the means of achieving both the parties' substantive objectives and the courts' justice, orderliness, and efficiency goals are broader and more flexible in the "civil" habeas corpus context than in criminal actions. Subject to a requirement of "fact" rather than "notice" pleading,[16] a greater degree of discretion on the part of the court than in other civil proceedings,[17] a greater capacity by the court to deny relief *sua sponte* in advance of adversary proceedings,[18] and stringent penalties for procedural defaults occurring in the state courts before federal litigation is initiated,[19] the tools available to habeas corpus judges and litigants include the full range of civil procedural devices — *e.g.*, sophisticated pleading, motions practice, summary judgment, magistrate judge practice, pretrial conferences, a range of fact-development procedures, pre- and post-trial briefs, proposed factfindings and legal conclusions, and fully developed written opinions.[20]

Third, flexibility is enhanced yet more by the equitable principles and broad adjudicative and interpretive powers that characterize habeas corpus practice. With the possible exception of some recent applications of the procedural default doctrine mentioned above, the remedy has not been characterized "by simple, rigid rules which, by avoiding some abuses, generate others,"[21] nor by "interpretations ... that would suffocate ... or hobble [the writ's] effectiveness with the manacles of arcane and scholastic procedural requirements."[22] Rather, "[t]he very nature of the writ demands that it be administered with the initiative and flexibility essential to ensure that miscarriages of justice within its reach are surfaced and corrected"[23] and that preclusive doctrines and formalities "yield to

---

[16] *See infra* § 11.6.

[17] *Compare, e.g.*, Rule 6 of the Rules Governing § 2254 Cases (discovery available only upon an order of the court) *with, e.g.*, FED. R. CIV. P. 26-37 (party-initiated discovery). *See generally* Granberry v. Greer, 481 U.S. 129 (1987) (confirming habeas corpus courts' powers to insist on certain nonjurisdictionally required procedures that both parties would prefer to forgo); *infra* Chapter 19.

[18] *Compare, e.g.*, Rule 4 of the Rules Governing § 2254 Cases (court may *sua sponte* dismiss petition on pleadings without requiring answer by respondent) *with, e.g.*, FED. R. CIV. P. 12 (mandatory answer; defendant-initiated motions for judgment on pleadings). *See generally infra* § 15.2.

[19] *See infra* Chapter 26.

[20] *See supra* note 4; *infra* Chapters 11, 17-21, 29. *See generally* Rules 2-8 of the Rules Governing § 2254 Cases.

[21] Brown v. Allen, 344 U.S. 443, 498 (1953) (Frankfurter, J., for the Court).

[22] Hensley v. Municipal Court, 411 U.S. 345, 349-50 (1973).

[23] Harris v. Nelson, 394 U.S. 286, 291 (1969). *See id.* (habeas corpus review affords federal courts the "ability to cut through barriers of form and procedural rules"); Frank v. Mangum, 237 U.S. 309, 346 (1915) (Holmes, J., dissenting).

the imperative of correcting ... fundamentally unjust incarceration."[24] Even when procedures are contemplated that are novel or out of the ordinary, or when procedural obstacles to an apparently just outcome arise, the federal courts retain the statutory power and the duty to "dispose of the matter as law and justice require."[25]

Finally, because federal habeas corpus litigants and courts have the power to mobilize labels as contradictory as "criminal" and "civil," "collateral" and "appellate," "legal" and "equitable," and "statutory" and "common law" — and to mobilize doctrines as flexible as those on the right side of each of those dichotomies — the descriptions of the writ discussed here leave considerable uncertainty and unpredictability about the purpose and uses of the writ.[26] In the next four sections, therefore, we search for a unified conceptual framework for the writ that moves beyond mere labels. We conclude that a unified framework *has* seemed to characterize the American writ for at least the first 207 years of its existence, surviving important statutory and judicial revisions of habeas corpus practice in, *e.g.*, 1833, 1867, 1886, 1915-1923, 1948, 1966, and 1989. Some circuit courts, however, have recently interpreted a provision of the Antiterrorism and Effective Death Penalty Act of 1996[27] — 28 U.S.C. § 2254(d)(1) — to abandon that longstanding framework.[28] Whether the statute warrants that construction — and, if so, whether it is constitutional — is discussed briefly in §§ 2.4b and 2.4d[29] and in detail in §§ 30.2c and 30.2d.

§ 2.3. The broad rhetoric and applications of the writ.[1]

The dry jurisprudential labels discussed in section 2.2 should not obscure the substantive importance of the Great Writ of Habeas Corpus in Anglo-American jurisprudence. To fill out the picture a bit, we present some authoritative descriptions of the writ over three centuries and more and refer to some examples of

---

[24] Engle v. Isaac, 456 U.S. 107, 135 (1982).

[25] 28 U.S.C. § 2243 (1994).

[26] *See, e.g., supra* note 9 (discussing contradictory views reached in separate opinions in *Withrow v. Williams, supra,* on basis of same label of habeas corpus as "equitable").

[27] Pub. L. 104-132, 110 Stat. 1214 (1996).

[28] *See infra* § 30.2c nn.35-37 (citing decisions).

[29] *See infra* § 2.4d nn.316-23 and accompanying text.

§ 2.3. [1] On the history of habeas corpus, in addition to the sources cited *supra* § 2.1 n.1, see generally W. CHURCH, A TREATISE ON THE WRIT OF HABEAS CORPUS (1893); WILLIAM F. DUKER, A CONSTITUTIONAL HISTORY OF HABEAS CORPUS (1981); 1 WILLIAM S. HOLDSWORTH, HISTORY OF ENGLISH LAW 202, 227-28 (1922); 9 *id.* at 109-25 (1926); 10 *id.* at 397, 658-72 (1938); ROLLIN C. HURD, A TREATISE ON THE RIGHT OF PERSONAL LIBERTY, AND ON THE WRIT OF HABEAS CORPUS (1876); DANIEL J. MEADOR, HABEAS CORPUS AND MAGNA CARTA — DUALISM OF POWER AND

its application over three decades and more. Doing so suggests what we set out to prove in section 2.4 — that breadth and continuity, not historical expansion and recent contraction, are the principal characteristics of the writ's function in our legal tradition.

Consider, for example, the 17th century English view of the writ as assuring that "[n]o freeman shall be imprisoned without due process of law" and that "the cause of ... commitment be just or legal."[2] And consider Blackstone's 18th

---

LIBERTY (1966); RONALD P. SOKOL, FEDERAL HABEAS CORPUS 3-21, 308-40, 346-47 (1969) (collecting sources); ROBERT S. WALKER, THE AMERICAN RECEPTION OF THE WRIT OF LIBERTY (1961); ROBERT S. WALKER, THE CONSTITUTIONAL AND LEGAL DEVELOPMENT OF HABEAS CORPUS AS THE WRIT OF LIBERTY (1960); Zechariah Chafee, Jr., *The Most Important Human Right in the Constitution,* 32 B.U. L. REV. 143 (1952); Maxwell Cohen, *Habeas Corpus Cum Causa: The Emergence of the Modern Writ,* 18 CANADIAN B. REV. 10 (1940); Maxwell Cohen, *Some Considerations on the Origins of Habeas Corpus,* 16 CANADIAN B. REV. 92 (1938); Rex A. Collings, Jr., *Habeas Corpus for Convicts — Constitutional Right or Legislative Grace?,* 40 CALIF. L. REV. 335 (1952); William F. Duker, *The English Origins of the Writ of Habeas Corpus: A Peculiar Path to Fame,* 53 N.Y.U. L. REV. 983 (1978); Eric M. Freedman, *The Suspension Clause in the Ratification Debates,* 44 BUFF. L. REV. 451 (1996); Christian G. Fritz, *A Nineteenth Century "Habeas Corpus Mill": The Chinese Before the Federal Courts in California,* 32 AM. J. LEGAL. HIST. 347 (1988); Edward Jenks, *The Story of Habeas Corpus,* 18 L.Q. REV. 64 (1902); George F. Longsdorf, *The Federal Habeas Corpus Acts Original and Amended,* 13 F.R.D. 407 (1953); Lewis Mayers, *The Habeas Corpus Act of 1867: The Supreme Court as Legal Historian,* 33 U. CHI. L. REV. 31 (1965); Dallin H. Oaks, *Habeas Corpus in the States — 1776-1863,* 32 U. CHI. L. REV. 243 (1965); Dallin H. Oaks, *Legal History in the High Court — Habeas Corpus,* 64 MICH. L. REV. 451 (1966); Francis Paschal, *The Constitution and Habeas Corpus,* 1970 DUKE L.J. 605; Jordan Steiker, *Incorporating the Suspension Clause: Is There a Constitutional Right to Federal Habeas Corpus for State Prisoners?,* 92 MICH. L. REV. 862 (1994).

[2] Darnell's (the Five Knights') Case, 3 St. Trials 1 (K.B. 1627) (argument of counsel) (quoted in MEADOR, *supra* note 1, at 15); Habeas Corpus Act, 1641, 16 Car. 1, ch. 10. *See* MEADOR, *supra* note 1, at 25 (by mid-17th century, habeas corpus was *"the* mode for vindicating the liberty of the subject by protecting him against confinement contrary to the due process of law" (emphasis in original)). The passage of the 1641 Act at the beginning of the struggle between Parliament and King Charles I reveals the writ's long usage as a method by which one branch of government checks another's exercise of arbitrary power. Note also Professor Sokol's discussion of the law and equity courts' frequent reliance on habeas corpus in the 15th through 17th centuries as a weapon "in the power struggle" between the two systems. SOKOL, *supra* note 1, at 6-8. As in this country since the Civil War, this "inter-court competition" (*id.* at 7) was played out in England through one court system's invocation of the writ as a quasi-appellate mechanism for reviewing decisions of the other system. In this country, however, the acceptance of the supremacy of federal over state law and of the supremacy of federal judicial — or, at least, Supreme Court — interpretations of federal law over state judges' interpretations makes habeas corpus look less like a chronic source of intercourt friction and competition and more like a constitutionally sanctioned device for using appellate, intercourt review as a check on the abusive parochial tendencies of local governments and courts. *See generally* Liebman & Ryan, supra § 2.1 n.2. The history of the writ in 17th and 18th Century England is discussed in more detail in LIEBMAN, *supra* § 2.1 n.1, § 2.2b nn.5, 6 and authorities cited there.

century description of the writ as "efficacious ... in all manners of illegal confinement."[3] And Alexander Hamilton's statement in *The Federalist* that habeas corpus should be (and in the Suspension Clause of the proposed Constitution[4] was) "provided for in the most ample manner" as a bulwark against "arbitrary methods of prosecuting pretended offenses, and arbitrary punishment upon arbitrary convictions."[5] Consider also the Supreme Court's 1830 understanding of the statutory habeas corpus remedy available in this country as "in the nature of a writ of error, to examine the legality of the commitment" and "to liberate an individual from unlawful imprisonment";[6] the lower federal courts' antebellum interpretation of habeas corpus as a privilege designed to ensure that no "arbitrary authority might act without warrant, or 'due process of law'" as the latter words were used in the 5th Amendment (1861);[7] and the Supreme Court's various post-bellum characterizations of the writ as a judicial remedy "for every possible case of privation of liberty contrary to the National Constitution, treaties or laws," whose scope "is impossible to widen" (1867);[8] a remedy available whenever a state prisoner "is held in custody in violation of the

---

[3] WILLIAM BLACKSTONE, COMMENTARIES 129 (6th ed. 1775).

[4] *See* U.S. CONST., art. 1, § 9, cl. 2. On the Suspension Clause, see generally Collings, *supra* note 1; Steiker, *supra* note 1; *infra* § 7.2d.

[5] THE FEDERALIST No. 83, at 499 (A. Hamilton) (Clinton Rossiter ed. 1961). *See also id.* No. 83, at 499 (arguing that jury trials and habeas corpus, by themselves, were sufficient protections against "judicial despotism" in criminal cases so that additional protections of sort later included in Bill of Rights were unnecessary); *id.* No. 84, at 511-12 (habeas corpus assured to redress "arbitrary imprisonments"). *The Federalist* is authority for more than just the constitutional importance of habeas corpus, including (1) the replacement of the States with individuals as the fundamental constituents of the nation, *see id.* Nos. 15, 16, 22, 23; (2) the need for national institutions to protect national law and individual liberties against local predispositions to subordinate them, *see id.* Nos. 3, 9, 10, 46, 51, 60 — with the Supreme Court and the *lower* federal judiciary listed prominently among those national institutions, *see id.* Nos. 10, 15, 21, 22, 39, 47-49, 51, 78, 80-82; (3) the recognition that state judges were not equal to federal judges in their disposition and ability to protect national law and individual liberties, *see id.* Nos. 10, 15-17, 22, 31, 33, 47-49, 51, 65, 78, 79, 81, 82; and (4) the recognition that state constitutions and governments lacked the structural protections for minority rights built into the national Constitution and government, thus presaging the post-Civil War Amendments' extension to the States of the Constitution's protection of minorities, *see id.* Nos. 44, 49-51, 58, 63, 65, 78.

[6] Ex parte Watkins, 28 U.S. 193, 202, 203 (1830) (discussed in Peller, *supra* § 2.1 n.1, at 611-12; *infra* § 2.4d nn.92-109 and accompanying text).

[7] In re McDonald, 16 F. Cas. 17, 21 (E.D. Mo. 1861) (No. 8,751).

[8] Ex parte McCardle, 73 U.S. (6 Wall.) 318, 325-26 (1867). *McCardle* interpreted the Habeas Corpus Act of 1867, many important provisions of which, with only technical modifications, remain in the habeas corpus statute today. Act of Feb. 5, 1867, ch. 28, § 1, 14 Stat. 385, *codified with amendments at* 28 U.S.C. §§ 2241-2243, 2254(a). *See infra* § 2.4d nn.114-26 and accompanying text.

Fourteenth Amendment ... in that the State thereby deprives him of liberty without due process of law ... [or abridges] his privileges and immunities as a citizen of the United States, ... [or denies him] the equal protection of the laws" (1890);[9] an assurance that the petitioner "was not deprived of his liberty without due process of law, ... so as to violate the provisions of the Fourteenth Amendment to the Federal Constitution" (1906);[10] a procedure for "securing to the petitioners their constitutional rights" (1923);[11] the means "by which the legality of the detention of one in the custody of another [court] could be tested judicially" (1934);[12] a mechanism "to test the constitutional validity of a conviction for crime" (1942);[13] a remedy giving "the final say" to the federal courts as to whether or not "State Supreme Courts have denied rights guaranteed by the United States Constitution" (1953);[14] and a federal judicial authority "conferred by the allegation of an unconstitutional restraint [that] is not defeated by anything that may occur in the state court proceedings" (1963).[15] Consider that the Court continues today to treat habeas corpus as a forum "for litigating constitutional claims generally" (1976),[16] a procedure in which "a state prisoner's challenge to the trial court's resolution of dispositive federal issues is always fair game [for] federal [review]" (1977),[17] a remedy designed "'to interpose the federal courts between the States and the people, as guardians of the people's federal rights — to protect the people from unconstitutional action'" (1984),[18] a procedure for resolving "all dispositive constitutional claims

---

[9] In re Converse, 137 U.S. 624, 631 (1890).

[10] Felts v. Murphy, 201 U.S. 123, 129 (1906). *Accord, e.g.,* Harlan v. McGourin, 218 U.S. 442, 445, 447 (1910) ("The writ of *habeas corpus* [is] to determin[e] whether the person restrained of his liberty is detained without authority of law" or whether there has been "a denial of a right secured under the Federal Constitution"). *See infra* § 2.4d nn.154-97 and accompanying text.

[11] Moore v. Dempsey, 261 U.S. 86, 87-88, 91 (1923) (Holmes, J., for the Court). *See infra* 2.4d nn.211-38 and accompanying text.

[12] McNally v. Hill, 293 U.S. 131, 136 (1934).

[13] Waley v. Johnson, 316 U.S. 101, 104-05 (1942) (*per curiam*). *See also* United States v. Kennedy, 157 F.2d 811, 813 (2d Cir. 1947) (L. Hand, J.) ("The writ is available, not only to determine points of jurisdiction, stricti juris, and constitutional questions; but whenever else resort to it is necessary to prevent a complete miscarriage of justice"); Ex parte Craig, 282 F. 138, 155-56 (2d Cir. 1922) (L. Hand, J., dissenting). *See infra* § 2.4d nn.239-60 and accompanying text.

[14] Brown v. Allen, 344 U.S. 443, 500, 510 (1953) (opinion of Frankfurter, J., for the Court). *See infra* § 2.4d nn.239-60 and accompanying text.

[15] Fay v. Noia, 372 U.S. 391, 426 (1963).

[16] Stone v. Powell, 428 U.S. 465, 495 n.37 (1976) (discussed *infra* §§ 2.4d nn.280-89 and accompanying text, 9.2).

[17] Wainwright v. Sykes, 433 U.S. 72, 79 (1977).

[18] Reed v. Ross, 468 U.S. 1, 10 (1984) (quoting Mitchum v. Foster, 407 U.S. 225, 242 (1972)).

presented in a proper procedural manner" (1991),[19] "'today, as it has always been, a fundamental safeguard against unlawful custody ... [that is available to cure any] detention ... "in violation of the Constitution or laws or treaties of the United States""'" (1993),[20] a remedy whose "most basic traditions and purposes" are to "avoid a grievous wrong — holding a person 'in custody in violation of the Constitution ... of the United States'" — and "thereby both [to] protect[ ] individuals from unconstitutional convictions and [to] help[ ] to guarantee the integrity of the criminal process by assuring that trials are fundamentally fair" (1995);[21] and a remedy that "'has been for centuries esteemed the best and only sufficient defense of personal freedom,'" which, if withdrawn, "risk[s] injury to an important interest in human liberty" (1996).[22] And consider, finally, the vast array of violations of fundamental federal norms in the course of incarcerating individuals that habeas corpus has stood to redress over the last several decades, some of which are collected in section 11.2c *infra*, and the high rate (42 percent of the published cases, 47 percent of the cases subject to review if the unpublished cases are included) at which habeas corpus relief has been granted to capitally sentenced petitioners over the last two decades.[23]

---

[19] McCleskey v. Zant, 499 U.S. 467, 479 (1991).

[20] Withrow v. Williams, 507 U.S. 680, 697-98 (1993) (O'Connor, J., concurring in part and dissenting in part) (quoting Fay v. Noia, 372 U.S. 391, 449 (1963) (Harlan, J., dissenting)). *See, e.g.*, McFarland v. Scott, 512 U.S. 849, 872 (1994) (Thomas, J., dissenting) ("the habeas statute provides federal courts with exceptional powers"); *Withrow v. Williams, supra* at 715 (Scalia, J., concurring in part and dissenting in part) (habeas corpus jurisdiction is "sweeping in its breadth"); Herrera v. Collins, 506 U.S. 390, 403 (1993) (habeas corpus is available to provide relief for "*any* constitutional violation which had occurred at the first trial" (emphasis added)); Teague v. Lane, 489 U.S. 288, 306 (1989) (plurality opinion) (noting "'broad scope of constitutional issues cognizable on habeas'" (citation omitted)); *infra* §§ 2.4b, 2.4d nn.261-315 and accompanying text.

[21] O'Neal v. McAninch, 513 U.S. 432, 442 (1995).

[22] Lonchar v. Thomas, 517 U.S. 314, 324 (1996) (quoting Ex parte Yerger, 75 U.S. (8 Wall.) 85, 95 (1869)). *See also* Bousley v. United States, 118 S. Ct. 1604, 1610 (1998) (among "'principal functions of habeas corpus [is] "to assure that no man has been incarcerated under a procedure which creates an impermissibly large risk that the innocent will be convicted"'" (citations omitted)).

[23] Brief *Amici Curiae* of Benjamin Civiletti, *et al.*, in Support of Respondent in *Wright v. West*, No. 91-542, 505 U.S. 277 (1992) (filed Mar. 4, 1992), at App. B (upon finally reviewing 357 state capital judgments between July 1, 1976 and May 31, 1991, published opinions of federal habeas corpus courts found reversible constitutional error affecting the conviction or the death sentence in 149 (42%) of the cases; the rate of violations found was essentially the same during both halves of the period studied — 42% between 1978 and 1984; 41% between 1985 and 1991; when unpublished cases also are included, the proportion of cases in which reversible constitutional error was found on habeas corpus review rises to 47% (191/404); in the 70 Georgia capital judgments reviewed during the period, constitutional violations were found in 46 (66%) of the cases). *See* Liebman & Ryan, *supra* § 2.1 n.2, at 865 n.802 (reporting initial results of extension of same study through first Monday in October, 1995, which reveals that reversal rate between 1976 and 1995

These descriptions and applications of habeas corpus give the impression, at least, that for centuries the writ has served the same essential function, at essentially the same intergovernmental and intercourt junctions in the Anglo-American system of criminal justice,[24] of judicially ferrying persons whom the government, through restraints, has separated from their rights under the fundamental Law of the Land to the safe harbor afforded by that Law. It may not be accurate, then, to say (as the current orthodoxy holds[25]) that the same ferry boat, traversing the same constitutional crossing, was not previously a ferry boat — simply because the amount of its cargo and frequency of its trips have increased over time.

§ 2.4. A surrogate for Supreme Court review as of right.[1]

a. *Introduction.* This section describes the parity that has long existed in this country between direct Supreme Court and habeas corpus review of state

was 38.5% (232/603) and in 1995 was 42.9% (9/21)). *See also* McFarland v. Scott, 512 U.S. 1256, 1263 (1994) (Blackmun, J., dissenting from denial of *certiorari*) ("Of the capital cases reviewed in federal habeas corpus proceedings between 1976 and 1991, nearly half (46%) were found to have constitutional error.... The total reversal rate of capital cases at all [appellate as well as postconviction] stages of review during the same time period was estimated at 60% or more." (citing James S. Liebman, *More Than "Slightly Retro": The Rehnquist Court's Rout of Habeas Corpus Jurisdiction in* Teague v. Lane, 18 N.Y.U. REV. L. & SOC. CHANGE 537, 541 n.15 (1990-1991) (discussing initial results of study reported in Civiletti *Amici Curiae* Brief, *supra*)); Whitmore v. Arkansas, 495 U.S. 149, 170-71 (1990) (Marshall, J., dissenting) (collecting numerous studies revealing modern post-trial reversal rates of anywhere from 30% to 70% in capital cases compared to similar reversal rate of 6.5% in noncapital cases). The high rate at which habeas corpus petitions are filed in capital cases (close to 100%) and the high rate at which relief is granted on those petitions contrasts dramatically with the very low rates of filing and relief in noncapital cases. *Compare* Meltzer, *supra* § 2.1 n.1, at 2524 (roughly estimating that only three to four of every thousand persons convicted in state prosecutions and committed to custody in any given year actually file habeas corpus petitions and that only 3.2% of petitions filed by 7.3% of petitioners result in relief; thus, "out of every 100,000 persons committed to state custody, no more than about 30 [.03%] obtain federal habeas relief") *with, e.g.,* Heck v. Humphrey, 512 U.S. 477, 480 (1994) (calling habeas corpus a "fertile source[] of federal-court prisoner litigation").

[24] *See supra* note 2.

[25] *Cf. infra* § 2.4c nn.39-44 and accompanying text (currently orthodox description of habeas corpus as having steadily expanded since latter half of 19th century and, particularly, since 1915 (or, sometimes, 1953)).

§ **2.4.** [1] Secondary sources are collected *supra* § 2.1 n.1 (general theories of habeas corpus), 2.3 n.1 (history of habeas corpus); *infra* §§ 2.4d n.276 (claimed contraction in writ over last several decades), 2.5 n.1 (relevance of innocence in habeas corpus proceedings), 2.6 n.1 (role of habeas corpus in capital cases). This section originally appeared in a somewhat different form in Liebman, *supra,* § 2.1 n.1, and is reproduced here with the permission of the *Columbia Law Review. See* Liebman & Ryan, *supra* § 2.1 n.2, at 882-84. *Cf.* Schlup v. Delo, 513 U.S. 298, 318 n.33 (1995) ("[T]here have been 'divergent discussions of the historic role of federal habeas corpus.' One

prisoners' constitutional attacks on their convictions and sentences (subsection b); summarizes the two standard but conflicting academic descriptions of the history and function of habeas corpus, criticizing both (subsection c); presents our own description, and the two centuries of legal precedent supporting that description, of habeas corpus as one of several methods — and now the preferred method — of assuring federal court appellate review as of right of all constitutional challenges to incarceration (subsection d); and discusses the logic of direct appeal/habeas corpus parity and the remarkable stability of federal review as of right of the constitutionality of incarceration over 200-plus years, contrary to claims that the writ currently provides wider federal review than historically was available (subsection e). We also briefly consider here (in subsection b and at the end of subsection d), and §§ 30.2c and 30.2d more comprehensively consider, whether a provision of the Antiterrorism and Effective Death Penalty Act of 1996 (AEDPA)[2] purports to — and, if so, whether it constitutionally may — depart from this centuries-old approach to the writ.

b. *Direct appeal/habeas corpus parity.* As just mentioned, analysis of the relationship between direct appeal and habeas corpus is complicated by AEDPA's ambiguities. In the following discussion, we show that centuries of pre-AEDPA law (which continues to govern in all cases filed on or before April 24, 1996, and also in some cases filed after that date[3]) had created a process of federal habeas corpus review of the constitutionality of criminal convictions that largely correlated with the review that such convictions would have received on direct appeal to the Supreme Court.[4] Although questions about the proper

---

recent commentator has offered a new perspective on the history of the writ. Liebman, Apocalypse Next Time?: The Anachronistic Attack on Habeas Corpus/Direct Review Parity, 92 Colum. L. Rev. 1997 (1992)." (quoting Wainwright v. Sykes, 433 U.S. 72, 77 n.6 (1977)).

[2] Pub. L. 104-132, 110 Stat. 1214 (1996). For a general overview of AEDPA, see *infra* § 3.2.

[3] *See infra* § 3.4.

[4] Pre-AEDPA decisions *equating* direct appeal and habeas corpus standards of review include, *e.g.,* Thompson v. Keohane, 515 U.S. 99, 109 (1995) (citing direct appeal decision in Culombe v. Connecticut, 367 U.S. 568 (1961) in support of standard of review that governs in habeas corpus proceedings); Romano v. Oklahoma, 512 U.S. 1, 10, 12 (1994) (citing habeas corpus decisions in Estelle v. McGuire, 502 U.S. 62 (1991); Donnelly v. DeChristoforo, 416 U.S. 637 (1974) to define substantive legal standards Court applies on direct review); Victor v. Nebraska, 511 U.S. 1, 19 (1994) (relying on habeas corpus decision in Ylst v. Nunnemaker, 501 U.S. 797, 801 (1991) to define scope of Court's direct review of claims rejected by state courts on basis of "independent and adequate state grounds"); Schiro v. Farley, 510 U.S. 222, 232 (1994) (citing direct appeal decision in Cichos v. Indiana, 385 U.S. 76, 79-80 (1966) as establishing standard of review of state court factfindings on habeas corpus); Coleman v. Thompson, 501 U.S. 722, 729-32 (1991) (relying in part on Supreme Court's direct review cases to define scope of habeas corpus review of claims rejected by state courts on basis of "independent and adequate state grounds" (discussed *infra*

interpretation of AEDPA, and about the statute's constitutionality under certain interpretations, preclude definitive conclusions about the statute's precise effects, we argue here, and in more detail in § 30.2, that AEDPA preserves the preexisting parity between direct appeal and federal habeas corpus review.

The nature and extent of parity between direct and habeas corpus review are best illustrated by comparing the federal review available on petition for a writ of *certiorari* to the Supreme Court and on petition for a writ of habeas corpus to the district court in the case of the same state prisoner — say, one convicted and incarcerated on the basis of a confession he unsuccessfully challenged in the state courts on the ground that it was obtained in violation of the 5th and 14th Amendment ban on coerced confessions. This subsection will use this fact pattern to compare the two stages of review, differentiating, where appropriate, between those federal habeas corpus cases that are, and those that are not, governed by AEDPA.

The jurisdictional and related requirements for *certiorari* review by the Supreme Court and federal habeas corpus review by a federal district court are identical. To establish Supreme Court jurisdiction, the prisoner's *certiorari* petition must show (1) that he has been deprived of a "right ... under the constitution, treaties or statutes of ... the United States" and (2) that he has exhausted his state remedies with regard to the federal claim — *i.e.*, is asking the Court to review a "judgment[] ... rendered by the highest court of a State in which a decision [on the claim] could be had" as of right.[5] To establish district court jurisdiction, the prisoner's habeas corpus petition must show (1) that he "is in custody in violation of the Constitution or laws or treaties of the United States,"[6] and (2) that he has exhausted his state remedies with regard to the

---

§ 26.1 nn.20-31 and accompanying text)); Mu'Min v. Virginia, 500 U.S. 415, 428-29 (1991) (direct appeal case citing habeas corpus decision in Patton v. Yount, 467 U.S. 1025 (1984) as establishing governing standard of review); *id.* at 450-52 (Kennedy, J., dissenting) (relying, in direct appeal case, on habeas corpus concept denying deference to state court factual findings following incomplete or unfair state court factfinding procedure); Arizona v. Fulminante, 499 U.S. 279, 287 (1991) (direct appeal case citing habeas corpus decision in Miller v. Fenton, 474 U.S. 104 (1985), as establishing governing standard of review of mixed question of law and fact); *Miller v. Fenton, supra* at 114 (treating as identical the questions of what level of review of legal and "mixed legal/factual" questions federal habeas corpus courts should apply to state court determinations and of what level of review of similar questions federal appellate courts should apply to lower federal court determinations). *See also* HART AND WECHSLER, 2d ed., *supra* § 2.1 n.1, at 1486 (it is "impossible" to draw a "logical distinction in kind between direct review and review on habeas corpus"); decisions cited *supra* § 2.2 n.5.

[5] 28 U.S.C. § 1257(a) (1994). *See* ROBERT L. STERN, EUGENE GRESSMAN, STEPHEN M. SHAPIRO & KENNETH S. GELLER, SUPREME COURT PRACTICE §§ 3.10-3.14 (7th ed. 1993).

[6] 28 U.S.C. § 2241(c)(3) (1994); 28 U.S.C.A. § 2254(a) (West 1994 & Supp. 1998).

federal claim by raising it either on direct or postconviction review in the state courts in the highest state court that is required to hear such claims.[7]

If *certiorari* review is granted by the Supreme Court, or if habeas corpus review is sought from the district court, the type and scope of review in both courts is virtually identical, as follows:

- The Supreme Court would engage in "independent" review of a state court's resolution of every relevant "pure" legal question (such as, for example, whether certain kinds of promises leading to a confession can be the basis for a claim of unconstitutional coercion) and every relevant "mixed question of fact and law" (such as the "voluntariness" of the confession).[8] A federal district court in a pre-AEDPA habeas corpus case would consider both types of questions *de novo* — meaning, from scratch, or without regard to the state court's prior decision of the same question in the same case.[9] In conducting

---

[7] *See id.* §§ 2254(a)-(b); Castille v. Peoples, 489 U.S. 346, 350-51 (1989). *See infra* Chapter 23 (exhaustion of state remedies requirement). In regard to AEDPA's preservation of preexisting jurisdictional requirements, see *infra* §§ 20.2c n.73 and accompanying text, 30.2a nn.11-12 and accompanying text.

[8] **Direct review authority in regard to "pure" legal questions:** *See, e.g., Arizona v. Fulminante, supra,* 499 U.S. at 287. **Direct review authority in regard to "mixed" legal questions:** *See, e.g., id.*; Spano v. New York, 360 U.S. 315, 316, 320, 321 & n.2 (1959) (direct appeal case deriving *de novo* review rule from habeas corpus decisions in Brown v. Allen, 344 U.S. 443 (1953) and Leyra v. Denno, 347 U.S. 556 (1954)); Norris v. Alabama, 294 U.S. 587, 589-90 (1935); STERN ET AL., *supra* note 5, § 3.25, at 159-61 (collecting cases); authority discussed *infra* § 2.4d nn.198-205 and accompanying text.

[9] **Habeas corpus authority in regard to "pure" legal questions:** *See, e.g., Schiro v. Farley, supra,* 510 U.S. at 232; Kimmelman v. Morrison, 477 U.S. 365, 373-83 (1986); *Miller v. Fenton, supra,* 474 U.S. at 112-13, 115; Townsend v. Sain, 372 U.S. 293, 318 (1963). **Habeas corpus authority in regard to "mixed" legal questions:** *See, e.g.,* Thompson v. Keohane, 515 U.S. 99, 111-16 (1995) (citing numerous cases); Kyles v. Whitley, 514 U.S. 419, 441 (1995); Withrow v. Williams, 507 U.S. 680, 693-94 (1993); Brecht v. Abrahamson, 507 U.S. 619, 650-51 (1993) (White, J., dissenting); Wright v. West, 505 U.S. 277, 300-06 (1992) (O'Connor, J., concurring in the judgment); *id.* at 309 (Kennedy, J., concurring in the judgment); Estelle v. McGuire, 502 U.S. 62, 70-73 (1991); Penry v. Lynaugh, 492 U.S. 302, 322-26 (1989); *Miller v. Fenton, supra,* 474 U.S. at 113-14; Francis v. Franklin, 471 U.S. 307, 314 (1985); Strickland v. Washington, 466 U.S. 668, 698 (1984); Rushen v. Spain, 464 U.S. 114, 120 (1983) (*per curiam*); Maggio v. Fulford, 462 U.S. 111, 118 (1983) (*per curiam*) (White, J. concurring); Marshall v. Lonberger, 459 U.S. 422, 430 (1983); Sumner v. Mata, 455 U.S. 591, 597 (1982) (*per curiam*); Sumner v. Mata, 449 U.S. 539, 543-44 (1981); Cuyler v. Sullivan, 446 U.S. 335, 341-42 (1980); Jackson v. Virginia, 443 U.S. 307, 318-22 (1979); Rose v. Mitchell, 443 U.S. 545, 561 (1979); Wainwright v. Sykes, 433 U.S. 72, 87 (1977); Castaneda v. Partida, 430 U.S. 482 (1977); Brewer v. Williams, 430 U.S. 387, 403-04 (1977); Neil v. Biggers, 409 U.S. 188, 193 n.3, 199 (1972); Pate v. Robinson, 383 U.S. 375 (1966); Boles v. Stevenson, 379 U.S. 43 (1964) (*per curiam*); Fay v. Noia, 372 U.S. 391 (1963); Townsend v. Sain, 372 U.S. 293, 312, 318 (1963); Irvin v. Dowd, 366 U.S. 717, 723 (1961); Douglas v. Green, 363 U.S. 192 (1960); United States ex rel. Jennings v. Ragen, 358 U.S. 276

independent review on direct appeal, the Supreme Court would rely primarily on its existing constitutional precedents, consistent with the degree of freedom to deviate from those precedents that it exercises under applicable prudential doctrines, mainly *stare decisis*.[10] In conducting *de novo* review on habeas corpus, the district court in a pre-AEDPA case would rely on the same Supreme Court precedents, as well as its own and those of the appropriate circuit court of appeals, consistent with the degree of freedom to deviate from those precedents that the court could exercise under the applicable prudential doctrines, mainly the nonretroactivity principle.[11] In a case governed by AEDPA, the federal district court would provide a form of review even more closely parallel to that available on direct review by the Supreme Court in the same case. AEDPA thus (1) replaces the prior system of truly *de novo* review of the petitioner's legal claims, without regard to the state court's resolution of the same claims, with independent review (as on direct appeal) of the state court "decision," and (2) limits relief to a "decision [that] was contrary to, or involved an unreasonable application of, clearly established Federal law, as determined by the Supreme Court of the United States."[12] In the latter regard, the new statute's limitation of independent review to "clearly established Federal law, as determined by the Supreme Court" has the effect of assuring, even more effectively than the preexisting nonretroactivity doctrine, that the legal principles the federal

---

(1959); Thomas v. Arizona, 356 U.S. 390, 393 (1958) (indiscriminately citing direct appeal and habeas corpus cases in defining standard of review); Leyra v. Denno, 347 U.S. 556 (1954); Brown v. Allen, 344 U.S. 443, 458 (1953) (opinion for the Court of Reed, J.); *id.* at 506-08 (opinion for the Court of Frankfurter, J.); Hawk v. Olsen, 326 U.S. 271, 276 (1945); Moore v. Dempsey, 261 U.S. 86 (1923); Felts v. Murphy, 201 U.S. 123, 129-30 (1906); Ex parte Royall, 117 U.S. 241, 247, 253 (1886); authority cited *infra* §§ 20.3d, 30.2. *See also supra* § 2.2 n.6 & *infra* § 28.2a (apparently anomalous failure of *res judicata* principles to bar federal habeas corpus actions from reaching conclusions contrary to those reached in regard to same parties and issues in state courts evaporates when "original proceeding" conception of habeas corpus gives way to "appellate" conception, because *res judicata* does not bar appellate court's reconsideration of issues decided by lower court). On the truly "*de novo*," or "from scratch," quality of the federal habeas corpus court's pre-AEDPA reconsideration of legal and "mixed" federal questions that previously had been resolved in the state courts in the same case, see Stone v. Powell, 428 U.S. 465, 477 (1976) (habeas corpus requires "full reconsideration of ... constitutional claim"); *Brown v. Allen, supra* at 458 (in habeas corpus proceedings, state court decision in case is not focus of review and has no more bearing than "the conclusion of [any other] court of last resort of another jurisdiction").

[10] *See, e.g.*, Payne v. Tennessee, 501 U.S. 808, 827-30 (1991).

[11] *See, e.g.*, Teague v. Lane, 489 U.S. 288, 305-07 (1989) (plurality opinion); *infra* notes 26, 28 and accompanying text; *infra* § 2.4d nn.306-10, 311-15 and accompanying text; *infra* Chapter 25.

[12] 28 U.S.C.A. § 2254(d)(1) (West 1994 & Supp. 1998). For a detailed explanation of the process of review under AEDPA and defense of this interpretation of section 2254(d)(1) over others that have been offered, see *infra* § 30.2.

district court applies are no broader (nor any narrower) than those the Supreme Court would have applied in the case had it granted *certiorari* immediately following direct appeal in the state courts.

- If the analysis of a mixed question of fact and law turns on a historical fact (for example, if the determination of the voluntariness of the confession turns on whether a certain promise was or was not made by the police), both the Supreme Court and the federal district court (in either an AEDPA or non-AEDPA case) would defer to the state courts' findings with regard to that fact[13] unless (1) there *is* no finding,[14] (2) the finding is inadequate or (in AEDPA's locution) "unreasonable" (*e.g.*, because there is no or too little evidence to support it[15] or because the factfinding procedure was unfair[16]),

---

[13] **Direct review authority:** *See, e.g.*, *Arizona v. Fulminante*, *supra*, 499 U.S. at 287; Watts v. Indiana, 338 U.S. 49, 50-52 (1949) (plurality opinion); Haley v. Ohio, 332 U.S. 596, 597-98 (1948); Lisenba v. California, 314 U.S. 219, 238 (1941); STERN ET AL., *supra* note 5, § 3.25, at 158-59 (citing cases); *infra* § 37.3b nn.8, 15 and accompanying text. **Habeas corpus authority:** 28 U.S.C.A. § 2254(e)(1) (West 1994 & Supp. 1998) (AEDPA provision establishing that adequate state court factfinding is presumed correct absent showing "by clear and convincing evidence" that it is erroneous); 28 U.S.C. § 2254(d) (1994) (pre-AEDPA provision, establishing equivalent standard but characterizing requisite showing in terms of "convincing evidence"). *See, e.g.*, *Schiro v. Farley*, *supra*, 510 U.S. at 232; Burden v. Zant, 498 U.S. 433, 436-37 (1991) (*per curiam*); Parker v. Dugger, 498 U.S. 308, 320 (1991); *Sumner v. Mata*, *supra*, 449 U.S. at 550; *Townsend v. Sain*, *supra*, 372 U.S. at 318; *infra* Chapter 20; *infra* §§ 30.2, 31.3.

[14] **Direct review authority:** *See, e.g.*, Beck v. Ohio, 379 U.S. 89, 92-93 (1964); Ashcraft v. Tennessee, 322 U.S. 143, 147-48 (1944); Carlson v. Washington ex rel. Curtis, 234 U.S. 103, 106 (1914); REYNOLDS ROBERTSON & FRANCIS R. KIRKHAM, JURISDICTION OF THE SUPREME COURT OF THE UNITED STATES § 112 (Richard F. Wolfson & Philip B. Kurland eds., 2d ed. 1951) ("A state court cannot, by omitting to pass upon evidence or to make findings of fact, deprive a litigant of the benefit of a federal right ...."). **Habeas corpus authority:** *See, e.g.*, 28 U.S.C.A. § 2254(e)(1) (West 1994 & Supp. 1998) (AEDPA cases); 28 U.S.C. § 2254(d) (1994) (non-AEDPA cases); Ford v. Wainwright, 477 U.S. 399, 410-11 (1986) (plurality opinion); *Townsend v. Sain*, *supra*, 372 U.S. at 314, 320; *infra* § 20.3c.

[15] **Direct appeal authority:** *See, e.g.*, Vachon v. New Hampshire, 414 U.S. 478, 480 (1974) (*per curiam*); Cox v. Louisiana, 379 U.S. 536, 545-49 (1965); *Lisenba v. California*, *supra*, 314 U.S. at 238 ("[W]e accept the determination of the triers of fact, unless it is so lacking in support in the evidence that to give it effect would work that fundamental unfairness which is at war with due process."); STERN ET AL., *supra* note 5, § 3.25, at 158-59; authority discussed *infra* § 2.4d nn.198-205. *See also* Burden v. Zant, 510 U.S. 132, 133 (1994) (*per curiam*) (reversing factfinding by federal court of appeals in habeas corpus case on basis of "manifest mistake," given evidence "strongly supporting" opposite finding). **Habeas corpus authority:** *See, e.g.*, 28 U.S.C.A. §§ 2254(d)(2), 2254(e)(1) (West 1994 & Supp. 1998) (in cases governed by AEDPA, no deference due state court factfindings that are not "[]reasonable ... in light of the evidence presented in the State court proceeding" or that are shown by "clear and convincing evidence" to be erroneous); 28 U.S.C. §§ 2254(d)(8), 2254(d) (1994) (in non-AEDPA cases, no deference due state court factfindings "not fairly supported by the record" or shown "by convincing evidence" to be "erroneous"); *Parker v. Dugger*, *supra*, 498 U.S. at 320; Cabana v. Bullock, 474 U.S. 376, 389-90

or (3) the finding was made in the process of applying an improper legal standard.[17] If one of these exceptional circumstances is present and the existing record permits, the Supreme Court may, and a federal district court on habeas corpus will have to, make its own finding in service of a final resolution of the case.[18] (The Supreme Court also may remand the case to a lower court to find the facts.) If through no fault of the petitioner, the record is too incomplete to permit such a new finding, either court will relegate to the next nearest responsible tribunal with the capacity to find the facts

---

(1986); *Townsend v. Sain, supra,* 372 U.S. at 316. A direct appeal version of the habeas corpus standard is codified in FED. R. CIV. PRO. 52(a), which requires federal appellate courts to accept the factfindings of lower federal courts in civil cases except upon a conclusion that those findings are "clearly erroneous." *See* Alfred Hill, *The Inadequate State Ground,* 65 COLUM. L. REV. 943, 946-47 (1965) (Supreme Court properly has given same treatment to state and lower federal court factfindings); *infra* §§ 20.3h & 31.3 (habeas corpus standard for overcoming adequate state court factfindings and FED. R. CIV. P. 52(a)'s "clearly erroneous" locutions are justifiably equated with same, "clear and convincing," plateau).

[16] **Direct appeal authority:** *See, e.g.,* Mu'Min v. Virginia, 500 U.S. 415, 450-52 (1991) (Kennedy, J., dissenting) (on direct appeal of state court judgment, deference is not due state court factfindings that are based on incomplete or unfair hearing); Graham v. Gill, 223 U.S. 643, 644-45 (1912) *(mem.)* (rejecting state factfindings based on evidence inadmissible as matter of federal law); Dower v. Richards, 151 U.S. 658, 667 (1894) (similar). *See also* Inwood Laboratories v. Ives Laboratories, 456 U.S. 844, 857 n.19 (1982) *(dicta)* (lower federal court's failure to "consider relevant evidence would have been an error of law" requiring remand). **Habeas corpus authority:** *See, e.g.,* 28 U.S.C.A. § 2254(d)(2) (West 1994 & Supp. 1998) (no deference due state court factfinding that was not "[]reasonable determination" of facts "in light of the evidence presented in the State court proceeding"); 28 U.S.C. § 2254(d)(6) (1994) (in non-AEDPA cases, no deference due state court factfinding resulting from hearing that was not "full, fair, and adequate"); Keeney v. Tamayo-Reyes, 504 U.S. 1, 10 (1992); *id.* at 15-16 (O'Connor, J., dissenting); *Ford v. Wainwright, supra,* 477 U.S. at 410-11, 416-18; *id.* at 427 (Powell, J., concurring); *id.* at 430-31 (O'Connor, J., concurring); Blackledge v. Allison, 431 U.S. 63, 74-75, 78 (1977); *infra* § 20.3e.

[17] **Direct appeal authority:** *See, e.g.,* Haynes v. Washington, 373 U.S. 503, 516-18 (1963); Rogers v. Richmond, 365 U.S. 534, 547 (1961) ("Historical facts 'found' in the perspective framed by an erroneous legal standard cannot plausibly be expected to furnish the basis for correct conclusions if and merely because a correct standard is later applied to them."); *Lisenba v. California, supra,* 314 U.S. at 236. *See also* Thornburg v. Gingles, 478 U.S. 30, 79 (1986) (Civil Procedure "Rule 52(a) 'does not inhibit an appellate court's power to correct ... a finding of fact ... predicated on a misunderstanding of the governing rule of law.'" (citation omitted)); *infra* § 37.3b nn.13-18, 21-22 and accompanying text. **Habeas corpus authority:** *See, e.g., Townsend v. Sain, supra,* 372 U.S. at 315 n.10; cases collected *infra* §§ 20.3c (para. (6)), 20.3d (para. (2)).

[18] **Direct appeal authority:** *See, e.g.,* Beck v. Ohio, *supra,* 379 U.S. at 92-93; Ashcraft v. Tennessee, 322 U.S. 143, 145 (1944) (Court makes its own factual analysis because "record discloses that neither the trial court nor the Tennessee Supreme Court actually held as a matter of fact that petitioners' confessions were 'freely and voluntarily made'"); *infra* § 37.3b nn.19, 23 and accompanying text. *See also* Brooklyn Sav. Bank v. O'Neil, 324 U.S. 697, 703 (1945); Carlson v. Washington ex rel. Curtiss, 234 U.S. 103, 106 (1914). **Habeas corpus authority:** *See, e.g., Parker v. Dugger, supra,* 498 U.S. at 320; *Townsend v. Sain, supra,* 373 U.S. at 310-12.

(which, in the case of the district court on habeas corpus, is itself or, more often, a federal magistrate judge) the task of doing so and then of resolving the remaining legal and mixed legal-factual issues on that basis.[19] If the record is incomplete for reasons that *are* the petitioner's fault (for example, he failed to present all the evidence he had, contrary to state procedural rules), and if the state courts did not inquire further because of that default (for example, those courts noted the existence of a legal issue not resolvable on the facts before them, but did not address it because the defendant waived the inquiry), either court will deny relief because of the state procedural ground, assuming the court finds it to be "adequate" and "independent of federal law."[20]

---

[19] **Direct appeal authority:** *See, e.g.*, STERN ET AL., *supra* note 5, § 3.25, at 161 ("Court may leave open the factual issue, allowing the state court to make the necessary findings on remand following reversal for error of law." (citing cases)). *See also* United States Postal Serv. Bd. of Gov. v. Aikens, 460 U.S. 711, 717 (1983). **Habeas corpus authority:** *See, e.g.*, Hull v. Freeman, 932 F.2d 159, 170 n.9 (3d Cir. 1991); Smart v. Scully, 787 F.2d 816, 821 (2d Cir. 1986); Grigsby v. Mabry, 637 F.2d 525, 528-29 (8th Cir. 1980); J. Skelly Wright & Abraham D. Sofaer, *Federal Habeas Corpus for State Prisoners: The Allocation of Fact-Finding Responsibility*, 75 YALE L.J. 895, 906-19 (1966); *infra* § 7.1b n.48. *See also infra* § 18.1b (especially broad use of magistrate judges to hear habeas corpus cases); *infra* Chapter 20 (federal habeas corpus hearings).

[20] **Direct appeal authority:** *See, e.g.*, James v. Kentucky, 466 U.S. 341, 348-52 (1984); Michigan v. Long, 463 U.S. 1032, 1037-44 (1983); Hathorn v. Lovorn, 457 U.S. 255, 262-63 (1982). **Habeas corpus authority:** *See, e.g.*, Lambrix v. Singletary, 117 S. Ct. 1517, 1522-23 (1997) (equating "adequate and independent state grounds" doctrines that apply on direct appeal and habeas corpus in all but "technical[ ]" respects; doctrine is applied in habeas corpus so that "federal district court or court of appeals would [not] be able to review claims that this Court would have been unable to consider on direct appeal"); *Keeney v. Tamayo-Reyes, supra*, 504 U.S. at 5-9, 10 n.5; Coleman v. Thompson, 501 U.S. 722, 729-32 (1991); Harris v. Reed, 489 U.S. 255, 263-64 (1989); *infra* §§ 20.3e n.106 and accompanying text, 26.1. *See generally* First Options of Chicago, Inc. v. Kaplan, 514 U.S. 938, 947-49 (1995) ("ordinary" rule is that court reviewing decision of another court must "accept[ ] findings of fact that are not 'clearly erroneous' but decid[e] questions of law *de novo*"; courts generally should follow "ordinary" rule and resist "special standards" of review because "it is undesirable to make the law more complicated by proliferating review standards"). The availability of counsel is another point of direct appeal/habeas corpus parity. *Cf.* Wright v. West, 505 U.S. 277, 291-94 (1992) (plurality opinion). This is because habeas corpus is not a surrogate for direct appeal to *state* supreme courts, which are constitutionally obliged to provide counsel to indigent criminal defendants, *see* Douglas v. California, 372 U.S. 353, 355-58 (1963), but rather for direct appeal to the *United States* Supreme Court, which is not constitutionally required to provide counsel, *see* Ross v. Moffitt, 417 U.S. 600 (1974). The statutory right to counsel on habeas corpus — which becomes mandatory only if a hearing is ordered, *see* Rule 8(c) of the Rules Governing § 2254 Cases; *infra* § 12.3b — thus is a near-perfect replica of the Supreme Court's practice of providing counsel to indigent *certiorari* petitioners only if *certiorari* is granted. *See infra* § 39.3b.

There are, of course, some differences between the review of claims of unconstitutional incarceration secured by the few state prisoners whose direct review *certiorari* petitions are granted by the Supreme Court and by the many state prisoners whose petitions are reviewed by federal district courts on habeas corpus. Each of these differences, however, is the product of the application of the same *appellate review* principles by courts with different practical capacities.[21]

First, unlike federal district courts, which must resolve all habeas corpus petitions over which they have jurisdiction,[22] the Supreme Court only reviews cases it chooses to review.[23] The special statutory capacity of the Court to determine its own docket is, however, simply the product of the special *in*capacity of its nine members to review the number of cases they would face were review available as of right, and of any "Highest Court in the Land" to fulfill its peculiar unifying and concluding duties with more members than is consistent with efficient *en banc* proceedings. Because these latter incapacities do not affect the numerically more elastic lower federal courts, those courts may more easily be *required* to exercise jurisdiction (on application by the aggrieved party) over all constitutional issues arising in state criminal courts.[24]

---

[21] *See supra* § 2.2 n.6. *See also* Liebman & Ryan, *supra* § 2.1 n.2, at 882-84; *infra* § 2.4d nn.275-315 and accompanying text.

[22] *See, e.g.,* McFarland v. Scott, 512 U.S. 849, 859 (1994) ("criminal defendants are *entitled* to challenge their conviction and sentence in habeas corpus proceedings" (emphasis added)); Collins v. Byrd, 510 U.S. 1185, 1185 (1994) (opinion of Scalia, J., respecting Court's denial of application to vacate stay of execution) (court of appeals properly rejected district court's claim to have discretion not to hear a habeas corpus petition over which it had jurisdiction and properly interpreted existing habeas corpus law to "*require* District Court consideration of the habeas petition on its merits, and to [require the lower court to] stay the execution pending that consideration" (emphasis added)).

[23] *See generally* STERN, ET AL., *supra* note 5, §§ 4.1-4.17, at 162-95.

[24] Characterizing habeas corpus review as a surrogate for the review the Supreme Court ideally should, but in practice is unable to, provide all state criminal defendants on direct appeal, are, *e.g.,* Reed v. Farley, 512 U.S. 339, 348-49 (1994) (plurality opinion); *id.* at 362-63 (Blackmun, J., dissenting); Rose v. Mitchell, 443 U.S. 545, 561 (1979); Brown v. Allen, 344 U.S. 443, 456-67 (1953) (opinion for the Court of Reed, J.); *id.* at 493-94 (opinion for the Court of Frankfurter, J.); Darr v. Burford, 339 U.S. 200, 214-15, 229-31 (1950); *id.* at 229 (Frankfurter, J., dissenting); Geagan v. Gavin, 181 F. Supp. 466, 469 (D. Mass. 1960) (Wyzanski, J.), *aff'd,* 292 F.2d 244 (1st Cir. 1961), *cert. denied,* 370 U.S. 903 (1962); Bator, *supra* § 2.1 n.1, at 516-17; Brennan, *supra* § 2.1 n.1, at 420; Cover & Aleinikoff, *supra* § 2.1 n.1, at 1041-44; Friedman, *supra* § 2.1 n.1 (four articles); Friendly, *supra,* § 2.1 n.1, at 154-55; Hart, *supra* § 2.1 n.1, at 106-07; Higginbotham, *supra* § 2.1 n.1, at 1009-10; Mishkin, *supra* § 2.1 n.1, at 86-87; Weschsler, *supra* § 2.1 n.1, at 181; Wright & Sofaer, *supra* note 19, at 897; Developments, *supra* § 2.1 n.1, at 1061. *See also* 28 U.S.C. § 2244(c) (1994) (only prior judgments given what amounts to *res judicata* effect in habeas corpus are prior judgments of the United States Supreme Court). The Supreme Court and its individual members often combine denials of *certiorari* with reminders of the availability of habeas

Second, the lower federal judiciary on habeas corpus has less freedom than the Supreme Court on direct review to deviate from existing Supreme Court precedent. In cases governed by AEDPA, the statute specifies that the issue to be determined is whether the state court decision "was contrary to, or involved an unreasonable application of, clearly established Federal law, as determined by the Supreme Court of the United States."[25] In non-AEDPA cases, a common law "nonretroactivity" bar similarly prevents habeas corpus petitioners from obtaining relief on the basis of "new rules of law," although this common law rule permits consideration of decisions of the lower federal courts and it does not strictly limit federal review to legal rules in effect when the state court decided the case.[26] As previously noted, however, when properly applied, these rules actually *preserve* parity between direct and habeas corpus review. By cutting off access to legal developments after a specified date (in AEDPA cases, the date of the state court decision;[27] in non-AEDPA cases, the date on which the prisoner's direct appeal *certiorari* petition was denied[28]), the habeas corpus rules maintain direct review/habeas corpus parity by assuring that the fortuitous delay in federal review occasioned by the Supreme Court's denial of *certiorari* gives the prisoner no *more* (but also no less) review on habeas corpus than he would have received on direct review.

Third, in the tiny proportion of cases that turn on unresolved factual issues requiring evidentiary procedures as opposed to mere factfinding,[29] the Supreme

---

corpus as an alternative. *See, e.g.,* Wills v. Texas, 511 U.S. 1097 (1994) (*mem.*) (O'Connor, J., concurring in denial of *certiorari*); Spencer v. Georgia, 500 U.S. 960 (1991) (*mem.*) (Kennedy, J., concurring in denial of *certiorari*) ("This case appears to present important questions of federal law, and if I thought our [caselaw] ... would prevent us from reaching those issues on federal habeas review, I would have voted to grant certiorari."); Irvin v. Indiana, 353 U.S. 948, 948 (1957) (*per curiam*) (denying *certiorari* "without prejudice to filing for federal habeas corpus after exhausting state remedies"); opinions cited *infra* § 25.1 n.31. *See also* Barber v. Tennessee, 513 U.S. 1184 (1995) (opinion of Stevens, J., respecting denial of *certiorari*) (concurring in Court's refusal to review state court direct appeal decision affirming "plainly impermissible" capital sentencing instruction because "Court's denial of certiorari does not constitute a ruling on the merits" that would bar subsequent correction of error by some other court).

[25] 28 U.S.C.A. § 2254(d)(1) (West 1994 & Supp. 1998). For a detailed discussion of this statutory provision and the standard it creates, see *infra* § 30.2.

[26] *See* Teague v. Lane, 489 U.S. 288, 305-07 (1989) (plurality opinion); *infra* § 2.4d nn.306-08, 311-15 and accompanying text; *infra* Chapter 25.

[27] *See* 28 U.S.C.A. § 2254(d)(1) (West 1994 & Supp. 1998) (confining review to legal rules that were "clearly established" at time of state court decision); *infra* § 30.2.

[28] *See, e.g.,* Sawyer v. Smith, 497 U.S. 227, 233 (1990); Saffle v. Parks, 494 U.S. 484, 488-89 (1990).

[29] *See* Report of the Subcommittee on the Role of the Federal Courts (Richard A. Posner, Chair), *in* 1 FEDERAL COURTS STUDY COMMITTEE, WORKING PAPERS AND SUBCOMMITTEE REPORTS 468-515 (July 1, 1990) (district courts hold hearings in only 1.17% of all habeas corpus cases).

Court on *certiorari* must remand to some other court to take evidence, while the federal district court on habeas corpus must hear the evidence itself (or, more usually, assign a magistrate judge to hear it). This is not a discrepancy between direct and habeas corpus review, however, but one between courts with only appellate capacities and those that also have original (evidence-taking) capacities.[30] Whether on direct or habeas corpus review, the Supreme Court must remand questions requiring evidentiary proceedings, as must the federal courts of appeals on habeas corpus. Nor is it an important disparity in principle that the Supreme Court on direct appeal remands the evidence-taking duties to *state* evidence-taking courts, while the Supreme Court and federal courts of appeals on habeas corpus remand those duties to *federal* evidence-taking courts. In both cases, the governing principle is the same: the generally applicable interest in expeditious resolution mandates that the highest court with evidence-taking capacities in the chain of courts that have exercised responsibility over the case resolve all outstanding evidentiary issues.[31]

---

[30] *See, e.g.,* Beck v. Ohio, 379 U.S. 89, 100-01 (1964) (Harlan, J., dissenting) (noting comparative advantage of federal district courts on habeas corpus over Supreme Court on direct review in obtaining "demeanor evidence" and "adjudging credibility"); Townsend v. Sain, 372 U.S. 293, 322 (1963); Wright & Sofaer, *supra* note 19, at 897. Consider also social security cases, in which federal district judges exercise significant appellate, as well as original, jurisdiction. *See, e.g.,* 42 U.S.C. § 405(g) (1994). As for the constitutional propriety of Congress' giving the inferior federal courts "[e]very variety and form of appellate jurisdiction within the sphere of the [constitutional] power [over federal questions], extending as well to [review of] the courts of the States as to those of the nation," with "no distinction ... between civil and criminal causes," see The Mayor v. Cooper, 73 U.S. (6 Wall.) 247, 252-53 (1867); Martin v. Hunter's Lessee, 14 U.S. (1 Wheat.) 304, 338 (1816); *supra* § 2.3 n.5 (discussing *The Federalist*).

[31] *See also* 1 LIEBMAN, *supra* § 2.1 n.1, at § 28.1 nn.23-46 and accompanying text (discussing other reasons for requiring district courts on habeas corpus, but not Supreme Court on direct review, to redetermine facts in lieu of remand to state courts, including: (1) desire to avoid making trier of fact the sole reviewer of its own findings, as would occur if Supreme Court found facts but does not occur when district court does so; (2) avoiding district court orders remanding cases to state courts for hearings which, if not appealable, would have serious federalism implications, *see, e.g.,* Purkett v. Elem, 514 U.S. 765, 776 (1995) (Stevens, J., dissenting) (as "Court's opinion today implicitly ratifies," when state court failed to make determination critical to resolution of constitutional question, federal habeas corpus court was justified in making decision "on its own" rather than "grant[ing] the writ conditioned on a proper [determination of issue] ... in the state ... court"); Grigsby v. Mabry, 637 F.2d 525, 527-29 (8th Cir. 1980); *infra* § 7.1b n.48, and if appealable would drastically lengthen and complicate habeas corpus proceedings; and (3) desire for "speedy" relief from unlawful custody, Browder v. Director, 434 U.S. 257, 271 (1978); *infra* § 21.1b, which trumps state interest in conducting hearings, given that (a) facts presented in petition, if true, would render prisoner's incarceration unconstitutional, *see* Rule 4 of the Rules Governing § 2254 Cases; *infra* § 15.2c; (b) petitioner — typically at substantial cost in terms of time spent in prison or otherwise "in custody," *see infra* § 8.2 — previously gave state trial and appellate courts the opportunity to adjudicate same factual allegations before asserting them in federal court, *see infra* §§ 23.3a, 23.3c (factual component of exhaustion requirement); and (c)

Finally, as a result of the Court's 1993 decision in *Brecht v. Abrahamson*,[32] the standard of harmless error applicable in habeas corpus proceedings (whether the error lacked substantial injurious effect) differs from the standard that long has applied on direct review of state court determinations in the Supreme Court (whether the error was harmless beyond a reasonable doubt).[33] Even assuming that *Brecht*'s downgrading of the harmless error standard applicable in habeas corpus proceedings is not a prelude to a similar downgrading of the harmless error standard applicable on direct review,[34] *Brecht* still can be seen as preserving, rather than defeating, direct appeal/habeas corpus parity. Thus, a more forgiving harmless error rule on habeas corpus review helps avoid a windfall that successful habeas corpus petitioners otherwise might receive in comparison to defendants who prevail on direct appeal. Because the time lapse between trial and retrial is usually significantly longer in the case of a successful habeas corpus petitioner than in the case of a successful direct appellant, the likelihood is greater in the habeas corpus context that a more favorable outcome on retrial will flow, not from removal of the violation that prompted the retrial, but instead from the staleness of the evidence of guilt.[35] *Brecht* neutralizes this disparity by increasing the requisite degree of certainty in habeas corpus proceedings that the error actually affected the original trial and, thus, that any improved outcome on retrial flows from the removal of the error and not the staleness of the evidence.

Putting aside these modest differences (all pragmatic and all stemming either from the comparative functional advantages and disadvantages of trial, appellate, and "highest" courts or from timing concerns) and assuming the courts construe

---

prerequisite for federal court redetermination of facts is conclusion that state courts' treatment of facts was not sufficiently full, fair, and complete to rule out petitioner's claim that he is illegally imprisoned, *see infra* § 20.3e).

[32] 507 U.S. 619 (1993).

[33] *See generally infra* Chapter 32.

[34] *But cf. infra* § 32.1 n.22 and accompanying text (hints in *Brecht* that its harmless error standard may eventually be extended to direct appeal cases).

[35] *See* O'Neal v. McAninch, 513 U.S. 432, 443 (1995) (one "legitimate and important" purpose of harmless error rule in habeas corpus cases is to "avoid retrials, some of which, held so late in the day, may lead to freedom for some petitioners whose initial convictions were in fact unaffected by the errors that took place at their initial trials"); *Brecht, supra,* 507 U.S. at 637 ("Retrying defendants whose convictions are set aside ... imposes significant 'social costs,' including ... the 'erosion of memory' and 'dispersion of witnesses' which accompany the passage of time and make obtaining convictions on retrial more difficult .... And since there is no statute of limitations governing federal habeas ..., retrials following grants of habeas relief ordinarily take place much later than do retrials following reversal on direct review." (citations omitted)). *See also infra* §§ 2.4d nn.311-15 (arguing that further expansion of *Brecht* rule, beyond policy discussed here, is unwarranted), 32.1 (similar criticism of broad interpretation of *Brecht* rule).

AEDPA in the manner we anticipate,[36] the federal review of state criminal cases available in the Supreme Court on direct review currently is the same in substance and scope as that available in the federal courts as a whole on habeas corpus. In each instance, state prisoners have access to a *limited* form of *appellate* review. The review is "limited" because only issues arising under the federal constitution, laws, and treaties are cognizable. The review is "appellate" in the sense that one (federal) court is called upon to review the decisions of another (state) court or set of courts[37] and, as is characteristic of American common law appellate procedures, the reviewing court is obliged to defer to the lower court's historical-factual determinations (assuming that they are "adequate and independent") but not to its legal and mixed legal-factual determinations.[38]

     c. *The two standard descriptions of the writ.* The foregoing conception of parity between direct appeal and habeas corpus is thought by some to be controversial, due mainly to the claim that it deviates from a historical *dis*parity between the two modes of review.[39] The most frequently cited basis for this claim is a 1963 article by Paul Bator[40] that presents one of the two competing analyses of the history and function of the writ that have dominated recent

---

[36] As explained *infra* § 2.4d nn.316-23 and § 30.2, ambiguities in certain key provisions of AEDPA make it difficult to reach definitive conclusions about the relationship between direct appeal and habeas corpus review under AEDPA. The textual analysis assumes that the courts will interpret AEDPA in the manner that § 2.4d nn.316-23 and § 30.2 suggest. As § 30.2 explains, the construction we advocate is not only dictated by the wording of the statute but also by the need to avoid an unconstitutional reading of the statute.

[37] *See, e.g., O'Neal v. McAninch, supra,* 513 U.S. at 440, 442 (federal court's function in habeas corpus proceedings is to "review errors in state criminal trials" (emphasis omitted)); Ex parte Yerger, 75 U.S. (8 Wall.) 85, 97 (1868) ("an appellate jurisdiction [is one] to be exercised ... in the revision of judicial decisions"); *supra* § 2.2 n.5; *infra* § 2.4d nn.84-91 and accompanying text.

[38] The juxtaposition of non-deferential review of "legal" questions and deferential review of "factual" questions is a principal defining trait of American appellate practice, which distinguishes American appeals both from English "appeals" prior to the American Revolution and modern European appeals, pursuant to both of which, review of legal *and* factual is *de novo. See* Mirjan R. Damaska, *Structures of Authority and Comparative Criminal Procedure,* 84 YALE L.J. 480, 490 (1975) (European appellate practice); Liebman, *supra* § 2.1 n.1, at 2009 n.51 (English appellate practice before American Revolution).

[39] *See, e.g.,* Heck v. Humphrey, 512 U.S. 477, 491 (1994) (Thomas, J., concurring) ("It has long been recognized that we have expanded the prerogative writ of habeas corpus ... far beyond the limited scope that [it] ... was originally intended to have."); Withrow v. Williams, 507 U.S. 680, 718-20, 722-23 (1993) (Scalia, J., concurring in part and dissenting in part); Wright v. West, 505 U.S. 277, 285-87 & n.3 (1992) (plurality opinion).

[40] Bator, *supra* § 2.1 n.1.

judicial opinions and scholarship.[41] The other leading analysis also took shape in 1963, in Justice William Brennan's opinion for the Court in *Fay v. Noia*,[42] though it waited two decades to receive a comprehensive academic defense, from Gary Peller.[43] Both analyses deserve attention because of their influence,[44] and also because of their inadequacies as discussed below.

According to Professor Bator, the range of claims cognizable in habeas corpus expanded in stages from 1789 to 1953. The 1789 Judiciary Act gave federal courts the power to grant writs on behalf of federal prisoners "for the purpose of an inquiry into the cause of commitment."[45] In Bator's view, the Supreme Court took this phrase to require something like a competent judicial forum's finding of probable cause to detain the petitioner, which meant that proof of conviction by a court of competent jurisdiction ended the inquiry by providing sufficient evidence of probable cause to detain.[46] Applied to habeas corpus review of post-trial incarceration, Bator argued, the 1789 Act left nothing for review save the competency — *i.e.*, the subject matter and personal jurisdiction — of the convicting tribunal.[47]

In Bator's view, this state of affairs continued until the 1870s, when the Court modestly expanded the writ to permit its use to remedy unconstitutional sentences and incarceration under unconstitutional penal laws but not any other constitutional violations such as a court's denial of a petitioner's right to trial by

---

[41] *See generally* Woolhandler, *supra* § 2.1 n.1, at 582-87. Other historical treatments of habeas corpus are collected *supra* § 2.1 n.1; *supra* § 2.3 n.1.

[42] 372 U.S. 391 (1963), *questioned in* Wainwright v. Sykes, 433 U.S. 72, 87-88 (1977), *and overruled in* Coleman v. Thompson, 501 U.S. 722, 750-51 (1991).

[43] *See* Peller, *supra* § 2.1 n.1.

[44] Adopting the Bator analysis are, *e.g.*, Schlup v. Delo, 513 U.S. 298, 317-18 (1995); Custis v. United States, 511 U.S. 485, 493-94 (1994); *id.* at 509-10 (Souter, J., dissenting); McCleskey v. Zant, 499 U.S. 467, 477-78 (1991); Kuhlmann v. Wilson, 477 U.S. 436, 445-46 (1986) (plurality opinion of Powell, J.); Wainwright v. Sykes, 433 U.S. 72, 78-81 (1977); Stone v. Powell, 428 U.S. 465, 475-77 (1976); Schneckloth v. Bustamonte, 412 U.S. 218, 254-56 (1973) (Powell, J., concurring); opinions cited *supra* note 39. Adopting the Brennan-Peller analysis is, *e.g.*, Wright v. West, *supra*, 505 U.S. at 297-300 (O'Connor, J., concurring in the judgment). *See generally Schlup v. Delo, supra* at 318 n.33 ("As this Court noted in *Wainwright v. Sykes*, there have been 'divergent discussions of the historic role of federal habeas corpus.'" (citing Wainwright v. Sykes, 433 U.S. 72, 77 (1977)).

[45] Act of Sept. 24, 1789, ch. 20, § 14, 1 Stat. 73, 81-82.

[46] *See* Bator, *supra* § 2.1 n.1, at 466.

[47] *See id.* at 471-74. *See also* HART & WECHSLER, 3d ed., *supra* § 2.1 n.1, at 1427-28, 1465-66. Early cases approving the writ's use to test post-, as well as pre-, conviction incarceration are, *e.g.*, Bushell's Case, 124 Eng. Rep. 1006 (1670); Ex parte Bollman, 8 U.S. (4 Cranch.) 74, 91-92, 100 (1807) (Marshall, C.J.); Ex parte Kearney, 20 U.S. (7 Wheat.) 38, 41-42 (1822) (Story, J.).

jury.[48] According to Bator, even Congress' 1867 supplementation of the 1789 Act's "cause of commitment" language with a power to use the writ to cure a state prisoner's detention "in violation of the Constitution, or of any treaty or law of the United States"[49] had little effect because of the Court's adoption, apparently by fiat, of a *Catch 22* preclusion doctrine in 1886 in *Ex parte Royall*.[50] As described by Bator, *Royall*'s so-called "exhaustion of state remedies" doctrine required state prisoners to challenge unconstitutional incarceration in state trial and appellate courts before alleging it on habeas corpus, but then made the state courts' resolution of the issues *res judicata* in subsequent habeas corpus proceedings unless the detaining court lacked jurisdiction, had convicted the petitioner under an unconstitutional statute, or had imposed an unconstitutional sentence.[51]

Only in 1915 in *Frank v. Mangum*[52] and in 1923 in *Moore v. Dempsey*[53] did the Court again (modestly) expand the writ, by limiting *Royall*'s *res judicata* doctrine to federal claims as to which "full and fair" corrective process was actually available in the state courts.[54] And only in a series of Supreme Court decisions beginning in the 1930s and culminating in the 1953 decision in *Brown v. Allen*[55] did the Court finally expand the writ broadly to reach *all* constitutional claims.[56]

Bator focused mainly on the range of claims that historically were cognizable in habeas corpus proceedings. In important but largely ignored passages, however, he also considered the question of the scope of review historically available on habeas corpus, concluding that the Court exercised *de novo* review of legal claims (*i.e.*, "ordinary review on the merits") from the moment it acquired jurisdiction under the 1867 habeas corpus act in 1885.[57] Although Bator opposed *de novo* review of mixed questions of law and fact by *the Supreme Court on direct review*, he argued forcefully that, if such review was available on direct

---

[48] *See* Bator, *supra* § 2.1 n.1, at 471-73.

[49] Act of Feb. 5, 1867, ch. 28, § 1, 14 Stat. 385.

[50] 117 U.S. 241 (1886). *See* Bator, *supra* § 2.1 n.1, at 478-80.

[51] *See* Bator, *supra* § 2.1 n.1, at 478-83.

[52] 237 U.S. 309 (1915).

[53] 261 U.S. 86 (1923).

[54] *See* Bator, *supra* § 2.1 n.1, at 486-87, 489.

[55] 344 U.S. 443 (1953).

[56] Bator, *supra* § 2.1 n.1, at 493-500 (discussing, *e.g.*, Johnson v. Zerbst, 304 U.S. 458 (1938) and *Brown v. Allen*, *supra*).

[57] *Id.* at 479. *See id.* at 444 & n.4, 462, 474, 500. *See also* HART & WESCHSLER, 2d ed., *supra* 2.1 n.1, at 1465, 1486; Liebman, *supra* § 2.1 n.1, at 2010-36.

review, it also, in fairness, should be available (and that it historically had been equally available) in habeas corpus review.[58]

Justice Brennan and Professor Peller offer a sharply different view of the "cognizability of claims" (but not the "scope of review") question, arguing that habeas corpus had always been a forum for providing specified classes of prisoners with review of the legality of their detention under existing standards of due process.[59] This result occurred naturally under the "cause of commitment" language, which emerged from proto-due process notions stretching back to the Magna Carta. The 1867 act simply expanded the range of cognizable claims from those drawing upon due process notions to constitutional claims of all sorts.[60]

Recognizing that the Court's relatively infrequent grants of review and relief represent too small a proportion of its habeas corpus jurisprudence to make the above description complete, Justice Brennan and Professor Peller identify three limitations that, they claim, frequently led the Court to deny the writ. First, because Article III withheld original jurisdiction over criminal and habeas corpus cases from the Supreme Court, and Congress withheld appellate jurisdiction in criminal cases,[61] the Court felt constrained from using habeas corpus as a substitute for the criminal jurisdiction it so clearly had been denied. Thus, the theory goes, only the lower federal courts, with potentially unlimited "original" jurisdiction, could exercise unlimited jurisdiction to issue the writ.[62] Second, until the incorporation movement of the 1940s-1960s, the constitutional due process right that was fully enforceable in habeas corpus meant no more than a "competent" forum — one with subject matter and personal jurisdiction — proceeding according to the applicable positive or common law and (a later requirement) the right to notice and a chance to be heard.[63] Thus, what Professor Bator treats as the *writ's* limitation was instead the outer reach of contemporary interpretations of the Due Process Clause and the Constitution. Finally, Justice Brennan and Professor Peller interpret many of the Court's decisions as relief-

---

[58] *See* Bator, *supra* § 2.1 n.1, at 502-11.

[59] *See* Fay v. Noia, 372 U.S. 391, 401-02, 409-10, 418 (1963); Peller, *supra* § 2.1 n.1 at 661-63.

[60] *See Fay v. Noia, supra,* 372 U.S. at 404-10; Peller, *supra* § 2.1 n.1, at 618-22, 629-30.

[61] U.S. CONST. art. III, § 2.

[62] *See Fay v. Noia, supra,* 372 U.S. at 391, 429-30; Peller, *supra* § 2.1 n.1, at 612-13 (discussing In re McDonald, 16 F. Cas. 23 (E.D. Mo. 1861) (No. 8,751)). *See also* Stephen A. Saltzburg, *Habeas Corpus: The Supreme Court and the Congress,* 44 OHIO ST. L.J. 367, 370-72 (1983).

[63] *See* Wright v. West, 505 U.S. 277, 297-300 (1992) (O'Connor, J., concurring in the judgment); *Fay v. Noia, supra,* 372 U.S. at 412-14; Peller, *supra* § 2.1 n.1, at 628-29.

delaying but not — as Professor Bator would have it — relief-*denying* applications of the exhaustion doctrine.[64]

Neither the Bator nor the Brennan-Peller thesis accurately describes the history of habeas corpus in this country. The Bator thesis (1) ignores the Court's repeated statements that state court review need only occur "in the first instance," or "in advance of" habeas corpus review — as if a "second instance" of federal review was to occur in the *wake* of state court review;[65] (2) cannot explain a number of 19th and early 20th century cases, including the celebrated decision in *Yick Wo v. Hopkins*,[66] that undeniably decided the merits of constitutional claims that were not premised on the detaining authority's lack of jurisdiction or application of an unconstitutional statute or sentence;[67] (3) cannot explain an even larger number of cases *denying* habeas corpus review on claims that manifestly *did* challenge the jurisdiction of the convicting court;[68] and (4) cannot explain the contrary outcomes on identical facts in *Frank v. Mangum* and *Moore v. Dempsey*, only the former of which provides any support for the Batorian view that, at the time, habeas corpus relief was available only on constitutional claims that prisoners had no full and fair opportunity to litigate in the state courts.[69]

---

[64] *See Fay v. Noia, supra,* 372 U.S. at 418-22; Peller, *supra* § 2.1 n.1, at 640-41.

[65] *See, e.g.,* Urquhart v. Brown, 205 U.S. 179, 181-82 (1907); Whitten v. Tomlinson, 160 U.S. 231, 240 (1895); Cook v. Hart, 146 U.S. 183, 195 (1892).

[66] 118 U.S. 356 (1886) (discussed in Liebman, *supra* § 2.1 n.1, at 2045).

[67] *See, e.g.,* Felts v. Murphy, 201 U.S. 123, 129 (1906); Davis v. Burke, 179 U.S. 399, 403-04 (1900); Bergemann v. Backer, 157 U.S. 655, 656-68 (1895); In re Duncan, 139 U.S. 449, 454-61 (1891); In re Converse, 137 U.S. 624, 631 (1891); Crowley v. Christensen, 137 U.S. 86, 92-94 (1890); other cases discussed *infra* § 2.4d nn.92-95, 104-06, 131-45, 184-85, 219-20, 245-47 and accompanying text.

[68] *See, e.g., Whitten v. Tomlinson, supra,* 160 U.S. at 240, 245-47 (refusing to address merits of petitioner's claims that Connecticut convicting court did not have jurisdiction over him because it (1) extradited him from Massachusetts in violation of federal extradition statute which only permitted extradition of "fugitive[s] from justice" (which Whitten claimed not to be), (2) arrested Whitten, a domiciliary of Massachusetts, under Connecticut statute only authorizing arrest of local residents, and (3) arrested Whitten pursuant to warrant that expired months before arrest); In re Tyler, 149 U.S. 164, 181 (1893) (citing cases) (Court would not review habeas corpus claim based on absence of sufficient amount in controversy to give federal convicting court jurisdiction over lawsuit that resulted in injunction and contempt conviction and incarceration for party's violation of injunction); Liebman, *supra* § 2.1 n.1, at 2054; cases discussed *infra* §§ 2.4d nn.96-98, 142-45, 178 and accompanying text.

[69] The Court denied relief in *Frank* but granted it in *Moore* on identical claims, which the prisoners in both cases had the same opportunity to litigate in the state courts — *i.e.,* trials allegedly dominated by mobs, followed by seemingly regular proceedings on motion for a new trial and appeal. *See* Moore v. Dempsey, 261 U.S. 86, 89 (1923); *id.* at 97-98 (McReynolds, J., dissenting); Frank v. Mangum, 237 U.S. 309, 312-17 (1915).

The Brennan-Peller thesis (1) ignores recurring language in the Court's late 19th and early 20th century cases that *"leave[s]* the petitioner to the usual and orderly course of proceeding" through the state process and "by writ of error from this court";[70] (2) inaccurately attributes important denials of the writ to (a) limitations on the Supreme Court's jurisdiction over criminal appeals, notwithstanding that the Court explicitly rejected that theory on numerous occasions[71] and contracted, as opposed to expanding, the writ when Congress gave the Court jurisdiction over criminal appeals in 1891,[72] and (b) to the limited reach of contemporary constitutional law, notwithstanding the Court's simultaneous grants of relief on similar constitutional claims on direct review;[73] and (3) cannot explain the divergent outcomes in *Frank* and *Moore* because the narrow constitutional interpretation to which Brennan and Peller attribute the denial of relief in *Frank* would have required the same outcome on identical facts in *Moore*.[74]

---

[70] *Whitten v. Tomlinson, supra,* 160 U.S. at 242 (relying on New York v. Eno, 155 U.S. 89, 93-95 (1894); Ex parte Royall, 117 U.S. 241, 251-53 (1886)) (emphasis added). *See, e.g., Urquhart v. Brown, supra,* 205 U.S. at 181-83; Tinsley v. Anderson, 171 U.S. 101, 104-05 (1898). *See also* Liebman, *supra* § 2.1 n.1, at 2047-48 (additional criticisms of Brennan-Peller's treatment of exhaustion doctrine).

[71] Justice Johnson twice unsuccessfully argued that, by withholding direct appellate jurisdiction in criminal cases, Congress also intended to withhold habeas corpus jurisdiction to review court-ordered incarceration. Ex parte Bollman, 8 U.S. (4 Cranch.) 74, 104-07 (1807) (Johnson, J., dissenting); Ex parte Watkins, 32 U.S. (7 Pet.) 567, 578-80 (1833) (Johnson, J., dissenting). *See also* Ex parte Wells, 59 U.S. (18 How.) 307, 329 (1855) (Curtis, J., dissenting). The Court rejected Johnson's view in the cited cases and in Ex parte Siebold, 100 U.S. 371, 377 (1879). The Court repeatedly held that the habeas corpus provision in the 1789 Judiciary Act was a sufficient grant to the Court under Article III of the Constitution of "appellate" jurisdiction to review court-ordered incarceration. *See, e.g.,* In re Kaine, 55 U.S. (14 How.) 103, 120-21 (1852) (Curtis, J., concurring); In re Metzger, 46 U.S. (5 How.) 175, 190-91 (1847); *Ex parte Bollman, supra* at 95-97. *See generally* Liebman, *supra* § 2.1 n.1, at 2043-44; *supra* § 2.2 nn.5, 6 and accompanying text; *infra* §§ 2.4d nn.84-91 and accompanying text, 40.2.

[72] *In re Tyler, supra,* 149 U.S. at 173, 180-81 (rejecting argument that Congress' authorization of criminal appeals had removed any "obstacle" to use of writ to "inquir[e] into the sufficiency of the evidence on which the judgment was founded and into errors of law beyond jurisdictional errors" and holding that habeas corpus was available only "when *no* writ of error or appeal will lie" (emphasis added)). *See* Liebman, *supra* § 2.1 n.1, at 2051-52.

[73] *See, e.g.,* In re Wood, 140 U.S. 278, 283-90 (1891) (denying relief on scrupulously preserved, impeccably pleaded, and, if allegations were true, patently meritorious jury discrimination claim of sort that had been cognizable on direct review in Supreme Court since Neal v. Delaware, 103 U.S. 370, 397 (1880)).

[74] If, as Brennan and Peller claim, Frank lost because the full and fair *appellate* affirmance of his guilt gave him all the process he was due, notwithstanding an unfair *trial*, there is no good reason why the *Moore* petitioners won after receiving the *same* appellate treatment. *See supra* note 69.

d. *History and function of the writ: 1789-1998.* A more accurate description of the writ's history and current function in this country is as follows:

> Federal habeas corpus is not a substitute for a *general* writ of error or other direct appeal as of right. Since 1789, however, it has provided statutorily specified classes of prisoners with a *limited* and *substitute* federal writ of error or appeal as of right. That appellate procedure has been *limited* because it has lain only to hear claims of particular national importance — a category of claims that Congress has delineated with greater specificity over time, but that has consistently been interpreted to include recognized constitutional claims. It has been a *substitute* because it has served only in the absence of Supreme Court review as of right.[75]

---

[75] *See, e.g.*, Brown v. Allen, 344 U.S. 443, 501, 510 (1953) (opinion for the Court of Frankfurter, J.) (through the writ, Congress has empowered "district courts to be the organ of the higher law rather than a Court of Appeals, or exclusively this Court" and "has told the District Judge to act on those occasions, however rare, when there are meritorious causes in which habeas corpus is the ultimate and only relief and designed to be such"); Waley v. Johnston, 316 U.S. 101, 105 (1942) (writ "extends ... to those exceptional cases where the conviction has been in disregard of the constitutional rights of the accused, and where the writ is the only effective means of preserving his rights"); In re Tyler, 149 U.S. 164, 180 (1893) (discussed in Liebman, *supra* § 2.1 n.1, at 2051-55) ("The writ of habeas corpus is not to perform the office of a writ of error of appeal; but *when no writ of error or appeal will lie*, if a petitioner is imprisoned under a judgment of [a court] ... which had no jurisdiction of the person or of the subject matter, or authority to render the judgment complained of, then [habeas corpus] relief may be accorded." (emphasis added)); Ex parte Parks, 93 U.S. 18, 21 (1876) (writ "is one of the modes in which this court exercises supervisory power over inferior courts and tribunals; but it is a special mode, and confined to a limited class of cases"). Our approach tracks Justice Gray's conscientious effort in Whitten v. Tomlinson, 160 U.S. 231 (1895), to locate a comprehensive analysis of the writ in both the statutory and caselaw context of federal question jurisdiction as a whole. According to Gray, "three different methods have been provided by statute for bringing before the courts of the United States proceedings begun in the courts of the States" when "necessary to secure the supremacy of the Constitution, laws and treaties of the United States." *Id.* at 238. The first two extended respectively to judgments allegedly contrary to, and to claims arising under, "the Constitution, laws or treaties of the United States." They were direct Supreme Court review on writ of error under section 25 of the Judiciary Act of 1789 and section 2 of the Act of February 5, 1867, and removal to the lower federal courts under a series of acts passed during periods of inter-sectional domestic crisis in 1815-1817, 1833, and 1863-February 5, 1867. As to writ of error review, see *id.* (citing, *e.g.*, Act of Sept. 24, 1789, ch. 20, § 25, 1 Stat. 73, 85; Act of Feb. 5, 1867, ch. 28, § 2, 14 Stat. 385, 385-86; Cohens v. Virginia, 19 U.S. (6 Wheat.) 264 (1821); Martin v. Hunter's Lessee, 14 U.S. (1 Wheat.) 304 (1816)). As to removal, see *id.* (discussing, *e.g.*, Act of Feb. 4, 1815, ch. 31, § 8, 3 Stat. 195, 198-99; Act of Mar. 2, 1833, ch. 57, § 3, 4 Stat. 632, 633-34; Act of Mar. 3, 1863, ch. 81, § 5, 12 Stat. 755, 756-57; Act of Apr. 9, 1866, ch. 31, § 3, 14 Stat. 27 (amended, *e.g.*, Act of Feb. 5, 1867, ch. 27, 14 Stat. 385)). Third was habeas corpus, the development of which Justice Gray traced from the 1789 Judiciary Act, to the same act by which Congress had enlarged federal

The *limited* class of nationally important claims cognizable in habeas corpus has changed over time under the influence of (1) constitutional and statutory limitations on the federal courts' jurisdiction — claims arising under state law, even if jurisdictional, have never been cognizable;[76] (2) caselaw identifying the legal defects in *civil* cases that are subject to collateral attack;[77] and (3) developing notions of due process and constitutional law.[78] At no time was the line between jurisdictional and nonjurisdictional claims a good proxy for the line between important and unimportant claims.

As a *substitute* for federal direct appeal, habeas corpus has never duplicated, but has always mirrored the scope of, Supreme Court review on direct appeal. Although the line between legal and factual questions has changed over time, the scope of both modes of review has always been *de novo* on legal claims and deferential-to-nonexistent on factual findings. "Innocence" claims and their close cousins, claims that the penal statute was not intended to reach the particular prisoner's conduct, are both nationally unimportant because *sui generis*, and subject to no or little review because aimed at the central fact determination at

---

removal jurisdiction in 1833, to section 1 of the same February 5, 1867 act cited in Justice Gray's writ of error discussion. *Id.* at 239 (quoting Act of Sept. 24, 1789, ch. 20, § 14, 1 Stat. 73, 82; citing, *e.g.*, Act of Mar. 2, 1833, ch. 57, § 7, 4 Stat. 632, 634-35; Act of Feb. 5, 1867, ch. 28, § 1, 14 Stat. 385, 385-86 (other citations omitted)). Under the 1874 Revised Statutes' unified codification of all prior habeas corpus provisions, federal judges and courts had the "power to grant writs of *habeas corpus* ... [to] any prisoner ... 'in custody in violation of the Constitution, or of a law or treaty of the United States;' and '... shall forthwith award a writ of *habeas corpus*, unless it appears from the petition itself that the party is not entitled thereto.'" *Id.* at 239-40 (quoting and paraphrasing Rev. Stat., tit. 13, ch. 13, §§ 751-755, 761, 18 Stat. 142-43 (1878) (recodified and amended at 28 U.S.C. §§ 2241(a)-(c), 2243)). According to Justice Gray, however, the habeas corpus statutes did not "compel [federal] courts ... to draw to themselves, *in the first instance*, the control of all criminal prosecutions commenced in state courts" and, instead, gave the courts "discretion as to the *time and mode* in which it will exert the powers conferred upon it." *Id.* at 240-42 (quoting Ex parte Royall, 117 U.S. 241, 251-53 (1886) (emphasis added)). Out of concern for "'relations existing ... between the judicial tribunals of the Union and of the States,'" the Court accordingly had directed the lower federal courts, "except in ... peculiar and urgent cases," to exercise their discretion so as "generally [to] leave the [habeas corpus] petitioner to" other, preferred modes of federal review (generally, the Supreme Court's writ of error review) if, but only if, such modes of review were available *as of right*. *Id.* at 240-42 (quoting Ex parte Royall, 117 U.S. at 251 (emphasis added)).

[76] *See, e.g.*, In re Converse, 137 U.S. 624, 630-31 (1891).

[77] *See, e.g.*, Cuddy, Petitioner, 131 U.S. 280, 284-85 (1889); Ex parte Lange, 85 U.S. (18 Wall.) 163, 177-78 (1873); Ex parte Watkins, 28 U.S. (3 Pet.) 193, 203-07 (1830); Woolhandler, *supra* § 2.1 n.1, at 587-96.

[78] *See, e.g.*, Frank v. Mangum, 237 U.S. 309, 326-28 (1915); Yick Wo v. Hopkins, 118 U.S. 356, 369-70, 373-74 (1886); *Ex parte Lange, supra*, 85 U.S. (18 Wall.) at 176-77; Peller, *supra* § 2.1 n.1, at 628-29; Woolhandler, *supra* § 2.1 n.1, at 596-629.

trial. For these reasons, the Court has been particularly careful to exclude such claims from habeas corpus.[79]

Federal question review under the 1789 Judiciary Act. The fount of all federal question jurisdiction is the First Judiciary Act of 1789. Section 25 of that act extended writs of error as of right to state prisoners (and other state litigants) who, within the preceding five years, had been denied relief "in the highest court of law ... of a State in which a decision in the suit could be had" on claims challenging a state statute or other state authority "on the ground of [its] being repugnant to the constitution, treaties or laws of the United States" or questioning "the construction of ... the constitution, ... a treaty, or statute of ... the United States."[80] Only errors that "appear[ed] *on the face* of the record" were cognizable.[81] Although section 25 provided without limitation that the state court "*judgment* ... may be *re-examined* and reversed or affirmed,"[82] the Court followed common law *appellate* practice, which only permitted *de novo* review of *legal* claims and forbade review of factual determinations.[83]

Sections 9 and 11 of the 1789 Act gave federal district and circuit courts jurisdiction to try criminal cases arising under federal penal statutes, but the Act granted no court direct appellate jurisdiction in criminal cases.[84] Section 14 of the 1789 Act did, however, give federal prisoners, but expressly withheld from state prisoners, the right to petition for writs of habeas corpus to review the "cause of commitment."[85] Although the statute did not expressly give the Supreme Court itself — only its individual Justices (along with lower federal courts and judges) — the power to issue the writ, the Court quickly held that the statute accorded the entire Court the power to grant habeas corpus relief.[86] In so holding, Justice Marshall rejected the Government's claims that the Court, as a court, had no habeas corpus jurisdiction because, citing *Marbury v. Madison*,[87] the Constitution's strict limits on the Court's original jurisdiction forbade the Court to hear habeas corpus petitions filed directly before it and because the 1789 statute failed to authorize appeals from lower federal courts in habeas

---

[79] *See infra* notes 96-98, 104-06, 142-50, 186 and accompanying text; *infra* § 2.5.

[80] Act of Sept. 24, 1789, ch. 20 § 25, 1 Stat. 73, 85-86.

[81] *Id.* § 25, 1 Stat. at 86-87 (emphasis added).

[82] *Id.* § 15, 1 Stat. at 85-86 (emphasis added).

[83] *See, e.g.*, Wiscart v. D'Auchy, 3 U.S. (3 Dall.) 320, 327 (1796). *See also supra* § 2.4b n.38.

[84] *See* Act of Sept. 24, 1789, ch. 20, §§ 9, 11, 1 Stat. 73, 76-79.

[85] *Id.* § 14, 1 Stat. at 81-82.

[86] *See* Ex parte Bollman, 8 U.S. (4 Cranch.) 75, 96, 100 (1807). The *Bollman* Court accepted the proposition that habeas corpus in this country is a statutory remedy and that "federal courts have no inherent power to issue the writ." Schlup v. Delo, 513 U.S. 298, 350 (1995) (Scalia, J., dissenting). *See supra* § 2.2 n.10 and accompanying text.

[87] 5 U.S. (1 Cranch.) 137 (1803).

corpus cases, thus denying the constitutionally required authorization of appellate power.[88] In a ruling that reverberated throughout the Court's 19th century habeas corpus cases, the Court avoided both claims by ruling (1) that habeas corpus was "clearly appellate" because it involved "the revision of a decision of an inferior court, by which a citizen has been committed to jail," and (2) that Congress through section 14 had given the full Court the constitutionally requisite authorization, in the exercise of its *appellate* jurisdiction, to adjudicate habeas corpus petitions originating in the Court.[89] Essentially until 1885, therefore, the Court routinely heard habeas corpus petitions arising in one of two postures — filed initially in the Supreme Court with no lower court action on habeas corpus,[90] or filed in a lower federal court followed by the filing in the Supreme Court of an "original" habeas corpus petition and a petition for a writ of *certiorari* to bring the lower court's record before the Court.[91]

The 1789 Act's authorization to inquire into the "cause of commitment" powered the Court's entire habeas corpus jurisprudence between 1789 and at least 1874.[92] Contrasting the nine federal-prisoner habeas corpus cases during the period in which the Court granted review, including the six in which it granted relief, with the two in which it denied review based on substantive limits on the scope of the writ[93] reveals that the 1789 Act cases did not limit habeas corpus review either to jurisdictional claims or to claims attacking pretrial as opposed to postconviction detention. In three of the cases in which the Court granted relief, and in at least one of those in which it granted review but denied

---

[88] *See Ex parte Bollman, supra*, 8 U.S. (4 Cranch.) at 96-101.

[89] *Id.* at 100-01. *See, e.g.*, Ex parte Siebold, 100 U.S. 371, 374 (1879); Ex parte McCardle I, 73 U.S. (6 Wall.) 318, 324 (1867); Ex parte Watkins II, 32 U.S. (7 Pet.) 568, 572-73 (1833); *supra* §§ 2.2 nn.5-6 and accompanying text, 2.4c n.71 and accompanying text; *infra* § 40.2.

[90] *See, e.g.*, Ex parte Kearney, 20 U.S. (7 Wheat.) 39-44 (1822). *Cf.* In re Metzger, 46 U.S. (5 How.) 176, 191-92 (1847) (forbidding review of petitions originally filed in Supreme Court and challenging executive detention because case was not appellate (*i.e.*, was not one court's review of actions of another court) and thus was beyond Court's constitutionally specified original jurisdiction).

[91] *See, e.g.*, Ex parte Yerger, 75 U.S. (8 Wall.) 85, 99-101 (1868); In re Kaine, 55 U.S. (14 How.) 103, 116 (1852).

[92] *See infra* notes 127-30 and accompanying text (gradual replacement of 1789 Act by 1867 Act during 1874-1885 period).

[93] Granting habeas corpus review and relief are: United States v. Hamilton, 3 U.S. (3 Dall.) 17 (1795); Ex parte Burford, 7 U.S. (3 Cranch.) 448 (1806); Ex parte Bollman, 8 U.S. (4 Cranch.) 75 (1807); Ex parte Watkins II, 32 U.S. (7 Pet.) 568 (1833); Ex parte Milligan, 71 U.S. (4 Wall.) 2 (1866); Ex parte Lange, 85 U.S. (18 Wall.) 163 (1873). Granting review but denying relief are: Ex parte Milburn, 34 U.S. (9 Pet.) 704 (1835); In re Kaine, 55 U.S. (14 How.) 103 (1852); Ex parte Wells, 59 U.S. (18 How.) 307 (1855). Denying review based on substantive limits on the scope of the writ are: Ex parte Kearney, 20 U.S. (7 Wheat.) 38 (1822); Ex parte Watkins, 28 U.S. (3 Pet.) 193 (1830).

relief, the detaining authority clearly had jurisdiction to detain the petitioner.[94] And in two of the cases in which it granted relief, the Court overturned what amounted to criminal *convictions*.[95] On the other hand, in the famous case of *Ex parte Watkins*,[96] the Court *denied* habeas corpus *review* of two challenges to the *jurisdiction* of the detaining Court — that the petitioner's conduct lay outside the proscription of the federal statute under which he was convicted, hence outside the detaining court's subject-matter jurisdiction, and that the petitioner's actions took place in another state, thus depriving the court of personal jurisdiction.[97] Nor did *Watkins* and the Court's other cases *claim* to limit habeas corpus review to jurisdictional claims, but instead identified as equally critical whether the detaining court acted without "authority" or "unlawfully."[98]

Instead, the Justices freely granted relief during this period on the basis of any and all legal claims of national (meaning, at the least, constitutional) importance — including whether the court that ordered the petitioner's arrest lacked probable cause to believe a crime had been committed, in violation of the 4th Amendment;[99] whether a court convicted the petitioner without the rudiments of

---

[94] Granting relief on nonjurisdictional claims are: *Ex parte Lange*, *supra*, 85 U.S. (18 Wall.) at 175 (curing double jeopardy violation); *Ex parte Bollman*, *supra*, 8 U.S. (4 Cranch.) at 135 (overturning lower court's arrest warrant for lack of probable cause); *United States v. Hamilton*, *supra*, 3 U.S. (3 Dall.) at 18 (similar). Hearing but denying relief on a nonjurisdictional claim is: *Ex parte Milburn*, *supra*, 34 U.S. (9 Pet.) at 710 (denying relief on alleged double jeopardy violation committed by court with unchallenged jurisdiction).

[95] *See Ex parte Milligan*, *supra*, 71 U.S. (4 Wall.) at 122-23 (civilian's conviction by military court violated constitutional right to trial by jury before life-tenured judge); *Ex parte Burford*, *supra*, 7 U.S. (3 Cranch.) at 453 (summary incarceration and fine imposed by justices of peace after finding petitioner to be of "ill fame" overturned for lack of "regular" proceedings).

[96] 28 U.S. (3 Pet.) 193 (1830).

[97] *Id.* at 197, 201 (alleging "that no offence was charged in the indictments, which was within the jurisdiction of the circuit court for the county of Washington" and "that the indictment charges no offense for which the prisoner was punishable in that court, or of which that court could take cognizance; and consequently, that the proceedings are *coram non judice*").

[98] *See, e.g.*, *Ex parte Lange*, *supra*, 85 U.S. (18 Wall.) at 166 ("whether th[e detaining] court has exceeded its authority"); *Ex parte Milligan*, *supra*, 71 U.S. (4 Wall.) at 116, 118 ("lawfulness of ... imprisonment"); *In re Metzger*, 46 U.S. (5 How.) 176, 191 (1847) ("legality of the commitment"); *Ex parte Watkins*, *supra*, 28 U.S. (3 Pet.) at 202 (same). *See also infra* note 105 (in 19th century, claim that act was "unlawful" or without "authority" was equivalent to constitutional claim that act violated due process).

[99] The dissenting judge in the lower court in *Bollman*, whose conclusion the Supreme Court accepted on appeal, *see supra* note 94 (summarizing *Bollman*), described the claim in that case as arising under the 4th Amendment. United States v. Bollman, 24 F. Cas. 1189, 1192 (C.C.D.C. 1807) (No. 14,622) (Cranch, J., dissenting). *See also* Ex parte Milburn, 34 U.S. (9 Pet.) 704, 705 (1835) (district attorney's issuance of arrest warrant violated 4th Amendment requirement of action by magistrate); *Ex parte Burford*, *supra*, 7 U.S. (3 Cranch.) at 452, 453 (granting relief in part "for want of [a warrant] stating some good cause certain, supported by oath").

a trial, or at least without a jury and a life-tenured judge as required by Article III and the 6th Amendment;[100] whether the detaining court had twice placed the petitioner in jeopardy by imposing two punishments for a single offense, in violation of the 5th Amendment;[101] and whether the statute under which the petitioner was convicted was unconstitutional.[102] When the Court denied relief on the merits, it did so only after satisfying itself that no constitutional violation had occurred.[103]

Furthermore, in the two cases in which the Court denied review, in both cases saying that the writ could not substitute for a plenary appeal,[104] it did so expressly on the ground that habeas corpus instead provided review that, although concededly "in the nature of a writ of error," only reached a *limited* range of cases.[105] And its holdings demarcate that limit precisely according to the *national importance* — as shown *inter alia* by the constitutional status — of the claims involved. Thus, the Court refused to hear even jurisdictional claims that merely challenged the sufficiency of the evidence to convict or asserted that

[100] *See, e.g., Ex parte Milligan, supra,* 71 U.S. (4 Wall.) at 122; *Ex parte Burford, supra,* 7 U.S. (3 Cranch.) at 452, 453 (apparently treating lack of jury trial as reason to grant writ and order trial "*de novo*" with "regular" proceedings); United States v. Hamilton, 3 U.S. (3 Dall.) 17 (1795). *See also* Ex parte Randolph, 20 F. Cas. 242, 254-55 (C.C.D. Va. 1833) (No. 11,558) (Marshall, C.J., Circuit Justice) (assuming cognizability of claim that statute violated Article III and the 4th, 5th, 6th, and 7th Amendments).

[101] *See Ex parte Lange, supra,* 85 U.S. (18 Wall.) at 169.

[102] *See Ex parte Randolph, supra,* 20 F. Cas. at 253-56 (*dicta* by Marshall, Circuit Justice).

[103] Ex parte Wells, 59 U.S. (18 How.) 307, 310-15 (1855) (denying relief on merits because President's pardoning power authorizes commutation of death sentence on condition that petitioner accept life imprisonment); In re Kaine, 55 U.S. (14 How.) 103, 110 (1852) (federal statute constitutionally permitted foreign government to move in court to extradite petitioner without President's concurrence); *Ex parte Milburn, supra,* 34 U.S. (9 Pet.) at 708-10 (denying relief on merits because no double jeopardy violation occurred).

[104] *See* Ex parte Watkins, 28 U.S. (3 Pet.) 193, 203 (1830); Ex parte Kearney, 20 U.S. (7 Wheat.) 38, 44-45 (1822).

[105] *Ex parte Watkins, supra,* 28 U.S. (3 Pet.) at 202-03. The understanding of habeas corpus presented here explains the puzzling juxtaposition of statements that habeas corpus does not comprehend the "power to examine the proceedings, on a writ of error" but is "in the nature of a writ of error, to examine the legality of the commitment." *Id.* Chief Justice Marshall was not contradicting himself. Habeas corpus did not substitute for an appeal, because it did not require the reviewing court to "examine [all] the proceedings" for even technical compliance with unimportant aspects of the law. Instead, habeas corpus required the court to review only a limited set of issues arising under the rubric of "the legality of the commitment" — a phrase corresponding to the era's definition of due process. *See* Woolhandler, *supra* § 2.1 n.1, at 627 nn.310, 312. As to the latter set of especially important issues, however, the *scope* of review was "in the nature of a writ of error."

the particular conduct for which the petitioner had been convicted fell outside the penal statute.[106]

Moreover, the *scope* of review that the Court afforded on habeas corpus precisely tracked that available on direct appeal. Thus, as section 25 expressly required on writ of error review,[107] the Court limited its habeas corpus review to *reexamination* of *legal* determinations[108] appearing "*on the face*" of the record.[109]

In short, as interpreted by the Court, the 1789 Act used habeas corpus as a substitute for the Court's direct review of nationally important questions when the latter review was not meaningfully available to incarcerated individuals. Having withheld from federal prisoners any right to a plenary direct appeal, the Act granted them instead the more limited, but still appellate, remedy of habeas corpus review of fundamental (including all constitutional) legal claims. Having granted state prisoners a writ of error as of right to challenge the state court's adverse constitutional decisions, the Act explicitly withheld substitute habeas corpus review.

The antebellum removal and habeas corpus acts. In 1815-1817 and 1833, when the New England States and then South Carolina threatened to "nullify" national revenue legislation by arresting and prosecuting federal officers who enforced it, Congress suddenly found that forcing this class of *state* prisoners to await their postconviction and postappeal writ of error remedies would indeed nullify nationally important laws. Congress accordingly authorized federal officers detained by state courts for acts undertaken "in pursuance of a law of the United States" to seek either removal or habeas corpus redress in the lower federal courts in advance of their inadequate writ of error remedies.[110] Moreover,

---

[106] *See, e.g.*, Ex parte Watkins II, 32 U.S. (7 Pet.) 568, 574 (1833) (refusing review of claim that statutorily permissible $3000 fine was excessive); *Ex parte Watkins, supra*, 28 U.S. (3 Pet.) at 207 (refusing review of claims that federal penal law did not comprehend charged embezzlements, and that crime of paying out money in Boston and New York embezzled from government in Washington did not take place in Washington); *Ex parte Kearney, supra*, 20 U.S. (7 Wheat.) at 45 (refusing to review lower court's finding that witness was in contempt for refusing to answer questions).

[107] *See supra* notes 81-83 and accompanying text.

[108] *See, e.g.*, Ex parte Milligan, 71 U.S. (4 Wall.) 2, 112-13, 118 (1866); *Ex parte Watkins, supra*, 28 U.S. (3 Pet.) at 203-07; *Ex parte Kearney, supra*, 20 U.S. (7 Wheat.) at 42 (reviewing *de novo* question whether "commitment was made by a court of competent jurisdiction ... in the exercise of an unquestionable authority"); Ex parte Bollman, 8 U.S. (4 Cranch.) 75, 114, 125, 135-36 (1807) (defining scope of review as "do[ing] that which the court below ought to have done," Court "fully examine[d] and attentively consider[ed]" whether probable cause existed).

[109] *See, e.g.*, Ex parte Lange, 85 U.S. (18 Wall.) 163, 176 (1873); *Ex parte Watkins, supra*, 28 U.S. (3 Pet.) at 202-03.

[110] Act of Mar. 2, 1833, ch. 57, §§ 3, 7, 4 Stat. 632, 633-34.

in the 1850s, when state prosecutions of federal marshals threatened the enforcement of the Fugitive Slave Act, the lower federal judiciary, often acting through Supreme Court Justices on circuit, repeatedly interpreted the 1833 habeas corpus provisions to permit review *de novo*[111] — *after* conviction as well as before[112] — of the officials' "pursuance of federal law" defenses. For the first time, moreover, habeas corpus review was understood to permit inquiry beyond the face of the commitment papers, into the substance of the federal officials' "pursuance" claims.[113]

Reconstruction-era accretions to writ of error, removal, and habeas corpus jurisdiction. With the use of the 1833 habeas corpus and removal powers to enforce the hated Fugitive Slave Law fresh in its members' minds, the Reconstruction Congress adapted both techniques to its own purposes in a series of acts passed in 1863, 1866, and on February 5, 1867. One of the two acts passed on this last day also broadened the Supreme Court's writ of error jurisdiction to review federal questions arising in state courts.[114] Through these acts, Congress made a series of parallel expansions of all three modes of federal court review of state court criminal actions.

The legislation widened the range of claims cognizable in all three types of proceedings up to Article III's federal-question maximum.[115] The new removal and habeas corpus provisions expanded the range of prisoners protected to *all* those with federal claims.[116] The new habeas corpus and writ of error provisions expressly overturned caselaw (in the case of habeas corpus) and legislation (in

---

[111] *See, e.g.*, Ex parte Sifford, 22 F. Cas. 105, 107-08 (S.D. Ohio 1857) (No. 12,848) (citing cases); Ex parte Robinson, 20 F. Cas. 965, 966, 968 (S.D. Ohio 1856) (No. 11,934); Ex parte Jenkins, 13 F. Cas. 445, 447 (E.D. Pa. 1853) (No. 7,259) (Grier, Cir. Justice); *id.* at 451, 459-60 (Kane, D.J.).

[112] *See, e.g.*, Electoral College Case, 8 F. Cas. 427, 431, 433, 434 (S.C. 1876) (No. 4336) (Bond, Cir. Justice); *Ex parte Robinson, supra,* 20 F. Cas. at 965-66 (granting relief after conviction); *Ex parte Jenkins, supra*, 13 F. Cas. at 451 (granting relief pretrial and saying that same result would occur post-trial).

[113] *See* authority cited *supra* note 112. The Supreme Court later validated these interpretations of the 1833 Act. *See* In re Neagle, 135 U.S. 1, 42, 53, 69-74 (1890).

[114] *See supra* note 75 (discussing *Whitten v. Tomlinson*).

[115] *See* Civil Rights Act of 1866, ch. 31, §§ 1, 3, 14 Stat. 27 (removal right available to all persons seeking to enforce "full and equal benefit of all laws and proceedings" for enforcement of various civil rights); Act of Feb. 5, 1867, ch. 28, § 1, 14 Stat. 385 (claims cognizable on habeas corpus expanded to include "*all* cases where *any* person may be restrained of his or her liberty in violation of the constitution, or of any treaty or law of the United States" (emphasis added)); *id.* § 2, 14 Stat. at 386-87 (broadening claims cognizable on writ of error in ways catalogued in HART & WECHSLER, 2d ed., *supra* § 2.1 n.1, at 439-40 & nn.2-5).

[116] *See supra* notes 75, 115 and accompanying text. The February 5, 1867 removal act was particularly designed to facilitate the use of the procedure by criminal defendants, as opposed to other litigants with federal claims. *See* Act of Feb. 5, 1867, ch. 27, 14 Stat. 385.

the case of writs of error) that previously had limited those modes of review to federal "error ... as appears on the face of the record."[117] Accordingly, what the Supreme Court said of the February 5, 1867 habeas corpus legislation when it first interpreted it that same year might just as well have been said of all three types of legislation that Congress passed that day: "This legislation is of the most comprehensive character.... *It is impossible to widen this jurisdiction.*"[118]

Congress' desire to save Reconstruction from judicial invalidation in the famous *Ex parte McCardle*[119] affair prompted its 1868-1885 withdrawal of the Supreme Court's jurisdiction under the 1867 habeas corpus provision.[120] Still, the Court's few initial interpretations of the provision around that period confirmed the Constitution-wide range of claims and the broad scope of review available under the provision.[121] The provision's breadth also is confirmed by its (sparse) legislative history,[122] the lower federal courts' early interpretations of it — as having "clothed the district and circuit court judges of the United States with power to annul the criminal processes of the states, to reverse and set aside by habeas corpus the criminal judgments of the state courts, to pass finally and conclusively upon the validity of the criminal codes, the police regulations, and

---

[117] Act of Sept. 24, 1789, ch. 20, § 25, 1 Stat. 73, 86-87, *repealed by* Act of Feb. 5, 1867, ch. 28, § 2, 14 Stat. 385, 386-87 (discussed in HART & WECHSLER, 2d ed., *supra* § 2.1 n.1, at 440 & n.7). *See* Act of Feb. 5, 1867, ch. 28, § 1, 14 Stat. 385-86. *See also* Frank v. Mangum, 237 U.S. 309, 330-32 (1915) (discussing impact of 1867 habeas corpus act's jettisoning of "face of the record" limitation).

[118] Ex parte McCardle, 73 U.S. (6 Wall.) 318, 325-26 (1867) (emphasis added).

[119] 74 U.S. (7 Wall.) 506 (1868).

[120] *See* Act of March 27, 1868, ch. 34, 15 Stat. 44, *repealed by* Act of March 3, 1885, ch. 353, 23 Stat. 437.

[121] *See* Yick Wo v. Hopkins, 118 U.S. 356, 366, 373-74 (1886); Ex parte Royall, 117 U.S. 241, 247-53 (1886) (discussed *infra* notes 159-69 and accompanying text); Ex parte Tom Tong, 108 U.S. 556, 560 (1883); Ex parte Yerger, 75 U.S. (8 Wall.) 85, 106 (1868); *Ex parte McCardle*, *supra*, 73 U.S. (6 Wall.) at 325-26; Ex parte Bridges, 4 F. Cas. 98, 106 (N.D. Ga. 1875) (No. 1,862) (Bradley, Cir. Justice).

[122] *See* CONG. GLOBE, 39th Cong., 1st Sess. 4151 (1866) (Rep. Lawrence) (habeas corpus provision is designed to "enforce the liberty of all persons .... It is a bill of the largest liberty, ... [not] restrain[ing] the writ of *habeas corpus* at all"). *See also id.* at 4229-30 (Sen. Davis) (statement by opponent of 1867 Act that its purpose was "to secure to the people of the United States the constitutional rights of all persons"). Congress apparently assumed that its creation (via the Civil Rights Acts and the 14th Amendment) of constitutional rights enforceable against the States required a federal judicial forum in which to enforce those rights. *See id.* at 4229 (Sen. Trumbull) ("Now, a person might be held under a state law in violation of the Constitution and laws of the United States, and he ought to have ... the benefit of the writ and ... recourse to United States courts to show that he was illegally imprisoned in violation of the Constitution and laws of the United States."). *See generally* Lee, *supra* § 2.1 n.1, at 178-89.

even the constitutions of the states"[123] — and the broader historical context of the Reconstruction Congress' reconstruction of federal judicial power.[124]

The most important confirmation, however, is the *immediate* statutory context — Congress' February 5, 1867, simultaneous expansion of all *three* modes of reviewing state court determinations of federal questions in criminal cases. Taken together, the writ of error, removal, and habeas corpus provisions adopted that day leave little doubt as to Congress' goal. Article III defines the maximum constitutional extent of jurisdiction with which Congress may invest the federal courts on review of state court determinations of federal questions. The writ of error, removal, and habeas corpus provisions all used language tracking the same constitutional maximum to ensure enforcement in actions "begun in the courts of the States"[125] of the myriad of constitutional provisions and federal laws just then taking effect. Whatever ambiguities one might endeavor to read into the words of the habeas corpus portion of the second Act of February 5, 1867, no one has ever suggested that the almost identical words in the writ-of-error portion of the same Act permit anything less than plenary appellate review of alleged violations of "any title, right, privilege, or immunity ... claimed under the constitution, or any treaty or statute of ... the United States."[126] Through all three modes of review, Congress sought to assure prisoners of one full opportunity to enforce their newly given national rights in a national court, whether via expanded writ of error review on appeal in the Supreme Court, or — lest the state courts' expected systematic resistance negate rights before writ of error remedies matured — via the extension to *all* prisoners of full-fledged, pre-writ-of-error habeas corpus and removal protections.

Broad post-Reconstruction federal-prisoner habeas corpus review. Congress' 1874 adoption of the Revised Statutes united all preexisting habeas corpus legislation in one set of sections.[127] This revision encouraged federal prisoners, who technically had access to the Supreme Court under only the 1789 Act,[128] to rely as well — with the Court's tacit acquiescence — on portions of the revised statutes from the 1867 Act. Federal prisoner access to the 1867 Act's grant of authority over constitutional claims and claims not visible on the face of the

---

[123] Seymour D. Thompson, *Abuses of the Writ of Habeas Corpus*, 6 ABA REPORTS 243, 260-63 (1883). *See also* Seymour D. Thompson, *Annotation*, 18 F. 68, 81-86 (1883) (comprehensive review of the 1867-1883 habeas corpus cases in the lower federal courts).

[124] *See* William M. Wiecek, *The Reconstruction of Federal Judicial Power 1863-1875*, 13 AM. J. LEGAL HIST. 333, 342-48 (1969).

[125] Whitten v. Tomlinson, 160 U.S. 231, 238 (1895) (discussed *supra* note 75).

[126] Act of Feb. 5, 1867, ch. 28, § 2, 14 Stat. 385, 386.

[127] Act of June 22, 1874, ch. 13, §§ 755-766 (originally codified as Rev. Stat. §§ 751-766).

[128] *See supra* notes 119-20 and accompanying text (Congress' withdrawal of Court's jurisdiction under 1867 Act in *Ex parte McCardle* affair).

record[129] thus ushered in the Golden Age of federal prisoner habeas corpus review. This trend lasted until 1891, when the onset of federal prisoner writs of error as of right largely superseded habeas corpus review.[130]

The Court's treatment of the federal prisoner habeas corpus cases during this period paralleled that in the 1789-1874 period, although here the larger number of cases provides a much clearer picture of the Court's inclinations and particularly of its location of the line between fundamental (including all constitutional) and nonfundamental claims that it used to distinguish cognizable and noncognizable claims.[131] The Court continued to hold itself out as addressing claims questioning not only the detaining court's jurisdiction but also, and distinctly, the "lawfulness" of the detaining court's actions, its "authority to give the judgment it did," and whether it acted "beyond the powers conferred upon it."[132] During this period, moreover, the line between lack of jurisdiction and lack of constitutionality sometimes blurred entirely, as when the Court held that a "sentence given was beyond the jurisdiction of the court, because it was against an express provision of the Constitution, which bounds and limits all jurisdiction."[133] In other instances, the Court went directly to the

---

[129] Early references in federal-prisoner cases to claims arising under the Constitution include Ex parte Crow Dog, 109 U.S. 556, 572 (1883); Ex parte Siebold, 100 U.S. 371, 374 (1879); Ex parte Jackson, 96 U.S. 727, 728 (1877). Early examples of review going beyond the face of the record include Ex parte Clarke, 100 U.S. 399, 401 (1879); Ex parte Virginia, 100 U.S. 339, 343 (1879); *Ex parte Jackson, supra* at 736-37 (*dicta*). *But see* In re Snow, 120 U.S. 274, 281, 286 (1887); Ex parte Bigelow, 113 U.S. 328, 331 (1885) (emphasizing need for cognizable violations to be visible from record).

[130] *See infra* notes 191-97 and accompanying text.

[131] Professor Woolhandler independently identified this same common sense distinction between important (or "fundamental") and unimportant (or nonfundamental) claims as determining the claims the Supreme Court recognized as constitutional and nonconstitutional during this period not only on habeas corpus but also on direct review of state decisions. *See* Woolhandler, *supra* § 2.1 n.1, at 623-29. The distinction is rough, of course, but, as is revealed by the congruence between the analysis here and Professor Woolhandler's analysis, it clearly is the distinction that the Court used during this period. *See id.* at 628.

[132] Ex parte Yerger, 75 U.S. (8 Wall.) 85, 99 (1868). *Accord* In re Bonner, 151 U.S. 242, 256 (1893); Nielsen, Petitioner, 131 U.S. 176, 184 (1889); Ex parte Parks, 93 U.S. 18, 23 (1876). *See also* In re Mills, 135 U.S. 263, 265-69 (1890) (review justified "[i]f it appears ... *apart from* any questions as to jurisdiction ..., detention ... is in violation of the laws of the United States" (emphasis added)); Ex parte Wilson, 114 U.S. 417, 420-21 (1885) (habeas corpus relief available if "the sentence exceeds the jurisdiction of th[e] court *or* there is no authority to hold him under the sentence" (emphasis added)).

[133] *Nielsen, Petitioner, supra,* 131 U.S. at 185. *See also In re Bonner, supra,* 151 U.S. at 257 (equating "jurisdiction to render a particular judgment" with "keep[ing] within the limitations prescribed by the law, customary or statutory" which in turn is equated, *e.g.,* with taking action that Constitution "specifically prescribe[s]"); *Ex parte Wilson, supra,* 114 U.S. at 422 ("if the crime of which the petitioner was accused was an infamous crime, within the meaning of the Fifth

constitutional point, using habeas corpus to enforce "the positive and restrictive language of the great fundamental instrument by which the government is organized"[134] and, through Justice Bradley, rejecting any distinction between "a conviction and punishment under an unconstitutional law" and "an unconstitutional conviction and punishment under a valid law."[135]

What the Court *did* during this period was to award habeas corpus review and, when merited, relief on claims that a penal statute or an action by the detaining court or official violated the prisoner's 1st,[136] 4th,[137] 5th,[138] or 6th[139] Amendment rights, 11th Amendment or other constitutional federalism principles,[140] or an applicable federal statute.[141] Faced with a parade of claims that the detaining court acted without subject matter jurisdiction by convicting the petitioner of conduct that federal law did not prohibit, the Court also found it necessary to draw a line separating these uniformly "jurisdictional" claims into

---

Amendment of the Constitution, no court of the United States had jurisdiction to try ... him except upon ... indictment by a grand jury").

[134] Ex parte Bain, 121 U.S. 1, 6 (1887).

[135] *Nielsen, Petitioner, supra,* 131 U.S. at 183. *See, e.g.,* Ex parte Terry, 128 U.S. 289, 301 (1888); Callan v. Wilson, 127 U.S. 540, 541 (1888).

[136] *See, e.g.,* Davis v. Beason, 133 U.S. 333, 342-45 (1890) (free exercise claim); Ex parte Curtis, 106 U.S. 371, 372-73 (1882) (reviewing law forbidding political activity by federal employees); Ex parte Jackson, 96 U.S. 727, 736-37 (1877) (free press claim).

[137] *See, e.g., Ex parte Jackson, supra,* 96 U.S. at 733 (illegal search claim).

[138] Decisions granting relief include Counselman v. Hitchcock, 142 U.S. 547, 585 (1892) (self-incrimination); *Nielsen, Petitioner, supra,* 131 U.S. at 188 (double jeopardy); United States v. DeWalt, 128 U.S. 393 (1888) (right to indictment); *Ex parte Bain, supra,* 121 U.S. at 5-6, 12-13 (same); *Ex parte Wilson, supra,* 114 U.S. at 422-26 (same). Decisions granting review but denying relief include *Ex parte Terry, supra,* 128 U.S. at 311-14 (due process claim of inadequate notice and violation of right to be present when convicted of contempt); In re Coy, 127 U.S. 731, 753-55 (1888) (due process claim that penal statutes must require proof of intent).

[139] Decisions granting relief include In re Bonner, 151 U.S. 242, 257-59 (1893) (jury clause); Horner v. United States, 143 U.S. 207, 213-14 (1892) (trial in district in which offense occurred); *Callan v. Wilson, supra,* 127 U.S. at 549-57 (same).

[140] *See, e.g.,* In re Ayers, 123 U.S. 443, 485-87, 507-08 (1887) (unlawful contempt conviction for violating injunction that offended 11th Amendment); Ex parte Rowland, 104 U.S. 604, 616-18 (1881) (unlawful contempt conviction for violating injunction requiring state officials to act outside their statutory powers); Ex parte Siebold, 100 U.S. 371, 374-77 (1879) (reviewing but denying relief on claim that federal conviction of state officials for actions in pursuance of state law is unconstitutional).

[141] *See, e.g.,* In re Mills, 135 U.S. 263, 269-70 (1890) (violation of statute reserving penitentiary for individuals with sentences greater than one year); *Ex parte Wilson, supra,* 114 U.S. at 422 (1885) (alleged violation of statutory right to indictment); Ex parte Crow Dog, 109 U.S. 556, 571-72 (1883) (violation of statutory exemption for intratribal crimes).

ones that were and ones that were not cognizable.[142] The Court's distinction neatly modeled its more general distinction between important and unimportant questions of federal law: The Court *would* decide on habeas corpus whether entire broad "classes" of conduct fell within the court's jurisdiction under a penal statute — whether, for example, actions occurring outside a courtroom could constitute contempt,[143] or whether different classes of conspiracies fell within a penal statute[144] — but would *not* decide whether conduct falling within "a well defined class of offenses" over which a criminal statute generally gave the court jurisdiction actually fit within the particular elements of the statutorily defined crime.[145] When the Court denied review, it did so on manifestly unimportant, typically *sui generis* claims — whether, for example, the indictment in question was "defective in form" or pleaded with sufficient specificity,[146] the evidence was sufficient to convict,[147] or the trial court's allocution at sentencing contained a "technical defect."[148] As to claims the Court considered, its review was *de novo* on the law,[149] deferential on the facts.[150]

With access to federal question review as wide as permitted by the Constitution, and with no available alternative mode of federal appellate review as of right, federal prisoner habeas corpus was in its heyday in the 1874-1890

---

[142] *See, e.g.*, *In re Coy, supra*, 127 U.S. at 755. *See also* In re Sawyer, 124 U.S. 200, 220-21 (1888) (denying review of jurisdictional insufficient-amount-in-controversy claim).

[143] *See* Cuddy, Petitioner, 131 U.S. 280, 284-86 (1889).

[144] *See* Ex parte Yarbrough, 110 U.S. 651, 657 (1884). *See also* Ex parte Virginia, 100 U.S. 339, 346-49 (1879) (whether state judge may be prosecuted under federal statute prohibiting discrimination in jury selection).

[145] *In re Coy, supra*, 127 U.S. at 758. *See* In re Bonner, 151 U.S. 242, 257 (1893). *Compare* In re Mayfield, 141 U.S. 107, 112-16 (1891) (reviewing whether victimless crimes by Indians should be treated under statute proscribing certain acts by one Indian against another or by statute proscribing certain acts by Indian against non-Indian) *and In re Coy, supra*, 127 U.S. at 755 (reviewing question whether federal penal statute required proof of intent) *with* Ex parte Parks, 93 U.S. 18, 23 (1876) (refusing to review claim that document on which petitioner forged bankruptcy official's signature fell outside proscription of federal statute forbidding forgery of certain specified documents in course of bankruptcy proceedings).

[146] *See, e.g.*, *In re Coy, supra*, 127 U.S. at 759; *Ex parte Yarbrough, supra*, 110 U.S. at 654. *See generally* Woolhandler, *supra* § 2.1 n.1, at 625-26.

[147] *See, e.g.*, In re Wight, 134 U.S. 136, 148-49 (1890); Ex parte Carll, 106 U.S. 521, 523 (1882).

[148] *See, e.g.*, Ex parte Wilson, 114 U.S. 417, 428-29 (1885).

[149] *See* decisions cited *supra* notes 136-41, 143-44.

[150] *See, e.g.*, Cuddy, Petitioner, 131 U.S. 280, 286 (1889); Savin, Petitioner, 131 U.S. 267, 276 (1889); Ex parte Terry, 128 U.S. 289, 299-300, 305 (1888).

period. Grants of review outstripped denials by a ratio of about four to one, and grants of *relief* occurred in over a third of the cases.[151]

Post-Reconstruction limits on state-prisoner removal and habeas corpus review. On the state-prisoner front, the Reconstruction-era consensus that writs of error, although available, were systematically inadequate, and that other modes of review accordingly were necessary, began to fade as Reconstruction ended. In an important 1879 decision, *Virginia v. Rives*,[152] the Supreme Court interpreted the post-war federal question removal statutes narrowly, ending their availability as a meaningful method of securing review and expressly relegating litigants to their state and federal writ-of-error remedies.[153]

Beginning in 1885, Congress and the Court jointly undertook a parallel scaling back of habeas corpus. That year, Congress repealed the *McCardle* act's restriction on the Court's appellate jurisdiction under the 1867 statute.[154] Because the 1874 codification had implicitly made the 1867 Act's cognizable claims and admissible evidence procedures available to federal prisoners in the Supreme Court, the restoration of jurisdiction simply extended the same type of review to state prisoners whose cases reached the Supreme Court.

Although expanding the *Supreme Court's* habeas corpus jurisdiction, Congress' 1885 action was intended to limit habeas corpus review as a whole. At the time, Congress had before it a number of proposals to repeal the 1867 habeas corpus law entirely or at least "to curtail and restrain to a certain extent the powers assumed by the Federal judges under the act ...."[155] Fearful that "[t]he special causes which were deemed to suffice to make the act of 1867 necessary" — the inability of African-Americans "to get fair and impartial justice at the hands of local tribunals" — "may exist yet to some extent," Congress decided for the time being "to do no more than to recommend the restoration of the right of appeals to the Supreme Court."[156] Through this mechanism, Congress sought to assure that any "overthrow of the final judgments of the State courts of general jurisdiction, by the *inferior* Federal judges, ... thus making them a court of errors over the highest tribunals of the States," would not "be final" and instead could occur only with the concurrence of the *Supreme Court.*[157] Thus, while acknowledging the need to "extend to [emancipated African-Americans] *as far as possible under the Constitution*, the protection of the Federal courts,"

---

[151] *See* decisions cited *supra* notes 132-50.

[152] 100 U.S. 313 (1879).

[153] *See id.* at 319, 322.

[154] *See* Act of March 3, 1885, ch. 353, 23 Stat. 437.

[155] H.R. REP. No. 730, 48th Cong., 1st Sess., at 5 (1884).

[156] *Id.* at 3, 5-6.

[157] *Id.* at 5.

Congress also invited the Supreme Court, "[w]ith this right of appeal restored [to define] the true extent of the act of 1867, and the true limits of the jurisdiction of the Federal courts and judges under [the act]," so that it could "then be seen whether further legislation is necessary."[158]

Ex parte Royall,[159] the Court's first state-prisoner habeas corpus decision under the 1885 act, did indeed identify "the true extent of the act of 1867." "The grant ... of jurisdiction to issue writs of habeas corpus," Justice Harlan concluded for the Court, "is in language as broad as could be well employed."[160] On cognizability, this meant "that it was the purpose of Congress to invest the courts of the Union ... with power ... to restore to liberty any person ... who is held in custody, by whatever authority, in violation of the Constitution of the United States."[161] A contrary state determination, the Court continued, expressly endorsing the long extant rule of *de novo* review, "cannot affect the question, of the power or jurisdiction of the Circuit Court to inquire into the cause of his commitment, and to discharge [the prisoner] if he be restrained of his liberty in violation of the Constitution."[162]

Having held (by reversing the lower court's contrary conclusion) that Congress left the federal courts with no choice but to review all constitutional and other federal law claims arising in state criminal courts, Justice Harlan then reached *Royall*'s more famous conclusion that the federal courts *do* have "discretion" as to the "time *and* mode" of that review.[163] Heeding Congress' invitation to see that "further legislation [was not] necessary" — thus giving the Court's actions more the feel of a delegated judicial rulemaking than the fiat traditionally assumed — and also heeding Congress' desire that the Court itself, and not "the inferior Federal judges," be the statutorily mandated "court of errors over the highest tribunals of the States," Justice Harlan identified the preferred "mode" of federal review as its own "writ of error from the highest court of the State."[164] That preference as to "mode" dictated an additional preference as to "timing," namely — as the writ of error statute required[165] — that federal review

---

[158] *Id.* at 3, 6.

[159] 117 U.S. 241 (1886).

[160] *Id.* at 247.

[161] *Id.* at 248.

[162] *Id.* at 249. *Accord* In re Ah Fong, 1 F. Cas. 213, 215 (C.C.D. Cal. 1874) (No. 102) (Field, Circuit Justice) ("The decision of ... the supreme court of the state, although entitled to great respect and consideration from the acknowledged ability and learning of the[] judges is not binding upon this court.").

[163] *Ex parte Royall, supra*, 117 U.S. at 251 (emphasis added).

[164] *Id.* at 253.

[165] *See supra* note 80 and accompanying text.

wait until "the State court[s] shall have finally acted upon the case."[166] By preference, that is, the Court simply substituted its own *de novo* review of constitutional claims, under section 2 of the February 5, 1867 act, for like review by lower federal courts under section 1 of the same act.[167]

Probably spurred on by an alarming bulge in the Court's habeas corpus docket — from two to four cases a year during the preceding decade to at least fourteen cases in 1890 and eight in 1891[168] — the Court transformed what was announced in *Royall* as a discretionary rule of preference[169] into a near-mandatory rule of practice. In the 1893 case of *In re Frederich*,[170] the Court announced that state prisoners henceforth would be left to their federal writ of error remedy.[171] In *New York v. Eno*,[172] the next year, the Court made the concomitant[173] exhaustion-of-*state*-remedies doctrine mandatory.[174] And in *Tinsley v. Anderson*[175] in 1898, the Court made clear that writ of error review, if at least

---

[166] *Ex parte Royall, supra*, 117 U.S. at 253.

[167] Paralleling its conclusion in *Royall* that it may choose between duplicative federal writ of error and habeas corpus remedies without frustrating Congress' will, the Court more recently has made a similar choice between otherwise duplicative habeas corpus and section 1983 remedies. *See, e.g.*, Prieser v. Rodriguez, 411 U.S. 475, 488-90 (1973) ("habeas corpus is the exclusive remedy for a state prisoner who challenges the fact or duration of his confinement and seeks immediate or speedier release, even though such a claim may come within the literal terms of [42 U.S.C. §] 1983"); Heck v. Humphrey, 512 U.S. 477, 487 (1994) (extending *Preiser* rule to bar section 1983 actions challenging the legality of conviction, even if only damages are sought, if "judgment in favor of the plaintiff would necessarily imply the invalidity of his conviction or sentence").

[168] *See* the 1890 and 1891 cases cited *infra* notes 169, 176-77, 184-86.

[169] *See Ex parte Royall, supra*, 117 U.S. at 252-53. Contributing substantially to the 1890-1891 bulge, the Court often ignored the exhaustion rules prior to 1892, but almost never afterwards. *See, e.g.*, In re Rahrer, 140 U.S. 545 (1891); Crowley v. Christensen, 137 U.S. 86 (1890); Minnesota v. Barber, 136 U.S. 313 (1890); Savage, Petitioner, 134 U.S. 176 (1890); Ex parte Harding, 120 U.S. 782 (1887); Yick Wo v. Hopkins, 118 U.S. 356 (1886).

[170] 149 U.S. 70 (1893).

[171] *See id.* at 77-78. *See, e.g.*, Baker v. Grice, 169 U.S. 284, 290-91 (1898); In re Eckart, 166 U.S. 481, 484-85 (1897); In re Belt, 159 U.S. 95, 100 (1895) ("Ordinarily the writ will not lie where there is a remedy by writ of error or appeal."); Andrews v. Swartz, 156 U.S. 272, 276 (1895); In re Chapman, 156 U.S. 211, 217-18 (1895); Pepke v. Cronan, 155 U.S. 100, 101 (1894).

[172] 155 U.S. 89 (1894).

[173] Suggesting that the main purpose of exhaustion of state remedies was to satisfy the prerequisite to writ of error review are, *e.g.*, Urquhart v. Brown, 205 U.S. 179, 181-83 (1907); United States ex rel. Drury v. Lewis, 200 U.S. 1, 6-7 (1906); Davis v. Burke, 179 U.S. 399, 401-02 (1900).

[174] *New York v. Eno, supra*, 155 U.S. at 96-98. *See also United States ex rel. Drury v. Lewis, supra*, 200 U.S. at 6-7; Minnesota v. Brundage, 180 U.S. 499, 500-01, 503, 505 (1901).

[175] 171 U.S. 101 (1898).

initially available, was exclusive.[176] From the mid-1890s onward, therefore, state prisoners were precluded from receiving subsequent federal consideration if they either sought writ of error review or waived it (for example, by waiving the state appeals that had to be exhausted in order to permit direct Supreme Court review).[177] *Pace* Bator, these rules applied without distinction to claims challenging the detaining court's jurisdiction, a penal statute's constitutionality, or the lawfulness of a sentence.[178]

The Court did not reject habeas corpus review, however, but only replaced it whenever possible with its own review on the merits as of right.[179] Clearly revealing the commensurability and the substitutability of writ of error and habeas corpus review[180] are the three exceptional situations in which the Court regularly afforded habeas corpus review — when (1) a writ of error remedy was not meaningfully available,[181] (2) exhausting State remedies prefatory to federal review would unduly delay federal review,[182] or (3) state remedies were exhausted before the case reached the Supreme Court so that dismissal in preference for a writ of error would simply require the meaningless gesture of

---

[176] *See id.* at 104-05. *See also* United States ex rel. Kennedy v. Tyler, 269 U.S. 13, 17 (1925); Reid v. Jones, 187 U.S. 153, 154 (1902); Fitts v. McGhee, 172 U.S. 516, 533 (1899). Contributing to the 1890-1891 bulge in its case load, the Court prior to 1892 (but not afterwards) occasionally granted habeas corpus review of claims previously rejected on writ of error. *See, e.g.*, McElvaine v. Brush, 142 U.S. 155, 157-60 (1891); In re Wilson, 140 U.S. 575, 583-84 (1891); In re Duncan, 139 U.S. 449, 449-50 (1891); In re Converse, 137 U.S. 624, 624-25 (1891).

[177] *See, e.g.*, Ex parte Spencer, 228 U.S. 652, 660-61 (1913); Glasgow v. Moyer, 225 U.S. 420, 429-30 (1912); In re Wood, 140 U.S. 278, 286-87, 289-90 (1891).

[178] *See, e.g.*, Knewel v. Egan, 268 U.S. 442, 445-46 (1925) (denying review of jurisdictional and unconstitutional-statute claim); *Minnesota v. Brundage, supra*, 180 U.S. at 500-01 (unconstitutional-statute claim); *Tinsley v. Anderson, supra*, 171 U.S. at 104-06 (jurisdictional claim); In re Eckart, 166 U.S. 481, 483-85 (1897) (same); In re Belt, 159 U.S. 95, 99-100 (1895) (unconstitutional-statute claims are not an exception to rule preferring writ of error review).

[179] The Court repeatedly justified its preference for writ of error review based on the writ of error's availability *as of right*. *See, e.g.*, Urquhart v. Brown, 205 U.S. 179, 182-83 (1907); Markuson v. Boucher, 175 U.S. 184, 185-87 (1899).

[180] *See* In re Chapman, 156 U.S. 211, 216-18 (1895) (characterizing habeas corpus and direct review as alternative "modes" of "appellate jurisdiction").

[181] *See, e.g.*, Pettibone v. Nichols, 203 U.S. 192, 202 (1906) (interlocutory extradition proceedings); Felts v. Murphy, 201 U.S. 123, 128-30 (1906) (petitioner could not afford to pay for transcript necessary to permit exhaustion of state, then federal writ-of-error, remedies); *In re Chapman, supra*, 156 U.S. at 216-18 (if, after exhaustion, Court deemed that writ of error statute did not apply to District of Columbia courts, habeas corpus review would be permitted).

[182] *See, e.g.*, Storti v. Massachusetts, 183 U.S. 138, 142-43 (1901) (apparent need for immediate review of impending execution); Baker v. Grice, 169 U.S. 284, 293 (1878) (*dicta*).

substituting writ of error papers for the habeas corpus papers already before the Court.[183]

In the significant number of cases during the period in which habeas corpus review remained available, the Court continued to apply its longstanding rules distinguishing fundamental — including all constitutional[184] — claims, which *were* cognizable,[185] from nonfundamental and state law claims, which were not,[186] and affording *de novo* review of legal,[187] but little or no review of factual,[188] determinations. Exemplifying the cognizability of constitutional claims on undisputed facts is the Court's grant of relief in *Yick Wo v. Hopkins*;[189]

---

[183] *See, e.g.*, Rogers v. Peck, 199 U.S. 425, 434-36 (1905); Davis v. Burke, 179 U.S. 399, 401-02 (1900).

[184] *See, e.g.*, *Pettibone v. Nichols, supra*, 203 U.S. at 201; *Felts v. Murphy, supra*, 201 U.S. at 130; *Rogers v. Peck, supra*, 199 U.S. at 433-34, 435 ("When a prisoner is in jail he may be released upon habeas corpus when held in violation of his constitutional rights"). *See also* In re Converse, 137 U.S. 624, 624-25, 631 (1891) ("unconstitutional conviction and punishment under a valid law would be as violative of a person's constitutional rights as a conviction and punishment under an unconstitutional law"); *supra* notes 159-61 and accompanying text.

[185] Among the fundamental claims litigated during this period were the applicability to the States of the 5th, 6th, and 8th Amendments (the Court's answer uniformly being negative), *see, e.g.*, *Davis v. Burke, supra*, 179 U.S. at 401-04; McElvaine v. Brush, 142 U.S. 155, 158-59 (1891); Ex parte Harding, 120 U.S. 782, 783-84 (1887); the scope of the 14th Amendment due process protection, *see, e.g.*, Valentina v. Mercer, 201 U.S. 131, 132, 138-39 (1906) (right to instruction on self-defense and voluntary manslaughter); *Felts v. Murphy, supra*, 201 U.S. at 124-26, 129-30 (constitutionality of convicting deaf prisoner in proceedings he could not understand); Andrews v. Swartz, 156 U.S. 272, 275 (1895) (right to appeal in capital cases); *Bergemann v. Backer, supra*, 157 U.S. at 656-58 (right to notice in indictment of degree of murder being charged); *In re Converse, supra*, 137 U.S. at 628 (constitutionality of procedures used to take guilty plea); and the scope of the 14th Amendment right to equal protection, *see, e.g.*, Crowley v. Christensen, 137 U.S. 86, 92-94 (1890); and ex post facto claims, *see, e.g.*, Medley, Petitioner, 134 U.S. 160, 171-73 (1890).

[186] *See, e.g.*, Storti v. Massachusetts, 183 U.S. 138, 138-39, 142 (1901) (governor's power to stay execution under state law); In re Eckart, 166 U.S. 481, 482-83 (1897) (sufficiency of form and legal meaning of indictment under state law); Kohl v. Lehlback, 160 U.S. 293, 299-300 (1895) (propriety under state law of seating alien on grand jury); In re Jugiro, 140 U.S. 291, 292-93, 297 (1891) (variance between indictment (alleging stab wound in breast) and proof (showing stab wound in neck)). *See also* Woolhandler, *supra* § 2.1 n.1, at 629 n.321 (during period, Supreme Court accorded same treatment to state law claims on direct appeal and habeas corpus).

[187] *See* cases cited *supra* notes 181-84.

[188] *See, e.g.*, Crossley v. California, 168 U.S. 640, 642 (1898) (sufficiency of evidence); *In re Jugiro, supra*, 140 U.S. at 297-98 (determination that no jury discrimination occurred); *In re Converse, supra*, 137 U.S. at 631 (determination that prisoner understood he was pleading guilty to felony and not, as he claimed, a misdemeanor).

[189] 118 U.S. 356, 374 (1886) (discussed in Liebman, *supra* § 2.1 n.1, at 2045; *supra* § 2.4c n.66 and accompanying text).

exemplifying the lack of review of state court factual determinations is the Court's denial of review of the jury discrimination claim in *In re Wood*.[190]

Late 19th century adoption of federal-prisoner appeals and contraction of federal-prisoner habeas corpus. Congress dramatically rearranged the appellate map in 1891 by, for the first time, affording federal criminal defendants writ of error review in the Supreme Court.[191] Then, in 1897, Congress routed appeals as of right in noncapital cases (and in 1911 in capital cases) through the newly created Circuit Courts of Appeals to the Supreme Court on *certiorari*.[192] Drawing an analogy to the exhaustion of *state* remedies doctrine, the Court immediately created an exhaustion of *federal* appellate remedies doctrine, requiring resort to direct review in the Supreme Court (and, after 1897, in the courts of appeals) on writ of error when meaningfully available.[193] Judgments attained on writ of error in the Court precluded subsequent habeas corpus review,[194] while the failure to appeal waived habeas corpus review of claims that could have been appealed.[195] In cases in which habeas corpus remained available for lack of meaningful appellate remedies,[196] exhaustion of lower federal court habeas corpus remedies was required before coming to the Supreme Court.[197] The Golden Age of federal prisoner habeas corpus consideration had passed.

---

[190] 140 U.S. 278, 285-87 (1891) (discussed *supra* § 2.4c n.73). *Pace* Bator, *Wood* is not a case in which the Court treated the state court's *judgment* as *res judicata*, *cf. supra* § 2.4c n.73 and accompanying text, but rather one in which it treated as unreviewable the state court's *factual* determination that no discrimination in the selection of the jury had occurred, *see Wood, supra,* 140 U.S. at 285-86, precisely the same treatment the Court at the time accorded the same type of claim *on direct review, see, e.g.,* Thomas v. Texas, 212 U.S. 278, 281-82 (1909); cases cited in Benno Schmidt, *Juries, Jurisdiction, and Race Discrimination: The Lost Promise of* Strauder v. West Virginia, 61 TEX. L. REV. 1401, 1462-72 (1983); Woolhandler, *supra* § 2.1 n.1, at 618 n.259.

[191] *See* Act of Mar. 3, 1891, ch. 517, § 5, 26 Stat. 826, 827-28. Congress gave capital prisoners a right of appeal two years earlier. Act of Feb. 6, 1889, ch. 113, § 6, 25 Stat. 655, 656.

[192] *See* Act of Jan. 20, 1897, ch. 68, 29 Stat. 492; Act of Mar. 3, 1911, ch. 231, §§ 128, 238, 36 Stat. 1087, 1133-34, 1157.

[193] *See, e.g.,* In re Lincoln, 202 U.S. 178, 182 (1906) ("ordinary procedure for the correction of errors in criminal cases is by writ of error, and that method should be pursued unless there be special circumstances calling for a departure therefrom"); Riggins v. United States, 199 U.S. 547, 548-50 (1905); In re Lancaster, 137 U.S. 393, 395 (1890).

[194] *See* cases cited *supra* notes 175, 176.

[195] *See, e.g.,* Craig v. Hecht, 263 U.S. 255, 277 (1923); Glasgow v. Moyer, 225 U.S. 420, 429-30 (1912); Toy Toy v. Hopkins, 212 U.S. 542, 548-49 (1909) (waiver for failure to appeal; no exception for jurisdictional claims).

[196] *See, e.g.,* Ex parte Hudgings, 249 U.S. 378, 379-80, 384 (1919); Dimmick v. Tompkins, 194 U.S. 540, 541, 546 (1904) (challenge to conditions of confinement); In re Schneider, 148 U.S. 162, 166 (1893) (no writ of error available to District of Columbia courts).

[197] *See, e.g., Ex parte Hudgings, supra,* 249 U.S. at 379-80, 384; In re Huntington, 137 U.S. 63, 64 (1890); Ex parte Mirzan, 119 U.S. 584, 586 (1887).

The impact on habeas corpus of expanded but "certiorarified" writ of error review — Frank *and* Moore. In 1912, the Supreme Court substantially expanded the scope of its appellate review of federal questions arising in the state courts by developing two doctrines that let it review *de novo* questions previously denominated as "factual" and, as such, given no review. Henceforth, the Supreme Court would independently review findings of facts (1) "'where a Federal right has been denied as the result of a finding shown by the record to be without evidence to support it,'" or (2) "'where a conclusion of law as to a Federal right and a finding of fact are so intermingled as to make it necessary, in order to pass upon the Federal question to analyze the facts.'"[198]

For a time, the Court applied the two doctrines exclusively in civil cases.[199] Only in *Fiske v. Kansas*[200] in 1927 and in *Norris v. Alabama*[201] in 1935 did the Court explicitly use the doctrines to expand the scope of its direct review of state criminal cases,[202] although, as is discussed below, Justice Holmes presaged these developments in 1915 and 1923.

From the beginning, the Court justified both doctrines on the ground that the questions affected were not "factual" at all but were "legal" questions masquerading as factual ones, and that preservation of the Court's power to settle the meaning of national law and rights required it to be able to look through the "factfinding" disguise.[203] The Court recognized, that is, that there may be some "factual" concepts — the voluntariness of confessions, for example — that are so difficult to define once for all time and so dependent for their

---

[198] ROBERTSON & KIRKHAM, *supra* § 2.4b n.14, § 108, at 198-99 (quoting Fiske v. Kansas, 274 U.S. 380, 385-86 (1927), and citing Cedar Rapids Gas Light Co. v. Cedar Rapids, 223 U.S. 655 (1912) (Holmes, J.), and Creswill v. Knights of Pythias, 225 U.S. 246, 261 (1912), as originating first exception, and Kansas City S. Ry. v. C.H. Albers Comm'n Co., 223 U.S. 573, 591 (1912), as originating second exception (footnotes omitted)).

[199] *See, e.g.,* Aetna Life Ins. Co. v. Dunken, 266 U.S. 389, 394 (1924); Ward v. Board of County Comm'rs, 253 U.S. 17, 22-23 (1920); Truax v. Corrigan, 257 U.S. 312, 324-25 (1921); New York & Queens Gas Co. v. McCall, 245 U.S. 345, 348-49 (1917); Norfolk & W. Ry. v. West Virginia, 236 U.S. 605, 609-10 (1915).

[200] 274 U.S. 380, 385-86 (1927).

[201] 294 U.S. 587, 589-90 (1935) (reviewing *de novo* question whether state officials discriminated against blacks in composing jury venire). *Cf.* In re Wood, 140 U.S. 278, 285-86 (1891) (discussed *supra* § 2.4c n.73 & *supra* note 190 and accompanying text).

[202] *See, e.g.,* Pierre v. Louisiana, 306 U.S. 354, 358 (1939) (jury discrimination); Brown v. Mississippi, 297 U.S. 278, 286-87 (1936) (voluntariness of confession).

[203] *See, e.g.,* Gallegos v. Nebraska, 342 U.S. 55, 61 (1951); *Norris v. Alabama, supra,* 294 U.S. at 590 (*de novo* review of mixed question required so that "appropriate enforcement of the federal right may be assured"; "[o]therwise, review by this Court would fail of its purpose in safeguarding constitutional rights"); *Ward v. Board of County Comm'rs, supra,* 253 U.S. at 22; *Kansas City S. Ry. v. C.H. Albers Comm'n Co., supra,* 223 U.S. at 591, 594.

evolution on a constant progression of new fact situations, that giving lower courts unreviewable authority not only to find the historical facts but also to determine whether the facts satisfy the definition is tantamount to giving those courts the power to define the concept — and make the law.[204] Even when a legal rule turns on the existence of a more readily and permanently definable fact, the prior court's "finding" of that fact in the absence of any evidence suggests that the prior court's definition of that fact must differ from the reviewing court's — hence that the prior court made a mistake of law.[205]

At the same time as the *scope* of direct review was expanding, its availability as of right was contracting. In 1914, after a quarter century of modest erosion in the Supreme Court's mandatory writ of error and appeal jurisdiction and accretion to its discretionary *certiorari* jurisdiction,[206] and of greater erosion in the number of cases actually granted plenary, as opposed to summary, review on writ of error,[207] Congress enacted the first in a series of laws that almost entirely replaced direct Supreme Court review as of right on writ of error with discretionary direct review on writ of *certiorari*. The 1914 law allowed litigants aggrieved by decisions of the state courts *in favor of* federal rights to seek review by *certiorari*.[208] A 1916 law made review of state court decisions in favor of *or against* a claim of federal right reviewable only on *certiorari*, unless the party seeking review attacked the "authority" of the state or federal governments to act as opposed to the constitutionality of an action within the authority of the official actor.[209] And a 1925 law located *all* requests for review within the Court's *certiorari* review, save requests for review of state court decisions striking down federal or upholding state statutes under the Constitution.[210]

Given the Court's prior treatment of direct Supreme Court review as of right, when available, as a preferred alternative to habeas corpus, and, when not

---

[204] *See* Miller v. Fenton, 474 U.S. 104, 113-18 (1985); Henry P. Monaghan, *Constitutional Fact Review*, 85 COLUM. L. REV. 229, 261-62, 271-76 (1985).

[205] *See, e.g.*, Cox v. Louisiana, 379 U.S. 536, 545 n.8 (1965); Stein v. New York, 346 U.S. 156, 182 (1953).

[206] *See* Judiciary Act of 1891, ch. 517, § 6, 26 Stat. 826, 828; *supra* note 192 and accompanying text.

[207] *See, e.g.*, Ex parte Frank, 235 U.S. 694 (1914) *(mem.)*; In re Kemmler, 136 U.S. 436, 438 (1890); Spies v. Illinois, 123 U.S. 131, 164 (1887).

[208] *See* Act of Dec. 23, 1914, ch. 2, 38 Stat. 790. Previously, the Supreme Court could not review such decisions at all.

[209] *See* Act of Sept. 6, 1916, ch. 448, § 2, 39 Stat. 726.

[210] *See* Act of Feb. 13, 1925, ch. 229, § 237, 43 Stat. 936, 937. In 1928, Congress renamed the residual right to review as of right an "appeal" rather than a "writ of error," but the scope of the right remained the same as in 1925. Act of Jan. 31, 1928, ch. 14, 45 Stat. 54; HART & WECHSLER, 3d ed., *supra* § 2.1. n.1, at 501-03; Liebman, *supra* § 2.1 n.1, at 2009 n.51.

available, as a model for proceedings under the writ, the early 20th century decrease in the as-of-right availability, and increase in the scope, of direct Supreme Court review should have expanded the use *and* widened the scope of habeas corpus review. And so they did in *Frank v. Mangum*[211] in 1915 and, especially, in *Moore v. Dempsey*[212] in 1923.

Frank and *Moore* are puzzles, given their similar facts and different outcomes — relief being denied in *Frank* on a Jewish man's claim that the jury that convicted him had been intimidated by a mob, and relief being granted in *Moore* on several African-Americans' identical claim.[213] In both cases, the presence of a mob threatening the courtroom was admitted, and the evidence supporting the petitioners' allegation of mob influence on the judge and jury was substantial.[214] In both cases, the trial court under cooler circumstances denied new trial motions on the basis that the mob's influence had not affected the proceedings.[215] In both, the state supreme court affirmed, finding, in effect, that the mob had not influenced the verdict.[216] In both, the petitioners unsuccessfully sought direct appeal review in the United States Supreme Court[217] before seeking and being denied habeas corpus relief in the lower federal courts.[218] On appeal from the denial of habeas corpus in both cases, the Supreme Court treated "the writ of habeas corpus [as available] ... only in case the judgment under which the prisoner is detained is shown to be absolutely void,"[219] but clearly and repeatedly said that all due process and constitutional violations sufficed to void the detention and to warrant habeas corpus relief.[220] In both, the Court concluded that due process also demanded a fair "corrective process" either at trial or on

---

[211] 237 U.S. 309, 329-32 (1915).

[212] 261 U.S. 86, 90-92 (1923).

[213] Leo Frank almost certainly was innocent of the rape and killing for which he was convicted and lynched. *See* Wendell Rawls, Jr., *After 69 Years of Silence, Lynching Victim Is Cleared*, N.Y. TIMES, Mar. 8, 1982, at A12. For a more complete discussion of *Frank* and *Moore*, see Liebman, *supra* § 2.1 n.1, at 2075-81.

[214] *See Frank, supra*, 237 U.S. at 332-34; *Moore, supra*, 261 U.S. at 87-90.

[215] *See Frank, supra*, 237 U.S. at 333; *Moore, supra*, 261 U.S. at 91-92; *id.* at 96-99 (McReynolds, J., dissenting).

[216] *See Frank, supra*, 237 U.S. at 313-14; *Moore, supra*, 261 U.S. at 91.

[217] *See* Ex parte Frank, 235 U.S. 694 (1914) (*mem.*); Moore v. Arkansas, 254 U.S. 630 (1920) (*mem.*).

[218] *See Frank, supra*, 237 U.S. at 311, 317; *Moore, supra*, 261 U.S. at 87.

[219] *Frank, supra*, 237 U.S. at 327. *See Moore, supra*, 261 U.S. at 91-92.

[220] *Frank, supra*, 237 U.S. at 326, 328, 330, 331, 335, 345 (habeas corpus lies to relieve petitioner "shown to have been deprived of any right guaranteed to him by the Fourteenth Amendment or any other provision of the Constitution or laws of the United States"); *Moore, supra*, 261 U.S. at 87-88 ("question [is] whether their constitutional rights have been preserved").

appeal in which to litigate a claim that trial by mob had occurred, and that habeas corpus was available to redress the absence of a fair corrective process.[221] And the Court found the same state corrective process in both cases — a new trial proceeding followed by an appeal, neither affected by a mob — which it ruled adequate in *Frank*[222] and did not clearly rule *in*adequate under the same circumstances in *Moore*.[223]

An understanding of habeas corpus as a surrogate for Supreme Court review as of right when Supreme Court review is unavailable explains *Frank*'s and *Moore*'s three puzzles: (1) why *both* decisions abandoned the Court's practice of treating its direct review as preferred over and preclusive of later habeas corpus review; (2) why the Court denied relief under the aggravated circumstances of *Frank*; and (3) why it then granted relief under the same circumstances in *Moore*.

In *Frank*, the majority and dissent clearly describe not only the exhaustion of *state* remedies doctrine but also the exhaustion of *Supreme Court* remedies doctrine as only preliminary to, and not preclusive of, later federal habeas corpus review.[224] The *Moore* Court proceeded according to the same rule. Clues to why the Court suddenly departed from its previously preclusive doctrine requiring exhaustion of Supreme Court review are found in (1) the Court's one-line summary memoranda reporting its denial of Frank's writ of error application and of the Moore petitioners' *certiorari* petition on direct review,[225] and (2) Justice Holmes' revelation in dissent in *Frank* that he and Justice Hughes had voted to grant Frank's writ of error application and thereby to afford him plenary review rather than just a summary denial.[226] Taken together, the denials of direct review in both *Frank* and *Moore* and the two Justices' internal dissent from the denial in *Frank* exemplify the unofficial (in *Frank*) and then official (in *Moore*) "certiorarification" of direct Supreme Court review. In both cases, the Court's plenary review on habeas corpus revealed its recognition that, by then, it could no longer supply the plenary review as of right that previously had permitted a preference for its own direct review over a lower federal court's habeas corpus consideration.

---

[221] *Frank, supra*, 237 U.S. at 335; *Moore, supra*, 261 U.S. at 91.

[222] *Frank, supra*, 237 U.S. at 335-36.

[223] *See Moore, supra*, 261 U.S. at 91-92.

[224] *See Frank, supra*, 237 U.S. at 328-29 ("the writ in the absence of very special circumstances, ought not to be issued *until* the state prosecution has reached its conclusion, and not even then *until* the Federal questions arising upon the record have been brought before this court upon writ of error") (emphasis added); *id.* at 348 (Holmes, J., dissenting).

[225] *See* Moore v. Arkansas, 254 U.S. 630 (1920) (*mem.*); In re Frank, 235 U.S. 694 (1914) (*mem.*).

[226] *Frank, supra*, 237 U.S. at 346 (Holmes, J., dissenting).

The *Frank* Court itself answered the second question — why it denied relief: The Georgia Supreme Court's legally dispositive determination that the mob had not intimidated the jury was one of fact, hence beyond the Court's power to overturn unless it was tainted by an independent constitutional violation, namely, the denial of an adequate procedure for litigating that factual issue.[227] Although the passage containing this holding is one of the most fought-over texts in American habeas corpus jurisprudence, its meaning is clear as long as the writ is understood to back-stop and replicate direct Supreme Court review. In the passage, Justice Pitney recognized that a trial "*in fact* dominated by a mob so that the jury is intimidated and the trial judge yields" violates due process as long as the "state suppl[ies] no corrective process [and] carr[ies] into execution" the judgment produced thereby.[228] Justice Pitney then explicitly rejected the argument that the Georgia courts' legal determination that there was no due process violation ought to be "*res judicata*" in habeas corpus proceedings, noting the absence of precedential support for the position and refusing to "limit[] in the least degree the authority of the United States in investigating an alleged violation by a state of the due process of law guaranteed by the Fourteenth Amendment."[229] Then, however, following standard *appellate* practice, the Court noted that the inapplicability of *res judicata* "does not mean that [the state] decision may be ignored or disregarded"[230] and proceeded to defer to the portion of the Georgia Supreme Court decision — but *only* the portion — that "upon a full review, decided appellant's allegations of fact ... to be unfounded."[231] A jury dominated by a mob cannot, without violating due process, adjudicate the defendant's guilt. And a judge dominated by a mob cannot, without violating due process, vitiate the first violation by "finding" on the spot that no mob domination occurred. But an appellate court that was not even arguably threatened by a mob can (and here did) *disprove* the first violation

---

[227] *See id.* at 335-36 (majority opinion).

[228] *Id.* at 335 (emphasis added).

[229] *Id.* at 334.

[230] *Id.*

[231] *Id.* at 335 (emphasis added). The Court explained:

> [W]e hold that such a determination of the *facts* as was thus made by the court of last resort of Georgia respecting the alleged interference with the trial through disorder and manifestations of hostile sentiment cannot in this collateral inquiry be treated as a nullity, but must be taken as setting forth the *truth of the matter*, certainly until some reasonable ground is shown for an inference that the court which rendered it either was wanting in jurisdiction, or at least erred in the exercise of its jurisdiction; and the mere assertion by the prisoner that the *facts of the matter* are other than the state court, upon investigation determined them to be, will not be deemed sufficient to raise an issue respecting the correctness of that determination ....

> *Id.* at 335-36 (emphasis added).

by finding, "upon a full review," free of any independent due process violation, that "in point of fact" no mob domination occurred.[232]

For Justice Holmes in dissent, the problem was that the majority's decision characterized as a matter of *fact* what he considered partly a matter of *law*.[233] "[T]he whole structure" of the majority opinion, Justice Holmes pointed out, rested on the view "that in no case would it be permissible, on the application for habeas corpus to override the *findings of fact* by the state courts."[234] He rejected this view "as a removal of what is perhaps the most important guaranty of the Federal Constitution."[235] In his view, supported by citation to the decision establishing the Court's *de novo* review doctrine for "mixed questions," "[w]hen the decision of the question of fact is so interwoven with the decision of the question of constitutional right that the one necessarily involves the other, the Federal court must examine the facts. Otherwise, the right will be a barren one."[236]

The decisive issue in *Frank* thus was not, as Bator argued, whether habeas corpus review reached all constitutional issues (which nine Justices assumed to be the case) nor, as Brennan-Peller argued, whether the Constitution's proscription of due process violations reached mob dominated jury verdicts upheld on appeal (which all nine Justices also assumed to be the case). Rather, the decisive issue was whether independent federal appellate review reached mixed factual and legal determinations or only purely legal ones. In resolving this issue, Justice Pitney looked backwards to the pre-1912 days in which fact review, of any sort, meant (in effect) "no review." Justice Holmes looked forward to the importation of the Court's mixed-question and no-evidence doctrines into the realm of personal, as well as economic, liberties.

Frank thus naturally flowed from (1) the certiorarification of the Court's direct appellate docket, (2) the resulting shift (back) to the lower federal courts on habeas corpus of the federal courts' statutory obligation to conduct review as of right of the constitutionality of state detention, and (3) the consequent shift from direct appeal to habeas corpus of the battleground over the scope of appellate review of questions of "constitutional fact." Justice Holmes' opinion for the Court in *Moore* then simply finished the fight begun in *Frank* over the application in criminal cases of the *de novo* review doctrine governing appellate review of factual questions determinative of the meaning of federal consti-

---

[232] *Id.* at 344.

[233] *See id.* at 348 (Holmes, J., dissenting).

[234] *Id.* at 347 (emphasis added).

[235] *Id.* at 348.

[236] *Id.* at 347-48 (citing, *e.g.*, Kansas City S. Ry. v. C.H. Albers Comm'n Co., 223 U.S. 573, 591 (1912)).

tutional law. Remanding the case to the lower court to examine the dispositive "fact" of mob influence, in order to see whether there was an uncorrected "wrong" denying "the petitioners constitutional rights," Justice Holmes ordered that examination to proceed *de novo*: "We shall not say more concerning the corrective process afforded to the petitioner" — as, in *Frank*, a new trial and appeal proceeding[237] — "than that it does not seem to us sufficient to allow a judge of the United States to escape the duty of *examining the facts for himself* when, if true as alleged, they make the trial absolutely void."[238]

Moore *to* Brown: *criminal procedure revolution; direct review devolution.* Just as the Court's mixed question and allied fact review doctrines expanded the *scope* of review on habeas corpus between *Frank* and *Moore*, so did the Court's emerging Criminal Procedure Revolution expand the reach of the constitutional claims *cognizable* on habeas corpus in the 30 years between *Moore* and *Brown v. Allen*[239] — both trends impelled by the shift from the Court to the lower federal courts of cases in which the Court's discretionary review was unavailable or denied. On the federal prisoner side, the Court's recognition of a group of constitutional rights whose violation created exceptions to the otherwise preclusive exhaustion-of-appellate-remedies doctrine[240] set off a second Golden Age of federal-prisoner review. The Court soon concluded, for example, that prisoners denied their newly recognized right to counsel could not be blamed for failing to pursue timely and complete appeals;[241] that prisoners coerced into pleading guilty typically could not be understood to have thereby waived an appeal;[242] and that prisoners convicted on the basis of government-tolerated perjury could not be expected to discover that fact in time to make it the basis of a timely appeal.[243] The result was a set of Supreme Court remands for *de novo* review in cases in which lower federal courts, applying preexisting exhaustion

---

[237] See *supra* notes 215-16 and accompanying text.

[238] Moore v. Dempsey, 261 U.S. 86, 92 (1923).

[239] 344 U.S. 443 (1953).

[240] For statements of the exhaustion of appellate remedies doctrine, see Sunal v. Large, 332 U.S. 174, 177-78 (1947); Craig v. Hecht, 263 U.S. 255, 277 (1923).

[241] *See, e.g.,* Adams v. United States ex rel. McCann, 317 U.S. 269, 274-75 (1942); Walker v. Johnston, 312 U.S. 275, 286-87 (1941); Johnson v. Zerbst, 304 U.S. 458, 465, 467 (1938).

[242] *See, e.g.,* Waley v. Johnston, 316 U.S. 101, 104-05 (1942).

[243] *See Sunal v. Large, supra,* 332 U.S. at 177-78 (*dicta*). *See also Adams v. United States ex rel. McCann, supra,* 317 U.S. at 272-73 (nonexhaustion excused where prisoner could not afford transcript needed to perfect appeal); Bowen v. Johnston, 306 U.S. 19, 26 (1939) ("rule requiring resort to appellate procedure" suspended in order to resolve conflict among courts on important question of federal jurisdiction); Escoe v. Zerbst, 295 U.S. 490, 494 (1935) (excusing exhaustion of other remedies in challenge to parole revocation because none exist).

and constitutional doctrine, had denied review altogether.[244] As before, the Court consistently described the range of claims cognizable on habeas corpus as all constitutional claims[245] — only occasionally with a bow in the direction of the "jurisdiction"-withdrawing effect of such violations[246] — and when, instead of remanding, it conducted review itself, it did so *de novo* on the law but deferentially on the facts.[247]

On the state-prisoner side, the range of available constitutional rights grew as slowly as incorporationism, but all rights that did exist were enforced on habeas corpus, as on appeal,[248] with *de novo* legal review.[249] Accordingly, when Congress undertook to codify existing habeas corpus practice in the new Judicial Code of 1948, it made all constitutional claims cognizable, adopted no qualifications on the traditional scope of review of legal and factual questions, and made exhaustion of *state* remedies a matter of timing, not preclusion.[250]

---

[244] *See, e.g.*, United States ex rel. McCann v. Adams, 320 U.S. 220, 222 (1943); *Waley v. Johnston, supra*, 316 U.S. at 105; *Walker v. Johnston, supra*, 312 U.S. at 287; *Johnson v. Zerbst, supra*, 304 U.S. at 469.

[245] *See, e.g.*, United States v. Hayman, 342 U.S. 205, 212 (1952); *Sunal v. Large, supra*, 332 U.S. at 178-79; *Waley v. Johnston, supra*, 316 U.S. at 105. *See also* Salinger v. Loisel, 265 U.S. 224, 232-33 (1924) (6th Amendment); Baender v. Barnett, 255 U.S. 224, 226 (1921) (5th Amendment and Article I, § 8); Ex parte Hudgings, 249 U.S. 378, 379 (1919) (5th Amendment).

[246] *See, e.g., Bowen v. Johnston, supra*, 306 U.S. at 23-24 (citing cases); *Johnson v. Zerbst, supra*, 304 U.S. at 467-68. Noting the amorphous quality of the jurisdictional-violation concept during this period is Custis v. United States, 511 U.S. 485, 507-10 (1994) (Souter, J., dissenting).

[247] *See, e.g., Bowen v. Johnston, supra*, 306 U.S. at 28 (*de novo* legal review); *Escoe v. Zerbst, supra*, 295 U.S. at 492-93 (same); Matter of Gregory, 219 U.S. 210, 214 (1911) (no review of insufficiency of evidence claims); Harlan v. McGourin, 218 U.S. 442, 448, 451-52 (1910) (*de novo* review of claim that prisoner's sentence violated federal statute but no review of insufficiency of evidence claim).

[248] *See, e.g.*, Darr v. Burford, 339 U.S. 200, 203 (1950) ("The writ ... command[s] general recognition as the essential remedy to safeguard a citizen against imprisonment by State or Nation in violation of" apparently all of "his constitutional rights."); Wade v. Mayo, 334 U.S. 672, 677 (1948); Hawk v. Olson, 326 U.S. 271, 278-79 (1945) (when "[p]etitioner states a good cause of action ... that through denial of asserted constitutional rights he has not had the kind of trial in a state court which the due process clause of the Fourteenth Amendment requires," and when he "prove[s] his allegations," relief is required); Mooney v. Holohan, 394 U.S. 103, 112 (1935) (*per curiam*) (recognizing constitutional bar to prosecutorial reliance on perjured testimony and cognizability of claim on habeas corpus); Ashe v. United States ex rel. Valotta, 270 U.S. 424, 425-26 (1926).

[249] *See, e.g., Darr v. Burford, supra*, 339 U.S. at 216-18; *Hawk v. Olsen, supra*, 326 U.S. at 276 ("When ... error, in relation to the federal question of constitutional violation, creeps into the record, we have the responsibility to review the proceedings.").

[250] *See* Act of June 25, 1948, ch. 646, part VI, ch. 153, §§ 2241-55, 62 Stat. 869, 964-68 (current version at 28 U.S.C. §§ 2241-2255); H.R. REP. No. 308, 80th Cong., 1st Sess. A177-78

The defining issue for the Court during this period was one that *Moore* implicitly decided but did not explicitly settle: If direct Supreme Court review on the merits as of right precluded subsequent federal review on habeas corpus, what, then, was the effect of the Court's newly certiorarified direct appeal? As did *Moore*, some pre-*Brown* cases assumed or concluded that the Court's denial of *certiorari* did not supply the statutorily mandated review as of right, which, accordingly, only habeas corpus could afford.[251] Other decisions did give effect to the denial of *certiorari*, although, in keeping with the newly established successive-habeas-corpus-petition principle of *Salinger v. Loisel*[252] and *Wong Doo v. United States*,[253] it was only a partial, and not a full, *res judicata* effect.[254]

Contrary to the received Batorian view,[255] the Supreme Court's 1953 decision in *Brown v. Allen*[256] worked no revolution when it recognized the cognizability on habeas corpus of all federal constitutional claims presented by state prisoners. True, as is discussed in detail elsewhere,[257] *Brown*'s two majority opinions nicely catalogue the long-governing habeas corpus principles, including the cognizability of all constitutional claims[258] and especially the right (as on direct

---

(1947) (1948 codification of habeas corpus provisions not intended to make substantive changes in existing practice); *infra* note 266 and accompanying text.

[251] *See, e.g., Wade v. Mayo, supra,* 334 U.S. at 677-78; White v. Ragen, 324 U.S. 760, 764-65 (1945); Mooney v. Holohan, 394 U.S. 103, 115 (1935) (*per curiam*) (*dicta*); *supra* notes 224-26 and accompanying text.

[252] 265 U.S. 224, 231-32 (1924).

[253] 265 U.S. 239, 241 (1924) (habeas corpus courts may "exercise sound discretion" but not "inflexible doctrine of *res judicata*" in denying single petitioner's second or successive habeas corpus petition).

[254] *See, e.g.,* Brown v. Allen, 344 U.S. 443, 456-57 (1953) (opinion of Reed, J.) (discussing *Salinger, supra*); Darr v. Burford, 339 U.S. 200, 214-15 (1950) (same); Ex parte Hawk, 321 U.S. 114, 118 (1944) (*per curiam*) (same).

[255] *See* authority cited *supra* § 2.4c nn.40, 46.

[256] 344 U.S. 443 (1953).

[257] *See* Liebman, *supra* § 2.1 n.1, at 2019-29.

[258] *See, e.g., Brown, supra,* 344 U.S. at 465 (opinion of Reed, J., for the Court) (habeas corpus lies to determine whether "petitioners received [trials] consonant with standards accepted by this Nation as adequate to justify their convictions" because they "lie in the compass of the Due Process and Equal Protection Clauses of the Fourteenth Amendment"); *id.* at 508-09 (opinion of Frankfurter, J., for the Court) ("District Judge [must] decide constitutional questions presented by a State prisoner even after his claims have been carefully considered by the State courts" because Congress "has seen fit to give this Court power to review errors of federal law in State determinations, and in addition to give to the lower federal courts power to inquire into federal claims, by way of habeas corpus.").

appeal) to *de novo* review of legal and mixed legal-factual claims.[259] But those principles already were long established, to anyone with the patience to search them out from among the literally hundreds of individually unimportant cases in which they lay dispersed. The only "revolution" *Brown* worked, therefore, was one that seems so obvious today that we can hardly imagine anyone having thought the law different — its holding that denial of *certiorari* on direct review

---

[259] *See id.* at 456-58 (opinion for the Court of Reed, J.) (compendium of progressively more rigorous standards of review in different habeas corpus contexts, ranging from total deference due state court decisions premised on adequate and independent state grounds, to substantial deference due fairly achieved state court determinations of fact, to "some" deference due prior *federal* determinations of same claim in earlier petition in same case, to no deference due *legal* claims previously adjudicated by *state* courts ("the state [legal] adjudication carries the weight that federal practice gives to the conclusion of a court of last resort of another jurisdiction on federal constitutional issues. It is not *res judicata.*")); *id.* at 458-59 & n.9 (indiscriminately annotating discussion of standard of review of state legal determinations with citations of Supreme Court cases on habeas corpus and direct review of state criminal judgments (citing Malinski v. New York, 324 U.S. 401 (1945) (direct review); Ex parte Hawk, 321 U.S. 114 (1944) (habeas corpus); Mooney v. Holohan, 294 U.S. 103 (1935) (*per curiam*) (same))); *id.* at 459 ("recogniz[ing] the power of the District Court to *reexamine* federal constitutional issues even after trial and review by a state" (emphasis added)); *id.* at 475; *id.* at 465-87 (affording *de novo* review of coerced-confession issue before Court); *id.* at 500 (opinion of Frankfurter, J., for the Court) ("The prior State determination may guide [the habeas corpus judge's] discretion in deciding upon the appropriate course to be followed in disposing of the application before him" but that determination "cannot foreclose consideration of such a claim, else the State court would have the final say which the Congress, by the Act of 1867, provided it should not have." (emphasis added) (citation omitted)); *id.* at 506-08 (compendium of habeas corpus standards of review: when faced with prior "denial of relief by a *federal* court," district court "may, [but] need not inquire anew" into the previously adjudicated factual and legal questions; "[w]hen ... the issue turns on basic *facts* ... [, u]nless a vital flaw be found in the process of ascertaining such facts in the *State* court, the District Judge may accept their determination in the State proceeding and deny the application"; but when case "calls for interpretation of the legal significance" of the historical facts, "District Judge *must exercise his own judgment* .... [S]o-called mixed questions or the application of constitutional principles to the facts as found *leave the duty of adjudication with the federal judge*"; likewise, state court determinations of purely legal questions "cannot, under the habeas corpus statute, be accepted as binding. It is precisely these questions that the federal judge is commanded to decide" (emphasis added)); *id.* at 507-08 (in adjudicating due process/fundamental fairness claim, district court must rely on state courts for historical facts, "[b]ut it is for the federal judge to assess on the basis of such historical facts the fundamental fairness of a conviction ... in the circumstances"); *id.* at 508 ("Although there is no need for the federal judge, if he could, to shut his eyes to the State consideration of such issues, *no binding weight* is to be attached to the State determination.... The State court cannot have the last say when it, though on fair consideration ..., may have *misconceived* a federal constitutional right." (emphasis added)). *Accord* United States ex rel. Smith v. Baldi, 344 U.S. 561, 565-70 (1953) (affording *de novo* review to case decided same day as *Brown*).

was not a ruling on the merits, hence could not serve in lieu of review as of right on habeas corpus.[260]

Brown did serve a critical confirming function, however. For years following Congress' 1885 warning and the Court's 1886 response in *Royall*, the Court had largely shut down habeas corpus by giving itself the federal review-as-of-right burden the Reconstruction Congress previously had encouraged the Court to share with the lower federal courts on habeas corpus and removal. It took the Court time to come to grips with the fact that the certiorarification of its direct appeal docket made the *Royall* compromise untenable. Although *Frank* and especially *Moore* adumbrated the Court's eventual resolution, only *Brown* forthrightly adopted it: All prisoners deserve one federal-court appeal as of right of their federal constitutional claims, if not on direct review in the Supreme Court, then on habeas corpus in the lower federal courts. As in other appeals, the scope of review was to be *de novo* on the law, deferential on the facts. In the federal prisoner context, the appeal generally would be a direct appeal to a United States Court of Appeals, unless the prisoner could not reasonably be expected to raise his claims in the immediate wake of trial. In the state-prisoner context, with direct Supreme Court review on the merits as of right having been limited to but a few cases each year, the bulk of the review responsibility would fall to the lower federal courts (and, at times, the Supreme Court) on habeas corpus.

Congressional affirmation: the 1966 amendments. "In 1966, Congress carefully reviewed the habeas corpus statutes and amended their provisions, ... weigh[ing] the interests of the individual prisoner against the sometimes contrary interest of the State."[261] In doing so it confirmed and strengthened the parity between and substitutability of direct and habeas corpus review. To begin with, just as in 1867, 1885,[262] 1948,[263] and at least 28 times between 1968 and 1992,[264] Congress between 1953 and 1966 repeatedly refused to withdraw the

---

[260] On this point, the Court's holding is in Justice Frankfurter's opinion. Justice Reed dissented. *See Brown, supra,* 344 U.S. at 489-97 (opinion of Frankfurter, J.); *id.* at 456-57 (Reed, J., dissenting).

[261] Kuhlmann v. Wilson, 477 U.S. 436, 449 (1986) (plurality opinion).

[262] *See supra* notes 155-62 and accompanying text.

[263] *See, e.g.,* REPORT OF THE JUDICIAL CONFERENCE 22-23 (1943) (proposing that state determinations of law and fact be conclusive unless prisoner could show that state law provided no "adequate remedy" for his constitutional claims); REPORT OF THE JUDICIAL CONFERENCE 22 (1944) (renewing recommendations made in 1943 report); S. 1451, 79th Cong., 1st Sess. (1945) (adopting Judicial Conference proposal); S. 20, 80th Cong., 2d Sess. (1948) (same); John J. Parker, *Limiting the Abuse of Habeas Corpus,* 8 F.R.D. 171 (1948).

[264] *See* Brief *Amicus Curiae* of Joseph Biden & Don Edwards at 10-16, Wright v. West, 505 U.S. 277 (1992) (No. 91-542) (cataloguing 1968-1992 proposals).

lower federal judiciary from *de novo* review of some or all state and federal court constitutional determinations in criminal cases.[265] The 1966 amendments instead left intact the 1948 codification of the 1867 act, which provided that district courts "shall entertain" applications "on the ground that [the applicant] is in custody in violation of the Constitution or laws or treaties of the United States" and "shall forthwith award the writ ... unless ... the applicant ... is not entitled thereto."[266]

The 1966 amendments qualified the rule of mandatory review of constitutional and other federal legal claims in three ways. First, Congress provided that, with one exception, a prisoner whose unconstitutional-incarceration claims the Supreme Court previously had rejected on the merits on appeal or *certiorari* shall *not* have the writ. Thus, although rarely granted, review by the Supreme Court on direct appeal is preferred and, once it occurs, *res judicata*.[267] Second, Congress provided that, with one exception, a prisoner whose claims to be in state custody in violation of the Constitution a federal habeas corpus court had previously heard and denied on the merits "need not" — but, in the discretion of the court, may — have the writ.[268] Thus, although not *res judicata*, prior review by another federal court on habeas corpus is generally a sufficient reason for a court to deny relief on a second or successive petition. Third, Congress provided that, with eight exceptions relating to the "full[ness] and fair[ness]" of the prior proceeding, a prisoner whose claims to be in state custody in violation of the Constitution a state court had previously heard and denied on the basis of a determinative finding of historical *fact* must be denied the writ except on a showing "by convincing evidence" that the finding is erroneous.[269] A prior "full and fair" determination of the facts by a state court thus is due the same deference the "clearly erroneous" rule affords factfindings

---

[265] The bills and the hearings and debates on them are summarized in Civiletti *Amici Brief*, *supra* § 2.3 n.23, at 15-28; Biden/Edwards *Amicus* Brief, *supra* note 264, at 7-8; Bruce W. Ewing, Habeas Corpus Legislation in the United States Congress, 1955-1966 (Jan. 28, 1992) (unpublished manuscript, on file with the authors); Liebman, *supra* § 2.1 n.1, at 208 & n.527.

[266] *See* 28 U.S.C. §§ 2254(a), 2241(c)(3), 2243.

[267] *See* 28 U.S.C. § 2244(c). The one exception occurs when "the applicant ... shall plead and the [habeas corpus] court shall find the existence of a material and controlling fact which did not appear in the record of the proceeding in the Supreme Court and the court shall further find that the applicant for the writ of habeas corpus could not have caused such fact to appear in such record by the exercise of reasonable diligence." *Id.*

[268] *See id.* § 2244(b). The one exception arises when "the application alleges and is predicated on a factual or other ground not adjudicated on the hearing of the earlier application for the writ, and ... the court, justice, or judge is satisfied that the applicant has not on the earlier application deliberately withheld the newly asserted ground or otherwise abused the writ." *Id.*

[269] *Id.* § 2254(d).

in other appellate settings.[270] As is evident from the discussion above, these three qualifications simply codified doctrines that had long been part of the habeas corpus caselaw. The first qualification codified the *Royall-Frederich-Eno* rule, "leaving" prisoners to their appellate remedies in the United States Supreme Court when available as of right.[271] The second qualification codified the Court's post-*Moore* successive petition rule announced in *Salinger v. Loisel*.[272] And the third qualification codified the 200-year-old rule, applied, for example, in *Frank*, requiring deferential habeas corpus review of issues of "pure fact."[273]

Once engrafted onto the 1948 recodification of the 1874 codification of the 1867 statute, therefore, the 1966 amendments either confirmed or left intact what the caselaw had long established — that habeas corpus review of the constitutionality of incarceration stands in for and replicates direct Supreme Court review when Supreme Court review is not available, but will not duplicate Supreme Court review when it *is* independently available. A prisoner in "custody in violation of the Constitution" accordingly "shall" have the writ unless the Supreme Court previously said the prisoner was not in custody in violation of the Constitution, in which case the Court's decision is conclusive on "all issues of *fact or law*"; or unless another federal court in a prior habeas corpus proceeding said the same thing, in which case the prior court's decision often will control the *facts and law*, although it is not quite conclusive; or unless a state court fully and fairly found facts that are inconsistent with unconstitutional incarceration, in which case, the state court's decision is dispositive *on the facts* as long as it is not clearly erroneous.[274]

---

[270] *See infra* §§ 20.3h, 30.1, 37.3b.

[271] *See supra* notes 163-77 and accompanying text.

[272] 265 U.S. 224 (1924). *See supra* notes 252-54 and accompanying text.

[273] *See supra* notes 106, 147, 150, 188, 231, 249 and accompanying text.

[274] By requiring a federal habeas corpus court to defer only to a state court's "determination ... of *factual* issues," 28 U.S.C. § 2254(d) (emphasis added), Congress left intact the preexisting rule of *de novo* review of legal questions. *See generally* Midlantic Nat'l Bank v. New Jersey Dep't of Envtl. Protection, 474 U.S. 494, 501 (1986) ("The normal rule of statutory construction is that if Congress intends for legislation to change the interpretation of a judicially created concept, it makes that intent specific"). This is clear, given (1) the juxtaposition in the 1966 amendments of the requirements in sections 2244(b) and 2244(c) that federal courts defer entirely or partially to prior Supreme Court or lower federal court determinations of fact *and law* and of the lesser requirement in section 2254(d) that federal courts defer to state court determinations of only "*factual* issues"; (2) the intent of the 1966 amendments to restore direct appeal/habeas corpus parity after three Supreme Court decisions in 1963 had afforded *more* review on habeas corpus than was available on direct appeal, *see* H.R. REP. No. 1892, 89th Cong., 2d Sess. 6 (1966); 110 CONG. REC. 14680 (1964) (statement of Rep. Wyman); *infra* notes 275-76 and accompanying text, and to codify Justice Harlan's dissenting views in those cases (Justice Harlan objected to deviations from parity but endorsed the preexisting rule of *de novo* review of legal and "mixed" questions, *see*

Temporary expansion and contraction — the mid-1960s to the mid-1990s. In the mid-1960s, the Supreme Court expanded habeas corpus beyond parity — giving it broader scope than direct appeal — only to have Congress in the 1966 amendments[275] and the Court itself in the 1976-1993 period pare back that expansion to the point that parity now has been restored and solidified.[276] For

---

Sanders v. United States, 373 U.S. 1, 23-32 (1963) (Harlan, J., dissenting); Fay v. Noia, 372 U.S. 391, 460-68 (1963) (Harlan, J., dissenting); Townsend v. Sain, 372 U.S. 293, 325-27 (1963) (Stewart, J., dissenting, joined by Harlan, J.)); (3) the absence of any other reasonably available standard of review of legal questions, *see* Liebman, *supra* § 2.1 n.1, at 2089 & n.551; and (4) the legislative history, which reveals that (a) the 1966 amendments were drafted by a Judicial Conference Committee explicitly in order to block an anticipated proposal by the state chief justices that would have required deference to state court determinations of *mixed questions* of fact, H.R. Rep. No. 1384, 88th Cong., 2d Sess. 1-3, 6, 22-23 (1964) (appending and adopting the analysis of the Judicial Conference report); (b) the view of the drafting committee that the state chief justices' proposal "would be *wholly incompatible with the duty of Federal courts to determine Federal constitutional questions,*" *id.* at 23 (emphasis added), a duty the committee, quoting *Brown*, defined as affording state court legal determinations "'the weight that federal practice gives to the conclusion of a court of last resort of another jurisdiction on federal constitutional issues,'" that is, "'respectful attention to [its] reasoning and conclusion,'" but *not* deference, *id.* at 24 (quoting Brown v. Allen, 344 U.S. 443, 458 (1953); Pennekamp v. Florida, 328 U.S. 331, 335 (1946)); (c) the committee's view that "'[t]he duty of the Federal district court on habeas is no less exacting'" when it comes to mixed questions of fact and law than the Supreme Court's "'duty to determine constitutional questions'" on direct appeal as defined in the Court's classic decisions establishing the *de novo* review rule for such questions, *id.* at 24 (quoting *Townsend v. Sain, supra* at 316; Blackburn v. Alabama, 361 U.S. 199, 205 (1960)); (d) a bottom-line exchange between two members of Congress and the Judicial Conference's spokesperson, Judge Orie Phillips, who, when asked whether the proposal that ultimately became the 1966 amendments "would result in curbing the right to the great writ on a meritorious case" or, if it would not "abrogate it ... [or] actually disturb the right," answered, "I do not think that [the bill] changes present practice," *Habeas Corpus: Hearings before Subcomm. No. 3 of the House Comm. on the Judiciary*, 86th Cong., 1st Sess. 18 (1959); *see also* 105 Cong. Rec. 14635-36 (1959) (statement of Rep. Feighan, appending letter of Chief Justice Carl W. Weygandt); and (e) the House Judiciary Committee's conclusion in approving the 1966 amendments that "[t]he substitute [bill] ... creates reasonable presumptions and fixes the party on whom the burden of proof, as to certain *factual* issues, shall rest in such proceedings, *without impairment of any of the substantive rights of the applicant,*" H.R. Rep. No. 1892, 89th Cong., 2d Sess. 3 (1966) (emphasis added). *See* S. Rep. No. 1797, 89th Cong., 2d Sess. 3, 6 (1966).

[275] *See, e.g.,* 28 U.S.C. § 2244(b) (as interpreted in McCleskey v. Zant, 499 U.S. 467 (1991), partially overruling Sanders v. United States, 373 U.S. 1 (1963)); 28 U.S.C. § 2254(d) (limiting Townsend v. Sain, 372 U.S. 293 (1963)); *supra* note 274.

[276] *See, e.g.,* Spencer v. Kemna, 118 S. Ct. 978 (1998) (suggesting that Court is reconsidering its expansion of definition of "custody" in such cases as Evitts v. Lucey, 469 U.S. 387 (1985) and Sibron v. New York, 392 U.S. 40 (1968)); Brecht v. Abrahamson, 507 U.S. 619 (1993) (overruling, *e.g.,* Anderson v. Nelson, 390 U.S. 523 (1968) (*per curiam*)); Keeney v. Tamayo-Reyes, 504 U.S. 1 (1992) (overruling in part Townsend v. Sain, 372 U.S. 293 (1963)); Coleman v. Thompson, 501 U.S. 722 (1991) (overruling Fay v. Noia, 372 U.S. 391 (1963)); McCleskey v. Zant, 499 U.S. 467 (1991) (overruling in part Sanders v. United States, 373 U.S. 1 (1963)); Teague

example, from the mid-1960s to the mid-1970s, the Court repeatedly assumed that, although not constitutionally compelled, the prophylactic exclusionary rule created in *Mapp v. Ohio*[277] to discourage police from violating the 4th Amendment proscription against certain unreasonable searches and seizures[278] applied on habeas corpus as well as direct review.[279] But in 1976 in *Stone v. Powell*,[280] citing "the established rule with respect to nonconstitutional claims" that they "can be raised on collateral review only if the alleged error constituted

---

v. Lane, 489 U.S. 288 (1989) (overruling Linkletter v. Walker, 381 U.S. 618 (1965)); Smith v. Murray, 477 U.S. 527 (1986); Kuhlmann v. Wilson, 477 U.S. 436 (1986) (overruling in part *Sanders, supra*); Wainwright v. Sykes, 433 U.S. 72 (1977) (overruling in part *Fay, supra*); Stone v. Powell, 428 U.S. 465 (1976) (overruling in part, *e.g.*, Mancusi v. DeForte, 392 U.S. 364 (1968)). Noting the recent contraction of the writ are, *e.g.*, Callins v. Collins, 510 U.S. 1141 (1994) (Blackmun, J., dissenting from denial of *certiorari*) (because, since 1976, "the Court has 'erected unprecedented and unwarranted barriers' to the federal judiciary's review of the constitutional claims of capital defendants" on habeas corpus, "I no longer can state with any confidence ... that the federal judiciary will provide meaningful oversight to the state courts as they exercise their authority to inflict the penalty of death" (quoting Sawyer v. Whitley, 505 U.S. 333, 351 (1992) (Blackmun, J., concurring in the judgment)); Brecht v. Abrahamson, 507 U.S. 619, 656 (1993) (O'Connor, J., dissenting) (puzzling over majority's adoption of complicated new harmless error rule for habeas corpus cases; concluding that, because rule "does not decrease [and probably increases] the burden of identifying ... cases that warrant relief" but does "permit more errors to pass uncorrected," majority's motivation must be simply to "reduce[] the number of cases in which relief will be granted"); Herrera v. Collins, 506 U.S. 390, 439 (1993) (Blackmun, J., dissenting) (reviewing Court's recent innovations in habeas corpus doctrine and concluding that "[t]he only principle that would appear to reconcile these ... positions is the principle that habeas relief should be denied whenever possible"); Lockhart v. Fretwell, 506 U.S. 364, 387-89 (1993) (Stevens, J., dissenting) (puzzling over habeas corpus retroactivity rules that almost automatically deny the petitioner, but automatically give the State, the benefit of new and favorable legal rules); Gilbert S. Merritt, *Access to Federal Courts in Habeas Corpus Cases,* 58 TENN. L. REV. 145 (1990); Kathleen Patchel, *The New Habeas,* 42 HASTINGS L.J. 939 (1991); Richard A. Powers III, *State Prisoners' Access to Federal Habeas Corpus: Restrictions Increase,* 25 CRIM. L. BULL. 444 (1989); Frank J. Remington, *Change in the Availability of Federal Habeas Corpus: Its Significance for State Prisoners and State Correctional Programs,* 85 MICH. L. REV. 570 (1986); Frank J. Remington, *Restricting Access to Federal Habeas Corpus: Justice Sacrificed on the Altars of Expediency, Federalism and Deterrence,* 16 N.Y.U. REV. L. & SOC. CHANGE 339 (1988); Ira P. Robbins, *Whither (or Wither) Habeas Corpus?: Observations on the Supreme Court's 1985 Term,* 111 F.R.D. 265 (1986); Yale L. Rosenberg, *Kaddish for Habeas Corpus,* 59 GEO. WASH. L. REV. 362 (1991); Mark V. Tushnet, *Judicial Revision of the Habeas Corpus Statutes: A Note on Schneckloth v. Bustamonte,* 1975 WIS. L. REV. 484, 487-91; Robert Weisberg, *A Great Writ While it Lasted,* 81 J. CRIM. L. & CRIMINOLOGY 9 (1990).

[277] 367 U.S. 643 (1961).

[278] *See* Stone v. Powell, 428 U.S. 465, 482, 484 (1976) ("The exclusionary rule was a judicially created means of effectuating the rights secured by the Fourth Amendment" that was "justified ... principally on the belief that exclusion would deter unlawful police conduct").

[279] *See* cases cited in *id.* at 518-19 (Brennan, J., dissenting).

[280] 428 U.S. 465 (1976).

"'a fundamental defect which inherently results in a complete miscarriage of justice,'"[281] the Court held that the *Mapp* rule generally would not thenceforth be enforced on habeas corpus.[282] In so holding, however, the Court carefully noted that "[o]ur decision today is *not* concerned with the scope of the habeas corpus statute as authority for litigating *constitutional* claims" but only with the writ's availability to litigate claims arising under "the exclusionary rule [which] is a judicially created remedy rather than a personal constitutional right."[283] *Stone* thus is not at odds with, but is part and parcel of, the Court's centuries old "fundamentality" jurisprudence with regard to the cognizability of claims on habeas corpus.[284] Since *Stone*, the Court has confirmed this view by declining to extend *Stone* to bar the enforcement on habeas corpus of (1) *any* constitutional claim,[285] (2) *any* federal statutory claims,[286] and (3) and at least some other subconstitutional, "merely prophylactic," claims. In the last regard, the Court's 1993 decision in *Withrow v. Williams*[287] held that the rule of *Miranda v. Arizona*[288] is sufficiently fundamental to be enforceable in habeas corpus proceedings, notwithstanding that it (like the 4th Amendment exclusionary rule) is a "merely prophylactic" and *sub*constitutional rule, because the *Miranda* rule (*un*like the 4th Amendment exclusionary rule) serves to protect a personal constitutional right of the criminal defendant (the 5th Amendment privilege against self-incrimination) and because its enforcement actually prevents some violations of that constitutional right.[289] Between them, *Stone* and *Withrow* thus

---

[281] *Id.* at 477 n.10 (quoting Davis v. United States, 417 U.S. 333, 346 (1974) (quoting Hill v. United States, 368 U.S. 424, 428 (1962))).

[282] *Id.* at 494-95 (only exclusionary rule claims as to which "the State has [not] provided an opportunity for full and fair litigation" are cognizable on habeas corpus).

[283] *Id.* at 495 n.37 (emphasis added). *See also* Arizona v. Evans, 514 U.S. 1, 10-11 (1995) ("'The question whether the exclusionary rule's remedy is appropriate in a particular context has long been regarded as an issue separate from the question whether the Fourth Amendment rights of the party seeking to invoke the rule were violated by police conduct.' The exclusionary rule operates as a judicially created remedy designed to safeguard against future violations of Fourth Amendment rights.... As with any remedial device, the rule's application has been restricted to those instances where its remedial objectives are thought most efficaciously served." (quoting Illinois v. Gates, 462 U.S. 213, 223 (1983); other citations omitted)).

[284] *See, e.g., supra* notes 92-106, 131-50, 184-90 and accompanying text; *infra* Chapters 9, 27.

[285] *See* Reed v. Farley, 512 U.S. 339, 348 & n.7 (1994) (collecting cases); *infra* 9.2.

[286] *See Reed v. Farley, supra,* 512 U.S. at 354; *infra* §§ 9.1 n.41, 9.2 nn.33-34 and accompanying text.

[287] 507 U.S. 680 (1993).

[288] 384 U.S. 436 (1966).

[289] *Withrow, supra,* 507 U.S. at 689-91 (discussed *infra* § 9.2 nn.24-32 and accompanying text). *Accord* Thompson v. Keohane, 516 U.S. 99, 107 n.5 (1995).

reaffirm that not only all constitutional rights but also all "fundamental," even if *sub*constitutional, federal rights are cognizable in habeas corpus proceedings.

In *Reed v. Farley*[290] in 1994, the Court further confirmed and clarified what 200-plus years of habeas corpus history already had established: Although all constitutional claims are cognizable on habeas corpus,[291] some subconstitutional claims are *not* cognizable (notwithstanding the statute's reference without limitation to "custody in violation of the Constitution *or laws or treaties* of the United States"[292]). And the cognizability of subconstitutional claims depends upon the national importance of redressing or deterring the particular violations at issue (given, *e.g.*, an especially high likelihood of state court nullification of the federal law at issue or the particular need for national uniformity) or the libertarian fundamentality of the rights at stake (given, *e.g.*, their near-constitutional status or the prejudice their violation causes). A unanimous Court thus concluded that habeas corpus lies to cure any federal statutory violation that constitutes "'a fundamental defect which inherently results in a complete miscarriage of justice, [or] an omission inconsistent with the rudimentary demands of fair procedure,'" which includes any "'failure to comply with the formal requirements' of [a federal statute]" that "'occurred in the context of other aggravating circumstances.'"[293] The Court also seemed to agree unanimously that "aggravating circumstances" warranting habeas corpus cognizability include: (1) prejudice to important interests of the petitioner[294] and (2) violation of an important or fundamental statutory right that, for example, "'effectuates a constitutional right' [such as] the Sixth Amendment guarantee of a speedy trial."[295] And seven members of the Court seemed to include among the "aggravating factors" warranting cognizability: (3) "willful or egregious"

---

[290] 512 U.S. 339 (1994).

[291] On this point, the Court in *Reed* was unanimous. *See id.* at 353 (assuming full cognizability unless "mere statutory violations are at issue"); *id.* at 357 (Scalia, J., concurring in part) (habeas corpus review is available for "class of procedural rights that are ... guaranteed by the Constitution (which includes the Due Process Clauses)"); *id.* at 365-66 (Blackmun, J., concurring) (all statutory and constitutional claims are cognizable on habeas corpus).

[292] 292 28 U.S.C. § 2254(a) (emphasis added).

[293] *Reed, supra,* 512 U.S. at 348, 350 (plurality opinion) (quoting Hill v. United States, 368 U.S. 424, 428, 429 (1962)); *id.* at 356-57 (Scalia, J., concurring in part); *id.* at 363-64 (Blackmun, J., dissenting) (Congress so rarely applies federal statutory mandates to state criminal proceedings that, when it does, the statutory right created is sufficiently important to be enforced on habeas corpus).

[294] *See id.* at 357 (Scalia, J., concurring in part) (interpreting plurality opinion to permit, and agreeing that there ought to be, habeas corpus enforcement given "circumstances that cause additional prejudice to the defendant, thereby elevating the error to a fundamental defect or a denial of rudimentary procedural requirements").

[295] *Id.* at 339 (majority opinion).

violations of federal law by a particular state judge,[296] (4) the existence of some "reason to suppose" that state judges in general may "undermine" or "be hostile to the federal law ... at stake,"[297] and (5) statutes as to which "nationally uniform interpretation" is important.[298]

The Court's recent exhaustion decisions also preserve parity, in this case by assuring that habeas corpus petitioners, like direct appellants, cannot seek the reviewing court's consideration before seeking the prior court's judgment. Most importantly, the Court's 1982 "total exhaustion" decision in *Rose v. Lundy*[299] assured that habeas corpus petitioners, like direct appellants, have only a single *unified* review of all their claims, not many piecemeal reviews following claim-by-claim exhaustion in the state courts.[300] *Rose*'s "total exhaustion" rule having required habeas corpus petitioners, like direct appellants, to aggregate *all* their claims in proceedings in the prior courts before bringing *any* of their claims to the federal courts, Justice Kennedy's successive-petition decision in *McCleskey v. Zant*,[301] then required habeas corpus petitioners, like direct appellants, to aggregate all their now exhausted claims in one federal review.

Likewise, the Court's procedural default cases — for example, *Wainwright v. Sykes*,[302] and *Coleman v. Thompson*[303] — have adopted a "cause and prejudice/manifest miscarriage" test that approximates the analogous "adequate and independent state grounds" doctrine on direct appeal,[304] to restore the direct appeal/habeas corpus parity that *Fay v. Noia* abolished in this respect in 1963.[305] And the Court's nonretroactivity decision in *Teague v. Lane*[306] overruled

---

[296] *Id.* at 357 (Scalia, J., concurring in part and concurring in the judgment) (declining to join plurality opinion's suggestion that federal statutes are cognizable on habeas corpus in "circumstances that make the trial judge's behavior more willful or egregious," as where trial judge commits "statutory violation [that] was not waived" and to which defendant vigorously objected).

[297] *Id.* at 355 (plurality opinion).

[298] *Id.* at 348. For further discussion, see *infra* § 9.1 nn.38-53 and accompanying text.

[299] 455 U.S. 509 (1982).

[300] *See id.* at 520.

[301] 499 U.S. 467 (1991).

[302] 433 U.S. 72 (1977).

[303] 501 U.S. 722 (1991).

[304] *See* Hart, *supra* § 2.1 n.1, at 118-19 (proposing precisely this solution 30 years before Court adopted it); *supra* § 2.4b n.20 and accompanying text; *infra* § 26.1 nn.22-31 and accompanying text.

[305] Fay v. Noia, 372 U.S. 391, 429-34, 438-39 (1963) (allowing habeas corpus courts to ignore adequate and independent state grounds for state court's determination except those premised on the prisoner's deliberate waiver of federal rights). *See* Wechsler, *supra* § 2.1 n.1, at 178 (severely criticizing *Fay* precisely because it gave habeas corpus petitioners more review than direct appellants).

[306] 489 U.S. 288 (1989).

Linkletter v. Walker[307] and other 1960s cases in which the Court had held that federal habeas corpus petitioners could take advantage of many newly created legal rights that did not exist at the time of their direct appeal proceedings. *Teague's* nonretroactivity doctrine restores parity by ensuring that the sum total of the law upon which the prisoner can draw in seeking release on habeas corpus is the same as would have been available on direct appeal in the Supreme Court.[308] Finally, in *Brecht v. Abrahamson*,[309] by rejecting precedent going back to the late 1960s that had applied the same standard of harmless error on habeas corpus as on direct appeal, the Court limited the potential advantage that successful habeas corpus petitioners might have over successful direct appellants due to the greater passage of time before retrial is ordered, hence the greater likelihood of acquittal on retrial caused not by the removal of the constitutional error but by the staleness of the evidence.[310]

In the last two regards (*i.e.*, nonretroactivity and harmless error), emanations from the Court's decisions threaten to go *beyond* restoring direct appeal/habeas corpus parity to the point that the scope of the writ is narrower than the scope of direct Supreme Court review. In *dicta*, at least,[311] the Court at times has defined "new rules" — *i.e.*, ones that were not in effect at the time of the prisoner's direct appeal to the Supreme Court and thus that cannot apply retroactively in habeas corpus — so broadly as to risk removing claims from habeas corpus that any court applying then-existing law almost assuredly would have found meritorious at the time of the prisoner's direct appeal.[312] Moreover, the *Brecht*

---

[307] 381 U.S. 618 (1965).

[308] See *supra* § 2.4b nn.26, 28 and accompanying text.

[309] 507 U.S. 619 (1993).

[310] See *supra* § 2.4b nn.32-35 and accompanying text.

[311] See *infra* § 25.5 nn.82-85 and accompanying text (most of Court's nonretroactivity holdings, as opposed to its language, are explainable as conclusions that asserted constitutional right did not exist, even at time case reached Court on habeas corpus, rather than as conclusions that newly created constitutional rights did not apply on habeas corpus review).

[312] See, e.g., Johnson v. Texas, 509 U.S. 350, 377-79 (1993) (O'Connor, J., dissenting); Butler v. McKellar, 494 U.S. 407, 414 (1990); *infra* § 25.5 nn.76-78 and accompanying text. The Court sometimes seems to define a rule as "new" if it gives criminal defendants more protection than the rule on which all reasonable judges could have agreed as of the date when the prisoner's direct appeal process ended, thus limiting habeas corpus petitioners to the rule of law that the *most prosecution-prone* "reasonable judge" would have identified as the law on the relevant date. A preferable definition would give habeas corpus petitioners the benefit of the rule that the *average* "reasonable jurist" would have understood to be the law at the relevant time. See, e.g., Desist v. United States, 394 U.S. 244, 263-64 (1969) (Harlan, J., dissenting). Although the former rule discourages federal judges from skating as close as they can to the Court's law-making function, it dangerously allows state judges to skate as close as they can to unconstitutionally prosecution-favoring rules. See *infra* § 25.5.

rule could have significantly undermined direct appeal/habeas corpus parity had it been held to transfer the burden of proof on the harmlessness question from the state to the petitioner, thereby importing something like a "prejudice" element into every constitutional claim pursued on habeas corpus (unlike on direct review). In *O'Neal v. McAninch*,[313] however, the Court reaffirmed its prior allocation to *the state* of the duty to persuade the court that proven error was harmless.[314] As illustrated by *O'Neal*, there are some indications, that, having restored the writ to its pre-1963 condition, the Court is now prepared to defend and preserve the status quo.[315]

---

[313] 513 U.S. 432 (1995).

[314] *Id.* at 435. *See id.* at 442 (rejecting allocation to petitioner of burden of proving harmfulness because doing so would be "contrary to the writ's most basic traditions and purposes"). *See also id.* at 443 ("our rule avoids the need for judges to ... determine prejudice in every habeas case").

[315] In Withrow v. Williams, 507 U.S. 680 (1993), and in Wright v. West, 505 U.S. 278 (1992), the Court turned away proposals by, respectively, Justice Scalia (joined by Justice Thomas) and Justice Thomas (joined by Chief Justice Rehnquist and Justice Scalia) to extend *Stone v. Powell*'s nonreviewability rule to most constitutional claims and to jettison the *de novo* review rule for mixed questions. Justices O'Connor and Kennedy, who wrote some of the most important decisions cutting back on the Court's mid-1960s habeas corpus cases, *see, e.g.*, Coleman v. Thompson, 501 U.S. 722 (1991) (opinion for the Court of O'Connor, J.); McCleskey v. Zant, 499 U.S. 467 (1991) (opinion for the Court of Kennedy, J.); Saffle v. Parks, 494 U.S. 484 (1990) (opinion for the Court of Kennedy, J.); Teague v. Lane, 489 U.S. 288 (1989) (opinion for the Court of O'Connor, J.), more recently have suggested that the Court has done enough to narrow habeas corpus review. *See Wright v. West, supra* at 302-06 (O'Connor, J., concurring in the judgment); *id.* at 306-10 (Kennedy, J., concurring in the judgment); Keeney v. Tamayo-Reyes, 504 U.S. 1, 14-16 (1992) (O'Connor, J., dissenting); *id.* at 24 (Kennedy, J., dissenting). *See also Brecht, supra* at 650 (O'Connor, J. dissenting) ("decisions [cutting back] the Great Writ 'warrant restraint,' for we ought not take lightly alteration of that "'fundamental safeguard against unlawful custody'"" (citations omitted)). And Justices Stevens, Souter, and Ginsburg recently have favored maintenance of the writ's current scope. *E.g.*, McFarland v. Scott, 512 U.S. 849, 855-58 (1994) (opinion for the Court of Blackmun, J., joined by Stevens, Kennedy, Souter, and Ginsburg, JJ.); Reed v. Farley, 512 U.S. 849, 855-58 (1994) (plurality opinion of Ginsburg, J.); *Withrow v. Williams, supra* at 686-89 (opinion for the Court of Souter, J., joined by White, Blackmun, Stevens, Kennedy, JJ.). *Cf.* Crawford-El v. Britton, 118 S. Ct. 1584, 1596 (1998) (in context of section 1983 suits by indigent prisoners, Court concludes that "[e]ven assuming that a perceived problem with suits by inmates could justify the creation of new rules by federal judges, Congress has already fashioned special rules to cover these cases.... If there is a compelling need to frame new rules of law..., presumably Congress either would have dealt with the problem in the [Prison Litigation] Reform Act, or will respond to it in future legislation."); *id.* at 1598 (Kennedy, J., concurring) ("I am in full agreement with the Court ... that the authority to propose ... far-reaching solutions lies with the Legislative Branch, not with us."). These same impulses may explain the Court's early decisions interpreting the Antiterrorism and Effective Death Penalty Act, Pub. L. 104-132, 110 Stat. 1214 (1996), which have tended to preserve the status quo prior to the Act's adoption, even when the text or other aspects of the statute invited a more radical interpretation. *See supra* § 2.2 n.13; *infra* § 3.2 nn.38-42 and accompanying text.

Congressional revisions of 1996. In 1996, Congress passed, and the President signed, the Antiterrorism and Effective Death Penalty Act (AEDPA),[316] which changed federal habeas corpus procedures in a number of ways that are described in later chapters of this book.[317] Most of the changes modify (or, in some instances, merely codify) preexisting procedures and do not affect the longstanding relationship of parity between direct review and habeas corpus. One provision of AEDPA, however — amended section 2254(d)(1) — could either enhance or substantially undermine the parity relationship, depending upon how the provision is interpreted. Under section 2254(d)(1), a state prisoner's habeas corpus application

> shall not be granted with respect to any claim that was adjudicated on the merits in State court proceedings unless the adjudication of the claim ... resulted in a decision that was contrary to, or involved an unreasonable application of, clearly established Federal law, as determined by the Supreme Court of the United States.[318]

If the Supreme Court were to interpret this provision (as some lower courts have)[319] — to require federal court deference to state court determinations of legal and/or mixed legal-factual questions that, in the independent judgment of federal habeas courts, were erroneous, AEDPA would dramatically alter not only direct review/habeas corpus parity but also the preexisting relationship between the federal and state courts. For that interpretation would forbid federal judges to exercise or to effectuate their independent judgment on issues of federal law and, instead, would require them to give effect to state court decisions that are inconsistent with the supreme law of the land. For reasons that we develop later in the book,[320] the wording of the statute, its legislative history, and the rules of statutory construction call for a different interpretation, one that requires deference to a state court decision only *if* and *after* the reviewing federal court determines that the state court's decision neither (1) contravened any Supreme Court precedents that at the time established a rule governing claims of the type before the state court nor (2) unreasonably constructed a rule to govern such claims in the absence of governing Supreme Court precedent.[321] AEDPA thus

---

[316] Pub. L. 104-132, 110 Stat. 1214 (1996).

[317] Section 3.2 provides an overview of the changes effected by AEDPA and contains cross-references to more detailed discussions elsewhere in the book. Section 3.5b outlines the federal habeas corpus review process in cases governed by AEDPA, as well as in cases governed by pre-AEDPA law.

[318] 28 U.S.C.A. § 2254(d)(1) (West 1994 & Supp. 1998).

[319] *See infra* § 30.2c n.32.

[320] *See infra* §§ 30.2c, 30.2d.

[321] *See infra* § 30.2c nn.32-95 and accompanying text.

calls for greater respect for state court decisions than the federal habeas corpus process previously provided, but it accomplishes this result by (1) abolishing the preexisting standard of *de novo* review regardless of the state court decision, (2) replacing it with an independent-review standard that makes the state decision the focus of federal court consideration and controlling as long as it is consistent with supreme law, and (3) significantly strengthening the nonretroactivity doctrine of *Teague v. Lane*.[322] Under this reading, AEDPA actually enhances the degree to which habeas corpus review resembles a federal appeal of a state court determination of a federal claim.[323] If this view of the statute is wrong, the ramifications are profound. As we explain in § 30.2d, a broad requirement of federal court deference to, or remedial impotence in the face of, erroneous state court decisions of law would render section 2254(d) unconstitutional under Article III and the Supremacy Clause.

e. *Conclusions: Federal review as of right, 1789-1998; the logic of direct appeal/habeas corpus parity.* For over three decades, analyses of habeas corpus have tended to ask — and to answer affirmatively — the question whether habeas corpus has expanded substantially over the course of American history. As shown above, both the question and answer are historically inaccurate. The more appropriate question is whether the reach and scope of *federal court review as of right of the legality of custody under constitutional law* has expanded. And the answer is that it has *not* done so. From the adoption of the Judiciary Act of 1789 until today, Congress has authorized and the federal courts have provided federal appellate review as of right of all fundamental (including all constitutional) questions raised by the government's or a state's decision to incarcerate an individual. When meaningfully available, federal appellate review as of right in the Supreme Court on writ of error has been the preferred mode of federal review, at least for state prisoners. But when Supreme Court review as of right on writ of error has been unavailable or has provided insufficient protection of federal law against state court resistance, Congress has authorized the federal courts to employ habeas corpus, along with removal and (in the federal-prisoner context) appeals as of right to the United States Courts of Appeals, as surrogates for the Court's direct review as of right.[324]

---

[322] 489 U.S. 288 (1989) (discussed *infra* Chapter 25). *See supra* § 2.4b nn.8-12 and accompanying text; *infra* § 30.2c nn.21-30 and accompanying text.

[323] *See supra* §§ 2.2 n.6, 2.4b n.12 and accompanying text; *infra* § 30.2c.

[324] Treating removal as a form of writ of error is, *e.g.*, McKee v. Rains, 77 U.S. (10 Wall.) 22, 25-26 (1869); *see also* Martin v. Hunter's Lessee, 14 U.S. (1 Wheat.) 304, 319-20, 349-50 (1816); treating the writ of error as a form of removal is, *e.g.*, Dower v. Richards, 151 U.S. 658, 665 (1894); treating habeas corpus as "in the nature of a writ of error" is, *e.g.*, Ex parte Watkins, 28 U.S. (3 Pet.) 193, 202 (1830); treating habeas corpus as a form of removal is, *e.g.*, Ex parte

On the state prisoner side, Supreme Court writ of error review sufficed for all prisoners from 1789 until 1815 and 1833. At these points, state court threats to nullify federal duties and tariffs by prosecuting their collectors led Congress to give federal employees removal and habeas corpus rights, lest hostile state proceedings indeed nullify federal law before an opportunity for federal review became available. In 1867, Southern courts' threats to nullify newly given federal rights led the Reconstruction Congress to extend the federal courts' removal and habeas corpus authorizations to intervene in, rather than await the end of, state court proceedings whenever necessary to protect any prisoner's federal rights.

With Reconstruction's close and a strong signal from Congress in 1885, the Court restored the preference for its own review as of right — in the habeas corpus context, by requiring state prisoners to exhaust the Court's writ of error remedy *when meaningfully available*. The moment Supreme Court review as of right was *not* meaningfully available, however, following the Court's unofficial, then Congress' official, certiorarification of the Court's appellate docket, the Court reinvigorated habeas corpus review. This reinvigoration began in *Frank* and *Moore* in 1915 and 1923 and culminated in *Brown*'s 1953 acknowledgment and Congress's 1966 confirmation that the Court's *certiorari* denial did not supply the requisite review on the merits and that habeas corpus review — commensurate in substance and scope with the Court's unavailing direct review — would have to fill the breach.[325]

Bollman, 8 U.S. (4 Cranch.) 75, 97-98 (1807); treating removal and habeas corpus as substitutes is, *e.g.*, HART & WECHSLER, 2d ed., *supra* § 2.1 n.1, at 423; treating removal and writs of error as substitutes is, *e.g.*, The Mayor v. Cooper, 73 U.S. (6 Wall.) 247, 253-54 (1867); treating habeas corpus and writs of error as substitutes is, *e.g.*, In re Chapman, 156 U.S. 211, 216-18 (1895).

[325] The analysis here reveals the fallacies in four arguments frequently advanced for the proposition that the writ has irrationally expanded and ought to be scaled back. First, the writ was never limited to jurisdictional claims, nor did it ever reach all such claims. *See, e.g., supra* § 2.4d nn.92-98, 104-06, 131-45, 159-61, 178, 184-85, 195, 219-20, 245-47, 258 and accompanying text. Although the jurisdiction-only description of claims historically cognizable on habeas corpus is Professor Bator's most enduring contribution to the debate over the writ, it is a shibboleth. Second and relatedly, the writ (and the other modes of federal review as of right for which the writ substitutes) have always lain at the least to enforce constitutional defects in state-imposed incarceration, *see, e.g., id.* — with most expansions in available relief over time occurring because of the expanded reach of the Constitution. *Compare, e.g.*, Felts v. Murphy, 201 U.S. 123, 129-30 (1906) (Court "regretted" that deaf habeas corpus petitioner did not understand proceedings at which he was convicted of murder but held that procedure did not "violate the provisions of the Fourteenth Amendment to the Federal Constitution") *with, e.g.*, Pate v. Robinson, 383 U.S. 375, 377, 385 (1966) (Due Process Clause — whether enforced on direct Supreme Court review, *see, e.g.*, Drope v. Missouri, 420 U.S. 162, 172, 174-75 (1975), or on habeas corpus — affords criminal defendants the right to understand proceedings against them and to assist in their defense). Third, the widening scope of review of mixed questions on habeas corpus was not due to the writ's expansion but only to its mirroring of expanded appellate review generally. *See supra* § 2.4d

On the federal prisoner side, the story is similar, if simpler. In lieu of federal appellate rights, Congress in 1789 afforded habeas corpus review, which for a century the Court consistently used to remedy violations of fundamental (including all constitutional) rights in criminal trials. The onset of federal appellate rights in 1891 (first on writ of error in the Court itself; later, in the newly created courts of appeal), and the Court's immediate conclusion that those rights, *when meaningfully available*, superseded the writ, diminished federal-prisoner habeas corpus until the Criminal Procedure Revolution of the 1930s and 1940s expanded the number of situations in which appellate remedies were understood to be inadequate, and surrogate review in the lower courts on habeas corpus was understood to be necessary.

Since 1789, therefore, Congress has consistently entitled federal and state prisoners incarcerated in violation of any fundamental legal principle to one meaningful federal court review as of right. The model for that review, and its preferred "mode" when available, has been direct review on the merits as of right in the Supreme Court on writ of error or appeal. When direct federal appellate review has not been meaningfully available, habeas corpus has consistently filled the breach. Filling the breach has meant filling it all — providing the same review that the Court itself would have provided on direct review had it been able to do so.

---

nn.198-238 and accompanying text. *Compare, e.g.*, In re Wood, 140 U.S. 278, 286 (1891) (deferring to state trial court's questionable determination that it had not improperly excluded blacks from petitioner's jury because question whether jury discrimination had occurred was one of fact that state court "was entirely competent to decide" without second-guessing by reviewing court) *with, e.g.*, Castaneda v. Partida, 430 U.S. 482, 500 (1977) (question whether jury discrimination occurred is one of law, not fact, subject to *de novo* federal review, whether on direct Supreme Court review, *see, e.g.*, Pierre v. Louisiana, 306 U.S. 354, 358 (1939), or on habeas corpus). Finally, it is not true that, as late as the mid-1940s — the usual reference is Ex parte Hawk, 321 U.S. 114, 118 (1944) (*per curiam*), which, in turn, cites Salinger v. Loisel, 265 U.S. 224, 230-32 (1924) — the Supreme Court was giving a kind of *res judicata* deference in habeas corpus proceedings to prior state court legal judgments. The only prior legal determinations to which *Hawk* and *Salinger* require deference are *federal*, not *state*, determinations of the merits of the petitioner's constitutional claims. *See Hawk, supra* at 118 (deferring to Court's prior denial of *certiorari* on Hawk's direct appeal); *Salinger, supra* at 231 (deferring to lower federal court's denial of Salinger's prior habeas corpus petition challenging same incarceration). Except for the Court's hardly controversial rejection a few years after *Hawk* of that decision's treatment of denials of *certiorari* as prior federal adjudications of the merits, *see Brown v. Allen, supra*, 344 U.S. at 407 (opinion for the Court of Frankfurter, J.), *supra* § 2.4d nn.251-54, 260 and accompanying text, the Court has been consistent over the years in according deference to prior federal adjudications, at the same time as it has given no deference to prior *state* court legal determinations. *See supra* § 2.4d nn.107-09, 111-13, 149-50, 187-88, 247, 259, 274 and accompanying text.

The rule of direct review/habeas corpus substitutability and parity thus has the virtue of longevity.[326] It also, however, has the virtue of logic. In a federal system that for the most part disperses the responsibility to adjudicate questions of national law among a massive collection of generalist state judiciaries, the most sensible rule might be to allocate to the relatively small and expert lower national judiciary the unifying and concluding function with respect to *all* such national legal questions that the Supreme Court ideally should, but in practice cannot manage to, review itself.[327] Even thus dispersed, however, this unifying and concluding function far outstrips the capacities of the federal judiciary as a whole, requiring some method of rationing the federal judiciary's performance of that function by concentrating it on only *some* cases of *particular* national interest. The "custody" requirement[328] provides a sensible rationing principle. Given (1) the nationally important (*i.e.*, typically, constitutional) nature of the federal questions arising in criminal cases, (2) the individually important libertarian interests jeopardized by those questions' adverse adjudication, and (3) the strong pressures on local communities to subordinate national interests and individual rights when serious criminal behavior has threatened the community's cohesion and security (particularly when, as often is the case, the criminally accused are poor, members of racial or ethnic minorities, and geographic

---

[326] Together with the Suspension Clause — U.S. CONST., art. I, § 9 ("The Privilege of the Writ of Habeas Corpus shall not be suspended, unless when in Cases of Rebellion or Invasion the public safety may require it") — this longevity suggests that federal review as of right of the constitutionality of incarceration is constitutionally mandated. *See generally* the Collings, Duker, Paschall, and Steiker works cited *supra* § 2.3 n.1. Congress' consistent, centuries-long, course of conduct since the Founding suggests *that body's* interpretation of the Clause as obliging it to make available federal court review as of right of constitutional and other fundamental federal questions arising in the course of the government's (including the States') incarceration of individuals. Moreover, the courts might well treat Congress' interpretation as authoritative (including even in reviewing any sudden congressional departure from its prior practice), given (1) the Founders' location of the Suspension Clause in Congress', not the courts', article, (2) Congress' longstanding and frequent exercise of responsibility in regard to habeas corpus and related modes of federal review, *see supra* § 2.4d nn.262-66 and accompanying text, and (3) the lengthy pedigree that the body's interpretation now has acquired. *See* Archibald Cox, *The Role of Congress in Constitutional Determinations*, 40 U. CIN. L. REV. 199 (1971). *See also* Collings, *supra* § 2.3 n.1 (scope of protection afforded by Suspension Clause is best left to congressional determination); *infra* § 7.2d. *See generally Schlup v. Delo, supra*, 513 U.S. at 343 (Scalia, J., dissenting) (suggesting that "the very broad limits set by the Suspension Clause" may constrain Court's power to curtail habeas corpus review of state convictions).

[327] *See* Martin v. Hunter's Lessee, 14 U.S. (1 Wheat.) 304, 336-39 (1816); Paul J. Mishkin, *The Federal "Question" in the District Courts*, 53 COLUM. L. REV. 157, 158 & n.11 (1953) ("[T]he exercise of federal question jurisdiction by lower federal tribunals presumably permits the Supreme Court to confine itself ... to the solving of new problems rather than the policing of old solutions, without the loss that might otherwise be entailed in the effectuation of national rights.").

[328] *See infra* § 8.2.

outsiders to the community),[329] the jurisdictional prerequisite of "custody" (meaning, usually, criminal custody prior to or following conviction of a serious criminal infraction), provides a sensible proxy for the nationally important questions whose prior resolution has in fact jeopardized nationally important interests.[330] Assuming only a congressional conclusion that questions of national law on which the lives and liberties of individuals depend deserve final resolution in national courts, this system of direct appeal/habeas corpus parity is logical. It gives all state prisoners the same limited appellate review, but spreads out that review among the entire federal judiciary, allocating a small number of obviously important and difficult cases to the Supreme Court on direct review; a smaller number of less obviously important and difficult cases to that Court at the end of the habeas corpus review process; and the rest to federal district courts with the intermediate possibility of final review in the courts of appeals in cases exhibiting intermediate levels of importance and difficulty.[331]

Once this appellate understanding of habeas corpus — so long obscured by Professor Bator's flawed *tour de force*[332] — emerges from the writ's history in this country, so does the reason for using the writ to provide federal review as of right of fundamental federal legal questions. That reason is the one Justice Story gave in *Martin v. Hunter's Lessee*,[333] not for habeas corpus review, but for its model and mentor, writ of error review of federal questions as of right:

> It is further argued, that no great public mischief can result from a construction which shall limit the appellate power of the United States to cases in their own courts ... because state judges are bound by an oath to support the constitution of the United States, and must be presumed to be men of learning and integrity .... [A]dmitting that the judges of the state courts are, and always will be, of as much learning, integrity, and wisdom, as those of the courts of the United States, (which we very cheerfully admit,) it does

---

[329] The last of these three justifications for using "custody" as the proxy for federal court review as of right is developed more fully *infra* §§ 2.5 nn.8-15 and accompanying text, 2.6 nn.7-14 and accompanying text.

[330] *See* 28 U.S.C. §§ 2241(c), 2254(a). *See generally* O'Neal v. McAninch, 513 U.S. 432, 440, 442 (1995) (noting high "stakes involved in a habeas proceeding"; "errors being considered by a habeas corpus court occurred in a *criminal* proceeding, and therefore, although habeas is a civil proceeding, someone's custody, rather than mere civil liability, is at stake"; as such, habeas corpus relief "avoid[s] a grievous wrong — holding a person 'in custody in violation of the Constitution ... of the United States'" (quoting 28 U.S.C. § 2241(c)(3), 2254(a))).

[331] *See infra* § 35.4 (limitation on habeas corpus appeals, which require certificate of probable cause based on substantiality of question presented). *See also infra* § 37.3b n.12 and accompanying text.

[332] *See supra* § 2.4c.

[333] 14 U.S. (1 Wheat.) 304, 349 (1816).

not aid the argument. It is manifest that the constitution has proceeded upon a theory of its own .... The constitution has presumed ... that state attachments, state prejudices, state jealousies, and state interests, might sometimes obstruct, or control, or be supposed to obstruct or control, the regular administration of justice.... In respect to ... cases arising under the constitution, laws, and treaties of the United States ...., reasons of a higher and more extensive nature, touching the safety, peace, and sovereignty of the nation, might well justify a grant of [final, federal] ... jurisdiction.[334]

Federal law is supreme, as is federal adjudication of that law if and when mandated by Congress. Throughout the nation's history, Congress *has* mandated final federal adjudication of important federal law whenever life or liberty has depended on the outcome. By preference, this adjudication as of right has been the Supreme Court's on direct appeal. By necessity, however, it also has been the lower federal courts' on habeas corpus. Nothing in this system of personal rights and judicial responsibilities seems strange to us. But were it strange, it nonetheless is the system towards which "the constitution has proceeded upon a theory of its own."[335]

§ 2.5. The relevance of innocence.[1]

There are two historically unassailable answers to the question Judge Henry Friendly used as the title of his famous article on habeas corpus: "Is Innocence

---

[334] *Id.* at 346-47. *See also* Arizona v. Evans, 514 U.S. 1, 8-9 (1995) ("State courts, in appropriate cases, are not merely free — they are bound — to interpret the United States Constitution. In doing so, they are *not* free from the final authority of this Court." (citing Cohens v. Virginia, 19 U.S. (6 Wheat.) 264 (1821)); The Mayor v. Cooper, 73 U.S. (6 Wall.) 247, 253 (1867) (same justification for federal-question removal jurisdiction).

[335] *Martin v. Hunter's Lessee, supra,* 14 U.S. (1 Wheat.) at 346. *See* Liebman & Ryan, *supra* § 2.1 n.2, at 884-87 & n.902; *infra* § 30.2d.

§ 2.5. [1] *See generally* Vivian Berger, Herrera v. Collins*: The Gateway of Innocence for Death-Sentenced Prisoners Leads Nowhere,* 35 WM. & MARY L. REV. 943 (1994); Eric M. Freedman, *Innocence, Federalism, and the Capital Jury: Two Legislative Proposals for Evaluating Post-Trial Evidence of Innocence in Death Penalty Cases,* 18 N.Y.U. REV. L. & SOC. CHANGE 315 (1990-91); Stephen P. Garvey, *Death-Innocence and the Law of Habeas Corpus,* 56 ALB. L. REV. 225 (1992); Bruce S. Ledewitz, *Habeas Corpus as a Safety Valve for Innocence,* 18 N.Y.U. REV. L. & SOC. CHANGE 415 (1990-91); Bruce S. Ledewitz, *Procedural Default in Death Penalty Cases: Fundamental Miscarriage of Justice and Actual Innocence,* 24 CRIM. L. BULL. 379 (1988); Tom Stacy, *The Search for the Truth in Constitutional Criminal Procedure,* 91 COLUM. L. REV. 1369, 1383-85 (1991); Jordan Steiker, *Innocence and Federal Habeas,* 41 UCLA L. REV. 303 (1993); Daniel M. Bradley, Jr., Comment, Schlup v. Delo*: The Burden of Showing Actual Innocence in Habeas Corpus Review and Congress' Efforts at Reform,* 23 NEW ENG. J. ON CRIM. & CIV. CONFINEMENT 463 (1997); Note, *Responding to* Herrera v. Collins*: Ensuring that Innocents Are Not Executed,* 45 CASE W. RES. L. REV. 603 (1995); other authority cited *supra* §§ 2.1 n.1, 2.3 n.1.

Irrelevant?"[2] The first answer is "yes," innocence is indeed irrelevant. As Justice Powell stated — albeit in arguing that history should be contravened in this instance — "history reveals no exact tie of the writ of habeas corpus to a constitutional claim relating to innocence or guilt."[3] Justice Powell might have left out the word "exact," for the history of the Court's efforts over the years to preserve a boundary around an already broad remedy is a history of holdings that, whatever else it is, habeas corpus is not a means of curing factually erroneous convictions.[4] In Justice Holmes' words, "what we have to deal with is

---

[2] Friendly, *supra* § 2.1 n.1.

[3] Schneckloth v. Bustamonte, 412 U.S. 218, 257 (1973) (Powell, J., concurring). *Accord* Kimmelman v. Morrison, 477 U.S. 365, 380 (1986) ("The constitutional rights of criminal defendants are granted to the innocent and the guilty alike," and the "scope" of those rights is not "altered ... simply because the[y are] asserted on federal habeas review rather than on direct review"); Jackson v. Virginia, 443 U.S. 307, 323-24 (1979) ("constitutional ... [protections are] not confined to those defendants who are morally blameless"); Mullaney v. Wilbur, 421 U.S. 684, 697-98 (1975) (habeas corpus relief available, though petitioner could not "exonerate" himself); Irvin v. Dowd, 366 U.S. 717, 722 (1961) (habeas corpus relief available to redress due process violations "regardless of the heinousness of the crime ... [and] the apparent guilt of the offender"); Ex parte Milligan, 71 U.S. (4 Wall.) 2, 118-19 (1866) ("[I]t is the birthright of every American citizen when charged with a crime, to be tried and punished according to law. The power of punishment is alone through the means which the laws have provided for that purpose, and if they are ineffectual, there is an immunity from punishment, no matter how great an offender the individual may be, or how much his crimes may have shocked the sense of justice of the country, or endangered its safety. By the protection of the law, human rights are secured; withdraw that protection, and they are at the mercy of wicked rulers, or the clamors of an excited people."); Walberg v. Israel, 766 F.2d 1071, 1078 (7th Cir.) (Posner, J.), *cert. denied*, 474 U.S. 1031 (1985) ("Guilty as [petitioner] undoubtedly is — unworthy member of the community as he undoubtedly is — he was entitled to a better procedure."); Coleman v. Kemp, 778 F.2d 1487, 1543 n.27 (11th Cir. 1985), *cert. denied*, 476 U.S. 1164 (1986) ("the law requires that even the obviously guilty are entitled to a fair trial").

[4] *See, e.g.,* S. REP. No. 1526, 80th Cong., 2d Sess. 2 (1948) (as codified in current statute, "habeas corpus ... is not a determination of guilt or innocence of the charge upon which petitioner was sentenced. Where a prisoner sustains his right to discharge in habeas corpus, it is usually because some right ... has been denied which reflects no determination of his guilt or innocence but affects solely the fairness of his earlier criminal trial"); Herrera v. Collins, 506 U.S. 390, 400, 401 (1993) (citing cases) ("federal habeas corpus courts sit to ensure that individuals are not imprisoned in violation of the Constitution — not to correct errors of fact"; "[f]ew rulings would be more disruptive of our federal system than to provide for federal habeas review of free-standing claims of actual innocence"); Barefoot v. Estelle, 463 U.S. 880, 887 (1983) ("Federal courts are not forums in which to relitigate state trials." (quoted in McFarland v. Scott, 512 U.S. 849, 859 (1994)); Jackson v. Virginia, 443 U.S. 307, 314, 324 (1979) (short of inquiry, derived from due process right to proof beyond a reasonable doubt, whether rational trier could have found petitioner guilty beyond a reasonable doubt, "question of evidentiary 'sufficiency'" is not cognizable in habeas corpus because it implicates no constitutional right); Mackey v. United States, 401 U.S. 667, 693-95 (1971) (Harlan, J., concurring in part and dissenting in part) ("adherence to precedent ... must ineluctably lead one to the conclusion that it is not a principal purpose of the writ to inquire whether a criminal convict did in fact commit the deed alleged"); Eagle v. Samuels, 329 U.S. 304,

not the petitioners' innocence or guilt but solely the question whether their constitutional rights have been preserved."[5] The Supreme Court accordingly has not hesitated to grant habeas corpus relief when there was little question that the constitutionally wronged petitioner was guilty,[6] or to deny such relief when there was reason to believe the petitioner was innocent but when no constitutional error was found in the process by which conviction came to pass.[7]

It is in fact arguable that a habeas corpus petitioner's apparent guilt should *heighten*, not cut off or diminish, the scrutiny of the procedures by which he was convicted and sentenced. As used in this country, habeas corpus has been an important means by which the availability of federal court review of the constitutionality of state-imposed incarceration checks "the prevalency of a local spirit" and the dangers to federal law and right inherent in granting "jurisdiction of national causes" to "state judges, holding their office during pleasure, or from year to year [who are] too little independent" of the local spirit "to be relied upon for the inflexible execution of the national laws."[8] Moreover, the Bill of

---

311 (1946); United States v. Tod, 264 U.S. 131, 133 (1924); Craig v. Hecht, 263 U.S. 255, 277 (1923) (citing cases); Glasgow v. Moyer, 225 U.S. 420, 428-29 (1912); Harlan v. McGourin, 218 U.S. 442, 445, 448-49 (1910) (citing cases); Hyde v. Shine, 199 U.S. 62, 84 (1905) ("it is well settled that upon *habeas corpus* the court will not weigh the evidence"); Ex parte Debs, 158 U.S. 564, 600 (1895); In re Frederich, 149 U.S. 70, 75 (1893); Ex parte Terry, 128 U.S. 289, 305 (1888) (on "writ of *habeas corpus* ... the[] facts [regarding guilt] cannot be re-examined"); Ex parte Lange, 85 U.S. (18 Wall.) 163, 177 (1873) (that "judgment [of conviction] ... is erroneous" is irrelevant to writ's constitutional concerns); Ex parte Watkins, 28 U.S. (3 Pet.) 193, 203 (1830). *Cf. infra* § 9.1 n.21 (discussing question whether newly discovered evidence of innocence, by itself, can ever rise to level of constitutional violation cognizable in habeas corpus). *See generally supra* § 2.4d.

[5] Moore v. Dempsey, 261 U.S. 86, 87-88 (1923) (approvingly quoted in *Herrera v. Collins*, *supra*, 506 U.S. at 400-01).

[6] *See, e.g.*, decisions cited *supra* note 3. *See also* O'Neal v. McAninch, 513 U.S. 432, 447, 451-52 (1995) (Thomas, J., dissenting) ("overwhelming majority of the innocent will never reach the habeas stage"; in most cases in which habeas corpus relief is granted under existing rules, "it ... will not be true that ... the state will have unjustly imprisoned an innocent person"; "when the Court discusses erroneous imprisonments and executions [in habeas corpus context], it is not addressing questions of innocence or guilt").

[7] *See, e.g.*, Herrera v. Collins, 506 U.S. 390 (1993) (discussed *infra* notes 22-25 and accompanying text).

[8] The quotations are from THE FEDERALIST, *supra* § 2.3 n.5, No. 81, at 486 (A. Hamilton). Hamilton's ideas are linked to habeas corpus in Amsterdam, *supra* § 2.1 n.1, at 823-25 and *supra* § 2.3 n.5. *See* Reed v. Farley, 512 U.S. 339, 355 (1994) ("concern that state courts might be hostile to ... federal law" is relevant in determining scope of writ); Reed v. Ross, 468 U.S. 1, 10 (1984) ("There can be no doubt that in enacting § 2254, Congress sought to interpose the federal courts between the States and the people, as guardians of the people's federal rights — to protect the people from unconstitutional action." (internal quotations and citation omitted)); Rose v. Mitchell, 443 U.S. 545, 563 (1979) ("Federal habeas corpus review is necessary to ensure that constitutional defects in the state judiciary's ... procedure[s] are not overlooked by the very state judges who operate that system"; to "reveal flaws not appreciated by state judges perhaps too close to the day-

Rights — among the most fundamental of the "national laws" and the principal source of habeas corpus claims — was added to the Constitution (simultaneously with Congress' adoption of the first habeas corpus statute), then extended 78 years later to the States (simultaneously with the extension of the habeas corpus remedy to state prisoners), in part at least to protect unpopular persons, causes, and classes, from just this "prevalency of a local spirit."[9] Consider, finally, the principle that "[i]n proportion to the grounds of ... distrust of the [local] tribunals ought to be the facility ... of [federal] appeals"[10] — and, accordingly, the facility of habeas corpus review, which has been understood in this country from the beginning as a "clearly appellate" mechanism for reviewing incarceration and as a substitute for Supreme Court review of such incarceration when Supreme court review is not available as of right.[11]

Nothing, of course, is more likely to arouse a "local spirit" against an individual than his apparent commission of a crime that seriously jeopardizes or destroys the health, well-being, and safety of the community and its citizens.[12] Notwithstanding the justifiability of that reaction, our system of government requires that even as unpopular an individual as this be protected by an "inflexible execution of the national laws" that safeguard his — and our — liberties.[13] Accordingly, even though that system of government recognizes "a

---

to-day operation of their system to be able properly to evaluate claims that the system is defective"; and to perform an "educative and deterrent" function "since the state officials who operate the system ... may be expected to take note of a federal court's determination that their procedures are unconstitutional and must be changed"); Stone v. Powell, 428 U.S. 465, 494 n.35 (1976); Fay v. Noia, 372 U.S. 391, 431 (1963); Brown v. Allen, 344 U.S. 443, 500 (1953) (Frankfurter, J.); Brown v. Kuhlmann, 142 F.3d 529, 543 (2d Cir. 1998) (**citing FHCPP**); Stephen B. Bright & Patrick J. Keenan, *Judges and the Politics of Death: Deciding Between the Bill of Rights and the Next Election in Capital Cases*, 75 B.U. L. REV. 759 (1995); Cover & Aleinikoff, *supra* § 2.1 n.1, at 1050-52; Liebman & Ryan, supra § 2.1 n.2, at 764-73; Peller, *supra* § 2.1 n.1, at 666-67. The classic explanation of the need for federal court review of controversial questions of federal law lest they be left to unsympathetic state courts is Burt Neuborne, *The Myth of Parity*, 90 HARV. L. REV. 1105 (1977). More recently reviewing the debate over state court/federal court parity is Woolhandler, *supra* § 2.1 n.1, at 633-35 & nn.341-54.

[9] *See* authority cited *supra* note 8.

[10] THE FEDERALIST *supra* § 2.3 n.5, No. 81 at 486 (A. Hamilton).

[11] Ex parte Bollman, 8 U.S. 75, 100-01 (1807) (Marshall, C.J.). *See supra* §§ 2.2 nn.5 & 6, 2.4c n.71 and accompanying text, 2.4d nn.84-91 and accompanying text. *See generally supra* § 2.4.

[12] *See, e.g.,* Moore v. Dempsey, 261 U.S. 86 (1923); Frank v. Mangum, 237 U.S. 309 (1915); Coleman v. Kemp, 778 F.2d 1487 (11th Cir. 1985), *cert. denied,* 476 U.S. 1164 (1986).

[13] *See, e.g.,* Joint Anti-Fascist Refugee Committee v. McGrath, 341 U.S. 123, 170 (1951) (Frankfurter, J., concurring) ("The heart of the matter is that democracy implies respect for the elementary rights of men, however suspect or unworthy; a democratic government must therefore practice fairness."); Watts v. Indiana, 338 U.S. 49, 55 (1949) (plurality opinion) ("Law triumphs when the natural impulses aroused by a shocking crime yield to the safeguards which our civilization has evolved for an administration of justice at once rational and effective."); Hill v.

necessity for confiding the *original* cognizance of [criminal] causes [implicating] ... those laws to [the state courts]," it recognizes "a correspondent necessity for leaving the door of [federal] appeals as wide as possible" — and wider yet, "[i]n proportion to the grounds of ... distrust" of the "local spirit."[14] Guilt, therefore, or at least its appearance, may pose the classic circumstance in which substitute federal appellate review under the writ is especially necessary.[15]

The second historically correct answer to Judge Friendly's question is that, "no," innocence is of course not "irrelevant." The fear that an innocent person's liberty or, worse, his life may be forfeited because of unfair proceedings has long been recognized as one, among other, circumstances that makes issuance of the writ most felicitous.[16] Indeed, it would not be surprising to learn (if we somehow

---

Texas, 316 U.S. 400, 406 (1942) ("Not the least merit of our constitutional system is that its safeguards extend to all — the least deserving as well as the most virtuous."); decisions cited *supra* note 3. *Cf.* Crawford-El v. Britton, 118 S. Ct. 1584, 1598 (1998) (Kennedy, J., concurring) (despite the prevalence of "frivolous" and even "farcical" section 1983 actions by indigent prisoners, rules regulating such actions must reflect central consideration that "even as to prisoners the Government must obey always the Constitution").

[14] THE FEDERALIST, *supra* § 2.3 n.5, No. 81, at 486 (A. Hamilton) (emphasis added).

[15] *See* Carter v. Rafferty, 621 F. Supp. 533, 560 (D.N.J. 1985), *aff'd,* 781 F.2d 993 (3d Cir. 1986) (granting writ to remedy conviction "rest[ing] upon racial stereotypes, fears and prejudices": "Although extended appeals in criminal matters have been widely criticized, the need for [habeas corpus] review is amply demonstrated by this matter. There is a substantial danger that our society, concerned about the growth of crime, will retreat from the safeguards and rights accorded to the accused by the constitution.").

[16] *See, e.g.,* Bousley v. United States, 118 S. Ct. 1604, 1610 (1998) ("one of the 'principal functions of habeas corpus [is] "to assure that no man has been incarcerated under a procedure which creates an impermissibly large risk that the innocent will be convicted."'"); O'Neal v. McAninch, 513 U.S. 432, 442 (1995) ("basic purposes underlying the writ of habeas corpus" include curing "error of constitutional dimension — the sort that risks an unreliable trial outcome and the consequent conviction of an innocent person"); Schlup v. Delo, 513 U.S. 298, 324-25 (1995) ("[T]he individual interest in avoiding injustice is most compelling in the context of actual innocence. The quintessential miscarriage of justice is the execution of a person who is entirely innocent. Indeed, concern about the injustice that results from the conviction of an innocent person has long been at the core of our criminal justice system." (footnote omitted; citing numerous authorities)); *id.* at 326 ("paramount importance of avoiding the injustice of executing one who is actually innocent"); *id.* at 326 n.42 ("fundamental injustice would result from the erroneous conviction and execution of an innocent person"); Jacobs v. Scott, 513 U.S. 1067, 1067-70 (1995) (Stevens, J., dissenting from denial of stay, joined by Ginsburg, J.) (prosecutor admittedly made inconsistent arguments at petitioner's trial and at his sister's trial about whether petitioner or sister actually committed the capital murder, and "[i]f prosecutor's statements at the [sister's] trial were correct, then [petitioner] is innocent of capital murder"; case accordingly presents "self-evident" and "deeply troubling" "injustice" warranting stay of execution to consider petitioner's claims); Withrow v. Williams, 507 U.S. 680, 700 (1993) (O'Connor, J., concurring in part and dissenting in part) (discussing "the ultimate equity on the prisoner's side — a sufficient showing of actual innocence"); *id.* at 718 (Scalia, J., concurring in part and dissenting in part) ("The most significant countervailing equitable factor [on which habeas corpus petitioner may seek to rely is] possibility

could learn) that the subset of habeas corpus cases in which relief actually is granted includes more than its proportionate share of the cases in which innocent persons have been convicted.[17] Nor can this second answer be passed off entirely as reflecting a lawless willingness to find constitutional violations in cases involving the apparently innocent, when no violations would be found were the petitioners more obviously guilty. The courts properly ought to take the fact that an innocent person may have been convicted (or that a blameworthy person has been convicted of an offense other than the one for which he is to blame) as one, among other, indicators that an unconstitutional breakdown in the process has occurred.[18] Accordingly, as a matter of fact and law, the petitioner's possible innocence is clearly "relevant," and counsel for a petitioner with a colorable claim of innocence or in whose case the state may have violated a right tied to the accurate ascertainment of guilt is obliged to make that fact plain to the habeas corpus court.

The Supreme Court continues today to give *both* of the above answers to Judge Friendly's question. By now, however, its decisions have largely harmonized the apparently paradoxical answers.

First, rejecting a possible implication of earlier *dicta* in *Stone v. Powell*,[19] the modern Court repeatedly has declined "the suggestion that criminal defendants should not be allowed to vindicate through federal habeas review their right[s]" absent a constitutional violation "'bearing on the guilt or innocence of the defendant.'"[20] Accordingly, except to the limited extent that actual or possible

---

that the assigned error produced the conviction of an innocent person ...."); Brecht v. Abrahamson, 507 U.S. 619, 652 (1993) (O'Connor, J., dissenting) (citing authority) ("If there is a unifying theme to this Court's [recent] habeas jurisprudence, it is that the ultimate equity on the prisoner's side — the possibility that an error may have caused the conviction of an actually innocent person — is sufficient by itself to permit plenary review of the prisoner's federal claim."). *See generally* Weidner v. Thieret, 932 F.2d 626, 631 (7th Cir. 1991), *cert. denied*, 502 U.S. 1036 (1992) (**citing FHCPP**).

[17] *See, e.g., infra* § 11.2c (para. (3) — *Carter, Brown, Chavis, Miller & Jent* cases; para. (5) — *Wallace* case; para. (9) — *Mason* case; para. (10) — *Kelly* case); William Styron, *Death Row*, N.Y. Times, May 10, 1987, at E25, col. 6 (habeas corpus relief based on prosecutorial suppression of evidence leads to freeing of petitioner who came within hours of being executed); Reitz, *supra* § 2.1 n.1, at 497 ("But for federal habeas corpus, these two men [the petitioners in Leyra v. Denno, 347 U.S. 556 (1954)] would have gone to their deaths for crimes of which they were found not guilty"); Note, *Federal Habeas Corpus Review of State Convictions: An Interplay of Appellate Ambiguity and District Court Discretion*, 68 YALE L.J. 98, 101 n.13 (1958); authority cited *supra* note 1.

[18] *See, e.g.,* United States v. Tod, 264 U.S. 131, 133 (1924).

[19] 428 U.S. 465, 490 (1976).

[20] Kimmelman v. Morrison, 477 U.S. 365, 379 (1986) (quoting Stone v. Powell, 428 U.S. 465, 490 (1976)) (habeas corpus relief available, although basis for ineffective assistance claim at issue was counsel's failure to object to admission of reliable and inculpatory evidence seized in violation

innocence forms an element of the underlying constitutional right itself[21] — in which case the innocence-focused element would apply equally on direct and habeas corpus review — a claim's bearing on innocence is irrelevant in determining the claim's cognizability in habeas corpus.

Second, in *Herrera v. Collins*,[22] the Court held that habeas corpus is not available "absent an independent constitutional violation occurring in the underlying state criminal proceeding," and that "a claim of 'actual innocence' is not itself a constitutional claim."[23] By itself, that is, innocence is not ordinarily a sufficient basis for habeas corpus relief. The *Herrera* Court, however, expressly left open the possibility that "in a capital case a truly persuasive demonstration of 'actual innocence' made after trial would render the execution of a defendant unconstitutional, and warrant federal habeas relief if there were no state avenue open to process such a claim."[24]

Third, as again is most clearly stated in *Herrera*, the Court has restricted its concern for "actual innocence" primarily to situations in which a petitioner

---

of 4th Amendment; Court has "never intimated" that vindication of constitutional rights on habeas corpus "is conditioned upon actual innocence"). *Accord Withrow v. Williams, supra*, 507 U.S. at 692 (rights deserve to be enforced on habeas corpus though they may be "divorced from [concerns for] the correct ascertainment of guilt"); Rose v. Mitchell, 443 U.S. 545, 563 (1979) (absence of direct relationship to correct ascertainment of guilt does not bar enforcement on habeas corpus of constitutional ban on jury discrimination); *Brecht v. Abrahamson, supra*, 507 U.S. at 655 (O'Connor, J., dissenting) (rejecting "rule requiring the [habeas corpus] courts to distinguish between errors that affect accuracy and those that do not"); *supra* § 2.4d nn.280-89 and accompanying text; *infra* § 9.2.

[21] *See* Jackson v. Virginia, 443 U.S. 307 (1979) (minimal constitutional standard for assessing sufficiency of evidence presented at trial); *infra* § 9.1 n.21 (collecting decisions on either side of question whether newly discovered evidence of innocence by itself and apart from some other constitutional violation can ever be so strong as to give a petitioner a constitutional right to relief from conviction or at least a death sentence). *Cf.* United States v. Bagley, 473 U.S. 667, 681-82 (1985) (plurality opinion) (in order to establish violation of government's due process obligation not to suppress "material" evidence, defendant must show that there is a "reasonable probability" the evidence would have affected the outcome of trial"); Strickland v. Washington, 466 U.S. 668, 695 (1984) (to establish constitutionally ineffective assistance of counsel, defendant must show, *inter alia*, that there is "reasonable probability" that but for counsel's ineffectiveness, outcome of trial would have differed).

[22] 506 U.S. 390 (1993).

[23] *Id.* at 400, 404.

[24] *Id.* at 417. *Accord* Schlup v. Delo, 513 U.S. 298, 314 n.28 (1995) ("In *Herrera*, we assumed for the sake of argument 'that in a capital case a truly persuasive demonstration of "actual innocence" made after trial would render the execution of a defendant unconstitutional, and warrant federal habeas corpus relief if there were no state avenue open to process such a claim.'" (citation omitted)); *Herrera v. Collins, supra*, 506 U.S. at 419-21 (O'Connor, J., concurring); *id.* at 429 (White, J., concurring in the judgment); *id.* at 434-35 (Blackmun, J., dissenting). *See infra* § 9.1 n.21. *See also infra* § 2.6.

seeking relief on a potentially meritorious constitutional claim faces an otherwise dispositive procedural bar to review or relief, and the petitioner proffers a colorable claim of innocence in order to defeat the bar:

> This is not to say that our habeas jurisprudence casts a blind eye towards innocence.... [W]e have held that a petitioner otherwise subject to defenses of abusive or successive use of the writ may have his federal constitutional claim considered on the merits if he makes a proper showing of actual innocence. This rule, or fundamental miscarriage of justice exception, is grounded in the "equitable discretion" of habeas courts to see that federal constitutional errors do not result in the incarceration of innocent persons.... But this body of our habeas jurisprudence makes clear that a claim of "actual innocence" is not itself a constitutional claim [of the sort needed to establish habeas corpus jurisdiction], but instead *a gateway through which a habeas petitioner must pass to have his otherwise barred constitutional claim considered on the merits.*[25]

---

[25] *Herrera, supra*, 506 U.S. at 404 (emphasis added; citations omitted). *See id.* at 416 ("Our federal habeas cases have treated claims of 'actual innocence,' not as an independent constitutional claim, but as a basis upon which a habeas petitioner may have an independent constitutional claim considered on the merits, even though his habeas petition would otherwise be regarded as ... abusive."). Illustrating the uses of innocence to trump procedural bars to relief are, *e.g., Schlup v. Delo, supra*, 513 U.S. at 314-17 ("Schlup's claim of innocence does not by itself provide a basis for relief. Instead, his claim for relief depends critically on the validity of his [constitutional] claims. Schlup's claim of innocence is thus 'not itself a constitutional claim, but instead a gateway through which a habeas petitioner must pass to have his otherwise barred constitutional claims considered on the merits.'" (footnote omitted; quoting *Herrera, supra*, 506 U.S. at 404)); Sawyer v. Whitley, 505 U.S. 333, 339 & n.5 (1992) (exception to successive petition and procedural default bars to claims arising at guilt/innocence phase of trial if prisoner "show[s] a fair probability that, in light of all the evidence, including that alleged to have been illegally admitted (but with due regard to any unreliability of it) and evidence tenably claimed to have been wrongly excluded or to have become available only after the trial, the trier of the facts would have entertained a reasonable doubt of his guilt" (quoting Kuhlmann v. Wilson, 477 U.S. 436, 455 n.17 (1986) (plurality opinion)); exception to same bars to claims arising at death-sentencing phase if petitioner "show[s] by clear and convincing evidence that but for a constitutional error, no reasonable juror would have found him eligible for the death penalty under the applicable state law"). *See infra* § 26.4. *See also* Weidner v. Thieret, 932 F.2d 626, 631 (7th Cir. 1991), *cert. denied*, 502 U.S. 1036 (1992) (**citing FHCPP**) (extending "substantial injustice" exception to "law of the case" doctrine (discussed *infra* § 37.3a n.7); "'substantial injustice' obviously includes the continued detention of an innocent petitioner; it is less apparent that it includes other errors that do not raise doubts about the correctness of the outcome reached at the state trial or the denial of the petition by the district court"). In *Schlup v. Delo, supra*, the Court concluded that the difference between using innocence as a basis for relief and, instead, as a "gateway" through an otherwise preclusive procedural defense justifies a lower standard of proof in the latter situation. *See Schlup v. Delo, supra*, 513 U.S. at 314-17, 329 & n.48 (petitioner making "gateway" use of innocence "need carry less of a burden" than petitioner asserting constitutional violation based on innocence because latter petitioner's

The Court's recognition of an "actual innocence" gateway through defenses to habeas corpus relief is neither surprising nor controversial. More troubling, however, would be a *limitation* of such gateways to innocence claims.[26] Making innocence the only way around procedural obstacles to habeas corpus relief would deviate from: the historical recognition of a variety of exceptions to defenses to habeas corpus review;[27] the clear legislative intent of section 2254 to place legal matters concerning the "violation of the constitution or laws ... of the United States" at the *top* of the hierarchy of reviewability and "determination[s] of ... factual issue[s]" (which, of course, the guilt determination more clearly than any other conclusion at trial is) at the *bottom*;[28] the broader history of the writ which, however available for other kinds of claims, has not in this country been "used as a ... demurrer to the evidence";[29] the best uses of federal judicial expertise, which is not particularly well suited to ascertaining guilt or innocence of state offenses;[30] Judge Friendly's own analysis;[31] and sound policy, given the

---

"evidence of innocence would have ... to be strong enough to make his execution 'constitutionally intolerable' *even if* his conviction was the product of a fair trial" while former petitioner only "must establish sufficient doubt about his guilt to justify the conclusion that his execution would be a miscarriage of justice *unless* his conviction was the product of a fair trial"; consequently, "a *Herrera*-type claim would have to fail unless the federal habeas court is itself convinced that those new facts unquestionably establish [the prisoner's] innocence" whereas use of innocence as "gateway" through procedural bar is established "if the habeas court were merely convinced that those new facts raised sufficient doubt about [petitioner's] guilt to undermine confidence in the result of the trial"; whereas "gateway" is present if petitioner demonstrates "legal" innocence (trier's inability to find guilt beyond a reasonable doubt), *Herrera* standard may require proof of "factual innocence" (focused not on what jury might be willing or able to conclude at trial beyond a reasonable doubt but, instead, on whether federal judge is convinced that petitioner is innocent).

[26] While on the Court, Justice Powell advocated such an approach, although he never attracted more than two other adherents to his view. *See, e.g., Vasquez v. Hillery*, 474 U.S. 254, 282 & n.16 (1986) (Powell, J., dissenting, joined by Burger, C.J., and Rehnquist, J.); *Rose v. Lundy*, 443 U.S. 545, 579 (1979) (Powell, J., concurring, joined by Rehnquist, J.); *Schneckloth v. Bustamonte*, 412 U.S. 218, 250 (1973) (Powell, J., concurring, joined by Burger, C.J., and Rehnquist, J.).

[27] *See infra* note 34 and accompanying text; authority cited *infra* notes 35-46.

[28] 28 U.S.C. §§ 2254(a), 2254(e)(1) (West 1994 & Supp. 1998). *See supra* § 2.4d nn.261-315 and accompanying text.

[29] *Ex parte Craig*, 282 F. 138, 156 (2d Cir. 1922) (L. Hand, J., dissenting), *aff'd sub nom. Craig v. Hecht*, 263 U.S. 255 (1923). *See supra* note 4.

[30] *See Herrera supra*, 506 U.S. at 401; Cover & Aleinikoff, *supra* § 2.1 n.1, at 1052; *Developments in the Law, supra* § 2.1 n.1, at 1060-61.

[31] Judge Friendly identified four "considerable" situations in which "collateral attack is readily justified irrespective of any question of innocence" — (1) when there is a "'failure to complete the court'" or "the criminal process itself has broken down," as, for instance, when "the defendant ... lacked the assistance of counsel," there was "racial discrimination in the selection of the jury," or the "jury was subjected to improper influences by a court officer or had been overcome by excessive publicity"; (2) "where a denial of constitutional rights is claimed on the basis of facts

various ways that the inherently elastic "innocence" concept would be stretched were it the only way to avoid procedural defenses.[32]

---

which 'are *dehors* the record and their effect on the judgment was not open to consideration and review on appeal,'" as when "pleas of guilty [are] obtained by improper means, or on evidence known to the prosecution to be perjured, or where it later appears that the defendant was incompetent to stand trial"; (3) "where the state has failed to provide proper procedure for making a defense at trial and on appeal"; and (4) when "[n]ew constitutional developments" are held to "be fully retroactive." Friendly, *supra* § 2.1 n.1, at 151-52, 168.

[32] The "innocence" concept may refer either to (1) the *individuals* permitted to avoid certain defenses, *e.g.*, only those who, irrespective of the claims they seek to raise, can show that they may be innocent (*e.g.*, McCleskey v. Zant, 499 U.S. 467, 498 (1991) ("ends of justice" exception to successive petition ban available to "petitioner [who] supplements a constitutional claim with a 'colorable showing of factual innocence'")), or (2) the *constitutional violations* as to which defenses will be excused, *e.g.*, only those that, irrespective of their effect in the individual case, tend to undermine reliable guilt/innocence determinations (*e.g.*, Teague v. Lane, 489 U.S. 288, 313 (1989) (plurality opinion) (exception to nonretroactivity defense for new rules requiring "procedures without which the likelihood of an accurate conviction is seriously diminished")); or (3) *both* the individual and the violation, *e.g.*, only to petitioners who can demonstrate a constitutional violation that is itself responsible for their having been convicted despite being innocent (*cf.* Strickland v. Washington, 466 U.S. 668, 687 (1984) (discussed *supra* note 21 and accompanying text)). *See generally* Cover & Aleinikoff, *supra* § 2.1 n.1, at 1088-91. Moreover, the innocence concept begs the question, "Innocent of what?" The Court, for example, has struggled to define "innocence of the death penalty" for purposes of the innocence exception to procedural defenses, *see, e.g.*, Sawyer v. Whitley, 505 U.S. 333 (1992) (discussed *supra* note 25); *infra* § 26.4 nn.17-22 and accompanying text, and has also struggled with the relationship between "factual innocence" and "legal innocence," *see infra* § 26.4 n.15. Another difficulty surrounds the question of just *how* likely it must be that the petitioner is "innocent" or that the right violated in her case undermines accuracy. The Court's verbalizations diverge, ranging from a requirement of proof by "clear and convincing evidence that, but for a constitutional error, no reasonable juror would have found the petitioner eligible ... under the applicable state law" for the verdict imposed, *Sawyer v. Whitley, supra* at 336, to proof that "it is more likely than not that no reasonable juror would have convicted him in the light of the new evidence," Schlup v. Delo, 513 U.S. 298, 327 (1995) (discussed *infra* § 26.4 nn.9-15 and accompanying text), to Justice Black's concern — whence came the innocence idea in the first place, *see* Friendly, *supra* § 2.1 n.1, at 163 — for "the kind of constitutional claim that casts some *shadow of a doubt* on his guilt," Kaufman v. United States, 394 U.S. 217, 242 (1969) (Black, J., dissenting) (emphasis added). Finally, if in order to adjudicate exceptions to defenses, federal judges must ascertain the innocence or guilt of convicted habeas corpus petitioners, they must decide how much deference to give the state court verdict on the matter. Although section 2254(e)(1) would seem to create a presumption of correctness for guilt determinations, that presumption only arises if the factfinding procedure employed was "reasonable," *i.e.*, was adequate to afford a full and fair hearing. 28 U.S.C.A. § 2254(d)(2) (West 1994 & Supp. 1998). *See infra* §§ 20.3e, 30.3. In this regard, petitioners would face the following difficulty: Under section 2254(e)(1), petitioners cannot show that they are innocent-in-fact (*i.e.*, cannot overcome the presumption that their guilty verdicts are correct) until they first show that the proceedings at their trials were unconstitutional, unreasonable, or unfair; yet, in the face of an otherwise valid defense to which innocence is an exception, petitioners cannot show that the

At first glance, the Court's emphasis on innocence in delineating the exceptions it recognizes to otherwise preclusive procedural bars does seem to be unduly preclusive of other considerations.[33] Most particularly, the Court has limited the long-recognized "manifest miscarriage of justice" exception to petitioners who can demonstrate a probability of innocence, notwithstanding that the exception has had a broader meaning historically in the habeas corpus context and continues today to have a broader meaning in most other areas of the Court's criminal law jurisprudence.[34] Closer analysis reveals, however, that the Court recognizes a range of exceptions to its various preclusion doctrines in habeas corpus, including but not limited to innocence, and that the overall *collection* of recognized exceptions is not very different from the meaning the Court has assigned to "manifest miscarriage of justice" in other contexts. For example, in one or another context, the Court supplements its willingness to sidestep procedural obstacles upon a showing of the petitioner's probable innocence with a willingness to do the same when necessary:

(1)   to assure federal court redress for:
    (a)   "'structural defects in the constitution of the trial mechanism'";[35]

---

proceedings at their trials were unconstitutional or unfair (given their previous default of that claim) until they first show that they are innocent.

[33] *See supra* note 25 and accompanying text.

[34] *See* Schlup v. Delo, 513 U.S. 298, 321-22 (1995) ("To ensure that the fundamental miscarriage of justice exception would remain 'rare' and would only be applied in the 'extraordinary case,' while at the same time ensuring that the exception would extend relief to those who were truly deserving, this Court explicitly tied the miscarriage of justice exception to the petitioner's innocence.... Explicitly tying the miscarriage of justice exception to innocence thus accommodates both the systemic interests in finality, comity, and conservation of judicial resources, and the overriding individual interest in doing justice in the 'extraordinary case.'" (citations omitted)); United States v. Olano, 507 U.S. 725, 736-37 (1993) (comparing limitation of "manifest miscarriage of justice" exception in habeas corpus context to "conviction or sentencing of an actually innocent defendant" and interpretation of concept in other contexts to reach any error that "'seriously affect[s] the fairness, integrity or public reputation of judicial proceedings'... [including] independently of the defendant's innocence" (citations omitted)); *infra* § 26.4. *See also* Steiker, *supra* note 1, at 336-41 (criticizing Court's recent emphasis on innocence because it deviates from broader meanings assigned to "miscarriage of justice" in habeas corpus and other contexts).

[35] Brecht v. Abrahamson, 507 U.S. 619, 629 (1993) (quoting Arizona v. Fulminante, 499 U.S. 279, 280 (1991)). *See* Rose v. Clark, 478 U.S. 570, 577-78 (1986) (cataloguing constitutional rights that "require reversal without regard to the evidence in the particular case ... [because they] render a trial fundamentally unfair"); Johnson v. Zerbst, 304 U.S. 458, 468 (1938) (habeas corpus lies to assure that no defendant forfeits life or liberty without basic structure of fair trial); Friendly, *supra* § 2.1 n.1, at 152 ("where the attack concerns the very basis of the criminal process, few would object to allowing collateral attack regardless of the defendant's probable guilt"); Walter V. Schaefer, *Federalism and State Criminal Procedure*, 70 HARV. L. REV. 1, 8 (1956); *infra* § 32.3. *See also* Hadley v. Groose, 1994 WL 14855, at *5 n.1 (W.D. Mo. Jan. 19, 1994), *rev'd on other*

    (b)   violations of "fundamental," "bedrock," or "watershed" rules that undermine the fundamental fairness of the proceeding;[36]

    (c)   procedures that "had the effect of foreclosing meaningful exploration of ... defenses," "precluded the development of true facts [or] resulted in the admission of false ones," or "serve[d] to pervert the jury's deliberations concerning the ultimate question";[37]

    (d)   constitutional "errors" occurring under circumstances — for example, in the absence of effective assistance of counsel — that "so upset the adversarial balance ... that the trial was rendered unfair and the verdict rendered suspect";[38] and

---

grounds, Hadley v. Caspari, 36 F.3d 51 (8th Cir. 1994) (*per curiam*) (*dicta*) ("alternative ground for asserting a basic miscarriage of justice [and thereby avoiding habeas corpus preclusion based on a procedural default] would be a constitutional violation undermining 'the structural integrity of the criminal tribunal itself'" (quoting Vasquez v. Hillery, 474 U.S. 254, 263 (1986)).

[36] Sawyer v. Smith, 497 U.S. 227, 241-44 (1991). *See Brecht v. Abrahamson, supra,* 507 U.S. at 633 ("writ of habeas corpus has historically been regarded as ... 'a bulwark against convictions that violate "fundamental fairness"'" (quoting Engle v. Isaac, 456 U.S. 107, 126 (1982) (quoting Wainwright v. Sykes, 433 U.S. 72, 97 (1977) (Stevens, J., concurring)))); *infra* § 25.7.

[37] Smith v. Murray, 477 U.S. 527, 538 (1986). *See infra* § 26.3b (defining "objective impediments"). *See also* 28 U.S.C. § 2244(d)(1)(B) (West 1994 & Supp. 1998) (usual triggering date for habeas corpus statute of limitations is delayed if "applicant was prevented from filing by ... State action" that was "in violation of the Constitution or laws of the United States"); *id.* § 2254(b)(1)(B) (requirement of exhaustion of state remedies is suspended if "there is an absence of available State corrective process" or if foregone state "process [is] ineffective to protect the rights of the applicant"); *id.* § 2254(d)(2) (preclusive effect of state court adjudication of merits is overcome if state court "decision ... was based on an unreasonable determination of the facts in light of the evidence presented in the State court proceeding"); *id.* § 2254(e)(1) (presumption of correctness of state court factfindings is overcome if findings are shown "by clear and convincing evidence" to be erroneous); *id.* § 2264(a)(1) (West Supp. 1998) (special procedural default rule for capital cases in "opt-in" States is suspended if default was "result of State action in violation of the Constitution or laws of the United States"); *id.* § 2266(b)(1)(C) (time limit on federal district court's resolution of habeas corpus petition is suspended if adhering to it would prevent adequate and effective adversarial treatment of issues).

[38] Kimmelman v. Morrison, 477 U.S. 365, 374 (1986). *Accord, e.g.,* Coleman v. Thompson, 501 U.S. 722, 752-53 (1991); Murray v. Carrier, 477 U.S. 478, 496 (1986). *See infra* §§ 20.3e nn.115-19, 133-35 and accompanying text, 26.3b nn.34-41 and accompanying text. *See also* 28 U.S.C. §§ 2261(b), 2261(c) (West Supp. 1998) (special limitations on habeas corpus review in capital cases confined to States that provide competent and adequately funded representation to indigent capital prisoners in state postconviction proceedings); *id.* § 2266(b)(1)(C)(ii)(III) (time limit on federal district court's resolution of habeas corpus petition is suspended if adhering to it "would deny counsel for the applicant ... the reasonable time necessary for effective preparation ..."). *Cf. id.* § 2261(e) (authorizing court to appoint "different counsel" *sua sponte* "or at the request of the prisoner, at any phase of State or Federal post-conviction proceedings on the basis of the ineffectiveness or incompetence of counsel in such proceedings").

    (e)   "deliberate and especially egregious error[s] of the trial type, or one[s] that [are] combined with a pattern of prosecutorial misconduct [that] so infect the integrity of the proceeding[s] as to warrant the grant of habeas relief";[39]

(2) shield individuals from criminal punishment, or from particular types of punishment, for "'certain kinds of primary, private individual conduct [that the Constitution or laws place] beyond the power of the criminal law-making authority to proscribe'" or beyond its power to punish with particular penalties, such as death;[40]

(3) provide a means by which "evolving standards of decency" and the most fundamental aspects of due process may be made available to persons incarcerated at an earlier, less "enlightened" time;[41]

(4) assure federal court review whenever "objective impediments" to the vindication of constitutional rights have undermined the capacity of the state courts to redress constitutional violations,[42] including via:

---

[39] *Brecht v. Abrahamson, supra*, 507 U.S. at 638 n.9 (citing Greer v. Miller, 483 U.S. 756, 769 (1987) (Stevens, J., concurring in the judgment)). *See* Reed v. Farley, 512 U.S. 339, 348-49 (1994); *infra* § 32.5.

[40] Teague v. Lane, 489 U.S. 288, 307 (1988) (plurality opinion) (quoting Mackey v. United States, 401 U.S. 667, 692 (1971) (Harlan, J., concurring in part and dissenting in part)). *Accord* Penry v. Lynaugh, 492 U.S. 302, 329 (1989). *See infra* § 25.7.

[41] Trop v. Dulles, 356 U.S. 86, 101 (1958) (plurality opinion); Weems v. United States, 217 U.S. 349, 378 (1910). *See* Kuhlmann v. Wilson, 477 U.S. 436, 447 (1986) (plurality opinion) ("The Court uniformly has been guided by the proposition that the writ should be available to afford relief to those 'persons whom society has grievously wronged' in light of modern concepts of justice." (quoting Fay v. Noia, 372 U.S. 391, 440-41 (1963))); Friendly, *supra* § 2.1 n.1, at 153 (certain "[n]ew constitutional developments relating to criminal procedure are another special case" in which habeas corpus should be available, regardless of innocence); *infra* § 25.7. *See also* 28 U.S.C. § 2244(b)(2)(A) (West 1994 & Supp. 1998) (bar to successive petitions suspended if "applicant shows that the claim [presented in second or successive petition] relies on a new rule of constitutional law, made retroactive to cases on collateral review by the Supreme Court, that was previously unavailable"); *id.* § 2244(d)(1)(C) (usual triggering date for habeas corpus statute of limitations is delayed if "right [on which the petitioner's claim relies] has been newly recognized by the Supreme Court and made retroactively applicable to cases on collateral review"); *id.* § 2254(e)(2)(A)(i) (bar to hearings on facts that petitioner failed to develop in state court suspended if, *inter alia*, petitioner's claim relies on "new rule of constitutional law, made retroactive to cases on collateral review by the Supreme Court, that was previously unavailable"); *id.* § 2264(a)(2) (West Supp. 1998) (special procedural default rule for capital cases in "opt-in" States is suspended if default was "result of the Supreme Court's recognition of a new Federal right that is made retroactively applicable").

[42] *Murray v. Carrier, supra*, 477 U.S. at 488-89. *See, e.g.*, Amadeo v. Zant, 486 U.S. 214, 222 (1988) ("If the district attorney's memorandum [revealing his instructions to jury commissioner to underrepresent blacks on county's juries] was not reasonably discoverable because it was concealed by Putnam County officials, and if that concealment, rather than tactical considerations,

    (a)   the use of procedures that are hostile or insufficiently hospitable to the vindication of federal rights;[43]

    (b)   the absence in the state courts of an "opportunity for full and fair litigation" of constitutional claims;[44] and

    (c)   the claimed "denial of constitutional rights ... on the basis of facts which 'are *dehors* the record' ([hence] ... not open to consideration and review on [direct] appeal)";[45] and

  (5)   avoid excessive prejudice to individual petitioners' constitutional rights as well as to their interest in an accurate verdict.[46]

---

was the reason for the failure of petitioner's lawyers to raise the jury challenge ..., then petitioner established ample cause to excuse his procedural default."); *infra* § 26.3b. *See also* statutory provisions cited *supra* note 37.

[43] *See infra* § 26.2d. *See also* statutory provisions cited *supra* note 37.

[44] Stone v. Powell, 428 U.S. 465, 494-95 & n.37 (1976). *See infra* §§ 7.1b nn.41-46 and accompanying text, 20.3e, 23.4a, 27.3. *See also* statutory provisions cited *supra* note 37.

[45] Friendly, *supra* § 2.1 n.1, at 152 (quoting Waley v. Johnston, 316 U.S. 101, 104-05 (1942)). *See, e.g.*, Coleman v. Thompson, 501 U.S. 722, 753 (1991) ("'showing that the ... legal basis for a claim was not reasonably available to counsel'" at earlier points in petitioner's challenges to conviction when error might have been, but was not, raised permits claim to be raised for first time in habeas corpus); Parker v. Dugger, 498 U.S. 308, 320, 324-25 (1991) (state factfinding ignored because it was "not fairly supported by the record in this case"); Wilwording v. Swenson, 404 U.S. 249, 249-50 (1971) (exhaustion of unfair state court proceedings is not required); Townsend v. Sain, 372 U.S. 293, 312 (1963) (state determinations of fact not binding in federal habeas corpus proceeding if not based on "full and fair" factfinding procedures); Young v. Ragen, 337 U.S. 235, 239 (1949); Marino v. Ragen, 332 U.S. 561, 564 (1947) (Rutledge, J., concurring); Frank v. Mangum, 237 U.S. 309, 335 (1915); Bator, *supra* § 2.1 n.1, at 444-62; *infra* §§ 20.3, 23.4a, 26.2d, 27.3. *See also* 28 U.S.C. § 2244(b)(2)(B)(i) (West 1994 & Supp. 1998) (bar to successive petitions suspended if, *inter alia*, "the factual predicate for the claim [presented in second or successive petition] could not have been discovered previously through the exercise of due diligence"); *id.* § 2244(c) (Supreme Court's resolution of claim on direct review bars later habeas corpus consideration of same claim "unless the applicant shall plead and the court shall find the existence of a material and controlling fact which did not appear in the record of the proceeding in the Supreme Court and the court shall further find that the applicant for the writ of habeas corpus could not have caused such fact to appear in such record by the exercise of reasonable diligence"); *id.* § 2244(d)(1)(D) (usual triggering date for habeas corpus statute of limitations is delayed if "date on which the factual predicate of the claim or claims presented could [not previously] have been discovered through the exercise of reasonable diligence"); *id.* § 2254(e)(1) (discussed *supra* note 37); *id.* § 2254(e)(2)(A)(ii) (bar to hearings on facts that petitioner failed to develop in state court suspended if, *inter alia*, petitioner's claim relies on "factual predicate that could not have been previously discovered through the exercise of due diligence"); *id.* § 2264(a)(3) (West Supp. 1998) (special procedural default rule for capital cases in "opt-in" States is suspended if defaulted claim is "based on a factual predicate that could not have been discovered through the exercise of due diligence in time to present the claim for State or Federal post-conviction review").

[46] *See, e.g.*, Reed v. Farley, 512 U.S. 339, 347-49 (1994); *id.* at 356 (Scalia, J., concurring in the judgment in part); Brecht v. Abrahamson, 507 U.S. 619, 622-23 (1993) (emphasis added); Yates v. Evatt, 500 U.S. 391, 404-05 (1993); Kotteakos v. United States, 328 U.S. 750, 778

Likewise, the Antiterrorism and Effective Death Penalty Act of 1996 (AEDPA),[47] which makes various changes in habeas corpus procedures,[48] permits prisoners to use a strong showing of probable innocence as a "gateway" through certain procedural impediments to habeas corpus relief — in large measure codifying, but at times extending, preexisting doctrine.[49] For example, under AEPDA, a showing of "innocence" constitutes part of the presentation a petitioner may make to (1) obtain a federal evidentiary hearing despite a default that resulted in the state courts' failure to develop the material facts;[50] and (2) file a same-claim successive petition.[51] Although AEDPA tracks preexisting Supreme Court doctrine in sometimes making a showing of probable innocence a prerequisite for avoiding certain procedural obstacles to relief, it, too, recognizes a number of noninnocence-based ways of avoiding those obstacles.[52]

Thus, innocence clearly is relevant in habeas corpus proceedings. Innocence is not, however, a necessary condition of habeas corpus relief, although it is a necessary condition of some (but not all) "gateways" through otherwise preclusive defenses to habeas corpus relief. Nor is innocence a sufficient condition of habeas corpus relief (except, perhaps, in a very narrow category of

---

(1946); *infra* §§ 26.3c, 32.4d. *See also* 28 U.S.C. § 2266(b)(1)(C) (West Supp. 1998) (time limit on federal district court's resolution of habeas corpus petition is suspended if adhering to it would unduly prejudice petitioner).

[47] Pub. L. 104-132, 110 Stat. 1214 (1996).

[48] For an overview of the ways in which AEDPA changes the federal habeas corpus process, see *infra* §§ 3.2, 3.3.

[49] *See* Calderon v. Thompson, 118 S. Ct. 1489, 1502 (1998) (*dicta*) (pointing out similarities between AEDPA's use of innocence as gateway and Court's "miscarriage of justice" doctrine).

[50] *See* 28 U.S.C.A. § 2254(e)(2) (West 1994 & Supp. 1998) ("If the applicant has failed to develop the factual basis of a claim in State court proceedings, the court shall not hold an evidentiary hearing on the claim unless the applicants shows [*inter alia*] that ... (B) the facts underlying the claim would be sufficient to establish by clear and convincing evidence that but for constitutional error, no reasonable factfinder would have found the applicant guilty of the underlying offense"). For discussion of this standard, see *infra* § 20.2b nn.23-25, 33-38 and accompanying text.

[51] *See* 28 U.S.C.A. § 2244(b)(2)(B) (West 1994 & Supp. 1998) (new-claim successive petition may be filed if "the factual predicate for the claim could not have been discovered previously through the exercise of due diligence; and ... the facts underlying the claim, if proven and viewed in light of the evidence as a whole, would be sufficient to establish by clear and convincing evidence that, but for constitutional error, no reasonable factfinder would have found the applicant guilty of the underlying offense"). *See also* Calderon v. Thompson, *supra*, 118 S. Ct. at 1502 (*dicta*) (discussing innocence showing required by 28 U.S.C. § 2244(b)(2)(B)). For further explanation of the innocence standard established by AEDPA in this regard, see *infra* § 28.3e nn.134-40 and accompanying text.

[52] *See* statutory provisions cited *supra* notes 37, 38, 41, 45, 46.

capital cases[53]), although innocence may provide a sufficient basis for avoiding otherwise preclusive defenses to habeas corpus relief.

§ 2.6. The writ's role in capital cases.[1]

The policies favoring a meaningful federal habeas corpus remedy for state prisoners apply with particular force in capital cases. If the adverse "custodial" consequences of any misdemeanor or felony conviction, including the consequences accompanying parole, probation, and release on recognizance are sufficient to justify federal habeas corpus review as of right,[2] then such review would seem to be of infinitely greater importance when the adverse consequence is death. The Supreme Court frequently has recognized that imposition of the death penalty is such a uniquely final and draconian step from the viewpoints of society and the condemned individual that it must be attended with a special set of procedural protections.[3] Those protections must assure both that the courts

---

[53] *See supra* note 24 and accompanying text.

§ 2.6. [1] *See generally* Smith v. Murray, 477 U.S. 527, 541-50 (1986) (Stevens, J., dissenting); Anthony G. Amsterdam, *In Favorem Mortis: The Supreme Court and Capital Punishment*, 14 A.B.A. SEC. INDIVIDUAL RTS. & RESP. 14 (1987); Robert Batey, *Federal Habeas Corpus Relief and the Death Penalty: "Finality with a Capital F,"* 36 U. FLA. L. REV. 252, 262-66 (1984); Hugo A. Bedau & Michael L. Radelet, *Miscarriages of Justice in Capital Cases*, 40 STAN. L. REV. 21, 71-75 (1987); Robert A. Burt, *Disorder in the Court: The Death Penalty and the Constitution*, 85 MICH. L. REV. 1741 (1987); Evan Caminker & Irwin Chemerinsky, *The Lawless Execution of Robert Alton Harris*, 102 YALE L.J. 225 (1992); Robert S. Catz, *Federal Habeas Corpus and the Death Penalty: Need for a Preclusion Doctrine Exception*, 18 U.C. DAVIS L. REV. 1177 (1985); Jack Greenberg, *Capital Punishment as a System*, 91 YALE L.J. 908 (1982); Joseph Hoffman, *Starting From Scratch: Rethinking Federal Habeas Review of Death Penalty Cases*, 20 FLA. ST. U. L. REV. 133 (1992); Bruce S. Ledewitz, *Procedural Default in Death Penalty Cases: Fundamental Miscarriage of Justice and Actual Innocence*, 24 CRIM. L. BULL. 379 (1988); Daniel J. Meltzer, *State Court Forfeitures of Federal Rights*, 99 HARV. L. REV. 1128, 1223-25 (1986); John T. Noonan, *Horses of the Night:* Harris v. Vasquez, 42 STAN. L. REV. 1011 (1993); John T. Noonan, *Should State Executions Run on Schedule?*, N.Y. TIMES, Apr. 27, 1992, at A17, col. 5; Stephen Reinhardt, *The Supreme Court, the Death Penalty, and the* Harris *Case*, 102 YALE L.J. 102 (1992); Ira P. Robbins, *Toward a More Just and Effective System of Review in State Death Penalty Cases*, 40 AM. U. L. REV. 1 (1990); Ronald J. Tabak, *Capital Punishment: Is There Any Habeas Left in this Corpus?*, 27 LOY. U. CHI. L.J. 523 (1996); Diane Wells, *Federal Habeas Corpus and the Death Penalty: A Need for a Return to the Principles of* Furman, 80 J. CRIM. L. & CRIMINOLOGY 427 (1989); Note, *The Reform of Federal Habeas Corpus in Capital Cases*, 29 DUQ. L. REV. 61 (1990); Note, *Summary Process and the Rule of Law: Expediting Death Penalty Cases in the Federal Courts*, 95 YALE L.J. 349 (1985); authority cited *infra* §§ 4.2 n.1, 7.1 n.2, 7.2 n.1.

[2] *See supra* § 2.4e; *infra* § 8.2d.

[3] *See, e.g.*, Herrera v. Collins, 506 U.S. 390, 405 (1993) ("We have, of course, held that the Eighth Amendment requires increased reliability of the process by which capital punishment may be imposed."); Murray v. Giarratano, 492 U.S. 1, 8-9 (1989) (plurality opinion of Rehnquist, C.J.) (collecting cases); *id.* at 21-22 nn.9-10 (Stevens, J., dissenting) (collecting cases); Turner v.

have reliably identified individuals who are guilty of a capital crime and for whom execution is an appropriate sanction and that the death sentence is "and appear[s] to be, based on reason rather than caprice or emotion."[4] Because habeas corpus review helps assure that the state courts have provided due process and that the guilt and sentencing decisions of those courts are reliable,[5] it follows that habeas corpus review is especially critical in capital cases because of the high constitutional standard of due process and the particular need for reliability in such cases.[6]

Additionally, capital cases present the situation in which the clash in the state courts between parochial interests and emotions on the one hand and national law and liberties on the other is most likely to favor the former and threaten the latter — precisely the situation in which the Framers saw a need for a federal appellate check on "a local spirit" and on a state judicial system "too little independent" of that spirit "to be relied upon for the inflexible execution of the national laws."[7] Consider a generalized fact pattern often encountered in capital cases:[8] An outsider only recently arrived in a community — often a rural or

---

Murray, 476 U.S. 28, 35-36 (1986); Strickland v. Washington, 466 U.S. 668, 686-87 (1984); California v. Ramos, 463 U.S. 992, 998-99 (1983); Zant v. Stephens, 462 U.S. 862, 885 (1983); Eddings v. Oklahoma, 455 U.S. 104, 117-19 (1982) (O'Connor, J., concurring); Beck v. Alabama, 447 U.S. 625, 637-38 (1980); Rummel v. Estelle, 445 U.S. 263, 271-72 (1980); Lockett v. Ohio, 438 U.S. 586, 604 (1978); Woodson v. North Carolina, 428 U.S. 280, 305 (1976); Reid v. Covert, 354 U.S. 1, 45-46, 71, 77 (1957) (Frankfurter and Harlan, JJ., concurring); Williams v. Georgia, 349 U.S. 375, 391 (1955); Stein v. New York, 346 U.S. 156, 196 (1953); Griffin v. United States, 336 U.S. 704, 708 (1949); Andres v. United States, 333 U.S. 740, 752 (1948); Powell v. Alabama, 287 U.S. 45, 71 (1932).

[4] Gardner v. Florida, 430 U.S. 349, 358 (1977).

[5] *See supra* § 2.5.

[6] *See* McFarland v. Scott, 512 U.S. 849, 855, 859 (1994) ("by providing indigent capital defendants with a mandatory right to qualified legal counsel in these proceedings, Congress has recognized that federal habeas corpus has a particularly important role to play in promoting fundamental fairness in the imposition of the death penalty" and "that quality legal representation is necessary in capital habeas corpus proceedings in light of 'the seriousness of the possible penalty and ... the unique and complex nature of the litigation'" (quoting Murray v. Giarratano, 492 U.S. 1, 14 (1989) (Kennedy, J., concurring in the judgment)). On the high rate at which reversible constitutional violations are found in capital habeas corpus cases, see *supra* § 2.3 n.23 and accompanying text.

[7] THE FEDERALIST, *supra* § 2.3 n.5, No. 81 at 486 (A. Hamilton) (discussed *supra* § 2.5 nn.8-15 and accompanying text).

[8] *See, e.g.,* Penry v. Lynaugh, 492 U.S. 302 (1989); McClesky v. Kemp, 481 U.S. 279 (1987); Darden v. Wainwright, 477 U.S. 168 (1986); Turner v. Murray, 476 U.S. 28 (1986); Strickland v. Washington, 466 U.S. 668 (1984); Gregg v. Georgia, 428 U.S. 153 (1976); Mitchell v. Kemp, 762 F.2d 886 (11th Cir. 1985); Spinkellink v. Wainwright, 578 F.2d 582 (5th Cir. 1978), *cert. denied,* 440 U.S. 976 (1979). *See also* Singleton v. Norris, 108 F.3d 872, 875 (8th Cir. 1997) (Heaney, J., concurring) ("At every stage, I believe the decision of who shall live and who shall die for his

small-town community — is charged with taking the life of a local citizen. Typically, the outsider is young, poor, urban, male, and African-American or Latino;[9] if he is white, he is probably a drifter and probably has a criminal record in another State. The victim, on the other hand is probably white,[10] a respected member of the community, most usually a merchant or law enforcement officer. The accused and the victim do not know each other; the latter had no particular reason to expect that the crime would occur as and when it did; in all likelihood, the homicide occurred in the course of some other serious felony, usually a robbery. The evidence against the accused seems strong.[11]

Such an offense obviously will shock, frighten, and enrage the community. That of course is why the community reserves its most severe punishment for such offenses. But inherent in the "local spirit" aroused by such egregious crimes against the community at the hands, apparently, of someone so thoroughly outside the community is the temptation — indeed, at times, the compulsion — for the legal arm of that community to move more swiftly and directly toward that punishment than "an inflexible execution of the national laws"[12] permits.[13] It is particularly for such cases, therefore, that a postconviction system of appeals to the federal courts needs exist.[14]

From time to time, these bases for applying a rule *in favorem vitae* of broad habeas corpus review of capital cases have led federal judges to endorse and exercise a level of consideration in capital cases that they generally would not endorse or exercise in noncapital cases.[15] Nonetheless, the Supreme Court thus

---

crime turns less on the nature of the offense and the incorrigibility of the offender and more on inappropriate and indefensible considerations: the political and personal inclinations of prosecutors; the defendant's wealth, race, and intellect; the race and economic status of the victim; the quality of the defendant's counsel; and the resources allocated to defense lawyers.").

[9] Fifty percent of the inmates on death row in this country are nonwhite; 98 percent are male. NAACP Legal Defense and Educational Fund, Death Row, U.S.A. 1 (Spring 1998).

[10] *See id.* at 5.

[11] As strong as it may seem at trial and during state appeals, the evidence against capitally sentenced petitioners occasionally evaporates during habeas corpus proceedings. *See* authority cited *supra* § 2.5 n.1; *supra* § 2.5 n.17 and referenced cases.

[12] THE FEDERALIST, *supra* § 2.3 n.5, No. 81, at 486 (A. Hamilton).

[13] *See, e.g.,* Coleman v. Kemp, 778 F.2d 1487, 1538-39 (11th Cir. 1985), *cert. denied,* 476 U.S. 1164 (1986). The high rate at which the federal courts in recent years have found constitutional defects in capital convictions and sentences provides empirical support for this proposition. *See supra* § 2.3 n.23 and accompanying text.

[14] *See supra* § 2.5 nn.8-15 and accompanying text. *See also infra* §§ 4.2, 7.2, 12.3b, 13.2, 13.3b, 19.4e, 20.1c, 26.3b nn.21-25 and accompanying text, 27.1 nn.7-15 and accompanying text.

[15] *See, e.g.,* Calderon v. Thompson, 118 S. Ct. 1489, 1507 (1998) (Souter, J., dissenting) ("however true it is that the en banc rehearing process cannot effectively function to review every three-judge panel that arguably goes astray in a particular case, surely it is nonetheless reasonable to resort to en banc correction that may be necessary to avoid a constitutional error standing

between a life sentence and an execution. It is, after all, axiomatic that this Court cannot devote itself to error correction, and yet in death cases the exercise of our discretionary review for just this purpose may be warranted."); O'Dell v. Netherland, 117 S. Ct. 1969, 1980 n.3 (1997) (Stevens, J., dissenting) ("we have long recognized that sentencing procedures, as well as trials, must satisfy the dictates of the Due Process Clause, and that the unique character of the death penalty mandates special scrutiny of those procedures in capital cases"); Angelone v. Bennett, 117 S. Ct. 381, 381 (1996) (*mem.*) (Stevens, J., dissenting) ("Given the irreparable consequences of error in a capital case, I believe we should steadfastly resist the temptation to endorse procedural shortcuts that can only increase the risk of error."); Kyles v. Whitley, 514 U.S. 419, 422 (1995) (because "there is reason to question whether the Court of Appeals evaluated the significance of ... evidence [suppressed by the prosecution] under the correct standard" and "[b]ecause '[o]ur duty to search for constitutional error with painstaking care is never more exacting than it is in a capital case,' we granted certiorari and now reverse" (quoting Burger v. Kemp, 483 U.S. 776, 785 (1987); citation and footnote omitted)); *id.* at 455 (Stevens, J., concurring) (responding to claim that grant of *certiorari* in case was "wholly unprecedented" and inappropriate because "petitioner claim[ed] only that a concededly correct view of the law was incorrectly applied to the facts," *id.* at 456 (Scalia, J., dissenting), Justice Stevens' concurring opinion argues that Court's "duty to administer justice occasionally requires busy judges to engage in a detailed review of the particular facts of a case, even though our labors may not provide posterity with a newly minted rule of law. The current popularity of capital punishment makes this 'generalizable principle' especially important.... Sometimes the performance of an unpleasant duty conveys a message more significant than even the most penetrating legal analysis."); Jacobs v. Scott, 513 U.S. 1067, 1070 (1995) (Stevens, J., dissenting from denial of stay, joined by Ginsburg, J.) ("'heightened need for reliability' in capital cases ... underscores the gravity of th[e] questions in the circumstances of this case," providing additional reason why Court should grant stay "so that we may carefully consider [habeas corpus petitioner's] claims by way of our ordinary procedure respecting petitions for certiorari" (quoting Caldwell v. Mississippi, 472 U.S. 320, 323 (1985))); McFarland v. Scott, 512 U.S. 849, 855, 859 (1994) (quoted *supra* note 6); Campbell v. Wood, 511 U.S. 1119 n.3 (1994) (Blackmun, J., dissenting from denial of stay of execution and denial of *certiorari*) (if capital habeas corpus cases presents "a fundamental constitutional question," Court should not await conflict among circuits before granting *certiorari*); Callins v. Collins, 510 U.S. 1141 (1994) (Blackmun, J., dissenting from denial of *certiorari*) ("my willingness to enforce the capital punishment statutes enacted by the States and the Federal Government '... has always rested on an understanding that ... the federal judiciary's power to reach and correct claims of constitutional error on federal habeas review[] would ensure that death sentences are fairly imposed'" (quoting Sawyer v. Whitley, 505 U.S. 333, 358 (1992) (Blackmun, J., concurring in the judgment))); Grubbs v. Delo, 506 U.S. 1301 (1992) (statement of Blackmun, J., on granting stay of execution pending *certiorari* to review lower court's rejection of habeas corpus petition) ("With an execution so irrevocable, I ... choose to err, if at all, on the side of the applicant."); Herrera v. Collins, 506 U.S. 390, 416-17 (1993) (in capital, but no other, criminal cases, strong showing of innocence, by itself, might amount to independent constitutional violation curable in habeas corpus proceedings); *id.* at 419-22 (O'Connor, J., concurring) (similar); *id.* at 429 (White, J., concurring in the judgment) (similar); *id.* at 433-35 (Blackmun, J., dissenting) (similar); Dobbs v. Zant, 506 U.S. 358, 360 (1993) (*per curiam*) (Scalia, J., concurring in the judgment) ("As a general matter, I agree ... that '[i]t is not appropriate for this Court to expend its scarce resources crafting opinions that correct technical errors in cases of only local importance where the correction in no way promotes the development of the law,'... I am willing to make an exception from that rule in capital cases — but only where there is a realistic likelihood that the 'technical error' affected the conviction or the sentence." (quoting Anderson v. Harless, 459 U.S. 4, 12 (1982) (Stevens, J., dissenting))); Schiro v. Indiana, 493 U.S. 910, 911 (1989) (Stevens, J., concurring in the denial of *certiorari*) ("The burdens associated with the delay in the date of execution" as result of grant of stays pending habeas corpus review "are more than offset by the benefit of complete and adequate [habeas corpus] review of the decision to impose a death sentence."); Murray v. Giarratano, 492 U.S. 1, 21 (1989) (Stevens, J., dissenting, joined by Brennan, Marshall and Blackmun, JJ.) (nature of death penalty cases requires additional and more scrupulous postconviction review procedures than in noncapital cases); *id.* at 14 (Kennedy, J., concurring in the judgment) (because of "complexity" of capital cases and because "it cannot be denied that collateral relief proceedings are a central part of the review process for prisoners sentenced to death," special forms of legal assistance that are not required in noncapital cases may constitutionally be required in capital postconviction review proceedings); Clemmons v. Delo, 100 F.3d 1394, 1399 n.5 (8th Cir. 1996) (accepting *pro se* brief in addition to brief filed by counsel, in contravention of "Court's normal practice," in part because "this is a death-penalty case"); Sidebottom v. Delo, 46 F.3d 744, 757 (8th Cir.), *cert. denied*, 516 U.S. 849 (1995) (although court of appeals generally treats claims that are not adequately argued in brief as abandoned, court exercises discretion to consider petitioner's claims "because this is a death penalty case, and because this is Sidebottom's first federal habeas petition"); Foster v. Delo, 39 F.3d 873, 878 (8th Cir. 1994) (*en banc*), *cert. denied*, 514 U.S. 1075 (1995) (because petitioner's claims relate to "propriety of his execution," court, upon granting state's petition for rehearing *en banc* of sole claim on which it lost in panel decision, also decides to rehear 24 claims on which petitioner lost but as to which he did not seek rehearing, notwithstanding general rule that court will "ordinarily consider on rehearing only those issues specifically raised in a petition, and will depart from the rule only on the rarest of occasions"); Siripongs v. Calderon, 35 F.3d 1308, 1310 (9th Cir. 1994), *cert. denied*, 513 U.S. 1183 (1995) ("In a capital case, a habeas petitioner who asserts a colorable claim to relief, and who has never been given the opportunity to develop a factual record on that claim, is entitled to an evidentiary hearing in federal court."); Harris v. Vasquez, 901 F.2d 724, 727 (9th Cir. 1990) (Noonan, J.) (order granting stay of execution) ("If speedy justice in capital cases is a desideratum, we should amend the Constitution to make it attainable. As the Constitution stands, the federal courts are committed to a process in which speed is sacrificed to thoughtful examination, and rough and ready justice for heinous crimes has been replaced by deliberate examination and dispassionate review."); Bass v. Estelle, 696 F.2d 1154, 1161 (5th Cir. 1983) (Goldberg, J., concurring) (fastidious trial procedures and meticulous scrutiny on post-trial review are mandated before the death penalty may be carried out); Davis v. Johnson, 8 F. Supp. 2d 897, 900 (S.D. Tex. 1998), *app. denied*, 1998 WL 733731 (5th Cir. Oct. 21, 1998) (reaching merits although death-sentenced petitioner's habeas corpus petition should be time-barred for failure to file it until approximately one year after expiration of extension court had previously granted, because state failed to raise statute of limitations in timely fashion and because "the government's taking a person's life should invoke the most awesome governmental accountability"); authority cited *infra* § 7.1b n.83. *See also* Monge v. California, 118 S. Ct. 2246, 2252 (1998) (direct review case) ("'capital proceedings [must] be policed at all stages by an especially vigilant concern for procedural fairness and for the accuracy of factfinding.'"); Barefoot v. Estelle, 463 U.S. 880, 888 (1983) (noting that "death sentence cannot be carried out by the State while substantial legal issues remain outstanding" and admonishing federal habeas corpus courts in such cases "to give non-frivolous claims of constitutional error the careful attention they deserve"); Williams v. Chrans, 50 F.3d 1358, 1360 (7th Cir. 1995) (*per curiam*) ("This court is well aware of its responsibilities not to interfere unduly with the sovereign power of the state to enforce criminal laws that pass constitutional muster. It is also aware of its own right and responsibility to conduct its judicial work in a manner that reflects the seriousness of inflicting the death penalty upon a

far has refused to allow these *ad hoc* dispensations to mature into formal rules raising the standard of review or lowering procedural obstacles in capital, as opposed to noncapital, habeas corpus cases.[16]

The Antiterrorism and Effective Death Penalty Act of 1996 (AEDPA),[17] which revises the federal habeas corpus process in various respects,[18] also distinguishes between capital and noncapital cases in an important respect. AEDPA establishes a series of "Special Habeas Corpus Procedures" that apply to capital prisoners incarcerated by qualifying "opt-in" States.[19] These procedures provide qualifying States with various procedural benefits (including, among other things, accelerated deadlines for the filing and resolution of federal habeas corpus petitions) as a *quid pro quo* for providing affected capital prisoners with certain meaningful procedural advantages during the state postconviction process.[20] Whether the overall package of protections AEDPA

---

human being."); Peterson v. Murray, 949 F.2d 704, 705 (4th Cir. 1991) ("any capital case is a matter of the utmost gravity and, even at the eleventh hour, a court must once again assure itself that no fundamental miscarriage of justice is taking place"). *But cf. Kyles v. Whitley, supra* at 457-58 (Scalia, J., dissenting) ("The greatest puzzle of today's decision is what could have caused *this* capital case to be singled out for favored treatment [*i.e.*, for careful review of the state court's application of established constitutional law to the facts of the case]. Perhaps it has been randomly selected as a symbol, to reassure America that the United States Supreme Court is reviewing capital convictions to make sure that no factual error has been made. If so, it is a false symbol, for we assuredly do not do that ... [and] we do nothing but encourage foolish reliance to pretend otherwise.").

[16] *See, e.g., Herrera v. Collins, supra*, 506 U.S. at 405 ("[W]e have 'refused to hold that the fact that a death sentence has been imposed requires a different standard of review on federal habeas corpus.'"); Penry v. Lynaugh, 492 U.S. 302, 314 (1989) (refusing to create capital case exception to nonretroactivity defense); *Murray v. Giarratano, supra*, 492 U.S. at 9 (plurality opinion) (Court has "refused to hold that the fact that a death sentence has been imposed requires a different standard of review on federal habeas corpus"); Smith v. Murray, 477 U.S. 527, 538 (1986) (rejecting "suggestion 'that [procedural default] principles apply differently depending on the nature of the penalty a State imposes for the violation of its criminal laws'"). *See also* Whitmore v. Arkansas, 495 U.S. 149, 161 (1990) (refusing to recognize capital-case exception to Article III's "case or controversy" requirement for establishing federal jurisdiction to hear case on direct appeal). *But cf. Schlup v. Delo, supra*, 513 U.S. at 326-27 (seeming to limit to capital cases Court's adoption of "somewhat less exacting" standard and rejection of "more stringent ... standard" for establishing "miscarriage of justice" sufficient "to avoid a procedural bar to the consideration of the merits of [petitioner's] constitutional claims." (discussed *infra* § 26.4)).

[17] Pub. L. 104-132, 110 St. 1214 (1996).

[18] For an overview of the ways AEDPA changes the federal habeas corpus process, see *infra* §§ 3.2, 3.3.

[19] Antiterrorism and Effective Death Penalty Act § 107, Pub. L. 104-132, 110 Stat. 1214, 1221 (1996) (creating new Chapter 154 of the Judicial Code, entitled "Special Habeas Corpus Procedures in Capital Cases," 28 U.S.C.A. §§ 2261-66 (West 1994 & Supp. 1998)).

[20] For discussion of AEDPA's "opt-in" provisions, including the prerequisites for their application, their effects, and the States to which they apply, see *infra* § 3.3.

provides to capital prisoners in "opt-in" contexts is more or less substantial than the protections afforded other prisoners depends on how successfully the States augment the fairness of their state postconviction proceedings in return for more truncated federal habeas corpus proceedings.

Chapter 3

OVERVIEW OF THE FEDERAL HABEAS CORPUS
PROCESS UNDER AEDPA

§ 3.1. Introduction.

This chapter provides an overview of the Antiterrorism and Effective Death Penalty Act of 1996 (AEDPA), the changes it has made in habeas corpus and section 2255 practice and procedure, and the categories of cases to which AEDPA does and does not apply. Section 3.2 provides a brief overview of the legislation, with cross-references to subsequent sections of the book that more comprehensively discuss specified topics. Section 3.3 provides a detailed explanation of AEDPA's "opt-in" provisions, which restrict the range of habeas corpus consideration available to capital petitioners in States that "opt in" to those restrictions by providing competent counsel and other support to indigent capital prisoners during state postconviction proceedings. Section 3.4 discusses AEDPA's applicability to cases in which a federal habeas corpus petition was filed (or some other relevant event occurred) prior to the time the legislation took effect — what loosely may be called the "retroactivity" question. Section 3.5 provides an outline of the habeas corpus process in those cases that are, and those that are not, governed by AEDPA.

§ 3.2. Overview of AEDPA.

On April 24, 1996, President Clinton signed into law the Antiterrorism and Effective Death Penalty Act of 1996 (AEDPA).[1] Title I of the Act makes important changes in the statutes governing federal habeas corpus practice for

---

§ 3.2 [1] Pub. L. 104-132, 110 Stat. 1214 (1996). *See generally* Marshall J. Hartman & Jeanette Nyden, *Habeas Corpus and the New Federalism After the Anti-Terrorism and Effective Death Penalty Act of 1996*, 30 J. MARSHALL L. REV. 389 (1997); Andrea D. Lyon, *New Opportunities for Defense Attorneys: How Record Preservation Requirements After the New Habeas Bill Require Extensive and Exciting Trial Preparation*, 30 J. MARSHALL L. REV. 389 (1997); Michael O'Neill, *On Reforming the Federal Writ of Habeas Corpus*, 26 SETON HALL L. REV. 1493 (1996); Ronald J. Tabak, *Habeas Corpus as a Crucial Protector of Constitutional Rights: A Tribute Which May Also Be a Eulogy*, 26 SETON HALL L. REV. 1477 (1996); Larry W. Yackle, *A Primer on the New Habeas Corpus Statute*, 44 BUFF. L. REV. 381 (1996); Note, *The Avoidance of Constitutional Questions and the Preservation of Judicial Review: Federal Court Treatment of the New Habeas Provisions*, 111 HARV. L. REV. 1578 (1998); David Blumberg, Note, *Habeas Leaps from the Pan and Into the Fire: Jacobs v. Scott and the Antiterrorism and Effective Death Penalty Act of 1996*, 61 ALB. L. REV. 557 (1997); Andrea A. Kochan, Note, *The Antiterrorism and Effective Death Penalty Act of 1996: Habeas Corpus Reform?*, 52 WASH. U. J. URB. & CONTEMP. L. 399 (1997); Note, *Rewriting the Great Writ: Standards of Review for Habeas Corpus Under the New 28 U.S.C. § 2254*, 110 HARV. L. REV. 1868 (1997); Kimberly Woolley, Note, *Constitutional Interpretations of the Antiterrorism Act's Habeas Corpus Provisions*, 66 GEO. WASH. L. REV. 414 (1998); other authority cited *supra* § 2.2 n.2; *infra* § 30.2c n.39.

state prisoners and section 2255 practice for federal prisoners,[2] enacts a new set of statutes to govern federal habeas corpus procedures in capital cases in "opt-in" States,[3] and amends Rule 22 of the Federal Rules of Appellate Procedure[4] and the statutory provisions for appointment and compensation of counsel for indigent habeas corpus petitioners and section 2255 movants.[5]

The Conference Committee report (there are no committee reports) describes AEDPA's effects in the following manner:

> This title incorporates reforms to curb the abuse of the statutory writ of habeas corpus, and to address the acute problems of unnecessary delay and abuse in capital cases. It sets a one year limitation on an application for a habeas writ and revises the procedures for consideration of a writ in federal court. It provides for the exhaustion of state remedies and requires deference to the determinations of state courts that are neither "contrary to," nor an "unreasonable application of," clearly established federal law.
>
> The revision in capital habeas practice also sets a time limit within which the district court must act on a writ, and provides the government with the right to seek a writ of mandamus if the district court refuses to act within the allotted time period. Successive petitions must be approved by a panel of the court of appeals and are limited to those petitions that contain newly discovered evidence that would seriously undermine the jury's verdict or that involve new constitutional rights that have been retroactively applied by the Supreme Court.
>
> In capital cases, procedures are established for the appointment of counsel, conduct of evidentiary hearings, and the application of the procedures to state unitary review systems. Courts are directed to give habeas petitions in capital cases priority status and to decide those petitions within specified time periods. These procedures apply both to state and federal capital cases.[6]

Upon signing the bill, the President issued a Statement declaring that AEDPA was intended to "streamline Federal appeals for convicted criminals sentenced to

---

[2] 28 U.S.C.A. §§ 2241-55 (West 1994 & Supp. 1998). Appendix A contains the text of the amended statutes and shows the precise changes that AEDPA made to the preexisting statutes.

[3] These statutes are codified as 28 U.S.C.A. §§ 2261-66 (West Supp. 1998). Appendix A contains the text of these new statutes.

[4] AEDPA amends FED. R. APP. P. 22 with respect to the procedures for seeking federal habeas corpus relief from a United States Court of Appeals. Appendix B(3) contains Appellate Rule 22, as amended.

[5] AEDPA amends a provision of the Anti-Drug Abuse Act of 1988 (21 U.S.C. § 848(q)) and the Criminal Justice Act, 18 U.S.C. § 3006A. Appendix C(1) contains the amendments to these provisions.

[6] H.R. Conf. Rep. 104-518, 94th Cong., 2d Sess. 111 (1996).

the death penalty" but not to make substantive changes in the standards for granting the writ.[7] The President stated that he would not have "signed this bill" if he thought the federal courts would "interpret[] [it] in a manner that would undercut meaningful Federal habeas corpus review."[8] He called upon "the Federal courts ... [to] interpret these provisions to preserve independent review of Federal legal claims and the bedrock constitutional principle of an independent judiciary."[9]

Part of AEDPA is devoted to amending provisions of the preexisting habeas corpus statute, which have long been codified in Chapter 153 of the Judicial Code and govern habeas corpus actions filed by state prisoners (including, at least on one theory, state capital prisoners subject to the "special procedures" discussed just below[10]) as well as section 2255 motions filed by federal prisoners.[11] AEDPA also, however, creates a new Chapter 154 of the Judicial Code containing a set of "Special Habeas Corpus Procedures in Capital Cases."[12] These special procedures and standards (which tend to restrict access to habeas corpus relief and include, among other things, accelerated deadlines for the filing and resolution of federal habeas corpus petitions) apply only to habeas corpus petitions filed by capital prisoners in the custody of States that "opt in" to the special provisions by establishing, in a statutorily specified way, a "mechanism for the appointment, compensation, and reimbursement of [state postconviction] counsel" that satisfies certain statutory standards.[13] In essence, States that "opt in" receive certain advantages in the way of restricted federal habeas corpus review of their capital prisoners as a *quid pro quo* for their having provided the

---

[7] Statement of the President of the United States upon Signing the Antiterrorism Bill, 1996 WL 203049 (White House, April 24, 1996). Appendix D contains the President's Statement.

[8] *Id.*

[9] *Id.*

[10] For discussion of instances in which the provisions of Chapter 153 do not or may not apply to capital "opt in" cases, see *infra* note 34; *infra* § 3.3c n.69 and accompanying text.

[11] *See* 28 U.S.C.A. §§ 2241-55 (West 1994 & Supp. 1998).

[12] Antiterrorism and Effective Death Penalty Act § 107, Pub. L. 104-132, 110 Stat. 1214, 1221 (1996) (creating new Chapter 154 of the Judicial Code, entitled "Special Habeas Corpus Procedures in Capital Cases," 28 U.S.C.A. §§ 2261-66 (West Supp. 1998)).

[13] 28 U.S.C.A. § 2261(b) (West Supp. 1998). *See* Calderon v. Ashmus, 118 S. Ct. 1694, 1696 (1998) (Chapter 154, which "provides for an expedited review process in proceedings brought against qualifying States," applies to "capital cases only if the state meets certain conditions. A State must establish 'a mechanism for the appointment, compensation, and payment of reasonable litigation expenses of competent counsel' in state post-conviction proceedings, and 'must provide standards of competency for the appointment of such counsel.' § 2261(b) (States with separate postconviction review proceedings); § 2265(a) (States with unitary review procedures). The State must offer counsel to all capital defendants, and the state court must enter an order concerning appointment of counsel. § 2261(b); § 2265(b)."); Lindh v. Murphy, 117 S. Ct. 2059, 2065 (1997). For more detailed discussion of these provisions described in *Ashmus*, see *infra* § 3.3.

affected capital prisoners with certain procedural advantages during state postconviction proceedings. As of the writing of this third edition of the book (August 1998), no State has been held to have qualified for opt-in status (although a number of States are assiduously attempting to qualify on the basis of new legislation and/or actions by the state courts), and a number of States have acknowledged that they do not qualify for that status or have been held not to qualify by the courts.[14] The discussion in this and later sections will use the terms "opt-in procedures," "opt-in provisions," or "Chapter 154 provisions [procedures]" interchangeably to refer to the special procedures that apply to States that have "opted in" by adopting qualifying state postconviction procedures, and will refer to those States as "opt-in States."

The Supreme Court summarized the effect of Title I of AEDPA as follows:

> Title I of the Act stands more or less independent of the Act's other titles in providing for the revision of federal habeas practice and does two main things. First, in §§ 101-106, it amends § 2244 and §§ 2253-2255 of chapter 153 of Title 28 of the United States Code, governing all habeas corpus proceedings in the federal courts. 110 Stat. 1217-1221. Then, for habeas proceedings against a State in capital cases, § 107 creates an entirely new chapter 154 with special rules favorable to the state party, but applicable only if the State meets certain conditions, including provision for appointment of postconviction counsel in state proceedings.[15]

AEDPA changes the longstanding provisions of the federal habeas corpus statute — i.e., those long codified in Chapter 153 of the Judicial Code — in the following ways:

- *Statute of limitations*: AEDPA establishes a one-year period of limitations for the filing of habeas corpus petitions. In many cases, the petition's limitations period runs from the date on which the judgment of conviction and sentence became final upon the completion of direct review. In other cases, the petition's limitations period runs from some later date — *e.g.*, the date on which an unconstitutional impediment to filing a claim in the petition was removed, or the date on which the legal or factual bases for a claim in the petition first became discoverable through the exercise of due diligence. The statute of limitations is tolled while properly filed state postconviction proceedings are pending.[16]

---

[14] *See* cases cited *infra* § 3.3a n.1.

[15] Lindh v. Murphy, *supra*, 117 S. Ct. at 2063 (footnotes omitted). *See also Calderon v. Ashmus*, *supra*, 118 S. Ct. at 1696.

[16] *See* 28 U.S.C.A. § 2244(d)(1)(A)-(D) (West 1994 & Supp. 1998) (discussed *infra* § 5.1b). As explained *infra* § 3.3, capital habeas corpus petitions by prisoners subject to AEDPA's "opt-in" provisions are subject to an accelerated statute of limitations.

- *Provision of counsel and support resources*: AEDPA sets a maximum hourly fee for counsel appointed to represent indigent petitioners in federal habeas corpus proceedings in capital cases. AEDPA also amends the procedures that indigent capital and noncapital prisoners must use to secure leave to hire and to secure compensation for court-funded investigators, expert witnesses, and other providers of support services by (1) requiring that lawyers who wish to make an *ex parte* request for funding for support services first make a "proper showing" of the "need for confidentiality"; and (2) setting a general limit on the amount of funds available for such support services in each case, while providing procedures for obtaining additional funds in appropriate cases.[17]

- *Exhaustion of state remedies*: AEDPA amends the preexisting rules governing exhaustion of state remedies in two modest respects: (1) If a federal habeas corpus petition contains an unexhausted claim that otherwise would require dismissal for nonexhaustion,[18] and if the court ascertains that all the claims in the petition are without merit, the court may deny the petition on the merits rather than dismissing for nonexhaustion. (2) The federal courts' authority to consider unexhausted claims when the state waives the exhaustion requirement is limited to express waivers by the state.[19]

- *Effect of state court factfindings; federal hearing standards*: AEDPA simplifies but does not substantially alter the preexisting provisions governing the effect in federal habeas corpus proceedings of state court findings of fact. AEDPA does substantially alter the standard for obtaining a federal evidentiary hearing when the petitioner's default was responsible for the state courts' failure to develop the material facts. Under the new standard, a petitioner who defaulted on the facts in the state courts may not obtain a federal evidentiary hearing to develop those facts except upon a showing of "cause" and "innocence."[20]

- *Federal court treatment of legal claims previously adjudicated by a state court*: AEDPA regulates a federal habeas corpus court's resolution of federal claims that previously were adjudicated by a state court. If the state court fairly adjudicated the legal merits of the federal claim and adequately explained its decision, the federal court may not grant relief unless the state court's adjudication of the claim either was "contrary to ... clearly established [Supreme Court] law" or "involved an unreasonable application

---

[17] *See* 21 U.S.C.A. § 848(q) (West 1994 & Supp. 1998) (discussed *infra* § 12.3b).

[18] *See infra* §§ 23.1, 23.5.

[19] *See* 28 U.S.C.A. § 2254(b)(2)-(3) (West 1994 & Supp. 1998) (discussed *infra* §§ 23.1, 23.2a, 23.5).

[20] *See id.* §§ 2254(d)(2), 2254(e) (discussed *infra* § 20.2b).

of[] clearly established [Supreme Court] law."[21] Although the relevant provision of AEDPA is sometimes said to require federal court "deference" to even erroneous state court determinations of law and of mixed questions of law and fact, the relevant provision of the statute does not contain the word "deference," does not appear to require substantive deference, and might be unconstitutional if it did.[22]

- *Successive petitions*: AEDPA alters both the procedures and standards for filing successive habeas corpus petitions. (1) Procedurally, the statute requires the petitioner to apply to a circuit panel for authorization to file a successive petition in the district court. The circuit panel may authorize the filing of a successive petition only upon the petitioner's *prima facie* showing that the petition satisfies AEDPA's new successive petition standards. The circuit panel has a limited time frame in which to act on the motion for leave to file the petition in the district court, and rehearing and *certiorari* review of the panel's determination are barred, although certain other forms of review are not barred.[23] (2) AEDPA's new successive petition standards prohibit same-claim successive petitions and limit new-claim successive petitions to cases in which the petitioner can make an adequate showing either that the legal rule on which she relies is new and retroactively applicable to her case or that the facts on which she relies previously were unavailable and that she probably is innocent.[24]

- *Appeals*: The legislation conditions appeals by petitioners on their obtaining a "certificate of appealability." The procedures and standards for seeking such a certificate are roughly equivalent to the preexisting rules for obtaining "certificates of probable cause to appeal" except in the following respects. (1) The certificate must indicate not only that the case as a whole, but also that a specific "issue or issues," satisfy the requisite standard (a "substantial showing of the denial of a constitutional right"). Although the relevant provision does not say so, some courts have read it to limit the claims the court of appeals may address on appeal to those that the certificate identifies as having satisfied the standard. (2) One provision of AEDPA seems to require a circuit judge or Supreme Court Justice — and thus to forbid a district court judge — to issue a certificate of appealability, although a neighboring provision (consistent with preexisting law and practice) seems to empower district judges to rule on requests for certificates and to require

---

[21] *Id.* § 2254(d)(1) (discussed *infra* § 30.2).

[22] *See infra* § 30.2.

[23] *See* 28 U.S.C.A. § 2244(b)(3) (West 1994 & Supp. 1998); Felker v. Turpin, 518 U.S. 651 (1996) (both discussed *infra* § 28.3d nn.120-24 and accompanying text).

[24] *See* 28 U.S.C.A. §§ 2244(b)(1), 2244(b)(2) (West 1994 & Supp. 1998) (discussed *infra* §§ 28.3, 28.4a).

that they generally do so in the first instance. Nearly all circuit courts have held that district courts may — and generally should — rule on certificates of appealability in the first instance.[25]

AEDPA also modifies the procedures and standards governing section 2255 motions by federal prisoners.[26] Those motions are subjected to provisions that roughly correspond to (but often do not precisely track) the following habeas corpus revisions that are discussed above: the one-year statute of limitations; limits on compensation of counsel, investigators, and experts; the requirement of a preliminary showing to justify an *ex parte* application for support services; restrictions on successive filings; and the requirement of a "certificate of appealability" (which for the first time limits the right of section 2255 movants to appeal adverse rulings).[27] AEDPA does not adopt any new restrictions on evidentiary hearings or on the federal courts' treatment of legal issues previously decided on direct appeal.

As noted, AEDPA applies a set of "Special Habeas Corpus Procedures" to capital prisoners incarcerated by qualifying opt-in States.[28] There are four sets of "special procedures":

(1) The habeas corpus petition must be filed within six months after the completion of direct appeal in the state courts, unlike other habeas corpus petitions which must be filed within a year after the conclusion of direct review. The six-month statute of limitations is tolled while state postconviction proceedings are pending, and the filing deadline may be extended up to 30 days upon a showing of "good cause."[29]

(2) The petition may only present claims that were previously raised and decided on the merits in state court, unless the petitioner can show that unconstitutional state interference prevented her from raising the claim in state court, that the legal rule on which the claim relies is new and retroactively applicable to the case, or that the factual bases of the claim were not previously available through the exercise of due diligence.[30]

---

[25] *See id.* § 2253; FED. R. APP. P. 22(b) (both discussed *infra* § 35.4b).

[26] AEDPA generally does not apply to federal prisoner habeas corpus actions under 28 U.S.C. § 2241 (1994). *See, e.g.,* Valona v. United States, 138 F.3d 693, 694-95 (7th Cir. 1998); Bradshaw v. Story, 86 F.3d 164, 166 (10th Cir. 1996); Leyva v. Meissner, 1998 WL 113901, at *834 (C.D. Ill. Feb. 9, 1998). *See also infra* §§ 28.3b n.35 (filing of section 2241 petition does not render subsequent section 2255 motion "successive" for purposes of AEDPA's successive motions bar), 41.2a n.28 (potential availability of section 2241 remedy when AEDPA's bar to successive motions precludes section 2255 relief).

[27] *See* 28 U.S.C. §§ 2253, 2255 (discussed *infra* §§ 41.1-41.7).

[28] *See supra* notes 12-14 and accompanying text; *infra* § 3.3.

[29] *See* 28 U.S.C.A. § 2263 (West Supp. 1998) (discussed *infra* § 3.3c nn.40-44).

[30] *See id.* § 2264(a) (West Supp. 1998) (discussed *infra* § 3.3c nn.65-91).

(3) In order to obtain a stay of execution, the petitioner must demonstrate that the petition makes a "substantial showing of the denial of a federal right."[31]

(4) The statute requires federal district courts and courts of appeals to resolve petitions and appeals within narrow time frames.[32]

Section 3.3 *infra* discusses the requirements States must satisfy in order to qualify for opt-in status and provides a more detailed discussion of the special opt-in procedures.

AEDPA does not clearly specify the relationship between its special procedures for capital cases in opt-in States (the Chapter 154 procedures) and the standards and procedures the amended habeas corpus statutes impose on all or other habeas corpus cases (the Chapter 153 procedures). On one theory, the Chapter 154 procedures apply *in addition to all* of the Chapter 153 procedures listed above, with the more specific Chapter 154 procedures modifying the more generally applicable Chapter 153 procedures when the two conflict (for example, Chapter 154 imposes a six-month statute of limitations but Chapter 153 imposes a one-year statute of limitations).[33] On another theory, the Chapter 154 standards apply *in addition to only some (explicitly incorporated), but in lieu of other (even nonconflicting),* Chapter 153 procedures.[34]

---

[31] *See id.* § 2262 (West Supp. 1998) (discussed *infra* § 3.3c nn.55-60).

[32] *See id.* § 2266 (West Supp. 1998) (discussed *infra* § 3.3c nn.45-54). The 4th Circuit has adopted accelerated time frame requirements for *non*opt-in capital habeas corpus cases similar to those that AEDPA's opt-in provisions apply to capital habeas corpus appeals in opt-in states. *See* Truesdale v. Moore, 142 F.3d 749, 758 (4th Cir. 1998).

[33] *Cf.* Edmond v. United States, 117 S. Ct. 1573, 1578 (1997) ("Ordinarily, where a specific provision conflicts with a general one, the specific governs.").

[34] Under 28 U.S.C.A. § 2261(a) (West Supp. 1998), the new "chapter [154] shall apply to cases arising under section 2254 brought by prisoners in State custody who are subject to a capital sentence" if the State in question satisfies the "opt-in" conditions set out in *id.* §§ 2261(b), 2261(c). *See also id.* §§ 2261(e), 2262(a), 2262(b)(1), 2262(b)(3), 2263(a), 2264(b) (all treating opt-in cases as having been filed pursuant to or under section 2254). Section 2254 is only one of several provisions in Chapter 153 of the Judicial Code. Arguably, by referring only to "section 2254" and not, for example, to "Chapter 153," section 2261(a) intends to add Chapter 154's "special procedures" *only* to the procedures established by section 2254 itself (*i.e.*, the procedures governing exhaustion, evidentiary hearings and the effect of state court findings of fact and legal determinations, *see supra* notes 18-22 and accompanying text), and intends to *substitute* the Chapter 154 procedures for the procedures established by other portions of Chapter 153 that are *not* cited in section 2261(a), such as sections 2244 (governing, *inter alia*, statutes of limitations and successive petitions, *see supra* notes 16, 23-24 and accompanying text) and section 2253 (governing certificates of appealability, *see supra* note 25 and accompanying text). This understanding avoids the conflict between Chapter 153's one-year statute of limitations, 28 U.S.C. § 2244(d)(1), and Chapter 154's six-month limitations period, *id.* § 2263(a), that would arise if all Chapter 153 provisions applied to all Chapter 154 cases. Although two of the opt-in provisions also refer to section 2244(b), *see id.* §§ 2262(c) (discussed *infra* § 28.3a n.14), 2266(b)(3)(B), both

As of the writing of this edition of the book, it is too early to gauge the impact of AEDPA on federal habeas corpus practice. Many of the early decisions construing AEDPA addressed primarily the issue whether the legislation could be applied "retroactively" to cases filed before its enactment, and a substantial number of these decisions were subsequently overruled when the Supreme Court held in *Lindh v. Murphy*[35] that the statute can*not* be applied to cases filed before its enactment date of April 24, 1996.[36] Decisions interpreting the more novel and important provisions amending Chapter 153 of the Judicial Code (applicable to most or all habeas corpus cases) often either assimilate those provisions to prior doctrine or are so significantly in conflict with each other that the provisions' ultimate effect remains uncertain pending Supreme Court resolution of the conflicts. Finally, litigation concerning the "opt-in" provisions for specified capital cases has focused on whether particular States qualify for the application of these provisions (*i.e.*, whether the States have adequately "opted-in") and, thus far, has consistently resulted in rulings that the States do *not* qualify.[37]

In the Supreme Court's early decisions construing and applying AEPDA, however, four important trends are apparent. As is most clearly revealed by the 1998 decisions in *Stewart v. Martinez-Villareal*[38] and *Hohn v. United States*,[39] (1) the Court is very reluctant to interpret AEDPA to deny a habeas corpus petitioner or section 2255 movant at least "one full bite," *i.e.*, at least one meaningful opportunity for postconviction review in a district court, court of appeals, and, via *certiorari*, the Supreme Court; (2) the Court will eschew a literal reading of the statute in order to assure one full opportunity for postconviction review — something dissenting Justices Scalia and Thomas chastised the majority for doing in both those cases;[40] and (3) the Court is

---

can be read to do so only in order to incorporate particular standards or procedures in section 2244(b) into particular opt-in contexts and not as reflecting Congress' intent that section 2244(b) (or section 2244 as a whole) apply across the board in opt-in situations. For discussion of the possibility that 28 U.S.C. § 2264(b) additionally selects among the *subparts* of section 2254 that apply in capital opt-in cases and excludes the exhaustion provisions in 28 U.S.C. § 2254(b) and (c), see *infra* § 3.3c nn.65-73 and accompanying text.

[35] 117 S. Ct. 2059 (1997).

[36] See *infra* § 3.4 for discussion of *Lindh* and its implications both for cases filed before and after AEDPA's enactment date of April 24, 1996.

[37] *See infra* § 3.3a n.1.

[38] 118 S. Ct. 1618 (1998).

[39] 118 S. Ct. 1969 (1998).

[40] *See Hohn v. United States, supra*, 118 S. Ct. at 1979 (Scalia, J., dissenting) ("Today's opinion permits review where Congress, with unmistakable clarity, has denied it. To reach this result, the Court ignores the obvious intent of the Antiterrorism and Effective Death Penalty Act of 1996 (AEDPA), Pub.L. 104-132, 110 Stat. 1214, distorts the meaning of our own jurisdictional statute, 28 U.S.C. § 1254(1), and overrules a 53-year-old precedent ...."); *Stewart v. Martinez-Villareal, supra*, 118 S. Ct. at 1623 (Scalia, J., dissenting) ("[t]he Court today flouts the

strongly disposed to interpret AEDPA as merely codifying preexisting, judge-made habeas corpus doctrine.[41] *Martinez-Villareal* and *Hohn* also affirmed —

---

unmistakable language of the statute"); *id.* at 1624 (Thomas, J., dissenting) (Court "disregard[s] ... the plain language of the statute").

[41] The issue in *Martinez-Villareal* was whether AEDPA's restrictions on successive petitions apply to a prisoner who previously raised the claim in an earlier habeas corpus petition that was dismissed without a ruling on the merits on the ground that the claim was premature. As the majority essentially acknowledged, a literal reading of the words of the statute, which imposes restrictions on any "'second or successive'" application for federal habeas corpus relief, would have compelled the conclusion that the restrictions applied to Martinez-Villareal's numerically "second" petition. *See Stewart v. Martinez-Villareal, supra,* 118 S. Ct. at 1621. The Court noted, however, that a literal interpretation of the statute would produce the "far-reaching and seemingly perverse" consequence (*id.* at 1621) that some habeas corpus petitioners would never "receive an adjudication of [their] ... claim[s]" in federal court (*id.* at 1622). To avoid this result — which the Court pointedly criticized on the ground that "none of *our cases* expounding this [successive petition] doctrine ha[s] ever suggested" it — and to permit one full round of habeas corpus review under the circumstances, the Court read the statute to incorporate the not-entirely-numerical definition of improperly multiple petitions that federal courts had developed under pre-AEDPA law. *See id.* at 1621-22 (emphasis added) (discussed in detail *infra* § 28.3b nn.29-35 and accompanying text). In dissent, Justice Scalia declared: "The Court today flouts the unmistakable language of the statute to avoid what it calls a 'perverse' result.... There is nothing 'perverse' about the result that the statute commands, except that it contradicts pre-existing judge-made law, which it was precisely the purpose of the statute to change." *Id.* at 1623 (Scalia, J., dissenting).

The issue in *Hohn* was "whether the Court has jurisdiction to review decisions of the courts of appeals denying applications for certificates of appealability" under AEDPA. *Hohn v. United States, supra,* 118 S. Ct. at 1971. As Justice Scalia pointed out in his dissenting opinion, a strict construction of AEDPA would have required that the Court answer this question in the negative. *See id.* at 1979 (Scalia, J., dissenting) ("This Court's jurisdiction under 28 U.S.C. § 1254(1) is limited to '[c]ases in the courts of appeals.' Section 102 of AEDPA provides that '[u]nless a circuit justice or judge issues a certificate of appealability, an appeal may not be taken to the court of appeals from ... the final order in a habeas corpus proceeding under section 2255,' that is, a district court habeas proceeding challenging federal custody. Petitioner, who is challenging federal custody under 28 U.S.C. § 2255, did not obtain a certificate of appealability (COA). By the plain language of AEDPA, his appeal 'from' the district court's 'final order' 'may not be taken to the court of appeals.' Because it could not be taken to the Court of Appeals, it quite obviously was never in the Court of Appeals; and because it was never in the Court of Appeals, we lack jurisdiction under § 1254(1) to entertain it."). Eschewing a literal interpretation, the Court undertook a lengthy analysis of relevant precedents and jurisprudential considerations, which led it to preserve its pre-AEDPA practice of "grant[ing] writs of certiorari to review denials of certificate applications without requiring the petitioner to move for leave to file for an extraordinary writ ... and without requiring any extraordinary showing or exhibiting any doubts about our jurisdiction to do so" (a practice that, the Court acknowledged, was inconsistent with one of its prior precedents, which the Court in *Hohn* thereupon overruled). *Id.* at 1977-78 (discussed in detail *infra* § 35.4b nn.29-33 and accompanying text). In the course of this analysis, the Court interpreted AEDPA's "certificate of appealability" requirement as permitting issuance of a certificate by a panel of circuit judges and not just an individual judge. *See id.* at 1972-74. In this respect too, as Justice Scalia pointed out, the Court ignored the plain meaning of a provision of AEDPA. *See id.* at 1979 ("Most of the

again, over the vigorous dissents of Justices Scalia and Thomas — what the Court's 1996 and 1997 AEDPA decisions already had shown, namely, that (4) the Court rejects the view (adopted by some lower federal courts) that doubts about the meaning of AEDPA's ambiguous provisions should usually or presumptively be resolved in favor of interpreting the statute to limit habeas corpus review or relief.[42] Indeed, even in (*e.g.*, successive petition) situations in

---

Court's analysis is expended in the effort to establish that petitioner made his request for a COA to the Court of Appeals as such, rather than to the circuit judges in their individual capacity .... Even that effort is unsuccessful, since it comes up against the pellucid language of AEDPA to the contrary. Section 102 does not permit application for a COA to a court of appeals; it states that the application must be made to a 'circuit justice or judge.' That this means precisely what it says is underscored by § 103 of AEDPA, which amends Rule 22 of the Federal Rules of Appellate Procedure: 'If [a COA] request is addressed to the court of appeals, it shall be deemed addressed to the judges thereof and shall be considered by a circuit judge or judges as the court deems appropriate.'").

[42] *See Hohn v. United States, supra,* 118 S. Ct. at 1984 (Scalia, J., dissenting, joined by Thomas, J.) (majority's opinion directly conflicts with AEDPA's "not obscure" general "purpose ... to eliminate the interminable delays in the execution of state and federal criminal sentences, and the shameful overloading of our federal criminal justice system, produced by various aspects of this Court's habeas corpus jurisprudence" and "also not obscure" "purpose of the specific provision of AEDPA at issue here ... to end § 2255 litigation in the district court unless a court of appeals judge or the circuit justice finds reasonable basis to appeal. By giving literally unprecedented meaning to the words in two relevant statutes, and overruling the premise of Congress's enactment, the Court adds new, Byzantine detail to a habeas corpus scheme Congress meant to streamline and simplify."); *Stewart v. Martinez-Villareal, supra,* 118 S. Ct. at 1623 (Scalia, J., dissenting) (majority's opinion ignores AEDPA's underlying intention to "require extraordinary showings before a state prisoner can take a second trip around the extended district-court-to-Supreme-Court-federal track" and restores "regime that our habeas jurisprudence established and that AEDPA intentionally revised .... It is wrong for us to reshape that revision on the very lathe of judge-made habeas jurisprudence it was designed to repair."); *id.* at 1625 (Thomas, J., dissenting) (Court's reliance on pre-AEDPA law and practices ignores effects and implications of "enactment of the Antiterrorism and Effective Death Penalty Act of 1996"; Court's decision has "expanded the availability of the writ" even though "federal habeas corpus is a statutory right"). *See also* Lindh v. Murphy, 117 S. Ct. 2059, 2063-68 (1997) (rejecting 7th Circuit's presumption that Congress intended AEDPA to limit review of all habeas corpus cases, even ones that were already pending when the statute became law); Felker v. Turpin, 518 U.S. 651, 658-62 (1996) (discussed further *infra* note 43) (rejecting Georgia's claim that AEDPA's clear intention to cut off one form of Supreme Court review of denials of successive habeas corpus petitions should be understood as intended to cut off all forms of Supreme Court review). Lower court decisions apparently adopting a "when in doubt, limit review" presumption in interpreting AEDPA are, *e.g.,* Green v. French, 143 F.3d 865, 869 (4th Cir. 1998); Drinkard v. Johnson, 97 F.3d 751, 764-69 (5th Cir. 1996), *cert. denied,* 117 S. Ct. 1114 (1997).

Because *Martinez-Villareal* and *Hohn* were issued at the end of the 1998 term, just as this edition was being written, the lower court caselaw the edition discusses did not have the benefit of these recent, highly significant indicators of the Supreme Court's view of AEDPA. One might reasonably expect that lower courts in the coming period will take their cue from the Supreme

which the petitioner can be viewed as having previously had "one full bite," the Court has demonstrated a willingness to use its interpretive powers to moderate restrictions apparently effected by AEDPA and, in situations in which AEDPA undeniably cuts off review, to establish or reaffirm the continuing vitality of alternative means of judicial review to rectify serious systemic malfunctions.[43]

§ 3.3. AEDPA's "opt-in" provisions.

a. *Introduction; qualifying States.* As explained in § 3.2 *supra*, AEDPA's "opt-in" provisions — which establish a set of "special habeas corpus procedures in capital cases" including an accelerated schedule for the filing and consideration of petitions — apply only to capital cases from States that "opt in"

Court and construe AEDPA in a manner that maintains the core integrity of the federal habeas corpus remedy.

[43] In Calderon v. Thompson, 118 S. Ct. 1489 (1998), a case in which the petitioner, although still proceeding on a first petition, had "already had extensive review of his claims in federal and state courts" (*id.* at 1502) over the course of "13 years of state and federal review of [his] ... conviction and sentence" (*id.* at 1501), the Court granted *certiorari* to consider whether the court of appeals violated AEDPA's successive petition standards by *sua sponte* recalling the mandate and granting habeas corpus relief. The first issue the Court had to resolve was whether AEDPA applies to a situation such as the one presented in *Thompson*. Acknowledging that AEDPA undeniably applies to similar situations (*see* id. at 1500; *infra* § 38.2d nn.59-60 and accompanying text), the Court declined to find AEDPA applicable, stating that "the court's order recalling its mandate did not contravene the letter of AEDPA." *Id.* at 1500. *See also id.* at 1494 ("[t]he recall of the mandate was not controlled by the precise terms of AEDPA"). Having declared AEDPA inapplicable, the Court next had to fashion a standard for the circuit courts' exercise of their discretion in such situations. Although recognizing that AEDPA necessarily "'inform[s]'" the development of such a standard (*id.* at 1502), the Court drew heavily on its pre-AEDPA habeas corpus jurisprudence to create a standard that, in the Court's own words, is "somewhat more lenient" than AEDPA's new-claim successive petition rule (*id.* at 1502). The resulting test is actually considerably "more lenient" than the portion of AEDPA that would otherwise apply in situation such as Thompson's: the same-claim successive petition standard, which wholly forecloses relitigation of already-adjudicated claims. *See id.* at 1500 (comparing standards for same-claim and new-claim successive petitions).

In Felker v. Turpin, 518 U.S. 651 (1996), a successive petition case which presented the Court with its first opportunity to address the wording and implications of AEDPA, the Court concluded that the plain wording of the statute precludes *certiorari* review of a circuit court's denial of authorization to file a second or successive habeas corpus petition. *See id.* at 661 ("The Act does remove our authority to entertain an appeal or a petition for a writ of certiorari to review a decision of the court of appeals exercising its 'gatekeeping' function over a second petition."). Yet, the Court then went on to emphasize that a prisoner in such a situation retains the statutory right to file an original habeas corpus petition in the Supreme Court. *See id.* at 658 ("We conclude that although the Act does impose new conditions on our authority to grant relief [on successive habeas corpus petitions], it does not deprive this Court of jurisdiction to entertain original habeas petitions."); *id.* at 661 ("[t]he Act ... does not repeal our authority to entertain a petition for habeas corpus").

by providing certain procedural advantages to capital prisoners pursuing state postconviction remedies. As of the writing of this edition of the book (August 1998), a number of States have acknowledged that they do not qualify for opt-in status, and none of the States that has claimed to have opted-in has been found to have satisfied the statutory prerequisites for doing so.[1] Subsection b describes

---

§ 3.3 [1] The relevant decisions include:

- *Alabama*: Neelley v. Nagle, 138 F.3d 917, 921-22 & n.1 (11th Cir. 1998) (case before court was governed by Chapter 153 and therefore district court did not err in rejecting petitioner's request for "evidentiary hearing to determine whether Alabama has put in place the necessary counsel appointment mechanisms" to qualify for Chapter 154).

- *California*: Ainsworth v. Calderon, 138 F.3d 787, 790 (9th Cir. 1998) (at least as of time AEDPA was enacted, when petition was pending, California did "not meet the conditions requisite for applying" Chapter 154); Ashmus v. Calderon, 935 F. Supp. 1048, 1075 (N.D. Cal. 1996), aff'd, 123 F.3d 1199 (9th Cir. 1997), rev'd on other grounds, 118 S. Ct. 1694 (1998) (discussed *infra* § 3.3b n.13) (California does not qualify for opt-in treatment).

- *Florida*: Hill v. Butterworth, 170 F.R.D. 509, 519, 524 (N.D. Fla. 1997) (certifying death-sentenced prisoners' challenge to Chapter 154 as class action and "permanently enjoin[ing] [defendants Governor and other officials of State of Florida] from invoking, or asserting, in any state or federal proceeding, that the State of Florida may avail itself of the procedures in Chapter 154 of the Judicial Code, 28 U.S.C. §§ 2261-66, until such time as Defendants have demonstrated that they have satisfied all of the 'opt-in' provisions to that Chapter."); Hill v. Butterworth, 941 F. Supp. 1129, 1143-44, 1147 (N.D. Fla. 1996) (Florida does not qualify for opt-in treatment).

- *Georgia*: Fugate v. Turpin, 1998 WL 327718, at *6 n.1 (M.D. Ga. June 18, 1998) ("The State has not asserted that the new expedited measures should apply in this case, and the court now holds that they do not.").

- *Idaho*: Leavitt v. Arave, 927 F. Supp. 394, 396 (D. Idaho 1996) (State makes no claim that it qualifies for opt-in treatment).

- *Illinois*: Thomas v. Gramley, 951 F. Supp. 1338, 1341 n.3 (N.D. Ill. 1996) ("State does not argue that Illinois satisfies the conditions set forth in § 2261(b)-(d) — conditions a State must meet in order to invoke the additional provisions of Chapter 154, § 2261(a).").

- *Indiana*: Burris v. Parke, 95 F.3d 465, 468 (7th Cir. 1996) (*en banc*) ("Indiana concedes it [has not] satisfied certain [opt-in] conditions for the processing of capital cases within the state court system").

- *Louisiana*: Williams v. Cain, 942 F. Supp. 1088, 1092 (W.D. La. 1996) (Louisiana does not qualify for opt-in treatment "[a]t the least [because] ... the State had not established standards of competency for the appointment of counsel in post-conviction proceedings at the time [petitioner's] state claims were denied").

- *Maryland*: Booth v. Maryland, 112 F.3d 139 (4th Cir. 1997), cert. denied, 118 S. Ct. 2063 (1998) (reversing Booth v. Maryland, 940 F. Supp. 849, 852-53 (D. Md. 1996), which had enjoined state from claiming eligibility for Chapter 154 benefits in current and future cases; court of appeals holds that 11th Amendment bars injunctive relief of sort district court entered but invites plaintiff death row inmates to obtain ruling on Maryland's eligibility for Chapter 154 by "rais[ing] their contention during federal habeas corpus proceedings"); Colvin-El v. Nuth, 1998 WL 386403, at *4-*8 (D. Md.

July 6, 1998) (adopting conclusions reached in district court opinion in *Booth v. Maryland, supra,* court concludes that Maryland does not qualify for opt-in treatment because (1) by paying fees to appointed lawyers in state postconviction cases that are "substantially below the break-even point of doing business" as defined by average per-hour "overhead of running a law office in Maryland" ($50 per hour or more, in Maryland) and thus are "insufficient to meet expenses," State "does not pay reasonable attorneys fees," *i.e.,* fees "at least sufficient to ensure an adequate supply of competent counsel"; (2) by relying entirely on "'good faith'" of appointing authority to assure that competent counsel are appointed, State lacks "formal system" that Chapter 154 requires States to have "in place to assure that defendants as of right are provided with adequate representation" — "at a minimum" formal system must require that attorney be at least "minimally competent in post-conviction practice," *i.e.,* that "attorney ... have some [actual] experience," irrespective of criminal trial and appellate experience, in "extraordinarily complex body of law and procedure unique to post-conviction review"; (3) because State "does not permit a defendant who needs [state postconviction] counsel to go before a court and receive counsel," and instead relies upon nonjudicially administered process of providing counsel that takes, on average, 11 months to appoint state postconviction counsel following completion of direct review proceedings — during which Chapter 154's 180-day statute of limitations (which is not tolled while prisoner awaits appointment of counsel) expires — State does not satisfy Chapter 154's requirement of court order appointing counsel; and (4) overall, "Chapter 154 represents a bargain between Congress and the states to provide for expedited federal habeas review where the states provide certain safeguards to ensure accelerated state collateral review [and] Maryland has not lived up to its end of the deal").

- *Missouri*: Schlup v. Bowersox, No. 4:92CV443 JCH (E.D. Mo. May 2, 1996) (Missouri does not qualify for opt-in treatment).
- *Montana*: Langford v. Day, 110 F.3d 1380, 1386 n.2 (9th Cir. 1996), *cert. denied*, 118 S. Ct. 208 (1997) ("The separate death penalty provisions of Chapter 154 ... do not apply by their own terms because Montana has not established of record its qualification under the Act's section 2261.").
- *North Carolina*: Ward v. French, 989 F. Supp. 752, 757 (E.D.N.C. 1997) ("North Carolina does not qualify for application of Chapter 154's new standards"); Noland v. Dixon, No. 3:88CV217-MU (W.D.N.C. April 30, 1996) (North Carolina does not qualify for opt-in treatment).
- *Ohio*: Scott v. Anderson, 958 F. Supp. 330, 331-32 (N.D. Ohio 1997) (Ohio does not qualify for opt-in treatment because "an indigent defendant who requests state appointed counsel is not certain to receive such assistance at the post-conviction stage"); Morales v. Anderson, No. 1:95CV2674 (N.D. Ohio Nov. 8, 1996) (Ohio does not qualify for opt-in treatment); Hamblin v. Anderson, 947 F. Supp. 1179, 1180-82 (N.D. Ohio 1996) (Ohio does not qualify for opt-in treatment because "entitlement to counsel is made contingent, by statute, upon the discretion of the public defender" and because appointment of counsel does not occur "by an entry of an order by a court"; fact that public defender always appoints counsel in capital cases does not change conclusion); Zuern v. Tate, 938 F. Supp. 468, 471 n.1 (S.D. Ohio 1996) (Ohio does not qualify for opt-in treatment).
- *Oklahoma*: Moore v. Reynolds, 1998 WL 387452, at *4 (10th Cir. July 13, 1998) ("Oklahoma has not yet satisfied, or even argued it can satisfy, the requirements of [28 U.S.C.] §2261(b) and (c), [so that] the expedited habeas procedures set forth in chapter

154 are inapplicable to this case"); Duvall v. Reynolds, 139 F.3d 768, 776 (10th Cir. 1998) (Oklahoma has "conceded that it is not a qualifying state for purposes of the new capital habeas corpus provisions" (citing *Williamson v. Ward, infra*)); Williamson v. Ward, 110 F.3d 1508, 1513 n.5 (10th Cir. 1997) (Oklahoma "conceded ... that it is not a qualifying state for purposes of [Chapter 154]").

- *Pennsylvania*: Death Row Prisoners of Pennsylvania v. Ridge, 106 F.3d 35, 36 (3d Cir. 1997) ("Commonwealth ... declared that Pennsylvania does not meet the requirements of § 2261 as of January 31, 1997, and that it has not met them previously" and "[a]fter independent review, the Court declares that it accepts the ... declarations of counsel as valid and binding, and adopts them"; "determination as to whether Pennsylvania meets the criteria of § 2261 [is] ... one to be made by state-wide authority, not admitting of county-by-county or case-by-case determination"); Death Row Prisoners of Pennsylvania v. Ridge, 948 F. Supp. 1258, 1264-67 (E.D. Pa. 1996), *aff'd*, 106 F.3d 35 (3d Cir. 1997) (permitting class action by six death row inmates seeking declaratory judgment that Pennsylvania does not qualify for opt-in treatment).

- *Tennessee*: Austin v. Bell, 927 F. Supp. 1058, 1061-62 (M.D. Tenn. 1996) (discussed *infra* § 3.3b n.14 and accompanying text; Tennessee does not qualify for opt-in treatment); Rahman v. Bell, 927 F. Supp. 262, 266 (M.D. Tenn. 1996) (similar; State lacks requisite mechanism for appointing counsel).

- *Texas*: Cannon v. Johnson, 134 F.3d 683, 685 n.1 (5th Cir. 1998) (Chapter 154 does not apply because "Texas has not instituted a system of representation that complies with the relevant requirements"); Green v. Johnson, 116 F.3d 1115, 1120 (5th Cir. 1997) ("Texas has not yet qualified for the expedited procedures governing habeas petitions in capital cases"); Mata v. Johnson, 99 F.3d 1261, 1266-67 (5th Cir. 1996), *vac'd on other grounds*, 105 F.3d 209 (5th Cir. 1997) (Texas does not qualify for opt-in treatment; although provisions limiting attorneys to $7500 and expenses to $2500 are not "facially inadequate," pending showing by prisoner that resources "prove[d] inadequate in his case," State's procedures for appointment of counsel based on questionnaire listing counsels' qualifications do not satisfy Act's requirement of "explicit standards of competency"); Cockrum v. Johnson, 934 F. Supp. 1417, 1422 (E.D. Tex. 1996), *rev'd on other grounds*, 119 F.3d 297 (5th Cir. 1997) (Texas cases, at least of a certain vintage, do not qualify for opt-in treatment because, *inter alia*, lawyers in the past have not actually been available to state postconviction petitioners who asked for them).

- *Virginia*: Breard v. Pruett, 134 F.3d 615 (4th Cir. 1998), *cert. denied*, 118 S. Ct. 1352 (1998) (district court held that Chapter 154 does not apply because Virginia has not "satisf[ied] the 'opt-in' provisions of the AEDPA" and state did not appeal ruling); Weeks v. Angelone, 1998 WL 171121, at *3 (E.D. Va. April 1, 1998) ("Virginia has failed to meet the first 'opt-in' requirement ... of a comprehensive mechanism for the appointment, compensation, and payment of reasonable litigation expenses for counsel.... As Judge Payne held in *Satcher*[, *infra*], this requirement could only be satisfied by strict, rather than substantial compliance.... There has been no change in Virginia law, since the *Satcher* and *Wright*[,*infra*,] decisions, that would require a different outcome."); Royal v. Netherland, 1998 WL 234185, at *3 (E.D. Va. May 5, 1998) ("For the reasons set forth in Judge Payne's well-reasoned opinion in Satcher v. Netherland[, *infra*], Chapter 154 of the AEDPA is inapplicable to Royal's petition."); Wright v. Angelone, No. 2:96cv830 (E.D. Va. Oct. 22, 1996) (Virginia does not qualify for opt-in treatment because State lacks "a comprehensive mechanism which meets the

those prerequisites. Subsection c explains the special procedures that apply to States that do qualify.

b. *Prerequisites for opting in.* To qualify for the opt-in provisions, a State must "establish[] by statute, rule of its court of last resort, or by another agency authorized by State law" two types of protections for indigent capital prisoners in state postconviction proceedings:

- The State's statute or rule must create "a mechanism for the appointment, compensation, and payment of reasonable litigation expenses of competent counsel in State post-conviction proceedings brought by indigent prisoners whose capital convictions and sentences have been upheld on direct appeal to the court of last resort in the State or have otherwise become final for State law purposes."[2]
- The statute or rule must "provide standards of competency for the appointment of such counsel."[3]

Additionally, the "mechanism for the appointment, compensation, and reimbursement of [postconviction] counsel" must satisfy three conditions:

- It must "offer counsel to all State prisoners under capital sentence."[4]
- The State must "provide for the entry of an order by a court of record — (1) appointing one or more counsels to represent the prisoner upon a finding that the prisoner is indigent and accepted the offer or is unable competently to decide whether to accept or reject the offer; (2) finding, after a hearing if necessary, that the prisoner rejected the offer of counsel and made the

---

qualification outlined in [Act's] section 2261"); Satcher v. Netherland, 944 F. Supp. 1222, 1238-45 (E.D. Va. 1996), *aff'd in part & rev'd in part*, 126 F.3d 561 (4th Cir.), *cert. denied*, 118 S. Ct. 595 (1997) (Virginia does not qualify for opt-in treatment because state law lacks any formal compensation requirement and does not "affirmatively" make counsel available in all capital cases but, instead, requires prisoners to apply for counsel; "substantial compliance" will not suffice "to afford the States the very significant benefits conferred by Chapter 154"; rather, "strict interpretation is necessary meaningfully to effectuate the [Act's] quid pro quo arrangement"). *See also* Dubois v. Greene, 1998 WL 276282, at *6 n.3 (4th Cir. May 26, 1998) (*per curiam*) (vacating portion of district court's decision that held that Virginia has satisfied opt-in requirements).

[2] 28 U.S.C.A. § 2261(b) (West Supp. 1998). For numerous decisions discussing the requirements that States must satisfy in order to qualify for opt-in status under this and the other provisions described in this subsection, see *supra* § 3.2a n.1.

[3] 28 U.S.C.A. § 2261(b) (West Supp. 1998).

[4] *Id.* § 2261(c).

decision with an understanding of its legal consequences; or (3) denying the appointment of counsel upon a finding that the prisoner is not indigent."[5]

- The mechanism must ensure that "[n]o counsel appointed ... to represent a State prisoner under capital sentence shall have previously represented the petitioner at trial or on direct appeal in the case for which the appointment is made unless the prisoner and counsel expressly request continued representation."[6]

Although AEDPA preserves the preexisting rule[7] that "[t]he ineffectiveness of counsel during State or Federal post-conviction proceedings in a capital case shall not be a ground for [habeas corpus] relief," it makes clear that "[t]his limitation shall not preclude the appointment of a different counsel, on the court's own motion or at the request of the prisoner, at any phase of State or Federal post-conviction proceedings on the basis of the ineffectiveness or incompetence of counsel in such proceedings."[8]

Recognizing that some States have replaced the traditional state postconviction procedure with a procedure that consolidates the direct review and postconviction stages, the federal legislation also sets forth the prerequisites such a State would have to satisfy in order to qualify for the opt-in provisions. The statute provides that States with "a 'unitary review' procedure" (which the statute defines as "a State procedure that authorizes a person under sentence of death to raise, in the course of direct review of the judgment, such claims as could be raised on collateral attack") may qualify for the opt-in provisions if:

- "[T]he State establishes by rule of its court of last resort or by statute a mechanism for the appointment, compensation, and payment of reasonable litigation expenses of competent counsel in the unitary review proceedings, including expenses relating to the litigation of collateral claims in the proceedings."[9]
- "The rule of court or statute ... provide[s] standards of competency for the appointment of such counsel."[10]
- The "procedure ... include[s] an offer of counsel following trial for the purpose of representation on unitary review, and entry of an order, as provided in section 2261(c), concerning appointment of counsel or waiver or denial of appointment of counsel for that purpose."[11]

---

[5] *Id.*

[6] *Id.* § 2261(d).

[7] *See infra* § 26.3b n.36.

[8] 28 U.S.C.A. § 2261(e) (West Supp. 1998).

[9] *Id.* § 2265(a).

[10] *Id.*

[11] *Id.* § 2265(b) (incorporating *id.* § 2261(c)).

- The procedure ensures that "[n]o counsel appointed to represent the prisoner in the unitary review proceedings [has] ... previously represented the prisoner at trial in the case for which the appointment is made unless the prisoner and counsel expressly request continued representation."[12]

A State that fails to satisfy any of the statutory prerequisites is categorically prohibited from obtaining the benefits of the opt-in provisions. For example, a district court in California found (in a decision subsequently reversed on procedural grounds) that the State does not qualify for opt-in status, notwithstanding the existence of a state mechanism for appointing and compensating counsel in state postconviction proceedings, because the mechanism was not contained in a "rule of court or statute," it fails to "impose any binding or mandatory standards" for the appointment of counsel, and it does not "require counsel to have any experience or competence in bringing [state] habeas petitions."[13] Similarly, a district court in Tennessee concluded that the State does not qualify for opt-in treatment, despite the fact that "Tennessee provides for the appointment of counsel for indigent defendants ... and has standards for determining whether counsel has sufficiently performed," because the State's appointment mechanism fails to "ensure that only qualified, competent counsel will be appointed to represent habeas petitioners in capital cases."[14]

Although hypothetical as of this writing, a related question looms on the horizon. Suppose that a State passes new legislation satisfying AEDPA's opt-in prerequisites by giving capital state postconviction petitioners the required procedural advantages, then attempts to take advantage of Chapter 154's restrictions on habeas corpus relief in a *pending* capital habeas corpus case brought by a prisoner who pursued (or omitted to pursue) the State's

---

[12] *Id.* § 2265(b).

[13] Ashmus v. Calderon, 935 F. Supp. 1048, 1072 (N.D. Cal. 1996), *modified & aff'd*, 123 F.3d 1199 (9th Cir. 1997) (affirming district court decision except to extent it suggested that competency standards could not satisfy section 2261 unless they required lawyers to have previous experience in habeas corpus litigation), *rev'd on other grounds*, 118 S. Ct. 1694 (1998) (without addressing merits of lower courts' rulings that California does not qualify for "opt-in" treatment, Supreme Court reverses and remands on ground that district court lacked authority to adjudicate issues in context of class action for declaratory judgment and injunctive relief rather than in individual federal habeas corpus proceeding).

[14] Austin v. Bell, 927 F. Supp. 1058, 1061-62 (M.D. Tenn. 1996) (because Tennessee mechanism merely requires that appointed counsel be "a competent attorney licensed in this state," *i.e.*, one who has "passed the Tennessee bar examination," mechanism fails adequately to ensure that "only qualified attorneys [will] be appointed to represent habeas petitioners in capital cases," a requirement that "is crucial under the Act ... because the Act does not permit the ineffectiveness or incompetence of counsel during State or Federal post-conviction proceedings to be grounds for relief in a proceeding arising under section 2254"). *See also* other decisions cited *supra* § 3.2a n.1.

postconviction remedy at a time when none of the new procedural advantages was available. AEDPA's section 107(c), which provides that Chapter 154 (containing the opt-in provisions) "shall apply to cases pending on or after the date of enactment of this Act,"[15] does not answer this question because one of the provisions it makes applicable to pending cases is section 2261, which specifies the prerequisites for application of the rest of Chapter 154's provisions. If section 2261's prerequisites are not met, then that provision's application to the pending case would bar the application of the rest of the Chapter 154 provisions.

As the courts that have adverted to this issue have tended to conclude (albeit in all cases in *dicta*), the better interpretation seems to be that only those prisoners who actually had access to the procedural advantages the State is required to provide to capital state postconviction prisoners in order to qualify for opt-in status are subject to the disadvantages that Chapter 154 imposes on habeas corpus petitioners once those prerequisites are met.[16] As section 3.4c *infra* discusses, this interpretation avoids serious "retroactivity" problems that otherwise would arise and, if they did arise, would probably forbid the statute's application in this manner, regardless of the "normal rules of [statutory]

---

[15] *See infra* § 3.4a nn.6-7 and accompanying text.

[16] *See* Smith v. Moore, 137 F.3d 808, 812 n.1 (4th Cir. 1998) ("Section 107 of the AEDPA is ... inapplicable to this appeal. South Carolina 'contends that it became eligible for the procedures outlined in § 107 of the AEDPA as of June 18, 1996.' ... Even if true, Smith's state habeas petition was finally decided by the South Carolina Supreme Court prior to that date."); Gilbert v. Moore, 134 F.3d 642, 645 n.1 (4tn Cir. 1998) (*en banc*) (same as *Smith v. Moore, supra*); Howard v. Moore, 131 F.3d 399, 403-04 n.1 (4th Cir. 1997) (*en banc*) (same as *Smith v. Moore, supra*); Bennett v. Angelone, 92 F 3d 1336, 1342 (4th Cir.), *cert. denied*, 117 S. Ct. 503 (1996) (discussed *infra* notes 18-19 and accompanying text); Colvin-El v. Nuth, 1998 WL 386403, at *4 n.3 (D. Md. July 6, 1998) ("In determining whether Maryland has 'opted-in' for purposes of Chapter 154, the Court must of course evaluate those procedures for the appointment of counsel as they existed when Colvin-El's petition for post-conviction relief was finally denied by the Maryland Court of Appeals on August 23, 1996." (citing *Bennett v. Angelone, supra*)); Royal v. Netherland, 1998 WL 234185, at *3 (E.D. Va. May 5, 1998) (same as *Smith v. Moore, supra*); Williams v. Cain, 942 F. Supp. 1088, 1092 (W.D. La. 1996) (assuming that opt-in provisions apply to petitioner only if State satisfied opt-in requirements "at the time [petitioner's] state [postconviction] claims were denied"); Banks v. Horn, 939 F. Supp. 1165, 1168 (M.D. Pa. 1996) (opt-in treatment based on new state postconviction statute is not appropriate in petitioner's case because he did not receive benefit of new statute when his postconviction petition was proceeding in state court); *But cf.* Jackson v. Johnson, No. 96-CA-716 SS (W.D. Tex. Oct. 30, 1996), at 4 n.2 (although Texas does not now qualify for opt-in treatment, were it to qualify in the future, it would get the benefit of Chapter 154 even if the capital prisoner before the court did not "have ... the benefit of appointed counsel at his state habeas proceeding"; this reading "may be unfair, but that is a determination Congress has made").

construction."[17] This interpretation conforms to AEDPA's language, structure, and policy: To begin with, section 2261(c) requires that the various procedural advantages needed to qualify a State for opt-in treatment must be available "to *all* State prisoners under capital sentence" — a requirement that can hardly be satisfied if the very prisoner before the court did not have those advantages available to her. Second, "the Act establishes a *quid-pro-quo* relationship: A state seeking greater federal deference to its habeas decisions in capital cases must, by appointing competent counsel to represent indigent petitioners, further ensure that its own habeas proceedings are meaningful."[18] Requiring capital prisoners to forgo full federal habeas corpus review without having received the benefit of AEDPA's assurance that the State's own postconviction review mechanisms are meaningful "would upset the *'quid pro quo'* the Act was supposed to establish."[19] Finally, Congress' apparent conclusion that only those pending habeas corpus cases that are subject to the new Chapter 154 provisions, but no other pending cases, can fairly be subjected to AEDPA's new provisions[20] makes good sense only if the particular category of "pending" habeas corpus petitioners to whom AEDPA applies in this "retroactive" fashion is comprised exclusively of prisoners who already in fact have been compensated, via enhanced state postconviction review, for the habeas corpus procedures that AEDPA newly withdraws.[21]

---

[17] Lindh v. Murphy, 117 S. Ct. 2059, 2063 (1997) (discussed *infra* § 3.4c nn.62-65 and accompanying text).

[18] *Bennett v. Angelone, supra,* 92 F.3d at 1342 (citing and quoting H. REP. No. 23, 104th Cong., 1st. Sess. (1995)). *See id.* (AEDPA creates "'*quid pro quo* arrangement under which states are accorded stronger finality rules on federal habeas review in return for strengthening the right to counsel for indigent capital defendants'").

[19] *Id.* ("Virginia's disposition of Bennett's petition should not receive the added deference afforded by [Chapter 154 of] the Act, because, at the time it denied his petition, Virginia had not yet set up the appointment [of counsel] procedures the Act requires as the price of deference," so that "applying [Chapter 154] to Bennett's petition would upset the *'quid pro quo'* the Act was supposed to establish").

[20] *See infra* § 3.4.

[21] *See infra* § 3.4c nn.62-65 and accompanying text. If the opt-in limitations on habeas corpus review are deemed to apply to capital petitioners who were not afforded state-appointed competent counsel and the other advantages that States must provide in order to qualify for opt-in status under 28 U.S.C. § 2261, those petitioners would have a basis for arguing "cause and prejudice" as to many procedural defaults occurring in state postconviction proceedings with which the state attempts to charge the petitioners as a basis for denying relief. The state's failure to fulfill its statutory obligation to provide competent counsel arguably would constitute state obstruction of the sort that has been deemed to furnish "cause" under the pre-AEDPA doctrine of procedural default (*see infra* § 26.3b n.33 and accompanying text), which applies to *non*opt-in cases (*see, e.g.,* Truesdale v. Moore, 142 F.3d 749, 753 n.2 (4th Cir. 1998); Moleterno v. Nelson, 114 F.3d 629, 633-34 (7th Cir. 1997)) as well as to defaults in state court proceedings in opt-in states that took place *before* the state qualified for opt-in treatment (*see* Ortiz v. Stewart, 1998 WL 349467, at *4

AEDPA poses another important (but, as yet, hypothetical), interpretive problem as a result of an apparent gap in its opt-in provisions. Pursuant to the *quid pro quo* arrangement adopted by those provisions,[22] capital prisoners in qualifying States are given a right to (1) the appointment of competent and compensated state postconviction counsel[23] and (2) a federal court's issuance of an "automatic stay" of execution throughout an initial state postconviction proceeding,[24] in return for which the prisoners are subjected, *inter alia*, to (3) a truncated, 180-day limitations period (tolled during a "first" state postconviction proceeding[25]) within which they must file a federal habeas corpus petition.[26] Although AEDPA specifies the triggering date for the running of the 180-day period, namely, the date of the "final State court affirmance of the conviction and sentence on direct review or the expiration of the time for seeking such

---

(9th Cir. July 1, 1998)). Even under the modified procedural default rule created by the opt-in provisions (*see infra* § 3.3c nn.75-91 and accompanying text), the same conclusion would result. The opt-in procedural default rule excuses defaults made in state court and permits federal adjudication of the otherwise defaulted claim if the default was "the result of state action in violation of the ... laws of the United States." 28 U.S.C.A. § 2264(a)(1) (West Supp. 1998). Because section 2261 is a "law[] of the United States," and because section 2261 requires that qualifying opt-in States "*must* offer [competent postconviction] counsel to *all* State prisoners under capital sentence," *id.* § 2261(c) (emphasis added), a State's claim that section 2261 is in force (because the State has opted in), together with the State's failure in violation of that very section to have provided the particular "prisoner under capital sentence" with competent state postconviction counsel, would seem to make any default during state postconviction that was caused by the absence of competent counsel "the result of state action in violation of the ... laws of the United States." 28 U.S.C.A. § 2264(a)(1) (West Supp. 1998). Also supporting this interpretation is 28 U.S.C. § 2261(e), which states that "[t]he ineffectiveness or incompetence of counsel during State ... post-conviction proceedings in a capital case shall not be a *ground for relief*" (emphasis added) — the italicized phrase being one the statute consistently uses to refer to the underlying constitutional *claim* for relief. Section 2261(e), thus, does *not* keep incompetence of counsel from supplying an excuse to a procedural default. Assumedly, AEDPA did not intend to invite procedures (here, subjecting petitioners who received no procedural advantages in state court to limitations on federal review that are premised on the availability of those advantages) that its own explicit provisions would then define as a "violation of the ... laws of the United States" and, in turn, use to neutralize the invited procedures (by *broadening* federal review through the recognition of a new excuse for an otherwise preclusive default). The simple and obvious way to avoid this self-defeating set of events is to interpret section 2261 as it is written, *i.e.*, as insisting that the State "offer [qualifying] counsel to *all* State prisoners under capital sentence," *id.* § 2261(c) (emphasis added), before *any* of them is thereafter subjected to the opt-in limitations in federal court. *See supra* text following note 16.

[22] *See supra* notes 18-19 and accompanying text.

[23] 28 U.S.C.A. §§ 2261(b), 2261(c) (West Supp. 1998) (discussed *supra* notes 2-6 and accompanying text).

[24] *Id.* § 2262 (discussed *infra* § 3.3c nn.55-60 and accompanying text).

[25] *See id.* § 2263(b)(2) (discussed *infra* § 5.1b nn.99-102 and accompanying text).

[26] *See id.* § 2263 (discussed *infra* § 5.1b nn.92-122 and accompanying text).

review,"[27] AEDPA does not specify — and arguably authorizes a self-defeating — triggering date for the required appointment and compensation of state postconviction counsel and for the automatic stay of execution. Thus, in order for a State to opt-in under AEDPA, it "must offer counsel to all State prisoners under capital sentence and must provide for the entry of an order by a court of record ... appointing one or more counsels"[28] in all "State post-conviction proceedings brought by indigent prisoners whose capital convictions and sentences have been upheld on direct appeal to the court of last resort in the State or have otherwise become final for State law purposes."[29] But AEDPA does not say *when* "the entry of [that] order" must occur or *which court* must enter it — e.g., "the court of last resort in the State" that has "upheld [the capital judgment] on direct appeal," or the "State post-conviction court."[30] And AEDPA triggers the right to an automatic stay of execution upon the "entry in the appropriate State court of record of an order" appointing counsel[31] but does not specify the timing of that order or the "appropriate" court to enter it.

These provisions are not problematic, and the integrity of AEDPA's *quid pro quo* arrangement is preserved, as long as the statute is read to mandate the *same* triggering date and "appropriate court" for purposes of "the entry of an order" appointing counsel (and, thus, the onset of the automatic right to a stay of execution) as AEDPA clearly does specify for purposes of commencing the running of the 180-day limitations period — *i.e.*, if the statute is read to mean that, on the date on which "the court of last resort in the State" denies the direct appeal, that same court must enter an order appointing counsel, thus triggering both the automatic right to a federal stay of execution and the running of the statute of limitations. Severe problems would arise, however, and the integrity of AEDPA's *quid pro quo* arrangement would be destroyed, if the triggering date and appropriate court are *different* for purposes of the entry of an order appointing counsel and, thus, for the onset of the automatic right to a stay of execution, and for purposes of commencing the running of the statute of limitations.

Consider, for example, the result if the opt-in provisions are read (1) to authorize the *state postconviction court* to enter a qualifying order appointing counsel and (2) to permit that court to issue that order (and, thus, trigger the right to a federal stay of execution) whenever it chooses. Accepting that hypothesis, consider a case in which, upon the denial of the prisoner's direct appeal, an execution date is set for 30 days hence, and in which the state postconviction

---

[27] *Id.* § 2263(a).

[28] *Id.* § 2261(c)(1).

[29] *Id.* § 2261(b).

[30] *Id.*

[31] *Id.* § 2262(a).

court does not grant the prisoner's applications for appointment of counsel and a stay of execution within the 30 days prior to the execution date. In that event, AEDPA's "automatic stay" provision would never trigger, and the prisoner could be executed — notwithstanding that he has never received the state postconviction representation, "automatic" stay of execution, and attorney-assisted state postconviction and federal habeas corpus proceedings that the statute promises him. Or consider another case in which no state postconviction counsel is appointed upon the denial of direct appeal, and in which the state postconviction court waits six months before granting the prisoner's application for the appointment of counsel to assist in preparing and filing a state postconviction petition. Or suppose that the prisoner — acting without counsel and without notice of the federal statute of limitations — simply lets six months pass before filing either a request for counsel or a state postconviction petition. In either of these latter events, the entire limitations period would run, and the prisoner's federal habeas corpus rights would be extinguished, before he received the competent and compensated state postconviction attorney and the attorney-assisted state postconviction proceedings that are intended to supply the *quid pro quo* for subjecting the prisoner to the 180-day statute of limitations.[32]

To avoid these difficulties, it seems likely that the federal courts either will have to unify the triggering dates and "appropriate court" for all three purposes — the appointment of counsel, the onset of the right to an automatic stay, and the commencement of the 180-day limitations period — or will have to develop a complicated scheme for interim stays of execution (*e.g.*, under the jurisdiction-preserving aspect of the All Writs Act[33]) and for the "equitable tolling" of the limitations period when state postconviction counsel has not been appointed for reasons not attributable to the prisoner's inexcusable neglect.[34] In the meantime, unrepresented capital prisoners in opt-in States are strongly advised *immediately upon the denial of direct appeal* (or immediately upon learning at some point thereafter that they are subject to AEDPA's opt-in provisions) to file the following documents in the specified courts:

- The capital prisoner should file two applications for the appointment of qualifying counsel[35] — one in the court of last resort that denied the

---

[32] These latter two scenarios are likely to match the reality in States like Texas that have many more capital prisoners than available capital postconviction lawyers. Indeed, the Supreme Court confronted a hybrid of all three scenarios in McFarland v. Scott, 512 U.S. 849, 851-54 (1994); *see infra* § 5.1b nn.79-91 and accompanying text.

[33] 28 U.S.C. 1651(a) (1994).

[34] *See infra* § 5.1b nn.53-54 and accompanying text ("equitable tolling" doctrine).

[35] *See* 28 U.S.C.A. §§ 2261(b), 2261(c) (West Supp. 1998) (defining attributes that appointed counsel must have in order to permit the State to qualify for opt-in treatment (discussed *supra* notes 2-6 and accompanying text)).

prisoner's direct appeal and one in the court with jurisdiction to hear the prisoner's state postconviction petition.

- In order to toll the federal statute of limitations,[36] the capital prisoner should (as expeditiously as possible) prepare a "placeholder petition" and the other documents that are described in section 5.1(b) *infra*, and should file those documents in the court with jurisdiction to hear the prisoner's state postconviction petition.[37]

c. *Procedures in qualifying opt-in States.* If a State makes an adequate showing of its compliance with the statutory prerequisites for opting in, then the "special habeas corpus procedures" in Chapter 154 apply to federal habeas corpus petitions filed by capital prisoners from that State (or, at least, those prisoners who received the benefit of the state postconviction procedures needed to enable the State to opt in). As is explained in section 3.4 *infra*, although Chapter 154 contains an "effective date" clause stating that the Chapter "shall apply to cases [from qualifying opt-in States if the cases were] pending on or after the date of enactment of this Act," that clause probably is insufficient to require the Chapter's application to cases filed before AEDPA's effective date *if* applying the statute in that situation would impose so-called "retroactive" effects.[38] Readers accordingly should consult section 3.4 in regard to petitions filed before AEDPA's effective date (April 24, 1996) or in regard to other petitions as to which there is a suspicion that the statute's application might be "retroactive."

Chapter 154's "special procedures" either supplement or replace[39] the procedures applicable in other cases in regard to: (1) the time frames for filing and resolving the petition at the district court and appellate levels; (2) the standards and procedures for stays of execution; (3) the rules governing the amendment of a petition; and (4) the treatment of claims that were not raised and decided on the merits in state court. Each set of "special procedures" is discussed in turn below.

---

[36] *See id.* § 2263(b)(2) (discussed *infra* § 5.1b nn.99-102 and accompanying text).

[37] *See infra* § 5.1b nn.79-91 and accompanying text. Placeholder petitions might also be advisable for tolling purposes in cases in which state postconviction counsel has been appointed but in which the appointed attorney has good reason to fear that most or all of the 180-day limitations period will be exhausted while she investigates, prepares, and files a fully comprehensive state postconviction petition.

[38] Antiterrorism and Effective Death Penalty Act § 107(c), Pub. L. 104-132, 110 Stat. 1214, 1226 (1996); *see infra* §§ 3.4b nn.17-25 and accompanying text, 3.4c.

[39] On the question whether AEDPA superimposes the Chapter 154 procedures for opt-in cases on top of all of the procedures applicable to nonopt-in cases or whether, on the other hand, the Chapter 154 procedures supplant some of the procedures applicable to nonopt-in cases, see *supra* § 3.2 n.34 and accompanying text.

1. The opt-in provisions accelerate capital habeas corpus proceedings in the following respects:

- The deadline for the filing of a federal habeas corpus petition by capital prisoners in qualifying opt-in States is 180 days — in contrast to the one-year limitations period that applies to all noncapital habeas corpus petitions, capital habeas corpus petitions from nonopt-in States, and section 2255 motions.[40] The opt-in statute of limitations begins running on the date of the "final State court affirmance of the conviction and sentence on direct review or the expiration of the time for seeking such review."[41] The statute of limitations is tolled during the period when the United States Supreme Court is considering a petition for *certiorari* from the final state court judgment on direct review[42] and during the period when the state courts are considering the prisoner's "first petition for post-conviction review or other collateral relief."[43] The legislation also provides for an additional tolling period of up

---

[40] *See* 28 U.S.C.A. § 2263 (West Supp. 1998). For a fuller discussion of the statutes of limitations that apply to both opt-in and other cases, see *infra* § 5.1b.

[41] *See* 28 U.S.C.A. § 2263(a) (West Supp. 1998). This triggering event is another respect in which the 180-day statute of limitations for capital cases from opt-in States appears to differ from the one-year limitations period that applies to other habeas corpus and all section 2255 cases. The triggering event for the general one-year statute of limitations appears to be the United States Supreme Court's resolution of *certiorari* proceedings on direct review (or the expiration of the time for seeking *certiorari* review if a petition is not filed). *See infra* § 5.1b nn.59-63 and accompanying text. Although the statute of limitations in the opt-in provision treats the filing of a direct review *certiorari* petition as a basis for tolling the statute of limitations, *see infra* note 42 and accompanying text; *infra* § 5.1b nn.97-98 and accompanying text, it relies on the final ruling of the highest *state* court on direct review to trigger the running of that statute. As a result, any amount of time the defendant takes to prepare a *certiorari* petition (or to decide whether or not to file such a petition) following the denial of relief on direct review in the state courts counts against her 180-day limitations period (assuming no state postconviction proceedings are then pending).

In opt-in States with a "'unitary review' procedure" (*see supra* § 3.3b nn.9-12 and accompanying text), AEDPA takes into account the possibility that "a transcript of the trial proceedings [may be] ... unavailable" at the time the 180-day limitation period ordinarily would begin to run. 28 U.S.C.A. § 2265(c) (West Supp. 1998). In such circumstances, "the start of the 180-day limitation period ... shall be deferred until a transcript is made available to the prisoner or counsel of the prisoner." *Id.*

[42] *See* 28 U.S.C.A. § 2263(b)(1) (West Supp. 1998) (statute of limitations is tolled "from the date that a petition for certiorari is filed in the Supreme Court until the date of final disposition of the petition if a State prisoner files the petition to secure review by the Supreme Court of the affirmance of a capital sentence on direct review by the court of last resort of the State or other final State court decision on direct review").

[43] *Id.* § 2263(b)(2). In limiting the tolling provision to the "*first* petition for [state] post-conviction review or other collateral relief," the opt-in statute of limitations differs from the general

- to 30 days upon a showing of "good cause."[44]
- The district court must "render a final determination and enter a final judgment ... not later than 180 days after the date on which the application [for a writ of habeas corpus] is filed."[45] The statute permits the district court to extend this period for up to 30 days upon a finding that "the ends of justice that would be served by allowing the delay outweigh the best interests of the public and the applicant in a speedy disposition of the application."[46] The state can enforce these timing requirements by petitioning the court of appeals for a writ of mandamus; if a mandamus petition is filed, it must be resolved by the court of appeals within 30 days of filing.[47]
- If the federal district court's final order is appealed, the court of appeals must "render a final determination" of the appeal within 120 days of the filing of the reply brief (or, if no reply brief is filed, within 120 days of the filing of the answering brief).[48] A subsequent petition for rehearing or rehearing *en banc* must be decided within 30 days of its filing (or, in cases in which a responsive pleading is filed, within 30 days of the filing of the latter pleading).[49] If rehearing or rehearing *en banc* is granted, a final determination must be rendered within 120 days.[50] The state can enforce

---

statute of limitations, which apparently is tolled whenever *any* "properly filed" state postconviction petition is pending. *Id.* § 2244(d)(2) (discussed *infra* § 5.1b nn.99-102 and accompanying text).

[44] *Id.* § 2263(b)(3) (180-day limitations period may be tolled "during an additional period not to exceed 30 days, if (A) a motion for an extension of time is filed in the Federal district court that would have jurisdiction over the case upon the filing of a habeas corpus application under section 2254; and (B) a showing of good cause is made for the failure to file the habeas corpus application within the time period established by this section").

[45] *Id.* § 2266(b)(1)(A). The statute breaks down this 180-day period by specifying that "[a] district court shall afford the parties at least 120 days in which to complete all actions, including the preparation of all pleadings and briefs, and if necessary, a hearing, prior to the submission of the case for decision." *Id.* § 2266(b)(1)(B). District courts must "give[ ] priority" to capital federal habeas corpus petitions and section 2255 motions "over all noncapital matters." *Id.* § 2266(a).

[46] *Id.* § 2266(b)(1)(C)(i). In making this assessment, the district court may consider, *inter alia*, the risk of "a miscarriage of justice," the complexity of the case, and the amount of time a "duly diligent" attorney would reasonably need "for effective preparation," *id.* § 2266(B)(1)(C)(ii), but may not consider the "general congestion of the court's calendar," *id.* § 2266(b)(1)(C)(iii).

[47] *See id.* § 2266(b)(4)(B).

[48] *Id.* § 2266(c)(1)(A). Courts of appeals, like district courts, are required by the statute to give capital habeas corpus petitions and section 2255 motions "priority ... over all noncapital matters." *Id.* § 2266(a).

[49] *See id.* § 2266(c)(1)(B)(i).

[50] *See id.* § 2266(c)(1)(B)(ii).

these timing requirements by applying to the Supreme Court for a writ of mandamus.[51]

The timing requirements for action by the district court and the court of appeals apply not only to an initial federal habeas corpus petition but also to successive petitions and redeterminations following reversal and remand by a higher court.[52] AEDPA's timing requirements for judicial action are not an independent basis for a stay of execution,[53] and a violation of the timing rules is not a basis for habeas corpus relief.[54]

2. The opt-in chapter is the only portion of AEDPA that addresses stays of execution. The opt-in stay provisions distinguish among three stages of the process of litigating a capital habeas corpus petition:

- During the period prior to the filing of a federal habeas corpus petition, the legislation provides for what amounts to an "automatic stay": Upon the commencement of the state's postconviction review process, a federal court must grant an application to stay any "warrant or order setting an execution date for a State prisoner."[55]
- The "automatic stay" remains in effect only until the filing of the federal habeas corpus petition. At that time, the prisoner must establish her right to a further stay by "mak[ing] a substantial showing of the denial of a Federal right."[56] If no federal habeas corpus petition is properly filed (either because

---

[51] *See id.* § 2266(c)(4)(B). *See also* Truesdale v. Moore, 142 F.3d 749, 759 (4th Cir. 1998) (4th Circuit's accelerated timetable for judicial resolution of *non*opt-in cases, patterned after AEDPA's opt-in provisions, differs from AEDPA in that circuit rule for nonopt-in capital cases does not permit state to enforce timetable by means of mandamus).

[52] *See* 28 U.S.C.A. §§ 2266(b)(2) (West Supp. 1998) (district court), 2266(c)(2) (court of appeals).

[53] *See id.* §§ 2266(b)(3)(A) (district court), 2266(c)(3) (court of appeals).

[54] *See id.* §§ 2266(b)(4)(A) (district court), 2266(c)(4)(A) (court of appeals).

[55] *Id.* § 2262(a) ("Upon the entry in the appropriate State court of record of an order under [*id.*] section 2261(c) [*i.e.*, an order granting or denying appointment of counsel for state postconviction proceedings], a warrant or order setting an execution date for a State prisoner shall be stayed upon application to any court that would have jurisdiction over any proceedings filed under section 2254. The application shall recite that the State has invoked the post-conviction review procedures of this chapter and that the scheduled execution is subject to stay.").

[56] *Id.* § 2262(b)(3) ("A stay of execution granted pursuant to subsection (a) [the "automatic stay" provision] shall expire if ... a State prisoner files a habeas corpus petition under section 2254 within the time period required by section 2263 and fails to make a substantial showing of the denial of a Federal right"). For discussion of two precursors of section 2262(b)(3)'s "substantial showing" standard, see *infra* §§ 13.2d, 35.4c. AEDPA uses a similar standard to determine whether unsuccessful habeas corpus petitioners and section 2255 movants are permitted to appeal. *See* 28 U.S.C.A. § 2253(c)(2) (West 1994 & Supp. 1998) (discussed *infra* § 35.4b n.17 and accompanying

the prisoner fails to comply with the statute of limitations or makes a knowing, voluntary, and intelligent waiver of the right to seek federal habeas corpus relief), the "automatic stay" expires,[57] and the only avenue for obtaining a stay is to seek authorization from the court of appeals for the filing of a successive petition.[58]

•   If the petitioner fails to satisfy the substantive standard for obtaining a stay from the federal district court at the time the petition is filed, or if the habeas corpus petition is "denied ... in the district court or at any subsequent stage of review,"[59] "no Federal court thereafter shall have the authority to enter a stay of execution in the case, unless the court of appeals approves the filing of a second or successive application."[60]

---

text); *see also infra* § 35.4c (similar test under preexisting law governing access to habeas corpus appeals).

[57] *See* 28 U.S.C.A. §§ 2262(b) (West Supp. 1998) ("A stay of execution granted pursuant to subsection (a) [the "automatic stay" provision] shall expire if (1) a State prisoner fails to file a habeas corpus application under section 2254 within the time required in section 2263; (2) before a court of competent jurisdiction, in the presence of counsel, unless the prisoner has competently and knowingly waived such counsel, and after having been advised of the consequences, a State prisoner under capital sentence waives the right to pursue habeas corpus review under 2254").

[58] *See id.* § 2262(c). For discussion of AEDPA's provisions governing successive petitions, including the procedures for obtaining approval from the court of appeals for the filing of a successive petition, see *infra* §§ 28.3, 28.4a.

[59] 28 U.S.C.A. § 2262(b)(3) (West Supp. 1998).

[60] *Id.* § 2262(c). The Supreme Court's analysis in Felker v. Turpin, 518 U.S. 651 (1996), suggests that section 2262(c) would be unconstitutional under Article III of the Constitution if the provision were read to deprive the United States Supreme Court of any "authority to enter a stay of execution" — and thus of any effective authority to review the federal questions in the case — upon a district court's denial of a stay or upon a district court's or court of appeals' "deni[al of] relief." 28 U.S.C.A. §§ 2262(c), 2262(b)(3) (West Supp. 1998). *See Felker v. Turpin, supra* at 660-62; *see also id.* at 665-66 (Stevens, J., concurring); *id.* at 666-67 (Breyer, J. concurring). *Felker* accordingly suggests that, in order to avoid constitutional questions, a reviewing court would be obliged to interpret section 2262 to mean that no stay of execution could be granted following (1) the lower federal courts' *and the Supreme Court's* conclusion that (or the Supreme Court's denial of a petition to consider whether) the petitioner had "fail[ed] to make a substantial showing of the denial of a Federal right," (2) the Supreme Court's denial of a *certiorari* petition to review the court of appeals' denial of relief, or (3) the Supreme Court's determination following a grant of *certiorari* that a lower federal court properly denied a stay or relief. It also seems unlikely that the 5th Amendment Due Process Clause would permit the denial of a stay pending appeal to the court of appeals following a district court's "den[ial of] relief," if the district court or court of appeals had granted (or had been asked to issue but has declined to rule on) a certificate of appealability attesting to the substantiality of at least one issue on appeal and thus giving the petitioner a statutory right to appeal. *See* 28 U.S.C. § 2253 (West 1994 & Supp. 1998) (discussed *infra* § 35.4b); Barefoot v. Estelle, 463 U.S. 880, 893-94 (1983) (discussed *infra* § 36.2a nn.17-32). Here again, to avoid constitutional problems (and to make sense of the statute as a whole), section 2262 should be read to forbid a stay following the district court's denial of relief only if that

3. An opt-in provision narrowly restricts a capital habeas corpus petitioner's ability to amend a petition after the state answers it. Until the state files its answer,[61] the existing (liberal) rules for amendment continue to apply.[62] After the state answers, the statute forbids amendments unless they raise a "new claim" of the narrowly circumscribed sort that one of AEDPA's nonopt-in provisions permits a habeas corpus petitioner to raise in a second or successive petition.[63] As section 28.3e *infra* explains, a claim satisfies AEDPA's successive petition rules only if the claim could not previously have been raised because it depends upon either (1) a "new rule of constitutional law, made retroactive to cases on collateral review by the Supreme Court," or (2) newly acquired facts that "could not have been discovered previously through the exercise of due diligence" and that "if proven and viewed in light of the evidence as a whole, would be sufficient to establish by clear and convincing evidence that, but for constitutional error, no reasonable factfinder would have found the applicant guilty of the underlying offense."[64]

---

court and the court of appeals deny a certificate of appealability, or the latter court affirms the district court's denial of relief, and Supreme Court consideration is preserved as discussed above. It also seems unlikely (if only because such an interpretation might interfere with the Supreme Court's ability to hear the case) that a district court's denial of a stay of execution could constitutionally forbid a court of appeals to reverse the district court's denial of a stay upon concluding that the issues in the case are substantial or, at least, to grant a stay pending appeal to the Supreme Court upon concluding that the issues are substantial enough to require that the petitioner have a chance to seek Supreme Court review of the district court's denial of a stay.

For discussion of the standards and procedures for successive petitions, see *infra* §§ 28.3, 28.4a.

[61] For discussion of the state's answer, see *infra* § 16.1.

[62] For discussion of the preexisting rules governing the amendment of habeas corpus petitions (which continue to apply in noncapital cases as well as in capital nonopt-in cases), see *infra* § 17.2.

[63] 28 U.S.C.A. § 2266(b)(3)(B) (West Supp. 1998) ("No amendment to an application for a writ of habeas corpus under this chapter shall be permitted after the filing of the answer to the application, except on the grounds specified in section 2244(b).").

[64] *Id.* § 2244(b)(2)(B)(i) (discussed *infra* §§ 20.2b nn.32-38 and accompanying text, 28.3e nn.134-40 and accompanying text).

AEDPA does not define the phrase "due diligence" that appears in several of its provisions (*see id.* §§ 2244(b)(2), 2244(d)(1), 2254(e)(A)(ii), 2255, 2264(a)), and the phrase has no clearly accepted meaning in the habeas corpus context. The term *is* commonly used in other areas of the law, some of which may be deemed sufficiently analogous to justify reliance on the caselaw construing the phrase. *See, e.g.*, Lewis v. Alexander, 987 F.2d 392, 396-97 (6th Cir. 1993) (petitioner, who had filed untimely appeal from denial of habeas corpus relief, could obtain relief under FED. R. CIV. P. 60(b)(1) because petitioner's counsel had exercised "due diligence" (as required by Civil Rule 60(b)(1)) in attempting to comply with applicable time constraints notwithstanding counsel's error in misreading date-stamp on notice of appeal); United States v. Walus, 616 F.2d 283, 303-04 (7th Cir. 1980) (relief available under FED. R. CIV. P. 60(b)(2) provision for "newly discovered evidence which by due diligence could not have been discovered in time to move for a new trial under Rule 59(b)" because defendant did not previously know about

4. Finally, under section 2264(a), federal courts in opt-in cases "shall only consider a claim or claims that have been raised and decided on the merits in State courts" except in three exceptional circumstances.[65] Although this provision might be read in any of the three ways set out below, the third reading best avoids serious interpretive difficulties:

• Section 2264(a) might be interpreted as a limitation on cognizable claims.[66] This reading is problematic, however, because AEDPA's opt-in chapter does not purport to amend, and in fact explicitly incorporates by reference, the longstanding provision delineating the broad range of federal claims that are cognizable in federal habeas corpus proceedings.[67]

---

witnesses despite extensive search for proof of innocence). Additionally or alternatively, doctrines that have been developed in the habeas corpus context may be viewed as sufficiently similar in nature and purpose to the new "due diligence" standard to shed light on that standard. *See, e.g.,* Dobbs v. Zant, 506 U.S. 357, 358 (1993) (*per curiam*) (court of appeals should have permitted habeas corpus petitioner to supplement record on appeal with transcript that bore upon claim of ineffectiveness of counsel because counsel's delay in obtaining transcript "resulted substantially from the State's own erroneous assertions that closing arguments had not been transcribed"); McCleskey v. Zant, 499 U.S. 467, 496 (1991) (unavailability of evidence may be basis for showing "cause," and thus for avoiding state's defenses of procedural default and (pre-Act) writ abuse, as long as unavailability is judged according to "the principle that petitioner must conduct a *reasonable* and *diligent* investigation" (emphasis added)). For an early effort to apply AEDPA's "due diligence" language, *see* Bush v. Singletary, 99 F.3d 373, 375 (11th Cir. 1996).

[65] 28 U.S.C.A. § 2264(a) (West Supp. 1998) ("Whenever a State prisoner under capital sentence files a petition for habeas corpus relief to which this chapter applies, the district court shall only consider a claim or claims that have been raised and decided on the merits in State courts, unless the failure to raise the claim properly is [within one of three exceptions]").

[66] For discussion of the longstanding provisions governing the claims that are cognizable in habeas corpus proceedings, see *infra* Chapter 9.

[67] *See* 28 U.S.C.A. § 2264(b) (West Supp. 1998) ("Following review subject to subsection[ ] (a) ... of section 2254, the court shall rule on the claims properly before it."). AEDPA does not in any respect amend 28 U.S.C. § 2254(a) (1994), which provides that the "district court shall entertain an application for a writ of habeas corpus in behalf of a person in custody pursuant to the judgment of a State court ... on the ground that he is in custody in violation of the Constitution or laws or treaties of the United States." *See also* 28 U.S.C. § 2241(c)(3) (1994) (unamended provision establishing habeas corpus jurisdiction and cause of action). Additionally, one of the opt-in provisions, section 2262, describes opt-in cases as being "file[d] ... under section 2254" in a federal court with "*jurisdiction* over ... proceedings filed under section 2254." 28 U.S.C.A. §§ 2262(b)(2), 2262(a) (West Supp. 1998) (emphasis added). This language suggests that the claims over which federal habeas corpus courts have subject-matter "jurisdiction" in opt-in cases (as in all other habeas corpus cases) are those specified in "section 2254," meaning, specifically, in section 2254(a). More generally, the opt-in provisions repeatedly describe the actions to which they apply as ones "arising under section 2254." *Id.* § 2261(e); *see id.* §§ 2262(a), 2262(b)(1), 2262(b)(3), 2263(a).

- The provision might be read as a substitute for the preexisting rule governing the exhaustion of state remedies.[68] This reading is multiply problematic: The opt-in chapter does not purport to amend the exhaustion requirement and, indeed, seems to incorporate that requirement by reference;[69] section 2264(a) can be read in a manner that is entirely consistent with the exhaustion requirement;[70] and Congress would not likely have intended to abandon the exhaustion requirement and the related procedural advantages it gives to the States in a set of habeas corpus revisions that generally are designed to increase the States' procedural advantages.[71]

---

[68] This is the interpretation given in *dicta* in Lindh v. Murphy, 96 F.3d 856, 862 (7th Cir. 1996) (*en banc*), *rev'd*, 117 S. Ct. 2059 (1997), and endorsed by the dissenting Justices when *Lindh* was reviewed by the Supreme Court. *See* Lindh v. Murphy, 117 S. Ct. 2059, 2070-72 (1997) (Rehnquist, C.J., dissenting) ("Section 2264(b) ... makes sense in light of § 2264(a), which replaces the exhaustion requirement of §§ 2254(b) and (c) with a requirement that federal courts consider (subject to narrow exceptions) only those claims 'raised and decided on the merits in State courts.'"). The Supreme Court majority, however, expressed doubts about the dissent's interpretation, albeit without finally deciding the issue. *See infra* note 71.

[69] Under 28 U.S.C.A. § 2261(a)(1) (West Supp. 1998), the opt-in provisions "shall apply to [specified capital] cases *arising under section 2254*" (emphasis added). *See also supra* note 67 (citing various provisions stating that opt-in actions "arise under" section 2254). Because the exhaustion provisions are among those included in section 2254, *see* 28 U.S.C.A. §§ 2254(b), 2254(c) (West 1994 & Supp. 1998), and because section 2261(a)(1) places no limitations on the *parts* of section 2254 "under" which opt-in cases "aris[e]," there is no reason to read such a limitation into section 2264(a) by excluding the exhaustion provisions. Additionally, another opt-in provision provides that the statute of limitations that applies in opt-in cases "shall be tolled ... (2) from the date on which the first petition for post-conviction review or other collateral relief is filed until the final State court disposition of such petition." *Id.* § 2263. It would hardly make sense for a statute designed to speed up capital habeas corpus proceedings to treat what often amount to *years* of state postconviction proceedings as a safe harbor from AEDPA's *six-month* statute of limitations unless it was the statute itself that often required prisoners to file state postconviction proceedings in order to exhaust state remedies.

[70] Section 2264(a) states that (with three exceptions) "the district court shall only *consider* a claim or claims that have been raised and decided on the merits in State courts" (emphasis added). This language is in no way inconsistent with the without-prejudice *dismissal* (or even the holding in abeyance) of a petition containing unexhausted claims to enable the petitioner to exhaust state remedies. Indeed, 28 U.S.C.A. § 2263 (West Supp. 1998), which tolls the opt-in chapter's statute of limitations during state "post-conviction review," seems to invite just that outcome. *See supra* note 69. Thus, there is nothing in section 2264(a) that would forbid a federal court to take the steps required by the exhaustion provisions in 28 U.S.C.A. §§ 2254(b), 2254(c) (West 1994 & Supp. 1998).

[71] Section 2264(a) creates a preference for claims that only recently became available because of "the Supreme Court's recognition of a new Federal right that is made retroactively applicable," 28 U.S.C.A. § 2264(a)(2) (West Supp. 1998), or the recent discovery of "a factual predicate that could not [previously] have been discovered through the exercise of due diligence," *id.* § 2264(a)(3). *See infra* notes 80-81 and accompanying text. Claims that satisfy these provisions often will have been discovered after state direct appeal and even after the completion of state

postconviction proceedings. Absent an exhaustion requirement, prisoners often will have very little incentive — and very little time, given the short opt-in statute of limitations and its omission of any tolling provision for second and successive state postconviction proceedings, *see* 28 U.S.C.A. § 2263(a) (West Supp. 1998) (discussed *supra* notes 40-44 and accompanying text; *infra* § 5.1b nn.92-122 and accompanying text) — to raise these newly discovered claims in available state court proceedings. Accordingly, were section 2264(a) read to absolve petitioners of having to exhaust available state remedies for newly discovered claims, it would deprive the State of at least three important advantages that are available in nonopt-in habeas corpus cases because of the exhaustion requirement. Two of those advantages have been available to the States since 1886:

- The ability of state courts to consider, and, when applicable, to choose an appropriate remedy for, claimed constitutional violations before a federal court is authorized to do so. *See infra* § 23.1.
- The ability to have the state courts make factual findings that are presumptively binding in later federal habeas corpus proceedings. *See* 28 U.S.C.A. § 2254(e)(1) (West 1994 & Supp. 1998); *infra* §§ 20.2, 20.3, 30.3.

AEDPA gives States a third advantage that accrues only if the petitioner previously chose to raise a federal claim in state court:

- The limitation on federal habeas corpus adjudication of legal claims that previously were "adjudicated on the merits *in State court proceedings.*" 28 U.S.C.A. § 2254(d) (West 1994 & Supp. 1998) (emphasis added); *infra* § 30.2. Although AEDPA purports to extend this advantage to qualifying opt-in States, *see id.* 2264(b) ("Following review [in opt-in cases] subject to *subsection[ ] ... (d) ... of section 2254*, the court shall rule on the claims properly before it." (emphasis added)), opt-in petitioners could entirely neutralize the advantage section 2254(d) gives the state if section 2264(a) let them forgo exhaustion of state remedies. (The same arguably is true of a fourth procedural advantage, section 2254(e)(2)'s limitation of federal habeas corpus hearings. Section 2254(e)(2) purportedly applies in opt-in cases, *see id.* 2264(b) ("Following review [in opt-in cases] subject to *subsection[ ] ... (e) of section 2254*, the court shall rule on the claims properly before it" (emphasis added)), but might well be nullified if opt-in petitioners were under no obligation to present their evidence in state court and, thus, were not to blame for failing to do so. *See infra* § 20.2b.)

Reading the opt-in provisions to deprive States of the three (or four) advantages listed above would seriously undercut the effectiveness of those provisions. This is because opting-in is costly to States; it requires them to fund competent postconviction counsel in all capital state postconviction proceedings. *See supra* § 3.3b nn. 2-6, 15-21 and accompanying text. Because Congress may not force States to bear costs of this sort, *cf.* Printz v. United States, 117 S. Ct. 2365, 2383, 2384 (1997); New York v. United States, 505 U.S. 144 (1992), the only way Chapter 154 could induce them to do so was by giving them a series of procedural and substantive advantages in return for volunteering to bear the costs. Consequently, any reading of section 2264(a) that saddles qualifying States with a series of *dis*advantages would undermine AEDPA's incentive structure by making it more costly than not for States to volunteer. Based on this difficulty, a majority of the Court in *Lindh v. Murphy, supra,* while declining to rule finally on the proper interpretation of section 2264(a), recognized a strong argument against reading it to replace the exhaustion rule:

> There are reasons why the position that § 2264(a) replaces rather than complements §§ 2254(b) and (c) is open to doubt: ... [T]o read § 2264(a) as replacing the exhaustion requirement of §§ 2254(b) and (c) [c]ould mean that in important classes of cases (those in the categories of three § 2264(a) exceptions), the State would not be able to insist on

- Section 2264(a) is most easily and uncontroversially understood as a strict procedural default rule that (with three narrow exceptions) forbids federal consideration of a claim that, as a matter of state law, was not raised in the proper manner or at the proper time in the state courts. Under this reading, federal habeas corpus consideration is forbidden (subject to the three exceptions) if (but only if) the federal claim either: (1) was not previously *"raised ...* in the State courts," and state law prevents the petitioner from raising it now (thus presenting a default, not an exhaustion, problem[72]); or (2) was before the state courts but was not *"decided on the [federal] merits"* by those courts which, instead, denied the claim on the basis of a state procedural ground (*e.g.*, a violation of the State's "contemporaneous objection" rule).[73]

---

exhaustion in the state courts. In cases raising claims of newly discovered evidence, for example, the consequence could be that the State could not prevent the prisoner from going directly to federal court and evading § 2254(e)'s presumption of correctness of state court factual findings as well as § 2254(d)'s new, highly deferential standard for evaluating state court rulings. It is true that a State might be perfectly content with the prisoner's choice to go straight to federal court in some cases, but the State has been free to waive exhaustion to get that result. The State has not explained why Congress would have wanted to deprive the States of the § 2254 exhaustion tools in chapter 154 cases, and we are hard-pressed to come up with a reason, especially considering the Act's apparent general purpose to enhance the States' capacities to control their own adjudications. It would appear that the State's reading of § 2264(a) would also eliminate from chapter 154 cases the provisions of § 2254 that define the exhaustion requirement explicitly as requiring a claim to be raised by any and every available procedure in the State, 28 U.S.C. § 2254(c), that newly authorize federal courts to deny unexhausted claims on the merits, 28 U.S.C. § 2254(b)(2), and that newly require a state's waiver of exhaustion to be shown to be express, 28 U.S.C. § 2254(b)(3). No explanation for why Congress would have wanted to deny the states these advantages is apparent or offered by the parties, which suggests that no such effects were intended at all but that § 2264(a) was meant as a supplement to rather than a replacement for § 2254(b) and (c).

Lindh v. Murphy, supra, 117 S. Ct. at 2066 n.7.

[72] *See infra* §§ 23.1 nn.21-30 and accompanying text, 26.1 n.25 (distinguishing exhaustion and default doctrines).

[73] 28 U.S.C.A. § 2264(a) (West Supp. 1998) (emphasis added). *See infra* §§ 26.1 n.2, 26.2b, 26.2c (discussing procedural miscues that count as defaults as a matter of state law).

Section 2264(a) withholds federal habeas corpus consideration from "claims that have [not] been *raised and decided* on the merits in the State courts, unless the failure to *raise* the claim properly is [within one of three exceptions]." 28 U.S.C.A. § 2264(a) (West Supp. 1998) (emphasis added). It is doubtful that Congress intended the italicized language to enable state courts to deprive capital prisoners who properly "raised" their claims in state court of federal habeas corpus consideration by refusing — for no good state-or-federal-law reason — to "decide [the claim] on the merits." Doing so would be inconsistent with the longstanding rule that exhaustion occurs and procedural default is avoided when claims are properly *raised* in state court proceedings even if the state court chose not to address the claims on the merits. *See infra* §§ 23.3a nn.4-5 and

We proceed here on the assumption that the last of these readings is the most appropriate one and, accordingly, that section 2264(a) does not create a jurisdictional bar to the consideration of specified claims nor rescind the exhaustion doctrine in opt-in cases but, rather, forbids federal habeas corpus consideration of exhausted but defaulted claims. As such, the state may waive section 2264(a). And a federal court may not rely on it to bar either the state from demanding that an unexhausted claim be exhausted or the prisoner from seeking to exhaust a claim that is found not to be exhausted — assuming, in both cases, that the statute of limitations leaves time for exhaustion to occur.[74] On this

---

accompanying text, 26.2c. It also would raise serious constitutional questions under the Due Process Clauses of the Fifth and Fourteenth Amendments and under the Suspension Clause. The far more plausible explanation for the use of the "raised *and decided on the merits*" language — which also explains the provision's omission of any reference to the absence of a "*decision* on the merits" in the provision's immediately following "failure to *raise*" clause — is that the language is meant to keep petitioners from circumventing section 2264(a) by raising claims in state court that are defaulted under state law and then from arguing, notwithstanding the state court's denial of the claim on default (*i.e.*, *non*merits) grounds, that the claim had been "raised ... in the State courts."

[74] It is possible that a state remedy will remain available for a claim not previously exhausted in the state courts but that the petitioner will be unable to take advantage of the state remedy before the expiration of AEDPA's 180-day federal statute of limitations for opt-in cases. *See* 28 U.S.C.A. § 2263 (discussed *supra* notes 40-44 and accompanying text; *infra* § 5.1b). Thus, the prisoner could potentially be whip-sawed between the exhaustion and statute of limitations requirements. This possibility arises because the 180-day limitations period is only tolled during the *litigation* of "the *first* petition for [state] post-conviction review or other collateral relief" but not during the period needed to *prepare* a first state postconviction petition (or, after state postconviction proceedings are completed, to prepare a federal habeas corpus petition) or during the period needed to prepare *or* litigate a *second or subsequent* state postconviction petition permitted under state law. 28 U.S.C.A. § 2263(b)(2) (West Supp. 1998) (emphasis added). The combined application of the statute of limitations and exhaustion requirements to keep a petitioner from receiving habeas corpus consideration only rarely will be appropriate, however, given AEDPA's recodification of the longstanding exception to the exhaustion requirement for "circumstances ... that render [State corrective] process ineffective to protect the rights of the applicant," including, evidently, the applicant's federal habeas corpus "rights." *Id.*, § 2254(b)(1)(B)(ii) (discussed *infra* § 23.4). Were a situation to arise in which the exhaustion of an available state remedy could not occur within the 180-day statute of limitations, the federal court has at least five options: (1) The federal court may conclude that the exhaustion requirement does not apply because requiring exhaustion would bar federal habeas corpus consideration and thus is "ineffective to protect the [federal statutory — and, possibly, the federal constitutional —] rights of the applicant." *Id.* If, on the other hand, the court concludes that state court consideration in the first instance is important, *see* Granberry v. Greer, 481 U.S. 129, 131, 134-35 (1987); *infra* § 23.2a, the court may: (2) grant a 30-day extension of the 180-day limitations period for "good cause," as is permitted by 28 U.S.C.A. § 2263(b)(3) (West Supp. 1998) (discussed *supra* note 44 and accompanying text; *infra* § 5.1b nn.104-05 and accompanying text), assuming that doing so would provide sufficient time for exhaustion; (3) exercise the federal court's discretion to hold the unexhausted federal habeas corpus petition before it in abeyance, in federal court, pending exhaustion proceedings in the state courts (thus preserving the petition's original, and by hypothesis timely, filing date for purposes of the statute of

assumption, section 2264(a)'s procedural default rule is in some respects similar to the preexisting procedural default rule (which courts have continued to apply in noncapital cases, capital cases in nonopt-in States, and section 2255 proceedings[75]). Both the opt-in and preexisting rules are waiveable,[76] and both are unavailable in the event that (1) no default occurred because the petitioner "raised" the claim in state court in accordance with state procedural law,[77] (2) the state court explicitly "decided [the claim] on the merits,"[78] or (3) the state court implicitly decided the claim on the merits by deciding it on the basis of a "nonindependent" state procedural ground.[79]

Although similar, the opt-in procedural default rule and the preexisting rule differ in regard to the exceptions they recognize to the rule of preclusion for claims that were defaulted in the state courts. Under section 2264(a), federal

---

limitations), *see infra* §§ 13.3a, 13.3b; or (4) accept the state's express waiver of the exhaustion requirement (assuming an express waiver is made), as AEDPA authorizes, 28 U.S.C.A. § 2254(b)(3) (West 1994 & Supp. 1998); *see Granberry v. Greer, supra; infra* § 23.2a. Or (5) when appropriate under the circumstances, the court might find that the petitioner's failure to discover the unexhausted claim is inexcusable (a relatively unlikely event, given our assumption here that a state remedy remains open, because a prisoner's inexcusable neglect in discovering a claim typically renders state postconviction remedies *un*available) and, thus, that the petitioner himself is to blame for not "protect[ing his] rights" and that none of the previous four solutions to the problem is warranted. Obviously, if the federal court finds that an unexhausted claim fits within any of the exceptions to section 2264(a)'s default rule, *see infra* notes 80-81 and accompanying text, because the claim previously could not reasonably have been discovered or asserted, the fifth option above will not be available. The possibility addressed here illustrates why prisoners should avoid using up the entire 180-day period (notwithstanding how short it is) before filing a first federal habeas corpus petition, so as to leave some time to file a state postconviction petition and, thereafter, an amended federal habeas corpus petition in the event that the first petition is found to contain unexhausted claims.

[75] *See, e.g.*, Truesdale v. Moore, 142 F.3d 749, 753 n.2 (4th Cir. 1998) ("We reject Truesdale's novel suggestion that AEDPA somehow abolished procedural default in all cases not governed by Chapter 154."); Moleterno v. Nelson, 114 F.3d 629, 633-34 (7th Cir. 1997) ("the substantive changes in § 2254(d) made by the Antiterrorism and Effective Death Penalty Act of 1996 ... made no change in the procedural default rules"). For further discussion of AEDPA's apparent retention of the pre-AEDPA doctrine of procedural default, see *infra* § 26.1 n.10 and accompanying text.

[76] *See infra* § 26.2a.

[77] 28 U.S.C.A. § 2264(a) (West Supp. 1998); *see infra* §§ 26.2b, 26.2c.

[78] 28 U.S.C.A. § 2264(a) (West Supp. 1998); *see infra* § 26.2e.

[79] As is discussed *infra* § 26.2d nn.23-54 and accompanying text, some state procedural rules allow a default to be found only, *e.g.*, if the underlying claim is not sufficiently "fundamental," meaning that it does not present a constitutional violation. In such cases, a determination that the claim is defaulted at least impliedly embodies a conclusion that the claim does not present a constitutional violation. That conclusion amounts to a "deci[sion] on the merits" sufficient to avoid a default cognizable under section 2264(a).

habeas corpus consideration of a defaulted claim is available only if the petitioner shows that "the failure to raise the claim properly [in state court] is —

(1) the result of State action in violation of the Constitution or laws of the United States;

(2) the result of the Supreme Court's recognition of a new Federal right that is made retroactively applicable; or

(3) based on a factual predicate that could not have been discovered through the exercise of due diligence in time to present the claim for State or Federal post-conviction review."[80]

These three exceptions resemble some of the primary bases for establishing "cause" under the preexisting procedural default rule, which courts continue to apply in effect in nonopt-in cases and assuredly will influence the interpretation of the new opt-in default rule.[81] There are significant differences, however: The opt-in provisions' exception for obstruction by state law, state judges, or other state officials, unlike the analogue under the preexisting rule,[82] is limited to "State action" that amounts to "a violation of the Constitution or laws of the United States";[83] the opt-in provisions' exception for claims that previously were legally unavailable differs from its preexisting analogue[84] in that it can only be triggered by newly announced decisions of the Supreme Court and not by newly announced decisions of the lower federal courts; and the opt-in provisions' exception for previously unavailable factual bases, unlike its preexisting analogue,[85] incorporates a "due diligence" standard.[86] Although section

---

[80] 28 U.S.C.A. § 2264(a) (West Supp. 1998). For discussion of the "due diligence" standard, see *supra* note 64.

[81] *See infra* § 26.3b. For discussion of Congress' assumed retention of the preexisting procedural default rule in nonopt-in cases, see *supra* note 75 and accompanying text; *infra* § 26.1 n.10 and accompanying text.

[82] *See infra* § 26.3b n.33.

[83] 28 U.S.C.A. § 2264(a) (West Supp. 1998). Section 2264(a)'s "State action" language encompasses ineffective assistance of counsel in violation of the 6th Amendment, *see* Murray v. Carrier, 477 U.S. 478, 488 (1986); *infra* § 26.3b nn.34-37; *see also infra* § 26.3b nn.38-41, and also defaults found on the basis of "inadequate" state procedural rules, *see infra* § 26.2d nn.23-54 and accompanying text. Although only a subset of the bases for finding state procedural rules to be "inadequate" under the preexisting procedural default rule amount to violations of the United States Constitution or statutes, *see id.*, all of those bases are derived from longstanding federal common law. *See, e.g.*, Rogers v. Alabama, 192 U.S. 226 (1904); Daniel J. Meltzer, *State Court Forfeitures of Federal Rights*, 99 HARV. L. REV. 1128 (1986). Consequently, all such bases might qualify as "violation[s] of the ... laws of the United States." 28 U.S.C.A. § 2264(a) (West Supp. 1998).

[84] *See infra* 26.3b n.27.

[85] *See infra* § 26.3b n.28.

[86] For further discussion of AEDPA's "due diligence" standard, see *supra* note 64.

2264(a)'s list of exceptions is shorter than the roster of circumstances amounting to "cause" for a procedural default under the preexisting rule,[87] the opt-in rule, unlike the preexisting one, requires no showing of "prejudice" as a prerequisite for federal court review of a procedurally defaulted claim.[88] The opt-in rule also appears to omit the preexisting exception for manifest miscarriages of justice.[89] It remains to be seen, however, whether the federal courts will countenance the execution of a capital petitioner who defaulted a meritorious claim in state court but can demonstrate a manifest miscarriage of justice by showing that he was unconstitutionally convicted and is more likely than not innocent,[90] or that he was unconstitutionally condemned and is very likely is innocent.[91]

§ 3.4.   AEDPA's applicability to cases filed before and after April 24, 1996.

The applicability of the Antiterrorism and Effective Death Penalty Act's (AEDPA's) habeas corpus and section 2255 provisions to particular classes of cases is most effectively discussed by distinguishing among three categories of cases defined in part by whether or not they were filed on or before the date AEDPA was signed into law, April 24, 1996 (the "enactment date"), and in part by whether they are governed exclusively by Chapter 153 of the habeas corpus statute ("Chapter 153 cases") or instead are at least partly governed by Chapter 154 ("Chapter 154 cases").[1]

---

[87] *See infra* § 26.3b.

[88] For discussion of the "prejudice" requirement, see *infra* § 26.3c.

[89] *See infra* § 26.4.

[90] *Cf.* Calderon v. Thompson, 118 S. Ct. 1489, 1501-02 (1998) (relying, by analogy, on AEDPA provision relaxing procedural limitation in cases of innocence and on "AEDPA's central concern that the merits of concluded criminal cases not be revisited in the absence of a strong showing of actual innocence" to fashion common law "miscarriage of justice" standard (explicitly derived from Court's preexisting procedural default jurisprudence) to govern circuit court's consideration of whether to recall mandate *sua sponte* in federal habeas corpus cases not governed by AEDPA); Schlup v. Delo, 513 U.S. 298 (1995) (pre-AEDPA case defining common law "miscarriage of justice" standard for excusing procedural default by federal habeas corpus petitioner who is more likely than not innocent); *supra* §§ 2.5 (discussing impact of innocence on otherwise preclusive doctrines), 3.2 n.43 (discussing *Calderon v. Thompson*); *infra* §§ 26.4 (discussing standard for manifest miscarriages of justice), 38.2d (discussing recall of the mandate and *Calderon v. Thompson*).

[91] *Cf. Calderon v. Thompson, supra,* 118 S. Ct. at 1501-02 (discussed *supra* note 90); Sawyer v. Whitley, 505 U.S. 333 (1992) (pre-AEDPA case defining common law "miscarriage of justice" standard for excusing procedural default by habeas corpus petitioner who is "'actually innocent' of a death sentence" as revealed by clear and convincing evidence of his innocence); *supra* § 2.5; *infra* § 26.4.

§ 3.4 [1] For a description of the differences between Chapter 153 cases and Chapter 154 cases, see *supra* § 3.2. For discussion of whether Chapter 153 supersedes or incorporates Chapter 153, see *supra* § 32 n.34 and accompanying text.

a. *Chapter 153 cases filed on or before April 24, 1996.* The first category of cases consists of federal postconviction actions that were filed in a federal district court prior to April 24, 1996, and arise exclusively under the provisions of Chapter 153 of the habeas corpus statute[2] — meaning any and all preenactment applications for federal habeas corpus or section 2255 relief filed by state or federal prisoners *except* applications filed by state capital prisoners that challenge convictions or death sentences imposed by a State that has qualified for "opt-in" status as to that case.[3] As the Supreme Court ruled in *Lindh v. Murphy*,[4] Congress intended to immunize *all* cases falling within this large category of preenactment cases from the application of *all* the habeas corpus and section 2255 revisions made by AEDPA.[5]

---

[2] 28 U.S.C.A. §§ 2241-55 (West 1994 & Supp. 1998).

[3] For discussion of AEDPA's "opt-in" provisions and the States to which they apply, see *supra* § 3.2 nn.3, 28-34, and *supra* § 3.3.

[4] 117 S. Ct. 2059 (1997).

[5] *See id.* at 2063-68. Although *Lindh* was a section 2254 case, the Court's analysis in *Lindh* necessarily applies to section 2255 cases as well. *See, e.g.*, United States v. Marmolejos, 140 F.2d 488, 490 (3d Cir. 1998) (section 2255 movant "was not subject to the new restrictions on successive habeas petitions contained in the [AEDPA], because his second habeas petition was filed five days prior to the April 24, 1996, date on which the Act took effect."); Torres v. United States, 140 F.3d 392, 400 n.6 (2d Cir. 1998) ("petitioners like Torres who filed section 2255 motions before April 24, 1996 are not required to [follow AEDPA requirement of] obtain[ing] a Certificate of Appealability to appeal the denial of their motions"); United States v. Ramos-Rodriguez, 136 F.3d 465, 466-67 (5th Cir. 1998) ("Because Rodriguez filed both section 2255 motions prior to April 24, 1996, the [AEDPA] does not apply to his claims."); David v. United States, 134 F.3d 470, 473 n.1 (1st Cir. 1998) ("The Supreme Court has determined [in *Lindh*], in general, that AEDPA does not apply to habeas petitions that were pending on AEDPA's effective date.... We believe that this rationale applies to section 2255 motions (which are, after all, a species of habeas petitions). Thus, we measure the petitioner's case against pre-AEDPA benchmarks.").

Prior to the decision in *Lindh*, the lower courts were split on the question of AEDPA's applicability to the category of cases filed on or before April 24, 1996. *See* Love v. Morton, 944 F. Supp. 379, 380 n.1 (D.N.J. 1996) ("majority view on retroactivity" is that "1996 amendments should not apply to non[opt-in] actions pending on the date of enactment"); Satcher v. Netherland, 944 F. Supp. 1222, 1247 (E.D. Va. 1996), *aff'd in part & rev'd in part*, 126 F.3d 561 (4th Cir.), *cert. denied*, 118 S. Ct. 595 (1997) ("overwhelming majority of federal courts ... have held that [nonopt-in portions of Act] are not applicable to pending petitions"). Cases anticipating *Lindh's* holding include, *e.g.*, Jeffries v. Wood, 114 F.3d 1484, 1493-501 (9th Cir. 1997) (*en banc*), *cert. denied*, 118 S. Ct. 586 (1997); Jeffries v. Wood, 103 F.3d 827, 827 (9th Cir. 1996) (*en banc*); United States v. Martin, 1997 WL 57153, at *2 (10th Cir. Feb. 12, 1997); Cawley v. Dorsey, 1997 WL 57086, at *1 n.1 (10th Cir. Feb. 11, 1997); Colby v. Thomas, 1997 WL 57078, at *1 n.2 (10th Cir. Feb. 11, 1997); Wiedemer v. Marr, 1997 WL 44934, at *1 n.2 (10th Cir. Feb. 5, 1997); Johnson v. Hill, 1997 WL 9755, at *1 n.* (4th Cir. Jan. 13, 1997); United States v. Sanchez, 1997 WL 8842, at *1 n.1 (10th Cir. Jan. 10, 1997); United States v. Zeigler, 1997 WL 4281, at *1 n.1 (10th Cir. Jan. 7, 1997); United States v. Price, 1996 WL 709938, at *1 n.1 (10th Cir. Dec. 11, 1996); United States v. Fykes, 1996 WL 699762, at *1 n.1 (10th Cir. Dec. 5, 1996); Ontiveros v. Dorsey, 1996 WL 603276, at *1 n.1 (10th Cir. Oct. 22, 1996), *cert. denied*, 117 S. Ct. 1116 (1997);

Vann v. Oklahoma, 1996 WL 375355, at *3 n.1 (10th Cir., July 5, 1996); Vasquez v. Neal, 1996 WL 369452, at *3 n.1 (10th Cir. July 3, 1996), *cert. denied*, 117 S. Ct. 616 (1996); Burkett v. Love, 89 F.3d 135, 138 (3d Cir. 1996). Some of these decisions concluded that section 107(c) revealed Congress' intent to apply most portions of AEDPA only to newly filed cases. *See, e.g.*, *Jeffries v. Wood, supra* at 1494-97; Edens v. Hannigan, 87 F.3d 1109, 1112 n.1 (10th Cir. 1996) (followed in Williamson v. Ward, 110 F.3d 1508 (10th Cir. 1997); Sena v. New Mexico State Prison, 109 F.3d 652, 653 (10th Cir. 1997); Acker v Colorado, 1996 WL 731492, at *1 n.1 (10th Cir. Dec. 20, 1996); Marquez v. Dorsey, 1996 WL 639840, at *1 n.1 (10th Cir. Nov. 6, 1996); United States v. Capadona, 1996 WL 637226, at *1 (10th Cir. Nov. 5, 1996); Bouwkamp v. Shillinger, 1996 WL 582733, at *1 n.1 (10th Cir. Oct. 10, 1996)); Herrera v. United States, 96 F.3d 1010, 1011-12 (7th Cir. 1996); Williams v. Calderon, 83 F.3d 281, 286 (9th Cir. 1996) (followed in Moore v. White, 1996 WL 478681, at *2 & n.1 (N.D. Cal. Aug. 19, 1996)); Gentry v. Trippett, 956 F. Supp. 1320 (E.D. Mich. 1997); Brewster v. Kirby, 954 F. Supp. 1155, 1158-59 (N.D. W. Va. 1997); Belle v. Stepanik, 1996 WL 663872, at *3 n.2 (E.D. Pa. Nov. 14, 1996); Hamblin v. Anderson, 947 F. Supp. 1179, 1182-83 (N.D. Ohio 1996); Turner v. Love, 1996 WL 622762, at *1 n.2 (E.D. Pa. Oct. 24, 1996); *Satcher v. Netherland, supra* at 1246-49; Johnston v. Love, 940 F. Supp. 738, 743 n.2 (E.D. Pa. 1996), *aff'd*, 118 F.3d 1576 (3d Cir.), *cert denied*, 118 S. Ct. 425 (1997); Cockrum v. Johnson, 934 F. Supp. 1417, 1423-24 (E.D. Tex. 1996), *rev'd on other grounds*, 1997 WL 425940 (5th Cir. July 29, 1997); Wilkins v. Bowersox, 933 F. Supp. 1496, 1505-06 (W.D. Mo. 1996); Warner v. United States, 926 F. Supp. 1387, 1390 n.4 (E.D. Ark. 1996).

Other decisions concluded that Congress' intent in regard to the applicability of most of AEDPA's provisions to preenactment cases was unclear but that (i) a particular provision of the statute had a "retroactive" effect because it attached new consequences to events occurring before the statute went into effect, and thus that (ii) the provision was subject to the rule of Landgraf v. U.S.I. Film Prod., 511 U.S. 244 (1994), barring the application of new legislation when doing so would have a "retroactive" effect and when the statute in question (as is true of AEDPA's nonopt-in provisions) omits any clear directive to apply its provisions in that "retroactive" manner. *See, e.g.*, Lindh v. Murphy, 96 F.3d 856, 867 (7th Cir. 1996) (*en banc*), *rev'd on other ground*, 117 S. Ct. 2059 (1997) (new statute of limitations in 28 U.S.C. § 2244(d) cannot be applied to bar habeas corpus relief under certain circumstances because doing so would attach new consequences to preenactment event); Burris v. Parke, 95 F.3d 465, 468-69 (7th Cir. 1996) (*en banc*) (applications of successive petition restrictions in 28 U.S.C. § 2244(b) that would attach new consequences to preenactment events are barred); Reyes v. Keane, 90 F.3d 676, 679 (2d Cir. 1996), *overruled in part*, Nelson v. Walker, 121 F.3d 828 (2d Cir. 1997) (statute of limitations in 28 U.S.C. § 2244(d) cannot be applied to previously filed case because it would have "retroactive effect that Congress has not sanctioned," but restriction on habeas corpus appeals in *id.* § 2253 can be applied to a previously filed case because it attaches no new consequence to any preenactment event); Boria v. Keane, 90 F.3d 36, 37 (2d Cir. 1996) (application of adjudication standard in 28 U.S.C. § 2254(d) to pending case would have "retroactive" effect and is forbidden); Hill v. Straub, 950 F. Supp. 807, 808-09 (E.D. Mich. 1997) (same conclusion re: successive petition provision in 28 U.S.C. § 2244(b)(3)); Thatsaphone v. Class, No. 95-4244 (D.S.D. June 11, 1996), at 7 (same conclusion re: amendments governing adjudication standards and hearings in 28 U.S.C. §§ 2254(d) and 2254(e)); *see also* United States ex rel. Jones v. Gilmore, 945 F. Supp. 158, 161 (N.D. Ill. 1996) (because applying AEDPA's complicated provisions would require appointment of counsel to assist *pro se* petitioner, court decides not to apply Act to case filed before enactment date).

Cases concluding (contrary to the Supreme Court's subsequent holding in *Lindh*) that some or all of AEDPA's provisions *did* apply to nonopt-in cases filed before April 24, 1996, include:

Lindh's rationale is straightforward. AEDPA's section 107(c) explicitly provides that the statute's special procedures for the subset of *capital* prisoners

---

Martin v. Bissonette, 1997 WL 280602, at *4-*6 (1st Cir. May 29, 1997), *vac'd in light of* Lindh, 118 F.3d 871, 874 n.3 (1st Cir. 1997) (same as *Drinkard v. Johnson, infra*); Lozada v. United States, 107 F.3d 1011, 1016-17 (2d Cir. 1997) (applying Act's new certificate of appealability provision to appeal filed after enactment date in case filed before that date); Lyons v. Ohio Adult Parole Auth., 105 F.3d 1063, 1066-76 (6th Cir.), *cert. denied*, 117 S. Ct. 1724 (1997) (Congress' failure to specify effective date of legislation requires that reviewing court assess "whether applying [particular provision of AEDPA] to ... petition would have retroactive effect"; § 2253's certificate of appealability requirement does not have such an effect "at least so far as this case is concerned" and therefore may be applied; requiring petitioner to "meet a higher burden under the new Act would raise obvious retroactivity concerns under *Landgraf*"); United States v. Orozco, 103 F.3d 389 (5th Cir. 1996) (same as *Lozada v. United States, supra*; section 2255 case); Hunter v. United States, 101 F.3d 1565, 1568-73 (11th Cir. 1996) (*en banc*), *cert. denied*, 117 S. Ct. 1695 (1997) (AEDPA's omission of "clear legislative intent about [its] application ... to pending cases" requires analysis under *Landgraf* of whether particular provision would have impermissible retroactive effect; concluding that certificate of appealability provisions may be applied to cases that were pending on appeal or in which an application for certificate of probable cause was pending at time of enactment); Moore v. Johnson, 101 F.3d 1069, 1072-74 (5th Cir. 1996), *vac'd in light of* Lindh, 117 S. Ct. 2054 (1997) (applying *Drinkard v. Johnson, infra* to conclude that 28 U.S.C. § 2254(d) can be applied to case in which appeal from district court's grant of writ was pending at time of AEDPA's enactment); Drinkard v. Johnson, 97 F.3d 751, 765-66 (5th Cir. 1996), *cert. denied*, 117 S. Ct. 1114 (1997), *overruled*, United States v. Carter, 117 F.3d 262 (5th Cir. 1997) (because Congress has not "expressly prescribed" effective date of legislation, reviewing court must determine whether application of particular provision to case would have improperly retroactive effect; concluding that adjudication standard in 28 U.S.C. § 2254(d) does not have that effect, nor do appealability restrictions in *id.* § 2253 when applied to appeal filed after effective date of Act); *Lindh v. Murphy, supra,* 96 F.3d at 861-67 (adjudication standard in 28 U.S.C. § 2254(d)(1) applies to previously filed cases because its application does not have retroactive effect); *Reyes v. Keane, supra* at 679-80 (restrictions on appealability in 28 U.S.C. § 2253 apply to previously filed cases); Lennox v. Evans, 87 F.3d 431, 433 (10th Cir. 1996) (same as *Lozada v. United States, supra*); Scott v. Anderson, 958 F. Supp. 330, 334 (N.D. Ohio 1997) (application of adjudication standard in section 2254(d) would not have impermissible retroactive effect); Cowan v. Artuz, 1996 WL 631726, at *5 (S.D.N.Y. Oct. 24, 1996) (exhaustion provision in 28 U.S.C. § 2254(b) does not attach new consequences to preenactment events, hence may be applied to previously filed cases); Perez v. Marshall, 946 F. Supp. 1521, 1527-31 (S.D. Cal. 1996) (adjudication standard in 28 U.S.C. § 2254(d) applies to previously filed cases); Leavitt v. Arave, 927 F. Supp. 394 (D. Idaho 1996) (Act's overall policies call for retroactive application of all of its provisions).

As is revealed by the Supreme Court and 1st Circuit orders, noted above, vacating *Moore v. Johnson, supra,* and *Martin v. Bissonette, supra,* the decisions cited in the immediately preceding paragraph and other decisions relying on them are no longer good law on the proposition for which they are cited. *See also, e.g., United States v. Carter, supra* at 264 & n.1 (overruling decisions in *Drinkard v. Johnson, supra, United States v. Orozco, supra,* "and their progeny"); Tucker v. Johnson, 115 F.3d 276, 278-81 nn.3-4 (5th Cir.), *cert. denied*, 118 S. Ct. 605 (1997) (same); Holmes v. Wyoming Dep't of Corrections, 1997 WL 368331, at *1 & n.1 (10th Cir. July 3, 1997) (overruling *Lennox v. Evans, supra*); *see also Lindh, supra,* 117 S. Ct. at 2062, 2063-68 (rejecting holding and analysis of *Hunter v. United States, supra*).

in qualifying *opt-in States*, codified in Chapter *154* of the Judicial Code, "shall apply to cases pending on or after the date of enactment of this Act."[6] AEDPA does not state, however, that any of its amendments to the generally applicable habeas corpus and section 2255 provisions in Chapter *153* of the Judicial Code are similarly applicable to cases pending when the statute became law. By dividing AEDPA's habeas corpus and section 2255 reforms into two chapters (153 and 154), but making only one chapter (154) applicable to "cases pending on ... the date of enactment of [the 1996] Act," section 107(c) revealed Congress' intent to keep the other chapter (153) from applying to "cases pending on ... the date of enactment." As *Lindh* stated its holding:

> We read this provision of § 107(c), expressly applying [the capital opt-in] chapter 154 to all cases pending at enactment, as indicating implicitly that the amendments to chapter 153 were assumed and meant to apply to the general run of habeas cases [i.e., *non*opt-in cases] only when those cases had been filed after the date of the Act.[7]

Section 107(c)'s and *Lindh*'s straightforward distinction between preenactment cases arising under Chapter 153 (to which AEDPA does not apply) and preenactment cases arising under Chapter 154 (to which some, but not all, parts of AEDPA *do*, presumptively,[8] apply) makes for an easily administrable bright-line rule. Three principles must be followed, however, in order to keep the line bright:

- The line that section 107(c) and *Lindh* draw is between categories of *cases*, *not* categories of *statutory provisions*. If a preenactment federal postconviction case arises under Chapter 154 because it is (1) a capital case (2) to which the opt-in provisions in 28 U.S.C. § 2261-66 apply, then AEDPA presumptively applies to the case (*i.e.*, it applies absent unauthorized "retroactive" effects). Otherwise — *i.e.*, if the preenactment federal postconviction case arises exclusively under Chapter *153* (28 U.S.C. §§ 2241-55) — AEDPA does *not* apply. (It is not helpful to treat the bright

---

[6] Antiterrorism and Effective Death Penalty Act of 1996, § 107(c), Pub. L. 104-132, 110 Stat. 1214 (1996). Section 3.2 *supra* more comprehensively discusses the relationship and differences between Chapters 153 and 154 of the Judicial Code.

[7] *Lindh, supra*, 117 S. Ct. at 2063; *accord id.* at 2064 ("If, then, Congress was reasonably concerned to ensure that chapter 154 be applied to pending cases, it should have been just as concerned about chapter 153, unless it had the different intent that the latter chapter not be applied to the general run of [*i.e.*, nonopt-in] pending cases. Nothing, indeed, but a different intent explains [section 107(c)'s] different treatment [of Chapters 153 and 154].").

[8] *But cf. supra* §§ 3.2 n.34, 3.3c nn.65-73 and accompanying text (certain Chapter *153* provisions may not apply to certain preenactment (and postenactment) capital opt-in cases); *infra* § 3.4b (certain Chapter *154* provisions may not apply to certain preenactment (and postenactment) cases).

line as if it divides statutory provisions, rather than cases, nor to treat the line as always bright insofar as Chapter 154 cases are concerned. There may be some Chapter 153 amendments that *do* apply to preenactment capital opt-in cases (because they are incorporated by reference in, and thus are made retroactively applicable by section 107(c) of, Chapter 154),[9] and some Chapter 154 provisions that do *not* apply to preenactment Chapter 154 cases (because they have unauthorized "retroactive effects").[10])

- The only preenactment cases to which section 107(c) and *Lindh* permit AEDPA to apply are the subset of capital habeas corpus cases as to which the State has qualified for opt-in treatment. In other words, the bright line is *not* between noncapital and capital cases but between nonopt-in cases (some of which are noncapital, others of which are capital) and opt-in cases (all of which happen to be capital).[11] This point has an additional implication:

---

[9] *See infra* § 3.4c n.53 and accompanying text.

[10] *See infra* § 3.4c.

[11] In one passage in *Lindh* (reprised in the syllabus to the case, which, however, has no precedential significance), the Court uses the phrase "noncapital cases" as a proxy for "nonopt-in cases": "The issue in this case is whether that new section of the statute dealing with petitions for habeas corpus governs applications in *noncapital cases* that were already pending when the Act was passed. We hold that it does not." *Lindh*, *supra*, 117 S. Ct. at 2061 (emphasis added). This passage is accurate as far as it goes, because all noncapital cases also are nonopt-in cases. And the passage is sensible in context, because the *Lindh* petitioner was challenging a noncapital conviction. *See id.* at 2062 (Court's precedents must be interpreted in "context"). But the passage is an incomplete summary of section 107(c) and the remainder of the Court's analysis, which exempt all nonopt-in preenactment cases from AEDPA's provisions, including not only all noncapital preenactment cases but also a high proportion of capital preenactment cases. This point is clearly made in the two passages from *Lindh* quoted *supra* note 7 and accompanying text, and also a third passage:

> The upshot is that our analysis accords more coherence to § 107(c) and [28 U.S.C. §] 2264(b) than any rival we have examined. That is enough. We hold that the negative implication of § 107(c) is that the new provisions of chapter 153 generally apply only to *cases filed after the Act became effective.* Because Lindh's case is not one of these, we reverse the judgment of the Court of Appeals and remand the case for further proceedings consistent with this opinion.

Lindh, *supra*, 117 S. Ct. at 2068 (emphasis added). This passage, comprising the last paragraph of the majority opinion and containing its formal holding, applies that holding to *all* preenactment *nonopt-in* cases, *i.e.*, all "cases filed [before] the Act became effective" that are governed by "the new provisions of Chapter 153." It makes no distinction between capital and noncapital cases. (Its statement that the chapter 153 amendments "*generally* apply only to cases filed" after enactment simply recognizes a point made in text and developed *infra* § 3.4c n.53 and accompanying text: Although the Chapter 153 amendments apply to none of the general run of preenactment habeas corpus cases (*i.e.*, cases governed exclusively by Chapter 153), they may apply to some of the preenactment capital opt-in cases governed by Chapter 154's "Special Habeas Corpus Procedures.") *See also Lindh*, *supra*, 117 S. Ct. at 2063 (noting (i) that under section 107(c), only "'Chapter 154 ... shall apply to cases pending on ... the date of enactment'" and (ii) that Chapter

Because Chapter 154's opt-in provisions only apply to *state* prisoners, the bright line rule places all postconviction actions brought by *federal* prisoners (including federal *capital* prisoners) within the category of preenactment cases to which AEDPA does *not* apply.

• The bright line that section 107(c) draws distinguishes *"cases pending on ... the date of enactment* of this Act"[12] from cases that were not pending on that date but were filed thereafter. A federal habeas corpus or section 2255 "case []" was "pending" on a particular date as long as it was *filed* in the United States District Court on or before that date.[13] Thus, the new

154 is "applicable only if the State meets *certain conditions*, including provision for appointment of postconviction counsel in state proceedings" (emphasis added), thus making clear that the provisions section 107(c) makes applicable to preenactment cases govern only the *subset* of capital cases that "meet [specified] conditions"); *id.* at 2066-67 (distinguishing "pending case [that] is also an *expedited* capital case *subject to chapter 154*" (emphasis added) from all other pending cases — again making clear that the preenactment cases to which section 107(c) applies are not *all* capital cases but only the subset of capital cases that are "expedited" because "subject to [the qualifying conditions in] chapter 154"); *see also* Green v. Johnson, 116 F.3d 1115, 1119-20 (5th Cir. 1997) ("chapter 154 is apposite to capital cases *only* where states have elected to opt in and have qualified to participate by meeting the requirements of [28 U.S.C. § 2261]" (emphasis added)).

Court of appeals decisions applying *Lindh* to forbid AEDPA's application to capital nonopt-in cases filed before April 24, 1996, include, *e.g.*, Cannon v. Johnson, 134 F.3d 683, 684 & n.1 (5th Cir. 1998) (AEDPA does not apply to case because capital prisoner filed "petition in the district court before enactment of the AEDPA" and Texas has not qualified for opt-in treatment by "institut[ing] a system of representation that complies with the relevant requirements"); Noland v. French, 134 F.3d 208, 212 (4th Cir. 1998) ("Nothing in *Lindh* supports ... [State's] argument" that *Lindh* should be limited to noncapital cases; "*Lindh* requires us to use the pre-AEDPA standard of review in a capital case pending in federal court at the time the AEDPA was signed into law."); Gochicoa v. Johnson, 118 F.3d 440, 444 n.4 (5th Cir. 1997), *cert. denied*, 118 S. Ct. 1063 (1998) (*Lindh* renders AEPDA inapplicable to "cases not subject to chapter 154, whether capital or noncapital, pending on the date of enactment of the AEDPA"); Tucker v. Johnson, 115 F.3d 276, 278 (5th Cir.), *cert. denied*, 118 S. Ct. 605 (1997) ("Since the panel opinion was issued in this [capital] case ..., the Supreme Court has held ...[Chapter 153] of the Antiterrorism and Effective Death Penalty Act ("AEDPA") of 1996 (codified at 28 U.S.C. §§ 2244, 2253-2254), inapplicable to habeas corpus petitions filed before the act's effective date of April 24, 1996. As petitioner's habeas petition pre-dated the act, she is not subject to it." (citation and footnote omitted)); *Green v. Johnson, supra* at 1120 ("Because the State of Texas has not yet qualified for the expedited procedures governing habeas petitions in capital cases, chapter 154 does not apply to the instant case. Thus, in light of *Lindh*'s explication that 'the negative implication of § 107(c) is that the new provisions of chapter 153 generally apply only to cases filed after the act,' and given that Green filed the instant petition before the April 24, 1996, effective date of the [AEDPA], we apply pre-[AEDPA] habeas law to his claims." (citation and footnote omitted)).

[12] Antiterrorism and Effective Death Penalty Act of 1996, § 107(c), Pub. L. 104-132, 110 Stat. 1214 (1996).

[13] *See, e.g., Lindh, supra*, 117 S. Ct. at 2061 ("on July 9, 1992, [Lindh] *filed* a habeas corpus application in the *United States District Court*" (emphasis added)); *id.* at 2063 (AEDPA applies only to "such *cases* as were *filed* after the statute's enactment" (emphasis added)); *id.* at

provisions do not apply to nonopt-in cases that were filed in the district court before (and also, rather clearly, *on*) April 24, 1996,[14] whether or not the new

---

("amendments to chapter 153 were assumed and meant to apply to the general run of habeas *cases* only when those cases had been *filed* after the date of the Act" (emphasis added)); *id.* at 2068 ("new provisions of chapter 153 generally apply only to *cases filed* after the Act became effective" (emphasis added)). *See also, e.g.,* United States v. Marmolejos, 140 F.2d 488, 490 (3d Cir. 1998) (section 2255 movant "was not subject to the new restrictions on successive habeas petitions contained in the [AEDPA], because his second habeas petition was filed five days prior to the April 24, 1996, date on which the Act took effect."); Williams v. Vaughn, 1998 WL 217532, at *1 (E.D. Pa. March 18, 1998) (rejecting state's attempt to distinguish *Lindh* on ground that district court had not yet ruled on merits as of April 24, 1996, whereas *Lindh* case was already on appeal on that date; "[t]he Supreme Court's holding in *Lindh* is quite clear" and renders AEDPA inapplicable to any case "'filed'" on or before April 24, 1996); Whitmore v. Avery, 1998 WL 271800, at *3 (D. Neb. March 4, 1998) ("The district court clerk received Whitmore's second § 2254 motion on April 5, 1996, a few weeks before the AEDPA went into effect.... [H]owever, this petition was filed erroneously as part of a previous habeas corpus action, [and] was not correctly filed as a new cause of action ... until October 23, 1996.... Therefore, in accordance with the recent Supreme Court decision, Lindh v. Murphy, 117 S. Ct. 2059 (1997), I find that the AEDPA should not be applied to Whitmore's second petition, as that petition was pending when the AEDPA became effective."). *Cf.* United States v. Nguyen, 997 F. Supp. 1281, 1287-88 (C.D. Cal. 1998) (for purposes of calculating whether petitioner complied with AEDPA's statute of limitations, clerk's three-day delay in filing pleading could not be counted against petitioner). *See also infra* § 5.1b n.57 (discussing "mailbox rule" that governs determinations of date of filing of pleading by incarcerated prisoner).

[14] The status of a case filed *on* April 24, 1996 presents interesting questions. If the district court clerk indicated the *time* of day on which the petition was filed on April 24, 1996, and if that time is prior to the time of that day when the President signed AEDPA into law, the case would seem to have been "pending" when the Act became law. More broadly, the negative implication that *Lindh* draws from section 107(c)'s application of AEDPA to Chapter 154 "cases pending on ... the date of enactment" is that the new statute does *not* apply to Chapter 153 cases "pending" on that same "date." *See Lindh, supra,* 117 S. Ct. at 2063-68. Because April 24, 1996, is the "*date* of enactment," therefore, any Chapter 153 case filed on April 24, 1996 would seem to have been "pending *on* ... the date of enactment" and, thus, to be subject to the negative implication that Chapter 153 does not apply. By holding that "the amendments to chapter 153 were assumed and meant to apply to the general run of habeas cases only when those cases had been filed *after* the date of the Act," the *Lindh* Court rather clearly accorded cases filed *on* that date the same treatment as cases filed *before* that date. *Id.* at 2063 (emphasis added). This conclusion is supported by Fed. R. Civ. P. 6(a), which presumptively applies in habeas corpus cases and section 2255 cases, *see* Rule 11 of the Rules Governing § 2254 Cases; Rule 12 of the Rules Governing § 2255 Proceedings. Under Civil Rule 6(a), "[i]n computing any period of time prescribed or allowed by ... any applicable statute, the day of the ... event ... from which the designated period of time begins to run shall not be included." Under *Lindh,* the determinative event "after" which AEDPA applies is the day AEDPA became law, April 24, 1996. Civil Rule 6(a) thus seems to provide that nothing occurring that day may be considered in deciding whether a filing occurred "after" that event. *Cf.* Flannigan v. Johnson, 1998 WL 556280, at *6 (5th Cir. Sept. 1, 1998) (under Civil Rule 6(a), the day of AEDPA's adoption does not count in determining whether a petition was filed within one year after

the statute became law). For discussions of what day actually qualifies as the day habeas corpus or section 2255 papers are "filed" in the district court, see *infra* §§ 5.1b n.57, 35.2a.

The *Lindh* rule also would appear to render AEDPA inapplicable in cases in which an application for habeas corpus or section 2255 relief had *not* been filed on or before April 24, 1996, but in which an application for appointment of counsel under 21 U.S.C. § 848(q) *had* been filed on or before that date. In McFarland v. Scott, 512 U.S. 849 (1994), the Supreme Court concluded that "a habeas corpus proceeding is pending," as that phrase is used in the stay provision of Chapter 153 of the habeas corpus statute, 28 U.S.C. § 2251, if a petition for habeas corpus relief had been filed before that date *or* if an indigent capital prisoner's application for the appointment of counsel under section 848(q) (which makes the appointment of counsel mandatory in capital habeas corpus and section 2255 cases) had been filed as of that date. *See McFarland v. Scott, supra* at 859 ("We conclude that a capital defendant may invoke this right [under section 848(q)] to a counseled federal habeas corpus proceeding by filing a motion requesting the appointment of habeas counsel, and that a district court [then] has jurisdiction to enter a stay of execution [under section 2251's "habeas corpus proceeding is pending" language] where necessary to give effect to that statutory right."); *infra* §§ 12.3a, 12.3b, 13.1, 13.2a, 13.2b (discussing *McFarland*). There is no meaningful distinction between the "cases pending" language of section 107(c), which, as *Lindh* concluded, "implicitly" governs the applicability of "the amendments to chapter 153," *Lindh, supra*, 117 S. Ct. at 2063, and the "proceeding ... pending" language of Chapter 153's stay provision that was interpreted in *McFarland*. Consequently, *McFarland's* conclusion that a habeas corpus "proceeding" is "pending" when a capital prisoner's application for the mandatory appointment of counsel has been filed establishes, as well, that a habeas corpus (and section 2255) "case" also is "pending" on that date.

The foregoing analysis is reinforced by the Court's recent decision in Hohn v. United States, 118 S. Ct. 1969 (1998). In that section 2255 proceeding, the Court concluded that a preliminary pleading filed in a court should be treated, for jurisdictional purposes, as an indivisible part of the overall "case" in that court:

> We further disagree with the contention ... that a request to proceed before a court of appeals should be regarded as a threshold inquiry separate from the merits which, if denied, prevents the *case* from ever being in the court of appeals. Precedent forecloses this argument. In Ex parte Quirin, 317 U.S. 1 (1942), we confronted the analogous question whether a request for leave to file a petition for a writ of habeas corpus was a *case* in a district court for the purposes of the then-extant statute governing court of appeals review of district court decisions. See 28 U.S.C. § 225(a) First (1940 ed.) (courts of appeals had jurisdiction to review final decisions "[i]n the district courts, in all *cases* save where a direct review of the decision may be had in the Supreme Court"). We held the request for leave constituted a *case* in the district court over which the court of appeals could assert jurisdiction, even though the district court had denied the request. We reasoned, *"[p]resentation of the petition for judicial action is the institution of a suit.* Hence the denial by the district court of leave to file the petitions in these causes was the judicial determination of a case or controversy, reviewable on appeal to the Court of Appeals." 317 U.S., at 24, 63 S. Ct., at 9.

Id. at 1974-75 (emphasis added). *See also id.* at 1979-80 (Scalia, J., dissenting) (noting majority's holding "that a request pertaining to a case constitutes its own 'case'"). The Court's decision in *Hohn* also appears to firm up the analogy to *McFarland* by equating "case" with "proceeding" (118 S. Ct. at 1972), the latter word being the language from 28 U.S.C. § 2251 (permitting stays during pendency of a "habeas corpus proceeding") that *McFarland* held broad enough to encompass an application for counsel filed in advance of an actual habeas corpus petition. If, as *McFarland* concludes, an application for counsel is sufficient to cause "a habeas corpus proceeding [to be]

provision in question governs trial or appellate proceedings and whether or not the case in question was still pending in the district court or had progressed to an appellate court as of April 24, 1996.[15] Most particularly, because section 107(c) and *Lindh* make determinative the pendency of the "case" as a whole, and not, for example, the "appeal" or some other "stage" of the case, the statute's bright-line character is preserved only by treating the case's original filing date as determinative of the applicability of all portions of AEDPA to all stages of all nonopt-in cases. So, if the "case" was originally filed on or before April 24, 1996, then pre-AEDPA law governs at all stages of the case, including stages initiated *after* that day by the filing of (i) an appeal, (ii) an amendment to the original habeas corpus petition or

---

pending" for purposes of section 2251, and if, as *Hohn* seems to say, a habeas "proceeding" and a habeas "case" are the same thing, then that kind of motion also should cause the habeas "case" to be "pending." *But see* Holman v. Gilmore, 126 F.3d 876, 879-80 (7th Cir. 1997), *cert. denied*, 118 S. Ct. 1169 (1998) (date petition was filed, not earlier date *McFarland* application was filed, determines applicability of AEDPA); Williams v. Cain, 125 F.3d 269, 273-74 (5th Cir. 1997), *cert. denied*, 119 S. Ct. 144 (1998) ("Although *McFarland* might be argued to raise a question in this regard," court concludes that *McFarland* application for appointment of counsel does not constitute filing of "petition" for purposes of determining AEDPA's applicability under *Lindh*); Lott v. Coyle, 1998 WL 185318, at *2-8 (N.D. Ohio March 11, 1998) (pre-AEDPA filing of notice of intent to file petition and *McFarland* application for appointment of counsel were not sufficient to render case "a 'pending' habeas proceeding" at time of AEDPA's enactment and therefore AEDPA governs); United States ex rel. Franklin v. Gilmore, 993 F. Supp. 1162, 1168 n.2 (N.D. Ill. 1998) (following *Holman v. Gilmore, supra*); *cf.* Calderon v. United States Dist. Ct., 1998 WL 309923, *withdrawn & rehearing en banc ordered*, 1998 WL 351217 (9th Cir. 1998) (*McFarland* application does not constitute "petition" for purposes of AEDPA's statute of limitations).

[15] *See, e.g.*, Crowell v. Walsh, 1998 WL 412489, at *2 (D.C. Cir. July 24, 1998) ("§ 2253(c) does not apply to appeals of habeas petitions [if the petitions were] filed before the effective date of the Act," even if appeals were filed after that date); Tankleff v. Senkowski, 135 F.3d 235, 241 (2d Cir. 1998) (AEDPA does "not apply to a defendant who had filed his § 2255 petition [or § 2254 petition] before the effective date of the AEDPA, despite the fact that both the denial of his petition by the district court and the filing of his appeal occurred after this date"); United States v. Kunzman, 125 F.3d 1363, 1364 n.2 (10th Cir. 1997), *cert. denied*, 118 S. Ct. 1375 (1998) (joining "majority of circuits that have considered this issue" in holding that operative date in applying AEDPA is when "the underlying petition was filed," not when "notice of appeal was filed"); Nelson v. Walker, 121 F.3d 828, 833 (2d Cir. 1997) (similar to *Carter, infra*, and *Holmes, infra*; critical question is whether petitioner "filed his *petition* prior to the effective date of the" new Act (emphasis added)); United States v. Carter, 117 F.3d 262, 264 n.1 (5th Cir. 1997) (in case pending on appeal, interpreting provision of AEDPA applicable only to appeals, critical question under *Lindh* is whether "*petition* is *filed in the district court* [before or] after the [AEDPA's] effective date of April 24, 1996" (emphasis added)); Holmes v. Wyoming Dep't of Corrections, 1997 WL 368331, at *1 & n.1 (10th Cir. July 3, 1997) (in same kind of case, critical question under *Lindh*, is when "this § 2254 *petition* for habeas corpus was *filed*" (emphasis added)); *Tucker v. Johnson, supra*, 115 F.3d at 278 (in same kind of case, critical question under *Lindh* is whether "petitioner's habeas *petition* pre-dated the act" (emphasis added)); other authority cited *infra* note 16. *But see* Tiedeman v. Benson, 122 F.3d 518, 520-21 (8th Cir. 1997) (discussed *infra* note 16).

section 2255 motion, and even, apparently, (iii) an amended habeas corpus petition following the original petition's dismissal without prejudice for nonexhaustion.[16]

---

[16] One of AEDPA's Chapter 153 provisions amends the statute, 28 U.S.C. § 2253, governing the right to appeals in habeas corpus cases and for the first time extends the statute to reach section 2255 appeals. *See* 28 U.S.C.A. § 2253 (West 1994 & Supp. 1998). In addressing the applicability of the amendments to section 2253, a number of courts of appeals prior to *Lindh* had distinguished between nonopt-in habeas corpus and section 2255 cases in which *appeals* were filed before April 24, 1996 (to which AEDPA was deemed inapplicable) and nonopt-in habeas corpus and section 2255 cases in which *appeals* were filed on or after that date (to which AEDPA was deemed to apply, even if the case was originally *filed in the district court* well before that date). *Compare, e.g.,* United States v. Rocha, 109 F.3d 225, 228-29 (5th Cir. 1997) ("AEDPA's COA requirement does not retroactively apply to appeals in which the final judgment and notice of appeal were entered before the AEDPA's effective date"; petitioner "did everything necessary to invoke the jurisdiction of this court at the time he filed his notice of appeal. Nothing in the AEDPA suggests that Congress meant [courts] to dismiss appeals that were properly filed and pending as of the act's effective date") *and* Brown v. Cain, 104 F.3d 744, 748 (5th Cir.), *cert. denied*, 117 S. Ct. 1489 (1997) ("Brown had already obtained [right to appeal] before the [AEDPA] was enacted. Brown had requested and received the right to appeal; his 'settled expectation' was that he had successfully passed all procedural hurdles to this court's consideration of his claims.... Applying the [AEDPA's appeal] requirement[s] to Brown in a technical fashion would clearly raise retroactivity concerns. We therefore hold that the [appeal] requirement[ ] of the [AEDPA] will not apply to habeas appellants who have already obtained [certificates of probable cause to appeal under the preexisting statute].") *and* Johnson v. Cody, 1996 WL 622006, at *1 n.1 (10th Cir. Oct. 28, 1996) (Act's new certificate of appealability provision does not apply to case in which petition and appeal were filed prior to enactment date) *with, e.g.,* Fisher v. Young, 99 F.3d 1149 (10th Cir. 1996) (applying Act's new certificate of appealability provision to appeal of denial of petition, where petition was filed before enactment date but appeal was filed after enactment date) *and* Lozada v. United States, 107 F.3d 1011, 1016-17 (2d Cir. 1997) (same; section 2555 case) *and* United States v. Orozco, 103 F.3d 389 (5th Cir. 1996), *overruled,* United States v. Carter, 117 F.3d 262, 264 (5th Cir. 1997) (same) *and* Drinkard v. Johnson, 97 F.3d 751 (5th Cir. 1996), *cert. denied,* 117 S. Ct. 1114 (1997), *overruled, United States v. Carter, supra* at 264 (same; section 2254 case) *and* Lennox v. Evans, 87 F.3d 431, 433 (10th Cir. 1996) (same) *and see also* United States v. Lopez, 100 F.3d 113, 116-17 (10th Cir. 1996) (retroactivity analysis explicitly distinguishing between AEDPA's provisions regulating resolution of habeas corpus petitions at trial level, as to which determinative date is day petition or motion was filed, and statute's provisions regulating taking of appeals, as to which determinative date is day notice of appeal was filed) *and* Nickel v. Hannigan, 97 F.2d 403, 407 n.4 (10th Cir. 1996), *cert. denied,* 117 S. Ct. 1112 (1997) (similar).

The rationale for the foregoing cases, however, was not the statutory interpretation rationale employed by *Lindh* but a "retroactivity" concern — *i.e.,* that it was unfair to apply new appeal provisions to already filed appeals but not unfair to apply them to later-filed appeals. Because *Lindh*'s statutory interpretation holding supersedes any retroactivity analysis, *see Lindh, supra,* 117 S. Ct. at 2063; *infra* § 3.4b n.18 and accompanying text, *Lindh* overrules the above decisions insofar as they focus on the date the *appeal,* as opposed to the "*case,*" was filed. *See, e.g., United States v. Kunzman, supra,* 125 F.3d at 1364 n.2 (in part of opinion that was "circulated to the en banc court," 10th Circuit "unanimously agree[s]" to overrule *Lennox* [*v. Evans*] and [*United States* v.] *Riddick*[, 104 F.3d 1239 (10th Cir. 1997)] and any other of our cases," to "the extent ... [they] are inconsistent" with interpretation of *Lindh* as holding that operative date for determining whether amendments to section 2253 apply is when petition was filed, not when appeal was filed); *Nelson v. Walker, supra,* 121 F.3d at 832-33 ("Although we held in Reyes v. Keane, 90 F.3d 676, 680 (2d Cir.1996), that the ... requirement[s] of [new] § 2253(c)(3) (as amended) should be applied retroactively, that decision has been overruled by *Lindh,* 117 S. Ct. at 2068. Thus, because Nelson filed his petition prior to the effective date of the AEDPA, the ... requirement[s of amended section 2253 are] ... inapplicable."); *United States v. Carter, supra* at 264 ("By deciding that the chapter containing the new [section 2255 appeal] requirement applies only to cases filed after the [AEDPA's] effective date, *Lindh* overruled our previous holdings in *United States v. Orozco,* [*supra*], and *Drinkard v. Johnson,* [*supra*], and their progeny, regarding the applicability of the [AEDPA's appeal] requirement[s] to § 2254 and § 2255 appeals. Following *Lindh,* we hold that § 2255 appellants are not subject to [AEDPA's appeal] requirement[s] unless their § 2255 *petitions* were *filed in the district court* after the [AEDPA's] effective date of April 24, 1996." (emphasis added)); *id.* at 264 n.1 ("Of course, in keeping with our evolved consistency of treatment of the new [appeal] requirement[s] for both § 2254 and § 2255 actions, the Court's pronouncement in *Lindh* extends to § 2254 appeals as well ..., [so that] § 2254 litigation is also subject to the [new appeal] requirement[s] only when a § 2254 *petition* is *filed in the district court* after the [AEDPA's] effective date of April 24, 1996." (emphasis added)); *Holmes v. Wyoming Dep't of Corrections, supra,* 1997 WL 368331, at *1 & n.1 ("it is unnecessary for a defendant to obtain a certificate of appealability to prosecute his appeal" because, under *Lindh,* "amendments to 28 U.S.C. § 2253, which imposed the requirement of a certificate of appealability do not apply to cases filed prior to the statute's effective date," and "this § 2254 petition for habeas corpus was filed on March 17, 1995"; "Supreme Court's decision [in *Lindh*] overrules our decision in *Lennox v. Evans,* [*supra*], to the extent that *Lennox* held that the [AEDPA] provisions applied to §§ 2254 and 2255 cases filed prior to the [Act's] effective date."); *Tucker v. Johnson, supra,* 115 F.3d at 279 n.3 ("amended 28 U.S.C. § 2253 ... require[s] a certificate of appealability... before a final order in a habeas proceeding can be appealed" but "[i]n light of *Lindh v. Murphy* ... this requirement does not apply to habeas petitions filed prior to April 24, 1996"). In Dickey v. United States, 118 S. Ct. 2365 (1998) (*mem.*), the Supreme Court provided considerable support for this view of its holding in *Lindh* by vacating and remanding for reconsideration in light of *Lindh* a lower court decision applying AEDPA's amended section 2253 in a section 2255 case in which the appeal was filed after, but the section 2255 motion was filed before, April 24, 1996. *Cf. infra* § 3.4b n.46 (positing a more limited interpretation of *Dickey,* tying it to special "retroactivity" considerations that arise in section 2255, but not habeas corpus, cases, but finding that interpretation to be doubtful, given *Dickey*'s citation of *Lindh*).

Consistently with *Dickey,* most of the circuit courts now recognize that AEDPA is inapplicable to a case in which a federal habeas corpus petition or section 2255 motion was filed on or before April 24, 1996, regardless of the timing or status of the appeal at any point thereafter. The courts that follow this rule are the 1ST CIRCUIT (*see, e.g.,* Tejeda v. Dubois, 142 F.3d 18, 22 n.4 (1st Cir. 1998)); 2D CIRCUIT (*see, e.g.,* Torres v. United States, 140 F.3d 392, 400 n.6 (2d Cir. 1998); *Tankleff v. Senkowski, supra,* 135 F.3d at 242; United States v. Perez, 129 F.3d 255, 260 (2d Cir. 1997)); 5TH CIRCUIT (*see, e.g.,* Lara v. Johnson, 141 F.3d 239, 241 n.1 (5th Cir. 1998); Neal v. Cain, 141 F.3d 207, 209-10 (5th Cir. 1998); Moody v. Johnson, 139 F.3d 477, 480 n.1 (5th Cir. 1998); United States v. Ramos-Rodriguez, 136 F.3d 465, 466-47 (5th Cir. 1998); Cannon v. Johnson, 134 F.3d 683, 685 (5th Cir. 1998); United States v. Cervantes, 132 F.3d 1106, 1108 n.1 (5th Cir. 1998); Lucas v. Johnson, 132 F.3d 1069, 1072-73 (5th Cir. 1998); Muniz v. Johnson, 132 F.3d 214, 218 (5th Cir.), *cert. denied,* 118 S. Ct. 1793 (1998); Carter v. Johnson, 131 F.3d 452,

457-458 (5th Cir. 1997), *cert. denied*, 118 S. Ct. 1567 (1998); United States v. Roberts, 118 F.3d 1071, 1072 (5th Cir.1997); Green v. Johnson, 116 F.3d 1115, 1119-20 (5th Cir. 1997)); **6TH CIRCUIT** (*see, e.g.*, Norris v. Schotten, 1998 WL 261395, at *2-3 (6th Cir. May 26, 1998); Arredondo v. United States, 120 F.3d 639, 640 & n.1 (6th Cir. 1997)); **10TH CIRCUIT** (*see, e.g.*, Aragon v. Shanks, 1998 WL 251110, at *3 n.1 (10th Cir. May 19, 1998); Sellers v. Ward, 135 F.3d 1333, 1336 (10th Cir. 1998); Lucero v. Kerby, 133 F.3d 1299, 1303 n.1 (10th Cir.), *cert. denied*, 118 S. Ct. 1375 (1998)); and **D.C. CIRCUIT** (*see, e.g.*, Crowell v. Walsh, 1998 WL 412489, at *2 (D.C. Cir. July 24, 1998)). *See also* other authority cited *supra* note 15.

Shortly after *Lindh* was announced, and a year before it was clarified to an extent by *Dickey*, the 8th Circuit used what appeared to be "retroactivity" (rather than statutory intent) analysis to conclude that AEDPA's amendment of 28 U.S.C. § 2253 applies to cases in which a petition was filed before April 24, 1996, if the appeal was filed after that date. *See Tiedeman v. Benson, supra*, 122 F.3d at 520-21. In two subsequent decisions, however, 8th Circuit panels expressed discomfort with the *Tiedeman* approach, given its deviation from the rule followed in other circuits. (Both decisions predated the Supreme Court's decision in *Dickey*). *See* Ramsey v. Bowersox, 1998 WL 300520, at *9 (8th Cir. June 10, 1998) (noting "contrary cases from other circuits"; refusing to endorse *Tiedeman* rule except to extent that "[o]ne panel of this court is bound by the decisions of other panels"; and noting that petitioner "would be no better off" even if 8th Circuit followed other circuits' rule because circuit's pre-AEDPA law would produce same result as AEDPA on facts of case); Roberts v. Bowersox, 137 F.3d 1062 (8th Cir. 1998) (after noting views of other circuits in conflict with 8th Circuit rule, court concludes that there is "some doubt about whether the [relevant] issue is properly before us [because it was certified in accordance with pre-AEDPA standards]" and that it is therefore "prudent to consider its merits"). Subsequently, however, another 8th Circuit panel followed *Tiedeman*, albeit without taking note of either the Supreme Court's intervening decision in *Dickey* or the second thoughts expressed in *Ramsey* and *Roberts*. *See* Carter v. Hopkins, 151 F.3d 872, 874 (8th Cir. 1998).

In light of *Dickey*, it is hard to see how the 8th Circuit approach can long survive. This is so, notwithstanding that, in one of the *pre-Lindh* 8th Circuit cases applying the circuit's approach, the Supreme Court denied *certiorari* on the propriety of this practice while granting *certiorari* on other issues. *See* Hohn v. United States, 99 F.3d 892, 893 (8th Cir. 1996) (*per curiam*), *cert. granted in part & denied in part*, 118 S. Ct. 361 (1997), *vac'd & remanded*, 118 S. Ct. 1969 (1998). On review, the Supreme Court treated the case as if it were subject to AEDPA (*see Hohn v. United States, supra*, 118 S. Ct. at 1972), an action that was consistent with the Court's denial of *certiorari* on this particular issue, which rendered the 8th Circuit's ruling on the issue the "law of the case" without implying any Supreme Court validation of the ruling (*see infra* § 6.4c nn.23-24 and accompanying text). *See* Hohn v. United States, *supra*, 118 S. Ct. at 361 (framing issue on which *certiorari* was granted as: "In light of the fact that the Court of Appeals denied the petitioner's request for a Certificate of Appealability, does this Court have jurisdiction to grant certiorari, vacate and remand this case per the suggestion of the Acting Solicitor General?"). In resolving the issue on which *certiorari* was granted, the Court did not express or indicate any views on the propriety of the 8th Circuit's ruling on the applicability of AEDPA to the case and, indeed, framed its holding in terms that expressly covered pre-AEDPA certificates of probable cause as well as AEDPA certificates of appealability. *See id.* at 1977 (overruling House v. Mayo, 324 U.S. 42 (1945) (*per curiam*), which held that Court "lack[s] statutory certiorari jurisdiction to review refusals to issue certificates of probable cause"). Because *Hohn* is silent on the question at issue here, while the Court's later decision in *Dickey* suggests that the 8th Circuit's approach is inconsistent with *Lindh*, it seems likely that the Court eventually will reject the 8th Circuit's approach. *See also infra* § 3.4b n.46 (criticizing 8th Circuit approach because it invites retroactivity problems).

The rule suggested by *Dickey* and that a majority of the circuits follow would also preclude application of AEDPA to cases that were filed in district court prior to the effective date of the statute and then held in abeyance pending exhaustion of state remedies. *See* Brewer v. Johnson, 139 F.3d 491, 492-93 (5th Cir. 1998) (suggesting that district court has discretion to hold case in abeyance, rather than dismissing, during exhaustion proceedings, which might preserve pre-AEDPA filing date, but also suggesting that there is no blanket requirement that abeyance, rather than dismissal, be used). *See also* Stewart v. Martinez-Villareal, 118 S. Ct. 1618, 1624 (1998) (Thomas, J., dissenting) (stating that federal court may avoid AEDPA's jurisdiction-withdrawing results when a prior petition is dismissed and a new one filed some time later by "hold[ing] ... [a claim or petition] in abeyance" rather than dismissing it). Arguably, the same analysis would apply to a case that was filed in district court and then dismissed, rather than held in abeyance, while the petitioner exhausted remaining state remedies. *See, e.g.*, Peterson v. Brennan, 1998 WL 470139, at *8 (E.D. Pa. Aug. 11, 1998) (similar to *Morris v. Horn, infra*); Kethley v. Berge, 1998 WL 324585 (E.D. Wis. June 18, 1998) (following exhaustion (to permit which, court dismisses petition without prejudice), new petition shall "retain the benefit of the present case number and filing date," *i.e.*, the number and date of the original petition); *Williams v. Vaughn, supra*, 1998 WL 217532, at *9 (E.D. Pa. Mar. 19, 1998) (new, exhausted petition "would ... relate back to the original filing date" of unexhausted petition that court dismissed without prejudice to permit exhaustion (ruling reinforced and further explained, upon denial of state's Rule 60(b) Motion for Relief from Judgment or Order, in Williams v. Vaughn, 1998 WL 238466, at *2-*3, *5 (E.D. Pa. May 8, 1998))); Morris v. Horn, 1998 WL 150966, at *4 (E.D. Pa. Mar. 19, 1998) (dismissing mixed petition "without prejudice to petitioner's right to file an amended petition pursuant to Federal Rule of Civil Procedure 15(c)(2)," which petition, pursuant to Civil Rule 15's "relation back" principle, will then be treated as if it had been filed on date when original federal petition was filed). *Cf.* Morris v. Bell, 1997 WL 560055, at *3 (6th Cir. Sept. 5, 1997), *cert. denied*, 118 S. Ct. 1169 (1998) (rejecting, as too "speculative," petitioner's claim that district court's refusal to hold case in abeyance prejudiced him by placing him at risk of having to litigate case under AEDPA upon refiling after exhaustion of state remedies). *But cf.* Earhart v. Johnson, 132 F.3d 1062, 1066 n.4 (5th Cir. 1998) (*dicta*) (rejecting request of capital petitioner who filed pre-AEDPA petition to be allowed to return to state court to exhaust unexhausted claims despite state's waiver of exhaustion defense, in part because "dismissing Earhart's present claims would have the ultimate effect of requiring him to litigate his future federal habeas petition under the more stringent standards of the AEDPA"; court does not discuss possibility of holding petition in abeyance rather than dismissing it while petitioner exhaust state remedies).

Finally, the foregoing analysis strongly suggests that when a pre-AEDPA petition is amended after April 24, 1996 to add a new claim, the new claim is not subject to AEDPA even though it was added after the statute became effective. *See* Williams v. Vaughn, *supra*, 1998 WL 238466, at *1 (rejecting state's attempt to distinguish between stages of a federal habeas corpus proceeding in determining whether AEDPA is applicable; "[t]he Supreme Court holding in *Lindh* is quite clear" and renders AEDPA inapplicable if case was "'filed'" before effective date of Act). That conclusion also follows from the dictates of FED. R. CIV. P. 15, incorporated into habeas corpus procedure by Rule 11 of the Rules Governing § 2254 Cases, which provides that "[a]n amendment of a pleading relates back to the date of the original pleading." FED. R. CIV. P. 15. *See* Calderon v. Ashmus, 118 S. Ct. 1694, 1700 (1998) (Breyer, J., concurring) (under Habeas Rule 11, and unless otherwise expressly governed by the statute — as in the case of amendments in Chapter 154 opt-in cases — habeas amendments are governed by FED. R. CIV. P. 15); *Peterson v. Brennan, supra* at *8

b. *Chapter 153 cases filed after April 24, 1996.* Under *Lindh*, and a predecessor decision, *Landgraf v. U.S.I. Film Prod.*,[17] if the "normal tools of [statutory] construction" lead to the conclusion that Congress intended that a particular new statute should *not* apply to particular cases, Congress' intent controls.[18] By contrast, the fact that the usual tools of statutory construction would lead to the conclusion that Congress intended that a particular statute *should* apply to particular cases is *not* dispositive of the new statute's application to those cases. Rather, because of the unfairness that often accompanies the application of a new statute to defeat an individual's settled expectations, the courts have long applied, and *Landraf* and *Lindh* reaffirm, a rule forbidding the "retroactive" application of new legislation unless the new statute includes an "'express command,'" "'unambiguous directive,'" or "'clear statement'" requiring retroactive application.[19] If the new statute does not include a clear statement requiring its "retroactive" application, the courts will refuse to apply it in that fashion, even though the usual tools of statutory construction would lead to the opposite result.[20] *Landgraf* gives the following statement and explanation of this so-called "antiretroactivity presumption":

> [T]he presumption against retroactive legislation is deeply rooted in our jurisprudence, and embodies a legal doctrine centuries older than our Republic. Elementary considerations of fairness dictate that individuals should have an opportunity to know what the law is and to conform their conduct accordingly; settled expectations should not be lightly disrupted. For that reason, the "principle that the legal effect of conduct should

---

(applying Civil Rule 15's relation-back principle to shield habeas corpus petition originally filed before AEDPA's effective date from adverse consequences under AEDPA); *Morris v. Horn, supra* at *4 (similar; discussed above); *infra* § 17.2 nn.6-19 and accompanying text. *But cf.* Freeman v. Kaylo, 1998 WL 252144, at *1 (E.D. La. May 15, 1998) (at least where petitioner seeks to add entirely new claim, unrelated to any claim already in petition, date of amendment rather than date of petition governs for purposes of AEDPA's statute of limitations).

[17] 511 U.S. 244 (1994).

[18] Lindh v. Murphy, 117 S. Ct. 2059, 2062-63 (1997) (discussing *Landgraf, supra*).

[19] *Id.* (quoting *Landgraf, supra*, 511 U.S. at 263, 280 (majority opinion); *id.* at 286 (Scalia, J., concurring in judgment)). *Accord* Hughes Aircraft Co. v. United States ex rel. Schumer, 117 S. Ct. 1871, 1876 (1997) (courts must apply "time-honored presumption" "'against retroactive application' ... unless Congress has clearly manifested its intent to the contrary" (quoting *Landgraf, supra,* 511 U.S. at 265)).

[20] *See Lindh, supra,* 117 S. Ct. at 2063 ("if the application of a [new statute] would be retroactive as to [a particular litigant], the [statute] will not be applied, even if, in the absence of retroactive effect, we might find the [statute] applicable" pursuant to "our normal rules of construction"). *Accord Hughes Aircraft Co. v. United States ex rel. Schumer, supra,* 117 S. Ct. at 1876, 1878-79.

ordinarily be assessed under the law that existed when the conduct took place has timeless and universal appeal."

* * * * *

Since the early days of this Court, [therefore,] we have declined to give retroactive effect to statutes ... unless Congress had made clear its intent. Thus, in *United States v. Heth*, 7 U.S. (3 Cranch) 399 (1806), we refused to apply a federal statute reducing the commissions of customs collectors to collections commenced before the statute's enactment because the statute lacked "clear, strong, and imperative" language requiring retroactive application, *id.*, at 413 (opinion of Paterson, J.).[21]

Under *Lindh* and *Landgraf*, therefore, a new statute's applicability to a particular case depends upon the answers to two questions, once it is determined that the usual rules of statutory construction would require the statute's application: (1) whether "the application of ... [the new statute] would be retroactive as to" a particular litigant and, if so, (2) whether "requiring retroactive application ... [is] supported by a clear [congressional] statement."[22] If the answer to the first question is "yes" (because the statute's application would be retroactive) and the answer to the second question is "no" (because Congress has not clearly required that retroactive effect), then the statute does *not* apply, notwithstanding the dictates of the usual rules of construction. Otherwise, the statute does apply. Below, we lay out the tests the Court has adopted for each branch of this inquiry, then apply those tests to AEDPA as it potentially affects *nonopt-in* cases filed *after* April 24, 1996.

Recognizing that "[a]ny test of retroactivity will leave room for disagreement in hard cases, and is unlikely to classify the enormous variety of legal changes with perfect philosophical clarity," *Landgraf* defined a new provision as "retroactive" if it "attaches new legal consequences to events completed before its enactment."[23] The Court elaborated this test as follows:

> While statutory retroactivity has long been disfavored, deciding when a statute operates "retroactively" is not always a simple or mechanical task.... Justice Story offered an influential definition in *Society for Propagation of the Gospel v. Wheeler*, 22 F. Cas. 756 (No. 13,156) (CCDNH 1814).... [According to Justice Story,] the ban on retrospective legislation embraced "all statutes, which, though operating only from their passage, affect vested

---

[21] *Landgraf, supra*, 511 U.S. at 265, 270 (footnotes and citations omitted); *accord Lindh, supra*, 117 S. Ct. at 2062-63.

[22] *Lindh, supra*, 117 S. Ct. at 2062, 2063.

[23] *Landgraf, supra*, 511 U.S. at 270.

rights and past transactions." *Id.* [at 767] "Upon principle," Justice Story elaborated,

> "every statute, which takes away or impairs vested rights acquired under existing laws, or creates a new obligation, imposes a new duty, or attaches a new disability, in respect to transactions or considerations already past, must be deemed retrospective...." Ibid. (citing *Calder v. Bull*, 3 U.S. (3 Dall.) 386 (1798) and *Dash v. Van Kleek*, 7 Johns. 477 (N.Y.1811)).

> Though the formulas have varied, similar functional conceptions of legislative "retroactivity" have found voice in this Court's decisions and elsewhere.[24]

In *Lindh,* the Court narrowly defined the types of statutory language that qualify as a "clear statement" of Congress' intent to apply a statute retroactively:

> In *United States v. Nordic Village, Inc.*, 503 U.S. 30, 34-37 (1992), this Court held that the existence of "plausible" alternative interpretations of statutory language meant that that language could not qualify as an "unambiguous" expression of a waiver of sovereign immunity. And cases where this Court has found truly "retroactive" effect adequately authorized by a statute have involved statutory language that was *so clear that it could sustain only one interpretation.* See *Graham & Foster v. Goodcell*, 282 U.S. 409, 416-420 (1931) (holding that a statutory provision "was manifestly intended to operate retroactively according to its terms" where the tax statute spelled out meticulously the circumstances that defined the claims to which it applied and where the alternative interpretation was absurd); *Automobile Club of Mich. v. Commissioner*, 353 U.S. 180, 184 (1957) (finding a clear statement authorizing the Commissioner of Internal Revenue to correct tax rulings and regulations "retroactively" where the statutory authorization for the Commissioner's action spoke explicitly in terms of "retroactivity"); *United States v. Zacks*, 375 U.S. 59, 65-67 (1963) (declining to give retroactive effect to a new substantive tax provision by reopening claims otherwise barred by statute of limitations and observing that Congress had provided for just this sort of retroactivity for other substantive provisions by explicitly creating new grace periods in which otherwise barred claims could be brought under the new substantive law). Cf. *Seminole Tribe of Fla. v. Florida*, 517 U.S. 44, 47 (1996) (finding a clear statement of congressional abrogation of Eleventh Amendment immunity where the federal statute went beyond granting federal

---

[24] *Id.* at 268-69.

jurisdiction to hear a claim and explicitly contemplated "the State" as defendant in federal court in numerous provisions of the Act).[25]

As thus defined by the Supreme Court, the rule forbidding the "retroactive" application of new statutes absent a "clear congressional statement" requiring that application leads to the conclusion that, although AEDPA applies to many Chapter 153 cases filed after April 24, 1996 — given Congress' apparent intent that it apply to such cases, as revealed by the usual rules of statutory construction[26] — there are some situations in which AEDPA may *not* apply to such cases. This conclusion is a function of three subsidiary points: (1) The application of AEDPA's *nonopt-in* statute of limitations to cases filed *after* April 24, 1996, but in which the new limitations period expired *before* that date, almost certainly would have the "retroactive" effect that *Landgraf* forbids. (2) So, *Lindh* suggests, might application of AEDPA's new "standards of proof and persuasion" to certain postenactment cases. (3) *Lindh* also makes clear that AEDPA's habeas corpus and related provisions nowhere state Congress' intention to cause retroactive effects with sufficient clarity to permit either of those two apparently "retroactive" applications of AEDPA. We develop each of these three points below.

(1) AEDPA's one-year statute of limitations for nonopt-in cases attaches to a prisoner's failure to file a habeas corpus petition or section 2255 motion within a year after the completion of direct review proceedings (or within a year after one of the statute's other triggering dates) the new legal consequence of entirely forgoing federal habeas corpus or section 2255 review and relief.[27] If the expiration of the one-year period occurred prior to April 24, 1996, therefore, applying AEDPA's statute of limitations to preclude review would be improperly "retroactive," even if the petition was filed after that date, because it would attach the new legal consequence of denial of the petition to an event — the failure to file within one year — that was completed before enactment. The *Landgraf* rule, and a number of older Supreme Court cases involving newly enacted statutes of limitations, forbid statutes to be applied in this "retroactive" manner.[28]

---

[25] *Lindh, supra*, 117 S. Ct. at 2064 n.4 (emphasis added).

[26] *See Lindh, supra*, 117 S. Ct. at 2063 ("amendments to chapter 153 were assumed and meant to apply to the general run of habeas cases only when those cases had been filed after [April 24, 1996]"); *infra* note 49 and accompanying text.

[27] *See* 28 U.S.C.A. §§ 2244(d), 2255 (West 1994 & Supp. 1998) (discussed *infra* § 5.1b).

[28] *See, e.g.*, United States v. St. Louis, S.F. & T. Ry., 270 U.S. 1, 3 (1926); Fullerton-Krueger Lumber Co. v. Northern Pac. Ry., 266 U.S. 435, 437 (1925); Sohn v. Waterson, 84 U.S. (17 Wall.) 596, 598 (1873). The lower federal courts have nearly unanimously refused to apply AEDPA's new statute of limitations to cases filed relatively soon after AEDPA became effective in which the one-year period expired prior to April 24, 1996. *See, e.g.*, United States v. Lopez, 100 F.3d 113, 116-17

(2) Whether any of AEDPA's other provisions might likewise have "retroactive" effects when applied to nonopt-in cases filed after April 24, 1996, is a more difficult question. In *Lindh*, the Court characterized a number of AEDPA's provisions as having "change[d] standards of proof and persuasion in a way favorable to a state."[29] The Court went on to suggest that the Court's prior cases at least leave open (and, given *Lindh*'s statutory resolution of the case at hand, it also left open) the question whether such changes produce "new legal consequences" of the sort that qualify as retroactive when "attache[d] ... to events completed before [a new provision's] enactment":

> If [AEDPA] were merely procedural in a strict sense..., the natural expectation would be that it would apply to pending cases. *Landgraf*, 511 U. S., at 275 (noting that procedural changes "may often be applied in suits arising before their enactment without raising concerns about retroactivity"). But [AEDPA] does more, for in its revisions of prior law to change standards of proof and persuasion in a way favorable to a state, the statute goes beyond "mere" procedure to affect substantive entitlement to relief. See ... [the] revised legal standard of new [28 U.S.C.] § 2254(d)[ ]. *Landgraf* did not speak to the rules for determining the temporal reach of such a statute (having no need to do so). While the statute might not have a true retroactive effect, neither [is] it clearly "procedural" so as to fall

_____

(10th Cir. 1996) (followed in United States v. Simmonds, 111 F.3d 737, 745-46 (10th Cir. 1997); United States v. Martin, 1997 WL 57153, at *2 (10th Cir. Feb. 12, 1997); United States v. Sanchez, 105 F.3d 670 (10th Cir. 1997)); Lindh v. Murphy, 96 F.3d 856, 863 (7th Cir. 1996) (*en banc*), *rev'd on other grounds*, 117 S. Ct. 2059 (1997); Dubois v. Angelone, No. 96-10 (4th Cir. Aug. 27, 1996) (*dicta*); Reyes v. Keane, 90 F.3d 676, 679 (2d Cir. 1996), *overruled on other grounds*, Nelson v. Walker, 121 F.3d 828, 832-33 (2d Cir. 1997); Samuel v. Duncan, 1996 WL 413632, at *1 (9th Cir. July 8, 1996), *cert. denied*, 117 S. Ct. 1338 (1997) (*dicta*); Scire v. United States, 1997 WL 138991, at *5 (E.D.N.Y. March 24, 1997); Breard v. Angelone, 926 F. Supp. 546, 547 (E.D. Va. 1996); Mitcham v. Calderon, C-94-2854 SBA (N.D. Cal. Dec. 20, 1996); Trammell v. Coombe, 1996 WL 719384, at *1-2 (S.D.N.Y. Dec. 13, 1996); Laboy v. Demskie, 947 F. Supp. 733, 739 (S.D.N.Y. 1996); Rienzi v. United States, 1996 WL 605310, at *1 (E.D. Pa. Oct. 21, 1996); other cases cited *infra* § 5.1b nn.49, 51. *But see* Clarke v. United States, 955 F. Supp. 593, 595, 597 (E.D. Va. 1997), *vac'd*, 1998 WL 559754 (4th Cir. Sept. 2, 1998) (*per curium*); Curtis v. Class, 939 F. Supp. 703, 707 (D.S.D. 1996); United States v. Bazemore, 929 F. Supp. 1567, 1569-70 (S.D. Ga. 1996). For a more comprehensive discussion of the range of "retroactive" applications of AEDPA's statute of limitations that the *Landgraf* rule forbids, see *infra* § 5.1b nn.44-56 and accompanying text. As is discussed in § 5.1b, a desire to avoid retroactive effects and the unfairness that often would accompany the application of Chapter 153's new statute of limitations to cases in which the one-year limitations period expired fairly soon *after*, as well as *before*, AEDPA's effective date has led all circuit courts that have considered the question to deem timely, under Chapter 153, any habeas corpus petition or section 2255 motion filed within a year of AEDPA's enactment. *See infra* § 5.1b nn.51, 54 and accompanying text.

[29] *Lindh, supra*, 117 S. Ct. at 2063.

within the Court's express (albeit qualified) approval of applying such statutes to pending cases.[30]

The dissenting opinion in *Lindh* concluded that at least some of AEDPA's changed standards of review and persuasion do *not* produce "new legal consequences" of a sort that qualify as "retroactive" but instead are the sorts of rules that generally do *not* have retroactive effect because they are merely "procedural," qualify access to only "prospective forms of relief," or either are "jurisdictional" or "if ... not jurisdictional, ... share[ ] the most salient characteristic of jurisdictional statutes ... [because their] commands are addressed to courts rather than to individuals."[31]

Assuming for the sake of argument that AEDPA's new standards of review and proof *do* have "new legal consequences" in some situations, *Lindh* and *Landgraf* still would not presumptively forbid those consequences (*i.e.*, forbid them absent a clear statutory statement requiring them), unless it were the case that applying the new statute would "attach [those] new legal consequences to *events completed before [the statute's] enactment.*"[32] Because *Lindh*'s statutory interpretation holding forbids AEDPA's application to nonopt-in cases filed *before* April 24, 1996, we here are considering only whether the new statute's

---

[30] *Id.*

[31] *Id.* at 2070-72 (Rehnquist, C.J., dissenting). The *Lindh* majority did not respond to most of Chief Justice Rehnquist's "retroactivity" analysis, because it concluded that Congress intended to bar the statute's application in any manner that might be considered retroactive under the circumstances of the case. *Id.* at 2063-68 (majority opinion). The majority did, however, reject Chief Justice Rehnquist's reading of AEDPA's standard of review provision as "merely procedural." *See id.* at 2063 (quoted *supra* text accompanying note 30). Readers who wish to have a fuller understanding of the "retroactivity" issue that the dissenting Justices addressed in full in *Lindh* but that the majority only addressed in part may find it useful to read the following portions of the petitioner's opening and reply briefs in *Lindh*, which develop the argument that, as controversially interpreted by the 7th Circuit, AEDPA's changed standard of review of state court decisions resolving mixed questions of law and fact produces "new legal consequences" of a sort that qualify as "retroactive": Brief for Petitioner, 1997 WL 82672, at *30-50 (Parts III(A)-(B), at pp.73-107), Lindh v. Murphy, 117 S. Ct. 2059 (1997); Reply Brief for Petitioner, 1997 WL 163976, at *5-16 (Parts II(A)-(B), at pp.21-37), Lindh v. Murphy, 117 S. Ct. 2059 (1997). One of the authors of this treatise collaborated on both briefs. The cited portion of the petitioner's opening brief argues that one portion of AEDPA, 28 U.S.C.A. § 2254(d) (West 1994 & Supp. 1998), as stringently interpreted by the 7th Circuit in Lindh v. Murphy, 96 F.3d 856, 864-67 (7th Cir. 1996) (*en banc*), *rev'd on other grounds*, 117 S. Ct. 2059 (1997) (discussed *infra* §§ 30.2c, 30.2d), "attache[d] new legal consequences to events completed before [the new statute's] enactment" because of its destruction of a previously accrued and matured habeas corpus cause of action. The cited portion of the petitioner's reply brief responds to the argument, found persuasive by the dissenting Justices in *Lindh*, that AEDPA's changes may be applied without presenting serious retroactivity concerns because the changes are "merely" procedural, limitations of prospective relief, or quasijurisdictional.

[32] *Landgraf, supra*, 511 U.S. at 270 (emphasis added).

application to nonopt-in cases filed *after* that date is presumptively forbidden. It might seem unlikely that applying a new statute to cases filed after the statute became law would attach the statute's new legal consequences (if any) to *pre*enactment events. On their faces, however, several of AEDPA's provisions make events occurring during exhaustion proceedings in the state courts or during trial proceedings in federal criminal cases determinative of whether the new standard of review or proof applies to the case. Because those events almost always occur *prior* to the filing of the federal habeas corpus or section 2255 action, they sometimes will have occurred *before* AEDPA went into effect even though the habeas corpus or section 2255 case was filed after the act went into effect. If the changes worked by those provisions qualify as "new legal consequences," therefore, AEDPA's application arguably would "attach" those consequences "to events completed before [the new statute's] enactment," even though the federal habeas corpus or section 2255 action was filed *after* enactment. In that event, *Landgraf* would presumptively forbid AEDPA's application.[33]

---

[33] A number of the Supreme Court's retroactivity decisions appear to decide whether a statute's "new legal consequences" are attached to "events completed before [the new law's] enactment" by asking whether the statute's consequences affect rights that had "'vested'" or "'had matured and become unconditional'" when the new law became effective. *Landgraf, supra*, 511 U.S. at 269; Bennett v. New Jersey, 470 U.S. 632, 639 (1985); *see* Greene v. United States, 376 U.S. 149, 153, 160 (1964) (when "petitioner's rights ... matured and were asserted"); United States v. Magnolia Petr. Co., 276 U.S. 160, 162 (1928) (when "claims fixed in accordance with earlier provisions"); Crane v. Hahlo, 258 U.S. 142, 145 (1922) (when right to relief "became complete"); United States Fidelity & Guar. Co. v. United States ex rel. Struthers Wells Co., 209 U.S. 306, 315 (1908) (when "respective rights of the parties [were] settled"); *cf.* Ziffrin v. United States, 318 U.S. 73, 75 (1943) (new statute did not attach new legal consequences to completed pre-act events because applicant's right to requested permit had not matured at time new statute was passed but, rather, depended upon conditions as of later time, when ICC finally ruled on application). *But see Landgraf, supra*, 511 U.S. at 275 n.29 ("we do not restrict the presumption against statutory retroactivity to cases involving 'vested rights'"). Due to the "exhaustion" and "custody" prerequisites for habeas corpus relief, federal habeas corpus rights arguably do not mature and become unconditional until the date of a federal habeas corpus petition's *filing. See, e.g.*, Carafas v. LaVallee, 391 U.S. 234, 238 (1968) (petitioner's satisfaction of "custody" requirement is assessed as of moment habeas corpus petition is filed); *infra* § 8.2 (custody requirement), Chapter 23 (exhaustion requirement). On the other hand, a prisoner's loss of the right to file a *certiorari* petition in the Supreme Court (if that is the basis for a claim of "new consequences attached to pre-act events," *see infra* note 41) might become "unconditional" *prior* to the filing of a habeas corpus petition — *i.e.*, as of 90 days following the completion of direct appeal in the state courts. Because the cases have paid scant attention to the impact of this aspect of *Landgraf* on AEDPA's applicability to postenactment cases, *but cf. infra* § 5.1b n.49 (statute of limitations decisions), it is impossible to say for certain at this point whether the preenactment "events" to which *Landgraf* refers are limited to rights to relief that "vested" or "matured" before AEDPA's enactment or, instead, include all preenactment litigation events that occurred in state exhaustion proceedings and federal criminal trials and are made decisive of relief by AEDPA's new standards of review and proof.

The following are two examples[34] of provisions that might attach new legal consequences to preenactment events even when applied to postenactment cases:

---

[34] Arguments of the sort set out below also might apply to other portions of AEDPA, including, for example, the new successive petition limitations in 28 U.S.C.A. § 2244(b)(2) (West 1994 & Supp. 1998). *See, e.g.,* United States v. Ortiz, 136 F.3d 161, 166 (D.C. Cir. 1998) (*dicta*) ("[T]he new standards and procedures under AEDPA for filing § 2255 motions could ... be improperly retroactive as applied to Ortiz if he would have met the [preexisting] ... standard [for successive section 2255 motions] and previously would have been allowed to file a second § 2255 motion, but could not file a second motion under AEDPA."); In re Hanserd, 123 F.3d 922, 924, 930-31 (6th Cir. 1997) (where federal prisoner never had opportunity to include a claim under Bailey v. United States, 516 U.S. 137 (1995), in his initial section 2255 motion because that decision had not been announced, and where a second motion raising that type of claim was not barred at the time, applying AEDPA's section 2244(b) to bar a second 2255 motion (filed after April 24, 1996) raising that claim would attach new consequences to previously completed events and would be improperly retroactive absent a clear indication in the statute (which is not present) that a retroactive effect was intended). *Cf.* In re Green, 1998 WL 216793, at *2-4 (6th Cir. May 5, 1998) (limiting *In re Hanserd, supra,* to (i) situations in which there is "cause" or an "excuse" (namely, in *Hanserd,* the absence of any warning as to the later-announced *Bailey* "new law") for failing to raise claim in prior habeas petition or section 2255 motion, and if basis for "cause" is that rule relied on is "new law," (ii) situations in which new law is not *Teague*-barred from application because new law falls within one of *Teague* exceptions (as *Bailey* rule does)). *But cf.* In re Jones, 137 F.3d 1271, 1272 n.1 (11th Cir.) (*per curiam*), *cert. denied,* 118 S. Ct. 1351 (1998) (holding that retroactivity challenge to application of successive petitions limitations is "foreclosed" by *In re Medina, infra*); In re Medina, 109 F.3d 1556, 1561-63 (11th Cir. 1997) (at least in those cases in which petitioner cannot show "detrimental reliance" of sort presented in *Burris, infra,* application of successive petition limitations to petitioner who filed first petition prior to AEDPA's enactment is not improperly "retroactive").

Pre-*Lindh* decisions (some of which are partially superseded by *Lindh*) supporting the view that application of AEDPA's successive petition limitations to prisoners who filed their previous petition before the effective date of AEDPA may be improperly "retroactive" include United States v. Fykes, 1996 WL 699762, at *1 n.1 (10th Cir. Dec. 5, 1996); Burkett v. Love, 89 F.3d 135, 138 n.2 (3d Cir. 1996); Williams v. Calderon, 83 F.3d 281, 285 (9th Cir. 1996); Hill v. Straub, 950 F. Supp. 807, 808-09 (E.D. Mich. 1997); United States ex rel. Horton v. Detella, 1996 WL 543320, at *1 (N.D. Ill. Sept. 23, 1996); Moore v. White, 1996 WL 478681, at *2 (N.D. Cal. Aug. 19, 1996). *See also* In re Vial, 115 F.3d 1192, 1199-200 (4th Cir. 1997) (*en banc*) (Hall, J., dissenting, joined by Murnaghan and Michael, JJ.) (resolving retroactivity issue that majority declined to reach, *see id.* at 1198 n.13, and concluding that "[a]pplying the successive-motion provision to prisoners like Vial [whose first petition preceded AEDPA's enactment] ... offends the 'familiar considerations of notice, reasonable reliance, and settled expectations' that militate against retroactive application of a statute"); Burris v. Parke, 95 F.3d 465, 468 (7th Cir. 1996) (*en banc*) (refusing to apply AEDPA's new successive petition provisions because of retroactive effect of doing so under particular circumstances). *Cf.* Greenawalt v. Stewart, 105 F.3d 1268, 1273-76 (9th Cir.) (*per curiam*), *cert. denied,* 117 S. Ct. 794 (1997) (petitioner, whose pre-AEDPA successive petition was dismissed on nonexhaustion grounds and whose subsequent post-AEDPA refiling was subject to new successive petition standards, could claim no prejudice for purposes of Civil Rule 60(b) because his "plainly and concededly premature" initial pleading conferred no entitlement to proceed under pre-AEDPA law). *But see* Roldan v. United States, 96 F.3d 1013, 1014 (7th Cir.

- AEDPA's hearing provision explicitly makes a habeas corpus petitioner's "fail[ure] to develop the factual basis of a claim in *state court proceedings*" preclusive of the relevant facts' consideration in federal habeas corpus proceedings except upon proof of "cause" and "*innocence*."[35] Section 2255 premises a similar provision on a federal criminal defendant's failure to develop facts at or before the federal trial.[36] In cases in which these new provisions preclude the federal court from considering facts that otherwise would justify relief and as to which the petitioner can show either "cause" and "prejudice" *or* "innocence" (either of which avoided preclusion under pre-AEDPA law[37]) but as to which the petitioner cannot show "cause" *and* "innocence," the provision attaches the new legal consequence of preclusion of relief-warranting facts to the state prisoner's failure to present those facts in state court or the federal prisoner's failure to present them at trial. Because that failure is certain to have been "completed" prior to enactment if the habeas corpus petition was properly exhausted and then filed on or not too long after April 24, 1996, or if the section 2255 motion was filed not too long after that date, applying AEDPA in this manner would arguably have a "retroactive" effect of the sort that *Landgraf* bars absent a clear congressional statement.[38]

1996) (except in particular circumstances of *Burris, supra*, AEDPA's new standard for successive petitions applies to second petition filed before AEDPA became law); Williams v. Stegal, 945 F. Supp. 145, 147-48 (E.D. Mich. 1996) (similar; magistrate judge's recommendation).

For discussion of retroactivity problems that might accompany application of AEDPA's new certificate of appealability requirements to section 2255 (but not habeas corpus) cases in which the underlying motion was filed before, but the appeal was filed after, April 24, 1996, see *infra* note 46.

[35] 28 U.S.C.A. § 2254(e)(2) (West 1994 & Supp. 1998) (emphasis added) (discussed *infra* § 20.2b).

[36] *Id.* § 2255.

[37] See *infra* § 20.3e nn.103-08 and accompanying text.

[38] *Cf.* Breard v. Greene, 118 S. Ct. 1352, 1354 (1998) (*per curiam*) (Court treats section 2254(e)(2) as applicable to petition filed after AEDPA's effective date; although Court does not address retroactivity issue, Court's express finding that there was no "cause" for procedural default and implicit rejection of "innocence" establish that petitioner could not have shown "new legal consequence" described in text). *But cf.* Neelley v. Nagle, 138 F.3d 917, 921 (11th Cir. 1998) (rejecting petitioner's argument that "application of AEDPA to her petition would be fundamentally unfair and a violation of the Constitution's Ex Post Facto Clause, as AEDPA was not enacted until after she exhausted her state court remedies").

Pre-*Lindh* decisions that involve petitions filed before April 24, 1996, but with analysis supportive of the suggestion in text in regard to the retroactive effect of certain applications of section 2254(e)(2) to cases filed after that date in which state proceedings occurred before that date, include Jeffries v. Wood, 114 F.3d 1484, 1498 (9th Cir.) (*en banc*), *cert. denied*, 118 S. Ct. 586 (1997) (*dicta*) (application of section 2254(e)(2) would probably be "retroactive" under circumstances and thus would be barred by *Landgraf* because AEDPA's "restrict[ion]s [of] the

- Depending on how AEDPA's adjudication provision is interpreted, it might attach to a state court's denial of a meritorious legal claim the consequence that the claim "shall not be granted" in federal court,[39] although pre-AEDPA law provided that meritorious claims denied by the state courts *had to be* granted by a federal habeas corpus court.[40] Applying that interpretation would attach a "new legal consequence" (the substitution of a denial for a grant of relief) to an event that almost certainly was completed before enactment (the state court adjudication) if the habeas corpus petition containing a meritorious constitutional claim was exhausted in the state courts and filed on or not too long after April 24, 1996. *Landgraf* arguably forbids applications that would have this "retroactive" effect, absent a clear congressional statement.[41]

---

scope of federal review of mixed questions of fact and law ... fall within the very genre of intertwined procedural and substantive issues which compelled the *Landgraf* court to conclude that altering the right to a jury trial was not merely a procedural question"); Hernandez v. Johnson, 108 F.3d 554, 558 (5th Cir.), *cert. denied*, 118 S. Ct. 447 (1997) ("Application of § 2254 as amended is ... problematic for claims that were adjudicated in federal district court but not on the merits in state court before the passage of AEDPA."); Pitsonbarger v. Gramley, 103 F.3d 1293, 1306-07 (7th Cir. 1997) (reserving question of potential retroactive effects of section 2254(e)(2)); Thatsaphone v. Class, No. 95-4244 (D.S.D. June 11, 1996), at 7; *see also* Wilkins v. Bowersox, 933 F. Supp. 1496, 1504 n.3 (W.D. Mo. 1996).

[39] 28 U.S.C.A. § 2254(d)(1) (West 1994 & Supp. 1998) (discussed *infra* § 30.2).

[40] *See supra* §§ 2.4b n.9 and accompanying text, 2.4d nn.198-238 & 261-74 and accompanying text; *infra* §§ 20.3d, 25.5 nn.72, 101-38 and accompanying text, 30.2.

[41] *But cf. Neelley v. Nagle, supra*, 138 F.3d at 921 (discussed *supra* note 38). Pre-*Lindh* decisions reaching this conclusion in regard to cases filed before April 24, 1996, include *Jeffries v. Wood, supra*, 114 F.3d at 1498 (*dicta*) (discussed *supra* note 24); Boria v. Keane, 90 F.3d 36, 37 (2d Cir. 1996) (*dicta*) (if "new statute would require a different outcome, application of the new statute would be retroactive" and thus would be barred by *Landgraf*); Cockrum v. Johnson, 934 F. Supp. 1418, 1423-24 (E.D. Tex. 1996), *rev'd on other grounds*, 119 F.3d 297 (5th Cir. 1997); Thatsaphone v. Class, No. 95-4244 (D.S.D. June 11, 1996), at 7. *See also* Brief for Petitioner, 1997 WL 82672, at *30-50 (Parts III(A)-(B), at pp.73-107), Lindh v. Murphy, 117 S. Ct. 2059 (1997); Reply Brief for Petitioner, 1997 WL 163976, at *5-16 (Parts II(A)-(B), at pp.21-37), Lindh v. Murphy, 117 S. Ct. 2059 (1997) (both discussed *supra* note 31). *But see Lindh, supra*, 117 S. Ct. at 2070-72 (Rehnquist, C.J., dissenting) (discussed *supra* note 31 and accompanying text); Drinkard v. Johnson, 97 F.3d 751, 766-68 (5th Cir. 1996), *overruled in part*, United States v. Carter, 117 F.3d 262 (5th Cir. 1997); Lindh v. Murphy, 96 F.3d 856, 866-67 (7th Cir. 1996) (*en banc*), *rev'd*, 117 S. Ct. 2059 (1997); other decisions cited *supra* note 5 (fourth para.). Of course, if the constitutional claim is not meritorious, then applying AEDPA to deny the claim would not have a "retroactive" effect because the new statute attaches no "*new* legal consequence."

Federal habeas corpus petitioners with meritorious federal claims who decided to forgo post-direct-appeal *certiorari* petitions to the United States Supreme Court, which that Court has broad discretion to grant or deny, and state postconviction proceedings, which are subject to qualified "previously determined" bars, might have an additional argument for the proposition that applying AEDPA's new adjudication provision to them would have an improperly "retroactive" effect,

Below are three examples of nonopt-in provisions that are *not* likely to have an improperly "retroactive" effect when applied to cases filed after April 24, 1996:

- AEDPA's new provision permitting a court to deny a petition presenting only nonmeritorious claims, some of which are not exhausted,[42] rather than dismissing the petition without prejudice for nonexhaustion, attaches no new legal consequences to the filing of the nonmeritorious petition which, eventually, would have been denied under preexisting law.[43]

- AEDPA's modifications of the preexisting presumption of correctness of state court factfindings are sufficiently modest that they are unlikely to attach any new legal consequences to events (*e.g.*, the state court proceedings in which those factfindings were made) occurring before enactment.[44]

- The application of AEDPA's substantive standard for a "certificate of appealability"[45] to a habeas corpus petitioner's appeal filed after April 24, 1996 would not have a "retroactive" effect because that standard seems to be no more stringent than the standard previously applied to "certificates of

---

namely, that it would attach "new legal consequences" to their pre-AEDPA decision to pass up those remedies. At the time those decisions were made, the decisions had *no* adverse consequences because federal habeas corpus provided the prisoner with an unequivocally preferable — because *non*discretionary and *un*qualified — *right* to relief from the prisoners' unconstitutional incarceration. Insofar as AEDPA *forbids* relief on such claims, however, it becomes an unequivocally *less* attractive remedy than *certiorari* or state postconviction proceedings, which at least held out a possibility of relief and, accordingly, attaches to those pre-AEDPA decisions the new legal consequence of waiver of a meaningful and preferable right to seek relief from unconstitutional custody. See Brief for Petitioner, 1997 WL 82672, at *12-*14 (Part III(A)(3), at pp.44-46), Lindh v. Murphy, 117 S. Ct. 2059 (1997). *But see Lindh v. Murphy, supra*, 96 F.3d at 766-68.

[42] *See* 28 U.S.C.A. § 2254(b)(2) (West 1994 & Supp. 1998) (discussed *infra* §§ 23.1, 23.2a, 23.5).

[43] Decisions that support this conclusion (albeit in the context of pre-*Lindh* cases that were filed before April 24, 1996) are: Shute v. Texas, 117 F.3d 233 (5th Cir. 1997); Loving v. O'Keefe, 960 F. Supp. 46, 49-50 (S.D.N.Y. 1997); Cowan v. Artuz, 1996 WL 631726, at *4 (S.D.N.Y. Oct. 24, 1996) (magistrate judge's report). *But cf.* Cephas v. Gavin, 1997 WL 21385, at *2 n.2 (E.D.N.Y. Jan. 13, 1997) (declining to apply AEDPA's new exhaustion rule to petition filed before effective date of Act).

[44] 28 U.S.C.A. §§ 2254(d)(2), 2254(e)(1) (West 1994 & Supp. 1998) (discussed *supra* § 3.2 n.20 and accompanying text; *infra* § 20.2c). For a pre-*Lindh* decision concluding that AEDPA's modifications of the presumption of correctness did not have an improperly "retroactive" effect when applied to a case filed *before* April 24, 1996, see United States ex rel. Winston v. Page, 955 F. Supp. 952, 954 n.2 (N.D. Ill. 1997). The one aspect of AEDPA's presumption of correctness that might be sufficiently different from the preexisting presumption to have "retroactive" effects of the sort *Landgraf* forbids is discussed *infra* § 20.2c nn.79-81 and accompanying text.

[45] *See* 28 U.S.C.A. § 2253(c)(2) (West 1994 & Supp. 1998) (discussed *infra* § 35.4b).

probable cause to appeal" and because certificates of appealability seem to play the same role in habeas corpus appeals as was played previously by certificates of probable cause to appeal.[46]

---

[46] Among the pre-*Lindh* decisions reaching similar conclusions, albeit in cases filed before April 24, 1996, are Lyons v. Ohio Adult Parole Auth., 105 F.3d 1063, 1066-76 (6th Cir.), *cert. denied*, 117 S. Ct. 1724 (1997); United States v. Riddick, 104 F.3d 1239, 1240-41 (10th Cir. 1997); Hunter v. United States, 101 F.3d 1565, 1568-73 (11th Cir. 1996) (*en banc*), *cert. denied*, 117 S. Ct. 1695 (1997); Drinkard v. Johnson, 97 F.3d 751, 756 (5th Cir. 1996), *overruled in part*, United States v. Carter, 117 F.3d 262 (5th Cir. 1997); Reyes v. Keane, 90 F.3d 676, 679 (2d Cir. 1996), *overruled on other grounds*, Nelson v. Walker, 121 F.3d 828, 832-33 (2d Cir. 1997); United States v. Coyle, 944 F. Supp. 418, 419 (E.D. Pa. 1996); *see also* Herman v. Johnson, 98 F.3d 171, 173 (5th Cir. 1996), *cert. denied*, 117 S. Ct. 1262 (1997) (new certificate of appealability requirements apply to pending cases as long as they do not change preexisting standards for certificate of probable cause to appeal; reserving judgment on latter question); Sechrest v. Ignacio, 943 F. Supp. 1253 (D. Nev. 1996) (similar).

As is noted *supra* § 3.4a n.16 and accompanying text, nearly all circuit courts have held that *Lindh* forbids the application of AEDPA's new certificate of appealability provisions to appeals filed after April 24, 1996, as long as the underlying habeas corpus petition or section 2255 motion was filed in the district court on or before that date. In circuits reaching this conclusion, it is highly unlikely that any retroactivity issue relating to the application of the certificate of appealability provisions could arise, because there is not likely to be any *preenactment* event (meaning an event occurring before the underlying petition or motion was *filed*) to which new legal consequences are even arguably attached. The 8th Circuit follows a different rule, however, under which the date of the filing of the appeal, not the date of the filing of the underlying habeas corpus petition or section 2255 motion, controls the question whether AEDPA's appealability requirements apply to the appeal. *See supra* § 3.4a n.16. The 8th Circuit rule invites retroactivity claims of the sort addressed in the text accompanying this footnote. Although our analysis of the weakness of such claims applies to habeas corpus petitions, it does *not* apply to section 2255 motions. Prior to AEDPA, appeals of the denial of section 2255 relief (by contrast to appeals of the denial of section 2254 relief) were matters of right that did not require a certificate of probable cause to appeal. Applying AEDPA's new certificate of appealability requirements to a postenactment appeal of a section 2255 motion that was filed and litigated prior to AEDPA's enactment (as the 8th Circuit's approach requires) thus might raise serious retroactivity issues — *e.g.*, if the movant could show that her failure to demonstrate the substantiality of one of her claims in a page-limited brief filed in the district court prior to AEDPA's enactment had no adverse legal consequences vis-a-vis appeal of the sort that subsequently were imposed by AEDPA's adoption of a bar to the appeal of particular section 2255 claims that had not theretofore been shown to be "substantial." 28 U.S.C.A. § 2253(c)(3) (West 1994 & Supp. 1998) (discussed *infra* § 35.4b nn.16-18 and accompanying text). In Dickey v. United States, 118 S. Ct. 2365 (1998) (*mem.*), the Supreme Court vacated and remanded for reconsideration in light of *Lindh* a lower court decision applying AEDPA's amended section 2253 in a section 2255 action in which the appeal was filed after, but the section 2255 motion was filed before, April 24, 1996. *See supra* § 3.4a n.16. *Dickey*'s citation of *Lindh* suggests that the Court's difficulty with the lower court decision was a function of the statutory interpretation analysis in *Lindh*, and was not a function of retroactivity concerns of a sort that *Lindh* avoided. *See supra* note 18; *supra* § 3.4a n.5. If so, *Dickey*'s implications apply equally to habeas corpus and section 2255 cases. Nonetheless, *Dickey* might also be read as a reaction to the

(3) The final step in the *Lindh* and *Landgraf* analysis is to resolve the question whether AEDPA contains a clear statement requiring any "retroactive" effects that would be produced by its application to cases filed on or after April 24, 1996.[47] On this question, the answer is obvious. Because AEDPA nowhere delineates in specific terms the postenactment nonopt-in cases to which Congress insisted that the statute would apply, AEDPA does not achieve the clarity that the Court (as reprised in *Lindh*) has required in order to overcome the antiretroactivity presumption and to satisfy the Court's other "clear statement" rules.[48] Put another way, because *Lindh* found that AEDPA only "implicitly" established its inapplicability to *pre*enactment nonopt-in cases by negative implication from section 107(c), and because one would have to draw the same kind of negative implication in order to discern Congress' intent to apply the statute to *post*enactment nonopt-in cases,[49] AEDPA provides nothing approaching a "clear statement" on the latter question.

c. *Chapter 154 cases filed before or after April 24, 1996*. AEDPA's section 107(c) provides that "Chapter 154 ... shall apply to cases pending on or after the date of enactment."[50] Interpreted according to the Court's usual rules of statutory construction, this provision would suggest that AEDPA applies to all cases governed by Chapter 154 — *i.e.*, to all capital opt-in cases[51] — no matter when those cases were filed. Moreover, because Chapter 154 expressly incorporates two of the new Chapter 153 provisions (28 U.S.C. §§ 2254(d) and (e)),[52] section 107(c) would seem to apply those new provisions, as well, to all capital opt-in

---

retroactivity problems that the 8th Circuit's approach to the applicability of the new certificate of appealability requirements invites in section 2255, but not in habeas corpus, cases.

[47] *See supra* notes 19, 25 and accompanying text.

[48] *See supra* note 25 and accompanying text; *infra* § 3.4c n.57 and accompanying text.

[49] *Lindh, supra*, 117 S. Ct. at 2063-64, 2068; *see id.* at 2063 ("amendments to chapter 153 were assumed and meant to apply to the general run of habeas cases only when those cases had been filed after [April 24, 1996]"); *infra* § 3.4c n.57 and accompanying text. The argument proceeds as follows: Because the only preenactment cases to which section 107(c) makes AEDPA applicable are preenactment *opt-in* cases, that section implicitly makes the statute *in*applicable to preenactment *nonopt-in* cases. (This, of course, is the holding of *Lindh*.) Moreover, because section 107(c) implicitly makes AEDPA inapplicable to *preenactment* nonopt-in cases, it impliedly *does* intend for the statute to apply to *postenactment* nonopt-in cases. Whatever the validity of this analysis as a matter of the Court's "normal rules of construction," *id.* at 2063, it disproves the existence of a "clear congressional statement."

[50] Antiterrorism and Effective Death Penalty Act of 1996, § 107(c), Pub. L. 104-132, 110 Stat. 1214 (1996).

[51] *See supra* § 3.2 nn.11-14, 28-34 and accompanying text; *supra* § 3.3 (describing subset of capital, state-prisoner habeas corpus cases governed by Chapter 154).

[52] *See* 28 U.S.C.A. § 2264(b) (West Supp. 1998) (incorporating 28 U.S.C. §§ 2254(d), 2254(e) (West 1994 & Supp. 1998)).

cases, no matter when filed.[53] As the preceding discussion indicates, however, matters are not so simple. Although this outcome is likely to obtain in many Chapter 154 cases, it is not necessarily appropriate in all of them. Thus, (1) if any of the Chapter 154 (or incorporated Chapter 153) provisions has a "retroactive effect"[54] in a particular case filed before or after April 24, 1996, and (2) if section 107(c) falls short of a "clear statement"[55] requiring that retroactive effect, then those provisions would *not* apply to that case, regardless of the usual rules of statutory construction. Moreover, as noted above, *Lindh* itself contains *dicta* in regard to the first of these qualifications suggesting the possibility that some of the Chapter 154 (and incorporated Chapter 153) provisions have "retroactive effects."[56]

Lindh also has *dicta* in regard to the second of these qualifications that rather strongly suggest that AEDPA contains no "clear statement" requiring any retroactive effects that the Chapter 154 (and incorporated Chapter 153) provisions would have if applied to particular cases:

> [T]he terms of § 107(c) may *not* amount to the clear statement required for a mandate to apply a statute in the disfavored way,[4] [because] they ... [only] serve to make clear as a general matter that chapter 154 applies to pending cases when its terms fit those cases at the particular procedural points they have reached. (As to that, of course, there may well be difficult issues, and it may be that application of *Landgraf*'s default rule [forbidding retroactive application when Congress' intent is not "clear"] will be necessary to settle some of them).
>
> [4] *Landgraf* suggested that the following language from an unenacted precursor of the statute at issue in that case might possibly have qualified as a clear statement for retroactive effect: "[This Act] shall

---

[53] On the question whether some or all of the provisions of Chapter 153 of the habeas corpus statute that are *not* expressly incorporated in Chapter 154 apply to some or all cases governed by Chapter 154 (*i.e.*, to capital opt-in cases) — whenever those cases may have been filed — see *supra* § 3.2 n.34 and accompanying text. *If* unincorporated portions of Chapter 153 apply to capital opt-in cases, the question arises whether the 1996 amendments to the unincorporated portions of Chapter 153 apply to particular temporally defined classes of Chapter 154 cases. The answer to that question (again, making the assumption, *arguendo*, that the portions of Chapter 153 that are not explicitly incorporated in Chapter 154 nonetheless apply to Chapter 154 cases) is set out *supra* § 3.4a in regard to Chapter 154 cases filed *on or before* April 24, 1996, and is set out *supra* § 3.4b in regard to Chapter 154 cases filed *after* that date. In other words, the applicability to Chapter 154 cases of the unincorporated portions of Chapter 153 (assuming they apply at all) is determined by the same retroactivity rules as control the entire Act's applicability to Chapter 153 cases.

[54] *See supra* § 3.4b nn.21-24 and accompanying effect (defining "retroactive effect").

[55] *See supra* § 3.4b nn.19, 25, 47-49 and accompanying text (defining "clear statement").

[56] *See supra* § 3.4b nn.21-24 and accompanying text.

apply to *all* proceedings pending on or commenced after the date of enactment of this Act." *Landgraf*, 511 U.S., at 260 (emphasis added; internal quotation marks omitted). *But, even if that language did qualify, its use of the sort of absolute language absent from § 107(c) distinguishes it.* Cf. *United States v. Williams*, 514 U.S. 527, 531-532 (1995) (finding a waiver of sovereign immunity "unequivocally expressed" in language granting jurisdiction to the courts over "*[a]ny* civil action against the United States for the recovery of *any* internal-revenue tax alleged to have been erroneously or illegally assessed or collected") (emphasis in *Williams*) (internal quotation marks omitted).[57]

Given section 107(c)'s omission of the word "all" or "any," and given the importance of such clear language under the principles reprised in footnote 4 of the above passage, there is strong reason to conclude that section 107(c) does not amount to the necessary clear statement. If that is so, courts would have to apply *Landgraf*'s default rule forbidding the application of any of the Chapter 154 (and incorporated Chapter 153 provisions) found to have "retroactive effects" when applied to particular cases.

The determinative question, therefore, is likely to be whether application of any of Chapter 154's provisions, and any of the Chapter 153 amendments incorporated in Chapter 154, *has* "retroactive effects" in particular preenactment or postenactment cases. Certainly, the application of Chapter 154's 180-day statute of limitations to dismiss a case in which the limitations period expired before April 24, 1996 (whether or not the federal petition was filed after that date) would qualify as a retroactive effect.[58] So also (as the Court explicitly left open in *dicta* in *Lindh*[59]) might the application of the incorporated Chapter 153 provisions that govern the standard of review of legal and factual questions, assuming that their application resulted in the denial of a petition that would not have been denied under the preexisiting habeas corpus statute and did so because

---

[57] *Lindh*, *supra*, 117 S. Ct. at 2064 (some emphasis added).

[58] *See* Dubois v. Angelone, No. 96-10 (4th Cir. Aug. 27, 1996) (*dicta*) (discussed *infra* § 5.1b n.56); Breard v. Angelone, 926 F. Supp. 546, 547 (E.D. Va. 1996) ("The Court finds that § 2263 infringes on the privilege of habeas corpus in this case because prior to its passage, the petitioner would not have been time barred, yet upon its passage he was immediately time barred; the statute provides for no safe harbor or special exception. The law would require the petitioner, prior to the passage of § 2263, to have anticipated this effect. Section 2263 in the instant case is inadequate to test the legality of the petitioner's conviction and completely prevents any consideration of the equities of the case; therefore, § 2263 violates the suspension clause and is unconstitutional as applied. The Court thus interprets the Act's 180-day limitations period as commencing for purposes of this case on April 24, 1996, the effective date of the new § 2263."); *see also* other authority discussed *supra* § 3.4b n.28.

[59] *Lindh*, *supra*, 117 S. Ct. at 2063 (quoted *supra* text accompanying § 3.4b n.30).

of some *preenactment* event that occurred during exhaustion proceedings in state courts (again, whether or not the federal petition or motion was filed before or after enactment).[60] And so also might the application of Chapter 154's strict procedural default rule so as to deny relief on the basis of a preenactment default in state court that would not have resulted in a denial of federal relief under the preexisting habeas corpus statute.[61]

There is at least one other important implication of *Lindh*'s suggestions that certain Chapter 154 (and incorporated Chapter 153) provisions may not apply to particular cases because their application would have retroactive effects not clearly required by Congress. As is discussed in § 3.3, there are two ways the courts might interpret Chapter 154's *quid pro quo* mechanism, under which States that "opt-in" by upgrading their state postconviction procedures in capital cases (*e.g.*, by making competent counsel available to indigent petitioners) receive, in return, the benefit of narrowed and expedited federal habeas corpus procedures. The statute may reward States for providing the "opt-in" procedures in state postconviction proceedings by affording the States procedural advantages in federal habeas corpus proceedings involving either *only* those petitioners who *themselves* had access to the upgraded state postconviction procedures or *all* capital petitioners including even those who completed state postconviction before the upgraded procedures were made available.[62] Subjecting particular habeas corpus petitioners to a raft of disadvantages — including ones (*e.g.*, a narrowed statute of limitations and restrictive standards of review) of the sort that *Lindh* identified as presenting potential retroactivity problems — as a *quid pro quo* for procedural advantages in state court that those petitioners *did not receive*, on the ground that *other* prisoners will receive them in the future, would present precisely the fairness concerns that led *Landgraf* to reaffirm the antiretroactivity presumption:

> [R]etroactive statutes raise particular concerns. The Legislature's unmatched powers allow it to sweep away settled expectations suddenly and *without individualized consideration.* Its responsivity to political pressures poses a risk that it may be tempted to use retroactive legislation as a means of retribution against unpopular groups or individuals.... [Antiretroactivity rules are designed to] "restrict[] governmental power by restraining arbitrary and potentially vindicative legislation."[63]

---

[60] The basis for such a conclusion is the same as that developed *supra* § 3.4b nn.29-41 and accompanying text.

[61] *See* 28 U.S.C.A. § 2264(a) (West Supp. 1998) (discussed *supra* § 3.3c nn.65-73 and accompanying text).

[62] *See supra* § 3.3b nn.15-21 and accompanying text.

[63] *Landgraf, supra,* 511 U.S. at 266-67 (emphasis added; citation omitted).

Assuming (as *Lindh* strongly implies) that section 107(c) is not a "clear statement" of intent to impose retroactive effects,[64] the antiretroactivity presumption may well compel courts faced with "'plausible' alternative interpretations"[65] of Chapter 154 to reject the one that would attach these "new legal consequences" to state postconviction proceedings that the State has upgraded for *future* capital prisoners but did not afford the petitioner in question when *he* was suing in state court.

These matters remain conjectural because, as of this writing, no State has qualified for "opt-in" treatment in any capital case that is the subject of a published opinion.

§ 3.5. Overview of the habeas corpus process in non-AEDPA and AEDPA cases.

a. *Stages of the case prior to federal habeas corpus review; implications for federal habeas corpus*. The following chronology of a state criminal case identifies the various stages of the state trial, appellate, and postconviction processes that (1) may give rise to federal constitutional or statutory claims cognizable in federal habeas corpus proceedings and (2) may affect the availability of federal habeas corpus review of those claims because of the ways in which the claims were litigated or defaulted at the trial, appellate, or postconviction stages. For a detailed discussion of the principles governing the cognizability of claims in federal habeas corpus, including the extent to which state law claims may have federal implications and thus may be cognizable, see Chapter 9 *infra*. For additional examples of constitutional and statutory claims that have led to a federal court's grant of a writ of habeas corpus, see section 11.2c *infra*. For a detailed discussion of the ways in which the litigation of or failure to litigate claims in the state courts may affect the availability of habeas corpus review and relief, see Chapters 23, 26 *infra*. In addition to the substantive or procedural claims that may arise at each of the following stages, defense counsel's errors or omissions at one or more of these stages may give rise to a federal constitutional claim of ineffectiveness of counsel and may excuse defaults of claims.

Although the primary purpose of this chronology is to assist habeas corpus counsel in analyzing prior proceedings to determine whether they reveal possible claims cognizable on habeas corpus and to assess how the litigation of the claims during the prior proceedings is likely to affect the availability of habeas corpus review and relief, counsel at prior stages of the case also may find the discussion helpful in recognizing and preserving claims (*e.g.*, by means of timely object-

---

[64] *See supra* § 3.4b nn.19, 25; *supra* § 3.4c n.57 and accompanying text.

[65] *Lindh, supra*, 117 S. Ct. at 2064 n.4.

ions) for later presentation in habeas corpus proceedings. Sections 23.1 and 26.1 *infra* discuss the harmful effects on habeas corpus petitioners caused by the failure of counsel at prior stages to utilize available state remedies and fully preserve federal constitutional and statutory claims. Familiarity with local rules is essential because a violation of state procedural requirements (*e.g.*, deadlines for filing pretrial motions, contemporaneous objection rules, and requirements for perfecting appeals and presenting claims on appeal) may cause a procedural default that bars habeas corpus review.

For further discussion of the procedures followed in felony and misdemeanor trials and the constitutional issues that may arise, see generally 1-3 ANTHONY G. AMSTERDAM, TRIAL MANUAL FOR THE DEFENSE OF CRIMINAL CASES (5th ed. 1988-89). For an equivalent discussion of procedure and constitutional issues in juvenile delinquency trials, see generally 1-2 RANDY HERTZ, MARTIN GUGGENHEIM & ANTHONY G. AMSTERDAM, TRIAL MANUAL FOR DEFENSE ATTORNEYS IN JUVENILE COURT (1991).

In the following outline, "*infra*" cross-references refer to sections of this book. Section references designated "TM" refer to Anthony G. Amsterdam's TRIAL MANUAL FOR THE DEFENSE OF CRIMINAL CASES (5th ed.), *supra*.

(1) *Pretrial proceedings*:
  (a) Appointment of counsel (TM §§ 14, 45-46, 53, 130-32, 190-92);
  (b) Determination of probable cause to hold accused pending further proceedings, *see* Gerstein v. Pugh, 420 U.S. 103 (1975) (TM §§ 125-27, 131-33, 139-44, 363);
  (c) Preliminary Hearing (TM §§ 124-47);
  (d) Grand Jury proceedings (TM §§ 153-55, 158-67, 172);
  (e) Arraignment (TM §§ 45-49, 53, 173-78, 188-200, 422);
  (f) Investigation (TM §§ 106-22);
  (g) Assessment of competency to stand trial (TM §§ 120-22, 180-81; *see also infra* § 20.3d n.55);
  (h) Pretrial motions, including:
      (i)   Motions to challenge sufficiency of charging paper or procedures used in securing indictment (TM §§ 135-36, 153-54, 158, 172-78; *see also infra* § 9.1 nn.14, 19);
      (ii) Motions to dismiss charging paper or counts on double jeopardy grounds (TM §§ 177, 422; *see also infra* § 5.2 n.6);
      (iii) Motions for dismissal for prosecutorial misconduct (TM §§ 422, 445);
      (iv) Motions for severance or consolidation of counts or codefendants (TM §§ 259-64);
      (v)   Motions for change of venue (TM §§ 254-57);

      (vi) Pretrial motions to challenge jury selection procedures (motions to quash the venire, object to the array, and so forth) (TM §§ 158, 172, 319-24);

      (vii) Motions for recusal or disqualification of the judge (TM § 258);

      (viii) Motions to suppress tangible evidence for violations of the 4th, 5th, or 14th Amendments or federal statutes governing electronic surveillance and wiretapping (TM §§ 223-53; 1-5 WAYNE R. LaFAVE, SEARCH AND SEIZURE: A TREATISE ON THE FOURTH AMENDMENT (3d ed. 1996 & Supp. 1998); *see also infra* § 9.2 & *infra* Chapter 27 (limitations on federal habeas corpus review of 4th Amendment exclusionary rule claims));

      (ix) Motions to suppress confessions, admissions, or other statements of the accused for violations of the 4th, 5th, 6th, or 14th Amendments (TM §§ 9, 232-33, 239, 249, 363-67; *see also infra* § 9.2 (*Stone v. Powell* doctrine inapplicable to claims other than 4th Amendment exclusionary rule claims));

      (x) Motions to suppress identification testimony for violations of the 4th, 5th, 6th, or 14th Amendments (TM §§ 233, 374);

      (xi) Speedy trial motions (TM §§ 306-11; *see also infra* § 5.2 n.5);

      (xii) Motions for a continuance (TM §§ 53, 270(A), 304);

      (xiii) Motions or applications for state funds for investigators, expert witnesses, transcripts, or other resources or tools for preparing for trial (TM §§ 266, 299-301; *see also infra* §§ 7.2a, 7.2b, 19.3);

  (i)   Pretrial discovery (TM §§ 265-76);

  (j)   Defense use of compulsory process to secure witnesses for trial (TM §§ 270, 285-93);

  (k)   Interlocutory review of pretrial rulings by means of writs of mandamus or prohibition (TM §§ 312-14);

  (l)   Guilty pleas (TM §§ 195-97, 201-20).

(2) *Trial:*

  (a)   *In limine* motions and other preliminary rulings (invocations of rule on witnesses, motions to close the trial, to sequester the jury, and so forth) (TM §§ 224(D), 343, 346-49, 358);

  (b)   Jury selection (TM §§ 326-40);

  (c)   Opening statements (TM §§ 350-53; *see also infra* § 9.1 nn.17, 24, 25);

(d)   The prosecution's direct case: cross-examination of prosecution witnesses and evidentiary rulings during the direct case (TM §§ 354-69, 370-84, 411-22; *see also infra* § 9.1 nn.16, 23);

(e)   Motion for judgment of acquittal (TM §§ 385-87, 423-33; *see also infra* § 9.1 nn.15, 20);

(f)   The defense case: presentation of defense witnesses and evidentiary rulings during the defense case (TM §§ 388-410; *see also infra* § 9.1 nn.16, 23);

(g)   The prosecution's rebuttal case and defense surrebuttal case (*see* authorities cited *supra* para. (2)(d), (2)(f));

(h)   Renewal of the motion for acquittal (TM §§ 423-33; *see also infra* § 9.1 nn.15, 20);

(i)   Closing arguments (TM §§ 444-48; *see also infra* § 9.1 nn.17, 24, 25);

(j)   Jury instructions (TM §§ 434-43; *see also infra* § 9.1 nn.18, 27);

(k)   Jury deliberations and verdict (TM §§ 450-54).

(3) *Postverdict proceedings*:

(a)   Motions for acquittal or judgment N.O.V. or new trial on grounds of insufficiency of evidence (TM §§ 456-58; *see also infra* § 9.1 nn.15, 20);

(b)   Motions for a new trial based on newly discovered evidence (TM §§ 455-58).

(4) *Sentencing*:

(a)   Capital cases: The sentencing stage of a capital trial may give rise to a wide range of federal constitutional issues, including those relating to the constitutionality of the state death penalty statute on its face or as applied; the procedures for preparing and providing the defense with the presentence report; the procedures for affording indigent defendants the resources needed to prepare adequately for sentencing; the procedures employed at the sentencing hearing; evidentiary rulings at the hearing; conduct of the prosecutor or judge at the hearing; jury instructions; procedures employed in reaching the verdict; and the sufficiency of the verdict. *See generally* RANDALL COYNE & LYN ENTZEROTH, CAPITAL PUNISHMENT AND THE JUDICIAL PROCESS (1994). *See also* TM § 468-A; *infra* §§ 9.1 n.22, 11.2c (para. (11)(a), (13)(d)). For an out-of-date but still potentially useful list of claims, see 2 JAMES S. LIEBMAN, FEDERAL HABEAS CORPUS PRACTICE AND PROCEDURE App. E (1st ed. 1988).

(b)   Noncapital cases: Although the array of federal constitutional rights applicable to noncapital sentencing is not as extensive or as well-defined as in the capital context, a noncapital sentencing may give rise to federal constitutional claims regarding the procedures for preparing and disclosing the presentence report, state funding for expert witnesses, validity of sentencing statutes on their face or as applied, sentencing procedures (particularly with regard to the imposition of special sentencing enhancement provisions), and the imposition of multiple punishments in violation of double jeopardy prohibitions. *See generally* TM §§ 460-68, 469-71; ARTHUR C. CAMPBELL, LAW OF SENTENCING (2d ed. 1991 & Supp. 1997); MARCIA G. SHEIN & JANA L. JOPSON, SENTENCING DEFENSE MANUAL: ADVOCACY, PRACTICE, PROCEDURE (1988 & Supp. 1998); *infra* § 9.1 nn.28, 32-34 and accompanying text; *infra* §§ 11.2c (paras. (11)(b), 13(d)), 41.2b nn.20-22 and accompanying text.

(5) *Direct appeal:*

The description of the federal appellate process for federal habeas corpus cases in Chapters 35-38 *infra* provides a very rough guide to the appellate process for the direct review of criminal cases in the vast majority of States. (The requirement of a certificate for leave to appeal (termed a "certificate of probable cause to appeal" in cases that are not, and a "certificate of appealability" in cases that are, governed by the Antiterrorism and Effective Death Penalty Act, Pub. L. 104-132, 110 Stat. 1214 (1996) (AEDPA) (discussed *supra* §§ 3.1-3.4)), which is discussed in section 35.4 *infra* is peculiar to habeas corpus proceedings, however.) *See generally* JONATHAN H. PURVER & LAWRENCE TAYLOR, HANDLING CRIMINAL APPEALS (1980 & Supp. 1993). Local rules must be consulted for specific requirements (some of which may be jurisdictional) for initiating an appeal, identifying claims the appellant intends to present for appellate review, briefing and arguing a case on appeal, and responding to an adverse appellate ruling by seeking rehearing and/or appealing to a higher state court. In many States, there are specialized procedures for appeals in capital cases. Some of these States have adopted a "unitary review" process that consolidates the direct review and postconviction stages. *See generally supra* § 3.3b nn.9-12 and accompanying text. Familiarity with state and local appellate rules governing the timing and content of pleadings is essential because a violation of such rules may be deemed a procedural default that bars federal habeas corpus review. *See* Chapter 26 *infra*. Moreover, a failure to utilize an available appellate remedy may result in a finding of nonexhaustion of state remedies, *see infra* § 23.3b, which in turn may result in a finding of a procedural default, *see infra* §§ 23.1 nn.21-30 and accompanying text, 26.1 n.25.

All state court appeals "as of right" must be utilized to avoid a later argument that the prisoner failed to exhaust state remedies or, possibly, procedurally defaulted. *See infra* §§ 23.3b, 26.1. Utilization of appellate procedures that state law classifies as "discretionary" (which, in some states, may take the form of petitioning for review or *certiorari* by the highest state court following an intermediate appellate court's affirmance) may not be necessary to exhaust state remedies. *See id.* The safer course, however, is to take advantage of any such discretionary appellate remedies afforded by state law, both in order to avoid the risk of a later finding of nonexhaustion and to maximize the range of newly announced Supreme Court precedents that may be considered part of the body of applicable law under the *Teague* doctrine of nonretroactivity (*see infra* §§ 5.1a, 25.6) and, in AEDPA cases, section 2254(d)(1)'s standard for reviewing state court determinations of law (*see infra* § 30.2). In cases in which the intermediate appellate court affirmed a conviction, there is rarely any strategic benefit to be gained from bypassing opportunities for discretionary review by a higher state court, except perhaps when the intermediate appeals court ruled on the merits and the higher court instead may dispose of the case on procedural grounds that would bar federal habeas corpus review (*see infra* § 26.2e) or when a noncapital prisoner with a comparatively short sentence wants to avoid the delay involved in a state remedy that counsel and the client have determined to be unnecessary and unlikely to produce relief.

Following review by the highest state court to hear criminal appeals (or, when applicable, denial of review by the highest state court that has discretion to hear appeals of criminal convictions), a defendant may file a petition for a writ of *certiorari* in the Supreme Court of the United States pursuant to 28 U.S.C. § 1257(3) (1994). *See generally* ROBERT L. STERN, EUGENE GRESSMAN, STEPHEN M. SHAPIRO & KENNETH S. GELLER, SUPREME COURT PRACTICE §§ 3.1-4.25, 5.1-5.15, at 88-210, 222-62 (7th ed. 1993). *See also infra* § 6.4 (*certiorari* following state postconviction review); *infra* Chapter 39 (*certiorari* following federal habeas corpus review). A petition for *certiorari* is not necessary to exhaust state remedies (*see supra* § 2.4d nn.251-60 and accompanying text; *infra* § 23.3b) and a noncapital defendant who prefers to avoid delay may wish to proceed directly to state postconviction remedies (*see infra* § 6.4b). Here again, utilization of the remedy has the benefit of maximizing the range of "new rules" announced by the Supreme Court and lower federal courts that apply retroactively in habeas corpus proceedings under the *Teague* doctrine (*see infra* §§ 5.1a, 25.6), but a petition for *certiorari* apparently would not similarly extend the body of Supreme Court precedents deemed relevant by AEDPA's standard of review of state court determinations of law (*see infra* § 30.2). Counsel practicing in States that have qualified for "opt-in" treatment under AEDPA (*see supra* § 3.3) must bear in mind that the tolling provision of the applicable statute of limitations does not apply to the time devoted to the preparation of a petition for *certiorari* from the final state court judgment on direct review; tolling does not begin until the *certiorari* petition actually is filed (*see infra* § 5.1b). In nonopt-in cases governed by AEDPA, however — meaning all noncapital and federal prisoner cases and many state prisoner habeas corpus cases (*see supra* §§ 3.2, 3.3a, 3.3b) — the applicable one-year statute of limitations apparently *is* tolled while a timely *certiorari* petition is being prepared (*see infra* § 5.1b).

In cases in which the state appellate process is flawed or insufficiently hospitable to an appellant's claims, the appeal itself may give rise to federal constitutional claims that may be adjudicated in federal habeas corpus proceedings. *See infra* §§ 9.1 n.28, 33.4 n.2. The most common violation occurring on appeal is ineffective assistance of appellate counsel. Federal habeas corpus also may be available, however, to review aspects of a state's appellate procedure (as, for example, when a state violates equal protection by denying indigent appellants adequate legal representation or adequate funding for transcripts or other needed resources) or the actions of the state appeals courts in a particular case (as, for example, when a state court violates due process by relying on evidence outside the record or on legal theories of guilt not subsumed within the indictment or information, or when an appellate court withholds the kind of review of death sentences that the 8th Amendment requires).

(6) *State postconviction review*:

All States provide some form of postconviction review, which may be denominated "habeas corpus," "*coram nobis*," "postconviction relief," "relief from personal restraint," or the like. *See generally* Chapters 6 and 7 *infra*. In most States, the remedy is established by statute or court rules (which sometimes are based on the federal-prisoner postconviction remedy in 28 U.S.C.A. § 2255 (West 1994 & Supp. 1998), discussed *infra* Chapter 41), but in others it is authorized by common law. The scope of postconviction review, and the procedures by which it may be sought, vary widely from State to State. Familiarity with local rules is essential to assure exhaustion of state remedies and to avoid a procedural default barring federal habeas corpus review. *See infra* §§ 23.1, 23.3b (exhaustion), 26.1 (procedural default). A detailed State-by-State survey of postconviction procedures may be found in DONALD E. WILKES JR., STATE POSTCONVICTION REMEDIES AND RELIEF (1996). *See also* LARRY W. YACKLE, POSTCONVICTION REMEDIES § 13 (1981 & Supp. 1998). There is no substitute, however, for careful examination of state and local rules. Attorneys unfamiliar with local practice also should consult experienced practitioners within the jurisdiction (and, when appropriate, court clerks) to become familiar with the idiosyncrasies of practice in the local court.

As a general rule, state postconviction relief is limited to two types of claims — violations of the federal or state constitutions or federal and state law guarantees of "fundamental" rights; and other nonconstitutional violations that could not adequately be raised at trial or on direct appeal (because, for example, they depend upon evidence that was unavailable at the time). In many States, a petition for postconviction relief is filed in a trial-level state court, where an evidentiary hearing may be held on any claims that require factfinding. If the trial court denies postconviction relief, the ruling typically may be appealed to a higher state court. In some States, the appellate ruling may be appealed still further, either as of right or through discretionary review. Following the conclusion of the state postconviction process, a state prisoner may file a petition for a writ of *certiorari* in the Supreme Court of the United States to review the federal questions raised in the postconviction petition. *See infra* § 6.4. *See generally* STERN ET AL., *supra* at 106-87, 236-39. (Counsel in cases governed by AEDPA should be aware that the Act's statutes of limitations probably are *not* tolled while *certiorari* petitions following state postconviction proceedings are being prepared and litigated. Counsel accordingly may have to consider forgoing such *certiorari* petitions or filing them simultaneously with timely federal habeas corpus petitions. *See infra* § 5.1b.)

If a claim was adequately litigated on direct appeal, a prisoner generally need not present it again in state postconviction proceedings in order to satisfy the exhaustion requirement and avoid a procedural default. *See infra* § 23.3b. Moreover, many States restrict postconviction review of claims that were or could have been raised at trial or on appeal. If, however, exhaustive litigation was not possible or did not take place at the direct appeal stage, utilization of the state postconviction process may be essential to preserve the claim for federal habeas corpus review. *See infra* §§ 6.2, 41.4a nn.6-7 and accompanying text. Exceptions to state law preclusion doctrines for previously raised or previously defaulted claims often are available in such situations. *Cf. infra* § 26.2b. Moreover, there may be tactical reasons for resorting to state postconviction remedies even when a claim has been adequately litigated on direct appeal. *See infra* §§ 6.2, 23.4b.

For further discussion of state postconviction procedures, *see infra* §§ 6.1, 6.2. For discussion of the procedures for obtaining stays of execution during postconviction review, *see infra* § 6.3. For discussion of the strategic considerations involved in deciding whether to seek *certiorari* review in the Supreme Court following a denial of state postconviction relief, *see infra* § 6.4. For discussion of constitutional bases for insisting upon fuller state postconviction remedies and, possibly, for raising challenges to state postconviction proceedings as independent bases for federal habeas corpus relief (or, at least, for avoiding state defenses to habeas corpus relief), *see infra* §§ 7.1b, 7.2.

b. *Outline of federal habeas corpus proceedings.*

Note: The following outline distinguishes, when doing so is helpful, between federal habeas corpus cases that are not governed by the Antiterrorism and Effective Death Penalty Act, Pub. L. 104-132, 110 Stat. 1214 (1996) (AEDPA), cases that are governed by AEDPA's nonopt-in provisions, and cases that are governed by AEDPA's opt-in provisions. For an introduction to these three categories of cases and the rules that govern each, see supra §§ 3.2, 3.3a-b, 3.4. Rules set out below without qualifying language are applicable to all three types of cases.

PREPARATION AND FILING OF PETITION

(1) When to file petition:

 (a) After "total exhaustion" of state remedies on *all* claims in petition. *See infra* §§ 5.3, 11.1, 13.3, 23.5. (Under one, controversial reading of 28 U.S.C. § 2264(a), exhaustion of some claims is not required in AEDPA opt-in cases. *See supra* § 3.3c nn.65-79 and accompanying text.)

 (b) Early enough to avoid state's invocation of defense of "prejudicial delay" under Rule 9(a) of the Rules Governing § 2254 Cases. *See infra* § 5.1b; *infra* Chapter 24.

 (c) During period in which petitioner is "in custody" (including not only a term of incarceration but also parole, probation, and certain other types of restraint). *See infra* § 8.2.

 (d) Additional requirement in AEDPA cases: Statute of limitations:

  (i) Nonopt-in States: Petition must be filed within one year from date on which judgment of conviction and sentence became final upon completion of direct review (including *certiorari* proceedings in Supreme Court), or, in applicable cases, from date on which unconstitutional impediment to filing claim was removed or on which legal or factual bases for claim became discoverable through due diligence. Statute of limitations is tolled while properly filed state postconviction pro-

ceedings are pending. *See supra*
§ 3.2; *infra* § 5.1b.

(ii) Opt-in States: Petition must be filed
within 180 days from date of final
State court affirmance of conviction and sentence on direct review
or expiration of time for seeking
such review. Statute of limitations
is tolled while Supreme Court considers (but not during time taken to
prepare) petition for *certiorari* from
final state court judgment on direct
review and while state courts consider *first* petition for post-conviction review or other collateral relief. Upon showing of "good
cause," tolling period may be extended for up to 30 days. *See supra*
§ 3.3c; *infra* § 5.1b.

(2)	Obtaining assistance of counsel and support services in preparing petition, if prisoner is indigent:	(a) Capital cases: Statutory right to counsel in capital habeas corpus proceedings includes right to legal assistance, transcript, and investigative and expert services in preparing petition. *See infra* §§ 12.2, 12.3, 19.2, 19.3. Motions for appointment of counsel, transcript, and support services may be filed prior to, or simultaneously with, petition. *See infra* §§ 12.3a, 19.2, 19.3. *See generally infra* §§ 11.2, 11.3 (preparation of petition). In AEDPA cases, lawyers who wish to make request for support services *ex parte* must first make adequate showing of "need for confidentiality." *See* § 12.3b.
		(b) Noncapital cases: District court has discretion (which is rarely exercised) to appoint counsel prior to filing of petition to assist in its preparation. *See infra* § 12.3a (discussing tactical benefits and potential

disadvantages of seeking prefiling appointment of counsel in noncapital cases). *See also infra* §§ 19.2 (prefiling access to transcript), 19.3 (possible availability of prefiling investigative and expert services). *See generally infra* §§ 11.2, 11.3 (preparation of petition). Under AEDPA, special procedures for requesting support services *ex parte* apply to noncapital as well as capital cases. *See infra* § 12.3b.

(3) Obtaining stay of execution pending filing of petition in capital cases:

(a) Non-AEDPA cases: Prisoners who make *timely* prepetition request for appointment of counsel may secure stay of execution from district court to permit thorough investigation of claims. *See infra* §§ 13.1-13.2b. *See also infra* §§ 5.3, 6.3, 11.1, 13.3.

(b) AEDPA nonopt-in cases: Obtaining stay requires satisfaction of statute of limitations which, depending upon interpretation of ambiguous statutory provision, either may be accomplished by filing prepetition application for counsel before expiration of limitations period or may require filing of habeas corpus petition (apparently including "Placeholder Petition" intended to be amended later) within limitations period. *See infra* §§ 5.1b, 13.1, 13.2b.

(c) AEDPA opt-in cases: Statutorily required federal court stay of execution goes into effect during initial state postconviction proceeding and remains in effect until timely filing of federal habeas corpus petition (and thereafter if petition contains substantial federal claims, *see infra* para. (6)(e)); stay expires, however, and federal court generally may not grant subsequent stay, if capital prisoner (i) fails to file petition before expiration of 180-day limitations period; (ii) "waives the right to pursue habeas corpus review" after being advised by court and counsel of consequences; (iii) files petition that "fails to make a substantial showing of the denial of a Federal right"; or (iv) "is denied relief in the district court or at any subsequent stage of review" (*but cf. supra* § 3.3c n.60). *See supra* § 3.3c; *infra* §§ 5.1b, 13.1, 13.2b.

(4)	Where to file petition:	Federal district court with jurisdiction over: (a) location of court of conviction; or (b) location of confinement. Local rules may specify, or prisoner may have choice. *See infra* §§ 10.1, 10.2.
		Note: When filing "second or successive" habeas corpus petition in AEDPA nonopt-in case (and possibly also in AEDPA opt-in case), petitioner must first obtain leave from court of appeals. *See infra* para. (9). In non-AEDPA cases (and possibly also AEDPA opt-in cases), no such leave is needed but state may challenge propriety of successive application as affirmative defense. *See infra* para. (17)(c), (18)(d).
(5)	Whom to name as respondent:	Generally, warden of facility in which prisoner is or was confined. *See infra* § 10.1.
(6)	Papers to file to initiate proceeding:	(a) Petition for a Writ of Habeas Corpus by a Person in State Custody. *See infra* §§ 11.4-11.8.
		(b) Verification. *See infra* § 11.7b.

184

(c) Filing fee. *See infra* § 11.9c. If petitioner is indigent, appli7cation for leave to proceed *in forma pauperis*, including:

    (i) Affidavit of indigency;

    (ii) Warden's certification of petitioner's assets. *See infra* §§ 11.7, 11.9c, 12.1.

(d) Motion for appointment of counsel if petitioner is indigent. *See infra* §§ 12.2, 12.3. *See also infra* §§ 7.2 & 12.4 (possible constitutional arguments). Motion for appointment of counsel may be filed prior to petition to obtain assistance in preparing petition. *See supra* para. (2).

(e) Application for stay of execution in capital cases, with memorandum of law in support of application establishing substantiality of one or more federal claims in petition. *See infra* Chapter 13. *See also infra* §§ 5.3, 6.3, 11.1. In non-AEDPA cases and apparently also AEDPA nonopt-in cases, stay of execution pending filing of petition may be sought when prisoner files *timely* prepetition request for appointment of counsel. In AEDPA opt-in cases, automatic prepetition stay that is in effect during initial state postconviction proceeding remains in effect until federal habeas corpus petition is timely filed and also thereafter, if petition contains one or more substantial federal claims. Filing of qualifying petition suffices to preserve preexisting stay, so separate stay application is not required. Stay expires, however, upon filing of nonqualifying petition or upon subsequent denial of relief. *See supra* para. (3); *infra* §§ 5.1b, 13.1, 13.2b.

(f) Motion for evidentiary hearing (optional). *See infra* § 11.7d; *infra* Chapters 20, 21.

(g) Motion for discovery (optional). *See infra* §§ 19.1, 19.4, 19.5.

(h) Other fact development motions (optional). *See infra* Chapters 18-21.

---

(7) Contents of petition:

(a) Statement of petitioner's custody status, including current sentence and any relevant terms or conditions of sentence. *See infra* § 8.2. *See also infra* § 8.3.

(b) Conviction(s) and judgment(s) under which petitioner has been detained and sentenced. *See infra* § 11.4a.

(c) Proceedings in which petitioner's claims were exhausted (or reasons why claims are exhausted although they were not raised in previously available state proceedings). *See infra* §§ 11.1, 11.3b; *infra* Chapter 23.

(d) Claims for relief, including legal and factual bases for claims that custody or sentence is unlawful. For discussion of types of claims that can be raised, *see infra* §§ 9.1, 9.2. Discovery of claims, claim selection, and possible anticipatory pleading of responses to defenses are discussed *supra* § 3.5a and *infra* §§ 11.2, 11.3. "Fact" pleading is required; "notice" pleading is not sufficient. *See infra* § 11.6.

(e) Titles, citations, and dispositions of other federal habeas corpus petitions filed by petitioner to challenge conviction and/or sentence now challenged, with explanation of why present claims were not raised earlier. *See infra* § 11.3b; *infra* Chapter 28.

(f) Statement of relief sought. *See infra* § 11.8; *infra* Chapter 33.

(g) Verification by petitioner. *See infra* § 11.7b.

---

(8) Filing and service of petition:

(a) File original and required number of copies with clerk of appropriate district. *See infra* §§ 11.7b, 11.9b. *See also supra* para. (4).

(b) District court clerk is required to serve respondent with one copy of petition; courtesy service by petitioner's counsel is recommended. *See infra* § 11.9d.

(c) Filing fee required unless petition is filed *in forma pauperis* ("ifp") with appropriate application, affidavit of indigency, and warden's certificate of petitioner's assets. *See supra* para. (6)(c). If Prison Litigation Reform Act of 1996 applies to federal habeas corpus proceedings (as yet, an unresolved issue, *see infra* § 12.1), court must screen each claim of ifp petition and deny ifp status as to any claims that are frivolous or state no basis upon which relief may be granted. *See infra* § 12.1.

---

(9) Second or successive petition, additional requirements:

(a) AEDPA nonopt-in and perhaps also opt-in cases: Before filing petition in district court, petitioner must obtain leave to file from court of appeals panel by making *prima facie* showing that (i) legal rule on which she relies is new and retroactively applicable to case or (ii) facts on which she relies were unavailable previously and petitioner probably is "innocent" under applicable statutory standard. If court of appeals grants leave to file, district court conducts plenary review of propriety of second or successive application for federal habeas corpus relief, using same criteria. *See infra* § 28.3d.

(b) Non-AEDPA cases and perhaps also AEDPA opt-in cases: Petitioner need not obtain leave before filing second or successive petition but State may challenge propriety of second or successive filing as affirmative defense. *See infra* para. (17)(c), (18)(d); *infra* §§ 28.3c, 28.4b.

RESPONSIVE PLEADINGS AND SUMMARY PROCEEDINGS

(10) State's answer and petitioner's responses:

(a) State's answer: Required only if ordered by court. *See infra* Chapter 16.

(b) Reply or traverse by petitioner: Permitted but not required. *See infra* § 17.1 (rules and tactical considerations).

(c) Amendment of petition: In non-AEDPA and AEDPA nonopt-in cases, amendment is liberally available. *See infra* § 17.2. In AEDPA opt-in cases, general rule of liberal availability of amendment applies before state files answer, but post-answer amendment is permissible only if it presents "new claim" that could not previously have been raised because it depends upon new legal rule that is retroactively applicable to petitioner's case, or upon facts that previously were unavailable and enable petitioner to satisfy statutory "innocence" standard. *See supra* § 3.3c; *infra* § 17.2.

(11) Summary proceedings:

    (a) Summary dismissal of petition:

       (i) Available under Rule 4 of the Rules Governing § 2254 Cases if, upon review by court *sua sponte* or upon motion by state, court finds that all claims in petition are "patently frivolous" or "palpably false." *See infra* Chapters 15, 16.

       (ii) May be available in *in forma pauperis* cases pursuant to Prison Litigation Reform Act of 1996. *See supra* para. (8)(c).

    (b) State's motion to dismiss (optional): Adjudicated under rules discussed *supra* subpara. (a)(i). *See infra* § 16.1c.

    (c) State's motion for summary judgment (optional): Adjudicated under Fed. R. Civ P. 56(c); summary judgment required if (i) there are no genuine issues of material fact and (ii) petitioner does not have right to relief under applicable law. *See infra* § 16.1c.

    (d) Petitioner's motion for summary judgment (optional): Adjudicated under Fed. R. Civ P. 56(c); summary judgment required if (i) there are no genuine issues of material fact and (ii) petitioner has right to relief under applicable law. *See infra* § 17.3c.

FACT-DEVELOPMENT PROCEDURES

(12) Magistrate judge practice:

Nondispositive matters relating to fact development (*e.g.*, discovery; production of state court record) may be referred to magistrate judge for determination, subject to district court's review under "clearly erroneous" standard. *See infra* § 18.1a. Dispositive matters relating to fact development, including evidentiary hearings, may be referred to magistrate judge, subject to *de novo* review by district court of objected-to portions of magistrate judge's report. *See infra* §§ 18.1b, 18.2. To preserve *de novo* review by district court (and, often, by court of appeals), objections generally must be filed within 10 days of report and must be sufficiently specific. *See infra* § 18.2a.

(13)	Filing of record of prior proceedings and related materials:	(a) State record: State must provide district court with relevant portions of state court record. *See infra* § 19.2. Record sometimes may be obtained before petition is filed, for use in preparation of petition. *See supra* para. (2).
		(b) Expansion of record: Court *sua sponte* — or on motion of party — may order that record be expanded to include relevant documents, exhibits, or other materials filed with record by state (*see supra* subpara. (a)), revealed during discovery (*see infra* para. (15)), or prepared for litigation (*e.g.*, affidavits). *See infra* § 19.5. Rules of evidence may not apply. *See id. See also infra* § 21.2.
(14)	Financial assistance for factual investigation and development:	In some circumstances, indigent petitioners have statutory rights — and may also have constitutional rights — to financial assistance for investigators, experts, and other resources needed to investigate and litigate claims. *See infra* § 19.3. Support services may be available before petition is filed, for use in preparation of petition. *See supra* para. (2).

(15) Discovery:

Full panoply of federal discovery procedures available if district court or magistrate judge grants motion for leave to conduct discovery. *See infra* §§ 19.4, 19.5.

(16) Evidentiary hearing:

(a) Mandatory hearings: Evidentiary hearing is *required* when:

(i) State courts made no written or otherwise reliably reflected findings.

(ii) State courts' determination is not one of pure fact but instead one of law or a mixture of law and fact.

(iii) State courts' findings did not fully resolve merits of factual dispute.

(iv) State courts held no hearing on disputed factual issues.

(v) State courts failed adequately to develop material facts and inadequacy of hearing is not attributable to petitioner or counsel. If failure to develop material facts *is* attributable to petitioner or counsel, evidentiary hearing still must be held if:

(A) In non-AEDPA cases: petitioner shows (I) "cause" for and "prejudice" from failure; or (II) that denial of hearing will result in "fundamental miscarriage of justice."

(B) In AEDPA nonopt-in and opt-in cases: petitioner shows that (I) claim on which hearing is sought rests on new rule of law that is retroactively applicable to case or on previously unavailable facts that could not have been discovered with due diligence; and (II) facts underlying claim satisfy statutory "innocence" standard.

(vi) State courts' hearing was not "full and fair" for some other reason.

(vii) State courts' factual determination was not fairly supported by record.

(viii) Federal hearing is needed to permit petitioner to rebut presumption of correctness by showing (in AEDPA cases, by "clear and convincing evidence"; in non-AEDPA cases, "by convincing evidence") that state court determination is erroneous.

See infra §§ 20.2, 20.3.

(b) Discretionary hearings: Even when evidentiary hearing is not *required*, district court has discretion in some situations (fewer under AEDPA) to hold hearing to resolve factual dispute. *See infra* § 20.4 (situations in which district courts can, and commonly do, exercise discretion to conduct hearing).

(c) Petitioner's presence: Petitioner has right to be present at all evidentiary hearings. *See infra* § 21.3.

(d) Nature and conduct of hearing, including continuances, speedy hearing right, and evidence rules: *See infra* Chapter 21.

PROCEDURAL DEFENSES

(17) Petitioner previously failed to utilize available procedure to raise claim in state or federal court:

(a) *Nonexhaustion defense*: State asserts that petition must be dismissed without prejudice to refiling because petitioner failed to raise same claim or claims in requisite state proceedings (A) in a full set of state proceedings (*see infra* §§ 23.3a, 23.3b), and (B) in manner "substantially similar" legally and factually to claim(s) in federal petition (*see infra* §§ 23.3a, 23.3c). *See infra* §§ 23.1, 23.3, 23.5. Possible responses by petitioner:

(i) State waived defense. In AEDPA cases, this response is available only if State's waiver was express. *See infra* § 23.2.

(ii) Claim is exhausted because petitioner raised it in full set of state proceedings (*see infra* §§ 23.3a, 23.3b) and in manner "substantially similar" legally and factually to claim(s) in federal petition (*see infra* §§ 23.3a, 23.3c).

(iii) Case comes within exhaustion doctrine's statutory exception for unavailable or ineffective state corrective processes or within doctrine's nonstatutory exceptions grounded in justice, judicial economy, and federalism. *See infra* § 23.4.

(iv) AEDPA opt-in case is controlled by controversial reading of 28 U.S.C. § 2264(a) under which exhaustion of some claims is not required. *See*

193

supra § 3.3c nn.65-79 and accompanying text.

Notes:

(i)   If unexhausted state court remedy is no longer available, claim is exhausted, but state may be able to invoke procedural default defense. *See infra* § 23.1 nn.21-30 and accompanying text (relationship between nonexhaustion and procedural default); *infra* subpara. (b) (procedural default).

(ii) In non-AEDPA cases, result of finding of nonexhaustion is dismissal without prejudice pending exhaustion; same applies in AEDPA cases, except that court has discretion to deny unexhausted claim that is frivolous in lieu of dismissing entire petition to permit exhaustion of frivolous claim. *See infra* § 23.1 n.5.

(b) *Procedural default defense:* State asserts that petitioner's failure to raise claim in state court at time or in manner required by state law constitutes "procedural default" that bars federal court review of claim. *See infra* § 26.1. *See also infra* § 23.1. Possible responses by petitioner:

(i)   State waived defense. *See infra* § 26.2a.

(ii) Petitioner did not commit default because (A) alleged procedural requirement was not clearly applicable or (B) petitioner adequately complied with it. *See infra* §§ 26.2b, 26.2c.

(iii) State court decided claim on merits. *See infra* § 26.2e.

(iv) State court implicitly resolved merits of claim by rejecting it on "nonindependent" state procedural ground. *See supra* § 3.3c n.79 and accompanying text; *infra* §§ 26.2d, 26.2e.

(v) State rule is not "adequate" basis for denying federal court review. *See infra* § 26.2d. (This response may not be available in this form in AEDPA opt-in cases, but may be available in form discussed *infra* subpara. (vi)(B)(I). *See supra* § 3.3c.)

(vi) Default should be excused because:

  (A) In non-AEDPA and AEDPA nonopt-in cases: Petitioner has shown (I) "cause" for and "prejudice" from default (*see infra* § 26.3); or (II) that failure to reach merits would constitute "miscarriage of justice" (*see infra* § 26.4).

  (B) In AEDPA opt-in cases: Petitioner has shown that default resulted from (I) unconstitutional state action; (II) unavailability of legal rule subsequently recognized by Supreme Court and retroactively applicable to case; or (III) unavailability of facts, given that diligent investigation would not have uncovered them in time for presentation in state postconviction proceeding. *See supra* § 3.3c.

(c) *Abuse of the writ* (non-AEDPA and possibly also AEDPA opt-in cases): State asserts that petitioner's failure to raise claim(s) in prior *federal* habeas corpus petition constitutes "abuse of the writ," barring relief. *See infra* § 28.3c. Possible responses by petitioner:

(i) State waived defense. *See infra* § 28.3c.

(ii) Petition is not truly "successive" and accordingly is not subject to "abuse of the writ" defense. *See infra* § 28.3b.

(iii) Omission should be excused because petitioner has shown "cause" and "prejudice" or that failure to reach merits would constitute "miscarriage of justice." *See infra* § 28.3c.

Notes:

(i) As is described *supra* para. (9), in AEDPA nonopt-in cases and possibly also AEDPA opt-in cases, propriety of petitioner's filing of new-claim successive petition is litigated, under extremely stringent standards, at time of filing rather than by means of State's assertion of affirmative defense.

(ii) In non-AEDPA cases, petitioners also may be able to file same-claim successive petition, a remedy that is unavailable in AEDPA nonopt-in cases and possibly also in AEDPA opt-in cases. *See infra* para. (18)(d).

(18) Claim or aspect of it was previously resolved by state or federal court in manner that forecloses or limits review of claim:

(a) *Presumption of correctness of state court factfindings*: State asserts that federal court must defer to state court factfindings (not true defense; when applicable, presumption of correctness changes federal court's standard of review from *de novo* to "clearly erroneous" (*see infra* paras. (22), (23))). *See infra* §§ 20.1, 20.2, 30.1, 30.3. Possible responses by petitioner:

(i) State waived defense.

(ii) State court factfindings are not sufficiently apparent or definite.

(iii) State court "factfindings" are actually legal or "mixed," not factual, determinations. (As to effect of state court legal and "mixed" determinations, *see infra* subpara. (c), *infra* para. (22).)

(iv) State court factfindings are incomplete.

(v) State court factfindings were not made following evidentiary hearing.

(vi) State court factfindings were. not made in fair manner.

(vii) State court factfindings are not adequately supported by record (in non-AEDPA cases, "not fairly supported by the record"; in AEDPA cases, "unreasonable determination of the facts in light of the evidence presented in State court proceeding[]").

(viii) Federal court should deem presumption rebutted because petitioner has shown (in non-AEDPA cases, by "convincing evidence"; in AEDPA cases, by "clear and convincing evidence") that state court factfinding is erroneous.

See infra §§ 20.2, 20.3, 30.3.

(b) *Stone v. Powell defense*: State asserts that review of 4th Amendment exclusionary rule claim is barred by Stone v. Powell, 428 U.S. 465 (1976) because state courts afforded "full and fair" opportunity to litigate claim. *See infra* § 27.1. *See also infra* § 9.2 (*Stone* defense inapplicable to non-4th Amendment claims). Possible responses by petitioner:

(i) State waived defense. *See infra* § 27.2.

(ii) Opportunity to litigate in state court was not "full and fair" because, *e.g.*, state provides no corrective process, process was structurally flawed, or petitioner was precluded from utilizing process. *See infra* § 27.3.

(c) *Section 2254(d)(1) defense* (in AEDPA cases): State asserts that relief "shall not be granted" on claim because claim was "adjudicated on the merits in State court proceedings." *See infra* § 30.2. Possible responses by petitioner:

(i) State waived defense. *See infra* § 30.2a.

(ii) State court did not (A) fairly "adjudicate" claim, or did not do so (B) "on the merits," (C) in state "court proceeding[]," or (D) reflect its conclusion in "decision" of claim. *See infra* § 30.2b.

(iii)   State "decision" (A) "was contrary to ... clearly established Federal law, as determined by the Supreme Court of the United States," or (B) "was ... an unreasonable application of clearly established [Supreme Court] law." Courts currently are sharply divided on meaning of both these statutorily specified bases for avoiding section 2254(d)(1) defense. *See infra* § 30.2c.

(iv)   If both statutorily specified bases for avoiding section 2254(d)(1) bar set out in subpara. (iii) *supra* are interpreted narrowly, then provision is unconstitutional under Article III and possibly also Suspension Clause of Constitution. *See infra* § 30.2d.

Note: Section 2254(d)(1) also may be treated as new standard of review. *See infra* para. (22).

(d)   *Successive petition defense*: State asserts that review of claim is barred because petitioner previously raised same claim in another *federal* habeas corpus petition, and federal court rejected claim on merits. *See infra* § 28.4. Possible responses by petitioner in non-AEDPA cases and possibly also in AEDPA opt-in cases:

(i)   State waived defense. *See infra* § 28.4b.

(ii)   The criminal judgment under attack is not same one challenged in previous petition. *See infra* §§ 28.3b, 28.4b.

(iii)   Previous denial of claim was not on merits. *See infra* §§ 28.3b, 28.4b.

(iv) Relitigation of successive claim should be permitted because petitioner has shown (A) "cause" and "prejudice," (B) that failure to reach merits would constitute "miscarriage of justice," or (C) that "ends of justice" require relitigation. *See infra* § 28.4b.

Note: Filing of second or successive petition to relitigate claim that was previously rejected on merits is absolutely barred in AEDPA nonopt-in cases and possibly also in AEDPA opt-in cases. Possible responses to defense set out in subparas. (i)-(iv) *supra* thus apply only to non-AEDPA cases and possibly also to AEDPA opt-in cases. *See supra* § 3.2; *infra* § 28.4.

---

(19) Petitioner's delay in filing petition prejudiced state's ability to respond:

Prejudicial delay defense: State asserts that petitioner's delay in presenting claim in federal habeas corpus proceeding prejudiced state's ability to respond to claim. *See infra* § 24.1. Possible responses by petitioner:

(a) State waived defense. *See infra* § 24.2.

(b) Petitioner did not unreasonably delay setting in motion course of judicial events necessary to bring petition before federal court. *See infra* § 24.3.

(c) Petitioner exercised reasonable diligence in discovering and presenting claims in petition. *See infra* § 24.5.

(d) Delay did not prejudice state in its ability to defend petition. *See infra* § 24.4.

Note: AEDPA's strict timing requirements for federal habeas corpus petitions (*see supra* para. (1)(d); *infra* § 5.1b), will in practice moot most (and may legally supersede all) assertions by state of "prejudicial delay" defense, leaving defense to be applied primarily (or perhaps even exclusively) to non-AEDPA cases. *See infra* § 24.1.

---

(20) Petitioner's claim is barred because it would require retroactive application of "new rule" of federal constitutional law:

Nonretroactivity defense (non-AEDPA cases; possibly superseded in AEDPA cases): State asserts that petitioner's claim is premised on "new rule" of federal constitutional law not in effect when petitioner's conviction became "final." *Teague v. Lane*, 489 U.S. 288 (1989). *See infra* §§ 25.1, 25.2. Possible responses by petitioner:

(a)   State waived defense. *See infra* § 25.3.

(b)   Rule on which petitioner relies is not "new." *See infra* § 25.5.

(c)   Rule on which petitioner relies was announced before petitioner's conviction became "final." *See infra* § 25.6.

(d)   Rule on which petitioner relies comes within exceptions for:

   (i)   New rules of substantive criminal law that exempt individuals from prosecution or punishment. *See infra* § 25.7.

   (ii)   "Fundamental" rules of criminal procedure. *See infra* § 25.7.

Note: The section 2254(d)(1) defense under AEDPA (which also may be treated as new standard of review of state court adjudications of law) incorporates form of, and may otherwise supersede, foregoing *Teague* nonretroactivity defense. *See supra* para. (18)(c); *infra* para. (22).

ADJUDICATION OF MERITS

(21) Briefing merits of petition:

    (a) Timing of brief: *See infra* §§ 11.7d, 17.1, 17.3, 29.1.

    (b) Contents of brief: *See infra* Chapter 29.

---

(22) Standards of review:

    (a) Review of state courts' legal and mixed legal/factual determinations:

        (i) Non-AEDPA cases: *De novo* review. *See supra* § 2.4; *infra* §§ 20.2, 20.3d, 30.2.

        (ii) AEDPA nonopt-in and opt-in cases: AEDPA directs federal court to determine whether state court's "decision was contrary to, or involved an unreasonable application of, clearly established Federal law, as determined by the Supreme Court of the United States." Courts currently are sharply divided on nature, scope, and even constitutionality of review this standard requires. *See infra* § 30.2. (New standard of review also may be treated as defense as described *supra* para. (18)(c).)

    (b) Deferential review of state courts' fact-findings, as described *infra* para. (23)(b). *See infra* §§ 20.1, 20.2, 20.3, 30.1, 30.3.

---

(23) Burdens of pleading and proof:

    (a) Merits generally: Burden on petitioner to prove facts determinative of claims in chief by preponderance of evidence. Burden on state to prove facts determinative of affirmative defenses by preponderance of evidence. *See infra* § 31.2.

	(b)	Merits of factual issues as to which there are adverse state factfindings: Burden on petitioner to disprove state factfindings (in non-AEDPA cases, by "convincing evidence"; in AEDPA cases, by "clear and convincing evidence"). *See infra* §§ 20.2c, 30.3, 31.3.
(24) Assessment of harmless error:	(a)	Standard: Relief is not required if error lacked "'substantial and injurious effect or influence in determining the jury's verdict.'" *Brecht v. Abrahamson*, 507 U.S. 619, 623 (1993). *See infra* § 32.1. *See also infra* §§ 32.4 & 32.5.
	(b)	Burdens of pleading and proof: State has burden of pleading and also burden of persuasion. *See infra* §§ 32.2a, 32.2b.
	(c)	*Per se* prejudice: Errors that are "pre-judicial *per se*" (along with errors of equivalent type and degree) are not subject to "harmless error" determination and compel relief. *See infra* §§ 32.3, 32.5.
(25) Relief:		Possible remedies include: release; release unless state provides retrial, resentencing, or other previously flawed procedure within specified time period. *See infra* Chapter 33.
(26) Timing of decision:		In opt-in cases, AEDPA establishes specific timetable for district court's issuance of decision and entry of final judgment. *See supra* § 3.3c.

POSTJUDGMENT PROCEEDINGS; APPEALS

(27) District court reconsideration of adverse rulings on some or all claims:	Postjudgment motions that may be available in appropriate cases are: "Motion for a New Trial," "Motion to Alter or Amend," or "Motion for Relief from Judgment" pursuant to (respectively) FED. R. CIV. P. 52(b), 59, 60. *See infra* Chapter 34.

(28) Appeal to United States Court of Appeals:	Appeals generally follow normal appellate procedures set forth in FED. R. CIV. P. and FED. R. APP. P. *See infra* Chapters 35-38 (procedures on appeal, including timing and form of notice of appeal; application for *in forma pauperis* status; appointment of counsel; motion for release of petitioner on recognizance or surety; preparation and enlargement of record on appeal; briefing; standards of appellate review; petitions for rehearing and rehearing *en banc*; issuance and stay of mandate). *See also infra* Chapter 40 (original habeas corpus proceedings in court of appeals). Special requirements for federal habeas corpus appeals include:

    (a) Timely filing of objections to magistrate judge's report (if any) is prerequisite to appeal in many circuits; objections usually are required within 10 days of magistrate judge's issuance of recommended disposition; court may excuse default in interests of justice or due to plain error. *See infra* § 18.2.

    (b) Application for authorization to appeal (in non-AEDPA cases, termed "certificate of probable cause to appeal"; in AEDPA cases, termed "certificate of appealability"). In non-AEDPA cases, appeal is authorized if court certifies that at least one claim in petition is "substantial"; in nonopt-in AEDPA cases and possibly also in opt-in AEDPA cases, court must state whether each claim is "substantial." *See infra* § 35.4.

(c) Application for stay of execution. *See infra* §§ 36.2 (stay pending appeal), 38.2a (stay pending rehearing by court of appeals), 38.2b (stay of mandate and of execution pending *certiorari*). *See also supra* paras. (3)(c), (6)(e); *supra* § 3.3c (stay procedures in AEPDA opt-in cases).

(d) In opt-in cases, AEDPA establishes specific timetable for court of appeals' determination of appeal and any subsequent petitions for rehearing or rehearing *en banc*. *See supra* § 3.3c.

---

(29) Petitioning Supreme Court for writ of *certiorari:*

(a) Procedures for filing *certiorari* petition: File petition within 90 days of entry of final judgment by court of appeals or order denying timely rehearing motion, except in capital cases, in which court of appeals' issuance of 30-day or shorter mandate, together with state's setting of execution date, may require *certiorari* petition to be filed within 30 days or less as basis for Supreme Court stay; suggestion of rehearing *en banc* does not toll time to file *certiorari* petition, although motion for rehearing does. *See infra* Chapter 39. *See also infra* Chapter 40 (original habeas corpus proceedings in Supreme Court).

(b) Procedures for seeking stay of execution pending *certiorari*: *See infra* §§ 38.2b, 38.2c, 39.3c.

Chapter 4
THE CLIENT

§ 4.1. The client.

In many instances, counsel representing a prisoner in postconviction proceedings will not have represented the client at trial or on appeal. In such cases, it is entirely possible for the attorney to initiate the postconviction proceedings in advance of any face-to-face or even telephonic contact with the client. When the trial record and briefs on appeal arrive in counsel's office, the first inclination may well be to set immediately about preparing a petition from the paper record, perhaps after directing a perfunctory letter of introduction to the client. This mode of proceeding is a mistake not only from the standpoint of counsel's professional obligations to the client but also given the peculiarities and the tactical and strategic necessities of habeas corpus litigation.

First, being incarcerated and having recently learned that his conviction was affirmed on appeal, the client is certain to be discouraged about the case and confused about the legal proceedings that potentially lie ahead. If the transition from direct appeal to collateral review is accompanied by a change of counsel, the client also may feel abandoned and mistrustful. Counsel's first task, accordingly, is to establish personal contact with the client, to reassure him that his representation continues, to discover the client's objectives,[1] to explain and discuss the procedures that may help achieve those objectives, to outline the litigative and administrative remedies available (including parole, alternative conditions and locations of incarceration, job and education programs within the prison, and the like) and, generally, to begin building a relationship of trust.

Establishing contact and trust is more than a matter of courtesy or even professional obligation. It is more even than a matter of giving the client some semblance of control over his legal destiny. For should a decision to litigate be made, contact and trust are likely to be crucial in framing and litigating a petition successfully in the case. The client very often knows more about the relevant facts and proceedings than anyone else and may be the best or only source of

---

§ 4.1. [1] Discovering and helping clients discover their objectives in habeas corpus proceedings is more complicated than it may seem. Although most clients presumedly want their convictions reversed and, failing that, their sentences reduced, some are most interested in assuaging a sense of injustice about some specific aspect of the proceedings in the case or in raising a particular claim that has yet to be litigated. Particularly in capital cases, moreover, clients frequently express preferences about the priority of guilt/innocence and sentencing issues. In helping the prisoner sort through these matters, counsel needs to inform the client about the increasingly severe restrictions the courts place on second or "successive" federal habeas corpus petitions raising claims not previously litigated. *See infra* § 11.3b; Chapters 23, 24, 28. Given these restrictions, the client should be made aware that a decision now to proceed with only a single issue or set of issues may foreclose him from litigating other issues later on.

information about important issues on which the record of the case is ambiguous, incomplete, or wholly silent. As a result, absent intensive discussions with and probing of the client,[2] important issues in the case may never surface, including, for example, coerced confessions; post-arraignment use of jailhouse informers; ineffective assistance of counsel at trial, sentencing, or on appeal; underrepresentation of minorities or women on the petit jury venire or their systematic removal from the venire by prosecutorial peremptory challenges; excessive courtroom security; improper contacts between jurors and court officers or others during trial; prosecutorial suppression or misrepresentation of evidence; and, in a capital case, the excessiveness of the penalty given the circumstances of the offense and background and status of the client.

Furthermore, without trust and contact, counsel will be at a severe disadvantage in carrying out the critical task at an evidentiary hearing and in other proceedings in the case of making the habeas corpus judge aware that the liberty or life of a human being — who is worthy of empathy or at least sympathy, and whose testimony on crucial issues can be believed — is at stake in the case.

Counsel accordingly should establish personal contact with the client immediately upon entering the case. At that point or soon thereafter and before actually tackling the record in the case (perhaps, after becoming somewhat familiar with the case by reading the most recent briefs and latest judicial opinion), counsel should conduct a lengthy substantive interview with the client. This interview should explore the client's objectives in the case and the issues that the client believes, or, following discussions with counsel, comes to realize, are present in the case. Next, after carefully reading the record — keeping in mind the issues flagged by the client — counsel should hold another lengthy interview with the client about the issues the client identified and others that may be present in the record. This second major interview will help prepare counsel for an intensive field investigation.[3] The fruits of that investigation, as well as counsel's legal research, then should be the subject of at least one more substantive interview with the client before counsel is ready to begin drafting a petition. Asking the client to review carefully a near but not yet final draft of the petition also is likely to dislodge additional information from the client's memory, facilitate forthright relations between client and counsel, and generally improve the final product.

This protocol sets out a minimally adequate procedure for discovering substantial claims in the case. Attorneys who frequently represent incarcerated clients recognize that they often do not uncover the strongest extra-record claims in the case — which often turn out to be the strongest claims in the case as a

---

[2] *See infra* § 11.2. *See also* Mann v. Reynolds, 46 F.3d 1055, 1058 (10th Cir. 1995) (discussed *infra* § 4.2 n.5).

[3] *See id.*

whole — during the first or second interview. Typically, those claims surface only later, after cultural, racial, and class barriers between attorney and client are surmounted and the client's memory of details that are not obviously important or are especially painful is revived or dislodged.

Second in importance only to establishing contact with the client is doing the same with members of the client's family. Contact with family members will assist counsel in communicating and establishing a relationship of trust with the client, in understanding the client's situation both at the time of the alleged offense and at the time of the representation, in developing the facts of the case, and even in such mundane matters as delivering papers to the client on short notice when counsel's time can better be spent on other matters in the case. Frequently, too, attorneys are unable without the assistance of members of the client's family to cross the cultural barriers that separate themselves and the people upon whom their field investigations will focus. Finally, and perhaps most importantly, counsel's efforts to establish contact with family members also often reopens or reinforces contact between the family and the client, which serves an important function quite apart from the success of any postconviction litigation that occurs.

§ 4.2. The capital client.[1]

Capital clients are more anxious than other convicted prisoners. They are under extraordinary psychological pressure. They know that they may well be

---

§ 4.2. [1] *See generally* CHRISTOPHER DAVIS, WAITING FOR IT (1980); STEPHEN H. GETTINGER, SENTENCED TO DIE (1979); BRUCE JACKSON & DIANE CHRISTIAN, DEATH ROW (1980); ROBERT JOHNSON, CONDEMNED TO DIE (1981); DOUG MAGEE, SLOW COMING DARK (1980); ROGER PARLOFF, TRIPLE JEOPARDY: A STORY OF LAW AT ITS BEST — AND ITS WORST (1996); HELEN PREJEAN, DEAD MAN WALKING: AN EYEWITNESS ACCOUNT OF THE DEATH PENALTY IN THE UNITED STATES (1993); DAVID VON DREHLE, AMONG THE LOWEST OF THE DEAD: THE CULTURE OF DEATH ROW (1995) (reviewed in George P. Fletcher, *Condemned to Wait*, WASHINGTON POST Book World, Feb. 26, 1995, at 2); Harvey Bluestone & Carl L. McGahee, *Reaction to Extreme Stress: Impending Death by Execution*, 119 AM. J. PSYCHIATRY 393 (1962); Richard J. Bonnie, *Psychiatry and the Death Penalty: Emerging Problems in Virginia*, 66 U. VA. L. REV. 167 (1980); John L. Carroll, *Death Row: Hope for the Future*, in CHALLENGING CAPITAL PUNISHMENT 269-88 (Kenneth C. Haas & James A. Inciardi eds., 1988); Johnnie L. Gallemore & James H. Panton, *Inmate Response to Lengthy Death Row Confinement*, 129 AM. J. PSYCHOLOGY 167 (1972); Phyllis Goldfarb, *A Clinic Runs Through It*, 1 CLIN. L. REV. 65, 86-91 (1994); Robert Johnson, *Under Sentence of Death: The Psychology of Death Row Confinement*, 1979 LAW & PSYCHOLOGY REV. 141; Robert Johnson, *Warehousing for Death: Observations on the Human Environment on Death Row*, 26 CRIME & DELINQ. 545 (1980); J. Mark Lane, *Is There Life Without Parole?: A Capital Defendant's Right to a Meaningful Alternative Sentence*, 26 LOYOLA L.A. L. REV. 327 (1993); Tom Murton, *Treatment of Condemned Prisoners*, 15 CRIME & DELINQ. 94 (1969); Colin Turnbull, *Death by Decree*, 87 NAT. HIST. 51 (May 1978); J.H. Wright, *Life-Without-Parole: An Alternative to Death or Not Much of a Life at All*, 43 VAND. L. REV. 529 (1990); authority cited *infra* § 8.3 n.1.

executed, yet realize that years may pass before they learn with certainty whether they in fact will forfeit their lives, and, if so, when. In effect, they are sentenced to "life without much possibility of parole but with some possibility — however uncertain — of execution at some point, probably many years later."[2] Some also go through the torturous experience of having execution date after execution date set, almost arrive, then be stayed by executive or judicial action — often after they have been removed to a "death cell" near the execution chamber, had their heads shaved, and seen other similarly terrifying rituals observed.[3] The physical and mental state of capital clients is not aided by conditions on death row, which typically include at least 23 hours a day of confinement in a six-by-eight foot cell while nondeath-sentenced prisoners are at work on prison jobs and at recreation in athletic fields.[4]

Faced with these especially difficult psychological and physical conditions, capital clients need more support than other clients the attorney is likely to represent. To the capital client, a letter from the attorney is an important occasion, a visit even more important.[5] At a minimum, counsel promptly should

---

[2] *See* David Bruck, *On Death Row in Pretoria Central,* NEW REPUBLIC, July 13 & 20, 1987, at 18, 18-19 ("There are now more than 1,900 condemned prisoners on the death rows of 32 American states .... At current sentencing rates, it will take an execution a day, including Sundays and holidays, to eliminate our backlog of death-sentenced prisoners before the year 2000. (At half that pace the death row population will continue to grow rather than diminish.)"); NAACP Legal Defense and Education Fund, Inc., Death Row, U.S.A. (Spring 1998) (nation's death row population now stands at 3,387); *supra* § 2.3 n.23 and accompanying text. *See also* Gomez v. Fierro, 117 S. Ct. 285, 285 (1996) (Stevens, J., dissenting from summary vacation of judgment and remand) ("From the standpoint of the defendant, the delay [in "the execution of judgments imposing the death penalty"] can become so excessive as to constitute cruel and unusual punishment prohibited by the Eighth Amendment."; respondent death row inmates "have suffered under a 'sword of Damocles' since they were first sentenced to death in 1978 and 1979").

[3] *See* William Styron, *Death Row,* N.Y. TIMES, May 10, 1987, at E25, col. 6.

[4] *See, e.g.,* Groseclose ex rel. Harries v. Dutton, 594 F. Supp. 949, 959 (M.D. Tenn. 1984), *appeal dismissed sub nom.* Groseclose v. Dutton, 788 F.2d 356 (6th Cir. 1986) (leading death row conditions decision describing day-to-day environment facing death row inmate, who for a time had sought to end his appeals and be executed: "[T]he ventilation is so poor that cigarette smoke stains his cell walls and toilet odors frequently make it difficult for him to sleep. Also, fumes from the [prison's] use of oil-based paints result in difficulty in normal breathing.... Mr. Harries is confined in his cell for twenty-three hours per day.... [The prison] permit[s] him to exercise during the day for forty to forty-five minutes and to shower daily for ten to fifteen minutes. At all other times, including the taking of his meals, Mr. Harries remains within his cell .... [T]he temperature within Mr. Harries' cell may reach uncomfortable and potentially life threatening limits"); Ruiz v. Estelle, 503 F. Supp. 1265 (S.D. Tex. 1980) (prison conditions suit with death row component). *See also* Ford v. Wainwright, 497 U.S. 388, 402-04 (1986) (account of prisoner's becoming insane while on Florida's death row). *See generally* Johnson, *Under Sentence of Death, supra* note 1.

[5] *See* Mann v. Reynolds, 46 F.3d 1055, 1058 (10th Cir. 1995) (observing, in context of section 1983 civil suit challenging restrictions upon contact visits between death row inmates and

answer letters received from the death-sentenced client and visit the client at each important juncture in the case. Even if it is impossible, as it often will be, to tell the client what he wants to hear, the client deserves and will appreciate deeply a responsive letter or visit. If clients do not write frequently, counsel nonetheless should write to them periodically and should send clients copies of each document prepared on their behalf and each document filed by the state — preferably, for review and comment before filing or response.

Counsel occasionally will receive letters from the client complaining about prison conditions. In addition to seeking redress of untoward circumstances from prison authorities, counsel in States with pending class-action prison condition lawsuits should contact the attorneys prosecuting the lawsuit, advise death row clients of the suit's progress, and invoke the enforcement mechanisms such suits provide for alleviating unreasonable conditions facing the client.[6]

If the death-sentenced client has family or close friends who write or visit frequently, counsel should keep in touch with them as well and be responsive to their inquiries. Because family members and friends also are in a state of anxiety, they will appreciate any information the attorney can supply; and contact with them will facilitate contact with the client.[7]

Under the strain of death row detention and of years of waiting, some death row prisoners in the past have announced an intention to terminate the legal proceedings in the case, dismiss counsel, and seek early execution.[8] Almost without exception, a critical catalyst to such decisions is the fact that a despairing client has lost contact with his attorney.[9] Although most death row inmates who consider dropping their appeals ultimately decide otherwise,[10] they

---

postconviction counsel, that "death row attorneys have 'a particular need to establish trust and communication'" because inmates "have different counsel at each stage of their representation and thus would be expected to begin a new relationship with a ... post-conviction attorney in this setting" and given need "'to explore all avenues of possible trial error or mitigation,' in the process of habeas review," including "'painful and emotional past acts or occurrences ... which are not easily divulged to strangers'" (citations omitted)).

[6] *See generally* MICHAEL B. MUSHLIN, RIGHTS OF PRISONERS (2d ed. 1993 & Supp. 1997); SHELDON KRANTZ, THE LAW OF CORRECTIONS AND PRISONERS' RIGHTS IN A NUTSHELL (4th ed. 1994); decisions cited *supra* note 4.

[7] *See* PREJEAN, *supra* note 1; *supra* § 4.1.

[8] *See, e.g.,* Demosthenes v. Baal, 495 U.S. 731 (1990) (*per curiam*); Whitmore v. Arkansas, 495 U.S. 149 (1990); Lenhard v. Wolff, 443 U.S. 1306 (1979) (Rehnquist, Circuit Justice, in chambers); Gilmore v. Utah, 429 U.S. 1012 (1976); In re Zettlemoyer, 53 F.3d 24, 27-28 (3d Cir. 1995) (quoting death row prisoner's testimony explaining his reasons for seeking execution, which included harshness of death row conditions); secondary sources cited *infra* § 8.3 n.1. *See also* NORMAN MAILER, THE EXECUTIONER'S SONG (1979). *See generally infra* § 8.3.

[9] *See generally* Barbara A. Babcock, *Gary Gilmore's Lawyers,* 32 STAN. L. REV. 865 (1980).

[10] *See, e.g.,* Hammett v. Texas, 448 U.S. 725 (1980); Evans v. Bennett, 440 U.S. 1301 (1979) (Rehnquist, Circuit Justice, in chambers); Vickers v. Ricketts, 798 F.2d 369, 373 (9th Cir. 1986);

typically do so only after their attorneys belatedly undertake the difficult and time-consuming process of counseling and building or rebuilding the relationship of trust and confidence that should have been maintained from the beginning. Once a client announces such a decision, it becomes counsel's most fundamental professional responsibility to construct such a relationship in order adequately to advise the client of the gravity and implications of his announced decision for himself, his family, and others he cares about.[11] Conscientious efforts to maintain regular personal contact with the capital client, his family, and his friends accordingly may avoid difficult and unnecessary developments later on that take up far more of counsel's time, patience, fortitude, and stamina than periodic letters and trips to the prison.

Clark v. Louisiana State Penitentiary, 694 F.2d 75 (5th Cir. 1982); Hays v. Murphy, 663 F.2d 1004 (10th Cir. 1981); Potts v. Zant, 638 F.2d 727, 741-46 (5th Cir.), *cert. denied,* 454 U.S. 877 (1981); Massie v. Sumner, 624 F.2d 72 (9th Cir. 1980); Groseclose ex rel. Harries v. Dutton, 594 F. Supp. 949, 951 (M.D. Tenn. 1984), *appeal dismissed sub nom.* Groseclose v. Dutton, 788 F.2d 356 (6th Cir. 1986); Commonwealth v. McKenna, 383 A.2d 174 (Pa. 1978). *See also* Lonchar v. Thomas, 517 U.S. 314, 331 (1996) (petitioner, who had initially sought to be executed and successfully fought siblings' efforts to file third-party petitions, eventually elected to file petition to delay execution until state changed execution method from electrocution to lethal injection so he could donate his organs; in reversing lower courts' dismissal of petition as abusive, Supreme Court held that petitioner's motive for filing was not "critical"); Smith v. Armontrout, 865 F.2d 1514, 1516 (8th Cir. 1988) (petitioner changed mind multiple times).

[11] *See e.g.,* AMERICAN BAR ASSOCIATION, MODEL CODE OF PROFESSIONAL RESPONSIBILITY, Canon 7, EC 7-7 to 7-12 (1969); AMERICAN BAR ASSOCIATION, MODEL RULES OF PROFESSIONAL CONDUCT, Rule 2.1 & comments [1]-[5] (1983). *See also infra* § 8.3 ("next friend" habeas corpus petitions filed on behalf of inmate by another person, including when death row inmates seek to end their appeals and be executed). *Cf.* Lawson v. Dixon, 510 U.S. 1171 (1994) (Blackmun, J., dissenting from denial of *certiorari*) (*certiorari* should be granted on claim that trial counsel was constitutionally required to investigate mitigating evidence of capital client's mental problems and present such evidence at sentencing phase, notwithstanding client's wishes to contrary). *See generally* Florida Bar Staff Opinion 16247 (Feb. 23, 1993) (discussing some, but not nearly all, ethical questions faced by defense attorney whose client asks him to assist client in securing and executing death sentence).

PART II

TIMING OF A FEDERAL HABEAS CORPUS PETITION; STATE REMEDIES

Chapter 5

ORDER OF REMEDIES AND TIMING

§ 5.1. General ordering and timing rules.[1]

a. *Proceedings that ordinarily should precede federal habeas corpus.* Typically, a prospective federal habeas corpus petitioner should not file a petition until after completing nine prior litigative steps — (1) the guilt trial, (2) the sentencing hearing, (3) proceedings on a motion for a new trial, (4) appeals as of right within the state courts, (5) discretionary appeals within the state courts, (6) *certiorari* review in the United States Supreme Court of the determination on appeal, (7) state postconviction proceedings on all available and not theretofore fully litigated state and federal claims, (8) all available state postconviction appeals, and, depending on the circumstances, (9) *certiorari* review[2] in the United States Supreme Court of the state postconviction proceedings.[3] Most of these prefiling stages are briefly discussed in section 3.5a *supra*.

Petitioners who skip any of these steps, save only steps (6) and (9) — petitions for a writ of *certiorari* to the United States Supreme Court[4] — incur at least a possibility of legally mandated adverse consequences in later federal

---

§ **5.1.** [1] *See generally* AMERICAN BAR ASSOCIATION, TOWARD A MORE JUST AND EFFECTIVE SYSTEM OF REVIEW IN STATE DEATH PENALTY CASES: A REPORT CONTAINING DEATH PENALTY HABEAS CORPUS AND RELATED MATERIALS FROM THE AMERICAN BAR ASSOCIATION CRIMINAL JUSTICE SECTION'S PROJECT ON DEATH PENALTY HABEAS CORPUS 135-65 (Ira P. Robbins, Reporter 1990); WAYNE R. LaFAVE & JEROLD H. ISRAEL, CRIMINAL PROCEDURE § 28.5(c) (1992); LARRY W. YACKLE, POSTCONVICTION REMEDIES § 114 (1981 & Supp. 1998); David A. Bagwell, *Procedural Aspects of Prisoner § 1983 and § 2254 Cases in the Fifth and Eleventh Circuits,* 95 F.R.D. 435, 549 (1982); Charles Alan Wright, *Procedure for Habeas Corpus,* 77 F.R.D. 227, 234-36 (1978); Brian E. Moore, Note, *Too Late for the Truth? Retroactivity and Application of the Statute of Limitations for Filing 28 U.S.C. § 2255 Petitions,* 20 CAMPBELL L. REV. 157 (1997); Peter Sessions, Note, *Swift Justice? Imposing a Statute of Limitations on the Federal Habeas Corpus Petitions of State Prisoners,* 70 S. CAL. L. REV. 1513 (1997).

[2] *See infra* § 6.4.

[3] Rehearing procedures also may be available and advisable following steps (4)-(9). Counsel should consult the rules of the respective courts.

[4] *See* Fay v. Noia, 372 U.S. 391, 435-38 (1963) (no adverse habeas corpus consequence from failing to seek *certiorari* to review state court decisions); *supra* § 2.4d nn.251-60 and accompanying text; *infra* § 23.3b.

habeas corpus proceedings.[5] Among the adverse consequences may be dismissal of the federal petition without prejudice because one or more of the claims in it were not properly exhausted (which also may have adverse statute of limitations consequences in certain cases);[6] denial of relief on a claim because the petitioner waived or procedurally defaulted the claim in an available state forum;[7] and denial of a second or successive federal habeas corpus petition because the petitioner omitted the claims in it from an earlier federal petition.[8]

Nor may even *certiorari* stages (6) and (9) be skipped without risks to the prisoner. The *Teague* doctrine of nonretroactivity,[9] and section 2254(d)(1) as amended by the Antiterrorism and Effective Death Penalty Act of 1996 (AEDPA),[10] both limit the body of law a federal habeas corpus court may consider to that which was in existence at a certain time — for *Teague* purposes, at the time *certiorari* proceedings in the Supreme Court following direct appeal were completed;[11] for AEDPA purposes, at the time the direct appeal proceedings in the state court were completed.[12] Consequently, the last opportunity prisoners may have to argue to a federal court that they should get the benefit of new legal developments is on *certiorari* to the United States Supreme Court following direct appeal (step (6))[13] or, possibly, following state

---

[5] Adverse consequences may occur not only if a litigative step is forgone but also if the step is taken but an available federal claim is not then raised or is not *properly* raised.

[6] *See infra* Chapter 23. On the statutes of limitations that apply to cases governed by the Antiterrorism and Effective Death Penalty Act, Pub. L. 104-132, 110 Stat. 1214 (1996), see *infra* § 5.1b. On the statute of limitations problems that may arise upon the dismissal of a habeas corpus petition without prejudice for exhaustion purposes, see *infra* § 5.1b nn.57, 64 and accompanying text.

[7] *See infra* Chapter 26.

[8] *See infra* Chapter 28. *See generally* McFarland v. Scott, 512 U.S. 849, 860 (1994) (O'Connor, J., concurring in the judgment in part) (Supreme Court's "carefully crafted doctrines of waiver and abuse of the writ make it especially important that the first [federal habeas corpus] petition [and, thus, the state exhaustion proceedings that precede the first federal petition] set forth all of a state prisoner's colorable grounds for relief").

[9] *See generally infra* Chapter 25.

[10] Pub. L. 104-132, 110 Stat. 1214 (1996). *See* 28 U.S.C.A. § 2254(d)(1) (West 1994 & Supp. 1998). For an overview of AEDPA's provisions and an explanation of the categories of cases to which it applies, see *supra* §§ 3.2, 3.4. For discussion of amended section 2254(d)(1), see *infra* § 30.2.

[11] *See infra* §§ 25.1, 25.6.

[12] *See infra* § 30.2c.

[13] *See infra* § 25.1 nn.25-31 and accompanying text (discussing impact of *Teague*'s non-retroactivity rule on selection of claims for presentation in *certiorari* petitions following direct appeal).

postconviction proceedings (step 9)).[14] Moreover, at least with regard to the *Teague* rule, the pendency of timely filed *certiorari* proceedings following direct appeal (step (6)) and possibly following state postconviction (step (9)) postpones the point at which a case becomes "final" for nonretroactivity purposes,[15] thereby maximizing the set of constitutional rules in existence prior to the point of "finality." Accordingly, subject to the qualifications in the next paragraph, petitioners are well advised to file *certiorari* petitions at both stages and to focus the petitions, *inter alia*, on "new," or possibly "new," legal rules that warrant relief.[16]

In cases governed by AEDPA, the question whether (and when) prisoners should file *certiorari* petitions at stages (6) and (9) is complicated in three ways by the Act's statute of limitations and tolling provisions. First, the 180-day statute of limitations that applies in AEDPA "opt-in cases"[17] usually begins running prior to, and is not tolled during, the time taken to *prepare* a direct appeal *certiorari* petition at step (6) and is tolled only after the *certiorari* petition is filed, while the Supreme Court considers it.[18] Second, the 180-day opt-in limitations period is not tolled during *any* part of the *certiorari* stage following state postconviction review (step (9)), even, apparently, if the Supreme Court grants *certiorari*.[19] Third, although the one-year statute of limitations that applies in AEDPA "nonopt-in cases"[20] apparently does not affect the preference for seeking *certiorari* following direct appeal (step (6)) — because the limitations period apparently does not commence until *after* completion of Supreme Court *certiorari* review following direct appeal[21] — the nonopt-in statute of limitations period *does* commence, and may *not* be tolled at any time, during the *certiorari* stage following state postconviction review (step (9)).[22] In order to avoid these difficulties in cases that will be governed by AEDPA's opt-in provisions once they reach federal court, prisoners may be forced (i) to expedite the filing of a *certiorari* petition following direct appeal (step (6)) or to

---

[14] *See infra* § 25.6 nn.11-27 (discussing situations in which *Teague*'s nonretroactivity rule may allow federal habeas corpus petitioner to receive benefit of "new rule" that was not established until prisoner's case was pending in state postconviction proceedings).

[15] *See infra* § 25.6.

[16] *See infra* §§ 6.4, 25.1 nn.25-31.

[17] For an explanation of AEDPA's "opt-in" provisions and the types of cases to which they apply, see *supra* § 3.3.

[18] *See infra* § 5.1b nn.97-98 and accompanying text.

[19] *See infra* § 5.1b nn.101-02 and accompanying text.

[20] For an explanation of AEDPA's "nonopt-in" provisions and the types of cases to which they apply, see *supra* §§ 3.2, 3.4.

[21] *See infra* § 5.1b nn.57-63 and accompanying text.

[22] *See infra* § 5.1b n.65 and accompanying text.

pursue *certiorari* proceedings following direct appeal (step (6)) *simultaneously* with state postconviction proceedings (steps (7) and (8)); (ii) to pursue *certiorari* following state postconviction proceedings (step (9)) simultaneously with federal habeas corpus proceedings); or, in a pinch, (iii) to forgo *certiorari* proceedings — particularly, following state postconviction proceedings — altogether. In order to avoid these difficulties in cases that will be governed by AEDPA's nonopt-in provisions once they reach federal court, prisoners may be forced (i) to pursue *certiorari* following state postconviction review (step (9)) simultaneously with federal habeas corpus proceedings or, in a pinch, (ii) to skip the latter *certiorari* stage altogether. If a prisoner takes the "simultaneous filing" route, and if the Supreme Court grants *certiorari*, assumedly either that Court or the state or federal court in which the simultaneous proceeding is pending will stay that proceeding while the Supreme Court acts. Tactical difficulties with the "simultaneous filing" alternative are discussed in § 6.4c *infra*.

Prisoners occasionally may dispense with steps (7) and (8) (state trial and appellate postconviction proceedings), but only if the petitioner has exhausted[23] — *i.e.*, fully litigated — at trial and on direct appeal every potentially meritorious federal claim or variation thereof that is available to the petitioner and that under some reasonably imaginable scenario the petitioner might decide to raise in a federal habeas corpus petition.[24] This rule of practice only occasionally allows prisoners to skip steps (7) and (8). The exacting exhaustion and procedural default[25] doctrines that now prevail in the federal courts, together with the nearly impenetrable statutory and common law barriers to successive federal petitions raising claims that the petitioner did not include or thoroughly litigate in an earlier petition,[26] leave potential federal petitioners with no choice but to take literally the exhaustion of state remedies metaphor. In particular, the various federal preclusion doctrines, together with their state counterparts, almost never permit a prisoner to forgo the opportunity via steps (7) and (8) to raise and exhaust a federal claim in the state courts based on the good faith expectation or assumption that, if a first federal habeas corpus petition fails, claims omitted from it may be pursued later on in subsequent state postconviction proceedings followed by a second federal petition. Efforts accordingly must be taken as early in the course of proceedings as possible, and certainly when state postconviction procedures become available under state

---

[23] *See infra* Chapter 23 (exhaustion doctrine).

[24] *See infra* Chapter 9 (claims cognizable in habeas corpus); *infra* §§ 11.2 (discovering claims), 11.3 (claim selection).

[25] *See infra* Chapter 26 (procedural default doctrine).

[26] *See infra* Chapter 28 (rules for successive petitions).

law, to discover and litigate all available federal claims in the state courts before filing a habeas corpus petition in the federal courts.[27]

In moving to and through steps (7) and (8), however, prisoners once again have to take into account the complications and risks created by AEDPA's statutes of limitations and tolling provisions. In both opt-in and nonopt-in cases, the limitations period begins running before, and is not tolled while, the prisoner *prepares* a state postconviction petition.[28] In addition, although the one-year statute of limitations for AEDPA nonopt-in cases is tolled during all "properly filed" state postconviction proceedings, the 180-day statute of limitations for AEDPA opt-in cases is tolled only while a *first* state postconviction petition is adjudicated and not while any second or subsequent state postconviction petition is under review.[29] AEDPA thus creates strong incentives (i) to commence state postconviction proceedings (step (7)) as soon as possible after the completion of post-direct appeal *certiorari* proceedings (step (6)) in cases that will be governed by AEDPA's nonopt-in provisions when they reach the federal habeas corpus stage, and (ii) to commence state postconviction proceedings (step (7)) as soon as possible after the completion of state direct appeal (step (5)), and to plead every possibly meritorious state postconviction claim, in cases that will be governed by AEDPA's opt-in provisions when they reach federal habeas corpus.

Capital petitioners face particularly serious consequences if they forgo any of the nine steps listed above. In the capital context, the prisoner faces — in addition to an irreversible sanction — an especially virulent combination of inhospitable rules governing successive petitions,[30] strict standards for obtaining stays of execution pending adjudication of such petitions,[31] and a near presumption that unusual litigative steps are taken solely for the purpose of delay.[32] These factors counsel strongly against forgoing any reasonably available means of discovering and redressing constitutional violations that have contributed to a capital conviction or sentence and against risking even the remotest possibility that a federal court will forbid the petitioner to litigate the merits of a federal claim because of an exhaustion or procedural default problem

---

[27] *See infra* §§ 6.2, 7.1a, 11.2, 11.3 (all bearing on claim discovery and selection in state and federal postconviction proceedings).

[28] *See infra* § 5.1b nn.64, 99 and accompanying text.

[29] *See infra* § 5.1b n.101 and accompanying text. On the requirement that state postconviction proceedings be "properly filed" in order to toll the one-year statute of limitations, see *infra* § 5.1b n.66 and accompanying text.

[30] *See infra* Chapter 28.

[31] *See infra* §§ 13.2d, 36.2, 38.2, 39.3c.

[32] *See* Anthony G. Amsterdam, *In Favorem Mortis: The Supreme Court and Capital Punishment*, 14 ABA INDIVIDUAL RTS. & RESP. 14 (1987); Note, *Summary Process and the Rule of Law: Expediting Death Penalty Cases in the Federal Courts*, 95 YALE L.J. 349 (1985).

created by the failure previously to pursue the claim fully and properly in an available state forum.[33] Here again, however, as is discussed in preceding paragraphs, AEDPA complicates matters. Thus, in capital opt-in cases, the statute requires the expedited or simultaneous filing of post-direct-appeal *certiorari* proceedings (step (6)), limits prisoners to a single set of state postconviction proceedings (steps (7) and (8)), and fails to toll the applicable statute of limitations during any part of the *certiorari* proceedings following state postconviction proceedings (step (9)). The third of these difficulties may also arise in capital nonopt-in cases.

Prisoners or counsel attempting to pursue proceedings *prior* to the filing of a federal habeas corpus petition must be fully conversant with the "exhaustion of state remedies" doctrine discussed in Chapter 23 *infra*. Without an adequate understanding of the exhaustion doctrine, a prisoner or his attorney is not in a position to answer at least three important questions that arise when deciding what litigative steps the prisoner should take before filing a federal habeas corpus petition: whether to pursue state postconviction proceedings (steps (7) and (8) above); what claims to raise when *any* of the steps discussed above other than the *certiorari* steps ((6) and (9) above[34]) is taken; and how thoroughly to present claims at stages other than the two *certiorari* stages.

b. *Statutes of limitations.* Until 1996, there was no fixed statute of limitations for filing federal habeas corpus petitions.[35] The only constraint upon the timing of the petition was a flexible "prejudicial delay" rule, akin to the equitable doctrine of laches.[36]

The Antiterrorism and Effective Death Penalty Act of 1996,[37] which was signed into law by President Clinton on April 24, 1996, establishes two different statutes of limitations — a one-year limit on the filing of most federal habeas corpus petitions[38] and all section 2255 motions,[39] and a shorter, 180-day limit on

---

[33] *See infra* §§ 5.3, 11.1, 13.3 (all discussing procedures for securing federal court stay pending exhaustion of state remedies if state court stay is unavailable).

[34] Claim selection at the state postconviction *certiorari* stage is discussed *supra* note 16 and accompanying text; *infra* § 6.4 (*certiorari* following state postconviction proceedings); and *infra* § 25.1 nn.25-31. *See also infra* § 39.2d (claim selection at *certiorari* stage following lower court habeas corpus review).

[35] *See, e.g.*, Brecht v. Abrahamson, 507 U.S. 619, 637 (1993); Vasquez v. Hillery, 474 U.S. 254, 264 (1986); Heflin v. United States, 358 U.S. 415, 420 (1959) (Stewart, J., concurring); Chessman v. Teets, 354 U.S. 156, 165 (1957); United States v. Smith, 331 U.S. 469, 475 (1947) (*dicta*).

[36] *See infra* Chapter 24.

[37] Pub. L. 104-132, 110 Stat. 1214 (1996).

[38] 28 U.S.C.A. § 2244(d) (West 1994 & Supp. 1998).

[39] *Id.* § 2255.

habeas corpus petitions filed by capital prisoners in States that previously have "opted in" to the act's "Special Habeas Corpus Procedures in Capital Cases."[40] This subsection begins with a word on the application of the statutes of limitations to cases filed — or in which the limitations period expired — on or before or within a year after AEDPA became law. The subsection next describes the general one-year statute of limitations, which applies to all noncapital habeas corpus proceedings, to capital habeas corpus proceedings in States that have not qualified for application of AEDPA's opt-in provisions, and (with some minor differences[41]) to all section 2255 motions. The subsection then addresses the 180-day statute of limitations that applies in capital cases in States that previously satisfied the statute's opt-in requirements.

Applicability to cases filed on or before April 24, 1997. As is explained in section 3.4 *supra*, the Supreme Court in *Lindh v. Murphy*[42] read AEDPA's section 107(c), which makes the opt-in provisions applicable to "cases pending on or after the date of the enactment of this Act"[43] but does not similarly require courts to apply the *non*opt-in provisions to previously filed cases, as implicitly exempting nonopt-in cases filed on or before April 24, 1996 from all provisions of AEDPA, including the statute of limitations.[44]

As is also discussed in section 3.4 *supra*, *Lindh* and a predecessor decision, *Landgraf v. U.S.I. Film Products, Inc.*,[45] reaffirm the Court's longstanding presumption against "retroactive" applications of new legislation absent a "clear statement" of congressional intent to require such applications.[46] AEDPA lacks any such "clear statement" as to nonopt-in cases and probably lacks one as to opt-in cases.[47] A "retroactive effect" arises whenever a new statute's application would "attach[] new legal consequences to events completed before [the

---

[40] *Id.* § 2263. For a general description of the opt-in provisions and their relationship to the rest of AEDPA's habeas corpus provisions, see *supra* §§ 3.2, 3.3.

[41] Most importantly, the section 2255 statute of limitations is not tolled during exhaustion proceedings, given the absence of any exhaustion requirement in section 2255 cases.

[42] 117 S. Ct. 2059 (1997).

[43] Antiterrorism and Effective Death Penalty Act § 107(c), Pub. L. 104-132, 110 Stat. 1214, 1226 (1996).

[44] *Lindh, supra,* 117 S. Ct. at 2063-68; *see supra* § 3.4a.

[45] 511 U.S. 244 (1994).

[46] *Id.* at 265 (discussed *supra* §§ 3.4b nn.17-25 and accompanying text). *Accord* Hughes Aircraft Co. v. United States ex rel. Schumer, 117 S. Ct. 1871, 1876 (1997).

[47] *See supra* § 3.4b nn.19, 25, 47-49 and accompanying text (obvious absence of "clear statement" requiring retroactive applications of AEDPA to nonopt-in cases); *supra* § 3.4c n.57 and accompanying text (apparent absence of "clear statement" requiring retroactive applications of AEDPA to opt-in cases).

statute's] enactment."[48] Under this definition, applying the new statute of limitations to bar a nonopt-in habeas corpus petition or section 2255 motion filed within a reasonable period *after* April 24, 1996, but in which the limitations period expired *before* that date, would be improperly retroactive (given AEDPA's omission of a "clear statement" of congressional intent to require that effect). Applying the statute of limitations in that manner would attach the new legal consequence of denial of the habeas corpus or section 2255 action (its legal merit notwithstanding) to the prisoner's preenactment failure to have filed a petition within one year of a triggering date that AEDPA only later identified.[49]

---

[48] *Landgraf, supra,* 511 U.S. at 270. *See also Hughes Aircraft Co. v. United States ex rel. Schumer, supra,* 117 S. Ct. at 1876.

[49] *See supra* § 3.4b nn.26-28 and accompanying text. Decisions reaching this conclusion include, *e.g.,* Goodman v. United States, 151 F.3d 1335, 1337 (11th Cir. 1998) ("It would be unfair, and impermissibly retroactive, to apply § 2255's one-year 'period of limitation' to federal prisoners like Goodman, whose convictions became final prior to the effective date of ... AEDPA."); Gendron v. United States, 1998 WL 514668, at *3 (7th Cir. Aug. 20, 1998) (Supreme Court's reasoning in *Lindh v. Murphy, supra,* compels conclusion that "period of limitations does not begin to run until April 24, 1996, the AEDPA's enactment date"); Brown v. Angelone, 150 F.3d 370, 372, 375 (4th Cir. 1998) ("Under the Commonwealth's theory, ... [f]or many prisoners the long-established right to seek federal habeas corpus relief simply vanished at midnight on April 24, 1996" because "the time to file a federal petition had apparently lapsed days, months, or years, earlier, without any notice to the prisoner"; court rejects that "theory" and establishes grace period for filing because "[f]air notice obviously carries great import when limiting the time afforded a prisoner to seek a writ of habeas corpus, the 'fundamental instrument for safeguarding individual freedom against arbitrary and lawless state action'" (quoting Harris v. Nelson, 394 U.S. 286, 290-91 (1969)); Duarte v. Hershberger, 947 F. Supp. 146, 147-49 (D.N.J. 1996) (discussed *infra* note 51); United States v. Mead, 946 F. Supp. 4, 5 (D. Or. 1996); Flowers v. Hanks, 941 F. Supp. 765, 770-71 (N.D. Ind. 1996) ("The same considerations that make it inequitable and prejudicial to apply a new statute of limitations to a claim filed prior to the announcement of the new rule also counsel against applying such a rule to a cause of action which accrued prior to the rule .... [I]t would follow that for all § 2254 actions which accrued before the effective date of the AEDPA — April 24, 1996 — petitioners would be entitled to a grace period in the amount of the limitations period to file a timely suit."); other decisions cited *supra* § 3.4b n.28 & *infra* note 51. A number of pre-*Lindh* decisions relied on the antiretroactivity presumption to bar application of AEDPA's one-year nonopt-in statute of limitations to federal habeas corpus and section 2255 cases filed *before* April 24, 1996, as to which AEDPA's one-year period had expired before that date — cases that now are governed by *Lindh*'s statutory construction holding, even apart from "retroactivity" concerns. As noted by *Flowers v. Hanks, supra,* however, the logic of these pre-*Lindh* cases applies in a straightforward manner to cases filed *after* April 24, 1996, but as to which the one-year limitations period defined by AEDPA expired before that date. Decisions of this sort include, *e.g.,* United States v. Martin, 1997 WL 57153, at *2 (10th Cir. Feb. 12, 1997) ("[A]pplication of the one-year limit would attach new consequences to defendant's failure to file his motion earlier. The new legislation, therefore, does not operate retroactively to preclude defendant's appeal."); United States v. Sanchez, 1997 WL 8842, at *4 n.1 (10th Cir. Jan. 10, 1997) ("Because this [one-year filing] requirement for [section 2255 motions] would attach new legal consequences to events completed before its enactment, it does not operate to preclude this appeal."); Lindh v. Murphy, 96

This conclusion does not mean, however, that prisoners falling into this category (*i.e.*, prisoners who filed their applications after April 24, 1996, but as to whom AEDPA's one-year period expired before that date) face no statute of limitations. Rather, the fairness policies underlying the antiretroactivity presumption, as reflected in the "equitable tolling" doctrine discussed below,[50] suggest that such prisoners should be given (and nearly all courts that have considered the matter *have* given them) a "reasonable" time after April 24, 1996 — which in most courts means up to, but not more than, one year after that date — in which to file.[51]

F.3d 856, 863 (7th Cir. 1996) (*en banc*), *rev'd on other grounds*, 117 S. Ct. 2059 (1997) (discussed *infra* note 51); Samuel v. Duncan, 1996 WL 413632, at *1 (9th Cir. July 8, 1996), *cert. denied*, 117 S. Ct. 1338 (1997) (state waived statute of limitations bar by not raising it; "highly doubtful that the new statute of limitations could be applied retroactively to cut off an action that had been filed before the new statute was adopted"); Reyes v. Keane, 90 F.3d 676, 679-80 (2d Cir. 1996), *overruled on other grounds*, Nelson v. Walker, 1997 WL 442686, at *5 (2d Cir. Aug. 7, 1997) (court will not apply section 2244(d)'s statute of limitations to bar consideration of petition filed before AEDPA went into effect but after its one-year period had expired); Trammell v. Coombe, 1996 WL 719384, at *1-2 (S.D.N.Y. Dec. 13, 1996); Laboy v. Demskie, 947 F. Supp. 733, 739 (S.D.N.Y. 1996); Kelly v. Keane, 1996 WL 640892, at *1 (S.D.N.Y. Nov. 4, 1996); Rienzi v. United States, 1996 WL 605130, at *1 (E.D. Pa. Oct. 21, 1996) (application of AEDPA's one-year statue of limitations to movant's previously filed section 2255 motion would be "'entirely unfair and a severe instance of retroactivity'"); cases cited *supra* § 3.4b n.28; *see also* Dubois v. Angelone, No. 96-10 (4th Cir. Aug. 27, 1996) (discussed *infra* note 56 and accompanying text; applying same approach to AEDPA's 180-day statute of limitations for opt-in cases); Breard v. Angelone, 926 F. Supp. 546, 547 (E.D. Va. 1996) (same). *But see* United States v. Bazemore, 929 F. Supp. 1567, 1569-70 (S.D. Ga. 1996).

[50] *See infra* notes 53-54 and accompanying text.

[51] As of this writing, all of the courts of appeals and most of the district courts that have addressed the issue have concluded that AEDPA's statutes of limitation are not jurisdictional and are subject to equitable tolling. *See, e.g.*, Flanagan v. Johnson, 1998 WL 556280, at *4 (5th Cir. Sept. 1, 1998); *Goodman v. United States, supra*, 151 F.3d at 1337; *Brown v. Angelone, supra*, 150 F.3d at 374 ("We hold that a prisoner whose statutory right to seek federal habeas relief accrued prior to the AEDPA must receive a reasonable period of time after the statute's effective date to file his petition. This holding comports with that of every one of our sister circuits — six to date — to consider the proper application of the new limitations period found in § 2244(d) or § 2255"); Miller v. New Jersey State Dept. of Corr., 1998 WL 270110, at *1 & n.1 (3d Cir. May 26, 1998) ("This appeal ... presents the question whether the period of limitation set forth in 28 U.S.C. § 2244(d)(1) is subject to equitable tolling. We conclude that it is [for both section 2254 petitions and section 2255 motions] ...."); Miller v. Marr, 141 F.3d 976, 978 (10th Cir. 1998) ("§ 2244(d) is not jurisdictional and as a limitation may be subject to equitable tolling"); Calderon v. United States Dist. Ct., 128 F.3d 1283, 1287-89 (9th Cir. 1997) ("[e]very relevant signal — from the Act's plain language, to its legislative history, to its structure — points in the same direction: Section 101's one-year timing provision is a statute of limitations subject to equitable tolling, not a jurisdictional bar"); Henderson v. Johnson, 1998 WL 180610, at *3 (N.D. Tex. April 16, 1998) ("§ 2244(d)(1) is a statute of limitations that is subject to equitable tolling, not a jurisdictional bar"). *See also, e.g.*, Ross v. Artuz, 150 F.3d 97, 99-100 (2d Cir. 1998); United States v. Flores,

135 F.3d 1000, 1002-06 (5th Cir. 1998); Burns v. Morton, 134 F.3d 109, 111 (3d Cir. 1998); Young v. United States, 124 F.3d 794, 795-96 (7th Cir. 1997), *cert. denied*, 118 S. Ct. 2324 (1998); United States v. Simmonds, 111 F.3d 737, 746 (10th Cir. 1997); Unger v. United States, 1998 WL 337476, at *4 n.1 (E.D. Wis. June 22, 1998); Moore v. Hawley, 1998 WL 310520, at *3 (E.D. Mich. May 29, 1998); Cox v. Angelone, 997 F. Supp. 740, 743 (E.D. Va. 1998); Landa v. United States, 991 F. Supp. 866, 868 (E.D. Mich. 1998); Parker v. Johnson, 988 F. Supp. 1474, 1475 (N.D. Ga. 1998); United States v. Ortiz, 1997 WL 214934, at *5 (E.D. Pa. April 28, 1997); United States ex rel. Smith v. Page, 1997 WL 61446, at *21 n.5 (N.D. Ill. Feb. 6, 1997), *modified on other grounds*, 1997 WL 102530 (N.D. Ill. March 4, 1997). *Cf.* United States ex rel. Galvan v. Gilmore, 997 F. Supp. 1019, 1026 (N.D. Ill. 1998) ("since § 2244(d) does not affect this court's subject matter jurisdiction over habeas petitions, ... the state can [and, court concludes, did] waive the § 2244(d) timeliness issue by failing to raise it"). *But see* Harris v. United States, 1998 WL 264228, at *1 (S.D.N.Y. May 20, 1998) ("timeliness of a habeas corpus petition is jurisdictional in nature"); Giles v. United States, 1998 WL 217948, at *2-3 (E.D. Mich. April 28, 1998) (AEDPA's statute of limitations creates jurisdictional bar that cannot be equitably tolled or waived by government); Person v. United States, 1998 WL 226235, at *5-6 (D.R.I. April 21, 1998) ("Although the majority of those courts that have considered the issue subsequent to the Supreme Court's determination in Lindh, have provided litigants whose convictions became final prior to April 24, 1996, with varying degrees of relief from the AEDPA's time limitation provisions," court predicts that First Circuit will not do so and rejects equitable tolling argument); Kile v. Trent, 1998 WL 173144, at *1 (N.D. W. Va. March 30, 1998) (following *Clarke v. United States, infra*); Clarke v. United States, 955 F. Supp. 593, 595, 597 (E.D. Va. 1997) (denying review because "[p]etitioner filed his motion on October 21, 1996, more than five years after the limitation period ended on May 27, 1991," and Congress did not "provide[] a grace period in this portion of the AEDPA"); Curtis v. Class, 939 F. Supp. 703, 707 (D.S.D. 1996) (review denied where one-year period expired in December 1995, and "petitioner did not file his federal habeas petition until July 11, 1996, which is [10 weeks] after the Act's effective date").

The vast majority of courts that have addressed the issue of equitable tolling have concluded that prisoners must be afforded a full year from AEDPA's effective date (April 24, 1996) to file a habeas corpus petition or section 2255 motion in a nonopt-in case. *See, e.g., Flanagan v. Johnson, supra*, 1998 WL 556280, at *4; *Goodman v. United States, supra* at 1337; *Brown v. Angelone, supra*, 150 F.3d at 375 ("'reasonable period' means one year from the effective date of the AEDPA — i.e., ... prisoners whose convictions became final any time prior to the effective date of the AEDPA had until April 23, 1997, to file their § 2254 or § 2255 motion"; "[g]iven that Congress found it necessary to provide a habeas petitioner 'placed on notice of this time constraint' an entire year to prepare and file a habeas petition, it does not seem unreasonable to hold 'that petitioners whose state court proceedings concluded before April 24, 1996,' also deserve 'one year with notice.' ... Moreover, considering that the courts have now been 'grappl[ing] with the AEDPA and the time-bar limitation' for two years, it is not untoward to allow inmates one year to understand and comply with these new provisions"); *Miller v. Marr, supra* at 978 (prisoner, whose state postconviction petition was denied by state high court on October 4, 1993, was entitled to "additional year after the enactment of AEDPA" in which to file petition); *United States v. Flores, supra* at 1006 ("We ... join the Seventh, Ninth, and Tenth Circuits in holding that one year, commencing on April 24, 1996, presumptively constitutes a reasonable time for those prisoners whose convictions had become final prior to the enactment of the AEDPA to file for relief under 28 U.S.C. § 2255."); *Burns v. Morton, supra* at 111 ("[W]e hold that habeas petitions filed on or before April 23, 1997, may not be dismissed for failure to comply with § 2244(d)(1)'s time limit."); *Calderon v. United States Dist. Ct., supra* at 1287 (period of limitations "did not begin to run against any state prisoner prior to the statute's date of enactment," so "[n]o petition filed on or before April 23, 1997 ... may be dismissed for failure to comply with section 101's time limit"); *Young v. United States, supra,* 124 F.3d at 795-96 ("time limit does not apply to petitions filed before April 23, 1997"); *United States v. Simmonds, supra* at 746 ("prisoners whose convictions became final on or before April 24, 1996 must file their § 2255 motions before April 24, 1997"); *Lindh v. Murphy, supra,* 96 F.3d at 863 (court will not deny relief on basis of AEDPA's nonopt-in statute of limitations provisions as long as habeas corpus petition or section 2255 motion was filed within one year of enactment date, *i.e.,* on or before April 24, 1997) (followed in United States v. Hankins, 1996 WL 667839, at *1 (N.D. Ill. Nov. 13, 1996); United States ex rel. Centanni v. Washington, 1996 WL 556978, at *1 (N.D. Ill. Sept. 27, 1996) (under *Lindh, supra,* "not only any pre-Act petition ... but even any post-Act petition filed not later than April 23, 1997 is invulnerable to the Act's one-year limitation period")); *Duarte v. Hershberger, supra,* 947 F. Supp. at 147-49 (adhering to rule that "petitioners who are not time-barred under the prior limitations period, receive a grace period equal to the new limitations period," court holds that petitioner, who had completed direct review nearly 10 years earlier, "is not time-barred" because he filed federal habeas corpus petition "only thirteen days after the AEDPA was signed into law," long before expiration of "one-year grace period" on April 24, 1997); Smith v. United States, 945 F. Supp. 1439, 1441 (D. Colo. 1996) (rejecting Government's "literal reading of the statute, [which] would foreclose the Petitioner [who filed section 2255 motion two months after enactment of AEDPA and whose date of conviction was almost six years earlier] from filing any petition under § 2255" because any such "result would be intolerable and ... defendants whose date of conviction would per se preclude the filing of a petition pursuant to § 2255 under a literal reading of the amendment were surely meant to have one year from the date of the amendment to file their petitions"); *Flowers v. Hanks, supra,* 941 F. Supp. at 770-71 (applying rule that petitioners have one year from date of enactment of AEDPA to file petition, court holds that petitioner is not time-barred because he filed two months after AEDPA's enactment); Mitcham v. Calderon, C-94-2854 SBA (N.D. Cal. Dec. 20, 1996) (one-year limitations period, which court deems to begin running on date of enactment of AEDPA, was tolled until date counsel was appointed and further tolled during time that counsel devoted to preparing court-ordered brief on effect of AEDPA). *Cf.* United States v. Cuero-Gongora, 1997 WL 346722, at *1 (E.D. La. June 23, 1997) (dismissing section 2255 motion filed five years after conviction became final and over one year after effective date of AEDPA).

The 2d Circuit initially appeared to eschew the foregoing bright-line rule in favor of an approach that granted all prisoners a "reasonable time" after AEDPA's effective date to file a petition or section 2255 motion and left the determination of "reasonableness" to be made on a case-by-case basis. *See* Peterson v. Demske, 107 F.3d 92, 93 (2d Cir. 1997) ("We conclude that a habeas corpus petitioner is entitled to a reasonable time after the effective date of the AEDPA to file a petition, and that Peterson's petition, filed 72 days after the effective date was filed within a reasonable time.... In circumstances like Peterson's, where a state prisoner has had several years to contemplate bringing a federal habeas corpus petition, we see no need to accord a full year after the effective date of the AEDPA. At the same time, we do not think that the alternative of a 'reasonable time' should be applied with undue rigor."). *See also, e.g.,* Velasquez v. United States, 1998 WL 317806, *1-2 (S.D.N.Y. June 15, 1998); United States v. Amuso, 1998 WL 310123, at *1 (E.D.N.Y. June 4, 1998); Oppenheimer v. Kelly, 1997 WL 362216, at *1 (S.D.N.Y. June 27, 1997); Ojeda v. Artuz, 1997 WL 283398, at *2 (S.D.N.Y. May 29, 1997); Scire v. United States, 1997 WL 138991, at *5 (E.D.N.Y. March 24, 1997). In its recent decision in *Ross v. Artuz, supra,* however, the Second Circuit explained that its previous language in *Peterson v. Demskie, supra,* was merely *dicta,* and the court joined "[a]ll of our sister Circuits ... [in] conclud[ing] that a one-year grace period should be allowed." *Ross v. Artuz, supra,* 150 F.3d at 100. *See id.* at 102-03.

Accord Mickens v. United States, 1998 WL 350078, at *3-4 (2d Cir. June 24, 1998); Joseph v. McGinnis, 1998 WL 350075, at *1 (2d Cir. June 24, 1998) (*per curiam*); Rosa v. Senkowski, 1998 WL 334346, at *1 (2d Cir. June 24, 1998) (*per curiam*). As the court explained, the "lack of a clear and uniform grace period has led to diversity in district court decisions among petitioners in seemingly similar circumstances." *Mickens v. United States, supra* at *3-*4. *See also Ross v. Artuz, supra* at 101-02. The 2d Circuit's holding in *Ross v. Artuz, supra,* effectively overrules several district court decisions that relied on the *dicta* in *Peterson* in finding petitions untimely though they were filed less than one year after AEDPA's effective date. *See, e.g.*, Cole v. Kuhlmann, 1998 WL 274685 (S.D.N.Y. May 28, 1998) (petition filed April 13, 1997 untimely); Fernandez v. Artuz, 1998 WL 159171 (S.D.N.Y. April 2, 1998) (petition filed April 7, 1997 untimely); Robles v. Senkowski, 1998 WL 159177 (S.D.N.Y. April 2, 1998) (petition filed March 24, 1997 untimely); Alexander v. Keane, 991 F. Supp. 329 (S.D.N.Y. 1998) (petition filed March 21, 1997 untimely); Rashid v. Kuhlmann, 991 F. Supp. 254 (S.D.N.Y. 1998) (petition filed April 18, 1997 untimely); Hill v. Keane, 984 F. Supp. 157 (E.D.N.Y. 1997) (petition filed April 17, 1997 untimely).

Prior to the 2d Circuit's change of direction, some district courts in other jurisdictions relied on that Circuit's reasoning in *Peterson v. Demskie, supra,* to adopt a case-by-case approach to equitable tolling. *See, e.g.*, United States v. Timber, 1998 WL 289753, at *4 (N.D. Ga. May 29, 1998) ("court adopts the view of the Second Circuit [in *Peterson v. Demskie, supra*] that the determination of whether a motion was filed within a reasonable time after the effective date of the AEDPA should be made based upon the unique facts and circumstances present in each case. Without a showing that the motion was in preparation at, or was filed within a reasonable period after, the effective date of the AEDPA, a § 2255 motion filed after the passage of the AEDPA and more than one year after the Defendant's conviction became final is time barred."). Notwithstanding such holdings, the 2d Circuit's revision of its approach — and the remarkable consistency of the other circuits' treatment of this issue — suggest that the one-year rule is likely to emerge as the approach followed in all jurisdictions.

The courts that have adopted the bright-line one-year rule disagree about the precise date on which that year ends. Most courts simply declare, without analyzing the issue, that the date is April 23, 1997. One court, observing that it "fails to see the magic in April 23, 1997," selected the date of "April 25, 1997" instead. Alves v. Matesans, 1998 WL 199985, at *3 (D. Mass. April 14, 1998) (adopting "bright line" rule letting petitioners file within one year of effective date, but limiting ruling to cases in which one year otherwise would have expired before AEDPA became law). The only courts that have thus far engaged in a careful analysis of the subject, the 2d and 5th Circuits, have concluded that the deadline should be April 24, 1997. *See Flanagan v. Johnson, supra,* 1998 WL 556280, at *5-*6 (after noting that most circuit decisions simply announce "that the reasonable time period will expire on April 23 or April 24," court concludes that correct date is April 24, 1997 because FED. R. CIV. P. 6(a) "governs the computation of federal statutory periods of limitation" and requires that "April 24, 1996, the effective date of AEDPA, must be excluded from the computation of the one year post-AEDPA time period"); *Mickens v. United States, supra* at *4 (grace period ends on April 24, 1997 because "when a statute of limitations is measured in years, the last day for instituting the action is the anniversary date of the start of the limitations period"); *Ross v. Artuz, supra* at 103 (same as *Mickens v. United States, supra*). *See also* Housley v. United States, 1998 WL 668115, at *1*3 (M.D. Fla. Sept. 21, 1998) (rejecting 11th Circuit and other caselaw that "established 4/23/97 as the deadline ... without any analysis, much less a search for Congressional intent," and instead relying on 5th Circuit's reasoned approach in *Flanagan v. Johnson, supra,* as basis for holding that section 2255 motion filed on April 24, 1997 was timely); *supra* § 3.4a n.14.

In the vast majority of jurisdictions that employ the one-year rule, every prisoner has *at least* one year following AEDPA's effective date to file a petition. *See, e.g., Calderon v. Dist. Ct., supra,* 128 F.3d at 1287-1288 ("[n]o petition filed on or before April 23, 1997 — one year from the date of AEDPA's enactment — may be dismissed for failure to comply with the section 101's time limit"; "Beeler, along with many other prisoners, ... has at least until April 23, 1997, to file his habeas petition."). The question may arise in some cases, however, whether a prisoner is entitled to equitable tolling beyond a year following AEDPA's effective date. *See, e.g., id.* at 1288 ("The district court went one step farther and, based on its conclusion that AEDPA's one-year limit could be equitably tolled, extended Beeler's deadline to October 17, 1997."); *see also, e.g., Miller v. Marr, supra,* 141 F.3d at 976, 978 (prisoner, whose state postconviction motion was denied by state's high court on October 4, 1993, and who therefore "was required to file prior to April 24, 1997, one year after the enactment of the AEDPA," argues that equitable tolling should be extended to permit filing of petition on July 10, 1997). In resolving such claims, the courts generally have required prisoners seeking such additional tolling to show that (i) they "diligently pursue[d] claims" (*Miller v. Marr, supra* at 978; *accord Miller v. New Jersey State Dept. of Corr., supra,* 1998 WL 270110, at *3 ("petitioner must show that he or she 'exercised reasonable diligence in investigating and bringing [the] claims.' Mere excusable neglect is not sufficient.") and/or that (ii) "'extraordinary circumstances' beyond [the] prisoner's control ma[d]e it impossible to file [the] petition on time" (*Calderon v. United States Dist. Ct., supra,* 128 F.3d at 1289; *accord Miller v. New Jersey State Dept. of Corr., supra* at *3; *Henderson v. Johnson, supra* at *3). *Compare, e.g., Calderon v. United States Dist. Ct., supra* at 1289 (prisoner entitled to additional equitable tolling because "lead counsel, ... [who] had diligently pursued the preparation of Beeler's petition ... withdrew after accepting employment in another state, and much of the work product he left behind was not usable by replacement counsel — a turn of events over which Beeler had no control") *with Miller v. Marr, supra* at 978 (prisoner's argument that incarceration in private correctional facility deprived him of access to requisite statutes and case law deemed insufficient to justify additional tolling because "Mr. Miller has provided no specificity regarding the alleged lack of access and the steps he took to diligently pursue his federal claims"; court indicates that result would differ if prisoner "contend[ed], for example, that a constitutional violation has resulted in the conviction of one who is actually innocent or incompetent") *and with Miller v. New Jersey State Dept. of Corrections, supra* at *1, *3 (remanding to district court to determine whether prisoner's claim "that he was delayed in filing his petition because he was in transit between various institutions and did not have access to his legal documents until April 2, 1997, and ... did not learn of the new limitation period until April 10, 1997" justified tolling of limitations period to June 4, 1997). Drawing upon concepts of waiver and equity that the courts have applied in determining the applicability of other procedural defenses to habeas corpus relief (*see generally infra* § 22.1 nn.37-50 and accompanying text), one court has concluded that the state's excessive delay in invoking the statute of limitations is a ground for excusing a petitioner's failure to comply with the statute. *See* Davis v. Johnson, 1998 WL 351854, at *3 (S.D. Tex. June 2, 1998) (although death-sentenced petitioner's habeas petition should be time-barred because he failed to file it until approximately one year after expiration of previously-granted extension, court nonetheless reaches merits because: "Timing rules work both ways: if the state wants to kill a man because his filings are not on time, it should raise that issue promptly. If limitations applies to Davis, laches should apply to Johnson. Johnson waited until May 1998 to raise a point it knew of in May 1997. Responsible government's prompt objection would have saved everyone time and trouble, especially since the court, Davis, and Johnson are funded by the taxpayers. Because the government's taking a person's life should invoke the most awesome governmental accountability, the court will address the merits of the petition in an abundance of caution.").

Even prisoners as to whom AEDPA's one-year limitations period expired shortly *after* April 24, 1996, can argue that an application of the statute of limitations to bar their subsequently filed habeas corpus petition or section 2255 motion is improperly "retroactive"[52] — or, at the least, unfair — inasmuch as it would deny relief on the basis of a new statutory provision with which the prisoners did not have a reasonable amount of time to comply. It is precisely for such litigants that the well-established rule of "equitable tolling" of new statutes of limitations has developed. Under the "equitable tolling" doctrine, courts must afford litigants a "reasonable period" of time to comply with a newly enacted statute of limitations.[53] As applied to the situation under discussion, the rule

---

[52] *See, e.g., Burns v. Morton, supra,* 134 F.3d at 111 ("Applying § 2244(d) as of its effective date would require Burns to have filed his habeas petition before September 21, 1996, one year after his petition for certification was denied by the New Jersey Supreme Court, but less than five months after § 2244(d) became effective. Several other courts of appeals have held that applying § 2244(d) in this manner 'would impermissibly "attach new legal consequences to events completed before its enactment."' ... We agree that applying § 2244(d)(1) to bar the filing of a habeas petition before April 24, 1997, where the prisoner's conviction became final before April 24, 1996, would be impermissibly retroactive. Even under § 2241(d)(1)'s time limitation, would-be petitioners are afforded one full year to prepare and file their habeas petitions, and as of April 24, 1996, have been placed on notice of this time constraint. We reject the notion that petitioners whose state court proceedings concluded before April 24, 1996, should be afforded less than one year with notice." (citing *Calderon v. United States Dist. Ct., supra; United States v. Simmonds, supra*)); *Calderon v. United States Dist Ct., supra,* 128 F.3d at 128 (statute of limitations would be impermissibly "retroactive" both in case of prisoner whose year elapsed prior to AEDPA's effective date and in case of prisoner whose year elapsed shortly thereafter; in latter case, prisoner "would face dire consequences for having wasted the time prior to AEDPA's enactment: They would have to investigate, prepare and file a petition in however much time remained — perhaps as little as one day.").

If the "event" to which *Landgraf*'s "attachment of new legal consequences" test applies is the date on which AEDPA's one-year limitations period begins to run, and not the date on which that one-year period expires, AEDPA's statute of limitations provision arguably has a "retroactive" effect on any case in which direct review proceedings (*see* 28 U.S.C.A. § 2244(d)(1)(A) (West 1994 & Supp. 1998), discussed *infra* notes 60-62 and accompanying text) ended prior to April 24, 1996. The "equitable tolling" doctrine discussed below, *infra* notes 53-54 and accompanying text, provides a workable solution to any of the problems the statute of limitations poses for prisoners who completed direct review prior to April 24, 1996.

[53] *See, e.g.,* Texaco, Inc. v. Short, 454 U.S. 516, 527 n.21 (1982); Canadian Northern Ry. Co. v. Eggen, 252 U.S. 553, 562 (1920); Sohn v. Waterson, 84 U.S. (17 Wall.) 596, 599 (1873); Ockerman v. May Zima & Co., 27 F.3d 1151, 1157 (6th Cir. 1994) (citing cases); decisions cited *supra* note 51. In United States v. Brockamp, 117 S. Ct. 849 (1997), the Court concluded that the "statutory time (and related amount) limitations" of section 6511 of the Internal Revenue Code of 1986 could not be equitably tolled because (1) "[s]ection 6511's detail, its technical language, the iteration of the limitations in both procedural and substantive forms, and the explicit listing of exceptions, taken together indicate to us that Congress did not intend courts to read other unmentioned, open-ended, 'equitable' exceptions into the statute that it wrote"; (2) "[t]here are no counter-indications" of legislative intent to create equitable exceptions, given that "[t]ax law, after

requires that, notwithstanding AEDPA's provisions, *all* prisoners in nonopt-in situations be afforded a "reasonable period" after the date of enactment in which to file. Most courts of appeals and lower court cases have defined that "reasonable period" to be AEDPA's full one-year period, through April 24, 1997.[54]

---

all, is not normally characterized by case-specific exceptions reflecting individualized equities"; and (3) "[t]he nature and potential magnitude of the administrative problem" that reading an equitable exception into section 6511 would create "suggest that Congress decided to pay the price of occasional unfairness in individual cases (penalizing a taxpayer whose claim is unavoidably delayed) in order to maintain a more workable tax enforcement system. At the least it tells us that Congress would likely have wanted to decide explicitly whether, or just where and when, to expand the statute's limitations periods, rather than delegate to the courts a generalized power to do so whenever a court concludes that equity so requires." *Id.* at 850, 852. As the *Brockamp* decision reflects, analysis of the propriety of "equitable tolling" is situation-specific, requiring careful examination of the statute at issue and the surrounding legal context. *See also* United States v. Beggerly, 118 S. Ct. 1862, 1868 (1998) (emphasizing that "[e]quitable tolling is not permissible where it is inconsistent with the text of the relevant statute," *id.* (citing *Brockamp, supra*), Court rejects claim of equitable tolling because statute at issue, Quiet Title Act, "has already effectively allowed for equitable tolling" and furthermore establishes "unusually generous ... limitations time period," thereby rendering "additional equitable tolling ... unwarranted," and because equitable tolling would disadvantage landowners by "throw[ing] a cloud of uncertainty over the[ir] rights").

The factors upon which the Court relied in *Brockamp* tend to militate in favor of (or, at least, do not militate against) equitable tolling of AEDPA's general one-year limitations period for filing habeas corpus petitions. *See, e.g., Calderon v. United States Dist. Ct., supra*, 128 F.3d at 1288 n.4 (*Brockamp* "is not to the contrary [of court's conclusion that AEDPA's limitations period should be equitably tolled]. In *Brockamp*, the Court held that a time-limit on filing tax refund claims was a jurisdictional bar, not a tollable statute of limitations. The statute at issue there was, however, phrased in 'a highly detailed technical manner, that linguistically speaking, cannot easily be read as containing implicit exceptions.' 117 S. Ct. at 851. AEDPA's one-year limit is neither detailed nor technical; it reads like an everyday, run-of-the-mill statute of limitations. Moreover, *Brockamp* also relied heavily on the fact that in administering a tax system, it is sometimes necessary 'to pay the price of occasional unfairness in individual cases ... in order to maintain a more workable' regime. 117 S. Ct. at 852. While such 'occasional' injustices may be a necessary price of tax administration, they are decidedly not an acceptable cost of doing business in death penalty cases."); Beeler v. Calderon, CV 96-0606-RT (C.D. Cal. Feb. 28, 1997) ("None of the facts which militated against applying the doctrine of equitable tolling in *U.S. v. Brockamp* exist here. New Section 2244's time limitation is not set forth in an unusually emphatic or highly detailed, technical manner. The time limitation is not reiterated several times in several ways, nor are any substantive limitations imposed. Although new section 2244(d)(2) provides that the time during which a properly filed application for state postconviction or collateral review shall not be counted toward any period of limitation, this is not an exception to the basic time limit, but a description of a circumstance which would toll the running of the limitations period. Furthermore, criminal law, unlike tax law, is characterized by case-specific exceptions reflecting individual equities, and the potential magnitude of petitions for habeas relief in death penalty cases in which equitable tolling might be sought in no way approaches the potential magnitude of tax refund claims in which such relief might be sought.").

[54] See authorities discussed *supra* note 51.

Finally, as also is discussed in section 3.4 *supra*, even in opt-in cases, notwithstanding the opt-in chapter's "effective date" provision, applying the 180-day statute of limitations to bar habeas corpus consideration of cases in which that limitations period expired prior to April 24, 1996 — or even soon thereafter — would present serious constitutional, retroactivity, and statutory interpretation questions.[55] In order to avoid those questions, one court of appeals has ruled that "the beginning of the 180-day period ... must [in all cases] be calculated from April 24, 1996 — the day the new provisions were enacted into law."[56]

One-year statute of limitations for nonopt-in cases. The new federal legislation requires that all noncapital state prisoners and all capital prisoners incarcerated by nonopt-in States file federal habeas corpus petitions, and that all federal prisoners file section 2255 motions — or, apparently, that those state or federal prisoners give the appropriate pleadings to prison officials *for* filing — within one year of a statutorily specified triggering date.[57] AEDPA establishes a

---

[55] *See supra* § 3.4c nn.50-57 and accompanying text.

[56] Dubois v. Angelone, No. 96-10 (4th Cir. Aug. 27, 1996) (assuming *arguendo* that 180-day statute of limitations for opt-in cases, 28 U.S.C.A. § 2263 (West Supp. 1998), applies to Virginia capital cases, it would *not* apply to petitioner because doing so would mean he "became time barred prior to the passage of the new provisions"; because AEDPA's opt-in provisions do not "indicate a clear intent that the statute of limitations should be applied to prevent Dubois from filing a first federal petition," and because "constru[ing] ... § 2263 as operating prospectively avoids a serious question of its constitutionality," court announces rule that 180-day period can begin no earlier than April 24, 1996). *Accord* Breard v. Angelone, 926 F. Supp. 546, 547 (E.D. Va. 1996) (discussed *infra* note 122).

[57] 28 U.S.C.A. §§ 2244(d)(1), 2255 (West 1994 & Supp. 1998). As several courts have recognized, the so-called "prison mail box" rule for an incarcerated prisoner's filing of a notice of appeal — under which incarcerated prisoners are deemed to have filed papers on the day they deposit them for mailing in the prison's internal mailing system (*see* PROPOSED FED. R. APP. P. 4(c) (effective December 1, 1998, absent contrary congressional action); Houston v. Lack, 487 U.S. 266, 273 (1988); *infra* § 35.2a nn.11-12 and accompanying text) — should be used to identify the date on which a prisoner "filed" her habeas corpus petition or section 2255 motion for purposes of AEDPA's statute of limitations. *See, e.g.*, United States v. Boone, 1998 WL 77884, at *1 (4th Cir. Feb. 25, 1998) (*per curiam*) (following Burns v. Morton, *infra*, and holding that, for purposes of AEDPA's one-year statute of limitations, movant's section 2255 pleading was "deemed filed when Boone handed it to prison authorities for mailing — before the AEDPA's effective date"); Burns v. Morton, 134 F.3d 109, 112-13 (3d Cir. 1998) (*Houston v. Lack*'s mail box rule applies to determination whether habeas corpus petitions and section 2255 motions are timely filed under AEDPA: "Many have expressed their concern with the pro se prisoner's lack of control over the filing of documents, especially as compared to the control other litigants maintain .... [T]he Supreme Court's holding in *Houston* was founded on such concerns, and [they] are present with equal force where a pro se prisoner places his habeas petition in the hands of prison authorities for mailing."); United States ex rel. Gonzalez v. DeTella, 1998 WL 289757, at *2 (N.D. Ill. June 1, 1998) ("Although his petition was not received by the clerk of this court until August 7, 1997, Gonzalez has provided the court with a copy of a request for payment of postage, which

demonstrates that he delivered his petition to prison officials for mailing on July 30, 1997. Under the mailbox rule of *Houston v. Lack*, [*supra*] ... Gonzalez is deemed to have filed his petition on July 30, 1997"); Alves v. Matesans, 1998 WL 199985, at *2 (D. Mass. April 14, 1998) ("In accordance with *Houston v. Lack*, the court concludes ... that Alves' petition was 'filed' on April 24, 1997, when it was handed to prison officials."); United States ex rel. Washington v. Gramley, 1998 WL 171827, at *3 (N.D. Ill. Apr. 10, 1998) ("Habeas petitions are filed when they are given to prison officials for mailing, whether they are accompanied by a filing fee, a meritorious IFP petition or one that is not. That rule promotes the dual goals of preserving a bright-line statute of limitations and treating all habeas petitioners equally." (footnote omitted)); Hughes v. Irvin, 1997 WL 357947, at *2 (E.D.N.Y. June 25, 1997) (quoted *infra* note 64). *See also* United States v. Nguyen, 997 F. Supp. 1281, 1287-88 (C.D. Cal. 1998) ("The clerk of the court received and lodged Nguyen's motion on April 22, 1997, but did not file it until April 25, 1997. Ordinarily, for purposes of a statute of limitations, papers and pleadings are considered filed when they are placed in the possession of the court.... The Court finds no reason why this rule would be inapplicable here. Thus, the Court concludes that for purposes of the AEDPA's period of limitations, unless a movant is entitled to the benefit of constructive filing under *Houston v. Lack*, 487 U.S. 266 (1988), a § 2255 motion is deemed filed on the date it is received (and perhaps lodged) by the clerk of the court. The date of the filed' stamp is not conclusive. Nguyen's motion is timely."); United States v. Dorsey, 988 F. Supp. 917, 919-20 (D. Md. 1998) ("[T]he Fourth Circuit has consistently applied the "mailbox rule" to its cases involving pro se prisoner litigation .... On the whole, the reasoning in Houston ... applies equally to § 2255 as the AEDPA has amended it.... Accordingly, this Court treats Dorsey's motion as filed when it was delivered to prison authorities for forwarding by depositing it in the prison mailbox."). *Cf.* Whitmore v. Avery, 1998 WL 271800, at *3 (D. Neb. March 4, 1998) ("The district court clerk received Whitmore's second § 2254 motion on April 5, 1996, a few weeks before the AEDPA went into effect.... [H]owever, this petition was filed erroneously as part of a previous habeas corpus action, [and] was not correctly filed as a new cause of action ... until October 23, 1996.... Therefore, in accordance with the recent Supreme Court decision, Lindh v. Murphy, 117 S. Ct. 2059 (1997), I find that the AEDPA should not be applied to Whitmore's second petition, as that petition was pending when the AEDPA became effective.").

For reasons discussed *supra* § 3.4a n.14 and *infra* notes 79-91 and accompanying text, the date of the filing of an application for mandatory appointment of counsel in capital cases under 21 U.S.C. § 848(q) (1994) also seems to qualify as the date of the filing of the habeas corpus proceeding for statute of limitations purposes.

Suppose that a habeas corpus petition is timely filed but thereafter is found to contain one or more unexhausted claims that bar the petition from being adjudicated until available state court remedies are exhausted. *See infra* § 23.5 (requirement that state remedies on all claims in petition be exhausted before any claim may be adjudicated). In the past, a federal court's usual response to a petition containing unexhausted claims has been to dismiss it "without prejudice" pending exhaustion, with the expectation that the petitioner thereafter would file a new federal petition once state remedies were exhausted (assuming the state courts denied relief). *See infra* §§ 23.1 n.16, 23.5 n.3 and accompanying text. AEDPA's adoption of a statute of limitations, however, now creates the possibility that the petitioner's subsequent filing of a fully exhausted federal petition will be time-barred. This might happen, for example, if the petitioner filed his original federal petition when only a short amount of time remained before the one-year limitations period expired and then spends more than that amount of time preparing to file the state petition needed to exhaust his state remedies, or is later held to have pursued state proceedings in a manner that did not toll the federal statute of limitations. *See infra* note 64 and accompanying text (one-year statute of limitations is tolled only by "properly filed" state conviction proceedings). Indeed, because federal habeas corpus proceedings do not themselves toll AEDPA's statute of limitations, the time remaining on the limitations period may expire while the federal judge before whom the original federal petition is filed determines that the petition contains unexhausted claims. In that event, any petition that is filed thereafter and that does not "relate back" to the original petition will be time-barred. To avoid these difficulties and, in effect, preserve the original, timely filing date, some courts either (i) acknowledge that the prejudice avoided by the court's "without prejudice" dismissal includes prejudice from statute of limitations problems that otherwise might arise, or (ii) hold the original petition in "abeyance" — rather than dismissing it — pending exhaustion. *See, e.g.*, Peterson v. Brennan, 1998 WL 470139, at *8 (E.D. Pa. Aug. 11, 1998) ("in order to avoid potential problems with respect to the tolling of the AEDPA's statute of limitations during the pendency of the [state postconviction] proceedings, the Court will dismiss the Petition without prejudice to petitioner's right to file an amended petition after exhaustion of state remedies. The filing of such an amended petition would, pursuant to Federal Rule of Civil Procedure 15(c)(2), relate back to the original filing date of the habeas corpus petition because 'the claim ... asserted in the amended pleading arose out of the conduct, transaction, or occurrence set forth in the original pleading.' Fed. R. Civ. P. 15(c)(2). The one year statutory bar can therefore be avoided."); Kethley v. Berge, 1998 WL 324585, at *1-2, *3 (E.D. Wis. June 18, 1998) (ordering petition dismissed "without prejudice" and further ordering that "if petitioner chooses to reopen this federal petition when his state remedies are exhausted in accordance with 28 U.S.C. § 2254(c), he will be allowed to reopen this file under its present case number and with the benefit of the original filing date of April 5, 1995"; "I allow Mr. Kethley this option to foreclose the possibility that the present dismissal on procedural grounds will forever bar the petitioner from obtaining habeas review in a federal forum.... That the petitioner should be caught in a bind not of his own making ... violates the spirit and logic of several analogous interpretations of the AEDPA's intricate procedural rules (citing *Stewart v. Martinez-Villareal, infra*)); Williams v. Vaughn, 1998 WL 238466, at *2 & n.2 (E.D. Pa. May 8, 1998) (dismissing "mixed" petition that contained unexhausted claims but specifying that dismissal is "without prejudice to petitioner's right to file an Amended Petition under Federal Rule of Civil Procedure 15(c)(2)," so as to "protect the right of the petitioner to return to federal court" in case "there is a finding that his state court collateral proceeding was not properly filed" and "the limitations period ... expire[s] before petitioner could ... file a new petition"); Morris v. Horn, 1998 WL 150956, at *3 (E.D. Pa. March 19, 1998) (dismissing mixed petition "without prejudice to petitioner's right to file an amended petition pursuant to Federal Rule of Civil Procedure 15(c)(2) upon exhausting his state remedies," so that, in event petitioner's state postconviction petition is later deemed not to have been "properly filed" and limitations period expires, petitioner will not suffer "'unfair' result" of being "barred from federal court"). *See also* Stewart v. Martinez-Villareal, 118 S. Ct. 1618, 1621, 1622 (1998) (concluding that filing of habeas corpus petition or claim that is not yet "ripe," followed by refiling of petition or claim when it is ripe, constitutes only *one*, not *two*, petitions — as would refiling of "habeas petition ... dismissed for failure to exhaust state remedies ... and [then] returned to federal court" after exhaustion — thus implicitly recognizing that numerically second petition "relates back" to first petition); *id.* at 1624 (1998) (Thomas, J., dissenting) (stating that federal court may avoid AEDPA's jurisdiction-withdrawing results when a prior petition is dismissed and a new one filed some time later by "hold[ing] ... [a claim or petition] in abeyance" rather than dismissing it); United States v. Contreras, 1998 WL 317586, at *1 (10th Cir. June 15, 1998) (district court erred in denying section 2255 movant's request to stay proceedings on motion pending exhaustion of administrative remedies so as to avoid foreclosure of federal court relief through operation of successive motion bar); Brewer v. Johnson, 139 F.3d 491, 492-93 (5th Cir. 1998) (district court did not abuse discretion to dismiss without prejudice instead of holding petition in abeyance pending exhaustion,

number of triggering dates for the one-year period[58] and provides that the period "shall run from the latest of" those dates.[59] The triggering date likely to apply to

given that, on facts of case, there is no reason to believe that "AEDPA limitations period will preclude [petitioner's] ... refiling of his federal proceeding after he has properly exhausted his state remedies"); Morris v. Bell, 1997 WL 560055, at *3 (6th Cir. Sept. 5, 1997), cert. denied, 118 S. Ct. 1169 (1998) (district court did not abuse discretion in dismissing mixed petition rather than holding it in abeyance pending exhaustion of state remedies because, even if state courts deny relief, petitioner has ample time to refile petition in federal court without running afoul of statute of limitations). Cf. Earhart v. Johnson, 132 F.3d 1062, 1066 n.4 (5th Cir. 1998) (dicta) (rejecting request of capital petitioner who filed preAEDPA petition to be allowed to return to state court to exhaust unexhausted claims despite state's waiver of exhaustion defense, in part because "dismissing Earhart's present claims would have the ultimate effect of requiring him to litigate his future federal habeas petition under the more stringent standards of the AEDPA"; court does not discuss possibility of holding petition in abeyance rather than dismissing it while petitioner exhausts state remedies). Well-established "equitable tolling" doctrines provide a third possible way to avoid statute of limitations problems when a timely filed habeas corpus petition is dismissed on nonexhaustion grounds. See generally supra notes 53-54 and accompanying text. Recognizing the "abeyance" procedure, but refusing to use it — or to acknowledge the capacity of a "without prejudice" qualification or of equitable tolling — to avoid statute of limitations problems when a petition is dismissed on nonexhaustion grounds, are Parker v. Johnson, 988 F. Supp. 1474, 1476-77 (N.D. Ga. 1998) (holding petition in abeyance only for 45 days to allow petitioner, who "filed his pro se petition on the last possible day" and therefore would be time-barred as soon as petition is dismissed, to avoid dismissal by "amend[ing] his complaint so as to delete all unexhausted claims"; court notes that petitioner thereafter "is of course free to pursue state relief on his unexhausted claims" but expresses view that subsequent federal pleading containing those claims, once exhausted, will be treated as new petition that does not relate back to original petition and is time-barred); Anthony v. Cambra, 1998 WL 164971, at *2 (N.D. Cal. Feb. 18, 1998) (similar to Parker v. Johnson, supra: "The new statute of limitation on the filing of federal habeas corpus petitions requires that district courts provide prisoners who file mixed petitions with an opportunity to strike their unexhausted claims and amend or resubmit their petitions [with only exhausted claims] so that their amendment or resubmission can relate back to the date of the original filing and not be time-barred."). For further discussion of the abeyance procedure, see infra §§ 11.1 n.14 and accompanying text, 13.3b n.18 and accompanying text, 23.5 n.28 and accompanying text. For discussion of the related question whether AEDPA or pre-AEDPA law applies to a federal petition that originally was filed before AEDPA became law and then was refiled after AEDPA became law following dismissal without prejudice for nonexhaustion, see supra § 3.4a n.16.

For related caselaw bearing on the proper application of the statute of limitations to amendments of petitions and motions — and, specifically, on whether, for statute of limitations purposes, claims amended into petitions or motions "relate back" to the petitions' or motions' original filing dates — see supra § 3.4a n.16.

On the question whether the statute of limitations is satisfied by a federal court filing within the one-year period that does not itself constitute a habeas corpus petition or section 2255 motion, but that anticipates and may be necessary to permit the filing of such a pleading, see infra notes 84-91 and accompanying text.

[58] See 28 U.S.C.A. §§ 2244(d)(1)(A)-(D), 2255(1)-(4) (West 1994 & Supp. 1998) (discussed infra notes 67-78 and accompanying text).

[59] Id. §§ 2244(d)(1), 2255.

most habeas corpus cases (or, at least, to most claims in most such cases) is "the date on which the judgment became final by the conclusion of direct review or the expiration of the time for seeking such review."[60] The date likely to apply to most section 2255 motions (or to most claims in such motions) is "the date on which the judgment of conviction becomes final."[61] Although AEDPA does not define either version of its "becomes final" test, it appears to intend the following triggering events in both situations: (1) in cases in which the petitioner pursued a direct appeal to all courts to which such an appeal was available as of right within the state or federal system (and any discretionary appeals that were available within the state system and that the prisoner elected to pursue), the completion of *certiorari* proceedings in the United States Supreme Court following completion of direct appeal, or the expiration of the time for filing a petition for a writ of *certiorari* in cases in which *certiorari* was not sought;[62]

---

[60] *Id.* § 2244(d)(1)(A). By "judgment," AEDPA appears to mean the judgment determinative of the custody that the petitioner challenges. For example, in cases in which a prisoner's sentence, but not her conviction, was reversed and in which a new sentence thereafter was imposed and affirmed on appeal, it appears that the statute of limitations begins to run on the date the second sentencing judgment became "final." *See* Burris v. Parke, 95 F.3d 465, 467 (7th Cir. 1996) (*en banc*) ("With immaterial qualification the year runs from 'the date on which the judgment became final by the conclusion of direct review,' and we take 'judgment' to refer to the sentence rather than to the conviction."); *infra* §§ 11.4a, 28.3b nn.18-27 and accompanying text (preexisting habeas corpus doctrines that similarly define "judgment").

[61] 28 U.S.C.A. § 2255(1) (West 1994 & Supp. 1998). *See* Baskin v. United States, 998 F. Supp. 188, 189 (D. Conn. 1998) ("The AEDPA does not define when a judgment becomes 'final' for purposes of a § 2255 petition. However, the AEDPA statute of limitations for § 2254 claims specifically runs from 'the date on which the judgment became final by the conclusion of direct review or the expiration of the time for seeking such review.' 28 U.S.C § 2244(d)(1).... [There is] no reason to treat the time limit for Section 2255 motions differently from that applicable to Section 2254 habeas petitions ... The legislative history of the AEDPA reveals no Congressional intent to apply different time limits to habeas petitions and Section 2255 motions.... Thus, the one year statute of limitations for § 2255 petitions begins to run from 'the conclusion of direct review or the expiration of the time for seeking such review.' Where a request for a writ of certiorari from the United States Supreme Court has been denied, the limitation period begins to run from that denial."); United States v. Dorsey, 988 F. Supp. 917, 919 (D. Md. 1998) ("In the absence of any direct guidance from Congress, the consensus view has extended the prior case law on § 2255, which held that a conviction is not 'final' for the purposes of the statute until a petitioner has completed any direct appeal. The absence of specific language regarding 'finality' in the amended § 2255 suggests that Congress did not wish to disturb this line of authority, which essentially resolved a matter of judicial administration.... Accordingly, this Court concludes that a judgment of conviction becomes 'final,' for purposes of a 2255 motion, on the date that a petitioner can no longer pursue direct appeal.").

[62] *See, e.g.,* Flanagan v. Johnson, 1998 WL 556280, at *1 (5th Cir. Sept. 1, 1998) (state conviction became final, and AEDPA's one-year statute of limitations for state prisoners in nonopt-in cases began running, at expiration of 90-day period in which petitioner could have sought *certiorari* review following completion of state direct appeal); United States ex rel. Hardy v.

Washington, 1998 WL 603276, at *1 (N.D. Ill. Sept. 9, 1998) ("at least where the petitioner actually files a petition for a writ of *certiorari* ... the one-year clock in § 2244(d)(1)(A) begins to run when the United States Supreme Court denies a § 2254 petitioner's petition for a writ of *certiorari*, as the petitioner's case is alive until [then]"); United States v. Feinberg, 1998 WL 547284, at *1 (N.D. Ill. Aug. 27, 1998) (conviction became final on date of Supreme Court's denial of *certiorari*); Harris v. United States, 1998 WL 264228, at *2 (S.D.N.Y. May 20, 1998) ("Harris's judgment of conviction did not become final for purposes of the one-year period of limitation contained in 28 U.S.C. § 2255 until th[e] date" Supreme Court denied *certiorari*); *Baskin v. United States, supra*, 998 F. Supp. at 189 (discussed *supra* note 61); *United States v. Dorsey, supra*, 988 F. Supp. at 919 ("Dorsey had one year from October 7, 1996, the date on which the Supreme Court denied certiorari, in which to file his 2255 motion."); Hughes v. Irvin, 1997 WL 357947, at *2 (E.D.N.Y. June 25, 1997) ("The New York Court of Appeals denied petitioner leave to appeal his conviction on September 16, 1988 ... [so AEDPA's] one-year time limit would have begun to accrue on December 16, 1988, at the conclusion of the ninety days during which he could have sought certiorari in the United States Supreme Court."). *But cf.* Gendron v. United States, 1998 WL 514668, at *2, *3 nn.1-2 (7th Cir. Aug. 20, 1998) (*per curiam*) ("federal prisoners [proceeding under 28 U.S.C. § 2255] who decide not to seek *certiorari* with the Supreme Court will have the period of limitations begin to run on the date [court of appeals] ... issues the mandate in their direct criminal appeal"; reserving question "whether § 2244's 'direct review' includes the time a state prisoner, who files for leave to appeal to a state supreme court, is given to seek *certiorari* with the United States Supreme Court").

The phrase used in the statute, "the date on which the judgment becomes final by the conclusion of direct review or the expiration of the time for seeking such review" closely parallels the test the Supreme Court uses in applying its *Teague* doctrine to determine the point at which a prisoner's conviction "becomes final" such that any later-developed rules of constitutional law will not be applied "retroactively" in adjudicating the prisoner's federal habeas corpus petition. *See, e.g.,* Teague v. Lane, 489 U.S. 289, 305 (1989) (new rule applies in habeas corpus proceeding only if announced while petitioner's case was "'pending on direct review or not yet final'" (quoting Griffith v. Kentucky, 479 U.S. 314, 328 (1987)); *see also* Caspari v. Bohlen, 510 U.S. 383, 390 (1994) ("A state conviction and sentence become final for purposes of retroactivity analysis when the availability of direct appeal to the state courts has been exhausted and the time for filing a petition for a writ of certiorari has elapsed or a timely petition has been finally decided."); *infra* § 25.6. When Congress elects to use terminology that has become commonplace in court decisions in a particular field of law, the rules of statutory construction call for defining the statute's terms in accordance with that accepted judicial meaning. *See, e.g.,* Evans v. United States, 504 U.S. 255, 260 & n.3 (1992) ("It is a familiar 'maxim that a statutory term is generally presumed to have its common-law meaning.'... Or, as Justice Frankfurter advised, 'if a word is obviously transplanted from another legal source, whether the common law or other legislation, it brings the old soil with it.'" (quoting Taylor v. United States, 495 U.S. 575, 592 (1990); Felix Frankfurter, *Some Reflections on the Reading of Statutes*, 47 COLUM. L. REV. 527, 537 (1947))). As is explained *infra* § 25.6, the *Teague* caselaw generally defines the point of "finality" or "conclusion of direct review" as the date on which the Supreme Court denies a petition for *certiorari* following direct appeal proceedings in the state courts — or, in cases in which no such petition is filed, the date on which the time for filing has expired; or in cases in which the Supreme Court grants *certiorari*, the date on which the Court finally resolves the case. *Cf. infra* § 25.6 nn.20-27 (discussing occasions when "judgment" or "conviction" does not "become[ ] final" until completion of *certiorari* proceedings following *state postconviction* review — *e.g.,* when state law defines "finality" differently from above definition or when state law forbids defendants to raise certain kinds of claims (*e.g.,*

(2) if no direct appeal was sought, the expiration of the time for filing such an

ineffective assistance of counsel claims) on direct appeal and requires them to be raised for first time in state postconviction proceedings). Accordingly, the same definition should apply to AEDPA's use of the term "final." *See, e.g.*, United States v. Feinberg, 1998 WL 547284, at *1 (N.D. Ill. Aug. 27, 1998) ("there is no reason, and the government offers none" for employing different definitions of "finality" in *Teague* and AEDPA contexts).

Further evidence of the meaning of the "becomes final" language defining the principal triggering date for the nonopt-in statutes of limitations in sections 2244(d) and 2255 is provided by contrasting that language to the terms used to identify the triggering date for the opt-in statute of limitations in 28 U.S.C.A. § 2263(a) (West Supp. 1998). Whereas the nonopt-in limitations period generally begins running on "the date on which the judgment became final by the conclusion of direct review or the expiration of the time for seeking such review," 28 U.S.C.A. § 2244(d)(1)(A) (West 1994 & Supp. 1998), the opt-in limitations period begins running on the date of "final *State court* affirmance of the conviction and sentence on direct review or the expiration of the time for seeking such review." *Id.* § 2263(a) (West Supp. 1998) (emphasis added). This latter language demonstrates Congress' awareness that the courts would construe the phrase "final ... direct review" to encompass Supreme Court *certiorari* review unless the concept was limited by the qualifier "*State court affirmance* ... on direct review." *See* Rodriguez v. United States, 480 U.S. 522, 525 (1987) (*per curiam*) ("'"[W]here Congress includes particular language in one section of a statute but omits it in another section of the same Act, it is generally presumed that Congress acts intentionally and purposely in the disparate inclusion or exclusion.'"'" (quoting Russello v. United States, 464 U.S. 16, 23 (1983))).

Notice also that the opt-in statute of limitations treats the filing of a petition for *certiorari* "to secure review by the Supreme Court of the affirmance of a capital sentence on direct review by the court of last resort of the State" — but not the time taken to prepare a timely *certiorari* petition — as a basis for tolling the statute of limitations. 28 U.S.C.A. § 2263(b)(1) (West Supp. 1998). The fact that the nonopt-in statute of limitations contains no provision for "tolling" during direct review *certiorari* proceedings, while the opt-in provision *does* contain such a tolling provision, supports the conclusion that the nonopt-in statute of limitations is not intended to begin running until after (and thus could not sensibly be tolled by) *certiorari* proceedings. We reach this conclusion because the opt-in limitations period, including as extended by the opt-in tolling provisions, is obviously intended to be substantially *shorter* in all respects than the nonopt-in limitations period. *Compare, e.g., id.* §§ 2263(a), 2263(b)(2) (opt-in limitations period is only 180 days, always runs from completion of direct review, and is tolled during only "the *first* petition for [State] post-conviction review or other collateral relief" (emphasis added)) *with id.* §§ 2244(d)(1), 2244(d)(1)(B)-(D), 2244(B) (nonopt-in limitations period is one year, sometimes runs from dates long after completion of direct review, and is tolled during *all* "properly filed ... State postconviction or other collateral review proceedings," including second and successive proceedings). It would make little sense for the *opt-in* provision to keep its far more truncated limitations period from running while *certiorari* proceedings are pending if the nonopt-in provision let its designedly longer limitations period run during the time devoted to *certiorari* proceedings. This potential anomaly is avoided by giving the words that define the *nonopt*-in triggering provision their established meaning under the *Teague* doctrine, thus keeping the nonopt-in limitations period from commencing until after completion of *certiorari* proceedings. In that event, the opt-in provision would retain its characteristic quality of being more truncated than the nonopt-in provision because the opt-in provision would count the period needed to *prepare* a *certiorari* petition against its limitations period, but the less truncated nonopt-in provision would not do so. *See generally infra* notes 92-108 and accompanying text (more thoroughly canvasing differences between nonopt-in and opt-in statutes of limitations).

appeal; or (3) if direct appeal was taken to a state intermediate appellate court but an available direct appeal as of right to a higher state court was not sought, the expiration of the time for filing an appeal to the higher appellate court.[63]

The nonopt-in provision's one-year limitations period for habeas corpus (but not section 2255) cases is tolled by state postconviction or other collateral proceedings that are "properly filed" as a matter of governing state procedural law — but not by the period needed to *prepare* a state postconviction petition.[64]

---

[63] *See, e.g., Gendron v. United States, supra,* 1998 WL 514668, at *2, *3 nn.1-2 (*dicta*) (if state prisoner pursues state appeal as of right but fails to pursue discretionary second appeal within state system, AEDPA's nonopt-in statute of limitations apparently begins running upon expiration of time for filing discretionary second appeal); United States v. Cuero-Congora, 1997 WL 346722, at *1 (E.D. La. June 23, 1997) (movant's "conviction and sentence became final on August 29, 1992, when he failed to file his notice of intent to appeal his conviction and sentence" 10 days after sentence was imposed following guilty plea).

[64] 28 U.S.C.A. § 2244(d)(2) (West 1994 & Supp. 1998) ("The time during which a properly filed application for State post-conviction or other collateral review with respect to the pertinent judgment or claim is pending shall not be counted toward any period of limitation under this subsection."). *See, e.g.,* Brewer v. Johnson, 139 F.3d 491, 493 (5th Cir. 1998) ("The time during which a properly filed application for state post conviction or other collateral review with respect to Brewer's conviction is pending is not counted toward the limitations period."); Lovasz v. Vaughn, 134 F.3d 146, 148-49 (3d Cir. 1998) (because Congress, "in enacting AEDPA, of which § 2244(d)(2) is a part, ... intended to 'reduce federal intrusion into state criminal proceedings,'" successive petitions authorized by state law toll state of limitations even if federal law would not permit successive petitions in such situations); Tesack v. Trent, 1998 WL 329683, at *1 (S.D. W. Va. May 12, 1998) ("Tesack's petition is not time-barred because the statute was tolled for the time Tesack's state habeas petition was pending."). As an example of how section 2244(d)'s triggering and tolling provisions interact, consider the following passage from Hughes v. Irvin, 1997 WL 357947, at *2 (E.D.N.Y. June 25, 1997):

> The New York Court of Appeals denied petitioner leave to appeal his conviction on September 16, 1988. In petitioner's case, the one-year time limit would have begun to accrue on December 16, 1988, at the conclusion of the ninety days during which he could have sought certiorari in the United States Supreme Court.... But as of December 16, 1988, Hughes' [first postappeal state postconviction review] motion was already pending in state court, which operated to immediately toll the running of the statute of limitations. Until September 12, 1989, when petitioner's [second postappeal state postconviction review] motion was denied, Hughes had a continuous stream of postconviction applications pending in state courts. From September 12, 1989, the statute of limitations ran for four months, until January 11, 1990, when Hughes filed his [third postappeal] application for collateral review, thereby restarting the tolling provision. That motion was finally resolved against petitioner on August 5, 1996. Thus, on August 5, 1996, Hughes had eight months remaining, until April 1997, to file his habeas petition in compliance with the one-year time limit. Hughes is deemed to have filed the instant application when he delivered it to prison officials. See Houston v. Lack, 487 U.S. 266, 273 (1988). Thus, Hughes "filed" his habeas petition sometime between December 26, 1996, the date he signed his petition, and January 23, 1997, the date the action was filed with the Court, well before the application would have been time-barred.

The requirement that federal courts ascertain whether petitions were "properly filed" as a matter of governing state procedural law will enhance the already considerable extent to which federal courts must be conversant with state postconviction law and practice. *See infra* §§ 23.3b, 24.2, 25.6, 26.2a-26.2d (discussing how state procedural law bears on, respectively, exhaustion, delay, nonretroactivity, and procedural default issues). No matter how expert federal courts become in state procedural law, however, determining whether a state postconviction petition has been "properly filed" is likely to be a source of substantial litigation, given the phrase's ambiguity. Does the language demand compliance only with formal pleading, filing, and timing requirements? Or does it also demand compliance with "jurisdictional," substantive, and default-avoiding requirements? *Cf. Hughes v. Irvin, supra* at *3 ("The Court's research failed to unearth any case law construing 'a properly filed application,' as that term is used in § 2244(d)(2). Nor does the legislative history shed any light on what Congress intended .... In other contexts, the term 'properly filed' refers [only] to satisfying procedural requirements, such as timeliness and proper place of filing." (citing authority)). Consider, for example, a state postconviction statute that, like the federal habeas corpus statute, 28 U.S.C.A. §§ 2241(c)(3), 2254(a) (West 1994 & Supp. 1998), treats the existence of a constitutional violation as a "jurisdictional" requirement. If the state courts take up more than the one-year limitations period intensively adjudicating a "close" constitutional claim, eventually concluding that no constitutional violation occurred, would that conclusion mean that the petition was not "properly filed" in the first place because there was no subject-matter jurisdiction — and that the one-year period expired during state postconviction proceedings that did not toll its running? Obviously, any such reading would nullify the tolling provision for state postconviction proceedings because only prisoners who were sure that they would secure state postconviction relief — and thus would never need federal habeas corpus relief — would file a state postconviction petition. Indeed, any such reading would nullify the exhaustion of state remedies doctrine. Although that doctrine generally makes the state courts' determination that no constitutional violation has occurred a prerequisite for federal habeas corpus review, *see id.* § 2254(b)(1)(A), the doctrine has an established exception, recodified in AEDPA, for situations in which state proceedings are "ineffective to protect the rights of the applicant," *id.* § 2254(b)(1)(B)(ii). *See supra* § 3.3c n.74; *infra* § 23.4a nn.6-23 and accompanying text. Were the statute of limitations read to render state postconviction proceedings almost uniformly ineffective as a matter of federal law to protect the habeas corpus applicant's federal constitutional and statutory "rights" (because the petitioner's statutory right to habeas corpus review would almost always expire while state proceedings took place), the end of the exhaustion doctrine would be at hand. Some other interpretation of the "properly filed" language accordingly is required to make that language consistent with Congress' retention and recodification of the exhaustion doctrine, its evident intention to toll the statute of limitations during routine state postconviction proceedings, and the apparent purposes of the "properly filed" language — *i.e.*, to make clear that tolling does not occur during the period needed to *prepare* a state postconviction petition and to keep prisoners from making bad faith use of state postconviction proceedings to delay the onset of federal habeas corpus proceedings and the final adjudication of the legality of their convictions and sentences. One such interpretation of the "properly filed" limitation would tie it to state court determinations, made while the prisoner is at the *threshold* of some state postconviction procedure, that the procedure clearly is not available to the petitioner. On the theory that courts always have jurisdiction to determine their jurisdiction, petitions presenting questions (including state procedural questions) that are sufficiently controverted to require state court proceedings beyond the threshold would (on this interpretation) be "properly filed." Another, simpler, interpretation — which the vast majority of courts have adopted — limits the "properly filed" language to the petitioner's conformity with the timing requirements and procedural formalities for filing as set forth in state law. *See, e.g.*, Hoggro v. Boone, 1998 WL 340005, at *3 n.4 (10th Cir. June 24, 1998) (out-of-time state postconviction petition is not "properly filed" for purposes of § 2244(d)(2)'s tolling provision); *Lovasz v. Vaughn, supra* at 148-49 ("a 'properly filed application' is one submitted according to the state's procedural requirements, such as the rules governing the time and place of filing.... If a petitioner complies with these procedural requirements, or other procedural requirements the state imposes, his petition, even a second or successive petition, is 'a properly filed application' for purposes of § 2244(d)(2).... [W]e reject the notion that a meritless [state postconviction] petition cannot constitute a 'properly filed application' under § 2244(d)(2). Rather, in considering whether a petition for postconviction relief is properly filed, district courts should not inquire into its merits. A rule requiring an inquiry into the merits of a [state postconviction] ... petition in order to determine if it was properly filed could become problematic ...."); Souch v. Harkins, 1998 WL 661389, at *4*5 (D. Ariz. Sept. 22, 1998) (state application for postconviction relief is "properly filed" if "submitted in compliance with basic state filing requirements, such as the rules governing the time and place of filing," even if state court subsequently dismisses application on procedural default grounds); Joyner v. Vacco, 1998 WL 63664, at *3 (S.D.N.Y. Sept. 15, 1998) ("to be 'properly filed' under AEPDA the state application for collateral review must do no more than comply with procedural filing requirements, such as requirements that it be timely filed, be submitted in the proper forum, and include notice to the respondents."); Robinson v. Day, 1998 WL 524895, at *2 (E.D. La. Aug. 19, 1998) (state application for postconviction relief did not toll one-year limitations period because state supreme court denied application as "untimely filed"); Ellis v. Johnson, 11 F. Supp. 2d 695, 696-97, 698 (N.D. Tex. 1998) (following 3d Circuit's approach in *Lovasz v. Vaughn, supra*, and concluding that successive state petition that was eventually dismissed for abuse of writ was "properly filed" because "[s]tate law does not prohibit relief in subsequent habeas applications" and "sets no limits on the number of applications for writ of habeas corpus which may filed"); United States ex rel. Morgan v. Gilmore, 1998 WL 372060, at *3, *5-*7 (N.D. Ill. June 29, 1998) (untimely initial state postconviction petition did not toll limitations period but timely successive state petition *did* toll period even though claim in latter petition was "procedurally barred and thus ... frivolous"); *Hughes v. Irvin, supra* at *3 ("'[P]roperly filed,' as used in § 2244(d)(2), means [only] that in order to trigger the tolling mechanism, a petitioner's collateral review application must be submitted in accordance with any applicable procedural requirements, such as notice to the respondent, correct place of filing, and timeliness of the motion. The Court rejects the proposition that a seemingly frivolous collateral attack is not 'properly filed' for purposes of tolling the one-year statute of limitations.... The writ of habeas corpus would be emasculated if the ... determination of a state court [that petition lacks merit] could preclude a petitioner's access to federal court to challenge that very finding. Moreover, [contrary interpretation, which might depend on when state court made frivolousness determination, would leave] ... unclear at what point [state postconviction action] ... no longer qualified as 'properly filed.'"); Keeney v. McDaniel, CV-N-93-792-ECR (D. Nev. Oct. 3, 1996) ("properly filed" for purposes of section 2244 means "filed in compliance with the basic technical rules of the state court" and "does not depend on the eventual determination of the merits of the ... petition filed in state court"). *But cf.* United States ex rel. Washington v. Gramley, 1998 WL 171827, at *1 n.2 (N.D. Ill. April 10, 1998) (successive state postconviction petition dismissed by state courts as "waived" did not toll statute of limitations); Valentine v. Senkowski, 966 F. Supp. 239, 241 (S.D.N.Y. 1997) (suggesting that federal court must deny tolling based on any state postconviction petition it deems to have been frivolous under governing state and federal procedural and substantive law).

Although prisoners usually (and are always well-advised to) exhaust all state postconviction remedies on all federal claims before filing federal habeas corpus petitions, it sometimes occurs that

AEDPA does not make entirely clear whether that tolling period includes *certiorari* review by the United States Supreme Court of the state courts' denial of postconviction relief.[65] The tolling provision does, however, clearly encompass *all* "properly filed" petitions for state postconviction relief, including not only the *first* such petition but also any *second or successive* state

---

a federal habeas corpus petition is found to contain one or more unexhausted claims that must be exhausted in state postconviction proceedings before any of the other claims in the federal petition may be adjudicated. *See infra* § 23.5. On the statute of limitations implications of dismissals of federal petitions for nonexhaustion, and the subsequent commencement of state postconviction proceedings, see *supra* note 57.

[65] At the least, the tolling period includes the time during which the denial of a state postconviction petition is on appeal within the state judicial system — perhaps including the time following a trial court's denial of state postconviction relief and before a timely notice of appeal is filed. *See* Davis v. Keane, 1998 WL 345009, at *2 (S.D.N.Y. June 26, 1998) (under § 2244(d)(2)'s plain language and under basic habeas corpus policies, that provision tolls running of statute of limitations during entire period from date application for state postconviction relief is properly filed until application is finally denied by all state courts with jurisdiction over such cases, including time while appeal of application is pending; exhaustion and antisuccessive-petitions polices also "support excluding time until state collateral review is decided finally upon appeal").

With respect to a subsequent petition to the United States Supreme Court seeking *certiorari* review of the state courts' denial of postconviction relief, a comparison of the nonopt-in and opt-in statutes of limitations suggests that Congress may have intended the nonopt-in tolling mechanism to encompass the period during which the United States Supreme Court is reviewing a "properly filed" petition for *certiorari* from denial of state postconviction relief. The nonopt-in provision's tolling period includes "[t]he time during which a properly filed application for State post-conviction *or other collateral review* ... is pending." 28 U.S.C.A. § 2244(d)(2) (West 1994 & Supp. 1998). By contrast, the opt-in provision terminates its analogous tolling period for state postconviction relief upon "the final *State court disposition* of such petition." *Id.* § 2263(b)(2) (emphasis added). Given the opt-in provision's clear exclusion of federal (*i.e.*, Supreme Court) *certiorari* review from the tolling period, the omission of similar language from the nonopt-in provision indicates that Congress did not intend to impose a similar limitation on the nonopt-in tolling mechanism. *See, e.g., Rodriguez v. United States, supra*, 480 U.S. at 525 (quoted *supra* note 62); *see also supra* note 62 (other ways in which opt-in statute of limitations and tolling periods are consistently more truncated than nonopt-in counterparts). *See generally infra* notes 92-108 and accompanying text (more thoroughly canvasing differences between nonopt-in and opt-in statutes of limitations). *But see* United States ex rel. Gonzalez v. DeTella, 1998 WL 289757, at *2 (N.D. Ill. June 1, 1998) (construing statutory phrase "during which a properly filed application for State post-conviction or other collateral relief ... is pending" as limited to applications pending in state courts and ruling that statute of limitations was not tolled during 90-day period in which prisoner could have sought *certiorari* review of denial of state postconviction relief). Given the grave consequences of violating AEDPA's statute of limitations, and given the uncertainty surrounding whether the Act's nonopt-in statute of limitations is tolled during *certiorari* proceedings following state postconviction review, prisoners and their lawyers are well-advised to assume that such proceedings do *not* toll the statute of limitations and to follow the timing and ordering suggestions for such situations that are made in the text following § 5.1a n.22 *supra*.

postconviction petition that is "properly filed" as a matter of state procedural law.[66]

Although the completion of direct review upon the conclusion of *certiorari* proceedings is the presumptively applicable triggering date for the nonopt-in statute of limitations,[67] AEDPA postpones the date on which the limitations period commences to run when the prisoner was unable to file a petition or particular claims because of impediments created by state action or because the factual or legal bases for a claim were not previously available. Thus, under section 2244(d)(1), "[t]he limitation period shall run *from the latest of* —

(A)   the date on which the judgment became final by the conclusion of direct review or the expiration of the time for seeking such review;

(B)   the date on which the impediment to filing an application created by State action in violation of the Constitution or laws of the United States is removed, if the applicant was prevented from filing by such State action;

(C)   the date on which the constitutional right asserted was initially recognized by the Supreme Court, if the right has been newly recognized by the Supreme Court and made retroactively applicable to cases on collateral review; or

---

[66] *See, e.g., Lovasz v. Vaughn, supra,* 134 F.3d at 148 ("[I]f a state allows petitioners to file second or subsequent petitions for postconviction relief, federal courts should not undermine the state's decision by refusing to toll the one-year period of limitation of § 2244(d)(1) where a second or subsequent petition is pending in the state court system. Nor should we discourage petitioners from exhausting all their claims in state court, even by means of a second or subsequent petition for postconviction relief where permissible under state law, before seeking habeas review in federal court."); *United States ex rel. Morgan v. Gilmore, supra,* 1998 WL 372060, at *5-*7; *Ellis v. Johnson, supra,* 11 F. Supp. 2d at 698 (given that "Texas sets no limits on the number of applications for writ of habeas corpus which may be filed ... [and] [s]tate law does not prohibit relief in subsequent habeas applications," properly filed second application for state habeas corpus relief tolled federal statute of limitations); *Hughes v. Irvin, supra,* 1997 WL 357947, at *3 (quoted *supra* note 64) ("continuous stream of [state] post-conviction applications pending in state courts" tolls running of statute of limitations); *Keeney v. McDaniel, supra,* CV-N-93-792-ECR ("properly filed" second state postconviction petition, filed for purpose of exhausting unexhausted claim, will toll statute of limitations). *Compare* 28 U.S.C.A. § 2244(d)(2) (West 1994 & Supp. 1998) (nonopt-in statute of limitations is tolled while "properly filed application for State post-conviction or other collateral review ... is pending") *with id.* § 2263(b)(2) (opt-in statute of limitations is tolled only during pendency of *"first* petition for [state] post-conviction review or other collateral relief" (emphasis added)). *See generally supra* notes 62, 65 (import of Congress' inclusion of limiting language in one provision but exclusion of it from otherwise parallel provision). *See generally infra* notes 92-108 and accompanying text (more thoroughly canvasing differences between nonopt-in and opt-in statutes of limitations).

[67] *See supra* notes 57-63 and accompanying text.

(D) the date on which the factual predicate of the claim or claims presented could have been discovered through the exercise of due diligence."[68]

The last three of these provisions, which effectively postpone the "principal" triggering date for the limitations period that is set out in the first of the provisions,[69] closely resemble a number of the factors the Supreme Court considers when assessing "cause" for a procedural default[70] — although the legislation defines those factors somewhat more narrowly than preexisting law had defined "cause."[71] Indeed, the last three provisions very closely resemble the three exceptions to AEDPA's own procedural default rule (which is limited to opt-in cases[72]). Given this overlapping terminology and Congress' evident desire to draw upon the procedural default doctrine to define the circumstances that avoid what otherwise would constitute a federal "procedural default" as a result of the untimely filing of a federal habeas corpus petition, the courts are likely to rely heavily on preexisting "procedural default" caselaw to define these new statutory criteria.

Because the statutory scheme conditions the commencement of the limitations period in part on the date on which the petitioner or movant first gained access to the legal or factual bases for a particular "*claim*"[73] — and it also ties its tolling

---

[68] 28 U.S.C.A. § 2244(d)(1) (West 1994 & Supp. 1998) (emphasis added); *accord id.* §§ 2255(1)-(4). *See, e.g.,* Mannino v. United States, 1998 WL 67674, at *2 (S.D.N.Y. Feb. 19, 1998) (section 2255 movants complied with statute of limitations by filing within one year of date they learned that prosecutor had failed to disclose potentially exculpatory information prior to trial; motion is timely because petitioners "did not become aware of [witness's potentially exculpatory] alleged comments until January 10, 1997, and ... they could not discover the evidence earlier because of the Government's alleged misconduct"). For discussion of the "due diligence" standard that appears throughout AEDPA, see *supra* § 3.3c n.64.

[69] For discussion of what we loosely have called the "principal" triggering date for the nonopt-in statute of limitations, *id.* §§ 2244(d)(1)(A), 2255(1), see *supra* notes 62-63 and accompanying text.

[70] *See infra* § 26.3b. For discussion of Congress' retention of the preexisting procedural default rule in nonopt-in cases, see *infra* § 26.1 n.10 and accompanying text.

[71] For discussion of the respects in which these provisions are the same as the corresponding bases for "cause" under the procedural default rule and the respects in which they are narrower than those corresponding bases, see *supra* § 3.3c nn.81-91 and accompanying text.

[72] *See* 28 U.S.C.A. § 2264(a) (West Supp. 1998) (discussed *supra* § 3.3c nn.80-91 and accompanying text).

[73] *See id.* § 2244(d)(1)(C) (West 1994 and Supp. 1998) ("date on which the factual predicate of *the claim or claims* presented could have been discovered ..." (emphasis added)); *see also id.* § 2244(d)(1)(B) ("date on which the "*constitutional right* asserted was initially recognized ..." (emphasis added)). *But cf. id.* § 2244(d)(1)(B) ("date on which the impediment to filing an *application* ... is removed" (emphasis added)). The section 2255 statute of limitations has similar language in all these respects. *See id.* § 2255.

provision for state postconviction proceedings to proceedings "with respect to the pertinent ... *claim*"[74] — a petition or motion with multiple claims may have different triggering dates for its various claims. If so, two questions arise: Does the deadline for the filing of a habeas corpus petition or section 2255 motion vary from claim to claim, or is there a single deadline that applies to the entire petition or motion? And, if the latter, what is that single deadline — the earliest or the latest of the various claims' limitations periods, or some other date? Although AEDPA does not clearly resolve this issue, its language strongly suggests that the applicant has until the end of the *latest* of the claims' limitation periods to file the application. Thus, AEDPA provides that "[a] 1-year period of limitation shall apply to an *application* for a writ of habeas corpus" and "shall run from the *latest* of" the various possible time periods set forth in the statute.[75] This language strongly suggests Congress' intention both that a single filing date apply to the entire "application," and that the deadline be determined by the "latest" of the limitation periods for the claims raised in the petition.[76] Because prisoners and their lawyers can — and should — be highly risk averse when endeavoring to avoid expiration of AEDPA's statute of limitations, and because of the many risk-creating judgment calls that have to be made in favor of the prisoner in order to invoke any of the provision's later triggering dates (*e.g.*, that an impediment to filing constituted "State action in violation of the [federal] Constitution or laws" or that a claim could not theretofore "have been discovered through the exercise of due diligence"[77]), the safest course always is to file within one year after the conclusion of direct review.[78]

---

[74] *Id.* § 2244(d)(2) (emphasis added).

[75] *Id.* §§ 2244(d)(1), 2255 (emphasis added).

[76] This interpretation is further supported by the rule that statutes should be construed in light of the underlying purposes of the legislation. NORMAN J. SINGER, 2A SUTHERLAND'S STATUTES AND STATUTORY CONSTRUCTION § 45.09 (5th ed. 1992). Given Congress' objective of streamlining the habeas corpus process, it seems highly unlikely that Congress would have opted for a claim-by-claim approach that could require piecemeal habeas corpus litigation on a scale never before imagined. *Cf.* Rose v. Lundy, 455 U.S. 509, 520 (1982) (recognizing difficulties created by "piecemeal [habeas corpus] litigation"); *infra* §§ 23.1, 23.5.

[77] 28 U.S.C.A. §§ 2244(d)(1)(B), 2244(d)(1)(D) (West 1994 & Supp. 1998).

[78] The later triggering dates may bear on decisions whether to permit the amendment of timely filed petitions. Assuming that the original petition was timely filed, and that the petitioner's attempt to amend the petition also is timely in the sense that the proposed new claim is presented within a year of one of AEDPA's alternative triggering dates, there can be no doubt that the amendment satisfies the Act's statute of limitations. *See generally infra* §§ 17.2, 37.2 (discussing, respectively, amendment and supplementation of issues on appeal). For the view that amendments generally "relate back" to the date on which a timely habeas corpus petition or section 2255 motion was filed, see *supra* § 3.4a n.16; *supra* notes 57, 64.

The forgoing considerations determine the date by which an "application for a writ of habeas corpus"[79] must be filed. Attention is due, as well, to the types of pleadings that qualify as the requisite "application." In its pre-AEDPA decision in *McFarland v. Scott*,[80] the Supreme Court held that a capital prisoner's filing of a prepetition application for appointment of counsel under the Anti-Drug Abuse Act of 1988[81] (which mandates the appointment of counsel for all indigent capital petitioners[82]) is sufficient to initiate a "habeas corpus proceeding" and give the court jurisdiction to grant a motion for a stay of execution.[83] In cases in which an application for appointment of counsel is filed within the limitations period but newly appointed counsel does not (*e.g.*, because she cannot) file the actual petition before the expiration of the limitations period, the courts will have to decide whether the filing of a prepetition application for counsel is sufficient to satisfy AEDPA's one-year statute of limitations.

Supporting a conclusion that an application for appointment of counsel filed within the one-year period satisfies the statute of limitations is the fact that AEDPA leaves intact — indeed, it takes explicit cognizance of — the statutory provisions interpreted in *McFarland*,[84] that resulted in the Court's conclusion that "the filing of a death row defendant's motion requesting the appointment of counsel for his federal habeas corpus proceeding" has the effect of "commenc[ing]" a federal habeas corpus proceeding.[85] Given that "Congress legislated against th[e] legal backdrop" of *McFarland*,[86] it is reasonable to infer that Congress intended to preserve the *McFarland* procedure. On this reading, the "application for a writ of habeas corpus"[87] that typically "commence[s]"[88] habeas corpus proceedings — to which AEDPA's "1-year period of limitation shall apply"[89] — would encompass the application for counsel that *McFarland* recognized as also sufficient to "commence[ ]" habeas corpus proceedings.[90] The

---

[79] 28 U.S.C.A. § 2244(d)(1) (West 1994 & Supp. 1998).

[80] 512 U.S. 849 (1994).

[81] 21 U.S.C. § 848q (1994).

[82] *See infra* § 12.3b nn.46-52 and accompanying text.

[83] *See infra* §§ 13.2a, 13.2b.

[84] *See* 28 U.S.C.A. § 2254(h) (West 1994 & Supp. 1998) (leaving intact mandatory right to counsel in capital habeas corpus cases (citing 21 U.S.C. § 848 (1994))).

[85] *McFarland, supra*, 512 U.S. at 856-57.

[86] *Id.*

[87] 28 U.S.C.A. § 2244(d)(1) (West 1994 & Supp. 1998).

[88] *McFarland, supra*, 512 U.S. at 857-58 (discussed *infra* § 13.1 nn.18-21 and accompanying text).

[89] 28 U.S.C.A. § 2244(d)(1) (West 1994 & Supp. 1998).

[90] *See also supra* § 3.4a n.14 (date of filing of application for appointment of counsel in capital habeas corpus or section 2255 case determines when habeas corpus or section 2255 proceeding was

matter is sufficiently in doubt, however — in an area in which litigants are well advised to avoid all doubts — that the most appropriate procedure to follow in advance of an authoritative interpretation of AEDPA is the procedure that *McFarland* rejected as unnecessarily cumbersome: Along with an application for appointment of counsel filed within the one-year limitations period, indigent capital prisoners should file (1) a habeas corpus petition presenting at least one cognizable claim (*e.g.*, a constitutional claim that was presented and rejected on direct appeal) with a clear designation that the pleading is a "Placeholder Petition" that very likely does not contain all of the available claims, and (2) a motion for leave to amend the petition upon the statutorily mandated appointment of counsel and counsel's completion of the legal and factual investigation that (as Congress recognized in mandating the appointment of

---

"pending" for purposes of determining whether AEDPA or pre-AEDPA law applies). *Cf.* Hohn v. United States, 118 S. Ct. 1969, 1972, 1974-75 (1998) (discussed *supra* § 3.4a n.14); Moseley v. French, 961 F. Supp. 889, 892-93 (M.D.N.C. 1997) (rejecting argument that *McFarland* motion for appointment of counsel commences federal habeas corpus action for purposes of limitations period but recognizing that filing of *McFarland* motion "may justify application of equitable tolling should the time to file run out during the pendency of the motion"); Mitcham v. Calderon, C-94-2854 (N.D. Cal. Dec. 20, 1996) (rejecting argument that application for appointment of counsel constituted "application for writ of habeas corpus" but deeming limitations period to be equitably tolled between date of enactment and date counsel was appointed and further tolled during time that counsel devoted to preparing court-ordered brief on effects of AEDPA); *supra* notes 52-54 and accompanying text (equitable tolling doctrine and caselaw). *But cf.* Calderon v. United States Dist. Ct., 1998 WL 309923, *withdrawn & rehearing en banc ordered*, 1998 WL 351217 (9th Cir. 1998) (*McFarland* application does not constitute "petition" for purposes of AEDPA's statute of limitations and does not trigger equitable tolling doctrine); Holman v. Gilmore, 126 F.3d 876, 879-80 (7th Cir. 1997), *cert. denied*, 118 S. Ct. 1169 (1998) (date petition was filed, not earlier date *McFarland* application was filed, determines when habeas corpus petition was "pending" for purposes of deciding whether AEDPA or pre-AEPDA law applies); Williams v. Cain, 125 F.3d 269, 273-74 (5th Cir. 1997) ("Although *McFarland* might be argued to raise a question in this regard," court concludes that *McFarland* application for appointment of counsel does not constitute filing of "petition" for purposes of determining whether AEDPA or pre-AEDPA law applies); Lott v. Coyle, 1998 WL 185318, at *2-8 (N.D. Ohio Mar. 11, 1998) (AEDPA governs case, despite pre-AEDPA filing of both notice of intent to file petition and *McFarland* application for appointment of counsel; neither pleading was sufficient to render case "a 'pending' habeas proceeding" at time of AEDPA's enactment); United States ex rel. Franklin v. Gilmore, 993 F. Supp. 1162, 1168 n.2 (N.D. Ill. 1998) (following *Holman v. Gilmore, supra*).

In *McFarland*, the Court recognized that prepetition applications for appointment of counsel and a stay of execution were subject to a laches defense, which would bar stays of execution for "dilatory capital defendant[s]." *McFarland, supra*, 512 U.S. at 858; *infra* §§ 12.3b nn.46-52 and accompanying text, 13.2a, 13.2b. AEDPA's new statute of limitations in effect replaces this loose equitable constraint in *McFarland* situations.

---

counsel in capital cases) the indigent capital prisoner could not theretofore have reasonably conducted himself.[91]

180-day statute of limitations for opt-in cases. The statute of limitations for opt-in cases (*i.e.*, for capital cases arising in States that have qualified for opt-in treatment[92]) differs in several important respects from the statute of limitations for nonopt-in cases (*i.e.*, for all noncapital cases, all capital cases from States that have not opted-in, and all section 2255 motions).[93] First, the limitations period is shortened from one year to 180 days.[94] Second, rather than following the nonopt-in statute's approach of commencing the limitations period upon the conclusion of *certiorari* review by the Supreme Court,[95] the opt-in statute of limitations begins running on the date of "final *State court* affirmance of the conviction and sentence on direct review or the expiration of the time for seeking such review."[96] Although the opt-in statute tolls the limitations period while the Supreme Court is considering a petition for *certiorari* from the final state court judgment on direct review,[97] that tolling does not begin until the *certiorari* petition actually is filed and thus does not include the time needed to *prepare*

---

[91] *See, e.g.*, Calderon v. Ashmus, 118 S. Ct. 1694, 1700 (1998) (Breyer, J., concurring) (**citing FHCPP**) (recognizing that petitioners in nonopt-in situations can satisfy statute of limitations by filing "'bare bones' habeas petition" and amending it thereafter; same may not be true "in at least some [opt-in] cases," given restrictions upon amendments that apply in that situation (*see supra* § 3.3c nn.61-64 and accompanying text)). For *McFarland's* discussion of the procedure, *see McFarland, supra*, 512 U.S. at 851-53.

[92] For discussion of the criteria a State must satisfy in order to qualify for the opt-in provisions, see *supra* § 3.3b nn.2-6 and accompanying text.

[93] For additional discussion of the differences between the nonopt-in and opt-in statutes of limitations, see *supra* notes 62, 65, 66.

[94] 28 U.S.C.A. § 2263 (West Supp. 1998). As noted *supra* § 3.3c n.41, the opt-in statute of limitations takes account of procedural differences in "unitary review" States by providing that, in cases in which "a transcript of the trial proceedings is unavailable" when the 180-day limitation period ordinarily would begin to run, "the start of the 180-day limitation period ... shall be deferred until a transcript is made available to the prisoner or counsel of the prisoner." 28 U.S.C.A. § 2265(c) (West Supp. 1998). For an explanation of the "unitary review" procedure and further discussion of the legislation's treatment of States with such procedures, see *supra* § 3.3b nn.9-12.

A prisoner's failure to comply with the 180-day statute of limitations causes any stay of execution granted pursuant to the opt-in provisions to expire. *See* 28 U.S.C.A. § 2262(b)(1) (West Supp. 1998).

[95] *See supra* notes 57-63 and accompanying text.

[96] 28 U.S.C.A. § 2263(a) (West Supp. 1998) (emphasis added). On the questions whether, as of this same date, opt-in States are obliged to provide state postconviction counsel, and whether federal courts are obliged to grant stays of execution pending state postconviction proceedings, see *supra* § 3.3b nn.22-37 and accompanying text.

[97] 28 U.S.C.A. § 2263(b)(1) (West Supp. 1998).

(even a timely) *certiorari* petition.[98] Third, although the opt-in statute follows the nonopt-in statute's approach of tolling the limitations period while a "petition for post-conviction review or other collateral relief" is pending,[99] the opt-in statute (unlike its nonopt-in counterpart[100]) limits this tolling provision to the "first" petition for state postconviction review[101] and clearly excludes Supreme Court *certiorari* review of the state courts' denial of postconviction relief.[102] Fourth, unlike the nonopt-in statute of limitations,[103] the opt-in version does not recognize situations in which later filing is permitted because of state-created impediments to earlier filing or because the legal or factual bases for a claim were not previously available. The only basis for extending the filing deadline beyond the conclusion of Supreme Court *certiorari* review and state court postconviction review is to file a "motion for an extension of time in the Federal district court that would have jurisdiction over the case upon the filing of a habeas corpus application under section 2254."[104] Upon a showing of "good cause ... for the failure to file the habeas corpus application within the [statutory] time period," the "time requirements ... shall be tolled ... during an additional period not to exceed 30 days."[105] Fifth, the opt-in statute of limitations is

---

[98] The difference in approach leads to particularly divergent results in cases in which no *certiorari* petition is filed. In such cases, the nonopt-in statute postpones the commencement of the limitations period until the time for seeking *certiorari* has expired. *See supra* notes 57-63 and accompanying text. By contrast, the opt-in statute neither postpones the commencement of the limitations period nor tolls the running of the statute of limitations in that situation.

[99] 28 U.S.C.A. § 2263(b)(2) (West Supp. 1998). Like the nonopt-in statute of limitations (*see supra* note 64), the opt-in statute's provision for tolling the period of state postconviction review excludes the time devoted to the preparation of the state postconviction petition. *See id.* ("The time requirements ... shall be tolled ... from the date on which the first petition for postconviction review or other collateral relief *is filed* until the final State court disposition of such petition" (emphasis added)).

[100] *See supra* notes 64-66 and accompanying text.

[101] 28 U.S.C.A. § 2263(b)(2) (West Supp. 1998); *see supra* note 62 and accompanying text. Oddly, the opt-in tolling provision, unlike the nonopt-in provision, *see* 28 U.S.C.A. § 2244(d)(2) (West 1994 & Supp. 1998) (discussed *supra* note 64), contains no "properly filed" limitation on state postconviction proceedings.

[102] As is explained in the earlier discussion of the nonopt-in statute of limitations, it is not entirely clear whether that statute's provision for tolling during the period when "State post-conviction or *other collateral review* ... is pending" includes the time during which the Supreme Court is considering a petition for *certiorari* from the state courts' denial of postconviction relief. *See supra* note 65 and accompanying text. The opt-in statute explicitly states that the tolling period for state postconviction petitions ends at the time of "final *State* court disposition of such petition." 28 U.S.C.A. § 2263(b)(2) (West Supp. 1998).

[103] *See supra* notes 67-72 and accompanying text.

[104] 28 U.S.C.A. § 2263(b)(3) (West Supp. 1998).

[105] *Id.*

satisfied by the timely filing of "*[a]ny* application under this chapter for habeas corpus relief under section 2254,"[106] which arguably is slightly broader than the "application for a writ of habeas corpus" phrasing in the nonopt-in statute.[107] As such, *McFarland's* treatment of applications for the appointment of counsel as sufficient to initiate habeas corpus relief may be more likely to apply in opt-in cases — subject, however, to the *caveat*, discussed above, in favor of the filing of timely "placeholder petitions" along with applications for counsel until the *McFarland* question is authoritatively resolved.[108]

This explanation of how the opt-in statute of limitations is supposed to work should not be understood to suggest that the statute of limitations *can* work, in any minimally fair manner. That statute of limitations requires what in some — perhaps many — cases is impossible in any meaningful and realistic sense: Within the space of less than six months, capital prisoners must (1) prepare a direct appeal petition for *certiorari* to the United States Supreme Court, a petition that is capital prisoners' statutory right,[109] that litigants typically have 90 days to file,[110] and that is capital prisoners' *only* opportunity to present certain federal claims to a federal court for review;[111] (2) prepare a state postconviction petition, a petition that AEDPA continues to require in many or most instances in order to exhaust state remedies[112] and that state law typically gives prisoners a number of *years* in which to file; and (3) prepare a federal habeas corpus petition, a petition that at least in theory continues to be the prisoners' statutory

---

[106] *Id.* § 2263(a) (emphasis added).

[107] *Id.* § 2244(d)(1).

[108] *See supra* notes 79-91 and accompanying text; *see also supra* § 3.4a n.14.

[109] *See* 28 U.S.C. § 1257 (1994).

[110] *See id.*

[111] Under the *Teague* doctrine, *see infra* Chapter 25, as recodified and strengthened by 28 U.S.C.A. § 2254(d)(1) (West 1994 & Supp. 1998), *see infra* § 30.2, habeas corpus petitioners are barred from relying on new rules of federal constitutional law that were not clearly established at the time of direct review. The direct appeal *certiorari* petition accordingly is the first *and last* time that prisoners may advance such rules in a federal court. *See* Spencer v. Georgia, 500 U.S. 960 (1991) (Kennedy, J., concurring in the denial of *certiorari*) (Supreme Court has important additional responsibilities when criminal defendant presents constitutional claim in direct appeal *certiorari* petition that cannot thereafter be reviewed by lower federal courts in federal habeas corpus proceedings).

[112] *See* 28 U.S.C.A. § 2254(b) (West 1994 & Supp. 1998). The best (although not the only) reading of AEDPA is that the exhaustion requirement applies to opt-in cases. *See supra* § 3.3c n.71 and accompanying text. In many States, certain claims (often, *e.g.*, ineffective assistance of counsel claims) cannot be raised on direct appeal and are only cognizable (and thus are only capable of being exhausted) in state postconviction proceedings. *See infra* § 7.1b nn.77-83 and accompanying text; *infra* § 7.2e nn.87-99 and accompanying text; *infra* § 9.1 nn.21, 26, 28, 33, 34; *infra* § 25.4 nn.40-45; *infra* § 26.3b n.36 and accompanying text; *infra* § 33.4 nn.3 & 7 and accompanying text; *infra* § 41.4a nn.6-7 and accompanying text.

and also her constitutional right[113] — and that, in 40 percent of all capital habeas corpus cases over the last two decades, has been found to be meritorious.[114] Because the process of preparing *certiorari* and state and federal postconviction petitions requires intensive legal investigation, and the process of preparing the latter two petitions requires intensive *factual* investigation,[115] the likelihood that all three petitions can be prepared in a responsible and minimally competent fashion within the available time period — either by typically overloaded institutional capital attorneys or by private lawyers to whom such cases sometimes are assigned over and above their preexisting caseloads — is low.[116] The burden placed on counsel's shoulders by the opt-in statute of limitations is aggravated by its application only in capital cases, in which counsel's responsibilities are already the most onerous,[117] and by AEDPA's withdrawal of two previously available escape hatches for special or extraordinary cases. First, an opt-in provision forbids an "amendment to an application for a writ of habeas corpus ... after the filing of an answer to the application, except on ... grounds" sufficient to permit the filing of a successive petition under AEDPA's new successive petition statute.[118] Second, that new successive petition statute limits successive petitions to a point just short of nonexistence.[119]

---

[113] *See infra* §§ 7.2d, 30.2a nn.10-11 and accompanying text.

[114] *See supra* § 2.3 n.23. For the reasons discussed *supra* § 3.3c n.74, prisoners are well advised to file the initial petition significantly before the entire 180-day period has expired.

[115] *See infra* §§ 6.2, 6.4, 7.1a, 9.1, 11.2.

[116] *See infra* §§ 7.1a, 7.2f, 12.2. This is true notwithstanding that the opt-in provisions require capital prisoners to be represented by "competent" counsel at the latter two of these stages — but not the first. *Compare supra* § 3.3b nn.2-6, 15-21 and accompanying text (right to state postconviction counsel in opt-in settings) *and infra* § 12.3b nn.46-52 and accompanying text (right to federal habeas corpus counsel in capital cases) *with infra* § 39.3b (no right to counsel at *certiorari* stage). (Note, however, that it frequently will be the case that the volunteer attorney, if any, filing a *certiorari* petition will be different from the state-appointed state postconviction attorney, who will be different from the federally appointed federal habeas corpus attorney. This is especially so because, unlike volunteer *certiorari* attorneys, appointed state postconviction attorneys must meet certain competency requirements and because appointed federal habeas corpus attorneys must meet competency requirements that often are more stringent than those governing the appointment of state postconviction lawyers. The 180-day period accordingly will often have to include the period(s) needed for new counsel to acquaint themselves with the case.) The discussion here is premised upon the human limitations of highly experienced and competent counsel. Woe unto the capital prisoner who has less than that at either the state postconviction or federal habeas corpus stage.

[117] *See McFarland, supra,* 512 U.S. at 855-56; *infra* § 12.3a nn.15-19 and accompanying text.

[118] 28 U.S.C.A. § 2266(b)(3)(B) (West Supp. 1998) (discussed *supra* § 3.3c nn.61-64 and accompanying text).

[119] *Id.* § 2244(b) (discussed *infra* §§ 28.3, 28.4a).

As the Supreme Court has recognized for centuries, an unconstitutional suspension of the writ of habeas corpus[120] can occur by indirection as well as direction. "[F]or if the means be not in existence, the privilege [of the writ] itself would be lost, although no law for its suspension should be enacted."[121] Because the opt-in statute of limitations virtually assures that there will be situations in which "the means be not in existence" to pursue habeas corpus relief in a responsible and effective manner within the 180-day period, the statute of limitations is likely to stimulate considerable amounts of Suspension Clause (and, possibly, Due Process Clause) litigation.[122] In the meantime, counsel will have to resist, as best they can, AEDPA's inducement to use techniques that responsible lawyers eschew — corner-cutting legal and factual investigations, simultaneous pursuit of multiple remedies, boilerplate pleadings, verbatim repetition of pleadings developed for a different stage of the case, pleading of

---

[120] *See* U.S. Const. art. I, § 9, cl. 2 (Suspension Clause).

[121] Ex parte Bollman, 8 U.S. (4 Cranch) 75, 95 (1807); *see, e.g.*, Smith v. Bennett, 365 U.S. 708, 712-13 (1961); *infra* § 7.2d; *see also* Felker v. Turpin, 518 U.S. 651, 664 (1996) (assuming for argument's sake "that the Suspension Clause ... refers to the writ as it exists today" and interpreting Clause in light of "evolutionary process" that writ has undergone in 20th century).

[122] *See, e.g.*, Miller v. Marr, 141 F.3d 976, 977-78 (10th Cir. 1998) (recognizing, in context of *non*opt-in statute of limitations, that "[w]hether the one-year limitation period violates the Suspension Clause depends upon whether the limitation period renders the habeas remedy 'inadequate or ineffective' to test the legality of detention" and that "[t]here may be circumstances where the limitation period at least raises serious constitutional questions and possibly renders the habeas remedy inadequate and ineffective," but concluding that one-year nonopt-in statute of limitations did not have that effect in instant case); Rosa v. Senkowski, 1997 WL 436484, at *7 (S.D.N.Y. Aug. 1, 1997), *modified*, 1997 WL 724559 (S.D.N.Y. Nov. 19, 1997), *aff'd on other grounds*, 1998 WL 334346 (2d Cir. June 24, 1998) ("The application of the [*non*opt-in] time limit to Rosa's first habeas petition effectively deprives him of the ability to obtain any collateral review in a federal court of the merits of his claim that his confinement violates his constitutional rights. Such a deprivation constitutes an unconstitutional 'suspension' of the writ of habeas corpus."). *See also* Breard v. Angelone, 926 F. Supp. 546, 547 (E.D. Va. 1996) ("The Court finds that § 2263 infringes on the privilege of habeas corpus in this case because prior to its passage, the petitioner would not have been time barred, yet upon its passage he was immediately time barred; the statute provides for no safe harbor or special exception. The law would require the petitioner, prior to the passage of § 2263, to have anticipated this effect. Section 2263 in the instant case is inadequate to test the legality of the petitioner's conviction and completely prevents any consideration of the equities of the case; therefore, § 2263 violates the suspension clause and is unconstitutional as applied. The Court thus interprets the Act's 180-day limitations period as commencing for purposes of this case on April 24, 1996, the effective date of the new § 2263."). *Cf.* Triestman v. United States, 124 F.3d 361, 378-79 & n.21 (2d Cir. 1997) (interpreting successive petition limitations to bar section 2255 movant from raising claim that could not practicably have been raised earlier would produce "serious Eighth Amendment and due process" problems; court notes existence of, but declines to reach, Suspension Clause issue). *See generally infra* § 7.2d nn.74-80 and accompanying text (Suspension Clause litigation generated by provisions of AEDPA other than 180-day statute of limitations applicable to opt-in cases).

facts that have not been sufficiently investigated on "information and belief," and the like.[123]

c. *Exceptions to general ordering and timing rules.* The next two sections discuss exceptional circumstances in which the petition may or should be filed *earlier* than is indicated by the general rules above, including before trial,[124] and the occasional need in capital cases to file the federal petition early in order to give a federal court the power to grant a future-jurisdiction-preserving stay of execution.[125] A subsequent section discusses the proper course of action when for some reason the petitioner has completed all of the pre-federal habeas corpus proceedings discussed above but nonetheless has not properly exhausted state remedies as to one or more claims that the petitioner seeks to raise in the federal petition.[126]

§ 5.2. Pretrial petitions.

The ordering and timing rules and practices discussed in section 5.1 above govern the use of habeas corpus as a *post*trial means of challenging the legality of a *conviction* or *sentence*. In addition, however, federal habeas corpus provides criminal defendants with an important mechanism for challenging the legality of their confinement *before* trial on the basis of a limited set of constitutional claims.[1] Claims cognizable in pretrial habeas corpus petitions include that: the defendant is being held in custody illegally,[2] for example because the state did not afford the defendant the prompt postarrest probable cause hearing required

---

[123] *See infra* § 11.3b nn.12-15 and accompanying text (recommended pleading techniques when counsel excusably lacks ability to conduct sufficient investigation).

[124] *See infra* § 5.2.

[125] *See infra* § 5.3.

[126] *See infra* § 11.1.

§ 5.2. [1] *See* 1 ANTHONY G. AMSTERDAM, TRIAL MANUAL FOR THE DEFENSE OF CRIMINAL CASES §§ 32, 62, 67, 68, 70, 71, 134, 146, 149 (5th ed. 1988). *Cf.* Barker v. Estelle, 913 F.2d 1433, 1440 (9th Cir. 1990), *cert. denied,* 500 U.S. 935 (1991) (petitioner's due process challenge to pretrial detention, which should have been raised at pretrial stage, was rendered moot by subsequent conviction and imposition of sentence). For further discussion of the mootness doctrine and its exceptions, see *infra* § 8.2b. *See also infra* Chapter 9 (discussing wider range of claims cognizable in *post*trial habeas corpus proceedings). On the question whether conviction moots particular habeas corpus challenges to pretrial detention, see *infra* § 8.2b n.13.

[2] *See, e.g.,* Matta-Ballesteros v. Henman, 896 F.2d 255, 258-59 (7th Cir.), *cert. denied,* 498 U.S. 878 (1990) (adjudicating pretrial petition brought by petitioner whom federal marshals arrested in Honduras after escape from federal prison in United States and who alleged that arrest and transportation to United States violated Honduran and American Constitutions and international law).

by *Gerstein v. Pugh*;[3] the defendant is being abused by law enforcement authorities who have him in custody;[4] the trial court is depriving the defendant of his constitutional right to a speedy trial;[5] the contemplated trial violates the defendant's constitutional immunity against being placed in jeopardy twice;[6] the

---

[3] 420 U.S. 103, 114, 124-25 (1975). *See* Riverside v. McLaughlin, 500 U.S. 44 (1991) (constitutional proscription of unreasonable arrests requires judicial determination of probable cause "within 48 hours of the warrantless arrest; absent extraordinary circumstances, a longer delay violates the Fourth Amendment").

[4] *Cf.* Fassler v. United States, 858 F.2d 1016, 1017-18 (5th Cir.), *cert. denied,* 490 U.S. 1099 (1989) (federal prisoner's claim alleging coercion through pretrial detention should be brought under 18 U.S.C. § 3145; although not exclusive remedy, section 3145 actions are preferable to federal-prisoner habeas corpus actions).

[5] *See e.g.,* Braden v. 30th Judicial Cir. Ct., 410 U.S. 484, 492-93 (1973); United States v. Castor, 937 F.2d 293, 296 (7th Cir. 1991); Ojeda-Rios v. Wigen, 863 F.2d 196, 199-202 (2d Cir. 1988); Kane v. Virginia, 419 F.2d 1369 (4th Cir. 1970); Palmer v. Judge and District Attorney General, 411 F. Supp. 1029 (W.D. Tenn. 1976). *Cf.* Norton v. Parke, 892 F.2d 476, 478 n.5 (6th Cir. 1989), *cert. denied,* 494 U.S. 1060 (1990) (pretrial petition for federal habeas corpus properly brought under 28 U.S.C. § 2241, not 28 U.S.C. § 2254; alleged violation of 180-day speedy-trial provision in Interstate Agreement on Detainers (IAD) may provide proper basis for pretrial petition, if IAD violation is of type that creates subject-matter jurisdiction for statutory violations (*see infra* § 9.1 n.48)).

[6] *See, e.g.,* Harpster v. Ohio, 128 F.3d 322, 325 (6th Cir. 1997), *cert. denied,* 118 S. Ct. 1044 (1998) ("federal adjudication of double jeopardy claims raised on pretrial petitions for habeas corpus is appropriate when those claims have been raised and rejected in the state trial court and under state law there is no right to interlocutory appeal"); Laswell v. Frey, 45 F.3d 1011, 1014 (6th Cir.), *cert. denied,* 516 U.S. 874 (1995) (petitioner, who claimed that Double Jeopardy Clause precluded her being tried in adult court for crime to which she previously pled guilty in juvenile court, did not have to go through trial in adult court in order to exhaust state remedies); Malinovsky v. Court of Common Pleas, 7 F.3d 1263, 1269 (6th Cir. 1993), *cert. denied,* 510 U.S. 1194 (1994) (double jeopardy clause bars retrial of petitioner because first trial ended in mistrial, declared over petitioner's objection and without "manifest necessity"); Satter v. Leapley, 977 F.2d 1259, 1261 (8th Cir. 1992); Mannes v. Gillespie, 967 F.2d 1310, 1312 (9th Cir. 1992), *cert. denied,* 506 U.S. 1048 (1993) ("Because full vindication of the [double jeopardy] right necessarily requires intervention before trial, federal courts will entertain pretrial habeas petitions that raise a colorable claim of double jeopardy."); Mars v. Mounts, 895 F.2d 1348, 1351 n.3 (11th Cir. 1990) (permitting pretrial habeas corpus petition based on alleged double jeopardy violation stemming from second prosecution after prior acquittal); Reimnitz v. State's Attorney, 761 F.2d 405, 410 (7th Cir. 1985) ("there is no longer any doubt that a state criminal defendant who has a colorable double jeopardy claim" may litigate issue in federal habeas corpus petition even if that means postponing state trial); Benson v. Superior Ct., 663 F.2d 355, 358-59 (1st Cir. 1981); Drayton v. Hayes, 589 F.2d 117, 120-21 (2d Cir. 1979); United States ex rel. Webb v. Court of Common Pleas, 516 F.2d 1034, 1036-39 (3d Cir. 1975); Fain v. Duff, 488 F.2d 218, 221-23 (5th Cir. 1973), *cert. denied,* 421 U.S. 999 (1975). *Cf.* Foster v. Gilliam, 515 U.S. 1301 (1995) (Rehnquist, Circuit Justice) (denying state's application for stay of *en banc* 4th Circuit's order enjoining second state trial of petitioner pending federal courts' resolution of double jeopardy claim); Jacob v. Clarke, 52 F.3d 178 (8th Cir.), *cert. denied,* 516 U.S. 924 (1995) ("pretrial double jeopardy claim is not moot" even if brought after petitioner has already been retried and convicted); Stratton v. United States,

trial court has denied or unconstitutionally revoked pretrial bail;[7] other "special circumstances" create a substantial likelihood that proceeding with the pending state trial would irreparably violate the defendant's constitutional rights;[8] and, in "unusual or extraordinary circumstances," that the state penal statute under which the petitioner is about to be prosecuted is unconstitutional.[9]

Apart from claims such as those listed above, which challenge the constitutionality of the pretrial custody itself or of the irreparably injurious conditions or effects thereof and which do not exclusively attack the legality of any conviction or sentence that subsequently may result, the federal courts generally are reluctant for comity and federalism reasons[10] to interfere with ongoing state criminal proceedings.[11] For the same reasons, the federal courts scrupulously enforce the requirement that state remedies for the claims raised in pretrial habeas corpus petitions be properly exhausted.[12]

§ 5.3. Pre-exhaustion proceedings in capital cases.

It sometimes is necessary in capital cases for the petitioner to file a federal habeas corpus petition after trial but before exhausting one or more of the state posttrial, appellate, or postconviction proceedings delineated in the general

---

862 F.2d 7, 8 (1st Cir. 1988) (double jeopardy claim litigated and lost on merits at pretrial stage does not preclude postconviction habeas corpus consideration; "[a] pre-trial double jeopardy claim may fail where a post-trial one will succeed").

[7] *See, e.g.,* Atkins v. Michigan, 644 F.2d 543, 550 (6th Cir.), *cert. denied,* 452 U.S. 964 (1981).

[8] Turner v. Tennessee, 858 F.2d 1201, 1205 (6th Cir. 1988), *vac'd & remanded on other grounds,* 492 U.S. 902 (1989) ("special circumstances" needed to justify intervention in pending state criminal proceedings present when state attempted to retry petitioner rather than permit him to accept initial plea offer rejected in first instance due to ineffective assistance of counsel). *See also* Levine v. Torvik, 986 F.2d 1506, 1518-20 (6th Cir.), *cert. denied,* 509 U.S. 907 (1993) (affirming district court's stay of further state court civil commitment proceedings that effectively would have prevented petitioning mental patient from obtaining federal habeas corpus review of constitutionality of present commitment); Davis v. Lansing, 851 F.2d 72, 74 (2d Cir. 1988) (allegation of violation of rule of Batson v. Kentucky, 476 U.S. 79 (1986), governing prosecutorial exercise of peremptory challenges, heard by federal habeas corpus court before state trial ended despite serious reservations by court as to its jurisdiction to do so).

[9] Kolski v. Watkins, 544 F.2d 762, 766 (5th Cir. 1977) (*dicta*); Tooten v. Shevin, 493 F.2d 173 (5th Cir. 1974), *cert. denied,* 421 U.S. 966 (1975) (*dicta*).

[10] *See generally* Younger v. Harris, 401 U.S. 37 (1971).

[11] *But cf. Levine v. Torvik, supra,* 986 F.2d at 1518-20 (discussed *supra* note 8); *Davis v. Lansing, supra,* 851 F.2d at 74 (discussed *supra* note 8).

[12] *See, e.g.,* Mannes v. Gillespie, 967 F.2d 1310, 1316 n.6 (9th Cir. 1992), *cert. denied,* 506 U.S. 1048 (1993); United States v. Castor, 937 F.2d 293, 296-97 (7th Cir. 1991) ("federal courts ... may require, as a matter of comity, that ... [pretrial] detainees exhaust all avenues of state relief before seeking the writ"); *infra* Chapter 23 (exhaustion requirement).

ordering rule in section 5.1a *supra*. In particular, if an execution date is set and rapidly approaching and if the state courts and all other state sources of a stay of execution have either refused or failed after a reasonable time to stay or postpone the execution pending completion of state proceedings, the prisoner must immediately file a federal habeas corpus petition or, possibly, an application for the appointment of federal habeas corpus counsel to assist in the preparation of a federal petition, to give the federal courts jurisdiction to grant a stay.[1] The petitioner then may ask the federal court to stay the execution and to defer adjudicating the federal petition (*i.e.*, to "hold it in abeyance") pending completion of the unexhausted state proceedings among the proceedings delineated in the general rule in section 5.1a *supra*.[2] This procedure does not circumvent any of the prefederal habeas corpus proceedings in the state courts delineated in the general rule but, instead, allows the capital prisoner, having secured a jurisdiction-preserving federal stay of execution, to complete those steps. This procedure also is available when the capital petitioner, after completing the steps listed in section 5.1a but before filing a federal petition, discovers a new and unexhausted claim but is unable to secure a state stay of execution while he exhausts the new claim.[3]

---

[1] *See infra* §§ 11.1 (procedures to follow upon discovering unexhausted claims when federal habeas corpus petition is being prepared or after it is filed), 12.3a (prepetition applications for appointment of counsel in capital cases), 13.2b (prepetition stays of execution upon filing application for appointment of counsel), 13.2c (postfiling stays of execution pending litigation of nonfrivolous claims). The discussion here deals with the procedure to follow when a state stay of execution is unavailable pending completion of the *state* proceedings discussed *supra* § 5.1a. Regarding stays pending *certiorari* to the United States Supreme Court and pending federal habeas corpus proceedings, see *infra* §§ 6.3, 13.1-13.6, 36.2, 38.2, 39.3c.

[2] For discussion of the stay/abeyance procedure, *see infra* § 13.3. *See also supra* § 5.1b n.57; *infra* §§ 11.1 n.14 and accompanying text, 23.5 n.28 and accompanying text.

[3] *See generally infra* § 11.1. By including the unexhausted claim in a federal petition that otherwise contains exhausted claims, the petitioner invites the district court, under the "total exhaustion" rule, to dismiss the entire petition. *See infra* §§ 11.1, 23.5.

Chapter 6
STATE POSTCONVICTION REMEDIES

§ 6.1. Introduction.[1]

A wide variety of statutory and common law postconviction remedies is available in the States, including the common law writs of habeas corpus and of error *coram nobis,* various writs of error, motions to recall the remittitur, motions for new trial and for review or reduction of sentence, and modern "postconviction hearing" statutes. These procedures, which are too diverse and protean for easy generalization and cannot be mastered without substantial

---

§ 6.1. [1] *See also supra* § 3.5a. *See generally* EQUAL JUSTICE INITIATIVE OF ALABAMA, ALABAMA CAPITAL POSTCONVICTION MANUAL (3d ed. 1998); ILLINOIS INSTITUTE FOR CONTINUING LEGAL EDUCATION, COLLATERAL ATTACK ON STATE CONVICTION: STATE POST-CONVICTION HEARING ACT; WAYNE R. LaFAVE & JEROLD H. ISRAEL, CRIMINAL PROCEDURE §§ 28.01 (2d ed. 1992); JAMES S. LIEBMAN, FEDERAL HABEAS CORPUS PRACTICE AND PROCEDURE App. F (1st ed. 1988) (outlining procedures under Tennessee's postconviction procedures act); NAT'L ASS'N OF CRIMINAL DEFENSE LAWYERS DEATH PENALTY TASK FORCE, POST-CONVICTION REMEDIES IN CAPITAL CASES: A MANUAL 11-12 (May 1984); ROBERT POPPER, POST-CONVICTION REMEDIES IN A NUTSHELL 44, 49-50 (1978); IRA P. ROBBINS, THE LAW AND PROCESSES OF POST-CONVICTION REMEDIES (1982); DONALD E. WILKES, STATE POSTCONVICTION REMEDIES AND RELIEF (1996); LARRY W. YACKLE, POSTCONVICTION REMEDIES §§ 1-13, 64-66 (1981 & Supp. 1998); Charles F. Baird, *The Habeas Corpus Revolution: A New Role for State Courts?,* 27 ST. MARY'S L. REV. 297 (1996); James D. Bell, *Habeas Corpus: The "Great Writ" in Mississippi State Courts,* 58 MISS. L.J. 25 (1988); John P. Decker, *"Last Chance" State Judicial Review in Criminal Cases — Illinois' Collateral Attack Remedies: A Call for a Principled Jurisprudence,* 38 DE PAUL L. REV. 201 (1989); James C. Harrington & Anne More Burnham, *Texas's New Habeas Corpus Procedure for Death-Row Inmates: Kafkaesque — and Probably Unconstitutional,* 27 ST. MARY'S L.J. 69 (1995); Thomas A. Hett, *Section 2-1401: Post-Judgment Relief in Criminal Cases,* 75 ILL. B.J. 386 (1987); John M. Morris, *Postconviction Practice Under the "New 27.26",* 43 J. MO. B. 435 (1987); Stephen J. Perello, Jr. & Albert N. Delzeit, *Habeas Corpus in San Diego Superior Court (1991-1993): An Empirical Study,* 19 THOMAS JEFFERSON L. REV. 283 (1997); Marion T. Pope, *A Study of the Unified Appeal Procedure in Georgia,* 23 GEORGIA L. REV. 185 (1988); Morgan Prickett, *The Writ of Error Coram Nobis in California,* 30 SANTA CLARA L. REV. 1 (1990); Ira P. Robbins, *The Revitalization of the Common-Law Civil Writ of Audita Querela as a Post-Conviction Remedy in Criminal Cases: The Immigration Context and Beyond,* 6 GEO. IMMIGR. L.J. 643 (1992); Edward A. Tomlinson, *Post-Conviction in Maryland: Past, Present and Future,* 45 MD. L. REV. 927 (1986); Larry W. Yackle, *The Misadventures of State Postconviction Remedies,* 16 N.Y.U. REV. L. & SOC. CHANGE 359 (1988); Comment, Hunter v. State: *Availability of Post-Conviction Hearing Act Remedies,* 68 OR. L. REV. 269 (1989); Note, *Coram Nobis as a Post-Conviction Remedy: Flight of the Phoenix?,* 32 S.D. L. REV. 300 (1987); Note, *Protecting Guiltless Guilty: Material Witness Recantation and Modern Post-Conviction Remedies,* 21 NEW ENG. L. REV. 429 (1985-86); Brad Snyder, Note, *Disparate Impact on Death Row: M.L.B. and the Indigent's Right to Counsel at Capital State Postconviction Proceedings,* 107 YALE L.J. 2211 (1998); Note, *Substantive Justice and State Interests in the Aftermath of Herrera v. Collins: Finding an Adequate Process for the Resolution of Bare Innocence Claims Through State Postconviction Remedies,* 75 TEX. L. REV. 131 (1996); sources cited *infra* note 2.

familiarity with the governing statutes, rules, precedents, and practices in each State, are comprehensively surveyed elsewhere.[2]

This chapter focuses on a few aspects of state postconviction practice that are particularly relevant to federal habeas corpus and other modes of federal court review of state convictions. As is discussed below, the litigative choices a prisoner or counsel makes during state postconviction proceedings often determine whether federal habeas corpus review or relief is thereafter available. The decisive impact of state postconviction remedies is enhanced by the Antiterrorism and Effective Death Penalty Act of 1996 (AEDPA).[3] In addition to expanding the occasions on which defaults of one sort or another in state postconviction litigation may bar federal habeas corpus review and relief, AEDPA adopts two statutes of limitations — a one-year limitations period running from the denial of direct appeal *certiorari* proceedings, which applies in "nonopt-in cases"; and a 180-day limitations period running from the denial of direct appeal by the highest state court, which applies in capital cases in "opt-in" States — that sometimes make the pace with which a prisoner or lawyer employs state postconviction remedies decisive of whether federal review and relief are available.[4] Although both statutes of limitations are tolled for certain state postconviction proceedings (the nonopt-in statute of limitations is tolled for all "properly filed" state postconviction proceedings;[5] the opt-in version is tolled for "first" state postconviction proceedings[6]), neither is tolled while the state postconviction petition or the federal habeas corpus petition is being prepared

---

[2] Appendix A in WILKES, *supra* note 1, at 219-895, and section 13 in YACKLE, *supra* note 1, survey postconviction remedies in the 50 States and the District of Columbia. Outdated citations may be found in Case v. Nebraska, 381 U.S. 336, 338 nn. 1-3 (1965) (Clark, J., concurring); *id.* at 345 n.8 (Brennan, J., concurring); Curtis S. Reitz, *Federal Habeas Corpus: Post-Conviction Remedies for State Prisoners*, 108 U. PA. L. REV. 461, 469-70 (1960); Note, *Effect of the Federal Constitution in Requiring State Post-Conviction Remedies*, 53 COLUM. L. REV. 1143 (1953); Note, *State Post-Conviction Remedies*, 61 COLUM. L. REV. 681 (1961); Note, *State Post-Conviction Remedies and Federal Habeas Corpus*, 40 N.Y.U. L. REV. 154 (1965); Note, *State Post-Conviction Remedies and Federal Habeas Corpus*, 12 WM. & MARY L. REV. 149 (1970); Note, *The Uniform Post-Conviction Procedure Act*, 69 HARV. L. REV. 1289 (1956). *See also* AMERICAN BAR ASSOCIATION, STANDARDS RELATING TO POST-CONVICTION REMEDIES (1978) (collecting and analyzing modern approaches to state postconviction procedures); NATIONAL COMMISSIONERS ON UNIFORM STATE LAWS, UNIFORM POST-CONVICTION PROCEDURES ACT (1966) (model statute).

[3] Pub. L. 104-132, 110 Stat. 1214 (1996). For an overview of AEDPA, see *supra* § 3.2

[4] For citation of the AEDPA provisions that stiffen the penalties for defaults in the state courts, with cross-references to more detailed discussions elsewhere in the book, see *infra* § 6.2 n.12. For discussion of AEDPA's statutes of limitations, see *supra* § 5.1b. For an explanation of the range of cases subject to AEDPA and a definition of the statute's "nonopt-in" and "opt-in" categories, see *supra* §§ 3.2, 3.3, 3.4.

[5] *See supra* § 5.1b nn.64-66 and accompanying text.

[6] *See supra* § 5.1b nn.99-101 and accompanying text.

(unless some other tolling provision happens to apply), and neither is clearly tolled (and the opt-in version clearly is *not* tolled) during *certiorari* proceedings following state postconviction review.[7] Counsel and prisoners involved in preparing and litigating state postconviction petitions accordingly must (1) ascertain which of the two statutes of limitations applies, (2) take care not to exhaust the applicable limitations period while preparing the state postconviction petition, (3) file state postconviction pleadings in a timely and procedurally appropriate manner, (4) pursue *certiorari* proceedings following state postconviction review simultaneously with federal habeas corpus proceedings or forgo *certiorari* review altogether, and, most importantly, (5) make sure that enough of the limitations period remains after the state postconviction petition is filed that current or future counsel will have the time needed to investigate, prepare, and file a timely federal habeas corpus petition once state proceedings are completed — and, ideally, will have enough of a timing cushion even after the federal petition is filed (at least in nonopt-in cases) to permit the filing and litigation of a successive state postconviction petition in the event that one or more claims in the federal petition are found to be unexhausted.[8]

§ 6.2. Claim selection.

State law and practice determine the range of claims attacking the conviction and sentence that a prisoner may raise in state postconviction proceedings.[1] Federal law also plays a role in state postconviction issue selection in that the federal exhaustion[2] and procedural default[3] doctrines compel prisoners, when permitted by state law and practice, to include in their state postconviction

---

[7] *See supra* § 5.1b nn.64, 65, 99, 101-02 and accompanying text.

[8] For discussion of strategies for balancing the demands of competent prefiling investigation and time management, especially in cases governed by AEDPA, see *supra* § 5.1b nn.79-91, 123 and accompanying text, and *infra* § 11.3b nn.16-25 and accompanying text. For discussion of the statute of limitations implications of dismissal of a federal petition for nonexhaustion, see *supra* §§ 3.4a n.16 and accompanying text, 5.1b n.57 and accompanying text. For discussion of effects of AEDPA's statutes of limitations on *certiorari* proceedings to review the denial of state postconviction relief, see *supra* §§ 5.1a nn.17-22 and accompanying text, 5.1b nn.65, 102 and accompanying text; *infra* §§ 6.4a-6.4c.

§ 6.2. [1] *See* sources cited *supra* § 6.1 nn.1, 2.

[2] *See infra* Chapter 23. *See also infra* § 11.1 (impact of exhaustion doctrine on claim selection at federal habeas corpus stage).

[3] *See supra* § 3.3c nn.65-91 and accompanying text (special procedural default rule in cases governed by "opt-in" provisions of Antiterrorism and Effective Death Penalty Act, Pub. L. 104-132, 110 Stat. 1214 (1996) (discussed generally, *supra* § 3.2, and, in regard to its opt-in provisions, *supra* § 3.3)); *infra* Chapter 26 (procedural default doctrine, generally). On the necessity of raising unexhausted claims in time-limited state postconviction proceedings before seeking federal habeas corpus relief in order to avoid a procedural bar to the claims in federal court, see *infra* § 26.1 n.25.

applications all claims that might warrant federal habeas corpus relief and that were not exhaustively litigated at trial and on direct appeal in the same case.[4]

Even if it is likely that the state postconviction courts will deny relief on a claim because the prisoner either failed to, or already did, raise it at some earlier stage in the case or because the state courts consistently have rejected similar claims in the past, federal preclusion doctrines require the prisoner to give serious consideration to raising the claim in order (1) to avoid procedural default problems later on,[5] (2) to give the state courts the opportunity to lay aside state procedural obstacles to relief and reach the merits, thereby requiring the federal courts to do the same in subsequent habeas corpus proceedings,[6] and (3) to enable the state courts to reconsider their previous rejection of the claim. Federal preclusion doctrines even encourage the prisoner to consider (although they do not necessarily require) raising in state postconviction proceedings federal claims that already were litigated at trial and on direct appeal. In some cases, partial relitigation is necessary to assure that the claim and all its factual and

---

[4] See McFarland v. Scott, 512 U.S. 1256, 1261 (1994) (Blackmun, J., dissenting from denial of certiorari) ("State habeas corpus proceedings are a vital link in the capital review process, not the least because all federal habeas claims first must be adequately raised in state court ... [to avoid being denied in federal court as] procedurally defaulted or waived ...."); McFarland v. Scott, 512 U.S. 849, 860 (1994) (O'Connor, J., concurring in the judgment in part) (Supreme Court's "carefully crafted doctrines of waiver and abuse of the writ make it especially important that the first [federal habeas corpus] petition [and, thus, state exhaustion proceedings prior to first federal petition] set forth all of a state prisoner's colorable grounds for relief"); infra §§ 9.1, 11.2, 11.3 (types of claims that may be raised in federal habeas corpus proceedings; methods of identifying claims; claim selection when preparing federal habeas petition). See also McFarland v. Scott, supra, 512 U.S. at 855 (majority opinion) ("The services of investigators and other experts may be critical in the preapplication phase of a [postconviction] proceeding, when possible claims and their factual bases are researched and identified."); infra Chapter 19 (experts, investigators, discovery, and other fact-development procedures available in federal habeas corpus proceedings); infra §§ 7.1b & 7.2 (possible constitutional rights to adequate state postconviction proceedings and counsel). Cf. Saldana v. New York, 850 F.2d 117, 119 (2d Cir. 1988), cert. denied, 488 U.S. 1029 (1989) (even if federal court reaches merits of unexhausted claim, petitioner not precluded thereafter from seeking state relief on same claim).

[5] See, e.g., Keeney v. Tamayo-Reyes, 504 U.S. 1, 9-10 (1992) (absence of diligent efforts by petitioner to present evidence supporting claims in state court may bar petitioner from presenting evidence in federal habeas corpus proceedings); Smith v. Murray, 477 U.S. 527, 535 (1986) ("'perceived futility alone cannot constitute'" excuse for "procedural default" caused by counsel's decision not to raise claim on direct appeal because state courts consistently had rejected claim in past; capital prisoner denied relief and subsequently executed notwithstanding apparent 5th Amendment violation (quoting Engle v. Isaac, 456 U.S. 107, 130 & n.36 (1982))). See generally portions of this book cited supra note 3.

[6] See infra §§ 26.2c, 26.2e.

federal legal nuances and variations are fully exhausted,[7] to clarify the position of the state or the state courts on the matter, or simply to enable the state courts to rethink their position.[8] In addition to federal claims, the prisoner should consider pleading in state postconviction proceedings any cognizable state law issues in the case.[9]

As other sections of the book explain, the Antiterrorism and Effective Death Penalty Act of 1996[10] creates a number of new procedural defenses to federal habeas corpus consideration and relief and expands other defenses that already existed.[11] A number of these defenses are triggered by the type, scope, and quality of factual and legal adjudication that does and does not take place during state postconviction proceedings and by the party (*e.g.*, the prisoner or state actors) responsible for incomplete or faulty state postconviction adjudication.[12]

---

[7] *See Keeney v. Tamayo-Reyes, supra*, 504 U.S. at 9-10 (failure to present important aspects of evidence supporting claim in state courts may bar reliance on that evidence in federal habeas corpus proceedings); *infra* §§ 23.3a, 23.3c.

[8] Before pleading federal law claims in state postconviction proceedings, the prisoner or counsel should consult the rules governing pleading in federal habeas corpus petitions, *see infra* § 11.6, and the federal statutory and judge-made rules defining the detail with which claims need to be pleaded in the state courts in order to satisfy federal exhaustion of remedies requirements, *see infra* §§ 23.3a, 23.3c. In general, federal habeas corpus pleading and exhaustion rules require detailed pleading of the facts supporting the petitioner's claims and a comprehensive listing of the petitioner's legal theories. For the reasons discussed *infra* § 11.6 n.8, by far the safest course when pleading federal claims at the state postconviction stage is to adhere not only to state pleading rules but also to federal habeas corpus pleading and exhaustion rules, to the extent the federal rules are more demanding than the state rules.

[9] Some States limit postconviction proceedings to claims arising under the state and federal constitutions. *See generally* sources cited *supra* § 6.1nn.1, 2.

[10] Pub. L. 104-132, 110 Stat. 1214 (1996).

[11] *See supra* § 3.2 (summarizing AEDPA provisions, with cross-references to more detailed discussions elsewhere).

[12] *See, e.g.*, 28 U.S.C.A. § 2244(d)(1)(B) (West 1994 & Supp. 1998) (postponing running of "nonopt-in" statute of limitations if state court proceedings created unconstitutional or otherwise unlawful impediment to timely filing of federal petition (discussed *supra* § 5.1b nn.67-72 and accompanying text)); *id.* § 2244(d)(2) (tolling "nonopt-in" statute of limitations during litigation of "properly filed" state postconviction petition (discussed *supra* § 5.1b nn.64-66 and accompanying text)); *id.* §§ 2254(b)(2), 2254(b)(3) (making it easier for federal courts to deny relief on unexhausted claims, rather than to dismiss without prejudice pending exhaustion, and making it more difficult for federal courts to find that state waived exhaustion requirement (discussed *infra* §§ 23.1, 23.2a)); *id* § 2254(d)(1) (making scope of federal habeas corpus adjudication of legal issues turn on scope and quality of state court adjudication of same issues (discussed *infra* § 30.2)); *id.* §§ 2254(d)(2), 2254(e)(1) (modestly strengthening presumption of correctness of state court factfindings (discussed *infra* § 20.2c)); *id.* § 2254(e)(2) (making it more difficult for petitioner to secure federal evidentiary hearing on facts petitioner failed to develop in state court proceedings (discussed *infra* § 20.2b)); *id.* § 2263(b)(2) (West Supp. 1998) (tolling "opt-in" statute of limitations during litigation of "first" state postconviction petition (discussed *supra* § 5.1b

The upshot of the changes is that prisoners have even more reason than before to discover and include in their initial state postconviction petitions "every colorable ground[] for relief"[13] but have considerably less time than before in which to discover and plead those claims. The heightened need for comprehensive discovery and pleading of claims at the earliest possible time arises, *e.g.*, because AEDPA in some instances forbids federal habeas corpus petitions to be amended[14] and truncates the time available for post-filing federal habeas corpus litigation that otherwise would serve to flesh out the prisoners' claims,[15] and because AEDPA in most or all instances makes it difficult to secure a federal evidentiary hearing on facts that the petitioner failed to develop in state proceedings[16] and severely limits the range of successive habeas corpus petitions that can succeed.[17] Less time is available to discover and plead claims, *e.g.*, because of a one-year statute of limitations that AEDPA applies to federal habeas corpus petitions in noncapital cases and capital cases in "nonopt-in" States[18] and, particularly, because of a 180-day statute of limitations that the statute applies to federal habeas corpus petitions in capital cases in "opt-in" States[19] — neither of which statute tolls the limitations period during time spent investigating and preparing state postconviction and federal habeas corpus petitions, the time spent litigating "[im]properly filed" state postconviction petitions, and (at least in opt-in cases) the time spent preparing and litigating *certiorari* proceedings following state postconviction review, and the latter of which is not tolled by time spent preparing the direct appeal *certiorari* petition or time spent litigating second and successive state postconviction petitions. As a result of these changes, state postconviction counsel (especially in capital cases in opt-in States[20]) must be even more creative than before in carrying out

---

nn.100-01 and accompanying text)); *id.* § 2264(a) (more stringent procedural default rule for "opt-in" cases if claim was not "raised and decided on the merits in the State court" (discussed *supra* § 3.3c nn.65-79 and accompanying text)).

[13] McFarland v. Scott, 512 U.S. 849, 860 (1994) (O'Connor, J., concurring in the judgment in part).

[14] *See* 28 U.S.C.A. § 2266(b)(3)(B) (West Supp. 1998) (discussed *supra* § 3.3c nn.61-64 and accompanying text).

[15] *See id.* § 2266 (discussed *supra* § 3.3c nn.45-54 and accompanying text).

[16] *See id.* § 2254(e)(2) (discussed *infra* § 20.2b).

[17] *See id.* § 2244(b) (discussed *infra* §§ 28.3, 28.4a).

[18] *See id.* § 2244(d) (discussed *supra* § 5.1b nn.57-91 and accompanying text). For discussion of the difference between "nonopt-in" and "opt-in" cases, see *supra* § 3.2.

[19] *See* 28 U.S.C.A. § 2263 (West Supp. 1998) (discussed *supra* § 5.1b nn.92-123 and accompanying text).

[20] *See supra* § 5.1b nn.109-23 and accompanying text.

effective but time-limited legal and factual investigations and in pleading colorable claims as to which less is known than is desirable.[21]

§ 6.3. Stays of execution.[1]

The steps available to prevent capital prisoners from being executed while they attempt to exhaust federally mandated and other state postconviction proceedings vary widely from State to State, depending upon: the applicability of the "opt-in" provisions of the Antiterrorism and Effective Death Penalty Act of 1996 (AEDPA), which provide for what amounts to a federal court "automatic stay" during state postconviction proceedings;[2] the presence or absence of state statutory time limits for filing state postconviction petitions in capital and other postconviction proceedings (compliance with which assumedly staves off the setting of execution dates or at least assures the availability of stays); the branch of government responsible for setting execution dates; the statutory requirements and practices determining the interval between the setting of the date and the date set; the willingness of state officials to forgo seeking or setting execution dates until after completion of all proceedings leading up to and including an initial federal habeas corpus proceeding; the willingness of responsible state officials to stay any execution dates that *are* set during the pendency of state and in anticipation of federal judicial proceedings; and the effect on state stay practices of the Supreme Court's decision in *McFarland v. Scott*,[3] which ruled that an indigent capital prisoner denied appointment of counsel and a stay of execution in state postconviction proceedings was entitled to a federal court's appointment of counsel and imposition of a stay pending a factual and legal investigation and preparation of a federal habeas corpus petition.[4] A few generalizations about the availability of stays of execution pending state postconviction procedures are possible.

In a growing number of States, the courts or executive officials responsible for requesting or setting execution dates follow the practice of not seeking or setting execution dates as long as prisoners are preparing to challenge or are actively

---

[21] *See infra* § 11.3b nn.8-15 and accompanying text.

§ 6.3. [1] *See generally* RICHARD L. AYNES & MARGERY M. KOOSED (eds.), OHIO DEATH PENALTY MANUAL IX-33 to IX-35 (Ohio Death Penalty Task Force, Ohio Criminal Defense Lawyers Ass'n 1981); NATIONAL ASS'N OF CRIMINAL DEFENSE LAWYERS DEATH PENALTY TASK FORCE, POST-CONVICTION REMEDIES IN CAPITAL CASES: A MANUAL 14 (May 1984).

[2] 28 U.S.C.A. § 2262(a) (West Supp. 1998) (discussed *supra* § 3.3c nn.55-58 and accompanying text). For discussion of the cases to which AEDPA's "opt-in" provisions apply, see *supra* §§ 3.3a, 3.3b, 3.4c.

[3] 512 U.S. 849 (1994).

[4] *Id.* at 856-58 (discussed *infra* notes 5-10 and accompanying text; *infra* §§ 12.3a, 12.3b, 13.2a, 13.2b).

challenging their convictions or sentences in a proper forum. *McFarland* supplies a significant incentive for States to adopt such an approach. If a state stay is denied pending state postconviction proceedings, *McFarland* assures indigent capital prisoners (assuming a timely application is made) a federal stay of execution prior to the filing of a federal habeas corpus petition to enable counsel to be appointed and to conduct the kind of comprehensive legal and factual investigation that otherwise might have occurred in state postconviction proceedings had those proceedings been available.[5] Because that investigation is likely in many cases to uncover new and unexhausted claims, additional state proceedings will then be required prior to pressing ahead with the federal habeas corpus proceeding.[6] At that point, if state stays remain unavailable, the federal court is likely to take one of two steps. It might issue an order holding the federal petition in abeyance and maintaining the stay of execution pending exhaustion of state remedies[7] — a route that is available to the federal court even if the state tries to waive exhaustion, as long as the federal court concludes that it should not

---

[5] *See McFarland, supra,* 512 U.S. at 857-58; *infra* §§ 12.3a, 12.3b, 13.1, 13.2b (all discussing impact of *McFarland* on availability of appointment of counsel and stays of execution to enable prospective federal habeas corpus petitioner to investigate and prepare federal petition; also discussing requirement of timely application for federal stay and appointment of counsel). *See also infra* § 13.2a nn.26-33 and accompanying text (further discussion of incentive *McFarland* gives States to forgo setting execution dates). Federal stays often were available even before the announcement of *McFarland. See* Kyles v. Whitley, 498 U.S. 931, 932 (1991) (Stevens, J., concurring in denial of stay) ("On review of the disposition of ... application[s] [for stay of execution] by the District Court and the Court of Appeals, I regularly vote to stay any scheduled execution in order to be sure that a death row inmate may have the same opportunity to have his or her federal claims considered by this Court as does any other applicant."). *Cf.* Clark v. Collins, 502 U.S. 1052 (1992) (Stevens, J., dissenting from denial of application for stay of execution and denial of *certiorari*) ("This case ... presents an extreme example of why" "we should routinely grant the stay application in all first federal habeas corpus cases 'in order to be sure that a death row inmate may have the same opportunity to have his or her federal claims considered by this Court as does any other applicant.'... The compressed schedule has denied state and federal courts the opportunity to review filings with adequate time for reflection, much less to review the record.... Indeed, it is doubtful that counsel has had a fair opportunity to discharge his professional obligations.").

[6] *See McFarland, supra,* 512 U.S. at 870 (Thomas, J., dissenting) (suggesting possibility that prefiling investigation endorsed by majority may turn up new and unexhausted claims); *infra* §§ 11.1, 23.5, and accompanying text (discussing (1) rule that federal court may not finally adjudicate habeas corpus petition containing some or all unexhausted claims; (2) need for habeas corpus petitioners with at least some unexhausted claims to exhaust *all* claims in state courts — usually by postponing federal habeas corpus proceedings while state postconviction proceedings on unexhausted claims take place — before finally litigating *any* claims in federal habeas corpus proceedings; and/or (3) inadvisability of withdrawing potentially meritorious claims from first federal habeas corpus petition in what is almost assuredly a vain hope of pursuing claims in second or successive habeas corpus petition).

[7] For discussion of the stay/abeyance procedure, *see infra* § 13.3. *See also supra* § 5.1b n.57; *infra* §§ 11.1 n.14 and accompanying text, 23.5 n.28 and accompanying text.

accept the waiver.[8] Or the federal court might rule that, absent the availability of a state stay of execution, no state remedy is meaningfully available, hence that exhaustion has occurred.[9] This latter step would deprive the state of the benefit of the presumption of correctness of any state court factfindings that might have been made in state exhaustion proceedings and possibly other advantages.[10] Given that federal courts are likely to grant stays pending postconviction proceedings even if state courts deny them, and that the denial of state stays may disadvantage the state in federal habeas corpus litigation via the loss of access to presumptively correct state court factfindings, States have little to gain and much to lose from setting execution dates and refusing to stay them.

Counsel practicing in States that forgo setting an execution date during an initial, timely round of state and federal postconviction proceedings should contact the responsible state official[11] as soon as the United States Supreme Court denies *certiorari* following direct appeal. Ideally, the lawyers for both sides can then work out a reasonable schedule for succeeding state and federal litigative steps in the case.

Even in States in which the practice generally is not to hold off setting execution dates when the case is in or about to enter postconviction proceedings, counsel may find it possible and desirable for a number of reasons to reach agreement with the responsible state officials on an informal stay.[12] First, such stays are a matter of convenience for the state postconviction court. Absent issuance of a stay by some other authority, the postconviction court either must devote extensive resources to adjudicating a stay application or to expediting the postconviction review procedures that state law requires it to provide. State-federal comity concerns also are involved. An execution date that prevents a federal petitioner from fulfilling the exhaustion of remedies prerequisite to

---

[8] *See infra* § 23.2a.

[9] *See infra* §§ 23.3b, 23.5. The possible implications of *McFarland* for the allocation of litigation between state and federal courts following a state court's denial and a federal court's granting of a prepetition stay of execution prior to completion of state postconviction proceedings are discussed further *infra* § 13.3a n.6.

[10] *See infra* §§ 20.2, 20.3, 30.2, 30.3. *See also supra* § 3.3c n.71 and accompanying text (discussing difficulties States encounter when deprived of ability to insist upon exhaustion of state remedies).

[11] In States in which the Governor sets execution dates, counsel either should contact the responsible official in the Governor's office or should attempt beforehand to reach agreement with the lawyer likely to represent the State in the contemplated proceedings. In States in which execution dates are set judicially, counsel should negotiate with the state official (often a district attorney or assistant attorney general) responsible for requesting that the state court set an execution date. In the latter situation, counsel alternatively or simultaneously may ask the date-setting court to discuss the matter with counsel for both sides in chambers.

[12] *See supra* note 11.

federal habeas corpus relief may interfere with the jurisdiction of the federal courts or, at the least, necessitate a federal-jurisdiction-preserving stay pending completion of state proceedings.[13] Finally, informal stays are efficient. Particularly in cases involving the prisoner's first attempt to secure state and federal postconviction relief — and *most* particularly in so-called "opt-in cases" governed by AEDPA — a federal stay in all likelihood will be granted,[14] so that an informal stay saves the state as well as the courts and the petitioner the time and energy otherwise required to set, then formally to stay, an execution.

If the sentencing or some other judge is the date-setting official and already has set a date, the first potentially available means of securing a formal stay is by applying to that court based on: (1) if applicable, the petitioner's compliance with the statutory time limits for filing state postconviction actions challenging capital or other criminal judgments; (2) the comity and efficiency rationales discussed above; (3) whatever state stay of execution standards apply; (4) the stay requirement implicit in the provision under state law of judicial remedies that cannot be effectuated in the time remaining before the date set for the execution and also implicit in the requirement under federal law that available state remedies be exhausted before initiating federal habeas corpus remedies during the pendency of which a stay is statutorily available and likely to be granted;[15] and ultimately (5) the federal standards for stays pending exhaustion, including AEDPA's "automatic stay" provision for opt-in cases and the similar but more broadly applicable implications of the *McFarland* decision, which effectively control notwithstanding contrary state law.[16]

If the date-setting court denies a stay, does not have the authority to grant one, or in the past consistently has refused to grant stays, or if the Governor sets the execution date, the prisoner's next alternative is to request a stay from the state court with jurisdiction over state postconviction proceedings — if that court is different from the date-setting court. Thereafter, state appellate avenues for securing a stay must be pursued on an expedited schedule. Finally, if all state courts with jurisdiction have refused to grant a stay — or if they have failed to rule one way or the other on a timely stay application as of no later than a week or so before the date set for the execution — and if no other informal or formal

---

[13] *See supra* notes 7-10 and accompanying text; *infra* § 13.3.

[14] *See supra* note 4 and accompanying text; *infra* §§ 13.2a-13.2c, 13.3. If counsel is practicing in an "opt-in" State, the Antiterrorism and Effective Death Penalty Act of 1996 *requires* the federal court to grant a stay during proceedings on a first state postconviction petition. *See supra* note 2 and accompanying text. The *McFarland* decision has a similar effect even in nonopt-in cases. *See supra* notes 3-10 and accompanying text.

[15] *See, e.g.*, Modesto v. Nelson, 296 F. Supp. 1375, 1376-77 (N.D. Cal. 1969) ("miscarriage of justice" if execution occurs before remedies provided by law are exhausted); other authority cited *infra* § 13.3b.

[16] *See supra* notes 2-10, 14 and accompanying text; *infra* §§ 13.2, 13.3.

avenue is available in the State for staying the execution, a prisoner with potentially meritorious but unexhausted federal claims must file in federal court either (1) an application for appointment of counsel and for a stay of execution pending the filing of a habeas corpus petition[17] or (2) a habeas corpus petition itself,[18] as a basis for a jurisdiction-preserving federal stay. Such a stay is not meant to supersede or circumvent state exhaustion proceedings but, instead, to assure that there is time for them to take place.

§ 6.4. *Certiorari* review.[1]

a. *Introduction.* A federal habeas corpus petitioner need not petition the United States Supreme Court for a writ of *certiorari* in order to satisfy the exhaustion of remedies requirement.[2] Counsel and client nonetheless must decide whether it is advisable to seek *certiorari* review of state postconviction proceedings before filing a federal habeas corpus petition in district court. As is explained below, employment of the *certiorari* remedy in advance of federal habeas corpus review may be advantageous in some situations but may pose a risk of severely impeding the prisoner's ability to prepare and file a federal habeas corpus petition within the limitations period set by the Antiterrorism and Effective Death Penalty Act (AEDPA).[3] This section discusses some of the factors the prisoner or counsel should consider when deciding whether to seek *certiorari* review of state postconviction proceedings — or, at the least, whether to do so before (as opposed to doing so at the same time as) the petitioner pursues federal habeas corpus review.

b. *Noncapital cases.* In noncapital cases, the state postconviction *certiorari* petition often may be forgone in order to enable a prisoner serving a term of years to get on with federal review of the conviction and sentence. Because the Supreme Court so rarely grants *certiorari* to review noncapital state postconviction decisions,[4] the prisoner often will not forgo a meaningful

---

[17] *See supra* notes 2-5 and accompanying text; *infra* §§ 12.3a, 12.3b, 13.1-13.2b.

[18] *See infra* § 13.3 (federal stays of execution pending exhaustion).

§ 6.4. [1] *See generally* ROBERT L. STERN, EUGENE GRESSMAN, STEVEN M. SHAPIRO & KENNETH S. GELLER, SUPREME COURT PRACTICE § 4.25, at 207-10 (7th ed. 1993).

[2] *See supra* § 2.4d nn.239-60 and accompanying text; *infra* § 23.3b.

[3] Pub. L. 104-132, 110 Stat. 1214 (1996). *See infra* §§ 6.4b nn.11-12 and accompanying text, 6.4c nn.16-18 and accompanying text. For an overview of AEDPA's provisions and an explanation of the cases to which it applies, see *supra* §§ 3.2, 3.4.

[4] *See* Kyles v. Whitley, 498 U.S. 931, 932 (1990) (Stevens, J., concurring in denial of stay) ("Because the scope of the state's obligation to provide collateral review is shrouded in so much uncertainty, ... this Court rarely grants review at this stage of the litigation even when the application for state collateral relief is supported by arguably meritorious federal constitutional

opportunity for review by not filing a *certiorari* petition at that stage. Moreover, as is discussed below, forgoing *certiorari* review of state postconviction proceedings may avoid adverse statute of limitations consequences on the federal petition.

Circumstances may arise, however, in which a noncapital petitioner should consider filing a state postconviction *certiorari* petition. For example, if the Supreme Court recently has announced a decision that requires reversal of the petitioner's conviction or sentence on a ground pursued unsuccessfully in state postconviction proceedings, the most expeditious means of enforcing the rule of that decision may be to petition the Supreme Court to grant *certiorari,* vacate the state court decision summarily, and remand for reconsideration in light of the Court's recent pronouncement.[5] Likewise, the Supreme Court's recent grant of a petition for *certiorari* to review a claim similar to one in the petitioner's case may warrant the filing of a *certiorari* petition asking the Court to consider the petitioner's claim along with the one the Court already has agreed to hear. In this latter situation, although the Court is unlikely to grant the petitioner's *certiorari* petition, it may "hold" the petition until it disposes of the one to which it granted *certiorari,* then dispose of the "held" petition as warranted by its decision in the original case.[6]

---

claims."). Supreme Court grants of *certiorari* to review state postconviction decisions adverse to prisoners in noncapital cases are rare. *See, e.g.,* Wilde v. Wyoming, 362 U.S. 607 (1960). *But cf.* New Mexico ex rel. Ortiz v. Reed, 118 S. Ct. 1860, 1862 (1998) (*per curiam*) (summarily granting state's petition for *certiorari* and reversing state supreme court's affirmance of lower courts' grant of habeas corpus relief); Pennsylvania v. Finley, 481 U.S. 551 (1987) (*certiorari* granted to review state postconviction decision adverse to state).

[5] *See infra* § 39.2d (discussing *certiorari* petitions directed toward this grant-vacate-remand option). *But cf. infra* note 6 (discussing risks inherent in seeking *certiorari* in this situation). If a Supreme Court decision announces a "new rule of law," *see infra* § 25.5 (defining "new rules"), that rule applies retroactively to all other cases that had not become "final" as of the date on which the Court's decision was announced but generally does *not* apply retroactively to cases that *had* become final as of that date. *See infra* Chapter 25. Clearly, cases still pending on direct appeal or direct appeal *certiorari* in the State courts are not "final." *See infra* § 25.6. The Court has not yet decided whether to treat as "final" a case that has completed direct appeal proceedings (including *certiorari* proceedings following direct appeal) but is pending in state postconviction proceedings (including *certiorari* proceedings to review the state postconviction proceedings) when the new Supreme Court decision was announced. *See infra* § 25.6 nn.10-27 and accompanying text. Despite some indications that the Court views such cases as already having passed the point of "finality" (so that new law does not apply), there are reasons, particularly in regard to claims that do not become cognizable until state postconviction proceedings and in regard to States that treat postconviction proceedings as part of the criminal process, to conclude that cases pending in state postconviction proceedings are *not* final (and, thus, that new law does apply). *See id.*

[6] *See infra* § 39.2d. If the Supreme Court upholds the claim in the case before it, for example, it may remand the held case to the state courts for reconsideration in light of the Court's new decision. The courses of action described here pose risks to prisoners, because Supreme Court

As is discussed in section 5.1a *supra*, the Supreme Court's *Teague* rule of nonretroactivity[7] and similar restrictions embodied in AEDPA's standard of review of state court legal and mixed legal/factual determinations[8] give rise to another consideration weighing in favor of filing a *certiorari* petition to review an adverse determination of the highest state court with jurisdiction to consider the prisoner's postconviction claims. Both the *Teague* rule and AEDPA's standard of review limit the body of law a federal habeas corpus court may consider to decisions issued before a certain point in time (generally, for *Teague* purposes, the completion of *certiorari* proceedings in the Supreme Court following direct appeal[9] and, for AEDPA purposes, the announcement of the state court decision on direct appeal[10]). Accordingly, Supreme Court *certiorari* review of state postconviction proceedings may be the only practicably available federal forum to litigate a claim that relies on legal principles established after the cut-off points set by *Teague* and AEDPA or that seeks to establish wholly new legal principles.

In considering whether to seek *certiorari* review of state postconviction proceedings in advance of habeas corpus review, the prisoner and any counsel must weigh the potential advantages discussed above against the risk of a severe disadvantage. As is explained in § 5.1b *supra*, it is unclear whether AEDPA's one-year statute of limitations for "nonopt-in" (which includes all noncapital) cases is tolled while a prisoner is seeking *certiorari* from the state courts' denial of postconviction relief.[11] If the statute of limitations is *not* tolled during this

review of *certiorari* petitions is summary, quirky, and unexplained in the vast majority of cases. It is quite possible, therefore, that the Court will deny a petition, rather than granting and summarily remanding it, even though the case may be controlled by the recent favorable decision. Then, when the prisoner pleads the claim in her habeas corpus petition, the federal habeas corpus court may (although legally it should not, *see infra* § 6.4c nn.23-24 and accompanying text) take the Supreme Court's action to reflect negatively on the claim or perhaps on its retroactivity, *see supra* note 5; *infra* Chapter 25.

[7] *See generally infra* Chapter 25.

[8] *See generally infra* § 30.2.

[9] *See infra* §§ 25.1, 25.6. As is explained *supra* note 5, the point of "finality" for *Teague* purposes may not occur, at least in some situations, until the conclusion of state postconviction review. Even if a "new" rule (as defined *infra* § 25.5) is announced after the point of finality, the *Teague* doctrine contains two limited exceptions that may permit a federal habeas corpus court to rely on the new rule in granting relief. *See infra* § 25.7.

[10] *See infra* § 30.2. Unlike the *Teague* doctrine, AEDPA limits the body of federal law that may be considered to Supreme Court decisions. *See infra* § 30.2c nn.25-29 and accompanying text.

[11] *See supra* § 5.1b n.65 and accompanying text. Because the textual discussion here is limited to noncapital cases, it refers exclusively to AEDPA's "nonopt-in" statute of limitations and related provisions, which govern *all* noncapital cases. (The nonopt-in provisions also govern many capital cases, to which the textual discussion accordingly is relevant. *See infra* § 6.4c n.16 and accompanying text). On the *certiorari* implications of AEDPA's "opt-in" statute of limitations (and

period, and if *certiorari* review of state postconviction proceedings is undertaken prior to filing a federal habeas corpus petition, such review could consume more than the time that remains before the one-year period for filing the federal habeas corpus petition expires.[12] Obviously, the minute chance that a *certiorari* petition will be granted can never justify forgoing (on statute of limitations, or any other, grounds) the prisoner's statutory right to federal habeas corpus review. Accordingly, before deciding to proceed with a petition for *certiorari* review of state postconviction proceedings, a prisoner or counsel must determine whether the appropriate federal jurisdictions have held that AEDPA's one-year statute of limitations is tolled during *certiorari* proceedings following state postconviction review and, if not, must carefully weigh the impact of the untolled statute of limitations on later federal habeas corpus proceedings. As is discussed in § 5.1a *supra*, a prisoner can take advantage of *certiorari and* avoid adverse statute of limitations consequences by *simultaneously* seeking *certiorari* and federal habeas corpus review.

c. *Capital cases.* In capital cases, the cost-benefit analysis described in the preceding subsection is different. The impetus to file a petition for *certiorari* review of state court proceedings is greater because (1) the Court is somewhat more likely to grant *certiorari* review of a state postconviction or other decision in a capital case,[13] and (2) a capital case is somewhat more likely to present the kind of potentially meritorious claims based on newly established legal principles of the sort that, even in noncapital cases, make postconviction

---

the other aspects of AEDPA's "Special Habeas Corpus Procedures in Capital Cases"), see *infra* § 6.4c nn.17-18 and accompanying text. On the general operation of AEDPA and the difference between nonopt-in and opt-in cases, see *supra* §§ 3.2, 3.3.

[12] For further discussion of the "nonopt-in" statute of limitations, *see supra* § 5.1b.

[13] Although decades may pass between grants of *certiorari* by the Court to review noncapital state postconviction decisions, *see supra* § 6.4b n.4 and accompanying text, the Court has often granted *certiorari* in one, and sometimes even more than one, capital state postconviction case in a term. *See, e.g.,* Victor v. Nebraska, 511 U.S. 1, 18-19 (1994); Yates v. Evatt, 500 U.S. 391 (1991); Johnson v. Mississippi, 486 U.S. 578 (1988); Yates v. Aiken, 484 U.S. 211 (1988); Tison v. Arizona, 481 U.S. 137 (1987); Truesdale v. Aiken, 480 U.S. 527 (1987). *See also* Campbell v. Wood, 511 U.S. 1119, 1119 n.3 (1994) (Blackmun, J., dissenting from denial of stay of execution and denial of *certiorari*) (if capital habeas corpus case presents "fundamental constitutional question," Court should not await conflict among circuits before granting *certiorari*, particularly if inter-circuit conflict "is unlikely to emerge" because practice under challenge is used in only one circuit); Dobbs v. Zant, 506 U.S. 357, 360 (1993) (*per curiam*) (Scalia, J., concurring in the judgment) (notwithstanding general principle that Court should not "'expend its scarce resources crafting opinions that correct technical errors in cases of only local importance where the correction in no way promotes the development of the law,' ... I am willing to make an exception from that rule in capital cases — but only where there is a realistic likelihood that the 'technical error' affected the conviction or the sentence").

certiorari petitions advisable.[14] On the other hand, the impetus *not* to file a petition for *certiorari* review also is greater in capital cases, the higher stakes of which make it even more perilous to pursue a remedy that may substantially abridge the time available for investigating and preparing a federal habeas corpus petition or may cause such a petition to be untimely.[15] These hazards may arise in any capital case in which an unstayed execution date has been set (given the Supreme Court's reluctance to grant stays of execution pending its consideration of a petition for *certiorari* review of a state postconviction decision), in capital cases subject to AEDPA's nonopt-in statute of limitations for the reasons discussed in the preceding subsection,[16] and especially in cases governed by AEDPA's "opt-in" provisions, which create a much shorter, 180-day statute of limitations that clearly is not tolled during any part of the time taken to pursue *certiorari* review of state postconviction proceedings.[17] Assuming there is time to do so responsibly, a prisoner may avoid these problems by filing *certiorari* and federal habeas corpus proceedings *simultaneously*.[18]

If a prisoner *does* elect to pursue *certiorari* review of state postconviction proceedings prior to filing a federal habeas corpus petition, and if an execution date is imminent and no stay of execution is immediately in view (because the case is not subject to the "automatic stay" that applies to "opt-in" States[19] and because the state courts refuse to grant a stay of execution pending the filing and determination of a *certiorari* petition[20]), the prisoner's first priority is to secure a stay. To do so, the prisoner can: (1) ask the Supreme Court itself for a stay pending the disposition of a *certiorari* petition; (2) file a federal habeas corpus petition (or the legally equivalent papers discussed in sections 12.3a and 13.2b *infra*) in the district court as the basis for a stay, then request that the district

---

[14] *See supra* § 6.4b nn.7-10 and accompanying text. *See also infra* §§ 7.1b n.47 (discussing additional basis on which to seek *certiorari* following state postconviction review, particularly in capital cases), 7.2f.

[15] *See supra* § 6.4b nn.11-12 and accompanying text.

[16] *See supra* § 6.4b nn.11-12 and accompanying text.

[17] *See supra* § 5.1b nn.94, 102 and accompanying text. For discussion of the means by which States qualify for "opt-in" treatment, see *supra* §§ 3.3a, 3.3b.

[18] *See supra* §§ 5.1a nn.22-23 and accompanying text, 6.4b. *See also infra* notes 23-24 and accompanying text (discussing some of the dangers of this approach).

[19] *See supra* § 6.3 n.2 and accompanying text.

[20] Some States employ the irresponsible (and possibly unconstitutional, *see infra* § 7.1b) practice of routinely denying stays of execution pending state postconviction proceedings and requiring the proceedings to take place in the short period of time between the setting of the execution date and the date set. *See, e.g.,* McFarland v. Scott, 512 U.S. 849, 851-53 & n.1 (1994) (describing Texas' use of this approach). The Court's decision in *McFarland* provides States with a incentive for forgoing such practices. *See supra* § 6.3 nn.5-10 & accompanying text.

court hold that petition in abeyance pending the determination of a *certiorari* petition by the United States Supreme Court; (3) file the federal habeas corpus petition (or legally equivalent papers) as a basis for a stay of execution pending final disposition of the *habeas corpus* petition and simultaneously litigate both the habeas corpus petition and the *certiorari* petition; or (4) file *only* the federal habeas corpus petition (or legally equivalent papers) as a basis for a stay of execution pending disposition of the habeas corpus proceeding. The first option rarely succeeds,[21] and the second one, although more likely to succeed,[22] presents certain tactical dangers when it does *not* succeed. The third option may deplete time and resources in pursuing a *certiorari* remedy that is not likely to result in relief at a point when the need to secure a stay quickly from a federal habeas court, hence to prepare and file a habeas corpus petition and stay application (or equivalent papers), place time and resources at a premium. In addition, there is some modest reason to fear that a denial of *certiorari* on a claim that is simultaneously being litigated in a federal habeas corpus petition will have a prejudicial effect on the claim in the federal habeas corpus court. As a matter of law, the Supreme Court's denial of *certiorari* to review a state court's

---

[21] A measure of the Court's distaste for option (1) is its practice during the summer months, when it is out of session and generally forbears ruling on *certiorari* petitions, of not only summarily denying applications for stays of execution pending adjudication of *certiorari* petitions to review capital state postconviction proceedings but also summarily denying the underlying postconviction *certiorari* petitions. *See, e.g.,* Drew v. Texas, 512 U.S. 1265 (1994) (*mem.*); Jones v. Murray, 505 U.S. 1245 (1992) (*mem.*); Lane v. Texas, 505 U.S. 1233 (1992) (*mem.*).

[22] *See* Collins v. Byrd, 510 U.S. 1185, 1186-88 (1994) (*mem.*) (Scalia, J., dissenting from denial of application to vacate stay) (describing 6th Circuit order granting stay of execution pending federal habeas corpus proceedings which Court, over Justice Scalia's dissent, declined to vacate; 6th Circuit's order directed district court to grant stay of execution pending adjudication of federal habeas corpus petition and to hold petition "'in abeyance until the Supreme Court either grants or denies petitioner's request for certiorari [following state postconviction proceedings], as the Court's decision will be directly relevant to the resolution of one of petitioner's habeas claims'"; Justice Scalia acknowledges that district court has discretion to hold petition in abeyance pending Supreme Court's decision on state postconviction *certiorari* petition raising claim "relevant to" claim in habeas corpus petition but objects to appellate limitations on district court's exercise of discretion). Although potentially successful, as *Collins v. Byrd, supra,* indicates, option (2) has the tactical danger of inviting the federal district judge to make a premature ruling, in a particularly hostile setting, on whether the claims included in both the *certiorari* and habeas corpus petition merit a stay of execution. The procedure runs the risk that the district judge erroneously will assume that a conclusion that a stay pending *certiorari* is not warranted, given the low likelihood in any case that the Supreme Court will grant its discretionary *certiorari* review, controls the answer to the formally similar but substantively different question whether the claims in the federal petition are sufficiently substantial to justify a stay of execution pending federal *habeas corpus* review *as of right* pursuant to 28 U.S.C.A. § 2254 (West 1994 & Supp. 1998). *Compare infra* § 13.2 (standard for stays of execution pending habeas corpus proceedings) *with infra* §§ 38.2c & 39.3c (standard for stays pending *certiorari*).

disposition of a federal claim clearly has no legal or precedential effect on the merits of that claim when it subsequently is raised in a federal habeas corpus proceeding,[23] and the Supreme Court frequently has granted or affirmed habeas corpus relief on federal claims unsuccessfully raised in earlier *certiorari* petitions.[24] Nonetheless, having long since won the "no precedential value" battle on the legal front with regard to issues on which the Supreme Court has denied *certiorari*, federal habeas corpus petitioners still occasionally lose it on the psychological level, particularly if *certiorari* is denied in the midst of the habeas corpus proceeding. A capital prisoner accordingly should forgo a petition

---

[23] *See, e.g.,* Lackey v. Texas, 514 U.S. 1045, 1047 (1995) (memorandum of Stevens, J., respecting denial of *certiorari*) ("Court's denial of certiorari does not constitute a ruling on the merits"; "[o]ften, a denial of certiorari on a novel issue will permit the state and federal courts to 'serve as laboratories in which the issue receives further study before it is addressed by this Court'"; "[p]etitioner's claim, with its legal complexity and its potential for far-reaching consequences, seems an ideal example of one which would benefit from such further study" (quoting McCray v. New York, 461 U.S. 961, 963 (1983) (memorandum of Stevens, J., respecting denial of *certiorari*))); Barber v. Tennessee, 513 U.S. 1184 (1995) (opinion of Stevens, J., respecting denial of *certiorari*) ("Court's denial of certiorari does not constitute a ruling on the merits"; although petitioner's challenge to his death sentence may have "merit" because sentencing instruction was "plainly impermissible under this Court's holdings," denial of *certiorari* is supported by "valid reasons"); Hamilton v. Texas, 498 U.S. 908, 911 (1990) (Stevens, J., concurring in denial of *certiorari*) (denial of *certiorari* "does not evidence any lack of merit in the petition"); Hambsch v. United States, 490 U.S. 1054 (1989) (memorandum of Stevens, J., respecting the denial of *certiorari*) ("it is important to emphasize the fact that an order denying a petition for a writ of *certiorari* is not a ruling on the merits of any question presented by the petition"); Teague v. Lane, 489 U.S. 288, 296 (1989); United States ex rel. Smith v. Baldi, 344 U.S. 561 (1953); Brown v. Allen, 344 U.S. 443, 488-97 (1953) (opinion for the Court of Frankfurter, J.). *See also* Kyles v. Whitley, 498 U.S. 931, 932 (1990) (Stevens, J., concurring in denial of stay) ("The denial of the present application [for a stay] should not ... be construed as having been predicated on a determination that there is no merit in the claims asserted in the state collateral review process.").

[24] *See, e.g.,* Kyles v. Whitley, 514 U.S. 491 (1995); Richmond v. Lewis, 506 U.S. 40 (1992); Maynard v. Cartwright, 486 U.S. 356 (1988); Turner v. Murray, 476 U.S. 28 (1986); Estelle v. Smith, 451 U.S. 454 (1981); Roberts v. LaVallee, 389 U.S. 40 (1967); Sheppard v. Maxwell, 384 U.S. 333 (1966); Townsend v. Sain, 372 U.S. 293 (1963); Irvin v. Dowd, 366 U.S. 717 (1961); Rogers v. Richmond, 365 U.S. 534 (1961); Leyra v. Denno, 347 U.S. 556 (1954); Moore v. Dempsey, 261 U.S. 86 (1923). *See also* Knapp v. Arizona, 435 U.S. 908 (1978) (Blackmun, J., concurring) (denial of *certiorari* is without prejudice to petitioner's seeking relief by habeas corpus); Davis v. Balkcom, 369 U.S. 811 (1962) (Warren, C.J.) (denial of *certiorari* does not mean that petitioner is necessarily precluded from obtaining relief in some other appropriate proceeding); Cranor v. Gonzales, 226 F.2d 83 (9th Cir. 1955); Anthony G. Amsterdam, *In Favorem Mortis: The Supreme Court and Capital Punishment,* 14 ABA SEC. INDIVIDUAL RTS. & RESP. 14, 16 & n.8, 54-56 (1987); other authority cited *supra* § 2.4b n.24. *Cf.* In re McDonald, 489 U.S. 180, 187-88 (1989) (Brennan, J., dissenting) (citing Chessman v. Teets, 354 U.S. 156 (1957)) ("it is rare, but it does happen on occasion that we grant review and even decide in favor of a [habeas corpus] litigant who previously had presented multiple unsuccessful petitions on the same issue").

for *certiorari* in this situation unless there is some good reason to think that the Supreme Court will grant *certiorari* or if there is no reason to fear that a claim's inclusion in a *certiorari* petition that is denied will decrease the claim's likelihood of success in contemporaneous habeas corpus proceedings.

If *certiorari is* granted and the merits of the petition are decided adversely to petitioner by the Supreme Court, that decision generally is binding upon the petitioner in subsequent federal habeas corpus proceedings on all issues "actually adjudicated by the Supreme Court."[25] Thereafter, federal habeas corpus review of the claim is unavailable "unless the applicant for the writ of habeas corpus shall plead and the [federal] court shall find the existence of a material and controlling fact which did not appear in the record of the proceeding in the Supreme Court and the court shall further find that the applicant for the writ of habeas corpus could not have caused such fact to appear in such record by the exercise of reasonable diligence."[26] By its terms, this provision only bars federal habeas corpus relitigation of claims decided by the Supreme Court "at the instance" of a prisoner. Also by its own terms, the provision does not apply to issues the Supreme Court did not actually adjudicate when it granted *certiorari* and decided the case.[27]

d. Certiorari, *not appeal.* Although in cases involving the constitutionality of a state statute, the prisoner theoretically may seek the Supreme Court's *appellate* review of an adverse state appellate or postconviction decision,[28] without exception the prisoner instead should petition for *certiorari* review under 28 U.S.C. § 1257(3).[29] Despite appearances, the appellate route provides no advantages and has severe disadvantages.

Most importantly, although the denial of a *certiorari* petition has no precedential or legally binding significance in future postconviction proceedings,[30] the summary dismissal by the Supreme Court of an appeal does have precedential significance and is legally binding on all courts that later

---

[25] 28 U.S.C.A. § 2244(c) (West 1994 & Supp. 1998).

[26] *Id. See* Coleman v. Balkcom, 451 U.S. 949, 963 (1981) (Rehnquist, J., dissenting from denial of *certiorari*); Neil v. Biggers, 409 U.S. 188, 190-92 (1972).

[27] *See, e.g.,* Proffitt v. Wainwright, 685 F.2d 1227, 1261 (11th Cir. 1982) (Supreme Court's declaration on *certiorari* review of state direct appeal decision that capital sentencing statute is *facially* valid does not prevent petitioner thereafter from bringing a habeas corpus petition attacking statute *as applied*).

[28] *See* 28 U.S.C. § 1257(1) (1994).

[29] *See* Amsterdam, *supra* § 6.4c n.24, at 16 ("[N]o competent attorney for a death-sentenced inmate would take an appeal to the Supreme Court of the United States under ordinary circumstances; *certiorari* is the prescribed mode of review in virtually all capital cases.").

[30] *See supra* § 6.4c nn.23-24 and accompanying text.

review the case, including habeas corpus courts.[31] Accordingly, by contrast to a *certiorari* denial, an appellate dismissal almost assuredly forecloses federal habeas corpus consideration of the denied claim.[32] Moreover, the expectation that an appeal is more likely than a petition for a writ of *certiorari* to compel a full decision on the merits by the Supreme Court is unwarranted. The Court now summarily dismisses the vast majority of the appeals it receives "for want of a substantial federal question,"[33] giving the appellate route virtually no advantage over *certiorari* to counterbalance its overwhelming disadvantages.

---

[31] *See, e.g.,* Mandel v. Bradley, 432 U.S. 173, 176 (1977); Tully v. Griffin, 429 U.S. 68, 74 (1976); Hicks v. Miranda, 422 U.S. 332, 343-44 (1975); STERN, ET AL., *supra* note 1, §§ 4.28-4.29, at 215-21; Amsterdam, *supra* § 6.4c n.24, at 16 & nn.7, 8.

[32] *See* 28 U.S.C.A. § 2244(c) (West 1994 & Supp. 1998). *Cf.* Anderson v. Celebrezze, 460 U.S. 780, 784 n.5 (1983); *Mandel v. Bradley, supra,* 432 U.S. at 176; Fusari v. Steinberg, 419 U.S. 379, 390, 391-92 (1975) (Burger, C.J., concurring) (all discussing limitations on scope of ruling that Supreme Court's summary dismissal implies).

[33] Regarding the "certiorarification" of the appellate process, see STERN, ET AL, *supra* note 1, §§ 4.26-4.27, at 210-15, 385-86; Amsterdam, *supra* § 6.4c n.24, at 16.

Chapter 7

STATE REMEDIES: PROFESSIONAL AND CONSTITUTIONAL ISSUES

§ 7.1. "Full and fair"[1] proceedings.

a. *Counsel's responsibilities.*[2] Although state postconviction proceedings serve the essentially appellate function of reviewing prior criminal judgments, they are procedurally both less and more than appeals. On the one hand, as the Supreme Court — grossly overgeneralizing — has stated:

> [State] [p]ostconviction relief is even further removed from the criminal trial than is discretionary direct review. It is not part of the criminal proceeding itself, and it is in fact considered to be civil in nature. It is a collateral attack that normally occurs only after the defendant has failed to secure relief through direct review of his conviction.[3]

---

§ 7.1. [1] *See* Townsend v. Sain, 372 U.S. 293, 312 (1963) (state determinations of fact not binding in federal habeas corpus proceeding if not based on "full and fair" factfinding procedures). *See also* Keeney v. Tamayo-Reyes, 504 U.S. 1, 10 (1992) ("State must afford the petitioner a full and fair hearing on his federal claim" or else federal rehearing of the facts is required); Stone v. Powell, 428 U.S. 465, 494-95 & n.37 (1976).

[2] *See generally* Richard J. Bonnie, *Dilemmas in Administering the Death Penalty: Conscientious Abstention, Professional Ethics, and the Needs of the Legal System,* 14 L. & HUM. BEHAV. 67 (1990); James E. Coleman, *Litigating at the Speed of Light: Postconviction Proceedings Under a Death Warrant,* 16 LITIGATION 14 (Summer 1990); Marcia Coyle, Fred Strasser & Marianne Lavelle, *Trial and Error in the Nation's Death Belt,* NAT'L L.J., June 11, 1990, at 30; Luke DeGrand, *Representing the Condemned: Professional Responsibility and Death Row,* 78 ILL. B.J. 30 (1990); James M. Doyle, *The Lawyers' Art: "Representation" in Capital Cases,* 8 YALE J.L. & HUMAN. 417 (1996); Esther F. Lardent & Douglas M. Cohen, *The Last Best Hope: Representing Death Row Inmates,* 23 LOY. L.A. L. REV. 213 (1989); Sarah Lee, *Representation on Death Row,* 141 NEW L.J. 26 (Jan. 11, 1990); Andrea D. Lyon, *New Opportunities for Defense Attorneys: How Record Preservation Requirements After the New Habeas Bill Require Extensive and Exciting Trial Preparation,* 30 J. MARSHALL L. REV. 389 (1997); Anthony Paduano & Clive A. Stafford Smith, *The Unconscionability of Sub-Minimum Wages Paid Appointed Counsel in Capital Cases,* 43 RUTGERS L. REV. 281 (1991). This subsection discusses counsel's responsibilities mainly in regard to the thorough presentation of the law and the facts once the state postconviction petition has been prepared and filed. Counsel's no less important responsibilities in regard to conducting a thorough prefiling investigation of potential legal claims and their factual bases are discussed *supra* §§ 3.5a, 6.2. *See also infra* §§ 11.1-11.3, 12.3a (similar responsibilities in preparing federal habeas corpus petition).

[3] Pennsylvania v. Finley, 481 U.S. 551, 556-57 (1987) (citation omitted). The Court's statement is an overgeneralization because — as is also true of the federal postconviction remedy for federal prisoners, 28 U.S.C.A. § 2255 (West 1994 & Supp. 1998); *see infra* Chapter 41 — some state postconviction procedures are statutorily defined as criminal in nature, part of the original criminal proceeding, and subject to criminal rules of procedure. *See, e.g.,* Tennessee Post-Conviction Procedure Act, TENN. CODE ANN. §§ 40-30-201 to 40-30-222 (1997). *See also* Rules 1, 12 of the

So, too, as is explained in Chapter 6 *supra*, the range of claims cognizable in state postconviction often is more limited than the range of claims that may be raised on appeal.

On the other hand, precisely because the postconviction proceeding is a new and at least somewhat separate action, which the prisoner initiates and which is not wholly dependent on the record made at trial,[4] the postconviction petitioner has more ability than the appellant to shape the action both procedurally and substantively.[5] Similarly, state postconviction proceedings are not, like appeals, bound to the *written* word and to *legal* argumentation. Instead, as a matter of state law in most places[6] — and in order to qualify their conclusions for deferential treatment under federal habeas corpus law[7] — state postconviction proceedings must provide prisoners with whatever "factfinding procedures" are necessary to afford "a full and fair" hearing[8] on any disputed and controlling factual issue in the case.[9]

Accordingly, when necessary to assure the full and fair adjudication of the client's federal claims, postconviction counsel should request that the state postconviction case be conducted, and should be prepared to conduct it, as a civil trial proceeding, initiated by her on behalf of the client, complete with frequent and productive interaction with the client;[10] comprehensive prefiling and pretrial documentary, field, and legal investigation to identify and prepare to litigate the appropriate causes of action;[11] careful pleadings;[12] motions practice;[13]

Rules Governing § 2255 Cases; Advisory Committee Notes to *id. See infra* § 25.6 nn.15-18 and accompanying text. With increasing frequency, moreover, given the use of "unified appeal" procedures, state postconviction procedures partly precede and partly occur simultaneously with direct appeal.

[4] *Cf.* Riddle v. Dyche, 262 U.S. 333, 335-36 (1923) ("The writ of *habeas corpus* is not a proceeding in the original criminal prosecution but an independent civil suit").

[5] *See generally supra* §§ 1.1, 2.2.

[6] *See, e.g.*, TENN. CODE ANN. § 40-30-210 (1997).

[7] *See infra* notes 33-39 and accompanying text.

[8] Keeney v. Tamayo-Reyes, 504 U.S. 1, 10 (1992); Townsend v. Sain, 372 U.S. 293, 312 (1963). Prior to its amendment in 1996, 28 U.S.C. § 2254(d) explicitly stated that "a full and fair hearing" in state court is a prerequisite to federal deference to state court factfindings. Although the current version of the statute (28 U.S.C.A. §§ 2254(d)(2), 2254(e) (West 1994 & Supp. 1998)) no longer contains that language, the statute's requirement of "reasonable" state court factfinding procedures, *id.* § 2254(d)(2), encompasses the preexisting standard. *See infra* § 20.2b.

[9] *See also infra* § 7.1b (possible constitutional right to adequate state postconviction proceedings).

[10] *See supra* § 4.1.

[11] *See supra* § 6.2; *infra* §§ 11.2, 11.3.

[12] *See generally supra* §§ 3.5a, 6.2; *infra* §§ 11.2, 11.3, 11.6.

[13] *See generally infra* §§ 11.7c, 17.3; *infra* Chapters 19-21.

evidentiary hearings;[14] briefing;[15] and any other procedures that counsel might use in civil litigation on a plaintiff's behalf.[16] Because many of these investigative, preparatory, and other litigative responsibilities are expansive and time-consuming, counsel almost surely will find it necessary, in the typical case involving an indigent client, to seek the court's appointment, and thereby gain access to additional financial resources.[17]

Similarly, if, as often is the case, the prisoner cannot establish the factual predicates for a state or federal claim without financial assistance for experts, investigators,[18] travel expenses for critical witnesses, and the like, it becomes counsel's responsibility to ask the state court to provide that assistance as well.[19] Claims of racial discrimination in the selection of juries, for example, may require the assistance of experts to provide essential social scientific and statistical advice and testimony;[20] mental-disorder-based claims may require psychiatric examinations and proof;[21] claims that the state withheld or misrepresented exculpatory evidence may require the assistance of forensic

---

[14] *See generally infra* Chapters 19-21.

[15] *See generally infra* Chapter 29.

[16] *See generally supra* §§ 1.1, 2.2; *infra* § 19.1.

[17] *See infra* § 7.2 (discussing possible constitutional right to appointment of counsel in state postconviction proceedings). *See also supra* § 3.3b nn.2-6 and accompanying text (requirement that States seeking to secure especially favorable "opt-in" treatment in federal habeas corpus proceedings in capital cases (*e.g.*, strict statute of limitations, restrictions on amendments, broad procedural default rule, and time limits on adjudication, *see supra* § 3.3c) must provide all capital state postconviction petitioners with competent counsel and adequate support services); *infra* § 7.2a n.6 and accompanying text.

[18] *See* McFarland v. Scott, 512 U.S. 849, 855 (1994) ("The services of investigators and ... experts may be critical in the preapplication phase of a habeas corpus proceeding, when possible claims and their factual bases are researched and identified."); *id.* at 860 (O'Connor, J., concurring in the judgment in part) ("to be meaningful in the habeas context," "'investigative, expert or other services ... reasonably necessary for the representation of the defendant'" "must be available prior to the filing of a first habeas petition" (citations omitted)). *See also* McCall v. Delo, 31 F.3d 750, 752 n.3 (8th Cir. 1994), *cert. denied*, 514 U.S. 1052 (1995) ("Unfortunately, this case probably represents another example in the criminal justice system of what might be called unequal justice between the rich and the poor. Given the nature of the circumstantial evidence here, some of it questionable, if McCall were a person of wealth who could employ the best of counsel and the best of investigators, he might have presented a more effective defense to the prosecution's case.").

[19] *See* other sections of this book cited *supra* note 17.

[20] *See, e.g.*, Vasquez v. Hillery, 474 U.S. 254, 257, 262 (1986); Castaneda v. Partida, 430 U.S. 482, 486-87 (1977).

[21] *See, e.g.*, Ake v. Oklahoma, 470 U.S. 68, 79-80, 85 (1985); Barefoot v. Estelle, 463 U.S. 880, 896-905 (1983).

experts to analyze the evidence in question;[22] almost any fact-intensive claim based on matters outside the trial record (for instance, claims alleging the ineffective assistance of counsel, prosecutorial suppression of evidence, improper contact between court personnel and jurors, and the like) may require the aid of investigators;[23] and any claim on which the testimony of lay or expert witnesses is required may necessitate funds to reimburse the witnesses for their time and expenses.[24]

Counsel's responsibility to seek an appointment to represent the client, to ask for any essential discovery,[25] subpoenas, an evidentiary hearing, and the like, and to secure the necessary financial and other resources to enable her to conduct the litigation in an effective and meaningful manner has two sources. First, of course, it stems from the general professional obligation to represent the client zealously and effectively.[26] Effective assistance of counsel is necessary to "assure[] the fairness, and thus the legitimacy, of our adversary process";[27] and "effective investigation" and "careful preparation" "form the basis of effective representation."[28]

Second and more particularly, the structure and interaction of state and federal postconviction review in this country place important responsibilities on state postconviction counsel to discover, plead, and litigate fully all available federal law claims. Particularly as a result of recent legislation, and most particularly in certain types of capital cases adjudicated under that legislation, a federal habeas corpus petitioner is often precluded from raising or securing relief on legal

---

[22] *See* Stephens v. Kemp, 846 F.2d 642, 645-50 (11th Cir.), *cert. denied,* 488 U.S. 872 (1988); AMERICAN BAR ASSOCIATION, STANDARDS FOR CRIMINAL JUSTICE § 22-3.1 (and commentary), § 22-4.3 (and commentary) (2d ed. 1980 & Supp. 1986); *id.,* commentary to § 4-4.1 (3d ed. 1993).

[23] *See* authority cited *supra* notes 18, 22. *See generally* JEROME FRANK, COURTS ON TRIAL: MYTH AND REALITY IN AMERICAN JUSTICE 94 (1949).

[24] *See infra* § 19.3. *See also supra* § 3.3b nn.2-6 and accompanying text (requirement that States seeking to secure especially favorable "opt-in" treatment in federal habeas corpus proceedings in capital cases (*e.g.,* strict statute of limitations, restrictions on amendments, broad procedural default rule, and time limits on adjudication, *see supra* § 3.3c) must provide all capital state postconviction petitioners with competent counsel and adequate financial support services).

[25] Postconviction discovery is virtually unheard of in some States but is relatively common in others. At the least, counsel should seek leave and the resources necessary to depose witnesses outside the subpoena range of the relevant court. *See generally infra* § 19.4.

[26] *See* ABA STANDARDS FOR CRIMINAL JUSTICE, *supra* note 22, §§ 4-2.2, 4-4.1 (and commentary), 4-4.4, 22-3.1 (and commentary), 22-4.3 (and commentary). *See generally* AMERICAN BAR ASSOCIATION, MODEL CODE OF PROFESSIONAL RESPONSIBILITY, Canon 7, EC 7-1, EC 7-8, DR 7-101(a)(1) (1969); AMERICAN BAR ASSOCIATION, MODEL RULES OF PROFESSIONAL CONDUCT, Rules 1.1, 1.2(a), 1.3, 3.1 (1983).

[27] Kimmelman v. Morrison, 477 U.S. 365, 374 (1986). *See infra* §§ 7.2c, 7.2d, 12.3a.

[28] ABA STANDARDS FOR CRIMINAL JUSTICE, *supra* note 22, commentary to § 4-4.1 ("Duty to Investigate"). *See id.,* §§ 22-3.1, 22-4.3 (and commentary). *See generally infra* §§ 11.2, 19.1.

claims — or even particular aspects of legal claims, including aspects tied to previously undiscovered facts — if the claims were not previously discovered, pleaded and fully presented in state postconviction proceedings that *preceded* the petitioner's *first* federal habeas corpus proceeding.[29] A federal petitioner also often is precluded from *de novo* federal relitigation of controlling factual (and, possibly, controlling legal[30]) issues if those issues were resolved in state courts after "full and fair" proceedings.[31] A well-developed body of federal court caselaw construing the habeas corpus statute recognizes that state proceedings are not sufficiently "full and fair" if an indigent prisoner was denied an adequate opportunity to adduce the relevant facts or legal claims, was obstructed by state officials in other ways, or was subjected to otherwise deficient or unconstitutional procedures.[32]

---

[29] *See* McFarland v. Scott, 512 U.S. 1256, 1261 (1994) (Blackmun, J., dissenting from denial of *certiorari*) ("State habeas corpus proceedings are a vital link in the capital review process, not the least because all federal habeas claims first must be adequately raised in state court ... [to avoid being denied in federal court as] procedurally defaulted or waived ...."); McFarland v. Scott, 512 U.S. 849, 860 (1994) (O'Connor, J., concurring in the judgment in part) ("our carefully crafted doctrines of waiver and abuse of the writ make it especially important that the first [federal habeas corpus] petition adequately set forth all of a state prisoner's colorable grounds for relief"); *infra* Chapters 23 (exhaustion of remedies doctrine), 26 (procedural default doctrine), 28 (successive petitions doctrine). On the need to raise all available claims in state proceedings before commencing an initial federal habeas corpus proceedings, see *supra* §§ 3.5a, 5.1a, 6.2. The preclusive effect of inadequately litigating the factual and legal aspects of federal constitutional claims in state postconviction proceedings — and the importance, generally, of state postconviction proceedings in determining the scope of federal habeas corpus review — has been greatly enhanced by a variety of provisions in the Antiterrorism and Effective Death Penalty Act (AEDPA), Pub. L. 104-132, 110 Stat. 1214 (1996). *See* provisions cited *supra* § 6.2 n.12. For an overview of AEDPA's habeas corpus provisions, see *supra* § 3.2. For discussion of AEDPA's especially preclusive provisions governing capital cases from States that qualify for opt-in treatment, see *supra* § 3.3.

[30] *See infra* § 9.2 & Chapter 27 (discussing rule of Stone v. Powell, 428 U.S. 465, 482, 494 (1976), under which federal habeas corpus relitigation of legal claims arising under 4th Amendment exclusionary rule is barred if state courts provided an "opportunity for full and fair litigation" of claims); *infra* § 30.2 (discussing 28 U.S.C. § 2254(d)(1) (West 1994 & Supp. 1998), which to some — as yet controversial and ill-defined — extent limits federal habeas corpus relitigation of some — as yet controversial and ill-defined — set of federal legal claims that were adjudicated on merits in state court proceedings).

[31] *See* Schiro v. Farley, 510 U.S. 222, 232 (1994) (*dicta*); Wainwright v. Witt, 469 U.S. 412, 426-27 (1985); Sumner v. Mata, 449 U.S. 539, 545 (1981); Townsend v. Sain, 372 U.S. 293, 312-13 (1963). *See generally supra* §§ 2.4b, 2.4d; § 7.1 n.1; *infra* §§ 20.1-20.3, 30.1, 30.3.

[32] *See infra* Chapter 30 (discussing caselaw developed under now superseded 28 U.S.C. § 2254(d)(1)-(8) and explaining that standards established by that caselaw continue to apply under current version of statute, 28 U.S.C.A. §§ 2254(d)(2), 2254(e) (West 1994 & Supp. 1998), and that inadequacy of state court hearing or hearing procedures warrants federal habeas corpus hearing); *infra* Chapter 27 & § 30.2b (discussing situations in which inadequate state procedures for

Because state postconviction proceedings are prisoner-initiated, and particularly because of the unforgiving nature of federal statutes and caselaw forbidding meaningful federal habeas corpus review in the wake of a default in state court, the responsibility to conduct a "full and fair" state postconviction proceeding on all available claims — and, failing that, to construct a record demonstrating how the state proceedings were *not* "full and fair" and why the state or the state courts bear the entire blame for the deficiencies — belongs to the petitioner, hence to counsel. Should counsel inexcusably fail to ask the state courts for relief on a particular claim, or to request some procedure or resource needed to litigate and adjudicate the claim in a procedurally full and fair manner, a federal habeas corpus court may penalize the prisoner by denying him that relief or that procedure or resource or by adopting a state court's inadequately premised factfinding or even, possibly, its admittedly erroneous legal determination.[33]

It is counsel's statutory as well as professional obligation, therefore, to insist upon a "full and fair" state proceeding — as defined not only by state law but also by the federal statute[34] and caselaw[35] that specify the attributes of a state proceeding that is sufficiently "full and fair" to preclude *de novo* federal relitigation.[36] Notwithstanding that the requested procedure or resource is expensive, far from routine, not explicitly authorized by state law, or (as often will be the case) almost certain to be denied,[37] counsel has the responsibility to

---

adjudicating federal legal claims bars application of judge-made and statutory limitations on federal habeas corpus relitigation of those claims). *See also infra* § 7.1b (due process obligations of state postconviction courts); *infra* § 7.2 (addressing question whether there is constitutional right to counsel in state postconviction proceedings).

[33] *See, e.g.*, Breard v. Greene, 118 S. Ct. 1352, 1354 (1998) (*per curiam*) (petitioner's failure to seek state court hearing on claim of violation of Vienna Convention barred federal hearing and thereby prevented petitioner from establishing facts essential for prevailing on claim); Keeney v. Tamayo-Reyes, 504 U.S. 1, 9-10 (1992) (petitioner's failure to request state postconviction hearing to establish facts showing that non-English speaking defendant pled guilty without understanding proceeding because court-provided "interpreter" had only rudimentary knowledge of Spanish bars federal hearing). *See generally* McFarland v. Scott, 512 U.S. 1256, 1263-64 (1994) (Blackmun, J., dissenting from denial of *certiorari*) ("Even the best lawyers [for federal habeas corpus petitioners] cannot rectify a meritorious constitutional claim that has been procedurally defaulted or waived by prior inadequate counsel [in state postconviction proceedings].... [I]t is the capital defendant who pays for the failings of counsel ... — generally with his life."). *See generally infra* Chapters 20, 30.

[34] *See* 28 U.S.C.A. §§ 2254(d)(1), 2254(e) (West 1994 & Supp. 1998) (discussed *infra* § 20.2).

[35] *See* Townsend v. Sain, 372 U.S. 293 (1963); other caselaw cited *infra* § 20.3e.

[36] *See generally infra* Chapters 20, 30.

[37] *See, e.g.*, McFarland v. Scott, 512 U.S. 1256, 1262 (1994) (Blackmun, J., dissenting from denial of *certiorari*) (although Texas statute authorizes "[f]unds for experts and other expenses" in state postconviction proceedings, state courts almost never grant requests for funds). If later federal habeas corpus proceedings are contemplated, then the fact that a particular claim or procedure is

request it, if she concludes that it is necessary to the "full and fair" litigation of a claim. If the request is denied, counsel's responsibility extends to making certain that the record, both at the postconviction trial level and on appeal, (i) reveals that the absence of the requested procedure and, generally, of a "full and fair" state proceeding is the fault of the state or the state courts, not the petitioner, and (ii) includes a detailed account, often by way of oral or written proffer supported by whatever physical and documentary evidence and affidavits can be made available, of the evidence or argument that the prisoner would have presented had she been permitted to do so and the prejudice the prisoner sustained as a result of being denied a full and fair proceeding.[38]

At the outset of state postconviction proceedings, counsel should identify the procedures and resources necessary to investigate the case fully and fairly; discover meritorious claims; ascertain the expert and other analyses, evidence, and testimony that effective litigation of those claims will require; and present that information in a meaningful manner, whether by way of an evidentiary hearing or some other procedure. Thereafter, counsel should request, formally and in writing, each of the necessary procedures and resources and explain *with specificity* why each is essential, what claim it relates to, what evidence is likely to be generated thereby, and, generally, how the "full and fair" litigation of one or more claims in the petition requires the requested procedure or resource.[39] If

---

likely or even virtually certain to be denied in the state courts is *not* a basis for failing to present the claim or request the procedure in state proceedings. *See, e.g.*, Engle v. Isaac, 456 U.S. 107, 130 (1982) (failure to raise claim in state court bars federal habeas corpus review of claim, notwithstanding that it would have been futile to raise claim in state courts given their repeated refusal to grant relief on same claim raised in prior proceedings). *See generally infra* Chapter 26.

[38] Although counsel certainly should not be vexatious, she should keep in mind the disposition of some federal courts to deny federal review of apparently meritorious factual issues that were seemingly litigated with care in prior proceedings, on the ground that the issues nonetheless could and should have been litigated with even *more* zeal. *See, e.g.*, McCleskey v. Zant, 499 U.S. 467 (1991) (petitioner denied relief in second federal habeas corpus petition, and ultimately executed, despite probably meritorious constitutional claim because, at time of initial state postconviction proceeding, counsel accepted state officials' word during discovery that they had not planted jailhouse informant in petitioner's cell, when in fact they had done so — as further investigation following completion of first habeas corpus proceeding belatedly revealed); Ross v. Kemp, 785 F.2d 1467 (11th Cir. 1985) (remand to determine whether state postconviction counsel were inexcusably neglectful because they did not subpoena records from court clerk who assured counsel (falsely, it turned out) that records did not exist); *infra* §§ 11.2a n.5, 11.3a nn.12-15 and accompanying text.

[39] Counsel should file her own, experts', investigators', or the client's affidavit attesting to as many of these matters as possible based on the affiant's knowledge or even, as a last resort, on "information and belief." *See infra* § 11.3a nn.12-15 and accompanying text. If disclosure of the information in the affidavits would reveal petitioner's case to the state without any "reciprocal discovery" from the state, it is appropriate to file such an affidavit under seal. *See generally* Wardius v. Oregon, 412 U.S. 470, 472 (1973); Simmons v. United States, 390 U.S. 377 (1968);

unsuccessful at the trial level, counsel should assert the denial of the requested procedures and resources as error not only in any postconviction appeal available within the state but also, as is discussed in the next subsection, on *certiorari* review in the United States Supreme Court following state postconviction review and in subsequent federal habeas corpus proceedings.

b. *Constitutional considerations.*[40] The absence or ineffectiveness of state postconviction remedies overcomes four doctrines that otherwise may preclude or at least drastically limit subsequent federal habeas corpus review or relief — (1) the requirement that habeas corpus review be postponed pending exhaustion of state remedies,[41] (2) the "adequate and independent state ground," or procedural default, rule barring habeas corpus relief on claims that were not raised in the state courts in the manner required by state law,[42] (3) the outright proscription against litigating 4th Amendment exclusionary rule claims in habeas corpus proceedings and the (as yet ill-defined) limitations that recent legislation places on the litigation of other legal claims,[43] and (4) the presumption of correctness of state court factfindings.[44] Accordingly, if available state postconviction remedies on their face or as applied offer an "[in]adequate corrective process for the hearing and determination of claims of violation of federal constitutional guarantees,"[45] it is counsel's obligation to argue the point

---

infra §§ 12.3a, 19.3. Exemplifying the potentially disastrous effects of counsel's failure to take the recommended steps is 28 U.S.C. § 2254(e)(2), which, except in very limited circumstances, denies evidentiary hearings to federal habeas corpus petitioners who previously "failed to develop the factual basis of a claim in State court proceedings." *See infra* § 20.2b nn.20-21, 23-40 and accompanying text.

[40] *See generally* RONALD P. SOKOL, FEDERAL HABEAS CORPUS 197 & n.164 (2d ed. 1969); LARRY W. YACKLE, POSTCONVICTION REMEDIES §§ 64-66 (1981 & Supp. 1998); Note, *Effect of the Federal Constitution in Requiring State Post-Conviction Remedies,* 53 COLUM. L. REV. 1143 (1953); authority cited *infra* § 7.2 n.1.

[41] *See* 28 U.S.C.A. § 2254(b)(1)(A) (West 1994 & Supp. 1998); *infra* § 23.4a.

[42] *See, e.g.*, Michel v. Louisiana, 350 U.S. 91, 93 (1955); *infra* § 26.2d.

[43] *See infra* §§ 27.3 (discussing Stone v. Powell, 428 U.S. 465, 482, 494 (1976)), 30.2b.

[44] *See* 28 U.S.C.A. §§ 2254(d)(2), 2254(e)(1) (West 1994 & Supp. 1998); *supra* § 2.5 nn.42-46 and accompanying text; *infra* §§ 20.3, 30.3. *See also* Keeney v. Tamayo-Reyes, 504 U.S. 1, 10 (1992) ("State must afford the petitioner a full and fair hearing on his federal claim," else federal rehearing of the facts is required); *id.* at 14-16 (O'Connor, J., dissenting); Hopkinson v. Shillinger, 866 F.2d 1185, 1220 (10th Cir. 1989), *cert. denied,* 497 U.S. 1010 (1990) ("Any deficiency in the state procedure would affect the presumption of correctness accorded the state court's findings"); Coleman v. Zant, 708 F.2d 541, 548 (11th Cir. 1983). A fifth preclusion doctrine — the harmless error rule — also might apply with less force in federal habeas corpus proceedings if the state courts did not provide any — or, possibly, adequate — review of the harmlessness issue. *See infra* § 32.1 n.18 and accompanying text.

[45] Case v. Nebraska, 381 U.S. 336, 337 (1965).

in state postconviction proceedings at the trial level or whenever inadequacies in the process become apparent and in all subsequent state court appeals.[46] Doing so might convince the state courts to utilize fairer proceedings, and, if not, will provide important clarification for purposes of later federal habeas corpus proceedings that inadequacies in the state procedures were the state courts' and not the petitioner's fault and, thus, that the four preclusion doctrines listed above cannot be applied to the petitioner. Arguing to the state courts that the State's inadequate corrective process violates federal constitutional law may serve another purpose, however — namely, exhausting that argument at the state level. Once the claim is presented and rejected in the state postconviction proceedings, the petitioner may be able — and, if so, is strongly advised — to raise it as a separate and independent basis either for the United States Supreme Court's *certiorari* review of the state postconviction decision,[47] or for habeas corpus

---

[46] *See generally supra* § 7.1a.

[47] Various provisions of the Antiterrorism and Effective Death Penalty Act (AEDPA), Pub. L. 104-132, 110 Stat. 1214 (1996), *see* provisions cited *supra* § 6.2 n.12; *see generally supra* § 3.2, and especially the statute's opt-in provisions that apply in capital habeas corpus cases in qualifying States, *see generally supra* § 3.3, limit the scope of habeas corpus review and relief based on an assumption that state postconviction proceedings afforded the prisoner a full and fair remedy for violations of federal law that occurred at the prisoner's criminal trial. If that assumption is wrong, AEDPA's limitations on habeas corpus review may effectively deny the prisoner *any* meaningful state *or* federal postconviction remedy. This state of affairs suddenly makes it crucial that prisoners denied full and fair review in state postconviction proceedings consider arguing that point as a separate ground for United States Supreme Court review on *certiorari* of the state court proceeding. *See generally supra* § 6.4. Although the Supreme Court has repeatedly acknowledged that the question whether inadequate state postconviction procedures violate the Constitution's Due Process, Equal Protection, and Suspension Clauses is a substantial issue worthy of the Court's *certiorari* review, *see* cases cited *infra* notes 51, 59, the Court has consistently declined to address the question because, *inter alia*, "if the State ... should ... deny all remedies to individuals imprisoned within the state in violation of the Constitution of the United States, the federal courts would be available to provide a remedy to correct such wrongs." Woods v. Niersheimer, 328 U.S. 211, 216 (1948). *See* Case v. Nebraska, 381 U.S. 336, 246 (1965) (Brennan, J., concurring). The real possibility that AEDPA has removed — or that lawyers for the state will argue in federal habeas corpus proceedings that AEDPA has removed — the longstanding federal habeas corpus backstop for deficient state postconviction proceedings both increases the importance of Supreme Court review of the question pretermitted in *Woods* and *Case* and undermines the Supreme Court's previously asserted reason for pretermitting the question. Doubts about the existence of a federal habeas corpus or other lower federal court forum for litigating the constitutionality of state postconviction proceedings, *see infra* note 48, enhance the importance of Supreme Court review on *certiorari* following state postconviction proceedings. Requests for Supreme Court review, in which the deficiencies of state postconviction procedures are made manifest, also may account for, or bolster, the Court's disposition in its initial interpretations of AEDPA to construe AEPDA narrowly. *See supra* §§ 2.2 n.13 and accompanying text, 3.2 nn.38-43 and accompanying text. For a good example of a capital prisoner's petition to the United States Supreme Court for *certiorari* review on this ground, see Petition for a Writ of Certiorari to the Texas Court of Criminal Appeals,

relief (irrespective of the argument's capacity to avoid preclusion doctrines as to other habeas corpus claims) — assuming that a writ of habeas corpus is an appropriate mechanism for providing the relief sought by such a claim.[48]

Colella v. Texas, No. 98-6463 (filed October 16, 1998) (on file with the Texas Defender Service, Houston, Texas).

[48] *See generally infra* Chapter 33 (habeas corpus remedies). The first of two "appropriate relief" questions arises because the immediate remedy sought as a result of the contemplated claim is not that traditionally available in habeas corpus proceedings, *i.e.*, a change in the prisoner's custodial status, but instead an expansion of state corrective processes. *See* Gibson v. Jackson, 578 F.2d 1045, 1046-47 (5th Cir. 1978), *cert. denied*, 439 U.S. 1119 (1979). Some federal courts, however, have permitted analogous habeas corpus actions seeking access to state corrective processes adequate to recognize constitutional violations and to order the prisoner's release from custody when that relief is appropriate. *See* Preiser v. Rodriguez, 411 U.S. 475, 499 (1973) (*dicta*) (challenges to the conditions of confinement, including limitations on the access of prisoners to legal remedies — the issue in Johnson v. Avery, 393 U.S. 483 (1969) — are cognizable in federal habeas corpus proceedings); Ex parte Hull, 312 U.S. 546, 548-49 (1941); Byrne v. Roemer, 847 F.2d 1130, 1133 n.1 (5th Cir. 1988); Lowe v. Letsinger, 772 F.2d 308, 312 (7th Cir. 1985); *infra* §§ 9.1. 33.1, 33.4, 41.2b. *Cf.* Lynott v. Story, 929 F.2d 228, 232-33 (6th Cir. 1991) (adjudicating habeas corpus claim challenging constitutionality of parole revocation hearing at which parole was revoked); other similar authority cited *infra* § 33.4 n.2. Nonetheless, the 5th Circuit has held that claims alleging the constitutional inadequacy of state postconviction procedures are *not* cognizable in habeas corpus suits and must be brought under 42 U.S.C. § 1983. *See* Gibson v. Jackson, *supra*; Ardister v. Hopper, 500 F.2d 229, 233 (5th Cir. 1974). Other circuits have followed the 5th Circuit's lead. *See, e.g.,* Hale v. Lockhart, 903 F.2d 545, 548 (8th Cir. 1990) (claim that delayed state postconviction review violated due process after reporter took excessive amount of time to provide trial transcript is not cognizable in habeas corpus); Williams-Bey v. Trickey, 894 F.2d 314, 317 (8th Cir.), *cert. denied*, 493 U.S. 1012 (1990) ("Section 2254 only authorizes federal courts to review the constitutionality of a state criminal conviction, not infirmities in a state post-conviction relief proceeding"); Franzen v. Brinkman, 877 F.2d 26 (9th Cir.) (*per curiam*), *cert. denied*, 493 U.S. 1102 (1989); Hopkinson v. Shillinger, 866 F.2d 1185, 1199-20 (10th Cir. 1989), *cert. denied*, 497 U.S. 1010 (1990); Bryant v. Maryland, 848 F.2d 492, 493 (4th Cir. 1988). *See also* authority cited *infra* § 9.1 nn.33-34 and accompanying text (constitutional claims that do not affect duration of confinement may be more properly brought in section 1983 than in habeas corpus proceedings); *infra* § 33.4. *But see* Dickerson v. Walsh, 750 F.2d 150, 153-54 (1st Cir. 1984) (equal protection challenge to state postconviction review procedures is cognizable in habeas corpus). Three relatively recent Supreme Court decisions suggest that federal courts should treat a challenge to the procedures utilized in state postconviction proceedings as cognizable and reviewable in habeas corpus. First is Ford v. Wainwright, 477 U.S. 399 (1986) (discussed *infra* notes 80-81 and accompanying text), in which the Court adjudicated and granted relief on a federal habeas corpus claim that the Due Process Clause requires a fair state postconviction procedure for determining that a capital prisoner is sufficiently "sane" to be executed. *Id.* at 414-17. *See id.* at 423-25 (Powell, J., concurring). Second is Herrera v. Collins, 506 U.S. 390 (1993), in which the Court adjudicated the merits of (but denied relief on) a federal habeas corpus claim that due process requires a fair state postconviction procedure for adjudicating the propriety of continuing to incarcerate or, at least, of executing a prisoner who can be shown via newly discovered evidence to be innocent. *See id.* at 410-11. Third, is Heck v. Humphrey, 512 U.S. 477 (1993) (discussed *infra* § 9.1 n.6), in which the Supreme Court held that habeas corpus and not section 1983 proceedings are the proper

Alternatively to pursuing the claim in a federal habeas corpus petition, the

forum for actions that may have, as a direct *or collateral* effect, a determination that the moving party's incarceration, or the length of incarceration, violates federal law. *See generally infra* § 9.1 n.6.

If the jurisdictional hurdle is cleared, a petitioner challenging the adequacy of state postconviction remedies via habeas corpus has to overcome federal habeas corpus courts' traditional reluctance, on prudential grounds, to order state courts to hold hearings or provide otherwise unavailable procedures. *See, e.g.,* Hull v. Freeman, 932 F.2d 159, 170 n.9 (3d Cir. 1991) ("if an evidentiary hearing is necessary in a federal habeas case to resolve a disputed factual question, it should be held in federal district court, rather than state court.... In the habeas context, comity requires only that the state courts be given the first chance to review federal claims. 'There is no requirement, however, that they be given more than one opportunity to adjudicate these claims.'"); Keller v. Petsock, 853 F.2d 1122, 1129-30 (3d Cir. 1988) (when state fails to hold hearing, federal court should conduct hearing and has no authority to require state to hold one); Smart v. Scully, 787 F.2d 816, 821 (2d Cir. 1986); Grigsby v. Mabry, 637 F.2d 525 (8th Cir. 1980) ("preference" for providing missing procedure in federal courts instead of remanding to state court with directions to provide those procedures); Dixon v. Beto, 472 F.2d 598, 599 (5th Cir. 1973). *See also* Purkett v. Elem, 514 U.S. 765, 776 (1995) (Stevens, J., dissenting) (as "Court's opinion today implicitly ratifies," when state court failed to make determination critical to resolution of constitutional question, federal habeas corpus court properly made that determination "on its own" rather than "grant[ing] the writ conditioned on a proper [determination of issue] ... in the state ... court"); Love v. Johnson, 57 F.3d 1305, 1316 (4th Cir. 1995) (discussed *infra* § 33.4 n.2). *Cf.* Smith v. Wyrick, 693 F.2d 808 (8th Cir. 1982), *cert. denied,* 460 U.S. 1024 (1983). Federal courts, however, occasionally give state courts the choice of either providing adequate corrective procedures or releasing the prisoner from custody on a federal writ of habeas corpus. *See Gibson v. Jackson, supra,* 578 F.2d at 1048-49 (addendum of Rubin, J.) (citing cases); other authority cited *infra* note 72 and *infra* § 33.4 n.2 and accompanying text. *See also Preiser v. Rodriguez, supra* at 487-99 (habeas corpus preferred over section 1983 suit because former remedy's exhaustion requirement affords state courts initial opportunity to cure any illegality). In a well-known article discussing this and other issues, Judge J. Skelly Wright and Abraham D. Sofaer argued that the resolution of the question whether, in lieu of holding a full and fair hearing themselves, the federal courts may order the state courts to conduct a hearing, merges with the question whether there is a constitutional right to an adequate state postconviction procedure. J. Skelly Wright & Abraham D. Sofaer, *Federal Habeas Corpus for State Prisoners: The Allocation of Fact-Finding Responsibility,* 75 YALE L.J. 895, 906-19 (1966). Citing as examples Jackson v. Denno, 378 U.S. 368 (1964) (Due Process Clause requires that trial judges resolve question whether confessions are voluntary in hearings outside presence of jurors; ordering prisoner released unless state court holds proper hearing) and Rogers v. Richmond, 365 U.S. 534 (1961) (hearing and factfindings supporting determination that confession was voluntary were tainted by trial judge's application of unconstitutional legal standard; ordering prisoner released unless new hearing was held and new factfindings were made pursuant to correct legal standard), Wright and Sofaer point out that a determination that a procedure is important enough that the federal courts may require the state courts to use it amounts to a determination that the absence of the procedure violates the Due Process Clause or some other provision of the Constitution. Wright & Sofaer, *supra* at 906-19. This analysis suggests that reaching the conclusion advocated in text — that a constitutional right to adequate state postconviction proceedings exists — would compel the supplementary conclusion that the federal courts have the authority to order the state courts to conduct such proceedings.

petitioner might present the claim to a federal court in a separate (albeit, possibly, simultaneous) civil rights action under 42 U.S.C. § 1983.[49]

An "inadequate state corrective process" argument might arise, *inter alia*, if: (1) the State provides *no* postconviction means of raising all or certain kinds of federal constitutional issues;[50] (2) the state procedure does not afford indigent petitioners a transcript of the trial proceeding; (3) competent appointed counsel and adequate public funds for experts, witnesses, and investigators are not available to enable indigent prisoners to make a meaningful case for postconviction relief; (4) the state postconviction remedy does not include the right to an evidentiary hearing or to some other meaningful method of adjudicating dispositive factual allegations; (5) state law or the state courts unduly restrict the evidence that can be introduced at postconviction hearings; (6) state jurisdictional requirements, limitations on cognizable claims, pleading rules, briefing restrictions, procedural default doctrines, or other rules or procedures are insufficiently hospitable to the adequate development and litigation of federal constitutional claims;[51] or (7) in capital cases, the state

---

[49] There are important procedural differences between habeas corpus and section 1983 actions. In capital cases, for example, the habeas corpus route has the advantage of a more established procedure for granting stays of execution. *See* 28 U.S.C. § 2251 (1994). On the other hand, the section 1983 approach avoids the habeas corpus statute's requirement of exhaustion of state judicial remedies. *Compare* 28 U.S.C. § 2254(b)(1)(A) (West 1994 & Supp. 1998) *with* Monroe v. Pape, 365 U.S. 167, 183 (1961). Exhaustion nonetheless is recommended to avoid any suspicion that the section 1983 route was taken in order to avoid habeas corpus' exhaustion requirement, rather than being used to avoid the difficult relief questions discussed *supra* note 48. *See generally* Heck v. Humphrey, 512 U.S. 477 (1994); *Preiser v. Rodriguez, supra,* 411 U.S. at 487-99 & n.14; *infra* §§ 9.1 nn.33-34 and accompanying text, 33.4.

[50] *See, e.g.,* 28 U.S.C.A. § 2254(b)(1)(B)(i) (West 1994 & Supp. 1998); Young v. Ragen, 337 U.S. 235, 239 (1949); Carter v. Illinois, 329 U.S. 173, 176 (1946). *See also Ex parte Hull, supra,* 312 U.S. at 549 (voiding prison rule that hampered state prisoner's ability to file state and federal postconviction petitions).

[51] *See generally* Case v. Nebraska, 381 U.S. 336, 337-47 (1965) (Brennan and Clark, JJ., concurring); United States ex rel. Herman v. Claudy, 350 U.S. 116, 119 (1956); Young v. Ragen, 337 U.S. 235 (1949); Grigsby v. Mabry, 637 F.2d 525 (8th Cir. 1980); *Gibson v. Jackson, supra,* 578 F.2d at 1048-49 (addendum of Rubin, J.); Hart v. Eyman, 458 F.2d 334, 340 (9th Cir.), *cert. denied,* 407 U.S. 916 (1972); Buchanan v. United States ex rel. Reis, 379 F.2d 612 (5th Cir. 1967); other cases cited *infra* note 59; *infra* §§ 7.2, 12.4, 26.2d. Suggesting the invalidity of state procedural rules or devices that are designed or serve to frustrate the adequate litigation of federal constitutional claims, are, *e.g.,* Ford v. Georgia, 498 U.S. 411, 423 (1991) (refusing to recognize default of state procedural rule with which petitioner could not reasonably have been expected to comply); Terrell v. Morris, 493 U.S. 1, 2 (1989) (similar); Ward v. Commissioners of Love County, 253 U.S. 17, 22 (1920) ("It therefore is within our province to inquire ... whether the [federal] right was denied [by the state court] in substance and effect, as by putting forward nonfederal [procedural] grounds of decision that were without any fair or substantial support"); Enterprise Irrigation Dist. v. Canal Co., 243 U.S. 157, 164 (1917) (adjudication of federal claim

courts' practice of refusing stays of execution pending litigation of state postconviction petitions so truncates the proceedings as to render them incapable of providing orderly and effective review of meritorious federal claims.[52] Deficits in the state remedial process such as these seven might lead the Supreme Court or a lower federal court to find a violation of the 14th Amendment or perhaps the Suspension Clause[53] for the reasons that we outline in the next paragraph, or for the reasons developed at greater length in §§ 7.2b-7.2f *infra* for concluding that one particular deficit (the denial of state postconviction counsel and other financial assistance) is unconstitutional. The next paragraph and § 7.2 *infra* accordingly should be consulted by readers interested in the constitutionality of either a particular State's postconviction procedures or the procedures actually used in a particular state postconviction case. In the remainder of this section, we explain why the existence and scope of a constitutional right to fair state postconviction proceedings remains an open question, notwithstanding Justice, thereafter Chief Justice, Rehnquist's *dicta* in *Pennsylvania v. Finley*[54] for a majority of the Court and in *United States v. MacCollom*[55] and *Murray v. Giarratano*[56] for pluralities, that States have no 14th Amendment obligation to provide postconviction procedures.[57]

---

may not be frustrated by "mere device to prevent a review of the decision upon the federal question"); authority cited *infra* § 26.2d nn.23, 44-51, 54 and accompanying text.

[52] *See generally* McFarland v. Scott, 512 U.S. 849, 851-59 (1994) (describing and overturning certain 'Catch-22' aspects of Texas' and 5th Circuits' stay procedures in capital cases); Anthony G. Amsterdam, *In Favorem Mortis: The Supreme Court and Capital Punishment*, 14 A.B.A. SEC. INDIVIDUAL RTS. & RESP. 14 (1987); Note, *Summary Processes and the Rule of Law: Expediting Death Penalty Cases in the Federal Courts*, 95 YALE L.J. 349 (1985); *infra* note 60. For an example of a constitutional challenge, based on the third and sixth deficiencies listed in text, to a state postconviction proceeding, see Petition for a Writ of Certiorari to the Texas Court of Criminal Appeals in Colella v. Texas, *supra* note 47.

[53] U.S. CONST., art. I, § 9, cl. 2.

[54] 481 U.S. 551 (1987).

[55] 426 U.S. 317 (1976).

[56] 492 U.S. 1 (1989).

[57] *Giarratano*, *supra*, 492 U.S. at 10-11 (1989) (plurality decision) ("State collateral proceedings are not constitutionally required...."); *Finley*, *supra*, 481 U.S. at 557 ("States have no obligation to provide this [postconviction] avenue of relief, cf. United States v. MacCollom, 426 U.S. 317, 323 (1976) (plurality opinion)"); *MacCollom*, *supra*, 426 U.S. at 323 (plurality opinion) ("Due Process Clause of the Fifth Amendment does not establish any right ... to collaterally attack a final judgment of conviction" (citation and footnote omitted)). *See also* Williams-Bey v. Trickey, 894 F.2d 314, 317 (8th Cir. 1989), *cert. denied*, 495 U.S. 936 (1990) ("there is no federal constitutional requirement that states provide a means of post-conviction review of state convictions"); Smith v. Lockhart, 882 F.2d 331, 334 (8th Cir. 1989), *cert. denied*, 493 U.S. 1028 (1990) (similar).

The germinal bases for finding a constitutional right to full and fair state postconviction procedures are the concurring opinions by Justices Clark and Brennan in the Supreme Court's 1965 decision in *Case v. Nebraska*.[58] In *Case*, the Court granted a writ of *certiorari* precisely in order to decide whether the Constitution requires States to provide a postconviction remedy that offers an "adequate corrective process for the hearing ... of federal constitutional guarantees" and, if so, what constitutes an "adequate" process.[59] Because the Nebraska legislature passed a comprehensive postconviction statute after *certiorari* was granted, the Court dismissed the writ as improvidently granted. In their concurring opinions, however, Justices Clark and Brennan concluded that, and explained why, the Constitution mandates full, fair, and adequate state postconviction procedures.[60]

---

[58] 381 U.S. 336 (1965).

[59] Several earlier decisions had suggested that the Constitution, particularly the Due Process Clause of the 14th Amendment, mandates an "adequate corrective process." *See* United States ex rel. Herman v. Claudy, 350 U.S. 116, 119 (1956) (suggesting cognizability of claimed "denial of ... constitutional protections ... in a [state postconviction] proceeding"); Young v. Ragen, 337 U.S. 235, 239 (1949); Foster v. Illinois, 332 U.S. 134, 138 (1947) (State's withholding of judicial remedy for constitutional violations occurring at criminal trials that are provable only by extra-record evidence supports "new claim of denial of due process for want of such relief"); Carter v. Illinois, 329 U.S. 173, 174 (1946) ("A State must give one whom it deprives of his freedom the opportunity to open an inquiry into the intrinsic fairness of a criminal process even though it appears proper on the surface."); Woods v. Nierstheimer, 328 U.S. 211, 217 (1946) (granting *certiorari* to decide whether state court's summary dismissals deprived petitioner of adequate postconviction remedy; writ dismissed after Court determined that other state remedies remained); Mooney v. Holohan, 294 U.S. 103, 113 (1935); Frank v. Mangum, 237 U.S. 309, 334 (1915). *See also* Kyles v. Whitley, 498 U.S. 931, 932 (1990) (Stevens, J., concurring in denial of application for stay) ("scope of the state's obligation to provide collateral review is shrouded in ... uncertainty"); Ex parte Hull, 312 U.S. 546, 549 (1941); other decisions cited *infra* note 73-74, 80-83.

[60] *Case, supra*, 381 U.S. at 340-47 & nn.5-6 (Brennan, J., concurring); *id.* at 337-40 (Clark, J., concurring). The concurring opinions in *Case* suggest that, to be effective, the state postconviction remedy:

> should be sufficiently comprehensive to embrace all federal constitutional claims. In light of Fay v. Noia, [372 U.S. 391 (1963)], it should eschew rigid and technical doctrines of forfeiture, waiver, or default. *See* Douglas v. Alabama, 380 U.S. 415, 422-423 (1965); Henry v. Mississippi, [379 U.S. 443 (1965)]. It should provide for full fact hearings to resolve disputed factual issues, and for compilation of a record to enable federal courts to determine the sufficiency of those hearings. Townsend v. Sain, [372 U.S. 293 (1963)]. It should provide for decisions supported by opinions, or fact findings and conclusions of law, which disclose the grounds of decision and the resolution of disputed facts. Provision for counsel to represent prisoners, as in § 4 of the Nebraska Act, would enhance the probability of effective presentation and a proper disposition of prisoners' claims.

Case, supra at 347 (Brennan, J., concurring). *Accord id.* at 339 (Clark, J., concurring). *See* Gibson v. Jackson, 578 F.2d 1045, 1048-49 (5th Cir. 1978), *cert. denied*, 439 U.S. 1119 (1979) (addendum

Just as *Case* did not finally resolve the issue in favor of a constitutional right to postconviction procedures, neither have Justice/Chief Justice Rehnquist's three *dicta* authoritatively established the contrary. To begin with, none of the three cases presented the question whether there is a constitutional right to postconviction review of some sort. *MacCollom* (announced in 1976) presented only the constitutionality of a federal statute requiring indigent prisoners to plead a nonfrivolous claim before receiving a free transcript for use in federal postconviction proceedings.[61] *Finley* (announced in 1987) presented only the question whether a Pennsylvania statute that provides prisoners with an extensive postconviction remedy and a right to counsel was deficient in not also requiring appointed counsel and the trial judge to undertake a complex series of actions before concluding that a postconviction case was frivolous.[62] *Giarratano* (announced in 1989) presented only the question whether Virginia's provision of counsel through a prisoners' legal services office to death row inmates seeking state postconviction review satisfied the Constitution.[63] Second, only a minority of Justices joined the opinions in *MacCollom* and *Giarratano*, and the opinion for the Court in *Finley* offered no authority or analysis in favor of its acknowledged *dictum* other than a citation to the same author's plurality opinion in *MacCollom*.[64] Third, the *dictum* in the plurality opinion in *MacCollom* — the sole support for the *dictum* in *Finley* — based its "no due process right" conclusion on the (unexplained) view that the Suspension Clause alone, and never the Due Process Clause, controls "[t]he constitutional treatment of habeas corpus."[65] And the sum total of the analysis in the two later opinions (aside from *Finley*'s citation of *MacCollom* and *Giarratano*'s citation of *Finley*) is the conclusional sentence from each quoted in footnote 57 above. Because none of the opinions, nor any other decision of the Court, addresses the bearing of the Suspension Clause on state postconviction proceedings or moves beyond mere assertion in addressing the 14th Amendment question, and because the Court elsewhere has indicated that the Due Process Clause *does* sometimes determine the constitutionality of state postconviction proceedings,[66] the three opinions

---

of Rubin, J.); decisions cited *infra* note 72. *See generally* ABA STANDARDS FOR CRIMINAL JUSTICE, *supra* § 7.1a n.22, §§ 2-1.1 to 1.4 and commentary.

[61] *See MacCollom, supra*, 426 U.S. at 319.

[62] *See Finley, supra*, 481 U.S. at 554-55.

[63] *See Giarratano, supra*, 492 U.S. at 3-4. *See generally infra* § 7.2a.

[64] *Finley, supra*, 481 U.S. at 557 (citing *MacCollom, supra*, 426 U.S. at 323). *See id.* at 557, 558 (acknowledging *obiter dicta* quality of opinion's "no constitutional right" ruminations by proceeding to "assum[e *arguendo*] ... that the Due Process Clause *is* relevant" and to hold that Pennsylvania's extensive postconviction procedures "comport[] with fundamental fairness"). *See also infra* § 7.2a.

[65] *MacCollom, supra*, 426 U.S. at 323.

[66] *See* authority cited *supra* note 59 & *infra* notes 74-83 and accompanying text.

rather clearly did not authoritatively decide whether a right to state postconviction review exists under some provision of the Constitution. The three opinions' unnecessary, unsupported, and incomplete assertions — in the process of deciding cases that did not present the question and in which counsel did not address it — thus cannot be said to have resolved what the Court in *Case* identified as a substantial enough matter to merit plenary consideration following briefing and argument by interested parties.[67] At this point, therefore, the only conclusion that can be reached is the one Justice Stevens offered the year after *Giarratano*, namely that, as yet, "the scope of the state's obligation to provide collateral review is shrouded in ... uncertainty."[68]

Even if a State need never provide a postconviction means of challenging the constitutionality of a conviction or sentence, if it chooses to do so, the Due Process Clause might require that the chosen means be full and fair.[69] The

---

[67] *See supra* note 59 and accompanying text. *See also* Brown v. Wainwright, 785 F.2d 1457, 1458 n.2, 1467 (11th Cir. 1986) (indicating that question is substantial); *infra* § 7.2a.

[68] Kyles v. Whitley, 498 U.S. 931, 932 (1990) (Stevens, J., concurring in denial of application for stay) ("Because the scope of the state's obligation to provide collateral review is shrouded in so much uncertainty, ... this Court rarely grants review at this stage of the litigation even when the application for state collateral relief is supported by arguably meritorious federal constitutional claims.").

[69] *See, e.g.,* Goeke v. Branch, 514 U.S. 115, 120 (1995) (*per curiam*) (*dicta*) (discussed *infra* § 7.2e n.89); O'Connell v. Kirchner, 513 U.S. 1138 (1995) (O'Connor, J., dissenting from denial of stay) (assuming availability of some federal constitutional challenges to procedural fairness of state habeas corpus proceeding); O'Connell v. Kirchner, 513 U.S. 1303, 1304 (1995) (Stevens, J., Circuit Justice, denying motion to recall mandate and for stay) (addressing merits of applicants' "procedural due process theory" that state habeas corpus proceeding unconstitutionally denied them "liberty interest ... absent a full and fair hearing" but finding that "exhaustive proceedings in the [state] courts" gave applicants "all process due them under federal law"); Ford v. Wainwright, 477 U.S. 399, 428-31 (1986) (O'Connor, J., concurring) (citing cases); Evitts v. Lucey, 469 U.S. 387, 401 (1985) (although States need not provide appeals, if they do, Due Process Clause requires that appeals conform to dictates of fundamental fairness and, accordingly, that counsel be made available and render effective assistance); *id.* at 396 ("[W]hen a State opts to act in a field where its action has significant discretionary elements, it must nonetheless act in accord with the dictates of the Constitution — and, in particular, act in accord with the Due Process Clause."); Hicks v. Oklahoma, 447 U.S. 343, 346 (1979) (although Constitution does not mandate jury sentencing, when state statute adopts that procedure, it creates "substantial and legitimate expectation," protected by Due Process Clause, that defendants will be afforded its benefits); Douglas v. California, 372 U.S. 353 (1963); Blair v. Armontrout, 916 F.2d 1310, 1335 n.3 (8th Cir. 1990), *cert. denied,* 502 U.S. 825 (1991) (Heaney, J., concurring in part and dissenting in part) ("[w]hile there is no absolute right to the appointment of counsel in [postconviction] proceedings, ... the absence of a general right to appointment does not mean that once counsel is appointed, no restraints imposed by law remain on his representation"; petitioner "has persuasive grounds" for due process challenge based on [prior] counsel's "deception of him."); Gibson v. Jackson, 578 F.2d 1045, 1054 n.3 (5th Cir. 1978) (addendum of Rubin, J.), *cert. denied,* 439 U.S. 1119 (1979); Welch v. Beto, 355 F.2d 1016, 1020 (5th Cir.), *cert. denied,* 385 U.S. 839 (1966) ("Having

importance of fundamentally fair state proceedings is clear given that it is the "'solemn duty of [state] courts, no less than federal ones, to safeguard personal liberties and consider federal claims in accord with federal law.'"[70] Because the federal system entrusts state courts with initial and *primary* responsibility for enforcing federal constitutional rights in the course of administering the States' criminal justice systems,[71] the integrity of federal law arguably requires that state courts have the capacity to exercise a broad postconviction jurisdiction capable of fully and fairly adjudicating the federal claims of state prisoners. In recognition of these principles, lower federal habeas corpus courts occasionally have granted petitioners relief in the form of remands to the state courts to provide the postconviction procedures that, it is argued here, the Constitution requires — including adequate hearings and other devices necessary to meaningful factfinding.[72] And notwithstanding the availability of federal habeas corpus, the Supreme Court has reversed state court decisions that denied an

---

invoked the Texas statutes granting post-conviction hearings, [petitioner] had the right to be tried according to the substantive and procedural due process requirements of the Fourteenth Amendment."). *But cf.* Coleman v. Thompson, 501 U.S. 722, 755-57 (1991) (except possibly in limited circumstances, process due during state postconviction proceedings does not include right to effective assistance of counsel); *Finley, supra*, 481 U.S. at 556-59 (doubting whether procedural due process norms apply to state postconviction procedures but proceeding to "assume" that norms do apply and to find them satisfied by ample procedures in Pennsylvania's postconviction statute).

[70] Schneckloth v. Bustamonte, 412 U.S. 218, 259 (1973) (Powell, J., concurring) (citation omitted). *See* Mooney v. Holohan, 294 U.S. 103, 113 (1935) ("Upon the state courts [meaning, in the context of the case, state postconviction courts], equally with the courts of the Union, rests the obligation to guard and enforce every right secured by th[e] Constitution."). *See also* Caspari v. Bohlen, 510 U.S. 383, 394-96 (1994); Teague v. Lane, 489 U.S. 288, 309 (1989) (plurality opinion); Murray v. Carrier, 477 U.S. 478, 489 (1986) (quoting Rose v. Lundy, 455 U.S. 509, 518 (1982)); Carter v. Estelle, 677 F.2d 427, 441 (5th Cir. 1982).

[71] *See, e.g.*, McFarland v. Scott, 512 U.S. 849, 859 (1994) (quoting Barefoot v. Estelle, 463 U.S. 880, 887 (1983)); Brecht v. Abrahamson, 507 U.S. 619, 635 (1993) ("'In criminal trials [the States] hold the initial responsibility for vindicating constitutional rights.'" (quoting Engle v. Isaac, 456 U.S. 107, 128 (1982)); Rose v. Lundy, 455 U.S. 509, 518 (1982); Stone v. Powell, 428 U.S. 465, 494 n.35 (1976). For discussions of the essentially appellate, hence in that sense secondary, responsibility of the federal courts via habeas corpus to protect federal rights that already have been the subject of plenary consideration by the state courts, see *supra* §§ 2.2, 2.4.

[72] *See, e.g.*, United States ex rel. McQueen v. Wangelin, 527 F.2d 579, 581 (8th Cir. 1975); Hart v. Eyman, 458 F.2d 334, 340 (9th Cir.), *cert. denied*, 407 U.S. 916 (1972); Buchanan v. United States ex rel. Reis, 379 F.2d 612 (5th Cir. 1967). *But cf.* authority cited *supra* note 48 (suggesting that only habeas corpus writs actually or conditionally releasing prisoners from custody or, possibly, damages or injunctions under section 1983, and not habeas corpus remands, are statutorily available modes of redress for state postconviction inadequacies).

adequate hearing to state prisoners raising federal claims in state postconviction proceedings.[73]

Finally, even if the Constitution has nothing to say on the question whether States must provide state postconviction procedures or on whether any procedures they *do* provide must be minimally fair, the Constitution clearly does require that any — or at least the initial — direct appellate procedure that a State provides defendants as of right must meet minimal standards of fairness and due process.[74] And, in *dicta* in *Coleman v. Thompson*,[75] the Court recognized that those same constitutional norms also might apply to state postconviction procedures whenever it is the case that "state collateral review is the first place a prisoner can present a challenge to his conviction" and thus whenever "a state collateral proceeding may be considered" the prisoner's "'one and only appeal.'"[76] Because the law of a number of States requires "that some claims ordinarily heard on direct review" — most usually, ineffective assistance at trial or on appeal[77] — "be relegated to postconviction proceedings" and because

---

[73] *See, e.g.*, Johnson v. Mississippi, 486 U.S. 578 (1988) (discussed *infra* notes 82-83 and accompanying text); Yates v. Aiken, 484 U.S. 211 (1988) (state postconviction courts implicitly faulted for failure to provide remedy for constitutional violations identified in recent, retroactive United States Supreme Court decisions); Tison v. Arizona, 481 U.S. 137 (1987); Truesdale v. Aiken, 480 U.S. 527 (1987); Rogers v. Richmond, 365 U.S. 534 (1961) (discussed *supra* note 48); Wilde v. Wyoming, 362 U.S. 607 (1960); Sublett v. Adams, 362 U.S. 143 (1960); Cash v. Culver, 358 U.S. 633 (1959); Pennsylvania ex rel. Herman v. Claudy, 350 U.S. 116 (1956); Palmer v. Ashe, 342 U.S. 134 (1951); Hawk v. Olson, 326 U.S. 271 (1945); Pyle v. Kansas, 317 U.S. 213 (1942); Cochran v. Kansas, 316 U.S. 255 (1942); Smith v. O'Grady, 312 U.S. 329 (1941); other authority cited *supra* note 59.

[74] *See, e.g.*, Evitts v. Lucey, 469 U.S. 387, 393 (1985); Douglas v. California, 372 U.S. 353, 356 (1963); other authority cited *supra* note 69 & *infra* § 9.1 n.28.

[75] 501 U.S. 722 (1991).

[76] *Id.* at 755-56 (quoting *Douglas v. California, supra*, 372 U.S. at 357). *See infra* § 26.3b n.36 and accompanying text (further developing implications of *Coleman*'s failure to resolve this issue). The Court did not have to reach the question in *Coleman* because the petitioner clearly had been afforded the due process right at issue — the effective assistance of counsel — in the initial, trial-level, state postconviction proceeding, thus giving him all the process that was due in "his 'one and only appeal.'" In rejecting Coleman's right to relief based on ineffective assistance during his postconviction *appeal*, the Court concluded that, apart from state postconviction's possible service as a substitute "'one and only appeal,'" there is no constitutionally protected right to the effective assistance of counsel in state postconviction proceedings. *See id.* But *cf. supra* note 69 and accompanying text. Refusing to recognize a constitutional right to competent counsel in state postconviction proceedings that effectively serve as the prisoner's first posttrial opportunity to raise a claim are Mackall v. Anderson, 131 F.2d 442, 448-49 (4th Cir. 1997) (*en banc*), *cert. denied*, 118 S. Ct. 907 (1998) (over two dissents); Hill v. Jones, 81 F.3d 1015, 1025-26 (11th Cir.1996), *cert. denied*, 117 S. Ct. 967 (1997); Bonin v. Vasquez, 999 F.2d 425, 430 (9th Cir. 1993).

[77] *See generally infra* §§ 26.3b nn.32, 41, 41.4a n.7. State decisions prohibiting claims of ineffective assistance of counsel from being considered on direct appeal under any circumstances and relegating them to postconviction proceedings include: Champion v. State, 908 P.2d 454, 470

"some irregularities, such as prosecutorial misconduct, may not surface until after direct review is complete,"[78] there frequently *are* claims for which state postconviction necessarily serves as the prisoner's "'one and only appeal'" and, accordingly, as to which state postconviction procedures arguably ought to adhere to the constitutional norms of fairness and due process that apply on direct appeal.[79] The Supreme Court's 1986 decision in *Ford v. Wainwright*,[80] supports this analysis. In *Ford*, confronting a claim likely to arise for the first time only after direct appeal, the Court held both that the States may not constitutionally execute an individual who became insane following trial and that they must afford minimally adequate postconviction procedures for assessing the sanity of condemned prisoners prior to their execution.[81] And, addressing another claim typically litigated after direct appeal, the Court's 1988 decision in *Johnson v. Mississippi*[82] faulted Mississippi for lacking a

---

(Alaska App. 1995); State v. Goetis, 930 P.2d 1324, 1327 (Ariz. Ct. App. 1996), *app. denied*, 938 P.2d 1110 (Ariz. 1997); Jackson v. State, 654 A.2d 829, 832 (Del. 1995); Lawrence v. State, 691 So.2d 1068, 1074 (Fla. 1997); Connell v. State, 691 So.2d 1004, 1006-07 (Miss. 1997); State v. Hurt, 931 S.W.2d 213, 214 (Mo. Ct. App. 1996); Edwards v. State, 918 P.2d 321, 324 (Nev. 1996); State v. Malstrom, 672 A.2d 448, 450 (R.I. 1996); State v. Kornahrens, 350 S.E.2d 180, 184 (S.C. 1986), *cert. denied*, 480 U.S. 940 (1987); Roach v. Commonwealth, 468 S.E.2d 98, 105 n.4 (Va.), *cert. denied*, 117 S. Ct. 365 (1996). State decisions allowing the consideration of ineffectiveness claims on direct appeal only if all the facts necessary to adjudicate the claim are in the trial record, while relegating all other such claims to postconviction proceedings, include: State v. Silva, 864 P.2d 583, 592-93 (Haw. 1993); State v. Pugsley, 911 P.2d 761 (Ida. 1995); People v. Kunze, 550 N.E.2d 284, 296 (Ill. App. Ct.), *app. denied*, 132 Ill. 2d 550 (1990); State v. Dinkins, 553 N.W.2d 339, 340 (Iowa Ct. App. 1996); State v. Hernandez, 686 So.2d 92, 94 (La. Ct. App. 1996); State v. Jordan, 659 A.2d 849, 851-52 (Me. 1995); Hunt v. State, 583 A.2d 218 (Md. 1990), *cert. denied*, 502 U.S. 835 (1991); Commonwealth v. Adamides, 639 N.E.2d 1092, 1096 (Mass. App. Ct. 1994); State v. Courchene, 847 P.2d 271, 275-76 (Mont. 1992); State v. Dawn, 519 N.W.2d 249, 256 (Neb. 1994); State v. Sparano, 592 A.2d 608, 613 (N.J. Super. Ct. App. Div. 1991); People v. Alicea, 656 N.Y.S.2d 2 (N.Y. App. Div. 1997); State v. House, 456 S.E.2d 292, 297 (N.C. 1995); State v. Bengson, 541 N.W.2d 702, 703 (N.D. 1996); State v. Murhagan, 584 N.E.2d 1204, 1208 (Ohio 1992); State v. Pettypool, 676 P.2d 368, 368-69 (Or. 1984); State v. McGill, 536 N.W.2d 89, 94 (S.D. 1995); Curtis v. State, 909 S.W.2d 465, 468-69 (Tenn. Crim. App. 1995); M.B. v. State, 905 S.W.2d 344, 346 (Tex. Ct. Crim. App. 1995); Salt Lake City v. Grutepas, 874 P.2d 136, 138 (Utah Ct. App. 1994), *rev'd on other grounds*, 906 P.2d 890 (Utah 1995); State v. Bacon, 658 A.2d 54, 66 (Vt.), *cert. denied*, 516 U.S. 837 (1995); State v. Miller, 476 S.E. 535, 558 (W. Va. 1996).

[78] Murray v. Giarratano, 492 U.S. 1, 24 (1989) (Stevens, J., dissenting).

[79] *See generally infra* § 7.2e nn.94-96 and accompanying text; *infra* § 9.1 nn.21, 26, 28, 33, 34; *infra* § 25.4 nn.40-45 and accompanying text; *infra* § 26.3b nn.30, 32, 41; *infra* §§ 33.3 n.11, 33.4 n.2, 41.4a n.7 (all discussing claims likely to become reviewable for first time in state postconviction proceedings).

[80] 477 U.S. 399 (1986).

[81] *Id.* at 414-17. *See id.* at 423-25 (Powell, J., concurring).

[82] 486 U.S. 578 (1988).

postconviction procedure in which a prisoner could secure relief from a death sentence that was premised in part on a prior conviction later held to be unconstitutional.[83]

§ 7.2.   The indigent's right to counsel and financial assistance.[1]

a. *Introduction; Supreme Court views.* Section 7.1a *supra* discusses counsel's professional obligation in appropriate circumstances to seek an

---

[83] *Id.* at 587-88. *Ford* and *Johnson* may suggest that adequate state corrective processes are particularly important in capital cases. *See* Monge v. California, 118 S. Ct. 2246, 2252 (1998) ("'capital proceedings [must] be policed at all stages by an especially vigilant concern for procedural fairness and for the accuracy of factfinding.'"); McFarland v. Scott, 512 U.S. 1256, 1261 (1994) (Blackmun, J., dissenting from denial of *certiorari*) ("State habeas corpus proceedings are a vital link in the capital review process ...."); Murray v. Giarratano, 492 U.S. 1, 14 (1989) (Kennedy, J., concurring) ("It cannot be denied that collateral relief proceedings are a central part of the review process for prisoners sentenced to death."); Carey v. Garrison, 403 F. Supp. 395, 397 (W.D.N.C. 1975) (unlike in noncapital cases, state should have duty in capital cases to provide counsel to prisoner to assist in preparation of *certiorari* petition to United States Supreme Court). *See also* Gibson v. Jackson, 578 F.2d 1045, 1054 n.4 (5th Cir. 1978), *cert. denied*, 439 U.S. 1119 (1979) (addendum of Rubin, J.) (rulings about adequacy of state postconviction procedures in noncapital cases are not dispositive in capital cases). *But cf. supra* § 2.6 n.16 and accompanying text (Supreme Court's resistance to rules categorically requiring broader federal habeas corpus review in capital cases). *See generally* authority cited *supra* § 2.6 nn.3, 4, 6, 15 (in capital context, 8th Amendment requires especially high degree of procedural protection to assure that state courts accurately have singled out appropriate offenders for ultimate sanction).

§ 7.2. [1] *See generally* AMERICAN BAR ASSOCIATION, TOWARD A MORE JUST AND EFFECTIVE SYSTEM OF REVIEW IN STATE DEATH PENALTY CASES: A REPORT CONTAINING DEATH PENALTY HABEAS CORPUS AND RELATED MATERIALS FROM THE AMERICAN BAR ASSOCIATION CRIMINAL JUSTICE SECTION'S PROJECT ON DEATH PENALTY HABEAS CORPUS 49-76 (Ira P. Robbins, Reporter 1990); ANTHONY G. AMSTERDAM, TRIAL MANUAL FOR THE DEFENSE OF CRIMINAL CASES §§ 298-301 (5th ed. 1988-89); WAYNE R. LaFAVE & JEROLD H. ISRAEL, CRIMINAL PROCEDURE § 11.2 (2d ed. 1992); IRA P. ROBBINS, THE LAW AND PROCESSES OF POST-CONVICTION REMEDIES 82-84 (1982); RONALD P. SOKOL, FEDERAL HABEAS CORPUS 116-20, 214-15 (1969); LARRY W. YACKLE, POSTCONVICTION REMEDIES § 137 (1981 & Supp. 1998); Vivian Berger, *The Chiropractor as Brain Surgeon: Defense Lawyering in Capital Cases,* 18 N.Y.U. REV. L. & SOC. CHANGE 245 (1990-91); Vivian Berger, *Justice Delayed or Justice Denied? — A Comment on Recent Proposals to Reform Death Penalty Habeas Corpus,* 90 COLUM. L. REV. 1665 (1990); Stephen B. Bright, *The Death Sentence Not for the Worst Crime But for the Worst Lawyer,* 103 YALE L.J. 1835 (1994); Stephen B. Bright, *In Defense of Life: Enforcing the Bill of Rights on Behalf of Poor, Minority and Disadvantaged Persons Facing the Death Penalty,* 57 MO. L. REV. 849 (1992); Ruth E. Friedman & Bryan A. Stevenson, *Solving Alabama's Capital Defense Problems: It's A Dollars and Sense Thing,* 44 ALA. L. REV. 1 (1992); William S. Geimer, *A Decade of Strickland's Tin Horn: Doctrinal and Practical Undermining of the Right to Counsel,* 4 WM. & MARY BILL RTS. J. 91 (1995); John C. Godbold, Pro Bono *Representation of Death Sentenced Inmates,* 42 REC. ASS'N B. CITY N.Y. 859 (1987);

appointment to represent the state postconviction petitioner and to request other financial resources necessary to permit the full and fair adjudication of the

Stephen M. Goldstein, *Expediting the Federal Habeas Corpus Review Process in Capital Cases: An Examination of Recent Proposals*, 19 CAP. U. L. REV. 599 (1990); Bruce A. Green, *Lethal Fiction: The Meaning of "Counsel" in the Sixth Amendment*, 78 IOWA L. REV. 433 (1993); William W. Greenhalgh, *The Assistance of Counsel Clause in the Year 2000*, 25 CRIM. L. BULL. 86 (1989); Lissa Griffin, *The Right to Effective Assistance of Appellate Counsel*, 97 W. VA. L. REV. 1 (1994); Roscoe C. Howard, Jr., *The Defunding of the Post-Conviction Defense Organizations as a Denial of the Right to Counsel*, 98 W. VA. L. REV. 863 (1996); Richard D. Klein, *The Eleventh Commandment: Thou Shalt Not Be Compelled to Render the Ineffective Assistance of Counsel*, 68 IND. L.J. 363 (1993); Norman Lefstein, *Reform of Defense Representation in Capital Cases: The Indiana Experience and Its Implications for the Nation*, 29 IND. L. REV. 495 (1996); Joe Margulies, *Resource Deprivation and the Right to Counsel*, 80 J. CRIM. L. & CRIMINOLOGY 673 (1989); David Medine, *The Constitutional Right to Expert Assistance for Indigents in Civil Cases*, 41 HASTINGS L.J. 281 (1990); Michael A. Mello, *Facing Death Alone: The Post-Conviction Attorney Crisis on Death Row*, 37 AM. U.L. REV. 513 (1988); Michael A. Mello, *Is There a Federal Constitutional Right to Counsel in Capital Post-Conviction Proceedings?*, 79 J. CRIM. L. & CRIMINOLOGY 1065 (1989); Michael Millemann, *Capital Post-Conviction Petitioners' Right to Counsel: Integrating Access to Court Doctrine and Due Process Principles*, 48 MD. L. REV. 455 (1989); Paul E. Miller, *The Right to Counsel in Collateral Proceedings — Habeas Corpus*, 15 HOW. L.J. 200 (1969); Anthony Paduano & Clive A. Stafford Smith, *The Unconscionability of Sub-Minimum Wages Paid Appointed Counsel in Capital Cases*, 43 RUTGERS L. REV. 281 (1991); Michael L. Perlin, *"The Executioner's Face is Always Well-Hidden": The Role of Counsel and the Courts in Determining Who Dies*, 41 N.Y. L. SCH. L. REV. 201 (1996); Vicki Quade, *Put Yourself on Death Row*, 14 BARRISTER 24 (1987); Albert L. Vreeland II, *The Breath of the Unfee'd Lawyer: Statutory Fee Limitations and Ineffective Assistance of Counsel in Capital Litigation*, 90 MICH. L. REV. 626 (1991); Robert Weisberg, *Who Defends Capital Defendants?*, 35 SANTA CLARA L. REV. 535 (1995); Welsh S. White, *Effective Assistance of Counsel in Capital Cases: The Evolving Standard of Care*, 1993 U. ILL. L. REV. 323 (1993); Richard J. Wilson & Robert L. Spangenberg, *State Post-Conviction Representation of Defendants Sentenced to Death*, 72 JUDICATURE 331 (1989); *The Death Penalty in America: Special Report*, 14 HUM. RTS. 14 (1987); Comment, *Constitutional Law: Validity of Attorney Fee Caps in Indigent Cases — Mississippi's Challenge*, 9 MISS. C.L. REV. 373 (1989); Comment, *The Ohio Supreme Court's Move Toward Quality Control of Court-Appointed Counsel for Indigent Defendants Charged with Capital Offense Crimes*, 21 AKRON L. REV. 503 (1988); Comment, *The Right to Appointed Counsel at Collateral Attack Proceedings*, 19 U. MIAMI L. REV. 432 (1965); Comment, *Right to Counsel in Criminal Post-Conviction Review Proceedings*, 51 CALIF. L. REV. 970 (1963); Comment, *Sixth and Fourteenth Amendments — Constitutional Right to State Capital Collateral Appeal: The Due Process of Executing a Convict Without Attorney Representation*, 80 J. CRIM. L. & CRIMINOLOGY 1190 (1990); *Developments in the Law — Federal Habeas Corpus*, 83 HARV. L. REV. 1038, 1197, 1202 (1970); Note, *Criminal Procedure: Post-Conviction Right to Counsel*, 77 W. VA. L. REV. 571 (1975); Note, *Discretionary Appointment of Counsel at Post-Conviction Proceedings: An Unconstitutional Barrier to Effective Post-Conviction Relief*, 8 GA. L. REV. 434 (1974); Note, *The Eighth Amendment and Ineffective Assistance of Counsel in Capital Trials*, 107 HARV. L. REV. 1923 (1994); Note, *Racism in Our Courts: The Underfunding of Public Defenders and Its Disproportionate Impact Upon Racial Minorities*, 22 HASTINGS CONST. L.Q. 219 (1994); Note, *Right to Counsel in Federal Collateral Attack Proceedings: Section 2255*, 30 U. CHI. L. REV. 583 (1963); Brad Snyder, Note, *Disparate Impact on Death Row: M.L.B. and the Indigent's Right to*

petitioner's federal claims. Section 7.1b *supra* discusses the constitutional right to procedurally fair state postconviction proceedings, noting the role that the provision of competent counsel and financial support services plays in making such proceedings fair. A significant number of States have statutes giving courts the duty or discretion to appoint counsel to represent indigent applicants[2] and to provide them with necessary financial assistance for experts, investigators, and the like, at least if they can demonstrate that their claims cannot be adjudicated without an evidentiary hearing.[3] State caselaw permitting courts to provide

---

Counsel at Capital State Postconviction Proceedings, 107 YALE L.J. 2211 (1998); authority cited *supra* § 7.1a n.2.

[2] For somewhat outdated lists of statutes, see Murray v. Giarratano, 492 U.S. 1, 12 n.7, 30 n.26, 31 n.27 (1989); *id.* at 29-32 nn.26-28 (Stevens, J., dissenting) (also collecting statutes reflecting varying compensation and monitoring of state postconviction counsel); 1 JAMES S. LIEBMAN, FEDERAL HABEAS CORPUS PRACTICE AND PROCEDURE § 7.2 n.2 (1st ed. 1988); Paduano & Smith, *supra* note 1, Appendix (also collecting statutes reflecting varying compensation of state postconviction counsel). *See also* 18 U.S.C. § 3006A(a)(2)(B) (1994); 21 U.S.C.A. § 848(q)(4)(B) (West 1994 & Supp. 1998); Rules 6(a), 8(c) of the Rules Governing § 2254 Cases (all discussed *infra* § 12.3b). The value of statutes giving courts the discretion but not the duty to appoint counsel is limited. *See* McFarland v. Scott, 512 U.S. 1256, 1262 (1994) ("Although ... Texas [statute] ... gives state courts discretion to appoint and compensate counsel for state habeas corpus proceedings, 'this is almost never done.'" (quoting the Spangenberg Group, A Study of Representation in Capital Cases in Texas vii (March 1993)). Often, moreover, as is documented in Justice Stevens' opinion in *Giarratano*, *supra*, and in Paduano & Smith, *supra*, the statutory maximum an attorney can collect for representing an indigent petitioner, even in capital litigation, is so low as to be prohibitive. As late as 1991, for example, Arkansas, Louisiana, and South Dakota provided only a $1000 fee for capital defense representation; Alabama provided a $1000 fee for trial-level representation of any indigent; Illinois provided $1250 for capital representation; South Carolina provided $1500 for the same; and Mississippi placed a $2000 limit on counsel fees which counsel had to split if two or more attorneys were appointed (MISS. CODE ANN. § 99-15-17 (Cum. Supp. 1991)). *See also* Ex parte Grayson, 479 So. 2d 76, 79-80 (Ala.), *cert. denied*, 474 U.S. 865 (1985); Fred Strasser, *$1,000 Fee Cap Makes Death Row's 'Justice' a Bargain for the State*, 12 NAT'L L.J. 33 (June 11, 1990). A few state courts have struck down statutes imposing maximum fee limits on compensation of counsel in capital cases, at least insofar as the caps apply at the criminal trial level. *See* McFarland v. Scott, *supra* at 1258 n.1 (Blackmun, J., dissenting from denial of *certiorari*) (collecting cases from Arkansas, Florida, Oklahoma, and South Carolina).

[3] For a somewhat outdated list of statutes, see LIEBMAN, *supra* note 2, at § 7.2a n.3. *See also* 18 U.S.C. § 3006A(c)(1) (1994), 28 U.S.C.A. § 848(q)(9) (West 1994 & Supp. 1998) (both discussed *infra* § 19.3). Discretionary authority to grant funds for investigative and expert services is of limited value in some States. *See* McFarland v. Scott, *supra*, 512 U.S. at 1262 n.1 (Blackmun, J., dissenting from denial of *certiorari*) (although Texas statute provides for "[f]unds for experts and other expenses" in state postconviction proceedings, state courts rarely grant such funds). For a fairly comprehensive judicial discussion of the right to "support services" in capital postconviction proceedings and of the right to apply for such services *ex parte*, see Owens v. State, 1994 WL 112997 (Tenn. Crim. App. Mar. 25, 1994), *rev'd in part & remanded*, 908 S.W.2d 923 (Tenn. 1995).

prisoners legal and financial assistance in state postconviction proceedings[4] and the courts' inherent authority to conduct their affairs in a fair and orderly manner also provide avenues for seeking necessary resources.[5] Additionally, as explained in § 3.3 *supra*, the Antiterrorism and Effective Death Penalty Act of 1996 (AEDPA) permits States to obtain the benefit of restrictive procedures in capital habeas corpus proceedings by establishing a "mechanism for the appointment, compensation, and reimbursement of [state postconviction] counsel" that satisfies certain statutory standards.[6]

The question remains whether the United States Constitution affords indigent prisoners a right of some sort to counsel and necessary financial assistance in postconviction proceedings. The remainder of this section addresses that question. This subsection discusses the Supreme Court's treatment of two aspects of the issue — whether the procedural due process component of the Due Process Clause requires the appointment of counsel and whether the 6th Amendment right to counsel and to the effective assistance of counsel "[i]n all criminal prosecutions"[7] applies to state postconviction proceedings. After examining the negative answers to these questions that the Court has given, at least in *dicta*, this subsection concludes that, although strongly suggestive of the Court's current thinking, its treatment of the matter to date is not legally conclusive of a right to counsel under all potentially applicable provisions of the United States Constitution. The succeeding subsections then reach the conclusion that not only the procedural due process component of the Due Process Clause (discussed in subsection b), which the Court has recently addressed, but also the "meaningful access" component of the Due Process Clause (subsection c), the Suspension Clause (subsection d), and the Equal

---

[4] *See, e.g.*, State ex rel. Public Defender Comm'n v. Bonacker, 706 S.W.2d 449 (Mo. 1986); Commonwealth v. Finley, 440 A.2d 1183 (Pa. 1981); Cooper v. Haas, 170 S.E.2d 5 (Va. 1969); Long v. State, 745 P.2d 547 (Wyo. 1987). *See also* Giarratano v. Murray, 847 F.2d 1118, 1119 (4th Cir. 1988) (*en banc*), rev'd sub nom. *Murray v. Giarratano*, 492 U.S. 1 (1989) (Virginia practice); Commonwealth v. Priovolos, 715 A.2d 420, 422 (Pa. 1998) (right to effective assistance of counsel in Pennsylvania postconviction proceedings); Rothering v. McCaughtry, 556 N.W.2d 136, 137-38 (Wis. Ct. App. 1996) (similar); *infra* note 8 (state cases discussing constitutional right to counsel); *infra* § 12.3b (federal decisions discussing discretionary right to counsel in federal habeas corpus cases).

[5] The discussion here relates to the constitutional bases for appointment of both state and federal postconviction counsel. *See also supra* § 3.3b; *infra* Chapter 12; *infra* §§ 19.3, 36.1, 39.3b (all discussing appointment of counsel and provision of financial assistance at various stages of federal habeas corpus proceedings). References to 14th Amendment due process and equal protection requirements generally encompass the 5th Amendment due process and equal protection principles that apply to federal postconviction proceedings.

[6] 28 U.S.C. § 2261(b) (West Supp. 1998). For more detailed discussion of this aspect of AEDPA, see *supra* § 3.3b. For an overview of the legislation, see *supra* § 3.2.

[7] U.S. CONST., amend. VI.

Protection Clause (subsection e), none of which the Court has yet addressed, provide strong bases for concluding that counsel is required in at least some state postconviction proceedings. Subsection f then discusses the particularly strong basis for a constitutional right to counsel in capital postconviction proceedings.

Prior to 1987, a few state and lower federal court decisions had found a constitutional right to counsel or financial assistance in state or federal postconviction proceedings under at least some circumstances,[8] and a few other courts had concluded, at least in *dicta*, that no such right existed.[9] Beginning in 1987, the Supreme Court announced three decisions concluding that the particular constitutional provisions before the Court did not provide a right to counsel or effective assistance of counsel in state postconviction proceedings. In the first decision, *Pennsylvania v. Finley,*[10] the Court noted that it had "never held that prisoners have a constitutional right to counsel when mounting collateral attacks to their convictions" in the state courts, and the Court "decline[d] to so hold today."[11] In *Murray v. Giarratano*[12] in 1989, a four-person

---

[8] *See* Williams v. Martin, 618 F.2d 1021 (4th Cir. 1980); Giarratano v. Murray, 668 F. Supp. 511 (E.D. Va. 1986), *aff'd,* 847 F.2d 1118, 1122 (4th Cir. 1988) (*en banc*), *rev'd sub nom. Murray v. Giarratano,* 492 U.S. 1 (1989); Nichols v. State, 425 P.2d 247 (Alaska 1967); People v. Shipman, 397 P.2d 993 (Cal. 1965); Honore v. Washington State Bd., 466 P.2d 485 (Wash. 1970). *See also* Gibson v. Jackson, 443 F. Supp. 239 (M.D. Ga. 1977), *vac'd on other grounds,* 578 F.2d 1045 (5th Cir.), *cert. denied,* 439 U.S. 1119 (1978) (right to counsel in most capital cases). *Cf.* Johnson v. Avery, 393 U.S. 483, 488 (1969) (reserving question).

[9] *See, e.g.,* Meeks v. Cabana, 845 F.2d 1319, 1322 (5th Cir. 1988) (5th Circuit has "long held" that state not required to appoint counsel for indigents in all postconviction and collateral proceedings); Jones v. Estelle, 722 F.2d 159, 167 (5th Cir. 1983) (*en banc*), *cert. denied,* 466 U.S. 976 (1984) (*dicta*); Robinson v. Fairman, 704 F.2d 368, 371 (7th Cir. 1983) (*dicta*) (citing Laclair v. United States, 374 F.2d 486 (7th Cir. 1967) (section 2255 case)). *See also* Price v. Johnston, 334 U.S. 266, 292 (1948) ("prisoners ... act ... often as their own counsel in [federal] *habeas corpus* proceedings"); Heath v. United States Parole Comm'n, 788 F.2d 85, 88 (2d Cir. 1986) (citing Miranda v. United States, 455 F.2d 402, 404-05 (2d Cir.) (*per curiam*), *supplemented,* 458 F.2d 1179 (2d Cir.) (*per curiam*), *cert. denied,* 409 U.S. 874 (1972)) ("appointment of counsel on [a federal] appeal involving a [federal prisoner's] collateral attack on a conviction is a matter that rests within the discretion of the appeals court" under 18 U.S.C. § 3006A(a)(2)(B)) (1994)).

[10] 481 U.S. 551 (1987).

[11] *Id.* at 555 (citing Johnson v. Avery, 393 U.S. 483, 488 (1969)). *See id.* ("Our cases establish that the right to appointed counsel extends to the first appeal of right, and no further.... We think that since a defendant has no federal constitutional right to counsel when pursuing a discretionary appeal on direct review of his conviction, *a fortiori,* he has no such right when attacking a conviction that has long since become final upon exhaustion of the appellate process"). *See also id.* at 557 ("respondent has no underlying constitutional right to appointed counsel in state postconviction proceedings").

[12] 492 U.S. 1 (1989). *Giarratano* presented the question whether the legal services the State of Virginia provides to death sentenced inmates to assist them in pursuing state postconviction challenges to their convictions and sentences satisfy the Due Process Clause and afford adequate access to the courts. *See id.* at 3-4.

plurality opinion read *Finley* as having concluded that there is "no right to postconviction counsel,"[13] although a majority of the Court either avoided the issue[14] or questioned the extent to which *Finley* finally resolved it.[15] And in *Coleman v. Thompson*[16] in 1991, a capital case, a six-person majority read "*Finley* and *Giarratano* [to] establish[] that there is no right to counsel [or, thus, to effective assistance of counsel] in state collateral proceedings," except, possibly, "where state collateral review is the first place a prisoner can present a challenge to his conviction."[17]

As did the Supreme Court plurality in *Giarratano* and majority in *Coleman*, a number of lower courts have treated *Finley* as having fully and negatively resolved the question whether the Constitution provides a right to counsel in

---

[13] *Id.* at 7-8, 9-10 (plurality opinion) ("We held in *Finley* that the logic of *Ross v. Moffitt*[, 417 U.S. 600 (1974)] required ... that there was no federal constitutional right to counsel for indigent prisoners seeking state postconviction relief"; "no different[]" conclusion applies to capital postconviction proceedings). *See also id.* at 13 (O'Connor, J., concurring) (citing *Finley, supra* (joining plurality opinion and writing separately: "nothing in the Constitution ... requires that a State provide counsel in postconviction proceedings ..., nor does ... the Constitution require [] the States to follow any particular federal model in those proceedings").

[14] *Id.* at 14-15 (Kennedy, J., concurring) (not expressing opinion on right to counsel in noncapital state postconviction proceedings; concluding as to capital cases that "collateral relief proceedings are a central part of the review process for prisoners sentenced to death" and that the "complexity" of such cases might require States to provide legal assistance but that legal services Virginia provides death sentenced inmates constitutionally suffice because "no prisoner on death row in Virginia has been unable to obtain counsel to represent him in postconviction proceedings, and Virginia's prison system is staffed with institutional lawyers to assist in preparing petitions for postconviction relief"). Because there was no majority opinion in *Giarratano*, and because Justice Kennedy's concurrence provided the narrowest basis for the outcome the Court reached, his concurrence embodies the holding of the case. *See* Marks v. United States, 430 U.S. 188, 193 (1978) ("When a fragmented Court decides a case and no single rationale explaining the result enjoys the assent of five Justices, 'the holding of the court may be viewed as that of the position taken by those Members who concurred in its judgments on the narrowest grounds ....'" (citation omitted)).

[15] *Id.* at 19-20 & n.4 (Stevens, J., dissenting, joined by Brennan, Marshall, and Blackmun, JJ.) (distinguishing language in *Finley;* concluding that *Finley* may be limited to its facts; suggesting that question whether "it is permissible to leave an ordinary prisoner to his own resources in collateral proceedings" is open; concluding that "it is fundamentally unfair to require an indigent death row inmate to initiate collateral review without counsel's guiding hand").

[16] 501 U.S. 722 (1991).

[17] *Id.* at 755. This statement is *dicta* because the Court thereafter determined that Coleman did have effective representation in a sufficient portion of his state postconviction proceeding to assure that all his constitutional claims had been fully and fairly adjudicated in state postconviction proceedings. *See id.* at 755-57. In regard to the possible "exception to the rule of *Finley* and *Giarratano* in those cases where state collateral review is the first place a prisoner can present a challenge to his conviction," see *supra* § 7.1b nn.74-83 and accompanying text; *infra* § 7.2e.

some or all state postconviction proceedings.[18] A more accurate summary of the Court's treatment of the issue, however, is Justice Blackmun's conclusion in his last opinion before retiring — that the Court "thus far has declined to hold that indigent capital defendants have a right to counsel."[19] The bases for considering the issue open are, first, that none of the Court's three opinions that have touched on the subject recently has discussed a number of provisions of the Constitution that bear directly on the matter, including the "meaningful access" component of the Due Process Clause,[20] the Suspension Clause,[21] and the Equal Protection Clause.[22] In addition, *Coleman* left open the question whether there is a constitutional right to counsel in the not uncommon situation in which state postconviction proceedings are, in essence, the prisoner's "'one and only appeal'" of an issue within the state courts.[23]

Finally, *Finley*, which provides the single citation in support of the Court's subsequent discussion of the matter, did not actually present, nor did it decide, the question whether there is a constitutional right to appointment of counsel in some or all state postconviction proceedings.[24] For, as *required by Pennsylvania statute*, the state postconviction trial judge in *Finley appointed counsel* to represent the prisoner. The issue presented in *Finley* arose when appointed counsel, after reviewing the trial record and consulting the client, concluded that "there were no arguable bases for relief" and so informed the trial court in writing in a request to withdraw. "The trial court" thereafter "conducted an independent review of the record[,] ... agreed that there were no issues even arguably meritorious [and] ... dismissed the petition...."[25] On appeal, an intermediate state court reversed in an ambiguous decision mixing federal and

---

[18] *See, e.g.*, Kitt v. Clarke, 931 F.2d 1246, 1248 n.4 (8th Cir. 1991) (no constitutional right to effective assistance of counsel in postconviction proceedings); United States ex rel. Simmons v. Gramley, 915 F.2d 1128, 1136-37 (7th Cir. 1990); DeLuna v. Lynaugh, 873 F.2d 757, 760 (5th Cir.), *cert. denied,* 493 U.S. 900 (1989) ("there is no constitutional right to appointed counsel in collateral proceedings such as a habeas corpus petition"). *But cf.* Commonwealth v. Priovolos, 715 A.2d 420, 422 (Pa. 1998) (discussed *supra* note 4); Rothering v. McCaughtry, 556 N.W.2d 136, 137-38 (Wis. Ct. App. 1996) (same).

[19] McFarland v. Scott, 512 U.S. 1256, 1261 (1994) (Blackmun, J., dissenting from denial of *certiorari*).

[20] *See infra* § 7.2c. A plurality of the Court in *Giarratano* did discuss this aspect of the Due Process Clause (*see supra* note 12), but the issue was not presented in *Finley* and *Coleman*.

[21] *See infra* § 7.2d.

[22] *See infra* § 7.2e.

[23] *See supra* § 7.1b nn.74-83 and accompanying text; *infra* § 7.2e.

[24] *See Finley, supra,* 481 U.S. at 559 (Blackmun, J., concurring in the judgment).

[25] *Id.* at 553 (majority opinion). On direct appeal several years before, the Pennsylvania Supreme Court had unanimously denied the claims the petitioner sought to relitigate in her postconviction petition. *Id.*

state legal analyses.[26] The state court concluded that the full range of prophylactic requirements that the Supreme Court had developed in *Anders v. California*[27] to govern withdrawal of appointed counsel during direct appeals also applied in state postconviction proceedings in Pennsylvania. The state court accordingly ruled that, as required on direct appeal by *Anders,* the attorney's written statement to the trial court should have been sent to the client and should have included a discussion by counsel of matters in the record that he felt arguably might support relief.[28] The single question presented in *Finley,* therefore, was whether — having appointed postconviction counsel, having supervised the provision by that counsel of apparently conscientious services including review of the record, consultation with the client, and a written report to the court, and having thereupon independently reviewed the record itself, finding no "even arguably meritorious" claims — the postconviction trial court nonetheless violated the prisoner's constitutional rights by failing to require that the attorney notify the client and file a brief referring to matters that might possibly support relief.[29] The Supreme Court answered this question by stating simply that "[t]he procedures followed by respondent's [state] habeas counsel fully comported with fundamental fairness."[30]

Accordingly, although Chief Justice Rehnquist's majority opinion in *Finley* reveals his and four other Justices' current "think[ing]"[31] on the right to counsel in state postconviction proceedings, the Court's actual holding in the case does not resolve that question. Indeed, even the majority's less than conclusional

---

[26] Commonwealth v. Finley, 479 A.2d 568 (1984), *rev'd,* 481 U.S. 551 (1987). *See Finley, supra,* 481 U.S. at 561-63 (Brennan, J., dissenting) (ambiguous bases for state court decision).

[27] 386 U.S. 738 (1967).

[28] *Commonwealth v. Finley, supra,* 479 A.2d at 570.

[29] None of the questions on which *certiorari* was granted in *Finley* presented the issue whether there is a constitutional right to postconviction counsel. *See* Pennsylvania v. Finley, 55 U.S.L.W. 3099 (U.S., Aug. 12, 1986).

[30] *Finley, supra,* 481 U.S. at 556. *See also id.* at 559 ("States have substantial discretion to develop and implement programs to aid prisoners seeking to secure postconviction review. In Pennsylvania, the State has made a valid choice to give prisoners the assistance of counsel without requiring the full panoply of procedural protections that the Constitution requires be given to defendants ... at trial and on first appeal as of right. In this context, the Constitution does not put the State to the difficult choice between affording no counsel whatsoever or following the strict procedural guidelines enunciated in *Anders*"). As *Finley* notes, the *Anders* rule is not independently required by the 14th Amendment, but rather was designed as "a prophylactic framework" to protect the equal protection right of indigent criminal defendants to appointment of counsel on appeal. *Finley, supra,* 481 U.S. at 551. *See* Douglas v. California, 372 U.S. 353 (1963) (equal protection right to appointment of counsel on appeal). Limited to a holding that subconstitutional prophylactic procedures do not always apply in postconviction proceedings, *Finley* is unexceptionable. *See supra* § 2.4d nn.280-98 and accompanying text; *infra* § 9.2.

[31] *See supra* note 11.

phrasing of its *dictum* — which merely *"declin[ed]* to ... hold"[32] that the Constitution requires counsel in state postconviction cases — bespoke an understanding that the issue remains open for the day when the facts, the lower court opinions, and the parties actually have presented the issue and have thereby enabled interested parties, in the context of postconviction proceedings actually pursued without counsel, to provide the Court with considered analyses of the question.[33] Because *Giarratano* also did not resolve the issue — given the absence of a majority opinion[34] and given that a majority of concurring and dissenting Justices suggested that a right to postconviction counsel *does* exist in capital cases[35] — and because *Coleman* only rejected the weakest of the various legal theories for a right to counsel, namely, a 6th Amendment theory[36] and expressly reserved the possibility that a right to effective postconviction counsel might exist in limited circumstances under an alternative equal protection theory,[37] the *Finley dictum* remains a *dictum* that cannot be said to have resolved the issue. Moreover, in a still more recent decision, *McFarland v. Scott*,[38] a majority of the Court noted "that quality legal representation is necessary in capital habeas corpus proceedings in light of 'the seriousness of the possible penalty[,] ... the unique and complex nature of the litigation[,]' [and] ... '[t]he complexity of our jurisprudence in this area ....'"[39] And the three dissenting

---

[32] *Finley, supra*, 481 U.S. at 555 (emphasis added).

[33] *See* Giarratano v. Murray, 847 F.2d 1118, 1122 (4th Cir. 1988) (*en banc*), *rev'd sub nom. Murray v. Giarratano*, 492 U.S. 1 (1989) (because *"Finley* was not a meaningful access case, nor did it address the rule enunciated in Bounds v. Smith," 430 U.S. 817 (1977), and because *"Finley* did not involve the death penalty," court refuses to "read *Finley* as suggesting that ... counsel cannot be required under the unique circumstances of post-conviction proceedings involving a challenge to the death penalty"). Given that courts addressing this issue have drawn distinctions as to the scope of the constitutional right based upon a number of considerations — for example, the capital or noncapital nature of the case, the scope of the library and other services available to prisoners apart from counsel, whether the prisoner is seeking assistance in state as opposed to federal postconviction proceedings, the complexity of the legal and factual issues involved, the availability *vel non* of volunteer counsel, whether prefiling or postfiling assistance is sought — the issue hardly seems soluble in the abstract, apart from a particular factual context. *See Giarratano, supra*, 492 U.S. at 14-15 (Kennedy, J., concurring in the judgment); Giarratano v. Murray, 678 F. Supp. 511, 513 (E.D. Va. 1986), *aff'd*, 847 F.2d 1118 (4th Cir. 1988) (*en banc*), *rev'd sub nom. Murray v. Giarratano*, 492 U.S. 1 (1989); decisions cited *infra* § 12.3b.

[34] *See supra* notes 12-15 and accompanying text.

[35] *See infra* § 7.2e.

[36] *See* Coleman v. Thompson, 501 U.S. 722, 752-57 (1991) (addressing question whether ineffective assistance of appellate counsel in state postconviction proceedings violated 6th Amendment).

[37] *See supra* note 17 and accompanying text.

[38] 512 U.S. 849 (1994).

Justices in the same case concluded "that Congress expected that the States would ... shoulder some of the burden of providing pre[-federal habeas corpus] legal assistance to indigent death-sentenced prisoners" because "'[a] state that has elected to impose the death penalty should provide adequate funding for the procedures it has adopted to properly implement that penalty.'"[40] The way is open, therefore, for a fuller and more conclusive treatment of the issue than the Court has yet provided. The subsections that follow discuss a number of grounds on which a conclusion contrary to the *Finley dictum* might be reached in particular circumstances under either the Federal Constitution or analogous provisions of a state constitution.

b. *Procedural due process.* In *Ake v. Oklahoma*,[41] the Supreme Court held that "the Fourteenth Amendment's due process guarantee of fundamental fairness" requires the State to take steps to assure that criminal defendants have a fair opportunity to present their defense, including by providing them with funds for expert assistance. Although *Ake* addresses a criminal defendant's right to funds for expert psychiatric assistance at a criminal trial, the Court's due process analysis is not confined to the criminal setting and appears to apply whenever an indigent litigant's interest in the outcome of a proceeding is substantial.[42] *Ake* identifies three factors that must be weighed in order to determine whether due process and fundamental fairness considerations require a requested procedural safeguard in a given judicial forum in which an individual's liberty or property interest is threatened: (1) the private interest that will be affected by the action of the state; (2) the governmental interest that will be affected if the safeguard is provided; and (3) the probable value of the additional safeguard that is sought

---

[39] *Id.* at 855 (quoting 21 U.S.C. § 848(q)(8) and *Giarratano, supra*, 492 U.S. at 14 (Kennedy, J., joined by O'Connor, J., concurring in the judgment)).

[40] *Id.* at 870 (Thomas, J., dissenting) (quoting Hill v. Lockhart, 992 F.2d 801, 803 (8th Cir. 1993)).

[41] 470 U.S. 68, 76 (1985).

[42] *See id.* at 77 (citing, *e.g.,* Mathews v. Eldridge, 424 U.S. 319 (1976) (social security proceedings)); Blair v. Armontrout, 916 F.2d 1310, 1335 n.3 (8th Cir. 1990), *cert. denied,* 502 U.S. 825 (1991) (Heaney, J., concurring in part and dissenting in part) ("While there is no absolute right to the appointment of counsel in [postconviction] proceedings, ... the absence of a general right to appointment does not mean that once counsel is appointed, no restraints imposed by law remain on his representation.... Blair ... has persuasive grounds [for a due process challenge based on his prior] counsel's [alleged] deception of him."); Stephens v. Kemp, 846 F.2d 642, 645-50 (11th Cir.), *cert. denied,* 488 U.S. 872 (1988) (applying *Ake* to petitioner's request for ballistics expert at trial and in state habeas corpus proceedings but concluding that petitioner failed to make adequate showing that expert was needed); other authority cited *supra* § 7.1b nn.59, 60, 73-83 and accompanying text & *infra* notes 46, 52.

and the risk of an erroneous deprivation of the affected interest if the safeguard is not provided.[43]

Each of the *Ake* criteria arguably supports the provision of counsel and essential financial assistance to petitioners in state postconviction proceedings. First, the prisoner has a strong interest in having his constitutional claims fairly presented and adjudicated. "The private interest in the accuracy of a criminal proceeding that places an individual's life or liberty at risk" — the central concern in state postconviction proceedings — is "almost uniquely compelling."[44] To the extent that a prisoner can demonstrate that the effective assistance of counsel or some type of financial assistance is necessary to test the reliability and accuracy of the guilt and sentencing determinations at trial,[45] his "private interest" is similar to the one at stake in *Ake*.[46]

---

[43] *Ake, supra*, 470 U.S. at 77. *See also* O'Connell v. Kirchner, 513 U.S. 1303, 1304 (1995) (Stevens, J., Circuit Justice, denying motion to recall mandate and for stay) (addressing merits of applicants' "procedural due process theory" that state habeas corpus proceeding unconstitutionally denied them "liberty interest ... absent a full and fair hearing" but finding that "exhaustive proceedings in the [state] courts" gave applicants "all process due them under federal law"). The analysis here assumes the obvious — that the Due Process Clause applies to state postconviction proceedings because the purpose of such proceedings is to "give one whom [the state] deprives of his freedom the opportunity to open an inquiry into the intrinsic fairness of a criminal process," Carter v. Illinois, 329 U.S. 173, 174 (1946), and because the petitioner's "liberty" (and sometimes her "life") thus is at stake in those proceedings. In addition, now that most States have undertaken by statute to provide prisoners with state postconviction remedies, *see supra* § 6.1 nn.1-2 and accompanying text, and indeed, to provide state-funded counsel to indigent petitioners in those proceedings (and, particularly in capital state postconviction proceedings), *see supra* § 7.2a nn.3-6 and accompanying text, prisoners also may have a constitutionally protected "property" interest at stake in those proceedings, in the sense of a statutorily created expectation that they will receive the substantive benefits associated with the statutorily promised procedures. *See, e.g.*, Hicks v. Oklahoma, 447 U.S. 343, 346 (1979) (although Constitution does not mandate jury sentencing, when state statute adopts that procedure, it creates "substantial and legitimate expectation," protected by Due Process Clause, that defendants will be afforded its benefits); Petition for a Writ of Certiorari to the Texas Court of Criminal Appeals, Colella v. Texas, *supra* § 7.1b n.47. The only question that remains, therefore — the question addressed in the remainder of this subsection — is what process is constitutionally "due" prisoners in state postconviction procedures before they may be deprived of one or more of these protected, life, liberty, and property interests. *See, e.g.*, *Ake, supra*, 470 U.S. at 77; *Mathews v. Eldridge, supra*, 424 U.S. at 335.

[44] *Id.*

[45] *See, e.g.*, ABA STANDARDS FOR CRIMINAL JUSTICE, *supra* § 7.1a n.22, at 22-3.1, 22-4.3 (and commentary) (recommending appointed counsel for indigent inmates pursuing postconviction relief because "[i]t is a waste of judicial resources and an inefficient method of treating the substantive merits of applications for postconviction relief to proceed without counsel for applicants," and because "[e]xploration of the legal grounds for complaint, investigation of the underlying facts, and more articulate statement of the claims are functions of an advocate").

[46] *See infra* notes 49-54 and accompanying text; *infra* §§ 7.2c, 7.2d, 7.2f, 12.3a nn.11-20 and accompanying text, 12.3b nn.59-84 and accompanying text (all discussing critical importance of

The governmental interest adversely affected by the appointment of counsel or the provision of essential financial assistance is, of course, monetary — an interest generally held to be of secondary importance when compared to the constitutional rights enforced in state postconviction proceedings.[47] The fact that many States provide postconviction counsel and expert and other essential financial assistance to state prisoners belies any claim that providing such resources is preclusively expensive.[48]

The third *Ake* factor — the value of the procedural safeguard and the risk of erroneous deprivation of the affected interest absent the safeguard — also supports the appointment of counsel and provision of essential financial

counsel in some or all postconviction settings). A prisoner's need for legal assistance in mounting a substantial constitutional challenge to his conviction or sentence is analogous to the need for legal assistance on the part of other participants in the criminal justice system to whom the Court has extended a constitutional right of counsel. *See, e.g.,* Douglas v. California, 372 U.S. 353 (1963) (criminal appeals); Mempa v. Rhay, 389 U.S. 128 (1967) (sentencing proceedings); Coleman v. Alabama, 399 U.S. 1 (1970) (preliminary hearing); United States v. Wade, 388 U.S. 218 (1967) (line-up); Miranda v. Arizona, 384 U.S. 436 (1966) (custodial interrogation); Hamilton v. Alabama, 368 U.S. 52 (1961) (arraignment). *See Developments in the Law, supra* note 1, at 1203 & n.334. Moreover, the postconviction petitioner's interest is at least as important as a litigant's interest in avoiding a finding of paternity or establishing the right to disability benefits — interests at stake in civil cases in which a due process right to access to judicial forums has been held to prohibit barriers to access caused by the litigant's indigency. *See* Little v. Streater, 452 U.S. 1 (1981) (paternity); *Mathews v. Eldridge, supra* (disability); *infra* note 52 and accompanying text. In Pennsylvania v. Finley, 481 U.S. 551 (1987) (discussed *supra* § 7.2a), the Court distinguished direct criminal appeals from postconviction proceedings, pointing out that the latter "normally occur[] only after the defendant has failed to secure relief through direct review of his conviction." *Id.* at 557. Although this factor may argue against a blanket right to counsel in postconviction cases, it does not explain why prisoners who can demonstrate a substantial basis for doubting the validity of their convictions have less of an interest in the outcome than criminal appellants. *See generally supra* § 2.5 (various habeas corpus doctrines providing greater review in situations in which petitioner can make colorable showing of innocence, can show particularly high likelihood of prejudice, or otherwise can demonstrate that denial of relief would result in miscarriage of justice).

[47] *See, e.g., Ake, supra,* 470 U.S. at 79 (state has no legitimate interest in using its superior financial position for "maintenance of a strategic advantage"); Bounds v. Smith, 430 U.S. 817, 825 (1977) ("cost of protecting a constitutional right cannot justify its total denial"); Smith v. Bennett, 365 U.S. 708, 713 (1961) ("Financial hurdles must not be permitted to condition its [the writ of habeas corpus'] exercise."); Mickens v. Winston, 462 F. Supp. 910, 912 (E.D. Va. 1978), *aff'd,* 609 F.2d 508 (4th Cir. 1979).

[48] *See* authority cited *supra* § 7.2a nn.2, 3. *See also Ake, supra,* 470 U.S. at 77 (rejecting claim of "staggering economic burden" to state on ground that "[m]any States, as well as the Federal Government, currently make psychiatric assistance available to indigent defendants, and they have not found the financial burden so great as to preclude this assistance"); Powell v. Alabama, 287 U.S. 45, 73 (1932). Imposing a threshold requirement of a substantial federal claim, *see supra* notes 45-46 and accompanying text, also would reduce the cost to the state and limit that cost to situations in which the competing interests are particularly strong.

assistance for convicted persons. The value of the safeguard is, first, the likelihood that assistance of counsel or essential financial assistance will enhance the reliability of postconviction review, hence of the underlying criminal proceedings. In addition, constitutional and other claims will be articulated more ably and presented more thoroughly by counsel and expert witnesses than by the usual *pro se* petitioner proceeding without such assistance, thus reducing the burden of federal and state judges, who often are forced to piece together unaided the legal and factual bases for a *pro se* petition.[49]

Finally, representation by counsel inevitably will make postconviction review a more reliable device for correcting constitutional error.[50] The importance of counsel in criminal cases long has been acknowledged by the courts; indeed, the right to counsel was one of the first rights recognized as "fundamental."[51] Courts also have held that this right extends to complex civil cases brought by indigent prisoners[52] — which *a fortiori* includes many postconviction proceedings in which the prisoner's life or liberty is at stake. This is especially so given that the constitutional and other bases for challenging both convictions and sentences are often as difficult and sophisticated as the controlling theories in complex civil

---

[49] *See, e.g.,* McFarland v. Scott, 512 U.S. 849, 855-56 (1994); Haines v. Kerner, 404 U.S. 519, 520-21 (1972) (*per curiam*); Williams v. Kullman, 722 F.2d 1048, 1050-51 (2d Cir. 1983) (citing authority); *infra* §§ 11.6 n.9, 12.2 n.14, 15.1 nn.9-10, 15.2c nn.52-53, 26.3b nn.42-49, 35.2a nn.29-31, 35.2b n.54, 41.4b n.19 (all discussing difficulties prisoners and courts encounter when prisoners litigate *pro se*).

[50] *See* McFarland v. Scott, 512 U.S. 1256, 1262-64 (1994) (Blackmun, J., dissenting from denial of *certiorari*); Murray v. Giarratano, 492 U.S. 1, 14 (1989) (Kennedy, J., concurring in the judgment); *id.* at 27-29 (Stevens, J., dissenting). *See also* McFarland v. Scott, 512 U.S. 849, 859 (1994) ("By providing indigent capital defendants with a mandatory right to qualified legal counsel in these proceedings, Congress has recognized that federal habeas corpus has a particularly important role to play in promoting fundamental fairness in the imposition of the death penalty."). *See generally* Schneckloth v. Bustamonte, 412 U.S. 218, 236 (1973) (effective assistance of counsel at trial is uniquely "a right constitutionally guaranteed to protect a fair trial and the reliability of the truth-determining process").

[51] Gideon v. Wainwright, 372 U.S. 335 (1963). *See* Kimmelman v. Morrison, 477 U.S. 365, 377 (1986) (citing cases).

[52] *See, e.g.,* Maclin v. Freake, 650 F.2d 885, 886-89 (7th Cir. 1981) (section 1983 case: where indigent cannot investigate facts and claims are complex, "fundamental unfairness" results if counsel is not appointed); Gordon v. Leeke, 574 F.2d 1147, 1153 (4th Cir.), *cert. denied,* 439 U.S. 970 (1978) ("If ... *pro se* [section 1983] litigant has a colorable claim but lacks the capacity to present it, the district court should appoint counsel to assist him."); authority cited *infra* § 7.2c n.63 & *infra* § 12.3b. *See also* In re Gault, 387 U.S. 1 (1967) (due process right to counsel in "civil" juvenile proceedings); Case v. Nebraska, 381 U.S. 336, 347 (1965) (Brennan, J., concurring) (due process may require States to have adequate postconviction remedies available to redress violation of federal constitutional rights in criminal process); Williams v. Martin, 618 F.2d 1021 (4th Cir. 1980) (relying on right to "effective defense" as basis for ordering district court to provide habeas corpus petitioner with expert assistance to determine if rights were violated at trial).

cases and are not so obvious that a layperson would easily recognize them.[53] And, were the sophisticated nature of the substantive law not sufficiently daunting, the prisoner also is faced with a perplexing array of procedural pitfalls, such as the exhaustion doctrine, procedural default, nonretroactivity, and abuse of the writ.[54]

c. *Meaningful access to the courts.* The Supreme Court also has held that prisoners have a constitutional right to meaningful access to state postconviction courts.[55] The "right of access to the courts ... is founded in the Due Process Clause and assures that no person will be denied the opportunity to present to the judiciary allegations concerning violations of fundamental constitutional rights."[56] "It is clear that ready access to the Courts is one of, perhaps *the,* fundamental constitutional right."[57]

Pursuant to this due process right, the Court has held that the States may not deny indigents access to state postconviction remedies by charging them filing fees they cannot pay;[58] that the States must either extend legal aid services to prisoners or, alternatively, provide them with law libraries and access to

---

[53] *See* McFarland v. Scott, 512 U.S. 849, 855-56 (1994); *Murray v. Giarratano, supra,* 492 U.S. at 25-29 (Stevens, J., dissenting); Giarratano v. Murray, 668 F. Supp. 511 (E.D. Va. 1986), *aff'd,* 847 F.2d 1118, 1122 (4th Cir. 1988) (*en banc*), *rev'd sub nom.* Murray v. Giarratano, 492 U.S. 1 (1989) (constitutional right to appointment of counsel in postconviction capital cases based in part on "complexity and difficulty of the legal work"). *See also infra* § 7.2f n.111.

[54] *See* McFarland v. Scott, 512 U.S. 849, 855-56 (1994); *id.* at 860 (O'Connor, J., concurring in the judgment in part); *Murray v. Giarratano, supra,* 492 U.S. at 24-29 (Stevens, J., dissenting); *infra* § 22.1. *See also infra* §§ 7.2c, 7.2d, 7.2f, 12.3a nn.11-20 and accompanying text, 12.3b nn.55-80 and accompanying text, 26.3b n.43 (all discussing risks faced by prisoners litigating *pro se* in some or all postconviction situations). *See generally infra* Chapters 22-28.

[55] *See* Bounds v. Smith, 430 U.S. 817, 825 (1977) (due process right to "reasonably adequate opportunity to present claimed violations of fundamental rights to the courts"). *Accord* Lewis v. Casey, 518 U.S. 343, 350 (1996).

[56] Wolff v. McDonnell, 418 U.S. 539, 579 (1974).

[57] Cruz v. Hauck, 475 F.2d 475, 476 (5th Cir. 1973) (prison regulations may unreasonably invade prisoner's relationship to courts) (emphasis in original). *Accord* McCarthy v. Madigan, 503 U.S. 140, 153 (1992) ("Because a prisoner ordinarily is divested of the privilege to vote, the right to file a court action might be said to be his remaining most 'fundamental political right, because preservative of all rights.' *Yick Wo v. Hopkins,* 118 U.S. 356, 370 (1886)."). *See Bounds v. Smith, supra.*

[58] Smith v. Bennett, 365 U.S. 708 (1961). *See* M.L.B. v. S.L.J., 117 S. Ct. 555, 561 & n.4 (1996) (describing *Smith v. Bennett, supra* as part of "line of decisions" resting on "'fundamental' principle that 'avenues of appellate review, ... once established, ... must be kept free of unreasoned distinctions that can only impede open and equal access to the courts'" (quoting Rinaldi v. Yeager, 384 U.S. 305, 310 (1966)); *Lewis v. Casey, supra,* 518 U.S. at 350 (Court has protected "right of access to the courts ... by requiring state courts to waive filing fees ... or transcript fees ... for indigent inmates").

jailhouse lawyers;[59] and that "'[m]eaningful access' ... is the touchstone."[60] A number of courts have recognized that assistance by attorneys is an indispensable element of meaningful access to the courts, at least in circumstances in which access to law books and other resources short of counsel is insufficient due to the mental or physical status of the prisoners, the conditions of their confinement, or the nature of their legal claims.[61] Under this aspect of

---

[59] *Bounds v. Smith, supra*; Johnson v. Avery, 393 U.S. 483 (1969). *See Lewis v. Casey, supra*, 518 U.S. at 351 (explaining that "*Bounds* did not create an abstract, free-standing right to a law library or legal assistance" for prisoners, but rather required that states adopt these or other appropriate measures as "means for ensuring 'a reasonably adequate opportunity to present claimed violations of fundamental constitutional rights to the courts'"; thus, "[i]nsofar as the right vindicated by *Bounds* is concerned, 'meaningful access to the courts is the touchstone'" (quoting *Bounds v. Smith, supra*, 430 U.S. at 823, 825)); Murray v. Giarratano, 492 U.S. 1, 14-15 (1989) (Kennedy, J., concurring in the judgment); *Bounds v. Smith, supra*, 430 U.S. at 824 (state has "affirmative obligation" to enable prisoners to secure access to the courts); Carper v. Deland, 54 F.3d 613, 616-17 (10th Cir. 1995) (if "state ... elect[s] to provide legal assistance to inmates in lieu of maintaining an adequate prison law library," state must "supply[ ] 'adequate assistance from persons trained in the law,' ... such as inmate law clerks, paralegals, law students, volunteer attorneys, or staff attorneys ... to aid inmates in the preparation of state or federal petitions for writs of habeas corpus or initial pleadings in civil rights actions challenging conditions of current confinement"); Martin v. Davies, 917 F.2d 336, 340 (7th Cir. 1990), *cert. denied*, 501 U.S. 1208 (1991) (denial of meaningful access to courts presumed if access to jail library is restricted on "substantial and continuous basis"; no denial of access because prisoner was offered counsel but refused and, in any event, had significant access to library).

[60] *Bounds v. Smith, supra*, 430 U.S. at 823. *See also* Ex parte Hull, 312 U.S. 546, 549 (1941).

[61] *See, e.g.*, McFarland v. Scott, 512 U.S. 849, 855-56 (1994) ("Congress' provision of a right to counsel [in capital habeas corpus cases] under [21 U.S.C.] § 848(q)(4)(B) reflects a determination that quality legal representation is necessary in capital habeas corpus proceedings in light of 'the seriousness of the possible penalty and ... the unique and complex nature of the litigation.' An attorney's assistance prior to the filing of a capital defendant's habeas corpus petition is crucial, because '[t]he complexity of our jurisprudence in this area ... makes it unlikely that capital defendants will be able to file successful petitions for collateral relief without the assistance of persons learned in the law.' (quoting 21 U.S.C. § 848(q)(8) and *Murray v. Giarratano, supra*, 492 U.S. at 14 (Kennedy, J., concurring in the judgment)); *Murray v. Giarratano, supra*, 492 U.S. at 14-15 (Kennedy, J., concurring) (meaningful access principle of *Bounds* may extend to representation by counsel, at least in capital postconviction cases, but Virginia meets constitutional standard as to its death row inmates because "no prisoner on death row in Virginia has been unable to obtain counsel to represent him in [state] postconviction proceedings, and Virginia's prison system is staffed with institutional lawyers to assist in preparing petitions for postconviction relief"); *id.* at 20-29 (Stevens, J., dissenting) (meaningful access right extends in some circumstances to right to "counsel's guiding hand"; listing three reasons why "[m]eaningful access, and meaningful judicial review, would be effected in this case only if counsel were appointed, on request, in time to enable examination of the case record, factual investigation, and preparation of a petition containing all meritorious claims, which the same attorney then could litigate to its conclusion": (1) severity of sentence facing capitally sentenced petitioners in case and special process due prisoners facing death penalty to assure that their convictions and sentences are reliable bases for their execution; (2) importance of postconviction review in Virginia given that it

due process analysis, therefore, counsel and necessary financial assistance arguably are constitutionally required in those circumstances in which the petitioner or class of petitioners makes a particularized showing[62] that the denial of counsel and necessary financial assistance is tantamount to the denial of

---

is first point at which several important claims may be raised; and (3) unusual complexities and speed of capital postconviction litigation); Cornett v. Donovan, 51 F.3d 894 (9th Cir. 1995), *cert. denied*, 518 U.S. 1003 (1996) (constitutional right of access to court requires provision of attorneys or legal assistants to assist mentally ill patients involuntarily committed to state hospital in filing habeas corpus petitions and section 1983 complaints as well as replies to opposing parties' responsive pleadings; right to legal assistance does not extend beyond "pleading stage," at which point litigant has gained access to court and judge has authority to appoint or request counsel for indigent litigant if "circumstances so warrant"); Giarratano v. Murray, 668 F. Supp. 511 (E.D. Va. 1986), *aff'd*, 847 F.2d 1118, 1122 (4th Cir. 1988) (*en banc*), *rev'd sub nom. Murray v. Giarratano*, 492 U.S. 1 (1989) (lawyers required in capital state postconviction proceedings; discussed *supra* § 7.2a n.33); Smith v. Bounds, 610 F. Supp. 597, 603 (E.D.N.C. 1985), *aff'd*, 813 F.2d 1299 (4th Cir. 1987), *aff'd en banc & supplemented*, 841 F.2d 77 (4th Cir.) (*per curiam*), *cert. denied*, 488 U.S. 869 (1988) ("The best method to insure ... access would be to set up a prisoners legal services program or provide some other form of assistance of counsel."); 2 MICHAEL B. MUSHLIN, RIGHTS OF PRISONERS §§ 11.05, 11.06 (2d ed. 1993) (citing cases). *See also Lewis v. Casey, supra*, 518 U.S. at 356 (prison officials must devise suitable mechanisms to "ensure that inmates with language problems have a reasonably adequate opportunity to file nonfrivolous legal claims challenging their convictions or conditions of confinement"; mere physical access to the law library is insufficient because "it is th[e] capability [of filing suit], rather than the capability of turning pages in a law library, that is the touchstone"); Procunier v. Martinez, 416 U.S. 396, 419-22 (1974) (due process right of access to court violated by prison regulation forbidding law students and legal paraprofessionals employed by private attorneys to interview inmates); Peterkin v. Jeffes, 855 F.2d 1021, 1033-47 (3d Cir. 1988) (remanding to determine whether death row inmates' right to access to court under *Bounds* adequately satisfied by system of appointed and volunteer postconviction counsel (on remand, settled by consent decree, Peterkin v. Jeffes, No. CIV.A.83-0304, 1989 WL 140489 (E.D. Pa. Nov. 14, 1989))); *infra* § 7.2f n.111; authority cited *infra* § 12.3b. For the view that meaningful access to counsel requires the appointment of counsel prior to the point when postconviction claims must be factually and legally investigated and then pleaded, see *McFarland v. Scott, supra* at 856, 858 ("right to [habeas corpus] counsel necessarily includes a right for that counsel meaningfully to research and present a defendant's habeas claims," else there is "substantial risk that [petitioner's] habeas claims never would be heard on the merits"); *id.* at 860 (O'Connor, J., concurring in the judgment in part) ("It is almost meaningless to provide a lawyer to pursue claims on federal habeas if the lawyer is not available to help prepare the petition."); *id.* at 868 (Thomas, J., dissenting) ("legal assistance prior to the filing of a federal [habeas corpus] petition can be very valuable to a prisoner"); *infra* § 12.3a nn.11-20 and accompanying text.

[62] Case v. Nebraska, 381 U.S. 336, 347 (1965) (Brennan, J., concurring). *See Lewis v. Casey, supra*, 518 U.S. at 354-55 (to establish *Bounds* violation, prisoner must "demonstrate that the alleged shortcomings in the library or legal assistance program hindered his efforts to pursue a legal claim. He might show, for example, that a complaint he prepared was dismissed for failure to satisfy some technical requirement which, because of deficiencies in the prison's legal assistance facilities, he could not have known. Or that he had suffered arguably actionable harm that he wished to bring before the courts, but was so stymied by inadequacies of the law library that he was unable even to file a complaint"). *See also Bounds v. Smith, supra*.

meaningful access to postconviction remedies — *i.e.*, that, under the circumstances "[t]he right to be heard [will] be ... of little avail if it d[oes] not comprehend the right to be heard by counsel."[63]

d. *Suspension Clause.* Supportive of the due process right of access to state postconviction proceedings is the proscription in Article I, Section 9 of the Constitution against suspension of the writ of habeas corpus.[64] Although the Suspension Clause has prompted the Court to recognize "that 'there is no higher duty than to maintain [the writ] unimpaired,'"[65] the precise scope of the remedy preserved by the clause is uncertain.[66] Nonetheless, two propositions have

---

[63] Powell v. Alabama, 287 U.S. 45, 68-69 (1932). *Accord Lewis v. Casey, supra,* 518 U.S. at 354-55 ("Nearly all of the access-to-courts cases in the *Bounds* line involved attempts by inmates to pursue direct appeals from the convictions for which they were incarcerated ... or habeas petitions.... The tools [*Bounds*] requires to be provided are those that the inmates need in order to attack their sentences, directly or collaterally, and in order to challenge the conditions of their confinement."); Kimmelman v. Morrison, 477 U.S. 365, 374-75, 377-78 (1986) (citing cases). *See* Johnson v. Avery, 393 U.S. 483, 486 (1969) ("for the indigent as well as for the affluent prisoner, postconviction proceedings must be more than a formality"); Battle v. Anderson, 376 F. Supp. 402, 426 (E.D. Okla. 1974) ("To be meaningful, the right of access to the courts must include the means to frame and present legal issues and relevant facts effectively for judicial consideration"); Hooks v. Wainwright, 352 F. Supp. 163, 165-67 (M.D. Fla. 1972). *See generally* Gibson v. Jackson, 578 F.2d 1045, 1052-53 (5th Cir. 1978) (addendum of Rubin, J.), *cert. denied,* 439 U.S. 1119 (1979); Lane v. Henderson, 480 F.2d 544, 545 (5th Cir. 1973). Considerable authority supports the proposition that in factually or legally complex postconviction cases and in cases in which the petitioner is mentally incompetent or for some other reason unable to grapple with the issues, fundamental fairness requires the provision of counsel and other necessary financial assistance. *See* Walters v. Jago, 642 F.2d 194 (6th Cir. 1981); Williams v. Martin, 618 F.2d 1021 (4th Cir. 1980) (assistance of pathologist); Pedrero v. Wainwright, 590 F.2d 1383, 1390-91 n.6 (5th Cir.), *cert. denied,* 444 U.S. 943 (1979) (psychiatric experts); Norris v. Wainwright, 588 F.2d 130, 133 (5th Cir.), *cert. denied,* 444 U.S. 846 (1979) (*dicta*); Kreiling v. Field, 431 F.2d 638, 640 (9th Cir. 1970); Jacobs v. United States, 350 F.2d 571 (4th Cir. 1965) (psychiatrist); United States ex rel. Robinson v. Pate, 345 F.2d 691 (7th Cir. 1965), *aff'd,* 383 U.S. 375 (1966) (psychiatrist); McCollum v. Bush, 344 F.2d 672 (5th Cir. 1965), *aff'g* 231 F. Supp. 560 (N.D. Tex. 1964) (psychiatric witness); Green v. United States, 158 F. Supp. 804, 808 (D. Mass.), *aff'd per curiam,* 256 F.2d 483 (1st Cir. 1958); other authority cited *supra* note 61; *infra* § 12.3b nn.59-84 and accompanying text. *See generally* 2 AMSTERDAM, *supra* § 7.2a n.1, at §§ 299-300. For an argument of the sort contemplated in text, see Petition for a Writ of Certiorari to the Texas Court of Criminal Appeals, Colella v. Texas, *supra* § 7.1b n.47.

[64] U.S. CONST., art. I, § 9, cl. 2 ("The Privilege of the Writ of Habeas Corpus shall not be suspended, unless when in Cases of Rebellion or Invasion the public Safety may require it"). *See generally supra* § 2.4e n.326 (discussing, *inter alia,* sources collected *supra* § 2.3 n.1).

[65] Johnson v. Avery, 393 U.S. 483, 485 (1969) (quoting Bowen v. Johnston, 306 U.S. 19, 26 (1939)).

[66] *See, e.g.,* Felker v. Turpin, 518 U.S. 651, 663-64 (1996) (discussed *infra* notes 73-80 and accompanying text) (noting, without resolving, controversy concerning extent of habeas corpus writ that Suspension Clause protects but assuming *arguendo* that Clause protects writ in its

considerable support. First, the right of habeas corpus is lost if individuals are

---

modern, fully evolved form). *See generally* Jordan Steiker, *Incorporating the Suspension Clause: Is There a Constitutional Right to Federal Habeas Corpus for State Prisoners?*, 92 MICH. L. REV. 862, 863-74 (1994); authorities cited in *id.* at 863 nn.6, 8, 865 n.16; authorities cited *supra* §§ 2.3 n.1 & 2.4e n.326. The Suspension Clause seems to preserve access to some judicial means of attacking some types of illegality in the process by which some agents of government incarcerate individuals, but its terse words do not specify either (1) the *types* of illegality of confinement that must be redressable in court, (2) the particular government *agents* whose incarcerative acts are subject to review, or (3) the *courts* in which those lines of attack must be open. *See infra* notes 74-80 and accompanying text. As we briefly delineate *supra* § 2.4e n.326, the historical analysis in section 2.4 *supra* suggests both a methodological and a substantive approach to the problem of interpreting the Suspension Clause and, specifically, to answering the three questions listed just above. Methodologically, it is arguable that Congress' views about the writ over the course of the nation's history as reflected in its enactments should be authoritative. Substantively, the rule conveyed by Congress' consistent course of legislation from 1789 until today is that *all important federal questions* — including, but not limited to all constitutional questions — arising in the process by which *the federal or a state government* comes to imprison an individual are subject to *federal court review as of right*. Moreover, because state review is now a statutory prerequisite to the only existing method of statutory review as of right of the legality under fundamental federal law of the custody of state prisoners, *see* 28 U.S.C.A. § 2254(b)(1) (West 1994 & Supp. 1998), it is arguable that state review sufficient to exhaust federal remedies also now deserves the Clause's protection. *See infra* note 73 and accompanying text.

At the least, however, the longstanding Anglo-American reliance on habeas corpus as "the fundamental instrument for safeguarding individual freedom against arbitrary and lawless state action," Harris v. Nelson, 394 U.S. 286, 290-91 (1969); *see supra* § 2.3, suggests that any exercise of the governmental power to incarcerate that violates the Due Process Clause's protections against arbitrary governmental action must be judicially redressable in *some* court "unless when in Cases of Rebellion or Invasion" such redress would threaten "the public Safety." *See Johnson v. Avery, supra,* 393 U.S. at 487; Ex parte Bollman, 8 U.S. (4 Cranch.) 75, 95 (1807). *See also* Ex parte Hull, 312 U.S. 546, 548-49 (1941). The description of the Suspension Clause in THE FEDERALIST leads to a similar conclusion. There, Alexander Hamilton stated that, via the Suspension Clause, habeas corpus was "provided for in the most ample manner" in order to guard against "[a]rbitrary impeachments, arbitrary methods of prosecuting pretended offenses, and arbitrary punishments upon arbitrary convictions" and that, together with the right to jury trial, habeas corpus provided comprehensive protection against "judicial despotism" in criminal cases. THE FEDERALIST No. 83, at 499 (A. Hamilton) (Clinton Rossiter ed. 1961). Via the adoption of the 14th Amendment, moreover, the post-bellum Framers clearly recognized that state as well as federal criminal courts were capable of the "judicial despotism" and "[a]rbitrary impeachments, arbitrary methods of prosecuting pretended offenses, and arbitrary punishments upon arbitrary convictions" to which Alexander Hamilton referred in THE FEDERALIST, *supra*. And via the 1867 habeas corpus act, passed simultaneously with the adoption of the 14th Amendment, Congress extended the habeas corpus remedy to all state prisoners incarcerated in violation of the Constitution and that amendment. *See supra* § 2.4d nn.114-26 and accompanying text. These premises make it reasonable to conclude that the post-bellum Framers understood the 14th Amendment's creation of *federal* protections against "judicial despotism" by state criminal courts also to extend to state prisoners the Constitution's protection against the suspension of a *federal* habeas corpus remedy. *See* Steiker, *supra* at 888-913 (arguing that 14th Amendment incorporates Suspension Clause and affords state prisoners constitutional right to federal court review of all constitutional claims).

unable to petition at least *some* court for postconviction relief.[67] Second, as the Court long has recognized, the writ may be suspended indirectly as well as by repeal,[68] including by interposing financial obstacles to postconviction proceedings that indigent prisoners cannot surmount,[69] imposing onerous conditions on prisoners' ability to file applications seeking postconviction relief,[70] or denying prisoners access to legal assistance.[71]

Together, these principles imply that a State effectively may suspend the writ by refusing to provide lawyers or other financial assistance necessary under the circumstances to permit prisoners meaningfully to pursue state, then federal, postconviction proceedings. To begin with, the denial of counsel and necessary financial assistance in state postconviction proceedings effectively may deny a prisoner a meaningful ability to utilize available state procedures to test the

---

[67] *See supra* §§ 2.4d, 2.4e (discussing historic assurance in this country of some means of federal court post-trial review as of right of constitutionality of incarceration and of procedures leading to it, with particular means changing from period to period); *supra* note 66. *See also* Heck v. Humphrey, 512 U.S. 477, 480-90 (1994) (discussed *infra* § 9.1 n.6) (availability of habeas corpus remedy permits Court to limit prisoners' access to largely redundant remedy under Civil Rights Act, 42 U.S.C. § 1983 (1994)). *Cf.* Nichols v. United States, 511 U.S. 738, 765 (1994) (Ginsburg, J., dissenting) (question "*whether*[] the defendant could attack a prior conviction for constitutional infirmity" presents much more serious issue than "forum question" as to "*where*" (*i.e.*, which of several modes of attack to use in which of several courts) (emphasis added)); Custis v. United States, 511 U.S. 485, 497 (1994) (in withdrawing one method of challenging legality of federal sentence, Court emphasizes continued availability of "federal habeas review" to bring similar challenge).

[68] *See Ex parte Bollman, supra*, 8 U.S. (4 Cranch.) at 95 ("for if the means be not in existence, the privilege itself would be lost, although no law for its suspension should be enacted"); Davis v. Adult Parole Authority, 610 F.2d 410 (6th Cir. 1979) ("rule which would permit a court to dismiss an action for habeas relief without any consideration of the equities presented renders the habeas corpus process inadequate to test the legality of a person's conviction and, thereby, constitutes a prohibited suspension of the writ").

[69] *See, e.g.,* Smith v. Bennett, 365 U.S. 708, 713 (1961) ("[f]inancial hurdles must not be permitted to condition [the writ's] exercise").

[70] *See, e.g., Ex parte Hull, supra*, 312 U.S. at 548-49 (invalidating prison regulation forbidding prisoners to file applications for postconviction relief unless their papers were approved beforehand by prison officials; "state and its officers may not abridge or impair petitioner's right to apply to a federal court for a writ of habeas corpus").

[71] *See, e.g.,* Johnson v. Avery, 393 U.S. 483, 487 (1969) (writ is impaired by prison rule forbidding inmates to furnish assistance to other inmates in preparing habeas corpus petitions). *But cf. The Habeas Corpus Reform Act of 1982: Hearings on S. 2216 Before the Senate Comm. on the Judiciary*, 97th Cong., 2d Sess. 106 (1982) (citing Swain v. Pressley, 430 U.S. 372, 385-86 (1977) (Burger, C.J., concurring)) (statement of Assistant Attorney General Rose: "If Congress can wholly abolish the writ of habeas corpus as it applies to federal court collateral review of state convictions, it necessarily can limit the scope of the writ in such cases without wholly abolishing it").

legality of his conviction and sentence.[72] Moreover, the State's failure to provide counsel to represent prisoners in filing *state* petitions for postconviction relief and other necessary financial assistance substantially impairs their right to meaningful *federal* habeas corpus review because state prisoners are not permitted to pursue federal remedies until state remedies are properly exhausted, and state prisoners may lose their statutory right to habeas corpus review or at least seriously compromise that right if they fail to present claims and evidence in an appropriate manner in the state courts.[73] Accordingly, by frustrating all available collateral remedies, the denial of counsel and other essential assistance — particularly in legally or factually complex cases and in cases involving prisoners without the means to litigate substantial claims — effectively may suspend the writ under any reasonable interpretation of the Suspension Clause.

As it already has begun to do,[74] the Antiterrorism and Effective Death Penalty

---

[72] *See supra* § 7.2c. *See also* McFarland v. Scott, 512 U.S. 849, 856 (1994) ("Requiring an indigent capital petitioner to proceed without counsel [in habeas corpus proceedings] ... would expose him to the substantial risk that his habeas claims never would be heard on the merits."); Murray v. Giarratano, 492 U.S. 1, 14-15 (1992) (Kennedy, J., concurring in the judgment) (similar); *id.* at 26-29 (Stevens, J., dissenting) (similar).

[73] *See* McFarland v. Scott, 512 U.S. 1256, 1261-63 (1994) (Blackmun, J., dissenting from denial of *certiorari*) ("State habeas corpus proceedings are a vital link in the capital review process, not the least because all federal habeas claims first must be adequately raised in state court ... [to avoid being denied in federal court as] procedurally defaulted or waived ...."); McFarland v. Scott, 512 U.S. 849, 860 (1994) (O'Connor, J., concurring in the judgment in part) ("our carefully crafted doctrines of waiver and abuse of the writ make it especially important that the first [federal habeas corpus] petition [and, thus, the state exhaustion proceedings that precede it] adequately set forth all of a state prisoner's colorable grounds for relief"); *Murray v. Giarratano, supra*, 492 U.S. at 14 (Kennedy, J., concurring in the judgment) ("It cannot be denied that collateral relief proceedings are a central part of the review process for prisoners sentenced to death"); *id.* at 26 (Stevens, J., dissenting) ("State postconviction proceedings ... are the cornerstone for all subsequent attempts to obtain collateral relief. Once a [state] court determines that a claim is procedurally barred, a federal court may not review it unless the defendant can make one of two difficult showings .... If an asserted claim is tested in an evidentiary hearing, the state postconviction court's factual findings may control the scope of a federal court's review ... [on] habeas corpus."); Giarratano v. Murray, 678 F. Supp. 511, 513, 515 (E.D. Va. 1986), *aff'd*, 847 F.2d 1118 (4th Cir. 1988) (*en banc*), *rev'd sub nom.* Murray v. Giarratano, 492 U.S. 1 (1989); Gibson v. Jackson, 443 F. Supp. 239, 250 (M.D. Ga. 1977), *vac'd on other grounds*, 578 F.2d 1045 (5th Cir. 1978), *cert. denied*, 439 U.S. 1119 (1979); *supra* § 7.1a nn.29-33 and accompanying text.

[74] *See, e.g.*, Felker v. Turpin, 518 U.S. 651, 663-64 (1996); Gendron v. United States, 1998 WL 514668, at *3 (7th Cir.1998) (discussed *supra* § 5.1b n.49); Martinez-Villareal v. Stewart, 118 F.3d 628, 632 (9th Cir. 1997), *aff'd on other grounds*, 118 S. Ct. 1618 (1998) (interpreting AEDPA's successive petition provisions narrowly to avoid "'serious constitutional problems'" under Suspension Clause that broader interpretation would raise); *id.* at 635 (T.G. Nelson, J., concurring) (concluding that AEDPA's successive petition restrictions caused Suspension Clause violation under circumstances); Martin v. Bissonette, 1997 WL 280602 (1st Cir. May 29, 1997), *vac'd*, 1997 WL 374793 (1st Cir. July 11, 1997) (similar to *Lindh v. Murphy, infra*); In re Medina,

Act of 1996 (AEDPA)[75] is likely to generate substantial amounts of litigation under the Suspension Clause.[76] In so doing, it may force the resolution of questions that the Clause has long posed but that the federal courts have never authoritatively resolved, such as whether the "writ of habeas corpus" that the Clause protects is only the writ as it existed in 1789 (and, if so, what the 1789 writ entailed); whether the Clause protects only federal, or also state, prisoners; whether the Clause only forbids Congress to suspend such habeas corpus remedies as already happen to be available (*e.g.*, under preexisting federal or state statutory law) — or only such habeas corpus remedies as particular prisoners already happen to have invoked — but does not require Congress to provide access to the writ in the first place; and so forth.[77] Although the result of the Suspension Clause litigation that AEDPA invites is in doubt, the Supreme Court's first allusions to the issue, in *Felker v. Turpin*,[78] are consistent with a broad interpretation of the Clause to protect the writ "as it exists today" or as it has been affected by "th[e] evolutionary process" that the writ has undergone during the 20th century.[79] *Felker* by negative implication, and a number of lower

---

109 F.3d 1556, 1564 (11th Cir. 1997) (addressing but rejecting Suspension Clause attack on application of AEDPA's successive petition rules); Greenawalt v. Stewart, 105 F.3d 1268, 1277 (9th Cir. 1997) (*per curiam*), *cert. denied*, 117 S. Ct. 794 (1997) (similar); Denton v. Norris, 104 F.3d 166, 167 n.2 (8th Cir. 1997) (rejecting argument that AEDPA's "blanket ban on same-claim successive petitions, is unconstitutional as a suspension of the writ of habeas corpus" but acknowledging that, in light of Suspension Clause, "[t]here may be circumstances in which the statute should not be literally and woodenly applied" to preclude litigation of constitutional claims); Lindh v. Murphy, 96 F.3d 856, 867-68 (7th Cir. 1996) (*en banc*), *rev'd on other grounds*, 117 S. Ct. 2059 (1997) (considering Suspension Clause's implications for interpretation of amended 28 U.S.C. § 2254(d)(1)); Dubois v. Angelone, No. 96-10 (4th Cir. Aug. 27, 1996) (discussed *supra* § 5.1b n.56); Breard v. Angelone, 926 F. Supp. 546, 547 (E.D. Va. 1996) (finding Suspension Clause violation caused by application of AEDPA's statute of limitations to bar petition as to which limitations period ran before AEDPA became law); Perez v. Marshall, 1996 WL 607075, at *7-*8 (S.D. Cal. Oct. 7, 1996) (similar to *Lindh v. Murphy*, *supra*); other decisions cited *infra* note 80. *See also supra* § 5.1b nn.120-22 (discussing likelihood of Suspension Clause challenges to 180-day statute of limitations that applies to "opt-in" cases under AEDPA).

[75] Pub. L. 104-132, 110 Stat. 1214 (1996).

[76] *See supra* §§ 3.3c n.60, 5.1b nn.109-122 and accompanying text; *infra* §§ 28.4a nn. 12-19 and accompanying text, 30.2d.

[77] *See* Steiker, *supra* note 66 (discussing many open questions that Suspension Clause presents); *supra* note 66 (similar).

[78] 518 U.S. 651 (1996).

[79] *Id.* at 663-64 ("assum[ing]" for argument's sake "that the Suspension Clause ... refers to the writ as it exists today" and relying on "the compass of th[e] evolutionary process" that writ has undergone during 20th century to resolve suspension question); *see* Martinez-Villareal v. Stewart, 118 F.3d 628, 631 n.2 (9th Cir. 1997), *aff'd on other grounds*, 118 S. Ct. 1618 (1998) ("like the Supreme Court, we assume that 'the Suspension Clause of the Constitution refers to the writ as it

federal court cases decided since *Felker*, have suggested that a Suspension Clause violation might arise if a prisoner had no *postconviction* opportunity (either in the lower federal courts or on original writ to the Supreme Court, and either in an initial or numerically successive federal petition) to raise a particular constitutional claim.[80]

---

exists today, rather than as it existed in 1789,'" hence analysis is not controlled by "writ known to the Framers").

[80] *See Felker, supra*, 518 U.S. at 660-61, 663-64 (constitutional questions avoided by Court's conclusion that AEDPA did not foreclose original writ in Supreme Court); Miller v. Marr, 141 F.3d 976, 977-78 (10th Cir. 1998) (recognizing that "[w]hether the one-year [nonopt-in] limitation period violates the Suspension Clause depends upon whether the limitation period renders the habeas remedy 'inadequate or ineffective' to test the legality of detention" and that "[t]here may be circumstances where the limitation period at least raises serious constitutional questions and possibly renders the habeas remedy inadequate and ineffective," but concluding that statute of limitations did not have that effect in instant case); *Martinez-Villareal v. Stewart, supra*, 118 F.3d at 631-32 & nn.3-5 (finding "patent" "constitutional problem with" applying AEDPA to "preclu[de]" any federal postconviction opportunity, including on original writ to Supreme Court, to raise constitutional claim of incompetence to be executed (because claim was "premature" at time of first petition when execution was not imminent and because, read literally, AEDPA would bar numerically "'second'" petition raising same claim); Suspension Clause problems are avoided only when "res judicata" principles apply because petitioner did raise or could have raised claim in prior petition; "reject[ing] ... suggestion that direct review by the Supreme Court [on *certiorari*] of the state court's competency proceedings suffices to sustain [AEDPA] against constitutional attack" because "[c]ertiorari review does not amount to an adequate alternative form of collateral relief" (citing Swain v. Pressley, 430 U.S. 372, 381 (1977)); also rejecting literal interpretation of AEDPA's ban on "'second'" petitions and treating petition at issue as not "'second or successive'" in order to avoid "'serious constitutional problems'"); *id.* at 635 (T.G. Nelson, J., concurring) ("In my view, the 1996 Act unconstitutionally suspends the writ of habeas corpus as to competence to be executed claims ... in an unambiguous fashion, by prohibiting the consideration of claims in second or successive petitions that ... there was no earlier [federal postconviction] opportunity to [raise]. If the writ has not been suspended as to those claims, it is difficult to see how it can ever be suspended as to any class of claims."); In re Medina, 109 F.3d 1556, 1564 (11th Cir. 1997) (finding no Suspension Clause violation in situation similar to that in *Martinez-Villareal, supra*, but premising conclusion on assumption that claim was cognizable on original writ in Supreme Court); Camarano v. Irvin, 98 F.3d 44, 46-47 (2d Cir. 1996) (giving nonliteral interpretation to "'second or successive petition'" as used in AEDPA to permit petitioner whose initial petition had been dismissed without prejudice for failure to exhaust state remedies to secure adjudication of later petition containing same, but now exhausted, claims; otherwise, "application of ... [AEDPA's successive petition restrictions] to deny a resubmitted petition in cases such as this would effectively preclude any federal [postconviction] review"); Rosa v. Senkowski, 1997 WL 436484, at *7 (S.D.N.Y. Aug. 1, 1997), *modified*, 1997 WL 724559 (S.D.N.Y. Nov. 19, 1997), *aff'd on other grounds*, 1998 WL 334346 (2d Cir. June 24, 1998) ("The application of the [nonopt-in] time limit to Rosa's first habeas petition effectively deprives him of the ability to obtain any collateral review in a federal court of the merits of his claim that his confinement violates his constitutional rights. Such a deprivation constitutes an unconstitutional 'suspension' of the writ of habeas corpus."); Breard v. Angelone, 926 F. Supp. 546, 547 (E.D. Va. 1996) ("The Court finds that [new opt-in statute of limitations in] § 2263 infringes on the privilege of habeas corpus in this case

e. *Equal protection — claims available for first time in state postconviction proceedings.* In *Douglas v. California,*[81] the Supreme Court held that the Equal Protection Clause requires the States to provide appointed counsel for indigents pursuing first appeals as of right. The Court concluded that "where the merits of *the one and only appeal* an indigent has of right are decided without benefit of counsel, we think an unconstitutional line has been drawn between rich and poor."[82] In that situation,

> [t]here is lacking that equality demanded by the Fourteenth Amendment where the rich man, who appeals as of right, enjoys the benefit of counsel's examination into the record, research of the law, and marshalling of arguments on his behalf, while the indigent, already burdened by a preliminary determination that his case is without merit, is forced to shift for himself. The indigent, where the record is unclear or the errors are hidden, has only the right to a meaningless ritual, while the rich man has a meaningful appeal.[83]

---

because prior to its passage, the petitioner would not have been time barred, yet upon its passage he was immediately time barred; the statute provides for no safe harbor or special exception. The law would require the petitioner, prior to the passage of § 2263, to have anticipated this effect. Section 2263 in the instant case is inadequate to test the legality of the petitioner's conviction and completely prevents any consideration of the equities of the case; therefore, § 2263 violates the suspension clause and is unconstitutional as applied."); *infra* § 28.4a nn.7, 19 and accompanying text). *See also* Burris v. Parke, 95 F.3d 465, 468-69 (7th Cir. 1996) (*en banc*) (applying pre-AEDPA law and thereby avoiding injustice of applying AEDPA's stringent standards for successive petitions in manner that would have entirely deprived habeas corpus petitioner — who filed separate petitions to challenge conviction and penalty retrial but who could have consolidated claims in single petition if he had been given notice of AEDPA — of any forum in which to litigate constitutional attacks on resentencing); Rodriguez v. Artuz, 990 F.Supp. 275, 277-84 (S.D.N.Y. 1998) (declining to follow holding in *Rosa v. Senkowski, supra,* "that the AEDPA's one-year statute of limitations is in all cases an unconstitutional suspension of the writ," but recognizing that Suspension Clause issues may arise if, as result of AEDPA, "a petitioner could never have raised his or her claim" or federal review is unavailable for "a petitioner [who] can show he is actually innocent of the crime for which he is convicted"). *Compare* In re Vial, 115 F.3d 1192, 1197-98 (4th Cir. 1997) (*en banc*) (concluding that Suspension Clause challenge to successive petitions limitations that would preclude petitioner from raising claim that could not have been raised earlier "is foreclosed by the recent decision of the Supreme Court in *Felker*") *with* Triestman v. United States, 124 F.3d 361, 378 n.21 (2d Cir. 1997) (expressing doubts about, but declining to resolve, propriety of 4th Circuit's interpretation of *Felker* in *In re Vial, supra,* and noting that issue presented in *Vial* and also in *Triestman* "involves a situation that the *Felker* Court did not face: Congress has arguably cut off all postconviction relief for a claim of actual innocence that was based on the existing record and that could not have been effectively brought previously.").

[81] 372 U.S. 353 (1963).

[82] *Id.* at 357 (emphasis in original).

[83] *Id.* at 357-58. *See also* Roberts v. LaVallee, 389 U.S. 40, 42 (1967) ("differences in access to the instruments needed to vindicate legal rights, when based upon the financial situation of the

Even earlier, in *Smith v. Bennett*, the Court recognized that the Equal Protection Clause applies to state postconviction proceedings, holding that States may not constitutionally deny indigents access to state postconviction remedies by charging them filing fees they cannot pay.[84] *Douglas* did not address the question whether appointed counsel or other necessary financial assistance must be provided for a prisoner seeking postconviction review.[85] Its reasoning supports a right to counsel in some postconviction proceedings, however, because, as to certain kinds of claims, such proceedings are the equivalent of a first state appeal as of right.[86]

As noted in section 7.1b *supra*, in many situations, whether as a matter of state law or of fact, postconviction proceedings provide the first and only available state court forum in which prisoners may raise certain kinds of constitutional claims — including claims of ineffective assistance of counsel, suppression of evidence, improper contacts between jurors and third parties, and the like.[87] State postconviction review also is likely to be the first meaningful state court review of any sort in situations in which actions by state judges or other state officials or of incompetent defense attorneys have previously blocked access to state trial and direct appellate forums for presenting constitutional claims.[88] In such circumstances, the convicted inmate whom state law, the facts, the trial court, the prosecution, or defense counsel has denied a meaningful opportunity to advance constitutional claims at trial or on appeal "has not previously had 'an adequate opportunity to present his claims fairly in the

---

defendant, are repugnant to the Constitution.'"); Coppedge v. United States, 369 U.S. 438, 446-47 (1962); decisions cited *infra* note 84.

[84] 365 U.S. 708, 713-14 (1961). Also indicative of the Equal Protection Clause's application to state postconviction proceedings are Supreme Court opinions applying the Clause to discretionary state judicial proceedings that States choose, but are not constitutionally required, to afford to criminal defendants. *See, e.g.*, Ohio Adult Parole Auth. v. Woodard, 118 S. Ct. 1244, 1254 (1998) (O'Connor, J., concurring) ("scheme whereby a state official flipped a coin to determine whether to grant clemency, or in a case where the State arbitrarily denied a prisoner any access to its clemency process" would violate Equal Protection Clause); M.L.B. v. S.L.J., 117 S. Ct. 555, 556 (1996); Estelle v. Dorrough, 420 U.S. 534, 568 (1975) (*per curiam*); decisions cited *supra* note 83.

[85] *See Douglas, supra,* 372 U.S. at 356.

[86] *Smith* independently supports an equal protection right to state postconviction counsel, given that, in many or most postconviction proceedings, the denial of counsel is likely to be as preclusive of meaningful habeas corpus review as the procedure voided in *Smith*, namely, denying indigent prisoners the financial ability to file in the first place. *See* authority cited *supra* §§ 7.2c, 7.2d; *infra* § 12.3a nn.11-20 and accompanying text, 12.3b n.68 and accompanying text.

[87] *See supra* § 7.1b nn.77-83 and accompanying text; *infra* § 9.1 nn.21, 26, 28, 33, 34; *infra* § 25.4 nn.40-45 and accompanying text; *infra* § 26.3b nn.30, 32, 41; *infra* §§ 33.3 n.11, 33.4 n.2, 41.4a n.7 (all providing examples; citing authority).

[88] For examples, see *infra* §§ 20.3e, 26.3b.

context of the State's appellate process.'"[89] Accordingly, state postconviction proceedings in which the prisoner is raising claims that are then available for the first time in any state court are the functional equivalent of a first appeal as of right. In such circumstances, the right to counsel and essential financial assistance recognized in *Douglas* should apply.

In *Coleman v. Thompson*,[90] the Court recognized that the Equal Protection Clause[91] might afford a right to meaningful representation in state postconviction proceedings whenever, practically speaking, those proceedings serve as the prisoner's "'one and only appeal'" as of right in the state courts.[92] Under *Coleman*, when practical or state law reasons make "state collateral review ... the first place a prisoner can present a challenge to his conviction," the equal protection rules of "*Douglas v. California*, ... that an indigent criminal defendant has a right to appointed counsel in his first appeal as of right in a state court" and of "*Evitts v. Lucey*,[[93]] ... that this right encompasses a right to effective assistance of counsel for all criminal defendants in their first appeal as of right" might give the state postconviction petitioner a right to counsel in "his 'one and only appeal,' if that is what a state collateral proceeding may be considered."[94]

---

[89] Evitts v. Lucey, 469 U.S. 387, 402 (1985) (quoting Ross v. Moffitt, 417 U.S. 600, 616 (1974)). *See* Goeke v. Branch, 514 U.S. 115, 120 (1995) (*per curiam*) (under *Evitts v. Lucey*, *supra*, although "'convicted criminal has no constitutional right to an appeal,'" he does have "Due Process Clause[ ] guarantee [of] ... effective assistance of counsel on his first appeal as of right" (citation omitted)).

[90] 501 U.S. 722 (1991).

[91] The same argument might be made directly under the 6th Amendment right to counsel "[i]n all criminal prosecutions," on the theory that direct appeal, and postconviction substitutes for direct appeal, are parts of the criminal prosecution. *See infra* § 25.6 (Supreme Court caselaw suggesting that criminal prosecution only terminates following direct appeal).

[92] *Coleman, supra,* 501 U.S. at 755-57 (quoting Douglas v. California, 372 U.S. 353, 357 (1963) (emphasis omitted by Court)).

[93] 469 U.S. 387 (1985).

[94] *Coleman, supra,* 501 U.S. at 755-57. *See also* Murray v. Giarratano, 492 U.S. 1, 24 (1989) (Stevens, J., dissenting) (among reasons for concluding that appointment of postconviction counsel for Virginia's death sentenced inmates is constitutionally required are that: "Virginia law contemplates that some claims ordinarily heard on direct review will be relegated to postconviction proceedings," including, for example, claims that trial or appellate counsel provided constitutionally ineffective assistance; "some irregularities, such as prosecutorial misconduct, may not surface until after the direct review is complete"; and "new evidence even may suggest that the defendant is innocent"); *id.* at 14 (Kennedy, J., concurring in judgment) ("It cannot be denied that collateral relief proceedings are a central part of the review process for prisoners sentenced to death"); Henry J. Friendly, *Is Innocence Irrelevant? Collateral Attack on Criminal Judgments,* 38 U. CHI. L. REV. 142, 151-52 (1970) ("there are circumstances, such as post-trial discovery of the knowing use of material perjured evidence by the prosecutor or claims of coercion to plead guilty, where failure to provide [a reliable means of collateral attack] would deny due process of law"). The *Coleman* Court did not finally adopt the legal theory discussed in text because it determined that Coleman

Evitts and *Coleman* reveal the irrelevance in the situation contemplated here — in which claims are available for state court review for the first time in state postconviction proceedings — of the Court's analysis in *Pennsylvania v. Finley*.[95] Addressing a state postconviction pleading "rais[ing] the *same* issues that the Supreme Court of Pennsylvania had rejected on the merits" on direct appeal, the *Finley* majority refused to draw an analogy between direct appeals as of right and redundant state postconviction proceedings.[96] Instead, the Court drew an analogy between state postconviction proceedings and discretionary appeals following a first appeal as of right — in the latter of which, under *Ross v. Moffitt*,[97] there is no right to counsel.[98] But as *Evitts* and the *Coleman dicta* reveal, in circumstances different from those actually presented in *Finley* — for example, when substantial claims cognizable for the first time in any state court are presented — *Ross* does not control.[99]

---

received effective representation at the trial phase of his state postconviction proceeding, hence in what amounted to his "'one and only appeal'" — irrespective of his claim that he received ineffective assistance on his state postconviction *appeal. See Coleman, supra* at 755-56. *But cf.* lower court decisions cited *supra* § 7.1b n.76 (refusing to extend constitutional protection to prisoners denied competent counsel in state postconviction proceedings that served as functional equivalent of first appeal on issue presented).

[95] 481 U.S. 551 (1987) (discussed *supra* § 7.2a).

[96] *Id.* at 553, 555-57 (emphasis added).

[97] 417 U.S. 600 (1974). *Ross* considered whether North Carolina had to provide counsel to represent an indigent convicted of a minor offense in preparing both an application for discretionary review by the North Carolina Supreme Court and a petition for writ of *certiorari* to the United States Supreme Court. *Ross* is distinguishable from the situation contemplated here because (1) the procedures at issue there were discretionary, not as of right, and were not decided based on the "perceived correctness" of the decision below but instead on whether the subject matter of the appeal had substantial public significance, *id.* at 615, and (2) the claims presented had "'once [previously] been presented by a lawyer and passed upon by an appellate court,'" *id.* at 614 (quoting *Douglas, supra,* 372 U.S. at 356).

[98] *Finley, supra,* 481 U.S. at 555. *See also* Austin v. United States, 513 U.S. 5, 8 (1994) (*per curiam*) ("though indigent defendants pursuing appeals as of right have a constitutional right to a brief filed on their behalf by an attorney, *Anders v. California,* 386 U.S. 738 (1967), that right does not extend to forums for discretionary review. *Ross v. Moffitt,* 417 U.S. 600, 616-17 (1974).").

[99] *See Evitts, supra,* 469 U.S. at 402 (right to effective assistance of counsel in criminal appeals because such appeals "– unlike the discretionary appeal in *Ross* –" are not "contingent on a discretionary finding ... that the case involves significant public or jurisprudential issues," but instead are required "to determine whether the individual defendant has been lawfully convicted" and serve persons who have "not previously had 'an adequate opportunity to present [their] claims fairly in the context of the State's appellate process'"); *supra* notes 90-94 and accompanying text (discussing *Coleman's dicta* contemplating extension of *Evitts'* reasoning to initial postconviction proceeding when that proceeding is petitioner's first opportunity to present claim).

f. *Capital cases.* The basis for a constitutional right to counsel and to other necessary financial assistance is strongest in capital litigation.[100] The three due process factors set forth by the Supreme Court in *Ake v. Oklahoma*[101] illustrate the point.[102] The private interest involved is life itself. The governmental interest in ensuring that the death penalty is imposed only in appropriate cases is equally significant.[103] And the risk of harming both those interests is high. In the last regard, capital cases by their nature are more factually and legally complex and demanding of legal expertise than other cases, while the frequent need to litigate such cases quickly under threat of an unstayed execution date or stringent statutes of limitations, the especially confining custodial constraints placed on death row inmates in most prisons, and the psychological pressures associated with an impending execution all render condemned prisoners less capable than other prisoners of adequately representing themselves.[104] Moreover, if — but only

---

[100] Many capital prisoners in the past have secured volunteer representation. On the difficulty of securing volunteer counsel under current conditions, especially in States with large death row populations, see McFarland v. Scott, 512 U.S. 1256, 1262 (1994) (Blackmun, J., dissenting from denial of *certiorari*) (citing sources); Godbold, *supra* § 7.2a n.1; Lardent & Cohen, *supra* § 7.1a n.2; The Spangenberg Group, *supra* § 7.2a n.2; Wilson & Spangenberg, *supra* § 7.2a n.1; *infra* § 12.2 n.2 and accompanying text. *See also* McFarland v. Scott, 512 U.S. 849, 870 (1994) (Thomas, J., dissenting) ("it seems likely that Congress expected that the States would also shoulder some of the burden of providing pre[-federal habeas corpus] legal assistance to indigent death-sentenced prisoners" because "'[a] state that has elected to impose the death penalty should provide adequate funding for the procedures it has adopted to properly implement that penalty'" (quoting Hill v. Lockhart, 992 F.2d 801, 803 (8th Cir. 1993)). Although the "opt-in" provisions of the Antiterrorism and Effective Death Penalty Act, Pub. L. 104-132, 110 Stat. 1214 (1996), were designed to give States incentives to provide capital prisoners with competent state postconviction counsel, *see supra* § 3.3, the early evidence is not cause for optimism, both because so many States have failed to satisfy the statute's competent counsel requirements, *see supra* § 3.3a n.1 and accompanying text, and because of the serious difficulties encountered by those States that have tried to do so. *See* Petition for a Writ of Certiorari to the Texas Court of Criminal Appeals, Colella v. Texas, *supra* § 7.1b n.47 (Texas).

[101] 470 U.S. 68, 77 (1985).

[102] *See generally supra* § 7.2b.

[103] Gardner v. Florida, 430 U.S. 349, 357-58 (1977) ("It is of vital importance ... to the community that any decision to impose the death sentence be, and appear to be, based on reason rather than caprice or emotion.").

[104] *See* McFarland v. Scott, 512 U.S. 1256, 1257 (1994) (Blackmun, J., dissenting from denial of *certiorari*) ("The unique, bifurcated nature of capital trials and the special investigation into a defendant's personal history and background that may be required, the complexity and fluidity of the law, and the high, emotional stakes involved all make capital cases more costly and difficult to litigate than ordinary criminal trials."); McFarland v. Scott, 512 U.S. 849, 855 (1994) ("Congress' provision of a right to counsel [in capital habeas corpus cases] under [21 U.S.C.] § 848(q)(4)(B) reflects a determination that quality legal representation is necessary in capital habeas corpus proceedings in light of 'the seriousness of the possible penalty and ... the unique and complex nature of the litigation.'" (citations omitted)); Murray v. Giarratano, 492 U.S. 1, 14 (1989)

if[105] — adequate representation *is* available to prove it, the very strong possibility exists that a wrongful or illegal conviction or death sentence has occurred. For, as Justice Blackmun has observed, the rate of error in capital cases is staggeringly high:

> Of the capital cases reviewed in federal habeas corpus proceedings between 1976 and 1991, nearly half (46%) were found to have constitutional error.... The total reversal rate of capital cases at all [including state court] stages of review during the same time period was estimated at 60% or more.... This Court frequently has granted capital defendants relief in federal habeas corpus proceedings.[106]

Eighth Amendment due process concerns reinforce this conclusion. The 8th Amendment requires that a state's capital-sentencing procedures assure "the evenhanded, rational, and consistent imposition of death sentences under law."[107] Where a life is in the balance, these procedures must operate "so as to minimize the risk of wholly arbitrary and capricious action."[108] Because the "provision for counsel to represent prisoners" in habeas corpus cases undoubtedly "enhance[s] the probability of an effective presentation and a proper disposition of prisoners' claims"[109] and because the 8th Amendment

---

(Kennedy, J. concurring in the judgment) (discussed *infra* note 111); *id.* at 28 (Stevens, J., joined by Brennan, Marshall, and Blackmun, JJ., dissenting) (discussed in *id.*) ("[T]his Court's death penalty jurisprudence unquestionably is difficult even for a trained lawyer to master"); Degarmo v. Collins, 984 F.2d 142, 143 (5th Cir. 1993) (*per curiam*) ("[W]e are aware of the difficulties for counsel in death cases both for the state and habeas petitioners.... The law is complex and there is often little time"); Giarratano v. Murray, 668 F. Supp. 511 (E.D. Va. 1986), *aff'd*, 847 F.2d 1118, 1122 (4th Cir. 1988) (*en banc*), *rev'd sub nom. Murray v. Giarratano*, 492 U.S. 1 (1989); Gibson v. Jackson, 443 F. Supp. 239, 250 (M.D. Ga. 1977), *vac'd on other grounds*, 578 F.2d 1045 (5th Cir. 1978), *cert. denied*, 439 U.S. 1119 (1979); Carey v. Garrison, 403 F. Supp. 395, 397 (W.D.N.C. 1975). *See also* Gibson v. Jackson, 578 F.2d 1045, 1054 n.4 (5th Cir. 1978) (addendum of Rubin, J.), *cert. denied*, 439 U.S. 1119 (1979); In re Anderson, 447 P.2d 117 (Cal. 1968), *cert. denied*, 406 U.S. 971 (1972); *supra* § 4.2; *infra* §§ 12.3a nn.11-20 and accompanying text, 12.3b n.68 and accompanying text.

[105] *See* authority cited *supra* note 104; *supra* §§ 7.2c, 7.2d.

[106] McFarland v. Scott, 512 U.S. 1256, 1263 (1994) (Blackmun, J., dissenting from denial of *certiorari*) (citations omitted). *See also* Murray v. Giarratano, *supra*, 492 U.S. at 23-24 & n.13 (Stevens, J., dissenting); Jack Greenberg, *Capital Punishment as a System*, 91 YALE L.J. 908, 921 (1982); authority cited *supra* § 2.3 n.23.

[107] Jurek v. Texas, 428 U.S. 262, 276 (1976); authority cited *supra* § 2.6 n.3.

[108] Gregg v. Georgia, 428 U.S. 153, 189 (1976). *See* Monge v. California, 118 S. Ct. 2246, 2252 (1998) ("'capital proceedings [must] be policed at all stages by an especially vigilant concern for procedural fairness and for the accuracy of factfinding.'").

[109] Case v. Nebraska, 381 U.S. 336, 347 (1965) (Brennan, J., concurring). *See also* Powell v. Alabama, 287 U.S. 45, 68-69 (1932) ("The right to be heard would be, in many cases, of little avail if it did not comprehend the right to be heard by counsel."); *supra* §§ 7.2c, 7.2d.

requires that the probability of a proper disposition in capital cases be higher than that demanded by due process in other criminal cases,[110] the 8th and 14th Amendments' separate due process components together seem to require counsel at each step of a capital case's journey from trial and appeal through state postconviction proceedings to an initial set of federal habeas corpus proceedings.[111]

---

[110] *See* authority cited *supra* § 2.6.

[111] *See* authority cited *supra* note 104. *Compare* Murray v. Giarratano, 492 U.S. 1, 9-10 (1989) (four-person plurality opinion) ("We have ... refused to hold that the fact that a death sentence has been imposed requires a different standard of review on federal habeas corpus ... [and] think that ... the rule of *Pennsylvania v. Finley* [481 U.S. 551 (1987), which the plurality interpreted as denying right to state postconviction counsel in all circumstances] should apply no differently in capital cases than in noncapital cases"; plurality "therefore decline[s] to read either the Eighth Amendment or the Due Process Clause to require yet another distinction between the rights of capital ... defendants and those in noncapital cases") *with id.* at 14-15 (Kennedy, J., concurring in the judgment) (discussed *supra* § 7.2a n.14) ("collateral relief proceedings are a central part of the review process for prisoners sentenced to death," and "[t]he complexity of our jurisprudence in this area ... makes it unlikely that capital defendants will be able to file petitions for collateral relief without the assistance of persons learned in the law"; constitutional requirement of representation satisfied in this case, however, because "no prisoner on death row in Virginia has been unable to obtain counsel to represent him in postconviction proceedings, and Virginia's prison system is staffed with institutional lawyers to assist in preparing petitions for postconviction relief") *and id.* at 19-20 (Stevens, J., dissenting, joined by Brennan, Marshall and Blackmun, JJ.) ("even if it is permissible to leave an ordinary prisoner to his own resources in collateral proceedings, it is fundamentally unfair to require an indigent death row inmate to initiate collateral review without counsel's guiding hand"; "[l]egislatures conferred greater access to counsel on capital defendants than on persons facing lesser punishment even in colonial times"). *Cf. supra* § 2.6 (Supreme Court's willingness to provide additional process in capital habeas corpus cases only on occasional, *ad hoc*, but not categorical, basis).

PART III
HABEAS CORPUS JURISDICTION

Chapter 8
SUBJECT-MATTER JURISDICTION: CUSTODY

§ 8.1. Introduction to subject-matter jurisdiction.

To invoke habeas corpus review by a federal court, the petitioner must satisfy two jurisdictional requirements — (1) the status requirement that the petition be "in behalf of a person in custody pursuant to the judgment of a State court";[1] and (2) the substance requirement that the petition challenge the legality of that custody on the ground that it is "in violation of the Constitution or laws or treaties of the United States."[2] This Chapter discusses the status requirement — defining custodial statuses and describing the circumstances in which an individual who is *not* in custody may file a petition on behalf of someone who is. Chapter 9 discusses the substance requirement.[3]

§ 8.2. Definition of "custody."[1]

a. *Custody in general.* Historically, the federal courts limited habeas corpus review to prisoners who, at the moment the federal petition was actually

---

§ 8.1. [1] 28 U.S.C.A. § 2254(a) (West 1994 & Supp. 1998).

[2] *Id. See* Rule 1 of Rules Governing § 2254 Cases. *See also* 28 U.S.C. §§ 2241(c)(3), 2242-43, 2252 (1994); 28 U.S.C.A. §§ 2244, 2253 (West 1994 & Supp. 1998).

[3] *See also supra* § 2.4.

§ 8.2. [1] *See generally* Advisory Committee Note to Rule 1 of the Rules Governing § 2254 Cases; WAYNE R. LaFAVE & JEROLD H. ISRAEL, CRIMINAL PROCEDURE § 28.2(c) (2d ed. 1992); RONALD P. SOKOL, FEDERAL HABEAS CORPUS 38-50, 54-80 (2d ed. 1969); LARRY W. YACKLE, POSTCONVICTION REMEDIES §§ 41-51 (1981 & Supp. 1998); James A. Albert & Gregory A. Brodek, *Habeas Corpus — A Better Remedy in Visitation Denial Cases,* 41 MAINE L. REV. 239 (1989); Nobel F. Allen, *Habeas Corpus and Immigration: Important Issues and Developments,* 4 GEO. IMMIG. L.J. 503 (1990); Ira P. Robbins & Susan M. Newell, *The Continuing Diminished Availability of Federal Habeas Corpus Review to Challenge State Court Judgments:* Lehman v. Lycoming County Children's Services Agency, 33 AM. U.L. REV. 271 (1984); Robert J. Sharpe, *Habeas Corpus, Extradition and the Burden of Proof: The Case of the Man Who Escaped from Devil's Island,* 49 CAMBRIDGE L.J. 422 (1990); Comment, *Federal Habeas Corpus Jurisdiction — the Undeveloped Areas,* 41 WASH. L. REV. 327 (1966); Comment, *Federal Habeas Corpus: The Concept of Custody and Access to Federal Court,* 53 J. URB. L. 61 (1975); Comment, *The Mootness Question in Habeas Corpus Proceedings Where Petitioner Is Released Prior to Final Adjudication,* 1969 UTAH L. REV. 265; Andrea Lovell, Note, *The Proper Scope of Habeas Corpus Review in Civil Removal Proceedings,* 73 WASH. L. REV. 459 (1998); Trevor Morrison, Note, *Removed from the Constitution? Deportable Aliens' Access to Habeas Corpus Under the New Immigration Legislation,* 35 COLUM. J. TRANSNAT'L L. 697 (1997); Note, *Deportation and Exclusion: A Continuing Dialogue Between Congress and the Courts,* 71 YALE L.J. 760 (1962);

adjudicated,[2] were seeking release from actual physical confinement[3] by challenging the particular judgment of conviction or sentence that was responsible for that confinement.[4] More recently, however, "stifling formalisms" and "arcane and scholastic procedural requirements"[5] have given way, permitting the transformation of habeas corpus into a modern, generally available, and essentially appellate postconviction procedure.[6] As the law now stands, any person[7] who, as a result of action by a state or federal criminal court, is "subject to restraints 'not shared by the public generally'" — any person who

---

Note, *Extradition Habeas Corpus*, 74 Yale L.J. 78 (1964); Note, *Hensley v. Municipal Court: An Update on Habeas Corpus*, 6 Colum. Hum. Rts. L. Rev. 249 (1974); Annotation, *When Is Person "In Custody" so as to Make Him Eligible for Remedy, Under Federal Statutory Provisions for Habeas Corpus, for Violation of Federal Constitutional Rights — Supreme Court Cases*, 36 L. Ed. 2d 1012 (1974).

[2] *See, e.g.,* Parker v. Ellis, 362 U.S. 574 (1960) (petition filed while petitioner was in custody dismissed as moot because petitioner was released from custody prior to final adjudication of petition).

[3] *See, e.g., Parker v. Ellis, supra*; Weber v. Squire, 315 U.S. 810 (1942) (petitioner on parole not "in custody"); McNally v. Hill, 293 U.S. 131 (1934); Stallings v. Splain, 253 U.S. 339, 343 (1920) (petitioner on bail not "in custody"); Johnson v. Hoy, 227 U.S. 245, 248 (1913); Ex parte Baez, 177 U.S. 378, 389 (1900); Wales v. Whitney, 114 U.S. 564, 571-75 (1885) (confinement of naval officer "to the limits of the City of Washington" did not establish custody). *See generally* Dallin H. Oaks, *Legal History in the High Court — Habeas Corpus*, 64 Mich. L. Rev. 451, 468-71 (1966).

[4] *See, e.g., McNally v. Hill, supra* (forbidding habeas corpus challenges to sentences prisoner had not yet begun to serve).

[5] Hensley v. Municipal Ct., 411 U.S. 345, 350 (1973).

[6] The watershed Supreme Court decision in this respect was Jones v. Cunningham, 371 U.S. 236 (1963). This trend has continued recently. *See, e.g.,* Garlotte v. Fordice, 515 U.S. 39 (1995). *See also* Spencer v. Kemna, 118 S. Ct. 978, 983-85 (1998) (similar to *Maleng, infra*); Maleng v. Cook, 490 U.S. 488, 492 (1989) (*per curiam*) (Court has "very liberally construed the 'in custody' requirement for purposes of federal habeas" and found "custody" whenever "petitioner suffers [some] present restraint from a conviction"). *See generally supra* §§ 2.2 n.13, 2.4.

[7] Resident and nonresident aliens are "persons" for purposes of the habeas corpus and related statutes. *See, e.g.,* Jean v. Nelson, 472 U.S. 846, 849-50 (1985) (by implication); Brownell v. Tom We Shung, 352 U.S. 180, 183 (1956) (*dicta*); Harisiades v. Shaughnessy, 342 U.S. 580, 586 n.9 (1952) (*dicta*); Ex parte Betz, 329 U.S. 672 (1947) (by implication); United States ex rel. Turner v. Williams, 194 U.S. 279, 295 (1904) (Brewer, J., concurring); Yick Wo v. Hopkins, 118 U.S. 356 (1886) (by implication); cases cited *infra* § 8.2d n.46. *See also* 25 U.S.C. § 1303 (1994) (writ of habeas corpus extended to Native Americans seeking to test "legality of ... detention" by order of tribal court); In re Griffiths, 413 U.S. 717 (1973); Sugarman v. Dougall, 413 U.S. 634, 641-42 (1973) (14th Amendment applies, indeed affords special protection, to aliens); Graham v. Richardson, 403 U.S. 365 (1971). *See generally* Sokol, *supra* note 1, §§ 5.2, 5.3 at 56-62. Habeas corpus is not available to corporations. *See, e.g.,* Waste Management of Wisconsin, Inc. v. Fokakis, 614 F.2d 138, 140 (7th Cir. 1979).

cannot come and go as she pleases — meets the "status" jurisdictional requirement in the habeas corpus statute.[8]

b. *Mootness.* As long as the habeas corpus petition was filed in federal court at a time when the petitioner was in custody,[9] an action challenging that custody

---

[8] *Hensley v. Municipal Ct., supra,* 411 U.S. at 351 (quoting *Jones v. Cunningham, supra,* 371 U.S. at 240). *Accord Jones v. Cunningham, supra,* 371 U.S. at 243 (paroled petitioner is "in custody" because parole restrictions "significantly restrain petitioner's liberty to do those things which in this country free men are entitled to do"). *See* Dickerson v. Guste, 932 F.2d 1142, 1144 (5th Cir.), *cert. denied,* 502 U.S. 875 (1991) (custody for purposes of habeas corpus review is broader than custody sufficient to trigger speedy trial requirements; detainer lodged against prisoner serving sentence under prior conviction satisfies former, but not latter, definition of custody); Fernos-Lopez v. Figarella-Lopez, 929 F.2d 20, 21-23 (1st Cir.), *cert. denied,* 502 U.S. 887 (1991) (incarceration in jail for civil contempt for failure to comply with order to pay alimony would constitute custody for habeas corpus purposes); Steinberg v. Police Court, 610 F.2d 449, 453 (6th Cir. 1979). *See also* Picrin-Peron v. Rison, 930 F.2d 773, 775-76 (9th Cir. 1991) (possibility that INS in future might confine petitioner whom it previously incarcerated pursuant to exclusion proceedings, but whom it released at least temporarily, might qualify as "custody" under "voluntary cessation exception to the mootness doctrine"; court concludes, however, that INS was not "free to resume" incarceration, as required by "voluntary cessation" exception, because INS signed declaration eschewing further exclusion proceedings for one year, as long as petitioner did not become involved with criminal justice system). *See generally* Advisory Committee Note to Rule 1 of the Rules Governing Section 2254 Cases (citing and discussing cases); authority cited *infra* § 8.2d nn.32-42.

[9] In addition to the formal statutes of limitations which apply in all cases subject to the Antiterrorism and Effective Death Penalty Act of 1996 (AEDPA) (discussed *supra* § 5.1b), the last date on which the petitioner is in "custody" effectively serves as a time limit on filing habeas corpus petitions in both AEDPA and non-AEDPA cases. At least some courts are prepared to enforce the latter restriction inflexibly and harshly under the circumstances. *See, e.g.,* Scanio v. United States, 37 F.3d 858 (2d Cir. 1994) (prisoner, whose period of supervised release expired on day on which clerk's office was closed and who attempted to file petition on next business day, could not invoke Civil Rule 6(a)'s provision for extending motions filing period when deadline falls on weekend or holiday); Allen v. Dowd, 964 F.2d 745, 746 (8th Cir.), *cert. denied,* 506 U.S. 920 (1992) (incarcerated prisoner who mailed petition five days before expiration of sentence but whose petition did not reach clerk until two weeks later was not in "custody" at time of filing, notwithstanding rule that notices of appeal by incarcerated *pro se* prisoners are deemed "filed" at time of delivery to prison authorities for forwarding to court (*see infra* § 35.2a)); Weaver v. Pung, 925 F.2d 1097, 1098-99 (8th Cir.), *cert. denied,* 502 U.S. 828 (1991) (petitioner submitted petition to district court clerk on Nov. 9, 1988, together with filing fee and motion for *in forma pauperis* (*ifp*) status; in view of filing of *ifp* motion, clerk refused fee, telling petitioner "there was plenty of time for the fee if required"; magistrate denied *ifp* motion on Nov. 9, but letter notifying petitioner of denial did not reach petitioner until Nov. 12, after which petitioner promptly paid fee on Nov. 14; because petitioner's sentence fully expired on Nov. 10, however, and because "filing" does not occur until fee is paid or *ifp* motion is granted, petitioner did not "file" petition until Nov. 14, four days after petitioner's custody had terminated; petition dismissed for lack of jurisdiction). As *Allen* and *Weaver* illustrate, the impending termination of "custody" calls for close attention to timely

is not necessarily mooted by the petitioner's release from custody prior to final trial and appellate adjudication of the petition.[10] Albeit with a hint of a second thought recently, the Court for decades has justified this rule on the ground that persons who have completed serving sentences for criminal convictions may retain "a substantial stake in [overturning] the judgment of conviction which

---

and proper filing procedures and may call for the tendering (and insistence upon the clerk's acceptance) of a filing fee, even if an *ifp* motion also is filed.

[10] Carafas v. LaVallee, 391 U.S. 234 (1968) (overruling Parker v. Ellis, 362 U.S. 574 (1960)). *Accord, e.g., Spencer v. Kemna, supra,* 118 S. Ct. at 983 ("Spencer was incarcerated by reason of the parole revocation at the time the petition was filed, which is all the 'in custody' provision ... requires."); Maleng v. Cook, 490 U.S. 488, 492 (1989); Bryan v. Duckworth, 88 F.3d 431, 432-33 (7th Cir. 1996) ("If a prisoner, while in custody, files a petition for habeas corpus challenging the conviction that has led to his being in custody, and is then released while the petition is pending, the petition is not moot unless there is no possibility that the conviction will have 'collateral consequences,' which is to say an adverse effect on him at some future time, perhaps because the conviction could be used to enhance a sentence for a future crime.... So unlikely is a conviction to have no collateral consequences that it is the respondent's burden to plead and prove that the petitioner's conviction will not."; same rule applies to petitions challenging orders of segregation or other disciplinary sanctions, filed after period of enhanced confinement has ended); Jones v. Jerrison, 20 F.3d 849, 852 n.2 (8th Cir. 1994); Fraley v. United States Bur. of Prisons, 1 F.3d 924, 925 (9th Cir. 1993) (*per curiam*); DePompei v. Ohio Adult Parole Auth., 999 F.2d 138, 140 (6th Cir. 1993); White v. White, 925 F.2d 287, 290 (9th Cir. 1991); McVeigh v. Smith, 872 F.2d 725, 727 (6th Cir. 1989); Landry v. Hoepfner, 840 F.2d 1201, 1204 n.8 (5th Cir. 1988) (*en banc*), *cert. denied,* 489 U.S. 1083 (1989); Rutledge v. Sunderland, 671 F.2d 377, 379 (10th Cir. 1982); Graham v. Smith, 602 F.2d 1078, 1081 (2d Cir. 1979); Harrison v. Indiana, 597 F.2d 115, 118 (7th Cir. 1979); Mizell v. Attorney General, 586 F.2d 942, 948 (2d Cir. 1978), *cert. denied,* 440 U.S. 967 (1979); Pinnell v. Cauthron, 540 F.2d 938, 939 (8th Cir. 1976); other authority cited *infra* notes 11, 12. *See also* 28 U.S.C. § 2243 (1994) (authorizing "dispos[ition]" of habeas corpus cases "as law and justice require"); Picrin-Peron v. Rison, 930 F.2d 773, 775-76 (9th Cir. 1991) (under doctrine that incarcerating official's "voluntary cessation" of illegal conduct does not moot challenge to conduct if offending party is "free to resume" improper activity, INS's incarceration of petitioner at time petition was filed may be sufficient to maintain "custody" even after INS voluntarily, but perhaps only temporarily, released petitioner; court concludes, however, that INS was not "free to resume" incarceration because it signed declaration eschewing further exclusion proceedings for one year, as long as petitioner did not become involved with criminal justice system). *Cf.* DeLong v. Hennessey, 912 F.2d 1144, 1146 (9th Cir. 1990) (termination of short jail term for contempt moots later-filed habeas corpus action challenging contempt citation); Johnson v. Riveland, 855 F.2d 1477, 1480-81 (10th Cir. 1988) (petition seeking credit for preconviction custody mooted when petitioner released on parole). Courts occasionally misuse the "mootness" rubric (a *subject matter jurisdiction* concept) when discussing the impact on *personal jurisdiction* and *venue* of a prisoner's transfer from a prison in the jurisdiction in which she originally filed the petition to a prison in another jurisdiction. *See, e.g.,* Barden v. Keohane, 921 F.2d 476, 477 n.1 (3d Cir. 1990) (improper subsequent transfer of prisoner does not spoil jurisdiction of court in district where petitioner was incarcerated at time petition was filed); Miller v. Hambrick, 905 F.2d 259, 262 (9th Cir. 1990) (subsequent transfer does not "moot" action filed when prisoner was incarcerated in jurisdiction where petition originally was filed). *See generally infra* §§ 10.2b, 10.2c, 14.1, 36.3.

survives the satisfaction of the sentence."[11] Among the post-release consequences of convictions capable of avoiding mootness by release as long as the

---

[11] *Carafas v. LaVallee, supra*, 391 U.S. at 237 (citing Fiswick v. United States, 329 U.S. 211, 222 (1946)). *See Spencer v. Kemna, supra*, 118 S. Ct. at 983, 985 ("In recent decades, we have been willing to presume that a wrongful criminal conviction has continuing collateral consequences (or, what is effectively the same, to count collateral consequences that are remote and unlikely to occur).... [I]n the context of criminal conviction, the presumption of significant collateral consequences is likely to comport with reality. As we said in *Sibron* [*v. New York, infra*], it is an 'obvious fact of life that most criminal convictions do in fact entail adverse collateral legal consequences'"); Minnesota v. Dickerson, 508 U.S. 366, 371 n.2 (1993) (case not moot, despite dismissal of charges against defendant following completion of probation and prior to Court's ruling; although state statute under which defendant was convicted provides that dismissal of charges following completion of probation averts normal disqualifications and disabilities, statute also "provides ... that a nonpublic record of the charges dismissed pursuant to the statute 'shall be retained by the department of public safety for the purpose of use by the courts'" in event defendant has "'"future difficulties with the law,"'" thus establishing sufficient "collateral legal consequences" to assure that "live controversy remains" (citations omitted)); Pennsylvania v. Mimms, 434 U.S. 106, 108 n.3 (1977) (*per curiam*) (*dicta*) (discussing cases) (although prisoner had completed sentence before Pennsylvania Supreme Court overturned conviction, Supreme Court adjudicated merits of state's petition because "possibility of a criminal defendant's suffering 'collateral legal consequence' from sentence already served permits him to have his claims reviewed here" and, by like reasoning, "State's inability to impose such ... burden[s] following a reversal of the conviction ... must ... be sufficient to enable the State to obtain review of its claims on the merits"); Sibron v. New York, 392 U.S. 40, 50-58 (1968); Ginsburg v. New York, 390 U.S. 629 (1968); Leonard v. Nix, 55 F.3d 370, 373 (8th Cir. 1995) ("Collateral consequences are presumed to stem from a criminal conviction even after release."); Larche v. Simons, 53 F.3d 1068, 1069-71 (9th Cir. 1995) (although questioning rule of *Chacon v. Wood, infra*, which generally precludes finding of mootness by establishing "presumption of collateral damages [that] is irrebuttable, even in misdemeanor cases," court follows *Chacon* and holds that case is not moot though (1) petitioner's term of probation ended, (2) "[h]e is currently free from any restraint upon his liberty," and (3) he "has not alleged, nor made any showing, of collateral consequences"); Dawson v. Scott, 50 F.3d 884, 886 n.2 (11th Cir. 1995) (petitioner's completion of prison sentence did not render petition moot because "Dawson is still serving his term of supervised release, which is part of his sentence and involves some restrictions upon his liberty"); Chacon v. Wood, 36 F.3d 1459, 1463 (9th Cir. 1994) ("in this day of federal sentencing guidelines based on prior criminal histories, federal 'career criminal' statutes, and state repeat offender provisions," individual convicted of crime "remains forever subject to the prospect of harsher punishment for a subsequent offense as a result of federal and state laws that either already have been or may eventually be passed"; accordingly, "presumption is ... irrebuttable" that "'collateral consequences follow from *any* criminal conviction'" and that habeas corpus petition filed while petitioner is in custody "is never moot simply because, subsequent to its filing, the petitioner has been released from custody" (citations omitted)); Oyler v. Allenbrand, 23 F.3d 292, 294 (10th Cir.), *cert. denied*, 513 U.S. 909 (1994) (case not moot, despite postfiling reduction of sentence to term of probation and petitioner's completion of entire probationary term, because conviction could be used in later case for impeachment or to enhance sentence); Nakell v. Attorney General, 15 F.3d 319, 322-23 (4th Cir. 1994) (petition filed during custody challenging criminal contempt conviction that resulted in jail sentence and $500 fine not moot despite unconditional release from custody because petitioner's

"interest in the return of the $500 fine is a collateral consequence sufficient to prevent mootness"); McClain v. United States Bur. of Prisons, 9 F.3d 503, 504 (6th Cir. 1993) (*per curiam*) (case not moot despite petitioner's postfiling release from prison because resolution of claim could affect supervised release dates); Fraley v. United States Bur. of Prisons, 1 F.3d 924, 925 (9th Cir. 1993) (case not moot despite postfiling release from prison because claim of credit for time spent in pretrial detention could affect petitioner's "two-year term of supervised release"); DePompei v. Ohio Adult Parole Auth., 999 F.2d 138, 140 (6th Cir. 1993) ("mere possibility that such [collateral] consequences could exist is sufficient to preserve a live controversy"); United States v. Smith, 997 F.2d 674, 676 n.2 (10th Cir.), *cert. denied,* 510 U.S. 937 (1993); Armant v. Marquez, 772 F.2d 552, 555 (9th Cir. 1985), *cert. denied,* 475 U.S. 1099 (1986); Walker v. McLain, 768 F.2d 1181, 1183 (10th Cir. 1985), *cert. denied,* 474 U.S. 1061 (1986); Reimnitz v. State's Attorney, 761 F.2d 405, 408 (7th Cir. 1985); Maggard v. Florida Parole Comm'n, 616 F.2d 890, 891 (5th Cir. 1980); Martineau v. Perrin, 601 F.2d 1201 (1st Cir. 1979); Matthews v. Florida, 463 F.2d 679, 681 (5th Cir. 1972). *See also* Calderon v. Moore, 518 U.S. 149, 150 (1996) (*per curiam*) (appeal of district court's grant of conditional habeas corpus relief was not moot, notwithstanding state's compliance with condition that new trial be granted, because "decision in the State's favor would release it from the burden of [conducting] the ... trial," and "even the availability of a 'partial remedy,' is 'sufficient to prevent [a] case from being moot'"); Garlotte v. Fordice, 515 U.S. 39, 43, 47 & n.5 (1995) (discussed *infra* § 8.2c n.14 and nn.16-19 and accompanying text) (recognizing as collateral consequence in analogous context that prior conviction "continue[s] to postpone the date for which [petitioner] would be eligible for [release]" under sentence being served and that "[i]nvalidation of ... [prior] conviction would advance the date of [petitioner's] eligibility for release from present incarceration"); Demjanjuk v. Petrovsky, 10 F.3d 338, 355-56 (6th Cir. 1993) (relying on habeas corpus caselaw on mootness, court rules that Demjanjuk's acquittal and release in Israel did not moot claim of unlawful extradition because of "collateral consequence[]" of stigma of "being found by the district court to be Ivan the Terrible"). *Cf.* Maleng v. Cook, 490 U.S. 488, 492 (1989) (*dicta*) (reaffirming rule of *Carafas* that case filed while petitioner was in custody but not decided until after he was unconditionally released is not moot but explaining that "we rested that holding *not* on the collateral consequences ... but on the fact that the petitioner had been in physical custody under the challenged conviction at the time the petition was filed" (emphasis in original)). *Compare* D.S.A. v. Circuit Ct., 942 F.2d 1143, 1150 (7th Cir. 1991), *cert. denied,* 502 U.S. 1104 (1992) (petition by adjudicated juvenile delinquent not moot notwithstanding postfiling release from custody because state law would permit use of delinquency adjudication "in a presentence report to increase a subsequent sentence, to impeach her testimony, and in subsequent child custody proceedings" to determine "her custody, or, at a later date, the custody of her children") *and* Clay v. Director, 564 F. Supp. 206, 207 n.1 (N.D. Ill. 1983), *rev'd on other grounds,* 749 F.2d 427 (7th Cir. 1984), *cert. denied,* 471 U.S. 1108 (1985) (adjudicated delinquent's release from custody did not moot habeas corpus action because of "potential for harsher sentencing on any future convictions") *with* Morgan v. Juvenile and Domestic Relations Ct., 491 F.2d 456 (4th Cir. 1974) (relying on pre-*Carafas* authority, court concludes that adjudicated juvenile delinquent's release from custody mooted action because opprobrium attached to delinquency adjudications is not by itself sufficient to give petitioner stake in litigation).

In *Spencer v. Kemna, supra,* the Court held that the "presum[ption] that a wrongful criminal *conviction* has continuing collateral consequences" does not extend "to the area of *parole revocation.*" 118 S. Ct. at 983, 985-86 (emphasis added). Accordingly, if, after filing a petition challenging the legality of a parole revocation, the prisoner "complete[s] the entire term of imprisonment underlying the parole revocation," *id.* at 981, he must affirmatively demonstrate "concrete injuries-in-fact attributable to his parole revocation" in order to avoid a finding of

petitioner was in custody when the petition was filed are exclusion from the franchise, jury service, professional licenses, and certain jobs.[12] Because

___

mootness. *Id.* at 983, 985-86. In reaching this conclusion, the Court simultaneously (i) reaffirmed its well-established rule treating an incarcerated prisoner's filing of a habeas corpus petition challenging a conviction as sufficient to avoid mootness when the prisoner thereafter is released, on the ground that collateral consequences from the conviction are highly likely, *id.* at 983, 985, yet (ii) seemed to criticize the practice, *see id.* at 984-85. Apart from the latter *dicta*, however, the Court's holding in *Spencer* casts little doubt on the Court's prior practice in regard to petitions challenging convictions, given that the collateral consequences of convictions are so much more likely and obvious than the analogous consequences of parole revocations.

[12] *Carafas v. LaVallee, supra*, 391 U.S. at 237. *See Spencer v. Kemna, supra*, 118 S. Ct. at 983-85 ("collateral consequences of conviction" sufficient to avoid mootness include "concrete disadvantages or disabilities that had in fact occurred, that were imminently threatened, or that were imposed as a matter of law (such as deprivation of the right to vote, to hold office, to serve on a jury, or to engage in certain businesses)," including, for example, inability "'[to] serve as an official of a labor union for a specified period of time,'" risk of "deportation and denial of naturalization," risk of "revocation of [petitioner's] license to operate luncheonette business," and "increase [of] petitioner's sentence under state recidivist law"); *Nakell v. Attorney General, supra*, 15 F.3d at 322-23 (discussed *supra* note 11) (notwithstanding attorney's unconditional release and dismissal of grievance filed with state bar, petition not moot because "grievance may be revived"); *DePompei v. Ohio Adult Parole Auth., supra*, 999 F.2d at 140 (physician's unconditional release from parole did not moot petition because reversal of conviction would allow petitioner to seek reinstatement of medical license); Zal v. Steppe, 968 F.2d 924, 926 (9th Cir.), *cert. denied*, 506 U.S. 1020 (1992) (attorney's release from custody on contempt citations did not render petition moot because "Zal risks being disciplined by the California State Bar if his contempt citations are allowed to stand."); *D.S.A. v. Circuit Ct., supra*, 942 F.2d at 1150 (adjudicated juvenile delinquent has "substantial stake in the outcome of this case" notwithstanding release from custody because delinquency adjudication can be used for aggravation at sentencing in future criminal or juvenile cases, impeachment of testimony, and as adverse factor in child custody proceedings); *White v. White, supra*, 925 F.2d at 290 (petition challenging parole revocation on basis of sexual contact with minor filed while petitioner was incarcerated for parole violation is not moot, although petitioner is now incarcerated for prison misconduct, not parole violation, because parole revocation based on sexual contact with minor has collateral consequences of enhancing possible sentence upon subsequent conviction and because stigma may harm job prospects); Robbins v. Christianson, 904 F.2d 492, 494-96 (9th Cir. 1990) (petitioner can avoid dismissal for mootness following postfiling unconditional release from custody by satisfying "burden of demonstrating he will suffer actual harm" as result of prior conviction; burden met by citing potential sentencing consequences of prior conviction under federal Sentencing Guidelines and possible impact upon employment opportunities, neither of which "possibility of future harm ... is ... too ephemeral to constitute a collateral consequence for mootness purposes"); Minor v. Dugger, 864 F.2d 124, 125-27 (11th Cir. 1989) (petition filed day before unconditional release not moot because collateral consequences possible, namely, conviction could be used to enhance future sentence); United States v. Romero-Vilca, 850 F.2d 177, 179 (3d Cir. 1988) (potential for deportation due to conviction is adequate collateral consequence to preserve habeas corpus petition filed during detention); Green v. Arn, 839 F.2d 300, 302 (6th Cir. 1988), *cert. denied*, 489 U.S. 1034 (1989) ("mere possibility that such [adverse collateral] consequences may exist is sufficient to preserve a live controversy" created by petition's filing during custody even if petitioner himself argues that petition is moot); other authority cited *supra* notes 10, 11. *See also* Beecham v. United States, 511

conviction is understood to terminate pretrial detention, and because pretrial detention often has no collateral effect on postconviction detention, conviction often "moots" a habeas corpus action that challenges only pretrial custody, notwithstanding that the action was filed while the petitioner was incarcerated before trial and notwithstanding that the incarceration continued after the conviction.[13]

U.S. 368, 371 (1994) (whether incarcerated or not, defendants convicted of felony are subject to "disability" in that they cannot legally possess firearms and can be prosecuted for any such possession under federal firearms statute); Richardson v. Ramirez, 418 U.S. 24 (1974) (upholding constitutionality of disenfranchising convicted felons). Note that "collateral consequences," such as employment, voting, and jury-service disabilities, enhancement of a later sentence based on the existence of a prior conviction, and the possibility of a higher sentence if convicted again, although sufficient to prevent a petition *filed* when the petitioner was in custody from becoming moot thereafter, do *not* by themselves satisfy the requirement that the petitioner be "in custody" when the petition is first filed — even if those consequences have actually materialized. See Maleng v. Cook, *supra*, 490 U.S. at 492; *infra* § 8.2c nn.19-20 and accompanying text; *infra* § 8.2e. *But cf. Maleng v. Cook, supra,* 490 U.S. at 492-93 (petitioner may challenge legality of prior conviction for which sentence already has been served but which is being used to lengthen incarceration under subsequent conviction by bringing petition challenging subsequent conviction and sentence as enhanced by prior conviction); *infra* § 8.2c nn.19-20 and accompanying text.

[13] *See, e.g.,* Eckert v. Tansy, 936 F.2d 444, 450 (9th Cir. 1991) (conviction precludes habeas corpus relief on claim of unlawful extradition from one state to another to stand trial); Barker v. Estelle, 913 F.2d 1433, 1440 (9th Cir. 1990), *cert. denied,* 500 U.S. 935 (1991) (conviction of offense cuts off claims challenging constitutionality of *pretrial* detention; by implication, termination of pretrial detention moots action challenging that detention even if action originally was filed during course of pretrial detention and incarceration continued without break before and after conviction); Fassler v. United States, 858 F.2d 1016, 1018 n.3 (5th Cir. 1988), *cert. denied,* 490 U.S. 1099 (1989) (challenge to pretrial detention becomes moot when petitioner convicted because pretrial detention has no collateral consequences); *infra* § 8.2e n.61 and accompanying text. *See generally supra* § 5.2 (pretrial habeas corpus petitions). On the mooting effect of deportation on habeas corpus actions brought to challenge INS custody, see *infra* § 8.2d n.46. Certain kinds of habeas corpus claims that may be brought before trial — *e.g.*, double jeopardy and some kinds of speedy trial claims — are not mooted by conviction because they challenge not only the legality of the pretrial detention but also the legality of the postconviction detention or the fairness of the procedure that led to the conviction. *See, e.g.,* Stratton v. United States, 862 F.2d 7, 8 (1st Cir. 1988) (by implication). An analogous issue is the effect of the completion of an appeal on a habeas corpus action that was filed before the appeal was resolved and that challenges the tardiness of the appellate process. *Compare* Allen v. Duckworth, 6 F.3d 458, 459-60 (7th Cir. 1993), *cert. denied,* 510 U.S. 1132 (1994) (claim of denial of speedy appeal in state court was moot because state courts had resolved appeal in interim and petitioner was unable to point to any further relief available through habeas corpus rather than suit under 42 U.S.C. § 1983) *with* Burkett v. Fulcomer, 951 F.2d 1431, 1447-48 (3d Cir. 1991), *cert. denied,* 505 U.S. 1229 (1992) (despite resolution of state court appeal, court of appeals reviews claim of denial of speedy appeal and grants relief of reduction of sentence) *and* Mathis v. Hood, 851 F.2d 612, 614 (2d Cir. 1988) (habeas corpus challenge to state's delay in hearing appeal not mooted when appeal finally granted because petition sought unconditional release, a remedy still available). *See also infra* § 33.4 n.2.

c. *Sentences not being served.* A petitioner incarcerated under one conviction may file a habeas corpus petition challenging another conviction as long as the sentence on the challenged conviction has not yet been fully served and adds in some way to "the aggregate of the ... sentences" the petitioner eventually must serve.[14] The challenged conviction has sufficient adverse consequences to establish custody (assuming the sentence on it has not yet been fully served) if it (1) does or may affect the length or conditions of the current incarceration under another conviction, (2) subjects the petitioner to future incarceration in the same penal system in which the petitioner now is incarcerated, or (3) subjects the petitioner to future incarceration in another jurisdiction at least as long as the second jurisdiction has lodged a detainer with an official responsible for the petitioner's current incarceration.[15] Similarly, a prisoner incarcerated under consecutive

---

[14] Peyton v. Rowe, 391 U.S. 54, 64-65 (1968) (overruling McNally v. Hill, 293 U.S. 131 (1934)) (petitioner may challenge second of two convictions for which consecutive sentences were imposed, although he is still serving the term imposed for the first conviction). *See* Garlotte v. Fordice, 515 U.S. 39, 40 (1995) (habeas corpus statute "permits prisoners incarcerated under consecutive state court sentences to apply for federal habeas relief from sentences they had not yet begun to serve ... 'if any consecutive sentence [the prisoner] is scheduled to serve was imposed as a result of a deprivation of constitutional rights'"; all "consecutive sentences should be treated as [single sentence in] a continuous series" (quoting *Peyton v. Rowe, supra,* 391 U.S. at 64-65)); Custis v. United States, 511 U.S. 485, 497 (1994) (prisoner serving federal sentence but "who is still 'in custody' for purposes of his state convictions at the time of his federal sentencing ... may attack his state sentences ... through federal habeas review"); Maleng v. Cook, 490 U.S. 488, 493 (1989) (*dicta*) (reaffirming rule of *Peyton* and noting its application to situations in which prisoner is subject to more than one sentence in more than one jurisdiction, at least as long as sentence or sentences not yet being served are subject of detainer lodged with authorities holding prisoner under sentence being served); Walker v. Wainwright, 390 U.S. 335, 336-37 (1968) (petitioner may challenge conviction responsible for sentence he currently is serving even though relief from that conviction would not free him from incarceration due to second conviction for which consecutive sentence was imposed).

[15] *See* Maleng v. Cook, *supra,* 490 U.S. at 493 (reaffirming rule of *Braden, infra*); Lockhart v. Nelson, 488 U.S. 33 (1988) (by implication) (challenge to second of two consecutive sentences during pendency of first); Braden v. 30th Judicial Cir. Ct., 410 U.S. 484, 489 n.4 (1973) (petitioner in custody where: (1) petition filed by prisoner serving time in one State challenged constitutionality of judicial proceedings against him in another State; and (2) second ("demanding") State had filed detainer with warden of prison in "incarcerating" State, thereby making warden of incarcerating State "agent" of demanding State); Leacock v. Henman, 996 F.2d 1069, 1071 & n.4 (10th Cir. 1993) (federal prisoner could challenge state conviction and future sentence because state sentence was consecutive to current federal sentence and state lodged detainer); Whatley v. Morrison, 947 F.2d 869 (8th Cir. 1991); Dickerson v. Guste, 932 F.2d 1142, 1144 (5th Cir.), *cert. denied,* 502 U.S. 875 (1991) (*dicta*) (detainer establishes custody by authority filing detainer); Thompson v. Missouri Bd. of Parole, 929 F.2d 396, 398-401 (8th Cir. 1991) (detainer lodged by Missouri Parole Board with Minnesota prison gave board custody of petitioner and gave Minnesota district court jurisdiction to cure Missouri board's violation); Parette v. Lockhart, 927 F.2d 366, 366-67 (8th Cir. 1991) (Louisiana's detainer lodged with Arkansas prison

sentences, one or more of which has been fully served, may file a habeas corpus petition challenging the expired sentences[16] — at least as long as they "continue to postpone the date for which he would be eligible for [release]" under the unexpired sentences.[17] For purposes of the "custody" requirement, that is, "consecutive sentences should be treated as a continuous series," so that a prisoner "remains 'in custody' under *all* of his [consecutive] sentences until *all* are served."[18] On the other hand, a prisoner who is *not* now serving *and* challenging some part of a consecutive series of sentences cannot file a habeas corpus petition challenging another sentence that has been fully served or the conviction underlying the other sentence — even if the other conviction does or may affect the length or conditions of the prisoner's current sentence. Such a

---

where petitioner was incarcerated established custody by Louisiana); Whittlesey v. Circuit Ct., 897 F.2d 143, 147-48 (4th Cir.) (Phillips, J., dissenting), *cert. denied,* 498 U.S. 922 (1990) (petition should be adjudicated even though prisoner escaped from prison and escapee cannot be "in custody"; petitioner is now in prison in another state for other crimes and subject to detainer for conviction he seeks to challenge); Frazier v. Wilkinson, 842 F.2d 42, 45 (2d Cir.), *cert. denied,* 488 U.S. 842 (1988) (federal prisoner may challenge consecutive state sentence absent state detainer when "there is a reasonable basis to apprehend that the jurisdiction that obtained the consecutive sentence will seek its enforcement"); United States ex rel. Meadows v. New York, 426 F.2d 1176, 1179 (2d Cir. 1970), *cert. denied,* 401 U.S. 941 (1971) (federal prisoner under state detainer may challenge state conviction); Word v. North Carolina, 406 F.2d 352, 353-55 (4th Cir. 1969); authority cited *infra* § 8.2d nn.27-31. *Cf.* Scott v. Louisiana, 934 F.2d 631, 635 (5th Cir. 1991) (dismissing petition because "[w]e are shown no current possibility that Scott will suffer from" life sentences that are being served concurrently with sentence of life without possibility of parole, but specifying that dismissal is without prejudice to refiling "[i]f Scott can demonstrate at some future time that [the life sentences] ... affect his ability to have his life sentence commuted to a term of years, or if he can otherwise demonstrate adverse consequences"). *But cf.* Campillo v. Sullivan, 853 F.2d 593, 595-96 (8th Cir.), *cert. denied,* 490 U.S. 1082 (1988) (INS detainer not sufficient to establish custody by INS until after alien has finished serving federal prison term); other authority cited *infra* § 8.2d n.46 (variable treatment of INS detainers). On the question whether a detainer is always necessary to establish custody in regard to a sentence in another jurisdiction that is not currently being served, see *infra* § 8.2d n.30. *See generally* Reed v. Farley, 512 U.S. 339, 342 n.1 (1994) ("A detainer is 'a request filed by a criminal justice agency with the institution in which a prisoner is incarcerated, asking either to hold the prisoner for the agency or to notify the agency when release of the prisoner is imminent.'" (quoting Carchman v. Nash, 473 U.S. 716, 719 (1985)).

[16] *See, e.g., Garlotte v. Fordice, supra,* 515 U.S. at 43-47; Fawcett v. Bablitch, 962 F.2d 617, 618 (7th Cir. 1992); Bernard v. Garaghty, 934 F.2d 52, 55 (4th Cir. 1991); Fox v. Kelso, 911 F.2d 563, 568 (11th Cir. 1990).

[17] *Garlotte v. Fordice, supra,* 515 U.S. at 43. *See id.* at 47 & n.5 ("Invalidation of Garlotte's marijuana conviction [for which sentence has expired] would advance the date of his eligibility for release from present incarceration.... We therefore hold that Garlotte was 'in custody' under his marijuana conviction when he filed his federal habeas petition.").

[18] *Id.* at 41. *Accord id.* at 46 ("we view consecutive sentences in the aggregate, not as discrete segments"); Peyton v. Rowe, 391 U.S. 54, 67 (1968) ("prisoner serving consecutive sentences is 'in custody' under any one of them").

prisoner is not in "custody" under either the former sentence or a sentence "consecutive" to it.[19] Instead, the prisoner in that situation must challenge the former conviction's legality as a basis for enhancing or lengthening incarceration pursuant to the current sentence by filing a petition challenging the legality of the current sentence and asserting that the current sentence has been or may be unlawfully enhanced or lengthened by the allegedly illegal prior conviction.[20]

---

[19] *See, e.g., Garlotte v. Fordice, supra*, 515 U.S. at 45 (without more, "potential use of a conviction" for which sentence "has fully expired" "to enhance a sentence for subsequent offenses [does] not suffice to render a person 'in custody'"); *Custis v. United States, supra*, 511 U.S. at 512 & n.7 (Souter, J., dissenting) (**citing FHCPP**) (discussing *Maleng, infra*); *Maleng v. Cook, supra*, 490 U.S. at 492 (once sentence under conviction unconditionally and "fully expire[s]," federal courts have no jurisdiction over petition filed thereafter to challenge legality of that conviction even if collateral consequence of that conviction, namely, enhancement or lengthening of sentence under another conviction, actually has materialized); Allen v. Dowd, 964 F.2d 745 (8th Cir.), *cert. denied*, 506 U.S. 920 (1992); Hogan v. Iowa, 952 F.2d 224 (8th Cir. 1991); Hendrix v. Lynaugh, 888 F.2d 336, 338 (5th Cir. 1989) ("Enhancement is a collateral consequence insufficient to render the petitioner 'in custody' under the previous conviction"); Flittie v. Solem, 867 F.2d 1053, 1055 (8th Cir. 1988) (custody not present in challenge to prior conviction used to enhance current sentence under separate conviction); Hicks v. Duckworth, 856 F.2d 934, 935-36 (7th Cir. 1988) (challenge to prior conviction in other State used to enhance current conviction cannot be transferred to another State because petitioner is not in custody pursuant to prior conviction in that State; challenge to legality of prior conviction as basis for enhancing current incarceration must proceed in jurisdiction of current incarceration). *Maleng* reversed or overruled a number of cases treating the actual materialization of the collateral consequence of lengthened incarceration as sufficient to establish "custody" under an expired prior conviction. *See, e.g.,* United States v. Woods, 870 F.2d 285, 286 n.1 (5th Cir. 1989); Aziz v. Leferve, 830 F.2d 184, 186 (11th Cir. 1987). *But cf.* Bernard v. Garraghty, 934 F.2d 52, 54-55 (4th Cir. 1991) (distinguishing *Maleng* and finding that prisoner was "in custody" with regard to completed sentence because prisoner was still serving second of two consecutive sentences and "Virginia law treats Bernard's sentences, as it did Rowe's [in Peyton v. Rowe, 391 U.S. 54 (1968) (discussed *supra* note 14)] as one aggregate sentence").

[20] *See, e.g., Garlotte v. Fordice, supra*, 515 U.S. at 45 n.4 (*Maleng* "left open the possibility ... that the conviction underlying the expired sentence might be subject to challenge in a collateral attack upon the subsequent sentence that the expired sentence was used to enhance" (citing *Maleng v. Cook, supra*, 490 U.S. at 494)); *Custis v. United States, supra*, 511 U.S. at 512 & n.7 (Souter, J., dissenting) (**citing FHCPP**) (majority's opinion, discussed *infra*, "does not disturb uniform appellate case law holding that an individual serving an enhanced sentence may invoke federal habeas to reduce the sentence to the extent it was lengthened by a prior unconstitutional conviction"); *Maleng v. Cook, supra*, 490 U.S. at 493 (federal habeas corpus court has jurisdiction to hear petitioner's attack on sentence to extent it was enhanced by prior, unconstitutional conviction); United States v. Tucker, 404 U.S. 443 (1972) (in section 2255 action, Court orders reconsideration of federal sentence enhanced on basis of prior state convictions upon showing that state convictions were imposed unconstitutionally in absence of counsel); Brock v. Weston, 31 F.3d 887, 889-90 (9th Cir. 1994) (petitioner currently confined as "sexually violent predator" can challenge expired assault conviction if it served as predicate for subsequent commitment under "predator" statute); Smith v. Farley, 25 F.3d 1363, 1365-66 (7th Cir. 1994), *cert. denied*, 513 U.S.

1114 (1995) ("Because a person currently serving a sentence that was enhanced on the basis of a prior conviction is still in custody, he may [by filing petition seeking relief from current sentence] challenge the enhancing conviction as constitutionally invalid even though that prior conviction's original custodial term has expired."); Willis v. Collins, 989 F.2d 187, 189 (5th Cir. 1993) ("'positive and demonstrable nexus between ... current custody and the allegedly unconstitutional [prior] conviction' ... [is] 'sufficient to meet the jurisdictional requirements of § 2254(a)'" because expired conviction elevated two later convictions to felonies and thereby laid predicate for petitioner's present habitual offender sentence); Collins v. Hesse, 957 F.2d 746, 748 (10th Cir. 1992) (because "pro se petition should be construed liberally," petition construed as "challenging [petitioner's] present confinement even though the essence of his attack was the alleged unconstitutionality of the prior predicate convictions" used to enhance present sentence); Hogan v. Iowa, supra, 952 F.2d at 225 & n.2 (petition filed in Iowa district court to challenge expired conviction dismissed without prejudice to refiling in Nevada district court as challenge to death sentence imposed partly on basis of prior Iowa conviction); Clay v. Bronnenberg, 950 F.2d 486, 487 n.2 (7th Cir. 1991) (although pro se petitioner erroneously styled petition as challenge to expired sentence, "his petition, when taken together with his other submissions to the district court, sufficiently raised the issue of the constitutionality of his current confinement" as augmented by previous conviction); Harper v. Evans, 941 F.2d 1538 (11th Cir. 1991) (even though pro se petitioner erred by framing petition as attack on previous conviction rather than on current sentence as enhanced by prior conviction, district court should not have dismissed petition; however "the petition is framed ..., the reality is that Harper is 'in custody' as a result of a prior and alleged illegal conviction"); Lesko v. Lehman, 925 F.2d 1527, 1537-40 (3d Cir.), cert. denied, 502 U.S. 898 (1991) (petitioner entitled to habeas corpus relief from death sentence if sentence was based on "prior conviction" aggravating circumstance and if guilty plea leading to prior conviction was involuntary because entered with erroneous understanding that conviction could not be relied upon as basis for death sentence in later prosecution); Allen v. Collins, 924 F.2d 88, 88-89 (5th Cir. 1991) ("We have recognized a habeas petitioner's right to challenge a prior conviction for which sentence has been completed when that conviction is used to enhance a subsequent sentence" that petitioner is currently serving and that petitioner is challenging in petition before court; rejecting district court's limitation of such challenges to prior convictions that are "'void, and not merely voidable'"); Bailey v. Crowley, 914 F.2d 1438, 1439 & n.1 (10th Cir. 1990) ("liberally constru[ing]" petition styled as attack on constitutionality of two 1973 convictions for which sentences already had been served as instead attack on current sentences under 1984 convictions insofar "as [those sentences were] enhanced by the allegedly invalid prior convictions"); Gavin v. Wells, 914 F.2d 97, 98 (6th Cir. 1990); Fox v. Kelso, 911 F.2d 563, 567-68 (11th Cir. 1990) (petitioner could challenge felony sentence as enhanced by four prior misdemeanors, although misdemeanor sentences had been served, because misdemeanor convictions delayed onset of good time credits for time served under felony conviction); Crank v. Duckworth, 905 F.2d 1090, 1091 (7th Cir. 1990), cert. denied, 498 U.S. 1040 (1991) (upon proof that there is "'positive and demonstrable nexus'" between current custody and prior conviction and that prior conviction is invalid, petitioner can secure order requiring state to resentence petitioner without enhancement on basis of prior conviction; at least where same State imposed prior conviction and current sentence, hence has full incentive to defend prior conviction, prior conviction's invalidation forbids all subsequent uses of prior conviction and not simply its use to enhance existing sentence (quoting Young v. Lynaugh, 821 F.2d 1133, 1137 (5th Cir. 1987))); Feldman v. Perrill, 902 F.2d 1445, 1448-49 (9th Cir. 1990) (treating habeas corpus petition filed as challenge to prior state conviction as instead petition (under 28 U.S.C. § 2241(c)) challenging extension of existing parole term under subsequent federal conviction on basis of prior state conviction); Gamble v. Parsons, 898 F.2d 117,

d. *Custodial statuses.* Under the general principles set out in the preceding three subsections, a person is in custody — and her federal habeas corpus petition is and remains justiciable (*i.e.*, not moot) throughout the entire period required to adjudicate the petition at trial, on appeal, and on *certiorari*[21] — as

---

118 (10th Cir. 1990) (citing Clark v. Commonwealth, 892 F.2d 1142 (3d Cir. 1989), *cert. denied,* 496 U.S. 942 (1990); Taylor v. Armontrout, 877 F.2d 726, 727 (8th Cir. 1989)) (*Maleng* leaves open question whether one may attack expired conviction by challenging current sentence as enhanced by previous conviction; court follows rule of other circuits that prisoner may attack a current sentence as enhanced by prior conviction); Lowery v. Young, 887 F.2d 1309, 1311-13 (7th Cir. 1989) (construing petition as attack on current sentence as enhanced by prior convictions; noting availability of writ of error *coram nobis* to vacate conviction for which sentence had been completely served); Dunn v. Simmons, 877 F.2d 1275, 1279 (6th Cir. 1989), *cert. denied,* 494 U.S. 1061 (1990). *But cf.* Henderson v. Cohn, 919 F.2d 1270, 1271-73 (7th Cir. 1990) (state court's rejection, on laches grounds, of petitioner's challenge to two prior convictions from mid-1960s that were being used to enhance petitioner's current sentence creates procedural default bar to federal court's adjudication of petitioner's challenge to current sentence as enhanced by 1960s convictions).

Among the practical consequences of the rule discussed in text are that the petition: (1) must be framed as a challenge to the current conviction and sentence, not the former ones; (2) must be filed in a court with personal jurisdiction and venue to hear a challenge to the current sentence; and (3) must name the petitioner's current custodian as the proper party respondent. *See infra* §§ 10.1, 10.2. In *Custis v. United States, supra,* in the process of forbidding certain kinds of attacks *at the time of sentencing* on prior convictions then being used to enhance sentences on federal convictions, the Court "recognized ... that Custis, who was still 'in custody' for purposes of his state convictions at the time of his federal sentencing ... may attack his state sentences ... through federal habeas review" and suggested without deciding that "[i]f Custis is successful ... he [might] then apply for reopening of any federal sentence enhanced by the state sentences." 511 U.S. at 497. Although the Court limited this *dictum* to attacks made on prior convictions while "custody" under them continues, it did not express a view one way or another, as Justice Souter noted (see above), on the federal circuit courts' uniform practice of hearing federal habeas corpus challenges to prior convictions used to enhance current sentences in the course of adjudicating the legality of the current sentences, even after custody under the prior convictions has terminated. Some courts have understood *Maleng* to leave open the validity of this practice. *See, e.g., Gamble v. Parsons, supra.* In fact, *Maleng* recognized that federal courts have jurisdiction to utilize this practice and left open only the less consequential question whether, in the process of voiding a current sentence enhanced on the basis of an unconstitutionally imposed prior conviction as to which custody has terminated, the prior conviction "itself" may be voided, thus depriving it of other collateral consequences in addition to its effect on the sentence currently being served. *Maleng v. Cook, supra,* 490 U.S. at 493-94. *See Custis v. United States, supra,* 511 U.S. at 512 n.7 (Souter, J., dissenting) ("Court of Appeals decisions postdating *Maleng* have uniformly read it as consistent with the view that federal habeas courts may review prior convictions relied upon for sentence enhancement and grant *appropriate relief*" (emphasis added)).

[21] *See, e.g.,* Carafas v. LaVallee, 391 U.S. 234 (1968).

long as, at the time the federal petition was filed,[22] the petitioner was subject to at least one of the following kinds of restraint:

(1) Incarceration[23] pursuant to the conviction[24] or sentence[25] challenged in the petition.

(2) Incarceration under sentence of death and challenging either the capital conviction or capital sentence.[26]

(3) Incarceration pursuant to the first of two consecutive sentences although the petitioner challenges the second (as yet unserved) sentence or the conviction for which the second sentence was imposed,[27] or incarceration pursuant to the second of two consecutive sentences although the petitioner has finished serving the first sentence and is challenging that sentence or the conviction for which that sentence was imposed.[28]

---

[22] *See, e.g.,* Maleng v. Cook, 490 U.S. 488, 492 (1989). As long as petitioner had the requisite status when the petition was filed, subsequent changes in that status will not moot the petition. *See* authority cited *supra* § 8.2b nn.10-12. *But cf. supra* § 8.2b nn.9, 12, 13.

[23] "Incarceration" encompasses confinement *in prison* (*e.g.,* Withrow v. Williams, 507 U.S. 680 (1993); Fay v. Noia, 372 U.S. 391 (1963)), *in jail* (*e.g.,* Townsend v. Sain, 372 U.S. 293 (1963); Atkins v. Michigan, 644 F.2d 543, 545 (6th Cir.), *cert. denied,* 452 U.S. 964 (1981)), or *in a hospital, mental health facility, or some other state facility* (*e.g.,* Baxstrom v. Herold, 383 U.S. 107 (1966) (mental health facility); Wales v. Whitney, 114 U.S. 564, 571 (1885) (*dicta*); Brock v. Weston, 31 F.3d 887, 890 (9th Cir. 1994) (commitment to special penal facility for sexually violent predators); Levine v. Torvik, 986 F.2d 1506 (6th Cir.), *cert. denied,* 509 U.S. 907 (1993) (mental hospital); Kolocotronis v. Holcomb, 925 F.2d 278, 279-80 (8th Cir. 1991) (mental hospital); Turney v. O'Toole, 898 F.2d 1470, 1472 n.1 (10th Cir. 1990) (mental health facility); Francois v. Henderson, 850 F.2d 231, 235-36 (5th Cir. 1988) (mental hospital); Mercado v. Rockefeller, 363 F. Supp. 489, 490 (S.D.N.Y. 1973), *rev'd on other grounds,* 502 F.2d 666 (2d Cir. 1974), *cert. denied,* 420 U.S. 925 (1975) (juvenile facility)); *infra* note 50 and accompanying text.

[24] *See, e.g., Withrow v. Williams, supra;* Kimmelman v. Morrison, 477 U.S. 365 (1986); Jackson v. Virginia, 443 U.S. 307 (1979).

[25] *See, e.g.,* Barton v. Lockhart, 762 F.2d 712 (8th Cir. 1985); McAffee v. Procunier, 761 F.2d 1124 (5th Cir.), *cert. denied,* 474 U.S. 907 (1985); Collins v. Buckhoe, 493 F.2d 343 (6th Cir. 1974). *See also* Lynott v. Story, 929 F.2d 228, 232-33 (6th Cir. 1991) (incarceration following revocation of parole); White v. White, 925 F.2d 287, 290 (9th Cir. 1991) (same); authority cited *infra* §§ 9.1 nn.32 & 33, 33.4 n.2.

[26] *See, e.g.,* Richmond v. Lewis, 506 U.S. 40 (1992); Parker v. Dugger, 498 U.S. 308 (1991); Strickland v. Washington, 466 U.S. 668 (1984); Zant v. Stephens, 462 U.S. 862 (1983); Hopper v. Evans, 456 U.S. 605 (1982); Estelle v. Smith, 451 U.S. 454 (1981).

[27] *See, e.g.,* Garlotte v. Fordice, 515 U.S. 39, 40, 43-47 (1995); Nelson v. George, 399 U.S. 224 (1970); Peyton v. Rowe, 391 U.S. 54 (1968); Leacock v. Henman, 996 F.2d 1069, 1071 & n.4 (10th Cir. 1993); Word v. North Carolina, 406 F.2d 352, 353-55 (4th Cir. 1969). *See supra* § 8.2c nn.14-15 and accompanying text.

[28] *See, e.g., Garlotte v. Fordice, supra,* 515 U.S. at 44-47; *supra* § 8.2c nn.16-18 and accompanying text (citing additional authorities).

(4) Incarceration pursuant to the second of two sentences although the petitioner challenges the first sentence or conviction, as long as the earlier conviction may affect the length or conditions of the present incarceration *and* (1) the sentence under the first conviction has not been fully served or has not fully expired in which case the petitioner may challenge the *first* conviction and sentence *directly,* or (2) if the sentence under the first conviction *has* fully expired, the petitioner frames the petition as a challenge to the *second* sentence as enhanced, lengthened, or otherwise affected by the prior assertedly unlawful conviction.[29]

(5) Incarceration in one jurisdiction although the petitioner is challenging a conviction, sentence, or proceeding in another jurisdiction, as long as the second ("demanding") jurisdiction has filed a detainer with the first ("incarcerating") jurisdiction requiring the prisoner to be turned over to the demanding jurisdiction when the prison term in the incarcerating jurisdiction is completed.[30]

(6) Incarceration under concurrent sentences although the petitioner is challenging only one of the sentences, at least when the challenged sentence may adversely affect the length or conditions of the other sentence.[31]

---

[29] *See* authority cited *supra* § 8.2c n.20.

[30] *See* authority cited *supra* § 8.2c n.15. *But cf. infra* note 46 (certain INS detainers that do not assure continuous physical custody also may not establish "custody" for purposes of habeas corpus statute). The courts are split on whether a conviction is subject to habeas corpus challenge by a prisoner incarcerated in another jurisdiction on a different conviction when the demanding State has not formally filed a detainer with the incarcerating State. *Compare, e.g.,* Vargas v. Swan, 854 F.2d 1028, 1031-32 (7th Cir. 1988) ("However labelled, an action that has as part of its effect the 'holding' of a prisoner for a future custodian who has evidenced an intent to retake or to decide the prisoner's future status ... serves to establish custody for habeas purposes") *and* Frazier v. Wilkinson, 842 F.2d 42, 45 (2d Cir.), *cert. denied,* 488 U.S. 842 (1988) (federal prisoner may challenge consecutive state sentence absent state detainer when "there is a reasonable basis to apprehend that the jurisdiction that obtained the consecutive sentence will seek its enforcement") *with, e.g.,* Stacey v. Warden, 854 F.2d 401, 403 (11th Cir. 1988) (detainer must be issued by other jurisdiction in order to permit challenge to conviction in that jurisdiction by petitioner incarcerated elsewhere under different conviction). By authorizing petitions on behalf of any "applicant [who] is not presently in custody pursuant to the state judgment against which he seeks relief but *may* be subject to such custody in the future" (emphasis added), Rule 2(b) of the Rules Governing § 2254 Cases seems to render a detainer unnecessary.

[31] *See, e.g.,* Lockhart v. Nelson, 488 U.S. 33, 37-39 (1988) (by implication); other authority cited *supra* § 8.2c nn.14, 15. If the prisoner challenges the second of two consecutive sentences after the sentence under the first conviction has fully expired, the prisoner must frame the petition as a challenge to the *second* sentence as enhanced by the first conviction. *See* Maleng v. Cook, 490 U.S. 488, 493-94 (1989) (discussed *supra* § 8.2c nn.19-20 and accompanying text); Benton v. Maryland, 395 U.S. 784, 791 (1969). *Compare* Cramer v. Fahner, 683 F.2d 1376, 1380-81 (7th

(7) Probation[32] or parole.[33]

(8) Furlough from prison.[34]

Cir.), *cert. denied,* 459 U.S. 1016 (1982) (court should exercise its discretion to allow petitioner to attack sentence when challenged sentence may aggravate petitioner's custodial situation under a concurrent sentence) *and* United States ex rel. Hickey v. Jeffes, 571 F.2d 762, 764-65 (3d Cir. 1978) *with* Scott v. Louisiana, 934 F.2d 631, 635 (5th Cir. 1991) (discussed *supra* § 8.2c n.15) *and* Dennis v. Hopper, 548 F.2d 589 (5th Cir. 1977) (challenge to sentence rejected when petitioner fails to show specific detrimental effect of challenged sentence on concurrent sentence) *and* Tyler v. Wyrick, 540 F.2d 921 (8th Cir. 1976) *and* Van Geldern v. Field, 498 F.2d 400, 403-04 (9th Cir. 1974) *and* Weems v. Follette, 414 F.2d 417 (2d Cir. 1969), *cert. denied,* 397 U.S. 950 (1970).

[32] *See, e.g.,* Krantz v. Briggs, 983 F.2d 961, 962 n.1 (9th Cir. 1993); Olson v. Hart, 965 F.2d 940, 942-43 (10th Cir. 1992); Fawcett v. Bablitch, 962 F.2d 617, 618 (7th Cir. 1992); Frank v. United States, 914 F.2d 828, 829 n.1 (7th Cir. 1990); McVeigh v. Smith, 872 F.2d 725, 727 (6th Cir. 1989) (probation period commenced and stayed); Barry v. Brower, 864 F.2d 294, 296 (3d Cir. 1988); Landry v. Hoepfner, 840 F.2d 1201, 1204 n.8 (5th Cir. 1988) (*en banc*), *cert. denied,* 489 U.S. 1083 (1989) (petitioner still eligible for habeas corpus relief despite expiration of probation because petitioner filed petition while on probation); Bruno v. Greenlee, 569 F.2d 775, 776 n.2 (3d Cir. 1978); Coronado v. United States Bd. of Parole, 540 F.2d 216, 217 (5th Cir. 1976); Porth v. Templar, 453 F.2d 330, 332-33 (10th Cir. 1971); United States v. Re, 372 F.2d 641, 643 (2d Cir. 1967).

[33] *See, e.g., Maleng v. Cook, supra,* 490 U.S. at 491 (reaffirming rule of *Jones v. Cunningham, infra*); Jones v. Cunningham, 371 U.S. 236, 243 (1963); Dawson v. Scott, 50 F.3d 884, 886 n.2 (11th Cir. 1995) (custody present when petitioner "is still serving his term of supervised release, which is part of his sentence and involves some restrictions upon his liberty"); Jones v. Jerrison, 20 F.3d 849, 852 n.2 (8th Cir. 1994); United States v. Tunstall, 17 F.3d 245, 246 n.3 (8th Cir. 1994); DePompei v. Ohio Adult Parole Auth., 999 F.2d 138, 140 (6th Cir. 1993); Brewer v. Dahlberg, 942 F.2d 328, 335 (6th Cir. 1991); Feldman v. Perrill, 902 F.2d 1445, 1447-49 (9th Cir. 1990); Gordon v. Duran, 895 F.2d 610, 612 (9th Cir. 1990); Felts v. Estelle, 875 F.2d 785, 785 n.1 (9th Cir. 1989) (citing Tisnado v. United States, 547 F.2d 452, 455 (9th Cir. 1976)); Walberg v. United States, 763 F.2d 143 (2d Cir. 1985); Reimnitz v. State's Attorney, 761 F.2d 405, 408 (7th Cir. 1985) (release under "mandatory supervised" conditions); Clonce v. Presley, 640 F.2d 271, 273 (10th Cir. 1981); United States ex rel. Baker v. Finkbeiner, 551 F.2d 180, 182 (7th Cir. 1977); *Coronado v. United States Bd. of Parole, supra,* 540 F.2d at 217; United States ex rel. Meadows v. New York, 426 F.2d 1176, 1179 (2d Cir. 1970), *cert. denied,* 401 U.S. 941 (1971) (parole detainer warrant); Mercado v. Rockefeller, 363 F. Supp. 489, 490 (S.D.N.Y. 1973), *rev'd on other grounds,* 502 F.2d 666 (2d Cir. 1974), *cert. denied,* 420 U.S. 925 (1975) (parole from training school); authority cited *infra* § 9.1 n.33. *But cf.* Spencer v. Kemna, 118 S. Ct. 978, 985-86 (1998) (discussed *supra* § 8.2b n.11 and accompanying text) (if petition challenges constitutionality of parole revocation procedures rather than underlying conviction, prisoner's postfiling "complet[ion of] the entire term of imprisonment underlying the parole revocation" (*id.* at 981) may render petition moot unless petitioner affirmatively demonstrates "concrete injuries-in-fact attributable to his parole revocation").

[34] *See, e.g.,* Powell v. Florida, 579 F.2d 324, 328 (5th Cir. 1978); United States ex rel. Geisler v. Walters, 510 F.2d 887, 893-94 (3d Cir. 1975).

(9) Detention or parole warrant,[35] bail[36] or bond[37] pending trial or appeal.

(10) Release on recognizance pending trial, sentencing, or appeal.[38]

(11) Suspended or stayed sentence.[39]

(12) Detainer arising from the conviction or sentence being challenged, even though the petitioner is not actually incarcerated under the challenged conviction or sentence.[40]

---

[35] *See, e.g.,* Mars v. Mounts, 895 F.2d 1348, 1351 n.3 (11th Cir. 1989).

[36] *See, e.g.,* Lefkowitz v. Newsome, 420 U.S. 283, 286 (1975) (bail pending appeal); Hensley v. Municipal Ct., 411 U.S. 345 (1973) (release on recognizance after conviction); Turner v. Tennessee, 858 F.2d 1201, 1204 (6th Cir. 1988), *vac'd & remanded on other grounds,* 492 U.S. 902 (1989) (release on bail pending trial); United States v. Doherty, 786 F.2d 491, 500 n.13 (2d Cir. 1986) (bail following arrest pending extradition); United States ex rel. Scranton v. New York, 532 F.2d 292, 293-94 (2d Cir. 1976) (pretrial bail); Marden v. Purdy, 409 F.2d 784, 785 (5th Cir. 1969) (postconviction bail); Burris v. Ryan, 397 F.2d 553, 555 (7th Cir. 1968) (bail pending appeal of mistrial); Campbell v. Shapp, 385 F. Supp. 305, 306-07 (E.D. Pa. 1974), *aff'd,* 521 F.2d 1398 (3d Cir. 1975), *cert. denied,* 424 U.S. 912 (1976) (bail pending extradition).

[37] *See, e.g.,* Malinovsky v. Court of Common Pleas, 7 F.3d 1263, 1265 (6th Cir. 1993), *cert. denied,* 510 U.S. 1194 (1994) ("custody" requirement satisfied because petitioner "has been released on a personal recognizance bond"); Capler v. City of Greenville, 422 F.2d 299, 301 (5th Cir. 1970) (bond pending appeal). *But cf.* Lahey v. Floyd, 992 F.2d 234, 235-36 (9th Cir. 1993) (although recognizing that pretrial release on bond can constitute "custody" in appropriate circumstances, court finds that petitioner's pretrial release on bond to live in brother's home (later modified to own home) did not constitute "custody" because "[n]o serious impairment of [petitioner's] freedom was involved").

[38] *See, e.g., Hensley v. Municipal Ct., supra,* 411 U.S. at 351-52 (release on recognizance subject to conditions pending appeal); Oyler v. Allenbrand, 23 F.3d 292, 293-94 (10th Cir.), *cert. denied,* 513 U.S. 909 (1994) (release on bond pending appeal); Nakell v. Attorney General, 15 F.3d 319, 323 (4th Cir. 1994); Mieles v. United States, 895 F.2d 887, 888 (2d Cir. 1990); Saylor v. Cornelius, 845 F.2d 1401, 1403 n.2 (6th Cir. 1988) (obligation to appear for trial constitutes custody for habeas corpus purposes); Reimnitz v. State's Attorney, 761 F.2d 405, 408 (7th Cir. 1985) (release under "mandatory supervised" conditions pending appeal); United States ex rel. Scranton v. New York, 532 F.2d 292, 293-94 (2d Cir. 1976) (release on recognizance pending trial); United States ex rel. Smith v. Di Bella, 314 F. Supp. 446, 448 (D. Conn. 1970) (release on recognizance pending appeal).

[39] *See, e.g.,* McVeigh v. Smith, 872 F.2d 725, 727 (6th Cir. 1989) (stay of probation); Sammons v. Rodgers, 785 F.2d 1343, 1345 (5th Cir. 1986); Sawyer v. Sandstrom, 615 F.2d 311, 313 n.1 (5th Cir. 1980); United States ex rel. Wojtycha v. Hopkins, 517 F.2d 420, 423-24 (3d Cir. 1975); Choung v. California, 320 F. Supp. 625, 627-28 (E.D. Cal. 1970) (stayed sentence); Walker v. North Carolina, 262 F. Supp. 102, 104-05 (W.D.N.C. 1966), *aff'd per curiam,* 372 F.2d 129 (4th Cir.), *cert. denied,* 388 U.S. 917 (1967).

[40] *See, e.g.,* Braden v. 30th Judicial Cir. Ct., 410 U.S. 484 (1973); Nelson v. George, 399 U.S. 224 (1970); authority cited *supra* § 8.2c n.15; *supra* note 30. *But cf.* authority cited *infra* note 46 (uncertain effect of INS detainer).

(13) Sentence requiring payment of a fine *together with* incarceration or a threat of incarceration to compel payment of the fine.[41]

(14) Custody of an asylum State or country pursuant to another State's or country's extradition request.[42]

---

[41] *See, e.g.,* United States v. Keane, 852 F.2d 199, 203-04 (7th Cir. 1988), *cert. denied,* 490 U.S. 1084 (1989) (by implication); Hanson v. Circuit Ct., 591 F.2d 404, 407 n.6 (7th Cir.), *cert. denied,* 444 U.S. 907 (1979) *(dicta)*; Wright v. Bailey, 544 F.2d 737, 739 (4th Cir. 1976), *cert. denied,* 434 U.S. 825 (1977) *(dicta)*; Edmunds v. Won Bae Chang, 509 F.2d 39, 41 (9th Cir.), *cert. denied,* 423 U.S. 825 (1975) *(dicta)* (custody if confinement is imminent, save for stay); United States ex rel. Lawrence v. Woods, 432 F.2d 1072 (7th Cir. 1970), *cert. denied,* 402 U.S. 983 (1971) (by implication). *See also* Barry v. Bergen County Probation Dep't, 128 F.3d 152, 159-62 (3d Cir. 1997), *cert. denied,* 118 S. Ct. 1097 (1998) (requirement of community service which, if violated, would result in obligation to pay fine, constituted "custody" because community service obligation significantly restrained petitioner's liberty); United States v. Watroba, 56 F.3d 28, 29 & n.1 (6th Cir.), *cert. denied,* 516 U.S. 904 (1995) (monetary fine, standing alone, was insufficient to establish "custody" for purposes of section 2255 motion); *infra* § 8.2e n.53. *But see* Spring v. Caldwell, 692 F.2d 994, 999 (5th Cir. 1982) ("arrest warrant issued for willful refusal to pay a fine does not amount to custody").

[42] *See, e.g.,* Liu v. United States, 117 S. Ct. 1491 (1997) (Breyer, J., dissenting) (dissenting from denial of stay of mandate pending consideration of *certiorari* petition presenting habeas corpus claim that extradition to Hong Kong, for trial under laws of People's Republic of China after Hong Kong reverts to that nation, violates treaty with United Kingdom under which extradition was ordered, which requires receiving state to "'be[ ] competent to try and punish'" and forbids transfer to "third state" (quoting Terlinden v. Ames, 184 U.S. 270, 289 (1902) (defining minimum standards for "extradition," as that term is used in treaties)); case also raises question whether 18 U.S.C. §§ 3184, 3186 give Executive Branch exclusive power to interpret relevant provisions of treaty; availability of habeas corpus to challenge legality of extradition under federal law is not challenged); Ludecke v. United States Marshal, 15 F.3d 496, 497 (5th Cir. 1994); Coungeris v. Sheahan, 11 F.3d 726, 728 (7th Cir. 1993); Austin v. Healey, 5 F.3d 598, 600-01 (2d Cir. 1993), *cert. denied,* 510 U.S. 1165 (1994) (affording limited review of extradition order that is available on habeas corpus); In re Extradition of Howard, 996 F.2d 1320, 1325 (1st Cir. 1993); Martin v. Warden, 993 F.2d 824, 828 (11th Cir. 1993); Bovio v. United States, 989 F.2d 255, 257 n.2 (7th Cir. 1993) ("Extradition rulings are not directly appealable; one may challenge an extradition ruling by filing a petition for a writ of habeas corpus."); Bozilov v. Seifert, 983 F.2d 140, 143 (9th Cir. 1993) (similar to *Theron v. United States Marshal, infra*); Koskotas v. Roche, 931 F.2d 169, 171 (1st Cir. 1991); Spatola v. United States, 925 F.2d 615, 617-19 (2d Cir. 1991); Theron v. United States Marshal, 832 F.2d 492, 495 (9th Cir. 1987), *cert. denied,* 486 U.S. 1059 (1988) (habeas corpus review of extradition order; review subject to "clearly erroneous" standard and limited to whether (1) extradition court had jurisdiction over proceedings and fugitive, (2) offense charged is within valid and enforceable extradition treaty, and (3) some evidence warrants finding of reasonable belief that accused is guilty); United States v. Doherty, 786 F.2d 491, 495 (2d Cir. 1986); Artukovic v. Rison, 784 F.2d 1354, 1355 (9th Cir. 1986) ("A petition for habeas corpus is the only method of review of an order certifying [an international] extradition."); Demjanjuk v. Meese, 784 F.2d 1114 (D.C. Cir. 1986) (by implication) (international extradition); Demjanjuk v. Petrovsky, 776 F.2d 571, 576 (6th Cir. 1985), *cert. denied,* 475 U.S. 1016 (1986) (by implication). *See* Sokol, *supra* § 8.2a n.1, at 44-49; Note, *Extradition Habeas Corpus, supra* § 8.2a n.1. *Cf.*

(15) Restraint imposed by a military court.[43]

(16) Induction into the military.[44]

(17) Restraint imposed by an Indian tribal court.[45]

(18) Restraint pursuant to an exclusion or deportation order.[46]

Eckert v. Tansy, 936 F.2d 444, 450 (9th Cir. 1991) (conviction precludes habeas corpus relief on prisoner's claim of unlawful extradition from one state to another to stand trial).

[43] *See, e.g.*, Burns v. Wilson, 346 U.S. 137, 139-40 (1953) (military convictions subject to limited habeas corpus review); Gusik v. Schilder, 340 U.S. 128 (1950); Whelcher v. McDonald, 340 U.S. 122 (1950); Hiatt v. Brown, 339 U.S. 103 (1950); Wales v. Whitney, 114 U.S. 564, 571 (1885), *overruled on other grounds*, Hensley v. Municipal Ct., 411 U.S. 345 (1973) (*dicta*); Lips v. Commandant, 997 F.2d 808, 810-11 (10th Cir. 1993) (discussing limited scope of habeas corpus review of court martial convictions); Matias v. United States, 923 F.2d 821, 822-26 (Fed. Cir. 1990) (Court of Claims retains jurisdiction to hear collateral attacks on court martial convictions; discussing limited scope of such review); Dodson v. Zelez, 917 F.2d 1250, 1252-53 (10th Cir. 1990); Welch v. Fritz, 909 F.2d 1330, 1331 (9th Cir. 1990); Lundy v. Zelez, 908 F.2d 593, 594-95 (10th Cir. 1990). *See generally* SOKOL, *supra* § 8.2a n.1, at 42-45; Dwight H. Sullivan, *The Last Line of Defense: Federal Habeas Review of Military Death Penalty Cases*, 144 MIL. L. REV. 1 (1994).

[44] *See, e.g.*, Oestereich v. Selective Service System, 393 U.S. 233 (1968); Arbitman v. Woodside, 258 F. 441 (4th Cir. 1919); Ex parte Cohen, 254 F. 711 (E.D. Va. 1918); In re Carver, 103 F. 624 (C.C.D. Me. 1900); In re Falconer, 91 F. 649 (S.D.N.Y. 1898); United States v. Anderson, 24 F. Cas. 813 (C.C.D. Tenn. 1812) (No. 14,449); Girard v. Wilson, 152 F. Supp. 21 (D.D.C.), *rev'd on other grounds,* 354 U.S. 524 (1957); Ex parte Fabiani, 105 F. Supp. 139, 143-44 (E.D. Pa. 1952) (habeas corpus available to test induction, even before petitioner was actually in service); United States ex rel. Steinberg v. Graham, 57 F. Supp. 938, 941-42 (E.D. Ark. 1944), *appeal dismissed,* 149 F.2d 647 (8th Cir. 1945); United States ex rel. Altieri v. Flint, 54 F. Supp. 889 (D. Conn. 1943), *aff'd,* 142 F.2d 62 (2d Cir. 1944). *See* SOKOL, *supra* § 8.2a n.1, at 70-71.

[45] 25 U.S.C. § 1303 (1994). *See, e.g.*, Wetsit v. Stafne, 44 F.3d 823 (9th Cir. 1995) (sentence of incarceration and fine imposed by tribal court); Duro v. Reina, 495 U.S. 676, 679, 682, 709 (1990) (granting habeas corpus to nonmember Indian seeking to avoid criminal prosecution by Indian tribe). *See generally* SOKOL, *supra* § 8.2a n.1, at 62-65.

[46] *See, e.g.*, 8 U.S.C. §§ 1105(a)(9), 1105(b), 1252(a) (1994); Jean v. Nelson, 472 U.S. 846 (1985) (remanding for consideration of habeas corpus relief based upon statutory violations affecting parole rights of undocumented aliens); Brownell v. Tom We Shung, 352 U.S. 180, 183 (1956) (*dicta*); Shaughnessy v. United States ex rel. Mezei, 345 U.S. 206, 213 (1953); United States ex rel. Knauff v. Shaughnessy, 338 U.S. 537 (1950); The Japanese Immigrant Case, 189 U.S. 86 (1903); United States v. Jung Ah Lung, 124 U.S. 621, 626 (1888); Balogun v. INS, 9 F.3d 347 (5th Cir. 1993) (detention pending deportation); Picrin-Peron v. Rison, 930 F.2d 773, 775 (9th Cir. 1991) (exclusion order); Mayo v. Schiltgen, 921 F.2d 177, 178-80 (8th Cir. 1990) (exclusion order); Bal v. Moyer, 883 F.2d 45, 47-48 (7th Cir. 1989) (*per curiam*) (appeal of denial of deportation stay); Vargas v. Swan, 854 F.2d 1028, 1031-32 (7th Cir. 1988) (INS message to prison authorities requesting information on release date may be sufficient to establish INS custody); United States v. Romero-Vilca, 850 F.2d 177, 179 (3d Cir. 1988) (potential for deportation due to conviction is adequate collateral consequence to preserve jurisdiction over habeas corpus petition filed during petitioner's incarceration, notwithstanding petitioner's release thereafter); Chavez v. INS, 790 F.2d 544, 548 (6th Cir. 1986) (*dicta*); Azzouka v. Sava, 777 F.2d 68 (2d Cir. 1985), *cert. denied,* 479 U.S. 830 (1986); Garcia-Mir v. Smith, 766 F.2d 1478, 1481-82 (11th Cir. 1985), *cert.*

(19) Placement of children or other wards of the state in public orphanages or other public facilities.[47]

denied, 475 U.S. 1022 (1986) (exclusion case; review "narrowly limited"; exhaustion of state administrative remedies required); Dallo v. INS, 765 F.2d 581 (6th Cir. 1985); SOKOL, *supra* § 8.2a n.1, at 41-42; Gerald L. Neuman, *Habeas Corpus, Executive Detention, and the Removal of Aliens,* 98 COLUM. L. REV. 961 (1998); Note, *Deportation and Exclusion: A Continuing Dialogue Between Congress and the Courts, supra* § 8.2a n.1. *See also* National Center for Immigration Rights v. INS, 913 F.2d 1350, 1352 (9th Cir. 1990), *rev'd on other grounds,* 502 U.S. 183 (1991) (habeas corpus is appropriate method of challenging INS's delay in determining deportability in individual cases but is not appropriate method of bringing simultaneous challenge to delays affecting all potentially deportable individuals); Subias v. Meese, 835 F.2d 1288 (9th Cir. 1987) (petitioner detained in Mexico by unknown United States authorities is in custody for habeas corpus purposes, but personal jurisdiction lacking). Holding that deportation moots habeas corpus challenges to preceding INS custody are, *e.g.,* Roldan v. Racette, 984 F.2d 85, 89-91 (2d Cir. 1993) (no jurisdiction to review petition if petitioner already has been deported); Quezada v. INS, 898 F.2d 474, 475-76 (5th Cir. 1990) (similar); Ortez v. Chandler, 845 F.2d 573, 575 (5th Cir. 1988) (challenge to bond determination made in consequence of failure to appear at deportation hearing mooted when petitioner voluntarily deported).

A majority of circuits have held that, unlike most detainers, *see supra* § 8.2c n.15; *supra* note 30 and accompanying text, an INS detainer filed with prison officials does not establish custody. *See, e.g.,* Garcia v. Taylor, 40 F.3d 299, 303-04 (9th Cir. 1994); Prieto v. Gluch, 913 F.2d 1159, 1162 (6th Cir. 1990), *cert. denied,* 498 U.S. 1092 (1991); Orozco v. INS, 911 F.2d 539, 541 (11th Cir. 1990); Mohammed v. Sullivan, 866 F.2d 258, 260 (8th Cir. 1989); Vargas v. Swan, 854 F.2d 1028 (7th Cir. 1988); Campillo v. Sullivan, 853 F.2d 593 (8th Cir. 1988), *cert. denied,* 490 U.S. 1082 (1989); Fernandez-Collado v. INS, 644 F. Supp. 741 (D. Conn. 1986), *aff'd,* 857 F.2d 1461 (2d Cir. 1987). *See also Roldan v. Racette, supra* at 88 (reviewing caselaw); Guti v. INS, 908 F.2d 495, 496 (9th Cir. 1990) (noting, but not taking position on, circuit split on question whether INS detainer lodged against prisoner establishes INS custody). *But cf. United States v. Romero-Vilco, supra.* INS detainers are arguably distinguishable from detainers lodged by state or federal correction officials. Whereas the latter detainers contemplate continuous custody — the immediate and automatic transfer of the prisoner from one facility to another — INS detainers do not assure continuous custody because they merely give the INS the authority, at some point in the future, often well after the preceding prison custody has ended, to take custody over and deport the subject of the detainer. *See also Picrin-Peron, supra* at 775-76 (although INS's threat to reincarcerate petitioner might qualify as "custody" under doctrine that "voluntary cessation" of party's unlawful activity does not establish mootness if party is "free to resume" offending activity, custody was not present under circumstances because petitioner, who had been subject to exclusion proceedings by INS, was reparoled into United States and because INS signed declaration eschewing further exclusion proceedings for one year, as long as petitioner did not become involved with criminal justice system). *Cf.* Galaviz-Medina v. Wooten, 27 F.3d 487, 493 (10th Cir. 1994), *cert. denied,* 513 U.S. 1086 (1995) (custody requirement was satisfied because "record suggests not only that a detainer was lodged, but also that there is a final deportation order in place.... [I]t is reasonable to assume that the deportation order establishes conclusively the INS's right to custody following the expiration of his current prison term.").

[47] *See* Hemon v. Office of Public Guardian, 878 F.2d 13, 14-15 (1st Cir. 1989) (no habeas corpus jurisdiction to review state court order awarding custody of ward to private nonprofit organization operating nursing home; suggesting that habeas corpus jurisdiction might be appropriate to review ward's placement in state-operated facility). *See also* Lehman v. Lycoming

(20) Enslavement.[48]

(21) Incarceration pursuant to civil contempt judgment imposed, for example, for failure to comply with order to pay alimony.[49]

(22) Confinement in a mental institution as a result of a judgment of not guilty by reason of insanity or as a result of any other judicial or administrative order.[50]

(23) Disciplinary or administrative segregation in prison.[51]

County Children's Services Agency, 458 U.S. 502, 511 n.12 (1982) (reserving question of habeas corpus jurisdiction over challenge to state-court placement of child in state institution); In re Larch, 872 F.2d 66, 67 (4th Cir. 1989) (by implication) (child subject to competing custody orders issued by state and Indian tribal court is "in custody" for purposes of habeas corpus action; nonetheless, court could not award custody to Indian court by granting writ because no legal violation cognizable in habeas corpus was present); Amerson v. Iowa Dep't of Human Services, 59 F.3d 92 (8th Cir. 1995), cert. denied, 516 U.S. 1080 (1996) (although placement of neglected child in state institution that significantly restricts liberty might constitute "custody" for habeas corpus purposes, particular residential group homes and psychiatric facilities in which child was placed did not "restrain[ ] his liberty to a significantly greater extent than a parent's or foster parent's custody"). Cf. O'Connell v. Kirchner, 513 U.S. 1138 (1995) (O'Connor, J., dissenting from denial of stay) (discussing successful state habeas corpus action brought by biological parent seeking custody of child currently living with adoptive parents following invalidation of adoption decree); O'Connell v. Kirchner, 513 U.S. 1303, 1304 (1995) (Stevens, J., Circuit Justice, denying motion to recall mandate and for stay) (same); infra § 8.2e n.62 and accompanying text (official action placing children in private foster care does not constitute custody for habeas corpus purposes). See generally Albert & Brodek, supra § 8.2a n.1; Robbins & Newell, supra § 8.2a n.1.

[48] See United States v. Davis, 25 F. Cas. 775 (D.C.C.C. 1839) (No. 14,926).

[49] See, e.g., In re Ayers, 123 U.S. 443, 507-08 (1887); Ex parte Rowland, 104 U.S. 604, 616-18 (1881); Fernos-Lopez v. Figarella-Lopez, 929 F.2d 20, 21-22 (1st Cir.), cert. denied, 502 U.S. 887 (1991) (petitioner jailed for failure to comply with order to pay alimony would be in custody for habeas corpus purposes; doctrines forbidding federal jurisdiction in domestic relations matters and withholding habeas corpus jurisdiction in some child custody disputes do not apply); De Long v. Hennessey, 912 F.2d 1144, 1146 (9th Cir.), cert. denied, 498 U.S. 1001 (1990) (habeas corpus would have been appropriate method of attacking allegedly unconstitutional order jailing petitioner for violating court-ordered injunction if petitioner had still been in jail when petition was filed).

[50] See, e.g., Levine v. Torvik, 986 F.2d 1506 (6th Cir.), cert. denied, 509 U.S. 907 (1993); Kolocotronis v. Holcomb, 925 F.2d 278, 279-80 (8th Cir. 1991); Francois v. Henderson, 850 F.2d 231, 235-36 (5th Cir. 1988); other authority cited supra note 23.

[51] See, e.g., United States v. Harris, 12 F.3d 735, 736 (7th Cir. 1994) (assuming proper exhaustion of administrative remedies, federal prisoner could seek habeas corpus relief for due process claim of excessive administrative segregation pending prosecution for crime allegedly committed in prison; "[s]ince being locked in one's cell 23 hours of the day is qualitatively different from having, as it were, the run of the prison, Harris's situation was equivalent to that of someone who is incarcerated before charges are brought against him"); Harris v. Duckworth, 909 F.2d 1057, 1058-59 (7th Cir. 1990) (habeas corpus proper forum to challenge constitutionality of procedure by which State Conduct Adjustment Board found petitioner guilty of battery while in prison and, as punishment, transferred him to different prison, segregated him from other prisoners,

(24) Court-ordered community service or participation in a substance abuse rehabilitation program or other analogous program.[52]

e. *Noncustodial statuses.* A person is not in custody if, at the time the petition was filed, she was subject to only the following kinds of restraint:

(1) Sentence requiring payment of a fine, absent either incarceration or a threat of imminent incarceration for failure to pay the fine.[53]

(2) Suspension, revocation or denial of a driver's license[54] or of a professional, occupational, or other license by local, state, or federal authorities.[55]

(3) Professional discipline[56] or other adverse employment consequences.[57]

---

and withdrew earned good time credits). For other cases involving challenges to administrative or disciplinary segregation in prison, *see infra* § 9.1 n.34.

[52] *See, e.g.,* Barry v. Bergen County Probation Dep't, 128 F.3d 152, 159-62 (3d Cir. 1997), *cert. denied,* 118 S. Ct. 1097 (1998) (court-ordered community service constituted "custody," even though only consequence of violation of court order would be obligation to pay fine, because "individual who is required to be in a certain place — or in one of several places — to attend meetings or to perform services, is clearly subject to restraints on his liberty not shared by the public generally"); Dow v. Circuit Ct., 995 F.2d 922, 922-23 (9th Cir. 1993) (*per curiam*), *cert. denied,* 510 U.S. 1110 (1994) (petitioner, who was sentenced to "fourteen hours of attendance at an alcohol rehabilitation program," was "in custody" because sentence "significantly restrain[ed] ... [his] liberty to do those things which free persons in the United States are entitled to do").

[53] *See, e.g.,* United States v. Michaud, 901 F.2d 5, 6-7 (1st Cir. 1990) (outstanding $60,000 fine and possibility of incarceration for nonpayment insufficient restraint to establish custody); Spring v. Caldwell, 692 F.2d 994, 996-97, 999 (5th Cir. 1982) (citing authority); Hanson v. Circuit Ct., 591 F.2d 404-05 (7th Cir.), *cert. denied,* 444 U.S. 907 (1979); Wright v. Bailey, 544 F.2d 737 (4th Cir. 1976), *cert. denied,* 434 U.S. 825 (1977); Russell v. City of Pierre, 530 F.2d 791 (8th Cir.), *cert. denied,* 429 U.S. 855 (1976); Edmunds v. Won Bae Chang, 509 F.2d 39 (9th Cir.), *cert. denied,* 423 U.S. 825 (1975); Pueschel v. Leuba, 383 F. Supp. 576, 579 (D. Conn. 1974). *See also supra* § 8.2d n.41 and accompanying text. For general discussion of statuses that are not usually sufficient to establish custody, see Spencer v. Kemna, 118 S. Ct. 978, 983-86 (1998) (discussed *supra* § 8.2b n.11 and accompanying text).

[54] *See, e.g.,* Westberry v. Keith, 434 F.2d 623, 624-25 (5th Cir. 1970) (license revoked); Whorley v. Brilhart, 359 F. Supp. 539, 541 (E.D. Va. 1973) (license suspended).

[55] *See, e.g.,* Harvey v. South Dakota, 526 F.2d 840, 841 (8th Cir. 1975), *cert. denied,* 426 U.S. 911 (1976) (unable to pursue certain professions). *But cf.* Glover v. North Carolina, 301 F. Supp. 364, 367 (E.D.N.C. 1969) (cited in Advisory Committee Note to Rule 1 of the Rules Governing § 2254 Cases) (denial of vote, juror eligibility, and access to certain offices and professions establishes custody).

[56] *See generally Edmunds v. Won Bae Chang, supra,* 509 F.2d at 41.

[57] *See, e.g.,* Fleming v. Abrams, 522 F. Supp. 1203, 1205-06 (S.D.N.Y. 1981), *aff'd,* 697 F.2d 290 (2d Cir. 1982) (loss of employment as police officer). *But see Glover v. North Carolina, supra,* 301 F. Supp. at 367-68 (discussed *supra* note 55).

(4) Dignitary, reputational, "moral," or psychological harm.[58]

(5) Loss of the right to vote, to serve on juries, and the like.[59]

(6) Use of prior conviction or parole revocation for which sentence (including all consecutive sentences) has fully expired to enhance, or to deny earlier parole from, existing sentence imposed for subsequent conviction, if petition challenges prior conviction rather than existing sentence.[60]

---

[58] *See, e.g.,* St. Pierre v. United States, 319 U.S. 41 (1943), *overruled on other grounds,* Carafas v. LaVallee, 391 U.S. 234 (1964) (fact that prior conviction may impair petitioner's credibility as witness in future proceedings or morally stigmatize him does not establish custody); Diaz v. Henderson, 905 F.2d 652, 654 (2d Cir. 1990) (habeas corpus relief not available for "anxiety" and other harm of "personal nature"); Morgan v. Thomas, 321 F. Supp. 565, 573 (S.D. Miss. 1970), *rev'd on other grounds,* 448 F.2d 1356 (5th Cir 1971), *cert. denied,* 405 U.S. 920 (1972) (*dicta*) ("something more than moral restraint is necessary"). *But see Glover v. North Carolina, supra,* 301 F. Supp. at 367-68 (discussed *supra* note 55).

[59] *See* United States v. Morgan, 346 U.S. 502, 511 (1954) (although habeas corpus is not available, writ of *coram nobis* is available to challenge past federal conviction "under circumstances compelling such action to achieve justice"); Chresfield v. United States, 381 F. Supp. 301 (E.D. Pa. 1974) (citing authority). *But see Glover v. North Carolina, supra,* 301 F. Supp. at 367-68 (discussed *supra* note 55).

[60] *See* Spencer v. Kemna, 118 S. Ct. 978, 985-86 (1998) (discussed *supra* § 8.2b n.11 and accompanying text) (if petition challenges constitutionality of parole revocation procedures rather than underlying conviction, prisoner's postfiling "complet[ion of] the entire term of imprisonment underlying the parole revocation" (*id.* at 981) may render petition moot unless petitioner affirmatively demonstrates "concrete injuries-in-fact attributable to his parole revocation"; implying that petitioner's prefiling completion of term of imprisonment always moots petition); Maleng v. Cook, 490 U.S. 488, 492 (1989) (if sentence has unconditionally and "fully expired" as of the time petition challenging that conviction or sentence was filed, fact of collateral consequences themselves will not establish custody even if collateral consequence — in this case, use of prior conviction to enhance sentence on subsequent conviction — actually has "materialized"); *supra* § 8.2c nn.17-20 and accompanying text. *See also* United States v. Keane, 852 F.2d 199, 203-04 (7th Cir. 1988), *cert. denied,* 490 U.S. 1084 (1989) (after release and payment of fine, petitioner cannot bring habeas corpus action absent showing of concrete lingering civil disabilities and demonstration that error would have justified relief during term of imprisonment). *But cf. supra* § 8.2b (filing of habeas corpus petition challenging conviction (but not parole revocation) prior to completion of prison term prevents habeas corpus action from becoming moot upon completion of prison term); *supra* § 8.2c nn.16-18 and accompanying text (jurisdiction exists to hear challenge to prior sentence if petitioner is serving another sentence that was made "consecutive" to sentence being challenged); *supra* § 8.2c n.20 and accompanying text (jurisdiction exists to hear challenge to *current* sentence to extent that it is enhanced or lengthened by prior unlawful conviction).

(7)   Incarceration pursuant to conviction, if the petition challenges solely the legality of a period of pretrial detention that preceded the conviction.[61]

(8)   State action assigning custody over children or incompetent individuals to a parent, guardian, foster parents, private foster care agencies, or other private agencies.[62]

§ 8.3.   Petitions in behalf of persons in custody.[1]

a. *Introduction.* The federal habeas corpus statutes permit not only the person

---

[61] *See, e.g.,* Barker v. Estelle, 913 F.2d 1433, 1440 (9th Cir. 1990), *cert. denied,* 500 U.S. 935 (1991) (conviction of offense cuts off all claims concerning constitutionality of *pretrial* detention, hence continued incarceration under conviction does not prevent termination of pretrial detention from mooting action challenging that detention); Fassler v. United States, 858 F.2d 1016, 1018 n.3 (5th Cir. 1988), *cert. denied,* 490 U.S. 1099 (1989) (similar); *supra* § 8.2b n.13 and accompanying text.

[62] *See, e.g.,* Lehman v. Lycoming County Children's Services Agency, 458 U.S. 502, 511 n.12, 515-16 (1982) (child custody disputes are matters of local concern, hence involve insufficiently strong federal interest in liberty to warrant habeas corpus jurisdiction over claims that state courts improperly awarded custody over child to private foster parents or private foster agency); Amerson v. Iowa Dep't of Human Services, 59 F.3d 92 (8th Cir. 1995), *cert. denied,* 516 U.S. 1080 (1996) (various residential group homes and psychiatric facilities in which child was placed did not so severely restrict liberty as to qualify as "custody" for purposes of filing habeas corpus petition); Roman-Nose v. New Mexico Dep't of Human Services, 967 F.2d 435, 436 (10th Cir. 1992) (same); Hemon v. Office of Public Guardian, 878 F.2d 13, 14-15 (1st Cir. 1989) (*dicta*) (guardianship and child custody disputes involve state domestic law and are not within scope of federal habeas corpus jurisdiction); Sylvander v. New England Home for Little Wanderers, 584 F.2d 1103, 1111-13 (1st Cir. 1978) (same). *Cf.* O'Connell v. Kirchner, 513 U.S. 1138 (1995) (O'Connor, J., dissenting from denial of stay) (discussing successful *state* habeas corpus action brought by biological parent seeking custody of child currently living with adoptive parents following invalidation of adoption decree); O'Connell v. Kirchner, 513 U.S. 1303, 1304 (1995) (Stevens, J., Circuit Justice, denying motion to recall mandate and for a stay) (same); *supra* § 8.2d n.47 and accompanying text (placement of children or other wards of state in public orphanages or other public facilities may constitute custody). *See generally* Albert & Brodek, *supra* § 8.2a n.1; Robbins & Newell, *supra* § 8.2a n.1.

§ 8.3   [1] *See generally* RONALD P. SOKOL, FEDERAL HABEAS CORPUS § 5.1 (2d ed. 1969); Richard J. Bonnie, *Dilemmas in Administering the Death Penalty: Conscientious Abstention, Professional Ethics, and the Needs of the Legal System,* 14 L. & HUM. BEHAV. 67 (1990); Richard J. Bonnie, *Grounds for Professional Abstention in Capital Cases: A Reply to Brodsky,* 14 L. & HUM. BEHAV. 99 (1990); Stanley L. Brodsky, *Professional Ethics and Professional Morality in the Assessment of Competence for Execution: A Response to Bonnie,* 14 L. & HUM. BEHAV. 91 (1990); Linda E. Carter, *Maintaining Systemic Integrity in Capital Cases: The Use of Court-Appointed Counsel to Present Mitigating Evidence When the Defendant Advocates Death,* 55 TENN. L. REV. 95 (1987); Paul F. Enzinna & Jana L. Gill, *Capital Punishment and the Incompetent: Procedures for Determining Competency to Be Executed after Ford v. Wainwright,* 41 FLA. L. REV. 115 (1989);

"in custody"[2] but also "someone acting in his behalf" to file a habeas corpus petition.[3] Often called a "next friend" petition, an "application by one on behalf of another ... entitles the petitioner to such relief ... as might be given if the application were made by the person ... detained in his own name."[4] Although

---

David Luban, *Paternalism and the Legal Profession*, 1981 WIS. L. REV. 454; G. Richard Strafer, *Volunteering for Execution: Competency, Voluntariness and the Propriety of Third Party Intervention*, 74 J. CRIM. L. & CRIMINOLOGY 860 (1983); Melvin I. Urofsky, *A Right to Die: Termination of Appeal for Condemned Prisoners*, 75 J. CRIM. L. & CRIMINOLOGY 553 (1984); Welsh S. White, *Defendants Who Elect Execution*, 48 U. PITT. L. REV. 853 (1987); Note, *The Death Row Right to Die: Suicide or Intimate Decision*, 54 SO. CAL. L. REV. 575 (1981); Note, *The Eighth Amendment and the Execution of the Presently Incompetent*, 32 STAN. L. REV. 765, 799-800 (1980); Note, *Third Party Standing — "Next Friends" as Enemies: Third Party Petitions for Capital Defendants Wishing to Waive Appeal*, 81 J. CRIM. L. & CRIMINOLOGY 981 (1991); Annotation, *Right of Stranger to Writ of Habeas Corpus*, 9 L.R.A. 1173 (1907); authority cited *supra* § 4.2 n.1.

[2] *See supra* § 8.2.

[3] 28 U.S.C. § 2242 (1994) ("Application for a writ of habeas corpus shall be [made] ... by the person for whose relief it is intended or by someone acting in his behalf."). *See* 28 U.S.C.A. § 2254(a) (West 1994 & Supp. 1998) ("The ... court shall entertain an application for a writ of habeas corpus in behalf of a person in custody pursuant to the judgment of a State court."); Whitmore v. Arkansas, 495 U.S. 149, 163 (1990). American next-friend procedures track those recognized in England as long ago as the 17th century. *See* Habeas Corpus Act of 1679, 31 Car. 2, ch. 2, § 2 (authorizing next friend petitions); Ex parte Child, 139 Eng. Rep. 413 (C.P. 1854) (*dicta*); In re Parker, 151 Eng. Rep. 15 (Ex. 1839); Ashby v. White, 14 State Trials 695, 814 (H.L. 1704) ("every Englishman, who is imprisoned by any authority whatsoever, has an undoubted right, by his agents, or friends, to apply for, and obtain a Writ of Habeas Corpus, in order to procure his liberty by due course of law"). *See also* United States ex rel. Bryant v. Houston, 273 F. 915, 916 (2d Cir. 1921) (citing cases) ("The practice of a next friend applying for a writ is ancient and fully accepted."). For a brief history of the English and American treatment of "next friend" habeas corpus petitions, see *Whitmore v. Arkansas, supra* at 161-62 & nn.3, 4. The statutory basis for "next friend" habeas corpus petitions distinguishes such petitions from (1) nonstatutorily authorized "next friend" and analogous *certiorari* petitions (*see id.* at 154-61 (stringent Article III "standing" requirements preclude attempts by one prisoner to file *certiorari* petition raising claims, with possible indirect effects on him, that are available to another prisoner who has declined to seek *certiorari*, preferring to be executed); *id.* at 164-65 (reserving question "whether a 'next friend' may ever invoke the jurisdiction of a federal court absent congressional authorization" and concluding that "scope of any [nonstatutory] federal doctrine of 'next friend' standing is no broader than what is permitted by the habeas corpus statute")), and (2) other "next friend" proceedings (*see generally id.* at 163 n.4 (listing nonhabeas corpus uses of "next friend" actions on behalf of, for example, minors, mental incompetents, and others)).

[4] Ex parte Dostal, 243 F. 664, 668 (N.D. Ohio 1917). The detained person remains the real party in interest. *See, e.g., Whitmore v. Arkansas, supra*, 495 U.S. at 163 ("A 'next friend' does not himself become a party to the habeas corpus action in which he participates, but simply pursues the cause on behalf of the detained person, who remains the real party in interest" (citing *Morgan, infra; Hashimoto, infra*)); Nash ex rel. Hashimoto v. MacArthur, 184 F.2d 606, 607 (D.C. Cir. 1950), *cert. denied*, 342 U.S. 838 (1951). *See* Note, *The Eighth Amendment and the Execution of the Presently Incompetent, supra* note 1, at 800 n.138 (citing authority) ("A next friend is therefore

next friend petitions have been filed in a variety of contexts in the past,[5] the device has been utilized almost exclusively in the last quarter century in behalf of capitally sentenced defendants who have at least temporarily announced an intention to end the legal proceedings in their case and be executed "voluntarily."[6]

In determining whether a next friend petition is appropriate in the circumstances of a particular case, the courts have established two requirements, the first relating to the status of the third-party petitioner and the second relating to the status of the person in custody on whose behalf the third party is seeking to act.[7] The next friend requirements are jurisdictional, and the third-party

---

the legal equivalent of a guardian ad litem. Dacaney v. Mendoza, 573 F.2d 1075, 1076 n.1 (9th Cir. 1978). The only difference is the purely technical one that a person sues by his next friend and defends by a guardian ad litem."). *See also* Morgan v. Potter, 157 U.S. 195, 198 (1895) (child custody case); Groseclose ex rel. Harries v. Dutton, 589 F. Supp. 362 (M.D. Tenn. 1984) (appointment of guardian *ad litem* in behalf of death row inmate who originally announced, but thereafter disavowed, an intention to end legal appeals and be executed); *infra* §§ 8.3b n.21 and accompanying text, 8.3c n.50.

[5] *See, e.g.,* Whitmore v. Arkansas, supra, 495 U.S. at 163 & n.4 (collecting cases); United States ex rel. Toth v. Quarles, 350 U.S. 11, 13 n.3 (1955) (sister of ex-serviceman in military custody in Korea petitioning in district court in Washington D.C.); Collins v. Traeger, 27 F.2d 842, 843 (9th Cir. 1928) (on behalf of extraditee in peril of being "removed from the jurisdiction of the court before he could act in person"); United States ex rel. Bryant v. Houston, 273 F. 915 (2d Cir. 1921) (on behalf of prisoner "troubled with aphasia"); *Ex parte Dostal, supra,* 243 F. at 668 ("application ... made by a parent or guardian having a superior right to the custody and control of a person illegally detained, when such person might not himself obtain relief").

[6] *See, e.g.,* Demosthenes v. Baal, 495 U.S. 731 (1990) *(per curiam)*; Lenhard v. Wolff, 443 U.S. 1306 (1979) (Rehnquist, Circuit Justice, in chambers); Evans v. Bennett, 440 U.S. 1301 (1979) (Rehnquist, Circuit Justice, in chambers); Gilmore v. Utah, 429 U.S. 1012 (1976); authority cited *infra* § 8.3c n.50. *See also* Rees v. Peyton, 384 U.S. 312 (1966) *(per curiam)* (attorney resists effort by capital client to withdraw petition originally filed by client). *See generally supra* § 4.2 (professional responsibilities in this situation).

[7] *See, e.g.,* Whitmore v. Arkansas, supra, 495 U.S. at 163 (citing *Smith, infra; Weber, infra; Davis, infra;* Morris v. United States, 399 F. Supp. 720, 722 (E.D. Va. 1975)) ("Decisions applying the habeas corpus statute have adhered to at least two firmly rooted prerequisites for 'next friend' standing," namely (1) that "'next friend' ... provide an adequate explanation ... why the real party in interest cannot appear on his own behalf to prosecute the action," and (2) that "'next friend' ... be truly dedicated to the best interests of the person on whose behalf he seeks to litigate"); *Lenhard v. Wolff, supra,* 443 U.S. at 1308 (Rehnquist, Circuit Justice, in chambers); *Evans v. Bennett, supra,* 440 U.S. at 1302 (Rehnquist, Circuit Justice, in chambers); *Gilmore v. Utah, supra,* 429 U.S. at 1014 (Burger, C.J., concurring); Lonchar v. Zant, 978 F.2d 637, 641 (11th Cir. 1992), *cert. denied,* 507 U.S. 956 (1993); Smith v. Armontrout, 812 F.2d 1050, 1053 (8th Cir.), *cert. denied,* 483 U.S. 1033 (1987); Rumbaugh ex rel. Rumbaugh v. McKaskle, 730 F.2d 291, 293 (5th Cir. 1984); Weber v. Garza, 570 F.2d 511, 513-14 (5th Cir. 1978) (citing cases); Wilson v. Dixon, 256 F.2d 536, 537 (9th Cir.), *cert. denied,* 358 U.S. 856 (1958) ("The right of one person to sue for habeas corpus to secure the release of another person ... exists only when the application or complaint for the writ sets forth 'some reason or explanation satisfactory to the court showing why the detained person

petitioner bears the burden of proving that both requirements are satisfied.[8] Each requirement is discussed in turn below.

b. *The third-party petitioner.* To establish "next-friend" jurisdiction, the third-party petitioner first must establish that she is proceeding in the detained person's, and not her own or some other party's, behalf, *i.e.*, that she is prepared to conduct the litigation for the benefit of the detained person alone.[9] Although some courts have alluded to a requirement of a "close personal relationship" or a "significant[] ... connection"[10] between the third-party petitioner and the person in custody, other courts either have adjudicated "next friend" petitions filed by "strangers" to the detained persons[11] or have refused to adjudicate such petitions

---

does not sign and verify the complaint and who "the next friend" is.'" (quoting *United States ex rel. Bryant v. Houston, supra,* 273 F. at 916)); *Groseclose ex rel. Harries v. Dutton, supra,* 594 F. Supp. at 951-52; Davis v. Austin, 492 F. Supp. 273, 275 (N.D. Ga. 1980). A third requirement sometimes expressed is that the third-party applicant not be using the next friend vehicle to engage in the unauthorized practice of law. *See, e.g., Groseclose ex rel. Harries v. Dutton, supra,* 594 F. Supp. at 951-52 (citing cases).

[8] *See, e.g., Demosthenes v. Baal, supra,* 495 U.S. at 734-36; *Whitmore v. Arkansas, supra,* 495 U.S. at 164 (citing *Groseclose, infra*) ("The burden is on the 'next friend' clearly to establish the propriety of his status, and thereby justify the jurisdiction of the court"); *Smith v. Armontrout, supra,* 812 F.2d at 1053; *Groseclose ex rel. Harries v. Dutton, supra,* 594 F. Supp. at 952 (citing authority) ("The [third-party] petitioners must show that jurisdiction exists by a preponderance of the evidence." (citing cases)).

[9] *See* Whitmore v. Arkansas, 495 U.S. 149, 163 (1990) ("A 'next friend' does not himself become a party to the habeas corpus action in which he participates, but simply pursues the cause on behalf of the detained person"); *id.* at 163-64 (critical requirement is that the "'next friend' ... be truly dedicated to the best interests of the person on whose behalf he seeks to litigate"); Morris v. United States, 399 F. Supp. 720, 722 (E.D. Va. 1975); *supra* § 8.3a n.4 (discussing guardian *ad litem* analogy).

[10] Davis v. Austin, 492 F. Supp. 273, 275, 276 (N.D. Ga. 1980) ("close relatives, such as a parent, spouse, or sibling, who maintain a close personal relationship with the aggrieved"; brother more appropriate next friend than first cousin because former has "significantly greater connection" with prisoner). *See Whitmore v. Arkansas, supra,* 495 U.S. at 164 (citing *Davis, supra*) (noting but not endorsing "suggest[ion] that a 'next friend' must have some significant relationship with the real party in interest"); Gusman v. Marrero, 180 U.S. 81, 87 (1901) (*dicta*) (connection "special enough to furnish a cause of action"); Franz v. Lockhart, 700 F. Supp. 1005, 1006 (E.D. Ark. 1988) (*dicta* noting state supreme court's conclusion that taxpayer lacks sufficiently close relationship to qualify as "next friend"); Ex parte Dostal, 243 F. 664, 668 (N.D. Ohio 1917) ("parent or guardian having a superior right to the custody and control of a person illegally detained").

[11] *See, e.g.,* Rosenberg v. United States, 346 U.S. 273, 291-92 (1953) (Jackson, J., concurring) (questioning sufficiency of third-party petitioner's next friend status because he "is a stranger to the Rosenbergs and to their case," but concurring in Court's reaching merits); Collins v. Traeger, 27 F.2d 842, 843 (9th Cir. 1928) (no relationship discussed or appearing). *See also* Lenhard v. Wolff, 443 U.S. 1306, 1309 (1979) (Rehnquist, Circuit Justice, in chambers) (adjudicating petition brought by former attorneys); *Franz v. Lockhart, supra,* 700 F. Supp. at 1014, 1024-25 (unrelated

notwithstanding a blood relationship between the petitioner and the person in custody.[12] Lying behind these apparently inconsistent formulations is a uniform concern that third-party petitioners not be "'intruders or uninvited meddlers, styling themselves next friends,'"[13] and particularly that the intervening parties not be seeking to use the litigation to advance their own ideological, political, financial, or legal interests, as opposed to those of the prisoner.[14] The courts' concern, therefore, for "the relationship *and interest* of the would be 'next-friend'"[15] calls for a determination that the third-party petitioner is likely to safeguard and advance the interests of the person on whose behalf the petition is brought.[16] The third party may establish such a likelihood by demonstrating either her close relationship to the prisoner or, regardless of any relationship, her

---

death row prisoner might have standing to raise issue of fellow prisoner's competency to waive habeas corpus review); Singleton v. Lockhart, 635 F. Supp. 1114, 1125 (E.D. Ark. 1986) (*dicta*) (attorney-next friends in *Lenhard v. Wolff, supra,* "act[ed] under ethical and moral obligations" when they filed next-friend petition); Groseclose ex rel. Harries v. Dutton, 594 F. Supp. 949 (M.D. Tenn. 1984) (petition brought by fellow inmates).

[12] *See, e.g.,* In re Heidnik, 112 F.3d 105, 105 n.1, 108 n.2 (3d Cir. 1997) (granting next-friend status to daughter but denying it to woman who "appears to be [prisoner's] ex-wife" "because her relationship to [prisoner] remains unclear ... [and] it would not appear at present that she qualifies"); *Davis v. Austin, supra,* 492 F. Supp. at 276 (denying prisoner's first-cousin next friend status).

[13] Wilson v. Dixon, 256 F.2d 536, 538 (9th Cir.), *cert. denied,* 358 U.S. 856 (1958) (quoting United States ex rel. Bryant v. Houston, 273 F. 915, 916 (2d Cir. 1921) and citing Gusman v. Marrero, 180 U.S. 81 (1901)). *Accord Whitmore v. Arkansas, supra,* 495 U.S. at 164 (quoting passage in text from *Bryant v. Houston*).

[14] *See, e.g., Lenhard v. Wolff, supra,* 443 U.S. at 1312 (Rehnquist, J., Circuit Justice, in chambers) (*dicta*); *Rosenberg v. United States, supra,* 346 U.S. at 291-92 (Jackson, J., concurring) (questioning propriety of next friend petition filed by "stranger to the Rosenbergs and to their case" whose "purpose in getting himself into this litigation is not explained" and whose "record" suggests he would not "be a helpful ... champion"); Weber v. Garza, 570 F.2d 511, 514 (5th Cir. 1978) ("individuals not licensed to practice by law by the state may not use the 'next friend' device as an artifice for the unauthorized practice of law"); *United States ex rel. Bryant v. Houston, supra,* 273 F. at 917 (questioning propriety of application by woman whose petition did not "disclose ... who she is, or what relationship, if any, she bears" to prisoner in situation in which it did not appear that relief sought — trial by Coast Guard, not Navy, court-martial — "is a matter of the slightest concern" to prisoner); *Davis v. Austin, supra,* 492 F. Supp. at 275 (*dicta*) ("members of the public in general do not have a right to intercede as 'next friend' ... because they are morally or philosophically opposed to the death penalty").

[15] *Weber v. Garza, supra,* 570 F.2d at 513-14 (emphasis added). *Accord, e.g., United States ex rel. Bryant v. Houston, supra,* 273 F. at 917.

[16] *See Whitmore v. Arkansas, supra,* 495 U.S. at 163-64; *In re Heidnik, supra,* 112 F.3d at 108 n.2 (next friend "must be truly dedicated to the best interests of the person on whose behalf he or she seeks to litigate").

lack of an interest in the outcome of the litigation that differs from the best interests of the prisoner.[17]

Applying this standard, the courts have applied virtually a *per se* rule favoring next-friend petitions by parents and children,[18] spouses,[19] siblings and even siblings-in-law,[20] legal guardians,[21] and lawyers.[22] So close a blood, legal, or

---

[17] *See, e.g.,* Morris v. United States, 399 F. Supp. 720, 722 (E.D. Va. 1975) (permitting "next friend" petition by codefendant who was "clearly operating ... in the best interests" of person on whose behalf petition was filed). *See also* AMERICAN BAR ASSOCIATION, MODEL CODE OF PROFESSIONAL RESPONSIBILITY, EC 7-12 (1969) ("Any mental or physical condition of a client that renders him incapable of making a considered judgment on his own behalf casts additional responsibilities upon his lawyer .... If a client under disability has no legal representative, his lawyer may be compelled in court proceedings to make decisions on behalf of the client .... If the disability of a client and the lack of a legal representative compel the lawyer to make decisions for his client, the lawyer should consider all circumstances then prevailing and act with care to safeguard and advance the interests of his client."); *id.,* EC 7-9 ("In the exercise of his professional judgment on those decisions which are for his determination in the handling of a legal matter, a lawyer should always act in a manner consistent with the best interests of his client.").

[18] *See, e.g.,* Hamilton v. Texas, 497 U.S. 1016 (1990) (*mem.*) (mother); Demosthenes v. Baal, 495 U.S. 731 (1990) (*per curiam*) (parents); Evans v. Bennett, 440 U.S. 1301 (1979) (Rehnquist, Circuit Justice, in chambers) (mother); Gilmore v. Utah, 429 U.S. 1012 (1976) (mother); *In re Heidnik, supra,* 112 F.3d at 105 n.1, 108 n.2 (prisoner's daughter permitted to proceed as next friend); Amerson v. Iowa Dep't of Human Services, 59 F.3d 92, 93 n.3 (8th Cir. 1995), *cert. denied,* 516 U.S. 1080 (1996) (mother of child placed with state department of human services "was, and still is, a proper next friend to bring this petition on behalf of M.H., notwithstanding termination of her parental rights"); Brewer v. Lewis, 989 F.2d 1021 (9th Cir. 1993) (mother); Rumbaugh v. Procunier, 753 F.2d 395 (5th Cir.), *cert. denied,* 473 U.S. 919 (1985) (parents); Hays v. Murphy, 663 F.2d 1004, 1009 (10th Cir. 1981) (mother); Beavans v. Maggio, No. 81-3668 (5th Cir. Nov. 2, 1981) (mother); *Davis v. Austin, supra,* 492 F. Supp. at 276 n.1 (*dicta*) (mother); United States ex rel. Kirk v. Kirkpatrick, 330 F. Supp. 821, 822 & n.1 (E.D. Pa. 1971) (father); Ex parte Dostal, 243 F. 664, 668 (N.D. Ohio 1917) (*dicta*) (parent); In re Keeler, 14 F. Cas. 173, 174 (D. Ark. 1843) (No. 7,637) (father). *See also Demosthenes v. Baal, supra* at 737 ("We realize that last-minute petitions from parents of death row inmates may often be viewed sympathetically.").

[19] *See, e.g.,* In re Ferrens, 8 F. Cas. 1158 (S.D.N.Y. 1869) (No. 4,746) (wife).

[20] *See, e.g.,* United States ex rel. Toth v. Quarles, 350 U.S. 11, 13 n.3 (1955) (sister); Lonchar v. Zant, 978 F.2d 637, 641 (11th Cir. 1992), *cert. denied,* 507 U.S. 956 (1993) (sister); Smith v. Armontrout, 812 F.2d 1050, 1052 n.3 (8th Cir.), *cert. denied,* 483 U.S. 1033 (1987) (*dicta*) (brother); *Davis v. Austin, supra,* 492 F. Supp. at 276 (*dicta*) (brother); *Ex parte Dostal, supra,* 243 F. at 668 (brother-in-law). *See also* Lonchar v. Thomas, 58 F.3d 588 (11th Cir. 1995) (*per curiam*) (denying next-friend petition brought by brother because prisoner competently had decided to forgo remedies, but not questioning brother's ability to proceed in prisoner's behalf if prisoner were incompetent).

[21] *See, e.g.,* Groseclose ex rel. Harries v. Dutton, 594 F. Supp. 949 (M.D. Tenn. 1984) (court-appointed guardian *ad litem* as well as fellow inmates permitted to proceed with next friend petitions); *Ex parte Dostal, supra,* 243 F. at 668 (*dicta*); *In re Keeler, supra,* 14 F. Cas. at 174 (*dicta*). *See also supra* § 8.3a n.4; *infra* § 8.3c n.50.

ethically bound professional relationship leaves little room for doubt concerning the third-party petitioner's concern for the real party in interest. Petitions brought by children or grandparents presumedly fall in the same category.[23]

When the relationship between the third-party petitioner and the detained person is less close, or where none at all exists, the courts scrutinize the interests of the third-party petitioner more closely to determine whether they conflict with the interests of the person on whose behalf the petition is filed.[24] In so doing, the courts place the burden on the third-party petitioner to explain who she is, what relationship if any she bears to the detained person, and what interests she has in the case.[25] Following this approach, the courts on the one hand have rejected as

---

[22] *See, e.g.,* Lenhard v. Wolff, 443 U.S. 1306, 1310 (1979) (Rehnquist, Circuit Justice, in chambers), *stay of execution denied,* 444 U.S. 807 (1979), *stay of execution denied,* 444 U.S. 1301 (1979) (Rehnquist, Circuit Justice, in chambers) ("from a purely technical standpoint a public defender [who previously represented prisoner] may appear as a 'next friend' with as much justification as [a] mother"); Ex parte Dorr, 44 U.S. (3 How.) 103, 104-05 (1845) (prisoner's lawyer may bring habeas corpus petition, but not writ of error, on prisoner's behalf); Smith v. Armontrout, *supra,* 812 F.2d at 1052 n.3 (substituting public defender for brother who had initially filed petition); Lovelace v. Lynaugh, 809 F.2d 1136, 1137 (5th Cir. 1987) (by implication); United States ex rel. Funaro v. Watchorn, 164 F. 152, 153 (C.C.S.D.N.Y. 1908) (lawyer). *See also* Ford v. Wainwright, 477 U.S. 399 (1986) (adjudicating merits of successive habeas corpus petition brought to litigate constitutionality of executing petitioner after he had become insane; although no discussion of next friend issues, Court accepts as true the petitioner's allegations of insanity, hence, apparently of incapacity to proceed in own behalf); Rees v. Peyton, 384 U.S. 312 (1966) (*per curiam*) (attorney successfully resists effort by client to withdraw petition client previously filed); In re Zettlemoyer, 53 F.3d 24 (3d Cir. 1995) (*per curiam*) (denying next-friend petition brought by prisoner's former counsel because prisoner was competent to waive remedies and choose to be executed, but not questioning lawyer's ability to proceed in prisoner's behalf if prisoner were incompetent); Wells by and through Kehne v. Arave, 18 F.3d 656 (9th Cir. 1994) (similar); Minerva v. Singletary, 4 F.3d 938, 939 (11th Cir.), *cert. dismissed,* 509 U.S. 943 (1993) (former attorneys' next-friend petition denied on grounds other than attorneys' lack of fitness as next friends); Singleton v. Lockhart, 653 F. Supp. 1114, 1125 (E.D. Ark. 1986) ("ethical and moral obligations" may require attorney to file next friend petition on behalf of inmate "volunteering" to be executed).

[23] *See* 39 AM. JUR. 2D, *Habeas Corpus* § 117 (1968 & Supp. 1998) (citing cases) ("father, son, brother or aunt"); 39A C.J.S., *Habeas Corpus* § 163 (1976 & Supp. 1998) ("husband, wife, father, mother, grandparent, guardian, brother, child, relative, or next friend of the person restrained").

[24] *See* authority cited *infra* notes 25-38. *See also* Note, *The Eighth Amendment and the Execution of the Presently Incompetent, supra* § 8.3a n.1, at 799-800 n.137 ("per se rules permitting next-friend applications"). *Cf.* In re Zettlemoyer, 53 F.3d 24 (3d Cir. 1995) (*per curiam*) (denying next-friend petition brought by "mother of the individual murdered by Zettlemoyer" on ground that prisoner was competent to waive habeas corpus remedies; not reaching question whether victim's parent could adequately proceed on behalf of incompetent prisoner).

[25] Denying jurisdiction because of the petitioning parties' failure to explain who they are and why they brought the petition are, *e.g.,* Weber v. Garza, 570 F.2d 511, 514 (5th Cir. 1978); Wilson v. Dixon, 256 F.2d 536, 537-38 (9th Cir. 1958); United States ex rel. Bryant v. Houston, 273 F. 915, 916-17 (2d Cir. 1921). *See also* Rosenberg v. United States, 346 U.S. 273, 291 (1953)

next friends a first cousin,[26] a minister who infrequently counseled the inmate,[27] fellow inmates,[28] friends,[29] and apparent strangers[30] due to the third party's unexplained or suspect motives. On the other hand, the courts have permitted fellow inmates,[31] a codefendant,[32] and apparent strangers[33] to proceed in the prisoner's behalf upon a satisfactory showing of both the need to do so and of the third-party petitioner's commitment to pursuing the "best interests" of the person in custody.[34] The stronger the explanation of why the person in custody is not able or at least not as able as the third-party to bring the petition on his own,[35] the more likely the courts are to accord next friend status to the third-party petitioner.[36] Similarly, although the prisoner's express authorization of a third-party to proceed in his behalf is not required,[37] the fact that the real party in

---

(Jackson, J., concurring) ("What may be [the third-party's] purpose in getting himself into this litigation is not explained, although inquiry was made at the bar.").

[26] Davis v. Austin, 492 F. Supp. 273, 276 (N.D. Ga. 1980).

[27] Id. at 275-76.

[28] See, e.g., Wilson v. Dixon, 256 F.2d 536 (9th Cir. 1958). See also Johnson v. Avery, 382 F.2d 353, 357 (6th Cir. 1967), rev'd, 393 U.S. 483 (1969).

[29] See, e.g., United States ex rel. Bryant v. Houston, 273 F. 915 (2d Cir. 1921) (term "friend" may be used as term of art). See also In re Heidnik, 112 F.3d 105, 105 n.1, 108 n.2 (3d Cir. 1997) (discussed supra note 12).

[30] See, e.g., Gusman v. Marrero, 180 U.S. 81, 87 (1901); Weber v. Garza, 570 F.2d 511 (5th Cir. 1978). See also Rosenberg v. United States, 346 U.S. 273, 291 (1953) (Jackson, J., concurring) (discussed supra note 11).

[31] See, e.g., Franz v. Lockhart, 700 F. Supp. 1005, 1014, 1024-25 (E.D. Ark. 1988) (discussed supra note 11). See also Whitmore v. Arkansas, 495 U.S. 149, 163-64 (1990) (discussed in id. at 177 & n.4 (Marshall, J., dissenting)) (after granting certiorari to decide, inter alia, whether fellow prisoner has standing to file next-friend certiorari petition, Whitmore v. Arkansas, 492 U.S. 917 (1989), Court notes but does not rely upon argument that one prisoner cannot file next-friend petition on behalf of another prisoner); United States ex rel. Sero v. Preiser, 506 F.2d 1115, 1125-26 & n.8 (2d Cir. 1974), cert. denied, 421 U.S. 921 (1975) (class action); Groseclose ex rel. Harries v. Dutton, 594 F. Supp. 949 (M.D. Tenn. 1984).

[32] See, e.g., Morris v. United States, 399 F. Supp. 720, 722-23 (E.D. Va. 1975).

[33] See, e.g., Collins v. Traeger, 27 F.2d 842, 843 (9th Cir. 1928); authority cited supra note 31.

[34] Morris v. United States, supra, 399 F. Supp. at 722-23.

[35] See infra § 8.3c.

[36] See authority cited supra notes 31-34.

[37] See, e.g., Gilmore v. Utah, 429 U.S. 1012 (1976) (by implication); Ex parte Dorr, 44 U.S. (3 Haw.) 103, 105 (1845) (by implication); Rumbaugh v. Procunier, 753 F.2d 395 (5th Cir.) (dicta), cert. denied, 473 U.S. 919 (1985); Hays v. Murphy, 663 F.2d 1004 (10th Cir. 1981). As Dorr and Hays illustrate, the function of the next friend device — to permit attacks on the legality of custody by persons incapable of effectively bringing such attacks themselves — would be frustrated if the prisoner's consent were required. Ex parte Dorr, supra at 103, 105 (counsel allegedly denied access to client by state prison officials); Hays v. Murphy, supra at 109-13 (prisoner with lengthy history of alcoholism, suicidal tendencies, schizophrenia and brain damage). See also infra § 8.3c

interest has authorized a third-party to proceed in his behalf goes most of the way toward establishing the *bona fides* of the third-party's interests in bringing the action.[38]

c. *The prisoner.* The second jurisdictional requirement for "next friend" petitions is that there be some reason why the third-party is better placed than the prisoner to bring the lawsuit and control its prosecution.[39] In situations in which the prisoner either authorizes the third-party to proceed in his behalf or gives no indication of opposing the suit, the courts have recognized a number of reasons[40] why a third-party is better placed to proceed than the prisoner. These reasons include the prisoner's youth,[41] language difficulties,[42] illiteracy or poor education,[43] physical or mental impairment,[44] peculiarly isolating or isolated confinement,[45]

---

nn.50-69 and accompanying text (next friend petition warranted notwithstanding apparent opposition of prisoner to filing of petition on his behalf).

[38] *See, e.g.,* Rosenberg v. United States, 346 U.S. 273, 291-92 (1953) (Jackson, J., concurring); Collins v. Traeger, 27 F.2d 842, 843 (9th Cir. 1928); Groseclose ex rel. Harries v. Dutton, 594 F. Supp. 949, 951 (M.D. Tenn. 1984); *Morris v. United States, supra,* 399 F. Supp. at 722. *See also* authority cited *infra* § 8.3c nn.40-50. For example, some death row prisoners seeking to reverse course after announcing a desire to be executed prefer to authorize someone else to proceed in their behalf.

[39] *See* Demosthenes v. Baal, 495 U.S. 731, 733 (1990) (*per curiam*) (to establish jurisdiction, next-friend petitioners must "provide[] an adequate explanation of why [the prisoner] could not appear on his own behalf to prosecute th[e] action"); other authority cited *supra* § 8.3a n.7.

[40] United States ex rel. Bryant v. Houston, 273 F. 915, 916 (2d Cir. 1921) ("many ... circumstances under which it may not be ... feasible that the detained person" file habeas corpus petition on his own behalf).

[41] *See, e.g.,* Whitmore v. Arkansas, 495 U.S. 149, 163 n.4 (1990); United States ex rel. Sero v. Preiser, 506 F.2d 1115, 1126 n.8 (2d Cir. 1974), *cert. denied,* 421 U.S. 921 (1975); United States ex rel. Kirk v. Kirkpatrick, 330 F. Supp. 821, 822 & n.1 (E.D. Pa. 1971) (*dicta*); Ex parte Dostal, 243 F. 664, 668 (N.D. Ohio 1917); United States ex rel. Funaro v. Watchorn, 164 F. 152, 153 (C.C.S.D.N.Y. 1908) (*dicta*).

[42] *See, e.g., United States ex rel. Bryant v. Houston, supra,* 273 F. at 916 (*dicta*).

[43] *See, e.g., United States ex rel. Sero v. Preiser, supra,* 506 F.2d at 1126.

[44] *See, e.g.,* Demosthenes v. Baal, 495 U.S. 731, 734 (1990) (*per curiam*); *Whitmore v. Arkansas, supra,* 495 U.S. at 162 ("Most frequently, 'next friends' appear in court on behalf of detained prisoners who are unable, usually because of mental incompetence ..., to seek relief themselves."); *id.* at 163 & n.4 ("mental incompetence, or other disability"); *id.* at 164-65 ("mental disease, disorder, or defect that substantially affect[s prisoner's] capacity to make an intelligent decision"); Smith v. Armontrout, 812 F.2d 1050, 1054-55, 1058 (8th Cir.), *cert. denied,* 483 U.S. 1033 (1987); *United States ex rel. Bryant v. Houston, supra,* 273 F. at 916 (*dicta*); *United States ex rel. Funaro v. Watchorn, supra,* 164 F. at 153 (*dicta*); King v. McLean Asylum, 64 F. 325, 328 (1st Cir. 1894).

[45] *See, e.g., Whitmore v. Arkansas, supra,* 495 U.S. at 162 ("Most frequently, 'next friends' appear in court on behalf of detained prisoners who are unable, usually because of ... inaccessibility, to seek relief themselves."); *id.* at 163 (same); United States ex rel. Toth v. Quarles,

geographic remoteness from the court or from counsel,[46] inability to act with the dispatch necessary to file the necessary papers,[47] susceptibility to duress or other conditions, including inhumane prison conditions, that render the prisoner's own actions involuntary,[48] and simply the fact that the incarcerated prisoner is incarcerated and for that reason (especially if not represented by counsel) is less capable of effectively prosecuting a lawsuit.[49] When the prisoner opposes the filing of a next-friend petition, the courts have required a higher showing by the third-party petitioner — *i.e.*, that the prisoner is for some reason incapable of knowingly, intelligently, and voluntarily waiving the rights that the third-party seeks to enforce through the federal habeas corpus petition.[50]

---

350 U.S. 11, 13 n.3 (1955) (prisoner incarcerated in Korea); Ex parte Dorr, 44 U.S. (3 How.) 103, 105 (1845) (prisoner held *incommunicado*); *United States ex rel. Bryant v. Houston, supra*, 273 F. at 916 (*dicta*) ("impossibility of access"); Morris v. United States, 399 F. Supp. 720, 722 (E.D. Va. 1975) ("federal prison officials restricted [prisoner's] ability to communicate by mail or verbally with [person] who was assisting the petitioner in drafting his petition"). *Cf.* Gilmore v. Utah, 429 U.S. 1012, 1017 (1976) (Stevens, J., concurring) (next-friend petition is not appropriate if prisoner's "access to the court is unimpeded").

[46] *See, e.g., United States ex rel. Toth v. Quarles, supra*, 350 U.S. at 13 n.3 (prisoner incarcerated in Korea; next friend suing in Washington D.C.).

[47] *See, e.g.*, Collins v. Traeger, 27 F.2d 842, 843 (9th Cir. 1928) (prisoner "in peril of being removed from the jurisdiction of the court before he could act in person"); *United States ex rel. Funaro v. Watchorn, supra*, 164 F. at 153 ("it has been the frequent practice in this district to present habeas corpus petitions in deportation cases signed and verified by others than the person detained. In such cases, often for lack of time, ... it would be impossible to present a petition signed and verified by the person detained"); *Morris v. United States, supra*, 399 F. Supp. at 722 (E.D. Va. 1975) ("expediency may have required that [the third-party] sign and mail the complaint").

[48] *See, e.g., Smith v. Armontrout, supra*, 812 F.2d at 1054, 1058-59; Groseclose ex rel. Harries v. Dutton, 594 F. Supp. 949, 961 (M.D. Tenn. 1980) (inhumane "conditions of confinement inflicted on [the prisoner] are so adverse that they have caused him to waive his post-conviction remedies involuntarily"; "next friend petition filed on behalf of [the prisoner] is needed to protect his due process interests").

[49] *See, e.g., Whitmore v. Arkansas, supra*, 495 U.S. at 165 (next friend must show "that the real party in interest is unable to litigate his own cause due to mental incapacity, lack of access to court, or other similar disability"); Hacklin v. State, 427 P.2d 910, 911 (Ariz. 1967), *appeal dismissed*, 389 U.S. 143 (1967) (state law "provision ... permitting any person acting on behalf of the prisoner to file an application for a writ of habeas corpus ... is a practical realization that one confined to a cell, without ready access to a lawyer, often must depend on his family to [challenge] ... the legality of his incarceration"). *But cf.* Johnson v. Avery, 382 F.2d 353, 357 (6th Cir. 1967), *rev'd*, 393 U.S. 483 (1969) (prisoner's "inability to draft legal papers" is not sufficient reason for next-friend petition brought by fellow inmate with some experience filing legal papers).

[50] *See, e.g.*, Demosthenes v. Baal, 495 U.S. 731, 734 (1990) (*per curiam*); *Whitmore v. Arkansas, supra*, 495 U.S. at 154, 165 (discussing *Lenhard, infra; Evans, infra; Gilmore, infra*) (next-friend standing inappropriate "where an evidentiary hearing show[ed and the state court made finding] that the defendant ha[d] given a knowing, intelligent, and voluntary waiver of his right to proceed"); Lenhard v. Wolff, 443 U.S. 1306, 1308 (1979) (Rehnquist, Circuit Justice, in chambers); Evans v. Bennett, 440 U.S. 1301 (1979) (Rehnquist, Circuit Justice, in chambers);

Gilmore v. Utah, 429 U.S. 1012, 1013 (1976); Rees v. Peyton, 384 U.S. 312 (1966); In re Heidnik, 112 F.3d 105, 110-12 (3d Cir. 1997) (next-friend satisfied burden of proving that prisoner — a delusional paranoid schizophrenic — had not made knowing, intelligent, voluntary, and rational decision to give up appeals and be executed; although petitioner understood he was about to be executed, had substantial innate intelligence, and had developed delusional rationalization about why he was being executed, and accordingly might be found to have knowingly, intelligently, and voluntarily waived rights, he was incompetent nonetheless, because he lacked "'a reasonable degree of rational understanding — ... a rational as well as factual understanding of the proceedings against him'" (quoting Dusky v. United States, 362 U.S. 402 (1960) (*per curiam*))); Lonchar v. Thomas, 58 F.3d 588 (11th Cir. 1995) (*per curiam*) (denying next-friend petition brought by brother of prisoner who sought to be executed because prisoner had competently and voluntarily decided to forgo remedies; subsequent to court's decision, prisoner elected to file petition in own name and court of appeals barred petition as abuse of writ, but Supreme Court reversed, concluding that neither the writ abuse doctrine nor any equitable equivalent applies to first habeas corpus petitions, *see* Lonchar v. Thomas, 58 F.3d 590 (11th Cir.) (*per curiam*), *rev'd*, 517 U.S. 324 (1996)); In re Zettlemoyer, 53 F.3d 24 (3d Cir. 1995) (*per curiam*) (denying next-friend petition brought by "mother of the individual murdered by Zettlemoyer" and Zettlemoyer's former counsel because record supports district court's finding, on basis of two-day evidentiary hearing at which Zettlemoyer testified, that he was competent to waive remedies and choose to be executed); Wells by and through Kehne v. Arave, 18 F.3d 656 (9th Cir. 1994) (denying next-friend petition filed on behalf of death row inmate who wished to waive all further remedies because proposed next friend "presented no 'meaningful evidence' to cast doubt on the state court's determination" that inmate was mentally competent and had made knowing, intelligent, and voluntary waiver of right to seek further relief); Minerva v. Singletary, 4 F.3d 938, 939 (11th Cir. 1993) (denying next-friend status to former attorneys of death row inmate who "has repeatedly and expressly declined to take any steps to interfere with his scheduled execution" because proposed next friends "have failed to proffer meaningful evidence that Durocher is suffering from a mental disease, disorder, or defect that prevents him from understanding his legal position and the options available to him or that prevents him from making a rational choice among his options."); Brewer v. Lewis, 989 F.2d 1021, 1025-27 (9th Cir. 1993) (prisoner's mother failed to make adequate showing of incompetence by submitting "brief affidavits of two doctors who have never met" prisoner, which were refuted by reports of four psychological experts who personally examined prisoner, and by state court's determination of competence); Wilson v. Lane, 870 F.2d 1250, 1253-54 (7th Cir. 1989), *cert. denied*, 495 U.S. 923 (1990) (next-friend standing requires successful attack on prisoner's competency or capacity); Smith v. Armontrout, 865 F.2d 1514, 1515 (8th Cir. 1988) (unless prisoner's incompetence is established, he alone has standing to invoke any remedies, and next-friend petitions are not permitted); *Smith v. Armontrout, supra*, 812 F.2d at 1053; Lovelace v. Lynaugh, 809 F.2d 1136 (5th Cir. 1987) (prisoner's former attorney lacked standing to bring next-friend petition over objections of competent prisoner); Rumbaugh v. Procunier, 753 F.2d 395, 398-99 (5th Cir.), *cert. denied*, 473 U.S. 919 (1985); Hays v. Murphy, 663 F.2d 1004, 1008-09 (10th Cir. 1981); Franz v. Lockhart, 700 F. Supp. 1005, 1014, 1024-25 (E.D. Ark. 1988) (unrelated death row prisoner might have standing to raise issue of fellow prisoner's competency to waive habeas corpus review); Singleton v. Lockhart, 653 F. Supp. 1114, 1125-26 (E.D. Ark. 1986) (discussing authority) ("This court recently ... gave [a petitioner] the right to abandon his habeas corpus petition if the Court was convinced that [he] was competent and was making the decision with full knowledge of all the pertinent facts and circumstances. All that is needed is a knowing and intelligent decision made by a person whose competence has been firmly grounded.");

A federal court always has jurisdiction to determine whether a case falls within its subject-matter jurisdiction.[51] Accordingly, once the third-party petitioner alleges facts which, if true, would establish that the prisoner is incapable of knowingly, intelligently, or voluntarily waiving his rights, the court may not dismiss the next-friend petition until determining the validity of the allegations.[52] Consistent with the relatively stringent "fact pleading" requirements that apply in federal habeas corpus cases generally (by contrast to the less exacting "notice pleading" requirements in most other federal civil litigation),[53] the third-party petitioner's allegations regarding the prisoner's incompetency and the involuntariness of the prisoner's waiver of legal remedies must be specific and detailed. The courts are more likely to credit such allegations if they are supported by the affidavits of individuals (including experts) familiar with the prisoner or at least with his background and condition and by medical, institutional, educational, and other available records revealing the prisoner's mental and physical condition.[54] Nonetheless, if the allegations themselves are

---

Groseclose ex rel. Harries v. Dutton, supra, 594 F. Supp. at 953-54, 956-57; *Davis v. Austin,* 492 F. Supp. 273, 276 (N.D. Ga. 1980).

In cases in which the petitioner seeks his own execution and no one steps forward or qualifies as next friend, the court probably has a duty *sua sponte* to appoint a guardian *ad litem* or next friend if the court concludes that the petitioner is incompetent and, accordingly, probably has a duty *sua sponte* to inquire into the prisoner's competency if there is reason to doubt competency. *See Whitmore v. Arkansas, supra* at 177 n.4 (Marshall, J., dissenting) ("I cannot believe that this Court would ever hold that a defendant judged incompetent to waive his right to appeal could be executed without appellate review on the ground that no one with a sufficiently close relation to him had stepped forward to pursue the appeal. Rather, a court would be required to appoint someone to represent such a defendant"); *Franz v. Lockhart, supra* at 1011 n.2; *see supra* §§ 8.3a n.4, 8.3b n.21 and accompanying text. *See also Ford v. Wainwright,* 477 U.S. 399 (1986) (condemned prisoners have constitutional right not to be executed when they are mentally incompetent); *Drope v. Missouri,* 420 U.S. 162 (1975) (given defendants' nonwaivable constitutional right not to be tried when incompetent, trial courts have duty *sua sponte* to inquire into prisoner's competence whenever there is reason to question competency); *Smith v. Armontrout, supra,* 812 F.2d at 1056 (incompetent petitioner may prosecute case ineffectively or attempt to sabotage petition).

[51] *E.g.,* FED. R. CIV. P. 12(h)(3). *See* Rule 11 of the Rules Governing Section 2254 Cases (Civil Rules applicable where "not inconsistent with [Habeas] rules").

[52] *See, e.g., Rumbaugh v. Procunier, supra,* 753 F.2d at 397-98 (by implication); *Hays v. Murphy, supra,* 663 F.2d at 1013 (reversing district court's dismissal of "next friend" petition and remanding for "further physical examinations and mental evaluations" and hearing on third-party's allegations regarding prisoner's incompetency); *Beavans v. Maggio,* No. 81-3668 (5th Cir. Nov. 2, 1981) (same); *Groseclose ex rel. Harries v. Dutton, supra,* 594 F. Supp. at 951.

[53] *See infra* § 11.6.

[54] *Compare, e.g., Demosthenes v. Baal, supra,* 495 U.S. at 734-37 (denying stay to permit consideration of parents' next-friend petition on behalf of son seeking to be executed; given pretrial and posttrial findings of four psychiatrists and two state courts that prisoner was competent to understand and waive rights, "conclusory and equivocal" affidavit by "non-examining psychiatrist" that next friends submitted "was insufficient to warrant a psychiatric hearing or additional

sufficient, the court should not deny the petition without at least considering the full record of all prior proceedings in the case as it bears on the prisoner's competency or the voluntariness of his decision to forgo legal remedies. When appropriate, the court also must grant a stay of execution to enable it, perhaps with the help of its own experts, to evaluate the prisoner's competency.[55]

---

psychiatric examinations"; Court distinguishes *Rees v. Peyton, supra,* 384 U.S. at 313, in which "psychiatrist examined [prisoner] and 'filed a detailed report concluding that [prisoner] was mentally incompetent'") *and* Lenhard v. Wolff, 603 F.2d 91, 93 (9th Cir. 1979) (standing to proceed as next friends denied, where prisoner sought to end appeals and be executed, because "minimum showing of incompetence" did not appear in record) *with, e.g., Hays v. Murphy, supra,* 663 F.2d at 1009-1013 (dismissal of next friend petition reversed because of substantial allegations, supported by sworn statements of experts and relatives and documentary evidence, showing "suicidal tendencies, lengthy alcoholism, ... possibility of a concussion," and "delusions," as well as statements by experts that prisoner's competency could not finally be determined without more intensive evaluation than had occurred to that point) *and Groseclose ex rel. Harries v. Dutton, supra,* 594 F. Supp. at 951, 956 ("allegations and documentary evidence showing that the respondents' administration of drugs to [the prisoner] hampered his ability to appreciate the gravity of his decision to waive judicial relief" is sufficient to foreclose dismissal and require further inquiry). *Cf. Smith v. Armontrout, supra,* 865 F.2d at 1504-06 (after death row prisoner waived future remedies and federal evidentiary hearing determined him to be competent, next-friend petition challenging competency was not sufficient to overcome presumption of sanity despite new testimony from psychiatrists).

[55] *See, e.g.,* Whitmore v. Arkansas, 495 U.S. 149, 154 (1990) (stay of execution granted to permit petitioner to attempt (unsuccessfully, it turned out) to establish his right to file next-friend *certiorari* petition on behalf of prisoner scheduled to be executed); Lenhard v. Wolff, 443 U.S. 1306, 1310-13 (1979) (Rehnquist, Circuit Justice, in chambers); Evans v. Bennett, 440 U.S. 1301, 1306-07 (1979) (Rehnquist, Circuit Justice, in chambers) (granting temporary stay of execution based on third-party application in part to enable Court to consider full record concerning prisoner's competency); Gilmore v. Utah, 429 U.S. 1012, 1012-13 (1976), *vacating* 429 U.S. 989 (1976) (temporary stay of execution granted "pending the filing ... by the state ... of a response ... together with transcripts of various specified hearings in the Utah courts and Board of Pardons"; action withheld until "[a]fter carefully examining" record in case with regard to whether "Gary Mark Gilmore made a knowing and intelligent waiver of any and all federal rights he might have asserted ... and, specifically, [whether] the state's determinations of his competence knowingly and intelligently to waive any and all such rights were firmly grounded"); Mason v. Vasquez, 5 F.3d 1220, 1224-25 (9th Cir. 1993), *reviewed en banc & remanded to panel,* 5 F.3d 1226 (9th Cir. 1993) (discussed *infra* note 57); *Smith v. Armontrout, supra,* 865 F.2d at 1516 (after determination that prisoner was competent to forgo further remedies despite constant wavering, next-friend petition was denied with court's suggestion that, should petitioner change his mind, stay would be granted but prisoner would not be permitted to waive remedies again). *Cf. Demosthenes v. Baal, supra,* 495 U.S. at 734-37 (quoting Barefoot v. Estelle, 463 U.S. 880, 895 (1983)) (vacating stay that district court had denied and court of appeals had granted based on presumption of correctness of state court findings of competency (discussed *infra* note 56); for reasons Court does not explain, stay standard to which it adverts is standard for *successive* petitions — namely, whether petition "'reflect[ed] the presence of substantial grounds upon which relief might be granted'" — and not "nonfrivolousness" standard generally applied to initial petitions, *see infra* § 13.2c). *See generally Hays v. Murphy, supra,* 663 F.2d at 1013 n.17 ("Supreme Court has taken extreme precautions" to

If the third-party petitioner makes the requisite specific and detailed allegations of incompetency or involuntariness, and if a court determines that the allegations are not conclusively refuted by the record already developed in the case,[56] a determination of the prisoner's competency and of the voluntariness of his waiver of legal remedies generally requires the court to: (1) ascertain, by way of a preliminary hearing if necessary, what "examinations and evaluations [must] be undertaken and the appropriate commitment to be made to state or federal hospital facilities, under conditions indicated by information from ... experts," in order effectively to assess the prisoner's mental and physical condition; (2) permit such "examinations and evaluations by a reasonable number of experts

---

assure itself that next friend proceedings are not necessary whenever a death-row inmate announces an intention to forgo available legal remedies and be voluntarily executed, even when allegations of "possibility of incompetence" are thin).

[56] Demosthenes v. Baal, 495 U.S. 731 (1990) (*per curiam*), exemplifies the situation in which the putative next-friend's allegations are conclusively refuted by the record. There, the state court "held ... an evidentiary hearing just one week before the petitioners brought this [next-friend] petition"; heard the prisoner "testif[y] that he did not want to continue any post-conviction proceedings" and "that he knew the date he would be put to death, the reason he would be put to death, and that his waiver ... would result in his death"; heard both "psychiatrist who had the opportunity to observe and talk to Baal" and "state prison official who had observed Baal ... testif[y] as to Baal's competence"; "reviewed the reports of three psychiatrists who [two years earlier] had examined Baal and concluded that he was competent to stand trial"; and found "that Baal was aware of his impending execution and of the reason for it, and thus was sane under the test set forth in *Ford v. Wainwright*, 477 U.S. 399 (1986)" and "that Baal was in control of his faculties, was competent to choose to decline to pursue ... an appeal, and had made an intelligent waiver of his right to pursue post-conviction relief." *Demosthenes v. Baal, supra* at 733-35. These proceedings, the Supreme Court concluded, were sufficiently full and fair to endow the state court's findings with a presumption of correctness that the federal courts could not overturn except upon a showing by the petitioners that the findings were "not 'fairly supported by the record.'" *Id.* at 735 (quoting 28 U.S.C. § 2254(d)(8) (now superseded)). Moreover, the petitioners failed to make a sufficient showing at a hearing conducted by the district court either that the prisoner was incompetent or that the state court finding of competency was the result of unfair procedures or was unsupported by the record. *Id.* at 736 (at hearing, petitioners produced only one "equivocal" affidavit prepared by "non-examining psychiatrist" that was "'conclusory and lacking sufficient foundation or substance to warrant either a psychiatric hearing or additional psychiatric examination of the defendant'"; district court "reviewed the state court record and the transcript of the state court proceedings" and spoke "with Baal at length via telephone." (quoting district court's findings)). *See also* Hamilton v. Collins, 905 F.2d 825, 827 (5th Cir. 1990). *Cf.* Hamilton v. Texas, 497 U.S. 1016, 1019 (1990) (Brennan, J., dissenting from denial of stay of execution) ("it is clearly error for a federal court to accord deference to state-court findings [of competency to choose to be executed] when the state hearing [at which the finding was made] is procedurally inadequate"; in absence of adequate state-court hearing on competency, federal district court should have held its own hearing). On the question whether competency to waive rights is entirely a question of fact or, on the other hand, is partly a question of law — and, thus, whether a fairly adjudicated state court determination of the question is or is not entitled to a presumption of correctness — *see infra* note 68 & *infra* § 20.3d n.55.

designated by the petitioner, the State, and any [experts] appointed independently by the ... court"; (3) conduct a hearing at which the court may "consider the testimony of such experts ... and other witnesses"; (4) "make findings and conclusions pertinent to the competency [or voluntariness] issue and maintenance of th[e] action by [a third-party] as petitioner"; and (5) in capital cases, grant a stay of execution of sufficient duration to permit the above procedures to occur.[57]

Recognized bases for permitting a third-party petitioner to proceed against the apparent wishes of the prisoner include: (1) the prisoner's inability to proceed

---

[57] *Hays v. Murphy, supra*, 663 F.2d at 1013-14. *Accord, e.g., Rees v. Peyton, supra*, 384 U.S. at 314; In re Heidnik, 112 F.3d 105, 111 (3d Cir. 1997) (next friend has burden at "an evidentiary hearing ... [to show] that 'the defendant has given a knowing, intelligent and voluntary waiver of his right to proceed'"; in this case, given impending execution date, district court granted temporary stay and conducted "marathon hearings lasting until midnight" (citations omitted)); *Mason v. Vasquez, supra*, 5 F.3d at 1224-25 (commending district court for procedures employed to assess prisoner's competency, which included stay of execution to permit "[a]dequate time for preparation" and hearings, appointment of psychiatric experts, hearings at which "[a]ll interested parties were able to present all the relevant evidence ... [and had] full opportunity to examine the witnesses," and "thorough[] and careful[] questioning" of prisoner by judge); Beavans v. Maggio, No. 81-3668 (5th Cir. Nov. 2, 1981) (dismissal of third-party petition reversed; remanded "to conduct a full and meaningful hearing to determine the [prisoner's] mental competence ... to waive further legal actions ... in compliance with the requirements set out in ... Hays v. Murphy," *supra*); *Lenhard v. Wolff, supra*, 603 F.2d at 93 (*dicta*); Smith v. Armontrout, 632 F. Supp. 503 (W.D. Mo. 1986), *aff'd*, 812 F.2d 1050 (8th Cir.), *cert. denied*, 483 U.S. 1033 (1987); Groseclose ex rel. Harries v. Dutton, 594 F. Supp. 949, 951 & n.1 (M.D. Tenn. 1984) (stay of execution ordered; prison officials directed "to cease administration of drugs to [prisoner] so his ability to reason would not be impaired;" guardian *ad litem* appointed; "reasonable, unlimited and expedited discovery" authorized; and hearing ordered (discussing Groseclose ex. rel. Harries v. Dutton, 589 F. Supp. 362, 366 (M.D. Tenn. 1984))); Davis v. Austin, 492 F. Supp. 273, 276 (N.D. Ga. 1980). *See Demosthenes v. Baal, supra*, 495 U.S. at 733-35 (quoting *Whitmore, infra*) (next-friend petition properly denied because "'evidentiary hearing,'" discussed in detail *supra* note 56, "'show[ed] that the defendant has given a knowing, intelligent, and voluntary waiver of his right to proceed'"); *Whitmore v. Arkansas, supra*, 495 U.S. at 165 ("Although we are not here faced with the question whether a[n evidentiary] hearing ... is required by the United States Constitution whenever a capital defendant desires to terminate further proceedings, such a hearing will obviously bear on whether the defendant is able to proceed on his own behalf"; next-friend standing properly denied because state trial court held "competency hearing [required] as a matter of state law" and trial court found, and state supreme court affirmed, that real party in interest knowingly and intelligently waived further proceedings); *Smith v. Armontrout, supra*, 865 F.2d at 1506 (discussing procedures utilized in case to test competency of death-row prisoner volunteering for execution); authority cited *supra* note 55 (discussing stays of execution). *See also* Hamilton v. Texas, 497 U.S. 1016, 1017-20 (1990) (Brennan, J., dissenting from denial of stay of execution) (discussing "adequacy of the state procedures used to determine [the] competency" of prisoner seeking to end appeals and be executed); *Ford v. Wainwright, supra*, 477 U.S. at 418 (right to evidentiary hearing on competency to be executed); Dusky v. United States, 362 U.S. 402, 403 (1960) (right to develop evidence on question whether defendant was competent to stand trial).

competently on his own because of schizophrenia, manic depressive illness, and other mental disorders,[58] mental retardation,[59] alcoholism,[60] drug abuse or prison-administered drugs,[61] suicidal tendencies,[62] physical impairment, distress or duress caused, for example, by inhumane prison conditions[63] or medical problems;[64] and (2) the involuntariness of a nonetheless competent and rational

---

[58] See, e.g., Gilmore v. Utah, supra, 429 U.S. at 1015 n.5 (Burger, C.J., concurring); Rees v. Peyton, supra, 384 U.S. at 314 ("mental disease [or] disorder"); Smith v. Armontrout, 812 F.2d 1050, 1054-55 (8th Cir.), cert. denied, 483 U.S. 1033 (1987) (distinguishing "mental disease," "mental disorder," and "mental defect," but suggesting that any one of them could suffice to permit next friend petition); Rumbaugh v. Procunier, 753 F.2d 395, 402 (5th Cir.), cert. denied, 473 U.S. 919 (1985) (prisoner found to be "mentally ill" and to have "severe depression, with no hope of successful treatment which would reduce his current mental discomfort to a tolerable level"; next friend petition nonetheless dismissed based on court's conclusion that prisoner made "reasoned" determination that, given his mental condition, he was better off dead); Beavans v. Maggio, No. 81-3668 (5th Cir. Nov. 2, 1981) ("mental incompetence"); Hays v. Murphy, supra, 663 F.2d at 1009-11 (prior mental commitment to state hospital, "history of paranoid schizophrenia," and "possibly psychotic behavior"); Lenhard v. Wolff, supra, 603 F.2d at 93 (dicta) ("[ir]rational thought processes"); Groseclose ex rel. Harries v. Dutton, supra, 594 F. Supp. at 953-56 ("manic depressive illness").

[59] See, e.g., Rees v. Peyton, supra, 384 U.S. at 314. See also Hays v. Murphy, supra, 663 F.2d at 1012 ("intelligence tests" ordered).

[60] See, e.g., Hays v. Murphy, supra, 663 F.2d at 1009-10 & n.9 ("lengthy alcoholism" warrants inquiry into competency).

[61] See, e.g., Lenhard v. Wolff, 444 U.S. 807, 811 n.2 (1979) (Marshall, J., dissenting) (prisoner's prior drug addiction and current administration to him of "large daily dosage of tranquilizers" suggests incompetency); Groseclose ex rel. Harries v. Dutton, supra, 594 F. Supp. at 951 & n.1, 954 (hearing ordered to determine whether prison officials' "administration of drugs to [prisoner] hampered his ability to appreciate the gravity of his decision to waive judicial relief"; concluding that "when [the prisoner] was given the drug Sinequan, a manic phase was precipitated and he became very violent and angry"). Cf. Rumbaugh v. Procunier, supra, 753 F.2d at 397, 402-03 (persistence of prisoner's desire to be executed after termination of prison-administered drug treatment supports competency).

[62] See, e.g., Gilmore v. Utah, supra, 429 U.S. at 1015 & n.5 (Burger, C.J., concurring) (suicide attempt prompts inquiry into prisoner's mental state); Rumbaugh v. Procunier, supra, 753 F.2d at 397-98 (inquiry into whether prisoner's attempt in federal district court to force federal marshal to shoot prisoner in self-defense was proof of inability to waive judicial remedies competently); Hays v. Murphy, supra, 663 F.2d at 1009 & n.8.

[63] See, e.g., Lenhard v. Wolff, supra, 444 U.S. at 811 n.2 (Marshall, J., dissenting); Groseclose ex rel. Harries v. Dutton, supra, 594 F. Supp. at 955-56 ("sensory deprivation due to conditions of confinement which altered [prisoner's] level of consciousness" supports conclusion that prisoner was incompetent to waive judicial remedies).

[64] See, e.g., Hays v. Murphy, supra, 663 F.2d at 1009 & n.9 (concussion). Cf. Davis v. Austin, 492 F. Supp. 273, 277 (N.D. Ga. 1980) ("pain resulting from the complications of a bullet wound in the area of [prisoner's] mouth, fragments of a bullet lodged in his neck, some numbness in his right side, and some dizziness" prompt inquiry into incompetency; held that, under circumstances, pain did not "raise the specter of incompetency").

prisoner's waiver of legal remedies occasioned by prison-administered drugs,[65] physical duress,[66] or inhumane prison conditions.[67] With regard to the former incompetency ground, the Supreme Court in 1966 identified the applicable standard as "whether [the prisoner] has capacity to appreciate his position and make a rational choice with respect to continuing or abandoning further litigation or on the other hand whether he is suffering from a mental disease, disorder, or defect which may substantially affect his capacity in the premises."[68] Subsequent adjudication has refined both aspects of this formulation and recognized the propriety of analogies to the well-developed legal standards governing a defendant's competency — and the voluntariness of any decision he makes — to confess, plead guilty, or waive other constitutional rights.[69]

---

[65] *See supra* note 61 and accompanying text.

[66] *Cf. Gilmore v. Utah, supra,* 429 U.S. at 1017 (Stevens, J., concurring). *See generally* authority cited *supra* note 48.

[67] *See, e.g.,* Smith v. Armontrout, 812 F.2d 1050, 1054, 1058-59 (8th Cir.), *cert. denied,* 483 U.S. 1033 (1987) (*dicta*); Groseclose ex rel. Harries v. Dutton, 594 F. Supp. 949, 958-62 (M.D. Tenn. 1984) ("conditions of [prisoner's] confinement render involuntary his decision to waive his right to post-conviction habeas relief and [his] acceptance of his sentence of death"). *But cf.* Evans v. Bennett, 467 F. Supp. 1108, 1110 (S.D. Ala.) (*dicta*), *temporary stay granted,* 440 U.S. 1301 (Rehnquist, Circuit Justice, in chambers), *stay of execution denied,* 440 U.S. 987 (1979) (focusing exclusively on competency and not addressing voluntariness, court finds prisoner's decision to waive remedies and be executed to be "rational" response to prison conditions). *See generally* Singleton v. Lockhart, 653 F. Supp. 1114, 1123-26 (E.D. Ark. 1986) (discussing authority).

[68] Rees v. Peyton, 384 U.S. 312, 314 (1966). *Accord, e.g.,* Mason v. Vasquez, 5 F.3d 1220, 1224-25 (9th Cir. 1993), *reviewed en banc & remanded to panel,* 5 F.3d 1226 (9th Cir. 1993) (*en banc*) (applying *Rees*). The *Rees* standard, the relationship between its two clauses, and the degree to which it poses purely factual, or mixed factual-legal, questions has occasioned uncertainty. *Compare, e.g.,* Rumbaugh v. Procunier, 753 F.2d 395, 398-99, 402 (5th Cir.), *cert. denied,* 473 U.S. 919 (1985) (*Rees* presents "essentially a factual question" in three parts: (1) is prisoner suffering from mental disease or defect, (2) if so, does mental disorder prevent prisoner from understanding legal situation, and (3) if not, does mental disorder "nevertheless, prevent him from making a rational choice among his options"; court concludes that prisoner's decision to be executed, although product of mental disorder, is "reasoned" and accordingly that prisoner is competent) *with id.* at 403-04 (Goldberg, J., dissenting) ("determination of competency" is mixed question of law and fact which does not warrant "appellate abdication"; "[i]f a person takes logical steps toward a goal that is substantially the product of a mental illness, the decision in a fundamental sense is not his: He is incompetent"). *See also* Smith v. Armontrout, *supra,* 812 F.2d at 1057-58 ("it is not sufficient simply to determine whether a waiver decision has been arrived at logically"). With regard to the circuit split on the "fact versus mixed question" issue, and the inconclusiveness of the statement in Demosthenes v. Baal, 495 U.S. 731, 735 (1990) (*per curiam*) that competency is a fact question, see the detailed discussion *infra* § 20.3d n.55. With regard to both the voluntariness and competency prongs of the test, see the comprehensive discussion in *Groseclose ex rel. Harries v. Dutton, supra,* 594 F. Supp. at 953, 956-57 & n.4.

[69] *See, e.g.,* Hays v. Murphy, 663 F.2d 1004, 1013 & n.18 (10th Cir. 1981) (citing, *e.g.,* Suggs v. LaVallee, 570 F.2d 1092, 1109-12 (2d Cir.), *cert. denied,* 439 U.S. 915 (1978) (guilty plea

case)); Lenhard v. Wolff, 603 F.2d 91, 93 (9th Cir. 1979) (citing de Kaplany v. Enomoto, 540 F.2d 975 (9th Cir. 1976) (*en banc*), *cert. denied,* 429 U.S. 1075 (1977) (guilty plea case)); *Groseclose ex rel. Harries v. Dutton, supra,* 594 F. Supp. at 953, 956-57 (citing numerous authorities relating to waiver of various due process protections and waiver of rights not to testify, to counsel, to trial, and to trial by jury). *See also, e.g.,* Sieling v. Eyman, 478 F.2d 211, 214-15 & n.2 (9th Cir. 1973) (guilty plea case relying on *Rees v. Peyton, supra,* in delineating appropriate legal standard of competency). *See generally* ANTHONY J. AMSTERDAM, TRIAL MANUAL FOR THE DEFENSE OF CRIMINAL CASES §§ 195, 232, 233, 237, 316 (5th ed. 1988-89); WAYNE R. LAFAVE & JEROLD H. ISRAEL, CRIMINAL PROCEDURE §§ 6.2, 6.9, 11.3, 21.4(b), 21.5(a) (2d ed. 1992).

Chapter 9

SUBJECT-MATTER JURISDICTION: COGNIZABLE CLAIMS

§ 9.1. Violation of the Constitution, laws, or treaties.[1]

As section 8.1 *supra* explains, the federal habeas corpus statute establishes two jurisdictional prerequisites for federal habeas corpus review of state prisoners' convictions. The first prerequisite focuses on the status of the petitioner, who must be "in custody"; the second prerequisite focuses on the substance of the claim being asserted, which must challenge the legality of custody on the ground that it is, or was imposed, "in violation of the Constitution or laws or treaties of the United States."[2] Chapter 8 discusses the "custody"

---

§ 9.1. [1] See generally WAYNE R. LAFAVE & JEROLD H. ISRAEL, CRIMINAL PROCEDURE § 28.3 (2d ed. 1992); RONALD P. SOKOL, FEDERAL HABEAS CORPUS 341-43 (2d ed. 1969); LARRY W. YACKLE, POSTCONVICTION REMEDIES §§ 88-104 (1981 & Supp. 1998); James A. Albert & Gregory A. Brodeck, *Habeas Corpus — A Better Remedy in Visitation Denial Cases,* 41 MAINE L. REV. 239 (1989); Noble F. Allen, *Habeas Corpus and Immigration: Important Issues and Developments,* 4 GEO. IMMIGR. L.J. 503 (1990); Marc M. Arkin, *Speedy Criminal Appeal: A Right Without a Remedy,* 74 MINN. L. REV. 437 (1990); Vivian Berger, Herrera v. Collins: *The Gateway of Innocence for Death-Sentenced Prisoners Leads Nowhere,* 35 WM. & MARY L. REV. 943 (1994); John Flannery, *Habeas Corpus Bores a Hole in Prisoners' Civil Rights Actions — An Analysis of* Preiser v. Rodriguez, 48 ST. JOHN'S L. REV. 104 (1973); Luis Kutner, *World Habeas Corpus and Humanitarian Intervention,* 19 VAL. U. L. REV. 593 (1985); Warren Lupel, *Recanted Testimony: Procedural Alternatives for Relief from Wrongful Imprisonment,* 35 DEPAUL L. REV. 477 (1986); Gerald L. Neuman, *Habeas Corpus, Executive Detention, and the Removal of Aliens,* 98 COLUM. L. REV. 961 (1998); Robert Plotkin, *Rotten to the "Core of Habeas Corpus": The Supreme Court and the Limitations on a Prisoner's Right to Sue;* Preiser v. Rodriguez, 9 CRIM. L. BULL. 518 (1973); Ira P. Robbins, *The Revitalization of the Common Law Civil Writ of Audita Querela as a Post-Conviction Remedy in Criminal Cases: The Immigration Context and Beyond,* 6 GEO. IMMIGR. L.J. 643 (1992); Martin A. Schwartz, *The* Preiser *Puzzle: Continued Frustrating Conflict Between the Civil Rights and Habeas Corpus Remedies for State Prisoners,* 37 DEPAUL L. REV. 85 (1988); Robert J. Sharpe, *Habeas Corpus, Extradition and the Burden of Proof: The Case of the Man Who Escaped from Devil's Island,* 49 CAMBRIDGE L.J. 422 (1990); Scott Singer, *"To Be or Not to Be: What is the Answer?" The Use of Habeas Corpus to Attack Improper Prison Conditions,* 13 NEW ENG. J. ON CRIM. & CIV. CONFINEMENT 149 (1987); *Developments in the Law — Federal Habeas Corpus,* 83 HARV. L. REV. 1038, 1055-62, 1216 (1970); Andrea Lovell, Note, *The Proper Scope of Habeas Corpus Review in Civil Removal Proceedings,* 73 WASH. L. REV. 459 (1998); Trevor Morrison, Note, *Removed from the Constitution? Deportable Aliens' Access to Habeas Corpus Under the New Immigration Legislation,* 35 COLUM. J. TRANSNAT'L L. 697 (1997); Note, *The Effect of Violations of the Interstate Agreement on Detainers on Subject Matter Jurisdiction,* 54 FORDHAM L. REV. 1209 (1986); Note, *Federal Habeas Corpus Review of Nonconstitutional Errors: The Cognizability of Violations of the Interstate Agreement on Detainers,* 83 COLUM. L. REV. 975 (1983); Note, *Habeas Corpus, Section 1983, and State Prisoners' Litigation:* Preiser v. Rodriguez *in Retrospect,* 1977 U. ILL. L.F. 1053; Note, *State Prisoners' Suits Brought on Issues Dispositive of Confinement: The Aftermath of* Preiser v. Rodriguez *and* Wolff v. McDonnell, 77 COLUM. L. REV. 742 (1977).

[2] 28 U.S.C. § 2241(c)(3) (1994); 28 U.S.C.A. § 2254(a) (West 1994 & Supp. 1998).

requirement. This Chapter addresses the substance, or federal question, prerequisite.

As is developed in sections 2.3 and 2.4 *supra*, the federal courts have long interpreted the habeas corpus statute's federal question requirement — that the prisoner's custody be "in violation of the Constitution or laws or treaties of the United States"[3] — to reach all important federal law questions, including all federal constitutional claims and all "fundamental" (but not other) federal statutory claims arising in the process by which a prisoner comes to be, or is kept, in custody.[4] On the other hand, as has been the case historically,[5] the federal courts will dismiss any portion of an otherwise jurisdictionally sound petition that raises claims of the following types:

(1) Claims that do not "call into question the lawfulness of conviction or confinement" or challenge the fact, length, or conditions of the petitioner's custody or "seek immediate or speedier release";[6]

---

[3] 28 U.S.C. § 2241(c)(3) (1994); 28 U.S.C.A. § 2254(a) (West 1994 & Supp. 1998). *Accord* Withrow v. Williams, 507 U.S. 680, 715 (1993) (Scalia, J., concurring in part and dissenting in part) ("By statute, a federal habeas court has jurisdiction over any claim that a prisoner is 'in custody in violation of the Constitution or laws' of the United States." (citing *id.* §§ 2241(c)(3), 2254(a), 2255)); Dunne v. Henman, 875 F.2d 244, 248 (9th Cir. 1989) (district court had subject-matter jurisdiction because petition filed under 28 U.S.C. § 2241 alleged federal question).

[4] On the current treatment of federal constitutional claims, see *infra* notes 12-13, 19-29, 35-37 and accompanying text; on the current treatment of statutory claims, see *infra* notes 38-53 and accompanying text.

[5] *See, e.g., supra* § 2.4d nn.104-06, 142-46, 186 and accompanying text.

[6] Heck v. Humphrey, 512 U.S. 477, 481-83 (1994). *See, e.g.,* Otey v. Hopkins, 5 F.3d 1125, 1130-32 (8th Cir. 1993), *cert. denied,* 512 U.S. 1246 (1994) (divided panel concludes that due process challenge to clemency procedures is cognizable under 42 U.S.C. § 1983 but not in habeas corpus proceedings); Gibson v. Jackson, 578 F.2d 1045, 1050 (5th Cir.), *cert. denied,* 439 U.S. 1119 (1978) (claim seeking declaratory judgment that state was constitutionally required to afford petitioner appointed counsel and reasonable monetary assistance in state postconviction proceedings should have been brought under section 1983, not in habeas corpus petition); Ardister v. Hopper, 500 F.2d 229, 233 (5th Cir. 1974). *See also supra* § 7.1b n.48 (decisions discussing cognizability on habeas corpus of challenges to constitutionality of state postconviction procedures); *infra* note 33 & *infra* § 41.2b nn.20-23 (discussing varying approaches to cognizability of challenges to procedures by which parole, good time, and similar benefits are allocated when challenges do not directly seek modification of sentence); *infra* note 34 and accompanying text (challenges to physical conditions of confinement); *infra* Chapter 33 (relief). *Compare* Allen v. Duckworth, 6 F.3d 458, 459-60 (7th Cir. 1993), *cert. denied,* 510 U.S. 1132 (1994) (although habeas corpus petition properly challenged denial of speedy state court appeal, resolution of appeal in interim left petitioner with only damages claim litigable under 42 U.S.C. § 1983 but not in habeas corpus proceedings) *and* other authority cited *supra* § 8.2b n.13 *with* Burkett v. Fulcomer, 951 F.2d 1431, 1447-48 (3d Cir. 1991), *cert. denied,* 505 U.S. 1229 (1992) (petitioner deprived of speedy appeal in state court is entitled to habeas corpus relief of reduction of sentence) *and* other authority cited *supra* § 8.2b n.13.

On their faces, the habeas corpus statute and the Civil Rights Act of 1871, now codified in 42 U.S.C. § 1983 (1994), authorize overlapping sets of constitutional challenges to state action resulting in conviction and sentence. In its 1994 decision in *Heck v. Humphrey, supra*, however, the Court narrowed section 1983 by making habeas corpus — which, unlike section 1983, includes an exhaustion of state remedies doctrine, *see infra* Chapter 23 — the "exclusive remedy for a state prisoner who challenges the fact or duration of his confinement and seeks immediate or speedier release, even though such a claim may come within the literal terms of [42 U.S.C. §] 1983." *Heck v. Humphrey, supra* at 481 (discussing rule of Preiser v. Rodriguez, 411 U.S. 475, 488-90 (1973)). Rejecting *dicta* in Wolff v. McDonnell, 418 U.S. 529, 553-54 (1974), and numerous lower court holdings, *see, e.g.*, Simmons v. Reynolds, 898 F.2d 865, 868 (2d Cir. 1990); Bailey v. Faulkner, 765 F.2d 102, 105 (7th Cir. 1985), the Court in *Heck v. Humphrey, supra*, substantially expanded the range of claims that, although potentially covered by both remedies, are understood by the Court to be cognizable only in habeas corpus. Under *Heck*, habeas corpus is the exclusive remedy for all prisoner claims — including claims ostensibly brought as requests for damages or injunctive relief and not for speedier release — that "call into question the lawfulness of conviction or confinement." *Heck v. Humphrey, supra* at 482-83. *See id.* at 487 (habeas corpus is exclusive remedy for prisoner claims that, if successful, "would necessarily imply the validity of [moving party's] conviction or sentence"; only if "action, even if successful, will not demonstrate the invalidity of any outstanding criminal judgment against the plaintiff ... should [it] be allowed to proceed" under section 1983); *id.* at 498 (Souter, J., concurring in the judgment) (test asks whether, if prisoner's action succeeds, it could have effect of forcing speedier release due to ruling's collateral estoppel effect in later state or federal action for release or due to "state indemnification" rules giving States financial incentive to release unlawfully confined prisoners to avoid incurring additional financial obligations). *See also* Tavarez v. Reno, 54 F.3d 109, 110 (2d Cir. 1995) (*per curiam*) (*Heck*'s analysis of section 1983 damages actions applies equally to *Bivens* actions); *infra* Chapter 33 (types of remedies available in habeas corpus actions).

In *Heck*, the Court applied its new rule to claims by incarcerated prisoners seeking damages for allegedly unlawful convictions or sentences, ruling that such claims generally cannot be brought under section 1983 because they call into question the validity of convictions or sentences. *Heck v. Humphrey, supra* at 482-87. *See also* Edwards v. Balisok, 117 S. Ct. 1584, 1586-89 (1997) (reiterating rule of *Heck* that "state prisoner's claim for damages is not cognizable under 42 U.S.C. § 1983 if 'a judgment in favor of the plaintiff would necessarily imply the invalidity of his conviction or sentence,' unless the prisoner can demonstrate that the conviction or sentence has previously been invalidated"; applying rule broadly to forbid section 1983 action seeking nominal damages and declaration voiding procedures used to deny prisoner good time credits based on commission of disciplinary infraction even though prisoner made no request for restoration of credits nor claimed that he was "depriv[ed] ... of ... credits *undeservedly* as a substantive matter," given that certain claims made by prisoner necessarily implied invalidity of denial of credits; Court clearly found claim of biased decisionmaker sufficient to forbid section 1983 action under *Heck* because violation, if proved, would make denial of good time credits reversible error *per se*; Court strongly suggests that claim that prisoner "was completely denied the opportunity to put on a defense [to alleged disciplinary infraction] through specifically identified witnesses who possessed exculpatory evidence" also could not be heard in section 1983 action because, if proved, violation constitutes "obvious procedural defect, and state and federal courts have reinstated good-time credits (absent a new hearing) when [claim] is established"; suggesting that demand for "statement of the facts supporting the guilty finding against him" and for extension of pages for appeal might be cognizable in section 1983 action (assuming federal violation is proved) because their success would not necessarily imply invalidity of withdrawal of good time credits; concluding that "request[for] an injunction requiring prison officials to date-stamp witness statements at the time they are received" might be cognizable in section 1983 action (assuming federal violation is proved) because "[o]rdinarily, a prayer for such prospective relief will not 'necessarily imply' the invalidity of a previous loss of good-time credits"). *Compare* Spencer v. Kemna, 118 S. Ct. 978, 988 (1998) ("If, for example, petitioner [who filed habeas corpus petition to challenge constitutionality of process that resulted in revocation of his parole] were to [file section 1983 action and] seek damages 'for using the wrong procedures, not for reaching the wrong result,' see Heck, 513 U.S., at 482-83, and if that procedural defect did not 'necessarily imply the invalidity of' the revocation, see id., at 487, then Heck would have no application at all.") *and* Perez v. Sifel, 57 F.3d 503, 505 (7th Cir. 1995) (*per curiam*) (plaintiff's section 1983 "claims relating to an illegal search and an improper arrest may not be barred, as neither claim would *necessarily* undermine the validity of the conviction") *and* Mackey v. Dickson, 47 F.3d 744, 746 (5th Cir. 1995) (*per curiam*) (district court acted prematurely in dismissing section 1983 claim of unlawful arrests in criminal cases that were still pending, given that it was impossible to determine whether "a successful attack on Mackey's arrests will implicate the validity of his confinement"; proper course of action was to "stay proceedings in the section 1983 case until the pending criminal case has run its course, as until that time it may be difficult to determine the relation, if any, between the two") *with* Schilling v. White, 58 F.3d 1081 (6th Cir. 1995) (applying *Heck* retroactively to case pending at time of decision, court dismisses section 1983 claim of unconstitutional search and seizure until such time as claimant succeeds in setting aside state conviction; "statute of limitation does not begin to run" until state conviction is set aside) *and* Trimble v. City of Santa Rosa, 49 F.3d 583 (9th Cir. 1995) (*per curiam*) (applying *Heck* to dismiss section 1983 suit without prejudice because asserted violations of *Miranda* rule, Confrontation Clause, and guarantee of effective assistance of counsel "necessarily imply the invalidity of [plaintiff's] conviction") *and* Jackson v. Vannoy, 49 F.3d 175 (5th Cir.) (*per curiam*), *cert. denied*, 516 U.S. 851 (1995) (*Heck* requires dismissal without prejudice of section 1983 suit for unlawful arrest because plaintiff alleged that arrest resulted in revocation of previously imposed probation and parole, and judgment in plaintiff's favor "would necessarily imply the invalidity of the revocation of his probation and parole") *and* Schafer v. Moore, 46 F.3d 43, 45 (8th Cir. 1995) (applying *Heck* to dismiss, without prejudice, section 1983 suit for monetary damages for state's refusal to release prisoner despite compliance with preparole condition of participation in sexual offender program).

The only exception the Court recognized in *Heck* is if "the plaintiff can demonstrate that the conviction or sentence has *already* been invalidated" in *another* forum — *e.g.*, via "direct appeal, expunge[ment] by executive order, declar[ation of] ... a state tribunal authorized to make such determination, or ... a federal court's issuance of a writ of habeas corpus." *Id.* at 486-87 (emphasis added). *See id.* at 498 (Souter, J., concurring in judgment) (endorsing majority opinion insofar as it permits "state prisoner to seek federal-court § 1983 damages for unconstitutional conviction or confinement ... only if [the claimant] has previously established the unlawfulness of his conviction or confinement, as on appeal or on habeas"). The Court's rule requiring a prior declaration of unlawfulness before a prisoner can bring a section 1983 action for damages "avoids the knotty statute-of-limitations problem that arises if federal courts dismiss suits filed before an inmate pursues federal habeas and (because the statute-of-limitations clock does not start ticking until an inmate's conviction is set aside) it does so without requiring federal courts to stay, and therefore to retain on their dockets, prematurely filed 1983 suits." *Id.* at 499 (Souter, J., concurring in the judgment). *Accord* at 489-90 (majority opinion); *Schafer v. Moore, supra* at 45 (specifying that court's dismissal of section 1983 suit on *Heck* grounds is "without prejudice" and that plaintiff can "refile his complaint should he succeed in challenging the legality of his continued confinement through appropriate state or federal remedies").

(2) Claims properly addressed to the fact, length, or conditions of a petitioner's custody that, nonetheless, are premised exclusively on:

    (a)   State law grounds;[7]

Because *Heck* lay "at the intersection" of habeas corpus and section 1983, given that the claimant was in custody under the challenged conviction when the suit was brought, *Heck, supra* at 480, the *Heck* Court had no occasion to address whether section 1983 would be an appropriate mechanism for a first-instance challenge to the legality of a conviction or sentence, if the section 1983 action was filed *after* custody under the conviction or sentence had terminated. In an opinion concurring in the judgment, Justice Souter concluded that section 1983 actions *would* be appropriate in that event. *Id.* at 499 (Souter, J., concurring in the judgment). More recently, Justice Souter reiterated his view in a concurring opinion and secured the agreement of four other Justices. *See Spencer v. Kemna, supra* at 989-90 (Souter, J., concurring, joined by O'Connor, Ginsburg & Breyer, JJ.) ("[W]e are forced to recognize that any application of the favorable-termination requirement to § 1983 suits brought by plaintiffs not in custody would produce a patent anomaly: a given claim for relief from unconstitutional injury would be placed beyond the scope of § 1983 if brought by a convict free of custody (as, in this case, following service of a full term of imprisonment), when exactly the same claim could be redressed if brought by a former prisoner who had succeeded in cutting his custody short through habeas.... The better view, then, is that a former prisoner, no longer 'in custody,' may bring a § 1983 action establishing the unconstitutionality of a conviction or confinement without being bound to satisfy a favorable-termination requirement that it would be impossible as a matter of law for him to satisfy."); *id.* at 990 (Ginsburg, J., concurring) ("I have come to agree with Justice Souter's reasoning: Individuals without recourse to the habeas statute because they are not 'in custody' (people merely fined or whose sentences have been fully served, for example) fit within § 1983's 'broad reach.'"); *id.* at 992 n.8 (Stevens, J., dissenting) ("Given the Court's holding that petitioner does not have a remedy under the habeas statute [because his completion of the entire term of imprisonment imposed as a result of his parole revocation mooted his challenge to the revocation procedures], it is perfectly clear, as Justice Souter explains, that he may bring an action under § 1983.").

[7] *See, e.g.,* Gilmore v. Taylor, 508 U.S. 333, 342, 344 (1993) ("Outside of the capital context, we have never said that the possibility of a jury misapplying state law gives rise to federal constitutional error"; "instructional errors of state law generally may not form the basis for federal habeas relief"); *id.* at 348-49 (O'Connor, J., concurring in the judgment) ("mere error of state law, one that does not rise to the level of a constitutional violation, may not be corrected on federal habeas," but "jury instructions may be so erroneous under state law as to rise to the level of a constitutional violation"); Arave v. Creech, 507 U.S. 463, 477-78 (1993); Richmond v. Lewis, 506 U.S. 40, 46-47 (1992) (if definition of aggravating circumstance actually applied at trial satisfies Constitution, habeas corpus relief is not available even though state law required use of different definition); Estelle v. McGuire, 502 U.S. 62, 67-68, 70-73 (1991); Lewis v. Jeffers, 497 U.S. 764, 780 (1990); Sawyer v. Smith, 497 U.S. 227, 239 (1990) ("'the availability of a claim under state law does not of itself establish that a claim was available under the United States Constitution'") (quoting Dugger v. Adams, 489 U.S. 401, 409 (1989)); Pulley v. Harris, 465 U.S. 37, 41 (1984); Engle v. Isaac, 456 U.S. 107, 119 (1982); Smith v. Phillips, 455 U.S. 209, 221 (1982); Mullaney v. Wilbur, 421 U.S. 684, 690-91 (1975) (question whether state courts properly interpreted state statute); Gryger v. Burke, 334 U.S. 728, 731 (1948); Riggins v. McMackin, 935 F.2d 790, 795 (6th Cir. 1991) (district court erred in granting habeas corpus relief on ground that plea colloquy failed to conform to state rules; "district court's sole inquiry should have been ... whether ... [the] guilty plea comported with the protections of due process"); Stomner v. Kolb, 903 F.2d 1123, 1128-29

(7th Cir.), *cert. denied*, 498 U.S. 924 (1990) (incorrect application of state evidentiary rules provides no basis for habeas corpus relief unless fundamental unfairness occurred); Williams-Bey v. Trickey, 894 F.2d 314, 317 (8th Cir.), *cert. denied*, 495 U.S. 936 (1990) (alleged error in state postconviction proceedings is not cognizable because Constitution does not require States to provide postconviction remedies); Lusk v. Dugger, 890 F.2d 332, 342 (11th Cir. 1989), *cert. denied*, 497 U.S. 1032 (1990) (claim based on violation of Florida's jury-override scheme in capital cases is not cognizable unless result violates federal law because it is "arbitrary or discriminatory"); Tucker v. Makowski, 883 F.2d 877, 881 (10th Cir. 1989); Franzen v. Brinkman, 877 F.2d 26 (9th Cir.) (*per curiam*), *cert. denied*, 493 U.S. 1012 (1989) (similar to *Williams-Bey, supra*); Jones v. Butler, 864 F.2d 348, 361 (5th Cir. 1988), *cert. denied*, 490 U.S. 1075 (1989) (review limited to federal minimum standard of proof notwithstanding that state law imposed higher standard of proof); Bell v. Duckworth, 861 F.2d 169, 170 (7th Cir. 1988), *cert. denied*, 489 U.S. 1088 (1989) (habeas corpus review only extends to procedural errors that are "so harmful to the cause of truth that, singly or cumulatively, they make the defendant's conviction fundamentally unfair"); Swindle v. Davis, 846 F.2d 706, 707 (11th Cir. 1988) (newly discovered evidence claim that goes only to petitioner's guilt or innocence and does not bear on constitutionality of petitioner's detention is not cognizable in habeas corpus); Holtan v. Black, 838 F.2d 984, 986 n.4 (8th Cir. 1988) (state law question of what constitutes fair and just reason to withdraw plea is not cognizable); Brogdon v. Butler, 838 F.2d 776, 778 n.1 (5th Cir. 1988) (court's exercise, under state law, of discretion in selecting jurors is not cognizable); Lockett v. Montemango, 784 F.2d 78, 81 n.7 (2d Cir.), *cert. denied*, 479 U.S. 832 (1986); Toneyel v. Franzen, 777 F.2d 1224, 1228 (7th Cir. 1985) (allegation that state department of corrections improperly calculated release date pursuant to state's administrative "early release" provisions); Sanderson v. Rice, 777 F.2d 902, 904 (4th Cir. 1985), *cert. denied*, 475 U.S. 1027 (1986); Georgalis v. Dixon, 776 F.2d 261, 262 (11th Cir. 1985) (merits of state-law-defined affirmative defenses to state criminal charges). *See also* Smith v. McCotter, 786 F.2d 697 (5th Cir. 1986) (although exhaustion of state remedies was waived because of state courts' unreasonable delay in providing those remedies, petitioner could not rely on state-law theories in federal habeas corpus proceedings). *Compare* Robinson v. Ponte, 933 F.2d 101, 103-04 (1st Cir. 1991), *cert. denied*, 503 U.S. 922 (1992) (no constitutional right to retroactive application of new state court decision) *and* Murray v. Cowley, 913 F.2d 832, 833-34 (10th Cir. 1990), *cert. denied*, 498 U.S. 1098 (1991) (no constitutional right to retroactive application of new state statute) *and* Rumble v. Smith, 905 F.2d 176, 179 (8th Cir.), *cert. denied*, 498 U.S. 1014 (1990) (similar to *Robinson, supra*) *with* Hagan v. Caspari, 50 F.3d 542, 544-45 (8th Cir. 1995) (if state supreme court's overruling of decision of intermediate appellate court "was an unforeseeable change in state law," it may violate due process rule prohibiting "retroactive application of an unforeseeable interpretation of a criminal statute, if detrimental to a defendant") *and* Jones v. Arkansas, 929 F.2d 375, 377 n.6 (8th Cir. 1991) (sentencing petitioner under state habitual-offender statute that was not in effect, as matter of state law, at time he committed crime violates due process and is proper basis for habeas corpus relief) *and* Lopez v. McCotter, 875 F.2d 273, 277-78 (10th Cir.), *cert. denied*, 493 U.S. 996 (1989) (retroactive application of state law was so unexpected that it created due process claim cognizable in federal habeas corpus proceedings). *Compare also* Larsen v. Frazier, 835 F.2d 258, 259 (10th Cir. 1987) (except when in conflict with federal Constitution, validity of guilty pleas and plea bargaining is matter of state law) *with* Innes v. Dalsheim, 864 F.2d 974, 979-80 (2d Cir. 1988), *cert. denied*, 493 U.S. 809 (1989) (validity of plea bargain, in terms of precision, breach, and knowing and intelligent waiver of rights, is cognizable in habeas corpus proceedings) *and* Brunelle v. United States, 864 F.2d 64, 65 (8th Cir. 1988) ("Whenever the government breaches a plea agreement with respect to a sentence recommendation ... a substantive violation has occurred" even if sentencing judge did not take recommendation into account). *Cf.* Walker v. Deeds, 50 F.3d 670, 672-73 (9th Cir. 1995) (granting writ because sentencing judge violated Due Process Clause by failing to follow state law procedure — in which petitioner had constitutionally protected "liberty" interest — for determining applicability of "habitual criminal" sentence); Echols v. Thomas, 33 F.3d 1277 (11th Cir. 1994) (*per curiam*), *cert. denied*, 516 U.S. 1096 (1996) (granting habeas corpus review of petitioner's claim that sentence exceeded statutory maximum, even though it "ultimately turns on a question of State law ... because 'the eighth amendment bars a prison sentence beyond the legislatively created maximum'"); DeWitt v. Ventetoulo, 6 F.3d 32, 34-37 (1st Cir. 1993), *cert. denied*, 511 U.S. 1032 (1994) (although Constitution does not ordinarily prevent postsentencing increases of erroneous sentences to comply with state law, Due Process Clause prevented state court from imposing life sentence and reimprisoning petitioner six years after court reduced sentence in violation of state law); Jackson v. Ylst, 921 F.2d 882, 886-87 (9th Cir. 1990) (if state law, including decisional law, imposes substantive limitations on trial court's or other authority's exercise of official discretion — *e.g.*, by requiring trial judge to admit specified evidence — state law may create constitutionally protected liberty interest, and clear violation of state law may amount to denial of liberty without due process in violation of 14th Amendment; no violation found because state caselaw on which petitioner relied only gave trial court discretion to admit evidence); Aiken v. Blodgett, 921 F.2d 214, 217 (9th Cir. 1990) (suggesting that arbitrary denial of state-created right could violate due process, but finding no violation here); Cannon v. Lockhart, 850 F.2d 437, 439 (8th Cir. 1988) ("Although not a constitutional right itself, the ability to use a peremptory challenge, once granted by statute, falls within the mandate of the sixth amendment"). With respect to certain double jeopardy claims, it is a question of state law whether state statutes authorize cumulative punishments for multiple criminal offenses based on a single act. *See, e.g.*, Watts v. Bonneville, 879 F.2d 685, 687 (9th Cir. 1989); Smith v. Sowders, 848 F.2d 735, 738-39 (6th Cir.), *cert. denied*, 488 U.S. 866 (1988); Tarpley v. Dugger, 841 F.2d 359, 364 (11th Cir.), *cert. denied*, 488 U.S. 837 (1988); Brecheisen v. Mondragon, 833 F.2d 238, 240 (10th Cir. 1987), *cert. denied*, 485 U.S. 1011 (1988) (citing Tarrant v. Ponte, 751 F.2d 459 (1st Cir. 1985)).

Federal habeas corpus courts generally are bound by the state courts' interpretations of state law. *See, e.g.*, *Estelle v. McGuire*, *supra* at 67-68 ("Today we reemphasize that it is not the province of a federal habeas court to reexamine state court determinations on state law questions."); Rose v. Hodges, 423 U.S. 19 (1975); Mansfield v. Champion, 992 F.2d 1098, 1100 (10th Cir. 1993); McCullough v. Singletary, 967 F.2d 530, 535-36 (11th Cir. 1992), *cert. denied*, 507 U.S. 975 (1993) ("federal courts entertaining petitions for writs of habeas corpus are bound by the construction placed on a state's criminal statutes by the courts of the state except in extreme cases"); Coogan v. McCaughtry, 958 F.2d 793, 802 (7th Cir.), *cert. denied*, 506 U.S. 986 (1992); Watson v. Dugger, 945 F.2d 367, 369 (11th Cir. 1991) (state court of appeals' interpretation of state law, which was final ruling in case, "must be followed as the law of the State unless [federal court] ... is convinced 'that the highest Court of the State would decide otherwise'" (quoting West v. American Tel. & Tel. Co., 311 U.S. 223, 237 (1940)); Williamson v. Jones, 936 F.2d 1000, 1004 (8th Cir. 1991), *cert. denied*, 502 U.S. 1043 (1992); Bates v. McCaughtry, 934 F.2d 99, 102 (7th Cir.), *cert. denied*, 502 U.S. 875 (1991); Dickerson v. Guste, 932 F.2d 1142, 1145 (5th Cir.), *cert. denied*, 502 U.S. 875 (1991); Travis v. Lockhart, 925 F.2d 1095, 1097 (8th Cir. 1991); Woods v. Solem, 891 F.2d 196, 199 (8th Cir. 1989), *cert. denied*, 495 U.S. 920 (1990); Fierro v. Lynaugh, 879 F.2d 1276, 1278 (5th Cir. 1989), *cert. denied*, 494 U.S. 1060 (1990); Humanik v. Beyer, 871 F.2d 432, 436 (3d Cir.), *cert. denied*, 493 U.S. 812 (1989). *See also* Wisconsin v. Mitchell, 508 U.S. 476, 483 (1993) (on Supreme Court's direct review of state court judgment, "[t]here is no doubt that we are bound by a state court's construction of a state statute"). An exception to this rule applies when there is "reason to suspect that federal rights are being improperly obstructed" by the

(b)   Federal common law grounds[8] *other* than:

   (A) Federal "prophylactic" rules that the federal courts have fashioned to protect "personal" constitutional "trial rights";[9] or

   (B) Federal common law rules challenging some condition or aspect of "custody" that, as a matter of law or fact, could not have been attacked on direct appeal of the judgment of conviction or sentence responsible for the petitioner's custody and thus are available for the first time on postconviction review;[10] or

(c)   Any other basis apart from the federal Constitution, laws, or treaties.[11]

Applying these principles, the federal courts frequently have held that various categories of errors are not cognizable in federal habeas corpus proceedings absent a showing either that they violate a specific provision of the Bill of Rights or that they "so infected the trial with unfairness as to make the resulting

---

state court through its interpretation or reinterpretation of state law. Sanderson v. Rice, 777 F.2d 902, 904 (4th Cir. 1985), *cert. denied,* 475 U.S. 1027 (1986) (citing authority). *Accord, e.g.,* Peltier v. Wright, 15 F.3d 860, 862 (9th Cir. 1994) ("we are bound by the state's construction [of state law] except when it appears that its interpretation is an obvious subterfuge to evade the consideration of a federal issue"); Miller v. Rowland, 999 F.2d 389, 392 n.3 (9th Cir. 1993), *cert. denied,* 511 U.S. 1008 (1994); Powell v. Ducharme, 998 F.2d 710, 713 (9th Cir. 1993) ("Washington Supreme Court interpretations of Washington law are binding on this court unless we determine such interpretations to be untenable, or a veiled attempt to avoid review of federal questions."); Aponte v. Gomez, 993 F.2d 705, 707 (9th Cir. 1993). *See also Wisconsin v. Mitchell, supra* at 484 (on direct review of state court judgment, Court is bound by state court's interpretation of state statute, but if "[state] Supreme Court did not, strictly speaking, construe the [state] statute in the sense of defining the meaning of a particular word or phrase" but instead "merely characterized the 'practical effect' of the statute," then state court's "assessment does not bind us," and "we may form our own judgment as to [the statute's] operative effect"); McIntyre v. Caspari, 35 F.3d 338, 342 (8th Cir. 1994), *cert. denied,* 514 U.S. 1077 (1995) ("We are required in habeas matters to accept the state courts' interpretation of state law ... but we are not similarly bound as to the constitutional effect of that construction.").

[8] *See, e.g.,* Middleton v. Cupp, 768 F.2d 1083, 1085-86 (9th Cir. 1985), *cert. denied,* 478 U.S. 1021 (1986) (admission of testimony concerning polygraph verification, although arguably in violation of policy underlying federal rules of evidence, did not amount to constitutional error cognizable in federal habeas corpus proceedings).

[9] Withrow v. Williams, 507 U.S. 680, 690-92 (1993). *See infra* note 56 and accompanying text; *infra* § 9.2 nn.24-32 and accompanying text.

[10] *See infra* note 57 and accompanying text.

[11] *See, e.g.,* O'Bremski v. Maass, 915 F.2d 418, 423 (9th Cir. 1990) (claim that state parole board was equitably estopped from postponing parole release date is not cognizable in habeas corpus action under 28 U.S.C. § 2254, although claim may be cognizable under 28 U.S.C. § 2255 pursuant to federal sentencing court's supervisory power in regard to federal sentences); Smith v. Zimmerman, 768 F.2d 69, 71 (3d Cir. 1985) (denial of petitioner's request to waive jury trial).

conviction a denial of due process"[12] or, if they were mandated by statute or a well-established procedure, the statute or procedure violated due process because it ""'offend[ed] some principle of justice so rooted in the traditions and conscience of our people as to be ranked fundamental.'"'"[13] Among the claims that courts frequently characterize as *not* cognizable are: insufficiency of a state indictment or information;[14] insufficiency of the evidence;[15] and "mere" errors in the admission of evidence,[16] argument by counsel,[17] or jury instructions[18] that do not implicate any specific provision in the Bill of Rights.

---

[12] Donnelly v. DeChristoforo, 416 U.S. 637, 642 (1974). *Accord, e.g.*, Sawyer v. Smith, 497 U.S. 227, 235 (1990); Darden v. Wainwright, 477 U.S. 168, 181-83 (1986); Henderson v. Kibbe, 431 U.S. 145, 154 (1977); authority cited *infra* notes 14-18. *See also* Payne v. Tennessee, 504 U.S. 808, 825 (1991) (direct appeal case stating basic due process test as whether error "is so unduly prejudicial that it renders the trial fundamentally unfair"); *id.* at 831 (O'Connor, J., concurring) (similar); *id.* at 836 (Souter, J., concurring) (similar).

[13] Herrera v. Collins, 506 U.S. 390, 407-08 (1993) (quoting Medina v. California, 505 U.S. 437, 445-46 (1992) (quoting Patterson v. New York, 432 U.S. 197, 202 (1977))).

[14] *See, e.g.*, Ginsburg v. United States, 909 F.2d 982, 984 (7th Cir. 1990) (relief denied because indictment was not "'so defective on its face as not to charge an offense under any reasonable construction'"); United States v. Harper, 901 F.2d 471, 472 (5th Cir. 1990) (sufficiency of indictment is not cognizable in habeas corpus unless indictment is so defective that convicting court had no jurisdiction); Tucker v. Makowski, 883 F.2d 877, 881 (10th Cir. 1989) (*per curiam*) (challenge to joinder of charges in same indictment is not cognizable); Hopkinson v. Shillinger, 866 F.2d 1185, 1199 (10th Cir. 1989), *cert. denied*, 497 U.S. 1010 (1990) (citing Tijerina v. Estelle, 692 F.2d 3, 6 (5th Cir. 1982)); Lopez v. Riley, 865 F.2d 30, 32-33 (2d Cir. 1989) (grand jury errors not open to attack after conviction); Heath v. Jones, 863 F.2d 815, 821 (11th Cir. 1989); Spalla v. Foltz, 788 F.2d 400, 405 (6th Cir.), *cert. denied*, 479 U.S. 935 (1986) (challenge to denial of grand jurors' request for transcript during deliberations); Breeland v. Blackburn, 786 F.2d 1239, 1240 (5th Cir. 1986) (violation of state law concerning joinder of offenses is not cognizable); Alexander v. McCotter, 775 F.2d 595, 598-99 (5th Cir. 1985) (apart from due process claims based on inadequate notice of offenses charged and insufficiently specific charges, challenges to sufficiency of state indictment are not cognizable unless they allege that indictment is so defective that under no circumstances could valid conviction result from facts provable under indictment); Hamilton v. McCotter, 772 F.2d 171, 184 (5th Cir. 1985); Rubio v. Estelle, 689 F.2d 533, 536 (5th Cir. 1982) (variance between indictment and proof).

[15] *See, e.g.*, Young v. Kemp, 760 F.2d 1097, 1104-05 (11th Cir. 1985), *cert. denied*, 476 U.S. 1123 (1986); authority cited *supra* § 2.5 nn.3-4. *See also* Gilley v. Collins, 968 F.2d 465, 468 (5th Cir. 1992) (claim of insufficiency of evidence reviewed under due process standard of Jackson v. Virginia, 443 U.S. 307 (1979), *see infra* note 20, "'even if state law would impose a more demanding standard of proof'").

[16] *See, e.g.*, Marshall v. Lonberger, 459 U.S. 422, 438 n.6 (1983) ("Due Process Clause does not permit the federal courts to engage in a finely tuned review of the wisdom of state evidentiary rules"); Cupit v. Whitley, 28 F.3d 532, 536 (5th Cir. 1994), *cert. denied*, 513 U.S. 1163 (1995) ("A state court's evidentiary rulings present cognizable habeas claims only if they run afoul of a specific constitutional right or render the petitioner's trial fundamentally unfair (in which case sustaining the conviction would violate Petitioner's Fourteenth Amendment right to due process)."); Alderman v. Zant, 22 F.3d 1541, 1555 (11th Cir.), *cert. denied*, 513 U.S. 1061 (1994);

Peters v. Whitley, 942 F.2d 937, 940-41 (5th Cir. 1991), *cert. denied*, 502 U.S. 1113 (1992) (in reviewing trial court's determination of retarded complainant's competency to testify, federal court's "role is properly fulfilled by examining not whether [complainant] was a competent witness under state law, but whether her testimony was so grossly unreliable that ... it infected and fatally undermined the reliability of [petitioner's] conviction"); Carter v. Armontrout, 929 F.2d 1294, 1296-97 (8th Cir. 1991) (admission of inadmissible evidence is grounds for habeas corpus relief only if it renders whole trial fundamentally unfair and if, absent evidence, verdict probably would have been different; admission of hearsay is not grounds for relief because trial court sustained petitioner's objection and gave curative instruction and because properly admitted evidence provided overwhelming proof of guilt); Vigil v. Tansy, 917 F.2d 1277, 1280 (10th Cir. 1990), *cert. denied*, 498 U.S. 1100 (1991) (evidentiary ruling preventing expert witness from testifying is not cognizable because it did not render trial fundamentally unfair); Tinsley v. Borg, 895 F.2d 520, 530 (9th Cir. 1990), *cert. denied*, 498 U.S. 1091 (1991) ("incorrect" evidentiary rulings are not basis for federal habeas corpus relief); United States ex rel. Lee v. Flannigan, 884 F.2d 945, 953 (7th Cir. 1989), *cert. denied*, 497 U.S. 1027 (1990) (claim based upon "other crime" evidence is not cognizable because error did not violate fundamental fairness); Leverett v. Spears, 877 F.2d 921, 925 (11th Cir. 1989) (review of alleged hearsay violation is "limited to ascertaining whether the error is of such a magnitude as to render the trial fundamentally unfair and thus violative of due process"); Palmariello v. Superintendent, 873 F.2d 491, 494 (1st Cir.), *cert. denied*, 493 U.S. 865 (1989); Bundy v. Dugger, 850 F.2d 1402, 1422 n.29 (11th Cir. 1988), *cert. denied*, 488 U.S. 1034 (1989); Chavez v. Kerby, 848 F.2d 1101, 1102 (10th Cir. 1988); Givens v. Housewright, 786 F.2d 1378, 1381 (9th Cir. 1986); Johnson v. Blackburn, 778 F.2d 1044, 1051 (5th Cir. 1985) (hearsay); Gross v. Greer, 773 F.2d 116 (7th Cir. 1985) (numerous evidentiary issues not of constitutional nature); Fuson v. Jago, 773 F.2d 55, 59 (6th Cir. 1985) (habeas corpus jurisdiction does not ordinarily extend to state court rulings admitting evidence unless erroneous application of state law deprived petitioner of fundamental constitutional guarantees); Warden v. Wyrick, 770 F.2d 112, 116 (8th Cir.), *cert. denied*, 474 U.S. 1035 (1985) ("other crimes" evidence); Middleton v. Cupp, 768 F.2d 1083, 1085 (9th Cir. 1985), *cert. denied*, 478 U.S. 1021 (1986) (admission of polygraph evidence); Anderson v. Maggio, 555 F.2d 447, 451 (5th Cir. 1977) (absence of authentication); Bell v. Arn, 536 F.2d 123 (6th Cir. 1976) (dying declaration); Mercado v. Massey, 536 F.2d 107, 108 (5th Cir. 1976) (inflammatory photograph).

[17] *See, e.g.,* Sawyer v. Smith, 497 U.S. 227, 235 (1990) (merely "'potentially' misleading" prosecutorial arguments do not violate Due Process Clause; Court "warn[s] against 'holding every improper and unfair argument of a state prosecutor to be a federal due process violation'" (quoting *Donnelly v. DeChristoforo, supra,* 416 U.S. at 645 and Caldwell v. Mississippi, 472 U.S. 320, 338 (1985))); Darden v. Wainwright, 477 U.S. 168, 181 (1986) (quoting *Donnelly v. DeChristoforo, supra* at 642 (challenge to argument of prosecutor does not rise to level of constitutional claim unless it "'so infected the trial with unfairness as to make the resulting conviction a denial of due process'")); Ward v. Whitley, 21 F.3d 1355, 1364 (5th Cir. 1994), *cert. denied*, 513 U.S. 1192 (1995); Serra v. Michigan Dep't of Corrections, 4 F.3d 1348, 1354-56 (6th Cir. 1993), *cert. denied*, 510 U.S. 1201 (1994); Williams v. Kemp, 846 F.2d 1276, 1283 (11th Cir. 1988), *cert. dismissed*, 489 U.S. 1094 (1989), *cert. denied*, 494 U.S. 1090 (1990); Bridge v. Lynaugh, 838 F.2d 770, 772-74 (5th Cir. 1988), *vac'd & remanded on other grounds*, 494 U.S. 1013 (1990); Davis v. Wyrick, 766 F.2d 1197, 1203 (8th Cir. 1985), *cert. denied*, 475 U.S. 1020 (1986); Brooks v. Kemp, 762 F.2d 1383, 1400 (11th Cir. 1985), *vac'd & remanded on other grounds*, 478 U.S. 1016 (1986).

[18] *See, e.g.,* Gilmore v. Taylor, 508 U.S. 333, 342, 344 (1993) ("Outside of the capital context, we have never said that the possibility of a jury [being instructed to] misapply[] state law gives rise to federal constitutional error"; "instructional errors of state law generally may not form the basis

Because, however, a number of due process and other federal constitutional (and, in rare instances, statutory) rules do in fact regulate the form and substance of and the procedures the States use in securing indictments,[19] the

---

for federal habeas relief"); Estelle v. McGuire, 502 U.S. 62, 72-73 (1991) (because Due Process Clause provides only limited protection beyond that afforded by more specific constitutional guarantees, due process violation stemming from state trial court's instruction requires that there be reasonable likelihood that jury applied challenged instruction in improper manner and that instruction, considered in context of other instructions and of trial as whole, infected entire trial); Henderson v. Kibbe, 431 U.S. 145, 154 (1977); *Donnelly v. DeChristoforo, supra*, 416 U.S. at 643; Cupp v. Naughten, 414 U.S. 141, 146 (1973); Esquibel v. Rice, 13 F.3d 1430, 1433-34 (10th Cir. 1994); Leach v. Kolb, 911 F.2d 1249, 1257 (7th Cir.), *cert. denied*, 498 U.S. 972 (1990) (improper instruction can form basis for habeas corpus relief only if it caused "complete miscarriage of justice"); Blazic v. Henderson, 900 F.2d 534, 540-41 (2d Cir. 1990) (claim based on misstatement of state law is not cognizable absent independent violation of federal law); Woods v. Solem, 891 F.2d 196, 198, 200 (8th Cir. 1989), *cert. denied*, 495 U.S. 920 (1990); Harrison v. Dahm, 880 F.2d 999, 1002 (8th Cir. 1989) ("nothing short of a complete miscarriage of justice justifies federal habeas corpus relief based on erroneous instructions"); Conner v. Director, 870 F.2d 1384 (8th Cir.), *cert. denied*, 493 U.S. 953 (1989) ("improper jury instructions generally do not justify granting habeas relief"); Allen v. Redman, 858 F.2d 1194, 1197, 1200 (6th Cir. 1988) (erroneous jury instruction on burden of proof as to insanity defense is not cognizable in habeas corpus proceedings because sanity is not element of crime as defined by state law); Givens v. Housewright, 786 F.2d 1378, 1381 (9th Cir. 1986); Murphy v. Holland, 776 F.2d 470, 475-76 (4th Cir. 1985), *vac'd on other grounds*, 475 U.S. 1138 (1986) (jury-instruction challenge is not cognizable unless it so infected trial with unfairness as to make resulting conviction denial of due process). *Compare* Tata v. Carver, 917 F.2d 670, 671-72 (1st Cir. 1990) (noting conflict among circuits and holding that failure to provide instruction on lesser included offense in noncapital case is cognizable in habeas corpus only if failure resulted in fundamental miscarriage of justice, which is rare and was not present because of substantial evidence supporting offense of which petitioner was convicted) *and* Pitts v. Lockhart, 911 F.2d 109, 112 (8th Cir. 1990), *cert. denied*, 501 U.S. 1523 (1991) (similar) *and* Bagby v. Sowders, 894 F.2d 792, 795-97 (6th Cir.), *cert. denied*, 496 U.S. 929 (1990) (joining 8th, 9th, 10th and 11th Circuits in holding that failure to instruct on lesser included offenses in noncapital cases is not fundamental defect that inherently results in miscarriage of justice) *and* Chavez v. Kerby, 848 F.2d 1101, 1103 (10th Cir. 1988) (failure to instruct jury on lesser included offense in noncapital case is not cognizable when such failure does not lead to "fundamental unfairness" regardless of whether evidence supported lesser-included-offense finding under state definition of lesser offense) *and* Alexander v. McCotter, 775 F.2d 595, 601 (5th Cir. 1985) (failure to give instruction on lesser included offenses required by state law is not cognizable in habeas corpus) *with* Rice v. Hoke, 846 F.2d 160, 164-65 (2d Cir. 1988) (reserving question whether failure to instruct on lesser included offenses in noncapital case presents cognizable claim) *and* authority cited *infra* note 27 (decisions holding that denial of lesser included offense instruction in noncapital cases is cognizable claim).

[19] *See, e.g.*, Rose v. Mitchell, 443 U.S. 545 (1979) (permitting habeas corpus review of claim of discrimination in selection of grand jury forepersons); Harpster v. Ohio, 128 F.3d 322, 330 (6th Cir. 1997), *cert. denied*, 118 S. Ct. 1044 (1998) (granting writ because retrial of petitioner, whose previous trial ended in mistrial not compelled by manifest necessity, would violate double jeopardy); Forgy v. Norris, 64 F.3d 399 (8th Cir. 1995) (charging instrument's failure to specify predicate crime for burglary charge violated due process right to fair notice of charges); Sheppard

amount of evidence necessary to sustain a conviction[20] (and, possibly, the amount of newly discovered evidence necessary to overturn a conviction[21]),

---

v. Rees, 909 F.2d 1234, 1236-37 (9th Cir. 1989) (on rehearing) (due process violation found based on absence of notice of crime charged, because, having indicted petitioner for general crime of murder and having tried him exclusively on theory of premeditated homicide, prosecution at last minute secured instruction on felony murder as well as premeditated homicide, and jury entered general verdict); Mars v. Mounts, 895 F.2d 1348, 1351-52 (11th Cir. 1990) (granting relief due to double jeopardy violation based on prosecution under second indictment charging offense of which petitioner previously was acquitted); Heath v. Jones, 863 F.2d 815, 821 (11th Cir. 1989) (dicta) (sufficiency of state indictment is cognizable "if the indictment was so deficient that the convicting court was deprived of jurisdiction"); Olsen v. McFaul, 843 F.2d 918, 931-33 (6th Cir. 1988) (petitioner was denied due process because indictment deprived him of fair notice of criminal acts allegedly committed and appellate court did not give fair notice of what law would be applied to affirm conviction); Hamilton v. McCotter, 772 F.2d 171, 184 (5th Cir. 1985) (quoting Liner v. Phelps, 731 F.2d 1201, 1203 (5th Cir. 1984)) (dicta); Bozeman v. Lambert, 587 F.Supp. 1021 (M.D. Ala. 1984), aff'd, 762 F.2d 1022 (11th Cir. 1985).

[20] See, e.g., Herrera v. Collins, 506 U.S. 390, 401-02 (1993) ("federal habeas court may review a claim that the evidence adduced at a state trial was not sufficient to convict a criminal defendant beyond a reasonable doubt" under rule of Jackson v. Virginia, 443 U.S. 307 (1979), because any such conviction establishes "an independent constitutional violation"; in adjudicating claims under Jackson, "federal habeas courts act in their historic capacity — to assure that the habeas petitioner is not being held in violation of his or her federal constitutional rights"); Wright v. West, 505 U.S. 277, 295-97 (1992); Jackson v. Virginia, supra at 324; McBath v. Gomez, 1997 WL 449696, at *1 (9th Cir. Aug. 4, 1997), cert. denied, 118 S. Ct. 375 (1997) (granting writ because evidence underlying attempted burglary was insufficient to satisfy due process standard of Jackson v. Virginia, supra); Mitchell v. Prunty, 107 F.3d 1337 (9th Cir. 1997); Martineau v. Angelone, 25 F.3d 734, 739 (9th Cir. 1994); Evans-Smith v. Taylor, 19 F.3d 899 (4th Cir.), cert. denied, 513 U.S. 919 (1994); Bates v. McCaughtry, 934 F.2d 99, 102 (7th Cir.), cert. denied, 502 U.S. 915 (1991) ("The due process clause requires the state to prove, beyond a reasonable doubt, all of the elements of the offense it defines. When the state attempts to evade this obligation, the writ of habeas corpus will issue."); Singer v. Court of Common Pleas, 879 F.2d 1203, 1206-07 (3d Cir. 1989) (one element of offense (legality of arrest) was not submitted to jury, and, in any event, the evidence was constitutionally insufficient to support that element).

[21] Assuming there is enough evidence in the record to convince a rational factfinder beyond a reasonable doubt that the petitioner is guilty of the charge of which she was convicted, see Jackson v. Virginia, supra, the courts traditionally have held that proof — including newly discovered proof — of the petitioner's innocence does not make out a cognizable habeas corpus claim absent an independent constitutional violation such as prosecutorial suppression of exculpatory evidence. See, e.g., Herrera v. Collins, supra, 506 U.S. at 400 ("Claims of actual innocence based on newly discovered evidence have never been held to state a ground for federal habeas relief absent an independent constitutional violation occurring in the underlying state criminal proceeding."); id. at 427-28 (Scalia, J., concurring) ("There is no basis in text, tradition, or even in contemporary practice ... for finding in the Constitution a right to demand judicial consideration of newly discovered evidence of innocence brought forward after conviction." (citing lower court decisions)); Townsend v. Sain, 372 U.S. 293, 317 (1963) ("Where newly discovered evidence is alleged in a habeas application, ... such evidence must bear upon the constitutionality of applicant's detention; the existence merely of newly discovered evidence relevant to the guilt of a state

prisoner is not a ground for relief on federal habeas corpus."); Evans v. Muncy, 916 F.2d 163, 165-67 (4th Cir.), *cert. denied*, 498 U.S. 927 (1990); Boyd v. Puckett, 905 F.2d 895, 896-97 (5th Cir.), *cert. denied*, 498 U.S. 988 (1990); Swindle v. Davis, 846 F.2d 706, 707 (11th Cir. 1988). *See also* Guzman v. Lansing, 934 F.2d 80, 82 (5th Cir. 1991) (in assessing constitutional sufficiency of evidence, federal habeas corpus court "is limited to a review of the record evidence presented at trial"). Some lower courts, however, have discerned a constitutional right, enforceable in habeas corpus proceedings, to freedom from convictions later shown to be erroneous on the basis of newly discovered evidence or recanted confessions, or at least to a state procedure for the consideration of such evidence and its implications for the underlying conviction. *See, e.g.*, Lewis v. Erickson, 946 F.2d 1361, 1362 (8th Cir. 1991) ("We grant habeas relief based on newly discovered evidence if the evidence "'would probably produce an acquittal on retrial'""; "[r]ecanted testimony ... is grounds for relief from a conviction when it either bears on a witness's credibility or directly on the defendant's guilt"; granting relief on basis of rape victim's recantation of identification of codefendant at codefendant's trial, following petitioner's trial at which victim testified she could identify both petitioner and codefendant as her assailants (quoting Cornell v. Nix, 921 F.2d 769, 771 (8th Cir. 1990)); Dumond v. Lockhart, 911 F.2d 104, 106 (8th Cir. 1990) (discussing Mastrian v. McManus, 554 F.2d 813, 823 (8th Cir.), *cert. denied*, 433 U.S. 913 (1977)) (newly discovered evidence — in this case, an immunoglobulin allotype test of semen allegedly showing that petitioner did not commit rape of which he was convicted — provides basis for habeas corpus relief if evidence would produce acquittal on retrial); Sanders v. Sullivan, 863 F.2d 218, 222, 226 (2d Cir. 1988) (reaffirmed in Sanders v. Sullivan, 900 F.2d 601 (2d Cir. 1990)) (due process requires state postconviction courts to vacate convictions premised on subsequently recanted testimony, whether or not prosecution knew testimony was false, if recantation is credible and court firmly believes, that, but for recanted testimony, "defendant would most likely not have been convicted").

In *Herrera, supra*, the Supreme Court addressed at length but left in doubt the question whether newly discovered evidence of innocence can ever form the basis for an independent constitutional right, enforceable in habeas corpus, to freedom from an underlying conviction or, at least, to freedom from a death sentence based on that conviction. Although dismissive of any constitutional right to relief based on newly discovered evidence in a *noncapital* setting, at least absent recantation evidence (which the Court did not consider), a majority of the Court *was* willing at least to "*assume*[] for the sake of argument that a truly persuasive demonstration of actual innocence would render an[] ... *execution* unconstitutional and that federal relief would be warranted if no state avenue were open to process the claim." *Herrera v. Collins, supra* at 427 (emphasis added). *Accord* Schlup v. Delo, 513 U.S. 298, 314 n.28, 315-16 & n.32, 317 (1995) ("In *Herrera*, we assumed for the sake of argument 'that in a capital case a truly persuasive demonstration of "actual innocence" made after trial would render the execution of a defendant unconstitutional, and warrant federal habeas corpus relief if there were no state avenue open to process such a claim'"; "[i]n such a case, when a petitioner has been 'tried before a jury of his peers, with the full panoply of protections that our Constitution affords criminal defendants,' it is appropriate to apply an "'extraordinarily high'" standard of review" and to require "'truly persuasive demonstration of "actual innocence'""; "*Herrera*-type claim would have to fail unless the federal habeas court is itself convinced that those new facts unquestionably establish [the prisoner's] innocence" (citations and emphasis omitted)). *See also id.* at 324-26 & n.42 ("quintessential miscarriage of justice is the execution of a person who is entirely innocent"; it is of "paramount importance ... [to] avoid[ ] the injustice of executing one who is actually innocent"; "fundamental injustice would result from the erroneous conviction and execution of an innocent person" (footnote omitted; citing numerous authorities)). And other members of the Court concluded that, under some circumstances, newly discovered evidence of innocence *does* establish a constitutional right to relief from a death

the amount of evidence constitutionally required to sustain a capital or other sentence,[22] the admission and exclusion of evidence,[23]

---

sentence. *See id.* at 429 (White, J., concurring in the judgment); *id.* at 433-35, 441-43 (Blackmun, J., dissenting). *See also* Jacobs v. Scott, 513 U.S. 1067, 1067-70 (1995) (Stevens, J., dissenting from denial of stay, joined by Ginsburg, J.) (at petitioner's trial, in response to petitioner's claim that his confession to kidnapping and killing victim was false insofar as it implicated petitioner in killing victim, prosecutor said "'that [petitioner] and [petitioner] alone killed'" victim; at subsequent trial of petitioner's sister, whom petitioner at his trial had identified as the actual killer, same prosecutor said that "'the state had been wrong in taking the position in [petitioner's] trial that [petitioner] had done the actual killing'" because "'further investigation ... [revealed] that [sister], not [petitioner], had killed the victim'" and that petitioner "'did not in any way anticipate that the victim would be shot'"; stay should be granted to permit Court to consider petitioner's *certiorari* petition because: (1) "[i]f the prosecutor's statements at the [sister's] trial were correct, then [petitioner] is innocent of capital murder," (2) four members of Court previously had concluded that "a 'clear' due process violation" occurs when state fails to vacate criminal judgment although "'State now knows that the testimony of the only witnesses against petitioner was false'" and that "'[n]o competent evidence remains to support the conviction,'" and (3) "serious questions are raised 'when the sovereign itself takes inconsistent positions in two separate criminal proceedings against two of its citizens'" (quoting Durley v. Mayo, 351 U.S. 277, 290-92 (1956) (Douglas, J., dissenting); United States v. Powers, 467 F.2d 1089, 1097 (7th Cir.) (Stevens, J., dissenting), *cert. denied*, 410 U.S. 983 (1973))). The most stringent standard among those discussed in the various opinions in *Herrera* for establishing innocence based on newly discovered evidence (*i.e.*, the standard that, if satisfied in a capital case, would be most likely to make out a constitutional violation), is the standard Justice White advocated in a concurring opinion: "To be entitled to relief [from a death sentence on the basis of factual innocence] ... petitioner would at the very least be required to show that based on proffered newly discovered evidence and the entire record before the jury that convicted him, 'no rational trier of fact could [find] proof of guilt beyond a reasonable doubt.'" *Herrera, supra* at 429 (White, J., concurring in the judgment) (quoting *Jackson v. Virginia, supra,* 443 U.S. at 324). *See also supra* § 2.5 n.24 and accompanying text.

[22] *See* Arave v. Creech, 507 U.S. 463, 477-78 (1993) (same as *Richmond, infra*); Richmond v. Lewis, 506 U.S. 40, 47 (1992) ("[I]n federal habeas corpus proceedings, the state court's application of the narrowing construction [of an otherwise overbroad aggravating circumstance] should be reviewed under the 'rational factfinder' standard of *Jackson v. Virginia*, 443 U.S. 307 (1979)."); Parker v. Dugger, 498 U.S. 308, 322 (1991) (aggravating or mitigating circumstances critical to death sentencing determinations are reviewable on habeas corpus under standard of *Jackson v. Virginia, supra*, namely, whether rational factfinder, applying relevant burden of proof, could have found aggravating circumstance present or mitigating circumstance not present (discussing Lewis v. Jeffers, 497 U.S. 764, 765 (1990))).

[23] *See, e.g.,* Duncan v. Henry, 513 U.S. 364, 366 (1995) (*per curiam*) (assuming cognizability in federal habeas corpus proceedings of claim that an "evidentiary ruling ... denied [petitioner] the due process of law guaranteed by the Fourteenth Amendment" because "it was so inflammatory as to prevent a fair trial"); *id.* at 369 (Stevens, J., dissenting) (federal habeas corpus relief appropriate upon proof that state court allowed "testimony ... [that] was so inflammatory and irrelevant as to render [the] trial fundamentally unfair"); United States v. Dunnigan, 507 U.S. 87, 96 (1993) (direct review case) ("The right to testify on one's own behalf in a criminal proceeding ... is ... a right

implicit in the Constitution." (citing Rock v. Arkansas, 483 U.S. 44, 51-53 (1987); Nix v. Whiteside, 475 U.S. 157, 164 (1986)); Crane v. Kentucky, 476 U.S. 683 (1986); Miller v. Pate, 386 U.S. 1 (1967); Reck v. Pate, 367 U.S. 433 (1961); Snowden v. Singletary, 135 F.3d 732, 738 (11th Cir. 1998) (granting writ because prosecutor, in trial on charges of sexual abuse of child, presented and relied heavily on unreliable expert testimony that "99.5 % of children tell the truth" when making accusations of abuse); Lindh v. Murphy, 124 F.3d 899, 901-02 (7th Cir. 1997), *cert. denied*, 118 S. Ct. 739 (1998) (granting writ because judge violated Confrontation Clause by prohibiting petitioner's counsel from cross-examining state's psychiatrist on potential biases); Lyons v. Johnson, 99 F.3d 499, 503 (2d Cir. 1996) (denial of defense's request that jury view person whom defense claimed was actual perpetrator violated due process right to fair trial); Justice v. Hoke, 90 F.3d 43 (2d Cir. 1996) (exclusion of defense witnesses' testimony casting doubt on complainant's credibility and supporting defense theory of fabrication violated 6th Amendment right to present defense); Offor v. Scott, 72 F.3d 30 (5th Cir. 1995) (introduction of videotaped interview of child complainant violated Confrontation Clause); Wigglesworth v. Oregon, 49 F.3d 578 (9th Cir. 1995) (granting writ because statutorily authorized procedure of admitting certified copy of drug analysis report, subject to defendant's subpoenaing and cross-examining chemist who prepared report, violated Due Process Clause by "reliev[ing] the state of its burden of proof on an essential element of its case"); Webb v. Lewis, 44 F.3d 1387 (9th Cir. 1994), *cert. denied*, 514 U.S. 1128 (1995) (granting writ because introduction of videotaped interview of child victim of sexual abuse violated Confrontation Clause); Maurer v. Department of Corrections, 32 F.3d 1286, 1289-91 (8th Cir. 1994) (granting writ because admission of testimony by prosecution witnesses that "complainant seemed sincere when she said she was raped" rendered trial "fundamentally unfair" in violation of due process); Stoner v. Sowders, 997 F.2d 209, 212-13 (6th Cir. 1993) (granting habeas corpus relief because trial court violated Confrontation Clause by admitting videotaped deposition of key witnesses without adequate showing of witnesses' unavailability); McKinney v. Rees, 993 F.2d 1378, 1384-86 (9th Cir.), *cert. denied*, 510 U.S. 1020 (1993) (granting habeas corpus relief because erroneous admission of irrelevant prior crimes evidence violated due process by rendering trial "fundamentally unfair"); Henry v. Estelle, 993 F.2d 1423, 1427-28 (9th Cir. 1993) (same as *McKinney, supra*); Nichols v. Butler, 953 F.2d 1550 (11th Cir. 1992) (*en banc*) (granting habeas corpus relief based on trial counsel's failure to accede to petitioner's demand to testify); White v. White, 925 F.2d 287 (9th Cir. 1991) (granting habeas corpus relief based on petitioner's inability to confront adverse witnesses at parole revocation hearing); Manocchio v. Moran, 919 F.2d 770, 782-84 (1st Cir. 1990) (introduction of hearsay violated Confrontation Clause but was harmless); Rivera v. Director, 915 F.2d 280, 281-82 (7th Cir. 1990) (granting habeas corpus relief based on trial court's hearsay-based exclusion of codefendant's confession exculpating petitioner); Crane v. Sowders, 889 F.2d 715, 716-18 (6th Cir. 1989), *cert. denied*, 493 U.S. 1094 (1990) (exclusion of evidence regarding circumstances of confession violated right to present defensive evidence and was not harmless error); Tucker v. Makowski, 883 F.2d 877, 878, 881 (10th Cir. 1989) (*per curiam*) (improper admission of "other crimes" evidence rose to level of due process violation); Stidum v. Trickey, 881 F.2d 582, 583-84 (8th Cir. 1989), *cert. denied*, 493 U.S. 1089 (1990) (same); Osborn v. Shillinger, 861 F.2d 612, 630 (10th Cir. 1988) (sentencing judge improperly heard *ex parte* reports before sentencing petitioner to death); Dudley v. Duckworth, 854 F.2d 967 (7th Cir. 1988), *cert. denied*, 490 U.S. 1011 (1989) (admission of statement by witness that he had been threatened by unknown party constitutes fundamental miscarriage of justice justifying habeas corpus relief under circumstances of case); Jones v. Lockhart, 851 F.2d 1115, 1117 (8th Cir. 1988) (defense counsel's stipulation to prior felony convictions under enhancement statute, made without petitioner's voluntary and knowing agreement, violated due process); Amos v. Minnesota, 849 F.2d 1070, 1073 (8th Cir.),

arguments by defense counsel,[24] arguments by prosecutors,[25] other actions by

---

cert. denied, 488 U.S. 861 (1988) ("Questions concerning the admissibility of evidence are ... reviewable in federal habeas corpus proceedings to the extent that the alleged error infringed upon a constitutionally protected right or was so prejudicial that it constituted a denial of due process"); Brown v. Lynaugh, 843 F.2d 849, 850 (5th Cir. 1988) (reaching merits of claim based on state's use of trial judge as witness in habeas corpus proceedings); Cooper v. Sowders, 837 F.2d 284, 286 (6th Cir. 1988) (addressing claim based on police officer's expressed personal opinion that defendant was guilty); Clark v. Dugger, 834 F.2d 1561 (11th Cir. 1987), *cert. denied,* 485 U.S. 982 (1988) (fundamentally unfair state evidentiary rulings are basis for habeas corpus relief (citing Dickson v. Wainwright, 683 F.2d 348, 350 (11th Cir. 1982)); Thomas v. Lynaugh, 812 F.2d 225, 230 (5th Cir.), *cert. denied,* 484 U.S. 842 (1987) (*dicta*) (admission or exclusion of evidence may be actionable if affected evidence is "crucial, critical, or highly significant factor in the context of the entire trial"); Walker v. Engle, 703 F.2d 959, 963 (6th Cir. 1983), *cert. denied,* 464 U.S. 951 (1984) ("where the violation of a state's evidentiary rule has resulted in the denial of fundamental fairness, ... habeas corpus relief will be granted"); McMorris v. Israel, 643 F.2d 458 (7th Cir. 1981), *cert. denied,* 455 U.S. 967 (1982) (prosecutor's apparently bad faith failure to comply with state stipulation procedure for admitting polygraph evidence deprived petitioner of exculpatory polygraph evidence and violated Due Process Clause). *See also* Estelle v. McGuire, 502 U.S. 62, 70, 72-75 (1991) (reserving questions whether "it is a violation of due process guaranteed by the Fourteenth Amendment for evidence that is not relevant to be received in a criminal trial" and suggesting that instruction informing jury to consider evidence of prior crimes not found to have been committed by petitioner as proof that petitioner committed offense charged or informing jury to consider prior crimes evidence linked to petitioner as proof that he had "propensity" to commit offenses such as one charged would violate due process and justify habeas corpus relief); *id.* at 76-77 (O'Connor, J., dissenting) (discussed *infra* note 27) (also indicating sympathy for view that admission of prior crimes evidence solely to show propensity could be basis for habeas corpus relief).

[24] *See, e.g.*, Dobbs v. Zant, 506 U.S. 357, 358-59 & n.1 (1993) (closing argument by defense counsel may be important basis for ineffective assistance of counsel claims reviewable in habeas corpus proceedings).

[25] *See, e.g.*, O'Neal v. McAninch, 513 U.S. 432, 435-36 (1995) (accepting lower court's assumption that "'confusion' arising out of a trial court instruction about the state of mind necessary for conviction combined with a related statement by a prosecutor" required habeas corpus relief if "combined" error was not harmless); Romano v. Oklahoma, 512 U.S. 1, 12 (1994) (direct review case) (closing arguments generally are reviewable under *Donnelly* standard quoted *supra* text accompanying note 12); Sawyer v. Smith, 497 U.S. 227, 235 (1990) ("'potentially' misleading" prosecutorial arguments normally are subject to habeas corpus review under *Donnelly* test, *see supra* text accompanying note 12; in capital cases, however, such arguments may violate 8th Amendment if they create "unacceptable risk" of arbitrary death sentence); Caldwell v. Mississippi, 472 U.S. 320 (1985) (direct appeal case) (granting relief based on prosecutor's closing argument appearing inaccurately to shift capital sentencing responsibility from jurors to appellate courts); Gilbert v. California, 388 U.S. 263 (1967) (direct appeal case) (granting relief based on prosecutor's closing argument commenting on defendant's failure to testify); Agard v. Portuondo, 117 F.3d 696, 714 (2d Cir. 1997) (granting writ because prosecutor violated petitioner's rights to fair trial, confrontation, and testify in own behalf by stating, in closing argument, that petitioner's presence in courtroom during trial enabled him to tailor his testimony to what other witnesses said);

Driscoll v. Delo, 71 F.3d 701, 711-13 (8th Cir. 1995), *cert. denied*, 117 S. Ct. 273 (1996) (prosecutor's penalty phase closing argument violated rule of Caldwell v. Mississippi, 472 U.S. 320 (1985), by minimizing significance of jury's recommendation to judge); Gravley v. Mills, 87 F.3d 779, 786-90 (6th Cir. 1996) (prosecutor violated due process by repeatedly making improper references to petitioner's post-arrest silence in cross-examination and closing argument); Franklin v. Duncan, 70 F.3d 75 (9th Cir. 1995) (*per curiam*) (prosecutor's reference in closing argument to post-*Miranda* silence, coupled with jury instruction informing jury that silence could be construed as adoptive admission, violated 5th Amendment right to remain silent); Miller v. Lockhart, 65 F.3d 676, 682-85 (8th Cir. 1995) (prosecutor's closing argument at penalty phase, which included expression of personal belief in propriety of death sentence, played on jurors' fears, and improperly commented on petitioner's decision not to testify, violated due process); Antwine v. Delo, 54 F.3d 1357, 1361-64 (8th Cir. 1995), *cert. denied*, 516 U.S. 1067 (1996) (prosecutor violated 8th Amendment by inaccurately claiming, in penalty-phase closing argument, that gas chamber execution is "'instantaneous,'" thereby "diminish[ing] the jurors' sense of responsibility for imposing the death penalty" by allowing them to take comfort in "thought that the death would at least be ... painless and easy"; prosecutor also violated 8th Amendment by implying that execution was preferable because it would spare taxpayers from having to pay for life imprisonment); Davis v. Zant, 36 F.3d 1538 (11th Cir. 1994) (granting writ because prosecutor's "repeated and clearly intentional misrepresentations" in objection and closing argument rendered trial fundamentally unfair in violation of Due Process Clause); Martin v. Parker, 11 F.3d 613, 615-17 (6th Cir. 1993) (*per curiam*) (due process right to fair trial violated by combination of improper closing argument comparing petitioner to Hitler and improper references during cross-examination to petitioner's prior bad acts); Nelson v. Nagle, 995 F.2d 1549, 1555-58 (11th Cir. 1993) (prosecutor's improper closing argument, quoting 19th century appellate decision "which overwhelmingly discourages a jury from considering mercy," rendered capital sentencing proceeding fundamentally unfair, violating due process); Sizemore v. Fletcher, 921 F.2d 667, 670-73 (6th Cir. 1990) (prosecutor's repeated references in summation to petitioner's wealth and ability to hire multiple attorneys warranted habeas corpus relief because remarks were extensive and intentional, may have misled jury, and were permitted without admonition by trial judge and because proof of guilt was weak); Bradley v. Meachum, 918 F.2d 338 (2d Cir. 1990), *cert. denied*, 501 U.S. 1221 (1991); Mahorney v. Wallman, 917 F.2d 469, 472-73 (10th Cir. 1990) (because prosecutorial argument undermining presumption of innocence violates *specific* constitutional right, relief was warranted upon showing (made here) of *some* prejudice; petitioner accordingly need not satisfy test for *general* due process violation — that argument rendered whole trial fundamentally unfair); Floyd v. Meachum, 907 F.2d 347, 355 (2d Cir. 1990) (habeas corpus relief granted because prosecutor's summation inaccurately described burden of proof, commented on defendant's failure to testify, vouched for integrity of witness whose credibility had been attacked, and vouched for truth of state's allegations); Rogers v. Lynaugh, 848 F.2d 606, 609-12 (5th Cir. 1988) (prosecutorial arguments that countermand specific constitutional rights incorporated into 14th Amendment by Due Process Clause (in this case, violation of 5th Amendment guarantee against double jeopardy in argument during sentencing) are cognizable; given violation of specific constitutional provision, petitioner need not establish, in addition, that violation infected trial with unfairness); Williams v. Kemp, 846 F.2d 1276, 1283 (11th Cir. 1988) *cert. denied*, 494 U.S. 1090 (1990) (*dicta*) (prosecutorial comments are cognizable if they "render the entire sentencing proceeding 'fundamentally unfair'" because there is reasonable probability that, but for the prosecutor's offending remarks, outcome of sentencing hearing would have differed); McFarland v. Smith, 611 F.2d 414, 420 (2d Cir. 1979); Miller v. North Carolina, 583 F.2d 701, 708 (4th Cir. 1978); Manning v. Jarnigan, 501 F.2d 408, 413 (6th Cir. 1974).

prosecutors,[26] jury instructions,[27] various other trial, sentencing, and appellate

---

[26] *See, e.g.,* Kyles v. Whitley, 514 U.S. 419, 421 (1995) ("On habeas review, we follow the established rule that the state's obligation under *Brady v. Maryland,* 373 U.S. 83 (1963), to disclose evidence favorable to the defense turns on the cumulative effect of all such evidence suppressed by the government, and we hold that the prosecutor remains responsible for gauging that effect regardless of any failure by the police to bring favorable evidence to the prosecutor's attention. Because the net effect of the evidence withheld by the state in this case raises a reasonable probability that its disclosure would have produced a different result, Kyles is entitled to a new trial."); *id.* at 533-35 & n.7 (habeas corpus relief available if (1) "previously undisclosed evidence revealed that the prosecution introduced trial testimony that it knew or should have known was perjured" and "'there is any reasonable likelihood that the false testimony could have affected the judgment of the jury'" or (2) "favorable evidence is ... suppress[ed] by the government" and "'there is a reasonable probability that, had the evidence been disclosed to the defense, the result of the proceeding would have been different'"; as to latter theory "showing of materiality does not require demonstration by a preponderance that disclosure of the suppressed evidence would have resulted ultimately in the defendant's acquittal" or that "after discounting the inculpatory evidence, there would not have been enough left to convict" and only requires showing that "evidentiary suppression 'undermines confidence in the outcome of the trial'" (citations omitted)); Schlup v. Delo, 513 U.S. 298 (1995) (prosecutorial suppression of evidence entitles habeas corpus petitioner to relief if claim is not procedurally defaulted); ABF Freight System v. NLRB, 510 U.S. 317, 323-24 (1994) (*dicta*) (habeas corpus relief is available for due process claim that prosecutor knowingly used perjurious or false testimony (discussing *Mooney v. Holohan, infra*)); Mooney v. Holohan, 294 U.S. 103, 112 (1935) (prosecutorial subornation of perjury is basis for habeas corpus relief); *Gravley v. Mills, supra,* 87 F.3d at 786-90 (discussed *supra* note 25); Bemis v. United States, 30 F.3d 220, 221-23 (1st Cir. 1994) (section 2255 motion was available to challenge validity of guilty plea and sentence on ground that U.S. Attorney's Office had reneged on promise to place movant in witness protection program upon release from prison); Ringstaff v. Howard, 885 F.2d 1542 (11th Cir. 1989) (*en banc*), *cert. denied,* 496 U.S. 927 (1990) (adjudicating, but rejecting on merits, claim that state violated 6th Amendment by delaying trial for 16 months to await Supreme Court ruling on constitutionality of state's death penalty statute); Newman v. Frey, 873 F.2d 1092, 1093-94 (8th Cir. 1989) (*dicta*) (due process violation may arise from relationship between prosecutor and victim that renders trial fundamentally unfair); Walker v. Davis, 840 F.2d 834, 838-39 (11th Cir. 1988) (prosecutor's breach of advocate-witness rule violated due process because it was so egregious and prejudicial to fair trial as to undermine confidence in the outcome); authority cited *supra* note 7 (decisions discussing misconduct in negotiation and execution of plea agreements). *See also* United States v. Hyde, 117 S. Ct. 1630, 1633-34 (1997) (suggesting that FED. R. CRIM. P. 32(e) in federal prisoner cases or, possibly, Due Process Clause may hold government or state to "benefit of ... bargain" defendant struck in return for guilty plea and that failure of government or state to abide by plea agreement lets "defendant ... back out of his promised performance (the guilty plea), just as a binding contractual duty may be extinguished by the nonoccurrence of a condition subsequent"); Dickson v. Sullivan, 849 F.2d 403, 405-08 (9th Cir. 1988) (deputy sheriff's comment to two jurors about petitioner's past similar offenses justified habeas corpus relief because comment was "highly prejudicial" and there was reasonable possibility that comment influenced two jurors).

[27] *See, e.g.,* Hopkins v. Reeves, 118 S. Ct. 1895 (1998) (reviewing, but rejecting on constitutional merits, habeas corpus petitioner's claim that capital defendant has 8th Amendment

right to "lesser included offense" jury instruction on less serious offenses that are not, technically speaking, lesser included offenses of charged crime); Buchanan v. Angelone, 118 S. Ct. 757 (1998) (reviewing, but rejecting on constitutional merits, habeas corpus petitioner's claim that jury instruction on consideration of mitigating evidence in capital case violated 8th Amendment); *O'Neal v. McAninch, supra*, 513 U.S. at 435-36 (discussed *supra* note 25); Gilmore v. Taylor, 508 U.S. 333 (1993) (reviewing, but denying relief, on claim that trial instruction deprived petitioner of opportunity to present defense available under state law); *id.* at 348-49 (O'Connor, J., concurring in the judgment) ("Although the Court's opinion today might be read as implying that erroneous jury instructions may never give rise to constitutional error outside of capital cases, such an implication would misconstrue our precedent.... Some erroneous state-law instructions ... may violate due process and hence form the basis for relief, even in a noncapital case"; for example, "very fact that the Court scrutinized the instruction [at issue in *Estelle v. McGuire, infra*] belies any assertion that erroneous instructions can violate due process only in capital cases"; "clear" that "jury instructions may be so erroneous under state law as to rise to the level of a constitutional violation"); Estelle v. McGuire, 502 U.S. 62, 76-77 (1991) (O'Connor, J., dissenting) (concluding, contrary to majority, that there was reasonable likelihood that jury would have understood trial court's instruction to require it (1) to presume that habeas corpus petitioner was perpetrator of prior sexual abuse known to have been committed against homicide victim by someone and (2) to conclude that prior sexual abuser also was individual who killed victim; habeas corpus relief warranted on ground that instruction relieved state of burden of proving that petitioner committed killing); Yates v. Evatt, 500 U.S. 391, 401-02 (1991) (state postconviction case) (granting relief based on instruction shifting burden of persuasion to defendant); Penry v. Lynaugh, 492 U.S. 302 (1989) (granting relief because jury instructions limited jury's consideration of mitigating evidence in capital case); Maynard v. Cartwright, 486 U.S. 356 (1988) (granting relief, *inter alia*, because jury instructions failed to limit scope of "heinous, atrocious or cruel" aggravating circumstance in capital case); Hitchcock v. Dugger, 481 U.S. 393 (1987) (similar to *Penry, supra*); Rose v. Clark, 478 U.S. 570, 575 (1986) (similar to *Yates, supra*); Francis v. Franklin, 471 U.S. 307 (1985) (similar to *Yates, supra*); Mullaney v. Wilbur, 421 U.S. 684 (1975) (similar); McClain v. Calderon, 134 F.3d 1383, 1386 (9th Cir. 1998) (granting writ because instruction misled jury into believing that governor could commute death sentence on own when actually petitioner's record precluded commutation in absence of written recommendations from four state supreme court justices); Gallego v. McDaniel, 124 F.3d 1065, 1076 (9th Cir. 1997), *cert. denied*, 118 S. Ct. 2299 (1998) (granting writ because jury instruction concerning availability of executive clemency, although "not inaccurate as a general statement of the law, ... could have prompted the jury into making erroneous speculations about the kind of sentence [petitioner] might actually serve"); Smith v. Horn, 120 F.3d 400, 418-19 (3d Cir. 1997), *cert. denied*, 118 S. Ct. 1037 (1998) (granting writ because jury instructions on accessorial liability allowed jury to convict on first-degree murder without finding beyond reasonable doubt that petitioner had specific intent to kill); Hanna v. Riveland, 87 F.3d 1034 (9th Cir. 1996) (instruction on permissive inference unconstitutionally relieved prosecution of its burden on element of crime); Hennessey v. Goldsmith, 929 F.2d 511, 516-17 (9th Cir. 1991) (failure to instruct on element of crime violates due process; relief denied because violation was harmless); Wiggerfall v. Jones, 918 F.2d 1544, 1550 (11th Cir. 1990) (similar to *Allen v. Morris, infra*); Falconer v. Lane, 905 F.2d 1129, 1137 (7th Cir. 1990) (questioned in *Gilmore v. Taylor, supra*) (instruction omitting element of murder distinguishing it from voluntary manslaughter warrants habeas corpus relief); Monk v. Zelez, 901 F.2d 885, 888-90 (10th Cir. 1990) (despite limited scope of habeas corpus review of court martial convictions, court overturns military conviction due to faulty instruction on prosecution's burden of proof beyond reasonable doubt); Allen v. Morris, 845 F.2d 610, 617 (6th Cir. 1988), *cert. denied*, 488 U.S. 1011 (1989) (failure to

practices and procedures,[28] and even possibly the permissibility of accumulations of these and other kinds of errors that individually do not, but

---

instruct on lesser included offenses when evidence warrants instruction raises question cognizable on habeas corpus review even in noncapital cases); Vujosevic v. Rafferty, 844 F.2d 1023, 1027 (3d Cir. 1988) (failure to instruct on lesser included offense supported by evidence constitutes violation of due process even in noncapital cases) (citing Beck v. Alabama, 447 U.S. 625 (1980) and Bishop v. Mazurkiewicz, 634 F.2d 724 (3d Cir. 1980)); McKenzie v. Risley, 842 F.2d 1525, 1530 (9th Cir.), *cert. denied*, 488 U.S. 901 (1988) (presumption instruction undermining reasonable doubt standard is cognizable in habeas corpus proceedings). *See also* Sullivan v. Louisiana, 508 U.S. 275 (1993) (direct appeal case) (similar to *Cage, infra*); Cage v. Louisiana, 498 U.S. 39, 40-41 (1990) (*per curiam*) (direct review case) (due process review, on direct appeal, of state jury instruction on reasonable doubt). *But cf.* Victor v. Nebraska, 511 U.S. 1 (1994) (direct review case) (limiting reach of *Cage* rule); authority cited *supra* note 18 (reaching conclusion different from, or reserving question addressed in, *Wiggerfall v. Jones, supra, Allen v. Morris, supra,* and *Vujosevic v. Rafferty, supra*).

The Court has vacillated on the question of how certain a reviewing court must be that an instruction had an unconstitutional effect or conveyed to the jury an unconstitutional understanding of the law. Although previously the Court seemed prepared to reverse criminal judgments if jurors "could" have given the instruction an unconstitutional interpretation, *see, e.g., Yates v. Evatt, supra* at 401-02; *Cage v. Louisiana, supra* at 40-41; Mills v. Maryland, 486 U.S. 367, 375-76 (1988); Sandstrom v. Montana, 442 U.S. 510, 517-19 (1979), more recently the Court seems to have reversed only if the jurors "would" have done so, *see, e.g., Victor v. Nebraska, supra* at 6 ("proper inquiry is not whether the instruction 'could have' been applied in an unconstitutional manner, but whether the jury did so apply it"; "question ... is whether there is a reasonable likelihood that the jury understood the instructions to allow conviction based on proof insufficient to meet [due process] standard" (citation omitted)); *Estelle v. McGuire, supra* at 72 & n.4 (in analyzing ambiguous jury instructions that are susceptible to more than one interpretation, court must consider instruction "in the context of the instructions as a whole and the trial record" and determine "'whether there is a reasonable likelihood that the jury has applied the challenged instruction in a way' that violates the Constitution"; Court disapproves alternative formulations of the "standard of review for jury instructions" set forth in *Yates v. Evatt, supra* at 401, and *Cage v. Louisiana, supra* at 41); Boyde v. California, 494 U.S. 370, 380 (1990) (reversal required if "there is a reasonable likelihood that the jury has applied the challenged instruction in a way that" violates Constitution). Reflecting the blurred line between the "could" and "would" formulations is Johnson v. Texas, 509 U.S. 350, 367-68 (1993) (direct review case) ("Although the reasonable likelihood standard [of *Boyde v. California, supra*] does not require that the defendant prove that it was more likely than not that the jury was prevented... [from adhering to constitutional requirements], the standard requires more than a mere possibility of such a bar. In evaluating the instructions, we do not engage in a technical parsing of this language of the instructions, but instead approach the instructions in the same way that the jury would — with a 'common sense understanding of the instructions in light of all that has taken place at trial'" (citation omitted)).

[28] *See, e.g.,* Bracy v. Gramley, 117 S. Ct. 1793, 1797 (1997) (although "most questions concerning a judge's qualifications to hear a case are not constitutional ones" cognizable in habeas corpus and "in most cases ... [are governed] by common law, statute, or ... professional standards," nonetheless "Due Process Clause ... establishes a constitutional floor" that "clearly requires 'a fair trial in a fair tribunal' before a judge with no actual bias against the defendant or interest in the outcome of his particular case" (citations omitted); "there is no question that, if it could be proved,

... [a bribe-taking judge's] compensatory, camouflaging bias ... in [habeas corpus] petitioner's own case [designed to produce excessively harsh result in petitioner's case to hide or compensate for fact that judge was selling leniency in other cases] would violate the Due Process Clause"); Mach v. Stewart, 137 F.3d 630, 633-34 (9th Cir. 1998) (granting writ because jury was tainted by exposure during *voir dire* to repeated statements by prospective juror, a social worker, that children's claims of sexual abuse, like those in case on which jury was about to sit, had been confirmed in every case she had seen); Eslaminia v. White, 136 F.3d 1234 (9th Cir. 1998) (granting writ because jury's exposure to unadmitted, prejudicial statement of petitioner's brother, which was on reverse side of police audiotape introduced into evidence, deprived petitioner of rights to confrontation, cross-examination, and assistance of counsel); Lucero v. Kerby, 133 F.3d 1299, 1318-20 (10th Cir.), *cert. denied*, 118 S. Ct. 1375 (1998) (granting writ because crimes charged in separate counts overlapped for double jeopardy purposes and resulted in impermissible multiple punishments); Grigsby v. Blodgett, 130 F.3d 365, 369-70 (9th Cir. 1997) (granting writ because sentencing statute unconstitutionally penalized right to insist upon trial by jury, by permitting sentence of death or life without parole for defendants who opted for trial while prohibiting sentence greater than life with possibility of parole for those who pled guilty); Jones v. Vacco, 126 F.3d 408, 416-17 (2d Cir. 1997) (granting writ because trial judge improperly barred petitioner from conferring with counsel during overnight recess in midst of petitioner's cross-examination); Turner v. Marshall, 121 F.3d 1248, 1251 (9th Cir. 1997), *cert. denied*, 118 F.3d 1178 (1998) (granting writ because prosecutor's use of peremptory challenges to strike African-American members of venire was not justified by stated reason, which was determined to be pretext); Hochstein v. Hopkins, 113 F.3d 143, 147 (8th Cir.), *modified*, 122 F.3d 1160 (8th Cir.), *cert. denied*, 118 S. Ct. 388 (1997) (granting writ because petitioner was sentenced to death based on unconstitutionally vague "exceptional depravity" aggravating circumstance); Ayala v. Speckard, 89 F.3d 91 (2d Cir. 1996) (closure of courtroom to protect identity of undercover officer violated petitioner's right to public trial); Williams v. Singletary, 78 F.3d 1510 (11th Cir.), *cert. denied*, 117 S. Ct. 221 (1996) (cumulative sentences for single incident of criminal behavior violated Double Jeopardy Clause); Yohn v. Love, 76 F.3d 508 (3d Cir. 1996) (*ex parte* communication between prosecutor and state supreme court justice, resulting in trial judge's reversal of ruling that had originally favored defense, violated Due Process Clause and 6th Amendment right to counsel); Riggins v. Rees, 74 F.3d 732 (6th Cir. 1996) (state's refusal to provide petitioner with transcripts, rather than merely court reporter's tape recordings, of previous two trials which ended in mistrial violated Equal Protection Clause); Love v. Johnson, 57 F.3d 1305, 1312-16 (4th Cir. 1995) (trial judge violated Due Process Clause by quashing petitioner's pretrial subpoenas *duces tecum* for state agency records without first conducting *in camera* inspection of subpoenaed records to determine whether portions were material and favorable to defense); Riley v. Deeds, 56 F.3d 1117 (9th Cir. 1995) (readback of complainant's direct examination testimony, authorized by judge's law clerk in response to jurors' request and conducted in judge's absence, violated Due Process Clause); Walker v. Deeds, 50 F.3d 670, 672-73 (9th Cir. 1995) (granting writ because sentencing judge violated Due Process Clause by failing to follow state law procedure for determining applicability of "habitual criminal" sentence); Weston v. Kernan, 50 F.3d 633 (9th Cir.), *cert. denied*, 516 U.S. 937 (1995) (because trial judge granted mistrial over petitioner's objection and without adequate consideration of alternatives, Double Jeopardy Clause precludes retrial); Hagan v. Caspari, 50 F.3d 542, 544-45 (8th Cir. 1995) (if state supreme court's overruling of decision of intermediate appellate court "was an unforeseeable change in state law," it may violate due process rule prohibiting "retroactive application of an unforeseeable interpretation of a criminal statute, if detrimental to a defendant"); Echols v. Thomas, 33 F.3d 1277 (11th Cir. 1994) (*per curiam*), *cert. denied*, 516 U.S. 1096 (1996) (granting habeas corpus review of petitioner's claim that sentence exceeded statutory maximum, even though it "ultimately turns on a question of State law ... because 'the eighth amendment bars a prison sentence beyond the legislatively created maximum'"); Griffin v. Lockhart, 935 F.2d 926, 930-31 (8th Cir. 1991) (granting habeas corpus relief because trial court violated due process by failing to hold hearing on petitioner's competency to stand trial); Jones v. Arkansas, 929 F.2d 375, 377 n.6 (8th Cir. 1991) (sentencing petitioner under state habitual-offender statute that, as a matter of state law, does not apply to him violates due process and is proper basis for habeas corpus relief); Woods v. Dugger, 923 F.2d 1454, 1456-57 (11th Cir.), *cert. denied,* 502 U.S. 953 (1991) (granting habeas corpus relief based on prejudicial pretrial publicity coupled with presence of large number of uniformed spectators at trial for killing prison guard); Rector v. Clark, 923 F.2d 570, 571 (8th Cir.), *cert. denied,* 501 U.S. 1239 (1991) (granting habeas corpus review of petitioner's competency to be executed — whether he understands he is to be executed and that execution constitutes punishment); Grant v. Hoke, 921 F.2d 28, 31-32 (2d Cir. 1990) *(dicta)* (improper denial of motion to sever supplies basis for habeas corpus relief if denial rendered trial fundamentally unfair, *e.g.,* because, in order to believe core of testimony of one defendant, jury would have to disbelieve core of testimony of other defendant); McMiller v. Lockhart, 915 F.2d 368, 372 (8th Cir. 1990), *cert. denied,* 498 U.S. 1108 (1991) (reviewing constitutionality of trial court's denial of continuance, albeit under narrow, "abuse of discretion" standard); Larson v. Tansy, 911 F.2d 392, 396 (2d Cir. 1990) (absence of defendant during closing argument); *infra* §§ 20.3d n.55, 31.2 n.4 (discussing habeas corpus claims challenging competence of petitioner to stand trial). *See also* Hernandez v. Ylst, 930 F.2d 714, 718-19 (9th Cir. 1991) ("While alleged violations of state law per se are not cognizable in a federal habeas petition" and "[f]ederal courts are chary of entertaining habeas corpus [claims] premised upon asserted deviations from state procedural rules," federal habeas corpus courts "can and will review an application of state law for alleged constitutional violations"); McQueary v. Blodgett, 924 F.2d 829, 831 n.1 (9th Cir. 1991) ("writ of habeas corpus exists precisely to allow federal-based challenges to state law" and such challenges "fail not because they challenge *state laws* but rather because the *facts* alleged, even if proven, would not establish that such laws violate the laws or Constitution of the United States" (emphasis in original)); Lopez v. McCotter, 875 F.2d 273, 277-78 (10th Cir.), *cert. denied,* 493 U.S. 996 (1989) (similar to *Hagan, supra*); decisions collected *infra* § 11.2c.

As another set of examples, consider the following due process requirements that govern state appeals, violations of all of which are cognizable in habeas corpus: (1) the appellant must be represented by competent counsel, *see* Evitts v. Lucey, 469 U.S. 387 (1985); Hunt v. Vasquez, 899 F.2d 878, 879-91 (9th Cir. 1990); Lombard v. Lynaugh, 868 F.2d 1475, 1483-84 (5th Cir. 1989); *see also* Menefield v. Borg, 881 F.2d 696, 701 n.7 (9th Cir. 1989) (discussed *infra* § 33.4 n.2); (2) the appellate court must have before it a sufficient record of the trial proceedings, *see* Fullan v. Commissioner, 891 F.2d 1007, 1010 (2d Cir. 1989), *cert. denied,* 496 U.S. 942 (1990); United States v. Woods, 870 F.2d 285, 287 (5th Cir. 1989) *(dicta)*; Henderson v. Lockhart, 864 F.2d 1447, 1449, 1452 (8th Cir. 1989); (3) the appellate court must provide fair notice of the legal basis upon which it affirmed the conviction, *see* Olsen v. McFaul, 843 F.2d 918, 933 (6th Cir. 1988); (4) the appellate court must avoid undue delay in processing the appeal, *see, e.g.,* Harris v. Champion, 48 F.3d 1127, 1132 (10th Cir. 1995) (establishing general rule that "if the state has been responsible for a delay of more than two years in adjudicating the petitioner's direct criminal appeal," federal court should "presume ... prejudice necessary to support an independent constitutional claim of deprivation of an effective direct appeal because of delay"); Diaz v. Henderson, 905 F.2d 652, 653 (2d Cir. 1990); Simmons v. Reynolds, 898 F.2d 865, 868-69 (2d Cir. 1990) *(dicta)* (in this case, six-year delay in appeal "did not so taint the fairness of the state proceedings as to deny [petitioner] an adequate and effective appeal"; "[r]elease from custody" denied because release "is an

collectively may, make the proceeding fundamentally unfair,[29] generalizations about the cognizability of these issues in habeas corpus are dangerous and no

---

extraordinary remedy ... in delay-of-appeal case where release would in effect nullify a ... conviction on grounds unrelated to the merits"); Brooks v. Jones, 875 F.2d 30, 31-32 (2d Cir. 1989); Mathis v. Hood, 851 F.2d 612, 614 (2d Cir. 1988); decisions cited *supra* § 8.2b n.13 & *infra* § 33.4 n.2; Arkin, *supra* note 1; and (5) in capital cases in which a balancing of aggravating and mitigating factors determines the propriety of a death sentence, and in which the appellate court invalidated at least one aggravating circumstance, the appellate court must conduct "meaningful" and "individualized" appellate review of the probable impact that the invalid aggravating circumstances had on the sentencer's decision to impose death, in view of the mitigating circumstances present in the record, *e.g.,* Richmond v. Lewis, 506 U.S. 40, 50-52 (1993); Stringer v. Black, 503 U.S. 222 (1992); Parker v. Dugger, 498 U.S. 308, 320-22 (1991).

[29] *Compare Kyles v. Whitley, supra,* 514 U.S. at 421-22, 440-41 (in determining whether exculpatory evidence suppressed by state is sufficiently material to violate Due Process Clause, court is required to assess "cumulative" or "net" effect of all suppressed evidence and commits legal error if it only conducts piecemeal analysis of each item of suppressed evidence) *and O'Neal v. McAninch, supra,* 513 U.S. at 435-36 (discussed *supra* note 25) *and* Starr v. Lockhart, 23 F.3d 1280 (8th Cir. 1994) (reversal of death sentence required by cumulative prejudice of invalidity of aggravating factor and trial court's refusal to appoint expert) *and* Martin v. Parker, 11 F.3d 613, 617 (6th Cir. 1993) *(per curiam)* ("Here, the prosecutor's improper comments [in closing argument that compared petitioner to Hitler] and his repeated references [during cross-examinations] ... to [petitioner's prior bad acts] combined to deny [petitioner] his right to a fair trial.") *and* Derden v. McNeel, 978 F.2d 1453, 1454 (5th Cir. 1992) *(en banc)* ("[F]ederal habeas corpus relief may only be granted for cumulative errors in the conduct of a state trial where (1) the individual errors involved matters of constitutional dimension rather than mere violations of state law; (2) the errors were not procedurally defaulted for habeas purposes; and (3) the errors 'so infected the entire trial that the resulting conviction violates due process.'") *and* Mak v. Blodgett, 970 F.2d 614 (9th Cir. 1992) (cumulative effect of counsel's ineffectiveness and erroneous exclusion of evidence at penalty phase of capital trial required grant of habeas corpus relief with regard to death sentence) *and* Woods v. Dugger, 923 F.2d 1454, 1456-57 (11th Cir.), *cert. denied,* 502 U.S. 953 (1991) (due process violation found based on combined effect of prejudicial pretrial publicity and presence of large number of uniformed spectators at trial for killing prison guard) *and* Stomner v. Kolb, 903 F.2d 1123, 1128 (7th Cir.), *cert. denied,* 498 U.S. 924 (1990) (analyzing allegedly improper evidentiary ruling singly and in aggregate to determine if fundamental fairness was violated) *and* Bell v. Duckworth, 861 F.2d 169, 170 (7th Cir. 1988), *cert. denied,* 489 U.S. 1088 (1989) *(dicta)* (habeas corpus review extends to procedural errors that are "so harmful to the cause of truth that, singly *or cumulatively,* they make the defendant's conviction fundamentally unfair" (emphasis added)) *and* Walker v. Engle, 703 F.2d 959, 963 (6th Cir.), *cert. denied,* 464 U.S. 951 & 962 (1983) ("Errors that might not be so prejudicial as to amount to a deprivation of due process when considered alone, may cumulatively produce a trial setting that is fundamentally unfair;" granting relief on basis of cumulative errors) *with* Wainwright v. Lockhart, 80 F.3d 1226, 1233 (8th Cir.), *cert. denied,* 117 S. Ct. 395 (1996) ("Neither cumulative effect of trial errors nor cumulative effect of attorney errors are grounds for habeas relief.") *and* Wharton-El v. Nix, 38 F.3d 372, 375 (8th Cir. 1994), *cert. denied,* 513 U.S. 1162 (1995) (variety of sentencing-related errors, none of which violated constitutional guarantees or rendered proceeding fundamentally unfair, would not be considered cumulatively because "[w]e reject cumulative error as a basis for habeas relief") *and* Scott v. Jones, 915 F.2d 1188, 1191 (8th Cir. 1990), *cert. denied,* 499 U.S. 978 (1991) (cumulative errors are not cognizable in habeas corpus) *and* Lundy v. Campbell, 888 F.2d 467, 473-81 (6th Cir.

substitute for a careful analysis of the constitutional principles that govern the particular issue and of the factual circumstances recognized as implicating those principles.

The range of claims cognizable in federal habeas corpus proceedings is broad.[30] First, although cognizable claims must affect the fact, length, or (possibly) conditions of confinement, such claims include challenges to the legality of holding the petitioner in custody at all (*i.e.*, typically, the legality of the underlying conviction or of the procedures that produced it),[31] the type of sentence,[32] the duration of sentence (including on the basis of parole, good time,

---

1989), *cert. denied*, 495 U.S. 950 (1990) (alleged infractions must amount to separate violations of fundamental fairness; individually insufficient violations may not be weighed cumulatively; court, however, cumulatively analyzes "constitutional significance of the trial errors"). For a discussion of the potentially important effect of cumulative error on harmless error analysis, see Brecht v. Abrahamson, 507 U.S. 619, 638 n.9 (1993); *infra* § 32.4e n.64 and accompanying text.

[30] *See* Withrow v. Williams, 507 U.S. 680, 715 (1993) (Scalia, J., concurring in part and dissenting in part) (habeas corpus "jurisdiction ... is ... sweeping in its breadth."); Ex parte McCardle, 73 U.S. (6 Wall.) 318, 325-26 (1868) ("This legislation [the Habeas Corpus Act of 1867] is of the most comprehensive character. It brings within the *habeas corpus* jurisdiction of every court and of every judge every possible case of privation of liberty contrary to the National Constitution, treaties, or laws. It is impossible to widen this jurisdiction."); *supra* §§ 2.3-2.4.

[31] *See, e.g.*, Moore v. Dempsey, 261 U.S. 86 (1923); Singer v. Court of Common Pleas, 879 F.2d 1203, 1205-07 (3d Cir. 1989); Bateman v. United States, 875 F.2d 1304, 1306-10 (7th Cir. 1989) (*per curiam*) (conviction of nonexistent crime); Sheppard v. Louisiana Bd. of Parole, 873 F.2d 761, 761-62 (5th Cir. 1989) (*per curiam*) (challenge to confinement for failure to pay parole fees should be brought under habeas corpus, not 42 U.S.C. § 1983); most of the decisions cited *supra* notes 19-29. *See also* United States v. Dixon, 509 U.S. 688, 696 (1993) (direct review case) (delineating "constitutional protections ... [that] apply in nonsummary criminal contempt prosecutions, just as they do in other criminal prosecutions").

[32] *See, e.g.*, Stewart v. Martinez-Villareal, 118 S. Ct. 1618, (1998) (despite dissent's view that petitioner's claim of incompetence to be executed is not cognizable in habeas corpus because it attacks "when (or whether) the sentence can be carried out" and "not ... prisoner's underlying conviction or the legality of the sentence," *id.* at 1625 n.3 (Thomas, J. dissenting), majority "hold[s] that the Court of Appeals was correct in deciding that respondent was entitled to a hearing on the merits of his *Ford* [v. *Wainwright, infra*] claim in the District Court," *id.* at 1622); Herrera v. Collins, 506 U.S. 390, 406 (1993) ("[T]he issue of [in]sanity [at time of execution] is properly considered [in habeas corpus proceeding] in proximity to the execution."); Campbell v. Wood, 511 U.S. 1119 (1994) (Blackmun, J., dissenting from denial of stay of execution and denial of *certiorari*) (unconstitutionality of hanging as method of execution); Poyner v. Murray, 508 U.S. 931, 931-33 (1993) (Souter, J., respecting denial of *certiorari*) (discussing viability of challenge to constitutionality of electrocution as method of execution); Richmond v. Lewis, 506 U.S. 40, 52 (1992) (adjudicating and granting relief on claim challenging death sentence affirmed by state court after invalidating one aggravating circumstance without reweighing remaining aggravating circumstances against mitigating circumstances); Stringer v. Black, 503 U.S. 222 (1992) (similar); Parker v. Dugger, 498 U.S. 308, 320-22 (1991) (similar); Ford v. Wainwright, 477 U.S. 399 (1986) (adjudicating claim that death sentence is inappropriate punishment for insane prisoner); Turner v. Murray, 476 U.S. 28 (1986) (unconstitutional procedures leading to imposition of death sentence);

and other prison- or administratively, as opposed to court-administered rules)[33] or, in some cases (*e.g.*, ones challenging administrative segregation or other

Cabana v. Bullock, 474 U.S. 376 (1986) (adjudicating claim that death sentence is inappropriate punishment for prisoner without sufficient culpability); Moore v. Parke, 1998 WL 315952 (7th Cir. June 17, 1998) (granting writ because evidence supporting habitual offender determination was insufficient to satisfy state's burden of proof beyond reasonable doubt); Harris v. Pulley, 885 F.2d 1354, 1373 (9th Cir. 1988), *cert. denied,* 493 U.S. 1051 (1990) (challenge to death sentence based on discrimination against petitioner, not discrimination in general, in application of death penalty); Arauz v. Rivkind, 845 F.2d 271, 276 (11th Cir. 1988) (challenge to abuse of discretion by Board of Immigration Appeals in denying asylum); Mirchandani v. United States, 836 F.2d 1223, 1226 (9th Cir. 1988) (challenging extradition); Emami v. United States Dist. Ct., 834 F.2d 1444, 1449 (9th Cir. 1987) (same); Theron v. United States Marshal, 832 F.2d 492, 496-98 (9th Cir. 1987), *cert. denied,* 486 U.S. 1059 (1988) (same); authority cited *supra* note 22; capital punishment authority cited *supra* notes 25, 27. *See also* Trop v. Dulles, 356 U.S. 86 (1958) (nonhabeas corpus case concerning constitutionality of punishment of denaturalization); *infra* note 33 (discussing challenges to use of prior convictions to make petitioner eligible for particular sentence or to enhance sentence).

[33] *See, e.g.,* Edwards v. Balisok, 117 S. Ct. 1584, 1586-89 (1997) (discussed *supra* note 6) (suggesting cognizability on habeas corpus (and noncognizability in section 1983 action) of following claims resulting in denial of good time credits based on finding that prisoner committed disciplinary infraction: disciplinary officer's bias, concealment of exculpatory witness statements, denial to prisoner of opportunity to introduce exculpatory material and present defensive evidence, and absence of "some evidence" supporting decision that disciplinary infraction occurred (citing Superintendent v. Hill, 472 U.S. 445, 454 (1985) (due process right to some record evidence supporting findings used as basis for revoking good time credits)); also, however, questioning validity of decisions discussed *infra* this footnote, holding section 1983 portions of lawsuits in abeyance, rather than immediately adjudicating or dismissing them, pending exhaustion of remedies in regard to portions of suits that have been reformulated as habeas corpus actions: "absent some other bar to the suit, a claim either is cognizable under § 1983 and should immediately go forward, or is not cognizable and should be dismissed"); Young v. Harper, 117 S. Ct. 1148, 1150, 1154 (1997) (affirming grant of habeas corpus relief to petitioner whose "preparole" status was revoked without due process protections that Morrissey v. Brewer, 408 U.S. 471 (1972), assures individuals subject to parole revocation because "preparole" "program ... differed from parole in name alone"); Lynce v. Mathis, 117 S. Ct. 891, 897-98 (1997) (application to petitioner of 1992 statute retroactively withdrawing good time credits accumulated under regulations in effect at time of petitioner's 1986 offense and guilty plea violated *Ex Post Facto* Clause even though regulations were merely "provisional" measure to alleviate overcrowding; ordering restoration of some or all of five years' worth of "provisional" credits revoked under 1992 statute and, possibly, voiding petitioner's reincarceration following revocation of credits); Reno v. Koray, 515 U.S. 50, 52-54 & nn.1, 2 (1995) (adjudicating merits of, but rejecting, federal prisoner's habeas corpus petition claiming that federal statute required that he be given credit toward prison term for time spent while on bail confined in community treatment center; citing numerous cases adjudicating similar statutory claims; finding equal protection claim waived); *id.* at 65 (Ginsburg, J., concurring) (had petitioner not been adequately informed, when he agreed to pretrial confinement in community treatment center, that he would not be given credit against sentence for time spent in treatment center, due process violation cognizable in habeas corpus might have occurred); Garlotte v. Fordice, 515 U.S. 39, 44, 47 (1995) (claim "that, if successful, would advance [prisoners'] release dates" is "enough ... to permit them to invoke the Great Writ";

any claim that, if valid, "would advance the date of ... eligibility for release from present incarceration ... implicates the core purpose of habeas review" (citing Peyton v. Rowe, 391 U.S. 54, 66-67 (1968)); California Dep't of Corrections v. Morales, 514 U.S. 499, 504, 508-10 (1995) (adjudicating, but rejecting on merits, habeas corpus claim that *Ex Post Facto* Clause forbids state to substitute triennial parole suitability hearings for annual hearings required by statute in effect when petitioner committed crime; no violation because changed provision only affected procedures, and not standards or time-frames, determinative of parole eligibility and did not create "sufficient risk of increasing the measure of punishment attached to the covered crimes"); Lackey v. Texas, 514 U.S. 1045 (1995) (memorandum of Stevens, J., respecting denial of *certiorari*) (finding substantial "question whether executing a prisoner who has already spent some 17 years on death row violates the Eighth Amendment's prohibition against cruel and unusual punishment"); Custis v. United States, 511 U.S. 485, 493-94 (1994) (discussed below); Parke v. Raley, 506 U.S. 20, 27 (1993) (adjudicating, but rejecting on merits, due process challenge to State's allocation of burden of proof on question of validity of prior convictions used as predicates for recidivism statute, noting that "charge under a recidivism statute does not state a separate offense, but goes to punishment only"); Solem v. Helm, 463 U.S. 277 (1983) (8th Amendment cruel and unusual punishment challenge to lengthy sentence for minor crimes); Weaver v. Graham, 450 U.S. 24, 26-27, 31-33 (1981) (subjecting petitioner to new formula for calculating amount of "gain time" available to prisoners during periods of good behavior violated *ex post facto* bar); Wolff v. McDonnell, 418 U.S. 539, 554 (1974); Preiser v. Rodriguez, 411 U.S. 475, 500 (1973) ("when a state prisoner is challenging the very fact or duration of his physical imprisonment, and the relief he seeks is a determination that he is entitled to immediate ... or speedier release from that imprisonment, his sole federal remedy is a writ of habeas corpus"; suit seeking restoration of good time credits properly brought as habeas corpus action); McBride v. Johnson, 118 F.3d 432, 436-37 (5th Cir. 1997) (granting writ because Texas state parole board violated petitioner's right to confrontation by revoking parole on basis of detective's hearsay account of commission of crime despite petitioner's acquittal of same crime at trial and despite hearing officer's statement to petitioner that victim's presence at hearing would be secured); Walker v. Deeds, 50 F.3d 670, 672-73 (9th Cir. 1995) (sentencing judge violated due process by failing to follow state law procedure — in which petitioner had constitutionally protected "liberty" interest — for determining applicability of "habitual criminal" sentence); Jackson v. Vannoy, 49 F.3d 175 (5th Cir. 1995) (*per curiam*) (habeas corpus, not section 1983, is proper remedy in first instance for claim that revocation of previously imposed probation and parole was invalid because revocation was based on invalid arrest); Schafer v. Moore, 46 F.3d 43, 45 (8th Cir. 1995) (habeas corpus, not section 1983, is proper remedy in first instance for challenge to state's refusal to release prisoner after he complied with preparole condition of participation in sexual offender program); Williams v. Lee, 33 F.3d 1010 (8th Cir. 1994), *cert. denied*, 514 U.S. 1032 (1995) (denial of good-time credits on basis of statute enacted after petitioner's offense violated *Ex Post Facto* Clause); Kelly v. United States, 29 F.3d 1107 (7th Cir. 1994) (district court lacked jurisdiction to impose enhanced sentence for drug conspiracy conviction because government failed to comply with statutory requirement of prior notice to defendant and counsel); Nulph v. Faatz, 27 F.3d 451 (9th Cir. 1994) (*per curiam*) (state parole board violated *Ex Post Facto* Clause by calculating release date pursuant to statutes and regulations adopted after date of petitioner's offense, thereby increasing potential length of incarceration beyond that allowed by law in effect when crime was committed); Graham v. Lanfong, 25 F.3d 203 (3d Cir. 1994) (prisoner serving concurrent federal and territorial court sentences in Virgin Islands federal prison was improperly denied federal good-time credit for both sentences); United States v. Maybeck, 23 F.3d 888 (4th Cir. 1994) (section 2255 movant improperly sentenced as career offender under Federal Sentencing Guidelines based on erroneous classification of prior conviction as one involving violence); Duncan v. Gunter, 15 F.3d 989, 991 (10th Cir. 1994) (prisoner's section 1983 action for declaratory judgment regarding effect of earned time on release date should be brought as habeas corpus action after exhausting state remedies); Belk v. Purkett, 15 F.3d 803 (8th Cir. 1994) (parole revocation procedures violated due process); DeWitt v. Ventetoulo, 6 F.3d 32, 34-37 (1st Cir. 1993), *cert. denied*, 511 U.S. 1032 (1994) (although Constitution does not ordinarily prevent postsentencing increases of erroneous sentences to comply with state law, Due Process Clause prevented state court from imposing life sentence and reimprisoning petitioner six years after court reduced sentence in violation of state law); Ballard v. Estelle, 937 F.2d 453, 456 (9th Cir. 1991) (due process challenge to length of sentence on ground that trial court misapplied state statutes governing sentence enhancement); Taylor v. Wallace, 931 F.2d 698, 699 n.1 (10th Cir. 1991) (habeas corpus is proper method of challenging unconstitutional withdrawal of good time credits); Thompson v. Missouri Bd. of Parole, 929 F.2d 396, 399 n.6, 401 (8th Cir. 1991) (granting habeas corpus relief requiring parole board, which vindictively denied petitioner parole for two years, to credit him with two more years of parole service and to consider him for immediate release from parole); Lynott v. Story, 929 F.2d 228, 232-33 (6th Cir. 1991) (adjudicating habeas corpus claim challenging constitutionality of parole revocation hearing at which parole was revoked); Hart v. Marion Correctional Inst., 927 F.2d 256, 259 (6th Cir.), *cert. denied*, 502 U.S. 816 (1991) (granting habeas corpus relief requiring state to resentence petitioner in manner consistent with understanding conveyed to him at original plea proceedings of maximum sentence allowed by law); White v. White, 925 F.2d 287 (9th Cir. 1991) (granting habeas corpus relief based on petitioner's inability to confront adverse witnesses at parole revocation hearing); Stewart v. Scully, 925 F.2d 58, 62 (2d Cir. 1991) (granting habeas corpus relief requiring state to resentence petitioner to term with maximum not exceeding 20 years); Rizzo v. Armstrong, 921 F.2d 855, 861 (9th Cir. 1990) (granting habeas corpus relief requiring Parole Commission to hold hearing and exercise discretion it unlawfully denied having with regard to forfeiture of petitioner's "street time" for time served while on parole); Barden v. Keohane, 921 F.2d 476, 477-83 (3d Cir. 1990) (ordering petitioner released unless Bureau of Prisons exercised discretion it unlawfully denied having to designate state prison *nunc pro tunc* as place of confinement for federal sentence in order to enable petitioner to get credit against 20-year federal sentence for 10 years spent in state prison under sentence that state judge expressly made concurrent with federal sentence); Story v. Collins, 920 F.2d 1247, 1250 (5th Cir. 1991) (habeas corpus action under 28 U.S.C. § 2254, as opposed to *id.* § 2241, is appropriate means of challenging state officials' unconstitutional denial of administrative good time); Cox v. Warden, 911 F.2d 1111, 1114 (5th Cir. 1990) (challenge to imposition of mental-health-care requirement as condition of release cognizable in habeas corpus); Fox v. Kelso, 911 F.2d 563, 570 (11th Cir. 1990) (granting habeas corpus relief requiring state to award petitioner five months credit for time served; credit previously had been denied petitioner on basis of prior misdemeanor convictions held to be unconstitutional); Harrison v. Dahm, 911 F.2d 37, 39 n.1 (8th Cir. 1990) (state prisoner who directly attacks fact or length of confinement, seeking restoration of good time or money damages, must do so via habeas corpus action, not action under 42 U.S.C. § 1983, hence must satisfy exhaustion requirement; if unexhausted action is filed under section 1983, court should dismiss action or (to avoid statute of limitations problems) stay portions of action that are properly brought under section 1983 (such as portions seeking damages) pending exhaustion); Harris v. Duckworth, 909 F.2d 1057, 1058-59 (7th Cir. 1990) (habeas corpus is proper forum to challenge constitutionality of procedure by which State Conduct Adjustment Board found petitioner guilty of battery while in prison and, as punishment, transferred him to different prison, segregated him from other prisoners, and withdrew earned good time credits); Young v. Kenny, 907 F.2d 874, 875-78 & nn.2-4 (9th Cir. 1989), *cert. denied*, 498 U.S. 1126 (1991) (extensive discussion and citation of other circuits' decisions) (adopting rule followed in most other circuits requiring claims that could reduce period of incarceration to proceed in habeas corpus subject to exhaustion requirement and requiring request for damages under section 1983 to be held in abeyance (but *not* dismissed, given adverse effect dismissal would have on section 1983 statute of limitations) while exhaustion takes place; if restoration of credits would not reduce sentence, then suit may proceed under section 1983 without exhaustion of remedies); Fruit v. Norris, 905 F.2d 1147, 1148 n.3, 1150 n.6 (8th Cir. 1990) (undertaking habeas corpus (but denying section 1983) adjudication of claim that denial of good time credits for refusal to engage in hazardous prison work without protective clothing violated 8th Amendment; refusing to address claim that counsel representing petitioners in administrative hearing was ineffective because there is no right to effective assistance in civil actions); Prather v. Norman, 901 F.2d 915, 918-19 (11th Cir. 1990) (action for damages and other relief filed under section 1983 properly treated as habeas corpus action, subject to exhaustion requirement, because it could affect fact or duration of confinement; following caselaw concluding that stay of portions of action seeking damages under section 1983 may be more appropriate than dismissal pending exhaustion, because dismissal could have adverse statute of limitations consequences); Bressman v. Farrier, 900 F.2d 1305, 1306-09 (8th Cir. 1990) (claims attacking length of confinement and seeking to regain good time credits, including claims challenging legality of prison disciplinary proceedings that extend duration of confinement, must be brought in habeas corpus proceedings subject to exhaustion requirement); Bostic v. Carlson, 884 F.2d 1267, 1269 (9th Cir. 1989) (habeas corpus relief is available upon proof that state denied prisoner good time credits based upon improper disciplinary finding, expungement of which will speed grant of parole); Fender v. Thompson, 883 F.2d 303, 304-08 (4th Cir. 1989) (parole ineligibility determination); United States ex rel. D'Agostino v. Keohane, 877 F.2d 1167, 1168 (3d Cir. 1989) (challenge to release date); Mann v. Hendrian, 871 F.2d 51, 52 (7th Cir. 1989) (claim seeking to shorten length of imprisonment must be brought in habeas corpus action and is not properly brought under section 1983); Kalka v. Vasquez, 867 F.2d 546, 547 (9th Cir. 1989) (challenge to rate at which work-time credit awarded); Chatman-Bey v. Thornburgh, 864 F.2d 804, 806-07 & n.2, 813-14 (D.C. Cir. 1988) (challenge to erroneous determination of parole date "must be brought in habeas corpus," not mandamus); Williams v. Hayes, 846 F.2d 6, 7 (4th Cir. 1988) (*per curiam*) (challenge to application of pretrial jail credits to shorter of two concurrent sentences); Palmer v. Dugger, 833 F.2d 253, 255-57 (11th Cir. 1987) (challenge to denial of credit for time spent in custody in another state fighting extradition and for presentence time in custody due to inability to make bail); United States v. Kovic, 830 F.2d 680, 689, 691 (7th Cir. 1987), *cert. denied,* 484 U.S. 1044 (1988) (challenge to higher sentence allegedly imposed in retaliation for failure to give up 5th Amendment rights); Spina v. Aaron, 821 F.2d 1126 (5th Cir. 1987) (habeas corpus, not civil rights action, proper method of challenging denial of fair hearing affecting prisoner's eligibility for or entitlement to expedited release); North Carolina v. Smith, 501 F.2d 613, 615 (4th Cir. 1974) (challenge to higher sentence allegedly imposed in retaliation against defendant's successful appeal); *infra* §§ 33.4 n.10, 41.2b nn.20-21. *See also* Markham v. Clark, 978 F.2d 993 (7th Cir. 1992) (state prisoners seeking federal habeas corpus review of due process claim of improper reduction of good time credit following disciplinary proceeding must exhaust Indiana's "corrective process for prisoners aggrieved by disciplinary sanctions ... before turning to the federal courts"); *infra* §§ 23.1 nn.18-20, 41.2b n.29 (exhaustion of administrative remedies). *Cf.* Jones v. United States Bur. of Prisons, 903 F.2d 1178, 1185 (8th Cir. 1990) (Parole Commission decisions are reviewable only to determine whether proper procedures were followed and whether decision was within Commission's statutory authority (following Wallace v. Christensen, 802 F.2d 1539 (9th Cir. 1986) (*en banc*))); *infra* note 34.

Contrary to some of the decisions cited above, a number of other decisions have held that section 1983, not habeas corpus, provides the more appropriate method of challenging the *procedures* by which access to parole, good-time credits, and the like are made available, as long as the relief sought is not modification of the claimant's sentence. *See, e.g.,* Nelson v. Murphy, 44 F.3d 497, 499 (7th Cir.), *cert. denied,* 516 U.S. 1027 (1995) (challenge to mental health facility's across-the-board cancellation of off-grounds passes for insanity acquittees "is proper under § 1983, rather than 28 U.S.C. § 2254, because the scope of passes may be understood as a condition of confinement"); Akins v. Snow, 922 F.2d 1558, 1559 n.2 (11th Cir. 1991) (suit challenging parole board's procedures for determining eligibility for parole but not directly challenging denial of parole may properly be brought in section 1983 action without exhaustion of state remedies); Clark v. Georgia Pardons and Parole Bd., 915 F.2d 636, 638-41 (11th Cir. 1990) (although indirect consequence of relief sought in suit might be earlier release, suit seeking declaratory judgment that parole board could not treat petitioner's suits against prison officials as basis for denying parole was properly filed under section 1983 and need not be brought as habeas corpus action subject to exhaustion of state remedies requirement); Smith v. Maschner, 899 F.2d 940, 951 (10th Cir. 1990) (although challenge to disallowance of good time credits must be brought as habeas corpus action, related claims seeking money damages may proceed under section 1983 without exhaustion of state remedies); Greene v. Meese, 875 F.2d 639, 640-43 (7th Cir. 1989); Viens v. Daniels, 871 F.2d 1328, 1331-36 (7th Cir. 1989) (similar); Georgevich v. Strauss, 772 F.2d 1078, 1083 (3d Cir. 1985), *cert. denied,* 475 U.S. 1028 (1986). The validity of these decisions is called into question by the Supreme Court's 1994 decision in Heck v. Humphrey, 512 U.S. 477 (1994), discussed *supra* note 6. *Heck* extended the rule of *Preiser, supra,* making certain prisoner claims otherwise subject to overlapping habeas corpus and section 1983 jurisdiction cognizable *only* in habeas corpus proceedings, to include any claim (even if it ostensibly seeks damages or declaratory relief, not release) that, if successful, would "call into question the lawfulness of ... [the claimant's] confinement" or "would necessarily imply the invalidity of [the claimant's] ... sentence" or would "demonstrate the invalidity" of that sentence. *Heck v. Humphrey, supra* at 483, 487. *See infra* Chapter 33 (types of remedies available in habeas corpus actions). *Heck* thus appears to make habeas corpus the exclusive method for challenging procedures for allocating parole, good time, and other benefits if succeeding in such a challenge would call into question the validity of any administrative or other decision affecting the fact or length of the claimant's confinement. *Accord Edwards v. Balisok, supra,* 117 S. Ct. at 1586-89 (discussed *supra* note 6). *See also* Spencer v. Kemna, 118 S. Ct. 978, 988 (1998). The Court in *Heck* recognized that an exception to this general rule arises if a court (including on habeas corpus) or an executive or administrative official already has formally declared the incarceration unlawful. *See supra* note 6. In addition, as is explained *supra* note 6, five Justices have expressed the view — in a combination of separate opinions — that "a former prisoner, no longer 'in custody,' may bring a § 1983 action establishing the unconstitutionality of a conviction or confinement without being bound to satisfy a favorable-termination requirement that it would be impossible as a matter of law for him to satisfy [because his noncustodial status precludes his filing a habeas corpus petition]." *Spencer v. Kemna, supra,* 118 S. Ct. at 990 (Souter, J., concurring). *Accord id.* (Ginsburg, J., concurring) ("Individuals without recourse to the habeas statute because they are not 'in custody' (people merely fined or whose sentences have been fully served, for example) fit within § 1983's 'broad reach.'"); *id.* at 992 n.8 (Stevens, J., dissenting). For discussion of how the *Heck* rule helps avoid the statute-of-limitations problem with actions proceeding simultaneously under habeas corpus and section 1983 causes of action, see *supra* note 6.

A common use of habeas corpus and other post-trial review mechanisms is to challenge the validity of prior convictions used to establish a petitioner's eligibility for a particular sentence or otherwise to enhance the sentence the petitioner then is serving. *See, e.g.,* Custis v. United States, *supra,* 511 U.S. 485, 493-94 (*dicta*; habeas corpus); Johnson v. Mississippi, 486 U.S. 578 (1988)

incarcerative results of administrative disciplinary actions), the conditions under which that sentence is being served.[34]

(state postconviction challenge to death sentence imposed in part on basis of prior unconstitutional conviction); United States v. Tucker, 404 U.S. 443 (1972) (section 2255 challenge to use of uncounseled conviction to enhance sentence); Burgett v. Texas, 398 U.S. 109 (1967) (direct appeal challenge based on use of uncounseled conviction to enhance sentence). On the proper procedures for prosecuting such challenges in habeas corpus proceedings, and, most particularly, the need to frame such challenges as attacks on current confinement and not as attacks on prior convictions for which custody has lapsed, see *supra* §§ 8.2c nn.19-20 and accompanying text, 8.2d n.28 and accompanying text. For more recent direct appeal decisions limiting the grounds and the forums available for challenges to prior convictions used to enhance current sentences, see Nichols v. United States, 511 U.S. 738 (1994) (no constitutional violation occurs when uncounseled misdemeanor conviction for which no jail time was imposed is used to enhance sentence on subsequent conviction); *Custis v. United States, supra,* 511 U.S. at 490-92 (prior convictions used to enhance sentence under certain federal criminal statutes may not be collaterally attacked at time of sentencing, given availability of postconviction and habeas corpus challenges). *See also Parke v. Raley, supra,* 506 U.S. at 28 (reserving question whether "due process ... require[s] state courts to permit challenges to guilty pleas used for enhancement purposes at all"); Smith v. Farley, 25 F.3d 1363, 1365-70 (7th Cir. 1994), *cert. denied,* 513 U.S. 1114 (1995) (given "systemic concerns of both fairness and efficiency," federal habeas corpus review generally is available to challenge constitutionality of prior state conviction now being used to enhance new sentence but only to extent of examining whether procedures that produced prior conviction and sentence were "constitutionally deficient").

[34] *See, e.g., Preiser v. Rodriguez, supra,* 411 U.S. at 499-500 & n.15 ("habeas corpus may ... be available to challenge ... prison conditions"; habeas corpus is a "concurrent federal remed[y] in prison conditions cases" along with 42 U.S.C. § 1983) (citing Wilwording v. Swenson, 404 U.S. 249, 251 (1971); Johnson v. Avery, 393 U.S. 483 (1969)); United States v. Harris, 12 F.3d 735, 736 (7th Cir. 1994) (due process claim of excessive administrative segregation pending prosecution for crime allegedly committed in prison); Campbell v. Henman, 931 F.2d 1212, 1213-15 (7th Cir. 1991) (due process claim seeking release of exculpatory information in prison officials' investigatory file for use in prison disciplinary proceeding); Gomez v. United States, 899 F.2d 1124, 1125-27 (11th Cir. 1990) (revoking district court's grant of bail to prisoner with AIDS; challenge to conditions of confinement (inadequate medical treatment) is cognizable in habeas corpus proceedings but does not merit release); Bostic v. Carlson, 884 F.2d 1267, 1269 (9th Cir. 1989) (administrative segregation); Woodson v. Lack, 865 F.2d 107, 109-110 (6th Cir. 1989) (solitary confinement); D'Amato v. United States Parole Comm'n, 837 F.2d 72, 74 n.5 (2d Cir. 1988) (parole conditions); Sheley v. Dugger, 833 F.2d 1420, 1426, 1429 (11th Cir. 1987) (12-year solitary confinement); Willis v. Ciccone, 506 F.2d 1011, 1014 (8th Cir. 1974); Armstrong v. Cardwell, 457 F.2d 34, 35-36 (6th Cir. 1972); Coffin v. Reichard, 143 F.2d 443, 445 (6th Cir. 1944); authority cited *infra* § 41.2b nn.22, 23. *See also* Sandin v. Conner, 515 U.S. 472, 484-87 & n.10 (1995) (section 1983 decision revamping standard for determining whether imposition of prison discipline implicates "liberty interest" sufficiently so that Due Process Clause requires certain procedures before discipline may be imposed; rejecting prior decisions' focus on whether state statutes or prison regulations contain mandatory language suggestive of entitlement to freedom from discipline under specified circumstances and focusing instead on whether discipline "exceed[s] the sentence in ... an unexpected manner," "present[s] a dramatic departure from the basic conditions of [prisoner's] sentence," or "imposes atypical and significant hardship on the

Second, as discussed earlier,[35] federal "habeas corpus [is] ... a regime that permits the federal courts ... to vacate a final conviction [or sentence] on *any*

inmate in relation to the ordinary incidents of prison life"; unclear whether such "atypical hardship[s]" or "dramatic departure[s]" from normal prison conditions suffice or whether state law or prison regulations also must create relevant entitlement; holding that administrative segregation did not constitute "dramatic departure" under circumstances because most other prisoners were subject to similar forms of incarceration for nondisciplinary reasons in discretion of prison officials and because plaintiff's disciplinary record had been expunged and could not affect his parole prospects; more protective standards apply to pretrial detainees); Groseclose v. Dutton, 788 F.2d 356, 357-58 (6th Cir. 1986) (transformation of prison-conditions lawsuit from habeas corpus to section 1983 action); *infra* § 11.4b (class action petitions). *See generally* Plotkin, *supra* note 1; *Developments in the Law, supra* note 1, at 1084. A number of courts have strictly adhered to the rule that "[i]f a prisoner seeks by his suit to *shorten the term* of his imprisonment, he is challenging the state's custody over him and must therefore proceed under the habeas corpus statute with its requirement of exhaustion of state remedies, while if he is challenging merely the *conditions of his confinement* his proper remedy is under the civil rights law, which (with [one] ... exception) does not require exhaustion." Graham v. Broglin, 922 F.2d 379, 380-81 (7th Cir. 1991) (Posner, J.) (emphasis added); *see supra* note 33. In *Graham*, the court addressed the "difficult intermediate case ... where the prisoner is seeking not earlier freedom, but transfer from a more to a less restrictive form of custody." *Graham v. Broglin, supra* at 381. Noting that requests for probation, bond, or parole rather than incarceration must be brought in habeas corpus actions, *id.* (citing authority), and suggesting the same treatment of suits seeking furloughs, *id.* at 381, the court adopted the following rule:

> If the prisoner is seeking what can fairly be described as a *quantum* change in the level of custody — whether outright freedom, or freedom subject to the limited reporting and financial constraints of bond or parole or probation, or the run of the prison in contrast to the approximation to solitary confinement that is disciplinary segregation — then habeas corpus is his remedy. But if he is seeking a *different program or location or environment*, then he is challenging the conditions rather than the fact of his confinement and his remedy is under civil rights law, even if, as will usually be the case, the program or location or environment that he is challenging is more restrictive than the alternative that he seeks.

Id. at 381 (emphasis added). *See id.* (request for work release is "smack in the middle" of distinction between challenges to incarceration and to conditions of incarceration: held that request for work release challenges conditions of confinement, not length or type of confinement, hence is properly brought as civil rights, not habeas corpus, action). *See also* Falcon v. United States Bur. of Prisons, 52 F.3d 137 (7th Cir. 1995) (pretrial detainee's challenge to transfer to different prison on grounds that distance from counsel interfered with representation was not cognizable in habeas corpus because it "challeng[es] only his location within the [federal prison] system ... [and does not] request a 'quantum change in the *level* of custody'"; prisoner could seek relief through *Bivens* action for injunctive relief after exhaustion of administrative remedies or through pretrial motion in pending criminal case seeking retransfer); *Graham v. Broglin, supra* at 381-82 ("If a prisoner who should have asked for habeas corpus misconceives his remedy, brings a civil rights suit, and fails to exhaust his state remedies, his suit must be dismissed. But if, as in this case, he asks for habeas corpus when he should have brought a civil rights suit, all he has done is mislabel his suit, and either he should be given leave to plead over or the mislabeling should simply be ignored.").

[35] *See supra* §§ 2.3, 2.4.

properly preserved ground of federal constitutional error"[36] — including the various Bill of Rights and due process-based claims catalogued in the text and footnotes above.[37]

Third, as again is discussed in section 2.4d *supra*, the Supreme Court has interpreted 28 U.S.C. §§ 2241(c)(3) and 2254(a) to mean that important, but not other, federal statutory claims also are cognizable in federal habeas corpus proceedings. To be sufficiently important to qualify for habeas corpus review, a federal statutory claim either must (1) attack a fundamental defect which inherently "'resul[ts] in a "complete miscarriage of justice" or in a proceeding "inconsistent with the rudimentary demands of fair procedure"'" or (2) present exceptional circumstances "'rendering "the need for the remedy afforded by the writ of *habeas corpus* ... apparent."'"[38] In a series of decisions culminating for

---

[36] Solem v. Stumes, 465 U.S. 638, 653 (1984) (Powell, J., concurring) (emphasis added). *Accord, e.g.,* Herrera v. Collins, 506 U.S. 390, 400, 403 (1993) (affirming "principle that federal habeas corpus courts sit to ensure that individuals are not imprisoned in violation of the Constitution" and to provide relief "because of *any* constitutional violation which had occurred at the first trial" (emphasis added)); Wainwright v. Sykes, 433 U.S. 72, 79 (1977) ("state prisoner's challenge to the [state] trial court's resolution of dispositive federal issues is always fair game on federal habeas"); authority cited *supra* § 2.3 nn.6-22 and accompanying text. In regard to Justice Powell's "properly preserved" caveat, see *infra* Chapters 23, 24, 26, 28 (exhaustion, timeliness, procedural default, and successive petition doctrines). Retroactivity concerns provide an additional caveat to the "all constitutional claims" rule. *See infra* Chapter 25. For decisions setting forth additional caveats on the range of claims available in habeas corpus proceedings challenging custody by military, immigration, and Indian tribal officials and in extradition and other special contexts, see *supra* § 8.2d nn.43-47, 50 and accompanying text; *infra* §§ 41.2b, 41.3b.

[37] *See supra* notes 12-13, 19-29 and accompanying text. *See also infra* § 11.2c (collecting examples of successful habeas corpus claims).

[38] Reed v. Farley, 512 U.S. 339, 350 (1994) (plurality opinion) (quoting Hill v. United States, 368 U.S. 424, 428, 429 (1962)); Davis v. United States, 417 U.S. 333, 346 (1974) (quoting *Hill v. United States, supra* at 428). *See Reed v. Farley, supra* at 356-57 (Scalia, J., concurring in part); *id.* at 363-64 (Blackmun, J., dissenting) (discussed *infra* note 41); Duro v. Reina, 495 U.S. 676, 679, 682, 709 (1990) (nonmember Indian entitled to writ of habeas corpus to avoid criminal sanctions by Indian tribe; assertion of jurisdiction by tribe would violate equal protection guarantees of Indian Civil Rights Act, 25 U.S.C. § 1302 *et seq.*); United States v. Timmreck, 441 U.S. 780, 783-84 (1979); Stone v. Powell, 428 U.S. 465, 477 n.10 (1976); Bowen v. Johnston, 306 U.S. 19, 27 (1939) (when "need for the remedy afforded by the writ of habeas corpus is apparent" (quoted in *Reed v. Farley, supra* at 350 (plurality opinion)); Knox v. Wyoming Dep't of Corrections State Penitentiary Warden, 34 F.3d 964, 967-68 (10th Cir. 1994), *cert. denied,* 513 U.S. 1091 (1995); United States v. Roberson, 917 F.2d 1158, 1159 (9th Cir. 1990); Roberson v. United States, 901 F.2d 1475, 1477 (8th Cir. 1990); Adams v. Lankford, 788 F.2d 1493, 1500 (11th Cir. 1986); United States v. Bonnette, 781 F.2d 357, 361 (4th Cir. 1986); Shack v. Attorney General, 776 F.2d 1170, 1171-72 (3d Cir. 1985), *cert. denied,* 475 U.S. 1030 (1986); Kerr v. Finkbeiner, 757 F.2d 604 (4th Cir.), *cert. denied,* 474 U.S. 929 (1985); Bush v. Muncy, 659 F.2d 402, 407 (4th Cir. 1981), *cert. denied,* 455 U.S. 910 (1982); Hitchcock v. United States, 580 F.2d 964, 966 (9th Cir. 1978); authority cited *infra* § 41.3b nn.12-13 and accompanying text. *See also* Reno v. Koray, 515 U.S. 50, 52-55 & n.1 (1995) (discussed *infra* note 50); United States v. Smith, 32 F.3d 194, 196

the moment in the 1994 decision in *Reed v. Farley*,[39] the Court has further refined these descriptions both by applying them to permit habeas corpus relief from any "'failure to comply with the formal requirements' of [a federal statute]" that "'occurred in the context of other aggravating circumstance'"[40] and by identifying at least five exemplary "aggravating circumstances" that satisfy this test for what amount to "nontechnical" violations:[41]

(5th Cir. 1994) (claim of erroneous imposition of special parole term instead of supervised release, although "not ris[ing] to the level of a constitutional claim or jurisdictional magnitude," nonetheless is cognizable in section 2255 proceedings because "denying Smith's petition would result in a miscarriage of justice ... as the defendant is entitled to be sentenced under the correct law").

[39] 512 U.S. 339 (1994).

[40] *Id.* at 350 (plurality opinion) (quoting *Hill v. United States, supra*, 368 U.S. at 429).

[41] The Court's emerging jurisprudence harks back to an older jurisprudence in which the Court distinguished "nontechnical" from "technical" violations of federal statutory law for purposes of harmless error analysis. *See, e.g.*, Weiler v. United States, 323 U.S. 606, 611 (1944); Bruno v. United States, 308 U.S. 287, 293-94 (1939) (Frankfurter, J. for the Court) (without giving an "abstract, inclusive definition of 'technical errors,'" Court roughly defines them as "matters concerned with the mere etiquette of trials and with the formalities and minutiae of procedure"). *See also Reed, supra*, 512 U.S. at 363-64 & n.7 (Blackmun, J., dissenting) (interpreting Court's cases as endorsing "line between 'important' and 'merely technical' violations, [which] ... is not identical to the line between statutory and constitutional violations" and as requiring proof of a "serious or substantial error" as opposed to "failure to comply with ... technical requirements"); *Hill v. United States, supra*, 368 U.S. at 429 (no collateral relief is available where "all that is shown is a failure to comply with the formal requirements" of rule of criminal procedure). *See generally* James S. Liebman & William F. Ryan, *"Some Effectual Power": The Quantity and Quality of Decisionmaking Required of Article III Courts*, 98 COLUM. L. REV. 696, 784-85 n.399, 836 n.674 (1998).

As is discussed *supra* § 2.4d nn.294-98 and accompanying text, the *Reed* Court was unanimous as to two of the five factors delineated in text (factors (1) and (5)), and a majority of seven Justices (three in the plurality, four in the dissent) endorsed the other three factors. In Justice Blackmun's view, joined by Justices Stevens, Kennedy, and Souter, Congress so rarely applies federal statutory mandates to state criminal proceedings that, when it does, the statutory right created always is sufficiently important to be enforced on habeas corpus. *Reed, supra* at 363-64 (Blackmun, J., dissenting). By unanimously endorsing either the "fundamental defect" test of *Hill v. United States, supra, see Reed, supra* at 348 (plurality opinion); *id.* at 356 (Scalia, J., concurring in part and concurring in the judgment), or the rule that *all* federal statutory claims are cognizable, *id.* at 362-63 (Blackmun, J., dissenting), *Reed* also in effect rejected the lower court's view that federal statutory claims are subject to the rule of Stone v. Powell, 428 U.S. 465 (1976) (discussed *supra* § 2.4d nn.280-89; *infra* notes 58-59 and accompanying text; *infra* § 9.2), hence are never enforceable in habeas corpus proceedings as long as the State provides a formally adequate procedure for adjudicating the particular claim. *See Reed, supra*, 512 U.S. at 347-49 & n.7 (plurality opinion) (noting but not following Reed v. Clark, 984 F.2d 209, 213 (7th Cir. 1993), *aff'd on other grounds sub nom.* Reed v. Farley, 512 U.S. 339 (1994)). *Compare id.* at 348-49 (couching conclusion not as rejection of, but as failure to "adopt," *Stone v. Powell* approach) *with id.* at 363 n.5 (Blackmun, J., dissenting) (squarely rejecting *Stone* approach). By endorsing factors

(1)   Violation of an important or fundamental statutory right that, for example, "'effectuates a constitutional right' [such as] the Sixth Amendment guarantee of a speedy trial";[42]

(2)   The existence of some particular "'reason'" to fear that state judges in general may "'undermine'" or "be hostile to the federal law" that was violated;[43]

(3)   Violations of statutes as to which "nationally uniform interpretation" is particularly important;[44]

(4)   "Willful or egregious" violations of *any* federal law by particular state judges;[45]

---

(2)-(4) delineated in the text, a majority of the Court also rejected Justice Scalia's suggestion that "[t]he class of procedural rights that are not guaranteed by the Constitution (which includes the Due Process Clauses), but which nonetheless are inherently necessary to avoid 'a complete miscarriage of justice,' or [are] numbered among the 'rudimentary demands of fair procedure,' is no doubt a small one, if it is indeed not a null set." *Id.* at 357 (Scalia, J., concurring in the judgment in part).

[42] *Reed, supra*, 512 U.S. at 352 (majority opinion) (*dicta*). *See, e.g.*, decisions in *United States v. Ammar, United States v. Harper, United States v. Bigman, United States v. Popoola, Bateman v. United States,* and *Grimes v. United States*, discussed *infra* § 41.3b n.13.

[43] *Reed, supra*, 512 U.S. at 355 (plurality opinion). *Cf. id.* ("concern that state courts might be hostile to the federal law here at stake is muted" because Court "reserved the question whether federal habeas review is available to check violations of the [Interstate Agreement on Detainers'] speedy trial prescriptions when the state court disregards timely pleas for their application" and because the "IAD is both federal law, and the law of Indiana," thus moderating likelihood that Indiana judges will be hostile to it).

[44] *Id.* at 348. *See id.* at 348-49 (suggesting that Interstate Agreement on Detainers claims (*see infra* note 48 and accompanying text) might fit in this category because "[t]he IAD's purpose — providing a nationally uniform means of transferring prisoners between jurisdictions — can be effectuated only by nationally uniform interpretation" and because "argument that the compact would be undermined if a State's courts resisted steadfast enforcement, with total insulation from 2254 review is not without force"); *id.* at 361-62 & n.3 (Blackmun, J., dissenting) ("As a practical matter, this Court's direct review of state court decisions cannot adequately ensure uniformity."). *Cf. id.* at 358 (Scalia, J., concurring in the judgment in part) (because "Court's direct review of state and federal decisions will suffice for that [uniformity-preserving] purpose," concern of majority of Court for uniformity of federal laws "alter[s] the fundamental disposition that this Court, and not individual federal district judges, has appellate jurisdiction, as to federal questions, over the supreme courts of the States").

[45] *Id.* at 357 (Scalia, J., concurring in the judgment in part) (declining to join plurality opinion's suggestion that federal statutory violations are cognizable on habeas corpus in "circumstances that make the trial judge's behavior more willful or egregious," as where trial judge commits "statutory violation [that] was not waived" and to which defendant vigorously objected). *Cf. id.* at 348 & n.6 (plurality opinion) (violation at issue not cognizable because it was result of "unwitting judicial slip" that "ranks with the nonconstitutional lapses we have held not cognizable in a postconviction proceeding"; distinguishing decision in which relief granted on IAD claim after state court violated IAD notwithstanding petitioner's "repeated request[s] for compliance").

(5) Prejudice to important interests of the incarcerated petitioner.[46]

Federal statutes that may satisfy these requirements include Title III of the Omnibus Crime Control and Safe Streets Act (which restricts wiretapping and electronic surveillance by state and federal law enforcement officials),[47] the Interstate Agreement on Detainers (assuming, as a threshold matter, that the petitioner raised the claim in a timely manner that clearly drew to the attention of the responsible judge both the Agreement's technical requirements and the petitioner's desire to have those requirements enforced),[48] federal rules of

---

[46] *See id.* at 357 (Scalia, J., concurring in part) (interpreting plurality opinion to permit, and agreeing that there ought to be, habeas corpus enforcement in "circumstances that cause additional prejudice to the defendant, elevating the error to a fundamental defect or a denial of rudimentary procedural requirements"). *See also* decisions in *Gutknecht v. United States, Poyner v. United States Parole Comm'n,* and *Poor Thunder v. United States,* cited *infra* § 41.3b n.13. *Compare* Hill v. United States, 368 U.S. 424, 429 (1962) (no collateral relief is available when "all that is shown is a failure to comply with the formal requirements" of rule of criminal procedure in absence of showing of prejudice) *with* Davis v. United States, 417 U.S. 333, 347 (1974) (collateral relief is available to challenge conviction under Selective Service Act on theory that Act did not authorize criminal prosecution for conduct for which petitioner was convicted).

[47] 18 U.S.C. §§ 2510-20 (1994). *See, e.g.,* Adams v. Lankford, 788 F.2d 1493, 1495-97 (11th Cir. 1986) (*dicta*) (claims based on core concerns of Title III are cognizable in habeas corpus proceedings); Llamas-Almaguer v. Wainwright, 666 F.2d 191, 194 (5th Cir. 1982) (violations of Title III of the Omnibus Crime Control and Safe Streets Act, 18 U.S.C. § 2510 (1982), are cognizable in federal habeas corpus if they "constitute a 'complete miscarriage of justice'"); Hussong v. Warden, 623 F.2d 1185 (7th Cir. 1980); Alfano v. United States, 555 F.2d 1128 (2d Cir. 1977) (Title III claims are cognizable in federal postconviction proceedings); Vitello v. Gaughan, 544 F.2d 17 (1st Cir. 1976), *cert. denied,* 431 U.S. 904 (1977); Nauton v. Craven, 521 F.2d 876, 877 (9th Cir. 1975); Cruz v. Alexander, 477 F. Supp. 516, 520-21 (S.D.N.Y. 1979), *rev'd on other grounds,* 669 F.2d 822 (2d Cir. 1982). *See also infra* § 9.2 n.36 and accompanying text (inapplicability to Title III claims of *Stone v. Powell* doctrine limiting habeas corpus relief on 4th Amendment exclusionary rule claims). *See generally Developments in the Law, supra* note 1, at 1070-72.

[48] 18 U.S.C. § 2 (1994). In *Reed, supra,* the Court "granted certiorari ... to resolve a conflict among the Courts of Appeals on the availability of habeas review of IAD speedy trial claims," noting that the lower courts had taken various approaches, including (1) enforcing all IAD/speedy trial claims, *see, e.g.,* Birdwell v. Skeen, 983 F.2d 1332, 1341 (4th Cir. 1993); Cody v. Morris, 623 F.2d 101, 103 (9th Cir. 1980); United States ex rel. Esola v. Groomes, 520 F.2d 830, 839 (3d Cir. 1975); (2) enforcing such claims in habeas corpus under the test of Hill v. United States, 368 U.S. 424 (1962), upon a showing of actual prejudice, *see, e.g.,* Seymore v. Alabama, 846 F.2d 1355, 1359-60 (11th Cir. 1988), *cert. denied,* 488 U.S. 1018 (1989); Kerr v. Finkbeiner, 757 F.2d 604, 607 (4th Cir.), *cert. denied,* 474 U.S. 929 (1985); (3) refusing to enforce such claims because they can never rise to the requisite level of fundamentality under the test of *Hill v. United States, supra, see, e.g.,* Reilly v. Warden, 947 F.2d 43, 44-45 (2d Cir. 1991) (*per curiam*); Fasano v. Hall, 615 F.2d 555, 557 (1st Cir.), *cert. denied,* 449 U.S. 867 (1980); and (4) applying the rule of Stone v. Powell, 428 U.S. 465 (1976), and refusing to enforce any federal statutory violations for which a theoretically full and fair state court remedy exists, *see* Reed v. Clark, 984 F.2d 209 (7th Cir. 1993), *aff'd on other grounds sub nom.* Reed v. Farley, 512 U.S. 339 (1994). *Reed, supra,* 512

U.S. at 346 & n.6 (majority opinion). Although the Court did not resolve the conflict in its entirety, it did decide that "while the IAD is indeed state law, it is a law of the United States as well," hence potentially cognizable in habeas corpus, *id.* at 347 (plurality opinion); *id.* at 366-70 (Blackmun, J., dissenting); that the "fundamental defect" rule of *Hill v. United States, supra, see supra* notes 38-46 and accompanying text, governs the applicability of IAD and other federal statutory claims, thus rejecting the fourth approach (based on *Stone v. Powell, supra*) delineated above, *see supra* note 41; and that IAD/speedy trial violations are not enforceable if the petitioner did not forthrightly bring to the responsible judge's attention the precise time limits under the IAD that he wanted enforced (as opposed to couching his IAD requests in oblique language — which did not mention the specific time limits or the IAD provisions containing them — in the midst of extensive written pleadings, while forgoing multiple opportunities in court, in the midst of scheduling discussions, to request enforcement of IAD time limits), *id.* at 343-45 & n.3 (majority opinion); *see id.* at 346 n.6 (plurality opinion) (distinguishing case in which petitioner made "repeated request for compliance with the 180-day rule"). Although "reserv[ing] the question whether federal habeas review is available to check violations of the IAD's speedy trial prescriptions when the state court disregards timely pleas for their application," *id.* at 355 (plurality opinion), a majority of the Court seems amenable to the idea that IAD/speedy trial violations to which forthright objections are made are cognizable on the basis of criteria (1), (3), and (4) in text. *See supra* notes 42, 44, 45 and accompanying text. *See also* Knox v. Wyoming Dep't of Corrections State Penitentiary Warden, 34 F.3d 964, 967-68 (10th Cir. 1994), *cert. denied,* 513 U.S. 1091 (1995) (interpreting *Reed v. Farley, supra,* as recognizing IAD claims to be cognizable in habeas corpus proceedings if claim involves "prejudicial error that "'inherently results in a complete miscarriage of justice, [or] an omission inconsistent with the rudimentary demands of fair procedure'""). Pre-*Reed* Supreme Court opinions noting the conflict among the circuits on the cognizability of IAD/speedy trial and other IAD claims, many of which conflicts survive the Court's decision in *Reed,* include Fex v. Michigan, 507 U.S. 43, 55 n.1 (1993) (Blackmun, J., dissenting on other grounds) (discussing various means by which "prisoner aggrieved by a flagrant violation of the IAD" may secure relief; "Courts of Appeals have split over the question of an IAD violation's cognizability on habeas" (citing cases); "[a]t argument, the State and the United States, respectively, suggested that [some such violations] ... can be addressed through a 42 U.S.C. § 1983 suit or a mandamus action" (citations omitted)); Metheny v. Hamby, 488 U.S. 913, 913 nn.1, 2 (1988) (*mem.*) (White, J., dissenting from denial of *certiorari*) (citing decisions); Kerr v. Finkbeiner, 474 U.S. 929 (1985) (*mem.*) (White, J., dissenting from denial of *certiorari*). In addition to the decisions cited above, IAD claims have been enforced in habeas corpus proceedings in, *e.g.,* Gibson v. Klevenhagan, 777 F.2d 1056, 1058 (5th Cir. 1985); Shack v. Attorney General, 776 F.2d 1170, 1172 (3d Cir. 1985), *cert. denied,* 475 U.S. 1030 (1986); United States v. Woods, 775 F.2d 1059, 1060-61 (9th Cir. 1985); United States ex rel. Holleman v. Duckworth, 770 F.2d 690, 691 (7th Cir. 1985), *cert. denied,* 474 U.S. 1069 (1986); Cavallaro v. Wyrick, 701 F.2d 1273, 1275 (8th Cir.), *cert. denied,* 462 U.S. 1135 (1983); Bush v. Muncy, 659 F.2d 402, 407-09 (4th Cir. 1981), *cert. denied,* 455 U.S. 910 (1982); Mars v. United States, 615 F.2d 704 (6th Cir.) *cert. denied,* 449 U.S. 849 (1980). Decisions refusing to enforce such claims are, *e.g.,* Cooney v. Fulcomer, 886 F.2d 41, 43 (3d Cir. 1989) (technical violation of IAD is not basis for grant of habeas corpus relief; only antishuttling provision of IAD (Art. IV(e)) is sufficiently fundamental to warrant habeas corpus relief); Browning v. Foltz, 837 F.2d 276, 283 (6th Cir. 1988), *cert. denied,* 488 U.S. 1018 (1989) (citing other decisions). *See generally* 1 MICHAEL B. MUSHLIN, RIGHTS OF PRISONERS §§ 10.24-10.36 (2d ed. 1993); Note, *Federal Habeas Review of Nonconstitutional Errors, supra* note 1; Note, *The Effect of Violations of the Interstate Agreement on Detainers, supra* note 1.

criminal procedure affecting important interests of federal prisoners,[49] various federal statutes governing the computation of sentences and the onset of parole eligibility for federal prisoners based on such things as credit for pretrial detention and for good behavior in prison,[50] the federal statutes governing deportation and exclusion,[51] the federal statutes governing the induction into and the conduct of members of the military,[52] and the laws governing Native-American Indian tribes.[53]

Fourth, the federal habeas corpus statute allows challenges to state convictions and sentences insofar as they violate "treaties of the United States."[54]

---

[49] *See infra* § 41.3b n.11 and accompanying text; *cf.* United States v. Hyde, 117 S. Ct. 1630, 1633-34 (1997) (interpreting FED. R. CRIM. P. 32(e); discussed *supra* note 26).

[50] *See, e.g.*, Reno v. Koray, 515 U.S. 50, 52-55 & n.1 (1995) (adjudicating merits of federal prisoner's habeas corpus petition claiming that denial of credit toward service of prison term for time spent in pretrial detention in community treatment center violated 18 U.S.C. § 3585, which "determines when a federal sentence of imprisonment commences and whether credit against that sentence must be granted for time spent in 'official detention' before the sentence began"; citing lower federal court cases adjudicating claims under same statute). *See also supra* note 33; *infra* § 41.2b nn.20-22 and accompanying text (collecting some analogous cases).

[51] *See* 8 U.S.C. §§ 1105(a)(9), 1252(a) (1994); Jean v. Nelson, 472 U.S. 846 (1985); Blancada v. Turnage, 891 F.2d 688, 689-90 (9th Cir. 1989); Mohammed v. Sullivan, 866 F.2d 258 (8th Cir. 1989); other authority cited *supra* § 8.2d n.46.

[52] *See, e.g.*, authority cited *supra* § 8.2d nn.43-44.

[53] *See, e.g.*, Negonsott v. Samuels, 507 U.S. 99, 102 (1993) (adjudicating merits of, but rejecting, habeas corpus claim attacking state court conviction of Native American defendant on ground that two federal statutes deprived state of jurisdiction over particular offense committed on tribal lands (citing Indian Major Crimes Act, 18 U.S.C. § 1153; Kansas Act, 18 U.S.C. § 3243)); Duro v. Reina, 495 U.S. 676, 679, 682, 709 (1990) (discussed *supra* note 38); Ex parte Crow Dog, 109 U.S. 556, 571-72 (1883) (awarding habeas corpus relief based on violation of statutory exemption for intratribal crimes); In re Larch, 872 F.2d 66, 67-68 (4th Cir. 1989) (by implication) (Indian Child Welfare Act); authority cited *supra* § 8.2d n.45.

[54] 28 U.S.C. § 2241(c)(3) (1994); 28 U.S.C.A. § 2254(a) (West 1994 & Supp. 1998). *See, e.g.*, Breard v. Greene, 118 S. Ct. 1352, 1355 (1998) (*per curiam*) (claimed violation of Vienna Convention on Consular Affairs, which requires that incarcerating countries advise incarcerated foreign nationals of their right to contact their consulate, was cognizable in section 2254 proceedings, although "it is extremely doubtful that the violation should result in the overturning of a final judgment of conviction without some showing that the violation had a [prejudicial] effect on the trial"); *id.* at 1357 (Breyer, J., dissenting) (claimed treaty violation might be ground for relief if, for example, "Virginia's violation of the Convention 'prejudiced' [petitioner] by isolating him at a critical moment from Consular Officials who might have advised him to try to avoid the death penalty by pleading guilty"); Liu v. United States, 117 S. Ct. 1491 (1997) (Breyer, J., dissenting from denial of stay of mandate) (extradition treaty; discussed *supra* § 8.2d n.42); Murphy v. Netherland, 116 F.3d 97, 100 (4th Cir. 1997) ("Treaties are one of the first sources that would be consulted by a reasonably diligent counsel representing a foreign national [in habeas corpus proceedings]." (citing habeas corpus and related cases involving defendants' and prisoners' treaty claims)); Herrmann v. Meese, 849 F.2d 101, 102-03 (3d Cir.), *cert. denied*, 488 U.S. 867 (1988) (European Convention on Transfer of Sentenced Persons); Emami v. United States Dist. Ct., 834

Until the 1990s, this provision was not much used, but more recent litigation suggests that it may be more broadly applicable than was previously perceived. For example, the provision may provide a basis for habeas corpus review of claims that the practice of executing persons for offenses committed while they were children, mentally retarded, or insane violates human rights treaties to which the United States is a signatory.[55]

Fifth, even federal common law may form the basis for a challenge to a federal or state prisoner's custody in certain circumstances. The Supreme Court

---

F.2d 1444, 1449 (9th Cir. 1987) (extradition treaty); Theron v. United States Marshal, 832 F.2d 492, 496-98 (9th Cir. 1987), *cert. denied,* 486 U.S. 1059 (1988) (extradition treaty); other authority cited *supra* § 8.2d n.42 (extradition treaties). *See also* Matta-Ballesteros v. Henman, 896 F.2d 255, 259 (7th Cir.), *cert. denied,* 498 U.S. 878 (1990) (violation of international law in recapture of escaped prisoner not basis for habeas corpus relief). *Cf. Murphy v. Netherland, supra* at 99-100 (pretermitting question whether federal treaty (Vienna Convention on Consular Relations) establishes "individual rights (as opposed to setting out the rights and obligations of signatory nations)" that are enforceable in habeas corpus proceedings and denying appeal from district court's rejection of treaty claim, citing 1996 amendment to habeas corpus statute limiting appeals to claims involving "'substantial showing of the denial of a *constitutional* right'" (emphasis added)).

In *Breard v. Greene, supra,* the Supreme Court made clear that claims for federal habeas corpus relief based upon treaty violations are subject to the same procedural defenses as claims based upon federal constitutional violations and thus should be raised and litigated in state court in a timely and procedurally appropriate manner before being presented in a federal habeas corpus petition. *See Breard v. Greene, supra* at 1354-55 ("Breard procedurally defaulted his claim, if any, under the Vienna Convention by failing to raise that claim in the state courts.... [W]hile we should give respectful consideration to the interpretation of an international treaty rendered by an international court with jurisdiction to interpret such, it has been recognized in international law that, absent a clear and express statement to the contrary, the procedural rules of the forum State govern the implementation of the treaty in that State.... It is the rule in this country that assertions of error in criminal proceedings must first be raised in state court in order to form the basis for relief in habeas.... Claims not so raised are considered defaulted.").

[55] *See* International Covenant on Civil and Political Rights, art. 6(5), *entered into force* March 23, 1976, G.A. Res. 2200A, 21 U.N. GAOR, Supp. (No. 16) at 49, 52, U.N. Doc. A/6316 (1966) ("Sentence of death shall not be imposed for crimes committed by persons below eighteen years of age and shall not be carried out on pregnant women."); American Convention on Human Rights, *entered into force* July 18, 1978, O.A.S. Doc. OEA/SER. K/XVI/1.1 Doc. 65 (1970), reprinted in [1969] YEARBOOK ON HUMAN RIGHTS 390 (United Nations) ("Capital punishment shall not be imposed upon persons who, at the time the crime was committed, were under 18 years of age."). President Carter signed the American Convention on June 1, 1977, and the International Covenant on October 5, 1977. *International Human Rights Treaties: Hearings Before the Senate Comm. on Foreign Relations,* 96th Cong. 1st Sess. 506, 520 (1979). Both treaties were transmitted to the Senate for advice and consent on February 23, 1978, together with certain proposed reservations and understandings. *Id. See* David Weissbrodt, *United States Ratification of the Human Rights Covenants,* 63 MINN. L. REV. 35 (1978). *See generally* Victor L. Streib, *Death Penalty For Children: The American Experience With Capital Punishment For Crimes Committed While Under Age Eighteen,* 36 OKLA. L. REV. 613 (1983).

has recognized that even "merely 'prophylactic,'" hence nonconstitutional, rights are enforceable in habeas corpus if they simultaneously: safeguard "'a fundamental *trial* right'" (such as the 5th Amendment ban on the introduction at trial of coerced confessions); "serve some value" that is not "necessarily divorced from the correct ascertainment of guilt"; and discourage violations of the underlying "fundamental right" at trial on behalf of the defendant personally, rather than simply deterring future violations in other venues against individuals besides the defendant.[56] Nonconstitutional, non-"fundamental" rights also may provide a basis for a federal habeas corpus claim if the aspect of "custody" under challenge could not be attacked on direct appeal (for example, when the claim involves the manner in which prison authorities implement a sentence rather than the validity of the sentence itself or the underlying conviction).[57] In *Stone v. Powell*,[58] the Supreme Court held that one important federal common law or

---

[56] Withrow v. Williams, 507 U.S. 680, 690-92 (1993) (quoting United States v. Verdugo-Urquidez, 494 U.S. 259, 264 (1990) (emphasis added by Court)). *Withrow* held that the "prophylactic" rights established in Miranda v. Arizona, 384 U.S. 436 (1966), are enforceable in habeas corpus. *See infra* § 9.2 nn.24-32 and accompanying text (detailed discussion of *Withrow*). *Cf.* Brecht v. Abrahamson, 507 U.S. 619, 628-29 (1993) (discussing difference between constitutional and nonconstitutional prophylactic rights and placing rule of Doyle v. Ohio, 426 U.S. 610 (1976), "squarely" in category of full-fledged constitutional rights.).

[57] *See, e.g.*, Dunne v. Keohane, 14 F.3d 335, 336-37 (7th Cir.) (Posner, J.), *cert. denied*, 511 U.S. 1149 (1994) (prisoner sentenced in both state and federal courts and thereafter repeatedly transferred between state and federal facilities entitled to invoke section 2241 habeas corpus remedy to challenge conditions of confinement as violating federal common law right to continuous, uninterrupted service of sentence; although habeas corpus is limited to "defects of a constitutional or at least quasi-constitutional dignity" when used "as the vehicle for a collateral attack on a criminal judgment," error "need not be fundamental" when "habeas corpus is being used for a different purpose — here as a vehicle for direct review of an order of confinement that is not a part of the sentence — ... though it must be grave enough to warrant the remedy of releasing the petitioner from custody"); Waletzki v. Keohane, 13 F.3d 1079, 1080-82 (7th Cir. 1994) (Posner, J.) (**citing FHCPP**) (federal prisoner's nonconstitutional, nonstatutory claim of arbitrary deprivation of good-time credits cognizable in habeas corpus even though not "fundamental" because error is neither "harmless or merely technical" and "habeas corpus is simply the vehicle — and the only vehicle — for obtaining judicial review of administrative action"; limitations on federal habeas corpus jurisdiction, which are "motivated in large part by hostility to allowing collateral attacks on criminal judgments," are inapplicable when prisoner "is not mounting a collateral attack on his conviction or sentence"). *See also infra* § 41.2b. The foregoing cases involved petitions filed by federal prisoners pursuant to 28 U.S.C. § 2241 (1994). The court's rationale for deeming the claims cognizable in habeas corpus also might apply to similar petitions filed by a state prisoner pursuant to 28 U.S.C. § 2254 (West 1994 & Supp. 1998), on the theory that *Withrow v. Williams, supra* (discussed *supra* note 56) extends important federal common law principles to state prisoners. Depending upon the type of claim, a petitioner might be obliged to exhaust administrative remedies before seeking federal habeas corpus review. *See* Markham v. Clark, 978 F.2d 993 (7th Cir. 1992) (discussed *supra* note 33); *infra* §§ 23.1 nn.18-20, 41.2b n.29.

[58] 428 U.S. 465 (1976).

"prophylactic" rule — the 4th Amendment exclusionary rule — does not qualify under either of these rubrics and accordingly is not reviewable in habeas corpus cases unless its violation is compounded by the State's denial to the petitioner of the opportunity for "full and fair consideration" of the violation in the state court.[59] Because the *Stone* doctrine affects an important set of federal rights, but also because of the lengths the Supreme Court has gone to confine the doctrine to that single set of 4th Amendment exclusionary rule claims, the doctrine is discussed separately and in some detail in the next section.

A final consideration — and, possibly, a qualification — is posed by the Antiterrorism and Effective Death Penalty Act of 1996 (AEDPA).[60] AEDPA does not purport to alter the federal courts' habeas corpus jurisdiction over "violation[s] of the Constitution or laws or treaties of the United States" or in any way to amend the preexisting jurisdictional statutes.[61] AEDPA does, however, add or modify certain barriers to habeas corpus consideration and relief, which petitioners may surmount only by proving that the violations they allege have particular attributes.[62] For reasons that are not readily apparent — or, more probably, as a result of careless drafting — these barrier-avoiding provisions at times refer to violations of all types of "Federal right[s]" or to all types of "claim[s]" cognizable in habeas corpus,[63] but at other times refer only to

---

[59] *Id.* at 486 (prophylactic right created by Mapp v. Ohio, 367 U.S. 643 (1961), to exclude illegally seized evidence at trial is not enforceable in habeas corpus if State provides full and fair remedy for 4th Amendment exclusionary rule violations).

[60] Pub. L. 104-132, 110 Stat. 1214 (1996).

[61] *See, e.g.*, Felker v. Turpin, 518 U.S. 651, 658-64 (1996); Lindh v. Murphy, 96 F.3d 856, 865 (7th Cir. 1996) (*en banc*), *rev'd on other grounds*, 117 S. Ct. 2059 (1997); *supra* § 3.4b n.31. *Cf.* Lindh v. Murphy, 117 S. Ct. 2059, 2071 (1997) (Rehnquist, C.J., dissenting) ("There is a good argument that § 2254(d) is itself jurisdictional ... [and] even if it is not jurisdictional, it shares ... [a] salient characteristic of jurisdictional statutes ...."). As *Felker* points out, AEDPA does not amend the jurisdictional provisions in 28 U.S.C. §§ 2241(c)(3) or 2254(a).

[62] *See, e.g.*, provisions cited *infra* notes 63-66.

[63] 28 U.S.C.A. § 2262(b)(3) (West Supp. 1998) (opt-in stay of execution available upon "substantial showing of the denial of a *Federal right*" (emphasis added)); *id.* § 2264(a)(1) (exception to opt-in procedural default rule upon "Supreme Court's recognition of a new *Federal right*" (emphasis added)); *id.* § 2244(d)(1)(D) (running of nonopt-in statute of limitations postponed when "factual predicate for *the claim* ... could not have been discovered through the exercise of due diligence" (emphasis added)); *see, e.g., id.* § 2254(b)(1)(B)(ii) (exhaustion doctrine excused if state remedy is "ineffective to protect *the rights* of the applicant" (emphasis added)); *id.* § 2254(d)(1) (exception to rule governing adjudication of claims previously adjudicated on merits in state court for state "decision that was contrary to, or involved an unreasonable application of, clearly established *Federal law* as determined by the Supreme Court ...." (emphasis added)); *id.* § 2255(3) (running of section 2255 statute of limitations delayed by assertion of "*right*" only recently recognized by Supreme Court and made retroactive to cases on collateral review); *id.* § 2255(4) (section 2255 provision that otherwise is same as section 2244(d)(1)(D), *supra*); *id.*

"violation[s] of the Constitution or laws [but not treaties] of the United States"[64] or only to violations of "*constitutional* right[s]" or to "*constitutional* error."[65] The haphazard — and, at times, downright arbitrary[66] — nature of the discrepancies among these provisions, and between them and the habeas corpus statutes' unamended jurisdictional provisions, should make courts think twice, even in an era of "plain meaning" statutory interpretation, before placing too much emphasis on their nuances. The longstanding jurisdictional provisions in the habeas corpus statute have often been loosely described as creating a remedy for "constitutional violations"[67] — the type of violations that, indeed, make up the bulk of those remedied in habeas corpus cases.[68] Because such descriptions often serve as merely a rough shorthand for the jurisdictional headings in the

---

§ 2264(a)(3) (exception to opt-in procedural default rule on same basis as in section 2244(d)(1)(D), *supra*).

[64] *Id.* § 2244(d)(1)(B) (running of nonopt-in statute of limitations postponed when petitioner was impeded in seeking habeas corpus relief "by State action in violation of the *Constitution or laws* of the United States" (emphasis added)); *id.* § 2255(2) (same rule for section 2255 statute of limitations); *id.* § 2264(a)(1) (exception to opt-in procedural default rule on same basis).

[65] *Id.* § 2244(b)(2)(A) (successive petition permitted if it asserts violation of "new rule of *constitutional law,* made retroactive to cases on collateral review" (emphasis added)); *id.* § 2244(b)(2)(B)(ii) (successive petition permitted if "facts underlying the claim ... establish by clear and convincing evidence that, but for *constitutional error,* no reasonable factfinder would have found the applicant guilty ..." (emphasis added)); *id.* § 2244(d)(1)(C) (running of statute of limitations postponed until "date on which [new] *constitutional right* was initially recognized" (emphasis added)); *id.* § 2253(c)(2) (right to appeal denial of habeas corpus or section 2255 motion only upon "substantial showing of the denial of a *constitutional right*" (emphasis added)); *id.* § 2254(e)(2)(A)(i) (evidentiary hearing on facts defaulted in state court under circumstances described in section 2244(b)(2)(A) *supra*); *id.* § 2254(e)(2)(B) (evidentiary hearing on facts defaulted in state court under circumstances described in section 2244(b)(2)(B)(ii) *supra*).

[66] For example, there seems to be no good reason why the opt-in provisions, which by design are substantially *more* restrictive than the nonopt-in provisions, *see supra* §§ 3.2, 3.3c nn.41-44 & 61-64, 5.1b nn.94-103, require stays of execution to permit appeals upon a "substantial showing of the denial of a *Federal right*," *id.* § 2262(b)(3) (emphasis added), but appeals in nonopt-in habeas corpus and section 2255 cases are available only upon "a substantial showing of the denial of a *constitutional right*," *id.* § 2253(c)(2) (emphasis added). Nor is there any good reason why the statute of limitations in nonopt-in habeas corpus cases is postponed only by the Supreme Court's recognition of a new and retroactive "*constitutional right,*" *id.* § 2244(d)(1)(C) (emphasis added), and procedural defaults in the state courts bar evidentiary hearings in nonopt-in cases except upon the Court's recognition of "a new [and retroactive] rule of *constitutional law,*" *id.* § 2254(e)(2)(A)(i) (emphasis added), but the statute of limitations in nonopt-in section 2255 cases is postponed by the Court's recognition of any new and retroactive "*right,*" *id.* § 2255(3) (emphasis added), and procedural defaults in opt-in cases are excused by the "Court's recognition of a new *Federal right* that is made retroactive," *id.* § 2264(a)(2) (emphasis added)).

[67] *See, e.g.,* Herrera v. Collins, 506 U.S. 390, 403 (1993) (habeas corpus is available to remedy "any *constitutional* violation which had occurred at the first trial" (emphasis added)).

[68] *See infra* § 11.2c.

relevant, and unamended, provisions of the habeas corpus statute, namely, "violation[s] of the Constitution *or* laws *or* treaties of the United States," and because of the constitutional issues that might arise if AEDPA were read to bar all consideration of particular (at least properly preserved) violations of federal law, it seems appropriate to treat AEDPA's references to "constitutional error" (and the like) as serving a similar shorthand function.[69]

As a general rule, therefore, all properly exhausted and preserved federal constitutional claims challenging the legality of a State's or the Federal Government's holding the petitioner in custody, or the terms, duration, and possibly the conditions of that custody, are cognizable in habeas corpus. Also cognizable are custodial challenges premised on the limited set of federal statutes, treaties, and federal common law rights that bear on the propriety and conditions of criminal confinement by the States and that implicate important principles of national law or important individual liberty interests.

Although it is impossible comprehensively to catalogue all the federal claims that conceivably could fall within these rules, section 11.2c *infra* lists some of the claims on which habeas corpus relief has been granted in relatively recent cases. Sections 11.2b and 11.3 discuss the means of discovering claims cognizable in habeas corpus proceedings as well as issue selection and pleading.

§ 9.2.   *Stone v. Powell* — 4th Amendment exclusionary rule claims.[1]

As discussed above,[2] in *Stone v. Powell*[3] in 1976, the Supreme Court addressed "the specific question" whether "state prisoners — who have been

---

[69] 28 U.S.C. § 2241(c)(3) (1994), 28 U.S.C.A. § 2254(a) (West 1994 & Supp. 1998) (emphasis added). *See supra* §§ 2.2 n.13 and accompanying text, 3.2 nn.38-43 and accompanying text, 7.2d nn.78-80 and accompanying text (discussing (i) Supreme Court's reluctance to interpret AEDPA to bar all habeas corpus consideration of particular federal legal claims and/or (ii) constitutional questions posed by such proposed interpretations). *Compare* Murphy v. Netherland, 116 F.3d 97, 99-100 (4th Cir. 1997) (denying appeal from district court's rejection of habeas corpus claim based on violation of federal treaty (Vienna Convention on Consular Rights) because treaty claims do not involve "'substantial showing of the denial of a *constitutional* right'" as required by 28 U.S.C. § 2253(c)(2) (emphasis added)) *and* In re Blackshire, 98 F.3d 1293, 1294 (11th Cir. 1996) (refusing to grant leave to file successive petition because claim based on federal statutory law did not satisfy requirement of "new rule of *constitutional* law" in 28 U.S.C. § 2255 (emphasis added)) *with* In re Sylvester Rollins, No. 96-00269 (5th Cir. Oct. 7, 1996) (ordering briefing on question whether habeas corpus petitioner seeking certificate of appealability "must make a substantial showing of the 'denial of a constitutional right'" when claim being appealed is "not purely constitutional").

§ 9.2. [1] *See generally* WAYNE R. LaFAVE & JEROLD H. ISRAEL, CRIMINAL PROCEDURE §§ 28.3(b), 28.3(c) (2d ed. 1992); LARRY W. YACKLE, POSTCONVICTION REMEDIES §§ 96-100 (1981 & Supp. 1998); David A. Bagwell, *Procedural Aspects of Prisoner § 1983 and § 2254 Cases in the Fifth and Eleventh Circuits*, 95 F.R.D. 435, 458-59 (1982); Sam Boyte, *Federal Habeas Corpus After Stone v. Powell: A Remedy Only for the Arguably Innocent?*, 11 U. RICH. L. REV. 291 (1977);

afforded the opportunity for full and fair consideration of their reliance upon the exclusionary rule with respect to seized evidence by the state courts at trial and on direct review — may invoke their claim again on federal habeas corpus review."[4] The Court concluded "that where the state has provided an opportunity for full and fair litigation of a Fourth Amendment claim, a state prisoner may not be granted federal habeas corpus relief on the ground that evidence obtained in an unconstitutional search or seizure was introduced at his trial."[5]

The reasoning of *Stone v. Powell* and the Court's subsequent applications of the *Stone* doctrine[6] make apparent that the doctrine is limited to claims arising entirely under the 4th Amendment's exclusionary rule — *i.e.,* to claims in which the sole federal violation asserted is the state court's failure at trial to exclude evidence obtained from a search, seizure, or arrest that the 4th Amendment prohibits. As the Court remarked in *Withrow v. Williams,*[7] in rejecting the state's attempt to apply *Stone* to bar habeas corpus consideration of *Miranda* violations, "we have repeatedly declined to extend the rule in *Stone* beyond its original bounds."[8]

In *Stone* itself, the Supreme Court reviewed two lower court decisions. In the first, the 9th Circuit concluded that a state court should have suppressed a murder weapon the police discovered during a search incident to an unlawful arrest. In the second case, the 8th Circuit concluded that the state courts should have suppressed evidence of a bomb-manufacturing operation that had been seized pursuant to a defective warrant. In each case, the federal court ordered the state either to release the petitioner or to conduct a new trial at which the illegally obtained physical evidence would be excluded.[9] On its facts, *Stone* held only that — assuming an "opportunity for full and fair litigation" of the 4th Amendment claim at the state level — a federal court could not order a state

---

Henry J. Friendly, *Is Innocence Irrelevant? Collateral Attacks on Criminal Judgments*, 38 U. CHI. L. REV. 142 (1970); Philip Halpern, *Federal Habeas Corpus and the Mapp Exclusionary Rule After* Stone v. Powell, 82 COLUM. L. REV. 1 (1982); Note, *A Modest Proposal: Habeas Corpus, The Exclusionary Rule and the Supreme Court*, 7 MEM. ST. U. L. REV. 85 (1976).

[2] *See supra* sections 2.4d nn.277-89 and accompanying text, 9.1.

[3] 428 U.S. 465 (1976).

[4] *Id.* at 489.

[5] *Id.* at 494-95. *See also* Brecht v. Abrahamson, 507 U.S. 619, 635 (1993) (*dicta*) (pursuant to *Stone v. Powell,* "[c]laims under *Mapp v. Ohio,* 367 U.S. 643 (1961), are not cognizable on habeas as long as the state courts have provided a full and fair opportunity to litigate them at trial or on direct review"); Cardwell v. Taylor, 461 U.S. 571 (1983) (*Stone* preclusion doctrine applies regardless of form of fruits of asserted 4th Amendment violations).

[6] *See infra* notes 11-34 and accompanying text.

[7] 507 U.S. 680 (1993).

[8] *Id.* at 687 (quoted in Reed v. Farley, 512 U.S. 339, 348 (1994) (plurality opinion)).

[9] *Stone, supra,* 428 U.S. at 469-74.

court to apply the 4th Amendment exclusionary rule to suppress physical evidence that was the fruit of an illegal search, seizure, or arrest. *Stone*'s facts are important because the Supreme Court expressly limited its holding to those facts:

> Our decision today is *not* concerned with the scope of the habeas corpus statute as authority for litigating constitutional claims generally. We do reaffirm that the exclusionary rule is a judicially created remedy rather than a personal constitutional right, ... and we emphasize the minimal utility of the rule when sought to be applied to Fourth Amendment claims in a habeas corpus proceeding.... In sum, we hold only that a federal court need not apply the exclusionary rule on habeas review of a Fourth Amendment claim absent a showing that the state prisoner was denied an opportunity for a full and fair litigation of that claim at trial and on direct review. Our decision does not mean that the federal court lacks jurisdiction over such a claim, but only that the application of the rule is limited to cases in which there has been both such a showing and a Fourth Amendment violation.[10]

In 1979, three years after *Stone*, the Court twice rejected proposals to extend the *Stone* rule to claims not arising under the 4th Amendment exclusionary rule. In *Jackson v. Virginia*,[11] the Court refused to apply *Stone* to due process claims of insufficiency of the evidence, explaining that "[t]he question whether a defendant has been convicted upon inadequate evidence is central to the basic question of guilt or innocence" and "far different from the kind of issue that was the subject of the Court's decision in *Stone v. Powell*."[12] In *Rose v. Mitchell*,[13] the Court declared that *Stone* is inapplicable to claims that "direct[ly] question" the "integrity of the judicial system," such as equal protection challenges to racial discrimination in grand and petit jury selection.[14]

In 1986, in *Kimmelman v. Morrison*,[15] the unanimous Court again demonstrated its unwillingness to extend *Stone*'s holding to non-4th Amendment

---

[10] *Id.* at 494 n.37 (emphasis in original). *See also* Arizona v. Evans, 514 U.S. 1, 10-11 (1995) ("'The question whether the exclusionary rule's remedy is appropriate in a particular context has long been regarded as an issue separate from the question whether the Fourth Amendment rights of the party seeking to invoke the rule were violated by police conduct.' The exclusionary rule operates as a judicially created remedy designed to safeguard against future violations of Fourth Amendment rights.... As with any remedial device, the rule's application has been restricted to those instances where its remedial objectives are thought most efficaciously served." (quoting Illinois v. Gates, 462 U.S. 213, 223 (1983); other citations omitted)).

[11] 443 U.S. 307 (1979).

[12] *Id.* at 323.

[13] 443 U.S. 545 (1979).

[14] *Id.* at 563.

[15] 477 U.S. 365 (1986).

claims. In *Kimmelman,* New Jersey sought a ruling that "the restrictions ... announced in *Stone v. Powell* ... should be extended to Sixth Amendment claims of ineffective assistance of counsel where the principal allegation and manifestation of inadequate representation is counsel's failure to file a timely motion to suppress evidence allegedly obtained in violation of the Fourth Amendment."[16] The Court rejected the state's argument,[17] reiterating that *Stone* "rested its holding on prudential, rather than jurisdictional, grounds" tied directly to the 4th Amendment exclusionary rule's peculiar status as "merely" a "'judicially created' structural remedy 'designed to safeguard 4th Amendment rights ... through its deterrent effect'" and "'not a personal constitutional right'" arising directly under the Constitution.[18] The Court explained that the jurisprudential concerns that permitted the exclusion of claims arising under the subconstitutional and merely prophylactic 4th Amendment exclusionary rule[19] could not be squared with the different policies underlying the 6th Amendment requirement of effective assistance of counsel.[20]

In the wake of *Jackson, Rose,* and *Kimmelman,* it appeared that the only non-4th Amendment claim likely to be brought within the *Stone* preclusion doctrine was a violation of the subconstitutional, prophylactic rule of *Miranda v. Arizona.*[21] The Court had expressly reserved the question whether *Miranda*

---

[16] *Id.* at 374.

[17] *Id.* at 382-83. *Accord id.* at 391-93 (Powell, J., concurring).

[18] *Id.* at 379 n.4 (quoting *Stone, supra,* 428 U.S. at 486, 495 n.37 (quoting United States v. Calandra, 414 U.S. 338, 348 (1974))).

[19] Although consistently reaching all federal constitutional claims in habeas corpus cases, *see supra* §§ 2.3, 2.4, 9.1, the federal courts long before *Stone* assumed the discretion to limit their consideration of statutory and other subconstitutional federal claims to violations that are particularly important from the standpoint of the national interests or individual liberties at stake. *See Stone, supra,* 428 U.S. at 477 n.10; authority cited *supra* §§ 2.4d nn.104-06, 142-48, 186 and accompanying text, 9.1 nn.38-53 and accompanying text; *infra* § 41.3b. In this sense, *Stone* is a routine exercise of the federal courts' long-recognized discretion with regard to subconstitutional claims that is far less important for its impact on habeas corpus than for its denigration of the 4th Amendment exclusionary rule. *See* Reed v. Farley, 512 U.S. 339, 347 (1994) (plurality opinion) ("Our opinion in *Stone* concentrated on 'the nature and purpose of the Fourth Amendment exclusionary rule.' The Court emphasized that its decision confined the exclusionary rule, not the scope of [section] 2254 generally[.]" (quoting *Stone, supra,* 428 U.S. at 481)).

[20] *Kimmelman, supra,* 477 U.S. at 374 (6th Amendment "assures the fairness, and thus the legitimacy, of our adversary process"). *See also id.* at 380 ("The *constitutional* rights of criminal defendants are granted to the innocent and the guilty alike"; unlike subconstitutional remedy at issue in *Stone,* "the scope of [constitutional] right[s] is [not] altered ... simply because the right is asserted on federal habeas review rather than on direct review.").

[21] 384 U.S. 436 (1966).

claims are subject to *Stone* preclusion,[22] and two Justices had expressed the view that the reasoning of *Stone* required the same treatment for the subconstitutional rule of *Miranda* as *Stone* had given to the subconstitutional 4th Amendment exclusionary rule.[23] In its 1993 decision in *Withrow v. Williams*,[24] however, the Court declared that not even *Miranda* violations warrant application of the *Stone v. Powell* rule.[25] The State of Michigan, supported by the United States as *amicus curiae*, argued in *Withrow* that "*Miranda*'s safeguards are not constitutional in character, but merely 'prophylactic,' and that in consequence habeas review should not extend to a claim that a state conviction rests on statements obtained in the absence of those safeguards."[26] For purposes of deciding the case, the Court "accept[ed] ... [this] premise" and treated "the *Miranda* safeguards [as merely] 'prophylactic'" and subconstitutional.[27] This classification, however, did not suffice to "put[] *Miranda* on all fours with *Mapp*, or ... [to] render[] *Miranda* subject to *Stone*."[28] The Court explained that "*Miranda* differs from *Mapp* ... [in that] *Miranda* safeguards 'a fundamental trial right'" and that the values served by *Miranda* are not "necessarily divorced from the correct ascertainment of guilt."[29] Moreover "and most importantly," the Court observed, "eliminating review of *Miranda* claims would not significantly benefit the federal courts in their exercise of habeas jurisdiction"[30] or "advance

---

[22] *See* Duckworth v. Eagan, 492 U.S. 195, 201 n.3 (1989); Wainwright v. Sykes, 433 U.S. 72, 87 n.11 (1977).

[23] *Duckworth v. Eagan, supra*, 492 U.S. at 207-14 (O'Connor, J., joined by Scalia, J., concurring in the judgment).

[24] 507 U.S. 680 (1993).

[25] Discussing *Withrow*, as well as *Stone, Jackson, Rose*, and *Kimmelman* is Reed v. Farley, 512 U.S. 339, 348-49 & n.7 (1994) (plurality opinion).

[26] *Withrow, supra*, 507 U.S. at 690.

[27] *Id.* at 690-91. *See also id.* at 690 (explaining that "we have sometimes called the *Miranda* safeguards 'prophylactic' in nature" because *Miranda* warnings are only one of many ways — and thus not a constitutionally prescribed method — to protect the 5th Amendment interests at stake in a custodial interrogation).

[28] *Id.* at 691.

[29] *Id.* at 691-92.

[30] *Id.* at 693. The Court pointed out that "eliminating habeas review of *Miranda* issues" would not "do much of anything to lighten the burdens placed on busy federal courts" because a state prisoner could "simply convert[] his barred *Miranda* claim into a due process claim that his conviction rested on an involuntary confession." *Id.* at 693-94. Acknowledging that there was "no empirical basis for projecting" the magnitude of such an effect, the Court nevertheless "suppose[d]" that virtually all *Miranda* claims would simply be recast in this way." *Id.* at 693. The Court characterized as "beside the point" Justice O'Connor's statement in dissent that "many such [recast] claims would be unjustified" and identified the determinative issue as whether the extension of *Stone* would prevent *Miranda* claims from being alleged and adjudicated, not whether it would prevent them from resulting in relief. *Id.* at 693 n.5.

the cause of federalism in any substantial way."[31] Accordingly, the Court concluded, "the argument for extending *Stone* again falls short."[32] Then, in the Court's 1994 decision in *Reed v. Farley*,[33] the Court again remarked on the narrowness of the *Stone* doctrine and the Court's consistent refusal to extend it, and declined the invitation to extend the doctrine even to federal statutory claims.[34]

As the lower courts have recognized, the Court's post-*Stone* jurisprudence calls for limiting *Stone v. Powell* to its specific context: claims of violations of the 4th Amendment exclusionary rule. Following the Supreme Court's lead in *Jackson*, *Rose*, *Kimmelman*, *Withrow*, and *Reed* (and, in one instance, at least, finding support for an even greater limitation of *Stone* in recent legislation), the lower courts have steadfastly resisted efforts by the state to extend *Stone v. Powell* to other types of constitutional claims[35] or to claims of violations of

---

[31] *Id.* at 693. The Court acknowledged that "tension results between the two judicial systems whenever a federal habeas court overturns a state conviction on finding that the state court let in a voluntary confession obtained by the police without the *Miranda* safeguards." *Id.* at 694. The Court concluded, however, that such occurrences are not "frequent enough to amount to a substantial cost of reviewing *Miranda* claims on habeas or to raise federal-state tensions to an appreciable degree." *Id.* at 694-95.

[32] *Id.* at 688. *Accord* Thompson v. Keohane, 516 U.S. 99, 107 n.5 (1995). For further discussion, see *supra* § 2.4d nn.287-89 and accompanying text.

[33] 512 U.S. 339 (1994).

[34] *See id.* at 347-48 (plurality opinion) (*Stone* Court "emphasized that its decision confined the exclusionary rule, not the scope of [section] 2254" and "[w]e have 'repeatedly declined to extend the rule in *Stone* beyond its original bounds'"; "we do not adopt the [lower-court's] *Stone*-based rationale" for declining to review federal statutory claim before Court); *id.* at 363 n.5 (Blackmun, J., dissenting, joined by Stevens, Kennedy, Souter, JJ.) (*Stone* rule does not apply to statutory claims); *supra* § 9.1 n.41.

[35] *See, e.g.*, Stephens v. Attorney General, 23 F.3d 248, 249 (9th Cir. 1994) (*Stone* does not bar federal court consideration of claim that state court violated constitutional doctrine of collateral estoppel by refusing to give effect to suppression ruling in prior federal prosecution of petitioner for same incident); Cody v. Solem, 755 F.2d 1323, 1328 (8th Cir.), *cert. denied*, 474 U.S. 833 (1985) (claims alleging unconstitutional suppression of exculpatory evidence and use of improper procedure for selecting jurors); Baker v. Metcalfe, 633 F.2d 1198, 1200 (5th Cir.), *cert. denied*, 451 U.S. 974 (1981) (double jeopardy); Taylor v. Lombard, 606 F.2d 371, 375 (2d Cir. 1979), *cert. denied*, 445 U.S. 946 (1980) (knowing use by prosecution of perjured testimony); Swicegood v. Alabama, 577 F.2d 1322, 1325 (5th Cir. 1978) (suggestive identification procedure). For other cases in which the lower courts anticipated the Supreme Court's holding in *Withrow v. Williams*, *supra*, that *Stone* is limited to 4th Amendment exclusionary rule claims, see JAMES S. LIEBMAN, 1 FEDERAL HABEAS CORPUS PRACTICE AND PROCEDURE § 25.2 nn.25-36 (1st ed. 1988).

In the wake of Congress' recent enactment of the Antiterrorism and Effective Death Penalty Act of 1996 (AEDPA), one court has questioned whether a provision of AEDPA, 28 U.S.C. § 2254(d) (West 1994 & Supp. 1998) effectively abolishes the distinction that *Stone v. Powell* drew between 4th Amendment and other claims and thus requires that federal courts employ a single, uniform

federal statutory protections such as the electronic eavesdropping restrictions in Title III of the Omnibus Crime Control and Safe Street Act.[36]

Even with regard to 4th Amendment exclusionary rule claims, the *Stone* doctrine bars federal habeas corpus review only if the state properly invokes the defense and if the federal court determines that the state prisoner actually had a "full and fair opportunity" to litigate the claim in state court. These aspects of the *Stone* doctrine are discussed in Chapter 27 *infra* in the portion of the book devoted to procedural defenses to habeas corpus relief, rather than in this chapter on habeas corpus jurisdiction and the cognizability of claims. As the Court made clear in *Stone*, the bar to adjudicating such claims in habeas corpus proceedings is not a matter of jurisdiction or cognizability.[37] Rather, the *Stone* doctrine is in the nature of a court-made and prudentially based procedural defense that, if properly invoked by the state, may provide a basis for a federal court to decline to hear a 4th Amendment exclusionary rule claim.

---

standard for assessing all types of federal claims. *See* Carlson v. Ferguson, 1998 WL 345066, at *1, *3 (S.D. W. Va. June 24, 1998).

36 18 U.S.C. §§ 2510-20 (1994). *See e.g.*, Adams v. Lankford, 788 F.2d 1493, 1495 (11th Cir. 1986); Llamas-Almaguer v. Wainwright, 666 F.2d 191, 193 (5th Cir. 1982); Hussong v. Warden, 623 F.2d 1185 (7th Cir. 1980) (*dicta*). *See supra* § 9.1 n.47 and accompanying text. *Cf. Stone*, *supra*, 428 U.S. at 477 n.10 (some statutory claims are cognizable in habeas corpus).

37 *See Stone*, *supra*, 428 U.S. at 494 n.37 ("Our decision does not mean that the federal court lacks jurisdiction over such a [4th Amendment] claim [for which the petitioner was afforded "an opportunity for a full and fair litigation" in state court]). A claim is "cognizable" if it comes "'within [the] jurisdiction of [a] court or power given to [a] court to adjudicate [a] controversy.'" Federal Deposit Insurance Corp. v. Meyer, 510 U.S. 471, 476 (1994) (quoting BLACK'S LAW DICTIONARY 259 (6th ed. 1990)).

Chapter 10

PERSONAL JURISDICTION

§ 10.1. The respondent.[1]

The Rules Governing § 2254 Cases specify that the proper respondent in a federal habeas corpus petition on behalf of a state prisoner is "the state officer having custody of the applicant"[2] — *i.e.*, the petitioner's "immediate custodian"[3] or the "person having a day-to-day control over the prisoner ... who can directly produce 'the body' of the petitioner"[4] in court and who can release the prisoner from custody if ordered to do so.[5]

---

§ 10.1. [1] See generally Wayne R. LaFave & Jerold H. Israel, Criminal Procedure § 28.2(c) (2d ed. 1992); Ronald P. Sokol, Federal Habeas Corpus 80-91 (2d ed. 1969); Larry W. Yackle, Postconviction Remedies §§ 46, 113 (1981 & Supp. 1998); Charles Alan Wright, *Procedure for Habeas Corpus*, 77 F.R.D. 227, 229-34 (1978); *Developments in the Law — Federal Habeas Corpus*, 83 Harv. L. Rev. 1038, 1160-69 (1970).

[2] Rule 2(a) of the Rules Governing § 2254 Cases. *See also* 28 U.S.C. § 2243 (1994) ("The writ ... shall be directed to the person having custody of the person detained."); Braden v. 30th Judicial Cir. Ct., 410 U.S. 484, 494-95 (1973) (writ acts not upon prisoner who seeks the relief but upon individual who holds prisoner in unlawful custody); Reimnitz v. State's Attorney, 761 F.2d 405, 408-09 (7th Cir. 1985) (state's attorney who does not have custody over petitioner is not appropriate respondent); Hanahan v. Luther, 760 F.2d 148 (7th Cir. 1985); Mackey v. Gonzalez, 662 F.2d 712, 713 (11th Cir. 1981) (arresting officers and state's attorney are improper respondents because none of them had custody of petitioner); Bozeman v. Lambert, 587 F. Supp. 1021, 1023 (M.D. Ala. 1984), *aff'd*, 762 F.2d 1022 (11th Cir. 1985) (*mem.*). *See infra* § 41.4b (United States is proper party respondent in federal prisoner actions under 28 U.S.C. § 2255).

[3] Demjanjuk v. Meese, 784 F.2d 1114, 1115 (D.C. Cir. 1986) (Bork, J., in chambers). *See, e.g.*, Monk v. Zelez, 901 F.2d 885, 887 (10th Cir. 1990) (proper custodian in habeas corpus action challenging military conviction is "immediate custodian," namely in this case, Commandant of United States Disciplinary Barracks, Fort Leavenworth, Kansas) (discussing Monk v. Secretary of the Navy, 793 F.2d 364 (D.C. Cir. 1986)); *Braden v. 30th Judicial Cir. Ct., supra*, 410 U.S. at 494-95.

[4] Guerra v. Meese, 786 F.2d 414, 416 (D.C. Cir. 1986) (citing cases). *See, e.g.*, Ex parte Endo, 323 U.S. 283, 306 (1944); Billiteri v. United States Bd. of Parole, 541 F.2d 938, 948 (2d Cir. 1976); Holley v. Cheuvront, 351 F.2d 615 (9th Cir. 1965) (clerk of court not proper party respondent); Sanders v. Bennett, 148 F.2d 19, 20 (D.C. Cir. 1945); Diogenes v. Malcolm, 600 F. Supp. 815, 816 (E.D. Pa. 1985); *Bozeman v. Lambert, supra*, 587 F. Supp. at 1023; Scott v. United States, 586 F. Supp. 66, 68 (E.D. Va. 1984). *Cf.* Jones v. Cunningham, 371 U.S. 236, 243 (1963) (petitioner on parole is in custody of parole board within meaning of habeas corpus statute).

[5] *See* Miller v. Hambrick, 905 F.2d 259, 262 (9th Cir. 1990) (citing authority from various circuits) (although petitioner was temporarily transferred from federal prison in Texas to facility in California pursuant to writ of habeas corpus *ad testificandum*, proper custodian was warden of Texas prison; writ of habeas corpus *ad testificandum* "authorizes a trip not a change of custodians"). *Cf.* Garlotte v. Fordice, 515 U.S. 39, 42 (1995) (noting, without further comment, that prisoner in state penitentiary "filed a habeas corpus petition ... naming as respondent Kirk Fordice, the Governor of Mississippi" (footnote omitted)); Stephens v. Attorney General, 23 F.3d

If the petitioner is imprisoned, the petition should name either the warden of the facility in which the petitioner is incarcerated[6] or the state corrections commissioner, secretary, or director[7] — depending upon which officer best fits the general rule above. If there is any doubt as to which officer fits the bill, both the warden and state corrections commissioner should be named. The respondent should (but need not) be mentioned by name, as well as by title and office.[8] If the petitioner is in pretrial detention, not a postconviction incarceration facility, the proper respondent is the sheriff, jailer, or other official immediately responsible for administering the detention facility.[9] If the petitioner, although "in custody"

---

248 (9th Cir. 1994) (naming California Attorney General). *See generally* Wales v. Whitney, 114 U.S. 564, 574 (1885), *overruled on other grounds*, Hensley v. Municipal Ct., 411 U.S. 345 (1973). The custodian of the petitioner is determined by state law. *See, e.g.,* Jones v. Cunningham, 371 U.S. 236, 241-242 (1963); *Bozeman v. Lambert, supra*, 587 F. Supp. at 1023. The state attorney general is assumed to be in the best position to identify the proper respondent, and that attorney's failure, upon the filing of the petition, to object to the respondent named is evidence that the petitioner has identified the proper respondent. *See id.* at 1024.

[6] *See, e.g.,* Strickland v. Washington, 466 U.S. 668 (1984) (warden of Florida State Prison); Stanley v. California Supreme Court, 21 F.3d 359, 360 (9th Cir. 1994) (custodian to be named as respondent in habeas corpus petition "typically is the warden of the facility in which the petitioner is incarcerated"); *Monk v. Zelez, supra*, 901 F.2d at 887 (discussing Monk v. Secretary of the Navy, 793 F.2d 364 (D.C. Cir. 1986)) (habeas corpus petitioner incarcerated in military prison should name prison's commandant as party respondent). *See also* Advisory Committee Note to Rule 2 of the Rules Governing § 2254 Cases ("the warden of the institution in which the petitioner is incarcerated (Sanders v. Bennett, 148 F.2d 19 (D.C. Cir. 1945)) or the chief officer in charge of state penal institutions"). *But cf.* Williams v. Missouri Dep't of Corrections, 463 F.2d 993, 996 (8th Cir. 1972) (proper respondent is warden, not department of corrections that employs warden).

[7] *See, e.g.,* California Dep't of Corrections v. Morales, 514 U.S. 499 (1995); Wainwright v. Greenfield, 474 U.S. 284 (1986) (Secretary of Florida Department of Corrections); Smith v. Secretary of New Mexico Dep't of Corrections, 50 F.3d 801 (10th Cir.), *cert. denied*, 516 U.S. 905 (1995); Levine v. Commissioner of Correctional Services, 44 F.3d 121 (2d Cir. 1995), *cert. denied*, 117 S. Ct. 1112 (1997); Knox v. Wyoming Dep't of Corrections State Penitentiary Warden, 34 F.3d 964 (10th Cir. 1994), *cert. denied*, 513 U.S. 1091 (1995); Maurer v. Department of Corrections, 32 F.3d 1286 (8th Cir. 1994); Del Vecchio v. Illinois Dep't of Corrections, 31 F.3d 1363 (7th Cir. 1994), *cert. denied*, 514 U.S. 1037 (1995). *But cf. Garlotte v. Fordice, supra*, 515 U.S. at 42 (discussed *supra* note 5) (naming governor of State in which prisoner was incarcerated); Watson v. New Mexico, 45 F.3d 385, 386-88 (10th Cir. 1995) (naming state); *Stephens v. Attorney General, supra*, 23 F.3d at 248 (naming state attorney general).

[8] *E.g.,* James A. Collins, Director, Texas Department of Criminal Justice, Institutional Division; Robert Farley, Superintendent, Indiana State Prison; Harry K. Singletary, Secretary, Florida Department of Corrections.

[9] *See, e.g.,* Townsend v. Sain, 372 U.S. 293 (1963) (county sheriff named as respondent in case involving petitioner held in county jail). *See* authority cited *supra* § 5.2 (pretrial petitions). *See also* Yi v. Maugans, 24 F.3d 500, 507 (3d Cir. 1994) (respondent in petition by alien detained pending exclusion proceedings should be "warden that has day-to-day control over the prisoner and who can produce the actual body," not district director of INS).

for habeas corpus purposes, is not incarcerated,[10] the proper respondents generally are the person and agency immediately responsible for supervising the petitioner and assuring that his behavior conforms to those restraints on his liberty that render him in custody.[11] If, finally, the prisoner is serving a sentence in one State but attacking the legality of his future custody in another State pursuant to a subsequent conviction, he should name both the warden of the facility in which he is currently incarcerated and the attorney general of the state that convicted him on the subsequent charge.[12]

Even if the petitioner is not complaining about the actions of his immediate custodian but rather is challenging the actions of the custodian's superior officer or of officials in another agency — for example, when a federal prisoner incarcerated in a federal facility outside the District of Columbia complains that the United States Parole Commission in Washington, D.C. improperly denied

---

[10] *See supra* §§ 8.2a, 8.2d.

[11] If the petitioner is on probation or parole, the proper respondents generally are the petitioner's probation or parole officer and the supervising agency or parole board. *See, e.g.,* Advisory Committee Note to Rule 2 of the Rules Governing § 2254 Cases; Jones v. Cunningham, 371 U.S. 236, 243 (1963). *Cf.* Schuemann v. Colorado State Bd. of Adult Parole, 624 F.2d 172, 173 n.1 (10th Cir. 1980) (parole board is appropriate respondent if imprisoned petitioner seeks review of parole board's action and remedy sought is release from confinement on parole); Bozeman v. Lambert, 587 F. Supp. 1021, 1023 (M.D. Ala. 1984), *aff'd,* 762 F.2d 1022 (11th Cir. 1985) *(mem.)* (although under state law, proper custodian of parolee is warden of prison from which she is on parole, court deems parole office proper respondent as well "because the parole board is best situated to provide petitioners with the relief they desire"). If the petitioner has been released on bail pending final disposition, the proper respondent is the court that admitted the petitioner to bail and that can revoke it, *see, e.g.,* Reimnitz v. State's Attorney, 761 F.2d 405, 408-09 (7th Cir. 1985), or the attorney general of the State or his local representative, Advisory Committee Note to Rule 2 of the Rules Governing § 2254 Cases (applicants in custody other than jail, prison, other physical restraint, probation, or parole should name attorney general of the state wherein challenge action was taken).

[12] Advisory Committee Note to Rule 2 of the Rules Governing § 2254 Cases. *See infra* § 10.2b (proper court in which to file in this situation). *See also* Braden v. 30th Judicial Cir. Ct., 410 U.S. 484, 499-500 (1973) (when petitioner incarcerated in one State alleges that trial court in another State is violating his speedy trial rights, trial court in other State is proper party respondent). Examples of other proper respondents include Baxstrom v. Herold, 383 U.S. 107 (1966) (director of state mental hospital); United States ex rel. Toth v. Quarles, 350 U.S. 11 (1955) (Secretary of the Air Force in military habeas corpus petition); Eagles v. United States ex rel. Samuels, 329 U.S. 304 (1946) (commanding officer of military installation); Kolocotronis v. Holcomb, 925 F.2d 278 (8th Cir. 1991) (superintendent of state hospital); Monk v. Zelez, 901 F.2d 885, 887 (10th Cir. 1990) (commandant of military prison); Demjanjuk v. Meese, 784 F.2d 1114, 1115-16 (D.C. Cir. 1986) (if petitioner subject to deportation order is in custody of United States Marshal whose location and identity are unknown, proper party respondent is United States Attorney General); Jones v. Biddle, 131 F.2d 853, 854 (8th Cir. 1942), *cert. denied,* 318 U.S. 784 (1943) (warden of medical center for federal prisoners).

him parole[13] — the proper party respondent is the warden, director, or other official in charge of the facility in which the prisoner is actually physically incarcerated.[14] A rough rule of practice is that the closer the location of the individual in command who is named as respondent to the place where the petitioner is detained, the more likely that person will be deemed a proper party respondent.[15]

---

[13] *See, e.g.,* Guerra v. Meese, 786 F.2d 414, 416 (D.C. Cir. 1986); authority cited *supra* § 9.1 n.33.

[14] *See, e.g., Braden v. 30th Judicial Cir. Ct., supra,* 410 U.S. at 500 (Court, commenting on Ahrens v. Clark, 335 U.S. 188 (1948), states in *dicta* that aliens held on Ellis Island in New York should name local federal officials who detained them there, not Attorney General in Washington); Baxstrom v. Herold, 383 U.S. 107 (1966) (director of state hospital in which petitioner was confined); Ex parte Endo, 323 U.S. 283, 306 (1944) (writ should be directed to and served upon petitioner's jailer; petitioner excused from naming current jailer because of recent transfer to new wartime relocation facility); Dunne v. Henman, 875 F.2d 244, 245-50 (9th Cir. 1989) (state prisoner subject to state and federal sentences and serving both sentences in prison system of second State (pursuant to contract with sentencing State) alleged that he was "'being required to serve a federal sentence in installments' in violation of due process and the 'separation of powers doctrine'"; held that challenge is to execution, not imposition, of federal sentence, and that petition should name as respondent warden of institution in which petitioner actually is incarcerated); Chatman-Bey v. Thornburgh, 864 F.2d 804, 810-11 (D.C. Cir. 1988) (challenges to parole decisions should name as respondent the actual custodian (in this case, warden), not Parole Commission or Attorney General, and petition should be filed in district of incarceration rather than D.C. Circuit); United States v. Kennedy, 851 F.2d 689, 691 (3d Cir. 1988) (challenge to Parole Commission should name warden of prison as respondent); Mikolon v. United States, 844 F.2d 456, 460 (7th Cir. 1988) (same); *Guerra v. Meese, supra,* 786 F.2d at 416 (citing cases) (in federal prisoner case, proper party respondent is warden of incarcerating facility, and not, for example, President, Attorney General, Parole Commission with authority to release prisoner, or federal judge who convicted and sentenced prisoner and accordingly has power to reduce sentence); *Demjanjuk v. Meese, supra,* 784 F.2d at 1116 (Bork, J., in chambers) (except in "very limited and special circumstances," such as when location and custodian of prisoner are not known, immediate custodian of federal prisoner, and not, for example, Attorney General, is proper party respondent); Billiteri v. United States Bd. of Parole, 541 F.2d 938, 948 (2d Cir. 1976) (despite parole board's power to release petitioner, warden of prison in which petitioner is confined, not parole board, is proper respondent); Diogenes v. Malcolm, 600 F. Supp. 815, 816 (E.D. Pa. 1985) (similar); Brown v. Neagle, 486 F. Supp. 364, 365 (S.D.W. Va. 1979) (warden having custody of prisoner is only proper respondent in habeas corpus proceeding attacking conditions of confinement).

[15] Some decisions hold that an official or entity other than the director of the facility in which the petitioner is actually detained is a proper party respondent if the actual custodian serves as the "agent" of the named respondent, *Braden v. 30th Judicial Cir. Ct., supra,* 410 U.S. at 489 n.4 (out-of-state court which lodged detainer with warden of prison in which petitioner was incarcerated, requiring warden to turn over petitioner to court upon completion of sentence, was proper party respondent because warden was acting as that court's "agent"), or if the official is the "constructive custod[ian]" of petitioner, Ali v. Gibson, 572 F.2d 971, 972 n.1, 974 (3d Cir. 1978) (Virgin Islands Commissioner of Public Safety who transferred petitioner from Virgin Islands to United States is

The petitioner may cure mistakes in designating the respondent that do not affect the court's personal jurisdiction by filing an amendment to the petition; dismissal of the petition in such a case usually is regarded as improper.[16] If the federal court's personal jurisdiction or venue over the lawsuit depends upon the residence of the party respondent and the wrong party respondent is named, the court has no power to adjudicate the petition.[17] Here too, however, dismissal is

---

proper respondent because he retains "constructive custody" of petitioner). *See, e.g.,* Weeks v. Wyrick, 638 F.2d 690, 692 (8th Cir. 1981) (prior custodian is suitable respondent when transfer of petitioner out of state occurs after respondent is properly served). Although vigilant for forum shopping, the courts are not inclined to penalize petitioners for honest mistakes. *See, e.g.,* Bozeman v. Lambert, 587 F. Supp. 1021, 1024 (M.D. Ala. 1984), *aff'd.* 762 F.2d 1022 (11th Cir. 1985) (*mem.*) (discussed *infra* note 17).

[16] *See, e.g.,* Stanley v. California Supreme Court, 21 F.3d 359, 360 (9th Cir. 1994) (upon finding that petition erroneously failed to name warden as respondent, court of appeals remands case to district court to afford petitioner opportunity to "amend his petition to name the correct party as respondent"); West v. Louisiana, 478 F.2d 1026, 1029-31 (5th Cir. 1973), *adhered to en banc,* 510 F.2d 363 (5th Cir. 1975); Ashley v. Washington, 394 F.2d 125, 126 n.1 (9th Cir. 1968) (*dicta*); Davis v. California, 341 F.2d 982, 983 n.1 (9th Cir. 1965); *Bozeman v. Lambert, supra,* 587 F. Supp. at 1023-24 (improper party respondent is not jurisdictional defect and may be cured by amendment); Copeland v. Mississippi, 415 F. Supp. 1271, 1272 n.1 (N.D. Miss. 1976). *See* Wright, *supra* note 1, at 230 n.18; *infra* §§ 15.1, 17.2 (amendment to cure formal defects). *See also* FED. R. CIV. P. 21; Graham v. Broglin, 922 F.2d 379, 382 (7th Cir. 1991) (when petitioner makes mistake in form of habeas corpus pleading that has no impact on court's jurisdiction or treatment of case, "either he should be given leave to plead over or the mislabeling should simply be ignored"); Aschan v. Auger, 861 F.2d 520, 521 n.2 (8th Cir. 1988) (if custodian dies while petition is pending, acting custodian is automatically substituted as respondent pursuant to FED. R. CIV. P. 25(d)(1)). *But see* Olson v. California, 423 F.2d 1326 (9th Cir. 1970) (*dicta*) (improper party respondent is jurisdictional defect).

[17] *See* 28 U.S.C. § 2241(a) (1994); *infra* § 10.2 (personal jurisdiction and venue); Miller v. Hambrick, 905 F.2d 259, 260, 262 (9th Cir. 1990) (citing authority from various circuits) (transfer of prisoner who was permanently incarcerated in federal prison in Texas to California facility pursuant to writ of habeas corpus *ad testificandum* does not give California court jurisdiction either to stay prisoner's transfer back to Texas or to hear habeas corpus action challenging prisoner's original incarceration); Sabias v. Meese, 835 F.2d 1288 (9th Cir. 1987) (petitioner allegedly taken to Mexico by United States officials is in custody, but actual custodian, not Attorney General, is proper party respondent; because actual custodian is in Mexico, hence is not amenable to service or to power of court, personal jurisdiction is lacking); Monk v. Secretary of the Navy, 793 F.2d 364 (D.C. Cir. 1986) (improper custodian and absence of personal jurisdiction). *See also* Ex parte Hayes, 414 U.S. 1327, 1328 (1973) (Douglas, Circuit Justice, in chambers) (absence of person with custody over applicant in district of court entertaining petition is jurisdictional defect); Guerra v. Meese, 786 F.2d 414, 417 (D.C. Cir. 1986); Hanahan v. Luther, 760 F.2d 148, 151 (7th Cir. 1985) (petitioner transferred to facility outside of jurisdiction of district court after adjudication of petition may not reopen petition because district court lacks jurisdiction over new custodian). *But cf. Bozeman v. Lambert, supra,* 587 F. Supp. at 1023-24 (court with personal jurisdiction over respondent actually named — who is official most able to provide relief sought but whom state law does not identify as proper custodian of paroled petitioners — refuses to dismiss or transfer already adjudicated petition, because: (1) defect, if any, goes to venue, not jurisdiction, (2) state originally

not appropriate. Instead, assuming the state has properly preserved the issue, the petition should be transferred to the appropriate court.[18]

§ 10.2. Personal jurisdiction, venue, transfer.[1]

a. *Introduction.* The federal habeas corpus statutes allow "the Supreme Court, any justice thereof, the district courts and any circuit judge" to grant writs of habeas corpus *"within their respective jurisdictions."*[2] The following discussion addresses the question of what those "respective jurisdictions" are, and, more specifically, which federal courts have personal jurisdiction to hear, and which court is the appropriate venue for, a federal habeas corpus petition.[3]

b. *Personal jurisdiction.* In 1948, in *Ahrens v. Clark,*[4] the Supreme Court held that personal jurisdiction over a federal habeas corpus petition lies exclusively in the single federal judicial district in which *both* the custodian of the prisoner *and* the prisoner reside. In *Braden v. 30th Judicial Circuit Court,*[5] the Supreme Court acted to heal the "self-inflicted judicial wound"[6] worked by *Ahrens'* unusual, plaintiff-focused limitation on personal jurisdiction. Recognizing that the writ of habeas corpus is directed at the person who allegedly has detained the prisoner

---

admitted in its answer that respondent named was proper custodian and did not change its mind until after court granted relief, (3) any defect was inadvertent and "understandable," and (4) dismissal would be wasteful of judicial resources and would delay granting relief to which petitioners are entitled; petitioners ordered to amend petition to name party deemed proper custodian under state law).

[18] *See infra* § 10.2c. *But cf. Chatman-Bey v. Thornburgh, supra,* 864 F.2d at 814 (failure by government to raise naming of improper respondent at correct time waives personal jurisdiction issues); Aziz v. Leferve, 830 F.2d 184, 186 (11th Cir. 1987) (state cannot raise personal jurisdiction defense after previously requesting and obtaining transfer of case on *forum non conveniens* grounds); *infra* § 10.2b n.10.

§ 10.2. [1] *See generally* Note, *Review and Appeal of Forum Non-Conveniens and Venue Transfer Orders,* 59 GEO. WASH. L. REV. 715 (1991); authority cited *supra* § 10.1 n.1.

[2] 28 U.S.C. § 2241(a) (1994) (emphasis added).

[3] Regarding petitions filed with a circuit judge, a Supreme Court Justice, or the Supreme Court itself, see *infra* note 8; *infra* Chapter 40.

[4] 335 U.S. 188 (1948) (although petitioners properly named United States Attorney General as respondent and sued in District of Columbia, district court there has no jurisdiction over habeas corpus action brought by aliens held on Ellis Island in Eastern District of New York). *But cf.* Braden v. 30th Judicial Cir. Ct., 410 U.S. 484, 499-500 (1973) (reinterpreting *Ahrens* as based on *forum non conveniens,* not personal jurisdiction, grounds).

[5] 410 U.S. 484 (1973).

[6] United States ex rel. Sero v. Preiser, 506 F.2d 1115, 1128 (2d Cir. 1974), *cert. denied,* 421 U.S. 921 (1975). *See* Wright, *supra* § 10.1 n.1, at 232.

unlawfully,[7] *Braden* held that a federal court with jurisdiction over the custodian of the prisoner has personal jurisdiction over the petition even if the petitioner is incarcerated outside that court's jurisdiction.[8] In general, therefore, once a federal district judge determines that some appropriate custodian[9] of the

---

[7] *See Braden v. 30th Judicial Cir. Ct., supra,* 410 U.S. at 494-95. *See also* Wales v. Whitney, 114 U.S. 564, 574 (1885), *overruled on other grounds,* Hensley v. Municipal Ct., 411 U.S. 345 (1973); Hanahan v. Luther, 760 F.2d 148, 151 (7th Cir. 1985).

[8] *Braden v. 30th Judicial Cir. Ct., supra,* 410 U.S. at 494-95 (petition was properly filed in Kentucky even though petitioner was incarcerated in Alabama because Kentucky court had filed detainer requiring Alabama officials to give it custody over petitioner when he completed his Alabama sentence and petition challenged Kentucky's violation of speedy trial guarantees). *See* Miller v. Hambrick, 905 F.2d 259, 262 (9th Cir. 1990) (citing authority from various circuits) (although prisoner who was permanently incarcerated in federal prison in Texas was transferred to California facility pursuant to writ of habeas corpus *ad testificandum,* prisoner remained in custody in Northern District of Texas, hence should have filed habeas corpus petition there; writ of habeas corpus *ad testificandum* "authorizes a trip not a change of custodians"); Feldman v. Perrill, 902 F.2d 1445, 1450 (9th Cir. 1990); Dunne v. Henman, 875 F.2d 244, 245-50 (9th Cir. 1989) (when state prisoner who is subject to state and federal sentences and is serving both sentences in prison system of second State (pursuant to contract with sentencing state) alleges that he is "'being required to serve a federal sentence in installments' in violation of due process and the 'separation of powers doctrine,'" challenge is to execution, not imposition, of federal sentence, and petitioner accordingly should file petition in district of actual incarceration; 28 U.S.C. § 2241(d) is not applicable to prisoner serving sentence in State other than State of conviction and sentence); United States ex rel. Meadows v. New York, 426 F.2d 1176, 1179-83 (2d Cir. 1970), *cert. denied,* 401 U.S. 941 (1971); *supra* § 10.1 (defining "custodian"). *See also* Schlanger v. Seamans, 401 U.S. 487, 491 (1971) (federal court in Arizona had no jurisdiction over petition brought by serviceman on temporary duty orders placing him in that State, when neither his commanding officer nor anyone else in chain of command was in the State); Ex parte Endo, 323 U.S. 283, 307 (1944) (court with jurisdiction over proper respondent does not lose jurisdiction when petitioner is removed to another circuit pending appeal from denial of the writ); *infra* §§ 14.1, 36.3 (transfer of prisoner from one facility to another during pendency of proceeding).

Section 2241(a) authorizes "the Supreme Court, any justice thereof, ... and any circuit judge" to grant writs of habeas corpus "within their respective jurisdictions." As interpreted in *Braden v. 30th Judicial Cir. Ct., supra,* this provision gives circuit judges authority to grant writs of habeas corpus directed at custodial officials located anywhere within their judicial circuit and gives Supreme Court Justices and the Supreme Court authority to grant such writs directed at custodial officials located anywhere within the United States and its territories. *See, e.g.,* Demjanjuk v. Meese, 784 F.2d 1114, 1115 (D.C. Cir. 1986) (Bork, J., in chambers). *See generally infra* Chapter 10 (petitions to circuit judges, Supreme Court justices, and Supreme Court).

[9] Although typically the district judge will apply this test to the person the petition names as respondent, mistakes in naming the party respondent are not by themselves jurisdictional. If the petition names the wrong respondent but the court has jurisdiction over at least one proper respondent, the appropriate relief is not dismissal but an order directing that the petition be amended to name the correct respondent. *See, e.g.,* West v. Louisiana, 478 F.2d 1026, 1029, 1031 (5th Cir. 1973), *adhered to en banc,* 510 F.2d 363 (5th Cir. 1975); Ashley v. Washington, 394 F.2d 125, 126 n.1 (9th Cir. 1968); Bozeman v. Lambert, 587 F. Supp. 1021, 1023-24 (M.D. Ala. 1984),

petitioner resides within *the State* in which that judge sits, *Braden* gives the court personal jurisdiction over the petition regardless of where the petitioner actually is detained.[10]

In rare circumstances in which (1) an agency with nationwide authority has custody over the petitioner, (2) the petitioner's nominal custodian resides outside the State in which the petitioner resides, and (3) the petitioner's residence provides the most convenient forum, the courts have concluded that the petitioner's, not the custodian's, residence determines the court with personal jurisdiction.[11] In other circumstances, as when a prisoner is incarcerated in one State but subject to a detainer issued by another State — the facts of *Braden* itself — federal courts in more than one State may have concurrent personal jurisdiction over the action.[12]

---

aff'd, 762 F.2d 1022 (11th Cir. 1985) (*mem.*); Copeland v. Mississippi, 415 F. Supp. 1271, 1272 n.1 (N.D. Miss. 1976); *supra* § 10.1 nn.16-18 and accompanying text. *But see* Olson v. California Adult Parole Auth., 423 F.2d 1326 (1970) (*dicta*).

[10] *See* FED. R. CIV. P. 4(k); Rule 11 of the Rules Governing § 2254 Cases (appropriate and "not inconsistent" Federal Rules of Civil Procedure apply in habeas corpus); United States ex rel. Ruffin v. Mancusi, 300 F. Supp. 686, 687 (E.D.N.Y. 1969); authority cited *supra* note 8. A petition filed in a district court in the State in which the prisoner is in custody is within the personal jurisdiction of that court, although it may not be filed in the proper venue. *See, e.g., Bozeman v. Lambert, supra,* 587 F. Supp. at 1023; *infra* § 10.2d. Venue lies only in the judicial district in which the prisoner either was convicted or currently is in custody. Mistakes as to both jurisdiction and venue are cured by transfer, not dismissal. *See infra* §§ 10.2c, 10.2d. The respondent waives the defenses of lack of personal jurisdiction and improper venue by failing to assert the defenses at the appropriate time. *See* Chatman-Bey v. Thornburgh, 864 F.2d 804, 813 (D.C. Cir. 1988) (to avoid waiver, respondent must raise personal jurisdiction or venue issue in pre-answer motion (*see* FED. R. CIV. P. 12(b)) or in responsive pleading (*see* FED. R. CIV. P. 12(h)(1))); Aziz v. Leferve, 830 F.2d 184, 186 (11th Cir. 1987) (state cannot raise personal jurisdiction defense in transferee court after successfully seeking transfer of case to that court on *forum non conveniens* grounds).

[11] *See* Strait v. Laird, 406 U.S. 341, 344-46 (1972) (inactive army reservist residing in California properly brought habeas corpus petition in that State seeking discharge as conscientious objector, although his commanding officer resided in Indiana; officer in Indiana held to be acting through officers in California); Eisel v. Secretary of Army, 477 F.2d 1251, 1263-66 (D.C. Cir. 1973).

[12] When, for example, a prisoner incarcerated in State A is challenging a subsequent conviction or other restraint imposed by State B, federal courts in the proper venues (see *infra* § 10.2d) in both State A and State B may have "concurrent habeas corpus jurisdiction." *Braden v. 30th Judicial Cir. Ct., supra,* 410 U.S. at 499 n.15. *See, e.g.,* Thompson v. Missouri Bd. of Parole, 929 F.2d 396, 398-401 (8th Cir. 1991); Parette v. Lockhart, 927 F.2d 366, 366-67 & n.2 (8th Cir. 1991) (Arkansas federal court improperly concluded that it lacked jurisdiction to hear Arkansas prisoner's habeas corpus challenge to detainer filed by Louisiana with Arkansas prison officials; transfer to Louisiana court for convenient-forum reasons might be appropriate). *Compare Braden v. 30th Judicial Cir. Ct., supra,* 410 U.S. at 493-501 (federal court in State B has jurisdiction when officials of that State have lodged a detainer against petitioner with prison officials in State A, thereby placing prisoner in putative custody of State B) *with* Nelson v. George, 399 U.S. 224

In most other circumstances, federal district courts outside the State in which the custodian of the petitioner resides do not have personal jurisdiction over

---

(1970) (federal court in State A has jurisdiction when prison officials in State A rely on challenged State B conviction to deny parole). Some courts have held, however, that a writ issued by the federal courts in State A only binds the officials in State A with custody of the prisoner and does not bind officials in State B. *See, e.g.,* Norris v. Georgia, 522 F.2d 1006, 1011 (4th Cir. 1975); Wingo v. Ciccone, 507 F.2d 354, 356-57 (8th Cir. 1974). *But cf. Norris v. Georgia, supra* at 1011 n.10 (jurisdiction over out-of-state warden might be obtained if in-state warden were served in capacity as agent for out-of-state warden). Under this view, an action brought in federal court in State B only results in the issuance of the writ to officials in State B and does not bind officials in State A. *See, e.g.,* Marks v. Rees, 715 F.2d 372, 374 (7th Cir. 1983) (Kentucky prisoner attacking constitutionality of prior Indiana conviction to prevent its use to increase Kentucky sentence must bring action in federal court in Kentucky, as only that court has jurisdiction to issue order binding Kentucky officials); Harris v. Ingram, 683 F.2d 97, 98 (4th Cir. 1982); Hanson v. Cir. Ct., 591 F.2d 404, 409 (7th Cir.), *cert. denied,* 444 U.S. 907 (1979); Noll v. Nebraska, 537 F.2d 967, 970 (8th Cir. 1976) *(per curiam);* Craig v. Beto, 458 F.2d 1131, 1134 (5th Cir. 1972). *See also* Sammons v. Rodgers, 785 F.2d 1343, 1345 (5th Cir. 1986) *(dicta).* A persuasive argument can be made that the above view is an unduly narrow interpretation of *Braden* and that the writ should bind officials in both states. *See Norris v. Georgia, supra* at 1014-19 (Winter, J., dissenting). Nonetheless, if petitioner's goal is to forestall officials in State A from relying in some way on an unconstitutional conviction in State B, the petitioner should file in federal court in State A after exhausting judicial remedies in the courts of State A. *See* Feldman v. Perrill, 902 F.2d 1445, 1448, 1450 (9th Cir. 1990); Lowery v. Young, 887 F.2d 1309, 1311 (7th Cir. 1989); *Nelson v. George, supra; Sammons v. Rodgers, supra;* Cooper v. Lockhart, 489 F.2d 308, 311-12 (8th Cir. 1973). If the petitioner's action in the federal court in State A succeeds, the federal court in State A thereupon should order officials in that State to give no effect to both the State B conviction and any detainer filed with them by State B based on the challenged conviction. *Cf. Cooper v. Lockhart, supra* at 317 n.16 (State A officials not forbidden to notify State B officials of prisoner's release date, enabling State B officials to secure petitioner's arrest and extradition after his release in State A). The preference for suing in a district court in the State of incarceration, not in the State that imposed the prior conviction, is reinforced by the Supreme Court's ruling in Maleng v. Cook, 490 U.S. 488 (1989) *(per curiam),* discussed *supra* § 8.2c, that there is no subject matter jurisdiction over a prisoner's challenge to a prior conviction if custody under that conviction has terminated. In the wake of *Maleng,* the lower federal courts have required petitions attacking prior convictions for which custody has lapsed but that are being used in some way to lengthen current custody under another conviction to challenge the *current* custody as enhanced by the allegedly improper prior conviction. *See supra* §§ 8.2c, 8.2d n.29 and accompanying text. On the other hand, if as in *Braden* itself, the prisoner seeks an order forbidding officials in State B to incarcerate petitioner there upon his release from prison in State A, he should bring the action in the federal court in State B after exhausting judicial remedies in the courts of State B.

Concurrent jurisdiction also may exist if more than one law-enforcement, military, or other official fairly can be said to be the petitioner's custodian and if the various custodians reside in different States. *See, e.g., Braden v. 30th Judicial Cir. Ct., supra,* 410 U.S. at 499-500 (immigration officials) (discussing Ahrens v. Clark, 335 U.S. 188 (1948)); Strait v. Laird, 406 U.S. 341, 342-46 (1972) (military officials); authorities cited *supra* § 10.1 n.17.

---

habeas corpus actions brought by the petitioner.[13] If a petitioner properly brings a habeas corpus action in a particular district, then, for reasons not related to the petition, the petitioner is transferred to a district in another state while the petition is pending, the court in which the petition originally was filed retains personal jurisdiction and remains the appropriate venue.[14]

---

[13] *See, e.g.*, Schlanger v. Seamans, 401 U.S. 487, 487-92 (1971) (federal court in Arizona had no jurisdiction to hear habeas corpus petition of enlisted man on temporary duty in that State because no one in chain of command resided there); Brittingham v. United States, 982 F.2d 378, 379-80 (9th Cir. 1992); Hogan v. Iowa, 952 F.2d 224, 225 & n.2 (8th Cir. 1991); United States v. Gabor, 905 F.2d 76, 78 & n.2 (5th Cir. 1990); *Feldman v. Perrill, supra*, 902 F.2d at 1448, 1450; Dunne v. Henman, 875 F.2d 244, 245-50 (9th Cir. 1989); *Chatman-Bey v. Thornburgh, supra*, 864 F.2d at 810-11 (personal jurisdiction lacking because petitioner filed challenges to parole decisions in Washington, D.C. and named Parole Commission and Attorney General as respondents, rather than filing petition in district of incarceration and naming actual custodian as respondent); Sabias v. Meese, 835 F.2d 1288 (9th Cir. 1987) (petitioner allegedly taken to Mexico by United States officials is in custody, but actual custodian, not Attorney General, is proper party respondent; because actual custodian is in Mexico, hence not amenable to service or to power of court, personal jurisdiction is lacking); Hanahan v. Luther, 760 F.2d 148, 151 (7th Cir. 1985) (petitioner seeking sentence credit based on prior custody in Illinois after *certiorari* was denied on Illinois habeas corpus claim must file new petition naming present custodian in Indiana, over whom Illinois federal court lacks jurisdiction); Guerra v. Meese, 786 F.2d 414, 415-417 (D.C. Cir. 1986) (because named respondent parole commission cannot properly be characterized as custodian, and no other custodians can be found in District of Columbia, federal courts in D.C. Circuit lack personal jurisdiction over petitioner). *See also Feldman v. Perrill, supra*, 902 F.2d at 1450 (if petitioner is challenging administration of parole, personal jurisdiction lies only in district courts in State — and venue lies only in district court in district — in which agency administering parole is located; petitioner's residence in another State, and fact that petition challenges legality of prior conviction in another State that is being used to extend parole, does not give personal jurisdiction or venue to district court located where petitioner resides or where prior conviction occurred).

[14] *See Ahrens v. Clark, supra*, 335 U.S. at 193, *overruled on other grounds*, Braden v. 30th Judicial Cir. Ct., 410 U.S. 484 (1973); Jackson v. Brennan, 924 F.2d 725, 727 n.2 (7th Cir. 1991); Barden v. Keohane, 921 F.2d 476, 477 n.1 (3d Cir. 1990) (unauthorized transfer — *i.e.*, transfer absent application pursuant to FED. R. APP. P. 23(a) — does not affect court's jurisdiction to hear petition as long as court had jurisdiction on date when petition originally was filed); Miller v. Hambrick, 905 F.2d 259, 262 (9th Cir. 1990) (filing of petition in Northern District of Texas, where petitioner was permanently incarcerated, would have preserved jurisdiction there, notwithstanding petitioner's transfer to prison in California pursuant to writ of habeas corpus *ad testificandum;* although petitioner, instead, improperly filed action challenging Texas incarceration in California court, latter court had authority to transfer case to Texas district court); Francis v. Rison, 894 F.2d 353, 354 (9th Cir. 1990); *Chatman-Bey v. Thornburgh, supra*, 864 F.2d at 806 n.1; Schiselman v. United States Parole Comm'n, 858 F.2d 1232, 1235 n.3 (7th Cir. 1988) (transfer of federal prisoner to state prison in different circuit does not affect jurisdiction); *infra* §§ 14.1, 36.3 (transfer). On the question of where to file a challenge to a prior conviction in a jurisdiction other than the jurisdiction of incarceration when the prior conviction is being used to enhance a current sentence in the jurisdiction of incarceration, see *supra* note 12; *supra* §§ 8.2c, 8.2d n.29 and accompanying text.

c. *Transfer, not dismissal.* If the petitioner files in a district court without personal jurisdiction, the appropriate remedy is not dismissal but transfer to the proper court.[15] This approach tracks the rule, applicable in federal civil cases generally, that a court's power to transfer a case to an appropriate forum exists even if the court does not have personal jurisdiction over the matter.[16]

d. *Venue and convenient forum.* Personal jurisdiction is only the first "proper forum" hurdle the petitioner must clear. It is possible that a given district court either (1) has personal jurisdiction over a habeas corpus petition yet must order

---

[15] *See, e.g.,* Miller v. Hambrick, 905 F.2d 259, 262 (9th Cir. 1990) (**citing FHCPP**) (after prisoner who was permanently incarcerated in Texas prison but was temporarily residing in California facility pursuant to writ of habeas corpus *ad testificandum* improperly filed petition in Central District of California, proper remedy was not to dismiss petition but instead to transfer it to Northern District of Texas; *sua sponte* transfer appropriate even though petitioner did not request it; although district court's decision not to transfer is reviewable only for abuse of discretion, abuse found because district court failed to exercise discretion; remand not needed because record before appellate court showed plainly that transfer rather than dismissal was in interests of justice); Aziz v. Leferve, 830 F.2d 184, 185 (11th Cir. 1987); Demjanjuk v. Meese, 784 F.2d 1114, 1115 (D.C. Cir. 1986) (Bork, J., in chambers) (transfer is usual response unless court concludes that petition is frivolous and a transfer pointless, in which case, dismissal on the merits is appropriate); Gist v. Henderson, 401 F. Supp. 819, 819 (W.D.N.Y. 1975); United States ex rel. Ayala v. Tubman, 366 F. Supp. 1268, 1270 (E.D.N.Y. 1973); United States ex rel. Ruffin v. Mancusi, 300 F. Supp. 686, 687 (E.D.N.Y. 1969); authority cited *supra* § 10.1. *See also* United States v. Ammar, 919 F.2d 13, 15 (3d Cir. 1990) (district court transferred habeas corpus petition filed in district of incarceration, which should have been filed as section 2255 motion in sentencing court, to sentencing district); United States ex rel. Sero v. Preiser, 506 F.2d 1115, 1128 (2d Cir. 1974), *cert. denied,* 421 U.S. 921 (1975) (transfer on convenience grounds); Meadows v. New York, 426 F.2d 1176, 1183 n.9 (2d Cir. 1970), *cert. denied,* 401 U.S. 941 (1971).

Respondent's waiver of personal jurisdiction or venue permits the court in which the petition originally is filed to hear a case notwithstanding a lack of personal jurisdiction or venue over the case. *See, e.g.,* authority cited *supra* § 10.2b n.10. *See also* United States v. Garcia-Gutierrez, 835 F.2d 585, 586 (5th Cir. 1988) (judicial economy warrants decision on merits by court without personal jurisdiction).

[16] *See, e.g.,* Goldlawr, Inc. v. Heiman, 369 U.S. 463, 466, 467 (1962) (dismissal is "time-consuming and justice-defeating"). *See* Federal Courts Improvement Act, 28 U.S.C. § 1631 (1994) (if federal court lacks personal jurisdiction, it "shall transfer" action to court with jurisdiction if doing so is in "interest of justice"); *Miller v. Hambrick, supra,* 905 F.2d at 262 (**citing FHCPP**) (applying section 1631 in habeas corpus case and noting that transfer, rather than dismissal, generally is in "interest of justice" to avoid delay and complication); In re McCauley, 814 F.2d 1350 (9th Cir. 1987); American Beef Packers Inc. v. ICC, 711 F.2d 388, 389 (D.C. Cir. 1988); United States ex rel. Ruffin v. Mancusi, 300 F. Supp. 686, 687 (E.D.N.Y. 1969). *Cf.* Hogan v. Iowa, 952 F.2d 224, 225 & n.2 (8th Cir. 1991) (because district court not only lacked personal jurisdiction but also lacked subject matter jurisdiction to consider challenge to expired sentence, *see supra* § 8.2c, petition dismissed without prejudice to refiling in proper district as challenge to current sentence as enhanced by prior conviction).

the case transferred to another district on statutory venue grounds;[17] or (2) has personal jurisdiction over the action and is a statutorily proper venue for it, but nonetheless will transfer the case to another court on grounds of convenience.[18]

---

[17] *See, e.g.,* Parette v. Lockhart, 927 F.2d 366, 366-67 (8th Cir. 1991) (*dicta*); Bozeman v. Lambert, 587 F. Supp. 1021, 1023 (M.D. Ala. 1984), *aff'd,* 762 F.2d 1022 (11th Cir. 1985) (*mem.*) (*dicta*); United States ex rel. Ruffin v. Mancusi, 300 F. Supp. 686, 686-687 (E.D.N.Y. 1969).

[18] *See, e.g.,* Braden v. 30th Judicial Cir. Ct., 410 U.S. 484, 499 n.15 (1973); United States ex rel. Meadows v. New York, 426 F.2d 1176, 1183 n.9 (2d Cir. 1970). If a petitioner properly brings a habeas corpus action in a particular venue, then, for reasons not related to the petition, is transferred to another venue while the petition is pending, the court in which the petition originally was filed remains the proper venue. *See supra* § 10.2b n.14 and accompanying text. A court may transfer a petition on convenience grounds *sua sponte.* The proper procedure in such cases is for the transferring court to issue an order to show cause prior to transferring the case in order to provide the parties an opportunity to respond and adduce evidence. *See* Chatman-Bey v. Thornburgh, 864 F.2d 804, 814 (D.C. Cir. 1988). Although orders transferring cases from one district to another pursuant to 28 U.S.C. § 1404(a) (1994) (*see infra* notes 24-27 and accompanying text (applicability of section 1404(a) in habeas corpus context)) are interlocutory hence not appealable until the case is finally decided, *see* Van Cauwenberghe v. Biard, 486 U.S. 517, 527 (1988); Roofing & Sheet Metal Services, Inc. v. La Quinta Motor Inns, Inc., 689 F.2d 982, 987 (11th Cir. 1982), the failure to consider the appropriate factors in ruling on a transfer motion or the failure to afford the aggrieved party notice of a proposed *sua sponte* transfer and an opportunity to respond with relevant evidence and argument may constitute clear error cognizable on mandamus. *See, e.g.,* Van Dusen v. Barrack, 376 U.S. 612, 622, 646 (1964) (transfer decision reversed on mandamus because "District Court ignored certain considerations which ... might have been considered controlling"); Hustler Magazine, Inc. v. United States Dist. Ct., 790 F.2d 69, 71 (10th Cir. 1986) (mandamus granted and district court's section 1404(a) decision overturned due to district court's failure to hold hearing and to consider "interests of justice and the convenience of the parties and the witnesses" as required by 28 U.S.C. § 1404(a)); *id.* at 73 (McKay, J., concurring) ("until the trial court affords petitioners a full hearing on the issue, and conscientiously considers the factors set forth in § 1404(a), it has not fulfilled its statutory duty" and "it is appropriate for us to invoke the extraordinary remedy of mandamus"); Roofing & Sheet Metal Services, Inc. v. La Quinta Motor Inns, Inc., supra at 987-88 (citing cases) ("courts of appeals have been particularly hospitable to petitions for mandamus challenging transfer orders entered, as the one in this case was, without a hearing"); In re Nine Mile Limited, 673 F.2d 242, 243-44 (8th Cir. 1982) (failure to give party aggrieved by *sua sponte* transfer opportunity to file reconsideration motion constitutes abuse of discretion justifying mandamus relief); Schwilm v. Holbrook, 661 F.2d 12, 16 (3d Cir. 1981) (section 1404(a) transfer decision by district court reversed because lower court considered improper factors and failed to consider proper ones); Starnes v. McGuire, 512 F.2d 918, 925-26 (D.C. Cir. 1974) ("statement of reasons" why district court transferred habeas corpus case is "essential when the basis for transfer cannot by inferred from the record with reasonable certainty"); Fine v. McGuire, 433 F.2d 499, 501, 502 (D.C. Cir. 1970) (habeas corpus case; similar to *Nine Mile Limited, supra*); Hite v. Norwegian Caribbean Lines, 551 F. Supp. 390, 393 (E.D. Mich. 1982) (*sua sponte* transfer is forbidden absent notice and opportunity to be heard); 15 CHARLES ALAN WRIGHT, ARTHUR R. MILLER & EDWARD H. COOPER, FEDERAL PRACTICE AND PROCEDURE (Civil) § 3844, at 338-39 (2d ed. 1986) (upon suggestion of transfer, "parties should be given an opportunity to make their views known and to oppose the motion"; hearing preferred "if

Ahrens, discussed in subsection b above, not only restricted personal jurisdiction, but also venue, confining both to the judicial district in which the prisoner was in custody. In 1966, Congress enacted 28 U.S.C. § 2241(d), which overruled *Ahrens* as to venue over petitions filed by a prisoner in a district court in the State — but not the judicial district — in which the prisoner is detained. Under section 2241(d), venue is appropriate in both the district in which the prisoner is in *custody* and the district in which he was *convicted and sentenced.*[19] After *Braden,* section 2241(d) is best understood, not as a statute limiting the federal courts' personal jurisdiction to something less than the scope of their power to effectuate service statewide under Rule 4(k) of the Federal Rules of Civil Procedure,[20] but rather as a provision designed to expand habeas corpus venue to include not only the district of incarceration (the *Ahrens* rule) but also the district of conviction and sentence.[21] Section 2241(d)'s legislative history

---

the evidence and arguments for and against transfer are in doubt"; court should "make findings specifically relating the evidence upon which it relies to the factors stated in § 1404(a)").

[19] 28 U.S.C. § 2241(d) (1994) ("Where an application for a writ of habeas corpus is made by a person in custody under the judgment and sentence of a State court of a State which contains two or more Federal judicial districts, the application may be filed in the district court for the district wherein such person is in custody or in the district court for the district within which the State court was held which convicted and sentenced him and each of such district courts shall have concurrent jurisdiction to entertain the application. The district court for the district wherein such an application is filed in the exercise of its discretion and in furtherance of justice may transfer the application to the other district court for hearing and determination."). *See, e.g.,* Dobard v. Johnson, 749 F.2d 1503, 1504 (11th Cir. 1985); Irving v. Breazeale, 265 F. Supp. 116, 120 n.9 (S.D. Miss. 1967), *modified on other grounds,* 400 F.2d 231 (5th Cir. 1968). *Compare* Story v. Collins, 920 F.2d 1247, 1250-51 (5th Cir. 1991) (state prisoner challenging denial of good-time credits may file either in district of incarceration or in district of conviction) *with* Feldman v. Perrill, 902 F.2d 1445, 1450 (9th Cir. 1990) (proper venue for petition challenging administration of parole is district in which agency administering parole is located) *with* Mikolon v. United States, 844 F.2d 456, 460-61 (7th Cir. 1988) (in challenge to Parole Commission decision, proper venue is district court of incarceration). *Cf.* Dunne v. Henman, 875 F.2d 244, 245-50 (9th Cir. 1989) (discussed *supra* § 10.2b n.8) (28 U.S.C. § 2241(d) (1994) is not applicable to prisoner serving sentence in State other than State of conviction and sentence; in such cases, proper venue is district of actual incarceration).

[20] FED. R. CIV. P. 4(k).

[21] *See, e.g.,* In re Green, 39 F.3d 582, 583-84 (5th Cir. 1994) (pursuant to 28 U.S.C. § 2241(d), petitioner had choice of filing petition in either district in which he was incarcerated or district in which trial and sentencing took place; statutory phrase "district within which the ... [petitioner was] convicted and sentenced" did not authorize filing of petition in third district in which indictment was filed but which did not serve as site of trial or sentencing); Thompson v. Missouri Bd. of Parole, 929 F.2d 396, 398-401 (8th Cir. 1991); *Parette v. Lockhart, supra,* 927 F.2d at 366-67 (subject to convenient-forum considerations, federal district court in either Arkansas or Louisiana is proper venue for petition filed by prisoner incarcerated in Arkansas challenging Louisiana detainer filed with Arkansas prison officials based on Louisiana conviction); United States ex rel.

makes clear that Congress intended the provision to *broaden* the number of federal courts available to hear habeas corpus petitions and thereby to allow a more even and efficient distribution of such cases among the federal courts in a given State and to enable those courts to choose the most convenient forum for conducting hearings.[22]

Before assuming that a prisoner incarcerated in a federal district different from the district of conviction has a choice of courts in which to file the petition, counsel or the prisoner should consult the local rules and prevailing practice in the relevant district courts. The local rules sometimes make the section 2241(d) choice *for* the petitioner, typically requiring the prisoner to file the petition in the federal judicial district — and even the division within that district — in which the prisoner was convicted.[23] Even if no local rule governs, the district court in which the petition is filed has "discretion" under section 2241(d) to transfer the petition to another appropriate venue "for hearing and determination."

Similarly, if the petition was filed in the less convenient of two districts with venue — for example, because critical witnesses reside in the other district or a court in the other district has granted a hearing on a claim similar to one of petitioner's claims where consolidation of the two cases is appropriate — a party may move under section 2241(d) to transfer the case to the more convenient forum.[24] In exercising its section 2241(d) discretion with regard to transfer, the court should rely on traditional *forum non conveniens* principles, which require the court to balance the interests of the parties, the witnesses, and the courts in

---

Sero v. Preiser, 506 F.2d 1115, 1127 (2d Cir. 1974) *cert. denied,* 421 U.S. 921 (1975); *Bozeman v. Lambert, supra,* 587 F. Supp. at 1023 (citing authority); Wright, *supra* § 10.1 n.1, at 231-32.

[22] *See* Silver v. Dunbar, 264 F. Supp. 177, 180 (S.D. Cal. 1967).

[23] *See infra* § 41.4c (venue rules under 28 U.S.C.A. § 2255 (West 1994 & Supp. 1998)). *See, e.g.,* E.D. CAL. RULE 191(g) ("Subject to the provisions of 28 U.S.C. § 2241(d), it is the policy of this Court that a petition should be heard in the district in which petitioner was convicted rather than in the district of petitioner's present confinement.").

[24] *See also* 28 U.S.C. § 1404(a) (1994) (court may transfer case from one proper venue to another "in the interest of justice"); Braden v. 30th Judicial Cir. Ct., 410 U.S. 484, 494 n.15 (1973); Brewer v. Swinson, 837 F.2d 802, 804 (8th Cir. 1988) (8th Circuit exercised its concurrent jurisdiction to hear claim of locally incarcerated petitioner who was named in class action pending in D.C. Circuit challenging Parole Commission decision, because parole rehearing date was fast approaching and D.C. case was far from resolved); Aziz v. Leferve, 830 F.2d 184, 186 (11th Cir. 1987) (New York prisoner's petition challenging prior conviction in Florida transferred to Florida on respondent's motion; respondent thereby waived Florida court's lack of personal jurisdiction or venue); Milstead v. Rison, 702 F.2d 216, 217 (11th Cir. 1983); Bell v. Watkins, 692 F.2d 999, 1013 (5th Cir. 1982), *cert. denied,* 464 U.S. 843 (1983); Noonan v. Smith, 375 F. Supp. 925, 926 (W.D.N.Y. 1974); United States ex rel. Hammen v. Mazurkiewicz, 303 F. Supp. 629, 630-31 (E.D. Pa. 1969). The circumstances described in text also support transfer from one division within a district to another or (if consolidation is appropriate) from one judge to another. *See infra* § 11.4b.

having the case adjudicated in one forum or the other.[25] Applying those principles, the courts have recognized the location of witnesses, the desire to hold the hearing closer to petitioner's place of incarceration,[26] the convenience of counsel, and other factors as justifying transfer.[27] The timeliness *vel non* of the motion to transfer also may affect the likelihood of court-ordered transfer.

---

[25] *See* Parker v. Singletary, 974 F.2d 1562, 1582 & n.118 (11th Cir. 1992) (when deciding whether to transfer habeas corpus petition under section 2241(d), district court should "giv[e] careful consideration to the convenience of witnesses"); *Parette v. Lockhart, supra,* 927 F.2d at 367 n.2. *See generally* 28 U.S.C. § 1404(a) (1994); American Dredging Co. v. Miller, 510 U.S. 443, 448 (1994) (in applying *forum non conveniens* doctrine, "'[i]mportant considerations are the relative ease of access to sources of proof; availability of compulsory process for attendance of unwilling, and the cost of obtaining attendance of willing, witnesses; possibility of view of premises, if view would be appropriate to the action; and all other practical problems that make trial of a case easy, expeditious and inexpensive'" (quoting Gulf Oil Corp. v. Gilbert, 330 U.S. 501 (1947)); Piper Aircraft Co. v. Reyno, 454 U.S. 235 (1981); Baris v. Sulpicio Lines, Inc., 932 F.2d 1540, 1549-52 (5th Cir.), *cert. denied,* 502 U.S. 963 (1991) (detailed review of criteria relevant to *forum non conveniens* analysis; applying 5th Circuit requirement that "district court ... set out its findings and conclusions supporting" dismissal or transfer on convenient-forum grounds to permit "meaningful appellate review"); Lockman Foundation v. Evangelical Alliance Mission, 930 F.2d 764, 767-71 (9th Cir. 1991) (reviewing *forum non conveniens* criteria; district court determination reviewed for abuse of discretion). Court "congestion alone is not sufficient reason for transfer." Starnes v. McGuire, 512 F.2d 918, 932 (D.C. Cir. 1974) (*en banc*). *Cf.* In re Chesson, 897 F.2d 156, 159 (5th Cir. 1990) (*per curiam*) (in direct appeal of criminal judgment, court holds that when deciding in which division of district to hold trial, "convenience of the defendant and the witnesses and the prompt administration of justice" must be balanced; latter factor includes consideration of court's docket as a whole); decisions cited *infra* note 27. An order granting or denying a motion to transfer on *forum non conveniens* grounds is not a collateral order subject to appeal as a final judgment under 28 U.S.C. § 1291 (1994). *See* Van Cauwenberghe v. Biard, 486 U.S. 517, 527-30 (1988); Michael v. INS, 48 F.3d 657, 661 (2d Cir. 1995) (transfer of habeas corpus petition to another district that "had jurisdiction over [petition] ... is an interlocutory order that is unappealable absent the necessary district court certification"); Van Orman v. Purkett, 43 F.3d 1201, 1202-03 (8th Cir. 1994) (district court's order transferring habeas corpus petition to district in which trial and sentencing took place over objection that witnesses were located in district of confinement was not "final, appealable order"; transfer order "may be reviewed ... for abuse of discretion in any appeal that Van Orman may take from the final disposition of his habeas petition"). Interlocutory review is available, if at all, pursuant to the certified appeal provision in 28 U.S.C. § 1292(b) (1994) and the extraordinary remedy of mandamus, *see supra* note 18.

[26] The prisoner has a statutory right to be present at evidentiary proceedings. *See* 28 U.S.C. § 2243 (1994); *infra* § 21.3.

[27] *See* Story v. Collins, 920 F.2d 1247, 1250 (5th Cir. 1991) (access to "necessary records and witnesses" and relief for courts with "inordinate proportion of habeas petitions" are legitimate grounds for choice of venue on basis of "convenient forum" considerations); Bell v. Watkins, 692 F. 2d 999, 1013 (5th Cir. 1982), *cert. denied,* 464 U.S. 843 (1983) (accessibility of evidence at site of conviction and overburdened court at site of incarceration are legitimate grounds for transfer); Wilkins v. Erickson, 484 F.2d 969, 973 (8th Cir. 1973) (availability of witnesses and records); Silver v. Dunbar, 264 F. Supp. 177 (S.D. Cal. 1967) (*dicta*) (redistribution of judicial workloads).

Should the petitioner file the petition in the wrong district or division, either because section 2241(d) does not provide for venue in that district, because a local rule prescribes a different venue, or because some other venue is found to be more convenient, the appropriate response is for the district court in which the petition was filed to transfer the petition to the appropriate district or division.[28] Dismissal is not appropriate in these circumstances.[29]

See also Developments in the Law, supra § 10.1 n.1, at 1160-61 (argument favoring transfer to district of conviction).

[28] *See* 28 U.S.C. § 2241(d) (1994); In re Green, 39 F.3d 582, 584 (5th Cir. 1994); *Parette v. Lockhart, supra,* 927 F.2d at 366-67 (*dicta*); United States ex rel. Sero v. Preiser, 506 F.2d 1115, 1128 (2d Cir. 1974), *cert. denied,* 421 U.S. 921 (1975); *supra* notes 24-27. *See generally* Wright, *supra* § 10.1 n.1, at 231-32.

[29] *See, e.g.,* Gist v. Henderson, 401 F. Supp. 819, 819 (W.D.N.Y. 1975); authority cited *supra* § 10.1 nn.16-18 and accompanying text. *See also American Dredging Co. v. Miller, supra,* 510 U.S. at 453 ("venue is a matter that goes to process rather than substantive rights"; same characterization applies to *forum non conveniens,* which "is nothing more or less than a supervening venue provision, permitting displacement of the ordinary rules of venue when, in light of certain conditions, the trial court thinks that jurisdiction ought to be declined").

Chapter 11

THE PETITION

§ 11.1. Exhaustion (reprise): implications for timing and claim selection.[1]

The "exhaustion of state remedies" doctrine generally forbids habeas corpus consideration of claims that the petitioner has not presented in the state courts.[2] The "total exhaustion" aspect of the doctrine generally forbids courts to review the federal habeas corpus petition as a whole if any single claim or part of a claim in it is not "exhausted."[3] This section briefly addresses the question of what a lawyer or prisoner investigating and selecting claims for inclusion in a federal habeas corpus petition should do upon discovering that some of the prisoner's colorable federal claims have not been exhausted (or fully exhausted) in state court proceedings.[4]

Several alternative procedures are or may be available in this situation:

(1) The prisoner may exhaust the new claims in state courts[5] before filing a federal petition.[6]

(2) In a capital case in which the prisoner is indigent and is unrepresented by counsel, or is represented by volunteer counsel who has not yet had the

---

§ 11.1. [1] The exhaustion doctrine is discussed *supra* §§ 5.1, 5.3, 6.2, 6.3 and, in detail, *infra* Chapter 23. Timing considerations are discussed at length *supra* Chapter 5.

[2] For a brief overview of the exhaustion doctrine and its exceptions, see *infra* § 23.1. For a comprehensive treatment, see Chapter 23 as a whole.

[3] *See infra* §§ 23.1 nn.3, 15-16 and accompanying text, 23.5. As these sections explain, a narrow exception to the rule of total exhaustion permits a federal court to reach — and reject — both exhausted and unexhausted claims if the court determines that all claims in the petition lack merit.

[4] By placing so much emphasis on the importance of a fresh and comprehensive investigation following state direct appeal and postconviction proceedings and in advance of preparing and filing a federal habeas corpus petition, and by authorizing district courts to appoint counsel in most *capital* cases even before a petition is filed so that a full prefiling investigation may occur, *see supra* § 5.1b nn.80-91 and accompanying text; *infra* §§ 12.3a, 13.1-13.2b, the majority in McFarland v. Scott, 512 U.S. 849, 854-59 (1994), clearly contemplated the possibility that entirely new, and thus probably unexhausted, claims will be discovered at this stage. *See id.* at 869-70 (Thomas, J., dissenting) (alluding to this assumption on majority's part). *See also* Collins v. Byrd, 510 U.S. 1185, 1185-88 (1994) (*mem.*) (Scalia, J., dissenting from denial of application to vacate stay) (describing 6th Circuit order, which majority of Court declined to vacate, directing district court to afford capital prisoner 120 days to investigate claims in addition to those pleaded in habeas corpus petition and 60 days to amend petition to include newly discovered claims).

[5] *See infra* Chapter 23.

[6] *See generally supra* § 5.1; *supra* Chapters 6, 7.

time or financial resources[7] needed to conduct a thorough prefiling investigation,[8] the prisoner may:

   (a)   seek federal court appointment of counsel[9] and, if necessary, a stay of execution[10] and, in cases covered by recent legislation creating a statute of limitations, file a federal "Placeholder Petition" within the statutorily specified filing deadline,[11]

   (b)   conduct the necessary investigation, and then

   (c)   choose between options (1) above and (3) below, basing the decision upon the need for a stay of execution and the potential impact additional state court litigation would have on the expiration of any applicable statute of limitations.[12]

  (3) The prisoner may file a federal petition that includes both exhausted and unexhausted claims and ask the court to hold the petition in abeyance while remaining state court remedies are exhausted. This approach is most commonly used in capital cases in which state officials have set and refused to stay an execution date. In that situation, the filing of a federal habeas corpus petition — even one that is not fully exhausted — gives the federal court with jurisdiction over the petition a basis for granting a jurisdiction-preserving stay of execution to permit exhaustion of remaining state remedies to occur while the federal petition is held in abeyance.[13] More recently, noncapital as well as capital prisoners who have filed federal petitions that are timely under recently enacted statutes of limitations, but who discover that claims in the petition are not fully exhausted, have been permitted to use the abeyance, or analogous, procedures to preserve their timely filing date while pursuing additional exhaustion proceedings in the state courts "without prejudice" from the statute of limitations.[14]

---

[7] *See infra* §§ 12.2-12.5, 19.3.

[8] *See infra* § 11.2.

[9] *See infra* §§ 12.2-12.5.

[10] *See infra* §§ 13.1-13.2b.

[11] *See supra* § 5.1b nn.84-91 and accompanying text.

[12] *See infra* notes 25-27.

[13] *See supra* §§ 5.3, 6.3.

[14] *See, e.g.,* Christy v. Horn, 115 F.3d 201, 207 (3d Cir. 1997) (approving procedure of "grant[ing] a stay and abeyance motion" rather than dismissing mixed petition when "state court has refused to grant a stay [of execution] pending its adjudication of a prisoner's federal constitutional claims"); Fetterly v. Paskett, 997 F.2d 1295, 1301-02 (9th Cir. 1993) (district court abused its discretion by refusing to hold federal proceedings in abeyance while petitioner returned to state court to litigate unexhausted claims; "it is understandable that [petitioner] wished to bring all his claims in one pending proceeding rather than move to dismiss and start again when he had

fully exhausted his new issues ... [and] [t]here is nothing at all in this record to suggest that the motion for a stay was brought to vex, or to harass, or that the request was an abuse of the writ"). *See also* Edwards v. Balisok, 117 S. Ct. 1584, 1589 (1997) (suggesting that federal courts are permitted to stay or hold in abeyance, rather than dismiss, previously filed judicial proceedings pending exhaustion of remedies that are prerequisite to final adjudication of previously filed proceedings); Lambrix v. Singletary, 117 S. Ct. 1517, 1522-23, 1523 (1997) (taking apparently approving notice of federal lower court's use of abeyance procedure); Burris v. Farley, 51 F.3d 655, 659 (7th Cir. 1995) (*dicta*) (analogizing to situation in "civil litigation when one or more legal theories is unripe," court suggests that habeas corpus petitioners with partially exhausted claims can "protect themselves" by "filing a petition raising all exhausted issues and asking the court for a stay [of federal proceedings] until the remaining issues have been exhausted"); Rowland v. Calderon, C-94-3037-EFL (N.D. Cal. April 21, 1997) (granting petitioner's request to amend petition to delete unexhausted claims and stay federal proceedings during exhaustion of state remedies). *Cf.* Greenawalt v. Stewart, 105 F.3d 1268, 1273-75 (9th Cir.) (*per curiam*), *cert. denied*, 117 S. Ct. 794 (1997) (district court did not abuse discretion in dismissing mixed petition instead of granting request to hold petition in abeyance pending exhaustion of unexhausted claim); Sterling v. Scott, 57 F.3d 451, 454 (5th Cir. 1995), *cert. denied*, 516 U.S. 1050 (1996) (district court did not abuse discretion in denying request to hold mixed petition in abeyance pending exhaustion of unexhausted claims). *But see* Victor v. Hopkins, 90 F.3d 276, 282 (8th Cir. 1996), *cert. denied*, 117 S. Ct. 1091 (1997) (district court has no authority to hold mixed petition in abeyance; proper procedure is to dismiss petition). Substantial caselaw, discussed *infra* § 13.3, permits the procedure outlined in text. *See also infra* note 28 (citing other references) (procedure if district court denies stay because petition mixes unexhausted and exhausted claims).

The abeyance procedure has most frequently been used by capital prisoners who are attempting to exhaust state remedies but have been denied state court stays of execution and accordingly need *federal* court stays pending exhaustion. *See infra* § 13.3. The procedure is now being used for an additional purpose — in both capital and noncapital cases — namely, to avoid problems created by the combination of the exhaustion rule (*see infra* Chapter 23) and recently enacted statutes of limitations governing the filing of federal habeas corpus petitions (*see supra* §§ 3.3c nn.68-71, 74 and accompanying text, 5.1b). For discussion of the propriety of holding a timely filed federal petition in abeyance pending exhaustion of state remedies when the effect of dismissing the unexhausted petition would or might be to render a subsequently filed federal petition *untimely*, see *supra* §§ 3.4a n.16, 5.1b n.57 and accompanying text; *infra* note 22 and accompanying text.

The prisoner's memorandum and affidavits supporting the motion described in text should explain the failure to exhaust the claim, emphasizing, to the extent possible, the petitioner's (even if not counsel's) lack of responsibility for the failure to exhaust. *See, e.g., Fetterly v. Paskett, supra* at 1301 (grant of petitioner's request to hold federal proceedings in abeyance pending exhaustion was particularly appropriate because failure to exhaust may have been attributable to ineffectiveness of counsel). *See also* McFarland v. Scott, 512 U.S. 849, 854-59 (1994) (acknowledging that counsel generally cannot conduct meaningful prefiling investigation under time and other constraints imposed by setting of execution date soon after prior proceedings ended and close to date set for execution). *See generally infra* § 26.3b (recognized excuses for analogous failures on part of prisoners).

In response to the procedure outlined in text, some attorneys for the state have undertaken to waive the nonexhaustion defense. *See, e.g.,* Felder v. Estelle, 693 F.2d 549, 554 (5th Cir. 1982). In Granberry v. Greer, 481 U.S. 129 (1987), the Supreme Court indicated that the courts may, but need not, accept such waivers. *See infra* note 24; *infra* § 23.2a.

(4) The prisoner may file a federal petition that includes only exhausted claims and simultaneously exhaust the omitted claims in the state courts with the intention of amending[15] the omitted claims into the federal petition after exhaustion proceedings are complete.

(5) The prisoner may file a federal petition that includes only exhausted claims and suspend activity on the omitted claims while the federal petition is adjudicated.[16]

In *noncapital* cases — leaving aside for a moment the statute of limitations issues that are considered below — option (1) is usually preferred. Option (2) is only available in capital cases, and the caselaw supporting option (3) is mainly confined to such cases. Moreover, given the doctrines prohibiting most second or successive federal habeas corpus petitions and their equivalents,[17] options (4) and (5) are strongly discouraged because they create a substantial probability that the claims omitted from the federal petition at the time it was filed will *never* receive federal habeas corpus consideration.[18] Apart from statute of limitations considerations, therefore, option (1) is almost certainly the best approach in noncapital cases, unless the unexhausted claims are so weak, or the length of the custody being challenged is so short, that the risk of losing a federal forum for the unexhausted claims via option (4) or (5) is bearable.[19]

---

[15] *See infra* § 17.2. *But cf.* amendment decisions cited *infra* note 28. On the difficulty of amending petitions filed by capital petitioners whose cases are governed by the "opt-in" provisions of the Antiterrorism and Effective Death Penalty Act of 1996, see *supra* § 3.3c nn.61-64 and accompanying text. *See generally supra* §§ 3.3, 3.4 (discussing AEDPA's "opt-in" provisions and describing cases to which they apply).

[16] The meager caselaw permitting this procedure and the extensive caselaw discouraging it are discussed *infra* §§ 23.5 nn.13-24 and accompanying text, 28.3c nn.95-97 and accompanying text.

[17] *See infra* §§ 17.2 n.17 and accompanying text, 34.3 nn.16-18 and accompanying text; *infra* Chapter 28.

[18] *See McFarland v. Scott, supra,* 512 U.S. at 860 (O'Connor, J., concurring in the judgment in part) ("our carefully crafted doctrines of waiver and abuse of the writ make it especially important that the first [federal habeas corpus] petition adequately set forth all of a state prisoner's colorable grounds for relief"). Additional state court proceedings are often advisable because they may avoid: (1) an exhaustion defense to the initial habeas corpus petition, *see infra* Chapter 23; (2) a successive petition defense to any subsequent habeas corpus petition or its equivalent that seeks to raise claims that were not presented at all or as well in the original federal petition, *see infra* Chapter 28; and also (3) procedural default problems, *see infra* Chapter 26, which additional state proceedings can avert in the ways discussed *infra* §§ 26.2b-26.2e. Additional state proceedings, however, can enhance the likelihood that the prisoner will face a "presumption of correctness" defense to efforts to overcome state court factfindings. *See infra* §§ 20.2, 20.3, 30.3. Statute of limitations problems that may arise if additional state court review is sought are discussed *infra* notes 20-22 and accompanying text.

[19] If the available claims include no claim that is clearly unexhausted but at least one claim that arguably is unexhausted, the prisoner must decide whether to submit *all* claims to the federal

Matters are considerably more complicated in cases governed by the Anti-terrorism and Effective Death Penalty Act of 1996 (AEDPA).[20] Due to AEDPA's statute of limitations — which, for noncapital cases, is one year, apparently begins running upon the completion (or noninvocation) of timely *certiorari* review following direct appeal, and is tolled only while a "properly filed" state postconviction petition is being adjudicated in the state courts but not while state postconviction and federal habeas corpus papers are being prepared — pursuing option (1) could have the extremely adverse consequence that the limitations period expires before the federal habeas corpus petition is filed.[21] Obviously, a significant risk of dismissal of an entire federal petition on statute of limitations grounds is too high a price to pay to permit exhaustion of some of its claims. Accordingly, upon discovering an unexhausted claim on the eve of filing a federal habeas corpus petition in a noncapital case governed by AEDPA, counsel or the prisoner must determine (i) whether there clearly is enough time remaining within the one-year limitations period (leaving a cushion, if possible) to prepare both a state postconviction petition and, following its adjudication (during which time the limitations period is tolled), a federal habeas corpus petition, and (ii) whether any state postconviction action needed to exhaust state remedies will be deemed "properly filed." If both conditions are met, option (1) is the preferred approach. If, however, there are doubts whether both petitions could be prepared within the time remaining before the limitations period expires, *or* whether state exhaustion proceedings would be "properly filed,"

---

district court in a single petition and to argue that each claim is in fact exhausted, or to postpone filing the federal petition and proceed first to litigate the possibly unexhausted claim(s) in the state courts. Relevant considerations include the seriousness of the exhaustion problem, the likelihood that the state will assert (or waive) the exhaustion defense, whether a state remedy clearly remains available, the amount of time remaining on the petitioner's sentence, the amount of time required to exhaust state remedies, whether exhaustion proceedings will or might cause any applicable statute of limitations governing the later filing of a federal habeas corpus petition to expire, the impact of additional state proceedings on the legal posture of the case, the relative strength of the exhausted and unexhausted claims, and the relevant federal courts' position on the questions whether claims may be withdrawn from a federal petition and simultaneously pursued in state proceedings and, if so, whether the withdrawn claim thereafter may be presented in a second federal petition without waiver problems. *See infra* §§ 23.5 nn.13-24 and accompanying text, 28.3c nn.95-97 and accompanying text. *See also infra* § 15.2d (procedure if petition is dismissed on exhaustion grounds). When the exhaustion problem is substantial and statute of limitations problems can be avoided, the preferred approach is usually to postpone federal proceedings and to pursue available state remedies in order to forestall exhaustion (as well as waiver and successive petition) problems.

[20] Pub. L. 104-132, 110 Stat. 1214 (1996). For a discussion of the cases to which AEDPA applies, see *supra* § 3.4.

[21] For discussion of the one-year statute of limitations that applies to all noncapital cases and the accompanying tolling provisions, see *supra* § 5.1b. For further discussion of the danger that AEDPA's limitations period will expire during the time required to prepare state postconviction pleadings, see *supra* 5.1a.

counsel or the prisoner should pursue either the noncapital variant of option (3) that courts have begun using to avoid statute of limitations problems under AEDPA, or pursue options (4) and (5), notwithstanding their serious "successive petition" risks.[22]

In *capital* cases, options (4) and (5) almost always are out of the question because they create so high a risk that the petitioner will forfeit her only opportunity to secure federal judicial consideration of particular "colorable grounds for relief."[23] The appropriateness of option (1)[24] turns on (i) whether the prisoner is indigent and needs the appointment of counsel for federal habeas corpus proceedings, (ii) whether the prisoner needs a federal court stay of execution while exhaustion of state remedies occurs, and (iii) whether in cases governed by AEDPA[25] (and particularly in AEDPA "opt-in" cases[26]), the one-year statute of limitations (or, in capital "opt-in" cases, the 180-day statute of limitations with its exceedingly narrow tolling provisions that, for example, do *not* apply to second or successive state postconviction proceedings) is likely to expire while the prisoner attempts to exhaust state remedies and then to prepare a federal habeas corpus petition.[27] If any of these three conditions is present, option (1) should be forgone in favor of option (2) or (3). Option (2) is appropriate if the prisoner needs a federal court appointment of counsel to assure that the resources needed for a thorough prefiling investigation are available. Option (3) is appropriate if a federal court stay of execution is needed and either a full investigation already has occurred (whether or not by counsel appointed by the

---

[22] For further discussion of the relevant strategic considerations, see *supra* §§ 5.1a, 6.1. For citation of caselaw discussing the noncapital variant of option (3), see *supra* §§ 3.4a n.16, 5.1b n.57.

[23] *McFarland v. Scott, supra,* 512 U.S. at 860 (O'Connor, J., concurring in the judgment in part) (quoted *supra* note 18).

[24] In cases in which the exhaustion problem is discovered *after* a habeas corpus petition already has been filed, but in which option (1) appears to be the preferred response (because the strategic or tactical advantages of further exhaustion proceedings outweigh their disadvantages), the petitioner may acknowledge the exhaustion problem, rather than resisting the state's exhaustion objection, or even alert the court to the exhaustion problem notwithstanding that the state has not done so, and recommend a dismissal without prejudice pending exhaustion. In order to assure that a stay of execution is in effect pending exhaustion and (in AEDPA cases) that statute of limitations problems are avoided, the petitioner might pursue option (3) as opposed to option (1) in this situation. Even if the state seeks to waive exhaustion (a waiver which, in cases governed by AEDPA, must be explicit), the federal court nonetheless has discretion to permit or require exhaustion. *See supra* note 14; *infra* § 23.2a.

[25] *See supra* § 3.4.

[26] For discussion of the "opt-in" and "nonopt-in" categories that AEDPA creates, and an explanation of the types of cases to which they apply, see *supra* §§ 3.2-3.4.

[27] *See supra* §§ 5.1a, 5.1b, 6.1.

federal court) or the petitioner is not indigent and thus is ineligible for appointment of counsel.[28]

§ 11.2. Identifying potential claims.

a. *Introduction*. This section discusses counsel's responsibility to discover federal claims that might be the basis for habeas corpus relief. Because the prisoner and her attorney, if any, typically must discover federal claims and present them to the state courts before including them in a federal habeas corpus petition, the discussion that follows applies as directly to the investigation preceding state postconviction proceedings[1] as to the investigation preceding the filing of the federal petition.

Investigating a postconviction case to discover meritorious federal claims often demands more lawyerly imagination and perspicacity than any other aspect of the litigation. It stands to reason — and the experience of skilled habeas corpus practitioners bears out — that the most blatant injustices ultimately revealed by habeas corpus cases are often the most difficult to discover.[2] It is

---

[28] If the federal district court refuses to grant a stay of execution based on a mixed petition and no state stay of execution pending exhaustion of state remedies is available, the prisoner should consider whether there is time to appeal the district court's denial of a stay of execution. *See infra* §§ 13.6, 15.2d. If there is insufficient time for an appeal or if an appeal has little chance of success, the petitioner then should either amend out the unexhausted claims or take a "without prejudice" dismissal of the mixed petition and file a new petition containing only the exhausted claims. *See, e.g.*, Parker v. Johnson, 988 F. Supp. 1474, 1476-77 (N.D. Ga. 1998) (holding petition in abeyance for 45 days so that prisoner, who filed mixed petition on last day of AEDPA-imposed limitations period, can "amend his complaint so as to delete all unexhausted claims" and proceed with federal habeas corpus proceedings on exhausted claims while, if he wishes, pursuing remaining state remedies with regard to unexhausted claims); Anthony v. Cambra, 1998 WL 164971, at *2 (N.D. Cal. Feb. 18, 1998) (same as *Parker v. Johnson, supra*). In this situation, the petitioner must make clear on the record, as appropriate under the circumstances, that (1) she does not intend to waive the omitted claims and has excised them only under compulsion of the impending execution date; (2) she intends to exhaust the unexhausted claims as quickly as possible and, if possible, to amend them into the pending federal petition after they are exhausted, *see infra* § 17.2 (amendment); *see also supra* § 3.3c nn.61-64 and accompanying text (difficulty of amendment in capital "opt-in" cases governed by AEDPA); *but cf.* Thomas v. Dugger, 846 F.2d 669, 673 (11th Cir. 1988), *cert. denied*, 493 U.S. 921 (1989) (refusing to remand to allow petitioner to amend into petition claim that became exhausted during pendency of appeal from district court; successive petition will be subject to abuse of writ principles); Kramer v. Butler, 845 F.2d 1291, 1295 (5th Cir.), *cert. denied*, 488 U.S. 865 (1988) (affirming district court's refusal to amend unexhausted claim into petition; reserving question whether future petition (petitioner's third) raising claim would be dismissed for abuse of writ); and (3) the failure previously to have exhausted the omitted claims is excusable, *see infra* §§ 23.4, 26.3, 28.3c. *See generally infra* § 15.2d.

§ 11.2. [1] *See supra* § 6.2. *See generally supra* Chapters 6, 7.

[2] *See infra* § 11.2c (cataloguing some of claims on which habeas corpus relief has been granted in past).

precisely "where the record is unclear or the errors are hidden" that the most pressing need for zealous advocacy arises.[3] The number of instances in which habeas corpus petitioners and attorneys uncover abuses[4] belies any pre-investigative assumption that the actors and events in the criminal process leading to a client's conviction and sentence are beyond constitutional reproach simply because the paper record looks clean.

The importance of discovering meritorious claims in the case as early as possible — preferably, before filing the *state* postconviction petition (indeed, if possible, before, during, or just after the state *trial*); at the latest, before the federal district court completes its consideration of the petitioner's *first* federal habeas corpus petition — is enhanced by the federal courts' exceedingly hostile attitude toward claims that were "procedurally defaulted" in the state courts before being raised in federal habeas corpus proceedings and toward successive federal habeas corpus petitions raising claims omitted from or incompletely litigated in earlier federal habeas corpus proceedings.[5] Although Congress and

---

[3] Douglas v. California, 372 U.S. 353, 358 (1963).

[4] Consider, for example, William Styron's description of the case of Shebaka Sundiata Waglini, convicted as Joseph Green Brown and sentenced to die in Florida in 1973. William Styron, *Death Row*, N.Y. Times, May 10, 1987, at E25 col. 6 (discussing Brown v. Wainwright, 785 F.2d 1457 (11th Cir. 1986)) (after Waglini came within 15 hours of being executed at commencement of his habeas corpus action, proof was developed showing that prosecutor had permitted key prosecution witness to lie on stand, suppressed FBI report concluding that alleged murder weapon could not have fired fatal shot, and intentionally misled jury in closing argument; Waglini was subsequently released). *See also* the lists of violations uncovered in recent federal habeas corpus litigation, in *Habeas Corpus Reforms, Hearing before the Senate Comm. on the Judiciary on S.238, A Bill to Reform Procedures for Collateral Review of Criminal Judgments, and for Other Purposes,* 99th Cong., 1st Sess. 92-93 (1985) (statement of Phylis Skloot Bamberger on behalf of the ABA); *id.* at 155 (letter from Professor Anthony G. Amsterdam to Hon. Strom Thurmond and Hon. Joseph Biden). *See also* MICHAEL L. RADELET, HUGO A. BEDAU & CONSTANCE E. PUTNAM, IN SPITE OF INNOCENCE: ERRONEOUS CONVICTIONS IN CAPITAL CASES (1992); Hugo A. Bedau & Michael L. Radelet, *Miscarriages of Justice in Potentially Capital Cases,* 40 STAN. L. REV. 21, 71-75 (1987); Hugo A. Bedau & Michael Radelet, *The Myth of Infallibility: A Reply to Markman and Cassell,* 41 STAN. L. REV. 161 (1988); Stephen J. Markman & Paul G. Cassell, *Protecting the Innocent: A Response to the Bedau-Radelet Study,* 41 STAN. L. REV. 121 (1988); Brief *Amicus Curiae* of Five Innocent Former Death Row Inmates and Centurion Ministries in Support of Petitioner in *Schlup v. Delo,* No. 93-7901 (filed May 27, 1994); decisions cited *infra* § 11.2c (paragraph (3), listing and describing cases in which prosecutorial or police suppression of evidence resulted in granting of writ); other authority cited *infra* § 11.2c n.99.

[5] *See, e.g.,* McCleskey v. Zant, 499 U.S. 467 (1991); *infra* Chapters 26, 28. *McCleskey* illustrates the critical importance of early discovery of the facts supporting constitutional claims. The district court had granted relief based upon a new-claim successive petition, finding that the state, before trial, had surreptitiously planted an informant in a cell next to the petitioner's, thereby securing inculpatory statements that were introduced against the petitioner at trial in violation of the petitioner's 6th Amendment right not to be interrogated by agents of the state in the absence of

the courts recognize occasional situations in which claims defaulted in the state courts may be litigated in federal court and in which successive federal habeas

counsel. Although the petitioner had suspected that the witness against him at trial was a police agent, and had so alleged in his state postconviction petition, his interviews of the responsible assistant district attorney, various jailers, and other government officials responsible for the informant's confinement produced a series of deceitful denials. Moreover, purporting to have turned over "a complete copy of the prosecutor's file" in the case during state postconviction proceedings, the state in fact withheld from the produced materials a 21-page statement by the informant documenting his surreptitious use as an agent of the prosecution. Having discovered no proof of a violation, the petitioner dropped the jailhouse-informant claim when he filed his first federal habeas corpus petition. Thereafter, a change in the state's open-records act permitted the petitioner for the first time to discover the informant's statement, which also contained the name of a jailer who, upon being interviewed by the petitioner's counsel, admitted that he had assisted in planting the informant in the petitioner's cell. Petitioner thereupon filed a second federal petition based upon the newly discovered evidence, and the district court held that there was no successive petition bar because "this is not a case where the petitioner has reserved his proof or deliberately withheld his claim for a second petition." McCleskey v. Zant, Civil Action No. C-87-1517A (N.D. Ga. Dec. 13, 1987), slip op. at 24, rev'd, 890 F.2d 342 (11th Cir. 1989), aff'd, 499 U.S. 467 (1991). The 11th Circuit reversed the district court's grant of relief, holding that a successive-petition bar existed because the investigation that the petitioner conducted before filing his first federal petition was "lacking" inasmuch as a diligent search at that time might have led to the discovery of the jailer, among the scores of other law enforcement officials who came into contact with the petitioner. McCleskey v. Zant, 890 F.2d 342, 349-50 (11th Cir. 1989), aff'd, 499 U.S. 467 (1991). The Supreme Court agreed with the 11th Circuit. 499 U.S. at 497-503. See also Strickler v. Pruett, 1998 WL 340420, at 5*-10* (4th Cir. June 17, 1998) (per curiam), cert. granted, 119 S. Ct. 40 (1998) (using McCleskey-type analysis to bar relief based on prosecutorial suppression of evidence on theory that, notwithstanding state's repeated (and false) statements that prosecution had turned over entire file, petitioner should have made blanket discovery request encompassing withheld documents during state postconviction proceedings).

The pressure that McCleskey places upon petitioners to conduct a thorough, no-stone-unturned, no-prosecutor-or-police-officer-believed investigation before filing her first federal habeas corpus petition has not been lost on the Supreme Court. See McFarland v. Scott, 512 U.S. 849, 856 (1994) (construing Congress' grant of a statutory entitlement to counsel in capital federal habeas corpus proceedings as encompassing a right to legal assistance in preparing a petition because "Congress legislated against th[e] legal backdrop" of decisions such as McCleskey v. Zant, supra, under which the dismissal of a pro se prisoner's first petition "would expose him to the substantial risk that his habeas claims never would be heard on the merits" because "any petition subsequently filed by counsel could be subject to dismissal as an abuse of the writ"); id. at 860 (O'Connor, J., concurring in the judgment in part) ("our carefully crafted doctrines of waiver and abuse of the writ make it especially important that the first petition adequately set forth all of a state prisoner's colorable grounds for relief"). Accord Brown v. Vasquez, 952 F.2d 1164, 1166-68 (9th Cir.), cert. denied, 503 U.S. 1011 (1992) (because, under McCleskey, "a prisoner applying for habeas corpus relief" has the "substantial burden" of "assert[ing] all possible violations of his constitutional rights in his initial application or run the risk of losing what might be a viable claim" and "will not be excused from failing to raise a claim in his first federal petition on the ground that his counsel had to prepare the first petition in haste and did not have time to become familiar with the case," court grants stay of execution and orders appointment of counsel to assist capital prisoner in investigating and preparing habeas corpus petition). See generally infra Chapter 28.

corpus petitions are appropriate,[6] the narrowness of those situations places an increasingly heavy burden of justification on prisoners seeking relief based on previously defaulted claims or through successive habeas corpus litigation. Likewise, the courts have shown a remarkable lack of solicitude for prisoners — including ones executed as a result — whose attorneys through no fault of the prisoners were not sufficiently versed in the law to recognize relatively novel or subtle but meritorious federal claims, did not consider the possibility that a claim long rejected by local, state, and federal courts nonetheless might succeed in the future or in a higher court, or simply failed to conduct enough of an investigation to discover facts supporting meritorious federal constitutional claims.[7]

These judicial practices place a heavy responsibility on counsel to undertake efforts sufficient to uncover hidden but meritorious claims in the case no later than the filing of the first postconviction petition. As a rule, counsel's prefiling investigatory activities should be directed preliminarily toward identifying every occurrence or nonoccurrence in the case that in some significant way seems untoward, unjust, abusive, inhospitable to the orderly, accurate, or reliable functioning of the criminal justice system, or "just not right." Obviously, many such occurrences do not amount to federal legal errors. But additional investigation may reveal clear legal violations of which the initially observed "red flag" was simply the most visible indication. And thorough and imaginative[8] legal research — the next critical step in the process of discovering habeas corpus claims — may reveal that occurrences that intuitively struck the lawyer as unjust or inappropriate did so precisely because they offend the Constitution, particularly in light of analogous legal developments elsewhere in the courts.[9]

Although counsel will have to conduct much of the necessary investigation informally, formal mechanisms are available for requiring the state to provide an indigent petitioner with a copy of all relevant portions of the record in the case, discovery, supplementation or expansion of the record, appointment of necessary experts and investigators, and subpoenaing witnesses and documents for trial. Some of these mechanisms are examined in the next section.[10] Others are addressed later, in Chapter 19's discussion of prehearing fact-development procedures.[11]

---

[6] See generally infra §§ 26.3, 28.1-28.4.

[7] See infra § 26.3b n.27.

[8] For a discussion of some of the types of claims that have prevailed in federal habeas corpus proceedings, see infra § 11.2c.

[9] See infra § 11.3 (choice of claims based on strength of facts and law).

[10] See infra § 11.2b nn.73, 84.

[11] See also infra Chapters 18, 20, 21.

b. *Potential sources of factual information.* Set out below is a nonexhaustive inventory of potential sources of factual information in support of claims for postconviction relief in state or federal court. The accompanying footnotes identify some of the types of claims about which the respective sources are likely to provide information.[12]

The inventory lists individuals whom counsel should interview as well as records and physical items that counsel should examine. When interviewing a potential source of factual information, counsel or the investigator always should ask the witness for any records or other physical items in that person's possession that may relate to the client or the case.

Potential sources of factual information include:

　(1)　The client.[13]
　(2)　Members of the client's family,[14] including:
　　　(a)　Family members in contact with the client since trial;[15]
　　　(b)　Family members who attended the trial (and/or pretrial hearings; the sentencing; post-verdict proceedings);[16]

---

[12] The footnotes identify the possible claims in very general terms. For more detailed discussion of the various constitutional claims, see generally 1-3 ANTHONY G. AMSTERDAM, TRIAL MANUAL FOR THE DEFENSE OF CRIMINAL CASES (5th ed. 1988-89); *infra* § 11.2c (cataloguing some of claims that have succeeded in habeas corpus proceedings).

[13] *See supra* Chapter 4 (claims about which the client is critical source of information; procedures for most effectively discovering and developing information known to client).

[14] *See supra id.* (claims about which client's family is important source of information).

[15] *Possible claims include:* inhumane conditions of confinement; inappropriate place or type of institutionalization; denial of timely release; denial of parole, "good time" credits, and the like; execution of the insane (*see* Ford v. Wainwright, 477 U.S. 399 (1986)).

[16] *Possible claims include:* competency to stand trial; excessive pretrial publicity; underrepresentation of minorities in the jury pool, prosecutorial use of peremptory challenges to remove members of minority groups from the jury, and other jury-selection claims; excessive security measures; improper raiment of the defendant (*e.g.,* in prison garb); improper influences on witnesses and jurors; prosecutorial misconduct; judicial misconduct; ineffective assistance of trial counsel.

Note — ineffective assistance of counsel claims: Under Strickland v. Washington, 466 U.S. 668 (1984), establishing ineffective assistance of counsel requires proof both that counsel's performance was not reasonably effective and that there is a reasonable probability that, but for counsel's derelictions, the outcome of the proceeding would have been different. *Id.* at 687. *See infra* §§ 26.3b nn.34-41, 26.3c n.63. In conducting a postconviction investigation, therefore, counsel must be vigilant for evidence supporting both the "performance" and the "prejudice" prongs of the test. Proving the latter prong often requires the petitioner to conduct a mini-trial at which she adduces the evidence that, but for trial counsel's unprofessional conduct, including his failure to investigate the case, would have been introduced at the original trial. As to ineffective assistance of counsel claims in particular, therefore, the postconviction investigation must proceed in virtually

(c)   Family members in contact with the client at the time of arrest and pretrial incarceration;[17]

(d)   Family members in contact with the client at the time of the offense;[18]

(e)   Family members in contact with the client at any time prior to the offense.[19]

(3) Participants in petitioner's defense,[20] including:

(a)   Trial counsel;[21]

---

the same manner and have the same scope as a conscientious pretrial investigation during the criminal proceeding itself. *See infra* note 21 (interviewing prior counsel).

[17] *Possible claims include:* illegal search, seizure, arrest; unlawful interrogation in violation of the rule of Miranda v. Arizona, 384 U.S. 436 (1966), the 6th Amendment right to counsel, or other constitutional guarantees; improper extraction of evidence from the accused; line-ups; show-ups; competency to stand trial; prosecutorial suppression of exculpatory evidence uncovered through the investigatory techniques listed above or through polygraph examinations and the like; ineffective assistance with regard to above issues. The Supreme Court's decision in Stone v. Powell, 428 U.S. 465 (1976), establishes certain (not always insuperable) barriers to federal habeas corpus review of 4th Amendment exclusionary rule claims (*see supra* §§ 2.4d nn.277-89 and accompanying text, 9.2; *infra* §§ 27.1-27.3), but the Court has made clear that the *Stone* doctrine does not extend to other types of constitutional claims or even violations of the subconstitutional, prophylactic rule of *Miranda v. Arizona, supra* (*see supra* § 9.2).

[18] *Possible claims include:* ineffective assistance of counsel with regard to pretrial investigation of events surrounding the offense, mental disorder-based defenses, mitigation of punishment, and the like; competency to stand trial; prosecutorial suppression of evidence.

[19] *Possible claims include:* competency to stand trial; ineffective assistance of counsel with regard to pretrial investigation of mental disorder-based defenses, mitigation of punishment, and the like.

[20] *See infra* para. (12)(a)-(i) of the text (discussing files postconviction counsel should review at — and, if necessary, retrieve from — offices of client's former counsel). *See also* para. (10), (11), (13), (15)-(17) (various records and materials that may well be in former counsel's possession).

[21] Trial counsel often is as important a source of information as the client about various types of claims that are not obvious from the record (*see supra* Chapter 4). Postconviction counsel, moreover, should interview *all* the attorneys and paraprofessionals who represented petitioner or worked on the case at or before trial. Frequently, the second- or third-chair lawyer has more comprehensive information about the aspects of the case on which she worked and will have more time and greater inclination to discuss the case than the lead attorney.

Before interviewing the prior attorneys and paraprofessionals in the case, postconviction counsel should secure from the client a statement in writing in which the client — only insofar as is necessary to permit prior counsel fully to advise current counsel about the case — authorizes members of the prior defense team to disclose to petitioner's current counsel all pertinent information in the case, including the substance of all prior communications between the prisoner and members of the defense team, and all the files in the case. For a list of files and records that are particularly important to obtain, see *infra* para. (12) of the text. *See also* para. (10), (11), (13), (15)-(17) (various records and materials that may well be in former counsel's possession).

If counsel is not careful, adversarial relationships may develop based upon the prior attorney's fear that his performance in the case warrants or will beget an ineffective assistance claim. Of

   (b) Appellate counsel;[22]
   (c) Postconviction counsel;[23]
   (d) Paraprofessionals who assisted prior counsel;[24]
   (e) Investigators who assisted prior counsel;[25]
   (f) Expert witnesses consulted or presented in court by prior counsel or by the prosecution.[26]

---

course, if former counsel *was* ineffective, it is his responsibility to the client and the profession to cooperate in redressing the violation. *See, e.g.,* Deutscher v. Angelone, 16 F.3d 981, 984 (9th Cir. 1994) (prior attorney submitted declaration to district court admitting that he filed first federal habeas corpus petition without notifying petitioner or explaining appropriateness of having another attorney review counsel's representation of petitioner at trial, upon appeal, and in state postconviction proceedings); Rachel v. Bordenkircher, 590 F.2d 200, 203-04 (6th Cir. 1978) (prior attorney's confession of ineffective assistance). On the other hand, postconviction counsel should make it clear that she does not treat ineffective-assistance claims lightly and that the primary goal of the interview is simply to learn as much about the case as possible from the person with the most and best-organized information about it.

   In general, counsel should encourage the prior attorney to talk about the most troubling aspects of the case, and those — for example, a lack of cooperation from the state, the trial court's denial of a continuance or necessary investigative resources or expert assistance, insufficient access to the client before or during trial, surprise evidence presented by the prosecution, surprise rulings by the court, and the like — that, through no fault of prior counsel's own, hampered his efforts to represent the client effectively. Any such circumstances are fruitful sources of federal habeas corpus claims and of mechanisms for avoiding habeas corpus defenses, and former counsel's support (and, ultimately, testimony) as to such claims often will prove critical. Postconviction counsel also should endeavor to enlist prior counsel's ongoing assistance and advice with regard to approaching local witnesses in the case; ascertaining local police, prosecutorial, and court practices; and developing the legal theories with which trial counsel is familiar. In general, postconviction counsel should begin developing a relationship of mutual respect and trust with former counsel — presumedly a natural consequence, in any event, of both parties' loyalty to the client — and should invite and entreat the former counsel's assistance in all relevant aspects of the case.

[22] In reviewing the record to identify claims to raise on appeal, appellate counsel may well have made notes on constitutional claims in the case that were not appropriate for appellate consideration (for example, ineffective assistance of counsel, unobjected-to trial errors and the like) but that are ripe for postconviction consideration. Interviewing appellate counsel and reviewing her notes and files, therefore, should provide an effective introduction to the record of the case. *See generally supra* note 21.

[23] *See generally supra* notes 21, 22.

[24] *See generally id.*

[25] *Possible claims include:* prosecutorial suppression or misrepresentation of evidence; search, seizure and arrest; confession; ineffective assistance of counsel with regard to pretrial investigation.

[26] *Possible claims include:* competency of defendant to stand trial; ineffective assistance with regard to mental disorder-based and other available defenses; claims listed *supra* note 25.

(4) Codefendants, codefendants' trial counsel, and other members of codefendants' defense team.[27]

(5) Acquaintances of petitioner falling into categories (and with regard to claims) similar to those in paragraph (2) above, including:

    (a) Friends;

    (b) Companions at the time of the offense;

    (c) Teachers;

    (d) Counselors;

    (e) Coaches;

    (f) Employers and fellow employees;

    (g) Spiritual advisors and church members;

    (h) Medical doctors and other health professionals;

    (i) Mental health professionals;

    (j) Social workers and other government or private social service personnel;

    (k) Parole and probation officers;

    (l) Jail or prison officials.[28]

(6) Law enforcement personnel who prepared or presented the case for the state or were present at trial,[29] including:

    (a) Investigating police officers;[30]

---

[27] *Possible claims include:* search, seizure, and arrest; confession; improper joinder of parties; prosecutorial suppression or misrepresentation of evidence dealt with more forthrightly at codefendant's trial; threats, promises, agreements to induce inculpatory testimony; challenges to improper jury selection techniques or security measures common to petitioner's and codefendant's trial; ineffective assistance with regard to above-listed or other matters.

[28] In addition to interviewing officials at the jail or prison at which petitioner was held prior to trial for information supporting claims such as those discussed *supra* note 17 and *supra* § 11.2a n.5, counsel should interview officials at any jail or prison at which the petitioner was held prior to sentencing to uncover any good-conduct evidence that an effective attorney would have presented as mitigating evidence at a capital sentencing hearing (*see, e.g.,* Skipper v. South Carolina, 476 U.S. 1 (1986)).

Counsel should prepare, advise the client concerning, and, if the client is willing, have the client sign a waiver of any privileges or confidentiality requirements that the individuals listed above may cite as a basis for refusing to talk — or to release relevant documents — to counsel. *See infra* note 87.

[29] *See infra* para. (13) of the text (discussing files, documents, and other evidence counsel should seek from law enforcement personnel). If materials in police and other investigative files cannot be obtained informally, counsel should file appropriate motions with the relevant state and federal postconviction courts. The Freedom of Information Act (FOIA) also may provide a useful means of obtaining pertinent records. *See infra* note 84.

[30] *Possible claims include:* prosecutorial suppression or misrepresentation of evidence; search, seizure and arrest; confession; performance of inappropriate tests on or improper extraction of

(b) Officers in charge of retrieving or storing the physical evidence;[31]

(c) Personnel responsible for conducting forensic analyses for the state;[32]

(d) Secretarial personnel responsible for typing up waiver forms, confessions, witness statements, and the like;[33]

(e) Pathologist or medical examiner;[34]

(f) Prosecutors;[35]

---

evidence from defendant; line-ups; show-ups; witness intimidation; excessive security arrangements at trial; ineffective assistance with regard to above-listed matters and pretrial investigation.

The cases in which habeas corpus relief has been granted amply attest to the frequency with which police officers and other law enforcement officers withhold exculpatory evidence as well as the likelihood that counsel's uncovering of such misconduct will persuade a federal court to grant relief. *See infra* § 11.2c (para. (3)) (listing and describing cases in which prosecutorial or police suppression of evidence resulted in granting of writ). Counsel accordingly should try to interview the various officers responsible for investigating the case, arresting the petitioner, seizing, storing, and examining evidence, conducting petitioner's interrogation, conducting line-ups and show-ups, conducting polygraph and other examinations of the petitioner or others, and testifying at trial on any subject. Although the received wisdom among the defense bar is that police officers will not talk to a defense attorney or investigator, it has been the authors' experience in representing criminal defendants at both the pretrial and postconviction stages that law enforcement officials often *will* talk with a defense attorney or investigator if approached in a nonaggressive, respectful manner. *See also* 1 AMSTERDAM, *supra* note 12, at § 94; Eric M. Freedman, *Innocence, Federalism, and the Capital Jury: Two Legislative Proposals for Evaluating Post-Trial Evidence of Innocence in Death Penalty Cases*, 18 N.Y.U. REV. L. & SOC. CHANGE 315, 316 n.7 (1990-91). Moreover, when interviewed at the postconviction stage with appropriate open-ended questions, police officers frequently remember — and recount — what *actually* happened, not what they may have *testified* happened or what they may have told defense counsel at the time of the trial.

[31] *See supra* note 30.

[32] *See id.*

[33] *See id.*

[34] *See id.*

[35] *Possible claims include:* selective prosecution; prosecutorial misconduct; suppression or misrepresentation of evidence; procurement of absence of witnesses; absence of "reciprocal discovery" provided by prosecution after defense disclosures to prosecution; unfair balance of resources between prosecution and defense; unkept plea bargain; use of prosecutorial peremptories to strike members of minority groups; improper jury-selection procedures in the relevant court; abuse of prosecutorial discretion regarding decisions to charge, accept pleas, recommend sentences, or seek the death penalty; grand jury abuse; improper prosecutorial conduct before, or influence on, the grand jury; ineffective assistance of trial counsel; confession, search and seizure, line-ups, show-ups, and other pretrial investigative techniques.

Particularly in situations in which the state's trial attorney has left the state's employ or is no longer responsible for petitioner's case (for example, because she only has trial responsibilities within the office or because postconviction cases, as is typical, are handled by attorneys employed by the state attorney general's office and not the local district attorney), prosecutors are sometimes more willing to talk frankly with postconviction counsel than with defense counsel before trial. *See* Freedman, *supra* note 30, at 316 n.7. In addition to issues relating to the facts of the particular case,

        (g)   Jail personnel;[36]

        (h)   Courtroom security personnel;[37]

        (i)   Court marshal, bailiff, clerk, and court reporter.[38]

(7)   Prosecution and defense witnesses at trial as well as potential witnesses who were never called to the witness stand by either side.[39]

(8)   The jurors.[40]

(9)   Newspaper or media reporters falling into categories (and with regard to claims) similar to those in paragraph (2) above.

(10) The record in the case and in the cases of any codefendants,[41] including:

---

interviews with prosecutors should touch on matters of office policy with regard to the exercise of prosecutorial charging, plea bargaining, and capital and noncapital sentencing discretion, the disclosure to the defense of evidence in their files, the use of peremptory challenges, and the like.

[36] *Possible claims include:* confession; competency to stand trial; improper extraction of evidence; planting of police informants in violation of right to presence of counsel (*see supra* § 11.2a n.5.); prosecutorial suppression or misrepresentation of evidence (*see id.*); restrictions on access to counsel; line-ups; show-ups; ineffective assistance of counsel with regard to pretrial investigation and client contact. *See also supra* note 28.

[37] *Possible claims include:* improper contacts with jurors; excessive courtroom security, claims listed *supra* note 16.

[38] *See supra* note 37.

[39] *Possible claims include:* prosecutorial misconduct and suppression and misrepresentation of evidence; ineffective assistance with regard to pretrial investigation.

[40] Although post-trial inquiries of jurors are not favored, *see infra* § 21.2 n.14, they occasionally are critical in discovering constitutional errors. *See, e.g.,* Remmer v. United States, 347 U.S. 227 (1954) (remanding for hearing regarding effect of third-party's attempt to bribe jury foreman; although trial judge and prosecutor were apprised of attempt, prisoner's counsel did not discover it until after trial); Green v. Zant, 715 F.2d 551 (11th Cir. 1983), *cert. denied,* 469 U.S. 1098 (1984) (remanding for hearing into whether juror's refusal to vote for death sentence prompted other jurors to force her off jury for purported health reasons); United States v. Mauldin, 714 F.2d 854, 855 (8th Cir. 1983) (discussing cases) (hearing on juror incompetence required if movant produces substantial, even if not wholly conclusive, evidence of a juror's incompetence such as an adjudication of insanity made shortly before trial).

[41] "Record" is used in the broadest possible sense. First, as used here, the term includes any official or unofficial indication of what took place at some formal or informal proceeding in, or related to, the petitioner's criminal trial or that of any codefendant. Furthermore, if the petitioner was tried more than once for a given offense or for other related offenses, whether in the same or a different court, counsel should apply the protocol set forth here to the "record" of all such proceedings.

    Second, the "record" encompasses more than the record on appeal, which all too often omits critical sources of constitutional error, such as the transcripts of the coroner's inquest, the preliminary hearing, the *voir dire* of prospective jurors, the opening and closing arguments by counsel, and the trial exhibits. Indeed, counsel will sometimes have trouble ascertaining what the "record" in the broad sense includes (as to which, close questioning of the client, prior counsel, the prosecutor, the clerk, and the court reporter is in order), and frequently will discover that substantial portions of that "record" have never been transcribed from audio or court reporters'

(a) The "technical record," charging papers, clerk's file, motions file, briefs file, clerk's correspondence file, and the docket sheet;[42]

(b) Pretrial hearing and other transcripts, including the:

---

tapes and may well not be stored in any clerk's office but instead at a court reporter's office or home. *See, e.g.,* Dobbs v. Zant, 506 U.S. 357 (1993) (*per curiam*). In such circumstances, it is counsel's responsibility to ask that the record on appeal — which typically becomes part of the record of the postconviction proceeding (*see infra* § 19.2) — be supplemented with the appropriate transcripts, documents, and exhibits. *See infra* §§ 19.2, 19.5 (discussing means of obtaining necessary documents at state's expense and of supplementing and expanding the record). *See also* Dobbs v. Zant, *supra.*

When motions, petitions, briefs, and the like are obtained, counsel also should attempt to secure the relevant responding pleadings and papers.

[42] Counsel should scrutinize: (1) any motion made by the defendant and denied by the trial court and (2) any motion made by the state and granted by the trial court. Such papers are likely to be fruitful sources of possible constitutional error. Even when the defendant's or the state's motions were premised or resolved on state-law or discretionary, not explicitly constitutional, grounds, the possibility of a federal issue exists. Counsel should consider whether the Constitution provides potential or additional grounds for making the defense motions or opposing the state's motions and, if so, should consider "federalizing" or more completely "federalizing" the issue in state, then federal, postconviction proceedings, if that is possible. *See infra* §§ 23.3c (exhaustion requirement that claim be fairly presented to state courts before federal habeas corpus review), 26.2c n.16 (procedural default implications).

Potential federal issues that might appear in the context of defense motions denied by the trial court, or prosecution motions granted by the trial court, include, among many others, the actual or effective denial of: counsel; sufficient funds to allow effective legal representation; the right to self-representation or joint representation; counsel separate from the one representing a codefendant or a witness; the appointment of essential experts and investigators; other resources necessary to an effective defense; subpoenas for critical witnesses, and travel expenses for those who were indigent; immunity for exculpatory witnesses disposed to assert the privilege against self-incrimination; essential medical, psychiatric, or physical examinations; a change of venue; motions to dismiss based on prosecutorial misconduct, selective prosecution, grand jury abuse, racial or other discrimination or the use of procedures foreclosing a representative cross-section of the community in the selection of the grand jury; a motion to quash the petit jury panel on similar grounds; a motion to prescribe fair jury selection procedures (such as individual sequestered *voir dire*) or to proscribe the exercise of prosecutorial peremptory challenges to exclude members of minority groups; recusal of the judge; a request to ascertain the competency of the defendant to stand trial; severance or misjoinder motions (regarding parties or claims); motions for discovery, "reciprocal" prosecutorial discovery following disclosures the defense was required to make, the production of evidence, or access to witnesses or to evidence in the hands of the prosecution; any suppression motions with regard to statements made by petitioner to law enforcement officials, evidence seized by the police, line-ups or show-ups, the fruits of the illegal arrest of the petitioner, or forced disclosures by or involuntary tests performed on the petitioner; a continuance; motions *in limine* with regard to the admission or exclusion of certain kinds of evidence (including some forms of hearsay), or to various types of prosecutorial arguments and statements to the jury; a motion to sequester the jury; and requested jury instructions.

      (i)   Coroner's inquest;[43]

      (ii)   Grand jury proceedings;

      (iii)   Arraignment;[44]

      (iv)   Preliminary hearing;

      (v)   Bail hearing;

      (vi)   Pretrial suppression hearings;

      (vii) Evidentiary or other hearings on pretrial matters;[45]

(c)   Discovery documents, including deposition transcripts, interrogatory answers, witness statements, confessions, expert reports and underlying notes and records, physical evidence, and answers to discovery motions;

(d)   The record of proceedings on the petitioner's plea of guilty;[46]

(e)   The guilt/innocence trial record,[47] including:

      (i)   Transcript of introductory statements to, admonitions to, and *voir dire* of prospective jurors;[48]

---

[43] *Possible claims include:* prosecutorial suppression or misrepresentation of evidence; prosecutorial misconduct; grand jury abuse; selective prosecution; coerced statements by defendant; illegally seized evidence.

[44] *Possible claims include:* denial of counsel; joint representation; denial of self-representation; coerced statements; ineffective assistance.

[45] *See supra* note 42 (listing matters on which pretrial hearings may have been held). *See also infra* note 47 (matters to look for in transcripts).

[46] *Possible claims include:* competency to plead guilty, voluntariness of plea, ineffective assistance, unkept plea bargain. *See also infra* note 47.

[47] Counsel should pay especially close attention to the points in the trial record at which: (1) one of the attorneys asserts an objection or makes a motion; (2) the trial judge announces a ruling; and (3) the prosecutor makes statements in front of or to the jury. Constitutional issues are particularly likely to be embedded in such portions of the record. *See supra* note 42 and *infra* note 64 regarding the need for vigilance to discover federal issues hidden in matters treated at trial as if they involved only state law issues and to discover additional federal implications beyond those recognized at trial.

Counsel, however, should not confine the search for potential federal claims to those errors that trial counsel objected to at trial. First, the failure to object itself may reveal important ineffective assistance issues. *See infra* § 26.3b n.37. Second, even if counsel's failure to object does not rise to the level of ineffective assistance, the underlying error still may be of constitutional dimension and reviewable in state and federal postconviction proceedings notwithstanding the omission of a contemporaneous objection. *See infra* §§ 26.2a-26.2e, 26.3b-26.3d, 26.4. Counsel accordingly should note all trial errors, whether or not objected to, then explore the bases discussed *infra* Chapter 26 for securing postconviction review of such claims.

[48] *Possible claims include:* biased jurors; tainted jury panel; venue change; prosecutorial use of peremptories against members of minority groups; *Witherspoon* error in capital cases (*see* Witherspoon v. Illinois, 391 U.S. 510 (1968) (prohibiting exclusion of jurors who have scruples against the death penalty but who are able to follow the law at both phases of trial); *see also* Morgan v. Illinois, 504 U.S. 719 (1992); Gray v. Mississippi, 481 U.S. 648 (1987); Wainwright v.

(ii)   Transcript of opening statement of the court;[49]

(iii)   Transcript of opening arguments of counsel;[50]

(iv)   Transcript of evidence;[51]

(v)   Transcript of *voir dire* examinations of witnesses outside the presence of the jury;[52]

(vi)   Transcript of bench conferences;[53]

(vii)   Trial exhibits admitted into evidence and ones offered but excluded;[54]

(viii) Transcript of proceedings on motion for directed verdict;[55]

(ix)   Transcript of closing arguments of counsel;[56]

(x)   Transcript of conference on jury instructions;[57]

(xi)   Transcript of jury instructions;[58]

(xii) Written jury verdict;[59]

Witt, 469 U.S. 412 (1985)); ineffective assistance of counsel; prosecutorial misconduct; judicial or prosecutorial interference with jurors' duty to find the facts; improper influence on jurors; improper statements of law or allocation or definition of burden of proof.

[49] *Possible claims include:* judicial bias; improper comments on evidence; comments effectively directing a verdict on controversial issues; disparaging remarks about defendant or defense counsel; improper statements of law; improper allocation or definition of burden of proof; comments on defendant's silence.

[50] *Possible claims include:* claims listed *supra* note 49; ineffective assistance of counsel; prosecutorial misconduct.

[51] *Possible claims include:* judicial bias; evidentiary rulings with confrontation, compulsory-process, or due process implications; comments on defendant's post-arrest or in-court silence; shackling the defendant; improper raiment of the defendant (*e.g.,* in prison garb); excessive in-court security; prosecutorial misconduct or misrepresentation of evidence; ineffective assistance of counsel.

[52] *See supra* note 51.

[53] *See id.*

[54] *See id.*

[55] *Possible claims include:* constitutional insufficiency of the evidence; misallocation of the burden of proof; other claims noted *infra* note 57.

[56] *See supra* notes 48-50.

[57] *Possible claims include:* misstatements of law; failure to instruct on elements of offense; misallocation or misdefinition of burden of proof; denial of instruction not to rely on defendant's silence as evidence of guilt; failure to instruct on defenses, lesser included offenses, defense's theory of case, dangers of particular kinds of evidence or testimony; duty of jury to assess credibility of witnesses, documentary evidence, inculpatory statements by defendant, and the like; comments on defendant's failure to testify; comments effectively directing a verdict on disputed issues.

[58] *See supra* note 57.

[59] *Possible claims include:* denial of unanimity; absence of requisite number of jurors; improper influence on or *ex parte* communications with jurors; incompetent jurors; improper substitution of jurors.

    (xiii) Transcript of announcement of verdict and polling of jury;[60]

(f) Records of proceedings with regard to multiple or habitual offender status, use of firearm, and other enhancement issues, including analogues to the records delineated in subparagraphs (10)(a)-(e) above;[61]

(g) Record of proceedings on sentence, including:

    (i)   Presentence report;

    (ii)   Transcript of presentencing conference;

    (iii) Transcript of sentencing hearing, including analogues to the records delineated in paragraphs (10)(a)-(e) above;[62]

    (iv) Order imposing sentence or the transcript of announcement of sentence;

    (v)   Any post-trial or postsentencing reports that judges file in capital cases pursuant to a state statute or court rule;[63]

(h) Post-trial, preappeal records, including:

    (i)   Records relating to bail pending appeal and any hearing on the subject;

    (ii)   Records relating to indigence status on appeal;

    (iii) Records relating to request for stay of sentence or execution pending appeal;

    (iv) Records relating to motions for new trial, for reduction in sentence, and the like;[64]

---

[60] *See supra* note 59.

[61] *See supra* notes 41-60.

[62] In capital cases and other cases in which sentencing issues are tried to a jury, the sentencing record often is as large and as critical to a proper evaluation of the case as the guilt-innocence trial record. Especially in those cases, therefore, counsel should read the sentencing records and insist upon their completeness with as much assiduity as is exercised in regard to the guilt-innocence record.

[63] *See, e.g.,* Burden v. Zant, 498 U.S. 433, 435 & n.2 (1991) (*per curiam*) (discussing Georgia's statutory requirement that trial judges file a "post-trial report" in "every case in which the death penalty is imposed ... to facilitate review by the Georgia Supreme Court"). *See also* Burden v. Zant, 510 U.S. 132 (1994) (*per curiam*). *See infra* § 37.3b nn.21-24 and accompanying text (discussing *Burden v. Zant* decisions and significance of such "post-trial reports" as potential sources of state court findings of fact).

[64] Trial counsel is likely to have prepared the motion for a new trial soon after trial, when the proceedings were fresh in mind and prior to discriminating among claims based on trial counsel's assessment of their "appeal-worthiness." As a result, the new trial motion often provides the most comprehensive available index to the potential errors in the case that are known to trial counsel. Because some of the potentially "federalizable" issues presented in the new trial motion may have been based exclusively on state-law grounds or on only some of the available federal grounds, and because appellate counsel may not have raised some of the issues presented in the new trial motion on appeal, that motion may reveal potentially meritorious constitutional claims that counsel must

(i) Appellate records,[65] including:
    (i) Notice of appeal and any other formal statement of issues on appeal, assignment of errors, petition for appeal, petition for *certiorari,* application for permission to appeal, and the like;
    (ii) Motions to appellate court;
    (iii) Opening, reply, and supplemental briefs and letters containing supplemental authority or other communications by any party with the court;
    (iv) Transcript of oral argument;
    (v) Opinion and orders of appellate court;
    (vi) Motion for rehearing or reconsideration;
    (vii) Records relating to request for stay of sentence or execution pending subsequent appeal or the filing of a petition for a writ of *certiorari*;
(j) Petition for writ of *certiorari* to the United States Supreme Court and supporting documents, including applications for leave to proceed *in forma pauperis* and for stay of sentence or execution.[66]

---

litigate in state postconviction petitions in order to exhaust them (*see* Chapter 23) and to ameliorate or avoid procedural default problems (*see* Chapter 26). *See supra* note 42 (discussing the process of "federalizing" claims that were confined at trial or on the appeal to state law, discretionary, or incomplete federal grounds).

[65] Counsel should consult available records relating to each level of appeal undertaken by the petitioner.

The appellate record often reveals federal claims in their clearest and most well-developed form, including ones that are essentially transferable verbatim to the federal habeas corpus petition. As with the pretrial motions file, the transcript of trial objections and rulings, and the new trial motion, the appellate record may reveal meritorious federal claims that so far have been litigated exclusively as matters of state law or only incompletely as matters of federal law. The process of fully "federalizing" such claims is discussed *supra* note 42.

The appellate record, like the trial record, may be as interesting for what it does not include as for what it does include. As at trial, the failure on appeal properly to assert meritorious constitutional claims may constitute ineffective assistance of counsel on appeal. *See supra* § 9.1 n.28; *infra* § 26.3b nn.34-41. Even if appellate counsel's omission of a meritorious claim does not rise to the level of constitutionally cognizable error, counsel should not necessarily acquiesce in appellate counsel's often inadvertent or mistaken abandonment of such a claim. As discussed *supra* note 64 with regard to meritorious constitutional claims that were not properly asserted at trial, claims omitted on appeal may be recoverable in state and/or federal postconviction proceedings.

[66] The petition for a writ of *certiorari* is supposed to be confined to federal issues and thus is likely to reveal issues that are suitable for essentially verbatim inclusion in a federal habeas corpus petition. *But see supra* note 65. Moreover, because the petition for a writ of *certiorari* is supposed to demonstrate that it presents only issues already presented to the state courts, *see* S. Ct. R. 14.1(i), the petition itself and any response by the state, may clarify the extent to which the federal law aspects of the relevant issues have been exhausted in the state courts.

(11) The state postconviction record,[67] including:
    (a) Pleadings, answer, reply or traverse;
    (b) Motions;
    (c) Discovery requests and documents;
    (d) Hearing, argument, and proffer transcripts;
    (e) Exhibits;
    (f) Memoranda of law, briefs;
    (g) Orders, rulings, opinions;
    (h) Postconviction appellate record.

(12) Trial and appellate counsel's files,[68] including:
    (a) Correspondence with the client and the client's family;[69]
    (b) Correspondence with the prosecutor;[70]
    (c) Correspondence with witnesses and potential witnesses, including expert witnesses;[71]
    (d) Correspondence with the court;[72]
    (e) Other correspondence;
    (f) Notes from investigation;
    (g) Legal notes and memoranda;

---

[67] Because counsel ordinarily will have engaged in investigative efforts to discover claims prior to state postconviction proceedings, the types of records potentially generated during post-conviction which counsel should make a point of analyzing before filing the *federal* habeas corpus petition are only briefly sketched here. Apart from the claims discussed *supra* §§ 7.1b (denial of a full and fair state postconviction remedy) and 7.2 (denial of appointment of counsel, experts and investigator, and of essential financial assistance), possible ineffective assistance of state postconviction counsel (which generally does not violate the 6th Amendment but may do so under limited circumstances, *see supra* § 7.2e nn.87-94, *infra* § 26.3b n.36), and misconduct by the state (*e.g.,* via suppression of evidence), it is not very likely that *new* constitutional claims will arise (although any number of preexisting but previously hidden claims may surface) during state postconviction review. Instead, counsel's review of the state postconviction record is likely to reveal already formulated federal claims, claims requiring further "federalization" and exhaustion (*see supra* notes 42, 64-65), claims as to which counsel must be prepared to counter procedural default assertions and other procedural defenses likely to be asserted by the state, and, most importantly, claims as to which full *de novo* federal relitigation, including of factual issues, is required because of the state court's failure to provide a full, fair, and adequate means to adjudicate them (*see infra* Chapter 20; *infra* § 32.3).

[68] *See supra* note 21.

[69] *Possible claims include:* competency to stand trial; ineffective assistance with regard to pre-trial preparation, client contact, mental health and other defenses, mitigation of punishment; police misconduct; confessions; search and seizure; government informers in violation of right to counsel; access by counsel to client. *See supra* notes 14-19 and accompanying text; *supra* Chapter 4.

[70] *See supra* note 35.

[71] *Claims:* claims listed *supra* notes 26, 39.

[72] *Claims:* claims listed *supra* note 42.

(h)   Expert reports not utilized at trial;

(i)   Any other document, computer file, audiotape, or videotape generated in the case by former counsel.

(13) Law enforcement files, documents, and other evidence:[73]

(a)   Police reports;[74]

---

[73] In some instances, the state's attorney defending a postconviction case will provide the complete police and prosecution file in the case or portions of it. In other instances, local police officers or the local prosecutor, now that responsibility for the case has passed out of their hands, will be willing to do the same. *See supra* notes 30, 35. Counsel certainly should explore these informal means of access to the relevant law enforcement records.

On other occasions, counsel will have to invoke more formal means of securing access. A number of states provide by statute, caselaw, or local practice for discovery during postconviction proceedings either at counsel's behest or upon motion requesting that the court exercise its discretion to order production of documents, depositions, interrogations, and the like. Counsel should consult the postconviction statute, rules of court, and attorneys familiar with local practices in this regard. In federal habeas corpus proceedings, discovery is available upon motion to the court. *See infra* § 19.4.

Counsel also may assert the various available constitutional grounds for securing access to the relevant law enforcement files. The due process principle of Brady v. Maryland, 373 U.S. 83 (1963), as explained in United States v. Agurs, 427 U.S. 97, 103-07 (1976), and United States v. Bagley, 473 U.S. 667, 674-78 (1985), and Kyles v. Whitley, 514 U.S. 419 (1995), may apply in postconviction proceedings to require production of all materials in state officials' control that are exculpatory in the sense that their production would assist the prisoner in establishing that the conviction or sentence violates the Constitution. *See e.g.,* Walker v. Lockhart, 763 F.2d 942, 955 (8th Cir. 1985) (*en banc*), *cert. denied,* 478 U.S. 1020 (1986) (finding prosecutorial suppression of evidence violation based in part on police officer's post-trial suppression of evidence, including during state and federal postconviction proceedings). To the extent, moreover, that counsel can demonstrate that production of the requested materials is essential to the full, fair, and adequate adjudication of the constitutional claims in the case, the due process and "suspension of the writ" considerations discussed *supra* §§ 7.1b, 7.2 provide additional constitutional bases for demanding access to law enforcement files.

Finally, pursuant to the requirement of federal habeas corpus relitigation of factual issues as to which the state proceedings were not "full and fair" (*see infra* Chapter 20), any denial by the *state* postconviction court of access to important information in the state's control provides counsel with good reason to invoke the full panoply of *federal* fact-development devices, including discovery. *See generally infra* Chapters 19, 20. Reference to this federal statutory argument is sometimes sufficient to induce state postconviction courts to provide discovery they otherwise would deny and thereby to assure that any factfindings they make thereafter will hold up in subsequent federal habeas corpus proceedings. Even in those situations in which counsel is virtually certain that discovery will be denied by the state courts, counsel should request it if she considers discovery important to the full, fair, and adequate development of a constitutional claim. As is discussed in more detail, *supra* § 7.1a, counsel's failure to request discovery even in this "futile" situation may have adverse consequences in federal habeas proceedings. *See also infra* note 84 (Freedom of Information Act requests).

[74] *See supra* note 30.

(b)   Police, "911," arrest, property, inventory, and other logs;[75]

(c)   Police and prosecutors' witness interview notes and reports;[76]

(d)   Pathologist's, coroner's, polygraph examiner's, and other forensic reports and underlying data, notes and records, including as to experts or information *not* presented at trial;[77]

(e)   Examination of the property locker or cage, including for evidence not presented at trial;[78]

(f)   Photographs of the scene of the offense;[79]

(g)   Mug shots of the petitioner at the time of the arrest;[80]

(h)   Reports on medical, psychiatric, physical, or forensic examinations of or operations performed on petitioner;[81]

(i)   Jail records, especially regarding petitioner's location at relevant times; medical condition or treatment of petitioner, or drugs administered to her; and fact and frequency of visitation by trial counsel, law enforcement officials, witnesses, family members, friends, and others;[82]

(j)   Prosecutor's file on the case, including interview notes; notes on exercise of prosecutorial discretion to charge, accept plea, strike prospective jurors peremptorily, recommend sentence, or seek the death penalty; expert reports; correspondence with petitioner, witnesses, the victim's family;[83]

(k)   FBI, DEA, Bureau of Alcohol, Tobacco and Firearms, Secret Service, and other federal investigative files, including on cases tried in state courts;[84]

---

[75] *See id.*

[76] *See supra* notes 30, 35, 39.

[77] *See supra* note 30.

[78] *See id.*

[79] *See id.*

[80] *See id.*

[81] *See id.*

[82] *See supra* notes 17, 30.

[83] *See supra* note 35.

[84] *See supra* notes 30, 35. Increasingly, postconviction petitioners have used requests for documents under the Freedom of Information Act, 5 U.S.C. § 552 (1994) to secure valuable information in the hands of federal law enforcement officials who assisted state officials in the investigation and prosecution of the offense for which the petitioner was convicted. *See, e.g.,* United States Dep't of Justice v. Landano, 508 U.S. 165, 168 (1993). Sometimes, the FBI records even reveal exculpatory information developed, but suppressed, by local law enforcement officials. If there is any hint of federal involvement in the investigation of the case — on the part of the FBI, DEA, Bureau of Alcohol, Tobacco and Firearms, Secret Service, or other federal law enforcement

(l) Police or prosecutorial policy statements, manuals, files, logs, reports, statistical (especially racial, ethnic, gender, socio-economic, and geographic) data (not necessarily specific to any individual case) regarding exercise of prosecutorial discretion as to:[85]

   (i)   Who, and what reported offenses, to investigate;
   (ii)   Whether, when, and what offenses to charge;
   (iii) When to negotiate and what pleas to accept;
   (iv)   When to invoke "multiple or habitual offender," "use of firearm," and other enhancement possibilities;
   (v)   What sentencing alternatives to recommend;
   (vi)   When to seek the death penalty;
   (vii) How to exercise peremptory challenges of prospective jurors;
   (viii) How to select grand and petit juries;
   (ix)   When and how police officers and prosecutors suspected of abusive law-enforcement practices are disciplined;
   (x)   What information in law enforcement files is disclosed to defendants.

(14) Inspection of the scenes of the offense and of the arrest, police searches, and other investigatory procedures.[86]

(15) Records relating to the client's character and background,[87] including records relating to:

   (a) Elementary, secondary, vocational, college, graduate and other education;
   (b) Medical or physical condition;
   (c) Mental health;
   (d) Substance abuse;
   (e) Employment;
   (f) Contact with juvenile, child abuse, welfare, drug abuse, housing, employment, and other social service agencies;
   (g) Military, law enforcement, or other governmental service;
   (h) Incarceration or other institutionalization;
   (i) Parole, probation, or supervised release status;
   (j) Arrests, convictions, and sentences.

---

agencies — postconviction counsel routinely should request the relevant information through available means.

[85] See supra note 35.

[86] See supra note 30.

[87] See supra notes 14-19, 30, 35. To secure such records, counsel should have petitioner sign an affidavit authorizing release of such documents to counsel. See supra note 28. For an example of a release of information of this sort, see RANDY HERTZ, MARTIN GUGGENHEIM & ANTHONY G. AMSTERDAM, 1 TRIAL MANUAL FOR DEFENSE ATTORNEYS IN JUVENILE COURT § 5.11 (1991).

(16) Correspondence, photographs, and memorabilia relating to petitioner's childhood, family life, and background.[88]

(17) Newspaper articles and media audiotapes and videotapes regarding:

    (a)   The client's background and record;[89]

    (b)   The offense;[90]

    (c)   The police investigation, including confessions, line-ups, show-ups, physical examinations of the defendant or witnesses (including the taking of hair, fingernail, blood or other samples), fingerprints, gunpowder tests, handwriting samples, polygraph examinations, and the like;[91]

    (d)   Pretrial proceedings in the defendant's and codefendants' cases;[92]

    (e)   The trial in the defendant's and codefendants' cases;[93]

    (f)   Sentencing proceedings in the defendant's and codefendants' cases;[94]

    (g)   Post-trial proceedings in the defendant's and codefendants' cases;[95]

    (h)   Appellate oral arguments in the defendant's and codefendants' cases;

    (i)   Postconviction proceedings;[96]

    (j)   The setting of execution dates and stay of execution proceedings.

    c. *Examples of federal habeas corpus claims that have prevailed.* Because of the wide range of claims cognizable in federal habeas corpus proceedings[97] and the virtually infinite number of factual variations possible with regard to each claim, any list of the substantive grounds for federal habeas corpus relief is necessarily incomplete. Rather than attempting to inventory all, or even most, of the claims that could be raised in a federal habeas corpus petition,[98] this section provides a rough indication of the range and variety of substantive claims by listing and briefly describing some of the claims that have resulted in a federal

---

[88] *See supra* note 19.

[89] *See id.*

[90] *See supra* notes 19, 30, 35.

[91] *See supra* notes 30, 35.

[92] *See supra* notes 42-53.

[93] *See supra* notes 27, 42-61.

[94] *See supra* notes 27, 41-63.

[95] *See supra* notes 27, 64.

[96] *See supra* note 67.

[97] *See supra* §§ 2.3, 2.4, 9.1, 9.2.

[98] The first edition of this treatise contains a listing of the most common claims available at the time of the book's publication in 1988. *See* 2 JAMES S. LIEBMAN, FEDERAL HABEAS CORPUS PRACTICE AND PROCEDURE 709-36 (1st ed. 1988) (Appendices C and D).

court's granting of habeas corpus relief over the last 35 or 40 years.[99] The list is arranged in approximately the order in which the constitutional issues are likely to have arisen as a petitioner's case moved through the various stages of the underlying criminal proceeding from arrest through trial and appeal.[100] At the end of the list is a collection of cases in which a writ of habeas corpus was granted because of ineffective assistance of counsel at trial or upon appeal.

(1) Claims attacking a search or seizure, interrogation, identification procedure, or other investigative practice employed by a law enforcement official or other agent of the state:

- Withrow v. Williams, 597 U.S. 680 (1993) (affirming grant of habeas corpus relief because police used trickery in securing confession from petitioner).

- Miller v. Fenton, 474 U.S. 104 (1985) (petitioner convicted on basis of involuntary confession that police extracted by intensively interrogating him while he was in state of physical shock and by telling petitioner he would not be punished if he confessed).

- Brewer v. Williams, 430 U.S. 387 (1977) (police driving petitioner across Iowa after petitioner's arraignment and aware of petitioner's background as former mental patient and his deep religious convictions obtained confession by violating promise to counsel not to interrogate petitioner and by giving petitioner an impassioned speech stating that kidnapping victim was entitled to a "Christian burial").

- Davis v. North Carolina, 384 U.S. 737 (1966) (confessions obtained after petitioner held incommunicado for 16 days in small cell on meager diet that resulted in 15-pound weight loss).

- Jackson v. Denno, 378 U.S. 368 (1964) (denial of fair hearing and of reliable determination of voluntariness of confession).

- Fay v. Noia, 372 U.S. 391 (1963) (confession resulting from lengthy incommunicado police interrogation of petitioner).

- Washington v. DeMorales, 1997 WL 547990 (9th Cir. Aug. 28, 1997), cert. denied, 118 S. Ct. 853 (1998) (police violated Miranda rule following accused's assertion of right to silence).

---

[99] For other surveys of habeas corpus cases, see 1 JAMES S. LIEBMAN & RANDY HERTZ, FEDERAL HABEAS CORPUS PRACTICE AND PROCEDURE 7-13 (1993 Cum. Supp.) (including many of same cases listed below but also older and district court cases not cited below); Curtis R. Reitz, Federal Habeas Corpus: Postconviction Remedy for State Prisoners, 108 U. PA. L. REV. 460, 481-88 (1960) (citing 1950s cases); Michael Wells, Habeas Corpus and Freedom of Speech, 1978 DUKE L.J. 1307, 1349-51 (citing 70 cases decided in 15 years preceding article); Brief Amici Curiae of Benjamin Civiletti, et al., in Support of Respondent in Wright v. West, No. 91-542, 505 U.S. 277 (1992) (filed Mar. 4, 1992), App. B (listing 149 capital habeas corpus cases in which relief was granted between mid-1978 and mid-1991); authority cited supra § 11.2a n.4.

[100] For an overview of the chronology of a criminal case, see supra § 3.5a.

- Shillinger v. Haworth, 70 F.3d 1132 (10th Cir. 1995) (deputy sheriff's listening in on and reporting to prosecutor substance of defense counsel's jailhouse conversations with client violated 6th Amendment right to counsel).

- Roberts v. Maine, 48 F.3d 1287 (1st Cir. 1995) (although 6th Amendment right to counsel had not yet attached, police violated Due Process Clause by refusing to "honor [petitioner's] ... reasonable request to call an attorney" after giving him misleading information about consequences of refusal to take blood/alcohol test).

- Kordenbrock v. Scroggy, 919 F.2d 1091 (6th Cir. 1990) (*en banc*), *cert. denied*, 499 U.S. 970 (1991) (confession obtained after police ignored petitioner's statements that he did not want to talk and wanted interrogation to cease and after police threatened to arrest petitioner's girlfriend (against whom they had no evidence) and to send petitioner to Ohio where, police said, he could be held incommunicado for days and put through "an ordeal [he] may not forget for a long time").

- Cervi v. Kemp, 855 F.2d 702 (11th Cir. 1988), *cert. denied*, 489 U.S. 1033 (1989) (rule of Edwards v. Arizona, 451 U.S. 477 (1981), violated when Georgia police officer interrogated petitioner in Iowa jail after he requested appointment of counsel with regard to extradition to Georgia).

- Christopher v. Florida, 824 F.2d 836 (11th Cir. 1987), *cert. denied*, 484 U.S. 1077 (1988) (rule of Michigan v. Mosley, 423 U.S. 96 (1975), violated when police failed to terminate interrogation after petitioner asserted right to silence).

- Felder v. McCotter, 765 F.2d 1245 (5th Cir. 1985), *cert. denied*, 475 U.S. 1111 (1986) (police interrogated defendant after 6th Amendment right to counsel had attached and without adequate waiver of right to presence of counsel).

- Jurek v. Estelle, 623 F.2d 929 (5th Cir. 1980) (*en banc*), *cert. denied*, 450 U.S. 1001 (1981) (police obtained two vastly different confessions from mentally deficient petitioner during 42-hour period of interrogation without counsel; exculpatory version appeared voluntary and to be in defendant's words while inculpatory version (used at trial) was involuntary and in prose beyond defendant's ken).

(2) Claims attacking the validity of the charging paper or the underlying charge on procedural or substantive grounds:

- Vasquez v. Hillery, 474 U.S. 254 (1986) (grand jury selection process systematically excluded blacks).

- Crist v. Bretz, 437 U.S. 28 (1978) (double jeopardy violation).

- Castaneda v. Partida, 430 U.S. 482 (1977) (Mexican-American petitioner suffered intentional discrimination in grand jury selection process; only 39 percent of those summoned for grand jury service were Mexican-American although that group accounted for 79 percent of county population).

- Smith v. Goguen, 415 U.S. 566 (1974) (petitioner convicted under Massachusetts' vague flag-misuse statute).

- Harpster v. Ohio, 128 F.3d 322 (6th Cir. 1997), *cert. denied*, 118 S. Ct. 1044 (1998) (retrial would violate double jeopardy because previous mistrial based on potential juror bias was not compelled by manifest necessity).

- Love v. Morton, 112 F.3d 131 (3d Cir. 1997) (double jeopardy violation).

- Forgy v. Norris, 64 F.3d 399 (8th Cir. 1995) (charging instrument's failure to specify predicate crime for burglary charge violated due process right to fair notice of charges).

- Weston v. Kernan, 50 F.3d 633 (9th Cir.), *cert. denied*, 516 U.S. 937 (1995) (because trial judge granted mistrial over petitioner's objection and without adequate consideration of alternatives, Double Jeopardy Clause precludes retrial).

- McIntyre v. Caspari, 35 F.3d 338 (8th Cir. 1994), *cert. denied*, 514 U.S. 1077 (1995) (double jeopardy violation).

- Redner v. Dean, 29 F.3d 1495 (11th Cir. 1994), *cert. denied*, 514 U.S. 1066 (1995) (county licensing ordinance regulating "adult entertainment establishments" that feature nude dancing violated First Amendment).

- Malinovsky v. Court of Common Pleas, 7 F.3d 1263 (6th Cir. 1993), *cert. denied*, 510 U.S. 1194 (1994) (Double Jeopardy Clause bars retrial of petitioner because first trial ended in mistrial, declared over petitioner's objection and without "manifest necessity").

- Sabel v. Stynchcombe, 746 F.2d 728 (11th Cir. 1984) (overturning conviction under state statute criminalizing abrasive speech).

- Monroe v. State Ct., 739 F.2d 568 (11th Cir. 1984) (state flag desecration statute unconstitutional as applied to petitioner).

(3) **Claims attacking prosecutorial or police suppression of evidence or other discovery-related practices:**

- Kyles v. Whitley, 514 U.S. 491 (1995) ("Because the net effect of the evidence withheld by the State in this case raises a reasonable probability that its disclosure would have produced a different result, Kyles is entitled to a new trial.").

- Carriger v. Stewart, 132 F.3d 463 (9th Cir. 1997) (*en banc*), *cert. denied*, 118 S. Ct. 1827 (1998) (prosecutor failed to disclose information in state's files showing that prosecution's central witness — who later confessed to murder for which petitioner was tried, convicted and sentenced to death — had been previously committed to mental hospital for violent rages and threats against his family, had long history of prior crimes and assaultive acts, and had "long history of lying to the police and blaming others to cover up his own guilt").

- East v. Johnson, 123 F.3d 235 (5th Cir. 1997) (prosecutor suppressed information that would have led defense to discover report raising substantial questions about sanity and credibility of crucial sentencing hearing witness who claimed that petitioner robbed and raped her prior to murder for which petitioner was sentenced to die).

- Guerra v. Johnson, 90 F.3d 1075 (5th Cir. 1996) (police coerced two eyewitnesses, who initially told police that fatal shots were fired by petitioner's companion, into corroborating prosecution's theory that petitioner fired shots; police told one witness that her common-law husband was at risk of parole revocation if she did not cooperate and told other witness that her infant daughter could be taken from her if she refused to cooperate).

- Riggins v. Rees, 74 F.3d 732 (6th Cir. 1996) (state's refusal to provide petitioner with transcripts, rather than merely court reporter's tape recordings, of previous two trials which ended in mistrial violated Equal Protection Clause).

455

- Love v. Johnson, 57 F.3d 1305 (4th Cir. 1995) (trial judge violated Due Process Clause by quashing petitioner's pretrial subpoenas *duces tecum* for state agency records without first conducting *in camera* inspection of subpoenaed records to determine whether portions were material and favorable to the defense).

- Banks v. Reynolds, 54 F.3d 1508 (10th Cir. 1995) (prosecution suppressed evidence that at least three other men were previously arrested for crime with which petitioner was charged, that two of them had been positively identified by eyewitnesses, and that cell-mate of one of previously arrested suspects claimed that suspect had confessed to crime).

- Devose v. Norris, 53 F.3d 201 (8th Cir. 1995) (petitioner was entitled under Roviaro v. United States, 353 U.S. 53 (1957), to disclosure of identity of confidential informant, particularly given that informant was "eyewitness to the offense ... [and therefore] could have shed sorely needed light on the events that took place").

- Smith v. Secretary of New Mexico Dep't of Corrections, 50 F.3d 801 (10th Cir.), *cert. denied*, 516 U.S. 905 (1995) (prosecutor failed to disclose that individual whom defense claimed was actual murderer was found in possession of bloody clothes, made statements indicating motive for murders, was using false name, and had prior record under real name).

- Orndorff v. Lockhart, 998 F.2d 1426 (8th Cir. 1993), *cert. denied*, 511 U.S. 1063 (1994) (prosecutor failed to inform defense that key witness in favor of death penalty was hypnotized prior to trial, preventing fair cross-examination concerning discrepancies between witness's prehypnotic and posthypnotic statements to police).

- Jean v. Rice, 945 F.2d 82 (4th Cir. 1991) (prosecution suppressed tape recordings and records showing that both of prosecution's key witnesses changed their accounts before trial under hypnosis performed by police captain whose "only training in this area had been a two-week course in investigative hypnosis").

- Kordenbrock v. Scroggy, 919 F.2d 1091 (6th Cir. 1990) (*en banc*), *cert. denied*, 499 U.S. 970 (1991) (police suppressed tape-recorded version of confession and pieced together written statement that gave description of crime different from description in actual confession).

- McDowell v. Dixon, 858 F.2d 945 (4th Cir. 1988), *cert. denied*, 489 U.S. 1033 (1989) (police withheld fact that chief prosecution witness, who at trial identified petitioner, an African-American, as the assailant, told police the assailant was white).

- Troedel v. Dugger, 828 F.2d 670 (11th Cir. 1987), *aff'g* 667 F. Supp. 1426 (S.D. Fla. 1986) (prosecutor suborned testimony of expert witness at separate trials of two codefendants that each codefendant had to have been sole triggerman in single killing with which both were charged and for which Troedel was sentenced to death).

- Carter v. Rafferty, 826 F.2d 1299 (3d Cir. 1987), *cert. denied*, 484 U.S. 1011 (1988) (prosecution suppressed statement of its most crucial witness corroborating other witnesses' trial testimony favorable to defendant; on retrial, charges dropped and petitioner released).

- Bowen v. Maynard, 799 F.2d 593 (10th Cir.), *cert. denied*, 479 U.S. 962 (1986) (prosecutor suppressed sheaf of investigative reports establishing that someone other than petitioner had murdered victim and that investigating officer with grudge against petitioner had maliciously framed him).

- Brown v. Wainwright, 785 F.2d 1457 (11th Cir. 1986) (state deliberately withheld fact that chief witness against petitioner repeatedly failed polygraph test; petitioner thereafter released from prison after charges dropped).

- Lindsey v. King, 769 F.2d 1034 (5th Cir. 1985) (prosecutor concealed statements to police in which witness, who identified petitioner at trial as perpetrator, admitted he did not see perpetrator's face).

- Walker v. Lockhart, 763 F.2d 942 (8th Cir. 1985) (*en banc*), *cert. denied*, 478 U.S. 1020 (1986) (prosecutorial suppression of exculpatory evidence).

- Blake v. Kemp, 758 F.2d 523 (11th Cir.), *cert. denied*, 474 U.S. 998 (1985) (state's withholding of important evidence relating to petitioner's sanity until day before trial precluded meaningful opportunity to prepare and present insanity defense).

- Monroe v. Blackburn, 748 F.2d 958 (5th Cir. 1984), *cert. denied*, 476 U.S. 1145 (1986) (state failed to disclose that police obtained information after completion of trial that someone other than petitioner may have committed murder).

- Chaney v. Brown, 730 F.2d 1334 (10th Cir.), *cert. denied*, 469 U.S. 1090 (1984) (prosecution suppressed evidence showing that petitioner did not commit killing for which he was sentenced to death).

- White v. Estelle, 685 F.2d 927 (5th Cir. 1982) (prosecution concealed whereabouts of undercover police officer whose testimony would have created reasonable doubt as to petitioner's guilt).

- Chavis v. North Carolina, 637 F.2d 213 (4th Cir. 1980) (prosecutor suppressed corrected statement of crucial witness and witness's psychiatric records).

- Freeman v. Georgia, 599 F.2d 65 (5th Cir. 1979), *cert. denied*, 444 U.S. 1013 (1980) (police detective knowingly concealed whereabouts of eyewitness to crime, visited her frequently before and near time of trial, and married her one year after trial).

- Lockett v. Blackburn, 571 F.2d 309 (5th Cir.), *cert. denied*, 439 U.S. 873 (1978) (prosecutor paid two defense witnesses to leave jurisdiction).

- Barbee v. Warden, 331 F.2d 842 (4th Cir. 1964) (police suppressed results of fingerprint and ballistics tests that cast doubt upon whether gun allegedly used by petitioner was murder weapon).

- Lambert v. Blackwell, 962 F. Supp. 1521 (E.D. Pa. 1997), *vacated & remanded on nonexhaustion grounds*, 134 F.3d 506 (3d Cir. 1998) (petitioner "proved at least by clear and convincing evidence" "at least twenty-five" instances of "obstruction of justice, perjured testimony, the wholesale suppression of exculpatory evidence and the fabrication of inculpatory evidence" by prosecutors and police officers which resulted in "trial [that] was corrupted from start to finish by wholesale prosecutorial misconduct" and conviction of innocent woman; on appeal, circuit court vacates and remands for exhaustion of state remedies, commenting that exhaustion will let state courts correct their own errors).

- Miller and Jent v. Wainwright, Nos. 86-98-Civ.-T-13 and 85-1910-Civ.-T-13 (M.D. Fla. Nov. 13, 1987), at 7-8, 11-13 (prosecutor exhibited "callous and deliberate disregard for the fundamental principles of truth and fairness that underlie our criminal justice system" by suppressing police reports identifying numerous witnesses who were fishing at location where victim's body was found at only time when capitally sentenced petitioners (who otherwise had airtight alibi defenses) could have deposited victim's body and who saw nothing amiss; charges dropped on retrial).

(4) Claims relating to the denial of expert assistance:

- Starr v. Lockhart, 23 F.3d 1280 (8th Cir. 1994) (indigent petitioner denied expert needed to prove diminished capacity mitigating circumstance).
- Liles v. Saffle, 945 F.2d 333 (10th Cir. 1991), *cert. denied*, 502 U.S. 1066 (1992) (due process violated by denial of motion for psychiatric assistance in preparing and presenting insanity defense at trial and in refuting claim of future dangerousness at capital sentencing hearing).
- Smith v. McCormick, 914 F.2d 1153 (9th Cir. 1990) (trial judge violated rule of Ake v. Oklahoma, 470 U.S. 68 (1985), by denying request for defense expert and instead appointing court expert who would report directly to judge).
- Buttrum v. Black, 908 F.2d 695 (11th Cir. 1990) (trial court's limited grant of psychiatric assistance deprived petitioner of psychiatric testing and testimony needed to present adequate defense at capital sentencing hearing).

(5) Claims relating to accused's incapacity to stand trial:

- Blazak v. Ricketts, 1 F.3d 891 (9th Cir. 1993), *cert. denied*, 511 U.S. 1097 (1994) (trial court failed to conduct competency hearing despite petitioner's history of mental illness and finding of incompetency to stand trial at prior trial on unrelated charges).
- Lafferty v. Cook, 949 F.2d 1546 (10th Cir. 1991), *cert. denied*, 504 U.S. 911 (1992) (state trial court's finding of competency to stand trial relied on legal standard inconsistent with due process; because record contained evidence that would have permitted finding of incompetency under proper standard, court grants writ and vacates conviction and death sentence).
- Wallace v. Kemp, 757 F.2d 1102 (11th Cir. 1985) (capitally sentenced petitioner found to have been incompetent to assist attorney at trial; on retrial after being restored to sanity, petitioner was acquitted).
- Strickland v. Francis, 738 F.2d 1542 (11th Cir. 1984) (evidence did not support special jury's finding that petitioner was competent to stand trial; state violated due process by subjecting incompetent petitioner to trial).

(6) Claims challenging denial of a change of venue, jury-selection procedures, other jury-related practices, or neutrality of judge:

- Bracy v. Gramley, 520 U.S. 899 (1997) (because judge who presided at trial at which petitioner was convicted and sentenced to die took bribes in return for leniency in many cases besides petitioner's, sometimes exhibited bias against defendants like petitioner who did not pay bribes, and had incentive to compensate for leniency in cases in which bribes were paid by being excessively harsh in other cases, district court abused discretion in denying petitioner discovery of documents in government's control that might show that judge was biased in favor of state in petitioner's case).

- Amadeo v. Zant, 486 U.S. 214 (1988) (jury selection pursuant to deliberate scheme devised by district attorney and jury commissioners to underrepresent African-Americans and women; scheme memorialized in handwritten note found after trial and appeal in office of clerk of court).

- Turner v. Murray, 476 U.S. 28 (1986) (capital defendant charged with interracial crime entitled to have prospective jurors informed of victim's race and questioned on subject of racial bias).

- Sheppard v. Maxwell, 384 U.S. 333 (1966) (massive, pervasive and prejudicial pretrial publicity and circus-style atmosphere at trial).

- Irvin v. Dowd, 366 U.S. 717 (1961) (failure to grant second change of venue despite widespread and inflammatory publicity; 8 of 12 jurors seated admitted to belief that defendant was guilty).

- Mach v. Stewart, 137 F.3d 630 (9th Cir. 1998) (jury was tainted by exposure during *voir dire* to repeated statements by prospective juror, a social worker, that children's claims of sexual abuse, like those in case on which jury was about to sit, had been confirmed in every case she had seen).

- Turner v. Marshall, 121 F.3d 1248 (9th Cir. 1997), *cert. denied*, 118 F.3d 1178 (1998) (prosecutor's use of peremptory challenges to strike African-American members of venire was not justified by stated reason, which was found to be pretext).

- Ford v. Norris, 67 F.3d 162 (8th Cir. 1995) (prosecutor's intentional use of peremptory challenges to exclude African-Americans from jury violated rule of Swain v. Alabama, 380 U.S. 202 (1965)).

- Miller v. Lockhart, 65 F.3d 676 (8th Cir. 1995) (same as *Ford v. Norris, supra*).

- Devose v. Norris, 53 F.3d 201 (8th Cir. 1995) (prosecutor's use of peremptory challenges to exclude African-American venirepersons violated Batson v. Kentucky, 476 U.S. 79 (1986), because ostensibly "race-neutral" rationale for excluding venirepersons "was pretextual").

- Simmons v. Beyer, 44 F.3d 1160 (3d Cir.), *cert. denied*, 516 U.S. 905 (1995) (prosecutor's use of peremptory strikes to exclude African-American venirepersons violated *Batson v. Kentucky, supra*).

- Cochran v. Herring, 43 F.3d 1404 (11th Cir.), *modified*, 61 F.3d 20 (11th Cir. 1995), *cert. denied*, 516 U.S. 1073 (1996) (*Batson* violation).

- Johnson v. Vasquez, 3 F.3d 1327 (9th Cir. 1993) (prosecutor, who used peremptory challenge to exclude only African-American member of venire, was unable to provide credible race-neutral explanation).

- Pilchak v. Camper, 935 F.2d 145 (8th Cir. 1991) (deputy sheriff who investigated case also personally picked jury venire).

- Knox v. Collins, 928 F.2d 657 (5th Cir. 1991) (*per curiam*) (in exercising peremptory challenges, counsel reasonably relied on judge's subsequently withdrawn promise to instruct jury at sentencing about limited eligibility for parole in event of life sentence).

- Woods v. Dugger, 923 F.2d 1454 (11th Cir. 1991) (combination of extensive pretrial publicity and presence of numerous uniformed prison guards in audience to show solidarity with decedent, who was prison guard).

- Berryhill v. Zant, 858 F.2d 633 (11th Cir. 1988) (underrepresentation of women on master jury list).
- Coleman v. Kemp, 778 F.2d 1487 (11th Cir. 1985), *cert. denied*, 476 U.S. 1164 (1986) and Isaacs v. Kemp, 778 F.2d 1482 (11th Cir. 1985), *cert. denied*, 476 U.S. 1164 (1986) (petitioners tried in small town where prejudicial publicity compromised nearly every juror, many of whom attended victims' funeral).
- Davis v. Kemp, 752 F.2d 1515 (11th Cir.) (*en banc*) (*per curiam*), *cert. denied*, 471 U.S. 1143 (1985) (reinstating in pertinent part, Davis v. Zant, 721 F.2d 1478 (11th Cir. 1983)) (underrepresentation of African-Americans and women in traverse jury pool).
- Gibson v. Zant, 705 F.2d 1543 (11th Cir. 1983) (underrepresentation of African-Americans and women in venire for both grand and petit juries).
- Hance v. Zant, 696 F.2d 940 (11th Cir.), *cert. denied*, 463 U.S. 1210 (1983) (exclusion of two venirepersons violated rule of Witherspoon v. Illinois, 391 U.S. 510 (1968), because their "responses regarding the death penalty were not automatic and unequivocal" and "they expressed uncertainty about their convictions and ambiguity about their feelings").
- Thompson v. White, 680 F.2d 1173 (8th Cir. 1982), *cert. denied*, 459 U.S. 1177 (1983) (petitioners convicted by jurors handpicked by local sheriff).
- Machetti v. Linahan, 679 F.2d 236 (11th Cir. 1982), *cert. denied*, 459 U.S. 1127 (1983) (right to representative jury violated by procedure permitting women but not men to avoid jury service by sending notice to jury commissioners).
- Moore v. Estelle, 670 F.2d 56 (5th Cir.), *cert. denied*, 458 U.S. 1111 (1982) (rule of *Witherspoon v. Illinois, supra*, precluded exclusion of venireperson who expressed opposition to death penalty but said she would "do it right" if "you make me do it").
- Granviel v. Estelle, 655 F.2d 673 (5th Cir. 1981), *cert. denied*, 455 U.S. 1003 (1982) (venireperson's statements that he did not "think" he could vote in favor of death and did not "feel ... entitled to take another person's life" insufficient to justify exclusion under rule of Witherspoon v. Illinois, *supra*).
- Henson v. Wyrick, 634 F.2d 1080 (8th Cir. 1980), *cert. denied*, 450 U.S. 958 (1981) (similar to *Thompson v. White, supra*).
- Burns v. Estelle, 626 F.2d 396 (5th Cir. 1980) (*en banc*) (venireperson's statements about death penalty fell short of "unequivocal avowals disqualifying her" under rule of *Witherspoon v. Illinois, supra*).
- Bailey v. Henslee, 287 F.2d 936 (8th Cir.), *cert. denied*, 368 U.S. 877 (1961) (racial discrimination in selection of all-white jury for black petitioner sentenced to death for rape).

(7) Claims relating to a guilty plea:

- United States v. De La Fuente, 8 F.3d 1333 (9th Cir. 1993) (section 2255 motion granted on due process grounds because government breached plea agreement by refusing to accept below-minimum sentence after movant fulfilled his obligations by providing government with information about codefendant).
- United States v. Roberts, 5 F.3d 365 (9th Cir. 1993) (section 2255 motion granted because guilty plea colloquy did not satisfy requirement of FED. RULE CRIM. P. 11 that judge advise defendant of maximum possible penalty).

- Fair v. Zant, 715 F.2d 1519 (11th Cir. 1983) (state trial judge informed capitally sentenced petitioner that guilty plea could later be withdrawn upon hearing sentence, then refused to withdraw it on petitioner's request).

(8) **Claims relating to evidence, procedures, and practices at trial:**

- Wainwright v. Greenfield, 474 U.S. 284 (1985) (state permitted to use, as evidence of petitioner's guilt, fact that petitioner exercised right to silence after police officers thrice told him he could refuse to talk to them without suffering adverse consequences).

- Miller v. Pate, 386 U.S. 1 (1967) (prosecutor claimed at trial that principal item of evidence, a pair of shorts, was stained with blood when he knew that substance on shorts was in fact paint).

- Eslaminia v. White, 136 F.3d 1234 (9th Cir. 1998) (jury's exposure to unadmitted, prejudicial statement of petitioner's brother, which was on reverse side of police audiotape introduced into evidence, deprived petitioner of rights to confrontation, cross-examination, and assistance of counsel).

- Snowden v. Singletary, 135 F.3d 732 (11th Cir. 1998) (trial on charges of sexual abuse of child violated due process right to fair trial because prosecutor presented and relied heavily on inaccurate expert testimony that "99.5 % of children tell the truth" when making accusations of abuse).

- Jones v. Vacco, 126 F.3d 408 (2d Cir. 1997) (trial judge improperly barred petitioner from conferring with counsel during overnight recess in midst of petitioner's cross-examination).

- Lindh v. Murphy, 124 F.3d 899 (7th Cir. 1997), *cert. denied*, 118 S. Ct. 739 (1998) (at insanity phase of trial, judge violated Confrontation Clause by forbidding petitioner's counsel to cross-examine state's psychiatrist on biases created by threatened prosecution of psychiatrist for sexually abusing patients).

- Agard v. Portuondo, 117 F.3d 696 (2d Cir. 1997) (prosecutor violated petitioner's rights to fair trial, confrontation, and testify in own behalf by stating, in closing argument, that petitioner's presence in courtroom during trial enabled him to tailor his testimony to what other witnesses said).

- Lyons v. Johnson, 99 F.3d 499 (2d Cir. 1996) (denial of defense request that jury view person whom defense claimed was actual perpetrator violated due process right to fair trial).

- Justice v. Hoke, 90 F.3d 43 (2d Cir. 1996) (exclusion of defense witnesses' testimony casting doubt on complainant's credibility and supporting defense theory of fabrication violated 6th Amendment right to present defense).

- Ayala v. Speckard, 89 F.3d 91 (2d Cir. 1996) (closure of courtroom to protect identity of undercover officer violated petitioner's right to public trial).

- Gravley v. Mills, 87 F.3d 779 (6th Cir. 1996) (prosecutor violated due process by repeatedly making improper references to petitioner's post-arrest silence in cross-examination and closing argument).

- Delguidice v. Singletary, 84 F.3d 1359 (11th Cir. 1996) (introduction at trial of uncounseled statements petitioner made to psychiatrist during competency evaluation in another case, without notification or waiver of right to silence, violated rule of Estelle v. Smith, 451 U.S. 454 (1981)).

461

- Yohn v. Love, 76 F.3d 508 (3d Cir. 1996) (*ex parte* communication between prosecutor and state supreme court justice, resulting in trial judge's reversal of ruling that had originally favored defense, violated Due Process Clause and 6th Amendment right to counsel).

- Offor v. Scott, 72 F.3d 30 (5th Cir. 1995) (introduction of videotaped interview of child complainant violated Confrontation Clause).

- Franklin v. Duncan, 70 F.3d 75 (9th Cir. 1995) (*per curiam*) (prosecutor's reference in closing argument to post-*Miranda* silence, coupled with jury instruction informing jury that silence could be construed as adoptive admission, violated 5th Amendment right to remain silent).

- Riley v. Deeds, 56 F.3d 1117 (9th Cir. 1995) (read-back of complainant's direct examination testimony, authorized by judge's law clerk in response to jurors' request and conducted in judge's absence, violated Due Process Clause).

- Wigglesworth v. Oregon, 49 F.3d 578 (9th Cir. 1995) (statutorily authorized procedure of admitting certified copy of drug analysis report, subject to defendant's subpoenaing and cross-examining chemist who prepared report, violated Due Process Clause by "reliev[ing] the state of its burden of proof on an essential element of its case").

- Webb v. Lewis, 44 F.3d 1387 (9th Cir. 1994), *cert. denied*, 514 U.S. 1128 (1995) (introduction of videotaped interview of child victim of sexual abuse violated Confrontation Clause).

- Davis v. Zant, 36 F.3d 1538 (11th Cir. 1994) (prosecutor's "repeated and clearly intentional misrepresentations" in objection and closing argument rendered trial fundamentally unfair in violation of Due Process Clause).

- Maurer v. Department of Corrections, 32 F.3d 1286 (8th Cir. 1994) (admission of testimony by prosecution witnesses that "complainant seemed sincere when she said she was raped" rendered trial "fundamentally unfair" in violation of Due Process Clause).

- Vidal v. Williams, 31 F.3d 67 (2d Cir. 1994), *cert. denied*, 513 U.S. 1102 (1995) (trial court violated petitioner's Sixth Amendment right to public trial by closing courtroom, and excluding petitioner's parents, during undercover officer's testimony).

- Bonner v. Holt, 26 F.3d 1081 (11th Cir. 1994), *cert. denied*, 514 U.S. 1010 (1995) (jury was improperly exposed to inadmissible extra-record evidence when prosecutor stated to judge in jury's presence that petitioner was habitual offender).

- Martin v. Parker, 11 F.3d 613 (6th Cir. 1993) (*per curiam*) (due process right to fair trial violated by prosecutor's references to petitioner's prior bad acts and closing argument comparing petitioner to Hitler).

- Carter v. Sowders, 5 F.3d 975 (6th Cir. 1993), *cert. denied*, 511 U.S. 1097 (1994) (admission, at trial, of pretrial deposition of paid police informant violated petitioner's 6th Amendment right to confrontation because, contrary to findings of state court and district court, neither petitioner nor counsel validly waived petitioner's 6th Amendment right to attend deposition).

- Shaw v. Collins, 5 F.3d 128 (5th Cir. 1993) (Confrontation Clause violated by introduction of videotaped testimony of prosecution witness who did not testify at trial).

- Lowery v. Collins, 988 F.2d 1364 (5th Cir.), *supplemented on reh'g*, 996 F.2d 770 (5th Cir. 1993) (introduction of videotaped interview of child complainant violated petitioner's right to confrontation).

- Derden v. McNeel, 938 F.2d 605 (5th Cir. 1991) (petitioner denied fair trial by combination of judge's repeated admonitions to defense counsel and accused (thereby "encourag[ing] a predisposition of guilt by the jury"), prosecutor's failure to disclose impeachment evidence in violation of Brady v. Maryland, 373 U.S. 83 (1963), and prosecutor's violations of state law standards for *voir dire* questions and introduction of other crimes evidence).

- Gaines v. Thieret, 846 F.2d 402 (7th Cir. 1988) (*per curiam*) (introduction of hearsay statement of petitioner's brother, implicating petitioner as triggerman, violated Confrontation Clause).

- Brown v. Lynaugh, 843 F.2d 849 (5th Cir. 1988) (presiding judge took witness stand and provided prosecution's principal evidence against petitioner).

- Walker v. Lockhart, 763 F.2d 942 (8th Cir. 1985) (*en banc*), *cert. denied*, 478 U.S. 1020 (1986) (trial before biased judge).

- Albert v. Montgomery, 732 F.2d 865 (11th Cir. 1984) (petitioner convicted based on evidence of prior offense of which petitioner previously had been acquitted).

- Anderson v. Warden, 696 F.2d 296 (4th Cir. 1982) (*en banc*), *cert. denied*, 462 U.S. 1111 (1983) (judge took witnesses to chambers and pressed them to change their testimony).

- Chavis v. North Carolina, 637 F.2d 213 (4th Cir. 1980) (petitioner denied opportunity to cross-examine critical prosecution witnesses about special treatment witnesses received).

- Smith v. Smith, 454 F.2d 572 (5th Cir. 1971), *cert. denied*, 409 U.S. 885 (1972) (state law shifted burden of proving alibi defense to petitioner).

- MacKenna v. Ellis, 280 F.2d 592 (5th Cir. 1960), *cert. denied*, 368 U.S. 877 (1961) (advance of trial date without notice forced petitioner to trial without defense witnesses).

(9) Claims relating to the jury instructions, deliberations, and verdict:

  (a) Claims, arising under Sandstrom v. Montana, 442 U.S. 510 (1979), that jury instructions on malice or intent violated due process by relieving state of proving every element beyond reasonable doubt:

- Yates v. Evatt, 500 U.S. 391 (1991) (jury instructions on malice violated due process by relieving state of burden of proving every element of crime beyond reasonable doubt).

- Francis v. Franklin, 471 U.S. 307 (1985) (instruction that person "is presumed to intend the natural and probable consequences of his acts" unconstitutionally gave defendant burden of proof on element of intent to kill).

- Smith v. Horn, 120 F.3d 400 (3d Cir. 1997), *cert. denied*, 118 S. Ct. 1037 (1998) (jury instructions on accessorial liability allowed jury to convict on first-degree murder without finding beyond reasonable doubt that petitioner had specific intent to kill).

- Houston v. Dutton, 50 F.3d 381 (6th Cir.), *cert. denied*, 516 U.S. 905 (1995) (instruction shifting burden of disproving malice to defendant violated Sandstrom v. Montana, 442 U.S. 510 (1979), and was not harmless error because instruction infected jury's findings of premeditation and deliberation as well as malice).

- Corn v. Kemp, 837 F.2d 1474 (11th Cir.) *(per curiam)*, *cert. denied*, 486 U.S. 1023 (1988) (instruction shifting burden of proof of intent to kill to defendant was not harmless error because intent to kill was issue at trial notwithstanding insanity defense).

- Godfrey v. Kemp, 836 F.2d 1557 (11th Cir.), *cert. dismissed*, 487 U.S. 1264 (1988) (instruction shifting burden of proof of intent to kill to defendant was not harmless error because defendant "presented to the jury competent evidence tending to show a lack of mental capacity to form criminal intent").

- Dick v. Kemp, 833 F.2d 1448 (11th Cir. 1987) (instruction shifting burden of proof of intent to kill to defendant was not harmless error notwithstanding defendant's post-arrest statement admitting shooting, because intent was still at issue).

- Bowen v. Kemp, 832 F.2d 546 (11th Cir. 1987) *(en banc)*, *cert. denied*, 485 U.S. 940 (1988) (intent to kill) (similar to *Corn v. Kemp, supra*).

- Hyman v. Aiken, 824 F.2d 1405 (4th Cir. 1987) (instruction shifting burden of proof of malice to defendant was not harmless error because jury could have credited evidence that petitioner's intoxication at time of crime prevented him from forming intent to commit murder).

- Brooks v. Kemp, 809 F.2d 700 (11th Cir.) *(en banc)*, *cert. denied*, 483 U.S. 1010 (1987) (reinstating Brooks v. Kemp, 762 F.2d 1383 (11th Cir. 1985) *(en banc)*) (instruction that law "presumes every homicide to be malicious until the contrary appears" unconstitutionally gave defendant burden of proof on element of malice).

- Thomas v. Kemp, 800 F.2d 1024 (11th Cir. 1986) *(per curiam)*, *cert. denied*, 481 U.S. 1041 (1987) (reinstating, in part, Thomas v. Kemp, 766 F.2d 452 (11th Cir. 1985)) (instruction shifting burden of proof of intent to kill to defendant was not harmless error because defendant presented evidence that drug ingestion at time of crime prevented formation of intent to commit kidnapping and armed robbery, the alleged acts underlying charge of capital felony murder).

- Flowers v. Blackburn, 779 F.2d 1115 (5th Cir.), *cert. denied*, 475 U.S. 1132 (1986) (instruction that all participants in crime "'are principals, and equal offenders, and subject to the same punishment'" unconstitutionally gave defendant burden of proof by "permitt[ing] the State to secure a conviction by showing that *either* [petitioner or the co-perpetrator] ... had the requisite specific intent to kill").

- Drake v. Kemp, 762 F.2d 1449 (11th Cir. 1985), *cert. denied*, 478 U.S. 1020 (1986) (same instruction as one struck down in *Francis v. Franklin, supra*, unconstitutionally gave defendant burden of proof on intent to aid and abet armed robbery and murder).

- Clark v. Louisiana State Penitentiary, 694 F.2d 75 (5th Cir. 1982) (instruction on criminal conspiracy unconstitutionally gave defendant burden of proof on element of intent to kill or inflict great bodily harm by allowing jury to "attribute the murderous act of one conspirator to the other" even if conspiracy only related to underlying armed robbery and co-conspirator's "wanton act of murder" was not "foreseeable and necessary to the robbery").

- Mason v. Balkcom, 669 F.2d 222 (5th Cir. 1982), *cert. denied*, 460 U.S. 1016 (1983) (instructions that person is presumed to intend "natural and probable consequences of his conduct" and that person who kills with "a deadly weapon [is presumed to have] ... an intention to kill" unconstitutionally gave defendant burden of proof because defendant's claim of self-defense "admit[ted] the facts that activated these presumptions").

(b) Other claims relating to jury instructions:

- O'Neal v. McAninch, 513 U.S. 432 (1995) (accepting court of appeals' assumption that combination of invalid instruction and improper argument by counsel misstating mental element of offense warranted habeas corpus relief).

- Hanna v. Riveland, 87 F.3d 1034 (9th Cir. 1996) (instruction on permissive inference unconstitutionally relieved prosecution of its burden on element of crime).

- Harmon v. Marshall, 69 F.3d 963 (9th Cir. 1995) (*per curiam*) (failure to instruct on elements of offense was *per se* prejudicial error).

- Cordova v. Lynaugh, 838 F.2d 764 (5th Cir.), *cert. denied*, 486 U.S. 1061 (1988) (denial of jury instruction on lesser included noncapital offense violated Due Process Clause and 8th Amendment).

- Potts v. Kemp, 814 F.2d 1512 (11th Cir. 1987) (reinstating, in pertinent part, Potts v. Zant, 734 F.2d 526, 529-30 (11th Cir. 1984)) (failure to instruct on definition of essential element of capital murder violated due process).

- Vickers v. Ricketts, 798 F.2d 369 (9th Cir. 1986), *cert. denied*, 479 U.S. 1054 (1987) (trial court's refusal to give instruction on lesser included noncapital offense violated rule of Beck v. Alabama, 447 U.S. 625 (1980)).

- Carter v. Montgomery, 769 F.2d 1537 (11th Cir. 1985) (jury instruction relieved state of burden of proving all elements of the crime).

(c) Claims relating to jury deliberations or verdict:

- Lawson v. Borg, 60 F.3d 608 (9th Cir. 1995) (juror's statement to other jurors that petitioner had "reputation for violence" constituted harmful due process violation because "extrinsic information directly related to a material issue in the case: ... intent to commit robbery").

- Jimenez v. Myers, 40 F.3d 977 (9th Cir.), *cert. denied*, 513 U.S. 810 (1994) (trial judge coerced jury into convicting by twice requiring that jurors continue deliberations after they declared they were hopelessly deadlocked, inquiring into jurors' numerical division, and failing to give cautionary instruction not to succumb to majority pressure).

(10) Due process claim that evidence was constitutionally insufficient to sustain jury's verdict of guilty:

- McBath v. Gomez, 1997 WL 449696 (9th Cir. Aug. 4, 1997), *cert. denied*, 118 S. Ct. 375 (1997) (evidence was insufficient to sustain conviction of attempted burglary because only evidence offered to prove specific intent to steal was "the naked fact of an attempted entry").

- Mitchell v. Prunty, 107 F.3d 1337 (9th Cir.), *cert. denied*, 118 S. Ct. 295 (1997), *overruled in part by Santamaria v. Horsley*, 133 F.3d 1242 (9th Cir.), *modified*, 138 F.3d 1280 (9th Cir.), *cert. denied*, 1998 WL 334158 (U.S. Oct. 5, 1998) (insufficient evidence to sustain charges of aiding and abetting murder).

- Martineau v. Angelone, 25 F.3d 734 (9th Cir. 1994) (Nevada Supreme Court's ruling that evidence was insufficient to support petitioners' conviction of involuntary manslaughter of their infant child also compelled finding that evidence was insufficient to sustain conviction of child abuse for delay in seeking medical care for child).

- Evans-Smith v. Taylor, 19 F.3d 899 (4th Cir.), *cert. denied*, 513 U.S. 919 (1994) (although timing and circumstances of murder pointed to petitioner and he gave contradictory statements to police and apparently attempted to induce friends to support false alibi, prosecution's entirely circumstantial case was insufficient to allow rational trier of fact to find guilt beyond reasonable doubt).

- Kelly v. Roberts, 998 F.2d 802 (10th Cir. 1993) (petitioner convicted of aggravated robbery on aiding and abetting theory that he was getaway driver but "[o]ther than the prosecutor's speculative and unsupported arguments to the jury, the record is completely devoid of any fact linking a car [or petitioner] to the crime"; "Mr. Kelly has been in custody nearly ten years for a crime the State failed to prove.").

- Fagan v. Washington, 942 F.2d 1155 (7th Cir. 1991) (evidence was insufficient under Jackson v. Virginia, 443 U.S. 307 (1979), to sustain conviction of murder on aiding and abetting theory because there was no evidence in record that fatal shot fired during melee came from gun held by either petitioner or any member of his gang).

- Singer v. Court of Common Pleas, 879 F.2d 1203 (3d Cir. 1989) (conviction of aggravated assault on police officer in course of arrest violated *Jackson v. Virginia, supra,* because prosecution failed to present constitutionally sufficient evidence of statutory element of lawfulness of underlying arrest).

(11) Claims arising at sentencing:

(a) Capital cases:

(i) Claims of improper introduction of uncounseled statements to state psychiatrist:

- Estelle v. Smith, 451 U.S. 454 (1981) (state-employed psychiatrist permitted to testify at death penalty phase based on petitioner's pretrial statements that were not freely and voluntarily given and that were made without counsel or waiver of counsel).

- Vanderbilt v. Collins, 994 F.2d 189 (5th Cir. 1993) (at resentencing, state elicited statements petitioner made at time of first trial to psychiatrist appointed, at defense request, to assess petitioner's sanity and competency).

- Buttrum v. Black, 908 F.2d 695 (11th Cir. 1990) (state-hired psychiatrist's use of petitioner's uncounseled statements during competency evaluation to show future dangerousness violated *Estelle v. Smith, supra*).

- Muniz v. Procunier, 760 F.2d 588 (5th Cir.), *cert. denied*, 474 U.S. 934 (1985) (psychiatrist interviewed petitioner at direction of prosecutor without notice to defense counsel and without administering *Miranda* warnings, in violation of rule of *Estelle v. Smith, supra*).

- White v. Estelle, 720 F.2d 415 (5th Cir. 1983) (judge granted state's motion for psychiatric examination of petitioner but neither petitioner nor counsel was advised that statements might be used as proof of future dangerousness at capital sentencing hearing).

- Green v. Estelle, 706 F.2d 148 (5th Cir. 1983) (*per curiam*) (finding violation of rule of *Estelle v. Smith, supra*, despite absence of contemporaneous objection because of state law exception to procedural rule).

- Gholson v. Estelle, 675 F.2d 734 (5th Cir. 1982) (uncounseled statements elicited in court-ordered psychiatric examination and also in additional interview conducted by another state psychiatrist without notice to defense counsel or judge violated rule of *Estelle v. Smith, supra*).

- Battie v. Estelle, 655 F.2d 692 (5th Cir. 1981) (petitioner did not waive claim under *Estelle v. Smith, supra*, by requesting psychiatric examination to determine competency to stand trial and sanity at time of offense).

(ii) Claims relating to aggravating circumstances:

- Stringer v. Black, 503 U.S. 222 (1992) (petitioner sentenced to death based on unconstitutionally vague "especially heinous, atrocious, or cruel" aggravating circumstance; state supreme court affirmed after invalidating aggravating circumstance without reweighing remaining aggravating and mitigating circumstances).

- Maynard v. Cartwright, 486 U.S. 356 (1988) (petitioner sentenced to death based on unconstitutionally vague "especially heinous, atrocious, or cruel" aggravating circumstance).

- Hochstein v. Hopkins, 113 F.3d 143 (8th Cir.), *modified*, 122 F.3d 1160 (8th Cir.), *cert. denied*, 118 S. Ct. 388 (1997) (petitioner sentenced to death based on unconstitutionally vague "exceptional depravity" aggravating circumstance).

- McKenna v. McDaniel, 65 F.3d 1483 (9th Cir. 1995), *cert. denied*, 517 U.S. 1150 (1996) (instruction on "depravity of mind" aggravating circumstance was unconstitutionally vague).

- Houston v. Dutton, 50 F.3d 381 (6th Cir.), *cert. denied*, 516 U.S. 905 (1995) ("'heinous, atrocious or cruel'" jury instruction was "too vague and uninformative to properly guide the jury in reaching a death verdict").

467

- Wade v. Calderon, 29 F.3d 1312 (9th Cir. 1994) (sentence of death based on unconstitutionally vague special circumstance of torture-murder).

- Beam v. Paskett, 3 F.2d 1301 (9th Cir. 1993), *cert denied*, 511 U.S. 1060 (1994) (death sentence premised in part on trial judge's distaste for petitioner's prior history of nonviolent "abnormal sexual relationships," including homosexuality and relationships with women substantially younger and older than petitioner).

- King v. Puckett, 1 F.3d 280 (5th Cir. 1993) (death sentence rested upon Mississippi's unconstitutionally overbroad "especially heinous, atrocious or cruel" aggravating factor).

- Duest v. Singletary, 997 F.2d 1336 (11th Cir. 1993), *cert. denied*, 510 U.S. 1133 (1994) (death sentence premised on prior conviction that was overturned on appeal).

- Rust v. Hopkins, 984 F.2d 1486 (8th Cir. 1993) (three-judge capital sentencing panel violated due process by failing to apply state law rule that aggravating circumstances must be proven beyond reasonable doubt; error was not cured by Nebraska Supreme Court's reweighing of circumstances on appeal because such reweighing exceeded permissible scope of principle of *Stringer, supra*, and deprived petitioner of state-created two-tiered process of sentencing followed by appellate review).

- Smith v. Black, 970 F.2d 1383 (5th Cir. 1992) (on remand from Supreme Court in light of *Stringer v. Black, supra*, court concludes that use of Mississippi's vague "especially heinous, atrocious and cruel" aggravating circumstance rendered petitioner's death sentence unconstitutional).

- Moore v. Clarke, 951 F.2d 895 (8th Cir. 1991) (Nebraska's "heinous, atrocious, cruel, or manifest[ing] exceptional depravity" aggravating circumstance was unconstitutionally vague on its face and as construed by state supreme court).

- Davis v. Maynard, 911 F.2d 415 (10th Cir. 1990) (*per curiam*) (applying rule of *Maynard v. Cartwright, supra*, to reverse death sentence because of vagueness of Oklahoma's "especially heinous, atrocious or cruel" aggravating circumstance).

- Newlon v. Armontrout, 885 F.2d 1328 (8th Cir. 1989), *cert. denied*, 497 U.S. 1038 (1990) (Missouri's "depravity of mind" aggravating circumstance was vague on its face and as construed by state supreme court).

- Adamson v. Ricketts, 865 F.2d 1011 (9th Cir. 1988) (*en banc*), *cert. denied*, 497 U.S. 1031 (1990) (Arizona's "especially heinous" aggravating circumstance was unconstitutionally vague).

- Lewis v. Lane, 832 F.2d 1446 (7th Cir. 1987), *cert. denied*, 488 U.S. 829 (1988) (defense counsel stipulated to, then prosecutor based successful argument in favor of death sentence on, "prior convictions" that did not exist).

(iii) Claims relating to mitigating circumstances:

(A) Claims, arising under Lockett v. Ohio, 438 U.S. 586 (1978), that trial court improperly restricted consideration of nonstatutory mitigating factors:

- Hitchcock v. Dugger, 481 U.S. 393 (1987) (petitioner sentenced to die by jury unconstitutionally instructed that, in passing on sentence, it could not consider fact that petitioner was brain damaged, had cooperated fully with police, and was capable of rehabilitation).

- Rupe v. Wood, 93 F.3d 1434 (9th Cir.), cert. denied, 117 S. Ct. 1017 (1996) (trial court improperly excluded polygraph examination of state's key witness showing that witness bore greater culpability for killing than he admitted and that petitioner "did not play as great a role in the offense as the prosecution would like the jury to believe").

- Smith v. Singletary, 61 F.3d 815 (11th Cir. 1995) (per curiam), cert. denied, 516 U.S. 1140 (1996) (trial judge improperly excluded mitigating evidence, and instructions curtailed sentencer consideration of mitigating evidence that was admitted).

- Gore v. Dugger, 933 F.2d 904 (11th Cir. 1991) (per curiam), cert. denied, 502 U.S. 1066 (1992) (unconstitutional exclusion of nonstatutory mitigating evidence of alcohol and drug ingestion at time of killing).

- Jackson v. Dugger, 931 F.2d 712 (11th Cir.), cert. denied, 502 U.S. 973 (1991) (jury unconstitutionally instructed, and sentencing judge believed, that nonstatutory evidence of good record of military service could not be considered).

- Aldridge v. Dugger, 925 F.2d 1320 (11th Cir. 1991) (jury instruction limiting mitigating circumstances to statutory factors violated Hitchcock, supra, even though petitioner declined to present any non-statutory mitigating evidence because tactical choice was reasonable response to restrictive state law at time).

- Booker v. Dugger, 922 F.2d 633 (11th Cir.), cert. denied, 502 U.S. 900 (1991) (capital sentencing jury instructed that it could not take into consideration nonstatutory mitigating evidence of petitioner's schizophrenia and organic brain damage).

- Smith v. McCormick, 914 F.2d 1153 (9th Cir. 1990) (Montana death penalty statute, as applied, unconstitutionally limited nonstatutory mitigating circumstances to those "sufficiently substantial to call for leniency").

- Delap v. Dugger, 890 F.2d 285 (11th Cir. 1989), cert. denied, 496 U.S. 929 (1990) (instructions violated Hitchcock, supra, by precluding jury consideration of nonstatutory mitigating evidence of petitioner's organic brain damage).

- Knight v. Dugger, 863 F.2d 705 (11th Cir. 1988) (rule of *Lockett v. Ohio*, *supra*, violated because sentencing judge, prosecutor, and defense counsel believed that mitigating circumstances must be limited to statutory roster).

- Ruffin v. Dugger, 848 F.2d 1512 (11th Cir. 1988) (*per curiam*), *cert. denied*, 488 U.S. 1044 (1989) (judge unconstitutionally instructed jury to consider only statutory mitigating circumstances).

- Stone v. Dugger, 837 F.2d 1477 (11th Cir. 1988), *cert. denied*, 489 U.S. 1071 (1989) (jury unconstitutionally instructed, and sentencing judge believed, that mitigation was limited to statutory factors).

- Messer v. Florida, 834 F.2d 890 (11th Cir. 1987) (jury unconstitutionally instructed, and sentencing judge believed, that mitigating evidence of petitioner's mental problems could only be considered to extent it bore on statutory mitigating factor).

- Armstrong v. Dugger, 833 F.2d 1430 (11th Cir. 1987) (jury unconstitutionally instructed, and sentencing judge believed, that mitigating circumstances must be limited to statutory list).

- Hargrave v. Dugger, 832 F.2d 1528 (11th Cir. 1987) (*en banc*), *cert. denied*, 489 U.S. 1071 (1989) (jury unconstitutionally instructed, and sentencing judge believed, that nonstatutory mitigating evidence of steady employment, below-average intelligence, and history of drug abuse could not be considered).

- Songer v. Wainwright, 769 F.2d 1488 (11th Cir. 1985) (*en banc*), *cert. denied*, 481 U.S. 1041 (1987) (*per curiam*) (sentencing judge unconstitutionally limited mitigating circumstances to factors enumerated in statute).

- Washington v. Watkins, 655 F.2d 1346 (5th Cir. Unit A 1981), *cert. denied*, 456 U.S. 949 (1982) (jury instructions unconstitutionally prevented jury from giving weight to nonstatutory mitigating evidence of steady domestic relationship, fulfillment of parental responsibilities, and good employment history).

(B)   Other claims relating to mitigating circumstances:

- Parker v. Dugger, 499 U.S. 308 (1991) (trial court sentenced petitioner to death on basis of asserted absence of mitigating circumstances, though mitigating circumstances manifestly were present).

- Penry v. Lynaugh, 492 U.S. 302 (1989) (petitioner sentenced to die by jury unconstitutionally instructed in manner that prevented it from considering in mitigation, and only permitted it to consider in aggravation, fact that Penry was retarded).

- Mak v. Blodgett, 970 F.2d 614 (9th Cir. 1992) (*per curiam*) (unconstitutional exclusion of potentially mitigating evidence that petitioner was follower, rather than leader, in multiple murder).

- Kordenbrock v. Scroggy, 919 F.2d 1091 (6th Cir. 1990) (*en banc*), *cert. denied*, 499 U.S. 970 (1991) (jury instruction could have misled jury into believing that findings of mitigating circumstances must be unanimous).

- Smith v. McCormick, 914 F.2d 1153 (9th Cir. 1990) (Montana death penalty statute, as applied, unconstitutionally prevented sentencing judge from considering whether mitigating circumstances in aggregate provided basis for sentence less than death even if each individual mitigating factor was insufficient).

- Mayo v. Lynaugh, 893 F.2d 683 (5th Cir. 1990), *cert. denied*, 502 U.S. 827 (1992) (instructions prevented capital jury from considering petitioner's history of abuse by father, who repeatedly broke petitioner's bones without thereafter securing medical treatment).

- Kubat v. Thieret, 867 F.2d 351 (7th Cir.), *cert. denied*, 493 U.S. 874 (1989) (instruction apparently requiring findings of mitigating circumstances to be unanimous violated rule of Mills v. Maryland, 486 U.S. 367 (1988)).

- Dutton v. Brown, 812 F.2d 593 (10th Cir.), *cert. denied*, 484 U.S. 836 (1987) (trial court barred petitioner's mother from testifying as mitigation witness because she attended trial in violation of rule on witnesses).

- Magwood v. Smith, 791 F.2d 1438 (11th Cir. 1986) (sentencing judge's determination of inapplicability of two mitigating circumstances was not fairly supported by record and undermined reliability of capital sentencing process).

- Pickens v. Lockhart, 714 F.2d 1455 (8th Cir. 1983) (trial judge violated rule of *Lockett v. Ohio, supra,* by giving accessorial liability instruction that directed jury to punish petitioner "as if he were a principal," thereby negating mitigating circumstance of lesser participation in crime).

(iv) Improper prosecutorial argument or other misconduct at capital sentencing stage:

- Driscoll v. Delo, 71 F.3d 701 (8th Cir. 1995), *cert. denied*, 117 S. Ct. 273 (1996) (prosecutor violated rule of *Caldwell v. Mississippi*, 472 U.S. 320 (1985), by minimizing significance of sentencing recommendation to judge that state law required jury to make).

- Miller v. Lockhart, 65 F.3d 676 (8th Cir. 1995) (prosecutor's closing argument at penalty phase, which included expression of personal belief in propriety of death sentence, played on jurors' fears, and improperly commented on petitioner's decision not to testify, violated due process).

- Antwine v. Delo, 54 F.3d 1357 (8th Cir. 1995), *cert. denied*, 516 U.S. 1067 (1996) (prosecutor violated 8th Amendment by inaccurately claiming, in closing argument, that gas chamber execution is "'instantaneous,'" thereby "diminish[ing] the jurors' sense of responsibility for imposing the death penalty" by allowing them to take comfort in "thought that the death would at least be ... painless and easy"; prosecutor also violated 8th Amendment by implying that execution was preferable because it would spare taxpayers from having to pay for life imprisonment).

- Lesko v. Lehman, 925 F.2d 1527 (3d Cir.), *cert. denied*, 502 U.S. 898 (1991) (prosecutor's closing argument at penalty phase violated rule of Griffin v. California, 380 U.S. 609 (1965), by referring to petitioner's failure to talk about crime and failure to express remorse in penalty-phase testimony about mitigating aspects of his background, and also violated due process by appealing to jurors' passions and encouraging them to "[e]xhibit the same sympathy" that defendants displayed towards their victims).

- Newlon v. Armontrout, 885 F.2d 1328 (8th Cir. 1989), *cert. denied*, 497 U.S. 1038 (1990) (prosecutor violated 8th and 14th Amendments by arguing to jury personal belief that case deserved death penalty "'more than any other in ten years,'" and by comparing petitioner to infamous mass-murderers and appealing to jurors' personal fears and emotions).

- Mann v. Dugger, 844 F.2d 1446 (11th Cir. 1988) (*en banc*), *cert. denied*, 489 U.S. 1071 (1989) (prosecutor violated rule of Caldwell v. Mississippi, 472 U.S. 320 (1985), by arguing to jury that verdict would be merely advisory and that imposition of death penalty was "not on your shoulders").

- Potts v. Kemp, 814 F.2d 1512 (11th Cir. 1987) (reinstating, in pertinent part, Potts v. Zant, 734 F.2d 526, 535-36 (11th Cir. 1984)) (prosecutor violated due process by reading from state supreme court opinions during closing argument, thereby "plainly attempting to suggest to the jury that prior decisions of the state supreme court mandated the imposition of the death penalty in this case").

- Wheat v. Thigpen, 793 F.2d 621 (5th Cir. 1986), *cert. denied*, 480 U.S. 930 (1987) (prosecutor violated rule of *Caldwell v. Mississippi*, *supra*, by telling jurors that any mistakes they made would be corrected by appellate courts).

- Wilson v. Kemp, 777 F.2d 621 (11th Cir. 1985), *cert. denied*, 476 U.S. 1153 (1986) (prosecutor presented quotations from United States Supreme Court opinion in Gregg v. Georgia, 428 U.S. 153 (1976), and state supreme court opinion in misleading and highly prejudicial manner).

- Drake v. Kemp, 762 F.2d 1449 (11th Cir. 1985) (*en banc*), *cert. denied*, 478 U.S. 1020 (1986) (prosecutor read to jury from state supreme court opinions, thereby presenting his arguments "wrapped in the cloak of [the court's] ... authority").

- Hance v. Zant, 696 F.2d 940 (11th Cir.), *cert. denied*, 463 U.S. 1210 (1983), *modified sub nom. Brooks v. Kemp*, 762 F.2d 1383 (11th Cir. 1985) (*en banc*) (prosecutor's closing argument at penalty phase violated due process by "appeal[ing] to the fears and emotions of an already aroused jury"; "dramatic appeal to gut emotion ha[d] no place in the courtroom, especially in a case involving the penalty of death").

(v) Claims relating to other aspects of capital sentencing procedures:

- Sumner v. Shuman, 483 U.S. 66 (1987) (statute mandating death penalty for murder committed by prisoner serving life sentence without possibility of parole violated 8th and 14th Amendments).

- McClain v. Calderon, 134 F.3d 1383 (9th Cir. 1998) (instruction misled jury into believing that governor could commute death sentence on own when actually petitioner's record precluded commutation in absence of written recommendations from four state supreme court justices).

- Grigsby v. Blodgett, 130 F.3d 365 (9th Cir. 1997) (Washington sentencing statute unconstitutionally penalized right to trial by permitting sentence of death or life without parole for defendants who opted for trial while prohibiting sentence greater than life with possibility of parole for those who pled guilty).

- Gallego v. McDaniel, 124 F.3d 1065 (9th Cir. 1997), *cert. denied*, 118 S. Ct. 2299 (1998) (jury instruction concerning availability of executive clemency, although "not inaccurate as a general statement of the law, ... could have prompted the jury into making erroneous speculations about the kind of sentence [petitioner] might actually serve").

- Coleman v. McCormick, 874 F.2d 1280 (9th Cir.) (*en banc*), *cert. denied*, 493 U.S. 944 (1989) (imposition of death sentence at resentencing hearing, pursuant to death penalty statute not in effect at time of conviction and original sentencing, violated due process).

- Fitzpatrick v. McCormick, 869 F.2d 1247 (9th Cir.), *cert. denied*, 493 U.S. 872 (1989) (Double Jeopardy Clause precluded imposition of death sentence at resentencing after previous sentence of life imprisonment).

- Adamson v. Ricketts, 865 F.2d 1011 (9th Cir. 1988) (*en banc*), *cert. denied*, 497 U.S. 1031 (1990) (sentencing judge's imposition of death sentence was unconstitutionally arbitrary because based solely on petitioner's breach of plea agreement that had resulted in life sentence).

- Stockton v. Virginia, 852 F.2d 740 (4th Cir. 1988), *cert. denied*, 489 U.S. 1071 (1989) (in lunch break during jury's death sentencing deliberations, courtroom deputies allowed owner of restaurant in which jurors were eating to tell jurors "they ought to fry the son of a bitch").

- Godfrey v. Kemp, 836 F.2d 1557 (11th Cir.), *cert. denied*, 487 U.S. 1264 (1988) (Double Jeopardy Clause barred imposition of death at resentencing because sole aggravating circumstance was previously found insufficient to support death sentence).

- Elledge v. Dugger, 823 F.2d 1439 (11th Cir.) (*per curiam*), *amended*, 833 F.2d 250 (11th Cir. 1987) (*per curiam*), *cert. denied*, 485 U.S. 1014 (1988) (shackling of petitioner at sentencing hearing violated Due Process Clause because inadequate prior determination of dangerousness and need for restraints).

- Moore v. Kemp, 809 F.2d 702 (11th Cir.) (*en banc*), *cert. denied*, 481 U.S. 1054 (1987) (instructions unconstitutionally failed to inform jury of its discretion under Georgia law to impose life sentence despite existence of statutory aggravating circumstance).

- Bell v. Watkins, 692 F.2d 999 (5th Cir.), *cert. denied*, 464 U.S. 843 (1983) (instructions unconstitutionally failed to provide clear and objective standards to channel jury's discretion).

- Proffitt v. Wainwright, 685 F.2d 1227 (11th Cir. 1982), *cert. denied*, 464 U.S. 1002 (1983) (sentencing judge violated petitioner's right to confront witnesses by considering court-appointed psychiatrist's written report without permitting defense counsel to cross-examine expert about conclusions and underlying premises; judge also violated petitioner's 6th and 14th Amendment right to presence at all stages of criminal trial by taking testimony of another court-appointed psychiatrist in petitioner's absence).

- Jordan v. Watkins, 681 F.2d 1067 (5th Cir. 1982) (Mississippi's capital sentencing procedures failed to give jury adequate guidance in identifying and weighing aggravating and mitigating circumstances).

(b) **Noncapital cases:**

- Solem v. Helm, 463 U.S. 277 (1983) (petitioner given life sentence for uttering a "no account" check for $100 following six minor prior convictions).

- Moore v. Parke, 148 F.3d 705 (7th Cir. 1998) (evidence supporting habitual offender determination was insufficient to satisfy state's burden of proof beyond a reasonable doubt).

- Lucero v. Kerby, 133 F.3d 1299 (10th Cir.), *cert. denied*, 118 S. Ct. 1375 (1998) (crimes charged in separate counts overlapped, resulting in impermissible multiple punishments for same offense).

- Grigsby v. Blodgett, 130 F.3d 365 (9th Cir. 1997) (Washington sentencing statute unconstitutionally penalized right to trial by permitting sentence of death or life without parole for defendants who opted for trial while prohibiting sentence greater than life with possibility of parole for those who pled guilty).

- Williams v. Singletary, 78 F.3d 1510 (11th Cir.), *cert. denied*, 117 S. Ct. 221 (1996) (cumulative sentences for single incident of criminal behavior violated Double Jeopardy Clause).

- Walker v. Deeds, 50 F.3d 670 (9th Cir. 1995) (sentencing judge violated Due Process Clause by failing to follow state law procedure — in which petitioner had constitutionally protected "liberty" interest — for determining applicability of "habitual criminal" sentence).

- Kelly v. United States, 29 F.3d 1107 (7th Cir. 1994) (district court lacked jurisdiction to impose enhanced sentence for drug conspiracy conviction because government failed to comply with statutory requirement of prior notice to defendant and counsel).

- United States v. Maybeck, 23 F.3d 888 (4th Cir. 1994) (section 2255 movant improperly sentenced as career offender under Federal Sentencing Guidelines based on erroneous classification of prior conviction as one involving violence).

- DeWitt v. Ventetoulo, 6 F.3d 32 (1st Cir. 1993), *cert. denied*, 511 U.S. 1032 (1994) (although Constitution does not ordinarily prevent postsentencing increases of erroneous sentences to comply with state law, Due Process Clause prevented state court from imposing life sentence and reimprisoning petitioner six years after court reduced sentence in violation of state law).
- Boardman v. Estelle, 957 F.2d 1523 (9th Cir.) (*per curiam*), *cert. denied*, 506 U.S. 904 (1992) (sentencing judge violated due process by denying defendant's request to address court before imposition of sentence).

(12) Claims arising during the post-trial, appellate, or postconviction stages of a case:

- Young v. Harper, 117 S. Ct. 1148 (1997) (revocation of so-called "preparole" status, conducted without due process protections which Morrissey v. Brewer, 408 U.S. 471 (1972) assures individuals subject to parole revocation, violated Due Process Clause because "preparole" "program ... differed from parole in name alone").
- Lynce v. Mathis, 117 S. Ct. 891 (1997) (1992 statute's retroactive revocation of five years' worth of good time credits that petitioner accumulated under regulations in effect in 1986 when offense and guilty plea occurred, and petitioner's rearrest and reincarceration after being released based on accumulated credits, violated *Ex Post Facto* Clause).
- Richmond v. Lewis, 506 U.S. 40 (1992) (state supreme court's affirmance of death sentence unconstitutional and invalid because majority of state supreme court justices considered sentence to be constitutionally infirm).
- Blackledge v. Perry, 417 U.S. 21 (1974) (vindictive reprosecution following successful appeal).
- McBride v. Johnson, 118 F.3d 432 (5th Cir. 1997) (Texas state parole board violated petitioner's right to confrontation by revoking parole on basis of detective's hearsay account of commission of crime despite petitioner's acquittal of same crime at trial and despite hearing officer's statement to petitioner that victim's presence at hearing would be secured).
- Williams v. Lee, 33 F.3d 1010 (8th Cir. 1994), *cert. denied*, 514 U.S. 1032 (1995) (denial of good-time credits on basis of statute enacted after petitioner's offense violated *Ex Post Facto* Clause).
- Nulph v. Faatz, 27 F.3d 451 (9th Cir. 1994) (*per curiam*) (state parole board violated *Ex Post Facto* Clause by calculating release date pursuant to statutes and regulations adopted after date of petitioner's offense, thereby increasing potential length of incarceration beyond that allowed by law in effect when crime was committed).
- Graham v. Lanfong, 25 F.3d 203 (3d Cir. 1994) (prisoner serving concurrent federal and territorial court sentences in Virgin Islands federal prison was improperly denied federal good-time credit for both sentences).
- Belk v. Purkett, 15 F.3d 803 (8th Cir. 1994) (procedures used to revoke petitioner's parole violated due process requirements established in Morrissey v. Brewer, 408 U.S. 471 (1972); "Petitioner has been imprisoned for almost two years now based

upon revocation procedures which did not approach the most minimal requirements of due process or reliability.").

- Monroe v. Blackburn, 748 F.2d 958 (5th Cir. 1984), *cert. denied*, 476 U.S. 1145 (1986) (rule of Brady v. Maryland, 373 U.S. 83 (1963), required that State provide defense counsel with exculpatory information obtained by police after trial so that petitioner could use it in motion for new trial).

(13) **Ineffective assistance of counsel (before, at, or after, trial; at sentencing; or on appeal) and other claims relating to the right to counsel:**

(a) **Denial of counsel altogether or of counsel of one's choice:**

- Gideon v. Wainwright, 372 U.S. 335 (1963) (petitioner forced to trial without lawyer because he was indigent).
- Blankenship v. Johnson, 118 F.3d 312 (5th Cir. 1997) (petitioner was constructively denied counsel when his attorney, who was elected county attorney after representing petitioner in appeal to intermediate appellate court, failed to represent petitioner at, and did nothing to secure substitute counsel during, state-requested discretionary review by state's criminal court of last resort).
- Snook v. Wood, 89 F.3d 605 (9th Cir. 1996) (state appellate court's failure to advise *pro se* appellant of "dangers and disadvantages" of waiving appellate counsel violated right to counsel on appeal).
- Robinson v. Norris, 60 F.3d 457 (8th Cir. 1995), *cert. denied*, 517 U.S. 1115 (1996) (petitioner was functionally deprived of counsel when judge refused to replace trial counsel with new attorney to file posttrial motion for new trial on grounds of ineffective assistance of counsel).
- Bland v. California Dep't of Corrections, 20 F.3d 1469 (9th Cir.), *cert. denied*, 513 U.S. 947 (1994) (trial court violated 6th Amendment by summarily rejecting petitioner's request for discharge of appointed counsel and substitution of different attorney without inquiring into basis of petitioner's request).
- Bowen v. Maynard, 799 F.2d 593 (10th Cir.), *cert. denied*, 479 U.S. 962 (1986) (petitioner forced to trial without retained attorney who was injured the day before trial).

(b) **Ineffective assistance at trial:**

- Kimmelman v. Morrison, 477 U.S. 365 (1986) (petitioner convicted after attorney failed to make obvious and meritorious objection to tainted evidence forming basis of state's case).
- Brown v. Myers, 137 F.3d 1154 (9th Cir. 1998) (counsel failed to investigate and present available testimony supporting petitioner's alibi).
- Bloom v. Calderon, 132 F.3d 1267 (9th Cir.), *cert. denied*, 118 S. Ct. 1856 (1998) (counsel retained psychiatric expert for insanity defense only days before trial and failed to provide expert and others who evaluated petitioner with relevant, readily available information that would have made diagnoses more favorable to petitioner).

- Rickman v. Bell, 131 F.3d 1150 (6th Cir. 1997), *cert. denied*, 118 S. Ct. 1827 (1998) (counsel's "total failure to actively advocate his client's cause" and "repeated expressions of contempt for his client for his alleged actions" had effect of "provid[ing] [petitioner] not with a defense counsel, but with a second prosecutor").
- Groseclose v. Bell, 130 F.3d 1161 (6th Cir. 1997), *cert. denied*, 118 S. Ct. 1826 (1998) (counsel failed to develop defense theory and "to conduct any meaningful adversarial challenge, as shown by his failure to cross-examine more than half of the prosecution's witnesses, to object to any evidence, to put on any defense witnesses, to make a closing argument, and, at sentencing, to put on any meaningful mitigation evidence"; instead, counsel effectively abdicated client's case to counsel for codefendant, whose defense was antagonistic to petitioner's).
- Johnson v. Baldwin, 114 F.3d 835 (9th Cir. 1997) (counsel's failure to investigate adequately resulted in defense's presentation of weak, unbelievable alibi defense).
- Williamson v. Ward, 110 F.3d 1508 (10th Cir. 1997) (counsel, who received no funding for expert or investigative services and who was paid statutory maximum of $3200, failed to investigate videotaped statement by another person confessing to crime and also failed to investigate extensive evidence of petitioner's mental illness and likely incompetence to stand trial).
- Berryman v. Morton, 100 F.3d 1089 (3d Cir. 1996) (counsel failed to use inconsistent testimony to impeach complainant's identification, opened door to irrelevant and prejudicial evidence of police investigation of unrelated homicide and robbery, and failed to investigate potential defense witnesses).
- Freeman v. Class, 95 F.3d 639 (8th Cir. 1996) (counsel was ineffective in, *inter alia*, introducing police report that contained prejudicial hearsay, failing to request cautionary instruction regarding accomplice testimony, and failing to object or move for mistrial in response to prosecutor's comment on post-*Miranda* silence).
- Baylor v. Estelle, 94 F.3d 1321 (9th Cir. 1996), *cert. denied*, 117 S. Ct. 1329 (1997) (counsel was ineffective in failing to pursue adequate investigation of potential exculpatory serological evidence in sexual assault case).
- Luchenburg v. Smith, 79 F.3d 388 (4th Cir. 1996) (counsel was ineffective in failing to request instruction to clarify findings jury had to make in order to convict).
- Tippins v. Walker, 77 F.3d 682 (2d Cir. 1996) (counsel's sleeping for "numerous extended periods of time [at trial] during which the defendant's interests were at stake" was *per se* prejudicial deprivation of effective assistance).
- Deluca v. Lord, 77 F.3d 578 (2d Cir.), *cert. denied*, 117 S. Ct. 83 (1996) (counsel failed to conduct adequate investigation of possible defense of extreme emotional disturbance which could have reduced murder charge to first-degree manslaughter).
- Crotts v. Smith, 73 F.3d 891 (9th Cir. 1995) (trial counsel was ineffective in failing to object to highly prejudicial evidence which likely would have been excluded if objection had been made).

- Driscoll v. Delo, 71 F.3d 701 (8th Cir. 1995), *cert. denied,* 117 S. Ct. 273 (1996) (counsel was ineffective in failing to prepare to cross-examine prosecution serologist on critical evidence and in failing to impeach key prosecutorial eyewitness with prior inconsistent statements).

- Harris v. Wood, 64 F.3d 1432 (9th Cir. 1995) (counsel was ineffective in, *inter alia,* failing to interview majority of witnesses identified in police reports, advising defendant to provide statement to prosecution without receiving any promise of reduction of charges, failing to file suppression motions, failing to propose or object to jury instructions, and failing to raise and preserve meritorious issues for appeal).

- Williams v. Washington, 59 F.3d 673 (7th Cir. 1995) (counsel failed to seek out or interview witnesses other than two clients, did not visit scene of crime, and was insufficiently familiar with documents in case to make adequate judgments about whether to object to admission).

- Genius v. Pepe, 50 F.3d 60 (1st Cir. 1995) (counsel did not pursue potential insanity defense by seeking independent psychiatric examination; although petitioner had been found competent to stand trial, facts suggesting possibility of incompetency "should have flagged the possibility" of meritorious insanity defense).

- Tomlin v. Myers, 30 F.3d 1235 (9th Cir. 1994) (counsel failed to file identification suppression motion to challenge obvious violation of petitioner's right to counsel at lineup; "absent some indication the motion would have been lacking in merit[,] ... the failure to bring to the court's attention a major constitutional error in the prosecution's case is not the product of reasonable professional judgment").

- Sanders v. Ratelle, 21 F.3d 1446 (9th Cir. 1994) (counsel's failure to interview, subpoena, or take statement against penal interest from petitioner's brother, not-withstanding reliable indications that brother was actual perpetrator, was "unfathomable" and "evidenced a gargantuan indifference to the interests of his client").

- Mason v. Scully, 16 F.3d 38 (2d Cir. 1994) (counsel ineffective in failing to object, on hearsay and Confrontation Clause grounds, to critical testimony by police detective about inculpatory statement by nontestifying codefendant).

- Foster v. Lockhart, 9 F.3d 722 (8th Cir. 1993) (counsel's decision not to investigate potentially viable defense was unreasonable and could not be justified as "tactical decision" to focus exclusively on alternative defense).

- Gray v. Lynn, 6 F.3d 265 (5th Cir. 1993) (trial counsel was ineffective in failing to object to obvious defect in jury instruction on elements of offense).

- Pilchak v. Camper, 935 F.2d 145 (8th Cir. 1991) (ineffective assistance by attorney "suffering from Alzheimer's disease at the time of trial, leading to disorientation, loss of memory, inability to concentrate and peculiar exhibitions of judgment").

- Henderson v. Sargent, 926 F.2d 706 (8th Cir.), *amended,* 939 F.2d 586 (8th Cir. 1991), *cert. denied,* 502 U.S. 1050 (1992) (counsel's failure to pursue available theory that killing was committed by someone other than petitioner "cannot be justified as a strategic decision").

- Smith v. Dugger, 911 F.2d 494 (11th Cir. 1990) (counsel failed adequately to investigate possible grounds for moving to suppress petitioner's confessions, which were "critical to the state's case").

- Chambers v. Armontrout, 907 F.2d 825 (8th Cir.), *cert. denied*, 498 U.S. 369 (1990) (counsel failed to interview and call witness who would have supported petitioner's claim of self-defense).

- Magill v. Dugger, 824 F.2d 879 (11th Cir. 1987) (counsel, who took over case at last minute, did not prepare for trial and did not adequately study preceding counsel's file, thereby prejudicing sentencing verdict that was largely dependent on evidence and arguments at trial).

- Smith v. Wainwright, 799 F.2d 1442 (11th Cir. 1986) (death-sentenced petitioner's attorney failed to inform jury that only witness against petitioner — the admitted killer, who testified in return for lesser charge — did not link petitioner to murder in detailed confession to police).

- Summit v. Blackburn, 795 F.2d 1237 (5th Cir. 1986) (counsel's failure to invoke state law *corpus delicti* rule to prevent petitioner's conviction of attempted armed robbery solely on basis of uncorroborated confession prejudiced petitioner at penalty stage by permitting conviction for capital felony murder).

- Dillon v. Duckworth, 751 F.2d 895 (7th Cir.), *cert. denied*, 471 U.S. 1108 (1985) (because of inexperience, personal crises, and judge's denial of continuance request, counsel failed to pursue available avenues for investigation, waived alibi defense by failing to file notice in timely fashion, and never attempted to plea bargain).

- House v. Balkcom, 725 F.2d 608 (11th Cir.), *cert. denied*, 469 U.S. 870 (1984) (capitally sentenced petitioner's counsel filed no pretrial motions, sought no defense witnesses, failed to interview petitioner's family or state's witnesses, did not visit crime scene, made no use of possibly exculpatory evidence available from state's own scientific tests, and failed to move for new trial based on evidence that victims were alive after last time petitioner could have been in contact with them).

- Francis v. Spraggins, 720 F.2d 1190 (11th Cir. 1983), *cert. denied*, 470 U.S. 1059 (1985) (counsel's concession of client's guilt in closing argument could not be justified as strategic decision to maintain credibility at upcoming capital sentencing hearing).

- Goodwin v. Balkcom, 684 F.2d 794 (11th Cir. 1982), *cert. denied*, 460 U.S. 1098 (1983) (trial counsel knew jury-selection procedures were unconstitutional but failed to challenge them because he did not want to jeopardize relationship with trial judge).

- Young v. Zant, 677 F.2d 792 (11th Cir. 1982), *cert. denied*, 464 U.S. 1057 (1984) (counsel "adopted an unsupportable defense to all counts," "ignored the obvious defenses to the malice murder and armed robbery charges," and "conceded his client's guilt of all three crimes for which he was charged in the guilt phase of the trial ... [out of a] mistaken belief that such an action was strategically necessary in order to make a strong plea for mercy").

- MacKenna v. Ellis, 280 F.2d 592 (5th Cir. 1960), *cert. denied*, 368 U.S. 877 (1961) (inexperienced counsel, appointed over petitioner's protest, were seeking employment at time from district attorney and failed to interrogate witnesses, secure witnesses for trial, apply for continuance, or protect client from hasty trial).

(c)   Ineffective assistance with regard to guilty plea:

- Boria v. Keane, 99 F.3d 492 (2d Cir. 1996) (counsel was ineffective in failing to counsel client about wisdom of accepting plea bargain which would have substantially reduced sentence).

- Dickerson v. Vaughn, 90 F.3d 87 (3d Cir. 1996) (petitioners pled *nolo contendere* based on counsel's erroneous advice that pretrial ruling on double jeopardy could be appealed after plea).

- Agan v. Singletary, 12 F.3d 1012 (11th Cir. 1994) (counsel, whose client pled guilty, was ineffective in failing to "make an independent examination of the facts and circumstances" in order to "offer an informed opinion as to the best course to follow" (in that counsel "only spent seven (7) hours conducting any sort of external investigation of the case," ignoring a potentially fruitful lead that would have "created substantial questions as to the identity of the actual perpetrator(s)") and also ineffective in failing "to investigate [the] client's competency ... to plead guilty" (in that counsel ignored indications of mental unfitness because client refused to submit to psychiatric examination)).

- Osborn v. Shillinger, 861 F.2d 612 (10th Cir. 1988) (counsel did nothing to assist petitioner in efforts to withdraw guilty plea before sentencing and made statements to media indicating that motion to withdraw plea was meritless).

- Holtan v. Parratt, 683 F.2d 1163 (8th Cir. 1982), *cert. denied*, 459 U.S. 1225 (1983) (counsel failed to comply with petitioner's instruction to seek withdrawal of *nolo contendere* plea).

(d)   Ineffective assistance at sentencing:

- Austin v. Bell, 126 F.3d 843 (6th Cir. 1997), *cert. denied*, 118 S. Ct. 1526 (1998) (counsel "did not present any mitigating evidence because he did not think it would do any good"; counsel's "reasoning does not reflect a strategic decision, but rather an abdication of advocacy").

- Patrasso v. Nelson, 121 F.3d 297 (7th Cir. 1997) (counsel failed to investigate and do other preparation needed to challenge prosecution's case and present case in mitigation).

- Hall v. Washington, 106 F.3d 742 (7th Cir.), *cert. denied*, 118 S. Ct. 264 (1997) (finding of ineffective assistance at sentencing based on "first, counsels' total failure to contact [petitioner] in preparation for the sentencing hearing and their consequent failure to present his mitigation witnesses, and second, counsel's failure in his closing argument to offer any reason other than blatant disregard of Illinois law for sparing Hall's life").

- Emerson v. Gramley, 91 F.3d 898 (7th Cir. 1996), *cert. denied*, 117 S. Ct. 1260 (1997) (counsel failed to investigate mitigation and failed to warn petitioner that death sentence was virtually certain if no mitigating evidence was presented).

- Glenn v. Tate, 71 F.3d 1204 (6th Cir. 1995), *cert. denied*, 117 S. Ct. 273 (1996) (counsel "made virtually no attempt to prepare for the sentencing phase of the trial until after the jury returned its verdict of guilty," failed to provide experts with information that would have been helpful to defendant, and failed to draw jury's attention to mitigating aspect of defendant's mental condition).

- Clabourne v. Lewis, 64 F.3d 1373 (9th Cir. 1995) (counsel failed to call any witnesses or to introduce evidence of defendant's history of mental illness and "committed a commensurate error" by passing up opportunity to furnish prosecution experts with information that would have led to their diagnosing defendant's mental illness).

- Hendricks v. Calderon, 64 F.3d 1340 (9th Cir. 1995), *cert. denied*, 517 U.S. 1111 (1996) (despite evidence that defendant was mentally impaired, counsel failed to investigate defendant's mental condition as possible mitigating factor at sentencing).

- Antwine v. Delo, 54 F.3d 1357 (8th Cir. 1995), *cert. denied*, 516 U.S. 1067 (1996) (given indications in police report that petitioner "had been acting strangely a few days before the offense," trial counsel should not have credited result of court-ordered mental examination by state psychiatrist and should have invoked petitioner's state law right to "independent, second mental examination").

- Baxter v. Thomas, 45 F.3d 1501 (11th Cir.), *cert. denied*, 516 U.S. 946 (1995) (because trial attorneys did not obtain petitioner's school and hospital records, they failed to find and present evidence of petitioner's psychiatric problems and prior commitment to psychiatric institution).

- Jackson v. Herring, 42 F.3d 1350 (11th Cir.), *cert. denied*, 515 U.S. 1189 (1995) (counsel, who "had a small amount of information regarding possible mitigating evidence regarding Jackson's history, ... inexplicably failed to follow up with further interviews and investigation").

- Wade v. Calderon, 29 F.3d 1312 (9th Cir. 1994), *cert. denied*, 513 U.S. 1120 (1995) ("counsel abandoned a potentially forceful mitigating circumstance in favor of exclusive reliance on a theory which the jury had rejected twice before [on issues of guilt and insanity], and which was presented in a manner that clearly risked alienating the jury").

- Hill v. Lockhart, 28 F.3d 832 (8th Cir. 1994), *cert. denied*, 513 U.S. 1102 (1995) (although receiving information that petitioner was previously hospitalized, counsel made no effort to obtain medical records, which would have shown that petitioner had long history of mental problems and needed antipsychotic medication).

- Starr v. Lockhart, 23 F.3d 1280 (8th Cir. 1994) (incompetent counsel failed to make obviously meritorious challenge to legality of aggravating circumstance on which jury based death sentence).

- Deutscher v. Angelone, 16 F.3d 981 (9th Cir. 1994) (reaffirming previous determination in Deutscher v. Whitley, 884 F.2d 1152 (9th Cir. 1989), that counsel was ineffective in failing to investigate and present mitigating evidence of petitioner's mental problems).

481

- Mak v. Blodgett, 970 F.2d 614 (9th Cir. 1992) (*per curiam*) (counsel failed to present evidence that would have humanized petitioner, including available expert testimony regarding cultural conflicts experienced by young immigrants attempting to assimilate into new culture).

- Horton v. Zant, 941 F.2d 1449 (11th Cir. 1991), *cert. denied*, 503 U.S. 952 (1992) (ineffective attorney's pretrial investigation of mitigating circumstances consisted of phone call to petitioner's mother the night before penalty trial asking her if she planned to attend; in summation, attorney said that "the one you judge is ... a worthless man.... [I] hate my client").

- Kenley v. Armontrout, 937 F.2d 1298 (8th Cir.), *cert. denied*, 502 U.S. 964 (1991) (counsel failed to investigate available mitigating evidence of petitioner's mental problems because of erroneous belief that evidence was too old and insubstantial).

- Brewer v Aiken, 935 F.2d 850 (7th Cir. 1991) (counsel failed to investigate and find readily available mitigating evidence of petitioner's low I.Q., susceptibility to influence of companions, and disadvantaged background).

- Cunningham v. Zant, 928 F.2d 1006 (11th Cir. 1991) (counsel failed to present significant mitigating evidence regarding petitioner's mild retardation, limited education, and "poverty-stricken socioeconomic background").

- Chambers v. Armontrout, 907 F.2d 825 (8th Cir.), *cert. denied*, 498 U.S. 950 (1990) (counsel failed to interview and call witness who would have supported petitioner's claim of self-defense and thereby provided basis for mitigation).

- Harris v. Dugger, 874 F.2d 756 (11th Cir.), *cert. denied*, 493 U.S. 1011 (1990) (no mitigation investigation conducted because "[e]ach lawyer ... believed ... the other was responsible for preparing the penalty phase").

- Kubat v. Thieret, 867 F.2d 351 (7th Cir.), *cert. denied*, 493 U.S. 874 (1989) (counsel contacted only 2 of 15 possible character witnesses, did not present the two at sentencing, and failed to object to instruction that misstated state law by requiring findings of mitigating circumstances to be unanimous).

- Osborn v. Shillinger, 861 F.2d 612 (10th Cir. 1988) (counsel failed to investigate and prepare for sentencing hearing because he was confident he could negotiate sentence less than death).

- Evans v. Lewis, 855 F.2d 631 (9th Cir. 1988) (counsel failed to investigate available mitigating evidence of history of mental problems and prior hospitalizations).

- Middleton v. Dugger, 849 F.2d 491 (11th Cir. 1988) (counsel conducted only minimal investigation into petitioner's background despite strong indications of available mitigating evidence).

- Stephens v. Kemp, 846 F.2d 642 (11th Cir.), *cert. denied*, 488 U.S. 872 (1988) (counsel failed to investigate, present, or argue available mitigating evidence of petitioner's history of mental problems).

- Armstrong v. Dugger, 833 F.2d 1430 (11th Cir. 1987) (counsel failed to discover available witnesses because he limited investigation of case for mitigation to interviews of petitioner, his parents, and his parole officer).

- Woodard v. Sargent, 806 F.2d 153 (8th Cir. 1986) (counsel failed to request that jury be instructed on mitigating circumstance that was adequately supported by evidence in record).

- Thomas v. Kemp, 796 F.2d 1322 (11th Cir.), *cert. denied*, 479 U.S. 996 (1986) (incompetent attorney failed to discover, or seek sentence less than death based on, defendant's long and well-documented history of mental disorder).

- Jones v. Thigpen, 788 F.2d 1101 (5th Cir. 1986), *cert. denied*, 479 U.S. 1087 (1987) (counsel conducted no investigation in mitigation of death penalty and did not realize, or inform jury, that his client had an I.Q. below 41).

- Johnson v. Kemp, 781 F.2d 1482 (11th Cir. 1986) (*per curiam*), *aff'g* Johnson v. Kemp, 615 F. Supp. 355 (S.D. Ga. 1985) (in investigating case for mitigation, counsel only spoke to petitioner and his parents and did not ask them for names of witnesses or other specific sources of mitigating evidence).

- Blake v. Kemp, 758 F.2d 523 (11th Cir.), *cert. denied*, 474 U.S. 998 (1985) (counsel failed to prepare for penalty phase before trial and then could not obtain continuance of sentencing hearing after trial ended in conviction).

- Tyler v. Kemp, 755 F.2d 741 (11th Cir.) (*per curiam*), *cert. denied*, 474 U.S. 1026 (1985) (counsel only interviewed members of petitioner's family and failed to make clear that he was seeking mitigating evidence for sentencing and not just evidence relating to guilt phase).

- King v. Strickland, 748 F.2d 1462 (11th Cir. 1984), *cert. denied*, 471 U.S. 1016 (1985) (counsel did not search carefully for mitigating evidence or even discuss potential case for mitigation with client and counsel's closing argument "probably caused his client more harm than good").

- Douglas v. Wainwright, 739 F.2d 531 (11th Cir. 1984), *cert. denied*, 469 U.S. 1208 (1985) (reinstating, in pertinent part, Douglas v. Wainwright, 714 F.2d 1532, 1553-58 (11th Cir. 1983)) (defense counsel who was insufficiently familiar with capital sentencing law and procedures failed to prepare adequately for hearing, did not fully interview petitioner about possible mitigation witnesses or advise him about option of taking the stand, and told sentencing judge during conference in chambers that no mitigating evidence could be found).

- Pickens v. Lockhart, 714 F.2d 1455 (8th Cir. 1983) (counsel failed to investigate and present available mitigating evidence about petitioner's background and his cooperation with authorities in apprehension of triggerman).

(e) Ineffective assistance on appeal:

- Evitts v. Lucey, 469 U.S. 387 (1985) (ineffective assistance of counsel on appeal).

- Robbins v. Smith, 125 F.3d 831 (9th Cir. 1997) (appointed appellate counsel's "*Anders* brief" violated procedure established in Anders v. California, 386 U.S. 738 (1967) by "fail[ing] to identify any grounds that arguably supported an appeal").

- Mason v. Hanks, 97 F.3d 887 (7th Cir. 1996) (appellate counsel omitted apparently meritorious claim that "admission of testimony concerning the informant's statements was inadmissible hearsay under Indiana law"; "when we are convinced that a petitioner might well have won his appeal on a significant and obvious question of state law that his counsel omitted to pursue, we are compelled to conclude, as we do here, that the appeal was not fundamentally fair and that the resulting affirmance of his conviction is not reliable").

- Mayo v. Henderson, 13 F.3d 528 (2d Cir. 1994) (appellate counsel was ineffective because he "omitted [a] significant and obvious [state law] issue[] [from the appeal] while pursuing issues that were clearly and significantly weaker").

(f) **Ineffective assistance at postconviction by counsel who also represented petitioner at earlier stages of case:**[101]

- Deutscher v. Angelone, 16 F.3d 981 (9th Cir. 1994) (previous determination of ineffectiveness of counsel, Deutscher v. Whitley, 884 F.2d 1152 (9th Cir. 1989), not barred by abuse of writ because ineffective counsel, who represented petitioner in habeas corpus proceedings as well as at trial and upon appeal, filed first petition without "notifying [petitioner] or seeking his authorization ... [and without] explain[ing] the nature of federal habeas corpus proceedings, the risk that claims not raised might be barred as abuse of the writ, or the appropriateness of having other counsel file the petition").

(g) **Ineffective assistance due to conflict of interest:**

- Blankenship v. Johnson, 118 F.3d 312 (5th Cir. 1997) (attorney, who represented petitioner in appeal to intermediate appellate court, had irremediable conflict of interest at time of subsequent state-requested discretionary review by state's criminal court of last resort because, in interim, attorney had been elected county attorney).

- Edens v. Hannigan, 87 F.3d 1109 (10th Cir. 1996) (counsel, who represented petitioner and codefendant at joint trial, presented less aggressive defense for petitioner to avoid prejudicing codefendant and failed to pursue plea offer with condition of testimony against codefendant).

- Griffin v. McVicar, 84 F.3d 880 (7th Cir. 1996), *cert. denied*, 117 S. Ct. 1288 (1997) (counsel, who represented petitioner and codefendant at joint trial, rejected defense that was clearly favorable to petitioner but detrimental to codefendant in favor of untenable joint defense).

- Selsor v. Kaiser, 81 F.3d 1492 (10th Cir. 1996) (trial judge failed to inquire adequately into need for separate counsel for petitioner and codefendant, both of whom were represented by same public defender's office).

- Ciak v. United States, 59 F.3d 296 (2d Cir. 1995) (despite awareness that defense counsel had recently represented government witness and may have

---

[101] For discussion of the limited circumstances under which a petitioner can attack counsel's performance in postconviction proceedings as a violation of the constitutional right to counsel, *see infra* § 26.3b n.36.

had conflicting interests, trial judge failed to conduct inquiry into need for withdrawal).

- Lopez v. Scully, 58 F.3d 38 (2d Cir. 1995) (counsel had "actual conflict of interest" at time of sentencing because client had moved to vacate guilty plea on ground that counsel induced plea by threats and misinformation).

- United States v. Cook, 45 F.3d 388 (10th Cir. 1995) (although trial counsel's initial conflict of interest in representing section 2255 movant and codefendant was resolved by withdrawal from codefendant's case, counsel developed new conflict of interest when he complied with district court's mid-trial instruction to advise codefendant of consequences of failure to comply with testimony agreement that counsel negotiated on her behalf).

- Dawan v. Lockhart, 31 F.3d 718 (8th Cir. 1994) (counsel, who had previously represented defense witness when he was charged as codefendant, did not rehabilitate witness's in-court testimony by aggressively attacking his out-of-court inconsistent statements as perjurious).

- Burden v. Zant, 24 F.3d 1298 (11th Cir. 1994) (on remand from Burden v. Zant, 510 U.S. 132 (1994) (*per curiam*), court of appeals concludes that writ should be granted because attorney who represented petitioner prior to trial also represented another suspect and negotiated agreement for latter individual to testify against petitioner in exchange for transactional immunity).

- Sanders v. Ratelle, 21 F.3d 1446 (9th Cir. 1994) (counsel's previous representation of petitioner's brother, who admitted to counsel in course of representation that he committed murder with which petitioner was charged, created conflict of interest precluding effective representation of petitioner).

- United States v. Fulton, 5 F.3d 605 (2d Cir. 1993) (section 2255 motion granted on grounds of ineffectiveness of counsel because prosecution witness's allegation of criminal activity by counsel created *per se* prejudicial conflict of interest).

- Fitzpatrick v. McCormick, 869 F.2d 1247 (9th Cir.), *cert. denied*, 493 U.S. 872 (1989) (counsel represented petitioner at retrial after serving as counsel for co-defendant at petitioner's first trial).

- Ruffin v. Kemp, 767 F.2d 748 (11th Cir. 1985) (counsel divided his loyalties between two codefendants, soliciting testimony of one against other).

- Walberg v. Israel, 766 F.2d 1071 (7th Cir.), *cert. denied*, 474 U.S. 1031 (1985) (trial judge threatened to withhold payment and future appointments from appointed counsel because petitioner "was unworthy of the protracted efforts that the lawyer was making on his behalf" and insisted that petitioner's "lawyer owed his first allegiance to the judge as a family friend and benefactor").

- Westbrook v. Zant, 743 F.2d 764 (11th Cir. 1984) (petitioner's attorney also was counsel to county and thus was responsible for defending jury commission in lawsuits challenging selection of grand and traverse jury pools).

(h)   Denial of right to self-representation:

- Myers v. Johnson, 76 F.3d 1330 (5th Cir. 1996) (*per curiam*) (state appellate court's appointment of appellate counsel instead of standby counsel for *pro se* appeal, and counsel's refusal to provide client with transcript, violated appellant's right to self-representation on appeal).

- Williams v. Bartlett, 44 F.3d 95 (2d Cir. 1995) (trial court improperly denied petitioner's timely and unequivocal assertion of right of self-representation).

- Peters v. Gunn, 33 F.3d 1190 (9th Cir. 1994) (trial court improperly denied petitioner's right to self-representation on ground that petitioner lacked adequate legal acumen).

§ 11.3. Claim selection.

a. *Assembling potential claims.* Previous sections describe the types of federal claims a prisoner may assert in postconviction proceedings,[1] the process of identifying potential claims in the particular case,[2] and some of the types of claims that have previously prevailed on habeas corpus.[3] In selecting the claims to present in a habeas corpus petition, counsel or a *pro se* prisoner often will find it useful to begin by assembling a preliminary list of all the legal claims that possibly[4] are presented by the case. The preliminary list may be constructed in tabular form with parallel columns for present and future citations to materials relevant to each claim, including, for example, the appropriate portions of the notes, memoranda, and files of trial, appellate and postconviction counsel; the trial record; the briefs of both parties on direct appeal; the appellate decision(s); the *certiorari* petition and response; the postconviction petition, record, trial-level decision, appellate briefs, appellate decision(s), and *certiorari* petition; and the federal habeas corpus petition, motions and pleadings, record, decision, appellate briefs, and appellate decisions. The table also may include a column noting the procedural defenses the state has asserted in prior state proceedings or may assert against each claim in federal proceedings.[5] Such a chart serves both

---

§ 11.3.   [1] *See supra* §§ 2.3, 2.4, 9.1, 9.2.

[2] *See supra* §§ 11.2a, 11.2b.

[3] *See supra* § 11.2c.

[4] At this preliminary stage, "possibly" is used in a broad sense. The somewhat narrower standard for inclusion in petition is whether the claim is "colorable." *See* McFarland v. Scott, 512 U.S. 849, 860 (1994) (O'Connor, J., concurring in the judgment in part and dissenting in part) ("our carefully crafted doctrines of waiver and abuse of the writ make it especially important that the first petition adequately set forth all of a state prisoner's *colorable grounds* for relief" (emphasis added)); *supra* § 11.2a n.5 & *infra* § 11.3b nn.12-15 and accompanying text (discussing need created by McCleskey v. Zant, 499 U.S. 467 (1991), to utilize broad standard for inclusion of claims in habeas corpus petitions).

[5] *See infra* Chapters 23-28, 30, 32.

to array the potential claims for claim-selection and claim-ordering purposes early in the case and to index the record in a manner that will make it more easily accessible when drafting pleadings and briefs.

b. *Claim selection; selection and pleading implications of procedural defenses.* An earlier section discusses some general considerations relevant to claim selection at the state postconviction stage.[6] This subsection elucidates in more detail the considerations affecting claim selection at both the state and federal postconviction stages.

In deciding which of the available issues to raise in the petition and which to emphasize, counsel and the client must exercise discretion based on: (1) the relative strength of each issue given the law as it exists in the Supreme Court and the federal judicial circuit and as it is developing elsewhere — and, given "nonretroactivity" considerations and related constraints in recent legislation, the law as it existed in the Supreme Court at the end of direct appeal proceedings; (2) the actual or potential strength and "provability" of the factual bases for each claim; (3) the strength of the defenses the state potentially could assert against each claim and the likelihood that the state actually will assert the defense(s); and (4) the optimum length of the petition given, on the one hand, the limits on the time and patience of the judges who will hear the case and the danger of the chaff obscuring the grain and, on the other hand, the far greater reluctance on the part of judges to permit the prisoner later to file a successive petition raising a previously omitted claim that hindsight or intervening developments have strengthened.[7]

In regard to the last factor, it is fair to expect the courts' patience to be roughly proportional to the severity of the restraints the state has placed on the petitioner and the seriousness of the alleged constitutional violations.[8] Consistent

---

[6] *See supra* § 6.2.

[7] *See infra* Chapter 25 (nonretroactivity considerations); *infra* Chapter 28 (successive petition considerations); *infra* § 30.2 (discussing recent legislation limiting habeas corpus relief, in cases to which new Act applies, *see supra* § 3.4, to legal claims supported by "clearly established Federal law, as determined by the Supreme Court" as of date direct appeal ended).

[8] By "seriousness" is meant the impact of the violation both on the prisoner's federal rights and on the fair and accurate functioning of the criminal justice system as a whole. These terms are intentionally vague and will vary in content from one case to another, one court to another, and one era to another. It is fair to predict that some judges' patience will be inversely proportional to the severity of the crime and the likelihood that the petitioner committed it. *But cf. supra* §§ 2.5, 2.6. To the extent that this version of the judicial patience factor bears on the wheat/chaff concerns mentioned above, it must be considered. It must not be permitted, however, to interfere with counsel's responsibility zealously to litigate colorable federal claims in hopes that the legal process eventually will subordinate emotional considerations to federal constitutional rights. *See, e.g.,* Ford v. Wainwright, 477 U.S. 399 (1986) (seven Justices concur in judgment remanding case to afford

with this rule, cases involving minor offenses and short sentences call for greater selectivity among claims than, for example, capital cases, in which the enormity and irrevocability of the penalty,[9] the particularly limited opportunity for filing successive petitions,[10] and the quick pace of legal change[11] militate strongly in favor of including all possibly meritorious claims.

The Court's 1991 decision in *McCleskey v. Zant*[12] has an important bearing on issue selection, particularly in capital cases such as *McCleskey* itself. There, the Supreme Court dismissed a capital prisoner's second habeas corpus petition, which raised an apparently meritorious 6th Amendment objection to police officers' use of a jailhouse informant to secure inculpatory statements from petitioner in the absence of counsel. Although the petitioner had long suspected that a witness against him at trial was a planted informer, and had so alleged in a state postconviction petition, false denials by state officials during state postconviction proceedings thwarted efforts to prove the facts necessary to make out the 6th Amendment claim, and the petitioner accordingly dropped the claim when he filed his first federal habeas corpus petition. After the denial of the first petition, McCleskey's attorneys discovered a former jailer who admitted that he and other officials had planted the witness in McCleskey's cell. Presented with these facts, the Supreme Court forbade a second petition raising the 6th Amendment claim. Notwithstanding law enforcement officials' false denials during state postconviction proceedings that they planted an informant, the Court held that McCleskey's failure to discover the jailer prior to the resolution of the initial habeas corpus petition constituted negligence, which gave the state a defense to a successive petition raising the claim.[13] Under *McCleskey*, a

---

petitioner fair process in proving that he is currently insane, hence should not be executed, although three Justices, including one of seven who later voted to remand, expressed view two years earlier that claim was too frivolous to justify stay of execution, *see* Wainwright v. Ford, 467 U.S. 1220 (1984)); Coleman v. Kemp, 778 F.2d 1487 (11th Cir. 1985), *cert. denied,* 476 U.S. 1164 (1986) (reversing district court's denial of relief on particularly egregious fair-trial violation in case involving particularly horrifying offense); Spencer v. Kemp, No. CV179-247 (S.D. Ga. March 31, 1987) (ordering relief, upon remand with instructions from court of appeals, based on "obvious" and "clearly unconstitutional" underrepresentation of blacks and women on jury rolls, notwithstanding district judge's view that "a system [defended] on the ground that the meanest defendant is entitled to a trial wholly without constitutional infirmity" is "ludicrous").

[9] *See supra* § 2.6.

[10] *See infra* Chapter 28.

[11] *See* Jack Greenberg, *Capital Punishment as a System,* 91 YALE L.J. 908, 921 (1982).

[12] 499 U.S. 467 (1991).

[13] *See supra* § 11.2a n.5 (describing facts and proceedings in *McCleskey*, and providing citations). Apparently crucial to *McCleskey's* holding is the fact that counsel could have uncovered support for the claim, notwithstanding the state's statements that the claim was groundless and its false denials that relevant documents existed, by interviewing one or more witnesses whom counsel could easily have located and who apparently would have been willing to talk to counsel and reveal

reasonable, even if as yet unconfirmed, belief that a meritorious fact-based claim exists may oblige the prisoner and counsel, at least in a capital or other serious case, to raise the claim and to pursue it via, *e.g.*, court-funded investigation (in the case of an indigent petitioner), discovery, an evidentiary hearing, and other fact-development procedures[14] of the sort that often are not fully available to prisoners until they file a habeas corpus petition. Thus, as Justice O'Connor has stated, referring, *inter alia*, to *McCleskey*, the Court's "carefully crafted doctrines of waiver and abuse of the writ make it especially important that the first petition adequately set forth *all* of a state prisoner's *colorable grounds* for relief."[15]

---

the facts establishing the violation. For an extension of the *McCleskey* principle (albeit in a procedural default, not successive petition, context) to a case in which the state repeatedly denied the existence of exculpatory information that was *not* so clearly available from sources outside the prosecution team, see Strickler v. Pruett, 1998 WL 340420 at *5-*10 (4th Cir. June 17, 1998) (*per curiam*), *cert. granted*, 119 S. Ct. 40 (1998).

[14] *See infra* Chapters 18-21.

[15] McFarland v. Scott, 512 U.S. 849, 860 (1994) (O'Connor, J., concurring in the judgment in part) (emphasis added). *Accord id.* at 856 (majority opinion) (citing *McCleskey, supra*); other authority cited *supra* § 11.2a n.5.

If faced with this situation, counsel might consider a procedure that the Advisory Committee responsible for revising the Federal Rules of Civil Procedure suggested in connection with the 1993 revision of Civil Rule 11(b)(3). Under Rule 11(b)(3), counsel filing a pleading is understood to certify that "the allegations and other factual contentions have evidentiary support *or, if specifically so identified, are likely to have evidentiary support after a reasonable opportunity for further investigation or discovery*." *Id.* (emphasis added). Counsel considering this procedure should take note of the Advisory Committee's description of the appropriate conditions in which to use the proposed procedure and of the special responsibilities the procedure places on counsel to investigate and, if warranted, to withdraw a claim shown by investigation or discovery to be insupportable:

> The certification with respect to allegations and other factual contentions is revised in recognition that sometimes a litigant may have good reason to believe that a fact is true or false but may need discovery, formal or informal, from opposing parties or third persons to gather and confirm the evidentiary basis for the allegation. Tolerance of factual contentions in initial pleadings by plaintiffs or defendants when specifically identified as made on information and belief does not relieve litigants from the obligation to conduct an appropriate investigation into the facts that is reasonable under the circumstances ....

Advisory Committee Note to 1993 Amendment of FED. R. CIV. P. 11(b) and 11(c). *See id.* ("The certification is that there is (or likely will be) 'evidentiary support' for the allegation, not that the party will prevail with respect to its contention regarding the fact."). If evidentiary support for the claim is not forthcoming after counsel has utilized every "reasonable opportunity for further investigation or discovery" that is available, the petitioner should "not ... persist with th[e] contention." *Id.* If counsel suspects that evidence exists that supports the claim but has been thwarted in developing that evidence by actions of the court or the adversary (*e.g.*, by denials of necessary fact-development procedures or of the funds needed to utilize them, by police officers' refusal to provide information, or by the state's refusal to produce documents or other physical evidence, *see generally infra* §§ 26.3b n.33 and accompanying text), counsel should preserve the

As is discussed in Chapter 3 *supra*, the Antiterrorism and Effective Death Penalty Act of 1996 (AEDPA)[16] creates a number of new procedural defenses and expands others that already existed.[17] As a result, prisoners have even more reason than before to discover and include in their initial federal habeas corpus petitions every "colorable ground[ ] for relief"[18] but have considerably less time in which to discover and plead those claims. The need for comprehensive investigation and pleading of claims arises, *e.g.*, because AEDPA in some instances forbids habeas corpus petitions to be amended[19] and limits the time available for postfiling litigation that otherwise would serve to flesh out the prisoner's claims,[20] and because AEDPA severely limits the range of successive petitions that can succeed.[21] Less time is available to discover and plead claims, *e.g.*, because of the one-year statute of limitations that AEDPA applies to noncapital habeas corpus petitions, capital habeas corpus petitions in "nonopt-in" States, and section 2255 motions[22] and, particularly, because of a 180-day statute of limitations that AEDPA adopts for capital cases in "opt-in" States[23] — neither of which statutes of limitations is tolled during time spent investigating and preparing state postconviction or federal habeas corpus petitions, and the latter of which is not tolled during time spent preparing the direct appeal *certiorari* petition or litigating second or successive state postconviction petitions. Given these changes, counsel (especially in capital cases in opt-in States[24]) must be even more creative than the *McCleskey* decision already required in carrying out effective but time-limited legal and factual investigations and in pleading claims as to which less is known than is desirable.[25]

---

claim while appeals are prosecuted as to the propriety of the court's or the adversary's actions. When recalcitrant witnesses or other third-parties are responsible for counsel's inability to develop a claim believed to be meritorious, counsel should include in the pleading withdrawing the claim a detailed description of the obstacles that have prevented full exploration of the relevant facts.

[16] Pub. L. 104-132, 110 Stat. 1214 (1996).

[17] *See supra* § 3.2 (summary of provisions of AEDPA, with cross-references to more detailed discussions elsewhere).

[18] *McFarland v. Scott, supra*, 512 U.S. at 860 (O'Connor, J., concurring in the judgment in part).

[19] *See* 28 U.S.C.A. § 2266(b)(3)(B) (West Supp. 1998) (discussed *supra* § 3.3c nn.61-64 and accompanying text).

[20] *See id.* § 2266 (discussed *supra* § 3.3c nn.45-54 and accompanying text).

[21] *See* 28 U.S.C.A. § 2244(b) (West 1994 & Supp. 1998) discussed *infra* §§ 28.3, 28.4).

[22] *See id.* § 2244(d) (discussed *supra* § 5.1b nn.58-91 and accompanying text). For discussion of the difference between "nonopt-in" and "opt-in" cases, see *supra* § 3.2.

[23] *See* 28 U.S.C.A. § 2263 (West Supp. 1998) (discussed *supra* § 5.1b nn.92-123 and accompanying text).

[24] *See supra* § 5.1b nn.109-19 and accompanying text.

[25] *See supra* notes 8-15 and accompanying text.

Additional claim selection and pleading considerations regarding the strength of the potential claims and the defenses the state may assert against them are set out below:

(1) Certainly, all claims meriting relief under current Supreme Court precedent or that of the relevant federal circuit or district court should be raised as should claims as to which the law of the circuit is unsettled but as to which there is favorable law in other jurisdictions. Although, as is discussed in paragraph (3) below and in Chapter 25 and § 30.2 *infra*, the state may object to claims that rely on "nonretroactive" Supreme Court precedent that postdates direct review, or to claims that rely on even older lower court precedent absent directly supportive Supreme Court caselaw, the doctrines supporting such objections have prerequisites (including timely assertion by the state) and exceptions that often keep the objections from succeeding. The possibility that such an objection might be raised accordingly is rarely a reason to forgo presenting a claim.

(2) The appellate lawyer's instinct to exclude claims requiring further development of the factual record should be entirely discarded in habeas corpus proceedings. State and federal postconviction remedies are intended to permit meaningful fact-determination.[26] Accordingly, far from being a negative factor in trial-level postconviction proceedings, the demonstrable need for further factual development to prove (or even to establish the facts necessary to pursue[27]) the claim enhances the claim's substantiality insofar as avoiding summary dismissal, securing summary judgment,[28] obtaining appointed counsel,[29] staying a pending execution,[30] and other like matters are concerned. Moreover, given the non-retroactivity and "clearly established ... law" defenses to relief on habeas corpus claims premised on "new rules" of law,[31] the claims most likely to succeed are ones (*e.g.*, involuntary confession, suppression of evidence, and denial or ineffectiveness of counsel claims) premised on long-established legal principles that require careful and comprehensive development of the facts.

(3) Claims that have been rejected in other cases by a state court or a federal district court or court of appeals but upon which the Supreme Court has

---

[26] See *supra* Chapter 7; *infra* Chapters 19-21.

[27] See *supra* notes 12-15 and accompanying text.

[28] See *infra* § 15.2.

[29] See *supra* § 7.2; *infra* §§ 12.2-12.5, 36.1, 39.3b.

[30] See *infra* Chapter 13; *infra* §§ 36.2, 38.2, 39.3c.

[31] See *infra* notes 34-43 and accompanying text; *infra* Chapter 25; *infra* § 30.2.

not yet ruled should not automatically be omitted. Indeed, under the strict waiver and procedural default rules prevailing in the federal courts, the fact that a district court in the relevant circuit — including the one in which the petition will be filed — has rejected a claim or that some other federal circuit court, a district court in another circuit, or state courts within or without the circuit have done so deserves only modest weight at the claim selection stage.[32] Particularly when the basis for a court's rejection of a similar claim in another case was its assessment of the strength of the evidence favoring the claim or its understanding of the particular factual circumstances involved, counsel should scrutinize the facts of the instant case carefully for distinguishing circumstances.[33] When the basis for a court's rejection of a similar claim in another case was not the weakness of the evidence or the absence of facts needed to bring the case within the governing constitutional rule but, rather, the invalidity of the underlying legal principles, then counsel should take into account the nonretroactivity principles embodied in the Supreme Court's *Teague* doctrine[34] and AEDPA's standard of review of state court legal and mixed legal/factual claims.[35] The *Teague* doctrine generally (but not always) precludes federal habeas corpus relief on the basis of "new" legal rules announced after a conviction becomes "final" (which generally, but not always, occurs at the completion of *certiorari* review following direct appeal).[36] In cases governed by AEDPA,[37] the body of "federal law" a habeas corpus court may consider when reviewing a state court's decision is sometimes limited to legal rules that had already been "clearly established" by the Supreme Court at the time

---

[32] *See, e.g.,* Smith v. Murray, 477 U.S. 527, 533-35 (1986) (petitioner's death sentence upheld despite clear constitutional violation because former counsel failed to challenge offending procedure on appeal in Virginia Supreme Court; fact that Virginia Supreme Court previously had rejected all similar claims did not excuse default); *infra* Chapter 26.

[33] For example, the fact that the present petitioner is sentenced to die while the litigant denied relief by an apparently adverse precedent was not sentenced to death may supply a sufficient basis for distinguishing the two cases. *See, e.g.,* Turner v. Murray, 476 U.S. 28, 33-35 (1986) (capital case) (distinguishing Ristiano v. Ross, 424 U.S. 589 (1976) (noncapital case)); Beck v. Alabama, 447 U.S. 625, 637-38 (1980) (limiting holding to capital cases); Gardner v. Florida, 430 U.S. 349, 357-58 (1977) (limiting holding to capital cases). *See also* Caspari v. Bohlen, 510 U.S. 383, 391-96 (1994). As these cases reveal, this same type of scrutiny should be applied before omitting a claim because a prior Supreme Court decision rejects a similar claim.

[34] *See infra* Chapter 25.

[35] *See generally infra* § 30.2.

[36] *See infra* §§ 25.1, 25.5, 25.5, 25.7.

[37] For discussion of the cases subject to AEDPA, *see supra* §§ 3.2, 3.4.

the state court issued its decision.[38] In the past, when applying the *Teague* doctrine, the courts have looked to the existence of prior decisions denying a claim as evidence that the claim relies on a new rule;[39] although AEDPA has not been in effect long enough to gauge its precise effects, it seems likely that at least some federal courts will follow a similar approach in assessing whether a legal rule was "clearly established" at the time of the state court decision. These non-retroactivity rules should not, however, be viewed as creating an excessively high pleading threshold for claims as to which there is not absolute or even general unanimity, given the inevitable ambiguity and fluidity of the concepts on which the rules turn[40] and the Supreme Court's demonstrated willingness to define a legal principles as *not* "new" for *Teague* purposes even though some or most lower courts theretofore had rejected the principles.[41] The most that can be said without consideration of the particular claim and its susceptibility to nonretroactivity barriers is that counsel should try as accurately as possible to estimate the probability that the district court, court of appeals, and possibly the Supreme Court will find the claim meritorious on the basis of preexisting law. That probability increases, of course, if other federal or state courts have ruled favorably on the claim in the past.[42] That probability substantially increases, as well, to the extent that the claim can be — *and actually is* — pleaded in the petition and is briefed as simply the application (perhaps in a new factual context, perhaps not) of a well-established principle of law. Thus, while creativity, thoroughness, and persistence as to *factual theories* is likely to be rewarded in habeas corpus proceedings,[43] a more conservative approach to *legal theories* — one, *e.g.*, that prefers older to newer citations, and unremarkable statements of law to new and "interesting" ones — is most likely to bear fruit.

(4) The need, in properly pleading habeas corpus claims to include more detailed factual allegations than is required in other civil pleadings,[44] has

---

[38] *See infra* § 30.2.

[39] *See infra* § 25.5.

[40] *See infra* §§ 25.5, 30.2.

[41] *See* Stringer v. Black, 503 U.S. 222, 227-28 (1992) (discussed *infra* § 25.5 nn.44-59 and accompanying text); Penry v. Lynaugh, 492 U.S. 302, 314-15 (1989) (discussed *infra* § 25.5 nn.21-28 and accompanying text).

[42] *See generally* ROBERT L. STERN, EUGENE GRESSMAN, STEPHEN M. SHAPIRO & KENNETH S. GELLER, SUPREME COURT PRACTICE §§ 4.3-4.10, at 167-84 (7th ed. 1993); *infra* §§ 37.2, 39.2d.

[43] *See supra* notes 26-31 and accompanying text; *infra* Chapters 19-21.

[44] *See infra* § 11.6.

claim-selection implications. Certain claims — for example, ones based on the petitioner's past or present mental status and race discrimination claims — may require sophisticated psychiatric, statistical, social-scientific, or other expert analyses and proof. In cases involving indigent clients, it sometimes is difficult to plead such claims with complete specificity. Nonetheless, because state or federal postconviction proceedings may provide the wherewithal to develop the necessary facts,[45] such claims should not be omitted from the petition on this ground alone as long as (1) there is a basis at the pleading stage to predict that the necessary expert or other analyses will support the claim (for example, earlier analyses of the same subject in the same case, preliminary expert opinions or predictions, or studies completed elsewhere but in similar circumstances) and (2) the petitioner or counsel is prepared to pursue the necessary factual inquiry once the petition is filed. Such claims should be pleaded with as much precision and specificity as possible, informing the court in the pleadings both of the need for further analyses and of the bases for believing that such analyses will establish the alleged violation.[46]

(5) Claims that are susceptible to one or more of the procedural defenses available to the state in habeas corpus proceedings present special claim selection and pleading concerns. It is important, therefore, that counsel at the claim selection stage review carefully the discussion of the various defenses in later sections of this book.[47] Exhaustion *of remedies* considerations at the pleading stage are addressed in section 11.1 *supra* and 11.7 *infra*. *Statutes and limitations* and *prejudicial delay* considerations that may affect the timing of the petition are discussed in section 5.1b *supra*. *Nonretroactivity* considerations at the claim selection stage are briefly discussed in paragraphs (1) and (3) above and are discussed more comprehensively in Chapter 25 and § 30.2 *infra*. Additional claim selection and pleading considerations in anticipation of defenses are as follows:

(a) *Statute of limitations.* As is discussed in Chapters 3 and 5, *supra*, cases covered by AEDPA are subject to one of two statutes of

---

[45] *See supra* §§ 7.1, 7.2; *infra* §§ 19.3, 19.4; *infra* Chapters 20, 21.

[46] *See generally supra* notes 12-15 and accompanying text.

[47] *See infra* Chapters 22 (general discussion of defenses), 23 (exhaustion), 24 (prejudicial delay), 25 (nonretroactivity), 26 (adequate and independent state grounds/procedural default), 27 (*Stone v. Powell*), 28 (successive petitions), 32 (harmless error); *infra* §§ 20.3 & 30.3 (presumption of correctness of state factfindings); *infra* § 30.2 (effect of state court determinations of law and of mixed questions on federal habeas corpus proceedings).

limitations, each with its own triggering, tolling, and (in one case) extension provisions. Both statutes apparently create nonjurisdictional defenses that the *state* has the obligation to plead as a basis for denying relief. Nonetheless, because AEDPA may cause the calculation of timeliness to become a routine part of the process of determining whether to dismiss habeas corpus petitions, even summarily (a process described in Chapter 15 *infra*), the statute behooves counsel and prisoners proceeding *pro se* to determine before filing a federal habeas corpus petition: (i) whether AEDPA applies to the case (a matter covered in § 3.4 *supra*); (ii) if so, *which* of AEPDA's statutes of limitations applies, based on whether the case does or does not qualify for "opt-in" treatment (covered in §§ 3.2 and 3.3 *supra*); (iii) whether and how the petition as a whole — or, in certain circumstances, particular claims in the petition — satisfy the applicable statute of limitations, given its triggering and tolling provisions and the timing of prior proceedings in the case (covered in §§ 3.3c and 5.1b *supra*); and (iv) whether, although the applicable statute of limitations appears to render the petition or a claim in it untimely, the prisoner can avoid that problem by relying on the bar to the retroactive application of new legislation, some version of the "equitable tolling" doctrine, or a statutorily authorized extension of time (all also covered in §§ 3.3c and 5.1b *supra*). If the petition as a whole is evidently timely, counsel or the prisoner should include in the listing of prior proceedings in the case enough detail as to the filing and decision dates of proceedings relevant to the triggering and tolling of the applicable statute of limitations that a reviewing court can easily determine that the petition is timely. Local pleading rules should be consulted to determine whether, in addition, the petition must include an explicit demonstration that the number of days expended in prior proceedings during which the statute of limitations was "running" (*i.e.*, had been triggered and was not tolled) is less than the statutorily specified limitations period. If the petition, or some claim in it, presents a significant timeliness question, the petition should include (typically, in the place or places where prior proceedings are discussed) all of the facts needed to show that the petition or claim *is* timely or that the retroactivity bar or equitable tolling doctrine applies. In this situation, the petition or its accompanying documents also should request whatever evidentiary hearing or other fact-development procedures are needed to prove the facts on which the prisoner relies to demonstrate timeliness or an applicable exception.

Whether, in addition, the petition should acknowledge explicitly that there is a timeliness problem and explain why dismissal on timeliness grounds is impermissible (or, in "opt-in" cases, whether the petition or accompanying papers should ask for the statutorily authorized extension of time, if applicable) is a more difficult question, given (on the one hand) the state's obligation to raise timeliness defenses and the consequent waiveability of the issue and (on the other hand) the tendency of courts in the post-AEDPA issue to dismiss petitions they consider untimely without requiring the state to answer. Resolution of this question will turn on: local pleading rules, which may require an explicit discussion of timeliness; the obviousness of the timeliness problem; the obviousness, once the relevant facts are pleaded, of the prisoner's preferred solution to the timeliness problem; the practices of the relevant federal court, including in regard to summarily dismissing petitions, reacting to motions to dismiss filed by the state, the availability of motions to reconsider summary dismissals on timeliness grounds, and the like; the practices of the relevant state's attorney; the likelihood, in "opt-in" cases, that the timeliness problem can be avoided by the extension of time for which the statute of limitations explicitly provides; and other case-specific considerations. As is discussed in § 5.1b *supra*, although the nonopt-in statute of limitations is triggered by factors relevant to particular *claims* in the federal habeas corpus petition, the *latest* triggering date for the various claims in the petition may serve as the date for determining the timeliness of the petition as a whole. This attribute of the nonopt-in statute of limitations may accordingly provide an important reason *to* include a particular claim in a petition — because the claim's later triggering date may render timely other claims in the petition that have earlier triggering dates and as to which the statute of limitations otherwise would be deemed to have run. Rarely, however, will statute of limitations considerations militate *against* including particular claims in the petition. Because of the "all or nothing" effect that the statute of limitations bar typically has, a petitioner with a colorable argument that her petition is timely, or that an exception to the timeliness rule applies, will rarely find it appropriate to forgo filing a petition on the basis of timeliness concerns.

(b) *Procedural default.* After reviewing Chapter 26 *infra* (and, if challenging a conviction or sentence in a capital case governed by

AEDPA's "opt-in" provisions, section 3.3c *supra* as well[48]), counsel may conclude that an otherwise colorable claim is potentially susceptible to a procedural default defense. Given the myriad preconditions[49] and exceptions[50] to the Court's procedural default doctrine and the statutory and judicial preference that all available claims be fully litigated in a single progression of state and then federal proceedings,[51] counsel should proceed cautiously before deleting an otherwise meritorious claim from a petition based on procedural default or waiver grounds. Caution also is appropriate given that the respondent bears the burden of pleading and proving a procedural default and that the state sometimes forgoes asserting the default defense because it prefers a dispositive federal decision on the merits of a claim to a decision on procedural grounds that invites subsequent proceedings.[52] Without knowing more about the circumstances, omission of a claim in anticipation of a procedural default defense generally is warranted only if (i) the case includes a knowing and intelligent waiver of a federal claim by petitioner or a clear and unequivocal default of a claim in all state courts that were legally authorized to consider and grant relief on it, (ii) both the highest and last state courts to pass on the claim rejected it in a written opinion based solely on the default, (iii) the state is very likely to assert the default defense, (iv) all of the other prerequisites to the defense are clearly present, *and* (v) none of the exceptions to the defense is present. In many cases, petitioners need not raise responses to potential procedural default defenses in their initial pleadings and briefs because the burden to raise and prove the defenses is on the state.[53] Only after the respondent has pleaded and proved that a default occurred in the state courts do the Supreme Court's decisions indicate that the petitioner bears the burden of coming forward with an "explanation" sufficient to es-

---

[48] As is explained in § 3.3c *supra*, AEDPA's "opt-in" provisions establish a more restrictive procedural default doctrine than the doctrine that applies to noncapital cases and to capital cases in "nonopt-in" jurisdictions. For discussion of the capital cases to which AEDPA's "opt-in" provisions apply, see *supra* §§ 3.3a, 3.3b.

[49] *See infra* §§ 26.1, 26.2.

[50] *See infra* §§ 26.3, 26.4.

[51] *See, e.g.,* Kuhlmann v. Wilson, 477 U.S. 436, 448-52 (1986) (plurality opinion).

[52] *See infra* §§ 22.1, 26.2a.

[53] *See id.*

tablish "cause"[54] and with specific allegations of "actual prejudice."[55] In some circumstances, however, the state court record
— which is likely to come before the federal court fairly early in
the habeas corpus process[56] and can be a basis for summary dismissal even in advance of the state's answer[57] — may appear to
satisfy the state's burden. For example, the highest or last state
court to address the federal claim may have rejected it on state
procedural grounds. In this latter situation, the petitioner may be
well-advised to include *in the petition* an explanation of why relief
on the claim is not barred by the procedural default defense.[58]

(c)   Stone v. Powell — *4th Amendment exclusionary rule claims.* As
discussed in earlier sections, the Supreme Court's 1976 decision in
Stone v. Powell[59] limits the availability of habeas corpus con-

---

[54] Wainwright v. Sykes, 433 U.S. 72, 90-91 (1977). *See* Murray v. Carrier, 477 U.S. 478, 497 (1986) (no cause because petitioner "never alleged any"); Jones v. Dugger, 928 F.2d 1020, 1024 (11th Cir.), *cert. denied,* 502 U.S. 875 (1991); Teague v. Lane, 820 F.2d 832 (7th Cir. 1987) (*en banc*), *aff'd,* 489 U.S. 288 (1989); Allen v. Risley, 817 F.2d 68, 69 (9th Cir. 1987) (citing *Murray, supra* at 488).

[55] *See* United States v. Frady, 456 U.S. 152, 170 (1982); Jones v. Dugger, 928 F.2d 1020, 1024 (11th Cir.), *cert. denied,* 502 U.S. 875 (1991). Although the Court has not explicitly addressed the final burden of proof or persuasion on cause and prejudice, *see generally Wainwright v. Sykes, supra,* 433 U.S. at 84, the Court seems inclined to assign that burden to the petitioner. *See* Smith v. Murray, 477 U.S. 527, 537 (1986) ("We conclude ... that petitioner has not carried his burden of [explaining his] noncompliance with Virginia's rules of procedure."); *Murray v. Carrier, supra,* 477 U.S. at 488 ("existence of cause for a procedural default must ordinarily turn on whether the prisoner can show that some objective factor external to the defense impeded counsel's efforts to comply with the State's procedural rule"). *See also* Alexander v. Dugger, 841 F.2d 371, 374 (11th Cir. 1988) ("The burden is on the petitioner to demonstrate actual prejudice from the alleged constitutional violations" (citing *United States v. Frady, supra*)). If the state waives or concedes the issue of either "cause" or "prejudice," the petitioner only has to address the remaining requirement. *See, e.g.,* Amadeo v. Zant, 486 U.S. 214, 228 n.6 (1988) (rejecting state's argument that "even if cause is found to be established, petitioner suffered no cognizable prejudice," because state failed to dispute lower court findings that were tantamount to finding of "prejudice").

[56] *See infra* §§ 16.1b, 19.2.

[57] *See infra* § 15.2.

[58] *See, e.g.,* Glover v. Hargett, 56 F.3d 682, 684 (5th Cir. 1995), *cert. denied,* 116 S. Ct. 726 (1996) (declining to address petitioner's argument of "cause" for procedural default, which was raised for first time on appeal, because "Glover did not allege in his habeas petition that he had cause for his default or that it caused him actual prejudice, and he made no showing of cause or prejudice in the district court"). *But cf.* Doe v. United States, 51 F.3d 693, 699 (7th Cir.), *cert. denied,* 516 U.S. 876 (1995) (by asserting "cause" for default in reply brief on appeal though government had not previously asserted procedural default defense, section 2255 movant waived right to argue that government waived defense).

[59] 428 U.S. 465 (1976).

sideration of one kind of claim — 4th Amendment exclusionary rule claims.[60] The doctrine affects no other federal constitutional or statutory claim, however. Indeed, even ineffective assistance of counsel claims premised entirely on an attorney's failure to make a 4th Amendment exclusionary rule objection at trial are not barred by the *Stone* doctrine.[61] Moreover, as is developed in Chapter 27 *infra*, federal habeas corpus consideration and relief is available even as to claims premised exclusively on the 4th Amendment exclusionary rule if the petitioner can show that "the state has [not] provided an opportunity for full and fair litigation of [the] ... claim."[62] Although the "no full and fair opportunity" exception is narrow, it is broader than is suggested by the infrequency with which most habeas corpus lawyers plead 4th Amendment exclusionary rule claims. Substantial 4th Amendment claims should be seriously considered for inclusion whenever there is a reasonable basis of the sort discussed in Chapter 27 *infra* for concluding that the petitioner did not have an opportunity for full and fair litigation of the issue in the state courts. Although the state has the burden of pleading the *Stone* defense,[63] the defense's availability is so obvious that a federal court may not await its assertion by the state before denying relief on that basis.[64] In pleading 4th Amendment claims, therefore, the petition should set out the reasons why the

---

[60] *See id.* at 494-95; *supra* §§ 2.4d nn.277-89 and accompanying text, 9.2. The rule of *Stone v. Powell* is retroactive to all cases tried before the decision was announced. *See, e.g.,* Dupont v. Hall, 555 F.2d 15, 16-17 (1st Cir. 1977); United States ex rel. Saiken v. Bensinger, 546 F.2d 1292, 1294-95 (7th Cir. 1976), *cert. denied,* 431 U.S. 930 (1977); Roach v. Parratt, 541 F.2d 772 (8th Cir. 1976); Bracco v. Reed, 540 F.2d 1019 (9th Cir. 1976); Chavez v. Rodriguez, 540 F.2d 500 (10th Cir. 1976). The Supreme Court has never authoritatively applied the *Stone* defense in a capital case. *See infra* § 27.1 nn.7-15 and accompanying text. *Cf. supra* § 2.6 (bases for, but Supreme Court's resistance to, exempting capitally sentenced prisoners from habeas corpus preclusion doctrines).

[61] *See* Kimmelman v. Morrison, 477 U.S. 365 (1977) (discussed *supra* § 9.2 nn.15-20 and accompanying text). *See also supra* §§ 9.1 n.47 and accompanying text & 9.2 n.36 and accompanying text (*Stone* does not apply to claims arising under Title III of the Omnibus Crime Control and Safe Streets Act, 18 U.S.C. §§ 2510-20 (1994), which regulates electronic surveillance and is enforced through statutory exclusionary rule).

[62] *Stone, supra,* 428 U.S. at 495.

[63] *See infra* § 27.2 nn.1-2 and accompanying text.

[64] *See, e.g.,* Tart v. Massachusetts, 949 F.2d 490, 497 n.6 (1st Cir. 1991) (*dicta*) (cautioning habeas corpus petitioners that court will invoke *Stone* defense *sua sponte* even if state fails to assert it). *See also infra* § 27.2 n.2.

state court proceedings should not be regarded as having provided a "full and fair opportunity" to litigate the 4th Amendment claim.[65]

(d) *Successive petitions.* As previously noted, the law has become extremely hostile to habeas corpus petitions challenging criminal judgments that were the subject of a prior federal habeas corpus petition.[66] The rules governing successive petitions in non-AEDPA and AEDPA cases are discussed in Chapter 28 *infra*. Under the pre-AEDPA rules that still apply in certain cases,[67] the state has the burden to assert a successive petition defense in the first instance in its answer to the petition;[68] in such cases, longstanding law establishes that successive petition issues should not be disposed of based on the petitioner's pleading.[69] Nonetheless, given the pre-AEDPA rules requiring that a petitioner explain the use of a successive petition to litigate a claim[70] and the willingness of some courts to dismiss successive petitions *sua sponte*,[71] a prisoner is

---

[65] For example: "Petitioner did not have a full and fair opportunity to litigate this claim in the state courts because [briefly and generally state the reason — *e.g.,*] the courts do not permit hearings on the good faith of allegations made in affidavits accompanying search warrant requests; the state courts misallocated to petitioner the burden of proving that there was no probable cause; and the prosecution withheld critical evidence establishing the illegality of the seizure." *See infra* § 27.3.

[66] *See supra* § 11.1 nn.17-18 and accompanying text; *supra* notes 12-15 and accompanying text.

[67] *See supra* § 3.4.

[68] *See, e.g.,* Price v. Johnston, 334 U.S. 266, 292 (1948); authority cited *infra* § 28.3c.

[69] *See, e.g.,* Robinson v. Fairman, 704 F.2d 368, 371-72 (7th Cir. 1983); *infra* § 28.3c. *See also infra* § 11.5 (legislative history of Habeas Rule 2(c)).

[70] The pre-AEDPA Habeas Rules contain a model habeas corpus petition — with which Habeas Rule 2(c) requires "substantial" although not necessarily total conformity (*see infra* § 11.5) — directing petitioners to list the grounds raised in all previous petitions and to "give [the petitioner's] reasons for not presenting" in the earlier petition the claims that are now being raised. *See* Model Form for Use in Application for Habeas Corpus Under 28 U.S.C. § 2254, foll. Rules Governing § 2254 Cases, pts. (11)(a)(3), (11)(b)(3), 11(c)(3), 13; *infra* § 11.7a n.6 and accompanying text. The Habeas Rules also append a form that the district courts are invited to use to inform the petitioner of the possibility of dismissal on successive petition grounds and to elicit more information from petitioners in regard to the reasons for a claim's omission from a prior petition. *See* Model Form for Use in 28 U.S.C. § 2254 Cases Involving a Rule 9 Issue, foll. Rules Governing § 2254 Cases; *infra* § 11.7a n.6 and accompanying text.

[71] *See, e.g.,* United States v. Fallon, 992 F.2d 212, 213 (8th Cir. 1993); Urdy v. McCotter, 773 F.2d 652, 655 (5th Cir. 1985) (*dicta*); *infra* §§ 22.1 n.46, 28.3c nn.42-43 and accompanying text). Even the courts that have adopted this approach apparently adhere to the rule that dismissal on successive petition grounds must be preceded by ample notice to the petitioner of the likelihood of dismissal, an opportunity to explain why successive litigation has occurred, and, in some cases, the appointment of counsel to assist *pro se* petitioners in making their explanations. *See, e.g., United*

well-advised to supplement the statement of any claim that was or could have been included in a prior petition with a sentence or paragraph explaining the propriety of raising the claim in a successive petition. AEDPA establishes its own distinct procedure for filing a successive petition, which requires that the petitioner first obtain authorization from a circuit panel based upon a *prima facie* showing of satisfaction of AEDPA successive petition standards.[72] AEDPA's standards prohibit same-claim successive petitions altogether and limit new-claim successive petitions to cases in which the petitioner can make an adequate showing either that the legal rule on which she relies is new and retroactively applicable to her case or that the facts on which she relies were previously unavailable and that she probably is innocent.[73]

(e)   *Presumption of correctness of state court factfindings but not, apparently, state court legal determinations.* As is discussed in Chapters 20 and 30 *infra*, fact-dependent claims on which the state courts have made dispositive factfindings adverse to the petitioner in prior proceedings in the case are subject to denial on the basis of a rebuttable statutory presumption that the state court's findings are correct (assuming the state court findings were produced by a reasonable factfinding procedure and have reasonable support in the state court record).[74] State court legal determinations and mixed legal-factual determinations, on the other hand, traditionally have not been accorded such deference and do not appear to deserve such deference under the best interpretation of AEDPA (although some courts have interpreted AEDPA differently, to require deference to state court determinations of "mixed questions" in some situations).[75] Because a relatively wide array of state court determinations bearing on fact questions (i) mix legal and factual

---

States v. Fallon, supra, 992 F.2d at 213; authority cited *infra* § 28.3c nn.57-58 and accompanying text; *see also infra* § 17.1 (special requirement of responsive pleading or traverse following assertion of successive petition defense in state's answer).

[72] *See infra* § 28.3d.

[73] *See infra* § 28.3e.

[74] 28 U.S.C.A. § 2254(e) (West 1994 & Supp. 1998).

[75] Prior to AEDPA's enactment, state court legal determinations and mixed legal-factual determinations were subject to *de novo* review in federal habeas corpus proceedings. *See* § 30.2. That standard continues to control cases that are not governed by AEDPA. *See* § 3.4 (explaining the cases to which AEDPA does and does not apply). For discussion of AEDPA's as yet ill-defined and controversial standard of review of legal and mixed legal-factual determinations, see *infra* § 30.2.

issues,[76] (ii) are not entirely dispositive of the claim, (iii) do not qualify for the presumption of correctness given its prerequisites[77] and exceptions,[78] or (iv) are rebuttable,[79] the existence of adverse factfindings is not necessarily a basis for forbearance at the claim-selection stage. Careful consideration of the presumption of correctness doctrine and its nuances is required. The more prominent in the state court record and the more apparently comprehensive and dispositive are the adverse factfindings, and the less prominent are the bases for overcoming those findings or denying them the presumption of correctness, the more incentive there is to say something in the petition about the bases for overcoming the findings on denying them a presumption of correctness. Often, the necessary procedural facts can be pleaded affirmatively, rather than as an awkward response to a defense that has not yet been offered, by requesting an evidentiary hearing on the claim.[80] Because of the longstanding rule that legal and mixed state court determinations deserve no deference, AEDPA's apparent adherence to that rule, and the constitutional difficulties that would accompany any other approach — all discussed in § 30.2 *infra* — prisoners and counsel should not forbear raising claims in federal habeas corpus petitions based on any anticipated presumption of correctness of state court conclusions of law.

(f)   *Harmless error.* As is discussed in Chapter 32 *infra*, the harmless error defense that applies in habeas corpus cases is broader than the standard that governs the direct appeal stage.[81] The Supreme Court has made clear, however, that an assessment of the impact of constitutional error requires a careful analysis of the error's impact on the actual course of the trial.[82] As a result, harmless error considerations at the claim-selection stage are likely to merge with considerations going to the clarity and strength of the evidence of the violation — considerations discussed above.[83] Additionally, counsel will be hard-pressed to assess an error's impact without

---

[76] *See infra* § 20.3d.

[77] *See infra* §§ 20.3a-20.3d.

[78] *See infra* §§ 20.3e, 20.3f.

[79] *See infra* § 20.3h.

[80] *See infra* §§ 11.7c (motion for hearing filed with petition), 11.8 (prayer for relief).

[81] *See infra* § 32.1.

[82] *See infra* § 32.4d.

[83] *See supra* notes 32-43 and accompanying text.

knowing precisely how the court views the error — a matter that will remain invisible to counsel until after the claim's adjudication on the merits. Apart from factually or legally weak claims, therefore, harmless error considerations only rarely should lead to a colorable claim's omission from a habeas corpus petition.[84] Likewise, because "harmless error analysis is triggered only *after* the reviewing court discovers that an error has been committed,"[85] the harmless error defense would generally seem to be an inappropriate subject for discussion in the petition.[86] This is particularly so because the state bears both the burden of pleading the harmless error defense[87] and the ultimate burden of persuasion on the issue of harmless error.[88]

c. *Order of pleading.* It is impossible to generalize about the order of pleading. Among the possible ways to arrange the claims are: (1) chronologically with claims arising before trial appearing ahead of ones arising during and after trial, and claims attacking the conviction placed ahead of ones attacking the sentence; (2) strongest-to-weakest (not recommended); (3) clustered by subject matter, with the clusters of claims arranged either chronologically or based on the overall strength of the claims in each cluster;[89] (4) narratively, with the claims placed in the order that best tells the single integrated story (albeit with as many themes and subplots as necessary) of how the prisoner came to be convicted or sentenced unlawfully; and/or (5) clustered in what may be understood as a series of concentric circles, with each cluster consisting of a "core" legal claim (typically pleaded first within the cluster) that is based on clearly established and long-accepted law and, ideally, has fairly strong factual

---

[84] *See* Brecht v. Abrahamson, 507 U.S. 619, 650-56 (1993) (O'Connor, J, dissenting) (making harmless error defense broader will not limit burden on courts because doing so will only rarely cause petitioners to forgo raising meritorious constitutional claims).

[85] Lockhart v. Fretwell, 506 U.S. 364, 369 n.2 (1993). *Accord* Greer v. Miller, 483 U.S. 756, 761 n.3 (1987).

[86] Counsel should keep in mind, however, that proof of some constitutional claims — *e.g.*, ineffective assistance of counsel and prosecutorial suppression of evidence — requires (among other things) proof of "prejudice" or harm. *See infra* § 26.3c nn.62-63. As to such claims, the stringent pleading rules applicable in habeas corpus cases require a careful specification of the facts supporting the "prejudice" element, as well as every other element, of the claim. *See infra* § 11.6.

[87] *See infra* § 32.2a.

[88] *See infra* § 32.2b (discussing O'Neal v. McAninch, 513 U.S. 432 (1995)).

[89] In multiple-claim petitions, the clustering of stronger with weaker claims and the arrangement of the clusters on the basis of overall strength avoids the perceptible downhill slant that impairs the simple strongest-to-weakest approach.

support and is surrounded (*i.e.*, followed in the petition) by related claims that are based on progressively more sophisticated or novel legal reasoning.

§ 11.4. Joinder.[1]

a. *Joinder of claims.* If a single "petitioner desires to attack the validity of the judgments of two or more state courts under which he is in custody or may be subject to future custody ..., he shall do so by separate petitions."[2] A single prisoner may properly join claims attacking more than one judgment only if the petition seeks relief "against [two or more] judgments of a *single* state court (sitting in a county or other appropriate political subdivision)."[3] In the latter, multiple judgment/single court situation, one petition suffices even if two or more judges of the same court entered the judgments and if the judgments were entered at different times.[4] Although the Rules Governing § 2254 Cases *permit* a single petitioner to join claims attacking multiple judgments in "single court" situations, the rules do not *require* that course of action,[5] and it may not be advisable. Certainly, if the petitioner has exhausted state remedies as to one judgment but not as to the other(s),[6] and other considerations may compel or

---

§ 11.4.   [1] *See generally* WAYNE R. LAFAVE & JEROLD H. ISRAEL, CRIMINAL PROCEDURE § 28.3 (2d ed. 1992); LARRY W. YACKLE, POSTCONVICTION REMEDIES §§ 87-89 (1981 & Supp. 1998); *Developments in the Law — Federal Habeas Corpus,* 83 HARV. L. REV. 1038, 1169-73 (1970); Note, *Multiparty Federal Habeas Corpus,* 81 HARV. L. REV. 1482 (1968).

[2] Rule 2(d) of the Rules Governing § 2254 Cases. *See* Rule 2(c) of the Rules Governing § 2255 Proceedings. *See, e.g.*, Thompson v. Missouri Bd. of Probation and Parole, 39 F.3d 186, 189 (8th Cir. 1994), *cert. denied*, 514 U.S. 1113 (1995) (Rule 2(d) of the Rules Governing § 2254 Cases prohibited petitioner from "challeng[ing] both the Scott County conviction and the Butler County conviction in one § 2254 petition").

[3] Rule 2(d) of the Rules Governing § 2254 Cases (emphasis added). *See* Bianchi v. Blodgett, 925 F.2d 305, 308, 310-11 & n.7 (9th Cir. 1991) (petition properly dismissed because it challenged judgments of courts in two States; neither judicial economy nor fact that both judgments were entered pursuant to single interjurisdictional plea agreement obviates Rule 2(d)'s prohibition of joinder of claims attacking judgments of courts in different States; although waiver of objection by both States or potential for prejudice might warrant exception to Rule 2(d) — and consolidation procedures might be available after filing of separate petitions — no exception was appropriate here because one State objected to joinder, and petitioner could secure all relief he wanted by challenging only one judgment).

[4] Rule 2(d) of the Rules Governing § 2254 Cases; Advisory Committee Note to *id.*

[5] Advisory Committee Note to Rule 2(d) of the Rules Governing § 2254 Cases (Habeas Rule 2(d) "permits, but does not require, an attack in a single petition on judgments based upon separate indictment or on separate counts even though sentences were imposed on separate days by the same court").

[6] The total exhaustion rule, *see supra* § 11.1; *infra* § 23.5, applies only to individual judgments of conviction and sentence, else the state could use a succession of convictions of a single petitioner to deprive her of an opportunity to test the legality of the earlier convictions.

counsel the petitioner to proceed immediately to challenge only the first judgment, leaving the second one for a subsequent petition.[7]

b. *Joinder of petitioners.* It is permissible for two or more petitioners to file a single "joint" petition or for one or more petitioners to file a class action petition if all of the claims in the petition (1) challenge only the judgment or judgments of a single court,[8] or, perhaps, (2) raise only common questions of fact or law.[9]

---

[7] Under Habeas Rule 2(d)'s judgment-specific, not petitioner-specific, rule, a second petition filed by the same petitioner but challenging a different judgment is *not* a successive petition subject to the restrictive rules discussed *infra* Chapter 28. *See infra* § 28.3b.

[8] Rule 2(d) of the Rules Governing § 2254 Cases.

[9] *Joint petitions: See, e.g.,* Ruiz v. Lockhart, 754 F.2d 254 (8th Cir. 1985), *vac'd & remanded on other grounds,* 476 U.S. 1112 (1986); DeGrandis v. Fay, 335 F.2d 173 (2d Cir. 1964); Labat v. Sigler, 267 F.2d 307 (5th Cir. 1959), *vac'd & remanded on other grounds,* 361 U.S. 375 (1960); Bozeman v. Lambert, 587 F. Supp. 1021 (M.D. Ala. 1984), *aff'd,* 762 F.2d 1022 (11th Cir. 1985) (*mem*). *But cf.* United States ex rel. Carmona v. Ward, 416 F. Supp. 276 (S.D.N.Y. 1976) (challenge to mandatory-sentence laws for cocaine offenders; intervention granted as to cocaine offender but denied as to heroin offender because strategies might diverge).

Class action petitions: Death Row Prisoners of Pennsylvania v. Ridge, 948 F. Supp. 1258, 1264-68 (E.D. Pa. 1996), *aff'd,* 106 F.3d 35 (3d Cir. 1997) (permitting class action by six death row inmates seeking declaratory judgment that Pennsylvania does not qualify as "opt-in" State under Antiterrorism and Effective Death Penalty Act of 1996 (*see supra* §§ 3.2, 3.3) and thus that state officials may not seek to enforce 180-day statute of limitations against capital prisoners pursuant to Act's opt-in provisions; "*Younger* doctrine" does not require abstention, and court has authority to grant declaratory judgment and injunction); Brewer v. Swinson, 837 F.2d 802, 804 (8th Cir. 1988) (discussing class action challenging parole commission guidelines); Martin v. Strasberg, 689 F.2d 365 (2d Cir. 1982) (challenge to harsher treatment of juvenile pretrial detainees than juveniles adjudged guilty); United States ex rel. Morgan v. Sielaff, 546 F.2d 218 (7th Cir. 1976) (challenge to sexually dangerous persons statute allowing adjudication on preponderance of evidence, not reasonable doubt); United States ex rel. Sero v. Preiser, 506 F.2d 1115, 1125-27 (2d Cir. 1974), *cert. denied,* 421 U.S. 921 (1975) (class certification granted for young adult misdemeanants alleging harsher sentences than they would have received as adults; class members likely to be illiterate or poorly educated, hence incapable of individually seeking relief); Williams v. Richardson, 481 F.2d 358, 361 (8th Cir. 1973) (inmates and patients at the United States Medical Center); Knapp v. Cardwell, 513 F. Supp. 4 (D. Ariz. 1980), *aff'd,* 667 F.2d 1253 (9th Cir.), *cert. denied,* 459 U.S. 1055 (1982) (death row inmates challenging constitutionality of capital-sentencing statute); Jackson v. Justices, 423 F. Supp. 50 (D. Mass. 1976), *vac'd on other grounds,* 549 F.2d 215 (1st Cir.), *cert. denied,* 430 U.S. 975 (1977) (double jeopardy challenge by class of juveniles whose delinquency complaints had been dismissed and who then were indicted for offense charged in delinquency complaints); Adderly v. Wainwright, 58 F.R.D. 389 (M.D. Fla. 1972) (class of death row inmates certified because functional illiteracy and lack of counsel otherwise would deprive them of effective review). *See also* Groseclose v. Dutton, 788 F.2d 356, 357-58 (6th Cir. 1986) (transformation, at movants' behest, of multiparty habeas corpus petition into class action section 1983 complaint challenging prison conditions); Funchess v. Wainwright, 772 F.2d 683, 688 (11th Cir. 1985), *cert. denied,* 475 U.S. 1031 (1986) (discussing state habeas corpus class action litigation in Brown v. Wainwright, 392 So. 2d 1327 (Fla.), *cert. denied,* 454

Except, however, in cases challenging conditions of confinement or denial of access to the courts by prisoners at a single facility,[10] such multiparty devices have several important drawbacks, including the courts' reluctance to permit joint or class litigation in the typical situation in which each potential petitioner's case probably will require an appreciable degree of individual factual or legal analysis;[11] the binding effect of a decision in joint or class litigation on all the moving parties and class members[12] notwithstanding that they exercised less control over the multiparty petition than they would have exercised over a single-party action; the difficult issues posed by the total exhaustion rule in multiparty litigation;[13] and, most especially, the troubling possibility that individual petitions filed thereafter by one or more of the parties to the joint or class action, whether raising the same or new claims, will encounter preclusive successive petition problems.[14] Of course, should it become useful to consolidate two or more single-prisoner petitions or one or more claims in those petitions for discovery or a hearing, a party may propose that course by

---

U.S. 1000 (1981)). *See generally Developments in the Law, supra* § 11.4a n.1, at 1170-73. Although a strict reading of Rule 2(d) of the Rules Governing § 2254 Cases might seem to forbid multiple-party petitions unless all parties were convicted and sentenced in the same court, the legislative history reveals no intention to abrogate the well-established practice allowing such petitions in limited circumstances. *See, e.g., Brewer v. Swinson, supra; Martin v. Strasberg, supra; Knapp v. Cardwell, supra; United States ex rel. Carmona v. Ward, supra* (post-Habeas Rules decisions permitting multiparty litigation). Reading Rule 2(d) to govern joinder of claims, not parties, also is more consistent with the use of the singular "petition" in the second sentence of Rule 2(d).

[10] *See supra* § 9.1 & *infra* § 41.2 (prison-conditions habeas corpus litigation); *supra* § 7.2c (denial of access to courts).

[11] *See, e.g.,* Browne v. Estelle, 544 F.2d 1244, 1245 (5th Cir. 1977). *See also* National Center for Immigration Rights v. INS, 913 F.2d 1350, 1352 (9th Cir. 1990), *rev'd on other grounds,* 502 U.S. 183 (1991) (habeas corpus is appropriate procedure for challenging INS's delay in determining deportability in individual cases but is not appropriate method of bringing simultaneous challenge to delays on behalf of all potentially deportable individuals).

[12] *See, e.g.,* Funchess v. Wainwright, 772 F.2d 683 (11th Cir. 1985), *cert. denied,* 475 U.S. 1031 (1986) (petitioner's participation in prior class petition forecloses attempt to raise same issue in individual petition).

[13] Under the total exhaustion rule, each petitioner must have exhausted available state remedies as to all of the claims in the multiparty petition. *See generally infra* § 23.5.

[14] *See generally infra* Chapter 28. In certain circumstances, a petitioner may withdraw from a habeas corpus class action without prejudice to his rights asserted in the action. *See, e.g.,* Brewer v. Swinson, 837 F.2d 802, 804 (8th Cir. 1988) (permitting withdrawal from class action challenging parole commission guidelines because petitioner needed speedy resolution, and class suit was not close to resolution).

motion.[15] The authority permitting multiparty petitions[16] *a fortiori* support the less drastic consolidation procedure.

§ 11.5. Form.[1]

As originally promulgated, the Rules Governing § 2254 Cases required habeas corpus petitioners to use a form petition that the drafters attached to the Rules as an appendix.[2] Congress rejected this proposal, requiring instead that the petition "be in *substantially* the form annexed to" the Habeas Rules.[3] The Rules as adopted also, however, give district courts the power to prescribe their own forms by local rule,[4] and most district courts now require the use of court-approved forms,[5] at least when the petition is filed by the petitioner *pro se*.[6] Other courts allow petitioners, or at least those represented by counsel, to deviate from the specified form as long as the petition contains "substantially" the same information elicited by the court-approved form.[7]

Even in jurisdictions in which the petition must be filed in a specified form, attorneys representing prisoners should not hesitate to augment the form, then retype the petition as revised.[8] First, the forms often do not provide enough space

---

[15] *See generally supra* § 10.2d (transfer of petitions between courts or judges for consolidation).

[16] *See supra* note 9.

§ 11.5. [1] *See generally* RONALD P. SOKOL, FEDERAL HABEAS CORPUS 91-95 (1969); LARRY W. YACKLE, POSTCONVICTION REMEDIES §§ 111-15 (1981 & Supp. 1998); David A. Bagwell, *Procedural Aspects of Prisoner § 1983 and § 2254 Cases in the Fifth and Eleventh Circuits*, 95 F.R.D. 435, 453 & n.113 (1982); Charles Alan Wright, *Procedure for Habeas Corpus*, 77 F.R.D. 227, 236-40 (1978); *Developments in the Law — Federal Habeas Corpus*, 83 HARV. L. REV. 1038, 1173-79 (1970).

[2] Proposed Rule 2(c) of the Rules Governing § 2254 Cases. *See* Proposed Rule 2(b) of the Rules Governing § 2255 Proceedings; Model Forms for Use in Applications for Habeas Corpus Under 28 U.S.C. § 2254, foll. Rules Governing § 2254 Cases and for Motions Under 28 U.S.C. § 2255, foll. Rules Governing § 2255 Proceedings.

[3] Rule 2(c) of the Rules Governing § 2254 Cases (emphasis added). *See* Rule 2(b) of the Rules Governing § 2255 Proceedings; H.R. REP. No. 1471, 94th Cong., 2d Sess. 4 (1976), *reprinted in* 1976 U.S. CODE CONG. & AD. NEWS 2478, 2480; Wright, *supra* note 1, at 238-39. *See also* Franklin v. Rose, 765 F.2d 82, 83-84 (6th Cir. 1985) (describing form petition).

[4] Rule 2(c) of the Rules Governing § 2254 Cases; Rule 2(b) of the Rules Governing § 2255 Proceedings.

[5] *See, e.g.,* C.D. CAL. CT. R. 26.1; S.D. FLA. CT. 88.2.

[6] *See, e.g.,* D.D.C. CT. R. 204; N.D. ILL. CT. R. 23.

[7] *See, e.g.,* D. NEB. CT. R. 83.10.

[8] *Pro se* petitioners generally should use court-mandated forms. *Cf. infra* §§ 11.6 n.9, 15.1 nn.9-10 and accompanying text, 35.2b, 41.1b n.19 and accompanying text (all discussing liberal treatment of *pro se* pleadings).

for the information they request, much less for other information (for example, an introductory statement of facts), and a string of addenda will be difficult for the court to follow.[9] Second, as long as a petition drafted by counsel contains all the information demanded by the form petition, it is hard to imagine a court finding noncompliance with a rule requiring adherence to the form.[10] Third, as is discussed in Chapters 3 and 5 *supra* and in § 11.6 and Chapters 15, 22-28 *infra*, the doctrines based on which even apparently minor missteps in pleading claims and responding to defenses may result in denial of habeas corpus relief have become so pronounced recently, and the courts' application of them so finicky, that a policy of giving all appropriate explanations, even when they exceed the space provided on court-generated forms, is a matter of legal necessity. Finally, given the legislative history of the Habeas Rules, it is clear that, as with the form petition attached to the Rules, Congress did not authorize the district courts to mandate absolute compliance with their local forms, but only allowed them to insist upon substantial compliance.[11] Nonetheless, counsel should carefully examine the model forms appended to the Habeas Rules[12] as well as the local rules on the subject of form. Even if an attorney decides not to conform the petition as a whole to the prescribed form, problems inevitably will be avoided by strict adherence to the more technical aspects of the form. Scrupulous compliance is especially desirable given the authority granted literal-minded clerks by the Habeas Rules and the local rules of some district courts to refuse to file petitions they conclude are not in proper form.[13] At a minimum, the petition should follow the form in the Habeas Rules or in local rules insofar as it asks for

---

[9] *See* Wright, *supra* note 1, at 240 ("The use of forms for habeas corpus works well in routine cases in which the prisoner is without counsel and his grounds for habeas corpus are familiar .... But what is true in the routine case is not true in every case. In those cases in which the prisoner has a lawyer, a carefully drafted and lawyerlike petition is likely to be far more useful to the courts than will be a printed form. In addition, the form is simply inadequate for the unusual case in which the prisoner is relying on an innovative legal theory.").

[10] *Id.* at 240 ("A judge is hardly likely to order the return of a petition [that does not track the form but is] prepared by a lawyer or present[s] a novel theory when the petition will lighten the court's burden, not add to it.").

[11] *See id.* at 239 ("The only reasonable construction" of the legislative history of the Rules is that "the use of a particular form cannot be made mandatory; substantial compliance with the form will suffice"). *See also* Davis v. Mueller, 481 F. Supp. 888, 890 (D.N.D. 1979), *aff'd,* 643 F.2d 521 (8th Cir.), *cert. denied,* 454 U.S. 892 (1981); *infra* § 15.1.

[12] *See* Appendices of Forms to Rules Governing § 2254 Cases and § 2255 Proceedings, foll. Rules Governing § 2254 Cases and § 2255 Proceedings, foll. 28 U.S.C. §§ 2254, 2255.

[13] Rule 2(e) of the Rules Governing § 2254 Cases; Rule 2(d) of the Rules Governing § 2255 Proceedings.

routine information,[14] deviating elsewhere as necessary for a full presentation of the petitioner's factual and legal claims[15] and the arguments and explanations on such nonroutine issues as exhaustion[16] and successive petitions.[17] It bears repeating that, even when a filed petition deviates from the model petition as a *formal* matter, it must include all the *substantive* information that the model petition requests.

§ 11.6. Fact pleading.[1]

The habeas corpus statute and rules and the model petition attached to the Rules Governing § 2254 Cases require the petitioner to "specify all the grounds for relief which are available to the [petitioner] and of which he has or by the exercise of reasonable diligence should have knowledge and [to] *set forth in summary form the facts supporting each of the grounds thus specified*."[2] The italicized "fact pleading" requirement — which deviates from the "notice pleading" rules applicable in other federal civil cases[3] — deserves special

---

[14] *See* Model Form for Use in Applications for Habeas Corpus Under 28 U.S.C. § 2254, foll. Rules Governing § 2254 Cases, pts. (1)-(10), (14)-(17).

[15] *See id.* pt. (12); *infra* § 11.6.

[16] *See* Model Form for Use in Applications for Habeas Corpus Under 28 U.S.C. § 2254, foll. Rules Governing § 2254 Cases, pt. (11); *supra* § 11.1; *infra* § 11.7 n.5 and accompanying text; *infra* Chapter 23.

[17] *See* Model Form for Use in Applications for Habeas Corpus Under 28 U.S.C. § 2254, foll. Rules Governing § 2254 Cases, pt. (13); *supra* § 11.3b nn.66-73 and accompanying text; *infra* § 11.7 n.6 and accompanying text; *infra* Chapter 28.

§ 11.6. [1] *See generally* authority cited *supra* § 11.5 n.1.

[2] Rule 2(c) of the Rules Governing § 2254 Cases (emphasis added); Rule 2(b) of the Rules Governing § 2255 Proceedings (emphasis added). *See* 28 U.S.C. § 2242 (1994) (application for writ of habeas corpus "shall allege the facts concerning the applicant's commitment or detention"); Model Form for Use in Applications for Habeas Corpus Under 28 U.S.C. § 2254, foll. Rules Governing § 2254 Cases (discussed *supra* § 11.5).

[3] FED. R. CIV. P. 8. *See* McFarland v. Scott, 512 U.S. 849, 860 (1994) (O'Connor, J., concurring in the judgment in part) ("habeas petition, unlike a [civil] complaint, must allege the factual underpinnings of the petitioner's claims"). *Cf.* Wright, *supra* § 11.5 n.1, at 238 ("wholly anachronistic to preserve fact pleading for habeas corpus petitions, which are ordinarily prepared by persons unrepresented by lawyers and often poorly educated, while a far less exacting pleading requirement is made for ordinary civil actions"); *Developments in the Law*, *supra* § 11.5 n.1, at 1174 ("hard to imagine any type of proceeding where stringent pleading rules would be less appropriate"). There are two explanations for the anomalous retention of fact pleading in habeas corpus cases, both related to the essentially appellate nature of habeas corpus proceedings. *See generally supra* §§ 2.2, 2.4. First, although technically separate from earlier proceedings, *see supra* § 2.2, habeas corpus is designed to review and draws heavily on the record of prior state proceedings. *See* 28 U.S.C.A. §§ 2254(d), 2254(e) (West 1994 & Supp. 1998). As such, the habeas corpus petition can, and justifiably may be required to, serve a function more akin to that served by

attention[4] and mandates that the petitioner at least summarily plead specific facts supporting each claim for relief.[5]

Although the Habeas Rules do not require that every item of relevant evidence or every relevant legal authority be catalogued in the pleading,[6] especially given

---

opening appellate briefs than that served by initiatory pleadings in most civil cases. Second, fact pleading, like other habeas corpus rules and practices, enables courts further along in the appellate chain — taking advantage of the winnowing and clarifying effect of the prior proceedings — to separate substantial petitions from insubstantial ones quickly and without need of adversary proceedings. *See also infra* § 15.2.

[4] *See* Advisory Committee Note to Rule 4 of the Rules Governing § 2254 Cases (quoting Aubut v. State of Maine, 431 F.2d 688 (1st Cir. 1970)) ("notice pleading is not sufficient [in habeas corpus pleadings], for the petition is expected to state facts that point to a 'real possibility of constitutional error'").

[5] *See, e.g., McFarland v. Scott, supra,* 512 U.S. at 856 ("Habeas corpus petitions must meet heightened pleading requirements." (citation omitted)); Hill v. Lockhart, 474 U.S. 52, 60 (1986); McMann v. Richardson, 397 U.S. 759, 764 n.9 (1970); Wacht v. Cardwell, 604 F.2d 1245, 1247 (9th Cir. 1979); Romanello v. Wainwright, 363 F.2d 28 (5th Cir. 1966). *See generally* 7 JAMES W. MOORE, JO DESHA LUCAS & KENT SINCLAIR, JR., MOORE'S FEDERAL PRACTICE § 81.04[4] (2d ed. 1994) (notice versus fact pleading). *Cf.* Withrow v. Williams, 507 U.S. 680, 696 (1993) (using apparently imprecise language, Court frames question whether *Miranda* claim in petition sufficed to raise separate, due-process-based involuntariness claim as whether "habeas petition's reference to *Miranda* rights had given [the state] insufficient *notice* to address a due process claim" (emphasis added); in any event, Court finds pleading insufficient to raise due process claim). Illustrating the difference between "fact" and "notice" pleading, and the modern preference for the latter in most civil litigation save habeas corpus, is Leatherman v. Tarrant County Narcotics Unit, 507 U.S. 163, 168 (1993) (rejecting special pleading rules in section 1983 suits as contrary to intent of Civil Rule 8 to impose "liberal system of 'notice pleading'" that requires only "'short and plain statement of the claim showing that the pleader is entitled to relief,'" so as to "'give the defendant fair notice of what the plaintiff's claim is and the ground upon which it rests'" (quoting FED. R. CIV. P. 8; Conley v. Gibson, 355 U.S. 41, 47 (1957)). *But cf.* FED. R. CIV. P. 26(a)(1)(A), 26(a)(1)(B) (recently revised discovery rules giving litigants incentive to plead "disputed facts ... with particularity" so as to impose on opposing party an obligation, "without awaiting a discovery request," to produce certain valuable information otherwise available only through complicated discovery proceedings).

[6] *See, e.g.,* Jones v. Jerrison, 20 F.3d 849, 853 (8th Cir. 1994) ("No statute or rule requires that a petition identify a legal theory or include citations to legal authority." (**citing FHCPP**)); Johnson v. Puckett, 929 F.2d 1067, 1070 (5th Cir.), *cert. denied,* 502 U.S. 398 (1991) (allegation that "'discrimination in selection of the Grand Jury Foreman existed at the time of Petitioner's indictment'" and that historical absence of black grand jury foremen violated "'due process'" sufficed to assert equal protection claim); Pringle v. Court of Common Pleas, 778 F.2d 998, 1002 n.4 (3d Cir. 1985) (petition need not plead every prior decision supporting claim; notification of basic outlines of claim by citing Supreme Court opinion discussing like claim, was sufficient); Bonner v. Warden, 422 F. Supp. 11, 14 (N.D. Ill. 1976), *aff'd,* 553 F.2d 1091 (7th Cir.), *cert. denied,* 431 U.S. 943 (1977) (petition must allege facts supporting grounds for relief but need not contain evidentiary material). *See also* Porcaro v. United States, 784 F.2d 38, 41 (1st Cir. 1986) (where petitioner's section 2255 motion did not set out many details, but petitioner's accompanying motion to recuse trial judge did, circuit court avoided dismissal by incorporating

that many of the relevant facts may not surface until fact-development proceedings (for example, discovery and a hearing) are made available,[7] the rules do
require that the petitioner include in the statement of each claim enough
supporting facts to distinguish it from claims of its generic type,[8] and to justify a

---

latter into former); Kiendra v. Hadden, 763 F.2d 69, 71-72 (2d Cir. 1985) (missing factual
allegations supplied by petitioner's affidavit in opposition to respondent's answer).

[7] *Cf.* United States v. Rodriguez-Rodriguez, 929 F.2d 747, 752 (1st Cir. 1991) (any lack of
factual specificity caused by petitioner's failure to name potential witness in original petition was
cured by naming of witness in objections to magistrate's proposed decision). For a discussion of
counsel's obligation in at least some circumstances to plead specially fact-based claims as to which
there is a reasonable, but as yet unconfirmed, belief that the facts sufficient to prove the alleged
claim exist and may be uncovered through additional investigation and discovery of a sort that
cannot occur until after the petition is filed, see *supra* § 11.3b nn.12-15 and accompanying text
(circumstances in which petitioners should — and special responsibilities created if they do —
plead reasonably believed but unconfirmed fact-based claims, using less factual specificity than is
normally required and giving explanation therefor).

[8] *See, e.g., Hill v. Lockhart, supra,* 474 U.S. at 57-60 (general allegation of ineffective
assistance of counsel is insufficient; petitioner must allege specific facts establishing both
unreasonable-representation and prejudice prongs of ineffective assistance standard); Strickland v.
Washington, 466 U.S. 668 (1984) (absence of specific allegations of prejudice); Dorsey v. Kelly,
112 F.3d 50, 54 (2d Cir. 1997) (*pro se* petitioner adequately exhausted legal and factual bases of
ineffective assistance claim when he "(1) claimed that he had been denied effective assistance of
counsel in violation of the federal constitution, (2) indicated the exculpatory nature of the lab
reports, and (3) connected his ineffective assistance claim with his counsel's failure (a) to introduce
the lab reports and (b) to challenge those parts of the prosecution's evidence and summation that
were inconsistent with those reports"); United States v. Michaud, 925 F.2d 37, 39 (1st Cir. 1991);
Zettlemoyer v. Fulcomer, 923 F.2d 284, 298 n.12 (3d Cir. 1991) (petitioner's vague allegation that
some "unspecified and speculative testimony" that counsel failed to secure might have supported
defense is insufficient to plead, and to justify hearing on, ineffective assistance claim); United
States v. Smith, 915 F.2d 959, 963-64 (5th Cir. 1990) (to plead claim that government made extra-
record promises to induce guilty plea, movant should specify terms of promises and describe where
and when they were made and by whom); Adams v. Armontrout, 897 F.2d 332, 333-34 (8th Cir.
1990) (petition returned for failure to state facts "of sufficient detail to enable the court to
determine, from the face of the petition alone, whether the petition merits further ... review");
Santos v. Kolb, 880 F.2d 941, 943 (7th Cir. 1989), *cert. denied,* 493 U.S. 1059 (1990) (petitioner
pleading ineffective assistance of counsel must explain why he would not have pleaded guilty but
for counsel's error); Bridge v. Lynaugh, 838 F.2d 770, 773 (5th Cir. 1988), *vac'd & remanded,* 494
U.S. 1013 (1990) (petitioner's mere allegation of deficiency on part of counsel is insufficient to
plead ineffective assistance; affirmative description of resulting prejudice is also required);
Siciliano v. Vose, 834 F.2d 29, 31 (1st Cir. 1987) (proper to deny hearing and dismiss if pleadings
do not allege "'specific and detailed supporting facts'"); Heath v. United States Parole Comm'n,
788 F.2d 85, 90 (2d Cir. 1986); Smith v. Wainwright, 777 F.2d 609, 616 (11th Cir. 1985) (general
allegation of ineffective assistance of counsel is insufficient; petition must allege specific errors in
counsel's performance and facts showing prejudice; as to latter, allegation of circumstances
creating presumption of prejudice (*e.g.,* joint representation) suffices). *See* ROBERT POPPER, POST-
CONVICTION REMEDIES IN A NUTSHELL 153-54 (1978) ("insufficient, for example, for the prisoner
alleging that his plea of guilty was involuntary simply to assert that his plea was coerced, or that he

---

decision for petitioner once the alleged facts are proven.[9] Citation of the controlling constitutional, statutory, or other bases for relief for each claim also should be included.

---

was threatened by the prosecutor"; petitioner should state "name of the prosecutor who made the threat, what exactly the threat was, the date when the threat was made, the place where it was made, who, if anyone, was present at the time other than the defendant and the prosecutor, and why the defendant instead of not disclosing the threat to the judge, answered, 'No,' when asked in court if anyone had threatened him"); SOKOL, *supra* § 11.5 n.1, at 93-94 ("petitioner's 'naked assertion, without any background factual substantiation whatsoever ...' does not [suffice].... The following allegation is not sufficient: Petitioner's ten-year sentence for armed robbery was obtained in violation of the Due Process Clause of the Fourteenth Amendment to the Constitution in that an involuntary confession was used against him at his trial" (quoting Midgett v. Warden, 329 F.2d 185, 187 (4th Cir. 1964) (other citations omitted))). *See also* Withrow v. Williams, 507 U.S. 680, 696 (1993) (discussed *supra* note 5).

For reasons having more to do with the exhaustion and procedural default defenses than with federal pleading rules, "fact," as opposed to "notice," pleading is by far the safer practice at the state postconviction stage, regardless of the State's pleading rules. *See, e.g.,* Flieger v. Delo, 16 F.3d 878, 885 (8th Cir. 1994) (failure to raise certain instances of ineffectiveness in state appellate court was procedural default barring federal habeas corpus review of those claims); Givens v. Green, 12 F.3d 1041, 1043-44 (11th Cir. 1994) (*per curiam*) (dismissing, as unexhausted, instance of ineffectiveness not presented to state habeas corpus court); Maynard v. Lockhart, 981 F.2d 981, 984-85 & n.1 (8th Cir. 1992) (petitioner's failure to present some of allegations of counsel's ineffectiveness to state courts results in findings of nonexhaustion and procedural default as to previously omitted allegations); Footman v. Singletary, 978 F.2d 1207, 1211 (11th Cir. 1992) ("instances of ineffective assistance of counsel" that were not fairly presented to state courts are subject to dismissal for nonexhaustion); Mathis v. Zant, 975 F.2d 1493, 1497 (11th Cir. 1992) (reversing district court's posthearing grant of writ and remanding for determination whether petitioner's introduction of "additional evidence to bolster his claim of ineffective assistance of counsel at sentencing by developing and submitting evidence never presented to the state court" "amounted to the presentation of a separate claim of ineffective assistance of counsel not yet exhausted in the state courts").

[9] *See, e.g., Hill v. Lockhart, supra,* 474 U.S. at 61-62 (White, J., concurring) (pleading insufficient on unreasonable-representation prong of ineffective assistance claim because petitioner did not support allegation that counsel was remiss in failing to advise him of effect of prior conviction with allegation that counsel knew of prior conviction); Blackledge v. Allison, 431 U.S. 63, 75 n.7 (1977) (petition must "state facts that point to a 'real possibility of error'" (quoting Advisory Committee Note to Rule 4 of the Rules Governing § 2254 Cases)); Diaz v. United States, 930 F.2d 832, 835 (11th Cir. 1991) (despite liberal construction due *pro se* movant's allegations, dismissal was appropriate because movant did not allege "facts that, if proven, would entitle him to relief"); Wright v. Minnesota, 833 F.2d 746, 749 (8th Cir. 1987), *cert. denied,* 485 U.S. 1011 (1988) (dismissal of petition without hearing is proper if allegations, even if true, fail to state claim cognizable in federal habeas corpus); Heath v. United States Parole Comm'n, 788 F.2d 85, 90 (2d Cir. 1986); Demjanjuk v. Meese, 784 F.2d 1114, 1117-18 (D.C. Cir. 1986) (petition dismissed because alleged facts clearly showed petitioner was not entitled to relief); Smith v. Wainwright, 777 F.2d 609, 616 (11th Cir. 1985); Nail v. Slayton, 353 F. Supp. 1013, 1019 (W.D. Va. 1972) ("It is not the duty of federal courts to try to second guess the meanings of statements and intentions of petitioners. Rather the duty is upon the individual who asserts a denial of his constitutional rights

In general, although the pleading need not — and, for the most part, should not — argue the implications of each relevant fact and controlling legal principle, it should include at least a listing of the major facts and legal principles on which petitioner relies to establish each claim. A somewhat more flexible and potentially creative approach is to plead the claims in something like the way an appellate attorney might state an issue in a combined, one-paragraph "statement of facts" and "summary of argument" in a brief.[10] If counsel believes that discovery, expert analyses, an evidentiary hearing, or some other fact-development procedure is likely to reveal additional facts, the petition should plead on "information and belief" the facts counsel expects to find, providing as much detail as possible, and should note the fact-development procedures the petitioner later will seek.[11]

In pleading the legal bases for a claim, it is often efficient to cite one or more prior decisions that develop in detail the legal analysis on which petitioner will rely.[12] In addition, although petitioners should use the technique sparingly and only when necessary to keep the length of the petition within reasonable bounds,

---

to come forth with a statement of sufficient clarity and sufficient supporting facts to enable a court to understand his argument and to render a decision on the matter"). *See also* authority cited *infra* § 15.2c. *Cf.* Lozada v. Deeds, 498 U.S. 430, 430-32 (1991) (*per curiam*) (notwithstanding absence of allegation of prejudice, petitioner's allegations that trial counsel denied petitioner opportunity to appeal state court convictions by failing to file notice of appeal or to assist petitioner in securing alternate counsel or in filing appeal *pro se* warrants certificate of probable cause to appeal, hence, arguably, avoids dismissal for inadequate pleading, because courts are split on question whether prejudice is required in this situation). Before a court dismisses a petition without a hearing as insufficiently well pleaded to state a federal cause of action, the court must accept all the factual allegations as true, then conclude that the facts do not present a valid federal cause. *See* decisions discussed *infra* §§ 15.1 nn.9-10 and accompanying text, 15.2c nn.52-53 and accompanying text, 35.2b n.54 and accompanying text. Courts often accord *pro se* petitioners extra leeway when adjudicating the sufficiency of their factual pleadings. *See* McNeil v. United States, 508 U.S. 106, 113 n.10 (1993) (*dicta*) ("we have insisted that the pleadings prepared by prisoners who do not have access to counsel be liberally construed" (citing Estelle v. Gamble, 429 U.S. 97, 106 (1976); Hanes v. Kerner, 404 U.S. 591 (1972))); Guidroz v. Lynaugh, 852 F.2d 832, 834 (5th Cir. 1988); United States v. Mosquera, 845 F.2d 1122, 1124 (1st Cir. 1988); other decisions cited *infra* §§ 15.1 nn.9-10, 15.2c nn.52-53, 35.2b n.54, 41.1b n.19. *See also infra* § 26.3b nn.42-49 and accompanying text.

[10] *See supra* note 3 (kinship between habeas corpus petition and appellate brief). The recommendations in text suggest a more extensive presentation than once was thought appropriate. *Compare* SOKOL, *supra* § 11.5 n.1, at 91-93 *with, e.g.,* Hill v. Lockhart, *supra,* 474 U.S. at 59-60.

[11] *See supra* § 11.3b nn.12-15 and accompanying text. The petition also may point out briefly how the incompleteness or inadequacy of available state corrective procedures contributes to the need for additional fact development.

[12] *See* Pringle v. Court of Common Pleas, 778 F.2d 998, 1002 n.4 (3d Cir. 1985) (approving practice recommended in text).

it is sometimes possible to incorporate by reference a fuller statement of the claim in a brief or pleading attached to the petition.[13]

§ 11.7. Checklists of additional pleading requirements.

a. *Other matters to plead.* In addition to the claims for relief[1] and the matters in anticipation of the state's defenses that are discussed in sections 11.3b and 11.6 *supra*, the petition should include a discussion of the following matters, either tracking the requirements of the model form annexed to the Rules Governing § 2254 Cases, some other form prescribed by a local rule of court, or using counsel's own format:[2]

(1)   The petitioner's custody status, including his current sentence, and any relevant terms or conditions of the sentence, date set for petitioner's execution, etc.[3]

(2)   The conviction(s) and judgment(s) under which the petitioner has been detained and sentenced.[4]

(3)   The state court proceedings in which the petitioner's claims were exhausted (or the reasons why such proceedings were not necessary to exhaustion).[5]

(4)   The titles, citations, and dispositions of other federal habeas corpus petitions filed by the petitioner challenging the conviction and/or sentence now being challenged and an explanation of why the present claims were not made earlier.[6]

(5)   A statement of the relief sought.[7]

b. *Other formal requirements.* Other formal requirements are that the petition be:[8]

(1)   "[T]ypewritten or legibly handwritten."[9]

---

[13] *See* Porcaro v. United States, 784 F.2d 38, 40 n.1 (1st Cir. 1986); other authority cited *supra* notes 6, 7.

§ 11.7.   [1] *See supra* §§ 9.1, 9.2, 11.2, 11.3, 11.6.

[2] *See supra* § 11.5. This list does not include idiosyncratic matters required by local district court rules, which should be consulted. *See id.*

[3] *See generally supra* § 8.2.

[4] *See generally supra* § 11.4a.

[5] *See supra* § 11.1; *infra* Chapter 23.

[6] *See supra* § 11.3b nn.66-73 and accompanying text; *infra* Chapter 28.

[7] *See infra* § 11.8; *infra* Chapter 33.

[8] As is true of the preceding list, this one does not include idiosyncratic requirements of local district court rules, which should be consulted. *See supra* § 11.5.

[9] Rule 2(c) of the Rules Governing § 2254 Cases; Rule 2(b) of the Rules Governing § 2255 Proceedings. *See also* 28 U.S.C. § 2242 (1994).

(2) "[S]igned under penalty of perjury by the petitioner."[10] (This verification requirement, which provides a remedy of prosecution for perjury that is not available under the Civil Rules,[11] together with other protective procedures in the Habeas Rules and other aspects of habeas corpus law and

---

[10] Rule 2(c) of the Rules Governing § 2254 Cases; Rule 2(b) of the Rules Governing § 2255 Proceedings. *See* 28 U.S.C. § 2242 (1994); Hendricks v. Vasquez, 908 F.2d 490, 491 (9th Cir. 1990) ("The district court may refuse to file, or may dismiss, an unsigned and unverified petition.... However, the defect" does "not deprive the district court of jurisdiction" and "is one the district court may, if it sees fit, disregard"; district court accordingly did not commit reversible error in addressing merits of petition signed by counsel but not signed or verified by petitioner). The 1982 amendments to Rule 2(c) of the Rules Governing § 2254 Cases and Rule 2(b) of the Rules Governing § 2255 Proceedings dispensed with the requirement that the petition "be ... *sworn to* by the petitioner" and authorized petitioners to precede their signature at the end of the petition with the statement that: "I declare (or certify, verify, or state) under penalty of perjury that the foregoing is true and correct. Executed on (date)."

In capital cases in which an execution date is imminent, it may be impossible in the time available before the execution to obtain the prisoner's signature. In such cases, counsel should sign the petition "under penalty of perjury" on behalf of the petitioner and include a statement that the petitioner's signature will be forwarded forthwith. *See* 28 U.S.C. § 2242 (1994) (application "shall be ... signed and verified by the person for whose relief it is intended *or by someone acting in his behalf*" (emphasis added)); *supra* § 8.3 (petition may be filed on behalf of prisoners when shortness of time available to secure necessary relief warrants third-party action); *infra* § 12.1 (*in forma pauperis* proceedings). *See also* Lucky v. Calderon, 86 F.3d 923, 925 (9th Cir. 1996) (federal habeas corpus petition verified by counsel who could not reach imprisoned client before pending execution date was properly filed under 28 U.S.C. § 2242, which permits petitions filed on client's behalf; although circumstances of filing rebutted general presumption that lawyers act with clients' consent when filing petitions, prisoner's subsequently executed affidavit adequately established that attorney was "fully authorized to file and pursue" litigation); Deutscher v. Angelone, 16 F.3d 981, 984 (9th Cir. 1994) (petition signed and filed by "competent counsel" gives rise to presumption that petitioner knew of and approved claims; presumption rebutted under circumstances of case because counsel was ineffective and admitted that "he filed the petition without notifying Deutscher or seeking his authorization ... [and without] explain[ing] the nature of federal habeas corpus proceedings, the risk that claims not raised might be barred as abuse of the writ, or the appropriateness of having other counsel file the petition [so as to review and possibly challenge original counsel's effectiveness at trial and appeal]").

[11] *See, e.g.,* Dickinson v. Wainwright, 626 F.2d 1184 (5th Cir. 1980) (petitioner who subscribes to false statement under penalty of perjury may be prosecuted for perjury under 18 U.S.C. § 1621 just as if false statements were made under oath); Hosie v. Massey, 105 F.R.D. 426, 428-29 (N.D. Fla. 1989) (discussed *infra* note 12). *See also* Rowland v. California Men's Colony, Unit II Men's Advisory Council, 113 S. Ct. 716, 723 (1993) ("'One who makes this affidavit exposes himself "to the pains of perjury in a case of bad faith." .... This constitutes a sanction important in protection of the public against a false or fraudulent invocation of the statute's benefits.'" (quoting Adkins v. E.I. DuPont de Nemours & Co., 335 U.S. 331, 338 (1948) (quoting Pothier v. Rodman, 261 U.S. 307, 309 (1923)))).

practice, may render the penalty for abusive filings in Civil Rule 11 inapplicable in federal habeas corpus proceedings.[12])

---

[12] *See* Rule 11 of the Rules Governing § 2254 Cases ("The Federal Rules of Civil Procedure, *to the extent that they are not inconsistent with these rules*, may be applied, when appropriate, to petitions filed under these [Habeas] rules" (emphasis added)). *Cf.* Degarmo v. Collins, 984 F.2d 142, 143 (5th Cir. 1993) (*per curiam*) (*dicta*) ("we are aware of the difficulties of counsel in death [habeas corpus] cases both for the state and habeas petitioners.... The law is complex and there is often little time. In this environment, we are careful to read our rules in ways that will not chill vigorous advocacy.... Counsel proceeding in vigorous good faith representation need not fear sanctions"; requiring state to show cause why it should not be sanctioned for violating nonappeal stipulation because court "will not tolerate abuse or sharp practice by counsel"); Anderson v. Butler, 886 F.2d 111, 113-14 (5th Cir. 1989) (FED. R. CIV. P. 11 sanctions should be imposed in habeas corpus cases "only in the most egregious circumstances," when claim is "utterly frivolous and ... is asserted with no good faith belief in its validity"; standard rarely met, except, perhaps, in cases involving successive petitions; *pro se* petitioners should be treated leniently); United States v. Quin, 836 F.2d 654, 657-58 (1st Cir. 1988) (sanctions under FED. R. CIV. P. 11 for frivolous claim; dissent by Coffin, J., cautioning against sanctions that impede access to habeas corpus). In 1993, Civil Rule 11 was amended to modify the requirements and moderate the available sanctions (including by permitting litigants alleged to have committed Rule 11 violations to avoid sanctions by withdrawing the allegedly offending pleading). *See* FED. R. CIV. P. 11 (effective, December 1, 1993). *See also* 113 S. Ct. CCCVII (Scalia, J., dissenting) (opposing adoption of amendments of rule on ground that they inappropriately undercut existing sanctions); *supra* § 11.3b n.15 and accompanying text (procedure for handling claims based on facts reasonably believed to exist but not yet discovered).

In addition to guarding against false statements by imposing a verification requirement, the habeas corpus statute and the Rules Governing § 2254 Cases and § 2555 Proceedings establish numerous specific protections against frivolous filings. *See infra* §§ 12.1 (frivolousness standard for denying *in forma pauperis* status), 13.2c (frivolousness standard for denying preadjudication stays of execution), 15.2 ("patently frivolous" standard for summary dismissal), 35.4b (frivolousness standard for denying certificate of probable cause to appeal denials of habeas corpus relief). *See also Hosie v. Massey, supra*, 105 F.R.D. at 428-29 (penalties for knowingly false statements in habeas corpus petition include dismissal, assessment of costs, prosecution for perjury, and criminal contempt citation). Applying its Rule 39.8, the Supreme Court occasionally has responded to *pro se* prisoners' repeated frivolous filings by not only denying *in forma pauperis* status in the instant case but also prospectively directing the clerk to reject particular types of filings by the prisoner unless accompanied by the appropriate filing fees. *See infra* § 39.3a n.2. The Court's actions may be emboldening lower courts to take similar steps in habeas corpus and other actions. *See, e.g.,* DePineda v. Hemphill, 34 F.3d 946 (10th Cir. 1994) (*per curiam*); Smith v. McCleod, 946 F.2d 417 (5th Cir. 1991); Visser v. Supreme Ct., 919 F.2d 113, 114 (9th Cir. 1990); Romesburg v. Trickey, 908 F.2d 258, 260 (8th Cir. 1990); Abdul-Akbar v. Watson, 901 F.2d 329, 333 (3d Cir. 1990). *See also* Support Systems Int'l, Inc. v. Mack, 45 F.3d 185 (7th Cir. 1995) (*per curiam*) (sanctioning nonindigent litigant, who was delinquent in paying fines for frivolous filings, by instructing clerk to reject his future civil filings until fines are paid in full, but specifically exempting criminal filings and habeas corpus applications so as to avoid "imped[ing] him from making any filing necessary to protect him from imprisonment or other confinement").

(3)   Accompanied by two conformed copies of the petition.[13]

c. *Accompanying documents.* When appropriate, the petition and its two copies may be accompanied by the following documents:

(1)   Application for leave to proceed *in forma pauperis* (with attached affidavits).[14]

(2)   Proposed order permitting petitioner to proceed *in forma pauperis.*

(3)   Application for stay of execution (in capital cases in which an execution date is set) and memorandum of law in support of application.[15]

(4)   Proposed order granting stay of execution.

(5)   Application for appointment of counsel and memorandum of law in support of application. (This last document should be filed in capital cases involving unrepresented indigent petitioners because appointment of counsel is mandatory; additional considerations apply to noncapital cases, in which appointment of counsel is *not* mandatory, and are discussed in the next subsection.[16])

d. *Additional documents that may be filed with the petition, or later.* In addition to the documents listed above, which the petitioner is obliged to file with the petition, the petitioner may, but need not,[17] file other documents, including:

---

[13] Rule 3(a) of the Rules Governing § 2254 Cases; Rule 3(a) of the Rules Governing § 2255 Proceedings. The rules of some federal district courts require that fewer or more than two copies be filed. *See infra* § 11.9b. *See also* Wright, *supra* § 11.5 n.1, at 240 (rules requiring petitioner to file more than one copy are "anachronistic when court clerks have easier access to Xerox machines than do persons in prison"). Under Rule 4 of the Rules Governing § 2254 Cases, the district court has the responsibility to serve respondents and the attorney general by hand or by certified mail, and petitioners generally need not do so. *See infra* §§ 11.9d, 16.1. In a few districts, the local rules give the petitioner the responsibility to serve the petition. *See infra* § 11.9d.

[14] *See infra* § 12.1.

[15] *See infra* Chapter 13. Discussing the important situations in which the application for a stay of execution, in conjunction with an application for appointment of counsel, should *precede* the filing of the habeas corpus petition are *supra* § 5.1b nn.80-91 and accompanying text and *infra* §§ 12.3a, 13.1-13.2b. In capital cases in which a stay of execution is needed, both the petition itself and the application for a stay should convey the urgency of the matter by displaying a notice in prominent lettering of the following sort: "*THIS IS A CAPITAL CASE. EXECUTION IS IMMINENT.*"

[16] *See infra* §§ 12.2-12.5. Discussing the important situations — in *capital* cases only — in which the applications for appointment of counsel and a stay of execution should *precede* the filing of the habeas corpus petition are *supra* § 5.1b nn.80-91 and accompanying text and *infra* §§ 12.3a, 13.1-13.2b.

[17] *See generally* Bundy v. Wainwright, 808 F.2d 1410, 1414-17 (11th Cir. 1987) (if petition satisfies formal pleading requirements of Rule 2 of the Rules Governing § 2254 Cases and

(1)   A memorandum of law in support of the claims in the petition.[18]
(2)   All or parts of the state court record or a motion (and supporting memorandum) to require the state to provide petitioner and the court with a transcript of the prior proceedings in the case.[19]
(3)   A motion (and supporting memorandum) for appointment of essential experts or investigators or for other necessary financial assistance.[20]
(4)   A motion (and supporting memorandum) for discovery.[21]
(5)   A motion (and supporting memorandum) for leave to expand the record.[22]
(6)   A motion (and supporting memorandum) for an evidentiary hearing.[23]
(7)   A motion (and supporting memorandum) seeking reference of the petition to a magistrate.[24]
(8)   A motion (and supporting memorandum) for appointment of counsel.[25]
(9)   A motion (and supporting memorandum) for summary judgment on one or more of the claims in the petition.[26]

The considerations bearing on the decision whether to file these documents with the petition will differ from case to case. For example, a petitioner's indigence and lack of counsel[27] may prevent her from providing the court with the state record, even assuming the prisoner has access to it, and from preparing complex briefs and motions. In regard to the record, the "[p]etitioner is not required by statute or Rules to attach to his petition or to file a state court record in order to avoid a dismissal for facial insufficiency, although often in

---

substantive requirement of Habeas Rule 4 that it state claim that warrants relief, district court may not dismiss petition for failure to include information or documents not required by Habeas Rules). For additional discussion of the considerations bearing on the question of when to file the documents listed in this subsection, see *infra* §§ 17.1, 19.1, 29.1.

[18] *See infra* Chapter 29.

[19] *See infra* §§ 16.1b, 19.2. *See also* United States v. Connors, 904 F.2d 535, 536 (9th Cir. 1990) ("prisoner proceeding in forma pauperis on a habeas corpus petition is entitled to receive at government expense copies of court documents" but must file habeas corpus petition to trigger entitlement); Ruff v. Kincheloe, 843 F.2d 1240, 1242-43 (9th Cir. 1988) (if entire record is not supplied by parties, district court has duty to obtain record for itself).

[20] *See infra* § 19.3.

[21] *See infra* § 19.4.

[22] *See infra* § 19.5.

[23] *See infra* Chapter 20.

[24] *See infra* Chapter 18.

[25] *See infra* §§ 12.2-12.5. In capital cases involving unrepresented indigent petitioners, this application is more properly considered a matter of course than an optional filing. *See supra* note 16 and accompanying text.

[26] *See infra* § 17.3.

[27] *See infra* Chapter 12 (*in forma pauperis* proceedings; appointment of counsel).

summarizing the facts a petitioner necessarily or as a matter of convenience may refer to state court proceedings and even attach extracts therefrom."[28]

In regard to briefing, if some or all of the claims in the petition require further factual development, a comprehensive memorandum of law (item (1)) generally is not appropriate. Were the prisoner to file a comprehensive memorandum in these circumstances, it almost inevitably would be incomplete pending further exploration of the facts and might mislead the court into reaching the merits in advance of necessary factfinding procedures. If significant factual issues are present, the petitioner instead should consider filing one or more of the motions listed above that are designed to assist in developing the facts (items (2)-(7)), perhaps in conjunction with a summary judgment motion (item (9)) covering the remaining, nonfactual claims. A comprehensive memorandum also is likely to be premature and incomplete if counsel is uncertain about the defenses the state will assert. Because many of those defenses (for instance, exhaustion, prejudicial delay, procedural default, "full and fair opportunity" to litigate 4th Amendment claims, abuse of the writ, and the presumption of correctness of state fact-findings[29]) may present factual issues of their own that determine the extent to which federal factfinding procedures must supplant those at the state level, even the motions (2)-(7) and (9) above may be premature in advance of the state's answer.[30] On the other hand, if the petitioner fails to accompany the petition with a comprehensive memorandum on the merits or one or more fact-development motions and thereby forgoes the opportunity more extensively to explain the nature of the claims of constitutional error in the petition, the petitioner may increase the likelihood that the district court improperly will dismiss the petition summarily pursuant to Rule 4 of the Rules Governing § 2254 Cases.[31] In deciding how to balance the competing concerns in each case, the petitioner must assess the facial strength of the claims pleaded in the petition and, to the extent possible, become familiar with practices in the court in which the petition is filed.

At all events, it is important for the petitioner and counsel to be aware of the range of available mechanisms for drawing the court's attention to the strength

---

[28] Bundy v. Wainwright, 808 F.2d 1410, 1414 (11th Cir. 1987). *See id.* at 1415 (citing Advisory Committee Note to Rule 5 of the Rules Governing § 2254 Cases) ("The obligation to come forward with the state court record is squarely upon the respondent, not upon the petitioner. This makes common sense as well as legal sense — in some cases the petitioner has no copy of the state court proceedings, while the [Habeas] Rules recognize that generally the attorney general has access to them.").

[29] *See supra* §§ 11.3b; *infra* Chapters 20, 23, 24, 26-28; *infra* § 30.3.

[30] *See infra* § 16.1 (answer).

[31] *See, e.g.,* Hill v. Lockhart, 474 U.S. 52 (1985); Mulero v. LeFevre, 873 F.2d 534, 536 (2d Cir. 1989); *supra* § 11.6; *infra* § 15.2 (summary dismissal).

of the claims in the petition, including: (1) filing a memorandum of law that enhances the degree of factual detail and legal specificity with which the claims in the petition are pleaded;[32] (2) filing a motion for counsel or for summary judgment on some or all claims (motions (8) and (9) above) that emphasizes the strength of some or all of the claims in the petition and, possibly, the need for counsel to be appointed to assist in developing those claims; (3) filing with the petition one or more of motions (2)-(8) above with memoranda discussing the relevant factual claims and the reasons why they cannot fairly be determined without the requested factfinding procedure(s);[33] (4) awaiting the state's answer or motion to dismiss (assuming the court does not summarily dismiss the petition without calling for an answer[34]) and at that point filing a reply or traverse to the answer,[35] a comprehensive memorandum of law, or some or all of the motions listed above; and (5) in capital cases, including in the memorandum in support of the stay application filed with the petition a more extensive discussion of the factual and legal bases for individual claims, and, in particular, a more detailed statement of why each claim requires further factual development or otherwise is sufficiently substantial that it cannot be disposed of in advance of the date set for execution because additional factfinding procedures or briefing are necessary.[36]

§ 11.8. Prayer for relief.

The various remedies potentially available to successful habeas corpus petitioners are discussed in Chapter 33 *infra*. The discussion here is limited to the question of how to frame the prayer for relief at the pleading stage. Because a number of ultimate remedies are potentially available,[1] and because the appropriateness of each is likely to depend upon the particular constitutional violation proved, care must be taken to request the full range of remedies that might be appropriate given the constitutional violations alleged in the petition.

Certain conventions regarding the prayer have developed. If claims in the petition challenge the constitutionality of the prisoner's conviction, petitioners

---

[32] *See supra* § 11.6; *infra* Chapter 29.

[33] *See infra* Chapters 18-21.

[34] *See* Rule 4 of the Rules Governing § 2254 Cases; *infra* § 15.2.

[35] *See infra* § 17.1.

[36] *See infra* Chapter 13.

§ 11.8.   [1] *See generally* Carafas v. LaVallee, 391 U.S. 234, 239 (1968) ("mandate [of habeas corpus statute] is broad with respect to the relief that may be granted"); Peyton v. Rowe, 391 U.S. 54, 67 (1968) (prisoner serving consecutive sentences is in custody under any one of them for purpose of habeas corpus relief); Bland v. Alabama, 356 F.2d 8, 16 (5th Cir.), *cert. denied,* 383 U.S. 947 (1966) (courts "need not limit relief to cases where an immediate discharge of the petitioner is required, but should tailor the relief according to the requirements of law and justice"); authority cited *infra* Chapter 33.

often ask the court to "issue a writ of habeas corpus to have petitioner brought before it to the end that he may be discharged from his unconstitutional confinement and restraint." If the constitutionality of the sentence is challenged, petitioners often ask the court to "issue a writ of habeas corpus to have the petitioner brought before it to the end that he may be relieved of his unconstitutional sentence."

In addition to seeking the ultimate relief discussed above, it is often advisable to include requests for whatever types of intermediate relief (often in the form of adjudication procedures) the petitioner will seek during the course of the proceeding. Although the petitioner eventually should support each such request with a separate motion or application — some of which must be filed with the petition,[2] and some of which may be filed later[3] — it will prove helpful to the court and discourage premature dismissal of the petition to use the prayer to collect and preview the various intermediate orders the petitioner will ask the court to make.[4]

It is occasionally suggested — and in rare circumstances the petitioner may request — that a habeas corpus case be preliminarily "remanded to the state courts" to provide some previously neglected postconviction or other adjudicative procedure (usually an evidentiary hearing) by which the petitioner may obtain redress in the state courts for the violations alleged in the federal petition.[5] The federal statute seems to contemplate, however, and important "speedy determination" policies strongly support a rule that, once the petitioner has exhausted state remedies with regard to the claims in the petition, the proper remedy for any failure of the state courts to provide a "full and fair" corrective

---

[2] *See supra* §§ 11.3-11.7.

[3] *See supra* § 11.7d; *infra* Chapters 18-21.

[4] The following are examples: (1) "The Court, pursuant to Rule 5 of the Rules Governing § 2254 Cases, should order the respondent to produce the transcript of the trial, the transcript of the state postconviction hearing [if one was held], the record on appeal, the postconviction record, and other relevant records in the case" (*see infra* § 19.2); (2) "the Court should order discovery on behalf of petitioner, pursuant to Rule 6 of the Rules Governing § 2254 Cases" (*see infra* § 19.4); (3) "the Court should conduct a hearing at which evidence may be offered concerning the factual allegations in the petition" (*see infra* Chapters 20, 21); (4) "the Court should permit petitioner, who is indigent, to proceed without prepayment of costs or fees" (*see infra* § 12.1); (5) "the Court should appoint counsel to represent petitioner, who is indigent" (*see infra* §§ 12.2-12.5); (6) "the Court should appoint experts essential to litigating [specify the applicable claims], or provide other necessary financial assistance to petitioner, who is indigent" (*see infra* § 19.3); (7) "the Court should stay petitioner's execution pending final disposition of the petition, pursuant to 28 U.S.C. § 2251" (*see infra* Chapter 13); (8) "the Court, if it concludes that state remedies with regard to any claim in the petition have not been properly exhausted, should hold the petition in abeyance under a stay of execution, pending exhaustion of state remedies" (*see supra* § 11.1 n.28; *infra* § 13.3).

[5] *See, e.g.,* Grigsby v. Mabry, 637 F.2d 525, 528-29 (8th Cir. 1980) (*dicta*); other authority discussed *supra* § 7.1b n.48.

procedure with regard to those claims is to make fully available to the petitioner the federal habeas corpus mechanism itself.[6] In such situations, a remand to the state courts is not required nor, usually, appropriate; instead, the federal courts should proceed to address the claims in the petition.[7]

Finally, it is always advisable, paraphrasing the habeas corpus statute itself, to invite the court to "grant such other relief as may be appropriate and to dispose of the matter as law and justice require."[8]

§ 11.9. Filing and service.[1]

a. *Place of filing.* Section 10.2 above discusses the proper district in which to file for personal jurisdiction, venue, and convenient forum purposes. Once the appropriate district and division are identified, the actual place of filing generally is the office of the clerk of the appropriate district court and division.[2]

b. *Copies.* Rule 3(a) of the Rules Governing § 2254 Cases provides that the petitioner must file the original and two "conformed" (*i.e.,* exact duplicate) copies of the petition in the office of the clerk of the appropriate district court.[3] A number of district courts have promulgated local rules allowing petitioners to file fewer, and a few districts require petitioners to file more, than two copies.[4]

---

[6] *See* Townsend v. Sain, 372 U.S. 293 (1963); *supra* § 2.4b n.31 and accompanying text; *infra* § 21.1b (speedy determination concerns). A claim that the state corrective procedure is unconstitutional is an exception to this rule. *See supra* §§ 7.1b, 7.2.

[7] *See, e.g.,* Smart v. Scully, 787 F.2d 816, 821 (2d Cir. 1986); *Grigsby v. Mabry, supra,* 637 F.2d at 528; Dixon v. Beto, 472 F.2d 598, 599 (5th Cir. 1973); *supra* §§ 2.4b n.31 and accompanying text, 7.1b n.48.

[8] *See* 28 U.S.C. § 2243 (1994) (discussed *infra* Chapter 33).

§ 11.9.[1] *See generally* David A. Bagwell, *Procedural Aspects of Prisoner § 1983 and § 2254 Cases in the Fifth and Eleventh Circuits,* 95 F.R.D. 435, 453 (1982); Charles Alan Wright, *Procedure for Habeas Corpus,* 77 F.R.D. 227, 240-41 (1978).

[2] Rule 3 of the Rules Governing § 2254 Cases; Rule 3 of the Rules Governing § 2255 Proceedings. Individual district courts have idiosyncratic filing rules requiring, for example, that the petition be filed with a judge rather than, or in addition to, the clerk. In capital cases in which an execution date is imminent and in which the judge sits in a location some distance from the clerk's office, counsel may need to submit copies of the petition both to the clerk and to the judge directly.

[3] Rule 3(a) of the Rules Governing § 2254 Cases; Rule 3(a) of the Rules Governing § 2255 Proceedings.

[4] The Advisory Committee Note to Rule 3 of the Rules Governing § 2254 Cases seems to permit this issue to be "dealt with by local rule or practice." *See also* Rule 2(c) of the Rules Governing § 2254 Cases (district courts may prescribe habeas corpus forms).

c. *Filing fee.* Habeas Rule 3(a) provides that the statutory filing fee (at present $5)[5] must be paid at the time of filing. Habeas Rule 3(a), however, provides an exemption for petitions filed *in forma pauperis* by indigent prisoners.[6] In order to file a petition *in forma pauperis,* Habeas Rule 3(a) requires that the petition be accompanied by the petitioner's affidavit of indigence in the form prescribed by 28 U.S.C. § 1915, as well as a certificate from the appropriate prison official describing the amount of money the prisoner has on deposit with the prison. The required forms may be obtained from the clerk of the district court and usually are attached to the form petition provided by the clerk upon request.[7] As section 12.1 *infra* explains, the recently enacted Prison Litigation Reform Act of 1996 (PLRA)[8] may require prisoners who have little money but are not entirely indigent to pay a partial fee at the time of filing[9] and the submission of additional documentation regarding the amount of money in the prisoner's account.[10] The applicability of the PLRA to federal habeas corpus cases is still in doubt, however.[11] Section 12.1 *infra* discusses the procedures that a petitioner or counsel should follow when seeking to file an ifp habeas corpus petition.

d. *Service.* Following long-established practice under 28 U.S.C. § 2243, Habeas Rule 4 provides that the petitioner need not serve a copy of the petition on respondent or on the legal officer likely to be representing respondent (typically the state attorney general).[12] Instead, it is the responsibility of the

---

[5] 28 U.S.C.A. § 1914(a) (West Supp. 1998) ("The clerk of each district court shall require the parties instituting any civil action, suit or proceeding in such court, whether by original process, removal or otherwise, to pay a filing fee of $150, except that on application for a writ of habeas corpus the filing fee shall be $5.").

[6] There is no filing fee for motions under 28 U.S.C.A. § 2255 (West 1994 & Supp. 1998). Advisory Committee Note to Rule 3 of the Rules Governing § 2255 Proceedings. *See infra* § 41.4b.

[7] *See supra* §§ 11.5 (form habeas corpus petition), 11.7c. *See generally infra* § 12.1 (*in forma pauperis* practice).

[8] Pub. L. 104-134, 110 Stat. 1321 (April 26, 1996).

[9] *See infra* § 12.1 nn.6-8, 20 and accompanying text.

[10] *See infra* § 12.1 n.21 and accompanying text.

[11] *See infra* § 12.1 nn.12-17 and accompanying text.

[12] *See* Rule 4 of the Rules Governing § 2254 Cases. *See also* Advisory Committee Note to *id.* ("copies of the court's orders to respondent will be mailed to petitioner"). The local rules in a few districts require habeas corpus petitioners and section 2255 movants to serve copies on respondents and the state attorney general or the U.S. Attorney. *See* S.D. & E.D.N.Y. Ct. R. 32(b); N.D.N.Y. Ct. R. 31(a). Such rules are of questionable validity given that the Advisory Committee Notes to the Rules Governing § 2254 Cases do not explicitly permit divergent local rules regarding service, as they do requiring filing. *See supra* § 11.9b n.4 and accompanying text.

court to serve respondent and the state's attorney general by certified mail.[13] For this reason, the local rules of many districts require the petitioner to file duplicates of the petition.[14]

Although petitioners *need* not serve respondents, they generally *should* do so, unless their indigence or custodial status renders service unduly burdensome. Service helps expedite the matter and is a courtesy to opposing counsel. Certainly, in any capital case in which expeditious action on an application for a stay of execution is required, counsel should serve the state's attorney representing respondent.[15] If the petitioner serves respondent, counsel should so indicate to the clerk and the court by means of a certificate of service accompanying the petition. When time is of the essence, counsel also should emphasize in a cover letter to the clerk or the court that she served the appropriate papers on the state.[16]

---

[13] Curiously, Rule 3(b) of the Rules Governing § 2254 Cases, although entitled *"Filing and service,"* says nothing about service. Instead, Habeas Rule 3(b) provides that "[t]he filing of the petition shall not require the respondent to answer the petition or otherwise move with respect to it unless so ordered by the court," and the Advisory Committee Note to Rule 3 states that "under Rule 3(b), the respondent receives a copy of the petition whether an answer is required or not." Habeas Rule 4 makes clear that it is the clerk's duty to serve the respondent by certified mail. *See infra* § 16.1 (state's answer). *See generally* Bundy v. Wainwright, 808 F.2d 1410, 1414-16 (11th Cir. 1987).

The habeas corpus statute has long required that, upon a prisoner's filing a petition, the federal court was obliged either to grant the writ or direct the respondent to "show cause why the writ should not be granted, unless it appears from the application that the applicant or person detained is not entitled thereto." 28 U.S.C. § 2243 (1994). Section 2243 authorized the court to give respondent no less than three and no more than 23 days to respond by "certifying the true cause of the detention" and required a hearing within five days after respondent's return date. *Id. See id.* § 2252. Habeas Rule 4 dispenses with section 2243's strict time limits; more explicitly provides a limited *sua sponte* summary dismissal procedure prior to service on respondent (*see generally infra* § 15.2); provides that, in the event that summary dismissal does not occur, "the judge shall order the respondent to file an answer or other pleading within the period of time fixed by the court or to take such other action as the judge deems appropriate"; and requires "[i]n every case [that] a copy of the petition and any order shall be served [by the clerk] by certified mail on the respondent and the attorney general of the state involved."

[14] *See supra* §§ 11.7b n.13, 11.9b.

[15] The appropriate person to serve generally will be a member of the state attorney general's legal staff. If counsel does not know who the appropriate staff attorney is, she may serve the attorney in the office who handled the state postconviction proceedings in the case or the attorney in charge of federal habeas corpus proceedings generally. Otherwise she may serve the attorney general in an envelope indicating in prominent lettering on the cover the urgency of the matter and the caption of the case. For example: *"THIS IS A CAPITAL CASE. EXECUTION IS IMMINENT."*

[16] *See also infra* § 16.1 (service of petition as relates to answer).

PART IV

ANCILLARY AND SUMMARY PROCEEDINGS
UPON FILING

Chapter 12

INDIGENTS AND APPOINTMENT OF COUNSEL

§ 12.1. *In forma pauperis* proceedings.[1]

The federal *in forma pauperis* ("ifp") statute, 28 U.S.C. § 1915, permits indigent litigants, upon authorization from the court, to "commence[], prosecut[e] or defen[d] ... any suit, action or proceeding, civil or criminal, or appeal therein, without prepayment of fees or security," based upon an affidavit that the litigant "is unable to pay such fees or give security."[2] In addition to

---

§ 12.1. [1]*See generally* WAYNE R. LAFAVE & JEROLD H. ISRAEL, CRIMINAL PROCEDURE § 11.2 (2d ed. 1992); RONALD P. SOKOL, FEDERAL HABEAS CORPUS 205-27 (2d ed. 1969); LARRY W. YACKLE, POSTCONVICTION REMEDIES §§ 161, 162 (1981 & Supp. 1998); Harry A. Blackmun, *Allowance of In Forma Pauperis Appeals in § 2255 and Habeas Corpus Cases,* 43 F.R.D. 343 (1967); Robert S. Catz & Thad M. Guyer, *Federal In Forma Pauperis Litigation: In Search of Judicial Standards,* 31 RUTGERS L. REV. 655 (1978); Stephen M. Feldman, *Indigents in the Federal Courts: The In Forma Pauperis Statute — Equity and Frivolity,* 54 FORDHAM L. REV. 413 (1985); Elmo B. Hunter, *Post-Conviction Remedies,* 50 F.R.D. 153, 174-77 (1970); *infra* §§ 35.3 (*in forma pauperis* proceedings in habeas corpus appeals), 39.3a (*in forma pauperis* proceedings in the Supreme Court).

[2] 28 U.S.C.A. § 1915(a) (West 1994 & Supp. 1998). *See* Rowland v. California Men's Colony, Unit II Men's Advisory Council, 506 U.S. 194, 197 (1993); Denton v. Hernandez, 504 U.S. 25, 31 (1992) ("In enacting the federal *in forma pauperis* statute, Congress 'intended to guarantee that no citizen shall be denied an opportunity to commence, prosecute, or defend an action, civil or criminal, in any court of the United States, solely because ... poverty makes it impossible ... to pay or secure the costs' of litigation"); Neitzke v. Williams, 490 U.S. 319, 324 (1989) (section 1915 is "designed to ensure that indigent litigants have meaningful access to the federal courts"); *id.* at 329 ("Congress' over-arching goal in enacting the *in forma pauperis* statute [was] 'to assure equality of consideration for all litigants'"(quoting Coppedge v. United States, 369 U.S. 438, 447 (1962))); Roman v. Jeffes, 904 F.2d 192, 195-96 (3d Cir. 1990) (section 1983 action) (court may not "accord[] disparate treatment to indigent litigants"). *Cf. Rowland v. California Men's Colony, Unit II Men's Advisory Council, supra* at 211-12 (section 1915(a) gives individual indigent litigants, but not associations of indigents, right to proceed ifp; because section 1915(a) ifp status is prerequisite to appointment of counsel under 28 U.S.C. § 1915(d), rule barring ifp status for associations may effectively bar them, if they cannot secure volunteer counsel, from bringing federal suit at all because of rule that association or "corporation may appear in the federal courts only through licensed counsel"; in order to secure ifp status and counsel, therefore, members of association must file "not in the [association's] name, as such, but under the title, '*X, Y, and Z, known as the Council v. Rowland,*' [and] X, Y, and Z would each need to file an affidavit stating that he met the indigence requirements of § 1915"); *id.* at 218 (Thomas, J., dissenting) ("When a ... person seeks

---

dispensing with the filing fee, an ifp order establishes a predicate for the appointment of counsel and the provision of other forms of essential financial assistance.[3]

In the Prison Litigation Reform Act of 1996 (PRLA),[4] Congress amended 28 U.S.C. § 1915 to establish special procedures for a specific category of indigent litigants: "prisoner[s] seeking to bring a civil action or appeal a judgment in a civil action or proceeding."[5] Litigants falling into this category are "required to pay the full amount of a filing fee"[6] (and, if the prisoner is unable to do so at the time of filing, to pay a partial filing fee supplemented by monthly installments from the litigant's prison account[7]), although the statute makes clear that prisoners may not be prevented from bringing a civil action because they have no assets at the time of filing.[8] The PLRA also establishes a mechanism for *sua sponte* judicial screening of ifp complaints to assess whether they are frivolous or state no basis on which relief may be granted, and, if so, to deny ifp status as to the offending petition or claim.[9]

---

the benefit of § 1915, a court often will allow that person to proceed *in forma pauperis* but refuse to appoint counsel.").

[3] *See infra* §§ 12.2-12.5.

[4] Pub. L. 104-134, 110 Stat. 1321 (April 26, 1996). *See* Crawford-El v. Britton, 118 S. Ct. 1584, 1596 (1998) (generally describing PLRA).

[5] 28 U.S.C.A. § 1915(a)(2) (West 1994 & Supp. 1998). The statute defines the term "prisoner" as "any person incarcerated or detained in any facility who is accused of, convicted of, sentenced for, or adjudicated delinquent for, violations of criminal law or the terms and conditions of parole, probation, pretrial release, or diversionary program." *Id.* §§ 1915(h), 1915A(c).

[6] *Id.* § 1915(b)(1).

[7] *Id.* §§ 1915(b)(1)-(2) ("The court shall assess, and when funds exist, collect, as a partial payment of any court fees required by law, an initial partial filing fee of 20 percent of the greater of — (A) the average monthly deposits to the prisoner's account; or (B) the average monthly balance in the prisoner's account for the 6-month period immediately preceding the filing of the complaint or notice of appeal.... After payment of the initial partial filing fee, the prisoner shall be required to make monthly payments of 20 percent of the preceding month's income credited to the prisoner's account. The agency having custody of the prisoner shall forward payments from the prisoner's account to the clerk of the court each time the amount in the account exceeds $ 10 until the filing fees are paid.").

[8] *Id.* § 1915(b)(4) ("In no event shall a prisoner be prohibited from bringing a civil action or appealing a civil or criminal judgment for the reason that the prisoner has no assets and no means by which to pay the initial partial filing fee.").

[9] *Id.* § 1915A(a)-(b) ("The court shall review, before docketing, if feasible or, in any event, as soon as practicable after docketing, a complaint in a civil action in which a prisoner seeks redress from a governmental entity or officer or employee of a governmental entity.... On review, the court shall identify cognizable claims or dismiss the complaint, or any portions of the complaint, if the complaint — (1) is frivolous, malicious, or fails to state a claim upon which relief may be granted; or (2) seeks monetary relief from a defendant who is immune from such relief.").

Prior to the enactment of the PLRA, indigent habeas corpus petitioners sought and obtained ifp status like all other indigent litigants in federal civil and criminal cases. As the courts long have recognized, indigent prisoners may not be denied access to statutory habeas corpus remedies because of an inability to pay fees or costs.[10] The Rules Governing § 2254 Cases, adopted prior to the PLRA's enactment, provide for the waiver of a filing fee if a "petitioner applies for and is given leave to prosecute the petition in forma pauperis ... [pursuant to] 28 U.S.C. § 1915."[11]

The courts are somewhat divided on the question whether the PLRA's category of "prisoner[s] seeking to bring a civil action or appeal a judgment in a civil action or proceeding" includes habeas corpus petitioners, but the vast majority of courts have held that habeas corpus petitioners are *not* included.[12] The reasoning supporting the majority approach is convincing. Although habeas corpus actions qualify as "civil" in a technical sense, they actually are a hybrid of civil, criminal, and (principally) appellate procedures[13] for which Congress has previously developed a specialized and, by most accounts, quite efficient screening mechanism.[14] Because the PLRA does not purport to amend the preexisting screening mechanism for habeas corpus cases, but instead largely duplicates that mechanism with procedures designed, in the main, with section 1983 actions in mind, and because Congress also left intact the Habeas Rules' longstanding policy of giving "prompt attention ... to [a] ... request to proceed *in forma pauperis*,"[15] the PLRA is appropriately understood to exclude ifp motions in habeas corpus cases.[16] Even were the PLRA deemed to apply to habeas corpus

---

[10] *See* Smith v. Bennett, 365 U.S. 708, 709 (1961) (to "interpose any financial consideration between an indigent prisoner ... and his exercise of a [statutory] right to sue for his liberty is to deny that prisoner the equal protection of the laws"). *See also* Rinaldi v. Yeager, 384 U.S. 305 (1966). If two or more petitioners file a joint petition (*see supra* § 11.4b (joint and class action petitions)), any one of them who is indigent may proceed ifp as to his "proportionate part of the costs." Adkins v. E.I. DuPont de Nemours & Co., 335 U.S. 331, 340 (1948).

[11] Rule 3(a) of the Rules Governing § 2254 Cases.

[12] 28 U.S.C.A. § 1915(a)(2) (West 1994 & Supp. 1998). *See* cases discussed *infra* note 16.

[13] *See supra* § 2.2.

[14] *See infra* note 31. *See also infra* § 15.2.

[15] Advisory Committee Note to Rule 3 of the Rules Governing § 2254 Cases. *See* Weaver v. Pung, 925 F.2d 1097, 1099 (8th Cir.), *cert. denied*, 502 U.S. 828 (1991) ("The advisory committee notes to the Rules Governing Section 2254 Cases indicate that rule 3(b) contemplates prompt attention will be given to applications to proceed *in forma pauperis*."). *See also* Neitzke v. Williams, 490 U.S. 319, 324 (1989) (dismissal of ifp application on grounds of false or insufficient allegation of poverty, frivolity, or malice may occur "*sua sponte*" prior to issuance of process "so as to spare prospective [respondents] the inconvenience and expense of answering such complaints"); Sills v. United States Bur. of Prisons, 761 F.2d 792, 794 (D.C. Cir. 1985) (similar).

[16] *See, e.g.*, Blair-Bey v. Quick, 151 F.3d 1036, 1039-42 (D.C. Cir. 1998) (applying circuit's rule that PLRA is inapplicable to habeas corpus petitions and rejecting government's argument that

cases, it apparently could not be applied retroactively to cases filed prior to the effective date of the legislation.[17]

PLRA should apply at least to petitions challenging denial of parole); Davis v. Fechtel, 150 F.3d 486, 488-90 (5th Cir. 1998) (PLRA does not apply to habeas corpus petitions filed pursuant to either 28 U.S.C. § 2241 or § 2254 or to motions filed pursuant to 28 U.S.C. § 2255); Kincade v. Sparkman, 117 F.3d 949, 951-52 (6th Cir. 1997) ("filing fee provisions of the Prison Litigation Reform Act do not apply to actions brought pursuant to § 2254 or § 2255"; "[b]y exempting § 2254 and § 2255 from the [PLRA] provisions of § 1915(b) and the three strikes provision of § 1915(g) (as this provision has a comparable provision in 28 U.S.C. § 2244(b)), we provide a prisoner the ability to seek § 2254 and § 2255 relief as a pauper under § 1915(a)(1). This conclusion requires that the prisoner submit an affidavit of indigence in compliance with § 1915(a)(1). However, a prisoner is not required to file a trust account statement because the information contained in the trust account is only necessary for the payment formula of § 1915(b)."); Martin v. Bissonette, 1997 WL 280602 (1st Cir. May 29, 1997), *vac'd but reaffirmed on this point*, 118 F.3d 871, 874-75 & n.3 (1st Cir. 1997) ("[a]ll the circuits that have addressed this question to date have agreed that the PLRA does not apply to habeas petitions"); Carson v. Johnson, 112 F.3d 818, 820 (5th Cir. 1997) (PLRA does not apply to "habeas petitions under § 2254"); Smith v. Angelone, 111 F.3d 1126, 1129 (4th Cir.), *cert. denied*, 118 S. Ct. 2 (1997) (similar); Anderson v. Singletary, 111 F.3d 801, 804-05 (11th Cir. 1997) (classification of habeas corpus proceedings as "'civil' is ... somewhat illusive, as habeas corpus actions are not purely (and thus not plainly) 'civil actions'" (**citing FHCPP**)); United States v. Simmonds, 111 F.3d 737, 741-44 (10th Cir. 1997) (PLRA inapplicable to habeas corpus cases because they are not "civil actions" for purposes of 28 U.S.C. § 1915); Naddi v. Hill, 106 F.3d 275, 277 (9th Cir. 1997) ("We hold that the [PLRA] provisions relating to prisoner civil actions and appeals do not apply to habeas proceedings."); United States v. Cole, 101 F.3d 1076, 1077 (5th Cir. 1996) (PRLA is inapplicable to section 2255 motions because "Congress distinguished procedures to be followed in habeas actions from those used in other civil litigation"); Santana v. United States, 98 F.3d 752, 755-56 (3d Cir. 1996) (PLRA does not apply to habeas corpus cases unless claim raised in petition is analogous to section 1983 claims for relief from unconstitutional prison conditions); Thurman v. Gramley, 97 F.3d 185, 186 (7th Cir. 1996) (PLRA is inapplicable to habeas corpus action under 28 U.S.C. § 2241 unless action challenges prison conditions); Martin v. United States, 96 F.3d 853, 855 (7th Cir. 1996) (although habeas corpus and section 2255 proceedings are "technically civil proceedings," they are not subject to PLRA "since the simultaneously enacted antiterrorism act deals comprehensively with habeas corpus, since habeas corpus is more accurately regarded as being *sui generis* ... than being either civil or criminal, and since postconviction relief and prisoner civil rights relief are analytically very different and the [PLRA] is addressed to the latter"); Reyes v. Keane, 90 F.3d 676, 678 (2d Cir. 1996), *overruled on other grounds*, Nelson v. Walker, 121 F.3d 828, 832-33 (2d Cir. 1997) (PLRA does not apply to habeas corpus cases; "PLRA was aimed primarily at prisoners' suits challenging prison conditions, many of which are routinely dismissed as frivolous. There is nothing in the text of the PLRA or its legislative history to indicate that Congress expected its filing fee payment requirements to apply to habeas corpus petitions."). *But see* Van Doren v. Mazurkiewicz, 935 F. Supp. 604, 605-06 (E.D. Pa. 1996) (disagreeing with *Reyes, supra*, and holding that PLRA applies to habeas corpus cases).

[17] *Compare* White v. Gregory, 87 F.3d 429, 430 (10th Cir.), *cert. denied*, 117 S. Ct. 528 (1996) (nonhabeas case; PLRA does not apply to previously filed appeal) *and* Zimmer v. Bork, 1996 WL 470323, at *1 n.1 (10th Cir. Aug. 20, 1996) (same) *with* Covino v. Reopel, 89 F.3d 105, 106-08 (2d Cir. 1996), *cert. denied*, 117 S. Ct. 1265 (1997) (nonhabeas case; PLRA does apply to

To secure an ifp order, the prisoner should append the following documents to the petition:

(1)   An application for leave to proceed ifp.

(2)   A proposed order granting ifp status.

(3)   A recent affidavit of indigence signed by the client.[18]

---

previously filed appeal). *See generally supra* §§ 3.4, 5.1b (discussing retroactivity of new legislation affecting habeas corpus cases).

[18] *See Neitzke v. Williams, supra,* 490 U.S. at 324 (section "1915(a) allows a litigant to commence a civil or criminal action in federal court *in forma pauperis* by filing in good faith an affidavit stating, *inter alia,* that he is unable to pay the costs of the lawsuit"); Wrenn v. Benson, 490 U.S. 89, 90 (1989) (*per curiam*); Kincade v. Sparkman, 117 F.3d 949, 952 (6th Cir. 1997) ("any prisoner seeking § 2254 and § 2255 relief in the district court as a pauper is required to file an affidavit that includes a list of all assets that the prisoner possesses and a statement that the prisoner is unable to pay the required filing fee.... [But] the prisoner is not required to file a trust account statement.").

The form of the affidavit is specified in 28 U.S.C.A. § 1915 (West 1994 & Supp. 1998) and Rule 3(a) of the Rules Governing § 2254 Cases. A knowingly false affidavit subjects the affiant to prosecution for perjury. *See* Rowland v. California Men's Colony, Unit II Men's Advisory Council, 506 U.S. 194, 205 (1993) ("'One who makes this affidavit exposes himself "to the pains of perjury in a case of bad faith."'... The perjury sanction thus serves to protect the public against misuse of public funds by a litigant with adequate funds of his own, and against the filing of 'frivolous or malicious' lawsuits funded from the public purse." (quoting Adkins v. E.I. DuPont de Nemours & Co., 335 U.S. 331, 338 (1948) (quoting Pothier v. Rodman, 261 U.S. 307, 309 (1923))))).

In addition, "§ 1915(d) authorizes federal courts to dismiss a claim filed ifp 'if the allegation of poverty is untrue.'" *Neitzke v. Williams, supra,* 490 U.S. at 324 (quoting 28 U.S.C. § 1915(d)). *See, e.g.,* Romesburg v. Trickey, 908 F.2d 258, 260 (8th Cir. 1990) (section 1983 action) ("a district court has the discretion to dismiss a case with prejudice where a plaintiff has in bad faith filed a false affidavit of poverty," but "dismissal with prejudice is a drastic sanction which should be exercised sparingly"); Matthews v. Gaither, 902 F.2d 877 (11th Cir. 1990) (section 1983 action) (minimal inaccuracy in prisoner's statement of prison account assets did not justify dismissal of complaint under § 1915(d) because "[t]here is no evidence that the misstatement was made in bad faith in order to qualify ... for *in forma pauperis* status"; "purpose of section 1915(d) is not to punish litigants whose affidavits contain insignificant discrepancies, but to weed out the litigants who falsely understate their net worth in order to obtain *in forma pauperis* status when they are not entitled to that status based on their true net worth").

As a result of statutes of limitations that apply to habeas corpus petitions subject to the Antiterrorism and Effective Death Penalty Act of 1996 (AEDPA), a court's dismissal of a timely petition based on technical problems with the ifp motion may have the drastic consequence of wholly foreclosing federal habeas corpus relief because the limitations period may expire while the steps needed to cure the defects in the ifp motion are taken. *See, e.g.,* United States ex rel. Palaggi v. Page, 1998 WL 547300 (N.D. Ill. Aug. 27, 1998) (dismissing *pro se* petition as untimely even though it was filed within statutory limitations period because it was unaccompanied by either filing fee or ifp application and prisoner's subsequent tendering of filing fee occurred after expiration of limitations period); United States ex rel. Barnes v. Gilmore, 987 F. Supp. 677, 682 (N.D. Ill. Dec. 29, 1997) (concluding that affidavit of indigence that accompanied petition was not "in good faith" and that petitioner's subsequent payment of filing fee had no legal effect because

(4) "[A] certificate of the warden or other appropriate officer of the institution in which the prisoner is confined as to the amount of money or securities on deposit to the petitioner's credit in any account in the institution."[19]

If the PLRA is deemed to apply to habeas corpus cases (and, pending a definitive determination of this issue, in those jurisdictions in which the courts have held that the Act applies), a petitioner also must pay a partial fee at the time of filing if she is able to do so[20] and submit "a certified copy of the trust fund account statement (or institutional equivalent) for the prisoner for the 6-month period immediately preceding the filing of the complaint or notice of appeal, obtained from the appropriate official of each prison at which the prisoner is or was confined."[21]

In some cases, there may be so great a need for immediate filing of a habeas corpus petition that counsel does not have sufficient time to secure a recent affidavit from the client and the requisite documentation of the amount of money in the client's prison account(s) before filing the petition. This may be the case, for example, when there is an impending execution date[22] or the limitations period set by the applicable statute of limitations is about to expire[23] or the petitioner's imminent release from "custody" could result in a loss of subject matter jurisdiction on the ground that "custody" ended prior to the filing of the petition.[24] In such cases, counsel should attempt to substitute the following

---

statutory limitations period had already terminated); *supra* §§ 3.2, 3.3a, 3.3c nn.40-44 and accompanying text, 3.4, 5.1b (discussing cases to which AEDPA applies and act's statutes of limitations). *See also supra* § 11.7c.

[19] Rule 3(a) of the Rules Governing § 2254 Cases. The district court must afford the petitioner "reasonable opportunity to see and respond to [prison] account information" relied upon by the state to oppose an ifp motion. Jones v. Zimmerman, 752 F.2d 76, 79 (3d Cir. 1985). Local rules often specify the forms that must be used, copies of which are available on request from the clerk.

[20] *See supra* notes 6-8 and accompanying text.

[21] 28 U.S.C.A. § 1915(a)(2) (West 1994 & Supp. 1998). As some of the courts that have found the PLRA inapplicable to habeas corpus cases have concluded, *see supra* note 16, the PLRA's establishment of a requirement that already exists in the Rules Governing § 2254 Cases (*see supra* note 19) is another indication that Congress did not intend the PLRA to apply to habeas corpus petitioners.

[22] *See supra* § 11.1; *infra* Chapter 13.

[23] *Cf.* United States ex rel. Barnes v. Gilmore, 987 F. Supp. 677 (N.D. Ill. 1997) (discussed *supra* note 18). For discussion of the recently enacted statutes of limitations that govern most habeas corpus cases, see *supra* § 5.1b.

[24] *See, e.g.,* Weaver v. Pung, 925 F.2d 1097, 1098-99 (8th Cir.), *cert. denied,* 502 U.S. 828 (1991) (petition dismissed for lack of jurisdiction because petitioner failed to complete "filing" by paying filing fee or obtaining ifp status prior to expiration of sentence, even though petitioner attempted to file in timely manner and was frustrated by clerk's initial refusal of filing fee and by delay in receipt of magistrate's ruling on ifp motion). *See supra* § 8.2b.

documents for the client's affidavit and officials' attestations about the client's prison account(s):

(1) Counsel's own affidavit attesting to the client's indigence.

(2) If available, a copy of an indigence affidavit filed by the client in, for example, a prior state postconviction proceeding.

(3) If available, a copy of an earlier order granting the petitioner ifp status.

(4) A statement in the application and any transmitted letter that an updated affidavit from the client and the necessary documentation of the amount of money and securities in the client's prison account(s) will be provided forthwith.

If good cause is shown, the clerk generally will accept these documents temporarily in lieu of the petitioner's affidavit and the documentation from the prison.[25] If the clerk or the court resists accepting a substitute affidavit, counsel should not jeopardize the client by delaying the filing of the petition until the necessary documentation can be obtained. Instead, counsel should pay the filing fee and move at a later date, when the documents are available, to have an ifp order entered.

Indigence is established if the prisoner is unable to pay the necessary filing fee and the costs of the action.[26] Absolute destitution is not necessary, and a person is functionally indigent if she "cannot ... pay or give security for the costs ... and still be able to provide himself and [his] dependents with the necessities of life."[27] Nor may prisoners be forced to forgo "those small amenities of life

---

[25] *See* Pothier v. Rodman, 261 U.S. 307, 309 (1923) ("supporting affidavit may properly be made by the counsel," although prisoner's obligation to file affidavit himself is not thereby excused).

[26] 28 U.S.C.A. § 1915(a) (West 1994 & Supp. 1998); Rule 3(a) of the Rules Governing § 2254 Cases. *See* Neitzke v. Williams, 490 U.S. 319, 324 (1989).

[27] Rowland v. California Men's Colony, Unit II Men's Advisory Council, 506 U.S. 194, 203 (1993); Adkins v. E.I. DuPont de Nemours & Co., 335 U.S. 331, 339 (1948). *Accord, e.g.,* Hardy v. United States, 375 U.S. 277, 289 n.7 (1964) (Goldberg, J., concurring); Barry v. Brower, 864 F.2d 294, 299-300 (3d Cir. 1988) (indigence established because defendant had fines exceeding equity in house and was unable to gain access to equity immediately; "[i]ndigence is not equivalent to total destitution"; "accused with assets may be indigent"); United States v. Cohen, 419 F.2d 1124, 1127 (8th Cir. 1969); Jefferson v. United States, 277 F.2d 723, 725 (9th Cir.), *cert. denied,* 364 U.S. 896 (1960). *See also Rowland v. California Men's Colony, Unit II Men's Advisory Council, supra,* 506 U.S. at 203 ("Poverty, in its primary sense is a human condition, to be '[w]anting in material riches or goods; lacking in the comforts of life; needy,' and it was in just such distinctly human terms that this Court [in *Adkins, supra*] ... established the standard of eligibility" under section 1915 (citing Webster's New International Dictionary 1919 (2d ed. 1942); *Adkins v. E.I. DuPont de Nemours & Co., supra,* 335 U.S. at 339 (other citations omitted)). The Advisory Committee notes to the Rules Governing § 2254 Cases explain that "[t]he standards of indigency [for appointment of counsel in habeas corpus cases] are less strict than those regarding eligibility to prosecute a petition *in forma pauperis* and thus many who cannot qualify to proceed

which they are permitted to acquire in a prison ...."[28] On the other hand, a number of district courts have local rules or practices providing that if the prisoner has more than a given amount in his prison account, *e.g.*, $100, he does not qualify as indigent.

An ifp litigant must satisfy a statutory test of "nonfrivolousness," but the applicable standard and the procedure for making the determination vary, depending upon whether the PLRA applies to the case. With respect to cases that are not governed by the PLRA, the statute provides that "the court shall dismiss the case at any time if the court determines that ... the action or appeal ... is frivolous or malicious ... [or] fails to state a claim on which relief may be granted."[29] To meet this standard, the petitioner need only show that one or more of the claims in the petition state a legal cause of action, that the facts alleged

---

under 28 U.S.C. § 1915 will be entitled to the benefit of counsel" in habeas corpus cases. Advisory Committee Note to Rule 8 of the Rules Governing § 2254 Cases. *See infra* § 12.3a n.6.

[28] Bullock v. Suomela, 710 F.2d 102, 103 (3d Cir. 1983). *Cf.* Wrenn v. Benson, 490 U.S. 89, 90 & n.4 (1989) (*per curiam*) (petitioner with four dependents does not qualify for ifp status given his salary of $1,073 per month, $8,400 per year in retirement benefits, $61 in cash, and a home worth $72,000); Weaver v. Pung, 925 F.2d 1097, 1099 n.4 (8th Cir.), *cert. denied*, 502 U.S. 828 (1991) (district court did not abuse discretion in denying ifp status to petitioner whose "income for the preceding twelve months was estimated at $26,000 to $30,000"); Jones v. Zimmerman, 752 F.2d 76, 79 (3d Cir. 1985). The 5th Circuit has held that a prisoner qualifies as indigent when the filing fee amounts to 40% of his assets. Green v. Estelle, 649 F.2d 298, 302 (5th Cir. 1981).

[29] 28 U.S.C.A. § 1915(e)(2) (West 1994 & Supp. 1998). *See Neitzke v. Williams, supra*, 490 U.S. at 324; Morrow v. FBI, 2 F.3d 642, 643 (5th Cir. 1993); Sills v. United States Bur. of Prisons, 761 F.2d 792, 794 (D.C. Cir. 1985); Franklin v. Murphy, 745 F.2d 1221, 1226-27 (9th Cir. 1984); Corgain v. Miller, 708 F.2d 1241, 1247 (7th Cir. 1983); Maclin v. Freake, 650 F.2d 885, 887 (7th Cir. 1981); Louisiana ex rel. Purkey v. Ciolino, 393 F. Supp. 102, 106 (E.D. La. 1975); Foley v. Massachusetts, 310 F. Supp. 1330, 1331 (D. Mass. 1970); Gilland v. Hyder, 278 F. Supp. 189, 190 (E.D. Tenn. 1967); Allison v. Wilson, 277 F. Supp. 271, 273 (N.D. Cal. 1967). *See also* Professional Real Estate Investors, Inc. v. Columbia Pictures Industries, Inc., 508 U.S. 49, 67 (1993) (question "whether the suit at issue here was objectively baseless is purely one of law, which [appellate court is] ... obliged to consider *de novo*"); *infra* § 20.3d n.71 and accompanying text.

The Supreme Court traditionally had allowed all individuals to petition that Court under 28 U.S.C. § 1915 and S. Ct. R. 39, upon a finding, adjudicated on a case-by-case basis, that the petitioner qualifies for ifp status: "Each year, we permit the vast majority of persons who wish to proceed *in forma pauperis* to do so; last Term, we afforded the privilege ... to about 2,300 persons. Paupers have been an important — and valued — part of the Court's docket, *see, e.g., Gideon v. Wainwright,* 372 U.S. 335 (1963), and remain so." In re McDonald, 489 U.S. 180, 184 (1989) (*per curiam*). In 1991, however, the Court amended Rule 39 to provide for denial of ifp status when the Court is "satisfied that a petition for a writ of *certiorari,* jurisdictional statement, or petition for an extraordinary writ ... is frivolous or malicious." In re Amendment to Rule 39, 500 U.S. 13, 14 (1991) (amendment effective July 1, 1991). *See also* S. Ct. R. 39.8 (as amended, July 26, 1995). The Court's application of Rule 39, and criticism of the rule and its application by dissenting Justices, is discussed *infra* § 39.3a n.2. *See also supra* § 11.7b n.12.

support that cause of action, and that there is no obvious and wholly sufficient legal defense to the claims raised.[30] The statute does not specify the stage of the

---

[30] *See* Denton v. Hernandez, 504 U.S. 25, 33 (1992) ("court may dismiss a claim as factually frivolous only if the facts alleged are 'clearly baseless,' ... a category encompassing allegations that are 'fanciful,' ... 'fantastic,' ... and 'delusional,' .... As those words suggest, a finding of factual frivolousness is appropriate when the facts alleged rise to the level of the irrational or the wholly incredible, whether or not there are judicially noticeable facts available to contradict them. An *in forma pauperis* complaint may not be dismissed ... simply because the court finds the plaintiff's allegations unlikely. Some improbable allegations might properly be disposed of on summary judgment, but to dismiss them as frivolous without any factual development is to disregard the age-old insight that many allegations might be 'strange, but true; for truth is always strange, Stranger than fiction.'" (quoting Lord Byron, *Don Juan*)); *Neitzke v. Williams, supra*, 490 U.S. at 322-25 (dismissal for frivolousness is permissible "'only if the petitioner cannot make any rational argument in law or in fact, which would entitle him or her to relief'"; standard is "'more lenient' than that of [FED. R. CIV. P.] Rule 12(b)(6)"; proper "formulae for evaluating frivolousness under § 1915(d) [are] close variants of the definition of legal frivolousness which [was] articulated in the Sixth Amendment case of *Anders v. California*, 386 U.S. 738[, 744] (1967)," namely, that a legal claim "is frivolous where '[none] of the legal points [are] arguable on their merits'"; complaint is frivolous if it "lacks an arguable basis either in law or in fact," a standard embracing an "inarguable legal conclusion" and a "fanciful factual allegation" (quoting Williams v. Faulkner, 837 F.2d 304 (7th Cir. 1988))); *id.* at 327 (section 1915(d) "accords judges not only the authority to dismiss a claim based on an indisputably meritless legal theory, but also the unusual power to pierce the veil of the complaint's factual allegations and dismiss those claims whose factual contentions are clearly baseless"; examples of former "are claims against which it is clear that the defendants are immune" and "claims of infringement of a legal interest which clearly does not exist"; examples of latter "are claims describing fantastic or delusional scenarios"); *id.* at 327-29 (dismissal appropriate if "it is clear that no relief could be granted" but not if there is chance that claim could be clarified to conform to requirements of valid legal cause of action); Weeks v. Jones, 100 F.3d 124, 127-28 (11th Cir. 1996) (*per curiam*) (claims in federal habeas corpus petition, which were "arguable, although ultimately unsuccessful," could not be deemed "frivolous"); Johnson v. Gibson, 14 F.3d 61, 63-64 (D.C. Cir. 1994) (*per curiam*) (section 1983 action) (district court erred in dismissing *pro se* complaint that did not make "fanciful allegations" and that could be "generous[ly] read[]" to assert arguably meritorious legal claim; section 1915(d) establishes more "stringent standard" for dismissal than FED. R. CIV. P. 12(b)(6)); Johnson v. Bi-State Justice Center, 12 F.3d 133, 135 (8th Cir. 1993) (section 1983 action) ("This is not a suitable case for a § 1915(d) dismissal" because prisoner's § 1983 claim is "neither irrational nor wholly incredible."); Koetting v. Thompson, 995 F.2d 37, 40 (5th Cir. 1993) (*per curiam*) (notwithstanding vagueness of petitioner's claims and doubts whether he could prevail on merits, district court erred in dismissing petition as "frivolous" because "petition has an arguable basis in law"); Olson v. Hart, 965 F.2d 940, 942 n.3 (10th Cir. 1992) (*pro se* request for order of mandamus, which could be construed as either section 2254 petition or section 1983 complaint, could not be dismissed as "frivolous" because "[w]e cannot say that the appellant's claims are 'fantastic or delusional'"); McKeever v. Block, 932 F.2d 795, 798 (9th Cir. 1991) (section 1983 action) (complaint should not have been dismissed as frivolous because "facts alleged are not fanciful; they do not describe delusional scenarios.... If true, they state colorable legal claims"); Wilson v. Barrientos, 926 F.2d 480, 482 (5th Cir. 1991) (section 1983 action) ("Frivolousness in this context is not coterminous with failure to state a claim, but it is to be equated with the raising of a wholly insubstantial federal claim."); Frazier v. Dubois, 922 F.2d 560, 562 (10th Cir. 1990) (*Bivens* action) ("It is by now well established that an action may

process at which this determination must be made, and it has become customary in many jurisdictions for the clerk of court to issue an ifp order pending final action by the court.[31]

The PLRA (assuming it applies to habeas corpus cases) changes the nonfrivolousness standard for "prisoner[s] seeking to bring a civil action or appeal a judgment in a civil action or proceeding"[32] by requiring that the court screen each of the claims in the complaint and dismiss any that are "frivolous, malicious, or fail[] to state a claim upon which relief may be granted."[33] The PLRA additionally bars prisoners from filing an ifp "civil action or appeal [of] a judgment in a civil action or proceeding" if the prisoner has had three ifp complaints previously dismissed for frivolousness or for failure to state a

---

not be dismissed as frivolous unless it is beyond doubt that the petitioner can prove no facts in support of his claim which would entitle him to relief."); Clark v. Georgia Pardons and Paroles Bd., 915 F.2d 636, 639-40 (11th Cir. 1990) (section 1983 action) (district court should not have dismissed complaint as frivolous because it "states a claim upon which relief can be granted" and "facts asserted to support the claim are not fantastic"); Nance v. Kelly, 912 F.2d 605, 606 (2d Cir. 1990) (section 1983 action) ("district court should look with a far more forgiving eye in examining whether a complaint rests on a meritless legal theory for purposes of section 1915(d) than it does in testing the complaint against a Rule 12(b)(6) motion"); Guti v. INS, 908 F.2d 495, 496 (9th Cir. 1990) (habeas corpus petition should not have been dismissed as frivolous because "there is no controlling authority requiring a holding that the facts as alleged fail to establish even an arguable claim as a matter of law" and "there is some authority to support the plaintiff's position"); Adams v. Hansen, 906 F.2d 192, 193-94 (5th Cir. 1990) (section 1983 action) ("district court's equating failure to state claim with frivolousness was error"; because prisoner alleged "scenario that was not inherently implausible," complaint should not have been deemed frivolous); Williams v. White, 897 F.2d 942, 943-45 (8th Cir. 1990) (section 1983 action); Flick v. Blevins, 887 F.2d 778, 778-79 (7th Cir. 1989), cert. denied, 495 U.S. 934 (1990). See also Aiello v. Kingston, 947 F.2d 834, 836 (7th Cir. 1991) (district court erred in granting ifp status only on some claims while denying it on others; when complaint "states multiple theories of relief against the same defendants, ... [t]he district judge must grant or deny leave to proceed without prepayment of costs with respect to all claims ... [because] the additional theories of liability produce no incremental costs that solvent persons would have to prepay"); decisions discussed infra § 15.2c.

[31] See Advisory Committee Note to Rule 3 of the Rules Governing § 2254 Cases (inviting district courts to delegate this authority to clerk and explaining that rule "contemplate[s] that prompt attention will be given [by the clerk and the court] to the request to proceed in forma pauperis"); Adkins v. E.I. DuPont de Nemours & Co., 335 U.S. 339 (1948) ("affidavits ... written in the language of the statute ... should ordinarily be accepted ... particularly where unquestioned and where the judge does not perceive a flagrant misrepresentation"); Newsom v. Peyton, 341 F.2d 904, 905 (4th Cir. 1965) (pro se ifp application should be granted notwithstanding lack of "nicety of a lawyer's pleading"). See also Weaver v. Pung, 925 F.2d 1097, 1099 (8th Cir.), cert. denied, 502 U.S. 828 (1991) ("The advisory committee notes to the Rules Governing Section 2254 Cases indicate that rule 3(b) contemplates prompt attention will be given to applications to proceed in forma pauperis.").

[32] 28 U.S.C.A. § 1915(a)(2) (West 1994 & Supp. 1998).

[33] Id. § 1915A(b).

claim;[34] this statutory bar recognizes a limited exception for prisoners who are "under imminent danger of serious physical injury."[35] The PLRA changes the procedure by requiring that the judicial screening of claims take place "before docketing, if feasible or, in any event as soon as practicable after docketing."[36] In jurisdictions in which the PLRA is deemed to apply to habeas corpus cases, the practices of the federal districts that required substantive screening of ifp requests in habeas corpus actions even before enactment of the PLRA provide a useful model for implementing the PLRA in habeas corpus cases. A number of those courts have accommodated the Habeas Rules' "prompt attention" policy by allowing habeas corpus petitions to be filed without a fee (assuming the clerk determines that the accompanying indigence papers are in order), pending subsequent screening by the court at the same time and manner as it conducts the screening required by Habeas Rule 4.[37]

The courts treat a decision denying ifp status as a final judgment allowing an immediate appeal, else filing costs might preclude legitimate claims from being heard due to the prisoner's indigence.[38] If, however, the district court concludes that the *appeal* is not in "good faith," it may deny the prisoner's motion to prosecute the appeal ifp.[39] In that event, the petitioner must secure leave to appeal ifp by motion to the court of appeals.[40]

---

[34] 28 U.S.C.A. § 1915(g) (West 1994 & Supp. 1998). The statutory bar created by the PLRA parallels the Supreme Court's practice in recent years of prospectively barring ifp petitions for *certiorari* and extraordinary writs by litigants whose previous filings the Court determined to be "patently frivolous." *See supra* § 11.7b n.12; *supra* note 29; *infra* § 39.3a n.2.

[35] 28 U.S.C.A. § 1915(g) (West 1994 & Supp. 1998). Even if the PLRA is definitively found to apply to federal habeas corpus proceedings, *but cf. supra* notes 4-17 and accompanying text, the statutory exception for prisoners "under imminent danger of serious physical injury" might be read to encompass capital habeas corpus proceedings.

[36] 28 U.S.C.A. § 1915A(a) (West 1994 & Supp. 1998).

[37] *See supra* note 31 and accompanying text.

[38] *See* 28 U.S.C. § 1291 (1994); Roberts v. United States Dist. Ct., 339 U.S. 844, 845 (1950) (citing Cohen v. Beneficial Industrial Loan Corp., 337 U.S. 541, 546 (1949)); Advisory Committee Note to FED. R. APP. P. 24(a) (same). *See also* Roman v. Jeffes, 904 F.2d 192, 195-96 (3d Cir. 1990) (section 1983 action) (district court erred in dismissing complaint pursuant to § 1915(d) after service of complaint; "threat of § 1915(d) dismissal at any time in the course of litigation accords disparate treatment to indigent litigants").

[39] 28 U.S.C.A. § 1915(a) (West 1994 & Supp. 1998). *See* Coppedge v. United States, 369 U.S. 438, 445, 447-48 (1962) ("good faith ... demonstrated when [applicant] seeks appellate review of any issue not frivolous"; burden of proof "should, at all times, be on the party making the suggestion of frivolity"); Ragan v. Cox, 305 F.2d 58, 60 n.2 (10th Cir. 1962); *infra* § 35.3.

[40] *See, e.g.*, Oatess v. Sobolevitch, 914 F.2d 428, 430 n.4 (3d Cir. 1990) (section 1915 case); Borning v. Hymel, 764 F.2d 1041, 1041-42 (5th Cir. 1985). *See infra* § 35.3.

§ 12.2. Appointment of counsel: introduction.[1]

Retained, volunteer,[2] and legal services lawyers[3] occasionally represent habeas corpus petitioners from the moment postconviction proceedings are contemplated. Under a provision of the Anti-Drug Abuse Act of 1988[4] and the Supreme Court's interpretation of that provision in *McFarland v. Scott*,[5] appointed counsel is mandatory for all indigent *capital* prisoners and becomes available even before they file federal habeas corpus petitions when, as normally is the case, they need appointed counsel to assist them in investigating and presenting claims in their petitions.[6] In other cases, however, indigent (*i.e.*, nearly all) federal habeas corpus petitioners commence the proceedings either

---

§ 12.2. [1] Most of the relevant commentary is cited *supra* §§ 7.1a n.2, 7.2 n.1. In addition, *see* Comment, *Attorney Fees — Award of Attorney Fees to Pro Se Litigant Who is an Attorney — Jones v. Lujan*, 63 Temp. L. Rev. 865 (1990); Comment, *Mallard v. United States District Court: Section 1915(d) and the Appointment of Counsel in Civil Cases*, 51 Ohio St. L.J. 1001 (1990); Annotation, *Compensation Under Subsection (d) of the Criminal Justice Act of 1964 (18 U.S.C. § 3006A(d)), of Counsel Appointed for the Accused*, 9 A.L.R. Fed. 569 (1968).

[2] *See* John C. Godbold, Pro Bono *Representation of Death Sentenced Inmates*, 42 Rec. Ass'n B. City N.Y. 859 (1987). *But cf.* Giarratano v. Murray, 668 F. Supp. 511, 515 (E.D. Va. 1986), *aff'd*, 849 F.2d 1118 (4th Cir. 1988) (*en banc*), *rev'd sub nom. Murray v. Giarratano*, 492 U.S. 1 (1989) ("In the past, ... [a]ttorneys volunteered their services or were recruited to provide pro bono assistance and representation to death row prisoners. Those days are gone.... [F]ew — very few — attorneys are willing to voluntarily represent death row inmates in post conviction efforts"); Memorandum to all Judges, United States Court of Appeals, *et al.*, from Administrative Office of the United States Courts, Recent Judicial Conference Action Relating to the Criminal Justice Act (CJA) (Mar. 24, 1987), at 5 ("The CJA Committee [of the United States Judicial Conference] has been concerned about the possible difficulties which may be experienced by courts in recruiting qualified attorneys to accept appointments in death penalty cases."); Michael A. Kroll, *Death Watch*, California Law, Dec. 1987, at 26 (80% of 250 death row inmates in Texas lack attorneys); *Lawyers, Citing Financial Losses, Shun Death Row Appeals*, N.Y. Times, Sept. 22, 1986, at A15; authority cited *supra* § 7.2 n.1.

[3] Prisoners have a due process right to "'[m]eaningful access' to the courts" which includes the requirement that States which do not make legal services attorneys available to indigent prisoners provide adequate law libraries and permit "jailhouse lawyering" by prisoners on behalf of others. *See* authority cited *supra* § 7.2c nn.59-61 and accompanying text. These decisions have led a few States to fund prisoner legal services offices. *See* Giarratano v. Murray, *supra*, 668 F. Supp. at 514 (discussing adequacy of such offices).

[4] 21 U.S.C.A. § 848(q)(4)(B) (West 1994 & Supp. 1998) (discussed *infra* §§ 12.3a nn.2 & 18-20 and accompanying text, 12.3b nn.46-52 and accompanying text).

[5] 512 U.S. 849 (1994) (discussed *infra* §§ 12.3a nn.15-20 and accompanying text, 12.3b nn.46-52 and accompanying text).

[6] *Id.* at 2572-73. *Accord* Brown v. Vasquez, 952 F.2d 1164, 1165, 1167 (9th Cir.), *cert. denied*, 503 U.S. 1011 (1992) (discussed *infra* § 12.3a nn.13-14 and accompanying text); Coleman v. Vasquez, 771 F. Supp. 300, 302-04 (N.D. Cal. 1991) (discussed *infra* § 12.3a n.16). For discussion of the important issue of timeliness of a prepetition application for counsel and a stay of execution, see *infra* § 13.2b.

without legal assistance[7] or with only the aid of a fellow inmate[8] or a volunteer attorney who may be unable to proceed with the case in the absence of reimbursement for costs and time spent on the case.[9] In view of the present political and fiscal climates, it is likely that most habeas corpus petitions outside capital cases will continue to be litigated either *pro se* or by unpaid counsel. Even when appointments are made, moreover, the low maximum fees that are statutorily assured in noncapital cases, and the complex process required to secure a waiver of the presumptive maximum, will continue to prevent attorneys representing indigent prisoners from earning a living wage.[10]

---

[7] *See* Price v. Johnston, 334 U.S. 266, 292 (1948) ("prisoners ... act ... often as their own counsel in *habeas corpus* proceedings"). The courts do not allow *pro se* petitioners to collect attorney's fees even if they obtain relief. *See, e.g.,* Ewing v. Rodgers, 826 F.2d 967, 971 (10th Cir. 1987) (*rev'g* Ewing v. Rodgers, 621 F. Supp. 1366 (D. Colo. 1986)) (Equal Access to Justice Act, 28 U.S.C. § 2412(d)(1)(A), does not include habeas corpus within "civil action[s]" in which prevailing *pro se* litigants may receive attorney's fees); Lowe v. Letsinger, 772 F.2d 308, 315 (7th Cir. 1985) (denying habeas corpus petitioner's request for attorney's fees under 42 U.S.C. § 1988); Boudin v. Thomas, 732 F.2d 1107 (2d Cir. 1984). *Pro se* litigants' expenses are reimbursable, however. *See, e.g.,* United States v. Feldman, 788 F.2d 625, 626-27 (9th Cir. 1986), *cert. denied,* 479 U.S. 1067 (1987).

[8] If a State fails to afford prisoners free counsel in preparing postconviction petitions, it must permit "jailhouse" lawyers to assist in preparing such papers. *See, e.g.,* Bounds v. Smith, 430 U.S. 817, 823 (1977); Younger v. Gilmore, 404 U.S. 15 (1971), *aff'g* Gilmore v. Lynch, 319 F. Supp. 105 (N.D. Cal. 1970); Johnson v. Avery, 393 U.S. 483, 487 (1969); *supra* § 7.2c nn.59-61 and accompanying text.

[9] *See* Peterson v. Davis, 421 F. Supp. 1220 (E.D. Va. 1976), *aff'd,* 562 F.2d 48 (4th Cir. 1977).

[10] *See* 18 U.S.C. §§ 3006A(d)(2), 3006A(d)(3) (1994); United States ex rel. Kubat v. Thieret, 690 F. Supp. 725, 725 (N.D. Ill. 1988) (available fees for representation of indigent habeas corpus petitioners are not "meant to provide 'full compensation'" but only "'to ease the financial burden on the attorney who offers his services to a defendant as a professional public duty'" (citation omitted)); *infra* § 12.3c. *See also supra* § 7.2a n.2 (meager compensation levels in state postconviction cases). Regarding the unreasonableness of current compensation levels, compare *infra* § 12.3c ($750 presumptive maximum compensation) *with, e.g., supra* §§ 4.1, 7.1, 11.2; *infra* § 21.1 (all discussing counsel's weighty and difficult responsibilities in postconviction representation). *See also* Mercer v. Armontrout, 864 F.2d 1429, 1433 (8th Cir. 1988) ("average time that a competent lawyer labors in post-conviction review of a single death sentence is approximately one-quarter of a lawyer's billable hours for one year"); Spangenberg Group, Time and Expense Analysis in Post-Conviction Death Penalty Cases 11 (Feb. 1987) (similar); authority cited *supra* § 7.2 n.1. Attorneys whose clients prevail may be able to avoid the Criminal Justice Act's compensation limits by seeking attorney's fees under 28 U.S.C. § 2412(d)(1)(A) (1994), 42 U.S.C. § 1988 (1994), or other statutes authorizing attorney's fees for prevailing indigent civil litigants. *See* Caruth v. Pinkney, 683 F.2d 1044, 1049 (7th Cir. 1982), *cert. denied,* 459 U.S. 1214 (1983) (even if court is not disposed under Criminal Justice Act to compensate volunteer counsel representing indigent petitioner, court should appoint counsel in order to permit him to collect fees under section 1988 should petitioner succeed). *But cf.* decisions discussed *supra* note 7 (*pro se* habeas corpus petitioners may not collect attorney's fees even if they prevail; questioning

Nonetheless, attorneys involved in or contemplating such representation need not resign themselves to receiving *no* compensation for their services. Assuming that the client is indigent, there are various statutory[11] and constitutional[12] provisions that sometimes require and otherwise permit the district court to appoint and pay willing[13] counsel something for representing indigent prisoners in habeas corpus cases.[14]

§ 12.3. The statutory right to counsel.[1]

a. *Procedure and timing.* In capital cases, applications by indigent prisoners for appointment of counsel should be made pursuant to the Anti-Drug Abuse Act of 1988, which mandates the appointment of counsel for all indigent capital prisoners seeking habeas corpus or other federal postconviction relief.[2] In noncapital cases, applications should be made pursuant to the Criminal Justice

---

availability of attorney's fees in habeas corpus cases under various provisions other than Criminal Justice Act and Anti-Drug Abuse Act of 1988).

[11] *See infra* § 12.3.

[12] *See supra* § 7.2; *infra* § 12.4.

[13] A district court may not compel a particular attorney against the attorney's will to represent an indigent defendant pursuant to 28 U.S.C.A. § 1915(e) (1) (West 1994 & Supp. 1998). *See* Mallard v. United States Dist. Ct., 490 U.S. 296, 301-07 (1989). *Mallard* is not meant to relax the ethical obligations of attorneys to represent clients when requested by the court. *Id.* at 307-08. The decision also is limited to appointments under section 1915(e)(1) (codified as § 1915(d) at the time of the decision) and leaves open the possibility that representation could be compelled pursuant to 18 U.S.C. § 3005A (1994), other federal statutes (including, potentially, the habeas corpus attorney-appointment provisions of the Criminal Justice Act, *id.* § 3006A(a)(2)(B), and the Anti-Drug Abuse Act of 1988, 21 U.S.C.A. § 848(q) (West 1994 & Supp. 1998)), and the federal courts' implied general authority to provide counsel in appropriate cases. *Mallard v. United States Dist. Ct., supra,* 490 U.S. at 308 n.8, 310. Although arguing that section 1915 does permit district courts to compel representation, the four-member *Mallard* dissent notes four legitimate reasons for excusing an attorney from compelled performance: (1) conflict of interest, (2) engagement in another trial, (3) prior participation in more than a fair share of uncompensated cases, and (4) inadequate qualifications. *Id.* at 311-18 (Stevens, J., dissenting).

[14] *See also infra* §§ 36.1, 39.3b (appointment of appellate counsel). Appointed counsel serve the courts' as well as clients' interests. *See, e.g.,* Battle v. Armontrout, 902 F.2d 701, 702 (8th Cir. 1990) ("appointment of counsel would benefit ... the court by allowing counsel to develop Battle's arguments and focus the court's analysis"); Shields v. Jackson, 570 F.2d 284, 286 (8th Cir. 1978); Taylor v. Pegelow, 335 F.2d 147 (4th Cir. 1964) ("Innumerable difficult questions and inordinate waste of time of judges and [state] lawyers ... might ... have been avoided if the District Court had appointed counsel."); Russell v. Jones, 679 F. Supp. 949 (W.D. Mo. 1988) (extensive discussion). *See also* United States v. Pope, 251 F. Supp. 234, 241-42 (D. Neb. 1966).

§ 12.3.   [1] *See generally* sources cited *supra* §§ 7.2 n.1, 12.2 n.1.

[2] Pub. L. No. 100-690, 102 Stat. 4393-94 (1988), 21 U.S.C.A. §§ 848(q), 848(r) (West 1994 & Supp. 1998). *See infra* notes 18-20 and accompanying text; *infra* § 12.3b nn.46-52 and accompanying text.

Act,[3] which requires federal district courts to adopt appointment-of-counsel plans that grant judges authority to appoint lawyers to represent indigent habeas corpus petitioners.[4] The application should include a memorandum stating the legal and factual reasons why counsel should be appointed[5] and the various documents necessary to secure leave to proceed *in forma pauperis.*[6] Some courts require the use of specified appointment of counsel forms, copies of which are available from the clerk.

If the petitioner is in contact with an attorney familiar with the case who is willing to accept the case upon appointment, the petitioner properly may seek appointment of that attorney by name, or the attorney may file papers seeking her own appointment. In the former situation, the memorandum or affidavit supporting the application should state facts establishing that the specified attorney is willing to be appointed; an affidavit from the attorney is preferred. In both situations, the supporting documents should describe the attorney's familiarity with the case. Although the Criminal Justice Act requires that

---

[3] 18 U.S.C. § 3006A (1994).

[4] 18 U.S.C. § 3006A(a)(2)(B) (1994). *See infra* § 12.3b. Prisoners and volunteer counsel should consult the relevant district court's plan for the appointment of counsel for additional procedural requirements and, generally, for deviations from the Criminal Justice Act provisions that are discussed in this section. In some circumstances, applications also should rely upon Rules 6(a) and 8(c) of the Rules Governing § 2254 Cases as bases for the appointment of counsel. *See infra* notes 37-40 and accompanying text; *infra* § 12.3b nn.85-92 and accompanying text.

[5] *See infra* §§ 12.3b, 12.4. In capital cases, the memorandum need not be extensive because counsel is statutorily mandated as long as the prisoner is indigent and not otherwise represented by counsel willing to bear the cost of the representation. If *prefiling* representation is sought, the capital prisoner or volunteer lawyer should explain in some detail why additional factual and legal investigation is needed before a comprehensive petition can be filed. *See generally* McFarland v. Scott, 512 U.S. 849, 855-58 (1994); *infra* notes 11-20 and accompanying text. In situations in which a stay of execution is needed to permit a prefiling investigation to occur, the memorandum also should discuss the timeliness of the application. *See infra* § 13.2b. In noncapital cases, the memorandum may have to be more extensive because, in addition to discussing the prisoner's indigence and need for representation and the timing of the application, the memorandum must explain why the court should exercise its discretion to grant counsel or why the case is one of the relatively unusual ones in which appointment of counsel is required. *See infra* § 12.3b.

[6] *See supra* § 12.1. Under the Criminal Justice Act, a prisoner is indigent if he is "financially unable to obtain adequate representation." 18 U.S.C. § 3006A(a) (1994). As discussed *supra* § 12.1 nn.26-28 and accompanying text, "indigence" is a functional concept focusing on the petitioner's inability to pay the necessary fees and costs without giving up the necessities of life or the small amenities available to men and women in prison. It should be noted that "[t]he standards of indigency [for appointment of counsel under 18 U.S.C. § 3006A(a)(2)(B) (1994)] are less strict than those regarding eligibility to prosecute a petition *in forma pauperis* and thus many who cannot qualify to proceed under 28 U.S.C. § 1915 will be entitled to the benefits of counsel under 18 U.S.C. § 3000A(g) [*recodified as* 18 U.S.C. § 3006A(a)(2)(B) (1994)]." Advisory Committee Note to Rule 8 of the Rules Governing § 2254 Cases.

appointments be made according to a plan promulgated by the relevant court for assigning counsel,[7] many plans afford judges discretion to appoint attorneys whom they have specially selected, including ones who volunteer and are familiar with the case.[8] The local rules of court and appointment plan should be consulted.

More difficult, perhaps, than the question *whether*[9] and *how* to seek appointment of counsel is the question of *when* to do so.[10] A number of options are available, including the five discussed below:

(1) Prior to filing or even fully investigating and preparing the petition, the prisoner may apply to the court in the district in which the petition will be filed[11] for appointment of counsel to assist in bringing the action. Legal assistance at this early stage often is critical to enable unsophisticated prisoners to recognize meritorious claims, draft the petition in a formally and substantively proper manner, file the necessary documents with the petition (including, for instance, motions for essential fact development procedures), and litigate the initial phases of the case.[12] As the Ninth Circuit has noted, prospective federal habeas corpus petitioners are "often illiterate or poorly educated" and need prefiling representation to help them "decipher a complex maze of jurisprudence [and] ... determine which of [their] ... constitutional

---

[7] 18 U.S.C. § 3006A(a) (1994).

[8] *See* Memorandum, *supra* § 12.2 n.2, at 5-6 (March 1987 amendments to Judicial Conference Guidelines for appointing counsel create preference in capital habeas corpus cases for representation by attorney who either "has represented the petitioner during state court proceedings" or otherwise is "familiar with the issues and the ... state court record" and allow such appointments to deviate from usual procedure for selecting attorneys (quoting ADMINISTRATIVE OFFICE OF THE UNITED STATES COURTS, GUIDE TO JUDICIARY POLICIES AND PROCEDURES, GUIDELINES FOR THE ADMINISTRATION OF THE CRIMINAL JUSTICE ACT § 2.14)).

[9] *See supra* § 12.2.

[10] In capital cases, in addition to the considerations discussed below, see *infra* Chapter 13 (stays of execution).

[11] *See supra* §§ 10.2, 11.9a.

[12] Recognizing the importance of prefiling legal assistance, in addition to the decisions discussed *infra* notes 13-20 and accompanying text, are: Wolff v. McDonnell, 418 U.S. 539, 579 (1974) (due process right to "opportunity," via legal assistance inside the prison, "to present to the judiciary allegations concerning violations of fundamental rights"); Procunier v. Martinez, 416 U.S. 396, 419-22 (1974); Johnson v. Avery, 393 U.S. 483 (1969) (state may not forbid prisoners to assist each other in preparing motions for postconviction relief if no other legal assistance is available); Gilmore v. Lynch, 319 F. Supp. 105 (N.D. Cal. 1970), *aff'd per curiam sub nom. Younger v. Gilmore*, 404 U.S. 15 (1971) (prisoners entitled to "assistance necessary to file petitions and complaints which will in fact be fully considered by the courts"). *See generally supra* § 7.2; *infra* §§ 12.3b, 13.2c n.70.

rights, if any, may have been violated."[13] Prefiling representation is particularly important because "a prisoner applying for federal habeas corpus relief in federal court must assert all possible violations of his constitutional rights in his initial application or run the risk of losing what might be a viable claim."[14] Moreover, as the Supreme Court noted in its 1994 decision in *McFarland v. Scott*,[15] "[t]he services of investigators and other experts may be critical in the preapplication phase of a habeas corpus proceeding, when possible claims and their factual bases are researched and identified," thus necessitating the availability of counsel to engage and direct the investigator and experts.[16] In many circumstances, therefore, as Justice O'Connor has said, it will be "almost meaningless to provide a lawyer to pursue claims on federal habeas if the lawyer is not available to help prepare the petition."[17]

In *McFarland*, the Supreme Court concluded that prefiling appointment of counsel is appropriate in capital cases under the mandatory counsel provisions of the Anti-Drug Abuse Act of 1988,[18] and, indeed, is the preferred course

---

[13] Brown v. Vasquez, 952 F.2d 1164, 1165, 1167 (9th Cir.), *cert. denied*, 503 U.S. 1011 (1992) (decision's holding limited to capital cases).

[14] *Id. Accord* McFarland v. Scott, 512 U.S. 849, 860 (1994) (O'Connor, J., concurring in the judgment in part) ("our carefully crafted doctrines of waiver and abuse of the writ make it especially important that the first petition adequately set forth all of a state prisoner's colorable grounds for relief"); *id.* at 855-56 (majority opinion) (similar). *See generally supra* §§ 11.2a n.5, 11.3b nn.12-15 and accompanying text (explaining need to raise all possibly available claims in first federal habeas corpus petition, and recommending treatment of possibly viable fact-based claims that cannot be adequately investigated prior to filing petition).

[15] 512 U.S. 849 (1994) (decision's holding limited to capital cases).

[16] *Id.* at 855. *Accord* Coleman v. Vasquez, 771 F. Supp. 300, 302-04 (N.D. Cal. 1991) (decision's holding limited to capital cases) (prefiling appointment may be needed so counsel can "conduct ... a preliminary [*i.e.,* prefiling] factual investigation ... and ensure that all possible claims for relief have been uncovered and evaluated").

[17] *McFarland, supra,* 512 U.S. at 860 (O'Connor, J., concurring in the judgment in part). *Accord id.* at 857 (majority opinion) ("right to counsel necessarily includes a right for that counsel meaningfully to research and present a defendant's habeas claims"); *id.* at 868 (Thomas, J., dissenting) ("legal assistance prior to the filing of a federal petition can be very valuable to a prisoner").

[18] *Id.* at 856-57 & n.3 ("§ 848(q)(4)(B) [of the Anti-Drug Abuse Act of 1988] bestows upon capital defendants a mandatory right to counsel, including a right to preapplication legal assistance"; "language and purposes of § 848(q)(4)(B) and its related provisions [permitting appointed counsel to apply for funds for necessary investigative services] establish that the right to appointed counsel includes a right to legal assistance in the preparation of a habeas corpus application"; Court "conclude[s] that a 'post-conviction proceeding' within the meaning of § 848(q)(4)(B) [existence of which triggers right to counsel] is commenced by the filing of a death row defendant's motion requesting the appointment of counsel for his federal habeas corpus proceeding," even if that motion is filed before habeas corpus petition is filed). *Accord Brown v.*

when, as is usually the case, a comprehensive prefiling investigation has not yet occurred: "An attorney's assistance prior to the filing of a capital defendant's habeas corpus petition is crucial, because '[t]he complexity of our jurisprudence in this area ... makes it unlikely that capital defendants will be able to file successful petitions for collateral relief without the assistance of persons learned in the law.'"[19] The Court also ruled that federal district courts

---

Vasquez, supra, 952 F.2d at 1166-68; *Coleman v. Vasquez, supra*, 771 F. Supp. at 302-04 (in light of McCleskey v. Zant, 499 U.S. 467 (1991), "federal monies under section 848(q)(4)(B) ... [are] available to petitioner's counsel to conduct a *McCleskey* investigation" prior to filing habeas corpus petition, including "review[ing] the record, conduct[ing] a preliminary factual investigation, and ensur[ing] that all possible claims for relief have been uncovered and evaluated"; court-funded "research and investigation ... may touch on unexhausted claims"). *McFarland* overruled In re Lindsey, 875 F.2d 1518 (11th Cir. 1989) (Anti-Drug Abuse Act gives district courts no authority to appoint counsel to represent death-sentenced individual until petitioner files federal petition that complies with local district court rules) and In re Lindsey, 875 F.2d 1502, 1506-07 (11th Cir. 1989) (Anti-Drug Abuse Act does not authorize prefiling appointment of counsel to develop federal claims as to which state remedies are not exhausted because, in that event, prisoner "has not yet initiated a 'proceeding under Section 2254' as that term is used in subsection 848(q)(4)(B)"). *But cf.* In re Joiner, 58 F.3d 143 (5th Cir. 1995) (*per curiam*) (following *Sterling v. Scott, infra*, as precedent binding within circuit, although one member of panel expresses "uneas[iness]" with *Sterling's* holding, *id.* at 144 (King, J., concurring)); Sterling v. Scott, 57 F.3d 451, 458 & n.9 (5th Cir. 1995), *cert. denied*, 516 U.S. 1050 (1996) (although *McFarland v. Scott, supra* overruled second *In re Lindsey* decision, *supra*, first *In re Lindsey* decision, *supra*, correctly held that petitioner "has no right to appointed and paid counsel under § 848(q)(4)(B) for the purpose of exhausting his state postconviction claims"); Wilson v. Horn, 1997 WL 137343 (E.D. Pa. Mar. 24, 1997) (denying request for appointment of counsel under § 848(q) to pursue claims in state postconviction proceedings).

[19] *See id.* at 855-56 (quoting Murray v. Giarratano, 492 U.S. 1, 14 (1989) (Kennedy, J. concurring in the judgment)); *id.* ("Congress' provision of a right to counsel under § 848(q)(4)(B) reflects a determination that quality legal representation is necessary in capital habeas corpus proceedings in light of 'the seriousness of the possible penalty and ... the unique and complex nature of the litigation'" (quoting 21 U.S.C. § 848(q)(4)(B))); *supra* notes 15-17 and accompanying text (other discussion in *McFarland* indicating that prefiling appointment of counsel is not only appropriate but, generally, necessary). The *McFarland* Court noted, but did not favor, the option of filing a "skeletal" petition — *e.g.*, raising a single claim previously presented on direct appeal or in state postconviction proceedings — as the basis for appointing counsel to conduct a thorough investigation and file an amended petition. *See id.* at 852 n.1. *See also* Collins v. Byrd, 510 U.S. 1185, 1185-88 (1994) (*mem.*) (Scalia, J., dissenting from denial of motion to vacate stay of execution) (describing order issued by 6th Circuit, which Supreme Court declined to vacate, directing district court, following Byrd's filing of capital habeas corpus petition, to hold petition in abeyance for 120 days to permit counsel to conduct additional investigation and to give Byrd 60 days in which to amend petition); Scott v. Dugger, 891 F.2d 800, 802 (11th Cir. 1989) (*per curiam*), *cert. denied*, 498 U.S. 881 (1990) ("[T]he United States District Court for the Southern District of Florida stayed the execution and allowed the appellant to file an amended petition.... [T]he district court [thereafter] stayed all proceedings and allowed the appellant to file claims in state court for exhaustion purposes"); *infra* § 13.1. *See generally infra* § 17.2 (amendments).

have the authority and responsibility to grant stays of execution upon an indigent capital prisoner's timely filing of a prepetition motion for the appointment of counsel, in order to permit a thorough prepetition investigation of all available claims.[20] The new statutes of limitations that the Antiterrorism and Effective Death Penalty Act of 1996 (AEDPA)[21] adopts for capital cases in "nonopt-in" and "opt-in" situations[22] can only be satisfied by the timely filing of an "application" for habeas corpus relief, which may or may not include a *McFarland* application for appointment of counsel.[23] Until this ambiguity in the statutes of limitations is resolved, and given the importance of avoiding even the slightest risk of allowing the limitations period to expire before filing the appropriate document, capital prisoners are strongly advised to take the extra step described in section 5.1b *supra* (*i.e.*, the filing of a "placeholder petition" for habeas corpus relief along with the application for appointment of counsel) in order to comply with *McFarland* and AEDPA simultaneously.[24]

In noncapital habeas corpus cases, Rule 8(c) of the Habeas Rules makes clear that district judges have the discretion to order "the appointment of counsel under [the Criminal Justice Act] at *any stage of the case* if the interest of justice so requires."[25] In her concurring opinion in *McFarland*, Justice O'Connor concluded that this provision permits the appointment of counsel prior to the filing of a habeas corpus petition.[26] The difficulty with applying

---

[20] This aspect of the holding of *McFarland*, the definition of a "timely" filed motion, and the slightly higher (nonfrivolousness) standard likely to be applied in deciding whether to maintain stays in effect following counsel's filing of a comprehensive petition are discussed *infra* § 13.2b.

[21] Pub. L. 104-132, 110 Stat. 1214 (1996). For a general description of AEDPA, with cross-references to more detailed discussions, see *supra* § 3.2.

[22] *See* 28 U.S.C.A. § 2244(d) (West 1994 & Supp. 1998) (nonopt-in statute of limitations), *id.* § 2263 (West Supp. 1998) (opt-in statute of limitations). The difference between "nonopt-in" and "opt-in" cases is discussed *supra* § 3.2. The divergent statutes of limitations and tolling provisions that apply in the two types of cases are discussed *supra* § 5.1b.

[23] *See supra* §§ 3.4b n.14, 5.1b nn.79-90 and accompanying text.

[24] *See supra* § 5.1b n.91 and accompanying text.

[25] Rule 8(c) of the Rules Governing § 2254 Cases (emphasis added). *Accord* Rule 8(c) of the Rules Governing § 2255 Proceedings. *See, e.g.*, Weygandt v. Look, 718 F.2d 952, 954 (9th Cir. 1983) ("These [Habeas] rules do not limit the appointment of counsel ... at any stage" (discussing Rule 8(c) of the Rules Governing § 2254 Cases)); other authority cited *infra* § 12.3b n.58.

[26] *McFarland, supra*, 512 U.S. at 860 (O'Connor, J., concurring in the judgment in part). *Cf. Sterling v. Scott, supra*, 57 F.3d at 458 & n.9 (following first *In re Lindsey* decision, *supra*, in holding that Anti-Drug Abuse Act does not authorize use of federally funded counsel to exhaust available state postconviction remedies in "mixed petition" situations); *In re Lindsey, supra*, 875 F.2d at 1507-09 (Criminal Justice Act does not authorize appointment of counsel to assist petitioners in pursuing state postconviction proceedings necessary to exhaust state remedies); Wilson v. Horn, 1997 WL 137343 (E.D. Pa. Mar. 24, 1997) (denying request for appointment of

for appointment at this early, but often most critical, stage of the proceeding is that appointment of counsel is discretionary at this stage of a noncapital case.[27] Not until two later stages — stages that often are not reached before the petition is dismissed or denied — does the appointment of counsel become mandatory for indigent noncapital petitioners, namely, (a) when counsel is "necessary for effective utilization of [the] discovery procedures" that Habeas Rule 6 authorizes district courts to grant "in the exercise of [their] discretion and for good cause shown,"[28] or (b) when the district court determines that "an evidentiary hearing is required."[29] Strategic and tactical concerns also come into play at this stage. For example, a petitioner being satisfactorily assisted by volunteer counsel of the prisoner's choice risks the loss of that arrangement should an application for appointment of counsel prompt the court to appoint someone else pursuant to the local appointment plan.[30] Moreover, the petitioner must consider the possibility that an early application for appointment of counsel will dispose a cost-conscious federal judge[31] to dismiss a petition summarily that otherwise might survive dismissal. Statute of limitations considerations of the sort discussed in the next previous paragraph in regard to capital petitions, and also discussed in §§ 5.1a and 11.1 *supra*, might also come into play. In deciding whether to submit a prefiling application in light of these considerations, the petitioner should be attentive to local rules and practice.[32]

(2) The petitioner may file a motion for appointment of counsel simultaneously with the petition — with the possibility that an amended

---

counsel under § 848(q) to pursue claims in state post-conviction proceedings). Neither the majority nor the dissent in *McFarland* discussed Habeas Rule 8(c).

[27] *See infra* § 12.3b. On the other hand, the importance of prefiling legal assistance to the fairness and adequacy of postconviction proceedings may make the incipient *constitutional* right to counsel *strongest* at this stage. *See supra* notes 11-19 and accompanying text. *See generally supra* § 7.2; *infra* § 12.4.

[28] Rule 6(a) of the Rules Governing § 2254 Cases (discussed *infra* § 12.3b nn.85-90 and accompanying text). *Accord* Rule 6(a) of the Rules Governing § 2255 Proceedings. *See generally infra* § 19.4 (habeas corpus discovery).

[29] Rule 8(c) of the Rules Governing § 2254 Cases (discussed *infra* § 12.3b nn.91-92 and accompanying text). *Accord* Rule 8(c) of the Rules Governing § 2255 Proceedings. *See generally infra* Chapter 20 (mandatory and discretionary habeas corpus hearings).

[30] *Cf. supra* note 8. *See generally* Wilson v. Mintzes, 761 F.2d 275, 279 (6th Cir. 1985); Birt v. Montgomery, 709 F.2d 690, 694 (11th Cir. 1983), *cert. denied*, 469 U.S. 874 (1984) (both discussing right to counsel of choice in criminal cases).

[31] Under 18 U.S.C. § 3006A(a)(2)(B) (1994), the federal judiciary, not the State, reimburses appointed counsel.

[32] *See generally* Robinson v. Fairman, 704 F.2d 368, 372 & n.7 (7th Cir. 1983) (appointment of counsel valuable if *pro se* petition is ambiguous but "not beyond an explanation that might preclude" dismissal).

petition might thereafter be filed by an attorney should the court appoint one.[33] This procedure allows the prisoner to use filing of the petition (a) to satisfy any applicable statutes of limitations, (b) to demonstrate the substantiality of its claims, (c) to suggest the possibility of other claims that a lawyer would have the investigative resources and legal acumen to discern,[34] and (d) to reveal the need for legal representation in developing and arguing both sets of claims.[35] On the other hand, strategic and tactical considerations of the sort discussed in point (1) above may counsel against filing an application at this stage.[36]

(3) Volunteer counsel may prepare and sign the petition and file an application to be appointed pursuant to the Criminal Justice Act (or, in capital cases, the Anti-Drug Abuse Act of 1988) and the local appointment plan, if appropriate. Some of the tactical considerations mentioned in point (1) also would apply at this stage.

(4) Because in *noncapital* cases the statutory argument for the appointment of counsel is stronger once the court grants the petitioner discovery,[37] and is airtight once the court orders an evidentiary hearing, the noncapital petitioner or his volunteer counsel may decide to defer filing the application for counsel in a noncapital case until those stages of the case.[38] If the petitioner is proceeding *pro se* and if the local rules have not liberalized the applicable standards, an application at this stage is the most likely to succeed and the least likely to contribute to a premature dismissal of the case.[39] In cases involving volunteer counsel, this procedure may appear awkward because

---

[33] *See supra* note 19.

[34] *See* Fendler v. Goldsmith, 728 F.2d 1181, 1190 (9th Cir. 1983) (remanded with instructions to appoint counsel to assist petitioner in developing legal claim to which he vaguely alluded on appeal).

[35] *See* Bounds v. Smith, 430 U.S. 817, 827-28 (1977) (counsel is especially important when postconviction petitioner must conduct evidentiary hearing and brief legal points not previously made by counsel in brief on direct appeal).

[36] If the court denies the application at this or another stage, the petitioner may request that the denial be without prejudice to a later application. *See infra* § 12.5 (interlocutory appeals from denials of counsel that effectively foreclose meaningful access to the remedy).

[37] Rule 6(a) of the Rules Governing § 2254 Cases. *Accord* Rule 6(a) of the Rules Governing § 2255 Proceedings. *See infra* §§ 12.3b nn.85-90 and accompanying text, 19.4.

[38] Rule 8(c) of the Rules Governing § 2254 Cases. *Accord* Rule 8(c) of the Rules Governing § 2255 Proceedings. *See* Miller v. Solem, 758 F.2d 144, 145 & n.2 (8th Cir. 1985) (remanding for hearing and appointment of counsel); *Fendler v. Goldsmith, supra,* 728 F.2d at 1190; Lamb v. Estelle, 667 F.2d 492, 496-97 (5th Cir. 1982); Wood v. Wainwright, 597 F.2d 1054 (5th Cir. 1979); *infra* §§ 12.3b nn.91-92 and accompanying text, 19.4; *infra* Chapter 20. *See also Bounds v. Smith, supra,* 430 U.S. at 827-28 (discussed *supra* note 35).

[39] *See* Alford v. United States, 709 F.2d 418 (1st Cir. 1983) (no waiver of right to counsel by waiting until hearing is ordered to request counsel).

counsel theretofore proceeded without appointment. That consideration should not control, however. A request for *nonretroactive* appointment renders counsel's prior activities essentially irrelevant for appointment purposes, while an application for a *retroactive* appointment may be justified on the ground that a request for appointment properly awaited the court's determination that the claims in the case were sufficiently complex and substantial to warrant evidentiary proceedings.[40]

(5) The final option discussed here is for volunteer counsel to seek an award of costs and attorney's fees — and, as a prerequisite, an *ex post* appointment — *after* the case has been completed at the district court level, or even following an appeal.[41] Nothing in the relevant provisions of the Criminal Justice Act (or, in capital cases, in the Anti-Drug Abuse Act of 1988) forbids this procedure;[42] section 3006A(d)(3) of the Criminal Justice Act may well

---

[40] *See* Bell v. Watkins, 692 F.2d 999, 1014 (5th Cir. 1982), *cert. denied,* 464 U.S. 843 (1983) (pre-Anti-Drug Abuse Act capital case) (although capital prisoner was represented by volunteer counsel throughout lengthy prior proceedings, court of appeals directed lower court, having ordered hearing on petition, to appoint counsel retroactively "so that they could be remunerated in accordance with [Criminal Justice Act]" (citing Rule 8(c) of the Rules Governing § 2254 Cases)); authority cited *infra* § 12.3b n.92. *Cf.* Caruth v. Pinkney, 683 F.2d 1044, 1049 (7th Cir. 1982), *cert. denied,* 459 U.S. 1214 (1983) (court should not deny appointment of volunteer counsel "solely" because attorney who takes case may not be fully compensated for his efforts).

[41] *See, e.g.,* Dicks v. Dutton, 969 F.2d 207, 210-11 (6th Cir. 1992) (reversing district court's order denying request for attorney's fees pursuant to 18 U.S.C. § 3006A(d) and Anti-Drug Abuse Act, and remanding for evidentiary hearing to resolve factual questions regarding counsel's work on case); Simmons v. Lockhart, 931 F.2d 1226, 1229-31 (8th Cir. 1991) (retroactive appointment and compensation of counsel in capital case covering period after effective date of act authorizing appointment); Landano v. Rafferty, 859 F.2d 301, 302 (3d Cir. 1988) (contemplating retroactive appointment of counsel); Spivey v. Zant, No. 80-7243 (11th Cir. April 20, 1983) (granting *post hoc* motion for appointment of counsel and reimbursement); *Bell v. Watkins, supra,* 692 F.2d at 1014; *Caruth v. Pinkney, supra,* 683 F.2d at 1049 (*dicta*); Bozeman v. Lambert, No. 83-H-579-N (M.D. Ala. June 29, 1984) (discussed *infra* note 42); Washington v. Watkins, No. GC 79-93-K-P (N.D. Miss. Feb. 6, 1980); Carmona v. Ward, No. 75 Civ. 6219 (S.D.N.Y. 1979). *See also* United States v. Perry, 471 F.2d 1069 (D.C. Cir. 1972) (retroactive appointment of counsel in direct criminal appeal; appointment effective from date appeal taken); Miranda v. United States, 458 F.2d 1179, 1182 & n.2 (2d Cir.), *cert. denied,* 409 U.S. 874 (1972). *But cf.* Hill v. Lockhart, 992 F.2d 801, 803 (8th Cir. 1993) (although 21 U.S.C. § 848(q) clearly authorizes appointment and compensation of counsel involved in state clemency proceedings, "in most if not all cases, a § 848(q)(10) request for compensation for such state [clemency] proceedings should be made prior to performing the services."). Once an appointment is made by the district court, it extends through the appellate stages of the case. *See* 18 U.S.C. § 3006A(c) (1994); 6TH CIR. R. 12(a), 12(b); 8TH CIR. R. App. IV, Plan to Expedite Criminal Appeals, II.

[42] *See Bozeman v. Lambert, supra,* No. 83-H-579-N (habeas corpus provision of Criminal Justice Act "does not explicitly provide for retroactive appointment, but § 3006A(b), which governs appointment for criminal defendants, provides that "appointment may be made retroactive to include representation furnished ... prior to appointment"; retroactive appointment granted).

endorse it;[43] and the analogy to after-the-fact attorney's fees motions in civil rights cases is available.[44] In noncapital cases, in which motions seeking the discretionary appointment of counsel may increase the court's incentive to dispose of the case summarily rather than appoint counsel, this procedure has the advantage of keeping financial considerations as far as possible from the mind of the judge at the time she is adjudicating the petition, ruling on motions for discovery and evidentiary hearings, and the like.

b. *The statutory right.* Several statutory provisions *authorize* — and, in capital cases and in certain circumstances in noncapital cases, *require* — the appointment of counsel in habeas corpus proceedings brought by indigent prisoners.[45] Those provisions, which provide the initial points of reference in deciding whether to appoint counsel, are discussed below in the order in which they become important as the case proceeds.

Commencement of proceedings — capital cases. The Anti-Drug Abuse Act of 1988 mandates the appointment of counsel for any indigent petitioner seeking to vacate or set aside a death sentence in habeas corpus proceedings pursuant to 28 U.S.C. §§ 2254 or 2255.[46] The 1988 Act, as amended in 1996, establishes

---

[43] *See* 18 U.S.C. § 3006A(d)(3) (1994) (discussed *infra* § 12.3c) (retroactive increases in amount of compensation in cases involving "extended or complex representation"). The Anti-Drug Abuse Act of 1988 also contemplates appointment of counsel after the commencement of habeas corpus proceedings inasmuch as it authorizes appointment if the petitioner "is *or becomes* financially unable to obtain adequate representation." 21 U.S.C.A. § 848(q)(4)(A) (West 1994 & Supp. 1998) (emphasis added).

[44] *See* 42 U.S.C. § 1988 (1994) (Civil Rights Act attorney's fees provision); United States v. Feldman, 788 F.2d 625, 626 (9th Cir. 1986), *cert. denied,* 479 U.S. 1067 (1987) (noting analogy to section 1988, but pointing out that Criminal Justice Act, unlike section 1988, makes fees available to losing as well as winning applicants). *Cf. Caruth v. Pinkney, supra,* 683 F.2d at 1049 (even if court is not disposed to grant compensation under Criminal Justice Act to volunteer counsel representing indigent habeas corpus petitioner, court should appoint counsel in order to permit him to collect fees under section 1988 should petitioner succeed); *Bozeman v. Lambert, supra,* No. 83-H-579-N ("retroactive" appointment of counsel where "[p]etitioners have prevailed on their claims"). *See also* In re Barker, 693 F.2d 925, 927 (9th Cir. 1982); *supra* § 12.2 n.10. *But cf. supra* § 12.2 n.7.

[45] *See* 18 U.S.C. § 3006A(a)(2)(B) (1994) (noncapital cases); 21 U.S.C.A. §§ 848(q), 848(r) (West 1994 & Supp. 1998) (capital cases); Rules 6(a) and 8(c) of the Rules Governing § 2254 Cases and of the Rules Governing § 2255 Proceedings (noncapital cases). *See also* Murray v. Giarratano, 492 U.S. 1, 12 n.7 (1989) (listing States that automatically provide habeas corpus counsel for capital defendants); *id.* at 30 n.26 (Steven, J., dissenting) (similar).

[46] Anti-Drug Abuse Act of 1988, Pub. L. No. 100-690, 102 Stat. 4393-94 (1988), 21 U.S.C.A. §§ 848(q)-848(r) (West 1994 & Supp. 1998). *See, e.g.,* McFarland v. Scott, 512 U.S. 849, 854 (1994) (section 848(q)(4)(B) "grants indigent capital defendants a mandatory right to qualified legal counsel and related services '[i]n any [federal] post conviction proceeding'" (quoting 21 U.S.C. § 848(q)(4)(B))); In re Heidnik, 112 F.3d 105, 109, 112 (3d Cir. 1997) (after finding that

minimum qualifications for appointed counsel in capital habeas corpus cases,[47] provides for appointment of co-counsel as appropriate and necessary under the circumstances,[48] requires appointed counsel to continue representing the

---

next-friend had standing to proceed on behalf of capital defendant, court orders appointment of counsel to represent next-friend; "normal" rule "in favor of appointing counsel and granting a stay under *McFarland*" applies in next-friend situation); Weeks v. Jones, 100 F.3d 124, 127-28 (11th Cir. 1996) (*per curiam*) (district court erred in setting aside appointment of counsel based on court's assessment that claims in petition were frivolous; "[b]ecause § 848(1)(4)(B) mandates counsel for indigent prisoners *to prepare* federal habeas petitions, a substantive, merits assessment of the petition is irrelevant to the appointment of counsel."); Barnard v Collins, 13 F.3d 871, 879 (5th Cir. 1994) (district court erred in denying motion for appointment of counsel on ground that claims in petition lacked merit; "§ 848(q)(4)(B) does not condition the appointment of counsel on the substantiality or nonfrivolousness of petitioner's habeas claims"); Brown v. Vasquez, 952 F.2d 1164, 1166-68 (9th Cir.), *cert. denied,* 503 U.S. 1011 (1992); Coleman v. Vasquez, 771 F. Supp. 300, 302-04 (N.D. Cal. 1991). Indigence is present if the petitioner "is or becomes financially unable to obtain adequate representation or investigative, expert, or other reasonably necessary services." 21 U.S.C. § 848(q)(4)(B). *See also* AMERICAN BAR ASSOCIATION, GUIDELINES FOR THE APPOINTMENT AND PERFORMANCE OF COUNSEL IN DEATH PENALTY CASES (adopted Feb. 1989).

In the Antiterrorism and Effective Death Penalty Act of 1996, Pub. L. 104-132, 110 Stat. 1214 (1996), Congress confirmed the preexisting rule that the Anti-Drug Abuse Act mandates the appointment of counsel in capital habeas corpus proceedings. *See* 28 U.S.C.A. § 2254(h) (West 1994 & Supp. 1998) (stating that courts have discretion whether or not to appoint counsel for indigent petitioners in habeas corpus proceedings *other than* those governed by "section 408 of the Controlled Substances Act" (emphasis added)).

[47] 21 U.S.C.A. § 848(q)(6) (West 1994 & Supp. 1998) ("at least one [appellate-level] attorney ... must have been admitted to practice in the court of appeals for not less than five years, and must have had not less than three years' experience in the handling of appeals in that court in felony cases"). *See id.* § 848(q)(5) (analogous qualifications for trial-level attorney); McFarland v. Scott, *supra,* 512 U.S. at 851, 854 n.2 ("Congress created a right to *qualified* legal representation for capital defendants in federal habeas corpus proceedings" (emphasis added); "[c]ounsel appointed to represent capital defendants in postconviction proceedings must meet more stringent experience criteria than attorneys appointed to represent noncapital defendants under [the Criminal Justice Act,] 18 U.S.C. § 3006A."). *See also* Hunter v. Delo, 62 F.3d 271, 274 (8th Cir. 1995) (assessing petitioner's right to obtain discharge of originally appointed counsel and substitution of new attorney by applying Sixth Amendment requirement that petitioner justify request by "showing justifiable dissatisfaction with appointed counsel [such as] a conflict of interest, an irreconcilable conflict, or a complete breakdown in communication between the attorney and the defendant").

[48] 21 U.S.C.A. § 848(q)(7) (West 1994 & Supp. 1998) ("court, for good cause, may appoint another attorney whose background, knowledge, or experience would otherwise enable him or her to properly represent the defendant, with due consideration to the seriousness of the possible penalty and to the unique and complex nature of the litigation"). *See* Simmons v. Lockhart, 931 F.2d 1226, 1231 (8th Cir. 1991) (awarding attorney's fees to appointed counsel and four other lawyers who lent assistance "in this case off and on" but who were never "appointed by name to represent Simmons," because "[t]he new statute expressly sanctions the appointment of several lawyers in federal capital cases on direct and collateral review" and "Simmons's successive petition required a large amount of factual investigation, legal research, and intellectual effort in a complex area of the law"); In re Lindsey, 875 F.2d 1502, 1507 n.3 (11th Cir. 1989).

petitioner throughout "all available post-conviction process[es]" and even in state executive clemency proceedings thereafter,[49] makes provision for *ex parte* application by appointed counsel for and funding by the court of "investigative, expert, or other services [as] are reasonably necessary,"[50] including prior to the filing of the petition,[51] and provides for compensation to be fixed by the courts at "such rates or amounts as the court determines to be reasonably necessary" with explicit provision for higher rates than are generally applicable in noncapital cases.[52]

---

[49] 21 U.S.C.A. § 848(q)(8) (West 1994 & Supp. 1998) ("Unless replaced by similarly qualified counsel upon the attorney's own motion or upon motion of the defendant, each attorney so appointed shall represent the defendant throughout ... all available post-conviction process, together with applications for stays of execution and other appropriate motions and procedures, and shall also represent the defendant in such competency proceedings and proceedings for executive or other clemency as may be available to the defendant"). *See, e.g.,* Hill v. Lockhart, 992 F.2d 801, 803 (8th Cir. 1993) (district court erred in denying compensation for representation in clemency proceedings; "plain language of § 848(q) evidences a congressional intent to insure that indigent state petitioners receive 'reasonably necessary' competency and clemency services from appointed, compensated counsel"). The 8th Circuit has established the following requirements for compensation of counsel in clemency proceedings: (1) "the request is made as part of a non-frivolous federal habeas corpus proceeding"; (2) "state law provides no avenue to obtain compensation for these services"; (3) "in most if not all cases, a § 848(q)(10) request for compensation for such state [clemency] proceedings should be made prior to performing the services." *Id.*

[50] 21 U.S.C.A. § 848(q)(9) (West 1994 & Supp. 1998). Such services must be requested by "the defendant's attorney." *Id.* Section 19.3 *infra* describes the procedures for making *ex parte* applications for investigators and experts in capital federal habeas corpus proceedings. As that section explains, these procedures were changed by the Antiterrorism and Effective Death Penalty Act of 1996, Pub. L. 104-132, 110 Stat. 1214 (1996).

[51] *See McFarland v. Scott, supra,* 512 U.S. at 855 ("21 U.S.C. § 848(q)(9) ... entitles capital [postconviction petitioners] to a variety of expert and investigative services upon a showing of necessity.... The services of investigators and other experts may be critical in the preapplication phase of a habeas corpus proceedings, when possible claims and their factual bases are researched and identified.").

[52] 21 U.S.C.A. § 848(q)(10) (West 1994 & Supp. 1998) ("Notwithstanding the rates and maximum limits generally applicable to criminal cases and any other provision of law to the contrary, the court shall fix the compensation to be paid to attorneys appointed under this subsection and the fees and expenses to be paid for investigative, expert, and other reasonably necessary services ... at such rates or amounts as the court determines to be reasonably necessary to carry out the requirements" of Anti-Drug Abuse Act). "The language of this section by its terms authorizes federal courts to compensate attorneys appointed to represent capital defendants ... in an amount exceeding the $2,500 limit of § 3006A(d)(2) of ... [the Criminal Justice] Act." In re Berger, 498 U.S. 233, 234 (1991) (*per curiam*). The Administrative Office of the United States Courts has undertaken to set fee schedules pursuant to this provision. *See, e.g., id.* (quoting "Guidelines for Administration of Criminal Justice Act"). *See also Simmons v. Lockhart, supra,* 931 F.2d at 1229-30 (concluding that fee provisions of Anti-Drug Abuse Act should not be applied retroactively to work performed prior to Act's effective date of November 18, 1988). The Supreme Court has

Commencement of proceedings — noncapital cases. The least mandatory but most widely applicable counsel provision, available at every stage of a federal habeas corpus case, is 18 U.S.C. § 3006A(a)(2)(B), a provision of the Criminal Justice Act of 1964[53] as amended by the Criminal Justice Act Revision of 1986.[54] Section 3006A(a)(2)(B) requires district courts to promulgate plans for the appointment of counsel under which "representation may be provided for any financially eligible person" in a case arising under the federal habeas corpus statute "[w]henever the United States magistrate or the court determines that the interests of justice so require."[55] The Rules Governing § 2254 Cases, which were promulgated after section 3006A(a)(2)(B) first was added to the Criminal Justice

---

chosen to establish a flat rate of $5,000 for counsel in capital proceedings before the Court rather than employing "an individual case-by-case approach to counsel fees" because an individualized "inquiry is time consuming, its result necessarily imprecise, and it would lead us into an area in which we have little experience." *In re Berger, supra* at 236. As the 8th Circuit has observed, the *Berger* considerations have less weight when it comes to fee determinations by lower federal courts, which "have a long experience under the Criminal Justice Act with individualized attorneys' fees decisions" and which have developed practices for screening requests efficiently and "avoid[ing] imprecision." *Simmons v. Lockhart, supra*, 931 F.2d at 1233. *See also Hill v. Lockhart, supra*, 992 F.2d at 802 ("Because of disparities in the markets for legal services throughout the circuit, we conclude that it would frustrate the congressional purpose if we either imposed uniform circuit compensation standards or readily substituted our judgment for that of the district court.").

Capital federal habeas corpus proceedings "commenced" after the effective date of the Antiterrorism and Effective Death Penalty Act (AEDPA) — April 24, 1996 — are subject to new maximum compensation levels. AEDPA establishes a maximum rate of $125 per hour for compensation of counsel, 21 U.S.C.A. § 848(q)(10)(A) (West 1994 & Supp. 1998) (as amended), and limits expenditures for investigative and expert services to a total of $7500 unless the district court finds that a higher sum is warranted for "services of an unusual character or duration" and that finding is approved by the Chief Judge of the Circuit, *id.* § 848(q)(10)(B) (as amended). AEDPA also provides that the fees paid for counsel and support (*e.g.*, expert and investigative) services in capital habeas corpus commenced on or after April 24, 1996 shall be disclosed to the public "after the disposition of the petition." Antiterrorism and Effective Death Penalty Act, Pub. L. 104-132 § 903(b), 110 Stat. 1214, 1318 (1996). *See generally supra* § 3.4 (discussing cases to which AEDPA does and does not apply).

[53] 18 U.S.C. § 3006A (1994).

[54] Pub. L. 99-651, tit. I, § 102, 100 Stat. 3642 (1986).

[55] 18 U.S.C. § 3006A(a)(2)(B) (1994) (citing 28 U.S.C. § 2254 (1994)). *See* Ewing v. Rodgers, 826 F.2d 967, 971 (10th Cir. 1987); Powell v. Livesay, 660 F. Supp. 82, 84 (M.D. Tenn. 1987). The same provision applies to federal prisoner actions under 28 U.S.C. §§ 2241, 2255. *See infra* § 41.4b n.27 and accompanying text. *Cf.* In re Lindsey, 875 F.2d 1502, 1507-09 (11th Cir. 1989) (Criminal Justice Act does not authorize appointment of counsel to assist petitioners in pursuing state postconviction proceedings necessary to exhaust state remedies). The relevant district court's plan for the appointment of counsel should be consulted for provisions in addition to, or that deviate from, the ones discussed in this section.

Act[56] and supersede conflicting statutes,[57] expressly endorse the Act's allowance for counsel *at any stage* of a case "if the interest of justice so requires."[58]

The legislative histories of section 3006A(a)(2)(B) and the Habeas Rules call for a liberal and flexible construction of section 3006(a)(2)(B)'s "interests of justice" language in habeas corpus cases and place limitations, enforceable on appeal, on the district court's discretion to deny counsel.[59] The House report on section 3006A(a)(2)(B)'s predecessor, section 3006A(g),[60] recognizes that habeas corpus and similar proceedings often present "serious and complex issues

---

[56] *See* Pub. L. 91-447, § 1(b), 84 Stat. 916 (1970), *codified as* 18 U.S.C. § 3006A(g), *recodified,* 18 U.S.C. § 3006A(a)(2)(B) (1994).

[57] 28 U.S.C. § 2072 (1994).

[58] Rule 8(c) of the Rules Governing § 2254 Cases (discussed *supra* § 12.3a nn.25-27 and accompanying text) ("These rules do not limit the appointment of counsel under 18 U.S.C. § 3006A at any stage of the case if the interest of justice so requires"). *Accord* Rule 8(c) of the Rules Governing § 2255 Proceedings. *See, e.g.,* Hodge v. Police Officers, 802 F.2d 58, 60 (2d Cir. 1986) (*dicta*) ("In habeas corpus cases, counsel must be appointed for qualified indigents when a hearing is required; the court may appoint counsel at any earlier stage if it deems appointment desirable"); Franklin v. Rose, 765 F.2d 82, 85 (6th Cir. 1985) (remanded with suggestion that counsel be appointed if petitioner's claims are not "totally spurious"); Miller v. Solem, 758 F.2d 144, 145 (8th Cir. 1985); Fendler v. Goldsmith, 728 F.2d 1181, 1190 (9th Cir. 1983) (remanded with instructions to appoint counsel to assist petitioner in developing legal claim to which he vaguely alluded on appeal); Weygandt v. Look, 718 F.2d 952, 954 (9th Cir. 1983); Robinson v. Fairman, 704 F.2d 368, 372 & n.7 (7th Cir. 1983).

The Antiterrorism and Effective Death Penalty Act of 1996, Pub. L. 104-132, 110 Stat. 1214 (1996), confirms the preexisting rule that federal courts "may appoint counsel for an applicant [for a writ of habeas corpus] who is or becomes financially unable to afford counsel" and that such appointments "shall be governed by section 3006 of title 18." 28 U.S.C.A. § 2254(h) (West 1994 & Supp. 1998).

[59] *See* Williams v. Kullman, 722 F.2d 1048, 1050 (2d Cir. 1983) ("If the writ of habeas corpus is to continue to have meaningful purpose, it must be accessible not only to those with a strong legal background or the financial means to retain counsel, but also to the mass of uneducated unrepresented prisoners"). The statute that generally governs the appointment of counsel in civil cases, 28 U.S.C. § 1915(e)(1), which the Criminal Justice Act and Habeas Rules liberalize insofar as it applies to habeas corpus cases (*see supra* § 12.3a n.6; *infra* note 62), also creates a responsibility enforceable on appeal to appoint counsel in the interest of justice. *See, e.g.,* Hodge v. Police Officers, 802 F.2d 58 (2d Cir. 1986) (civil rights case; denial of counsel reversed and remanded for reconsideration under section 1915(d)); Whisenant v. Yuam, 739 F.2d 160, 163-64 (4th Cir. 1984); Maclin v. Freake, 650 F.2d 885, 886-87 (7th Cir. 1981) (discretion to deny counsel under section 1915 "'not left to a court's inclination, but to its judgment; and its judgment is to be guided by sound legal principles'"; denial of counsel reversed (quoting Albemarle Paper Co. v. Moody, 422 U.S. 405, 416 (1975))).

[60] Although the Criminal Justice Act Revision of 1986 moved the habeas corpus counsel provision from subsection (g) to subsection (a)(2)(B) of 18 U.S.C. § 3006A, it left the provision linguistically intact and reveals no intention to change the provision's well-established meaning and application.

of law and fact"[61] of a sort requiring the assistance of counsel. The House report on Habeas Rule 8(c) states, in turn, that the federal courts should make counsel available from the beginning of habeas corpus proceedings if the petition "raises a substantial legal issue."[62] Finally, in discussing the discretionary "may" language in section 3006A(a)(2)(B)'s predecessor provision, the congressional report on the provision states that the court "*should*" appoint counsel when "necessary to insure a fair hearing."[63]

In conformity with these expressions of congressional intent, the courts generally have endorsed the appointment of counsel to represent indigent and legally unsophisticated prisoners in:

(1) Capital cases, even before Congress in 1988 made the appointment of counsel mandatory,[64] given the especially wide range of difficult legal questions raised by such decisions as *Furman v. Georgia*[65] and *Gregg v. Georgia;*[66] the complex bifurcated nature of capital trials which makes

---

[61] H.R. REP. No. 1546, 91st Cong., 2d Sess. (1970), *reprinted in* 1970 U.S. CODE CONG. & ADMIN. NEWS 3982, 3993.

[62] H.R. REP. No. 1471, 94th Cong., 2d Sess. (1976), *reprinted in* 1976 U.S. CODE CONG. & ADMIN. NEWS 2478, 2481. *See also Franklin v. Rose, supra*, 765 F.2d at 85 (counsel should be appointed if claims are not "'totally spurious'" and require "'aid of competent counsel'" (quoting Deloney v. Estelle, 679 F.2d 372, 373 (5th Cir. 1982)). The right to counsel in habeas corpus cases under section 3006A(a)(2)(B) and Habeas Rule 8(c) is broader than in other civil cases, in which 28 U.S.C.A. § 1915(e) (1) (West 1994 & Supp. 1998) (discussed *supra* note 59) generally controls. *See Hodge v. Police Officers, supra*, 802 F.2d at 61 (citing cases) (under section 1915(d) but not section 3006A(a)(2)(B), indigent party must demonstrate inability to secure counsel willing to take case on contingent fee basis or voluntarily); Aldabe v. Aldabe, 616 F.2d 1089, 1093 (9th Cir. 1980) (stiff "exceptional circumstances" test under section 1915(d)); *supra* § 12.3a n.6 (stricter indigence standard under section 1915(d) than under section 3006A(a)(2)(B)). Because section 3006A(a)(2)(B) and Habeas Rule 8(c) apply exclusively to a population of mostly indigent and poorly educated and incarcerated persons facing society's severest restraints, those provisions reasonably may be understood to create a firmer presumption in favor of appointed counsel than does the more general and generally applicable counsel provision in section 1915. *See Hodge v. Police Officers, supra*, 802 F.2d at 60-61. Because the standards under section 1915(d) are no more and may be less demanding than those controlling appointment of counsel in habeas corpus cases, precedents requiring counsel under the former statute should be persuasive in habeas corpus cases and are cited here.

[63] H.R. REP. No. 1546, *supra* note 61, at 3993 (emphasis added).

[64] *See supra* notes 46-52 and accompanying text (mandatory right to counsel in capital habeas corpus cases since 1988).

[65] 408 U.S. 238 (1972).

[66] 428 U.S. 153 (1976). *See generally* Jack Greenberg, *Capital Punishment as a System*, 91 YALE L.J. 908, 921 (1982).

special demands on counsel not present in other cases;[67] and the especially stringent requirements of procedural due process and reliability that the 8th Amendment places on procedures leading to death sentences.[68]

(2) Cases that turn on substantial and complex procedural, legal or mixed legal and factual questions (*e.g.*, the fair composition of grand and petit juries, the voluntariness of confessions, and the effective assistance of counsel).[69]

---

[67] *See, e.g.*, Caldwell v. Mississippi, 472 U.S. 320 (1985); Estelle v. Smith, 451 U.S. 454 (1981); Bullington v. Missouri, 451 U.S. 430 (1981). *See also* Strickland v. Washington, 466 U.S. 668, 706 (1984) (Brennan, J., concurring).

[68] *See* authority cited *supra* §§ 2.6, 7.2f, 12.3a nn.13-20 and accompanying text. Decisions recognizing a special need for postconviction counsel in capital cases, or noting Congress' recognition of the same need in the Anti-Drug Abuse Act of 1988, are, *e.g.*, McFarland v. Scott, 512 U.S. 849, 859 (1994) ("By providing indigent capital defendants with a mandatory right to qualified legal counsel in these proceedings, Congress has recognized that federal habeas corpus has a particularly important role to play in promoting fundamental fairness in the imposition of the death penalty."); *id.* at 855-56 (quoted *supra* § 12.3a n.19 and accompanying text); Murray v. Giarratano, 492 U.S. 1, 14 (1989) (Kennedy, J., concurring in the judgment); *id.* at 26-29 (Stevens, J., dissenting); Brown v. Vasquez, 952 F.2d 1164 (9th Cir.), *cert. denied*, 503 U.S. 1011 (1992); Battle v. Armontrout, 902 F.2d 701, 702 (8th Cir. 1990) ("Of course, the complexity of the issues takes on an even greater significance in a case involving the death penalty."); Chaney v. Lewis, 801 F.2d 1191, 1196 (9th Cir. 1986) (petitioner's death sentence and court's holdings "placed the case in a different posture and increased the complexities of issues with which the district court must deal on remand"); Bell v. Watkins, 692 F.2d 999, 1014 (5th Cir. 1982), *cert. denied*, 464 U.S. 843 (1983); Hitchcock v. Eyman, 418 F.2d 1245, 1246 (9th Cir. 1969) (*per curiam*), *cert. denied*, 404 U.S. 946 (1971) (severity of sentence warrants appointment of counsel); Giarratano v. Murray, 668 F. Supp. 511 (E.D. Va. 1986), *aff'd*, 847 F.2d 1118, 1122 (4th Cir. 1988) (*en banc*), *rev'd sub nom.* Murray v. Giarratano, 492 U.S. 1 (1989) (capital cases present special difficulties because "inmate is required to rapidly perform the [especially] complex and difficult work necessary to file a timely petition [when] he is the least capable of doing so"); Jarrell v. Balkcom, No. C79-896A (N.D. Ga. Sept. 2, 1980) (appointment because "petitioner has been sentenced to death"); Gibson v. Jackson, 443 F. Supp. 239, 250 (M.D. Ga. 1977), *vac'd & remanded on other grounds*, 578 F.2d 1045 (5th Cir. 1978), *cert. denied*, 439 U.S. 1119 (1979); Carey v. Garrison, 403 F. Supp. 395, 397 (W.D.N.C. 1975); GUIDELINES, *supra* § 12.3a n.8, at §§ 2.14(B), 3.16 (discussed in Memorandum, *supra* § 12.2 n.2) (special efforts made to provide counsel in death penalty habeas corpus cases).

[69] *See, e.g.*, Reese v. Fulcomer, 946 F.2d 247, 264 (3d Cir. 1991), *cert. denied*, 503 U.S. 988 (1992) (citing cases) ("[f]actors influencing a court's decision [to appoint counsel in habeas corpus cases] include the complexity of the factual and legal issues in the case"; district court did not abuse discretion in denying counsel because issues in case "were neither factually nor legally complex" and petitioner "indicated that he fully comprehended the issues"); Hughes v. Joliet Correctional Center, 931 F.2d 425, 429 (7th Cir. 1991) (section 1915 case) ("In deciding whether to grant a motion for appointment of counsel, a district judge must be alert to the pitfalls that confront laymen in dealing with nonintuitive procedural requirements applied in a setting of complex legal doctrine."); *Battle v. Armontrout, supra*, 902 F.2d at 702 ("The factual and legal issues are sufficiently complex and numerous that appointment of counsel would benefit both

(3) Cases involving uneducated or mentally or physically impaired petitioners.[70]

(4) Cases likely to require the assistance of experts either in framing or in trying the claims.[71]

Battle and the court by allowing counsel to develop Battle's arguments and focus the court's analysis."); Hodge v. Police Officers, 802 F.2d 58, 61 (2d Cir. 1986) (section 1915 case) (complexity of issues is factor in deciding whether to appoint counsel (discussing Maclin v. Freake, 650 F.2d 885, 888-89 (7th Cir. 1981) (*per curiam*))); *Chaney v. Lewis, supra,* 801 F.2d at 1196; Weygandt v. Look, 718 F.2d 952, 954 (9th Cir. 1983) ("complex[] ... legal issues"); Wilson v. Duckworth, 716 F.2d 415, 418 (7th Cir. 1983); Merritt v. Faulkner, 697 F.2d 761, 764 (7th Cir.), *cert. denied,* 464 U.S. 986 (1983) (section 1915 case) (counsel required for particular claim because of "novelty and complexity"); Branch v. Cole, 686 F.2d 264, 266 (5th Cir. 1982) (*per curiam*) (section 1915 case); United States ex rel. Jones v. Franzen, 676 F.2d 261, 267 (7th Cir. 1982) ("allegations respecting withheld evidence, the admission of codefendant's statement and improper jury sequestration ... raise complex legal issues" which may require "the legal expertise of counsel"); Abduc v. Lane, 468 F. Supp. 33, 37 (E.D. Tenn.), *aff'd,* 588 F.2d 1178 (6th Cir. 1978) (counsel appointed following *prima facie* showing of discrimination in selection of grand jurors); *supra* notes 60-61 and accompanying text (discussing House Judiciary Committee Report on predecessor of section 3006A(a)(2)(B), which calls for appointment of counsel in habeas corpus proceedings presenting "serious and complex issues of law and fact"); authority cited *supra* § 7.2c & *supra* note 68. *Cf.* Terrovona v. Kincheloe, 912 F.2d 1176, 1177 (9th Cir. 1990), *cert. denied,* 499 U.S. 979 (1991) (narrow issues did not require appointment of counsel); Ferguson v. Jones, 905 F.2d 211, 214 (8th Cir. 1990) (motion to appoint counsel properly denied because issues were "straightforward and capable of resolution on the record").

[70] *See, e.g., Merritt v. Faulkner, supra,* 697 F.2d at 764 (section 1915 case) (as to "colorable" claim, counsel required because investigation of crucial facts of causation, treatment, and prognosis was beyond capacity of blind indigent prisoner; counsel required for another claim because of "novelty and complexity"); *Maclin v. Freake, supra,* 650 F.2d at 889-90 (section 1915 case) (because of "mental disease" and "confine[ment] to a wheelchair ... in constant pain," movant is incapable of "developing evidence"); Drone v. Hutto, 565 F.2d 543, 544 (8th Cir. 1977); Pike v. United States, 330 F.2d 53, 54 (5th Cir. 1964). *Cf.* Phelps v. United States Federal Gov't, 15 F.3d 735, 737-38 (8th Cir.), *cert. denied,* 511 U.S. 1114 (1994) (district court did not abuse discretion in refusing to appoint counsel for individual acquitted by reason of insanity who was committed to federal medical center because quality of filings and previous petitions demonstrated petitioner's intelligence and familiarity with legal standards, no evidentiary hearing was required, and petitioner apparently may not have been indigent); La Mere v. Risley, 827 F.2d 622, 626 (9th Cir. 1987) (request for counsel properly denied because petitioner had "good understanding of the issues and the ability to present forcefully and coherently his contentions"); Hudak v. Curators, 586 F.2d 105, 106 (8th Cir. 1978), *cert. denied,* 440 U.S. 985 (1979) (section 1915 case) (appointment of counsel denied former law professor).

[71] *See, e.g.,* Paradis v. Arave, 667 F. Supp. 1361, 1364-65 (D. Idaho 1987), *aff'd in part & rev'd in part on other grounds,* 954 F.2d 1483 (9th Cir. 1992), *vac'd & remanded,* 507 U.S. 1026 (1993); Grigsby v. Mabry, Nos. PB-C-78-32, PB-C-81-2, PB-C-80-429 (E.D. Ark. 1984) (claims and expert testimony described in Lockhart v. McCree, 476 U.S. 162 (1986)). *Cf.* The Anti-Drug Abuse Act of 1988, 21 U.S.C.A. § 848(q) (West 1994 & Supp. 1998) (providing fees for investigative, expert, and other reasonable necessary services); *supra* notes 50-51 and accompanying text; *supra* § 12.3a nn.15-16 and accompanying text. *See generally Hodge v. Police*

(5) Cases in which "the indigent is in no position to investigate crucial facts."[72]

(6) Factually complex cases, *e.g.*, ones involving "conflicting testimony," in which the truth is more likely to "be exposed where both sides are represented by those trained in the presentation of evidence."[73]

Officers, supra, 802 F.2d at 61 (inability of petitioner to present case under circumstances); *infra* § 19.3.

[72] *Maclin v. Freake, supra*, 650 F.2d at 887. *Accord, e.g.*, Abdullah v. Norris, 18 F.3d 571, 573 (8th Cir.), *cert. denied*, 513 U.S. 857 (1994) (factors to consider in determining whether to appoint counsel include "petitioner's ability to investigate and present his claim"); *Reese v. Fulcomer, supra*, 946 F.2d at 264 ("[f]actors influencing a court's decision [to appoint counsel in habeas corpus cases] include ... the pro se petitioner's ability to investigate facts and present claims"); *Battle v. Armontrout, supra*, 902 F.2d at 702 ("Battle's ability to investigate is seriously impaired by his incarceration."); *Hodge v. Police Officers, supra*, 802 F.2d at 61 (section 1915 case) ("substantial factual investigation" required and movant is "unable to conduct the investigation"); Jenkins v. Chemical Bank, 721 F.2d 876, 880 (2d Cir. 1983) (section 1915 case) ("[in]ability to gather and present crucial facts"); *Merritt v. Faulkner, supra*, 697 F.2d at 764 (section 1915 case) (discussed *supra* note 70); Ulmer v. Chancellor, 691 F.2d 209, 211 (5th Cir. 1982) (section 1915 case) (citing cases); Shields v. Jackson, 570 F.2d 284, 286 (8th Cir. 1978) (inmate is "not in a position to adequately investigate the cause"); Peterson v. Nadler, 452 F.2d 754, 758 (8th Cir. 1971) (section 1915 case); Hodge v. Huff, 140 F.2d 686, 687 (D.C. Cir.), *cert. denied*, 322 U.S. 733 (1944) (*dicta*); Richardson v. Miller, 721 F. Supp. 1087 (W.D. Mo. 1989) (extensive discussion of importance of appointing counsel in habeas corpus cases to investigate facts and thus either to avoid need for evidentiary hearing and facilitate dismissal of nonmeritorious claims or to prosecute potentially meritorious fact-based claims); Russell v. Jones, 679 F. Supp. 949, 950 (W.D. Mo. 1988) (counsel appointed and ordered "to make an appropriate factual investigation and to file a report of his investigation"); United States ex rel. Robinson v. Myers, 222 F. Supp. 845, 848 (E.D. Pa. 1963), *aff'd*, 326 F.2d 972 (3d Cir. 1964) (*dicta*). *See also* Jackson v. State, 1998 WL 469953, at *3 (Miss. Aug. 13, 1998) (mandating appointment of counsel for indigent prisoners in state postconviction proceedings because, *inter alia*, "[a]pplications for post-conviction relief often raise issues which require investigation, analysis and presentation of facts outside the appellate record ... [and] [t]he inmate is confined ... [and therefore] unable to investigate").

[73] *Maclin v. Freake, supra*, 650 F.2d at 888. *Accord, e.g., Hodge v. Police Officers, supra*, 802 F.2d at 61 (section 1915 case) ("conflicting evidence implicating the need for cross-examination will be the major proof presented"); Whisenant v. Yuam, 739 F.2d 160, 163 (4th Cir. 1984) (section 1915 case) (*pro se* litigant's version of events sharply conflicts with defendant's "so that the outcome of the case depends largely on credibility"); *Ulmer v. Chancellor, supra*, 691 F.2d at 213 (section 1915 case); Manning v. Lockhart, 623 F.2d 536, 540 (8th Cir. 1980) ("question of credibility of witnesses and ... case presents serious allegations of fact"). *See also Hughes v. Joliet Correctional Center, supra*, 931 F.2d at 429 (section 1915 case) ("layman's need for a lawyer is most acute when a case reaches the stage at which evidence must be obtained and presented"; "suit *had* reached that stage when the defendants moved for summary judgment, since by submitting evidence with their motion the defendants shifted to the plaintiff the burden of producing his own evidence"); United States ex rel. Marshall v. Wilkins, 338 F.2d 404, 406 (2d Cir. 1964) (appointment is appropriate if hearing is required); United States ex rel. Wissenfeld v. Wilkins, 281 F.2d 707, 715-16 (2d Cir. 1960) (complexity of facts makes legal assistance necessary to ensure

Some courts apply even more liberal appointment of counsel rules,[74] assigning attorneys in:

(7) Cases in which the petitioner "has a colorable claim but lacks the capacity to present it"[75] or in which the legal issues are difficult and the petitioner has not "demonstrated a workable knowledge of the legal process."[76]

(8) Cases involving at least one strong legal claim.[77]

---

fair presentation of claim). *Cf. Phelps v. United States Federal Gov't, supra,* 15 F.3d at 737 (district court did not abuse discretion in denying counsel because "it had yet to determine that an evidentiary hearing would be required"); McCann v. Armontrout, 973 F.2d 655, 661 (8th Cir. 1992), *cert. denied,* 507 U.S. 942 (1993) (district court did not abuse discretion in denying counsel because issues could be resolved without evidentiary hearing on basis of state court record).

[74] *See generally Hodge v. Police Officers, supra,* 802 F.2d at 60-61 (discussing competing standards under section 1915).

[75] Gordon v. Leeke, 574 F.2d 1147, 1153 (4th Cir.), *cert. denied,* 439 U.S. 970 (1978). *See Hughes v. Joliet Correctional Center, supra,* 931 F.2d at 429 (section 1915 case) ("Hughes had a colorable case, but without the assistance of a lawyer was likely to be tripped up by his opponents' lawyers"); Franklin v. Rose, 765 F.2d 82, 85 (6th Cir. 1985) (suggesting appointment if petitioner's claims not "'totally spurious'" (quoting *Deloney v. Estelle, infra*)); *Whisenant v. Yuam, supra,* 739 F.2d at 163 (section 1915 case); Robinson v. Fairman, 704 F.2d 368, 372 & n.7 (7th Cir. 1983) (ambiguous petition "is not beyond an explanation that might preclude" dismissal); Deloney v. Estelle, 679 F.2d 372, 373 (5th Cir. 1982); *Maclin v. Freake, supra,* 650 F.2d at 889-90; Abduc v. Lane, 468 F. Supp. 33, 37 (E.D. Tenn.), *aff'd,* 588 F.2d 1178 (6th Cir. 1978) (counsel appointed following *prima facie* showing of discrimination in selection of grand jurors).

[76] *Maclin v. Freake, supra,* 650 F.2d at 889. *See Whisenant v. Yuam, supra,* 739 F.2d at 163 (section 1915 case) (litigant "is relatively uneducated generally and totally uneducated in legal matters"). *See also Hodge v. Police Officers, supra,* 802 F.2d at 61 ("trial judge should be more inclined to appoint counsel if the legal issues presented are complex"); *Jenkins v. Chemical Bank, supra,* 721 F.2d at 880 ("complexity of the legal issues raised" affects need to appoint counsel); other authority cited *supra* notes 69, 70.

[77] One circuit court has established a *per se* rule under 28 U.S.C. § 1915(d) (now 28 U.S.C.A. § 1915(e)(1) (West 1994 & Supp. 1998)) (discussed *supra* notes 59, 62) "that when an indigent presents a colorable civil claim to a court, the court, upon request, should order the appointment of counsel from the bar." Hahn v. McLey, 737 F.2d 771, 774 (8th Cir. 1984) (citing Nelson v. Redfield Lithograph Printing, 728 F.2d 1003 (8th Cir. 1984)). *But see Jenkins v. Chemical Bank, supra,* 721 F.2d at 880 ("attorney need [not] be appointed in every case which survives a motion to dismiss"); *Maclin v. Freake, supra,* 650 F.2d at 887. Other courts, although not applying a *per se* rule, generally have held that a strong legal claim, especially one that may be stronger than a lay litigant is capable of establishing without assistance, provides a particularly appropriate occasion for appointing counsel. *See, e.g., Whisenant v. Yuam, supra,* 739 F.2d at 163; *Robinson v. Fairman, supra,* 704 F.2d at 372 & n.7; Branch v. Cole, 686 F.2d 264, 266 (5th Cir. 1982) (*per curiam*); *Maclin v. Freake, supra,* 650 F.2d at 889 (by implication); authority cited *infra* notes 83, 84. The same reasoning is implicit in cases establishing the converse proposition — that appointment of counsel is unnecessary if (1) all of the claims are so weak as to warrant summary dismissal (*see infra* note 79 and accompanying text; *infra* § 15.2) and (2) the court concludes that it

(9)   Analogous cases.[78]

Looked at from another angle, the decisions in which the courts of appeals have upheld the denial of applications for appointment of counsel at the outset of habeas corpus proceedings generally involve conclusions that the claims raised in the petition are frivolous, that summary judgment was appropriate, and that no further proceedings were required.[79] Taken together with the Habeas Rules discussed below,[80] the decisions under section 3006A(a)(2)(B) embody a presumption favoring appointment of counsel for legally unsophisticated prisoners as long as the petition (1) is not frivolous[81] — *i.e.,* as long as it survives summary dismissal pursuant to Habeas Rule 4[82] because it presents a

---

is not the petitioner's lack of legal acumen but instead his claims' lack of worth that accounts for the weakness. *See, e.g., Maclin v. Freake, supra,* 650 F.2d at 887 ("chances of success are extremely thin"); Miller v. Pleasure, 296 F.2d 283, 285 (2d Cir. 1961), *cert. denied,* 470 U.S. 964 (1962) (claims "so highly dubious that a judge [could] not properly ask a member of the bar to assume this thankless burden").

[78] *See, e.g., Hodge v. Police Officers, supra,* 802 F.2d at 62 ("any special reason ... why appointment of counsel would be more likely to lead to a just determination"); Schultz v. Wainwright, 701 F.2d 900, 901 (11th Cir. 1983) ("when the interests of justice or due process so require"); Pope v. Turner, 426 F.2d 783, 785 (10th Cir. 1970); Hitchcock v. Eyman, 418 F.2d 1245, 1246 (9th Cir. 1969), *cert. denied,* 404 U.S. 946 (1971) (severity of sentence); United States ex rel. Rebenstorf v. Pate, 417 F.2d 1222, 1226 (7th Cir. 1969); United States ex rel. Worlow v. Pate, 411 F.2d 972, 974 (7th Cir. 1969), *cert. denied,* 403 U.S. 921 (1971); Anderson v. Heinze, 258 F.2d 479, 481 (9th Cir.), *cert. denied,* 458 U.S. 889 (1958).

[79] *See, e.g.,* Heath v. United States Parole Comm'n, 788 F.2d 85, 88 (2d Cir. 1986); Travis v. Lockhart, 787 F.2d 409, 411 (8th Cir. 1986); *Schultz v. Wainwright, supra,* 701 F.2d at 901; Williams v. Missouri, 640 F.2d 140, 144 (8th Cir. 1981).

[80] *See* Rule 6(a) of the Rules Governing § 2254 Cases (appointment of counsel recommended if discovery ordered); Rule 8(c) of the Rules Governing § 2254 Cases (appointment of counsel required if hearing is ordered); *infra* notes 85-92 and accompanying text.

[81] *See* Franklin v. Rose, 765 F.2d 82, 85 (6th Cir. 1985) (if claims are not "'totally spurious'"(quoting Deloney v. Estelle, 679 F.2d 372, 373 (5th Cir. 1982))); Cullins v. Crouse, 348 F.2d 887, 889 (10th Cir. 1965) (if petition is not summarily dismissed); United States ex rel. Marshall v. Wilkins, 338 F.2d 404, 406 (2d Cir. 1964) (if petition is not frivolous); Farrar v. United States, 233 F. Supp. 264, 268 (W.D. Wis. 1964), *aff'd,* 346 F.2d 375 (7th Cir. 1965) (if petitioner's allegations are not "hopelessly frivolous"). *See also* 7TH CIR. R. 22(a)(5) (1988) (pre-Anti-Drug Abuse Act court rule requiring that counsel be appointed on request in capital habeas corpus appeals if issues raised are not frivolous); 7TH CIR. DISTRICT COURT RULES FOR THE DISPOSITION OF PETITIONERS FOR WRIT OF HABEAS CORPUS BROUGHT PURSUANT TO 28 U.S.C. § 2254 INVOLVING PETITIONERS UNDER SENTENCE OF CAPITAL PUNISHMENT § A(5) (same rule for district courts); *supra* note 62 and accompanying text (discussing House Judiciary Committee report on Habeas Rules, which calls for appointment of counsel if petition "raises a substantial legal issue").

[82] Rule 4 of the Rules Governing § 2254 Cases. *See infra* § 15.2c.

"triable" issue[83] or includes a "colorable claim"[84] — and (2) requires further significant or sophisticated factual or legal development.

Discovery ordered — noncapital cases. The Habeas Rules allow the district court in its discretion to order discovery upon request.[85] If discovery is ordered on behalf of an indigent petitioner, and if counsel is "necessary for effective utilization of discovery procedures," Habeas Rule 6(a) provides that "counsel *shall* be appointed."[86] As Professor Wright has remarked, and as the Advisory Committee Notes to the Habeas Rules recognize, it "ordinarily" *is* "true"[87] that counsel is necessary when discovery is granted, in order to "assist the petitioner who seeks to utilize discovery to stave off dismissal of his petition ... or to demonstrate that an evidentiary hearing is necessary."[88] In any event, numerous special circumstances in the discovery context — *e.g.*, that the petitioner is uneducated or mentally incompetent; that the discovery sought is complex; or that an incarcerated petitioner is unable to conduct the type of discovery ordered

---

[83] *See, e.g.,* Hahn v. McLey, 737 F.2d 771, 774 (8th Cir. 1984) (*per se* requirement of counsel under section 1915 in stated circumstance); *Cullins v. Crouse, supra,* 348 F.2d at 889; Dillon v. United States, 307 F.2d 445, 448 (9th Cir. 1962); United States ex rel. Wissenfeld v. Wilkins, 281 F.2d 707, 715 (2d Cir. 1960). *See* Charles Alan Wright, *Procedure for Habeas Corpus,* 77 F.R.D. 227, 245 (1978) (citing cases) ("better practice [is] to assign counsel for an indigent prisoner if the petition presents a triable issue of fact").

[84] Gordon v. Leeke, 574 F.2d 1147, 1153 (4th Cir.), *cert. denied,* 439 U.S. 970 (1978) (appointment required if *"pro se* litigant has a colorable claim but lacks the capacity to present it"). *Accord, e.g.,* Whisenant v. Yuam, 739 F.2d 160, 163 (4th Cir. 1984); *Hahn v. McLey, supra,* 737 F.2d at 774 (*per se* rule requiring appointment of counsel in stated circumstances). *See also* Mulero v. LeFevre, 873 F.2d 534, 536 (2d Cir. 1989) (denial of petition reversed "in the interests of justice" because counsel appointed to represent *pro se* petitioner mistakenly failed to brief claims prior to district court's dismissal); Shields v. Jackson, 570 F.2d 284, 286 (8th Cir. 1978) (counsel appointed because *pro se* litigant was unable adequately to investigate facts of claim which "states a cause of action"); *Dillon v. United States, supra,* 307 F.2d at 447 & nn. 8-11 (*dicta*) (extensive "authority indicating that counsel should be appointed in collateral attack proceedings whenever it appears probable that any substantial issue ... will be presented").

[85] Rule 6(a) of the Rules Governing § 2254 Cases. *Accord* Rule 6(a) of the Rules Governing § 2255 Proceedings. *See* Thomas v. Scott, 47 F.3d 713, 714-15 & n.1 (5th Cir. 1995); *infra* § 19.4 (discovery).

[86] Rule 6(a) of the Rules Governing Section 2254 Cases (emphasis). *Accord* Rule 6(a) of the Rules Governing Section 2255 Proceedings.

[87] Wright, *supra* note 83, at 246. *See* Weygandt v. Look, 718 F.2d 952, 954 (9th Cir. 1983). *Cf.* Porcaro v. United States, 832 F.2d 208, 210-11 (1st Cir. 1987) (district court properly may order *pro se* petitioner acting without counsel to secure affidavits to determine need for evidentiary hearing and to file affidavits pursuant to Rule 7 of the Rules Governing § 2254 Cases, and may deny relief when *pro se* petitioner fails to produce affidavits).

[88] Advisory Committee Note to Rule 6 of the Rules Governing § 2254 Cases.

(for example, depositions[89]) — suffice to require appointment of counsel as a matter of course.[90]

Hearing ordered — noncapital cases. Consistent with the Supreme Court's recognition that a postconviction petitioner's need for counsel is at its greatest when the prisoner must prepare for and conduct an evidentiary hearing,[91] the Habeas Rules make the appointment of counsel mandatory if an evidentiary hearing is granted during federal habeas corpus proceedings.[92]

c. *Compensation.* The Anti-Drug Abuse Act of 1988, as amended in 1996, contains special provisions, noted above, for compensation of counsel in capital habeas corpus litigation.[93] In noncapital cases, section 3006A(d)(1) of the Criminal Justice Act provides for presumptive compensation "at a rate not exceeding $60 per hour for time expended in court or before a United States magistrate and $40 per hour for time reasonably expended out of court, unless the Judicial Conference determines that a higher rate of not in excess of $75 per hour is justified for a circuit or for particular districts within a circuit, for time

---

[89] *Cf.* FED. R. CIV. P. 32(a)(3) ("A deposition taken without leave of court ... shall not be used against a party who demonstrates that, when served with the notice, it was unable through the exercise of diligence to obtain counsel to represent it at the taking of the deposition ...."); Rule 11 of the Rules Governing § 2254 Cases (Civil Rules apply in habeas corpus proceedings unless inconsistent with Habeas Rules).

[90] *See also* authority cited *supra* notes 64-78.

[91] Bounds v. Smith, 430 U.S. 817, 822-28 (1977). *See* authority cited *supra* note 73.

[92] Rule 8(c) of the Rules Governing § 2254 Cases ("If an evidentiary hearing is required the judge *shall* appoint counsel for" indigent petitioners. (emphasis added)). *Accord* Rule 8(c) of the Rules Governing § 2255 Proceedings. *See* Thomas v. Scott, 47 F.3d 713, 714-15 & n.1 (5th Cir. 1995); Swazo v. Wyoming Dep't of Corrections State Penitentiary Warden, 23 F.3d 332, 333 (10th Cir. 1994) ("there is a right to counsel in a habeas case when the district court determines that an evidentiary hearing is required"); Abdullah v. Norris, 18 F.3d 571, 573 (8th Cir.), *cert. denied*, 513 U.S. 857 (1994) ("If a district court conducts an evidentiary hearing on the petition, the interests of justice require that the court appoint counsel for the petitioner."); Rauter v. United States, 871 F.2d 693, 695-696 (7th Cir. 1989) (appointment of counsel mandatory if evidentiary hearing required in section 2255 proceeding (citing Rule 8(c) of the Rules Governing § 2255 Proceedings and citing cases)); Hodge v. Police Officers, 802 F.2d 58, 60 (2d Cir. 1986) (*dicta*); Bashor v. Risley, 730 F.2d 1228, 1234 (9th Cir.), *cert. denied*, 469 U.S. 838 (1984); Weygandt v. Look, 718 F.2d 952, 954 (9th Cir. 1983); Bell v. Watkins, 692 F.2d 999, 1014 (5th Cir. 1982), *cert. denied*, 464 U.S. 843 (1983); Lamb v. Estelle, 667 F.2d 492, 496-97 (5th Cir. 1982); Wood v. Wainwright, 597 F.2d 1054 (5th Cir. 1979); United States ex rel. Cadogan v. LaVallee, 502 F.2d 824, 826 (2d Cir. 1974) (by implication). *See also* Alford v. United States, 709 F.2d 418 (1st Cir. 1983) (petitioner did not waive right to counsel by failing to apply for counsel until after evidentiary hearing had been ordered). *See generally Developments — Federal Habeas Corpus,* 83 HARV. L. REV. 1038, 1197, 1202 (1970). *See generally infra* Chapters 20 & 21 (evidentiary hearings).

[93] *See supra* § 12.3b n.52 and accompanying text.

expended in court ... and for time expended out of court."[94] The same section allows recovery of "expenses reasonably incurred, including the costs of transcripts authorized by the ... court."[95] Because section 3006(A)(1) permits the Judicial Conference periodically to raise maximum hourly rates, the schedule of rates applicable in any given year should be consulted.

Hourly rates aside, section 3006A(d)(2) sets "$750 for each attorney in each proceeding" as the presumptive maximum compensation in habeas corpus cases.[96] Under section 3006A(d)(3), "[p]ayment in excess of [this] maximum amount ... may be made for extended or complex representation whenever the court in which the representation was rendered, or the United States magistrate if the representation was furnished exclusively before him, certifies that the amount of the excess payment is necessary to provide fair compensation and the payment is approved by the chief judge of the circuit."[97] Section 3006(d)(3) has

---

[94] 18 U.S.C. § 3006A(d)(1) (1994). On the question whether *pro se* petitioners or habeas corpus counsel may be compensated under 28 U.S.C. § 2412(d)(1)(A) (1994), 42 U.S.C. § 1988 (1994), or other statutes authorizing fees for prevailing civil litigants, see *supra* § 12.2 nn.7, 10.

[95] 18 U.S.C. § 3006A(d)(1) (1994). *See, e.g.,* United States v. Feldman, 788 F.2d 625, 626-27 (9th Cir. 1986), *cert. denied,* 479 U.S. 1067 (1987) (*pro se* litigant's photocopying and postage costs); Spivey v. Zant, No. 80-7243 (11th Cir. Apr. 20, 1983); United States v. Cook, 628 F. Supp. 38, 43 (D. Colo. 1985) (telephone and delivery expenses; computer-assisted legal research fees denied); Grigsby v. Mabry, Nos. PB-C-78-32, PB-C-81-2, PB-C-80-429 (E.D. Ark. 1984); United States v. Owens, 256 F. Supp. 861, 864 & n.1 (W.D. Pa. 1966) (travel, telephone, postage and other office expenses); United States v. Pope, 251 F. Supp. 234, 239 (D. Neb. 1966) (telephone, travel, and photocopying expenses reimbursed; meals for witnesses and family members and clothing for defendant to wear at trial not reimbursed); *Annotation, supra* § 12.2 n.1, at §§ 16-20. *See infra* note 100 (affidavit reflecting expenses required when reimbursement is sought).

[96] *See* United States ex rel. Kubat v. Thieret, 690 F. Supp. 725, 725 (N.D. Ill. 1988) ("The legislative history of the [Criminal Justice Act] makes clear ... that prescribed fee allowances were not meant to provide 'full compensation' but rather were 'intended to ease the financial burden on the attorney who offers his services to a defendant as a professional public duty'" (quoting H.R. REP. No. 91-1546, *supra* § 12.3b n.61)).

[97] 18 U.S.C. § 3006A(d)(3) (1994). *See United States ex rel. Kubat v. Thieret, supra,* 690 F. Supp. at 726 ("'If the legal or factual issues in a case are unusual, thus requiring the expenditure of more time, skill, and effort by the lawyer than would normally be required in an average case, the case is "complex." If more time is reasonably required for total processing than the average case, including pre-trial and post-trial hearings, the case is "extended."'" (quoting VII *Guide to Judiciary Policies and Procedures,* ch.2, ¶ 2.22 (1988))); *id.* ("'The following criteria, among others, may be useful in ... [determining whether case is "complex" and "extended"]: responsibilities involved measured by the magnitude and importance of the case; manner in which duties were performed; knowledge, skill, efficiency, professionalism, and judgment required of and used by counsel; nature of counsel's practice and injury thereto; any extraordinary pressure of time or other factors under which services were rendered; and any other circumstances relevant and material to a determination of a fair and reasonable fee'" (quoting same)); United States v. Bailey, 581 F.2d 984, 989 (D.C. Cir. 1978) (test is whether "legal or factual problems in the case, or the quantity or nature of the services are 'significantly' greater than average. The point of reference is the case commonly

permitted reimbursement substantially in excess of the $750 maximum and is likely to come into play in litigation involving, for example, multiple claims, extensive investigation or evidentiary proceedings, or complex briefing.[98] Because invocation of this reimbursement-enhancement provision requires the approval of the chief judge of the relevant circuit,[99] the practices of that judge as well as the relevant district judge should be explored when seeking enhancement. Counsel should keep and be prepared to present the court with an accurate and orderly record of the time spent on the case, the activities undertaken, and the expenses incurred.[100]

The Criminal Justice Act apparently does not limit the number of lawyers who may be appointed in a single federal habeas corpus case, as long as additional legal assistance would further "the interests of justice."[101] Section 3006A(e)

---

encountered, and the comparison must reveal enough margin of a difference to justify a confident conclusion that excess compensation is essential to fairness" (citing authority)).

[98] *See, e.g., Spivey v. Zant, supra,* No. 80-7243; *United States ex rel. Kubat v. Thieret, supra,* 690 F. Supp. at 726-28 (pre-Anti-Drug Abuse Act capital case) ($12,126 in fees and $648 in expenses for capital habeas corpus representation based on "[e]xhaustively and superbly articulated arguments ... presented by counsel attacking Kubat's convictions and death sentence"; "variety of significant and unique legal and factual issues"; "responsibilities of representing an individual whose life is at stake in the final stages of collateral review [which] impose[] extraordinary emotional and professional burdens"; and "quality of work performed and ... efficiency"; noting request in similar case for $168,000); *Grigsby v. Mabry, supra,* Nos. PB-C-78-32, PB-C-81-2, PB-C-80-429 (complex evidentiary proceedings, described in Lockhart v. McCree, 476 U.S. 162 (1986)); *Bozeman v. Lambert, supra,* No. 83-H-579-N ($4708 for one attorney; $882 for another; $750 for expenses); Carmona v. Ward, 75 Civ. 6219 (S.D.N.Y. 1979). *See also United States v. Bailey, supra,* 581 F.2d at 990 ($1750 awarded to criminal defense attorneys because difficult issues of law required extraordinary time and effort); United States v. Jordan, 812 F. Supp. 1235, 1238 (S.D. Ga. 1993) ($7530 for court time and nearly $4600 for expenses because criminal trial representation "was sufficiently extended and complex to warrant an excess payment"); United States v. Cook, 628 F. Supp. 38, 42-43 (D. Colo. 1985) ($6675 awarded to defense attorney in six-month drug conspiracy trial); United States v. Tutino, 419 F. Supp. 246 (S.D.N.Y. 1976) (awarding average of $7208 to six attorneys in a felony trial at time when statutory maximum was $1000); United States v. Hunter, 394 F. Supp. 997 (D.D.C. 1975) (average of $2516 to defense attorneys); United States v. Hunter, 358 F. Supp. 358 (D.D.C. 1974); United States v. James, 301 F. Supp. 107 (W.D. Tex. 1969); United States v. Aadal, 282 F. Supp. 664, 666 (S.D.N.Y. 1968); *Annotation, supra* § 12.2 n.1, at §§ 13-15.

[99] 18 U.S.C. § 3006A(d)(3) (1994).

[100] *See id.* § 3006A(d)(4) (counsel seeking reimbursement must file affidavit "specifying the time expended, services rendered, and expenses incurred while the case was pending"). Dicks v. Dutton, 969 F.2d 207, 210-11 (6th Cir. 1992) (reversing district court's order denying request for attorney's fees pursuant to 18 U.S.C. § 3006A(d) and Anti-Drug Abuse Act, and remanding for evidentiary hearing to resolve factual questions regarding counsel's work on case).

[101] *See* 18 U.S.C. § 3006A(a)(2)(B) (1994) (referring not to number of lawyers but to "representation" found to be "require[d]" by "interests of justice"). *See, e.g.,* Paradis v. Arave, 667 F. Supp. 1361, 1364-65 (D. Idaho 1987), *aff'd in part & rev'd in part on other grounds,* 954 F.2d

authorizes counsel to employ "investigative, expert, or other services necessary for adequate representation" either upon "ex parte application" or *without* prior approval if the cost does not exceed $300.[102]

§ 12.4. The constitutional right to counsel.

As described in the preceding section, there now is an established statutory right to counsel in all capital habeas corpus cases, in all habeas corpus cases of any kind in which an evidentiary hearing is ordered, and in many other habeas corpus proceedings that present a nonfrivolous or triable issue of fact or law.[1] In addition, although many of the federal courts that have considered the issue (albeit, typically, only in passing) have suggested otherwise,[2] there are

---

1483 (9th Cir. 1992), *vac'd & remanded*, 507 U.S. 1026 (1993) (two local attorneys appointed under 18 U.S.C. § 3006A to assist volunteer counsel from out-of-state pursuant to understanding that one local attorney would primarily assist in discovery and prehearing preparation and other local attorney would primarily assist at hearing); *Bozeman v. Lambert, supra*, No. 83-H-579-N (retroactively appointing two attorneys and multiplying presumptive maximum, before enhancement, times two). In multiple representation situations, the $750 maximum applies to each petitioner represented by counsel. *Bozeman v. Lambert, supra*.

[102] 18 U.S.C. § 3006A(e)(1) (1994) ("[c]ounsel for a person who is financially unable to obtain investigative, expert, or other services necessary for adequate representation may request them in an ex parte application"; court "shall authorize counsel to obtain the services" "if they are necessary"); *id.* § 3006(A)(e)(2) (discussing limited reimbursable investigative and expert services that appointed counsel may obtain without prior request). See *Grigsby v. Mabry, supra*, Nos. PB-C-78-32, PB-C-80-429 (social scientific and statistical experts); United States v. Pope, 251 F. Supp. 234, 241 (D. Neb. 1966) (psychiatrists; ballistics expert); *infra* § 19.3. *See also* 18 U.S.C. § 3006A)(e)(3) (limiting amounts to be paid individual experts, absent "certifi[cation] by the court").

In cases commenced on or after the effective date of the Antiterrorism and Effective Death Penalty Act of 1996 — April 24, 1996 — the fees paid for counsel and support services (*e.g.*, expert and investigative services) shall be disclosed to the public "after the disposition of the petition." Antiterrorism and Effective Death Penalty Act, Pub. L. 104-132 § 903(a), 110 Stat. 1214, 1318 (1996).

§ 12.4.[1] *See supra* § 12.3b.

[2] *See, e.g.*, Murray v. Giarratano, 492 U.S. 1 (1989) (discussed *supra* § 7.2a) (plurality of Justices concludes that there is no constitutional right to state postconviction counsel and suggests that same ruling would apply to federal postconviction proceedings; majority of Justices in concurring and dissenting opinions concludes that there may be right to postconviction counsel in capital cases); Reese v. Fulcomer, 946 F.2d 247, 264 (3d Cir. 1991), *cert. denied*, 503 U.S. 988 (1992) (there is no constitutional right to counsel in habeas corpus case); Deluna v. Lynaugh, 873 F.2d 757, 760 (5th Cir.), *cert. denied*, 493 U.S. 900 (1989) (there is "no constitutional right to appointed counsel in collateral proceedings such as a habeas corpus petition"); Giarratano v. Murray, 847 F.2d 1118, 1122 (4th Cir. 1988) (*en banc*), *rev'd on other grounds sub nom. Murray v. Giarratano*, 492 U.S. 1 (1989) (if death row inmates are provided with court-appointed attorneys in state postconviction proceedings, there is no constitutional right to counsel in subsequent federal habeas corpus proceedings); Hooks v. Wainwright, 775 F.2d 1433, 1438 (11th Cir. 1985) (there is

substantial reasons, discussed in detail in section 7.2 *supra*, why counsel may be *constitutionally* required at least under certain circumstances in state and federal postconviction proceedings.

§ 12.5. Denial and interlocutory appeal.[1]

If the district court denies an application for appointment of counsel but does not dismiss or deny the petition, the prisoner may consider appealing that order immediately rather than awaiting a ruling on the merits of the petition. In capital cases, the right to counsel is so clear that a mandamus action is appropriate in this situation and ought to succeed, regardless of the appealability of an order denying the appointment of counsel in a case that otherwise is not yet final.[2] The same may well be true in noncapital cases if counsel is denied after the district court determines that an evidentiary hearing is necessary, thus making the appointment of counsel mandatory.[3] By contrast, in those noncapital cases in which the appointment of counsel is only discretionary,[4] the appealability question — *i.e.*, whether the court of appeals has jurisdiction to hear an appeal from what is a nonfinal judgment — must be confronted. As of this writing, three circuits have held that the predecision denial of counsel in habeas corpus cases (at least if the denial is without prejudice to a subsequent request for

---

no "automatic constitutional right to legal representation in federal habeas corpus proceeding"); Williams v. Missouri, 640 F.2d 140, 143 (8th Cir.), *cert. denied,* 451 U.S. 990 (1981); Ardister v. Hopper, 500 F.2d 229, 233 (5th Cir. 1974); Hampton v. Oklahoma, 368 F.2d 9, 12 (10th Cir. 1966); Barker v. Ohio, 330 F.2d 594 (6th Cir. 1964); other decisions cited *supra* § 7.2a (there is no right to state postconviction counsel); *infra* § 39.3b. *See also* 28 U.S.C.A. § 2254(i) (West 1994 & Supp. 1998) ("[t]he ineffectiveness or incompetence of counsel during Federal or State collateral post-conviction proceedings shall not be a ground for relief in a [habeas corpus] proceeding"). *But see* authority cited *supra* § 7.2a n.8 (collecting state and federal decisions finding constitutional right to postconviction counsel in some situations).

§ 12.5. [1] *See generally* Comment, *Decisions Denying the Appointment of Counsel and the Final Judgment Rule in Civil Rights Litigation,* 86 Nw. U. L. REV. 782 (1992); Note, *Motions for Appointment of Counsel and the Collateral Order Doctrine,* 83 MICH. L. REV. 1547 (1985).

[2] *See generally* Barnard v. Collins, 13 F.3d 871, 879 (5th Cir. 1994) (district court erred in denying motion for appointment of counsel on ground that claims in petition lacked merit; "§ 848(q)(4)(B) does not condition the appointment of counsel on the substantiality or nonfrivolousness of petitioner's habeas claims"). *See also* authority cited *supra* § 12.3b nn.46-52. In capital cases, an appeal of a denial of an application for counsel under the Anti-Drug Abuse Act apparently does not require a certificate of probable cause to appeal or, assumedly, a certificate of appealability. *See, e.g.,* Weeks v. Jones, 100 F.3d 124, 127 n.6 (11th Cir. 1996) (*per curiam*); Barnard v. Collins, 13 F.3d 871, 878 n.6 (5th Cir.), *cert. denied,* 510 U.S. 1102 (1994).

[3] *See supra* § 12.3b nn.91-92 and accompanying text.

[4] *See supra* § 12.3b.

counsel) is not immediately appealable,[5] and a majority of circuits has reached the same nonappealability conclusion as to predecision denial of counsel in somewhat analogous civil rights[6] and Title VII[7] cases.[8] Other circuits, however,

---

[5] *See* Thomas v. Scott, 47 F.3d 713, 714-15 & n.1 (5th Cir. 1995) (rejecting argument that preliminary predecision denial of appointment of counsel is appealable under collateral order doctrine; leaving open possibility that interlocutory appeal may be available to challenge district court's denial of request for counsel in situations in which Rules 6(a) and 8(c) of the Rules Governing § 2254 Cases provide for appointment of counsel after court orders discovery or evidentiary hearing); Weygandt v. Look, 718 F.2d 952 (9th Cir. 1983) (*per curiam*) (discussed *infra* notes 17-18 and accompanying text) (denial of counsel "without prejudice" is not appealable); Miller v. Pleasure, 425 F.2d 1205 (2d Cir.), *cert. denied,* 400 U.S. 880 (1970) (*per curiam*). *Cf.* Landano v. Rafferty, 859 F.2d 301, 302 (3d Cir. 1988) (denial of retroactive appointment of habeas corpus counsel and compensation in excess of statutory maximum is not appealable because ruling is essentially administrative and not final). *But cf.* Waters v. Kemp, 845 F.2d 260 (11th Cir. 1988) (permitting appeal by state from denial of motion to disqualify appointed counsel); Welch v. Smith, 810 F.2d 40, 41 (2d Cir.), *cert. denied,* 484 U.S. 903 (1987) (civil rights action) (*Miller v. Pleasure, supra,* compels holding that denial of counsel request under 28 U.S.C. § 1915(d) is not appealable, but, were issue "one of first impression, we would find [it] of considerable intricacy, in light of the weighty competing interests involved and the varying resolutions of our sister circuits").

[6] 42 U.S.C. § 1983 (1994).

[7] 42 U.S.C. §§ 2000e–2000e-17 (1994).

[8] *See, e.g.,* Hodges v. Department of Corrections, 895 F.2d 1360, 1361-62 (11th Cir. 1990) (*per curiam*); Holt v. Ford, 862 F.2d 850 (*en banc*) (11th Cir. 1989); Wilborn v. Escalderon, 789 F.2d 1328 (9th Cir. 1986) (denial of counsel in civil rights action is not appealable); Kuster v. Block, 773 F.2d 1048 (9th Cir. 1985) (civil rights action); Henry v. City of Detroit Manpower Dep't, 763 F.2d 757 (6th Cir. 1985) (*en banc*) (vacating 739 F.2d 1109 (6th Cir. 1985)); Smith-Bey v. Petsock, 741 F.2d 22 (3d Cir. 1984) (overruling Ray v. Robinson, 640 F.2d 474 (3d Cir. 1981)); Appleby v. Meachum, 696 F.2d 145 (1st Cir. 1983); Randle v. Victor Welding Supply Co., 664 F.2d 1064 (7th Cir. 1981); Cotner v. Mason, 657 F.2d 1390 (10th Cir. 1981). *See also* Richardson-Merrell, Inc. v. Koller, 472 U.S. 424 (1985) (interlocutory order disqualifying retained counsel in civil case is not appealable); Flanagan v. United States, 465 U.S. 259 (1984) (interlocutory order disqualifying retained counsel in criminal case is not appealable); Firestone Tire & Rubber Co. v. Risjold, 449 U.S. 368 (1981) (interlocutory order refusing to disqualify counsel in civil case is not appealable). *Cf.* Note, *supra* note 1, at 1570 ("Although the Supreme Court has recognized few instances in which denying immediate appeal of an interlocutory decision made later vindication of an individual's claim impossible, courts ought to recognize such an instance in the case of a [civil rights, Title VII, or other civil] litigant whose motion to appoint counsel is denied"); *infra* notes 25-30 and accompanying text (issue of appealability of predecision denial of habeas corpus counsel is not resolved by either Supreme Court's nonappealability decisions in counsel context or various lower court decisions in civil settings other than habeas corpus). Most courts have held that "a district court's interim award of attorney's fees" and also its interim decision that fees of some sort are appropriate "is not appealable [prior to final decision] ... in part because the fee award is effectively reviewable after final judgment on the merits of the case is entered." Campanioni v. Barr, 962 F.2d 461, 463-64 (5th Cir. 1992) (discussing cases).

have permitted interlocutory appeals of the predecision denial of counsel in civil rights and Title VII cases.[9]

Pursuant to section 1291 of the Judicial Code, only "final decisions" of a district court may be appealed to the court of appeals.[10] "A 'final decision' generally is one which ends the litigation on the merits and leaves nothing for the court to do but execute the judgment."[11] In *Cohen v. Beneficial Industrial Loan Corp.*,[12] however, the Supreme Court recognized a "collateral order" exception to the usual requirement of a final adjudication of the merits. Applying that exception to permit an appeal from a decision denying a motion to require a plaintiff to post bond in a stockholder's derivative suit, the Supreme Court held that:

> This decision appears to fall in that small class which finally determine claims of right separable from, and collateral to, rights asserted in the action, too important to be denied review and too independent of the cause itself to require that appellate consideration be deferred until the whole case is adjudicated. The Court has long given this provision of the statute this practical rather than a technical construction.[13]

---

[9] *See, e.g.*, Lariscey v. United States, 861 F.2d 1267 (Fed. Cir. 1988); Jackson v. Dallas Police Dep't, 811 F.2d 260 (5th Cir. 1986) (*per curiam*); Robbins v. Maggio, 750 F.2d 405, 409-13 (5th Cir. 1985) (prisoner civil rights action); Slaughter v. City of Maplewood, 731 F.2d 587 (8th Cir. 1984) (employment discrimination action); Bradshaw v. Zoological Soc'y, 662 F.2d 1301 (9th Cir. 1981) (denial of counsel in Title VII case is immediately appealable); Hudak v. Curators, 586 F.2d 105 (8th Cir. 1978), *cert. denied*, 440 U.S. 985 (1979) (same); Caston v. Sears Roebuck & Co., 556 F.2d 1305, 1308 (5th Cir. 1977). *But see Thomas v. Scott, supra,* 47 F.3d at 714-15 & n.1 (rejecting petitioner's attempt to extend rationale of 5th Circuit's section 1983 and Title VII decisions in *Robbins v. Maggio* and *Caston v. Sears Roebuck & Co., supra,* to section 2254 context and holding that predecision denial of request for counsel in habeas corpus is not immediately appealable, except possibly when counsel is specifically provided for by Rules 6(a) and 8(c) of Rules Governing § 2254 Cases because court has ordered discovery or evidentiary hearing). Cataloguing the differing views of the circuit courts are, *e.g.*, Welch v. Smith, 484 U.S. 1036 (1987) (White, J., dissenting from denial of *certiorari*); Henry v. City of Detroit Manpower Dep't, 474 U.S. 1036 (1985) (White, J., dissenting from denial of *certiorari*); Marler v. Adonis Health Products, 997 F.2d 1141, 1142 & nn.1-3 (5th Cir. 1993); Comment, *supra* note 1, at 787-89.

[10] 28 U.S.C. § 1291 (1994). Statutory exceptions to the final judgment rule allow appeals (1) from nonfinal orders granting or denying injunctions, *id.* § 1292(a)(1), and (2) certified under stringent requirements by the district court and approved by the court of appeals, *id.* § 1292(b); FED. R. CIV. P. 54(B). The former exception does not and the latter exception rarely will allow appeals from orders denying appointment of counsel.

[11] Catlin v. United States, 324 U.S. 229, 233 (1945).

[12] 337 U.S. 541 (1949).

[13] *Id.* at 546. *See* Johnson v. Jones, 515 U.S. 304, 310-12 (1995) (detailed discussion of Court's "collateral order" doctrine); Swint v. Chambers County Comm'n, 514 U.S. 35, 42 (1995) (summarizing Court's "collateral order" doctrine; emphasizing that doctrine "'disallow[s] appeal

A year after *Cohen*, the Supreme Court in *Roberts v. United States Dist. Ct.*[14] held that the "collateral order" exception rendered appealable an order denying a state prisoner the right to proceed *in forma pauperis* in an action against prison officials.[15] More recently, in *Coopers & Lybrand v. Livesay*, the Court defined appealable collateral orders as ones that (1) "conclusively determine the disputed question," (2) "resolve an important issue completely separate from the merits of the action," and (3) are "effectively unreviewable on appeal from a final judgment."[16] The application of each factor to the question of the appealability of a predecision denial of habeas corpus counsel is discussed below in turn.

The district court may entertain applications to appoint habeas corpus counsel at various points in the proceeding, including when the petition is filed and if and when the court orders discovery or an evidentiary hearing.[17] In many cases, the tentative nature of a denial of counsel will foreclose an immediate appeal under the first *Cohen/Coopers* factor, which requires a *conclusive* determination of the disputed question.[18] To discover whether the district court intends a denial to be final, the petitioner may wish to accompany a motion for appointment of counsel with alternative proposed orders giving the court the options of (a) appointing counsel, (b) denying the appointment of counsel "without prejudice to renewal of the motion at a later point should further fact-development

---

from any decision which [was] tentative, informal or incomplete'" when rendered (quoting *Cohen, supra*, 337 U.S. at 546)); Puerto Rico Aqueduct and Sewer Auth. v. Metcalf & Eddy, Inc., 506 U.S. 139, 146-47 (1993) (concise summary of Court's "collateral order" doctrine under *Cohen, supra*). *Cf. Swint v. Chambers County Comm'n, supra* at 1212 (fact that appellate court properly may review one nonfinal order under *Cohen*'s "collateral order" doctrine does not give it "pendent" jurisdiction to review other nonfinal orders that otherwise would not qualify under "collateral order" doctrine, at least unless nonqualifying orders were "inextricably intertwined with" reviewable order or "review of the former ... [is] necessary to ensure meaningful review of the latter").

[14] 339 U.S. 844 (1950) (*per curiam*).

[15] *Id.* at 845 (citing *Cohen, supra*) ("denial by a District Judge of a motion to proceed *in forma pauperis* is an appealable order"). *See* Advisory Committee Note to FED. R. APP. P. 24(a); *supra* § 12.1 n.38 and accompanying text.

[16] 437 U.S. 468 (1978) (denial of class certification is not appealable collateral order). *See generally infra* §§ 13.6, 14.2 nn.14-18 and accompanying text, 35.1 (all discussing final decisions and collateral order exception in other habeas corpus contexts).

[17] *See supra* § 12.3a. *See also* Weygandt v. Look, 718 F.2d 952, 954 (9th Cir. 1983); *supra* § 12.3b.

[18] *See* Thomas v. Scott, 47 F.3d 713, 714-15 & n.1 (5th Cir. 1995) (denial of counsel for habeas corpus petitioner, which preceded decisions whether to authorize discovery or to order evidentiary hearing, did not "conclusively determine the issue of whether counsel will ultimately be appointed for the petitioner" because Rules 6(a) and 8(c) of Rules Governing § 2254 Cases, respectively, permit appointment of counsel if discovery is authorized and require appointment of counsel "if there is to be an evidentiary hearing"); *Weygandt v. Look, supra*, 718 F.2d at 954.

procedures be ordered," and (c) "with prejudice." If the court issues the last order, which conclusively resolves the counsel issue, the first *Cohen/Coopers* requirement is met.[19] That requirement also may be met if the court denies motions for discovery and a hearing at the same time as or after refusing to appoint counsel, revealing an unwillingness to order proceedings that the Rules Governing § 2254 Cases recognize as appropriate occasions for renewing a previously unsuccessful application for appointment of counsel.[20]

Roberts resolves affirmatively the question of whether the conclusive denial of habeas corpus counsel satisfies the second *Cohen/Coopers* requirement, *i.e.,* that the issues disposed of by the collateral order and those presented by the underlying merits of the suit be separable. The standard for appointment of counsel[21] focuses on two factors — (a) the petitioner's financial and litigative need for counsel, a factor "separate from the merits of the underlying litigation";[22] and (b) the "nonfrivolous" nature of the underlying claims, a factor that has the same relationship to the merits of the case as does the "good faith" or "nonfrivolous claim" standard[23] that governs *in forma pauperis* orders such as that held appealable in *Roberts.*[24]

Given the peculiarly circumscribed availability of appeals in habeas corpus cases, the denial of counsel also meets the third *Cohen/Coopers* requirement, because it so enhances "the likelihood that [the] litigant will not be able effectively to prosecute his claim or to appeal."[25] Unlike the situation in most other civil cases — including those in which various courts have dismissed

---

[19] *See, e.g.,* Henry v. City of Detroit Manpower Dep't, 763 F.2d 757, 762 (6th Cir. 1985) (*en banc*) (denial of counsel motion meets first *Cohen/Coopers* requirement if "district court's order was expressly made final"); Robbins v. Maggio, 750 F.2d 405, 412 (5th Cir. 1985).

[20] *See supra* §§ 12.3a, 12.3b.

[21] *See supra* § 12.3b.

[22] *Robbins v. Maggio, supra,* 750 F.2d at 412.

[23] *See* 28 U.S.C. § 1915(a) (West 1994 & Supp. 1998); PROPOSED FED. R. APP. P. 24(a) (effective December 1, 1998, absent contrary congressional action); *supra* § 12.3b; *infra* § 35.3.

[24] Henry v. City of Detroit Manpower Dep't, 763 F.2d 757, 762-63 (6th Cir. 1985) (*en banc*) and Miller v. Pleasure, 425 F.2d 1205 (2d Cir.), *cert. denied,* 400 U.S. 880 (1970) (*per curiam*), reject an analogy to *Roberts,* but do so in analyzing the *third,* not the *second, Cohen/Coopers* factor. *See infra* notes 25-30 and accompanying text. The decision in Weygandt v. Look, 718 F.2d 952 (9th Cir. 1983) (*per curiam*), rejects the appealability of a denial of counsel in habeas corpus (as opposed to other civil) proceedings without noting the analogy to *Roberts.*

[25] *Robbins v. Maggio, supra,* 750 F.2d at 413. *But see* Thomas v. Scott, 47 F.3d 713, 714-15 & n.1 (5th Cir. 1995) (distinguishing section 2254 context from circuit's section 1983 ruling in *Robbins v. Maggio, supra*), on ground that requirement of provision of counsel if evidentiary hearing is ordered in section 2254 cases "ameliorates the concern expressed in *Robbins* that an individual without counsel has little hope of prosecuting his case to a final resolution on the merits" (discussing Rule 8(c) of the Rules Governing § 2254 Cases)).

appeals from orders denying counsel in civil rights and Title VII cases[26] — an unsuccessful habeas corpus petitioner does not have an unqualified right to appeal. Rather, the petitioner must secure leave to appeal (traditionally termed "a certificate of probable cause to appeal" and renamed a "certificate of appealability" by the Antiterrorism and Effective Death Penalty Act of 1996) by demonstrating that there is a "substantial question" in the case.[27] "[W]hen a litigant unable to afford counsel and unable to present his case himself is forced to proceed *pro se,* there is little guarantee"[28] that the petitioner will prosecute his claims adequately enough to demonstrate their substantiality, or, therefore, that he will be permitted to appeal. Accordingly, because (a) appeals in habeas corpus cases depend upon the petitioner's ability to demonstrate some merit to his claims at the trial level and (b) that demonstration often requires the assistance of counsel,[29] making the denial of counsel unappealable renders the right to counsel under section 3006A(a)(2)(B) of the Criminal Code a "'right the legal and practical value of which could be destroyed if it were not vindicated before trial.'"[30] Because all three *Cohen/Coopers* requirements are satisfied by the predecision denial of appointed habeas corpus counsel, that denial qualifies as an appealable collateral order.

At whatever stage an appeal is prosecuted, the standard of review of a district court decision refusing to appoint counsel in a noncapital case, assuming appointment is sought under the general provisions of the Criminal Justice Act,[31] is abuse of discretion.[32] A stricter standard applies in capital cases, and in noncapital cases following a court's conclusion that an evidentiary hearing is required, in which event the Anti-Drug Abuse Act of 1988 and Habeas Rule 8(c),

---

[26] *See supra* note 8 and accompanying text.

[27] 28 U.S.C. § 2253 (West 1994 & Supp. 1998). *See* Barefoot v. Estelle, 463 U.S. 880 (1983); Rosoto v. Warden, 83 S. Ct. 1788 (1963) (Harlan, J., Circuit Justice, in chambers); *infra* § 35.4.

[28] *Robbins v. Maggio, supra,* 750 F.2d at 413. *But see Thomas v. Scott, supra,* 47 F.3d at 714-15 (rejecting effort to analogize circuit's section 1983 decision in *Robbins v. Maggio, supra,* to section 2254 context, in part because "our experience has been that pro se habeas petitioners are capable of perfecting, and very frequently do perfect, appeals from the denial of habeas relief").

[29] *See supra* §§ 7.2, 12.3b.

[30] Firestone Tire & Rubber Co. v. Risjord, 449 U.S. 368, 377 (1981) (quoting United States v. MacDonald, 435 U.S. 850, 860 (1978)). Cases holding that the denial of habeas corpus counsel is not immediately appealable have not discussed the "certificate of probable cause to appeal" requirement peculiar to such cases. *See* decisions cited *supra* note 5. Cases addressing this issue in the capital context have concluded that denials of appointment of counsel under the Anti-Drug Abuse Act do not require a certificate of probable cause to appeal or, assumedly, a certificate of appealability. *See supra* note 2.

[31] *See supra* § 12.3b nn.53-84 and accompanying text.

[32] *See, e.g.,* Reese v. Fulcomer, 946 F.2d 247, 253 (3d Cir. 1991); Battle v. Armontrout, 902 F.2d 701, 702 (8th Cir. 1990).

respectively, make the appointment of counsel mandatory.[33] The denial of counsel following an order authorizing discovery — at which point counsel is mandatory "[i]f necessary for the effective utilization of discovery procedures"[34] — would seem to belong in the latter category because there is a definite legal standard to apply, although the district court's determination on the "necessity" question deserves deference.

---

[33] *See, e.g.,* Barnard v. Collins, 13 F.3d 871, 879 (5th Cir. 1994) (by implication); Hill v. Lockhart, 992 F.2d 801, 803 (8th Cir. 1993) (by implication); *supra* § 12.3b nn.46-52 & 91-92 and accompanying text; *supra* notes 2-3 and accompanying text.

[34] Rule 6(a) of the Rules Governing § 2254 Cases. *See supra* § 12.3b nn.85-90 and accompanying text.

Chapter 13

STAYS OF EXECUTION

§ 13.1. Stay practice.[1]

In the past, the stay procedures discussed here have been among the most difficult for counsel and clients to pursue competently and with a reasonable degree of confidence in the fairness of the outcome. Often, lawyers have had far less time than was necessary to prepare adequately the stay application and other documents that had to accompany the stay application.[2] And counsel has had to

---

§ 13.1. [1] *See generally* Anthony G. Amsterdam, *In Favorem Mortis: The Supreme Court and Capital Punishment*, 14 A.B.A. SEC. INDIVIDUAL RTS. & RESP. 14 (1987); Steven G. Calabresi & Gary Lawson, *Equity and Hierarchy: Reflections on the Harris Execution*, 102 YALE L.J. 255 (1992); Evan Caminker & Erwin Chemerinsky, *The Lawless Execution of Robert Alton Harris*, 102 YALE L.J. 225 (1992); James E. Coleman, *Litigating at the Speed of Light: Postconviction Proceedings Under a Death Warrant*, 16 LITIG. 14 (1990); Arthur J. Goldberg, *The Supreme Court Reaches Out and Touches Someone — Fatally*, 10 HASTINGS CONST. L.Q. 7 (1982); Steven M. Goldstein, *Expediting the Federal Habeas Corpus Review Process in Capital Cases: An Examination of Recent Proposals*, 19 CAP. U. L. REV. 599 (1990); Patrick E. Higginbotham, *Stays of Execution: A Search for Predictability and Rationality*, 20 TEX. TECH. L. REV. vii (1989); Gailon W. McGowen, Jr., *An Opportunity to Address the Merits: Barefoot v. Estelle*, 17 COLUM. HUM. RTS. L. REV. 83 (1985); Michael Mello, *Facing Death Alone: The Post-Conviction Attorney Crisis on Death Row*, 37 AM. U. L. REV. 513 (1988); John T. Noonan, Jr., *Horses of the Night: Harris v. Vasquez*, 45 STAN. L. REV. 1011 (1993); Stephen Reinhardt, *Supreme Court, the Death Penalty, and the Harris Case*, 102 YALE L.J. 102 (1992); Ira P. Robbins, *Toward A More Just and Effective System of Review in State Death Penalty Cases*, 40 AM. U. L. REV. 1 (1990); Alvin Rubin, *Bureaucratization of the Federal Courts: The Tension Between Justice and Efficiency*, 55 NOTRE DAME L. REV. 648 (1980); Charles M. Sevilla & Michael D. Laurence, *Thoughts on the Cause of the Present Discontents: The Death Penalty Case of Robert Alton Harris*, 40 UCLA L. REV. 345 (1993); Note, *The Reform of Federal Habeas Corpus in Capital Cases*, 29 DUQ. L. REV. 61 (1990); Note, *Staying Death Penalty Executions: An Empirical Analysis of Changing Judicial Attitudes*, 84 GEO. L.J. 2543 (1996); Note, *Summary Process and the Rule of Law: Expediting Death Penalty Cases in the Federal Courts*, 95 YALE L.J. 349 (1985); Special Project, *Capital Punishment in 1984: Abandoning the Pursuit of Fairness and Consistency*, 69 CORNELL L. REV. 1129 (1984); other authority cited *supra* §§ 2.6 n.1, 7.2 n.1.

[2] Adding to the time pressure faced by counsel representing a petitioner subject to an execution date is the Supreme Court's suggestion that a court "may consider the last-minute nature of an application to stay execution in deciding whether to grant [the] equitable relief" sought by the petitioner. Gomez v. United States Dist. Ct., 503 U.S. 653, 654 (1992). *See also* McFarland v. Scott, 512 U.S. 849, 857-58 (1994) (discussed *infra* § 13.2b n.52 and accompanying text); McKenzie v. Day, 57 F.3d 1461, *aff'd en banc*, 57 F.3d 1493 (9th Cir.), *cert. denied*, 514 U.S. 1104 (1995) (applying *Gomez v. United States Dist. Ct.*, *supra*, to deny stay to petitioner who engaged in "abusive delay" by waiting until "eve of his execution" to raise claim that was available at time of previous habeas corpus petitions, "offered no reason for failing to raise the claim earlier," and failed to present "strong showing of likelihood of success on the merits"). In Lonchar v. Thomas, 517 U.S. 314, 320-21 (1996), the Supreme Court made clear that *Gomez* relied on the "eleventh hour" timing of the filing of a petition and the writ abuse doctrine as the basis for

carry out these tasks in a manner responsive to her own and the client's anxieties about the consequences of not succeeding. Moreover, when counsel did succeed — by making the district court aware of the urgency of the matter and of the need for a quick grant of interim relief in the form of a stay — she then faced the difficult task of immediately returning the litigation to the deliberate, nonemergent pace contemplated by the habeas corpus statutes and rules[3] and in particular by their goal of a "full and fair" adjudication of the legality of the petitioner's conviction and death sentence.[4]

---

denying a stay only because the case involved a successive habeas corpus petition. *Id.* at 328-29. "*Gomez* did not concern a first habeas petition, and ... did not discuss (or even cite)" the Court's established jurisprudence on stays of execution, "much less explicitly repudiate its rationale." *Id.* at 321. Nor did *Gomez* "authorize[ ] *ad hoc* departures from the Habeas Corpus Rules ... [or] purport to[ ] work a significant change in the law applicable to the dismissal of first habeas petitions." *Id.* at 328. Under *Lonchar*, therefore, the only effect that the petitioner's delay in filing and motive for filing may have on the district court's adjudication of an initial habeas corpus petition is procedural: "within the constraints of due process," federal district courts are "afforded substantial discretion to expedite proceedings in order quickly to dispose of meritless first petitions while at the same time preserving the important right of those raising serious questions to have their claims thoroughly considered by the district court." *Id.* at 320, 326. If, however, the petition is "substantial enough to prevent dismissal under Rule 4" of the Rules Governing § 2254 Cases, the district court "is obligated to address the merits and must issue a stay to prevent the case from becoming moot." *Id.* at 320. (discussed *infra* § 13.2c n.69). The short statutes of limitations imposed by the Antiterrorism and Effective Death Penalty Act of 1996, *see supra* § 5.1b, as well as AEDPA's stringent restrictions on successive petitions, *see infra* §§ 28.3, 28.4, are likely to solve most of the problems addressed by *Lonchar*, *Gomez*, and related cases. Compliance with AEDPA's statute of limitations, particularly in "nonopt-in" cases in which stays of execution are not automatic, *see supra* § 3.2; *cf. supra* § 3.3c nn.55-60 and accompanying text; *infra* § 13.2 nn.16-33 (discussing automatic stay of execution under AEDPA's "opt-in" procedures) may increase the time pressure imposed by stay litigation.

[3] *See, e.g.,* 28 U.S.C. §§ 2242, 2243, 2246-51 (1994); 28 U.S.C.A. §§ 2253, 2254(d)-(e) (West 1994 & Supp. 1998); Rules 1-8, 10, 11 of the Rules Governing § 2254 Cases.

[4] *See, e.g.,* Keeney v. Tamayo-Reyes, 504 U.S. 1, 10 (1992) ("State must afford the petitioner a full and fair hearing on his federal claim" or else federal rehearing of the facts is required); Townsend v. Sain, 372 U.S. 293, 312 (1963) (state determinations of fact not binding in federal habeas corpus proceeding if not based on "full and fair" factfinding procedures). *See also* Breard v. Greene, 118 S. Ct. 1352, 1357 (1998) (*per curiam*) (Stevens, J., dissenting) ("I respectfully dissent from the decision to act hastily rather than with the deliberation that is appropriate in a case of this character" and would "follow the procedures that we have adopted for the orderly disposition of noncapital cases"); *id.* (Breyer, J., dissenting) ("Virginia is now pursuing an execution schedule that leaves less time for argument and for Court consideration than the Court's rules provide for ordinary cases," a procedure "I can find no special reason" to adopt); *id.* at 1357 (Ginsburg, J., dissenting); Gosch v. Johnson, 118 S. Ct. 1072, 1072 (1998) (*mem.*) (statement of Souter, J, respecting the denial of *certiorari*) (explaining his and three other Justices' votes for temporary stay in case, which reached Court 90 minutes before scheduled execution, as being "in part because the grounds for relief raised by petitioner included claims under Strickland v. Washington, 466 U.S. 668 (1984), and Giglio v. United States, 405 U.S. 150 (1972), on each of which there were

Recently, stay practice has become considerably less prevalent and somewhat less pressured as a result of three circumstances — (1) the emerging practice in most, but not all, capital punishment States of forbearing to set, or almost automatically staying, execution dates pending the completion of an initial federal habeas corpus proceeding;[5] (2) Congress' adoption of a mandatory right to counsel in capital cases in the Anti-Drug Abuse Act of 1988 and the Supreme Court's 1994 holding in *McFarland v. Scott*[6] that stays of execution are available in some federal habeas corpus cases, even before a habeas corpus petition is filed, upon an indigent prisoner's timely request under the Act for appointment of counsel; and (3) Congress' adoption via the Antiterrorism and Effective Death Penalty Act of 1996 (AEDPA) of the statutory system described in § 3.3 *supra*, under which States can "opt-in" to a set of generally advantageous procedures and defenses (*e.g.*, a short statute of limitations, a strict procedural default rule, and time limits on federal habeas corpus adjudication), in return for providing indigent capital prisoners with competent counsel in state postconviction proceedings and for accepting an automatic stay of execution during state postconviction and federal habeas corpus proceedings.[7] Still, because of the high stakes and short time frames, special care is needed to observe all the applicable legal, procedural, and timing requirements.

---

potential evidentiary issues dependent on a state court record, subject to conditional deference by the District Court under 28 U.S.C. § 2253(e)" and in part because of question about "adequacy of less than a day's time (instead of the normal briefing and argument period) for th[e circuit] court to review the soundness of the District Court's reliance on the state court evidence and findings. Given the importance of adequate review on a first (and presumably, only) federal petition, I voted to stay the execution to allow further time to examine claims coming to us in such unusual circumstances."); Magouirk v. Phillips, 1998 WL 320934, at *15 (5th Cir. June 18, 1998) (remanding to district court with instructions to supplement record because "meaningful ... review" of sufficiency of evidence cannot be "conduct[ed] ... without a transcript of trial"); Bundy v. Wainwright, 808 F.2d 1410, 1412 (11th Cir. 1987) (denial of stay reversed; case remanded "for orderly, careful and deliberate consideration of the constitutional issues ... involved"). *See generally id.* at 1415 (orderly proceedings described).

[5] *See supra* § 6.3 (discussing, *inter alia*, reasons to expect Supreme Court's decision in McFarland v. Scott, 512 U.S. 849 (1994) to discourage setting of execution dates prior to initiation of federal habeas corpus proceedings); *infra* § 13.2a (similar). At the *end* of the initial habeas corpus procedure, the United States Supreme Court sometimes has been unwilling to grant stays of execution pending its discretionary *certiorari* review of lower federal courts' denial of the initial petition — and has even come into informal session during the summer solely to deny applications for stays of execution and underlying *certiorari* petitions. *See, e.g.*, Demouchette v. Collins, 505 U.S. 1246 (1992) (*mem.*); Jones v. Murray, 505 U.S. 1245 (1992) (*mem.*). *See also supra* § 6.4c n.21 and accompanying text; *infra* §§ 38.2c, 39.3b.

[6] 512 U.S. 849 (1994). For additional discussion of the impact of *McFarland* on stay practice, see *supra* § 6.3; *infra* § 13.2a.

[7] Pub. L. 104-132, 110 Stat. 1214 (1996). *See supra* § 3.3; *infra* § 13.2 nn.16-33 and accompanying text.

The first question confronting a capitally sentenced prisoner who anticipates or already is faced with an execution date that the state courts are expected to refuse — or already have refused — to stay pending federal habeas corpus proceedings is how to initiate the federal proceeding so that a federal district judge acquires jurisdiction to grant a stay of execution. This issue may arise at two points in the process of litigating the legality of a capital prisoner's conviction and death sentence after state officials set an execution date and refuse to stay it[8] — (1) prior to the initiation or completion of state post-conviction proceedings[9] that are needed to exhaust state remedies as a prerequisite for federal habeas corpus proceedings,[10] or (2) after completion of state postconviction proceedings but before a federal habeas corpus petition is filed.[11] In either situation, the filing in a federal court of an application for a stay of execution and supporting memorandum probably is *not* enough by itself, and without some other document sufficient to initiate habeas corpus proceedings, to give a federal court jurisdiction to grant a stay of execution.[12] This difficulty

---

[8] *See generally supra* § 3.5a (summarizing stages of criminal case leading up to habeas corpus stage); *supra* §§ 5.1 & 11.1 (discussing timing of federal habeas corpus petition and interaction with exhaustion of remedies doctrine); *supra* § 6.3 (state court stays of execution pending state postconviction proceedings).

[9] *See supra* Chapters 6 and 7.

[10] *See supra* § 11.1 (proper procedures if unexhausted claim is discovered on eve of filing federal habeas corpus petition); *infra* § 13.3 (federal court stays pending exhaustion of state remedies); *infra* Chapter 23 (exhaustion of remedies). The need for a stay is likely to arise after completion of state direct appellate procedures and subsequent *certiorari* proceedings because stays are automatically available from most state high courts and the United States Supreme Court during direct appellate processes. *See, e.g.,* Williams v. Missouri, 463 U.S. 1301 (1983) (Blackmun, Circuit Justice, in chambers).

[11] *See generally infra* § 13.2 (legal standards for federal court stays pending adjudication of federal habeas corpus petitions).

[12] *See McFarland, supra,* 512 U.S. at 860 (O'Connor, J., dissenting in part); *id.* at 873 (Thomas, J., dissenting). The All Writs Act, 28 U.S.C. § 1651(a) (1994), which empowers federal judges to issue orders necessary to preserve their jurisdiction, may give district courts jurisdiction to grant stays of execution before federal habeas corpus proceedings have been initiated when necessary to preserve the courts' jurisdiction to conduct such proceedings once they *are* initiated. *See* United States v. Shipp, 203 U.S. 563 (1906) (in advance of habeas corpus jurisdiction being established, Supreme Court had inherent jurisdiction to decide whether habeas corpus jurisdiction was appropriate; Court accordingly could issue stay of state court proceedings pending decision on whether habeas corpus jurisdiction had been established and thus could punish with contempt state officers who violated stay order by lynching prisoner after receiving stay order). *See also* Lenhard v. Wolff, 443 U.S. 1306 (1979) (Rehnquist, Circuit Justice, in chambers) (relying on All Writs Acts in granting temporary stay of execution; stay apparently granted based on stay application alone and in absence of *certiorari* petition by prisoner claiming he wanted to be executed without further judicial proceedings); Edwards v. New Jersey, 76 S. Ct. 538 (1956) (Harlan, Circuit Justice, in chambers) (granting stay to death-sentenced prisoners who had not filed *certiorari* petitions in order to enable them to do so and to preserve Supreme Court's not-yet-ripened jurisdiction to rule

arises because 28 U.S.C. § 2251, the federal habeas corpus stay provision, only authorizes stays by a federal judge "before whom a habeas corpus proceeding *is pending*."[13] Prior to or at the same time as the petitioner files an application for a stay of execution, therefore, he also must take some additional step sufficient to initiate a habeas corpus proceeding in the federal court from which a section 2251 stay is requested.[14]

There are two steps that may suffice to commence the habeas corpus proceeding and thus to give a federal court jurisdiction to grant a section 2251 stay. One step — which until 1994 had been the recommended step,[15] and may

on those petitions); Brown v. Vasquez, 952 F.2d 1164, 1165-69 (9th Cir.), *cert. denied*, 503 U.S. 1011 (1992). *Cf.* Delo v. Stokes, 495 U.S. 320, 323 (1990) (*per curiam*) (Kennedy, J., concurring) (All Writs Act gives Supreme Court jurisdiction to consider state's motion to vacate stay of execution if necessary "to protect the parties from the consequences of a stay entered without adequate basis" (citing authority)); Michael v. INS, 48 F.3d 657 (2d Cir. 1995) (reviewing caselaw on applicability of All Writs Act to deportation context and adopting 3d Circuit's rule that "in extraordinary cases, a court of appeals may invoke its injunctive powers under the All Writs Act so as to preserve its potential jurisdiction to review orders of deportation" (citing Reid v. INS, 766 F.2d 113, 116 n.9 (3d Cir. 1985); Dabone v. Karn, 763 F.2d 593, 597 n.2 (3d Cir. 1985)). *See generally* Turner Broadcasting Syst., Inc. v. FCC, 507 U.S. 1301, 1303 (1993) (Rehnquist, Circuit Justice, in chambers) (discussing caselaw governing Court's power to grant stays of execution of court judgments under All Writs Act).

There are three reasons why the All Writs Act alternative should be used only in the most extreme circumstances, when no other option exists. First, there is uncertainty as to the availability of the All Writs Act as a basis for a stay of execution to preserve a merely prospective jurisdiction and as a substitute for the more specific provision for habeas corpus stays in 28 U.S.C. § 2251 (1994). *See, e.g., McFarland, supra*, 512 U.S. at 863 n.* (O'Connor, J., dissenting in part) ("Because the habeas statute itself addresses when district courts may order a stay of state proceedings, the All Writs Act does not provide a residual source of authority for a stay." (citation omitted)); Steffen v. Tate, 39 F.3d 622, 625 (6th Cir. 1994). Second, there also is uncertainty as to whether All Writs Act stays are permitted by the Anti-Injunction Act, 28 U.S.C. § 2283 (1994), which sometimes forbids federal court stays of state-court proceedings. *Cf.* McFarland v. Collins, 7 F.3d 47, 48 (5th Cir. 1993), *rev'd on other grounds sub nom.* McFarland v. Scott, 512 U.S. 849 (1994). *But see* 28 U.S.C. § 2283 (1994) (exception to anti-injunction rule for federal-jurisdiction preserving stays). Finally, a federal court is unlikely to grant an All Writs Act stay absent proof that the court assuredly would lose jurisdiction if it insisted on the filing of even a "perfunctory habeas corpus petition ... reciting a single claim," *McFarland, supra*, 512 U.S. at 852 n.1, *see infra* note 17 and accompanying text, or some other pleading sufficient to establish jurisdiction for a stay under 28 U.S.C. § 2251 (1994), *see infra* notes 15-21 and accompanying text.

[13] 28 U.S.C. § 2251 (1994) (emphasis added). *See McFarland, supra*, 512 U.S. at 857.

[14] *See McFarland, supra*, 512 U.S. at 860 (O'Connor, J., dissenting in part) (clearly assuming that stay application itself does not commence habeas corpus proceeding and give court jurisdiction under section 2251 to issue stay); *id.* at 873 (Thomas, J., dissenting) (similar). *Cf. id.* at 859 (majority opinion) (not deciding question, because alternative mechanism for commencing habeas corpus proceeding was present).

[15] *See* JAMES S. LIEBMAN, FEDERAL HABEAS CORPUS PRACTICE AND PROCEDURE §§ 13.1-13.3 (1st ed. 1988).

once again have that distinction as a result of the operation of AEDPA's statutes of limitations — is to file a habeas corpus petition accompanied by an application for a stay of execution. Generally, a stay of execution at this juncture requires a showing by the petitioner that one or more claims in the filed petition is at least "colorable,"[16] although on occasion — typically when the prisoner lacked any or adequate prefiling representation — courts have concluded that even "a perfunctory habeas corpus petition ... reciting only a single claim" suffices pending appointment of counsel, counsel's conduct of the necessary prefiling investigation, and subsequent amendment of the petition to include a colorable or nonfrivolous claim.[17]

In *McFarland v. Scott*[18] in 1994, the Court endorsed a second procedure — the indigent capital prisoner's commencement of the habeas corpus proceeding by filing an application for the appointment of counsel under a mandatory-appointment-of-counsel provision of the Anti-Drug Abuse Act of 1988.[19] The Court concluded that the 1988 Act authorizes and, indeed, favors the appointment of counsel for indigent prisoners in capital cases "*prior* to the filing of a capital defendant's habeas corpus petition" — in order to enable "counsel meaningfully to research and present a defendant's habeas claims."[20] Reading the 1988 Act *in pari materia* with section 2251, the Court concluded that the filing of an application for appointment of counsel is sufficient to commence the

---

[16] *See McFarland, supra,* 512 U.S. at 860 (O'Connor, J., concurring in the judgment in part and dissenting in part) ("our cases have made it clear that capital defendants must raise at least some colorable federal claim before a stay of execution may be entered" (citing cases)); *infra* §§ 13.2a, 13.2c, 13.2d.

[17] *McFarland, supra,* 512 U.S. at 852 n.1 (describing "[t]raditional[]" practice in Texas capital habeas corpus proceedings). *See, e.g.,* Collins v. Byrd, 510 U.S. 1185, 1185-88 (1994) (*mem.*) (Scalia, J., dissenting from denial of motion to vacate stay of execution) (describing 6th Circuit order, which Supreme Court declined to vacate, directing district court following filing of habeas corpus petition to grant petitioner 120 days in which to conduct "'further investigation and discovery of possible habeas claims'" and 60 days in which to amend petition); Scott v. Dugger, 891 F.2d 800, 802 (11th Cir. 1989) (*per curiam*), *cert. denied,* 498 U.S. 881 (1990) ("[T]he United States District Court for the Southern District of Florida stayed the execution and allowed the appellant to file an amended petition.... [T]he district court stayed all proceedings and allowed the appellant to file claims in state court for exhaustion purposes"). *See generally infra* § 17.2 (amendments).

[18] 512 U.S. 849 (1994).

[19] *Id.* at 854-56 (interpreting 21 U.S.C.A. § 848(q)(4)(B) (West 1994 & Supp. 1998), which is discussed in detail *supra* §§ 12.2, 12.3).

[20] *Id.* at 855-58 (discussed in detail *supra* §§ 12.3a nn.11-20 and accompanying text, 12.3b nn.46-52 and accompanying text).

federal habeas corpus proceeding and thus to give a federal court jurisdiction to grant a stay of execution.[21]

The *McFarland* Court apparently assumed that this latter procedure applies only to indigent prisoners contemplating an *initial* (*i.e.*, not a second or successive) federal habeas corpus petition.[22] Although McFarland himself was entirely unrepresented at the time of his prepetition application for appointment of counsel, the procedure the Supreme Court endorsed would seem to be available to indigent capital prisoners who have identified attorneys willing to represent them in federal habeas corpus proceedings — including, for example, attorneys who have been appointed or have volunteered to represent the prisoners in prior proceedings.[23] Under *McFarland*, there are three prerequisites for a prepetition stay upon the appointment of counsel prior to the filing of an initial habeas corpus petition[24] — (1) the filing of an application for appointment of counsel,[25] (2) indigence,[26] and (3) a showing that a stay of execution is necessary "to give effect to th[e] right" to counsel in light of the absence thus far of a "meaningful[]" opportunity "to research and present a defendant's habeas claims."[27]

In any case involving a request for a stay of execution pending a second or successive habeas corpus petition or in which one of the three prerequisites

---

[21] *Id.* at 858 ("once a capital defendant invokes his right to appointed counsel, a federal court also has jurisdiction under § 2251 to enter a stay of execution"). *Accord* Brown v. Vasquez, 952 F.2d 1164, 1165 (9th Cir.), *cert. denied*, 503 U.S. 1011 (1992) (district court has power under 28 U.S.C. § 2251 to "stay the execution of a state prisoner in order to appoint counsel to assist the prisoner in preparing and filing a petition for federal habeas corpus relief"). Any other procedure, the *McFarland* Court concluded, would frustrate the Anti-Drug Abuse Act's policy of facilitating meaningful prefiling investigations by appointed counsel. *McFarland*, *supra*, 512 U.S. at 857-58.

[22] *See McFarland*, *supra*, 512 U.S. at 855-56.

[23] *See supra* § 12.3a. *But cf.* In re Parker, 49 F.3d 204 (6th Cir. 1995) (applying *Steffen v. Tate*, *infra*, court holds that prisoner, who was "already well-represented" by state-funded postconviction counsel "for years," could not rely on *McFarland* to "invoke the 'stay' jurisdiction of a federal court by seeking pre-petition appointment of counsel who already represents him" and thereby "stop all state proceedings against him indefinitely"); Steffen v. Tate, 39 F.3d 622, 623-28 (6th Cir. 1994) (prisoner, who "is, and has been for over two years now, ably defended by the Ohio Public Defender" and who was "not seeking a stay of execution in order to find counsel or to gain the time to file a habeas petition," could not invoke *McFarland* procedure to "delay indefinitely" both execution and filing of federal habeas corpus petition while petitioner "pursues any state procedure that he can conjure up, regardless of its merit").

[24] *See supra* note 22 and accompanying text. *See infra* § 28.3b (circumstances in which second or successive federal habeas corpus petition may qualify for treatment as initial petition).

[25] *See supra* § 12.3a.

[26] *See supra* §§ 12.1, 12.3b n.46.

[27] *McFarland*, *supra*, 512 U.S. at 858-59. This important requirement is discussed in detail *infra* § 13.2b.

above clearly is not satisfied, the petitioner's only safe option is to file a federal habeas corpus petition — or, in successive petition cases governed by AEDPA, a motion directed to the relevant federal *circuit court* for leave to file a second or successive habeas corpus petition — simultaneously with, or prior to, the filing of an application for a stay of execution.[28] Except in rare circumstances,[29] the petitioner should demonstrate in the application for a stay and accompanying memorandum that the filed petition presents claims sufficient to satisfy the postfiling standards for a stay of execution discussed in section 13.2c *infra* (in the case of initial petitions) or section 13.2d *infra* (in the case of second or successive petitions). Additionally, when there is a substantial basis for a conclusion that prerequisite (3) is not satisfied (*e.g.*, because a court might find that the petitioner already has had a meaningful opportunity to prepare the petition),[30] the petitioner is well-advised to file as comprehensive a petition as possible under the circumstances with the application for a stay — seeking to amend the petition thereafter if needed to make the petition complete.[31] Drafting and arguing prepetition applications for appointment of counsel and a stay that are reasonably likely to be denied and then have to be replaced with a full-fledged habeas corpus petition and *post*petition stay papers is not an efficient use of time in the days leading up to a pending execution date. In addition, the stakes are too high to invite a district or appellate court's ruling on the substantiality of the claims in the petition — as required in connection with a postpetition stay request — under the cloud of the district court's immediately prior determination that the petitioner or volunteer counsel previously was "dilatory" or "inexcusabl[y]" negligent in not having sought the prepetition appointment of

---

[28] *But cf. supra* note 12 (discussing tenuous option of seeking stay under All Writs Act rather than section 2251). AEDPA's requirement that petitioners seeking to file a second or successive habeas corpus petition first obtain permission to do so from the relevant circuit court is discussed *infra* §§ 13.2d, 28.3d. AEDPA's premising of stays pending successive litigation on the relevant circuit court's grant of permission to file a successive petition (thus often requiring the prisoner to apply to the relevant circuit court for the stay) is discussed *supra* § 3.3c n.58 and accompanying text; *infra* § 13.2d n.92 and accompanying text. For discussion of the cases to which AEDPA applies (in this context, any successive petition filed after April 24, 1996 is likely to be governed by the Act), see *supra* § 3.4. If AEDPA applies, the application for a stay of execution that is discussed in text should accompany the motion for leave to file a second or successive habeas corpus petition, and both pleadings should be filed in the relevant circuit court. The application and/or motion should demonstrate that AEDPA's stringent standards for successive litigation (which forbid all same-claim successive petitions and narrowly limit new-claim successive petitions) are satisfied. *See infra* § 28.3e.

[29] *See supra* note 17 and accompanying text (discussing situation of, *e.g.*, nonindigent prisoner represented by retained counsel who, through no fault of prisoner or counsel, has not had enough time to conduct meaningful investigation before filing petition that accompanies stay application).

[30] *See infra* § 13.2b nn.52-63 and accompanying text.

[31] *See id.*

counsel earlier than it *was* sought.[32] Only, therefore, when the petitioner or volunteer counsel feels sufficiently confident that the three prerequisites listed above are present is *McFarland*'s prepetition stay procedure recommended.

If an unstayed order setting a date for the prisoner's execution is in effect and a federal court stay of execution pending federal habeas corpus proceedings is determined to be necessary, the following documents must be filed:

(1) Either an application under the Anti-Drug Abuse Act of 1988 for appointment of counsel to represent an indigent capital prisoner together with a supporting memorandum and an application to proceed *in forma pauperis*,[33] or, if a prepetition application for a stay is not appropriate or desirable,[34] a petition for a writ of habeas corpus.[35]

(2) An application for a stay of execution.

(3) A memorandum of law in support of the stay application.

(4) A proposed order granting the stay of execution.

(5) Any other documents required by the rules of the relevant district and circuit court in connection with any of the documents listed above.[36]

Note, however, that the new statutes of limitations that AEDPA[37] adopts for capital cases in "nonopt-in" and "opt-in" situations[38] can only be satisfied by the timely filing of an "application" for habeas corpus relief, which may or may not

---

[32] *McFarland, supra,* 512 U.S. at 858 (stating as corollary to requirement (3) in text, *see supra* note 27 and accompanying text, that stay of execution might be denied if prepetition application for appointment of counsel is unduly and inexcusably delayed). *See also* In re Parker, 49 F.3d 204 (6th Cir. 1995) (discussed *supra* note 23); Steffen v. Tate, 39 F.3d 622, 623-28 (6th Cir. 1994) (discussed *supra* note 23); *infra* §§ 13.2b nn.52-63 and accompanying text, 13.2c.

[33] *See supra* § 12.3 (describing application for counsel in capital cases and contents of argument in supporting memorandum); *supra* §§ 12.1 & 12.3b n.46 (form and contents of *in forma pauperis* papers).

[34] *See supra* notes 28-32 and accompanying text; *infra* § 13.2b nn.52-63 and accompanying text.

[35] *See supra* Chapter 11 (preparation and contents of habeas corpus petition and accompanying documents).

[36] The local rules sometimes require a copy of the state court order to be stayed and a copy of all federal rulings arising out of petitioner's past efforts to litigate the matters in question in federal court. *See generally supra* §§ 10.2, 11.9 (discussing question of where to file federal habeas corpus proceedings and mechanics of filing).

[37] For a general description of AEDPA, with cross-references to more detailed discussions elsewhere in this book, see *supra* § 3.2.

[38] *See* 28 U.S.C.A. § 2244(d) (West 1994 & Supp. 1998) (nonopt-in statute of limitations); 28 U.S.C.A. § 2263 (West Supp. 1998) (opt-in statute of limitations). The difference between "nonopt-in" and "opt-in" cases is discussed *supra* § 3.2. The statutes of limitations that apply in the two kinds of cases are discussed *supra* § 5.1b.

include a *McFarland* application for appointment of counsel.[39] Until this ambiguity in the statutes of limitations is resolved, and given the importance of avoiding even the slightest risk of allowing the limitations period to expire before filing the appropriate document, capital prisoners are strongly advised to take the extra step described in section 5.1b *supra* (*i.e.*, the filing of a "placeholder petition" for habeas corpus relief at the same time as the application for appointment of counsel is filed) in order simultaneously to comply with *McFarland* and AEDPA.[40]

The stay memorandum (item (3)) should include a relatively brief statement of facts and description of the prior proceedings in the case from trial onward, notice of the date and time set for the execution, and a legal argument. In the case of a prepetition stay in conjunction with an indigent prisoner's application for appointment of counsel, the argument may be relatively brief and need only demonstrate the petitioner's conformity to the requirements of *McFarland* and, in particular, satisfaction of the three prerequisites listed above and discussed in section 13.2b *infra*.[41] In the case of a postpetition stay, the argument should include a discussion of some or all of the claims in the petition, giving the reasons why each claim is substantial enough to meet the standards for a stay described in section 13.2c *infra* (if a stay is sought pending adjudication of an *initial* federal habeas corpus petition) or section 13.2d (if a stay is sought pending adjudication of a *second or successive* petition[42]). In the postpetition situation, the memorandum generally should explain why one or more of the claims in the petition requires full-scale adjudication of its merits, why such adjudication necessitates further proceedings as well as the courts' considered deliberation — for example, discovery, an evidentiary hearing, or comprehensive briefing[43] — and, if necessary, an appeal,[44] and why that adjudication and those proceedings cannot occur in the time remaining before the date set for the execution.[45]

---

[39] *See supra* § 5.1b nn.79-90 and accompanying text.

[40] *See supra* § 5.1b n.91 and accompanying text.

[41] *See supra* notes 18-27 and accompanying text.

[42] *See infra* § 28.3b (circumstances in which second or successive federal habeas corpus petition may qualify for treatment as initial petition).

[43] *See generally infra* Chapters 18-21, 29.

[44] *See generally infra* Chapters 35-39.

[45] The stay memorandum might focus, for example, on claims that: were deemed meritorious by at least one state judge during prior proceedings; have been decided favorably in similar circumstances by other state or federal courts; are pending in other cases in the relevant district or on appeal in the relevant circuit court (*e.g.,* Goode v. Wainwright, 670 F.2d 941, 942 (11th Cir. 1982)); are similar to ones on which the Supreme Court has granted *certiorari* or that an appellate court has identified as presenting open questions; or that are for some other reason particularly compelling legally or factually. *See generally infra* § 35.4c.

In the *McFarland* (*i.e.*, the prepetition) situation, the court's role in ruling on a stay application is limited to assessing the presence of the three prerequisites listed above and discussed in section 13.2b *infra*. If all three prerequisites are present, a stay is required; if one or more prerequisite is *not* present, the stay decision lies in the court's discretion.[46] In the postpetition situation, the court generally must review summarily the claims in the petition to determine if they are so wholly lacking in merit as to fail to meet the applicable postpetition standard for a stay.[47] At this preliminary stage, the court need not and generally should not finally adjudicate claims that satisfy the appropriate stay standard.[48] The summary dismissal that is implicit in denying a stay of execution is inappropriate in this situation and will deprive the petitioner of the "full and fair" consideration of his claims that is required by the habeas corpus statute and rules.[49]

Once the necessary documents are filed, counsel immediately should inform the court, through the clerk, of the execution date and the need for expeditious consideration. In conjunction with Habeas Rule 4, the habeas corpus statute permits the district court to grant a stay *ex parte* without conducting an evidentiary hearing or awaiting a response from the respondent.[50] *Ex parte*

---

[46] *See infra* §§ 13.2b, 13.2d.

[47] *See infra* §§ 13.2c, 13.2d.

[48] Even in the rare instances in which the court fairly may adjudicate the merits of nonfrivolous claims without granting a stay — a procedure never appropriate when the facts remain in doubt — the court must afford petitioner notice and an opportunity to present written and oral argument on the merits. *See infra* § 36.2a. *See also* King v. McCotter, 795 F.2d 517, 517-18 (5th Cir. 1986) (citing cases) (district court summarily denying stay of execution and dismissing petition must provide "statement of reasons ... for the denial of each claim presented in [the condemned prisoner's] petition for a writ of habeas corpus"); Flowers v. Blackburn, 759 F.2d 1194, 1195 (5th Cir. 1985), *cert. denied,* 475 U.S. 1132 (1986) ("statement of reasons" requirement itself may "require temporarily staying the execution"); W.D. TEX. CT. R. CV-3(c)(3) (ruling denying stay "shall separately state each issue raised by the petition and rule expressly on each issue stating the reasons for each ruling made"). *Cf.* Bundy v. Wainwright, 808 F.2d 1410, 1417 & n.11 (11th Cir. 1987) (reversing denial of stay and dismissal of petition but reserving question "whether the petitioner, told by the court to present his arguments on motion to stay, was entitled to some word or indication that the court was taking the case under submission for decision on [the merits]").

[49] *See* Barefoot v. Estelle, 463 U.S. 880, 889 (1983) ("[a]pproving the execution of a defendant before his [petition] is decided on the merits would clearly be improper" if claim satisfies standard for stay of execution); *supra* note 4 and accompanying text. As revealed by a review of the applicable stay standards, *see infra* § 13.2, and the applicable summary dismissal standards, *see infra* § 15.2c ("patently frivolous" standard for summary dismissal), any claim sufficient to satisfy the standard for a stay also is sufficient to survive consideration of summary dismissal. *See* Bundy v. Wainwright, *supra*, 808 F.2d at 1420-21 (11th Cir. 1987) (interaction between summary dismissal and stay of execution rules).

[50] 28 U.S.C. § 2251 (1994); Rule 4 of the Rules Governing § 2254 Cases. Habeas Rule 4 authorizes the district court *ex parte* to make a preliminary judgment whether to proceed with or

proceedings are appropriate, *e.g.*, when one or more claims in the petition is clearly substantial, when necessary to preserve the court's jurisdiction against the mooting effect of an execution, or when the state fails either to make a timely response to a stay application or to supply the court with the portion of the state court record necessary for a judgment whether or not the claims raised are frivolous.[51]

§ 13.2. Legal standards.[1]

a. *Stays generally.* Section 2251 of the Judicial Code expressly gives federal judges the power to stay the execution of condemned prisoners whose habeas corpus proceedings are pending before that judge's court or a lower federal court.[2] Federal courts regularly grant stays pending disposition of capitally sentenced petitioners' federal claims.[3]

---

dismiss a habeas corpus petition. *See supra* note 49; *infra* § 15.2c (discussing summary dismissal standards under Habeas Rule 4).

[51] *See Bundy v. Wainwright, supra,* 808 F.2d at 1415-17; *infra* § 15.2 (necessity of transcript as prerequisite to summary dismissal); *infra* § 19.2 (state's duty to supply transcript).

§ 13.2. [1] *See generally* authority cited *supra* §§ 2.6 n.1, 7.2n.1, 13.1 n.1.

[2] 28 U.S.C. § 2251 (1994) (discussed *supra* § 13.1 n.13 and accompanying text) ("A justice or judge of the United States before whom a habeas corpus proceeding is pending, may, before final judgment or after final judgment of discharge, or pending appeal, stay any proceeding against the person detained in any State court or by or under the authority of any State for any matter involved in the habeas corpus proceeding"). *See* McFarland v. Scott, 512 U.S. 849, 858 (1994) ("Because § 2251 expressly authorizes federal courts to stay state court proceedings 'for any matter involved in the habeas corpus proceeding,' the exercise of this authority is not barred by the Anti-Injunction Act," 28 U.S.C. § 2283). *See also supra* § 13.1 n.12 (discussing possible availability of All Writs Act, 28 U.S.C. 1651(a) (1994), as basis for federal court stay in aid of court's jurisdiction).

[3] *See, e.g.,* Buchanan v. Angelone, 117 S. Ct. 1423 (1997) (*mem.*) (granting stay of execution pending ruling on prisoner's *certiorari* petition); Anderson v. Buell, 516 U.S. 1100 (1996) (*mem.*) (denying state's application to vacate lower court stay of execution); *McFarland v. Scott, supra,* 512 U.S. at 857-59; Collins v. Byrd, 510 U.S. 1185 (1994) (denying motion to vacate lower court stay of execution); Grubbs v. Delo, 506 U.S. 1301 (1992) (Blackmun, Circuit Justice, in chambers) (stay granted because, due to no "undue delay or procedural unfairness on the part of the applicant," "there just is not sufficient time for me adequately to consider the merits of the stay application" and "[w]ith an execution so irrevocable, I ... choose to err, if at all, on the side of the applicant"); Moore v. Blackburn, 479 U.S. 1048 (1987) (White, Circuit Justice, in chambers) (stay of execution pending Supreme Court's decision on application for a writ of *certiorari*); Moore v. Blackburn, 478 U.S. 1037 (1986) (White, Circuit Justice, in chambers) (stay of execution pending appeal to Court of Appeals); Darden v. Wainwright, 477 U.S. 168 (1986) (Powell, Circuit Justice, in chambers); James v. Wainwright, 475 U.S. 1074 (1986) (Powell, Circuit Justice, in chambers); Rook v. Rice, 474 U.S. 1112 (1986) (Burger, Circuit Justice, in chambers); Autry v. Estelle, 464 U.S. 1301 (1983) (White, Circuit Justice, in chambers); Lenhard v. Wolff, 443 U.S. 1306 (1979) (Rehnquist, Circuit Justice, in chambers); In re Heidnik, 112 F.3d 105, 112 (3d Cir. 1997) (granting stay of execution to permit next-friend to file habeas corpus petition on behalf of

In *McFarland v. Scott*,[4] the Supreme Court discussed capital prisoners' right to a stay of execution in *advance* of the filing of a habeas corpus petition when a stay is needed to assure a meaningful opportunity for investigation and preparation of a petition. *McFarland* holds that "the right to counsel" that Congress gave all indigent capital habeas petitioners through the Anti-Drug Abuse Act of 1988[5] "necessarily includes a right for that counsel meaningfully to research and present a defendant's habeas claims. If this opportunity is not afforded, '[a]pproving the execution of a defendant before his [petition] is decided on the merits would clearly be improper.'"[6]

The Court's leading decision on *post*petition habeas corpus stays is *Barefoot v. Estelle*.[7] Although focused primarily on postpetition stays pending appeal,[8] *Barefoot* more generally recognizes: that habeas corpus proceedings provide a limited but "important" means of "uncovering constitutional error" and "assuring that constitutional rights are observed;"[9] that federal courts

---

incompetent capital prisoner); Byrd v. Delo, 917 F.2d 1037, 1048 (8th Cir. 1990) ("stay of execution is generally appropriate where a petitioner has failed to exhaust state remedies"); Lesko v. Owens, 881 F.2d 44, 49 n.6 (3d Cir. 1989), *cert. denied,* 493 U.S. 1036 (1990); Julius v. Jones, 875 F.2d 1520, 1525-26 (11th Cir.), *cert. denied,* 493 U.S. 900 (1989); Mercer v. Armontrout, 864 F.2d 1429, 1431-32 (8th Cir.), *cert. denied,* 488 U.S. 900 (1988); Graham v. Lynaugh, 854 F.2d 715, 717 (5th Cir. 1988); Daugherty v. Dugger, 831 F.2d 231 (11th Cir. 1987); Smith v. Armontrout, 825 F.2d 182 (8th Cir. 1987); Bundy v. Wainwright, 808 F.2d 1410, 1413 (11th Cir. 1987); Fleming v. Kemp, 794 F.2d 1478 (11th Cir. 1986); Milton v. Procunier, 744 F.2d 1091, 1092 (5th Cir. 1984), *cert. denied,* 471 U.S. 1030 (1985); DeLaRosa v. Texas, 743 F.2d 299, 301 (5th Cir. 1984), *cert. denied,* 470 U.S. 1065 (1985); Ford v. Wainwright, 734 F.2d 538 (11th Cir.), *aff'd,* 467 U.S. 1220 (1984); Smith v. Kemp, 715 F.2d 1459 (11th Cir.), *application to vacate stay denied,* 463 U.S. 1344 (1983); Collins v. Lockhart, 707 F.2d 341 (8th Cir. 1983); Spinkellink v. Wainwright, 578 F.2d 582, 589 (5th Cir. 1978); authority cited *infra* notes 10-15; authority cited *infra* §§ 13.3b, 13.3c. *See also infra* § 36.2 (stays pending appeal); *infra* §§ 38.2c & 39.3c (stays pending *certiorari*).

[4] 512 U.S. 849 (1994).

[5] *See supra* §§ 12.2, 12.3, 13.1.

[6] *McFarland, supra,* 512 U.S. at 858 (quoting Barefoot v. Estelle, 463 U.S. 800, 889 (1993)). *See supra* §§ 6.3, 12.3a, 13.1 nn.6, 18-27, 37-40 and accompanying text; *infra* notes 26-33 and accompanying text; *infra* § 13.2b (all discussing *McFarland*'s impact on timing of applications for appointment of counsel).

[7] 463 U.S. 880 (1983).

[8] *Id.* at 887, 888. *See* Bundy v. Wainwright, 808 F.2d 1410, 1420-21 (11th Cir. 1987) ("[n]othing in *Barefoot* suggests that the Supreme Court intended to, if indeed it could, alter the ... obligations" in habeas corpus statute and rules regarding district court stays); *infra* §§ 36.2, 38.2, 39.3c (appellate stays).

[9] *Barefoot, supra,* 463 U.S. at 887-88. *Accord* Harris v. Nelson, 364 U.S. 286, 292 (1968) ("no higher duty of a court, under our constitutional system, than the careful processing and adjudication of petitions for writs of habeas corpus"). *See* Goode v. Wainwright, 670 F.2d 941, 942 (11th Cir. 1982).

consequently "need not, and should not ... fail to give nonfrivolous claims of constitutional error the careful attention that they deserve;"[10] and that a postpetition stay of execution usually is required to assure that habeas corpus petitions presenting nonfrivolous claims receive the careful processing they deserve[11] and to permit habeas corpus petitioners to "have their day in ... court before their lives are extinguished."[12] Clearly, "there would be a miscarriage of

---

[10] *Barefoot, supra,* 463 U.S. at 888. *See also* Anderson v. Collins, 495 U.S. 942, 942 (1990) (Brennan, J., dissenting from denial of stay of execution) (denial of stay pending habeas corpus *certiorari* petition imposes "needless burden on federal review of potentially meritorious capital claims [that] should not be sanctioned by this Court. Even the Judicial Conference's recent proposal for streamlined review in capital cases is premised on the view that a prisoner is entitled to 'one complete and fair course of collateral review in the state and federal system, *free from the time pressure of an impending execution*'" (emphasis in original)); Zant v. Stephens, 462 U.S. 862, 885 (1983) ("severity of the sentence [of death] mandates careful scrutiny in the review of any colorable claim of error"). *Cf.* Delo v. Stokes, 495 U.S. 320, 323 (1990) (Kennedy, J., concurring) ("Delay or default by courts in the federal system must not be allowed to deprive parties, including States, of the lawful process to which they are entitled.... Prompt review and determination is necessary to enable criminal processes to operate without undue interference from the federal courts, and to assure the proper functioning of the federal habeas procedure").

[11] *See Barefoot, supra,* 463 U.S. at 888-89, 898.

[12] Dobbert v. Strickland, 670 F.2d 938, 940 (11th Cir. 1982). *Accord, e.g.,* Lonchar v. Thomas, 517 U.S. 314, 320 (1996) ("[I]f the district court cannot dismiss the petition on the merits before the scheduled execution, it is obligated to address the merits and must issue a stay to prevent the case from becoming moot. That is, if the district court lacks authority to dispose of the petition on the merits, it would abuse its discretion by attempting to achieve the same result indirectly by denying a stay."); Clark v. Collins, 502 U.S. 1052, 1052-53 (1992) (Stevens, J., dissenting from denial of application for stay of execution and denial of *certiorari*) ("stay application[s]" should be "routinely grant[ed] ... in all first habeas corpus cases 'in order to be sure that a death row inmate may have the same opportunity to have his or her federal claims considered ... as does any other applicant'"); Kyles v. Whitley, 498 U.S. 931, 932 (1990) (Stevens, J., concurring in denial of stay) ("I assume that in ... a [federal habeas corpus] proceeding the District Court will routinely enter a stay of execution that will enable it to give full and deliberate consideration to the applicant's constitutional claims"; "[o]n review of the disposition of such an application by the District Court and the Court of Appeals, I regularly vote to stay any scheduled execution in order to be sure that a death row inmate may have the same opportunity to have his or her federal claims considered ... as does any other applicant"); Schiro v. Indiana, 493 U.S. 910, 911 (1989) (Stevens, J., concurring in denial of *certiorari*) ("In many of these [capital] cases review of the federal constitutional issues is more effectively administered in federal habeas corpus proceedings" than in Supreme Court *certiorari* proceedings reviewing state court judgments; "burdens associated with the delay in the date of execution" resulting from grants of stays pending habeas corpus review "are more than offset by the benefit of complete and adequate [habeas corpus] review of the decision to impose a death sentence," and "delay ... is manifestly not relevant to, and should have no impact on, petitioner's entitlement to consideration of his substantial federal claims by the federal [habeas corpus] courts"); McDonald v. Missouri, 464 U.S. 1306, 1307 (1984) (Blackmun, Circuit Justice, in chambers) (nonfrivolous petition statutorily entitles petitioner to habeas corpus review and "to have that review before paying the ultimate penalty"); Otey v. Hopkins, 972 F.2d 210, 212-13 (8th Cir. 1992) ("To vacate the stay would require summary disposition of issues the district court has

justice if the irremediable act of execution is taken"[13] before the petitioner's challenge to his conviction and sentence of death can be fairly heard and "finally adjudicated."[14] Accordingly, when a court is "unable to resolve the merits of [a federal habeas claim] before the scheduled date of execution, the petitioner is entitled to a stay of execution to permit due consideration of the merits."[15]

The Antiterrorism and Effective Death Penalty Act of 1996 (AEDPA)[16] amends stay practice in significant respects. In all cases governed by AEDPA,[17] the legislation makes the satisfaction of the applicable statute of limitations an explicit or effective prerequisite for a stay of execution.[18] In the subset of capital habeas corpus cases that qualify for "opt-in" treatment as described in § 3.3 *supra*, AEDPA establishes a right to an automatic federal court stay of execution during an initial state postconviction, as well as an initial federal habeas corpus, proceeding[19] but imposes new restrictions upon the federal courts' power to

---

held to be not frivolous and to require development of a record. When human life is at stake, we would be derelict in our judicial duty to so rule."); Mercer v. Armontrout, 864 F.2d 1429, 1431 (8th Cir. 1988) ("if the petition is not frivolous on its face, the *very essence of this court's duty is to study and research the points raised* .... No judge can digest, retain, or apply these principles to a voluminous state court record without reflective study and analysis. To suggest that a life or death decision can be made by simply reading a petition is to advocate dereliction of judicial duty" (emphasis in original)). Counsel should consult the rules of the relevant district and circuit court, a number of which (*e.g.*, in the Seventh Circuit) mandate stays pending adjudication of any capital petition presenting a nonfrivolous claim. *See also* Blackledge v. Allison, 431 U.S. 63, 76 (1977) (summary dismissal of petition appropriate only if petition is patently frivolous); *infra* § 15.2c (same).

[13] Modesto v. Nelson, 296 F. Supp. 1375, 1376-77 (N.D. Cal. 1969).

[14] Hill v. Nelson, 272 F. Supp. 790, 795 (N.D. Cal. 1967). *Accord Barefoot, supra,* 463 U.S. at 889; Evans v. Bennett, 440 U.S. 1301 (1979) (Rehnquist, Circuit Justice, in chambers); Williams v. Missouri, 463 U.S. 1301 (1983) (Blackmun, Circuit Justice, in chambers); Shaw v. Martin, 613 F.2d 487, 491-92 (4th Cir. 1980) (Phillips, J., in chambers).

[15] *Barefoot, supra,* 463 U.S. at 889. *Accord, e.g.*, Breard v. Greene, 118 S. Ct. 1352, 1357 (1998) (*per curiam*) (Stevens, J., dissenting) ("We have ... been deprived of the normal time for considered deliberation by the Commonwealth's decision to set the date of petitioner's execution for today. There is no compelling reason for refusing to follow the procedures that we have adopted for the orderly disposition of noncapital cases."); *id.* (Breyer, J., dissenting) ("Virginia is now pursuing an execution schedule that leaves less time for argument and for Court consideration than the Court's rules provide for ordinary cases. Like Justice Stevens, I can find no special reason here to truncate the period of time that the Court's rules would otherwise make available."); *id.* (Ginsburg, J., dissenting) (same). *Dobbert v. Strickland, supra,* 670 F.2d at 940.

[16] Pub. L. 104-132, 110 Stat. 1214 (1996). For an overview of the changes AEDPA makes in federal habeas corpus practice, see *supra* § 3.2.

[17] For discussion of the cases to which AEDPA does and does not apply, see *supra* § 3.4.

[18] *See supra* 5.1b nn.79-90 and accompanying text.

[19] 28 U.S.C.A. § 2262(a) (West Supp. 1998). *See supra* § 3.3c nn.55-60 and accompanying text.

grant stays. In the latter situation, AEDPA's opt-in provisions call for the expiration of any extant stay of execution and forbid the granting of a subsequent stay of execution[20] if the capital prisoner (1) fails to file a federal habeas corpus petition within the 180-day opt-in statute of limitations,[21] (2) knowingly and intelligently "waives the right to pursue habeas corpus review" after being advised by the court and counsel of the consequences of doing so,[22] (3) files a federal habeas corpus petition that "fails to make a substantial showing of the denial of a Federal right,"[23] or (4) "is denied relief in the district court or at any subsequent stage of review."[24] Once the "automatic stay" expires, the only avenue for obtaining a stay in an "opt-in" case is to seek the relevant federal *court of appeals'* authorization, under stringent standards, for the filing of a successive petition.[25]

The enactment of AEDPA in 1996, together with the Court's *McFarland* decision in 1994,[26] may substantially transform the nature of stay practice. Traditionally, stay litigation has served two purposes — (1) in the absence of statutes of limitations (which did not exist prior to AEDPA), to assure that capital prisoners expeditiously initiated and pursued federal habeas corpus challenges to their convictions and sentences,[27] and (2) to assure that the delay in

---

[20] 28 U.S.C.A. § 2262(c). *See supra* § 3.3c n.57 and accompanying text.

[21] 28 U.S.C.A. § 2262(b)(1) (West Supp. 1998). *See supra* § 3.3c nn.56-60 and accompanying text. For discussion of the statute of limitations that governs opt-in cases, *see supra* § 3.3c nn.40-54 and accompanying text, 5.1b nn.92-123 and accompanying text.

[22] 28 U.S.C.A. § 2262(b)(2) (West Supp. 1998). *See supra* § 3.3c nn.56-60 and accompanying text.

[23] 28 U.S.C.A. § 2262(b)(2) (West Supp. 1998). *See supra* § 3.3c nn.56-60 and accompanying text; *infra* note 24. This provision of AEDPA tightens the standard for stays of execution in capital opt-in cases by adopting something like the preexisting standard for stays of execution (and certificates of probable cause — or, in the new terminology, "certificates of appealability") pending appeal and for stays of execution pending the litigation of second and successive federal habeas corpus petitions. *See infra* §§ 13.2d, 35.4.

[24] 28 U.S.C.A. § 2262(b)(2) (West Supp. 1998). *See supra* § 3.3c nn.56-60 and accompanying text (discussing section 2262(b)(2) and caveats about its constitutionality if it truly means to extinguish statutorily conferred appellate rights and Supreme Court review following lower federal court's denial of stay or of relief); *infra* § 13.6b nn.24-25 (similar).

[25] 28 U.S.C.A. § 2262(c) (West Supp. 1998). For discussion of AEDPA's provisions governing successive petitions, including the new procedures for obtaining approval from the court of appeals for the filing of a successive petition, see *infra* §§ 28.3, 28.4.

[26] *See supra* §§ 6.3, 13.1; *supra* notes 4-6 and accompanying text; *infra* § 13.2b.

[27] *See, e.g., McFarland, supra,* 512 U.S. at 857-58; *id.* at 861-62 (O'Connor, J., concurring in the judgment in part and dissenting in part); Herrera v. Collins, 506 U.S. 390, 426 (1993) (O'Connor, J., concurring) (among equities court could consider in ruling on stay pending litigation of successive habeas corpus petition was that "[p]etitioner delayed presenting his new evidence [for years] ... without offering a semblance of a reasonable excuse for the inordinate delay"); Gomez v. United States Dist. Ct., 503 U.S. 653, 654 (1992) (discussed *supra* § 13.1 n.2);

the execution of state court judgments and the expenditure of federal judicial resources occasioned by habeas corpus litigation was warranted by the existence of at least one claim calling into question the legality of the procedures that led to the prisoner's conviction and condemnation.[28] By establishing short statutes of limitations with specific tolling provisions,[29] AEDPA assures expeditious filing of federal habeas corpus petitions and thereby obviates the need for stay litigation to accomplish this purpose. In addition, by providing prisoners with a "meaningful[]" prepetition opportunity[30] for the discovery of "all ... colorable grounds for relief,"[31] *McFarland* significantly increases the likelihood that capital habeas corpus petitions will include "colorable" claims.[32] As a result, federal judges are likely to assume that the granting of a prepetition stay under *McFarland* sets the stage in most cases for the stay's continuation throughout the remainder of the proceedings on an initial federal habeas corpus petition. Such practices, in turn, are likely to further the trend in the States, noted above,[33] toward forbearance from setting execution dates pending the completion of initial federal habeas corpus proceedings.

The next three subsections discuss the legal standards governing three types of stays of execution, each distinguished from the others by the stage of the habeas corpus proceeding at which the stay is requested — *pre*petition stays of execution to enable appointed counsel to investigate and prepare an *initial* federal habeas corpus petition (subsection b); *post*petition stays of execution pending the adjudication of an *initial* federal habeas corpus petition (subsection c); and *post*petition stays of execution pending the adjudication of a *second or successive* federal habeas corpus petition (subsection d). Thereafter, subsection e discusses the extent to which the district courts have discretion to grant stays even if the prerequisites for them are not met.

The discussion that follows will focus on the standards that govern non-AEDPA and AEDPA "nonopt-in" cases, although the variations in "opt-in" cases

---

Delo v. Stokes, 495 U.S. 320, 323 (1990) (Kennedy, J., concurring) (quoted *supra* note 10); *Barefoot, supra*, 463 U.S. at 887-88; Autry v. Estelle, 464 U.S. 1 (1983) (*per curiam*).

[28] *See, e.g., McFarland, supra*, 512 U.S. at 860 (O'Connor, J., concurring in the judgment in part and dissenting in part); *Barefoot, supra*, 463 U.S. at 894-95; *Autry v. Estelle, supra*, 464 U.S. at 2-3.

[29] *See generally supra* § 5.1b.

[30] *McFarland, supra*, 512 U.S. at 858.

[31] *Id.* at 860 (O'Connor, J., concurring in part). *See infra* § 13.2c.

[32] Even before the Court decided *McFarland*, it was rare for stay applications to be denied on the ground that they lacked any "colorable" claims. In a high proportion of these cases, the claims were not merely "colorable" but ultimately successful. *See supra* § 2.3 n.23 (high rate at which reversible constitutional error was discovered in capital habeas corpus proceedings between mid-1976 and 1995).

[33] *See supra* §§ 6.3 nn.5-11 and accompanying text, 13.1 n.5 and accompanying text.

will be mentioned. Section 3.3c *supra* provides a more detailed discussion of the ways in which AEDPA's "opt-in" provisions change existing stay practice.[34]

b. *Prefiling stays — first petition.* A provision of the Anti-Drug Abuse Act of 1988 affords all indigent capital prisoners a right to the appointment of counsel to investigate, prepare, file, and litigate federal habeas corpus petitions.[35] In its 1994 decision in *McFarland v. Scott*,[36] the Supreme Court interpreted the 1988 Act, in conjunction with the habeas corpus stay provision in 28 U.S.C. § 2251, to require a federal court stay of execution upon an indigent capital prisoner's filing of a *pre*petition application for appointment of counsel if a stay is needed to assure that there is sufficient time prior to the scheduled execution to permit appointed counsel meaningfully to research and present the prisoner's initial habeas corpus petition.[37] Under *McFarland*, there are three prerequisites for a prepetition stay of execution prior to the filing of an initial federal habeas corpus petition:[38]

(1) The filing of an application for appointment of counsel under the Anti-Drug Abuse Act.[39]

(2) Indigence, as defined by the Act and as demonstrated in an application to proceed *in forma pauperis*.[40]

(3) A showing that "a stay of execution is necessary to give effect to th[e] statutory right"[41] to counsel — a "right [that] ... necessarily includes a

---

[34] *See supra* § 3.3c nn.55-60 and accompanying text.

[35] 21 U.S.C.A. § 848(q) (West 1994 & Supp. 1998). *See* McFarland v. Scott, 512 U.S. 849, 854 (1994); *supra* §§ 12.3a, 12.3b, 13.1.

[36] 512 U.S. 849 (1994) (discussed *supra* §§ 13.1 nn.6 & 18-27 and accompanying text, 13.2a nn.4-6 and accompanying text).

[37] *Id.* at 857-59. *Accord id.* at 859 ("[A] capital defendant may invoke this right to a counseled federal habeas corpus proceeding by filing a motion requesting the appointment of habeas counsel, and ... a district court has jurisdiction to enter a stay of execution where necessary to give effect to that statutory right."). *See, e.g.*, In re Heidnik, 112 F.3d 105, 112 (3d Cir. 1997) (after finding that next-friend had standing to proceed on behalf of capital defendant, court orders stay of execution and appointment of counsel to represent next friend; "normal" rule "in favor of appointing counsel and granting a stay under *McFarland*" pending appointment of counsel and counsel's filing of petition applies in next-friend situation).

[38] *See supra* § 13.1 nn.22-32 and accompanying text. *McFarland*'s apparent assumption that prepetition stays are available only prior to an initial habeas corpus proceeding is discussed *supra* § 13.1 n.22 and accompanying text. *See also infra* § 28.3b (circumstances in which second or successive federal habeas corpus petition may qualify for treatment as initial petition).

[39] *See supra* § 12.3a.

[40] *See supra* §§ 12.1, 12.3b n.46.

[41] *McFarland, supra*, 512 U.S. at 859 ("We conclude that a capital defendant may invoke this right to a counseled federal habeas corpus proceeding by filing a motion requesting the

right for that counsel meaningfully to research and present a defendant's habeas claims."[42]

Potentially altering the *McFarland* procedures are the new statutes of limitations that the Antiterrorism and Effective Death Penalty Act of 1996 (AEDPA)[43] adopts for capital cases in "nonopt-in" and "opt-in" situations.[44] These statutes of limitations can only be satisfied by the timely filing of an "application" for habeas corpus relief, which may or may not include a *McFarland* application for appointment of counsel.[45] Until this ambiguity in the statutes of limitations is resolved, and given the importance of avoiding even the slightest risk of allowing the limitations period to expire before filing the appropriate document, capital prisoners are strongly advised to take the extra step described in section 5.1b *supra* (*i.e.*, the filing of a "placeholder petition" for habeas corpus relief at the same time as the application for appointment of counsel is filed) in order to comply with *McFarland* and AEDPA simultaneously.[46]

McFarland contemplates a stay in order to facilitate the investigation and discovery of federal habeas corpus claims.[47] It accordingly imposes no requirement tied to the existence or strength of the claims in the yet-to-be-prepared petition or in any placeholder petition that is filed as the basis for satisfying a statute of limitations.[48] Nor does it impose any requirement tied to

---

appointment of habeas counsel, and that a district court has jurisdiction to enter a stay of execution where necessary to give effect to that statutory right.").

[42] *Id.* at 858 ("[T]he right to counsel necessarily includes a right for that counsel meaningfully to research and present a defendant's habeas claims."). *See also infra* note 51 and accompanying text.

[43] Pub. L. 104-132, 110 Stat. 1214 (1996). For a general description of AEDPA, with cross-references to more detailed discussions elsewhere in this book, see *supra* § 3.2.

[44] *See* 28 U.S.C.A. §§ 2244(d) (West 1994 & Supp. 1998) (nonopt-in statute of limitations); *id.* § 2263 (West Supp. 1998) (opt-in statute of limitations). The difference between "nonopt-in" and "opt-in" cases is discussed *supra* § 3.2. The statutes of limitations that apply in the two kinds of cases are discussed *supra* § 5.1b.

[45] *See supra* § 5.1b nn.79-90 and accompanying text.

[46] *See supra* § 5.1b n.91 and accompanying text.

[47] *McFarland, supra*, 512 U.S. at 857-58.

[48] *See id.* at 861 (O'Connor, J., concurring in part and dissenting in part) ("Court's approach ... permits a stay of execution in the absence of any showing of a constitutional claim"); *id.* at 873 (Thomas, J., dissenting) ("[U]nder the Court's reading of the statute, a federal district court determining whether to enter a stay will no longer have to evaluate whether a prisoner has presented a potentially meritorious constitutional claim. Rather, the court's task will be to determine whether a 'capital defendant' who comes to federal court shortly before his scheduled execution has been 'dilatory' in pursuing his 'right to counsel.' If he has not been 'dilatory,' the district court presumably must enter a stay to preserve his 'right to counsel' and his 'right for that counsel meaningfully to research and present [his] habeas claims.'" (quoting *id.* at 858 (majority opinion))).

the strength of the federal claims presented in the prisoner's prior briefs and pleadings in the *state* courts.[49] Rather, if the three prerequisites listed above are present, the denial of a stay "'would clearly be improper.'"[50] If one or more of the prerequisites is *not* present, the decision whether to grant a stay lies within "the sound discretion of [the] federal court."[51]

The first two *McFarland* prerequisites are straightforward. In discussing the third prerequisite, the *McFarland* Court noted that the requirement is not satisfied if the petitioner has been "dilatory" in that he "inexcusably ignored" an opportunity for meaningful preparation of the federal petition and "flouted the available processes."[52] Rather, the prisoner must show that he has not yet had "sufficient time ... prior to his scheduled execution" (a) "to request the appointment of counsel," (b) "meaningfully to research and present a defendant's [federal] habeas claims," and (c) to "file a formal habeas corpus

---

[49] The *McFarland* Court undertook no inquiry into the federal nature, much less the strength, of the claims McFarland previously had raised in the state courts. As Justice Thomas' dissent makes clear, the majority squarely rejected the notion that, "[g]iven th[e] exhaustion requirement, ... by the time a death-sentenced prisoner reaches a federal court, 'possible claims and their factual bases' will already have been 'researched and identified.'" *Id.* at 870 (Thomas, J., dissenting) (citations omitted). *See also* Collins v. Byrd, 510 U.S. 1185, 1187 (1994) (*mem.*) (Scalia, J., dissenting from denial of motion to vacate stay of execution) (describing 6th Circuit order, which Supreme Court declined to vacate, directing district court to stay execution and give petitioner 120 days to conduct "'further investigation and discovery of possible habeas claims'"; expressing view, which Court evidently rejected, that stay should be vacated because "[r]espondent has had *six years* [during state postconviction proceedings] to 'investigate and discover possible habeas claims, and there is no justification for another four months' delay on that score" (emphasis in original; citations omitted)).

[50] *McFarland, supra,* 512 U.S. at 858 ("Where this opportunity [for the meaningful investigation and presentation by appointed counsel of the prisoner's habeas corpus claims] is not afforded, '[a]pproving the execution of a defendant before his [petition] is decided on the merits would clearly be improper.'" (quoting Barefoot v. Estelle, 463 U.S. 880, 889 (1983))).

[51] *Id.* at 858. *See infra* § 13.2e.

[52] *McFarland, supra,* 512 U.S. at 858 ("[I]f a dilatory capital defendant inexcusably ignores this opportunity [for meaningful investigation and preparation of petition] and flouts the available processes, a federal court presumably would not abuse its discretion in denying a stay of execution."). *See also* In re Parker, 49 F.3d 204 (6th Cir. 1995) (similar to *Steffen v. Tate, infra*); Steffen v. Tate, 39 F.3d 622, 627-28 (6th Cir. 1994) (prisoner, who was already represented and "is clearly able and ready, though definitely unwilling, to file a petition for writ of habeas corpus," could not invoke *McFarland* procedure to delay execution "indefinitely" on "pretense that a habeas proceeding is 'pending'" and will commence at some future time after completion of any unexhausted "state procedure that [prisoner] can conjure up, regardless of its merit"). *Cf.* Anderson v. Buell, 516 U.S. 1100, 1103 (1996) (*mem.*) (denying state's application to vacate stay of execution over Justice Scalia's dissent, which claimed that prisoner who obtained *McFarland* stay for purpose of "develop[ing] a claim, which may or may not be possible," had "twice engaged in dilatory maneuvers").

petition."[53] As the Court noted, "[u]nder ordinary circumstances," *i.e.*, under the procedure that prevails in most States, in which execution dates are not set unless a represented petitioner inexcusably neglects to pursue available state and federal capital review procedures in a deliberate and diligent manner,[54] "a capital defendant presumably *will* have sufficient time" following the termination of state proceedings and prior to the date set for the execution to secure the appointment of counsel, conduct the necessary research and investigation, and file a petition.[55] On the other hand, in cases like *McFarland* (which apparently were not unusual in Texas in the early 1990s[56]) — in which the termination of each prior proceeding under stay of execution typically is followed immediately by the setting of a new execution date only a few weeks in the future — *McFarland* holds that the "ordinary" situation does not prevail and that a stay of execution is required.[57] *McFarland* also makes clear that presumptively adequate representation at trial and on appeal by court-appointed counsel — which was available to McFarland himself — does not satisfy the "meaningful research and presentation" requirement.[58] Nor do state postconviction proceedings in which appointed counsel was unavailable to the indigent prisoner.[59] Rather, the

---

[53] *McFarland, supra,* 512 U.S. at 858.

[54] *See supra* §§ 6.3, 13.1 n.5 and accompanying text.

[55] *McFarland, supra,* 512 U.S. at 858 (emphasis added). *See also In re Parker, supra* (discussed *supra* note 52); *Steffen v. Tate, supra,* 39 F.3d at 627-28 (discussed *supra* note 52).

[56] *See McFarland, supra* at 852 n.1.

[57] *See id.* at 851-53, 859 (authorizing stay of execution to permit appointment of counsel and meaningful prefiling investigation in case in which execution date was set two months after termination of direct appeal and *certiorari* proceedings and in which interval between date on which execution was set and date set for execution (after being once extended) was approximately 10 weeks; prisoner unsuccessfully sought state, then federal, court appointment of counsel beginning approximately four and one-half weeks after date for execution initially was set and approximately one week prior to date initially set for execution).

[58] *See id.* at 851-53 (describing prior history of case); *id.* at 857 (making clear that procedures in McFarland's own case required stay: "Even if the District Court had granted McFarland's motion for appointment of counsel and had found an attorney to represent him, this appointment would have been meaningless unless McFarland's execution also was stayed.").

[59] *See id.* at 851-53 (discussing prior proceedings in case); *supra* note 58. Given the clear absence in McFarland's own case of full and fair state postconviction proceedings, the Court had no occasion to address whether such proceedings would suffice to establish that the prisoner previously had a "meaningful opportunity" to develop federal habeas corpus claims. *McFarland* makes clear, however, that, to qualify as full and fair, state postconviction proceedings would have to include the appointment of counsel for indigent prisoners, the provision of sufficient time to conduct a meaningful investigation of the factual and legal aspects of all of a petitioner's colorable federal claims, and the availability of necessary state-funded investigative and expert services. *See supra* notes 53, 57; *infra* notes 60-63 and accompanying text. On these and other conditions that must be present in order for state postconviction proceedings to qualify as "full and fair," see *supra* §§ 7.1b, 7.2; *infra* §§ 20.3e, 23.4, 26.2d.

requirement is satisfied only by the opportunity for a pre-habeas corpus investigation of "all of a state prisoner's colorable grounds for relief,"[60] including both the claims' "factual bases" (for which "[t]he services of investigators and other experts may be critical") and the legal and strategic implications of the Court's "'complex[] ... jurisprudence'" in capital cases.[61] *McFarland* indicates that the period between the termination of the prior state proceeding and the date set for execution must be a matter of months (and not simply a matter of weeks)[62] in order to qualify as "sufficient ... time to request the appointment of counsel" and "meaningfully to research and present a defendant's habeas claims."[63]

c. *Postfiling stays — first petition.* As noted in section 13.2a *supra*, in cases in which a prepetition stay of execution has previously been granted to enable appointed counsel to conduct a meaningful legal and factual investigation prior to filing an initial federal habeas corpus petition,[64] the assumption is likely to arise that the prepetition stay should remain in effect following the filing of the petition and until the petition is finally litigated.[65] In situations in which the question of a *post*petition stay of execution pending adjudication of an initial federal habeas corpus petition *does* arise, however, the Supreme Court's decision in *Barefoot v. Estelle*[66] will generally govern the availability of a stay in cases

---

[60] *McFarland, supra*, 512 U.S. at 860 (O'Connor, J., concurring in the judgment in part). *Accord id.* at 855-56 (majority opinion) (all "possible claims").

[61] *Id.* at 855-56 (quoting Murray v. Giarratano, 492 U.S. 1, 14 (1989) (Kennedy, J., concurring in the judgment)). *See supra* §§ 7.1a, 11.2 (describing necessary prefiling factual and legal investigation); *infra* § 19.3 (availability under Anti-Drug Abuse Act of funds for expert and investigative services). *See also* Collins v. Byrd, 510 U.S. 1185, 1185-88 (1994) (*mem.*) (Scalia, J., dissenting from denial of motion to vacate stay of execution) (discussed *supra* note 49; *infra* note 62).

[62] *See supra* note 57 (describing time frames in *McFarland* that Court deemed insufficient to permit meaningful prefiling preparation). *See also* Collins v. Byrd, *supra*, 510 U.S. at 1185-88 (Scalia, J., dissenting from denial of motion to vacate stay) (describing 6th Circuit order, which Supreme Court declined to vacate, directing district court to grant petitioner, who recently had filed apparently incomplete federal habeas corpus petition, 120 days for "'further investigation and discovery of possible habeas claims'"; petitioner was convicted in 1983, his direct appellate proceedings ended in 1988, and state court postconviction proceedings had terminated, although a *certiorari* petition to review those proceedings was pending when 6th Circuit ruled; Court rejected Justice Scalia's view that stay should have been vacated because "[r]espondent has had *six years* [of state postconviction proceedings] to 'investigate and discover possible habeas claims'" (emphasis in original; citations omitted)).

[63] *McFarland, supra*, 512 U.S. at 858.

[64] *See supra* §§ 13.1, 13.2b.

[65] *See supra* § 13.2a nn.26-33 and accompanying text.

[66] 463 U.S. 880 (1983). *See supra* § 13.2a nn.7-15 and accompanying text.

that are not governed by the Antiterrorism and Effective Death Penalty Act of 1996 (AEDPA)[67] and in cases that are governed by AEDPA's "nonopt-in" provisions.[68]

In *Barefoot*, the Court held that, as far as *district* court adjudication of a capital petitioner's *first* habeas corpus petition is concerned, "due consideration" requires "careful attention" to, hence usually a stay of execution pending resolution of, every "*non-frivolous* claim[] of constitutional error."[69] In recognition of the need to preserve the petitioner's life and the court's jurisdiction pending "examin[ation] to see whether [the petitioner's] trial and appeal ... measure[d] up to constitutional standards," the federal courts typically have required a district court stay whenever: (1) at least one of the claims in the petition is "not frivolous"[70] or is "colorable"[71]; (2) a claim necessitates further

---

[67] Pub. L. 104-132, 110 Stat. 1214 (1996). For a general description of AEDPA, with cross-references to more detailed discussions elsewhere in this book, see *supra* § 3.2.

[68] For discussion of the "nonopt-in" and "opt-in" categories of habeas corpus cases created by AEDPA, see *supra* § 3.2.

[69] *Barefoot, supra,* 463 U.S. at 888, 889 (emphasis added). *See also supra* § 13.2a nn.9-12 and accompanying text. In Lonchar v. Thomas, 517 U.S. 314 (1996), the Supreme Court affirmed *Barefoot*'s analysis in the strongest terms. Because "[d]ismissal of a first federal habeas petition is a particularly serious matter, for that dismissal denies the petitioner the protections of the Great Writ entirely, risking injury to an important interest in human liberty," and because "the interest in permitted federal habeas review of a first petition is quite strong," "if the district court cannot dismiss [a first] ... petition on the merits before the scheduled execution, *it is obligated to address the merits and must issue a stay to prevent a case from becoming moot.* That is, if the district court lacks authority to directly dispose of the petition on the merits, it would abuse its discretion by attempting to achieve the same result indirectly by denying a stay." *Id.* at 320, 324, 329 (emphasis added). By substantially rejecting the broad uses to which a number of lower courts had put the Supreme Court's prior decision in Gomez v. United States Dist. Ct., 503 U.S. 653 (1992), *see supra* § 13.1 n.2, *Lonchar* makes clear that the nonfrivolousness requirement for determining the propriety of a stay is *not* augmented in first-petition cases (although it may be augmented in successive petition cases) by considering the "eleventh hour" timing of, or the petitioner's motive for, filing the petition. *See id.* at 320-21, 328-29 (discussed *supra* § 13.1 n.2). The short statutes of limitations imposed by the Antiterrorism and Effective Death Penalty Act of 1996 (AEDPA), *see supra* § 5.1b, as well as AEDPA's stringent restrictions on successive petitions, *see infra* §§ 28.3, 28.4, are likely to solve most of the problems addressed by *Lonchar, Gomez,* and related cases.

[70] *See, e.g.,* E.D. CAL. RULE 191(h)(1) ("Upon the filing of a [capital] habeas corpus petition, unless the petition is patently frivolous, the District Court shall issue a stay of execution pending final disposition of the matter."); *id.,* RULE 191(h)(2)-(3) (temporary stay is appropriate when counsel in state court proceedings withdraws or is unavailable or unqualified to proceed and new counsel, unfamiliar with case, is appointed). *See* Otey v. Hopkins, 972 F.2d 210, 212-13 (8th Cir. 1992); Fleming v. Kemp, 794 F.2d 1478 (11th Cir. 1986); Goode v. Wainwright, 670 F.2d 941 (11th Cir. 1982) (cited approvingly in *Barefoot, supra,* 463 U.S. at 893).

In Neitzke v. Williams, 490 U.S. 319 (1989), the Supreme Court defined "frivolous" as used in 28 U.S.C. § 1915(d) to identify those civil complaints that are insufficient to justify a federal court's grant of *in forma pauperis* status to indigent litigants. That definition, which may be helpful

trial court proceedings;[72] (3) the petitioner's claims "are debatable among jurists of reason [and] a court *could* resolve the issues" favorably to the petitioner;[73] (4) "the questions [presented in the petition] are 'adequate to deserve encouragement to proceed further'";[74] or (5) the court is not "confident that [the claim]

---

by analogy in determining when a stay of execution is appropriate, is satisfied "'only if the petitioner cannot make any rational argument in law or in fact which would entitle him or her to relief.'" *Neitzke v. Williams, supra* at 322-23 (quoting court of appeals decision). *Accord* Denton v. Hernandez, 504 U.S. 25, 33 (1992) (under *Neitzke* standard, "finding of factual frivolousness is appropriate when the facts alleged rise to the level of the irrational or the wholly incredible"). *See also* O'Neal v. McAninch, 513 U.S. 432, 443 (1995) ("In a highly technical area such as this one, consistency [of rules] brings with it simplicity, a body of existing law available for consultation."); Keeney v. Tamayo-Reyes, 504 U.S. 1, 10 (1992) (recognizing value of employing analogous standards from other "area[s] of habeas law" so as to "advance[] uniformity in the law of habeas corpus"). The *Neitzke* standard is "more lenient" than that of FED. R. CIV. PRO. 12(b)(6) governing dismissal of a complaint for failure to state a claim on which relief can be granted. Frivolous claims include claims that are "based on an outlandish legal theory." *Neitzke v. Williams, supra* at 327. Frivolous claims do not, however, include "close but ultimately unavailing" claims or "[c]lose questions of federal law." *Id.* at 327-28. When *pro se* petitioners are involved, a finding of frivolousness is inappropriate if there is a chance that the claim could be "clarif[ied] ... to conform with the requirements of a valid legal cause of action." *Id.* at 329-30. *See also* Professional Real Est. Inves., Inc. v. Columbia Pictures Indus., Inc., 508 U.S. 49, 66-67 (1993) (Souter, J., concurring) (question "whether the suit at issue here was objectively baseless is purely one of law, which [appellate court is] ... obliged to consider *de novo*"); Holt v. Caspari, 961 F.2d 1370, 1372 (8th Cir.), *cert. denied*, 506 U.S. 865 (1992) (section 1983 action) ("Pro se complaints must be liberally construed and can be dismissed [as 'frivolous' under § 1915(d)] only if the face of the complaint shows an insuperable bar to relief."). *See generally supra* § 12.1 & *infra* §§ 15.2c, 35.4b (all discussing applications of similar "frivolousness" tests in other habeas corpus contexts).

[71] McFarland v. Scott, 512 U.S. 849, 860 (1994) (O'Connor, J., concurring in the judgment in part and dissenting in part) ("[O]ur cases have made it clear that capital defendants must raise at least some colorable federal claim before a stay of execution may be entered."). *See Lonchar v. Thomas, supra*, 517 U.S. at 320-21 (district court may deny stay *only* if court also is authorized to dismiss petition under Rule 4 of the Rules Governing § 2254 Cases, discussed *infra* § 15.2c, because "'it plainly appears ... that the petitioner is not entitled to relief in the district court'"; adopting *per se* rule that petitioner "could not be denied a stay unless his petition was properly subject to dismissal," so that stay must be granted if petitioner's "claims ... [are] substantial enough to prevent dismissal under Rule 4"); Zant v. Stephens, 462 U.S. 862, 885 (1983). *See also McFarland, supra*, 512 U.S. at 856 (majority opinion) ("substantial federal claim").

[72] *See, e.g., Otey v. Hopkins, supra*, 972 F.2d at 212-13; Mattheson v. Maggio, 714 F.2d 362, 365 (5th Cir. 1983).

[73] *Barefoot, supra*, 463 U.S. at 893 n.4. *See* Agan v. Dugger, 828 F.2d 1496, 1497 (11th Cir. 1987), *cert. denied*, 487 U.S. 1205 (1988). *See also* Lesko v. Owens, 881 F.2d 44, 49 n.6 (3d Cir. 1989), *cert. denied*, 493 U.S. 1036 (1990) (stay of execution granted after United States Supreme Court granted *certiorari* to consider constitutionality of jury instructions similar to those challenged by petitioner).

[74] *Barefoot, supra*, 463 U.S. at 893 n.4 (quoting Gordon v. Willis, 516 F. Supp. 911, 913 (N.D. Ga. 1980)).

is squarely foreclosed by statute, rule, or authoritative court decision, or is lacking in any factual basis in the record."[75]

In adopting tougher standards for stays pending appeals and second or successive petitions, *Barefoot* took pains to preserve the longstanding federal rule requiring *district* court stays of execution for all *first* petitions encompassing at least one "nonfrivolous" or "colorable claim of error."[76] The Court explicitly premised its imposition of a higher stay standard at subsequent stages on the assumption — justified in *Barefoot* by more than 13 months of district court proceedings under a stay of execution, an evidentiary hearing, and full briefing and argument prior to the request for a stay pending appeal at issue in the case — that the district court previously afforded the petitioner a stay and plenary consideration of all nonfrivolous claims.[77]

As is discussed in more detail elsewhere,[78] AEDPA's "opt-in" provisions governing capital habeas corpus proceedings in States that qualify for "Special" treatment[79] require habeas corpus petitioners to justify continuation of statutorily

---

[75] *Id.* at 894. *See* Evans v. Bennett, 440 U.S. 1301, 1306 (1979) (Rehnquist, Circuit Justice, in chambers); Goode v. Wainwright, 670 F.2d 941, 942 (11th Cir. 1982); Dobbert v. Wainwright, 670 F.2d 938, 940 (11th Cir. 1982) (citing cases); Shriner v. Wainwright, No. 80-5469 (11th Cir. Apr. 20, 1982); Antone v. Strickland, No. 82-5120 (11th Cir. Feb. 1, 1982); Shaw v. Martin, 613 F.2d 487, 491 (4th Cir. 1980) (Phillips, J., in chambers); Tilford v. Page, 395 F.2d 220 (10th Cir. 1968), *vac'd & remanded on other grounds*, 408 U.S. 939 (1972); Foster v. Wainwright, TCA 81-0047 (N.D. Ga. Jan. 19, 1982); Douglas v. Wainwright, 521 F. Supp. 790 (M.D. Fla. 1981); Adderly v. Wainwright, 272 F. Supp. 530, 532 (M.D. Fla. 1968); Hill v. Nelson, 271 F. Supp. 439 (N.D. Cal.), *modified on other grounds,* 272 F. Supp. 790 (N.D. Cal. 1967); Moorer v. South Carolina, 240 F. Supp. 529 (E.D.S.C. 1964). *See also* McCoy v. Lynaugh, 874 F.2d 954, 967 (5th Cir. 1989) (listing four factors to be considered for granting stay of execution: (1) applicant's probability of success on merits; (2) irreparability of injury if stay is not granted; (3) extent of harm to other parties if stay is granted; (4) public interest in grant or denial of stay (citing Selvage v. Lynaugh, 842 F.2d 89 (5th Cir. 1988), *vac'd & remanded on other grounds sub nom. Selvage v. Collins,* 494 U.S. 108 (1990))). The latter three stay standards listed in the text govern stays pending appeal and are higher standards than the "nonfrivolous" requirement for trial court/first petition stays. *See infra* § 13.2d. *See generally infra* § 36.2.

[76] *Barefoot, supra,* 463 U.S. at 888; Zant v. Stephens, 462 U.S. 862, 885 (1983). *Accord* Lonchar v. Thomas, 517 U.S. 314, 321 (1996) (*Barefoot*'s restrictive standard for ruling on stays of execution in successive petition cases does not apply when petition is prisoner's first, even if prisoner waited until "last minute" to seek stay). *See infra* §§ 13.2d (stays pending successive petition), 36.2 (pending appeal), 38.2 & 39.3c (pending *certiorari*).

[77] *Barefoot, supra,* 463 U.S. at 886-92. *See also* Alabama v. Evans, 461 U.S. 1301, 1302 (1983) (Powell, Circuit Justice, in chambers).

[78] *See supra* §§ 3.3c nn.55-60 and accompanying text; 13.2a nn.19-25 and accompanying text.

[79] For an explanation of AEDPA's "opt-in" provisions and the States to which they apply, see *supra* §§ 3.2, 3.3.

required "automatic stays"[80] by making a "substantial showing of the denial of a Federal right."[81] This language roughly emulates the standard that *Barefoot* reserved for stays pending appeals and second or successive petitions.[82]

d. *Postfiling stays — successive petition.* In *Barefoot v. Estelle*,[83] the Supreme Court concluded that the requisite "due consideration"[84] of a second or successive petition requires a stay whenever (1) Rule 9(b) of the Rules Governing § 2254 Cases does not compel dismissal on the basis of the successive petition defense to habeas corpus consideration[85] and (2) the petition "reflect[s] the presence of substantial grounds upon which relief might be granted."[86] A petition satisfies *Barefoot*'s requirement of "substantial grounds on

---

[80] In States that qualify for "opt-in" treatment, AEDPA establishes a right to an automatic federal court stay of execution during an initial state postconviction proceeding. *See supra* §§ 3.3c nn.55-60 and accompanying text, 13.2a nn.16-25 and accompanying text.

[81] 28 U.S.C.A. § 2262(b)(3) (West Supp. 1998).

[82] For further discussion of this standard, see *supra* § 3.3c n.56 and accompanying text; *infra* §§ 13.2d, 35.4c.

[83] 463 U.S. 880 (1983).

[84] *Id.* at 889. Although the Supreme Court has consistently recognized that a stay must remain in effect as long as necessary to afford "due consideration" of a petition, the Court has cautioned lower courts that "the grant of a stay of execution [on a second or successive petition] imposes on th[e] ... court the concomitant duty to take all steps necessary to ensure a prompt resolution of the matter, consistent with its duty to give full and fair consideration to all of the issues presented in the case." *In re* Blodgett, 502 U.S. 236, 240 (1992) (*per curiam*); *see also id.* at 237-40 (questioning need for "two-and-a-half-year stay of execution" pending Court of Appeals' resolution of successive petition and remanding to Court of Appeals with instruction to "determine how best to expedite the appeal," but denying state's petition for writ of mandamus directing Court of Appeals to issue its decision).

[85] *See, e.g.,* Delo v. Stokes, 495 U.S. 320, 321-22 (1990) (*per curiam*) (stay pending petitioner's fourth habeas corpus petition denied because petition raises claims that are "not novel" and "could have been raised in [petitioner's] first petition"; petition accordingly "constitutes an abuse of the writ" (quoting *Barefoot, supra,* 463 U.S. at 895)); Richley v. Norris, 32 F.3d 1237, 1239 (8th Cir. 1994) (stay pending petitioner's second habeas corpus petition denied because "all of Richley's claims are either successive or abusive and he has not demonstrated cause or prejudice or shown that a failure to review the claims will result in a fundamental miscarriage of justice"); Baldwin v. Maggio, 704 F.2d 1325, 1326 n.1 (5th Cir. 1983), *cert. denied,* 467 U.S. 1220 (1984). *See infra* Chapter 28 (discussing successive petition defense under Habeas Rule 9(b)). *See also* Hawkins v. Lynaugh, 862 F.2d 487, 489 (5th Cir. 1988), *vac'd & remanded sub nom. Hawkins v. Collins,* 494 U.S. 1013 (1990) (when stay of execution is sought based on successive petition defense, court may dispense with usual requirement that court give successive litigant notice of court's consideration of dismissal on "abuse of writ" grounds and opportunity to respond; either in petition or in stay of application, successive litigants seeking stay should explain why successive petition is not abusive; stay is appropriate if no abuse of writ found).

[86] *Barefoot, supra,* 463 U.S. 895. *See* Bowersox v. Williams, 517 U.S. 345 (1996) (*per curiam*) (vacating stay granted by court of appeals on third habeas corpus petition, because court of appeals

which relief might be granted" if it includes claims that "are debatable among jurists of reason" or that "are 'adequate to deserve encouragement to proceed further."'[87]

---

failed to identify "'substantial grounds upon which relief might be granted'" (citation omitted)); Herrera v. Collins, 506 U.S. 390, 425-26 (1993) (O'Connor, J., concurring) ("stays on 'second or successive federal habeas petition[s] should be granted only when there are "substantial grounds upon which relief might be granted,"' and only when the equities favor the petitioner" (citations omitted) (quoting *Delo v. Stokes, supra,* 495 U.S. at 321 (quoting *Barefoot, supra,* 463 U.S. at 895) and citing Gomez v. United States Dist. Ct., 503 U.S. 653, 654 (1992))); *Delo v. Stokes, supra,* 495 U.S. at 321 ("A stay of execution pending disposition of a second or successive federal habeas petition should be granted only when there are 'substantial grounds upon which relief might be granted'"); Buxton v. Collins, 925 F.2d 816, 819 (5th Cir.), *cert. denied,* 498 U.S. 1128 (1991); Waye v. Townley, 884 F.2d 762, 764 (4th Cir.), *cert. denied,* 492 U.S. 937 (1989) (denying stay after finding no merit to claims); Edwards v. Black, 876 F.2d 377 (5th Cir.), *cert. denied,* 491 U.S. 913 (1989) (*per curiam*) (similar); Fleming v. Kemp, 794 F.2d 1478 (11th Cir. 1986). *Compare* Demosthenes v. Baal, 495 U.S. 731, 737 (1990) (*per curiam*) (for reasons not explained, Court uses same standard — whether petition "'reflect[s] the presence of substantial grounds upon which relief might be granted'" — to ascertain propriety of stay requested by next-friend petitioners seeking to file initial habeas corpus petition on behalf of prisoner who wanted to end appeals and be executed (quoting *Barefoot, supra,* 463 U.S. at 895)) *with* Mercer v. Armontrout, 864 F.2d 1429, 1432 (8th Cir.), *cert. denied,* 488 U.S. 900 (1988) ("Concerns for comity to a sovereign state and finality to its judgments do not outweigh the absolute need to protect against the deprivation of an individual's constitutional rights which might invalidate the capital sentence"; applying same frivolousness test to govern stay pending successive petition as applies to stay pending first petition) *and* Selvage v. Lynaugh, 842 F.2d 89, 91 (5th Cir. 1988), *vac'd & remanded on other grounds,* 494 U.S. 108 (1990) (applying same test for stay pending appeal of denial of second petition as applies to stay pending appeal of denial of first petition). *See generally* Bowden v. Kemp, 474 U.S. 891 (1985) (*mem.*); Autry v. Estelle, 464 U.S. 1301 (1983) (White, Circuit Justice, in chambers); Moore v. Zant, 734 F.2d 585, 586-87 (11th Cir. 1984); Ford v. Strickland, 734 F.2d 538 (11th Cir.), *aff'd sub nom. Wainwright v. Ford,* 467 U.S. 1220 (1984); Smith v. Kemp, 715 F.2d 1455 (11th Cir.), *application to vacate stay denied,* 463 U.S. 1344 (1983); Gray v. Lucas, 710 F.2d 1048 (5th Cir.), *cert. denied,* 463 U.S. 1237 (1983); Baldwin v. Maggio, 704 F.2d 1325, 1326 (5th Cir. 1983), *cert. denied,* 467 U.S. 1220 (1984). A procedural concern for timeliness may augment *Barefoot's* substantive requirement of a substantial claim in determining the appropriateness of a stay in successive petition (but not first-petition) cases. *See* Lonchar v. Thomas, 517 U.S. 314, 320-21, 328-29 (1996) (discussed *supra* §§ 13.1 n.2, 13.2c n.69); *Herrera v. Collins, supra,* 506 U.S. at 426 (O'Connor, J., concurring) (among equities court could consider in ruling on stay pending litigation of successive habeas corpus petition is that "[p]etitioner delayed presenting his new evidence [for years] ... without offering a semblance of a reasonable excuse for the inordinate delay"); *Gomez v. United States Dist. Ct., supra* at 654 (discussed *supra* § 13.1 n.2); McKenzie v. Day, 57 F.3d 1461 (9th Cir.), *aff'd en banc,* 57 F.3d 1493 (9th Cir.), *cert. denied,* 514 U.S. 1104 (1995) (applying *Gomez v. United States Dist. Ct., supra,* to deny stay to petitioner who engaged in "abusive delay" by waiting until "eve of his execution" to raise claim that was available at time of previous habeas corpus petitions, "offered no reason for failing to raise the claim earlier," and failed to present "strong showing of likelihood of success on the merits").

[87] *Barefoot, supra,* 463 U.S. at 893 n.4 (quoting Gordon v. Willis, 516 F. Supp. 911, 913 (N.D. Ga. 1980)). The memorandum in support of a stay in a successive petition case must set out the

The enactment of the Antiterrorism and Effective Death Penalty Act of 1996 (AEDPA)[88] has significant implications for stay practice in successive petition cases. In "nonopt-in States,"[89] *Barefoot* remains the applicable standard for stays of execution in such cases, but AEDPA tightens the substantive standards, and imposes new and onerous procedures, for filing a successive petition.[90] In "opt-in" cases,[91] AEDPA conditions the granting of a stay of execution upon the petitioner's obtaining authorization from the court of appeals for the filing of a successive petition.[92]

e. *District court discretion in non-AEDPA, AEDPA nonopt-in, and AEDPA opt-in cases.* In cases that are not governed by the Antiterrorism and Effective Death Penalty Act of 1996 (AEDPA), [93] the habeas corpus statute gives district courts the discretion to grant stays at *any* time, even if the standards for mandatory stays set out above are not met.[94] In AEDPA "nonopt-in" cases,[95] the district court generally has such discretion but satisfaction of the applicable statute of limitations is likely to be treated as a prerequisite for the granting of a stay.[96] In AEDPA "opt-in" cases,[97] the statutorily-required "automatic" stay

---

reasons why there is no meritorious successive petition defense to habeas corpus consideration under Habeas Rule 9(b) or why that question cannot be decided without an evidentiary hearing. *See infra* Chapter 28. In the successive petition context, the discussion of the substantiality of the claims should be as exhaustive as possible under the circumstances. *See* Julius v. Jones, 875 F.2d 1520, 1525-26 (11th Cir.), *cert. denied,* 493 U.S. 900 (1989) (district court grants stay and certificate of probable cause to appeal on issue that court rejected on merits because state courts had erroneously refused to consider claim's merits, and district judge felt that more than one judge should pass on merits prior to prisoner's execution).

[88] Pub. L. 104-132, 110 Stat. 1214 (1996). For a general description of AEDPA, with cross-references to more detailed discussions elsewhere in this book, see *supra* § 3.2.

[89] For an explanation of AEDPA's "opt-in" provisions and the States to which they apply, see *supra* §§ 3.2, 3.3.

[90] *See infra* §§ 28.3, 28.4 (discussing 28 U.S.C.A. §§ 2244(b)(1), 2244(b)(2) (West 1994 & Supp. 1998)).

[91] *See supra* § 3.3c.

[92] 28 U.S.C.A. § 2262(c) (West Supp. 1998). *See supra* § 3.3c n.58 and accompanying text.

[93] Pub. L. 104-132, 110 Stat. 1214 (1996). For a general description of AEDPA, with cross-references to more detailed discussions elsewhere in this book, see *supra* § 3.2.

[94] *See* McFarland v. Scott, 512 U.S. 849, 858 (1994) ("Section 2251 ... dedicates the exercise of stay jurisdiction to the sound discretion of a federal court."). Barring an "abuse of discretion," such stays should stand up on appeal. *See* 28 U.S.C. § 2251 (1994); Smith v. Kemp, 463 U.S. 1344, 1345 (1983) (Powell, Circuit Justice, in chambers); *infra* § 36.2b.

[95] For an explanation of the "nonopt-in" and "opt-in" categories of cases that AEDPA creates, and the States to which each category applies, see *supra* §§ 3.2, 3.3.

[96] *See supra* §§ 13.1 nn.37-40, 13.2b nn.43-46.

[97] For an explanation of AEDPA's "opt-in" provisions and the States to which they apply, see *supra* §§ 3.2, 3.3.

during an initial state postconviction proceeding terminates, and (unless the stringent procedural and substantive standards for filing a successive habeas corpus petition are satisfied) the district court thereafter is prohibited from granting a stay of execution, if the capital prisoner: (1) fails to file a federal habeas corpus petition within the 180-day opt-in statute of limitations, (2) knowingly and intelligently "waives the right to pursue habeas corpus review" after being advised by the court and counsel of the consequences of doing so, (3) files a federal habeas corpus petition that "fails to make a substantial showing of the denial of a Federal right," or (4) "is denied relief in the district court or at any subsequent stage of review.[98]

§ 13.3. Pre-exhaustion stays.

a. *The stay/abeyance procedure.*[1] In cases in which a condemned prisoner is faced with an imminent execution date that the state courts have refused to stay pending exhaustion of state remedies, the petitioner must secure a pre-exhaustion stay from a district court.[2] A federal stay in this situation enables the district court to preserve its statutory habeas corpus jurisdiction pending exhaustion of state remedies. To secure a stay, the prisoner generally — *i.e.*, unless adherence to the requirement would almost certainly frustrate the federal court's jurisdiction[3] — must establish federal jurisdiction in one of two ways: Either the petitioner must file an application for appointment of federal habeas corpus counsel under the Anti-Drug Abuse Act of 1988,[4] assuming the petitioner is indigent and otherwise qualifies for a stay of execution prior to the filing of a

---

[98] 28 U.S.C.A. § 2262 (West Supp. 1998). *See supra* § 3.3c nn.55-60 and accompanying text (discussing section 2262 and caveats about its constitutionality if it truly means to extinguish statutorily conferred appellate rights and Supreme Court review following lower federal court's denial of stay or of relief); *infra* § 13.6b nn.24-25 (similar). *See also supra* §§ 3.3c n.58, 13.2d n.92 and accompanying text; *infra* §§ 28.3, 28.4 (limited circumstances in which stay is permissible under AEDPA's opt-in procedures pending successive federal habeas corpus litigation).

§ 13.3. [1] This section discusses the procedures for securing or maintaining a federal court stay of execution pending necessary state and federal court consideration of unexhausted claims when such claims are discovered after state postconviction proceedings have terminated, or when a stay of execution is unavailable in such proceedings and the filing of a federal petition pleading unexhausted claims is needed as a basis for securing or maintaining a federal court stay of execution. The chain of proceedings that ordinarily should precede federal habeas corpus is discussed *supra* § 3.5a and *supra* § 5.1. On the procedures to follow when unexhausted claims are identified just before or after a federal habeas petition is filed, apart from the procedures necessitated by the need to secure or maintain a federal court stay of execution, see *supra* § 11.1.

[2] For discussions of the various ways in which this situation might arise, see *supra* §§ 5.3, 6.3, 13.1 nn.8-10 and accompanying text; *infra* note 5 (discussing McFarland v. Scott, 512 U.S. 849 (1994)).

[3] *See supra* § 13.1 n.12.

[4] 21 U.S.C.A. § 848(q) (West 1994 & Supp. 1998).

federal habeas corpus petition, followed (after a sufficient prepetition investigation) by the filing of a comprehensive federal habeas corpus petition;[5]

---

[5] *See supra* §§ 12.1 (indigence and *in forma pauperis* proceedings), 12.2-12.3b (application for appointment of counsel under Anti-Drug Abuse Act of 1988), 13.1-13.2b (prerequisites for prepetition stay of execution). In regard to the sufficiency of the prepetition investigation, see *supra* §§ 11.2 (prefiling investigation and claim identification, generally), 13.2b (scope of prefiling investigation contemplated by *McFarland v. Scott, supra*). The Supreme Court approved the procedure discussed in text in McFarland v. Scott, 512 U.S. 849 (1994) (discussed *supra* §§ 12.2, 12.3a, 12.3b, 13.1, 13.2a, 13.2b). There, an unrepresented prisoner unable to take advantage of state postconviction proceedings because neither state-funded counsel nor a state stay of execution was available sought a federal district court's appointment of counsel and stay of execution pending investigation of claims and the filing of a federal habeas corpus petition that almost certainly would have included unexhausted claims. *See McFarland, supra* at 851-52. The *McFarland* Court reversed the district court's denial of the prisoner's request for prepetition counsel and a stay, reaching four conclusions along the way — (1) "a capital defendant may invoke his right to a counseled federal habeas corpus proceeding by filing a motion requesting the appointment of habeas counsel" even before a federal petition is filed, *id.* at 859; (2) "a district court has jurisdiction to enter a stay of execution where necessary to give effect to th[e] statutory right" to counsel, *id.*; (3) "the [statutory] right to counsel necessarily includes a right for that counsel meaningfully to research and present a defendant's habeas claims," *id.* at 858; and (4) meaningful research and presentation (a) may require the "services of investigators and other experts [because such services] may be critical in the preapplication phase of a habeas corpus proceeding, when possible claims and their factual bases are researched and identified," and (b) does require consideration of the Court's "complex[] ... jurisprudence" governing criminal and especially capital cases, *id.* at 855. *See also id.* at 860 (O'Connor, J., concurring in the judgment in part) (counsel's goal upon being appointed prior to filing federal petition is to assure "that the first [federal] petition adequately set[s] forth all of a state prisoner's colorable claims for relief"). Given that Frank McFarland had not been able to pursue any state postconviction proceedings due to the absence of counsel and a stay of execution, and given the comprehensive pre-federal habeas corpus petition investigation that the Court permitted, the only proper reading of *McFarland* is as endorsing a federal stay and appointment of federal counsel *before* state postconviction proceedings whenever a state stay and appointment of counsel are unavailable — notwithstanding that the almost inevitable effect of the procedure (as Justice Thomas suggested, *see id.* at 869-70 (Thomas, J., dissenting)) will be the identification and inclusion in the federal petition of new and entirely *unexhausted* claims. *See supra* § 13.2b nn.49, 59 and accompanying text.

Note, however, that the new statutes of limitations that the Antiterrorism and Effective Death Penalty Act of 1996 (AEDPA), Pub. L. 104-132, 110 Stat. 1214 (1996), adopts for capital cases in "nonopt-in" and "opt-in" situations can only be satisfied by the timing filing of an "application" for habeas corpus relief, which may not — although it probably does — include a *McFarland* application for appointment of counsel. *See supra* § 5.1b nn.79-90 and accompanying text; for discussion of the differences between "nonopt-in" and "opt-in" cases, see *supra* § 3.2. Until this ambiguity in the statutes of limitations is resolved, and given the importance of avoiding even the slightest risk of allowing the limitations period to expire before filing the appropriate document, capital prisoners are strongly advised to take the extra step described in section 5.1b *supra* (*i.e.*, the filing of a "placeholder petition" for habeas corpus relief at the same time as the application for appointment of counsel is filed) in order to comply with *McFarland* and AEDPA simultaneously. *See supra* § 5.1b n.91 and accompanying text.

or the petitioner must file a habeas corpus petition pleading the unexhausted claims together with an application for a stay of execution pending exhaustion of state remedies and a supporting memorandum asking the court to grant a stay and to hold the case in abeyance pending exhaustion.[6]

State courts can keep capital prisoners from skipping over state postconviction proceedings and moving (if only temporarily) to the federal courts by providing state postconviction counsel and stays of execution. *See McFarland, supra,* 512 U.S. at 870 (Thomas, J., dissenting) ("it seems likely that Congress expected that the States would ... shoulder some of the burden of providing preapplication legal assistance to indigent death-sentenced prisoners"; "'[a] state that has elected to impose the death penalty should provide adequate funding for the procedures it has adopted to properly implement that penalty'" (quoting Hill v. Lockhart, 992 F.2d 801, 803 (8th Cir. 1993)). The States' incentive to grant stays and appoint counsel may be limited, however, by the desire to shift to the federal courts the cost of adequate pre-postconviction legal representation and legal and factual investigation. If the States encourage cases to jump to federal court prior to state postconviction proceedings for purposes of prefiling investigation and preparation of petitions, there are three possible allocations of responsibility among state and federal courts that may ensue upon a prisoner's discovery of unexhausted claims: (1) By invoking their "exhaustion of state remedies" defense to federal relief, *see infra* Chapter 23, the State may successfully insist that the case return to the state courts for litigation of newly discovered claims, thereby ensuring that factfindings made during state postconviction proceedings will be accorded a presumption of correctness. *See infra* §§ 20.2, 20.3, 30.3. (2) If the prisoner opposes invocation of the exhaustion doctrine, a federal court might resist the State's effort to derive the benefit without bearing the costs of the exhaustion doctrine, by applying the rule that exhaustion of *inadequate* state remedies is *not* required and by finding that the absence of state-funded counsel and stays makes the State's postconviction remedy inadequate. *See infra* § 23.4. (3) If the prisoner and the federal court approve, the State may waive exhaustion and thus permit federal habeas corpus to supersede the state postconviction remedy. *See infra* § 23.2. Which of these procedures will become the norm(s) remains to be seen and may differ from State to State and case to case. For further exploration of these questions, *see supra* § 6.3 nn.5-10 and accompanying text. *But see* In re Joiner, 58 F.3d 143 (5th Cir. 1995) (*per curiam*) (following *Sterling v. Scott, infra,* as precedent binding within circuit, although one member of panel expresses "uneas[iness]" with *Sterling's* holding, *id.* at 144 (King, J., concurring)); Sterling v. Scott, 57 F.3d 451, 454-58 (5th Cir. 1995), *cert. denied,* 516 U.S. 1050 (1996) (neither *McFarland* nor Anti-Drug Abuse Act authorizes use of federally funded counsel for exhaustion of available state postconviction remedies in "mixed petition" situations; district court did not err in dismissing mixed petition and terminating appointment of counsel while petitioner exhausted remaining state remedies); In re Parker, 49 F.3d 204 (6th Cir. 1995) (similar to *Steffen v. Tate, infra*); Steffen v. Tate, 39 F.3d 622, 624-28 (6th Cir. 1994) (prisoner, who "is, and has been for over two years now, ably defended by the Ohio Public Defender" and who had already "proceeded through two complete rounds of litigation in the state courts," could not invoke *McFarland* procedure to stay execution "indefinitely" while petitioner pursues any unexhausted "state procedure that he can conjure up, regardless of its merit" because it was apparent that petitioner had no intention to file federal habeas corpus petition in foreseeable future and was "frantically attempting to *avoid* invoking the jurisdiction of the federal court"); Wilson v. Horn, 1997 WL 137343, at *5 (E.D. Pa. March 24, 1997) (denying request for appointment of counsel under 21 U.S.C. § 848(q)(8) to pursue state postconviction remedies).

[6] *See supra* §§ 13.1 (procedural prerequisites for stay, generally), 13.2a & 13.2c (substantive prerequisites for stay pending initial habeas corpus petition), 13.2d (substantive prerequisites for

In other cases, a condemned prisoner may, after exhausting state postconviction remedies on all known claims and before filing a federal habeas corpus petition, discover a new and unexhausted claim.[7] If the state courts will not grant a stay of execution pending exhaustion of the new claim, the broadly preclusive rules governing successive habeas corpus petitions force the condemned prisoner to include the new claim in the federal petition so as to avoid any charge that he waived the claim.[8] Because the total exhaustion rule forbids the federal court to reach the merits of any claim in a petition mixing exhausted and unexhausted claims (except in those narrow instances in which all claims in the petition lack merit and the court therefore can deny the entire petition on the merits),[9] the prisoner additionally must ask the district court to grant a federal stay of execution pending exhaustion of the new claim and to hold the petition in abeyance pending exhaustion. In such circumstances, the petition should be accompanied by an application for a stay pending exhaustion and a memorandum in support of that application.[10]

In still other cases, the respondent may convince the district court that the prisoner has not exhausted one or more of the claims that the prisoner believed to be exhausted. In this case, too, the court should hold the petition in abeyance under an existing or newly granted stay and permit the prisoner to complete the requisite state proceedings.[11]

Although the abeyance procedure has been used most frequently in capital cases to provide federal habeas corpus courts with jurisdiction to enforce stays of execution while exhaustion proceedings occur in the state courts, the same or a similar procedure has also been used more recently to permit federal habeas corpus courts to avoid difficulties caused by the combination of the exhaustion

---

stay pending successive habeas corpus petition); *infra* §§ 13.3b & 13.3c (legal authority for jurisdiction preserving stays pending exhaustion of state remedies).

[7] *See supra* § 11.1. *See also supra* note 6; *supra* §§ 13.1 n.17, 13.2b nn.49, 59 and accompanying text (all discussing Supreme Court's and other courts' contemplation of not uncommon situations in which federal habeas corpus petitioners discover new and unexhausted claims during legal and factual investigation that either precedes or immediately follows filing of federal habeas corpus petition).

[8] *See McFarland v. Scott, supra*, 512 U.S. at 860 (O'Connor, J., concurring in the judgment in part) ("our carefully crafted doctrines of waiver and abuse of the writ make it especially important that the first [federal] petition adequately set forth all of a state prisoner's colorable grounds for relief"); other similar authority discussed *supra* §§ 11.2a nn.5-7 & 11.3b nn.12-15 and accompanying text (discussing implications of McCleskey v. Zant, 499 U.S. 467 (1991)); *supra* § 12.3a nn.15-20 and accompanying text; *infra* Chapter 28 (successive petition doctrine).

[9] *See supra* § 11.1; *infra* § 23.5.

[10] The rules of some district and circuit courts require the petitioner to explain why he failed to exhaust state remedies. *See* Model Form for Use in Applications for Habeas Corpus Under 28 U.S.C. § 2254, pt. II(e), foll. Rules Governing § 2254 Cases.

[11] *See infra* § 15.2d.

requirement and recently adopted statutes of limitations. Thus, as is discussed in more detail elsewhere, the abeyance or an analogous procedure might serve to assure that a habeas corpus petition that was filed before the expiration of the limitations period is not rendered untimely by (i) the discovery in the petition of unexhausted claims, (ii) the petition's dismissal pending exhaustion of state remedies, and (iii) the petition's subsequent refiling after the statute of limitations has expired.[12]

b. *Legal authority.* The pendency or contemplation of state postconviction proceedings does not preclude a federal district court from taking or retaining jurisdiction over a habeas corpus petition and granting or extending a stay of execution pending exhaustion of state remedies.[13] Under the terms of 28 U.S.C. § 2254(b), exhaustion of state remedies is not a necessary precondition to the *filing* of a federal habeas corpus petition, but instead a condition that must be fulfilled before relief may be granted.[14] Exhaustion of state remedies, in other words, is not jurisdictional.[15] Accordingly, if a state court has refused to grant a

---

[12] *See supra* §§ 3.4a n.16 and accompanying text, 5.1b n.57 and accompanying text, 11.1 n.14 and accompanying text.

[13] *See, e.g.,* E.D. CAL. RULE 191(h)(5) (district court may grant stay of execution and stay of proceedings on current habeas corpus petition if petitioner indicates that unexhausted claim is still available; petitioner then has 60 days to file state exhaustion proceedings; once petitioner completes exhaustion proceedings, he may amend newly exhausted claim into federal petition). The courts of at least one State, however, will not adjudicate a state postconviction petition of a prisoner who has filed a petition in federal court challenging the same petition. *See* Rumbaugh ex rel. Rumbaugh v. McKaskle, 730 F.2d 291, 293 (5th Cir. 1994) (Texas practice).

[14] "An application for a writ of habeas corpus ... shall not be *granted* unless it appears that the applicant has exhausted the remedies available in the courts of the State." 28 U.S.C. § 2254(b) (1994) (emphasis added). *See, e.g.,* Sharpe v. Buchanan, 317 U.S. 238 (1942); Davis v. Jackson, 246 F.2d 268 (2d Cir. 1957). *Cf.* McNeil v. United States, 508 U.S. 106, 111 (1993) (exhaustion of administrative remedies under Federal Tort Claims Act, 28 U.S.C. § 2675(a), is prerequisite to *filing* an action, but only because Act's language — "[a]n action shall not be *instituted* ... unless the claimant shall have *first* presented the claim to the appropriate Federal agency and his claim shall have been *finally* denied by the agency" (emphasis added) — "unambiguous[ly]" requires pre*filing* completion of exhaustion); Coleman v. Vasquez, 771 F. Supp. 300, 303 (N.D. Cal. 1991) (federal court appointment of counsel in capital cases to investigate possible unexhausted claims "does no violence to the exhaustion doctrine, which is limited to the *adjudication* of constitutional claims"; as long as "the state courts [have the opportunity], in the first instance to pass upon and correct alleged violations of prisoners' federal constitutional rights[,] ... [t]he federal court in no way has trod on the state court's resolution of the federal constitutional issues" (emphasis in original)).

[15] *See, e.g.,* Granberry v. Greer, 481 U.S. 129, 131 (1987); Strickland v. Washington, 466 U.S. 668, 679 (1984); Duckworth v. Serrano, 454 U.S. 1, 3-4 (1981); Fay v. Noia, 372 U.S. 391, 415-20 (1963); Irvin v. Dowd, 359 U.S. 394, 404-05 (1959); Frisbie v. Collins, 342 U.S. 519, 521-22 (1952); Ex parte Royall, 117 U.S. 241, 249-51 (1886); Zettlemoyer v. Fulcomer, 923 F.2d 284, 309 (3d Cir. 1991), *cert. denied,* 502 U.S. 902 (1992); Prather v. Norman, 901 F.2d 915, 918 (11th Cir. 1990); Brown v. Rison, 895 F.2d 533, 535 (9th Cir. 1990) (judicially created requirement that

stay pending its adjudication of a prisoner's federal constitutional claims or if it may be difficult to obtain such a state court stay in time to preserve those claims, the district court is authorized to order a stay of execution (or to extend a stay already in effect).[16]

When a condemned prisoner faced with an unstayed execution date files a federal habeas corpus petition prior to the exhaustion of state remedies, it is proper for the district court to enter a stay of execution[17] and to hold the petition in abeyance pending exhaustion of remedies in the state courts.[18] In modifying a

---

federal prisoners exhaust administrative remedies before filing habeas corpus petition is not jurisdictional); Dispensa v. Lynaugh, 847 F.2d 211, 217 & n.3 (5th Cir. 1988); Pador v. Matanane, 653 F.2d 1277, 1278 n.1 (9th Cir. 1981); United States ex rel. Lockett v. Illinois Parole and Pardon Bd., 600 F.2d 116, 117 (7th Cir. 1979); Galtieri v. Wainwright, 582 F.2d 348, 354 (5th Cir. 1978) (*en banc*); Powell v. Keve, 409 F. Supp. 228, 231 (D. Del. 1976) (citing cases); other authority cited *infra* §§ 23.2a nn.6-7, 23.3b n.24, 23.5 n.8. *See generally infra* Chapter 23 (exhaustion doctrine).

[16] *See* authority cited *infra* notes 17-19.

[17] *See, e.g.,* Byrd v. Delo, 917 F.2d 1037, 1048 (8th Cir. 1990) ("stay of execution is generally appropriate where a petitioner has failed to exhaust state remedies"); Neuschafer v. Whitley, 860 F.2d 1470, 1472 & n.1 (9th Cir. 1988), *cert. denied,* 493 U.S. 906 (1989) (citing cases) (discussed *infra* note 18); Prejean v. Blackburn, 743 F.2d 1091, 1094 (5th Cir. 1984) (temporary stay granted to allow petitioner to present unexhausted claim to state court); Spencer v. Wainwright, 403 F.2d 778, 782 n.9 (5th Cir. 1968); Brent v. White, 398 F.2d 503, 507 (5th Cir. 1968), *cert. denied,* 393 U.S. 1123 (1969); Whitney v. Wainwright, 339 F.2d 275, 276 (5th Cir. 1964); Duffy v. Wells, 201 F.2d 503, 504 (9th Cir. 1952); Hill v. Nelson, 271 F. Supp. 439, 444 (N.D. Cal.), *modified on other grounds,* 272 F. Supp. 790 (N.D. Cal. 1967) (stay issued to permit amendment and further hearing of petition); Brown v. Brough, 248 F. Supp. 342, 344 (D. Md. 1965); Crawford v. Bailey, 234 F. Supp. 700, 702 (E.D.N.C. 1964); authority cited *infra* note 18 (similar). *See also* Collins v. Byrd, 510 U.S. 1185, 1185-88 (1994) (*mem.*) (Scalia, J., dissenting from denial of motion to vacate stay) (describing 6th Circuit order, which Supreme Court declined to vacate, directing district court to hold federal habeas corpus petition in abeyance pending United States Supreme Court's ruling on prisoner's petition for *certiorari* to review state courts' denial of postconviction relief); Herrera v. Collins, 506 U.S. 390, 424-25 (1993) (O'Connor, J., concurring) (suggesting by negative implication that federal court may grant stay pending state proceedings either (1) if state court's refusal to grant stay or other review of petitioner's claim violates federal Constitution or (2) if necessary to enable petitioner to "obtain[] relief — or even a hearing — through the state courts" on claims cognizable in state court but *not* thereafter cognizable in federal court; caveat to latter implication is that "District Court ... [must] order[] the habeas petition dismissed and the stay lifted once the state court action was filed, without further condition"). *Compare* Tinder v. Paula, 725 F.2d 801, 805 (1st Cir. 1984) (noncapital case) ("Whether jurisdiction over a claim for habeas relief should be retained pending exhaustion of state court remedies is generally a matter within the discretion of the [federal] court") *with* Nottlemann v. Welding, 861 F.2d 1087, 1088 (8th Cir. 1988) (*per curiam*) (noncapital case) ("When a petitioner fails to exhaust state remedies in a habeas corpus action it is not necessary or proper for the federal court to retain jurisdiction ... [and it] must decline to exercise jurisdiction until such time that state remedies are exhausted").

[18] *See e.g.,* Edwards v. Balisok, 117 S. Ct. 1584, 1589 (1997) (suggesting that federal courts are permitted to stay or hold in abeyance, rather than dismiss, previously filed judicial proceedings

pending exhaustion of remedies that are prerequisite to final adjudication of previously filed proceedings); Lambrix v. Singletary, 117 S. Ct. 1517, 1521-22, 1523 (1997) (in case in which petitioner brought claim based on recently announced Supreme Court decision to attention of 11th Circuit before which petitioner's case then was pending, Court notes with seeming approval that, "[r]ather than address this issue in the first instance ..., the Eleventh Circuit held its proceedings in abeyance to permit [petitioner] to present [the relevant claim] to the Florida state courts"); Christy v. Horn, 115 F.3d 201, 207 (3d Cir. 1997) (approving procedure of "grant[ing] a stay and abeyance motion" rather than dismissing mixed petition when "state court has refused to grant a stay pending its adjudication of a prisoner's federal constitutional claims"); Calderon v. United States Dist. Ct., 107 F.3d 756, 760 (9th Cir.), *cert. denied*, 118 S. Ct. 265 (1997) ("When a petitioner has not exhausted his state remedies before filing a federal habeas petition, a district court may hold the petition in abeyance, issue a stay of execution, and allow the petitioner an opportunity to exhaust his state remedies."); Burris v. Farley, 51 F.3d 655, 659 (7th Cir. 1995) (*dicta*) (analogizing to situation in "civil litigation when one or more legal theories is unripe," court suggests that habeas corpus petitioners with partially exhausted claims can "protect themselves" by "filing a petition raising all exhausted issues and asking the court for a stay [of federal proceedings] until the remaining issues have been exhausted"); Rowland v. Calderon, C-94-3037-EFL (N.D. Cal. April 21, 1997) (granting petitioner's request to amend petition to delete unexhausted claims and stay federal proceedings during exhaustion of state remedies); Fetterly v. Paskett, 997 F.2d 1295, 1301-02 (9th Cir. 1993) (district court abused discretion by refusing to hold federal proceedings in abeyance while petitioner returned to state court to litigate unexhausted claims; "it is understandable that [petitioner] wished to bring all his claims in one pending proceeding rather than move to dismiss and start again when he had fully exhausted his new issues ... [and] [t]here is nothing at all in this record to suggest that the motion for a stay was brought to vex, or to harass, or that the request was an abuse of the writ"); Scott v. Dugger, 891 F.2d 800, 802 (11th Cir. 1989), *cert. denied*, 498 U.S. 881 (1990) (*per curiam*) (district court stayed execution and stayed federal habeas corpus proceedings pending exhaustion of state remedies); Giarratano v. Procunier, 891 F.2d 483, 485 (4th Cir. 1989), *cert. denied*, 498 U.S. 881 (1990) (district court stayed judgment denying petitioner relief in order "to permit [petitioner] to present his lack of competency claim to the state courts"); Young v. Kenny, 887 F.2d 237, 238 (9th Cir. 1989); *Neuschafer v. Whitley*, *supra*, 860 F.2d at 1472 n.1 (citing cases) ("When a petitioner has not exhausted his state remedies before filing a federal habeas petition, a district court may hold the federal petition in abeyance, issue a stay of execution, and allow the petitioner an opportunity to exhaust his state remedies"); *id.* at 1482 (Alarcon, J., concurring) (if state fails to grant stay to permit newly appointed counsel time to review record and raise unexhausted claims, thereby forcing counsel to file federal petition without exhausting all claims, district court should grant stay for reasonable time in order to allow counsel to review record and inform district court whether any unexhausted claims remain that petitioner wishes to pursue; if necessary, district court should hold petition in abeyance under stay until all claims become exhausted and can be added to federal petition); Collins v. Lockhart, 754 F.2d 258, 260 (8th Cir.), *cert. denied*, 474 U.S. 1013 (1985); Arango v. Wainwright, 716 F.2d 1353, 1355 (11th Cir. 1983), *reh'g denied with opinion*, 739 F.2d 529 (11th Cir. 1984), *cert. denied*, 469 U.S. 1127 (1985) (stay of execution not involved); Thompson v. Wainwright, 714 F.2d 1495, 1499 (11th Cir. 1983), *cert. denied*, 466 U.S. 962 (1984); Collins v. Lockhart, 707 F.2d 341, 344 (8th Cir. 1983); Briley v. Hutto, No. 81-6261 (4th Cir. Apr. 23, 1981); Shaw v. Martin, 613 F.2d 487, 493 (4th Cir. 1980) (Phillips, J., in chambers); Chenault v. Stynchcombe, 581 F.2d 444, 448 (5th Cir. 1978); Thomas v. Teets, 205 F.2d 236, 240 (9th Cir.), *cert. denied*, 346 U.S. 910 (1953); Tyler v. James, No. C82-36A (N.D. Ga. Jan. 19, 1982); Modesto v. Nelson, 296 F. Supp. 1375, 1376 (N.D. Cal. 1969); Moorer v. South Carolina, 239 F. Supp. 180, 182 (E.D.S.C. 1965);

Ralph v. Pepersack, 203 F. Supp. 752, 754-55 (D. Md.), *cert. denied,* 369 U.S. 813 (1962); United States ex rel. La Marca v. Denno, 159 F. Supp. 486, 488 (S.D.N.Y. 1958). *See also* Wilton v. Seven Falls Co., 515 U.S. 277, 283 (1995) (when exercising discretion whether to adjudicate federal declaratory judgment action or withhold federal judicial action until state proceeding addressing related issues was completed, it was "of little moment" that federal court "stayed rather than dismissed the [federal] action" because, if state proceeding later turns out to "bind the parties" to federal action, dismissal of stayed federal proceeding can occur at that time); Carchman v. Nash, 473 U.S. 716, 722 (1985) (federal proceedings in noncapital case stayed pending exhaustion of state remedies); Oscar Mayer & Co. v. Evans, 441 U.S. 750, 764-65 (1979) (when plaintiff in Age Discrimination in Employment Act was found to have failed to exhaust administrative remedies as required by statute, proper result was to suspend federal proceedings rather than to dismiss; suspension rather than dismissal is particularly appropriate "in a statutory scheme in which laymen, unassisted by trained lawyers, initiate the process" (quoting Love v. Pullman Co., 404 U.S. 522, 526-27 (1972))); Mackey v. Dickson, 47 F.3d 744, 746 (5th Cir. 1995) *(per curiam)* (district court acted prematurely in dismissing section 1983 claim of unlawful arrests in criminal cases that were still pending, given that it was impossible to determine whether "successful attack on Mackey's arrests will implicate the validity of his confinement" and thus require dismissal of section 1983 under rule of Heck v. Humphrey, 512 U.S. 477 (1994); proper course of action was to "stay proceedings in the section 1983 case until the pending criminal case has run its course, as until that time it may be difficult to determine the relation, if any, between the two"); Simpson v. Camper, 927 F.2d 392, 393-94 (8th Cir. 1991) (state's appeal of grant of writ held in abeyance pending petitioner's exhaustion of state remedies that may still be available); Bliss v. Lockhart, 891 F.2d 1335, 1339 (8th Cir. 1989) (noncapital case) (suggesting that, following finding of nonexhaustion, district court may "continue" case pending exhaustion or dismissal without prejudice); Johnson v. Texas, 878 F.2d 904, 906 (5th Cir. 1989) (when habeas corpus and civil rights claims are joined in same complaint and civil rights claim is subject to statute of limitations, district court has discretion to hold petition in abeyance pending exhaustion of state remedies rather than dismissing petition; order holding petition in abeyance is appealable pursuant to collateral-order exception to final-judgment rule); Sheppard v. Louisiana Bd. of Parole, 873 F.2d 761, 762 (5th Cir. 1989) *(per curiam)* (similar); Blair v. California, 340 F.2d 741 (9th Cir. 1965); *Coleman v. Vasquez, supra,* 771 F. Supp. at 303 (discussed *supra* note 14); Johnson v. Lumpkin, 654 F. Supp. 592, 596 (S.D. Cal. 1987) (applying exception to rule requiring dismissal of unexhausted petitions in noncapital cases when "special circumstances" would make outright dismissal inappropriate; federal jurisdiction retained pending exhaustion so as to preserve federal order granting bail (citing Nelson v. George, 399 U.S. 224 (1970); Wade v. Wilson, 396 U.S. 282 (1970); Smith v. Wyrick, 558 F. Supp. 600 (W.D. Mo. 1983))); Rogers v. Britton, 466 F. Supp. 397, 403 (E.D. Ark. 1979); authority cited *supra* § 9.1 n.33 (collecting cases similar to *Johnson* and *Sheppard, supra,* permitting or requiring district courts to hold section 1983 claims in abeyance pending exhaustion of related habeas corpus claims in order to avoid losing jurisdiction over former claims by operation of statutes of limitations). *Cf.* Greenawalt v. Stewart, 105 F.3d 1268, 1273-75 (9th Cir.) *(per curiam), cert. denied,* 117 S. Ct. 794 (1997) (district court did not abuse discretion in dismissing mixed petition instead of granting request to hold petition in abeyance pending exhaustion of unexhausted claim). *But see* Victor v. Hopkins, 90 F.3d 276, 282 (8th Cir. 1996), *cert. denied,* 117 S. Ct. 1091 (1997) (district court does not have authority to hold mixed petition in abeyance and maintain stay pending exhaustion; proper procedure is to dismiss petition and lift stay); Sterling v. Scott, 57 F.3d 451, 454 (5th Cir. 1995), *cert. denied,* 516 U.S. 1050 (1996) (district court did not err in denying request to hold mixed petition in abeyance pending exhaustion of unexhausted claims); Smith v. Dugger, 888 F.2d 94, 95 (11th Cir. 1989) *(per curiam), cert.*

district court's dismissal of an unexhausted petition filed by a capital prisoner, for example, the 5th Circuit has stated that "[u]ntil the [state] courts make their ruling under the facts and circumstances of [the] case," a federal court should "retain jurisdiction for the purpose of continuing the stay of execution, provided [petitioner] immediately files and diligently prosecutes to a prompt conclusion his habeas corpus petition in the ... state courts."[19]

---

denied, 494 U.S. 1047 (1990) (court of appeals denies motion to hold appeal in abeyance pending exhaustion of newly discovered federal claim that petitioner sought to exhaust and then amend into petition).

In generally distinguishing federal court "abstention" from federal court "deferral" in the face of actual or potential action by a state court "exercising concurrent jurisdiction over the same subject matter" as that before the federal court, the Supreme Court has provided additional support for the stay/abeyance procedure described in text. *See* Growe v. Emison, 507 U.S. 25, 32 & n.1 (1993). As *Growe* points out, in those "rare circumstances" in which "principles of federalism and comity dictate" that a federal court forbear acting on a matter over which it exercises concurrent jurisdiction with the state courts, two alternative courses of action are possible: "a federal court ...[]either [may] abstain (*i.e.,* dismiss the case before it) []or defer to the state proceedings (*i.e.,* withhold action until the state proceedings have concluded)." *Id.* at 32. The Court's description of the "deferral" option accurately describes the exhaustion of state remedies doctrine in the habeas corpus context. According to *Growe,* deferral is appropriate in "circumstances ... that require postponing," rather than permanently refraining from, "consideration of [a suit's] merits." *Id.* at 32 n.1. Under the "deferral" option, as under the habeas corpus exhaustion doctrine, "a federal court ... 'stay[s] its hands' when a constitutional issue in the federal action ... will be mooted or presented in a different posture following conclusion of the state-court case" or when it is thought "that federal courts should not prematurely resolve the constitutionality of a state statute ... [or] prematurely involve themselves in [other constitutional adjudication affecting important state functions such as] redistricting." *Id.* at 32 & n.1 (quoting Railroad Comm'n v. Pullman Co., 312 U.S. 496, 501 (1941), and citing Scott v. Germano, 381 U.S. 407 (1965) (*per curiam*)). *Growe* suggests that "deferral" or abeyance, rather than "dismissal," is *an,* if not the *only,* appropriate procedure following a federal court's conclusion that state remedies in regard to claims raised in a federal habeas corpus petition have not been exhausted. This is so, given: (1) the Court's care in *Growe* to "bring out more clearly ... the distinction between those circumstances that require dismissal of a suit and those that [merely] require postponing consideration of its merits" until state action is completed; (2) the Court's care in *Growe* to characterize the latter set of doctrines as "deferral," and not, for example, as "abstention" doctrines, *id.* at 32 n.1; (3) the nearly perfect match between *Growe*'s "deferral" doctrines and the habeas corpus exhaustion requirement; and, finally, (4) the plain meaning of the "deferral" or "'stay[s] its hand'" terminology. In a somewhat analogous (declaratory judgment) situation, *Wilton v. Seven Falls Co., supra,* holds that a district court's decision whether to dismiss, stay, or proceed with a case presenting issues raised in related state court litigation was reviewable only for "abuse of discretion" and not "*de novo.*" *See Wilton v. Seven Falls Co., supra,* 515 U.S. at 283, 289-90.

For discussion of caselaw recognizing the propriety of holding a petition in abeyance pending exhaustion when the effect of dismissal may be to render a re-filed federal petition time-barred under AEDPA's statute of limitations, see *supra* § 5.1b n.57. *See also supra* §§ 3.4a n.16 and accompanying text, 11.1 n.14 and accompanying text, 13.3a n.12 and accompanying text.

[19] Clarke v. Grimes, 374 F.2d 550, 553 (5th Cir. 1967). *Accord, e.g., Fetterly v. Paskett, supra,* 997 F.2d at 1301-02; *Shaw v. Martin, supra,* 613 F.2d at 493 (Phillips, J., in chambers); Tyler v.

c. *Total exhaustion and stay/abeyance.* The total exhaustion rule of *Rose v. Lundy*[20] does not bar the stay/abeyance procedure.[21] In *Rose*, the Supreme Court recognized that a failure to exhaust is not a jurisdictional defect.[22] The Court held only that, if final *relief* on one or more claims is unavailable due to exhaustion, the district courts should withhold relief on all claims.[23] The total exhaustion rule is grounded in a judicial economy concern that all claims in the petition be adjudicated at once, not piecemeal.[24] Nothing in the rule prevents a district court from holding the *entire* petition in abeyance under a stay pending exhaustion, then adjudicating the *entire* petition once all claims are exhausted.[25] Rather, by permitting the petitioner to exhaust available state remedies with regard to all known claims before federal proceedings on the merits commence, the stay/abeyance procedure facilitates achievement of the policies underlying the total exhaustion rule.[26]

Rose implicitly supports the stay/abeyance procedure. First, *Rose* derived the total exhaustion rule from a similar requirement previously applied by the 5th Circuit;[27] and the 5th Circuit before *Rose* utilized the stay/abeyance procedure when necessary to preserve federal jurisdiction and protect federal rights against

---

James, *supra*, No. C82-36A. *See also* Williams v. Wyrick, 763 F.2d 363 (8th Cir. 1985). For an illustration, in another context, of the importance of ensuring that the federal court retain jurisdiction over the case by holding the petition in abeyance rather than dismissing it pending exhaustion, see Kokkonen v. Guardian Life Ins. Co., 511 U.S. 375, 377-82 (1994) (federal court lacked jurisdiction to enforce court-approved settlement agreement between parties because case had been dismissed and neither settlement agreement nor statute specifically provided for ongoing court jurisdiction). Given that stay standards are less stringent earlier and more stringent later in the habeas corpus process, *see supra* §§ 13.2b-13.2d, the standard governing stays pending exhaustion of state remedies should be no more stringent than the "nonfrivolous claim" requirement for post-exhaustion district-court stays in Barefoot v. Estelle, 463 U.S. 880 (1983). *See supra* § 13.2.

[20] 455 U.S. 509 (1982) (discussed *supra* § 11.1; *infra* § 23.5).

[21] In fact, by its very nature, the habeas corpus exhaustion doctrine seems at the least to invite the stay/abeyance procedure. *See supra* § 13.3b n.18.

[22] *Rose, supra,* 455 U.S. at 518. *Accord* Granberry v. Greer, 481 U.S. 129, 131 (1987); Strickland v. Washington, 466 U.S. 668, 684 (1984); other authority cited *supra* § 13.3b n.15 & *infra* §§ 23.2a nn.6-7, 23.3b n.24, 23.5 n.8.

[23] *Rose, supra,* 455 U.S. at 518-20. *See supra* § 13.3b n.14 and accompanying text.

[24] *Rose, supra,* 455 U.S. at 520.

[25] *See* post-*Rose* authority cited *supra* § 13.3b nn.17-19.

[26] *See* Fetterly v. Paskett, 997 F.2d 1295, 1301-02 (9th Cir. 1993) (discussed *supra* § 13.3b n.18).

[27] *See* Galtieri v. Wainwright, 582 F.2d 348, 355-60 (5th Cir. 1978) (*en banc*) (cited approvingly in *Rose, supra,* 455 U.S. at 513 n.5).

the mooting effect of the petitioner's premature execution.[28] Second, the federal courts best can advance *Rose*'s policy of achieving "a more focused and thorough review" of "all the prisoner's claims in a single [federal] proceeding" by ensuring that capital prisoners have an opportunity without threat of execution to exhaust all their claims before pursuing them in a single federal petition.[29]

§ 13.4. The stay hearing.[1]

Section 2251 of the habeas corpus statute and Rule 4 of the Rules Governing § 2254 Cases permit the federal courts to grant stays of execution summarily and *ex parte*.[2] In some circumstances, however, the district court will ask the state to respond to the stay application and the court may even order oral argument and an evidentiary hearing. At this point, counsel first must determine whether the date set for the filing of a written response or for the hearing will allow the district court enough time to rule and counsel enough time to appeal an unfavorable ruling.[3] If there is not enough time, petitioner should appeal immediately, following the procedure outlined in section 13.6b *infra*.

Although at a later point in the proceedings the petitioner may seek a full-blown evidentiary hearing on the merits,[4] such a hearing *never* is appropriate in considering the propriety of a *pre*petition stay of execution[5] and *generally* is not appropriate in *post*petition stay proceedings at this preliminary and time-constrained stage of the proceedings which typically is not amenable to the "full and fair" procedures contemplated by the habeas corpus statute.[6] As discussed above,[7] stays are required in cases involving nonfrivolous claims precisely so that the district court thereafter can afford such claims the "careful attention they

---

[28] *See, e.g.,* Stephens v. Zant, 631 F.2d 397 (5th Cir. 1980), *amended on reh'g,* 648 F.2d 446 (5th Cir. 1981), *rev'd on other grounds,* 462 U.S. 862 (1983); Chenault v. Stynchcombe, 581 F.2d 444, 448 (5th Cir. 1978).

[29] *Rose, supra,* 455 U.S. at 520. *See Fetterly v. Paskett, supra,* 997 F.2d at 1301-02 (discussed *supra* § 13.3b n.18); Arango v. Wainwright, 716 F.2d 1353, 1355 (11th Cir. 1983), *reh'g denied with opinion,* 739 F.2d 529 (11th Cir. 1984), *cert. denied,* 469 U.S. 1127 (1985) (abeyance procedure serves "interests of judicial economy"); Thompson v. Wainwright, 714 F.2d 1495, 1499 (11th Cir.), *stay of mandate denied,* 456 U.S. 988 (1983), *cert. denied,* 466 U.S. 962 (1984) (abeyance procedure "furthers the interests" underlying *Rose*).

§ 13.4. [1] *See generally infra* Chapters 20, 21 (hearings generally).

[2] 28 U.S.C. § 2251 (1994). *See supra* § 13.1 nn.50-51 and accompanying text.

[3] *See generally infra* Chapters 35-39 (appeal and *certiorari* procedures).

[4] *See generally infra* Chapters 20, 21.

[5] *See supra* § 13.2b nn.48-50 and accompanying text. *See generally supra* §§ 13.1-13.2b.

[6] *See supra* § 13.1 n.4 and accompanying text.

[7] *See supra* § 13.2a.

deserve" — attention that typically requires fact and law development procedures that cannot meaningfully occur in the short span of time remaining before the date set for execution.[8] In general, therefore, the stay hearing is designed to permit the district court to make a determination as to whether the petition may be dismissed summarily because it is "'patently frivolous,'"[9] barring which, a stay generally must be granted and the parties afforded time to utilize the fact and law development procedures provided by the Rules Governing § 2254 Cases.[10] Put another way, the Habeas Rules offer various means of resolving habeas corpus claims ranging from summary dismissal to a full-blown trial and briefing,[11] and, to require a stay, the petitioner need only convince the court at this stage that *some* further proceedings are necessary on at least *one* such claim.[12]

If the district court is disposed — albeit improperly — to treat the stay hearing as an occasion to reach the merits of nonfrivolous claims or to conduct a final evidentiary hearing on them, counsel who has not had sufficient time to prepare to present the legal and factual bases for those claims should object on the record to any final adjudication, describe the reasons why the petitioner is not prepared for a final hearing on the merits, and request a continuance and a temporary stay to allow adequate preparation and presentation of the factual and legal bases for the claims.[13] At the least, the petitioner should be permitted to limit the presentation at this preliminary stage to establishing a *prima facie* case on the relevant claims — which is still more than the applicable "nonfrivolousness" stay standard requires.[14] Likewise, unless the entire petition can be resolved "only [on] issues of law," counsel has the obligation, absent an informed waiver by the client, to insist that any hearing be postponed until the respondent produces the petitioner in the courtroom.[15] The habeas corpus statute imposes a

---

[8] *See* Barefoot v. Estelle, 463 U.S. 880, 888 (1983); authority cited *supra* §§ 13.2a, 13.2c.

[9] Blackledge v. Allison, 431 U.S. 63, 76 (1977) (quoting Pennsylvania ex rel. Herman v. Claudy, 350 U.S. 116, 119 (1956)).

[10] *See supra* §§ 13.2a, 13.2c. *See also* Rule 4 of the Rules Governing § 2254 Cases; *infra* § 15.2c ("patently frivolous" standard for summary dismissal). *See generally* Rules 5-8, 10, 11 of the Rules Governing § 2254 Cases; *infra* Chapters 18-21, 29-32. *Cf.* Wesson v. Oglesby, 910 F.2d 278, 282 (5th Cir. 1990) (section 1915 case) (in hearing to determine whether complaint should be dismissed as "frivolous" pursuant to 28 U.S.C. § 1915(d), district court must limit credibility assessments to determinations whether "the prisoner's version of the facts ... is inherently plausible and internally consistent"; "[i]t is only for the ultimate trier of fact to decide which party is more believable").

[11] *See generally infra* Chapters 15-21, 29-32.

[12] *See supra* §§ 13.1 n.49 and accompanying text, 13.2c n.69 and accompanying text.

[13] *See infra* § 21.1b (continuances).

[14] *See supra* §§ 13.2a, 13.2c.

[15] *See infra* § 21.3.

duty *on the respondent* to produce the petitioner in that situation.[16] The state also has the obligation at or before the stay hearing to produce for the district court all relevant portions of the state court record;[17] as long as the petition meets the formal and substantive requirements for avoiding dismissal,[18] any insufficiency in the record necessary to dispose of the matter may not be held against the petitioner.[19]

§ 13.5. Effectuating stays.

Once a stay is obtained, counsel has the responsibility to make sure that the respondent warden or corrections commissioner and the governor and attorney general are notified immediately. Lines of communication with these people should be established earlier so that the stay can be effectuated quickly and smoothly and so that there is no confusion about counsel's status as the client's representative. The state should not continue preparing for an execution while a stay is in effect.[1]

§ 13.6. Proceedings following denial.

a. *Explicit or implicit denial — prepetition stays.* As discussed in sections 13.1-13.2b *supra*, it sometimes is appropriate — subject to important statute of limitations concerns in cases governed by the Antiterrorism and Effective Death Penalty Act of 1996 — for capital prisoners to seek and for district courts to grant stays of execution even before a habeas corpus petition is filed, upon the appointment of counsel for an indigent prospective habeas corpus petitioner.[1] The purpose of both the appointment of counsel and the stay at this point are to enable the prisoner, through counsel, to conduct the necessary legal and factual investigation and to prepare a petition containing all of the prisoner's colorable

---

[16] 28 U.S.C. § 2243 (1994). *See infra* § 21.3.

[17] *See infra* § 19.2.

[18] *See supra* Chapters 8-11; *infra* Chapter 15.

[19] *See* Bundy v. Wainwright, 808 F.2d 1410, 1414-17 (11th Cir. 1987) ("obligation to come forward with the state court record is squarely upon the respondent, not upon the petitioner"; improper for district judge to deny stay and dismiss petition because of petitioner's "fail[ure] to supply him with supplemental information and materials other than the petition. This was a burden petitioner did not have so long as the petition was facially sufficient").

§ **13.5.** [1] *See, e.g.,* E.D. CAL. RULE 191(h)(7) ("Upon the granting of any stay of execution, the Clerk will immediately notify the warden of San Quentin Prison and the California Attorney General"); Smith v. Armontrout, 825 F.2d 182 (8th Cir. 1987).

§ **13.6.** [1] *See also supra* Chapter 12. In regard to the serious difficulties that the approach described in text (seeking a stay without filing a federal habeas corpus petition) may encounter as a result of the statutes of limitations adopted by the Antiterrorism and Effective Death Penalty Act of 1996, see *supra* §§ 5.1b n.91, 13.1 nn.37-40 and accompanying text.

federal claims.[2] If (1) such a stay is requested, (2) the district court appoints counsel but denies a stay, (3) appointed counsel concludes that the necessary prefiling investigation and preparation of a federal petition cannot occur prior to the date set for execution, and (4) there are no statute of limitations problems with taking additional prepetition steps, the proper procedures for appealing the district court's denial (including the seeking of a stay pending appeal) are described in subsection b *infra*. The legal bases for a stay at this stage, and thus for arguing on appeal that the district court erred when it denied a stay, are discussed in section 13.2b *supra*. If the district court denies the application for appointment of counsel as well as the stay request, and if the prisoner clearly is indigent[3] (the only prerequisite for the otherwise mandatory appointment of counsel for prospective capital habeas corpus petitioners[4]), then the appeal papers also might include an application for mandamus seeking enforcement of the district court's clear duty to appoint counsel.[5] If the district court has not acted on the stay application within a week to 10 days of the date set for execution notwithstanding a reasonable amount of time to consider the application, the procedures to follow are described in subsection c *infra*. The substantive principles that govern the propriety of a stay in this situation are covered in section 13.2b *supra*.

b. *Explicit denial — postpetition stays.* This subsection discusses available procedures if the district court promptly denies an application for a stay following submission of a federal habeas corpus petition and stay papers. (The next subsection discusses available procedures should the district court unduly delay ruling on a request for a stay following submission of the petition and stay papers.) This subsection's discussion will begin by describing the standards and procedures that apply to cases that are not governed by the Antiterrorism and Effective Death Penalty Act of 1996 (AEDPA)[6] and to cases governed by AEDPA's "nonopt-in"[7] provisions. Thereafter, the discussion will explain the different standards and procedures that apply in AEDPA "opt-in" cases.

Sometimes, the district court will deny a stay at the same time it denies relief on the merits and dismisses the petition. In this situation, the appellate

---

2 *See supra* §§ 12.3a, 13.1, 13.2b.

3 *See supra* §§ 12.1, 12.3b n.46.

4 *See supra* §§ 12.3a, 12.3b.

5 *See supra* § 12.5 (discussing propriety of mandamus action in this situation).

6 Pub. L. 104-132, 110 Stat. 1214 (1996). For an overview of the changes AEDPA makes in federal habeas corpus procedures, see *supra* § 3.2. For an explanation of the cases to which AEDPA applies, see *supra* § 3.4.

7 For an explanation of AEDPA's "nonopt-in" and "opt-in" categories of cases, see *supra* §§ 3.2, 3.3

procedures described in subsequent chapters are available to secure a stay pending appeal.[8] Because time is of the essence, an attorney who anticipates difficulty obtaining a district court stay should prepare appellate stay papers at the same time as the petition, stay application, and other papers filed in the district court.

Less frequently, the court will deny a stay but not rule on the merits of the petition. If this legally incoherent action[9] occurs, the petitioner immediately should appeal the denial of a stay to the court of appeals. Authority for appealing the denial of a stay is found in two statutory provisions.[10] First, 28 U.S.C. § 1291 allows appeals from any "final decision" of the district court. The courts have applied "'a practical rather than technical construction'" of finality,[11] the key element of which is an analysis of whether the district court's order — as a practical matter — precludes further litigation.[12] Because the denial of a stay permits the execution of petitioner to go forward, thereby "end[ing] the litigation on the merits" as a practical matter,[13] and manifestly "'[has] a final and irreparable effect on the rights of the parties,'"[14] such an order is "final" for purposes of section 1291.[15] Second, section 1292(a)(1) allows appeals of orders

---

[8] *See generally infra* Chapters 35-39. A number of circuit courts have local rules governing stay applications and appeals in this situation.

[9] The identical "frivolous claim" standard governs both summary dismissals (*see infra* § 15.2c) and stays of execution (*see supra* §§ 13.2a, 13.2c). *See supra* §§ 13.1 n.49 and accompanying text, 13.2c n.69 and accompanying text. The *non*frivolous claim" determination implied by the court's failure to dismiss accordingly renders the stay denial incoherent.

[10] *See generally* United States ex rel. Goins v. Sigler, 250 F.2d 128 (5th Cir. 1957).

[11] Gillespie v. U.S. Steel Corp., 379 U.S. 148, 152 (1964) (quoting Cohen v. Beneficial Industrial Loan Corp., 337 U.S. 541, 546 (1949)).

[12] *See, e.g.,* Roberts v. United States Dist. Ct., 339 U.S. 844, 845 (1950) (*per curiam*); Lummus Co. v. Commonwealth Oil Refining Co., 297 F.2d 80 (2d Cir. 1961), *cert. denied,* 368 U.S. 986 (1962). *See supra* § 12.5; *infra* §§ 14.2, 35.1.

[13] Dunlop v. Ledet's Foodliner, 509 F.2d 1387, 1389 (5th Cir. 1975).

[14] United States v. Cefaratti, 202 F.2d 13, 15 (D.C. Cir. 1952) (quoting *Cohen v. Beneficial Industrial Loan Corp., supra,* 337 U.S. at 545).

[15] *See* Harris v. Gibson, 322 F.2d 780, 781 (5th Cir. 1963), *cert. denied,* 376 U.S. 908 (1964) (pretrial order was sufficiently dispositive of rights to constitute appealable final order); United States v. Wood, 295 F.2d 772 (5th Cir. 1961), *cert. denied,* 369 U.S. 850 (1962) (order otherwise not appealable is appealable because delay would affect substantial rights of parties). *See generally, e.g.,* Vickers v. Trainor, 546 F.2d 739, 747 (7th Cir. 1976); In re Grand Jury Proceedings (U.S. Steel Clairton Works), 525 F.2d 151 (3d Cir. 1975); McSurely v. McClellan, 426 F.2d 664, 668 (D.C. Cir. 1970) (various orders staying and refusing to stay official state proceedings sufficiently final to allow section 1291 appeal).

"granting [or] refusing ... injunctions," including orders granting and denying stays of state proceedings.[16]

Although an appeal from the denial of habeas corpus relief requires a certificate of leave to appeal (termed a "certificate of probable cause to appeal" in non-AEDPA cases and a "certificate of appealability" in cases governed by AEDPA), this requirement apparently applies only to appeals of decisions on the merits of the claims in the petition.[17] Nonetheless, if there is time, counsel should attempt to secure the requisite certificate prior to appealing, not only to avoid having to litigate in the short time available the uncertain question whether a certificate is required in the situation, but also to attempt to clarify the meaning of the district court's ambiguous view of the merits of the petition.[18] After filing a notice of appeal in the district court,[19] counsel immediately should file the appeal with the clerk of the court of appeals,[20] along with a motion for expedited consideration, a motion to docket the appeal on certified copies of the record, an application for a stay pending appeal,[21] a memorandum in support of that application, and a brief on the merits of the appeal.[22]

In "opt-in" cases, AEDPA provides that if the district court denies a stay of execution, "no Federal court thereafter shall have the authority to enter a stay of execution in the case, unless the court of appeals approves the filing of a second or successive application."[23] As explained earlier,[24] the Supreme Court's

---

[16] 28 U.S.C. § 1292(a)(1) (1994). *See, e.g.,* Codex Corp. v. Milgo Electronic Corp., 553 F.2d 735 (1st Cir.), *cert. denied,* 434 U.S. 860 (1977) (denial of injunction); Johnson v. England, 356 F.2d 44 (9th Cir.), *cert. denied,* 384 U.S. 961 (1966) (orders dissolving stay).

[17] 28 U.S.C.A. § 2253 (West 1994 & Supp. 1998). *See infra* § 35.4.

[18] *See supra* note 9 and accompanying text. *See generally infra* § 35.4.

[19] *See infra* § 35.2.

[20] *See generally infra* Chapters 35, 36.

[21] *See infra* § 36.2. Before the court of appeals will rule on a motion for a stay pending appeal, the district court must have been presented with and either denied or refused to rule (*see infra* § 13.6c) on such a motion.

[22] *See generally infra* Chapters 35-39 (appeals and *certiorari* proceedings). If the district court denies a stay without ruling on the merits, counsel also simultaneously may file an "original" habeas corpus petition directed to a single circuit judge. *See infra* Chapter 40. Because of the uncertain status of original petitions, *id.,* filing such a petition in lieu of an appeal is not advised.

[23] 28 U.S.C.A. § 2262(c) (West Supp. 1998). For discussion of AEDPA's standards and procedures for the filing of successive applications, see *infra* §§ 28.3, 28.4. AEDPA's "opt-in" provisions also condition the granting of a stay of execution upon the satisfaction of the standards and procedures for successive petitions in those cases in which the prisoner failed to comply with the statute of limitations or made a knowing, voluntary, and intelligent waiver of the right to seek federal habeas corpus relief and in those cases in which the federal court denied the petition. *See supra* § 3.3c nn.55-60 and accompanying text.

[24] *See supra* § 3.3c n.60 and accompanying text.

analysis in *Felker v. Turpin*[25] strongly suggests that, in order to avoid constitutional questions, this statute has to be construed to provide for circuit court or at least Supreme Court review of a district court's determination that a stay of execution should be denied.

c. *Implicit denial — postpetition stays.* As an unstayed execution date approaches, counsel must keep in constant touch with the district court, typically through the clerk's office. If, as occasionally occurs,[26] the court has not acted on the stay application within a week to 10 days of the date set for execution notwithstanding a reasonable amount of time to consider the application, the steps outlined below become necessary.

First, counsel should communicate the urgency of the situation to the clerk of the district court in person or by telephone. That failing, counsel should file three alternative proposed orders and make a motion asking the court to sign either the proposed stay order that was filed with the stay application or one of the three new proposed orders. The three new orders should give the court the following options:

(1) Refuse to grant the stay now but set a prompt date for a hearing on the stay[27] (prompt generally meaning a week or more before the execution date).

(2) Refuse both to grant the stay now and to set a prompt date for a hearing on the stay, but set a later date for such a hearing[28] (later meaning less than a week before the execution date).

(3) Acknowledge that the court has received and considered requests to grant or deny a stay, but refuse to do so or to set a hearing on the application.

Once these papers have been filed, counsel should allow the court sufficient time to consider them (sufficiency varying according to the time remaining before the execution date). If the district court enters no order within a week of the execution, or if it enters order (2) above and counsel believes that the hearing date will not allow sufficient time before the execution to secure a stay from the court of appeals if necessary,[29] or, finally, if the district court enters order (3)

---

[25] 518 U.S. 651 (1996).

[26] *See, e.g.,* Hance v. Zant, No. 82-8336 (11th Cir. 1982) (discussed in Hance v. Zant, 696 F.2d 940, 945 (11th Cir. 1983)); Briley v. Hutto, No. 81-6261 (4th Cir. Apr. 23, 1981).

[27] Such an order should make clear that the hearing sought is solely on the stay application and not on the merits of the petition. *See supra* §§ 13.1, 13.4.

[28] This order should make clear that the hearing is on the stay only, not on the substantive claims in the petition. *See supra* §§ 13.1, 13.4.

[29] *See infra* §§ 36.2, 38.2, 39.3c.

above, the petitioner immediately should file a notice of appeal in the district court.[30] This appeal is not on the merits of petitioner's claims but rather challenges the district court's "action" on the stay application and should address the merits only to the limited extent necessary to establish that the petition is "nonfrivolous" and requires a stay.[31]

Simultaneously with the filing of the notice of appeal in the district court, counsel should file in the court of appeals: a copy of the notice of appeal, an application for a stay of execution pending the appeal and a supporting memorandum, a request for expedited consideration of the appeal, a motion to docket the appeal on certified copies of the record, and a short brief in support of the appeal.[32] Counsel should establish contact with the clerk of the court of appeals and explain the urgency of the situation.

Action or inaction by the district court which, *as a practical matter,* has ended the litigation or had an irreparable effect on one of the parties constitutes an appealable "final decision" under section 1291.[33] Accordingly, the appellate brief should describe the district court's action (if it signed an order) or its *inaction* (if it failed to sign any order), emphasizing that the district court's behavior effectively denies the petition by allowing the execution to occur before the petition is fully and fairly adjudicated.[34] The brief also should argue the merits of the stay but not of petitioner's claims.[35] It should discuss the district court's duty to grant the stay or at least to hold a prompt hearing on the

---

[30] *See infra* § 36.2.

[31] *See supra* §§ 13.2a, 13.2c (discussing "nonfrivolous claim" standard for stay prior to district court consideration of merits). This type of pre-adjudication appeal differs from an appeal after the petitioner has had a full and fair hearing on the merits in the district court. In the latter situation, the prior district court adjudication gives the appellate court the power in certain circumstances to address the motion for a stay pending appeal and the merits of the appeal itself simultaneously. By contrast, at the preliminary stage under discussion here, the petitioner's "nonfrivolous claims" are due "careful attention," which typically cannot occur simultaneously with an appellate court's summary, prebriefing, and pre-evidentiary hearing consideration of a stay application. *See* Barefoot v. Estelle, 463 U.S. 880, 888 (1983); *supra* §§ 13.2c, 13.2d; *infra* § 36.2.

[32] *See supra* § 13.6b nn.19-22 and accompanying text. The petitioner also should formally request that the district court forward the record in the case to the court of appeals. Should that request be denied, counsel will have to attach a copy of all of the relevant documents to the stay memorandum and brief and make a motion for leave to docket the appeal based on verified documents. *See generally infra* § 37.1 (record on appeal).

[33] 28 U.S.C. § 1291 (1994). *See supra* §§ 12.5, 13.6b nn.11-15 and accompanying text; *infra* § 35.1.

[34] The brief should discuss the filing of the petition, the stay application, the proposed order granting the stay application, and the three alternative proposed orders discussed above. Copies of these documents should be appended to the brief.

[35] *See supra* §§ 13.1, 13.4.

application if any claim presented is "nonfrivolous"[36] and should elucidate the nonfrivolousness of one or more of the claims in the petition. The brief should request that the court of appeals grant a stay of execution and remand the case to the district court with directions to adjudicate the merits[37] or, if the appellate court feels that a hearing on the stay application is necessary, that it grant a stay and remand to the district court for a hearing.[38] The court of appeals generally should not render a *final* decision on the merits of the petition at this time.[39]

If the court of appeals does not act expeditiously on these papers, a similar, but inevitably more compressed, procedure should be followed to secure a stay from the appropriate Justice of the Supreme Court. If the court of appeals denies the application for a stay pending appeal (regardless of its actions on the appeal itself), steps should be taken to secure a Supreme Court stay.[40]

---

[36] *See* authority cited *supra* §§ 13.2a, 13.2c.

[37] *See, e.g.,* Bundy v. Wainwright, 808 F.2d 1410, 1413 (11th Cir. 1987) ("The district court erred in denying a stay of execution, and it erred in denying the petition and ordering it dismissed. The judgment of the district court must be reversed and the case remanded for orderly, careful and deliberate consideration of the constitutional issues that are involved.").

[38] *Cf.* Fabian v. Reed, 707 F.2d 147, 149 (5th Cir. 1983) (after petitioner filed notice of appeal following dismissal of noncapital habeas corpus petition but neither applied for nor was granted or denied certificate of probable cause to appeal by district court, court of appeals retained jurisdiction over appeal, remanded to district court to allow petitioner to apply for certificate of probable cause, and set time limit for ruling by district court, after which period absence of ruling by district court would be treated as denial of application and as triggering application to court of appeals for certificate of probable cause).

[39] *See supra* §§ 13.1, 13.4.

[40] *See generally infra* §§ 38.2, 39.3c.

Chapter 14

MODIFICATION OF CUSTODY STATUS

§ 14.1. Transfer.

Transfer of the prisoner from one facility to another during the pendency of habeas corpus proceedings may destroy the district court's personal jurisdiction and venue over the action,[1] require substitution of a new party respondent,[2] and adversely affect judicial economy, the fairness of the proceeding, and the federal courts' ability to effectuate a remedy. Restrictions on the state's ability to transfer the prisoner during the pendency of habeas corpus proceedings are discussed in detail in section 36.3 *infra*.

§ 14.2. Release on recognizance or surety.[1]

Although the practice is not explicitly authorized by statute or rule,[2] "there is abundant authority that federal district judges in habeas corpus and section 2255 proceedings have inherent power to admit applicants to bail pending the decision of their cases."[3] "The federal court's authority to release a state prisoner on

---

§ 14.1. [1] *Cf. supra* § 10.2b n.14 and accompanying text (decisions resisting notion that transfers occurring after petition was filed in proper jurisdiction and venue undermine original court's authority to adjudicate petition). *See generally supra* § 10.2.

[2] *See generally supra* § 10.1.

§ 14.2. [1] *See generally* LARRY W. YACKLE, POSTCONVICTION REMEDIES § 123 (1981 & Supp. 1998); Note, *Detaining Successful Habeas Corpus Petitioners Due to Dangerousness:* Hilton v. Braunskill, 9 N. ILL. U. L. REV. 129 (1988). This section discusses release pending the district court's adjudication of the petition. Section 36.4 *infra* discusses release pending appeal or, if no appeal is taken from a conditional grant of relief, release pending retrial.

[2] *See e.g.*, Falconer v. Lane, 905 F.2d 1129, 1137 n.6 (7th Cir. 1990) (staying district court order releasing petitioner on recognizance, following grant of writ, pursuant to FED. R. APP. P. 23(c) and Hilton v. Braunskill, 481 U.S. 770, 774 (1987)); Marino v. Vasquez, 812 F.2d 499, 507-08 (9th Cir. 1987) (citing authority); Carter v. Rafferty, 781 F.2d 993, 995 (3d Cir. 1986); Cherek v. United States, 767 F.2d 335, 337 (7th Cir. 1985); United States ex rel. Thomas v. New Jersey, 472 F.2d 735, 741 (3d Cir.), *cert. denied*, 414 U.S. 878 (1973); Ballou v. Massachusetts, 382 F.2d 292, 293 (1st Cir. 1967). *Cf.* PROPOSED FED. R. APP. P. 23(b), 23(c) (effective December 1, 1998, absent contrary congressional action) (bail pending habeas corpus appeals); SUP. CT. R. 36.2, 36.3; *infra* § 36.4 (bail pending appeal). Neither the Federal Bail Reform Act of 1966, 18 U.S.C. §§ 3142-52 (1994), nor any other federal statute or rule (*e.g.*, FED. R. CRIM. P. 46) governing bail for federal defendants at trial or on direct appeal applies to federal postconviction proceedings under 28 U.S.C. §§ 2241-55 (West 1994 & Supp. 1998).

[3] *Cherek v. United States, supra*, 767 F.2d at 337. *See, e.g., Falconer v. Lane, supra*, 905 F.2d at 1137 n.6 (by implication); Dotson v. Clark, 900 F.2d 77 (6th Cir. 1990); Bliss v. Lockhart, 891 F.2d 1335, 1337 (8th Cir. 1989); Blair v. McCarthy, 881 F.2d 602, 603 (9th Cir. 1989), *vac'd & remanded on other grounds*, 498 U.S. 954 (1990); *Marino v. Vasquez, supra*, 812 F.2d at 507; Martin v. Solem, 801 F.2d 324, 329 (8th Cir. 1986); Bowen v. Maynard, 799 F.2d 593, 613-14 & n.12 (10th Cir.), *cert. denied*, 479 U.S. 962 (1986) (in light of (1) conditions of release imposed by

recognizance or surety in the course of a habeas corpus proceeding derives from the power to issue the writ itself" and thereby regulate the government's exercise of custody over its citizens.[4]

The exhaustion of remedies requirement usually assures that the prisoner reaches the federal district court in the posture of a convicted appellant whose constitutional claims previously have been considered and rejected by another court. Accordingly, as in most appeals, the likelihood of success is sufficiently low that release on surety or recognizance is not appropriate as a general matter.[5] Rather, the decisions reveal a "parsimonious exercise of the [bail] power."[6]

---

district court ($100,000 bond), (2) portion of FED. R. APP. P. 23(c) permitting release on recognizance or surety during certain habeas corpus appeals, and (3) directive in 28 U.S.C. § 2243 that district court "'dispose of the matter as law and justice require,'" court concludes "that the district court in these circumstances did not abuse its discretion in ordering the immediate issuance of the writ of habeas corpus" and immediate release of capital petitioner); Pfaff v. Wells, 648 F.2d 689, 693 (10th Cir. 1981); Ostrer v. United States, 584 F.2d 594, 596 n.1 (2d Cir. 1978); Jago v. United States Dist. Ct., 570 F.2d 618, 621-22 (6th Cir.), cert. denied, 439 U.S. 883 (1978); In re Wainwright, 518 F.2d 173, 175 (5th Cir. 1975) (per curiam); United States ex rel. Thomas v. New Jersey, supra, 472 F.2d at 743; Glynn v. Donnelly, 470 F.2d 95, 98 (1st Cir. 1972); Woodcock v. Donnelly, 470 F.2d 93, 94 (1st Cir. 1972) (per curiam); Baker v. Sard, 420 F.2d 1342, 1343 (D.C. Cir. 1969) (per curiam); Benson v. California, 328 F.2d 159, 162 (9th Cir. 1964); Jimenez v. Aristiguieta, 314 F.2d 649, 652 (5th Cir.), cert. denied, 373 U.S. 914 (1963); Johnston v. Marsh, 227 F.2d 528, 531 (3d Cir. 1955); United States v. Evans, 2 F. 147, 152 (C.C.W.D. Tenn. 1880). See also In re Wainwright, supra at 175 n.1 ("probably within the power of a United States Magistrate to enlarge a state prisoner on bail pending district court consideration of his habeas corpus action" (discussing 28 U.S.C. § 636(a)(1))). Cf. Gomez v. United States, 899 F.2d 1124, 1127 (11th Cir. 1990) (reversing bail grant because release is not appropriate ultimate remedy, hence is not appropriate interim remedy, for AIDS-infected petitioner alleging inadequate medical care).

[4] Marino v. Vasquez, supra, 812 F.2d at 507. Accord, e.g., Ostrer v. United States, supra, 584 F.2d at 597; Jago v. United States Dist. Ct., supra, 570 F.2d at 623-26; In re Wainwright, supra, 518 F.2d at 174, 175 n.1; United States ex rel. Thomas v. New Jersey, supra, 472 F.2d at 741-42; Woodcock v. Donnelly, supra, 470 F.2d at 94.

[5] See, e.g., Hilton v. Braunskill, supra, 481 U.S. at 773-74 (contrasting bail situations of pretrial detainee in criminal case and habeas corpus petitioner). See also Aronson v. May, 85 S. Ct. 3, 5 (1964) (Douglas, Circuit Justice, in chambers) ("It is obvious that a greater showing of special reasons for admission to bail pending review should be required in this [postconviction] case than would be required in a case where applicant had sought to attack by writ of habeas corpus an incarceration not resulting from a judicial determination.").

[6] Cherek v. United States, supra, 767 F.2d at 337 ("a power to be exercised very sparingly"). Accord, e.g., Ostrer v. United States, supra, 584 F.2d at 596 n.1 ("only in 'unusual cases'"); Argro v. United States, 505 F.2d 1374, 1377 (2d Cir. 1974) ("unusual cases"); Baker v. Sard, supra, 420 F.2d at 1343 ("heightened standard requiring a showing of exceptional circumstances"); Reiff v. United States, 288 F.2d 887, 888 (9th Cir. 1961) ("exceptional circumstance"). See Falconer v. Lane, supra, 905 F.2d at 1137 n.6 (court of appeals stays district court's order releasing petitioner on recognizance following grant of writ to give state time to decide whether to resentence petitioner for voluntary manslaughter or retry her).

Generally, to establish the right to release on recognizance or surety the petitioner must demonstrate: (1) that the petition presents a "substantial question" as to the constitutionality of the prisoner's detention;[7] (2) "that a denial of bail could leave the petitioner without remedy" given how much time will be expended in adjudicating his substantial claims[8] or given other "extraordinary circumstances ... that make the grant of bail necessary to make the habeas remedy effective";[9] and (3) that there is little risk that the petitioner will flee, given the surety or other conditions the court could impose.[10] If these criteria are satisfied, the state apparently may oppose release by showing that (4) the petitioner presents a "risk of danger to the community,"[11] or (5) release will

---

[7] *See, e.g., Aronson v. May, supra,* 85 S. Ct. at 5 (Douglas, Circuit Justice, in chambers) ("substantial questions"); United States v. Smith, 835 F.2d 1048, 1050 (3d Cir. 1987) ("strong showing" of likelihood of success on merits); Iuteri v. Nardoza, 662 F.2d 159, 161 (2d Cir. 1981) ("substantial claims"); *Pfaff v. Wells, supra,* 648 F.2d at 693 ("clear case on the merits"); *Ostrer v. United States, supra,* 584 F.2d at 596 n.1 (petitioner seriously "contest[s] the legality of his custody"); *Baker v. Sard, supra,* 420 F.2d at 1343-44 ("substantial issues"). *See also Hilton v. Braunskill, supra,* 481 U.S. at 776-79 (similar consideration for bail pending appeal). *Cf. Gomez v. United States, supra,* 899 F.2d at 1127 (bail is not appropriate where legal claim in petition, even if proven, does not justify release).

[8] *Marino v. Vasquez, supra,* 812 F.2d at 509 (bail pending appeal affirmed because state, by appealing, can exhaust "time remaining to be served on the petitioner's sentence"). *See Hilton v. Braunskill, supra,* 481 U.S. at 777-78 (bail pending appeal case; the less time that remains on prisoner's sentence, the stronger his interest in release pending further adjudication); LaFrance v. Bohlinger, 487 F.2d 506, 507 (1st Cir. 1973) *(mem.), cert. denied,* 419 U.S. 1080 (1974) (release pending appeal approved because petitioner "had served much, possibly most of his sentence," and "requiring him to serve ... more ... would be too harsh").

[9] *Iuteri v. Nardoza, supra,* 662 F.2d at 161. *See, e.g., Pfaff v. Wells, supra,* 648 F.2d at 693 ("exceptional circumstances"); *Ostrer v. United States, supra,* 584 F.2d at 596 n.1 (quoting Calley v. Callaway, 496 F.2d 701, 702 (5th Cir. 1974) *(per curiam));* Galante v. Warden, 573 F.2d 707, 708 (2d Cir. 1977) *(per curiam). See also Hilton v. Braunskill, supra,* 481 U.S. at 776-79 (similar consideration for bail pending appeal); *Aronson v. May, supra,* 85 S. Ct. at 4 (Douglas, Circuit Justice, in chambers) (whether bail is necessary in "interests of justice"). *Cf. Baker v. Sard, supra,* 420 F.2d at 1343-44 ("likelihood of success" itself may supply "forceful special circumstance").

[10] *See, e.g., Marino v. Vasquez, supra,* 812 F.2d at 508-09; Carter v. Rafferty, 781 F.2d 993, 995 (3d Cir. 1986); *LaFrance v. Bohlinger, supra,* 487 F.2d at 508; Jago v. United States Dist. Ct., 570 F.2d 618, 623 (6th Cir. 1978) *(per curiam);* Baker v. Sard, supra, 420 F.2d at 1344; Ballou v. Massachusetts, 382 F.2d 292, 293 (1st Cir. 1967) *(per curiam)* (bail denied because amount prisoner is willing to post is "totally inadequate") (all release-pending-appeal decisions).

[11] *Marino v. Vasquez, supra,* 812 F.2d at 509 (bail pending appeal). *See Hilton v. Braunskill, supra,* 481 U.S. at 777-78 ("if the state establishes that there is a risk that the prisoner will pose a danger to the public if released, the court may take that factor in consideration in deciding whether or not to enlarge him" pending appeal); Lewis v. Henderson, 356 F.2d 105, 106 (6th Cir. 1966) *(per curiam)* (similar); United States ex rel. Taylor v. Redman, 500 F. Supp. 453, 459 (D. Del. 1980); Sellars v. Estelle, 450 F. Supp. 1262, 1265 (S.D. Tex. 1978), *aff'd,* 591 F.2d 1208 (5th. Cir. 1979). Because the prisoner's conviction remains intact at the beginning of the habeas corpus proceeding, that conviction presumedly may bear on the "danger to the community" factor.

substantially interfere with "[t]he state's interest in ... rehabilitation pending a final determination of the case ...."[12] Because the assessment and application of these factors "contemplates individualized judgments in each case, the formula cannot be reduced to a set of rigid rules" and accords a good deal of discretion to the district court.[13]

Although there is contrary precedent,[14] the majority and better-reasoned view is that denials of bail are appealable final orders under the "collateral order" doctrine.[15] Otherwise, the fully resolved matter of bail, which is collateral to the

---

[12] *Hilton v. Braunskill, supra,* 481 U.S. at 776-79 (bail pending appeal). The "rehabilitation" factor is "strongest where the remaining portion of the sentence to be served is long, and weakest when there is little of the sentence remaining to be served." *Id.* at 777. *Hilton* recognizes an analogy between the factors listed above and those governing grants of injunctions pending judicial proceedings. The latter, more general, factors are (1) whether the applicant has shown a likelihood of success on the merits; (2) whether the applicant will be irreparably injured absent relief; (3) whether relief will substantially injure other parties to the proceeding; and (4) where the public interest lies. *Id.* at 776 (citing authority).

[13] *Id.* at 777. *See id.* at 775 ("broad discretion" accorded district court in bail pending appeal situations). *See also* Bliss v. Lockhart, 891 F.2d 1335, 1337 (8th Cir. 1989) (district court held hearing to enable petitioner to establish prerequisites to bail pending final resolution of petition in district court).

[14] *See, e.g.,* Woodcock v. Donnelly, 470 F.2d 93, 94 (1st Cir. 1972) *(per curiam). See also* Grune v. Coughlin, 913 F.2d 41, 43 (2d Cir. 1990) (discussing split in circuits and citing decisions); Dotson v. Clark, 900 F.2d 77, 78 (6th Cir. 1990) (citing 1st and 9th Circuit precedents). *Cf.* United States v. DiRusso, 548 F.2d 372, 374 (1st Cir. 1976) (denial of bail is not appealable final judgment but is reviewable via mandamus under All Writs Act, 28 U.S.C. § 1651(a)).

[15] *See, e.g.,* Lee v. Jabe, 989 F.2d 869, 870-71 (6th Cir. 1993) ("denial or granting of bail [pending disposition of habeas corpus petition] is appealable under the collateral order doctrine"); *Grune v. Coughlin, supra,* 913 F.2d at 43 (denial of bail pending habeas corpus proceedings is appealable collateral order and should be treated no differently from grant of bail (citing Iuteri v. Nardoza, 662 F.2d 159, 161 (2d Cir. 1981))); *Dotson v. Clark, supra,* 900 F.2d at 77-79 (district court decisions granting or denying bail to prisoners petitioning for federal habeas corpus relief are appealable pending district court's decision on merits of petition; holding is equally appealable whether petitioner is state or federal prisoner; noting split in circuits on issue: 1st and 9th circuits do not treat bail orders as appealable, but address underlying issues nonetheless by means of mandamus jurisdiction; 2d, 3d, 7th, 8th, and D.C. Circuits treat such orders as appealable (citing numerous decisions)); United States v. Smith, 835 F.2d 1048, 1049-50 (3d Cir. 1987) (denial of bail pending habeas corpus disposition reviewable on appeal); *Marino v. Vasquez, supra,* 812 F.2d at 507 n.10; Martin v. Solem, 801 F.2d 324, 328-29 (8th Cir. 1986); Cherek v. United States, 767 F.2d 335, 336-37 (7th Cir. 1985) (holding in Stack v. Boyle, 342 U.S. 1, 6 (1951), that denial of pretrial bail in criminal case is appealable final order applies to denial of postconviction bail); Luther v. Molina, 627 F.2d 71, 73 & n.1 (7th Cir. 1980) *(dicta). See also* Puerto Rico Aqueduct and Sewer Auth. v. Metcalf & Eddy, Inc., 506 U.S. 139, 143-44 (1993) (concise summary of Court's "collateral order" doctrine under *Cohen, infra*); Cohen v. Beneficial Industrial Loan Corp., 337 U.S. 541, 545-47 (1949); *supra* §§ 12.1, 12.5, 13.6b; *infra* § 35.1 (collateral order rule in other habeas contexts). *Cf.* Falconer v. Lane, 905 F.2d 1129, 1137 n.6 (7th Cir. 1990) (granting state's "emergency motion" to stay district court's order releasing petitioner on recognizance).

main issues in the litigation, would be essentially nonreviewable by way of appeal.[16] On appeal, review of the underlying historical fact determinations by the district judge (for example, the risk that a prisoner will flee or that his release will endanger the community) takes place under the "clearly erroneous" rule,[17] but the underlying legal issues (for instance, likelihood of success on the merits) and the ultimate balancing of the determinative factors are "question[s] of law ... reviewable de novo."[18]

If the district court releases the petitioner, "any recognizance, with or without surety, must in a habeas case run to and be filed with the federal court."[19] The federal courts accordingly may not order a state court to fix the amount of surety or to accept a personal recognizance from the prisoner either in an amount fixed

---

[16] *See, e.g., Grune v. Coughlin, supra,* 913 F.2d at 43-44 (denial of bail pending habeas corpus proceedings is appealable collateral order because it is effectively unreviewable after district court's final decision on merits; although merits are relevant to release determination, they are not finally decided, hence decisions on bail and on merits do not merge); *Cherek v. United States, supra,* 767 F.2d at 336-37. *See also Stack v. Boyle, supra,* 342 U.S. at 6 (pretrial bail decision). The cases rarely discuss whether a *grant* of bail at the outset of habeas corpus litigation is an appealable final order. *But cf.* Jago v. United States Dist. Ct., 570 F.2d 618, 619 (6th Cir.), *cert. denied,* 439 U.S. 883 (1978); In re Wainwright, 518 F.2d 173, 174 (5th Cir. 1975) (*per curiam*) (appellate review of pretrial grant of bail under All Writs Act, 28 U.S.C. § 1651(a)). The first two of the three collateral order requirements — (1) final resolution of (2) a collateral matter (*see generally* authority cited *supra* note 15; *supra* § 12.5; *infra* § 35.1) — support appealability of prehearing denials and grants of bail. The third factor — effective unreviewability of an issue posing serious risk of loss to the putative appellant — also supports appealability of *denials* of bail (the prisoner can never regain liberty lost during periods of unlawful incarceration) but does not obviously support appealability of *grants* of bail because such orders merely toll, but do not prevent, the prisoner's service of the sentence of incarceration. *See* LaFrance v. Bohlinger, 487 F.2d 506, 507 (1st Cir. 1973) (*mem.*), *cert. denied,* 419 U.S. 1080 (1974). *But see Grune v. Coughlin, supra,* 913 F.2d at 45 (Pratt, J., dissenting) (grants of bail pending habeas corpus proceedings are appealable collateral orders, but denials of bail should not be appealable). Only, therefore, if risk of flight and danger to the community often are the deciding issues in appeals from grants of bail should such grants constitute appealable final judgments. *Cf. Marino v. Vasquez, supra,* 812 F.2d at 509 (flight risk and danger to community are matters of fact, and court of appeals must defer to district court's determination). In any event, the state apparently can precipitate an appealable interlocutory order by seeking a stay of the district court's release order. *See* 28 U.S.C. § 1292(a) (1994) (stay denials appealable). *See also Hilton v. Braunskill, supra,* 481 U.S. at 773 & n.2 (review of court of appeals' interlocutory denial of stay of order releasing petitioner pending appeal).

[17] *Marino v. Vasquez, supra,* 812 F.2d at 509. *See generally infra* §§ 30.3, 37.3b.

[18] *Id.* at 507, 509. *See also Cherek v. United States, supra,* 767 F.2d at 337-38 (apparently *de novo* review). *Cf. Hilton v. Braunskill, supra,* 481 U.S. at 777 (in bail pending appeal situations, FED. R. APP. P. 23(d) creates "presumption of correctness of the [district court's] initial custody determination"). *See generally infra* §§ 20.3d, 30.2, 37.3a.

[19] United States ex rel. Thomas v. New Jersey, 472 F.2d 735, 743 (3d Cir.), *cert. denied,* 414 U.S. 878 (1973).

by the federal court as security or without the posting of security.[20] Before granting release, the court must conduct "a prompt hearing on notice to the petitioner."[21] At the hearing, the court must determine "the amount of any recognizance and the surety, if any, on any recognizance, which shall be required ... to assure (1) the petitioner's compliance with any district court order with respect to his availability and (2) the petitioner's compliance with any judgment which may be rendered" by the district court, the court of appeals, or the Supreme Court.[22] If, at any point after the district court grants release, circumstances substantially change with regard to the factors governing the initial grant, the district court may revise the release conditions or revoke the release order.[23]

---

[20] *Id.* at 741-44 (citing Johnston v. Marsh, 227 F.2d 528 (3d Cir. 1955)).

[21] *Id.* at 744.

[22] *Id. See, e.g., Marino v. Vasquez, supra,* 812 F.2d at 503 & n.2 ("order setting conditions for Marino's release ... and plac[ing] restrictions on the petition during his release"); Jago v. United States Dist. Ct., 570 F.2d 618, 619 & n.2 (6th Cir.), *cert. denied,* 439 U.S. 883 (1978) (order releasing petitioner "pending ... appeal on the condition that he post bail in the amount of $10,000, ten percent deposit"); LaFrance v. Bohlinger, 487 F.2d 506, 508 (1st Cir. 1973) *(mem.), cert. denied,* 419 U.S. 1080 (1974) (release conditioned on petitioner's execution of "bond agreeing to his being recognized on personal recognizance" and agreeing "that he will remain within the [federal judicial] District and answer all orders of [the] court").

[23] *See supra* notes 7-13 and accompanying text. *See generally* PROPOSED FED. R. APP. P. 23(d) (effective December 1, 1998, absent contrary congressional action) (release pending appeal; to justify modification, state must show "special reasons" other than those initially considered); Hilton v. Braunskill, 481 U.S. 770, 777-78 (1987) (Appellate Rule 23(d) creates rebuttable "presumption of correctness" of initial decision regarding bail).

Chapter 15

SUMMARY PROCEEDINGS

§ 15.1. Return of defective petitions.[1]

Rule 3(b) of the Rules Governing § 2254 Cases authorizes the clerk of the court, upon receipt of a habeas corpus petition and accompanying documents, to ascertain whether "the petition appears on its face to comply" with the rules dictating the form of the petition (*i.e.*, with Rules 2 and 3 of the Rules Governing § 2254 Cases). If the petition appears to comply with Habeas Rules 2 and 3, the clerk must file it.[2] If the petition does not appear to comply with those rules, the clerk must "promptly"[3] present it to a district judge who may authorize the clerk to "return" the defective application to the petitioner "together with a statement of the reason for its return."[4] Although a number of district courts now authorize the clerk *sua sponte* to return petitions deemed inadequate as to form, the Habeas Rules, as revised on precisely this point by Congress, clearly forbid the practice.[5]

---

§ 15.1. [1] This section discusses defects in the *form* of a petition; substantive defects are addressed *infra* § 15.2. *See infra* note 4. *See also supra* Chapters 8-11 (formal and substantive pleadings requirements).

[2] Rule 3(b) of the Rules Governing § 2254 Cases ("Upon receipt of the petition and the filing fee, or an order granting leave to the petitioner to proceed in forma pauperis, and having ascertained that the petition appears on its face to comply with rules 2 and 3, the clerk ... shall file the petition and enter it on the docket in his office.").

[3] *See* Rule 4 of the Rules Governing § 2254 Cases.

[4] Rule 2(e) of the Rules Governing § 2254 Cases ("If a petition received by the clerk of a district court does not substantially comply with the requirements of rule 2 or rule 3, it may be returned to the petitioner, if a *judge* of the court so directs, together with a statement of the reason for its return" (emphasis added)). *See* Advisory Committee Note to Rule 3(b) of the Rules Governing § 2254 Cases (nonconforming petitions "may be returned *in accordance with rule 2(e)*" (emphasis added)); Hendricks v. Vasquez, 908 F.2d 490, 491 (9th Cir. 1990) ("The district court may refuse to file, or may dismiss, an unsigned and unverified petition.... However, the defect is one that the district court may, if it sees fit, disregard," so district court did not commit "reversible error ... [by] address[ing] the merits of an unverified petition."). Habeas Rule 2(e)'s reference to "the requirements of rule 2 or rule 3" limits "return[]" of the petition to purely formal matters and does not authorize consideration (at that stage) of such substantive questions as whether the claims in the petition are colorable or whether the petition is timely. Matters such as those are governed by the summary dismissal rules and procedures discussed *infra* § 15.2.

[5] See the italicized portions of Rule 2(e) of the Rules Governing § 2254 Cases and Advisory Committee Note to Rule 3(b) of the Rules Governing § 2254 Cases, quoted *supra* note 4. Rule 2(e) originally empowered clerks *sua sponte* to return nonconforming applications. According to Professor Wright, Proposed Rule 2(e) "was too much for Congress. It believed that 'the rules as promulgated by the Supreme Court put too much emphasis upon a strict compliance with the forms, perhaps leading to a rejection of otherwise meritorious claims on the ground of failure to adhere strictly to the form.'" Charles Alan Wright, *Procedure for Habeas Corpus*, 77 F.R.D. 227, 238-39, 240 (1978) (quoting H.R. REP. No. 1471, 94th Cong., 2d Sess. 4 (1976), *reprinted in* 1976 U.S. CODE CONG. & ADMIN. NEWS 2478, 2480). *See id.* at 240 (it is "fortunate that Congress

The legislative history of Habeas Rule 2(e) also suggests that judges should use sparingly the power to reject petitions on formalistic grounds, particularly when return is likely to have a preclusive effect — *e.g.*, when it will mean denying or delaying a stay in a capital case or when the prisoner apparently lacks the literacy, education, or mental capacity to file scrupulously correct papers.[6] Congress' intent to give prisoners, particularly *pro se* prisoners, considerable leeway with respect to the form of their petitions is manifested by Congress': (1) rejection of proposed Habeas Rule 2 insofar as it would have required compliance with a specified form petition and delegated to court clerks the unsupervised power to return defective petitions; (2) forbidding "too much emphasis upon a strict compliance" with form, which might lead "to a rejection of otherwise meritorious claims on the ground of failure to adhere strictly to ... form";[7] and (3) countenancing return of a petition only if it "does not *substantially* comply" with the formal requirements in Habeas Rules 2 and 3.[8]

Interpreting Habeas Rule 2(e)'s "substantial compliance" language, the courts have heeded Congress' admonition against undue formalism and, especially in cases involving a *pro se* litigant when the court can deduce what the litigant intends by the pleading, have allowed rather wide deviations from the form petitions attached to the Habeas Rules and specified by some local rules as well as from the accepted captions, form, and causes of action of other analogous prisoner pleadings.[9] Such decisions conform to the traditional rule that *pro se*

---

amended Rule [2(e)], since a petition not [in] the prescribed form would have been returned routinely ..., while now the petition is to be returned only if the judge so directs"). As Professor Wright notes, "[h]aving concluded that the Supreme Court was in error in promulgating a rule that put too much emphasis on ... form[], it could not have been the intention of Congress to allow that undue emphasis to be restored in particular districts under the haphazard procedures by which local rules are made." *Id.* at 239 (footnote omitted). *See also supra* §§ 11.7b n.12, 12.1 n.34, *infra* 39.3a n.3 (all discussing Supreme Court decisions prospectively instructing Clerk of Court to reject petitions from certain individuals found to have abused right to petition Court).

6 In these circumstances, the appropriate response is to appoint counsel. *See supra* § 12.3b.

7 H.R. REP. No. 1471, 94th Cong. 2d Sess. 4 (1976), *reprinted in* 1976 U.S. CODE CONG. & ADMIN. NEWS 2478, 2480.

8 Rule 2(e) of the Rules Governing § 2254 Cases (emphasis added). *See supra* note 5 & *supra* § 11.5 (legislative history).

9 *See, e.g.,* Adams v. United States, 1998 WL 514679, at *1-*2 (2d Cir. Aug. 20, 1998) (describing widespread pre-AEDPA practice of liberally construing *pro se* federal prisoners' postconviction motions as section 2255 motions to "assist[] the prisoner-movant in dealing with legal technicalities"; modifying practice to guard against adverse consequences for petitioner that could arise because of AEDPA); Leacock v. Henman, 996 F.2d 1069, 1071 (10th Cir. 1993) (liberally construing vague section 2241 petition as section 2254 petition challenging state conviction and section 2255 motion challenging federal conviction); United States v. Johnson, 988 F.2d 941, 943 (9th Cir. 1993) (liberally construing *pro se* federal prisoner's Rule 35(a) motion to correct sentence as section 2255 motion); United States v. Weathersby, 958 F.2d 65, 66 (5th Cir. 1992) (*pro se* section 2255 petition challenging denial of credit for pretrial period spent on bond,

habeas corpus petitions should be viewed "with the greatest liberality" and that substance, not form, should govern the availability of habeas corpus relief.[10]

which should have been brought under section 2241, liberally construed as section 2241 petition); Pearson v. Gatto, 933 F.2d 521, 527 (7th Cir. 1991) (section 1983 action) (*pro se* prisoner's letter, filed shortly before expiration of statute of limitations and indicating intention to amend complaint, should have been "broadly constru[ed]" to be amended complaint so as to preserve jurisdiction); United States v. Jordan, 915 F.2d 622, 624-25 (11th Cir. 1990), *cert. denied,* 499 U.S. 979 (1991) (considering that movant was *pro se* and that FED. R. CRIM. P. 35(a) recently had been amended so as not to authorize relief sought by movant, court treats movant's Rule 35(a) "motion to correct illegal sentence" as section 2255 motion); United States v. Eatinger, 902 F.2d 1383, 1384-85 & n.3 (9th Cir. 1990) (similar to *United States v. Jordan, supra; pro se* documents "must be liberally construed" to invoke available procedures); Balisteri v. Pacifica Police Dep't, 901 F.2d 696, 699 (9th Cir. 1988) (section 1983 action) (federal court "has a duty to ensure that pro se litigants do not lose their right to a hearing on the merits of their claim due to ignorance of technical procedural requirements"); Kelley v. McGinnis, 899 F.2d 612, 616 n.8 (7th Cir. 1990) (*per curiam*) (section 1983 petition); Williams v. White, 897 F.2d 942, 944 (8th Cir. 1990) (same); Chitwood v. Dowd, 889 F.2d 781, 784 (8th Cir. 1989), *cert. denied,* 495 U.S. 953 (1990) (court permitted petitioner's "inartfully worded ... pro se ... petition" to be "clarified" after filing); Lowery v. Young, 887 F.2d 1309, 1311 (7th Cir. 1989) (waste of time to construe "*pro se* petition ... subject to reasonable interpretation" as improperly filed; "requiring [petitioner] to refile an identical petition would only serve to burden the court's and the parties' time and resources"); Rauter v. United States, 871 F.2d 693, 694-95 (7th Cir. 1989) (petitioner's letter to district court requesting withdrawal of guilty plea treated as section 2255 motion); United States v. Mosquera, 845 F.2d 1122, 1123 n.1 (1st Cir. 1988) (*pro se* prisoner's "motion for appropriate relief" construed as section 2255 motion); United States v. Zuleta-Molina, 840 F.2d 157, 158 (1st Cir. 1988) (*pro se* petitioner's improper Rule 35 motion treated as petition for relief under section 2255); Wilson v. Foti, 832 F.2d 891, 891-92 (5th Cir. 1987) (treating *pro se* petitioner's complaint, improperly filed under section 1983, as habeas corpus petition); Okot v. Callahan, 788 F.2d 631, 633 (9th Cir. 1986) (treating "Motion for Writ of Habeas Corpus" attached to motion to remove case from state to federal court as petition for habeas corpus); Franklin v. Rose, 765 F.2d 82, 84-85 (6th Cir. 1985) (liberally construing habeas corpus petition that was improper as to form); Johnson v. Onion, 761 F.2d 224, 225 (5th Cir. 1985) (prisoner who filed complaint seeking relief under section 1983, when habeas corpus petition was the proper pleading, permitted to refile habeas corpus action); Hanahan v. Luther, 760 F.2d 148, 150-51 (7th Cir. 1985) (prisoner's "motion" should have been treated as habeas corpus petition, as to which, however, district court lacked personal jurisdiction); Cook v. Wyrick, 428 F. Supp. 98 (E.D. Mo. 1977). *Cf.* Howard v. Lewis, 905 F.2d 1318, 1323 (9th Cir. 1990) ("'legal rules ... must not be "construed to derogate from the traditional liberality of the writ of habeas corpus"'" (quoting Johnson v. Lumpkin, 769 F.2d 630, 637 (9th Cir. 1985) (quoting Sanders v. United States, 373 U.S. 1, 11 (1963)))); nonetheless, summary dismissal of *pro se* habeas corpus petition under local district court rule providing that failure to respond to motion to dismiss constitutes assent to dismissal is appropriate unless prison officials interfered with petitioner's ability to respond to motion to dismiss).

[10] Wright, *supra* note 5, at 237-40 & n.46 (citing cases). *Accord, e.g.,* McNeil v. United States, 508 U.S. 106, 113 (1993) ("we have insisted that pleadings prepared by prisoners who do not have access to counsel be liberally construed" (citing Estelle v. Gamble, 429 U.S. 97, 106 (1976); Haines v. Kerner, 404 U.S. 519, 520-21 (1972)); Boag v. MacDougall, 454 U.S. 364, 365 (1982) (*per curiam*) (discussing need for liberal interpretation of *pro se* prisoner's pleading); Cooper v.

If the court decides to return a petition because of a defect in form, the court must accompany the return "with a statement of the reason for [the petition's] return," and the clerk must keep one copy of the petition on file with the court.[11] Return is not an appropriate response to defects discovered after the clerk has filed the petition. At that point, the proper procedure is to grant the petitioner leave to amend the petition and, should the prisoner refuse, to dismiss the petition.[12]

§ 15.2. Summary dismissal.[1]

a. *When appropriate.* After the petition is filed, there are several points at which the question may arise whether the court should dismiss the pleading summarily because the grounds for relief asserted are facially lacking in merit.

Pate, 378 U.S. 546 (1964); Pollard v. United States, 352 U.S. 354, 359 (1957); Durley v. Mayo, 351 U.S. 277, 282 n.3 (1956); Gibbs v. Burke, 337 U.S. 773, 779 (1949); Price v. Johnston, 334 U.S. 266, 292 (1948); Tomkins v. Missouri, 323 U.S. 485, 487 (1945); United States v. Mosquera, 845 F.2d 1122, 1124 (1st Cir. 1988) (courts should treat *pro se* petitioner's pleadings liberally); Williams v. Kullman, 722 F.2d 1048, 1050-51 (2d Cir. 1983) (same); Johnson v. Estelle, 625 F.2d 75, 76 (5th Cir. 1980) (*per curiam*); McCloud v. Wainwright, 508 F.2d 853 (5th Cir. 1975); Russell v. Knight, 488 F.2d 96 (5th Cir. 1973); *Developments in the Law — Federal Habeas Corpus,* 83 HARV. L. REV. 1038, 1174-75 (1970). *See also* authority cited *supra* note 9 (collecting authority liberally treating *pro se* prisoner and related trial-level pleadings filed in improper form, with improper caption, or under improper legal provision when proper provision was obvious to court); *supra* §§ 11.6 n.9 (collecting authority liberally assessing compliance of *pro se* habeas corpus petitions with fact pleading rules), 12.2 n.14 (decisions discussing value to courts of appointment of counsel for indigent prisoners); *infra* §§ 15.2c n.52 (collecting authority liberally construing substantive allegations in *pro se* habeas corpus and similar pleadings in determining propriety of summary dismissal), 15.2c n.53 (collecting authority applying different, more forgiving, rules and procedures to *pro se* prisoner and other litigants), 35.2b n.54 (collecting authority liberally construing formally improper *pro se* pleadings seeking to initiate appellate habeas corpus and related procedures), 41.4b n.19 (similar liberal treatment of *pro se* pleadings in section 2255 proceedings).

[11] Rule 2(e) of the Rules Governing § 2254 Cases. In light of (1) the above requirement, (2) the rule's formulation in terms of "return" rather than "dismissal," and (3) Congress' desire that formalities not lead to "a rejection of otherwise meritorious claims" (*see supra* note 7 and accompanying text), it appears that the court may retain jurisdiction over the case while the petition is returned for correction or amendment. *See, e.g.,* Adams v. Armontrout, 897 F.2d 332, 334 n.2 (8th Cir. 1990) (court orders return of formally defective petition but permits petitioner to refile because dismissal is without prejudice). This procedure is important in capital cases because it allows the court to grant or preserve a stay of execution notwithstanding the "return" of the petition. *See generally supra* § 13.3.

[12] *See, e.g.,* Byrd v. Martin, 754 F.2d 963, 965 (11th Cir. 1985). *See also Johnson v. Onion, supra,* 761 F.2d at 225; *infra* § 17.2 (amendments).

§ 15.2. [1] *See generally* RONALD P. SOKOL, FEDERAL HABEAS CORPUS 102-08 (2d ed. 1969); LARRY W. YACKLE, POSTCONVICTION REMEDIES §§ 116, 117 (1981 & Supp. 1998); David A.

First, if the Prison Litigation Reform Act of 1996 ("PRLA")[2] applies to federal habeas corpus proceedings — an issue that is subject to some doubt currently, though the strong majority view is that PLRA does *not* apply to such proceedings[3] — an *in forma pauperis* petition may be dismissed summarily if the petitioner fails to pay at least partial filing fees or if the court determines that the complaint is frivolous or states no basis on which relief may be granted.[4] Individual claims also may be dismissed for "frivolous[ness]" or "failure to state a claim upon which relief may be granted."[5] The PLRA requires that the courts screen complaints for compliance with the statutory standards "before docketing, if feasible or, in any event as soon as practicable after docketing."[6]

Second, Rule 4 of the Rules Governing § 2254 Cases requires the clerk, upon filing the petition, "promptly" to present it to a judge[7] who "shall examine[]" the petition to determine "[i]f it plainly appears from the face of the petition and any exhibits annexed to it[8] that the petitioner is not entitled to relief."[9] If the "plainly appears" standard is not met, "the judge shall order the respondent to file an answer or other pleading within the period of time fixed by the court or to take

---

Bagwell, *Procedural Aspects of Prisoner § 1983 and § 2254 Cases in the Fifth and Eleventh Circuits,* 95 F.R.D. 435, 454-61 (1982); Charles Alan Wright, *Procedure for Habeas Corpus,* 77 F.R.D. 227, 241 (1978); *Developments in the Law — Habeas Corpus,* 83 HARV. L. REV. 1038, 1173-79 (1970); *supra* Chapters 8-11 (formal and substantive habeas corpus requirements); *supra* § 15.1 ("return" of petitions due to defects in form).

[2] Pub. L. 104-134, 110 Stat. 1321 (April 26, 1996). *See* Crawford-El v. Britton, 118 S. Ct. 1584, 1596 (1998) (generally describing PLRA).

[3] *See supra* § 12.1 nn.12-17 and accompanying text.

[4] 28 U.S.C.A. § 1915 (West 1994 & Supp. 1998). *See supra* § 12.1 nn.4-9, 20-21, 32-37 and accompanying text. Among the bases for dismissing petitions, or at least included claims, as "frivolous" are obvious violations of applicable statutes of limitations. For discussion of recently enacted statutes of limitations, and of the cases to which they apply, see *supra* §§ 3.2, 3.3c, 3.4, 5.1b.

[5] 28 U.S.C.A. § 1915A(b) (West 1994 & Supp. 1998). *See supra* § 12.1 n.33 and accompanying text.

[6] 28 U.S.C.A. § 1915A(a) (West 1994 & Supp. 1998). *See supra* § 12.1 nn.36-37 and accompanying text.

[7] The particular judge to whom the petition is presented is determined by the local rules. Rule 4 of the Rules Governing § 2254 Cases. *See also infra* § 41.4c (assignment of motions under 28 U.S.C. § 2255 (West 1994 & Supp. 1998)).

[8] *See* decisions cited *infra* §§ 15.2c n.59, 16.1b n.15, 19.2, 20.3b.

[9] Rule 4 of the Rules Governing § 2254 Cases. *See* Lonchar v. Thomas, 517 U.S. 314, 320, 325 (1996); McFarland v. Scott, 512 U.S. 849, 856 (1994); O'Bremski v. Maass, 915 F.2d 418, 420 (9th Cir. 1990), *cert. denied,* 498 U.S. 1096 (1991). Among the bases for dismissing petitions or claims as "plainly" lacking merit are obvious violations of applicable statutes of limitations. For discussion of recently enacted statutes of limitations, and of the cases to which they apply, see *supra* §§ 3.2, 3.3c, 3.4, 5.1b.

such other action as the judge deems appropriate." If, on the other hand, the petition and annexed exhibits do "plainly" show that the petitioner is not entitled to relief, then Rule 4 provides that "the judge shall make an order for [the petition's] summary dismissal and cause the petitioner to be notified."[10] The court is not, however, authorized, absent notice to the petitioner and an opportunity to respond, to dismiss based on matters outside the petition and the papers attached to it, including, apparently, state court opinions.[11] In order to enable the court of appeals to determine that the various prerequisites for summary dismissal by the district court were satisfied, some courts of appeals require a written opinion by the district court reflecting the basis for the district court's summary dismissal.[12]

Rule 4 dismissal in advance of the state's answer is not a generally preferred course of action, and some federal courts of appeals have held — based on fairness[13] and efficiency[14] grounds — that district courts only rarely should

---

[10] Rule 4 of the Rules Governing § 2254 Cases. Whatever action it takes, the court must serve a copy of the petition and its order on the respondent and the attorney general of the involved State by certified mail. *Id.* Habeas Rule 4 essentially recodifies 28 U.S.C. § 2243 (1994), which requires the court to issue "an order ... to show cause why the writ should not be granted, unless it appears from the application that the applicant or person detained is not entitled thereto." *See* 28 U.S.C. § 2072 (1994) (Habeas Rules supersede prior inconsistent statutes). *See generally* Bundy v. Wainwright, 808 F.2d 1410, 1414-16 (11th Cir. 1987).

[11] *See, e.g.,* authority cited *infra* § 16.1c n.20. *Cf.* Denton v. Hernandez, 504 U.S. 25, 34 (1992) (reserving question whether "*pro se* litigant bringing suit *in forma pauperis* is entitled to notice and an opportunity to amend the complaint to overcome any [correctable] deficiency").

[12] *See, e.g.,* United States v. Marr, 856 F.2d 1471, 1472 (10th Cir. 1988) (summary dismissal of ineffective assistance claim is not appropriate unless district court states in written opinion that it reviewed entire record and that record conclusively shows no entitlement to relief).

[13] *See* FED. R. CIV. P. 56(c) (complaint should not be dismissed summarily without affording complainant notice that dismissal is contemplated and opportunity to demonstrate that dismissal is improper). For habeas corpus decisions identifying Civil Rule 56(c)'s requirements of notice and opportunity to respond in advance of summary judgment as proper procedure before dismissing a petition on successive petition or other grounds, see *infra* § 16.1c n.20.

[14] Requiring district courts in the first instance to interpret ambiguous *pro se* papers and to comb state court records often results in an unwise expenditure of judicial resources. *See* Franklin v. Oregon State Welfare Div., 662 F.2d 1337, 1341-42 (9th Cir. 1981) (improper for court *sua sponte* to dismiss cases over which court had jurisdiction because procedure eliminates traditional adversarial relationship, causes inefficiencies in judicial process, and gives appearance that judiciary is proponent rather than independent entity); Lewis v. New York, 547 F.2d 4, 5-6 (2d Cir. 1976); SOKOL, *supra* note 1, at 107; Daniel J. Meador, *Accommodating State Criminal Procedure and Federal Postconviction Review,* 50 A.B.A. J. 928 (1964); *Developments in the Law, supra* note 1, at 1178. Given the broad discretion granted the district court to decide how best to analyze the substantiality of the petition (*see infra* notes 16-28 and accompanying text) and in setting the time within which the state must answer the petition (*see* Advisory Committee Note to Rule 4 of the Rules Governing § 2254 Cases; Clutchette v. Rushen, 770 F.2d 1469, 1474 (9th Cir. 1985), *cert. denied,* 475 U.S. 1088 (1986); *infra* § 16.1), the Habeas Rules encourage federal courts at the

dismiss petitions for nonjurisdictional reasons before hearing from the state.[15] Habeas Rule 4 supports a cautious approach to summary dismissal. By giving the court the options of asking the state to file some "other pleading" besides or in

least to call upon the state's attorney to respond to ambiguous *pro se* allegations and to direct the court to relevant portions of the record. *See* Advisory Committee Note to Rule 5 of the Rules Governing § 2254 Cases ("attorney general has both the legal expertise and access to the record and thus is in a much better position to inform the court on [certain] matter[s]"). Appointment of counsel to represent the petitioner also may be appropriate. *See supra* § 12.3. On the other hand, the appellate nature of habeas corpus proceedings, *see supra* § 2.4, creates a greater likelihood in that setting than in traditional civil cases that the issues presented in the initiatory pleading will be clear and fully developed. There thus is reason to retain the capacity of habeas corpus judges in limited circumstances to rule summarily, without adversary proceedings. *See supra* § 11.6 n.3.

[15] *See, e.g.,* Cuadra v. Sullivan, 837 F.2d 56, 58-59 (2d Cir. 1988) ("'*sua sponte* dismissal of *pro se* prisoner petitions which contain non-frivolous claims without requiring service upon respondents or granting leave to amend is disfavored'" (quoting Moorish Science Temple of America, Inc. v. Smith, 693 F.2d 987, 990 (2d Cir. 1982))); Williams v. Kullman, 722 F.2d 1048, 1050-51 (2d Cir. 1983) (courts generally should await state's answer or permit amendment before summarily dismissing habeas corpus petition); United States ex rel. Jones v. Franzen, 676 F.2d 261, 267 (7th Cir. 1982) (courts should rarely dismiss before answer); Franklin v. Oregon State Welfare Div., supra, 662 F.2d at 1341; Lewis v. New York, 547 F.2d 4, 5-6 (2d Cir. 1976); Nichols v. Schubert, 499 F.2d 946, 947 (7th Cir. 1974). *See also* Benitez v. Wolff, 907 F.2d 1293, 1295 (2d Cir. 1990) (section 1983 action) ("*Sua sponte* dismissal of a *pro se* complaint prior to service of process is a 'draconian device,' ... which is warranted only when the complaint 'lacks an arguable basis either in law or in fact'"); authority cited *infra* § 15.2c n.44. *But cf.* Flick v. Blevins, 887 F.2d 778, 780-81 (7th Cir. 1989), *cert. denied,* 495 U.S. 934 (1990) (over dissent, court affirms district court's dismissal of petition as frivolous without requesting state's response); Franklin v. Murphy, 745 F.2d 1221, 1226 (9th Cir. 1984) (exception to Franklin v. Oregon State Welfare Div., supra, allowing *sua sponte* dismissal if claim is frivolous). *See generally* McCarthy v. Madigan, 503 U.S. 140, 153 (1992) (section 1983 case) (Among "'the principles that necessarily frame our analysis of prisoners' constitutional claims' is that 'federal courts must take cognizance of the valid constitutional claims of prison inmates.' Because a prisoner ordinarily is divested of the privilege to vote, the right to file a court action might be said to be his remaining most 'fundamental political right, because preservative of all rights.'" (quoting Turner v. Safley, 482 U.S. 78, 84 (1987); Yick Wo v. Hopkins, 118 U.S. 356, 370 (1886))).

If a petition has been dismissed improperly, summarily or otherwise, the petitioner may file a motion for reconsideration, *see infra* Chapter 34, or seek leave to appeal, *see infra* § 35.4; *see generally* Chapters 34-39. When summary dismissal occurs, district courts are encouraged to "provide a statement explaining the dismissal that facilitates 'intelligent appellate review....'" *Denton v. Hernandez, supra,* 504 U.S. at 34 (quoting Boag v. MacDougall, 454 U.S. 364, 365 n.* (1982) (*per curiam*)) (discussed *infra* § 15.2c n.50). Failure to explain the dismissal may warrant reversal. *See id.* Although the Court has held that summary dismissal under the general *in forma pauperis* provision of 28 U.S.C.A. § 1915(d) (West 1994 & Supp. 1998) (discussed *supra* § 12.1; *see also supra* notes 2-6) is committed to the discretion of the district court and is reviewed on appeal only for abuse of discretion, *Denton v. Hernandez, supra* at 34, its reasons for this holding — including that section 1915(d) dismissal, unlike Habeas Rule 4 dismissal, "is not a dismissal on the merits, but rather an exercise of the court's jurisdiction under the *in forma pauperis* statute," *id.* — do not apply to Rule 4 dismissal.

addition to an answer or of taking any "other action ... deem[ed] appropriate," Rule 4 affords the court "flexibility" to take actions short of outright dismissal, such as asking the state to produce additional portions of the state court record, inviting appropriate motions or explanations to clarify the allegations in the petition,[16] summarily dismissing only some of the claims, inviting the petitioner to amend the petition to flesh out incomplete or ambiguous statements of fact or law,[17] appointing counsel to assist the petitioner in formulating a more comprehensible petition,[18] and the like.[19]

Third, the respondent may move for summary judgment or dismissal, either on invitation by the court[20] or by motion filed simultaneously with or after an answer.[21]

---

[16] *See* Bundy v. Wainwright, 808 F.2d 1410, 1415 & n.9 (11th Cir. 1987).

[17] A number of courts have indicated a preference for amendments as an alternative to summary judgment. *See, e.g., Cuadra v. Sullivan, supra,* 837 F.2d at 58-59; Petty v. McCotter, 779 F.2d 299, 302 (5th Cir. 1986), *cert. dismissed as improvidently granted,* 480 U.S. 873 (1987); Byrd v. Martin, 754 F.2d 963, 965 (11th Cir. 1985); *Franklin v. Murphy, supra,* 745 F.2d at 1228 n.9 (citing cases); *Williams v. Kullman, supra,* 722 F.2d at 1051; Jarvis v. Nelson, 440 F.2d 13, 14 (9th Cir. 1971) (dismissal without leave to amend is improper unless no tenable claims can be pleaded); Hill v. Nelson, 271 F. Supp. 439, 443 (N.D. Cal. 1967). *See also Denton v. Hernandez, supra,* 504 U.S. at 34 (discussed *infra* § 15.2c n.50) ("if it appears that frivolous factual allegations could be remedied through more specific pleadings, a court of appeals reviewing a [28 U.S.C.] § 1915(d) disposition should consider whether the district court abused its discretion by dismissing the complaint with prejudice or without leave to amend"; Court reserves question whether "opportunity to amend ... to overcome any deficiency" is always required); Holiday v. Johnston, 313 U.S. 342, 350 (1941) (petitions not to be regarded meticulously; if insufficient, petitions may be amended); Porcaro v. United States, 832 F.2d 208, 210-12 (1st Cir. 1987) (because allegations in petition were barely sufficient, district court properly concluded that most expeditious course was to require petitioner to obtain and file supporting affidavits; thereafter, district court properly denied relief when *pro se* prisoner failed to file requested affidavits). *See infra* § 17.2 (amendments).

[18] *See* authority cited *supra* § 12.3b.

[19] *See* Advisory Committee Note to Rule 4 of the Rules Governing § 2254 Cases; *Williams v. Kullman, supra,* 722 F.2d at 1051 (listing alternatives to summary dismissal).

[20] *See* Advisory Committee Note to Rule 4 of the Rules Governing § 2254 Cases; *Bundy v. Wainwright, supra,* 808 F.2d at 1415 & n.9.

[21] *See* Advisory Committee Note to Rule 8 of the Rules Governing § 2254 Cases ("dismissal pursuant to a motion by the respondent"). Both motions to dismiss and motions for summary judgment are available in this context. *See* Advisory Committee Note to Rule 8 of the Rules Governing § 2254 Cases; Granberry v. Greer, 481 U.S. 129, 130 (1987) (Civil Rule 12(b)(6) motion); Browder v. Director, 434 U.S. 257, 269 n.14 (1978) (motion to dismiss); Blackledge v. Allison, 431 U.S. 63, 80 (1977) (summary judgment); *infra* §§ 16.1c, 16.2. The procedural requirements for motions for summary dismissal or summary judgment filed by the state are discussed *infra* § 16.1c n.20.

Fourth, the court has another opportunity to dismiss the petition *sua sponte* "after the answer and the petition are considered or after consideration of the pleadings and an expanded record."[22]

Fifth, after the parties file their initial papers and motions, Habeas Rule 8(a) authorizes the court to determine whether or not "an evidentiary hearing is required"[23] and, if not, to "make such disposition of the petition as justice shall require," including granting the writ,[24] authorizing fact development procedures short of a hearing, requesting briefing,[25] or dismissing the petition.[26] There "must ordinarily be an evidentiary hearing" if "there is some issue beyond the legal effect of undisputed facts";[27] otherwise, following briefing, the court should either grant relief or "dismiss[] the case under Habeas Rule 8(a)."[28]

In addition to the foregoing formal mechanisms for summary dismissal, there are various judicial determinations on other issues that may, as a practical matter, prevent a prisoner from proceeding with a federal habeas corpus petition. Even assuming that the PLRA does not apply to federal habeas corpus proceedings,[29] the court may deny *in forma pauperis* status under preexisting statutory authority[30] and thereby effectively end the action. The same is often true of rulings denying appointment of counsel[31] and, in capital cases, a stay of execution.[32]

b. *Tactical considerations.* Because *sua sponte* summary dismissal is considerably more likely in habeas corpus than in other federal civil litigation, the habeas corpus petitioner faces a number of special tactical decisions. Most

---

[22] Advisory Committee Note to Rule 8 of the Rules Governing § 2254 Cases. *See infra* § 19.5 (expansion of the record).

[23] *See infra* Chapter 20.

[24] *See* Advisory Committee Note to Rule 8 of the Rules Governing § 2254 Cases; *infra* § 17.3 (petitioner-initiated summary judgment motions).

[25] *See supra* § 11.7d; *infra* Chapters 19, 20.

[26] *See generally* Advisory Committee Note to Rule 8 of the Rules Governing § 2254 Cases.

[27] *See, e.g.,* Fontaine v. United States, 411 U.S. 213, 215 (1973) (*per curiam*); Townsend v. Sain, 372 U.S. 293 (1963); authority cited *infra* § 20.1b n.13.

[28] Bagwell, *supra* note 1, at 461 (citing Harris v. Oliver, 645 F.2d 327, 331 (5th Cir.), *cert. denied,* 454 U.S. 1109 (1981); Easter v. Estelle, 609 F.2d 756 (5th Cir. 1980); Cronnon v. Alabama, 587 F.2d 246 (5th Cir. 1979), *cert. denied,* 440 U.S. 974 (1980)). *See also* McBride v. Sharpe, 25 F.3d 962, 970-71 (11th Cir.) (*en banc*), *cert. denied,* 513 U.S. 990 (1994) (indicating, without deciding, that due process may require district court to give petitioner notice that it is considering dismissal of petition pursuant to Habeas Rule 8(a)).

[29] *See supra* notes 2-6.

[30] *See supra* § 12.1.

[31] *See supra* §§ 12.2-12.5.

[32] *See supra* Chapter 13.

particularly, the petitioner must decide whether to argue against summary dismissal more or less explicitly — in the petition itself, in some document accompanying the petition (such as a memorandum supporting an application for leave to proceed *in forma pauperis,* for appointment of counsel, for a stay of execution,[33] for discovery, or for an evidentiary hearing), or in a legal memorandum in support of the petition. An earlier section discusses the advantages and disadvantages of these means of forestalling summary dismissal.[34] Alternatively, the petitioner may let the petition speak for itself as to its substantiality,[35] relying on a motion to reconsider[36] if the district court unexpectedly dismisses the petition summarily.

The petitioner also should be aware of and prepared to respond to: (1) indications that the court is seriously considering summary dismissal, such as (a) court orders requiring further briefing or a hearing on applications for leave to proceed *in forma pauperis,* to appoint counsel, and to grant stays of execution,[37] and (b) orders setting a hearing on the question of dismissal, requiring petitioner to show cause why the petition should not be dismissed, or inviting the respondent to file a motion to dismiss;[38] as well as (2) pleadings filed by the state that may increase the likelihood of dismissal, including (a) the state's answer,[39] and (b) the state's response to the petitioner's requests for provision of transcripts, financial assistance, discovery, expansion of the record, an evidentiary hearing, or other procedures.[40] If dismissal of a claim or claims seems likely, the petitioner may seek to amend the petition if doing so might save it from dismissal.[41]

---

[33] Because the same "nonfrivolousness" standard governs applications for *in forma pauperis* status (*see supra* §§ 12.1, 15.2a nn.2-6, 30 and accompanying text), appointment of counsel (*see supra* § 12.3b), and a stay of execution pending adjudication of a first petition (*see supra* § 13.2c; *but see supra* § 13.2c nn.77-82 (higher stay standard in cases governed by the "opt-in" provisions of the Antiterrorism and Effective Death Penalty Act of 1996 (AEDPA)), all three applications generally invite discussion of the substantiality of the claims. *See also infra* § 35.4b (similar standard under AEDPA requirement of "certificate of appealability" and pre-AEDPA requirement of "certificate of probable cause to appeal").

[34] *See supra* § 11.7d.

[35] *See* Bundy v. Wainwright, 808 F.2d 1410 (11th Cir. 1987).

[36] *See infra* Chapter 34.

[37] *See supra* note 33 and accompanying text.

[38] *See* Advisory Committee Note to Rule 4 of the Rules Governing § 2254 Cases; *supra* § 15.2a nn.16-28 and accompanying text.

[39] *See infra* §§ 16.1 (answer), 17.1 (petitioner's traverse or reply to answer).

[40] *See supra* § 11.7d; *infra* Chapters 19, 20.

[41] *See infra* § 17.2 (amendments). *See also supra* § 11.6 (fact pleading).

c. *Legal standards.*

In general. Summary dismissal under Habeas Rule 4 is a drastic disposition, not generally available in other civil litigation[42] and disfavored even in habeas corpus cases in some circuits.[43] Under the applicable legal standards, *sua sponte* dismissal is appropriate only when the petition presents obviously untenable arguments that further factual development, legal explication, or the assistance of counsel cannot make tenable.[44] In *Blackledge v. Allison*,[45] the Supreme Court held that "the critical question" which must be answered affirmatively to justify summary dismissal is whether the "allegations, when viewed against the record [available to the court are] so 'palpably incredible,' so 'patently frivolous or false,' as to warrant summary dismissal."[46]

---

[42] *See Developments in the Law, supra* § 15.2a n.1, at 1178 (discussed in Advisory Committee Note to Habeas Rule 4) (answers almost always should be required).

[43] *See supra* § 15.2a nn.13-15 and accompanying text.

[44] *See, e.g.,* Cuadra v. Sullivan, 837 F.2d 56, 58-59 (2d Cir. 1988) (summary dismissal is appropriate only if petition establishes on face "'that petitioner can prove no set of facts to support a claim entitling him to relief'" (quoting Williams v. Kullman, 722 F.2d 1048, 1050 (2d Cir. 1983))). *See also* SOKOL, *supra* note 1, at 103 ("summary denial should be used ... only ... [i]f the petition has been competently drafted, the allegation is clear, and it is patently without merit."). Because the state can waive exhaustion of state remedies, *see infra* § 23.2, and because the appropriate remedy for nonexhaustion may be to hold the petition in abeyance rather than dismiss it, *see supra* §§ 11.1, 13.3, summary dismissal on nonexhaustion grounds in advance of an assertion of an exhaustion bar by the state in its answer and a response by the petitioner is almost never permissible. *See, e.g.,* McCartney v. Vitek, 902 F.2d 616, 617 (8th Cir. 1990) *(dicta)* (ordinarily, "habeas petition should not be dismissed for failure to exhaust state remedies before the state has responded" to petition because state may waive exhaustion); Prather v. Norman, 901 F.2d 915, 918 (11th Cir. 1990) ("The practice in this circuit is not to dismiss [summarily] habeas petitions containing claims that have not met the ... exhaustion requirement.... Because exhaustion is not jurisdictional and may be waived by the state, it is error to dismiss a petition [summarily, in advance of state's answer] solely on grounds of failure to exhaust."); *infra* § 16.1b n.13. The same rule might be thought to apply to other defenses to relief that may be waived by the state — including *e.g.*, violation of an applicable statute of limitations, *see supra* § 5.1b, nonretroactivity, *see infra* Chapter 25, and procedural default, *see infra* Chapter 26 — although there is less caselaw on those subjects. At the least, summary dismissal on the basis of a defense is not appropriate unless the defense is obviously meritorious and there clearly is no exception or response that might apply.

[45] 431 U.S. 63 (1977).

[46] *Id.* at 75-76 (quoting Machibroda v. United States, 368 U.S. 487, 495 (1962); Pennsylvania ex rel. Herman v. Claudy, 350 U.S. 116, 119 (1956)). *Accord, e.g.,* Herrera v. Collins, 506 U.S. 390, 441 (1993) (Blackmun, J., dissenting on other grounds) ("The district court is entitled to dismiss the petition summarily only if 'it plainly appears from the face of the petition and any exhibits annexed to it that the petitioner is not entitled to relief.'" (quoting Rule 4 of the Rules Governing § 2254 Cases)); Fontaine v. United States, 411 U.S. 213, 215 (1973) *(per curiam)* (summary dismissal was improper because record did not conclusively show that movant was entitled to no relief); United States ex rel. McCann v. Adams, 320 U.S. 220, 221 (1943); Chacon v.

Wood, 36 F.3d 1459, 1465 (9th Cir. 1994) (claim could not be dismissed summarily because it was not "'frivolous or incredible,'" as demonstrated "in part" by fact that "state has *never* denied the allegation in the more than three years of the federal habeas proceeding"); Houston v. Lockhart, 982 F.2d 1246, 1250-53 (8th Cir. 1993) (*en banc*); Tower v. Phillips, 979 F.2d 807, 811 (11th Cir. 1992); Murchu v. United States, 926 F.2d 50, 57 (1st Cir.), *cert. denied,* 502 U.S. 828 (1991) (summary dismissal of section 2255 motion is inappropriate because allegations that trial judge vindictively gave movant high sentence after movant refused to plead guilty "are not conclusory, contradicted by the record []or so inherently incredible as to permit them to be ignored"); Hendricks v. Vasquez, 908 F.2d 490, 491-92 (9th Cir. 1990) ("Summary dismissal is appropriate only where the allegations in the petition are 'vague [or] conclusory' or 'palpably incredible'"; summary dismissal was inappropriate here because claims were set forth with specificity, were documented with citations to record, and could "[]not be characterized as ... incredible or frivolous"; district court's "summary dismissal followed by the issuance of a certificate of probable cause is 'intrinsically contradictory' and warrants reversal"); United States v. Aiello, 900 F.2d 528, 534 (2d Cir. 1990) (summary dismissal is appropriate only if "motion and the files and records of the case conclusively show that the petitioner is entitled to no relief"); Dziurgot v. Luther, 897 F.2d 1222, 1225 (1st Cir. 1990) ("petition can be dismissed without a hearing if the petitioner's allegations, accepted as true, would not entitle the petitioner to relief, or if the allegations cannot be accepted as true because 'they are contradicted by the record, inherently incredible, or conclusions rather than statements of fact'" (quoting United States v. Mosquera, 845 F.2d 1122, 1124 (1st Cir. 1988))); United States v. Schmitz, 887 F.2d 843, 844 (8th Cir. 1989); United States v. Birdwell, 887 F.2d 643, 645 (5th Cir. 1989); Long v. United States, 883 F.2d 966, 968 (11th Cir. 1989); United States v. Popoola, 881 F.2d 811, 812 (9th Cir. 1989); Aleman v. United States, 878 F.2d 1009, 1012 (7th Cir. 1989); Myatt v. United States, 875 F.2d 8, 11 (1st Cir. 1989); Dory v. Commissioner, 865 F.2d 44, 45-46 (2d Cir. 1989) (summary dismissal reversed because district court granted certificate of probable cause, indicating that petition was not frivolous and hence was not susceptible to summary dismissal); Wright v. Minnesota, 833 F.2d 746, 749 (8th Cir. 1987), *cert. denied,* 485 U.S. 1011 (1988) (dismissal is "proper if the allegations, even if true, fail to state a claim cognizable in a federal habeas corpus proceeding"); Demjanjuk v. Meese, 784 F.2d 1114, 1115 (D.C. Cir. 1986) (Bork, J., in chambers) (dismissal ordered because it was "absolutely clear" that petitioner was not entitled to relief); Flowers v. Blackburn, 779 F.2d 1115, 1119 (5th Cir. 1986); United States v. Barboa, 777 F.2d 1420, 1422 n.2 (10th Cir. 1985); Sanderson v. Rice, 777 F.2d 902, 909-10 (4th Cir. 1985); O'Blasney v. Solem, 774 F.2d 925, 926 (8th Cir. 1985) ("petition ought not be summarily dismissed unless it appears without a doubt that the petitioner can prove no set of facts which would entitle him to relief" (citing Conley v. Gibson, 355 U.S. 41, 45-46 (1957))); Franklin v. Murphy, 745 F.2d 1221, 1228 (9th Cir. 1984) (summary dismissal requires allegations "of a wholly fanciful kind" (quoting Crisafi v. Holland, 655 F.2d 1305, 1307-08 (D.C. Cir. 1981))); United States ex rel. Jones v. Franzen, 676 F.2d 261, 264 (7th Cir. 1982); Alexander v. Harris, 595 F.2d 87, 91 (2d Cir. 1979) (summary dismissal requires "frivolous" petition); Burkhart v. Lane, 574 F.2d 346 (6th Cir. 1978); Allen v. Perini, 424 F.2d 134 (6th Cir.), *cert. denied,* 400 U.S. 906 (1970); United States ex rel. Darcy v. Handy, 203 F.2d 407 (3d Cir. 1953), *aff'd,* 351 U.S. 454 (1956); authority cited *infra* §§ 20.1b nn.13 & 28, 20.3e n.92, 20.4 nn.5-7. *See also* McFarland v. Scott, 512 U.S. 849, 856 (1994) ("Federal courts are authorized to dismiss summarily any habeas petition that appears legally insufficient on its face." (citation omitted)); Smith v. Phillips, 455 U.S. 209, 215 (1982); McLain v. Real Estate Bd., 444 U.S. 232, 246 (1980) ("It is axiomatic that a complaint should not be dismissed unless 'it appears beyond doubt that the [complainant] can prove no set of facts in support of his claim which would entitle him to relief'" (quoting *Conley v. Gibson, supra* at 45-46)).

The *Blackledge* standard generally does not permit summary dismissal simply because the claims in the petition are somewhat vague or conclusory.[47] Instead, appointment of counsel, leave to amend, or one of the other clarifying procedures discussed above[48] is the appropriate initial response to uncertain pleadings. For the "palpably incredible" and "patently frivolous" standard to be met, the petition's legal argument must be wholly foreclosed by prior precedent or wholly unreasonable[49] or the factual record actually before the court must absolutely preclude the court from finding facts, including ones not yet explored at a hearing, that would support the claim.[50]

---

[47] *See Blackledge, supra,* 431 U.S. at 75-76. *See also* Denton v. Hernandez, 504 U.S. 25, 31-34 (1992) (although summary dismissal of "delusional" claims via denial of *in forma pauperis* status may be permissible, summary dismissal of merely "unlikely" or "improbable" claims is not permitted).

[48] *See supra* § 15.2a nn.16-19 and accompanying text.

[49] *See, e.g.,* Norman v. McCotter, 765 F.2d 504, 509 (5th Cir. 1985) (dismissal is appropriate because claim is clear and is not one on which federal relief is available).

[50] *See, e.g.,* Herrera v. Collins, *supra,* 506 U.S. at 390, 441 (Blackmun, J., dissenting on other grounds) ("The district court is entitled to dismiss the petition summarily only if 'it plainly appears from the face of the petition and any exhibits annexed to it that the petitioner is not entitled to relief.' If, as is the case here, the petition raises factual questions and the State has failed to provide a full and fair hearing, the district court is required to hold an evidentiary hearing." (quoting Rule 4 of the Rules Governing § 2254 Cases; citing Townsend v. Sain, 372 U.S. 293, 313 (1963)); cautioning courts against "confus[ing] the question whether the petition may be dismissed summarily with the question whether petitioner is entitled to relief on the merits of his claim"); *Blackledge, supra,* 431 U.S. at 76-78 & n.16; McKenzie v. Risley, 915 F.2d 1396, 1398 (9th Cir. 1990); O'Blasney v. Solem, *supra,* 774 F.2d at 926 ("If the petition is not frivolous and alleges facts which, even though unlikely, would justify granting the writ, then the petitioner is entitled to have his allegations fairly tested."); Williams v. Kullman, 722 F.2d 1048, 1050 (2d Cir. 1983) ("Summary dismissal is appropriate only in those cases where the pleadings indicate that petitioner can prove no set of facts to support a claim entitling him to relief."); Franklin v. Oregon State Welfare Div., 662 F.2d 1337, 1347 (9th Cir. 1981) (although claim raised "may well turn out to be frivolous," summary dismissal was improper because claim was "not so wholly insubstantial" as to rule out any possibility of relief); Blair v. California, 340 F.2d 741, 742 (9th Cir. 1965). *See also* Professional Real Est. Inves., Inc. v. Columbia Pictures Indus., Inc., 508 U.S. 49, 66-67 (1993) (Souter, J., concurring) (question "whether the suit at issue here was objectively baseless is purely one of law, which [appellate court is] ... obliged to consider *de novo*"); Leatherman v. Tarrant County Narcotics Unit, 507 U.S. 163, 164 (1993) (section 1983 action) ("We review here a decision granting a motion to dismiss, and therefore must accept as true all the factual allegations in the complaint." (citing United States v. Gaubert, 499 U.S. 315, 327 (1991)); *Denton v. Hernandez, supra,* 504 U.S. at 32-33 ("a court may dismiss a claim as factually frivolous only if the facts alleged are 'clearly baseless,' ... a category encompassing allegations that are 'fanciful,' ... 'fantastic,' ... and 'delusional,' .... As those words suggest, a finding of factual frivolousness is appropriate when the facts alleged rise to the level of the irrational or the wholly incredible.... An *in forma pauperis* complaint may not be dismissed, however, simply because the court finds the plaintiff's allegations unlikely.... [T]o dismiss ["improbable allegations"] as frivolous without any factual development is to disregard the age-old insight that many allegations might be 'strange, but

Pro se *cases*. *Pro se* petitions are held to a less stringent summary dismissal standard than petitions filed by counsel. For "if habeas corpus is to continue to have meaningful purpose, it must be accessible ... to the mass of uneducated, unrepresented prisoners."[51] Accordingly, the courts have viewed *pro se* habeas corpus petitions and analogous pleadings "with the greatest liberality" in deciding whether or not to dismiss them summarily.[52] In some cases, the courts

true; for truth is always strange, Stranger than fiction.'" (quoting Neitzke v. Williams, 490 U.S. 319, 325, 327, 328 (1989); Lord Byron, *Don Juan*)); *Neitzke v. Williams, supra* at 322-25 (discussed *supra* §§ 12.1 n.30, 13.2c n.70 (discussing and defining "frivolousness" in different but related settings; claim is frivolous "'only if the petitioner cannot make any rational argument in law or in fact, which would entitle him or her to relief'")); United States ex rel. McCall v. O'Grady, 908 F.2d 170, 175 (7th Cir. 1990) (summary judgment on behalf of petitioner is inappropriate on ineffective assistance claim because of record's ambiguity on determinative factual issue). *Compare* United States v. Smith, 915 F.2d 959, 964 (5th Cir. 1990) (dismissal of ineffective assistance claim without hearing was warranted because petitioner did not make detailed and specific allegations, and record clearly contradicted allegations that were made) *and* United States v. Drummond, 910 F.2d 284, 285-86 (5th Cir. 1990), *cert. denied,* 498 U.S. 1104 (1991) (district court properly dismissed section 2255 motion alleging petitioner's incompetence to plead guilty because record of plea hearing revealed degree of lucidity on petitioner's part that clearly contradicted incompetence claim; given clarity of circumstantial evidence, neither direct (*e.g.,* psychiatric) evidence nor findings on competence issue were required) *with* Beaulieu v. United States, 930 F.2d 805, 808 (10th Cir. 1991) (dismissal on record was inappropriate because movant's ineffective assistance allegations dealt with counsel's actions outside of court) *and* United States v. Bigman, 906 F.2d 392, 394-95 (9th Cir. 1990) (overturning summary dismissal of section 2255 motion alleging that counsel misinformed petitioner on mental element of crime before petitioner pled guilty; although reflecting that counsel "discussed" plea with petitioner, record "does not conclusively establish that Bigman was [properly] apprised" of mental element). On the appropriateness of importing the "frivolousness" standard from *in forma pauperis* cases such as *Denton, supra* and *Neitzke, supra,* into the summary dismissal context, *see* O'Neal v. McAninch, 513 U.S. 432, 443 (1995) ("In a highly technical area such as this one, consistency [of rules] brings with it simplicity, a body of existing law available for consultation."); Keeney v. Tamayo-Reyes, 504 U.S. 1, 10 (1992) (promoting value of "uniformity in the law of habeas corpus"). *See also supra* §§ 12.1, 12.3b, 13.2c & *infra* § 35.4c (various uses in habeas corpus context of "frivolousness" standard).

51 *Williams v. Kullman, supra,* 722 F.2d at 1050. *See* United States ex rel. Sero v. Preiser, 506 F.2d 1115, 1126 (2d Cir. 1974); dissenting Supreme Court opinions cited *infra* § 39.3a n.2.

52 Wright, *supra* note 1, at 238 & n.46 (citing, *inter alia,* White v. Wyrick, 530 F.2d 818, 819 (8th Cir. 1976); Russell v. Knight, 488 F.2d 96, 97 (5th Cir. 1973); CHARLES ALAN WRIGHT & ARTHUR MILLER, FEDERAL PRACTICE & PROCEDURE § 1234 n.96 (1969)). *Accord, e.g.,* Denton v. Hernandez, supra, 504 U.S. at 34 (summary dismissal through denial of right to proceed *in forma pauperis* might constitute "abuse of discretion" if litigant "was proceeding *pro se*"); Maleng v. Cook, 490 U.S. 488, 493-94 (1989) (*per curiam*) (in order to establish subject matter jurisdiction, Court reads *pro se* petition as challenge to 1978 conviction as enhanced by 1958 conviction, rather than as challenge to 1958 conviction itself; petition only explicitly attacked 1958 conviction); *Neitzke v. Williams, supra,* 490 U.S. at 330 (indigent plaintiffs proceeding *pro se* often are "less capable of formulating legally competent initial pleadings," and courts reviewing *pro se* pleadings should be more reluctant than usual to dismiss; courts thus should not deny *in forma pauperis*

status to *pro se* complainants under 28 U.S.C. § 1915 based on "frivolousness" of complainants' claims if there is chance that claims could be "clarif[ied] ... to conform with the requirements of a valid legal cause of action"); Boag v. MacDougall, 454 U.S. 364, 365 (1982) (liberally construing prisoner's *pro se* complaint); Coulter v. Gramley, 93 F.3d 394, 396-97 (7th Cir. 1996) (reading *pro se* petition "generously" as raising issue that was properly preserved rather than related issue that was procedurally defaulted; "[a]lthough we agree that the petition is not a model of legal drafts-manship, it is important to construe *pro se* filings liberally."); Chacon v. Wood, 36 F.3d 1459, 1465 (9th Cir. 1994) (liberally construing factual allegation in *pro se* habeas corpus petition as presenting newly discovered evidence that necessitates evidentiary hearing); Brock v. Weston, 31 F.3d 887, 890 (9th Cir. 1994) (*pro se* petition by petitioner whose sentence had expired is liberally construed so as to give court jurisdiction over implied challenge to current confinement as enhanced by prior conviction); Jones v. Cowley, 28 F.3d 1067, 1069 (10th Cir. 1994) (liberally construing *pro se* petitioner's contention that his attorney erred in failing to file appeal as constituting claim of ineffective assistance of counsel); Jones v. Jerrison, 20 F.3d 849, 853 (8th Cir. 1994) (given "'liberal'" standard for interpreting *pro se* petitions and district court's consequent obligation "to analyze all alleged facts to determine whether they state a federal claim," magistrate judge erred in dismissing what appeared to be state law challenge to timeliness of filing of charging paper rather than construing it as cognizable federal due process claim); Myers v. Collins, 8 F.3d 249, 253 & n.9 (5th Cir. 1993) (state's motion for summary judgment should have been denied because *pro se* prisoner's petition, when "[v]iewed in a light most favorable to [petitioner], ... raise[d] a material issue of fact"); Osborn v. Shillinger, 997 F.2d 1324, 1328 & n.1 (10th Cir. 1993) (liberally construing *pro se* prisoner's attack upon validity of guilty plea as encompassing claims of ineffective assistance of counsel); United States v. Day, 969 F.2d 39, 42 (3d Cir. 1992) ("We must construe the allegations in Day's pro se [section 2255] petition liberally, and we must not subject his petition to the standards that we would apply to pleadings drafted by lawyers."); Collins v. Hesse, 957 F.2d 746, 748 (10th Cir. 1992) (applying rule that "*pro se* petition should be construed liberally," court interprets petition as "challenging [petitioner's] present confinement even though the essence of his attack was the alleged unconstitutionality of the prior predicate convictions" used to enhance present sentence); Clay v. Bronnenberg, 950 F.2d 486, 487 n.2 (7th Cir. 1991) (avoiding dismissal of *pro se* petition by liberally construing petitioner's attack on expired sentence as challenge to current sentence as augmented by previous conviction); Harper v. Evans, 941 F.2d 1538 (11th Cir. 1991) (even though *pro se* petitioner erred by framing petition as attack on previous conviction rather than current sentence as enhanced by prior conviction, district court should not have dismissed petition; however "petition is framed ..., the reality is that Harper is 'in custody' as a result of a prior and alleged illegal conviction"); Diaz v. United States, 930 F.2d 832, 835 (11th Cir. 1991); Ayala-Serrano v. Lebron-Gonzalez, 909 F.2d 8, 14-15 (1st Cir. 1990) (liberally construing prisoner's section 1983 complaint to avoid dismissal); Martin v. Kaiser, 907 F.2d 931, 935 (10th Cir. 1990) ("Because Martin's petition for a writ of habeas corpus is a pro se petition, and because a constitutional right is at stake, we construe his double jeopardy argument in its most favorable light."); Williams v. White, 897 F.2d 942, 944-45 (8th Cir. 1990) (court liberally construes *pro se* section 1983 complaint that "is handwritten and not drawn with legal finesse or understanding" and is not "conclusory" or obviously "frivolous"); Anderson v. Butler, 886 F.2d 111, 114 (5th Cir. 1989) (when considering sanctions for frivolous pleading, courts should treat *pro se* petitioners more leniently); Mulero v. Lefevre, 873 F.2d 534, 536 (2d Cir. 1989) (if counsel is appointed for *pro se* petitioner, district court generally should not summarily dismiss petition before hearing from counsel); Guidroz v. Lynaugh, 852 F.2d 832, 834 (5th Cir. 1988) (citing cases) (*pro se* petitions construed liberally; dismissal is inappropriate if petition "set[s] forth facts giving rise to the cause of action" or, though failing to raise ground of error explicitly, does so implicitly

have adopted a separate set of less stringent rules for *pro se* petitions;[53] in other cases, the courts have recognized the need to interpret *pro se* petitions creatively to determine if they encompass valid federal claims[54] or *sua sponte* to invite

---

or in accompanying document (quoting Bounds v. Smith, 430 U.S. 817 (1977)); Williams v. Lockhart, 849 F.2d 1134, 1138 (8th Cir. 1988) (*pro se* litigant's allegations should be liberally construed to include allegations of apparent facts); Cuadra v. Sullivan, 837 F.2d 56, 58-59 (2d Cir. 1988) (court "'should review habeas petition [filed *pro se*] with a lenient eye, allowing borderline cases to proceed'" (quoting *Williams v. Kullman, supra,* 722 F.2d at 1050)); Ewing v. Rodgers, 826 F.2d 967, 971 (10th Cir. 1987) ("pro se habeas petitions will be held 'to less stringent standards than formal pleadings drafted by lawyers'" (quoting Haines v. Kerner, 404 U.S. 519, 520 (1972) (*per curiam*))); Franklin v. Rose, 765 F.2d 82, 84-85 (6th Cir. 1985) (citing cases); United States v. Fiddler, 688 F.2d 45, 48-49 (8th Cir. 1982) ("inartful" pleading does not justify dismissing petition when court understands substantive argument being made); Burris v. United States, 430 F.2d 399, 400-01 (7th Cir. 1970); Coleman v. Peyton, 340 F.2d 603, 604 (4th Cir. 1965). *See also* authority cited *supra* §§ 11.6 n.9 (collecting authority liberally assessing compliance of *pro se* habeas corpus petitions with fact pleading rules), 12.2 n.14 (decisions discussing value to courts of appointment of counsel for indigent prisoners), 15.1 n.9 (collecting authority liberally treating *pro se* prisoner and related trial-level pleadings filed in improper form, with improper caption, or under improper legal provision when proper provision was obvious to court), 15.2c n.15 (authority generally recognizing need to construe *pro se* pleadings liberally); *infra* note 53 (collecting authority applying different, more forgiving, rules and procedures to *pro se* prisoner and other litigants); *infra* §§ 35.2b n.54 (collecting authority liberally construing formally improper *pro se* pleadings seeking to initiate appellate habeas corpus and related procedures), 41.4b n.19 (similar liberal treatment of *pro se* pleadings in section 2255 proceedings).

[53] *See, e.g.,* 7TH CIR. R. 51(b) (requiring notice of motion to dismiss *pro se* appeal); Frank v. Johnson, 968 F.2d 298, 300 (2d Cir.), *cert. denied,* 506 U.S. 1038 (1992) ("To alleviate the unreasonable burden placed on a *pro se* litigant by a waiver rule found only in case law, this Court requires the magistrate's report to warn the *pro se* litigant of the consequences of the failure to object"); Moore v. United States, 950 F.2d 656, 659 (10th Cir. 1991) (failure to object to magistrate's findings or recommendations will not be deemed waiver in *pro se* cases unless magistrate adequately advises petitioner of time for filing objections and consequences of failure to object); Lowery v. Young, 887 F.2d 1309, 1311 (7th Cir. 1989) (*pro se* petition "subject to reasonable interpretation" construed to name proper respondent because "construing it as improperly filed makes little practical sense"); United States ex rel. Leonard v. O'Leary, 788 F.2d 1238, 1240 (7th Cir. 1986) (district court should advise would-be appellant, particularly one proceeding *pro se,* that notice of appeal is untimely and that motion for extension of time may be filed); Burnside v. White, 760 F.2d 217, 221 n.4 (8th Cir. 1985) (less stringent requirement for pleading exhaustion in pro se petitions). *See also* Adams v. United States, 1998 WL 514679, at *1-*2 (2d Cir. Aug. 20, 1998) (because pre-AEDPA practice of routinely converting *pro se* federal prisoners' postconviction motions into section 2255 motions could have adverse consequences for prisoners under AEDPA, court of appeals adopts new procedure that includes advising prisoner of "potential adverse consequences of such recharacterization ... and offer[ing] the movant the opportunity to withdraw the motion rather than have it so recharacterized").

[54] *See, e.g.,* Leacock v. Henman, 996 F.2d 1069, 1071 (10th Cir. 1993); Kelley v. McGinnis, 899 F.2d 612, 616 n.8 (7th Cir. 1990) (*per curiam*); Chitwood v. Dowd, 889 F.2d 781, 784 (8th Cir. 1989), *cert. denied,* 495 U.S. 953 (1990); *Lowery v. Young, supra,* 887 F.2d at 1311; *Franklin v. Rose, supra,* 765 F.2d at 84-85; Kiendra v. Hadden, 763 F.2d 69, 72 (2d Cir. 1985); White v.

amendments;[55] and in all cases, the courts have exercised greater tolerance for vague and conclusory claims than they would in cases involving represented petitioners.[56] Indeed, the raft of costly special procedures used by the courts in *pro se* cases well illustrates the point made in section 12.2 *supra* that appointment of counsel in cases involving unsophisticated petitioners is as much a service to the courts as to indigent prisoners themselves.

Fact-bound cases. Unless patently false, the facts alleged in the petition must be presumed to be true for summary dismissal purposes.[57] If the facts alleged

---

Wyrick, 530 F.2d 818, 819 (8th Cir. 1976); authority cited *supra* note 52. *See also* Ratliff v. United States, 999 F.2d 1023, 1026 (6th Cir. 1993) (although *pro se* section 2255 movant did not specifically allege "cause" and "prejudice," court liberally construes motion to identify factual bases for both factors).

[55] *See, e.g., Williams v. Kullman, supra,* 722 F.2d at 1051; authority cited *supra* § 15.2a n.17. *See infra* § 17.2 (amendments). *See also* Bryan v. Duckworth, 88 F.3d 431, 434 (7th Cir. 1996) (district court erred in "fail[ing] to apprise Bryan, a nonrepresented prisoner litigant, of the consequences under Fed. R. Civ. P. 56(e) of failing to submit his own affidavit" in response to state's motion for summary judgment).

[56] *See, e.g.,* McBride v. Sharpe, 25 F.3d 962, 971 (11th Cir.) (*en banc*), *cert. denied,* 513 U.S. 990 (1994) (*pro se* petitioner's claim that improper denial of counsel precluded full and fair hearing, which did not indicate whether challenge related to state postconviction proceeding or federal district court, is liberally construed to challenge denial of counsel in both proceedings); Belk v. Purkett, 15 F.3d 803, 814-15 (8th Cir. 1994) (district court erred in treating ambiguity of *pro se* petitioner's objections to magistrate's report as basis for denying *de novo* review; precisely because *pro se* petitioners are "[n]ot versed in the law ... [and] may on occasion flounder in a sea of terminology and jurisprudence[,] ... hands-on *de novo* review is most needed" and "[i]t is in just such situations that our district courts must be most alert"). *See also, e.g.,* authority cited *supra* note 52.

[57] *See, e.g., Blackledge, supra,* 431 U.S. at 76; Cooper v. Pate, 378 U.S. 546 (1964); Machibroda v. United States, 368 U.S. 487, 495-96 (1962); Pennsylvania ex rel. Herman v. Claudy, 350 U.S. 116, 118-19 (1956); Cave v. Singletary, 971 F.2d 1513, 1516 (11th Cir. 1992); Diaz v. United States, 930 F.2d 832, 835 (11th Cir. 1991); Lesko v. Lehman, 925 F.2d 1527, 1536-37 (3d Cir.), *cert. denied,* 502 U.S. 898 (1991); Yordan v. Dugger, 909 F.2d 474, 478 (11th Cir. 1990); Panzardi-Alvarez v. United States, 879 F.2d 975, 985 n.8 (1st Cir. 1989), *cert. denied,* 493 U.S. 1082 (1990); Futch v. Dugger, 874 F.2d 1483, 1486 (11th Cir. 1989); Williams v. Lockhart, 849 F.2d 1134, 1138-40 (8th Cir. 1988) (generally, allegation of material facts establishing right to relief requires hearing); United States v. Mosquera, 845 F.2d 1122, 1124 & n.2 (1st Cir. 1988) (when disposing of application summarily, court must accept allegations as true unless allegations are "contradicted by the record, inherently incredible, or conclusions rather than statements of fact"); Valles v. Lynaugh, 835 F.2d 126, 127 (5th Cir. 1988); Rizzo v. Dawson, 778 F.2d 527, 530 (9th Cir. 1985); Edgemon v. Lockhart, 768 F.2d 252, 255 (8th Cir. 1985); United States v. Butt, 731 F.2d 75, 77 (1st Cir. 1984) (sworn *ex parte* statements by government do not justify summary dismissal in absence of full record of prior proceedings); Rogers v. Maggio, 714 F.2d 35, 37 (5th Cir. 1983); Wiley v. Wainwright, 709 F.2d 1412, 1413 (11th Cir. 1983); Johnson v. Estelle, 704 F.2d 232, 234-35, 239-40 (5th Cir. 1983), *cert. denied,* 465 U.S. 1009 (1984); Cain v. Smith, 686 F.2d 374, 380 (6th Cir. 1982); United States ex rel. Jones v. Franzen, 676 F.2d 261, 265 (7th Cir. 1982). *See also* Denton v. Hernandez, 504 U.S. 25, 32-33 (1992) (discussed and quoted *supra* note

"point to a 'real possibility of constitutional error,'" summary dismissal is not appropriate.[58] Consequently, summary dismissal generally is inappropriate in fact-bound cases until the court carefully examines all state court opinions, transcripts of state court hearings, and other records relevant to the petition.[59]

---

50). *Cf.* Compton v. Butler, 883 F.2d 27, 29 (5th Cir. 1989) (because state judges are presumed to have applied correct law, "bare allegation[s]," without any basis in record, that state judge did not know law are insufficient to stave off dismissal); Ouellette v. United States, 862 F.2d 371, 377-78 (1st Cir. 1988) (no hearing required because facts alleged were conclusively contradicted by record and postconviction court also was trial court and was familiar with the record); Tran v. Lockhart, 849 F.2d 1064, 1067-68 (8th Cir. 1988), *cert. denied,* 489 U.S. 1091 (1989) (no hearing required on petitioner's allegation of fact that was "'bare contradiction'" of statement he made at guilty plea hearing).

[58] *Blackledge, supra,* 431 U.S. at 75 n.7 (quoting Advisory Committee Note to Rule 4 of the Rules Governing § 2254 Cases). *Accord, e.g.,* Fontaine v. United States, 411 U.S. 213, 215 (1972) (*per curiam*); United States ex rel. McCann v. Adams, 320 U.S. 220, 221 (1943) (*per curiam*); authority cited *infra* § 20.1. *See also Denton v. Hernandez, supra,* 504 U.S. at 32-33 (discussed and quoted *supra* note 50) (summary dismissal by means of denial of *in forma pauperis* status is reversible abuse of discretion when district court "inappropriately resolved genuine issues of disputed fact"); Wesson v. Oglesby, 910 F.2d 278, 282 (5th Cir. 1990) (when frivolousness is test for dismissal, court may not summarily dismiss solely because it disbelieves prisoner's allegations and believes respondent's, unless prisoner's version of facts is inherently implausible or internally inconsistent).

[59] *See, e.g.,* Hamilton v. Vasquez, 882 F.2d 1469, 1471 (9th Cir. 1989) (if claim presents mixed question of law and fact, district court has *sua sponte* duty to obtain and review state record); United States v. Marr, 856 F.2d 1471, 1472 (10th Cir. 1988) (summary dismissal of ineffective assistance claim is not appropriate unless district court states in written opinion that it reviewed entire record and that record conclusively shows no entitlement to relief); *Williams v. Lockhart, supra,* 849 F.2d at 1137-38 (petition should not have been dismissed because factual allegations, although disputed by respondent, were sufficient on their face to warrant relief and because federal court did not yet have transcript of relevant state hearing); Thames v. Dugger, 848 F.2d 149, 151 (11th Cir. 1988) (dismissal premature because district court did not have complete record); Ruff v. Kincheloe, 843 F.2d 1240, 1242-43 & n.5 (9th Cir. 1988) (in order to determine if conceded error in burden of proof instruction was harmless, district court had to conduct complete and independent review of entire trial transcript; because neither party had supplied court with complete trial transcript, court had duty to obtain record *sua sponte*); Cuadra v. Sullivan, 837 F.2d 56, 60 (2d Cir. 1988) (predismissal review of jury charge required, hence dismissal of challenge to jury charge was inappropriate in absence of record); United States v. Kovic, 830 F.2d 680, 692 (7th Cir. 1987), *cert. denied,* 484 U.S. 1044 (1988); Bundy v. Wainwright, 808 F.2d 1410, 1414, 1417, 1419 (11th Cir. 1987) ("[p]etitioner is not required by statute or Rules to attach to his petition or to file a state court record in order to avoid a dismissal for facial insufficiency [under Habeas Rule 4], although often in summarizing the facts a petitioner necessarily or as a matter of convenience may refer to state court proceedings and even attach extracts therefrom"; district judge improperly dismissed petition "based ... on the fact that the petitioner had failed to supply him with supplemental information and [record] materials other than the petition" (footnote omitted)); Travis v. Lockhart, 787 F.2d 409, 410-11 (8th Cir. 1986); Richmond v. Ricketts, 774 F.2d 957, 961-62 (9th Cir. 1985); O'Blasney v. Solem, 774 F.2d 925 (8th Cir. 1985); Johnson v. Lumpkin, 769 F.2d 630, 636 (9th Cir. 1985) (citing Rheinhart v. Gunn, 598 F.2d 557, 558 (9th Cir. 1979) (*per curiam*));

For this reason, the Advisory Committee Note to Habeas Rule 4 states that summary dismissal should not occur in a fact-dependent case until the state makes all the relevant records (including "transcripts, sentencing records, and copies of state court opinions") available to the court pursuant to Habeas Rule 5.[60]

Although state court factfindings sometimes are due a presumption of correctness under section 28 U.S.C. § 2254(e)(1),[61] those findings only infrequently can furnish a basis for summary dismissal. In the first place, the court often does not have the state court record before it at this stage of the proceedings. Most petitioners do not have the ability to submit the record with the petition, and the statute and rules relieve them of any obligation to do so and require the state to furnish the record with the answer.[62] Absent the record, the court has no way to determine whether any state court factfindings apply and deserve a presumption of correctness.[63] Even if the petitioner furnishes the record, it often will lack factfindings on critical issues. This situation often arises, for example, when the basis for summary judgment contemplated by the court is a defense to relief such as a violation of an applicable statute of

---

United States v. Butt, supra, 731 F.2d at 77 (discussed *supra* note 57); *Williams v. Kullman, supra,* 722 F.2d at 1050-51; Williams v. Estelle, 681 F.2d 946, 948 (5th Cir. 1982); *United States ex rel. Jones v. Franzen, supra,* 676 F.2d at 265; Maes v. Patterson, 401 F.2d 200, 202 (10th Cir. 1968) (summary dismissal was not appropriate under circumstances until court reviewed transcript of state hearing). See *Blackledge, supra,* 431 U.S. at 76-78 & n.15; Durr v. Cook, 442 F. Supp. 487, 488 (W.D. La. 1977), *rev'd on other grounds,* 589 F.2d 891 (5th Cir. 1979); authority cited *supra* § 15.2a n.8 and accompanying text; *infra* §§ 16.1b n.15, 19.2, 20.3b. See also Yates v. Evatt, 500 U.S. 391, 405-06 & n.10, 409-10 (1991) (describing situations in which ruling on harmless error cannot be made in absence of review of entire trial record). *Cf.* Love v. Butler, 952 F.2d 10, 15 (1st Cir. 1991) (district court did not err in summarily dismissing under Rule 4 without reviewing trial transcript because "each of petitioner's arguments was readily susceptible to resolution without resort to the transcript" and petitioner submitted state court briefs and other pleadings and grand jury minutes); Maynard v. Dixon, 943 F.2d 407, 411 (4th Cir. 1991), *cert. denied,* 502 U.S. 1110 (1992) (district court did not err in granting summary judgment before state's submission of transcripts and other state court records because petitioner included all "relevant portions of the transcript" in petition); *Hamilton v. Vasquez, supra* at 1471 ("district court is under no obligation to obtain and review the state court record when disposing of purely factual questions").

[60] See *Williams v. Kullman, supra,* 722 F.2d at 1050 (preference for expansion of record under Habeas Rules 5 and 7 to summary dismissal under Habeas Rule 4).

[61] See 28 U.S.C.A. § 2254(e)(1) (West 1994 & Supp. 1998); *infra* §§ 20.2, 20.3; *infra* Chapter 30.

[62] See *Bundy v. Wainwright, supra,* 808 F.2d at 1414-19 (discussing Rule 5 of the Rules Governing § 2254 Cases); *infra* §§ 16.1 (answer); 19.2 (state court record).

[63] See, e.g., *Thames v. Dugger, supra,* 848 F.2d at 15; *Bundy v. Wainwright, supra,* 808 F.2d at 1416 (discussing 28 U.S.C. § 2254(d) (1994) (now superseded by 28 U.S.C.A. § 2254(e)(1) (West 1994 & Supp. 1998)) ("unusual" for petition to "contain sufficient state court record materials that a court can correctly find on the face alone (with any exhibits attached), that the § 2254(d) presumption applies and that it bars relief").

limitations, failure to exhaust, procedural default, or excessive delay.[64] Because factual matters controlling the outcome of such exclusively federal defenses usually are not addressed in the state courts, they typically may "not be disposed of on a motion to dismiss."[65]

Even when the court has the state record before it and the record contains factfindings contrary to the petitioner's allegations, those findings are not a sufficient basis for summary dismissal unless the pleadings and attachments establish as to each finding the prerequisites to the presumption of correctness — *i.e.,* that the findings were (1) made in writing or at a transcribed hearing, (2) by a court of competent jurisdiction, (3) in a proceeding to which the petitioner and state were parties, (4) following an evidentiary hearing on the merits of all the determinative factual issues, and (5) qualify as findings of historical fact rather than determinations of purely legal or mixed legal and factual issues.[66] And, even if the record is before the court and contains state court factfindings that satisfy these five requirements and are dispositive of all the controlling factual issues in the case, the presumption of correctness still affords no basis for summary judgment if the record indicates or the petitioner pleads facts which, if true, establish that either (6) the state court proceedings that produced those findings were not "full and fair,"[67] or (7) the state court factfinding is clearly wrong.[68] If, as is likely, the court cannot be certain on the basis of the state court factfindings and record that the findings are reliable, that they were the result of full and fair proceedings, *and* that they are impervious to even extra-record proof that they are clearly wrong, summary dismissal is not permissible.[69] Instead, further fact development proceedings must take place to determine what disposition is appropriate.[70]

---

[64] *See supra* § 5.1b; *infra* Chapters 22-28, 32.

[65] Black v. Brown, 513 F.2d 652, 654 n.6 (7th Cir. 1975). *See infra* § 20.1.

[66] *See Bundy v. Wainwright, supra,* 808 F.2d at 1416; *infra* §§ 20.2, 20.3, 30.3.

[67] Townsend v. Sain, 372 U.S. 293, 312-13 (1963); *Bundy v. Wainwright, supra,* 808 F.2d at 1416, 1418; *infra* § 20.3e.

[68] *See* 28 U.S.C.A. § 2254(e)(1) (presumption of correctness may be rebutted "by clear and convincing evidence"); Sumner v. Mata, 449 U.S. 539, 550 (1981); *infra* §§ 30.3, 31.3. The seven conditions listed in text clearly apply to cases filed before April 24, 1996; whether they apply in precisely this form to cases filed after that date is unclear. *See supra* §§ 3.2, 3.4; *infra* Chapters 20, 30.

[69] *See, e.g., Blackledge, supra,* 431 U.S. at 76-78 & n.16; Machibroda v. United States, 368 U.S. 487, 494-95 (1962); Thames v. Dugger, 848 F.2d 149, 151 (11th Cir. 1988) (without thorough review of state court record, district court could not properly determine whether state court hearing was full and fair); *Bundy v. Wainwright, supra,* 808 F.2d at 1416, 1418; Rose v. Duckworth, 769 F.2d 402, 405 (7th Cir. 1985) (summary dismissal is improper until court reviews entire record and determines that state factfindings are "fairly supported" by "record as a whole").

[70] *See* O'Blasney v. Solem, 774 F.2d 925, 927 (8th Cir. 1985) ("Even though the final decision of a state court is entitled to great deference, it is not to be accepted conclusively by a federal court

d. *Post-dismissal tactical considerations.*

Other than nonexhaustion grounds. If the court dismisses the petition on any ground other than nonexhaustion, the dismissal has a prejudicial — though not quite a *res judicata* or absolutely preclusive — effect on subsequent petitions challenging the legality of the conviction and sentence at issue in the dismissed petition.[71] Accordingly, if there are grounds for appealing the dismissal, that course is strongly preferred to filing a successive petition in the district court[72] or an original petition in a higher court.[73]

Nonexhaustion grounds. In contrast to most other dismissals, dismissal for failure to exhaust state remedies typically is "without prejudice" to the petitioner's ability to refile the petition after state remedies have been exhausted.[74] The "without prejudice" character of dismissal on nonexhaustion grounds gives petitioners a wider range of responses than they have to most other dismissals.

---

in a habeas corpus action without first determining that there is factual and legal support for that decision"); United States v. Fiddler, 688 F.2d 45, 48-49 (8th Cir. 1982); *infra* § 20.1c n.42 (decisions requiring evidentiary hearing to assess whether seven prerequisites set out above for presumption of correctness are present). An evidentiary hearing is not the only alternative to summary dismissal in fact-bound cases. Alternatives range from allowing the petitioner to submit legal arguments in writing on controverted issues, *e.g., Blackledge, supra,* 431 U.S. at 81-83; Franklin v. Murphy, 745 F.2d 1221, 1231 (9th Cir. 1984); Williams v. Kullman, 722 F.2d 1048, 1050 (2d Cir. 1983), to permitting discovery or other fact-development procedures short of a hearing, *see infra* Chapters 18, 19. *See generally supra* § 15.2a. Even if "a full evidentiary hearing is not required, [petitioners are] 'entitled to careful consideration and plenary processing of ... the relevant facts.'" *Blackledge, supra* at 82-83 (quoting Harris v. Nelson, 394 U.S. 286, 298 (1969) and citing David Shapiro, *Federal Habeas Corpus: A Study in Massachusetts,* 87 Harv. L. Rev. 321, 337-38 (1973)).

[71] *See infra* Chapter 28 (successive petition doctrine).

[72] *See infra* Chapters 35-39 (appeals).

[73] *See infra* Chapter 40 (original habeas corpus proceedings).

[74] *See, e.g.,* Ex parte Abernathy, 320 U.S. 219, 220 (1943); Woods v. Kemna, 13 F.3d 1244, 1246 (8th Cir. 1994); Ashker v. Leapley, 5 F.3d 1178, 1180 (8th Cir. 1993); Leacock v. Henman, 996 F.2d 1069, 1072 (10th Cir. 1993) ("If Petitioner has not exhausted his state remedies, the district court must dismiss the § 2254 petition without prejudice so that Petitioner can exhaust his remedies in state court."); Whatley v. Morrison, 947 F.2d 869, 870 (8th Cir. 1991) ("When a district court dismisses a habeas petition for petitioner's failure to exhaust state remedies, ... the dismissal should be without prejudice."); Johnson v. Lewis, 929 F.2d 460, 464 (9th Cir. 1991); Guizar v. Estelle, 843 F.2d 371, 372 (9th Cir. 1988) (*per curiam*); Irving v. Thigpen, 732 F.2d 1215, 1218 n.7 (5th Cir. 1984); Cole v. Hunter, 726 F.2d 434, 437 (8th Cir. 1984); Szeto v. Rushen, 709 F.2d 1340, 1341 (9th Cir. 1983); Powell v. Spalding, 679 F.2d 163, 165 & n.2 (9th Cir. 1982); Dirring v. Massachusetts, 459 F.2d 953, 955 (1st Cir. 1972). *But cf.* Jones v. Hess, 681 F.2d 688, 695-96 (10th Cir. 1982) (deletion of unexhausted claims from petition mixing unexhausted and exhausted claims risks foreclosing future federal consideration of deleted claim); *infra* notes 77-89 and accompanying text & *supra* § 11.1 (withdrawal of unexhausted claims from otherwise exhausted petition risks severe prejudice to later attempts to litigate withdrawn claims).

If the district court dismisses the petition on the ground that the petitioner failed to exhaust state remedies with regard to *every* claim in it, the petitioner has two options. First, the petitioner may undertake to exhaust the state remedies that are available to review the claims in the petition.[75] Alternatively, if there is a basis for an appellate court to conclude that the claims in the petition have been exhausted or that they fall within one of the recognized exceptions to the exhaustion rule,[76] the petitioner may appeal the dismissal. Statute of limitations considerations of the sort discussed *supra* §§ 5.1b and 11.1 may prompt petitioners who otherwise would pursue additional state proceedings to pursue an appeal instead.

Total exhaustion grounds — generally. If the district court dismisses the petition because it mixes some claims that were not exhausted with other claims that were exhausted, the petitioner has three options. First, he may elect to exhaust the assertedly unexhausted claims in the state courts; second, he may appeal dismissal of the petition; or third, he may refile the federal petition with only those claims that the district court found to be exhausted — at the same time, perhaps, as he proceeds to exhaust the deleted claims in the state courts.[77] As is discussed in section 11.1 *supra*, the first option may be perilous for statute of limitations reasons, and the third option *is* perilous unless for some unusual reason the petitioner can be sure that state exhaustion procedures will occur rapidly enough to allow him to amend the deleted claims, once exhausted, back into the federal petition before the district court adjudicates that petition.[78] The third option should not be invoked save in the rare circumstances discussed in section 11.1.

Total exhaustion grounds — capital cases. In a capital case in which an execution date has been set, the availability of a stay of execution largely governs the petitioner's choice among the possible responses[79] to dismissal on total exhaustion grounds. As is discussed in detail in earlier sections, the preferred procedure in this situation is for the federal court to grant a stay of execution, then hold the petition in abeyance while the petitioner expeditiously exhausts state remedies on the unexhausted claims.[80] This procedure both preserves the federal court's jurisdiction against the possibility that the petitioner will be executed prior to exhaustion and advances the policy enunciated in

---

[75] *See supra* Chapters 6, 7 (state postconviction procedures).

[76] *See infra* Chapter 23 (exhaustion standards and exceptions). *See also infra* Chapters 36-39 (appeals).

[77] *But see supra* § 13.3b n.13 (courts of at least one State forbid state proceedings simultaneous with federal proceedings).

[78] *See infra* § 17.2 (amendments).

[79] *See supra* notes 77-78 and accompanying text.

[80] *See supra* §§ 6.3, 11.1, 13.3.

Habeas Rules 2(c) and 9(b) and reiterated by the Supreme Court in *Rose v. Lundy*[81] favoring the simultaneous adjudication of all habeas corpus claims in a single federal action.[82] This approach is especially appropriate (1) because it may avoid statute of limitations problems and (2) given the stringent rules that now apply to discourage petitioners from litigating successive petitions raising claims omitted from earlier petitions for nonexhaustion reasons.[83] The option of withdrawing the federal petition in its entirety and returning to the state courts to exhaust the unexhausted claims also is available to the petitioner if he can secure a state stay of execution and if there are no statute of limitations obstacles to this approach.[84]

When there is a substantial question whether the petition includes unexhausted claims,[85] the district court, upon application by the petitioner for a certificate of probable cause to appeal (or, as the requirement recently has been reformulated, a certificate of appealability)[86] and a stay of execution pending appeal,[87] can protect the policies favoring preservation of federal jurisdiction and discouraging piecemeal adjudication by granting both applications and permitting the petitioner to appeal the nonexhaustion decision.

In the limited circumstance in which (1) the petition is dismissed on total exhaustion grounds in a capital case and (2) neither the state nor the federal courts will grant a stay of execution pending exhaustion proceedings or an appeal, the petitioner has little choice but to refile the federal petition with only those claims that have been found to be exhausted. In so doing, the petitioner should state on the record that he does not intend to waive the withdrawn claims but instead will exhaust them simultaneously in the state courts and thereafter seek to amend them into the federal petition.[88] The petitioner also should make

---

[81] 455 U.S. 509 (1982).

[82] *Id.* at 520. *See supra* §§ 5.3, 11.1, 13.3c.

[83] *See, e.g.,* Jones v. Estelle, 722 F.2d 159, 168 (5th Cir. 1983) (*en banc*), *cert. denied,* 466 U.S. 976 (1984) (given stringent successive petition rules, only way "petitioner who has both exhausted and unexhausted claims ... [can avoid] ... barrier to the federal prosecution of all his claims ... [is to] obtain dismissal of his federal writ, completely exhaust his claims, and, if unsuccessful, return to federal court"). In capital cases involving unstayed execution dates, effectuating the approach laid out in *Jones* requires that a federal stay of execution be granted during the pendency of exhaustion proceedings. *See generally supra* §§ 5.1b (statutes of limitations), 11.1; *infra* Chapter 28 (successive petitions).

[84] *See supra* §§ 5.1b, 6.3, 11.1.

[85] *See supra* § 11.1; *infra* Chapter 23.

[86] *See infra* § 35.4.

[87] If the district court grants a certificate of probable cause to appeal or a certificate of appealability, the court also generally must grant a stay pending appeal. *See* Barefoot v. Estelle, 463 U.S. 880, 893-94 (1983); *infra* § 36.2.

[88] *See infra* § 17.2 (amendments).

clear on the record that he has been compelled to submit his federal claims in this piecemeal fashion in order to assure a stay of execution and thereby preserve his life and the federal courts' jurisdiction pending final adjudication of his constitutional claims.[89]

---

[89] *Cf. infra* § 26.2d n.36 (citing United States v. Jackson, 390 U.S. 570 (1968), and Fay v. Noia, 372 U.S. 391 (1963), as examples of courts' recognition that waivers of constitutional rights are not "voluntary" when made to avoid execution).

Chapter 16

THE STATE'S RESPONSE

§ 16.1. Service and answer.[1]

a. *Service generally.* As is noted in an earlier chapter, the Rules Governing § 2254 Cases do not require the petitioner to serve the petition on the respondent.[2] Rather, Habeas Rules 3(b) (by implication) and 4 (explicitly) provide that, once the clerk files the petition[3] and the district court's initial review establishes that the petition either is or is not so "palpably frivolous" that summary dismissal is warranted,[4] the court must serve on the respondent and the state attorney general by certified mail a copy of the petition, any accompanying documents, and any orders in the case.[5]

b. *Answer generally.* Service of the petition does not by itself oblige the respondent to answer.[6] That duty arises only if the court, following an initial review of the petition, expressly orders respondent to answer it pursuant to Habeas Rules 3(b) and 4.[7] Nonetheless, the Habeas Rules invite, and a number of circuit courts have adopted, a practice of requiring answers unless the petition manifestly cannot be construed or revised to state a tenable cause of action.[8] As a result, states' attorneys in a number of States — particularly in capital cases — have adopted the practice of routinely answering petitions upon service.

---

§ 16.1. [1] *See generally* RONALD P. SOKOL, FEDERAL HABEAS CORPUS §§ 11.3, 12 (2d ed. 1969); LARRY W. YACKLE, POSTCONVICTION REMEDIES §§ 116-18 (1981 & Supp. 1998); David Bagwell, *Procedural Aspects of Prisoner § 1983 and § 2254 Cases in the Fifth and Eleventh Circuits,* 95 F.R.D. 435, 460-61 (1982); Charles Alan Wright, *Procedure for Habeas Corpus,* 77 F.R.D. 227, 241-242 (1978); *Developments in the Law — Federal Habeas Corpus,* 83 HARV. L. REV. 1038, 1178 (1970).

[2] *See supra* § 11.9d. A few federal district courts have adopted local rules requiring the petitioner to serve the petition on respondent. *See supra* § 11.9d n.12.

[3] *See supra* § 15.1.

[4] *See supra* § 15.2c.

[5] *See* Advisory Committee Note to Rules 3 and 4 of the Rules Governing § 2254 Cases. Even when the court summarily dismisses the petition, Habeas Rule 4 requires that the petition plus the dismissal order be served on respondent and the attorney general. *See supra* § 15.2a n.10 and accompanying text. *See also* 28 U.S.C. § 2243 (1994) (pre-Habeas Rules provision also utilizing judicial, not party, service, but requiring it only if petition was not dismissed); 28 U.S.C. § 2072 (1994) (Habeas Rules supersede prior inconsistent statutes); Advisory Committee Note to Rule 4 of the Rules Governing § 2254 Cases. *Cf. supra* note 2 & *supra* § 11.9d (situations in which petitioners are required or advised to serve respondent).

[6] Rule 3(b) of the Rules Governing § 2254 Cases. *Accord* Rule 3(b) of the Rules Governing § 2255 Proceedings.

[7] *See supra* § 15.2c (limited scope of court's pre-answer review).

[8] *See supra* § 15.2a nn.13-15 and accompanying text.

The district court must specify how long the respondent has for filing an answer[9] and must provide the petitioner with a copy of its order requiring and specifying the time for the answer.[10]

In the answer, the state must include the following information along with any other matters requested by the court when it orders an answer:[11]

(1)   A response to the allegations in the petition.[12]

---

[9] Rule 4 of the Rules Governing § 2254 Cases. *See* Advisory Committee Note to *id.* ("Rule 4, which contains no fixed time requirement, gives the court the discretion to take into account various factors such as the respondent's workload and the availability of transcripts before determining a time within which an answer must be made"); Bleitner v. Welborn, 15 F.3d 652, 654 (7th Cir. 1994) (district court has discretion under Habeas Rule 4 "to fix the deadline" for state's answer and under FED. R. CIV. P. 60(b)(2) to "grant an untimely motion to extend a deadline, provided the failure to file a timely motion was due to excusable neglect"); Garcia v. Powers, 973 F.2d 684, 686 (8th Cir. 1992) (district court has discretion to extend state's time for filing responsive pleading); Clutchette v. Rushen, 770 F.2d 1469, 1474-75 (9th Cir. 1985), *cert. denied,* 475 U.S. 1088 (1986) (Habeas Rule 4 gives judge discretion to grant state more time to answer than the 43 days allowed by FED. R. CIV. P. 81(a)(2)). *But see* E.D. CAL. RULE 191(i)(3) (answer to be filed within 30 days of service of petition in capital cases); Bagwell, *supra* note 1, at 461 & n.160 (FED. R. CIV. P. 81(a)(2) applies in habeas corpus cases in 5th and 11th Circuits, requiring answer within "'3 days unless for good cause shown additional time is allowed which ... shall not exceed 40 days'"). The state's failure to comply with the schedule set by the court generally is not considered a basis for granting the petition on default but may result in other sanctions. *See infra* note 18 and accompanying text.

[10] Rules 3, 4, and 5 of the Rules Governing § 2254 Cases govern service on respondents and the proper form and timing of the answer. These rules supersede 28 U.S.C. § 2243 (1994), which previously required the court "forthwith" either to grant the writ of habeas corpus or to order respondent (generally within three days and in no case within more than 20 days) to file "a return certifying the true cause of detention" and, in some cases, showing "cause why the writ should not be granted." *See* Advisory Committee Note to Rules 4 and 5 of the Rules Governing § 2254 Cases. *See also* 28 U.S.C. § 2072 (1994) (Habeas Rules supersede prior inconsistent statutes).

[11] *See* Advisory Committee Note to Rule 4 of the Rules Governing § 2254 Cases (district court may request information from state as alternative to immediate dismissal). *See also* Advisory Committee Note to Rule 5 of the Rules Governing § 2254 Cases (quoting *Developments in the Law, supra* § 16.1 n.1, at 1178) ("The answer plays an obviously important role in a habeas proceeding: '[I]t permits the court and the parties to uncover quickly the disputed issues; it may reveal to the petitioner's attorney grounds for release that the petitioner did not know; and it may demonstrate that the petitioner's claim is wholly without merit.'"); E.D. CAL. RULE 191(i)(1) (in capital cases, state must provide federal court with following documents within 20 days of service of petition: complete transcripts of state trial court proceedings; petitioner's and respondent's briefs on direct appeal to the California Supreme Court; petitioner's and respondent's briefs in any state court habeas corpus proceedings, and all opinions, orders, and transcripts of such proceedings; copies of all pleadings, opinions, and orders in any previous federal habeas corpus proceeding filed by petitioner that arose from the same conviction; and an index).

[12] Rule 5 of the Rules Governing § 2254 Cases. The answer must go beyond "a statement certifying the ... cause of detention, or a series of delaying motions to dismiss." Advisory Committee Note to Rule 5 of the Rules Governing § 2254 Cases (Habeas Rules supersede 28 U.S.C.

(2)   A statement as to "whether the petitioner has exhausted his state rem-
      edies including any postconviction remedies available to him under the
      statutes or procedural rules of the state and including also his right of
      appeal both from the judgment of conviction and from any adverse
      judgment or order in the postconviction proceeding."[13]

(3)   A discussion of "what transcripts ... are available, when they can be
      furnished, and also what proceedings have been recorded and not
      transcribed."[14]

---

§ 2243 (1994), which previously allowed state to limit its answer to statement of cause of
detention). *See also* Wright, *supra* § 16.1 n.1, at 242 (Rule 5 requires answer to have "more
specificity than the statute [section 2243] had required" and is "'intended to ensure ... a responsive
pleading'" (quoting Advisory Committee Note to Rule 5 of the Rules Governing § 2254 Cases)).
Cf. Advisory Committee Note to Rule 4 of the Rules Governing § 2254 Cases (court "may want to
authorize the respondent to make a motion to dismiss" in lieu of an answer which, "based upon
information furnished by respondent, ... may show that petitioner's claims have already been
decided on the merits in a federal court; that petitioner has failed to exhaust state remedies; [or]
that the petitioner is not in custody within the meaning of 28 U.S.C. § 2254"); Advisory Committee
Note to Rule 5 of the Rules Governing § 2254 Cases, quoted *infra* note 13 (nonexhaustion may be
raised by motion in lieu of answer); Bundy v. Wainwright, 808 F.2d 1410, 1415 n.9 (11th Cir.
1987). Although the applicability of FED. R. CIV. P. 11 in habeas corpus proceedings is in doubt,
see supra § 11.7b n.12 and accompanying text, counsel should be aware of amendments to that rule
(effective December 1, 1993) that, *inter alia*, place on civil respondents a duty (1) to make sure that
"denials of factual allegations" are "warranted by the evidence" or are "reasonably based on a lack
of information and belief," (2) to refrain from denying "an allegation [the respondent] knows to be
true," and (3) to withdraw a prior denial when "further investigation or discovery" reveals that "a
denial is no longer warranted." Advisory Committee Note to 1993 amendment to FED. R. CIV. P.
11(b) & 11(c). *See generally infra* note 18; *infra* § 22.1 n.47 (sanctions available against state for
dilatory or abusive conduct).

[13] Rule 5 of the Rules Governing § 2254 Cases. *See* McCartney v. Vitek, 902 F.2d 616, 617
(8th Cir. 1990) (*dicta*) (ordinarily, "habeas petition should not be dismissed for failure to exhaust
state remedies before the state has responded" to petition, because state may waive exhaustion);
Prather v. Norman, 901 F.2d 915, 918 (11th Cir. 1990) (summary dismissal on exhaustion grounds
in advance of state's answer is inappropriate because state's answer may waive exhaustion); *supra*
§ 15.2c n.44. *See also* Advisory Committee Note to Rule 5 of the Rules Governing § 2254 Cases
("exhaustion requirement is often not understood by the unrepresented petitioner" or easily
adjudicated by court, which lacks "attorney general['s] ... access to the record"; "alleged failure to
exhaust state remedies as to any ground in the petition may be raised by a motion by the attorney
general, thus avoiding the necessity of a formal answer as to that ground."); Granberry v. Greer,
481 U.S. 129, 134 (1987) ("When the state answers a habeas corpus petition, it has a duty to advise
the District Court whether the prisoner has, in fact, exhausted all state remedies."); Russell v. Rolfs,
893 F.2d 1033, 1038 (9th Cir. 1990), *cert. denied,* 501 U.S. 1260 (1991) (in answer, state must
choose between inconsistent defenses of nonexhaustion and procedural default and may not assert
both defenses). On the rules governing the state's ability to waive the exhaustion defense, see *infra*
§ 23.2a.

[14] Rule 5 of the Rules Governing § 2254 Cases. *See* Advisory Committee Note to *id.* (notice of
available transcripts "serve[s] to inform the court and petitioner as to what factual allegations can

(4) An attachment containing "such portions of the transcript as the answering party deems relevant," or "[i]f a transcript is neither available nor procurable, a narrative summary of the evidence."[15]

(5) If "the petitioner appealed from the judgment of conviction or from an adverse judgment or order in a postconviction proceeding," an attachment containing "a copy of the petitioner's brief on appeal and of the opinion of the appellate court, if any."[16]

Habeas "Rule 5 does not indicate who[m] the answer is to be served upon, but it necessarily implies that it will be mailed to the petitioner (or to his attorney if he is one). The number of copies of the answer required is left to the court's discretion."[17] "Although the Advisory Committee Note to Rule 5 says that the Rule 'is intended to ensure that a responsive pleading will be filed,'" Professor Wright correctly predicted that the Rules would make it "no more likely than before [their adoption] ... that the court will grant a default judgment and release the prisoner merely because the respondent has not made a timely answer."[18]

---

be checked against the actual transcripts" and should include references to "pretrial transcripts relating, for example, to pretrial motions to suppress; transcripts of the trial or guilty plea proceeding; and transcripts of any postconviction proceedings which may have taken place").

[15] Rule 5 of the Rules Governing § 2254 Cases. *See Bundy v. Wainwright, supra*, 808 F.2d at 1415 ("The obligation to come forward with the state court record is squarely upon the respondent, not upon the petitioner" (citing Advisory Committee Note to Rule 5 of the Rules Governing § 2254 Cases)). "The Court on its own motion or upon request of the petitioner may order that further portions of the existing transcripts be furnished or that certain portions of the non-transcribed proceedings be transcribed and furnished." Rule 5 of the Rules Governing § 2254 Cases. *See Vicks v. Bunnell*, 875 F.2d 258, 259-60 (9th Cir. 1989) (ordering district court to obtain state trial transcripts and to reexamine petitioner's allegation based on full record); *Ruff v. Kincheloe*, 843 F.2d 1240, 1242-43 & n.5 (9th Cir. 1988) (in order to determine if conceded error in instruction on burden of proof was harmless, district court must conduct complete and independent review of entire trial transcript; because neither party had supplied court with complete trial transcript, court had duty to obtain record *sua sponte*); *supra* §§ 15.2a n.8, 15.2c n.59; *infra* §§ 19.2, 20.3b. *See also Russell v. Jones*, 886 F.2d 149, 152-53 (8th Cir. 1989) (state, not federal courts, must pay cost of furnishing state transcripts for indigent habeas corpus petitioner). *But see Hamilton v. Vasquez*, 882 F.2d 1469, 1471 (9th Cir. 1989) ("petitioner who raises only questions of fact has the burden of providing the district court with the relevant portions of the state court record, or of showing his inability to do so"; "district court is under no obligation to obtain and review the state court record when disposing of purely factual questions").

[16] Rule 5 of the Rules Governing § 2254 Cases. *See also* Advisory Committee Note to *id.* (respondent also may file copy of respondent's brief).

[17] Advisory Committee Note to Rule 5 of the Rules Governing § 2254 Cases.

[18] Wright, *supra*, § 16.1 n.1, at 242 (quoting Advisory Committee Note to Rule 5 of the Rules Governing § 2254 Cases and citing prior cases). *See, e.g., Bleitner v. Welborn*, 15 F.3d 652, 653-54 (7th Cir. 1994) (district court did not abuse discretion in declining to impose default judgment when state missed deadline for filing answer to habeas corpus petition; appropriate response in such situations may be to deem procedural defenses waived and "proceed directly to the merits of

c. *Motions to dismiss or for summary judgment.* If the court orders the state to file an answer, a "motion to dismiss" typically is not by itself sufficient to respond to the court's order.[19] Nonetheless, the court will entertain motions to dismiss or for summary judgment which *accompany* the answer as long as they conform to the provisions in the Federal Rules of Civil Procedure that govern the notice and timing of such motions.[20]

---

the petition"); Gordon v. Duran, 895 F.2d 610, 612 (9th Cir. 1990) (default judgment was inappropriate because magistrate could decide case in absence of state's response); Stines v. Martin, 849 F.2d 1323, 1324-25 (10th Cir. 1988) (default judgment was inappropriate in circumstances of case; reserving question whether district court has power to grant default judgment based upon state's failure to file timely response); Aziz v. Leferve, 830 F.2d 184, 187 (11th Cir. 1987) (default judgment inappropriate; court should proceed as if state had responded); Clutchette v. Rushen, 770 F.2d 1469, 1474-75 (9th Cir. 1985), *cert. denied*, 475 U.S. 1088 (1986); Goodman v. Keohane, 663 F.2d 1044, 1047 n.4 (11th Cir. 1981); Broussard v. Lippman, 643 F.2d 1131, 1134 (5th Cir.), *cert. denied*, 452 U.S. 920 (1981). *See infra* § 16.2a n.11 (ethical obligations constraining state's bases for opposing relief); *infra* § 22.1 n.47 (courts' use of withdrawal of state's habeas corpus defenses as sanction short of outright dismissal for dilatory or other abusive conduct by states). *See also* Degarmo v. Collins, 984 F.2d 142, 143 (5th Cir. 1993) (*per curiam*) (other sanctions considered when dismissal or denial of defenses is not available).

[19] *See supra* § 16.1b n.12. *See also* Browder v. Director, 434 U.S. 257, 269 n.14 (1978) ("response to a habeas corpus petition is not like a motion to dismiss"); *infra* note 20 (procedural requirements for motions to dismiss and for summary judgment). *Cf.* White v. Lewis, 874 F.2d 599, 602-03 (9th Cir. 1989) (motion to dismiss is responsive pleading authorized under Rule 4 of the Rules Governing § 2254 Cases); *infra* § 16.2e (similar).

[20] *See, e.g.,* Teague v. Scott, 60 F.3d 1167, 1171-72 (5th Cir. 1995) (district court erred in granting summary judgment to state on ineffective assistance claim because, "[v]iewing the evidence in the light most favorable to the nonmoving party, as we must do in reviewing a summary judgment," petitioner's factual allegations were sufficient to permit reasonable factfinder to conclude that counsel's performance was deficient and that petitioner was prejudiced); Randle v. Scott, 43 F.3d 221, 226 (5th Cir.), *cert. denied*, 515 U.S. 1108 (1995) (rejecting petitioner's contention "that a summary judgment motion is inappropriate in a habeas corpus proceeding"); McKenzie v. Risley, 915 F.2d 1396, 1398 (9th Cir. 1990); Bassette v. Thompson, 915 F.2d 932, 934-35 (4th Cir. 1990) (affirming district court's grant of state's summary judgment motion); Howard v. Lewis, 905 F.2d 1318, 1323 (9th Cir. 1990) (district court permitted to grant state's motion to dismiss pursuant to local court rule treating failure to respond to motion to dismiss as assent to dismissal, unless *pro se* habeas corpus petitioner can prove that prison officials obstructed efforts to respond to motion to dismiss); Buxton v. Lynaugh, 879 F.2d 140, 141 (5th Cir. 1989), *cert. denied*, 497 U.S. 1032 (1990); Valles v. Lynaugh, 835 F.2d 126, 127 (5th Cir. 1988) (citing FED. R. CIV. P. 56(c)); King v. Brewer, 577 F.2d 435, 439 (8th Cir. 1978). *Cf.* Myers v. Collins, 8 F.3d 249, 252-53 (5th Cir. 1993) (district court erred in granting state's motion for summary judgment because case presented "material question of fact"); Cain v. Smith, 686 F.2d 374, 380 n.10 (6th Cir. 1982) (state criticized for filing summary judgment motion as to claim supported by considerable evidence); *supra* § 15.2a nn.20-21 and accompanying text.

Rule 56(c) of the Federal Rules of Civil Procedure is generally held to apply in habeas corpus proceedings pursuant to Rule 11 of the Rules Governing § 2254 Cases, *see* Allen v. Newsome, 795 F.2d 934, 938 n.11 (11th Cir. 1986), and requires that petitioners be given notice and an opportunity to respond to summary judgment and similar motions. *See, e.g.* Balogun v. INS, 9 F.3d

d. *Service and answer — capital cases.* The Habeas Rules give the court the responsibility to serve the respondent, to call for an answer, and to specify the time in which the answer must be filed.[21] In capital cases in which the petitioner faces imminent execution, however, counsel for the petitioner must pay close

---

347, 352 (5th Cir. 1993) (district court erred in dismissing petition on basis of exhibits attached to respondents' answer without first giving petitioner "notice that he was considering recommending summary judgment in favor of respondents ... [and] time to reply to respondents' memorandum"); McBride v. Sharpe, 981 F.2d 1234, 1235-36 (11th Cir.) (*per curiam*), *vac'd and reh'g en banc granted*, 999 F.2d 502 (11th Cir. 1993), *rev'd*, 25 F.3d 962 (11th Cir.) (*en banc*), *cert. denied*, 513 U.S. 990 (1994) ("When a district court considers matters outside of the pleadings in rendering judgment, the action is in the nature of an order granting summary judgment, ... and the court must comply with the summary judgment notice requirements of Federal Rule of Civil Procedure 56(c)," including 10-day notice rule); *Allen v. Newsome, supra* at 937-38 & n.11 (reliance on materials dehors pleadings transforms summary dismissal process into summary judgment procedure subject to FED. R. CIV. P. 56(c), which requires that party opposing motion have 10 days notice and opportunity to respond); Manning v. Warden, 786 F.2d 710, 711 (5th Cir. 1986) (procedure for summary dismissal on successive petition grounds); Urdy v. McCotter, 773 F.2d 652, 656 (5th Cir. 1985) (similar); Robinson v. Fairman, 704 F.2d 368, 371 (7th Cir. 1983) (similar); Hill v. Linahan, 697 F.2d 1032, 1034-35 (11th Cir. 1983) (requiring notice of motion 10 days before motion is heard and opportunity to present argument and evidence against summary judgment on successive petition grounds); McDonnell v. Estelle, 666 F.2d 246 (5th Cir. 1982) (procedure for summary dismissal on successive petition grounds). *See also* Bundy v. Wainwright, 808 F.2d 1410, 1416-17 & nn.10, 11 (11th Cir. 1987) (*dicta*) (appearing to criticize district court for summarily dismissing petition, without notice to petitioner, based on matters "outside the petition" including "published opinions of the Supreme Court of Florida in [petitioner's] litigation [that were] not attached to the petition"). *Cf.* McBride v. Sharpe, 25 F.3d 962, 967-70 (11th Cir.) (*en banc*), *cert. denied*, 513 U.S. 990 (1994) (10-day notice rule for motions for summary judgment pursuant to FED. R. CIV. P. 56(c) does not apply when court dismisses petition on pleadings pursuant to Habeas Rule 8(a) (*see supra* § 15.2a) without consideration of material outside record); Maynard v. Dixon, 943 F.2d 407, 412-13 (4th Cir. 1991), *cert. denied*, 502 U.S. 1110 (1992) (district court did not err in granting state's motion for summary judgment without first obtaining answer; petitioner had "ample notice" of summary judgment motion and "failed to respond ... within the allowed time, or for several months thereafter"); Dillard v. Blackburn, 780 F.2d 509, 515-16 (5th Cir. 1986) (lack of Civil Rule 56(c) notice deemed harmless). As final denials of relief, *grants* of summary judgment on all claims are appealable final orders. Generally speaking, however, *denials* and *partial grants* of summary judgment are neither appealable final orders nor nonfinal orders that are appealable under the "collateral order" rule. *See* Johnson v. Jones, 515 U.S. 304, 313-18 (1995) (section 1983 action); Swint v. Chambers County Comm'n, 514 U.S. 35, 41-42 (1995) (same). The "collateral order" rule is discussed *supra* §§ 12.1, 12.5, 13.6b, 14.2 nn.15-18 and accompanying text; *infra* §§ 17.3 nn.14-15 and accompanying text, 35.1. Motions to dismiss under FED. R. CIV. P. 12(b)(6) generally are not appropriate in habeas corpus. *See, e.g.,* O'Bremski v. Maass, 915 F.2d 418, 420 (9th Cir. 1990), *cert. denied*, 498 U.S. 1096 (1991) (affirming district court's grant of state's motion to dismiss but stating that motion was improperly filed under FED. R. CIV. P. 12(b)(6) and should have been filed under Rule 4 of the Rules Governing § 2254 Cases); White v. Lewis, 874 F.2d 599, 602-03 (9th Cir. 1989) (similar).

[21] *See supra* §§ 16.1a, 16.1b.

attention to the timing of the court's actions given the need to secure a timely stay. In this situation, counsel for the petitioner should serve respondent (and so notify the court) and may need to take measures to expedite the issuance of court orders calling for an answer to the stay application or the petition.[22]

The district court may act on the stay application *ex parte* without hearing from the state on either the stay application or the petition itself.[23] If, however, the district court refuses to rule on the stay application before hearing from the state, counsel may ask the court to require an expedited answer. Particularly when state officials announce an execution date a short time before the scheduled date, and then oppose the granting of a stay, it is reasonable for the court to require the state to act on an abbreviated schedule.

If the district court refuses to act immediately on the stay and grants the state an unreasonably long period of time for filing an answer, the petitioner should file a motion asking the court to shorten the time for the answer. The imminence of the date set for the execution and the need for time to file papers in the court of appeals and the Supreme Court justify expeditious proceedings in these circumstances. If the district court, in the face of an imminent execution date, refuses either to act on the stay application or to call for a prompt answer, the petitioner should consider invoking the procedures discussed in section 13.6c *supra* for securing prompt action by the district court or a prompt appeal challenging the district court's failure to act.

§ 16.2. Tactical considerations following answer.

a. *Introduction.* As in any civil action, the respondent in a federal habeas corpus case may oppose a claim in the petition on any of the following three grounds: (1) the facts alleged by the petitioner in support of a claim are untrue; (2) regardless of the truth of the petitioner's factual allegations, the claim is insupportable as a matter of law or is not legally cognizable in federal proceedings, including because the petitioner is not "in custody";[1] or (3) regardless of the factual or legal viability of the petitioner's claim, some defense bars relief.[2] Generally, the state will assert one or more of these responses to

---

[22] *See supra* § 16.1b. *See also supra* § 13.6c and *infra* §§ 36.2, 38.2, 39.3c (actions counsel may have to take to secure timely stay of execution from district court or court of appeals).

[23] *See supra* § 13.1 nn.50-51 and accompanying text.

§ 16.2. [1] *See supra* Chapters 8 (custody), 9 (cognizable claims); *infra* Chapter 33 (relief). *See generally supra* Chapter 2.

[2] Defenses include: lack of personal jurisdiction or improper venue, *see supra* § 10.2; wrong party respondent, *see supra* § 10.1; improper joinder of claims or parties, *see supra* § 11.4; petition improper as to form, *see supra* §§ 11.5-11.7, 15.1; nonexhaustion, *see supra* §§ 5.3, 11.1 & *infra* Chapter 23; violation of a statute of limitations or prejudicial delay in filing, *see supra* § 5.1

each claim in its answer or in a motion to dismiss or for summary judgment.[3]

Petitioners often do not seek summary judgment (or only seek partial summary judgment[4]) because the claims in a habeas corpus petition frequently cannot be proven without evidentiary proceedings of some kind.[5] For this same reason, petitioners often focus their attention (or much of it) on securing leave to utilize fact development procedures and accordingly oppose the state's efforts to have the entire case disposed of on motion at the outset of the case. To forestall final resolution of the case at this stage, petitioners may file (in addition to a response to any dispositive motions by the state) either a traverse to the answer,[6] or motions for fact development procedures,[7] or both.

There are four factors that generally affect the petitioner's response to, and the court's consideration of, a state's motion for dismissal or summary judgment. First, the petitioner has the right to notice and a 10-day opportunity to respond to a summary judgment motion.[8] Second, in adjudicating motions to dismiss or for summary judgment, the court must presume the truth of any of the petitioner's factual allegations that are not affirmatively disproved by records actually before the court.[9] Third, if there is any doubt whether dismissal or summary judgment is appropriate, the court should explore alternatives to dismissal — including, if it prefers, ones short of a full-blown evidentiary hearing such as production of the state court record, expansion of the existing record with new materials, or directing the state to address a certain issue in its answer or to employ other available means to clarify the record or prior proceedings in the case.[10] Finally,

---

(statutes of limitations) & *infra* Chapter 24 (prejudicial delay defense); waiver or procedural default, *see infra* Chapter 26; the bar to 4th Amendment exclusionary rule claims established in Stone v. Powell, 428 U.S. 465 (1976), *see supra* § 9.2 & *infra* Chapter 27; successive petitions, *see infra* Chapter 28; the presumption of correctness of state factfindings, *see infra* Chapter 20 & *infra* § 30.3, and (on one very controversial reading of recent legislation) the presumption of correctness of state court determinations of law or mixed questions, *see infra* § 30.2; and harmless error, *see infra* Chapter 32. *See generally infra* Chapter 22 (introduction to defenses).

[3] *See* Advisory Committee Note to Rule 5 of the Rules Governing § 2254 Cases; *supra* § 16.1.

[4] *But cf. infra* § 17.3 (petitioner-initiated proceedings for summary judgment on some or all claims).

[5] *See* Advisory Committee Note to Rule 8 of the Rules Governing § 2254 Cases; *infra* Chapter 31 (burdens of proof). *See also* Machibroda v. United States, 368 U.S. 487, 495 (1962) ("by the whole of the testimony must it be determined whether the petitioner has carried his burden of proof and shown his right to discharge"); *infra* Chapters 20, 30.

[6] *See infra* § 17.1.

[7] *See supra* §§ 11.7c, 11.7d; *infra* Chapters 19, 20.

[8] *See* authority cited *supra* § 16.1c n.20.

[9] *See* authority cited *supra* § 15.2c n.57; *infra* § 20.1b n.28.

[10] *See* authority cited *supra* § 15.2a nn.13-28 and accompanying text. *See also supra* § 16.1b (answer); *infra* §§ 19.2 (production of record), 19.5 (expansion of record).

states' attorneys, like counsel for other parties to federal civil actions, are ethically barred from moving for summary judgment when a factual dispute clearly is present.[11] Specific replies to the three types of responses available to the state are discussed below.

b. *Factual disputes.* If the state's response explicitly or implicitly disputes the petitioner's factual allegations, creating a "genuine issue as to [a] material fact," then summary judgment or dismissal is inappropriate.[12] In that event, the petitioner may respond to the state's pleadings by asking the court to authorize procedures to resolve the factual dispute, such as discovery, employment of experts or investigators, expansion of the record, an evidentiary hearing, or reference to a magistrate.[13] Accompanying the motions for leave to conduct factfinding procedures should be either a traverse (if the state has made its arguments in its answer) or a response (if the state has made its arguments in a motion to dismiss or for summary judgment) as well as a memorandum in support of the motions for factfinding procedures.[14] Even if only some of the claims raised in the petition or only some of the defenses raised by the state require factual development, the court may well conclude that the necessary factfinding procedures should go forward before the court rules on the other, strictly legal, issues. Deferring legal argument pending completion of factfinding procedures allows the legal issues thereafter to be addressed efficiently in a single round of briefing.[15]

c. *Legal disputes.* If the state disputes the legal merits of the claims,[16] the petitioner first should examine respondent's arguments for implicit factual assumptions that are untrue or in dispute and that require the factfinding pro-

---

[11] *See, e.g.,* Cain v. Smith, 686 F.2d 374, 380 n.10 (6th Cir. 1982). *See also supra* §§ 11.7b n.11-12, 16.1b n.18; *infra* §§ 22.1 n.47, 28.3c n.51.

[12] FED. R. CIV. P. 56(c). *See* Valles v. Lynaugh, 835 F.2d 126, 127 (5th Cir. 1988); *supra* §§ 15.2c nn.57-70 and accompanying text, 16.1c n.20; *infra* § 20.1b nn.13, 27.

[13] *See infra* Chapters 18-20.

[14] These papers should (1) identify factual disputes between the petitioner and the state; (2) discuss the strict summary dismissal standard, which forbids dismissal of factual claims that are not "patently frivolous," Blackledge v. Allison, 431 U.S. 63, 76 (1977) (quoting Pennsylvania ex rel. Herman v. Claudy, 350 U.S. 116, 119 (1956)); *see supra* § 15.2c; and (3) explain the need for the factfinding procedures requested by the petitioner, *see supra* §§ 11.7c, 11.7d; *infra* Chapters 18-20.

[15] *See supra* § 11.7d; *infra* Chapter 29 (briefing).

[16] *See supra* Chapters 8, 9 (petitioner must be in custody in violation of federal law and be seeking specified kinds of relief). *See generally supra* §§ 2.3-2.5.

cedures discussed in the preceding subsection.[17] If careful scrutiny reveals no factual disputes, the petitioner should ask the court to set a briefing schedule.[18]

d. *Defenses.* If the state asserts a procedural defense to relief on a claim or to the petition as a whole, the petitioner must scrutinize the state's assertions with care to identify factual disputes they present. Not infrequently, the defenses themselves and recognized responses to the defenses raise unresolved factual questions that may or may not be obvious on the face of the answer.[19] Generally, the court will find it efficient to allow the factfinding procedures to proceed simultaneously with respect to the petitioner's claims and the state's defenses.[20]

If the entire petition can be resolved on purely legal grounds — either because none of the defenses and no other issue in the case raises factual questions or because the state has raised at least one nonfactual defense that, if sustained, would result in dismissal of the entire petition[21] — then the petitioner generally should file a traverse or response comprehensively replying to the state's factually undisputed defenses.[22] If, on the other hand, the state's defenses, even if sustained, would not require dismissal of all of petitioner's claims, efficiency generally dictates that the court defer ruling on the legal issues presented by the defenses until completion of factfinding procedures on the factually disputed substantive claims.

e. *Motions to dismiss.* If the state requests that the court dismiss the petition or any of its claims without further proceedings, the petitioner immediately should ask the court to defer ruling pending receipt from the petitioner of a traverse, response, motion for factfinding procedures or (in rare circumstances) a counter-motion for summary judgment.

---

[17] *See infra* § 20.3.

[18] *See infra* Chapter 29 (briefing).

[19] *See infra* §§ 20.1c, 20.3. *See also supra* § 16.2b (response to factual disputes presented by answer). *See generally supra* § 5.1b & *infra* Chapters 22-28, 32 (defenses).

[20] *See, e.g.,* Smith v. Wainwright, 741 F.2d 1248, 1256 (11th Cir. 1984), *cert. denied,* 470 U.S. 1087 (1985) (simultaneous hearing on petitioner's ineffective assistance claim and on state's defense that state factfindings deserve presumption of correctness). *But cf. infra* § 17.3 (discussing petitioner-initiated motions for partial summary judgment on less than all claims in petition).

[21] *See supra* § 11.1 & *infra* § 23.1 (nonexhaustion); *supra* §§ 10.1 & 10.2 (improper party respondent, no personal jurisdiction or venue); *supra* Chapter 8 (petitioner not in custody); *supra* § 5.1b & *infra* Chapter 24 (violation of statute of limitations or prejudicial delay).

[22] *See supra* § 17.1 (traverse); *infra* Chapters 22-28, 32 (defenses).

Chapter 17

TRAVERSE, AMENDMENT, AND PETITIONER-INITIATED SUMMARY PROCEEDINGS

§ 17.1. Traverse.[1]

Before Congress enacted the Rules Governing § 2254 Cases in 1978, the controlling procedural statute provided that "the allegations of a return [*i.e.,* the answer] ..., if not traversed, shall be accepted as true except to the extent that the judge finds from the evidence that they are not true."[2] Accordingly, if respondent's answer alleged some fact or legal principle fatal to the petition or to some claim in the petition (for example, that the claims were not exhausted or that an allegedly coerced confession was in fact voluntary), the court could dismiss the petition or claim if the prisoner failed to file a "traverse" alleging a contrary fact or principle. The traverse was designed, albeit in a repetitive and hypertechnical manner, to provide the district court with a statement of the controverted issues.[3]

The Habeas Rules omit any reference to a traverse.[4] Explaining the omission, the Advisory Committee Note to Habeas Rule 5 states that a traverse no longer is required except when the respondent alleges in the answer that the petitioner has improperly filed a successive petition challenging the same conviction and sentence as were unsuccessfully challenged in an earlier habeas corpus petition.[5] Although the Habeas Rules dispense with the *requirement* of a traverse (except in successive petition situations), they do not forbid such a pleading, and the Advisory Committee Notes endorse a traverse or amendment[6] "where it will serve a truly useful purpose" or "is called for by the contents of the answer" filed

---

§ 17.1. [1] *See generally* Ronald P. Sokol, Federal Habeas Corpus 109-10 (2d ed. 1969); Charles Alan Wright, *Procedure for Habeas Corpus,* 77 F.R.D. 237, 242 (1978).

[2] 28 U.S.C. § 2248 (1994). *See* Advisory Committee Note to Rule 5 of the Rules Governing § 2254 Cases; Wright v. Dickson, 336 F.2d 878, 881 (9th Cir. 1964).

[3] The traverse requirement and its exception — when "'the judge finds from the evidence that ... [the allegations of the answer] are not true'" — occasioned "difficulty," Advisory Committee Note to Rule 5 of the Rules Governing § 2254 Cases (quoting 28 U.S.C. § 2248), and led some courts to ignore the requirement when disputed issues of fact were involved. *See, e.g.,* Stewart v. Overholser, 186 F.2d 339, 342 n.5 (D.C. Cir. 1950).

[4] *See* 28 U.S.C. § 2072 (1994) (Habeas Rules supersede contrary prior statutes).

[5] Advisory Committee Notes to Rule 5 of the Rules Governing § 2254 Cases (traverse not required, in interest of "streamlined and manageable" procedures (citing Advisory Committee Note to Rule 9 of *id.*)). *See supra* § 16.2a n.6 & *infra* § 28.3c (traverse of pre-AEDPA successive petition defense and possible use of traverse to respond to state's assertion of other defenses). *But cf.* Howard v. Lewis, 905 F.2d 1318, 1323 (9th Cir. 1990) (discussing practice under local district court rule of treating even *pro se* petitioner's failure to respond to state's motion to dismiss habeas corpus petition as assenting to dismissal, thus in effect re-adopting traverse requirement).

[6] *See infra* § 17.2 (amendments).

by respondent.[7] If the petitioner concludes that respondent's answer is misleading or otherwise necessitates reply, she may style the reply as a "Traverse to the Answer."

If the state's answer simply denies the petition's claims or the facts it alleges and is not accompanied by a brief, motion to dismiss, summary judgment motion, or the like, a traverse probably is not necessary.[8] In this situation, the more useful course is to file a motion or motions seeking further, post-pleading proceedings — including, when applicable, provision of the record of prior proceedings, funds to employ essential experts, investigators, and the like, discovery, expansion of the record, an evidentiary hearing, reference to a magistrate, briefing, or other fact or law development procedures.[9] In some cases, however, the state's answer may raise what on their face appear to be legally sufficient affirmative defenses to the petition or to individual claims or it may be accompanied by a brief, or a motion to dismiss or for summary judgment that, under the circumstances, seems likely to induce the court to dismiss the petition or claim without further proceedings.[10] In these circumstances, petitioner may find it necessary to file a prompt "Reply" or "Traverse to the Answer" in order to explain why the state's defenses are not meritorious.[11] If the

---

[7] Advisory Committee Note to Rule 5 of the Rules Governing § 2254 Cases. *See* E.D. CAL. RULE 191(i)(4) ("Within thirty (30) days after respondent has filed his answer, petitioner may file a traverse."); McBride v. Sharpe, 25 F.3d 962, 970 n.9 (11th Cir.), *cert. denied*, 513 U.S. 990 (1994) ("Had he wished to do so, McBride could have filed a traverse to the answer." (citing Advisory Committee Note to Rule 5 of the Rules Governing § 2254 Cases)); Thompson v. Missouri Bd. of Parole, 929 F.2d 396, 399 n.3 (8th Cir. 1991) (petitioner properly preserved claims by raising them for first time in "Traverse"). *Cf.* Cacoperdo v. Demosthenes, 37 F.3d 504, 507 (9th Cir. 1994), *cert. denied*, 514 U.S. 1026 (1995) (because "[a] Traverse is not the proper pleading to raise additional grounds for relief," district court properly excluded claims which petitioner raised for first time in traverse and which he declined to amend into petition despite district court's suggestion that he do so).

[8] *See* Advisory Committee Note to Rule 5 of the Rules Governing § 2254 Cases (traverse in this situation would be "mere pro forma refutation of the return, serving little if any expository function").

[9] *See supra* § 11.7d; *infra* Chapters 18-21, 29.

[10] *See supra* § 16.2a n.2 and referenced sections (cataloguing defenses); *infra* Chapter 22 (introduction to defenses).

[11] *See, e.g.*, Lowery v. Young, 887 F.2d 1309, 1311 (7th Cir. 1989) (traverse filed addressing state's argument that petitioner was not "in custody" for habeas corpus purposes; amendment to traverse filed asserting new claim). *See supra* § 16.2e (request that court defer ruling pending reply). *See also Thompson v. Missouri Bd. of Parole, supra*, 929 F.2d at 399 n.3 (discussed *supra* note 7); Jones v. United States Bur. of Prisons, 903 F.2d 1178, 1181 n.10 (8th Cir. 1990) (suggesting that traverse was appropriate method of alleging prejudice caused by respondent's allegedly improper delay in providing parole hearing). *But see* United States ex rel. Crist v. Dolan, 1997 WL 94736, at *1 (N.D. Ill. Feb. 28, 1997) (rejecting petitioner's "Reply to the Respondent's

state raises its defenses in a motion to dismiss or in a motion for summary judgment, the petitioner should file a written response to the motion and inform the court in advance that such a response will be filed. Rule 56(c) of the Federal Rules of Civil Procedure requires that the petitioner be given at least 10 days notice before the court hears the state's summary judgment motion and that the petitioner be given an opportunity to respond to the motion.[12]

§ 17.2. Amendment.[1]

The availability of the option of amending a petition depends in part on the applicability to the case of certain provisions of the Antiterrorism and Effective Death Penalty Act of 1996 (AEDPA)[2] and in part on the stage of the case at which the petitioner seeks to amend. The following discussion begins by examining the rules that apply to all cases other than those governed by AEDPA's provisions for capital cases in "opt-in" States.[3] Thereafter, the discussion addresses the special rules that apply to AEDPA "opt-in" cases.

Section 2242 of the Judicial Code provides that habeas corpus applications "may be amended or supplemented as provided in the rules of procedure applicable to civil actions."[4] Likewise, Rule 11 of the Rules Governing § 2254 Cases provides that "[t]he Federal Rules of Civil Procedure, to the extent that they are not inconsistent with these rules, may be applied, when appropriate, to the petitions filed under these rules." The Advisory Committee Note to Habeas Rule 5 points out, in turn, that "under [Habeas] rule 11 the court is given the discretion to incorporate Federal Rules of Civil Procedure when appropriate, so

---

Answer" in part because "'Section 2254 Rules' ... make no provision for any pleading beyond the respondent's Answer").

[12] *See supra* § 16.1c n.20. *See generally supra* § 15.2a, 16.2a, 16.2b; *infra* § 17.3.

§ 17.2. [1] *See generally* RONALD P. SOKOL, FEDERAL HABEAS CORPUS 105-07 (2d ed. 1969); Charles Alan Wright, *Procedure for Habeas Corpus*, 77 F.R.D. 227, 240 (1978); *Developments in the Law — Federal Habeas Corpus*, 83 HARV. L. REV. 1038, 1078-79 (1970).

[2] Pub. L. 104-132, 110 Stat. 1214 (1996).

[3] *See* Calderon v. Ashmus, 118 S. Ct. 1694, 1700 (1998) (Breyer, J., concurring) (**citing FHCPP**) (noting that AEPDA's new restrictions on amendment of petitions apply only to capital cases in "opt-in" States and that preexisting liberal standard for amendment continues to apply in all other cases). For an overview of the ways in which AEDPA changes standards and procedures in federal habeas corpus proceedings, see *supra* § 3.2. For an explanation of the rules that apply under AEDPA in "opt-in" and "nonopt-in" situations, and the cases to which those rules apply, see *supra* § 3.2, 3.3, 3.4. For discussion of the applicability of AEDPA when a petition is filed prior to the effective date of the statute but amended after the statute became effective, see *supra* § 3.4a n.16 and accompanying text.

[4] 28 U.S.C. § 2242 (1994).

civil rule 15(a) may be used to allow the petitioner to amend his petition ...."[5] Taken together, these provisions allow "amendment of the petition ... under the liberal standards of Civil Rule 15."[6]

Civil Rule 15(a) gives habeas corpus petitioners, like other civil complainants, the right to amend the petition once without leave of the court "at any time before [the state files] a responsive pleading."[7] After the petitioner files one pre-answer amendment or the respondent submits an answer or other responsive pleading, Civil Rule 15 permits amendment "by leave of court or by written consent of the adverse party."[8] "[L]eave [to amend] shall be freely given when justice so requires."[9]

---

[5] Advisory Committee Note to Rule 5 of the Rules Governing § 2254 Cases (discussing Rule 11 of *id.* and FED. R. CIV. P. 15(a)).

[6] Wright, *supra* note 1, at 240 (citing, *inter alia,* Holiday v. Johnston, 313 U.S. 342, 350 (1941); Jarvis v. Nelson, 440 F.2d 13 (9th Cir. 1971)). *See* Withrow v. Williams, 507 U.S. 680, 696 n.7 (1993) (**citing FHCPP** for proposition that "Rule 15 applies in habeas actions"); Gillette v. Tansy, 17 F.3d 308, 312 (10th Cir. 1994).

[7] *See, e.g.,* Willis v. Collins, 989 F.2d 187, 189 (5th Cir. 1993) (petitioner's written objection to state's motion to dismiss deemed timely amendment of petition under FED. R. CIV. P. 15(a) because "party may amend a pleading at any time before a responsive pleading is served" and "the government's motion [to dismiss for lack of jurisdiction] was not a responsive pleading").

[8] FED. R. CIV. P. 15(a). *Cf.* Bird v. Collins, 924 F.2d 67, 68 (5th Cir.) (*per curiam*), *cert. denied,* 501 U.S. 1213 (1991) (without "say[ing]" that a district judge lacks the authority to raise claims *sua sponte,* or that it is never prudent to do so," court of appeals vacates portion of district court opinion rejecting unexhausted claim that district court had amended into petition *sua sponte;* appellate court feared that, if not vacated, federal ruling might preclude petitioner from seeking state remedy). Civil Rule 15(b) also allows amendment by the express or implied consent of the parties following one party's assertion and the other party's acknowledgment of or failure to object to a claim or defense not raised in the asserting party's pleadings. FED. R. CIV. P. 15(b) ("When issues not raised by the pleadings are tried by express or implied consent of the parties, they shall be treated in all respects as if they had been raised in the pleadings. Such amendment of the pleadings as may be necessary to cause them to conform to the evidence and to raise these issues may be made upon motion of any party at any time, even after judgment; but failure so to amend does not affect the result of the trial of these issues."). In *Withrow v. Williams, supra,* the Court seemed to accept that Rule 15(b) applies in habeas corpus proceedings, but found the rule inapplicable on the facts before it because "[t]he record ... reveals neither thought, word, nor deed of [respondent] that could be taken as any sort of consent to the determination of a ... claim [not raised in the petition], and [respondent] was manifestly prejudiced by the District Court's failure to afford her an opportunity to present evidence bearing on the claim's resolution." 507 U.S. at 696 & n.7 (**citing FHCPP**). *See* Titcomb v. Virginia, 869 F.2d 780, 782-83 (4th Cir.), *cert. denied,* 493 U.S. 843 (1989) (Civil Rule 15(b) applies in habeas corpus proceedings). *See also* Miller v. Laird, 464 F.2d 533, 534 (9th Cir. 1972) (applying FED. R. CIV. P. 15(c)'s liberal "relation back" doctrine to habeas corpus amendment).

[9] FED. R. CIV. P. 15(a). *See, e.g.,* Sanders v. United States, 373 U.S. 1, 19 (1963) (although dismissal was proper, "better course might have been to direct petitioner to amend" (citing authority)); Holiday v. Johnston, 313 U.S. 342, 350 (1941); *Gillette v. Tansy, supra,* 17 F.3d at 312-13 (district court abused its discretion in denying petitioner leave to amend petition for second

Two situations recur in which petitioners seek and the courts usually grant leave to amend. The first situation, discussed in Chapter 15, arises when either the district court (acting through the clerk[10] or the judge) or respondent (for instance, in its answer or in a dismissal or summary judgment motion) suggests that the petition is defective in form[11] or that it fails to state a cause of action or to plead facts sufficient to justify relief.[12] The Advisory Committee Notes to the Habeas Rules invite amendments in these situations,[13] and the federal courts long have permitted such amendments that cure formal, procedural, or substantive defects in the petition and state tenable claims for relief.[14]

---

time, given that amendment would not have caused "undue delay" and "there is no evidence of bad faith by petitioner or prejudice to respondents"); Riley v. Taylor, 62 F.3d 86, 90, 92 (3d Cir. 1995) (district court's denial of leave to amend habeas corpus petition violated applicable FED. R. CIV. P. 15(a) standard of "freely giv[ing]" leave to amend); authority cited *infra* notes 14, 23-25. On the scope of appellate review of denials of leave to amend, see *Gillette v. Tansy, supra,* 17 F.3d at 312 (district court's ruling on motion to amend petition reviewed for abuse of discretion); Cox v. Warden, 911 F.2d 1111, 1114 (5th Cir. 1990) (district court's denial of motion to amend cannot be reversed without showing of prejudice, which was absent because courts consistently reject claim petitioner sought to amend into petition); Pelmer v. White, 877 F.2d 1518, 1521 (11th Cir. 1989) (district court's denial of motion to amend reviewed for abuse of discretion).

[10] *See supra* § 15.1 (questioning validity of local rules giving clerk power to return petitions without authorization from court).

[11] *See generally supra* note 7; *supra* § 11.5, 15.1.

[12] *See supra* Chapters 8, 9; *supra* § 11.6, 15.2. *See also supra* § 16.1, 16.2 (answer; dismissal and summary judgment motions).

[13] *See* Advisory Committee Note to Rule 5 of the Rules Governing § 2254 Cases (inviting amendments "called for by the contents of the answer"); Advisory Committee Note to Rule 4 of *id.* (procedures short of summary dismissal by which court may signal doubts about substantive sufficiency of petition and invite curative amendment); Williams v. Kullman, 722 F.2d 1048, 1050 (2d Cir. 1983) (court may grant leave to amend *sua sponte*); SOKOL, *supra* note 1, at 105-07 (court may issue "order to amend" with statement indicating defects in petition (citing authority)); *supra* § 15.2a n.17 and accompanying text. *See also* Rule 2(e) of the Rules Governing § 2254 Cases (court must accompany "return" of formally defective petition with statement of reasons for return).

[14] *See, e.g.,* Roman v. Estelle, 917 F.2d 1505, 1506 (9th Cir. 1990) (granting leave to amend petition to include only exhausted claims); Porcaro v. United States, 784 F.2d 38, 41 (1st Cir. 1986) (allegations in recusal motion prevented dismissal of previously filed and otherwise insufficient application); Johnson v. Onion, 761 F.2d 224, 225 (5th Cir. 1985); *Williams v. Kullman, supra,* 722 F.2d at 1050; Wilwording v. Swenson, 502 F.2d 844, 847 n.4 (8th Cir. 1974), *cert. denied,* 420 U.S. 912 (1975) (courts "welcome" amendments clarifying *pro se* petitions; amendments preferred because they avoid successive petitions and indicate whether hearing is necessary); Ham v. North Carolina, 471 F.2d 406, 407 (4th Cir. 1973); United States ex rel. Ellington v. Conboy, 459 F.2d 76, 79 (2d Cir. 1972); *supra* § 10.1 & 10.2 (amendments to cure nonjurisdictional mistakes as to party respondent). *See also* Pearson v. Gatto, 933 F.2d 521, 527 (7th Cir. 1991) (section 1983 action) (*pro se* prisoner's letter, filed shortly before expiration of statute of limitations and indicating intention to amend complaint, should have been "broadly constru[ed]" as amended complaint in order to preserve jurisdiction); Reynoldson v. Shillinger,

Second, amendments typically are appropriate when new claims become available for the first time after the petitioner files the federal petition.[15] Here again, the Habeas Rules support liberal resort to amendments. Habeas Rule 2(c) requires petitioners to "specify all the grounds for relief which are available to the petitioner and of which he has or by the exercise of reasonable diligence should have knowledge."[16] Along with (1) Habeas Rule 9(b), which discourages "second or successive petition[s],"[17] (2) the Supreme Court's recognition in *McFarland v. Scott*[18] that the successive petition and related doctrines "make it especially important that the first petition adequately set forth all of a state prisoner's colorable grounds for relief"[19] and its admonition in *Rose v. Lundy*[20] against piecemeal adjudication of a single petitioner's claims,[21] and (3) Habeas Rule 11's incorporation of the liberal amendment doctrine of Civil Rule 15(a),[22] Habeas Rule 2(c) strongly suggests that, at least prior to entry of the district

---

907 F.2d 124, 125-26 (10th Cir. 1990) (liberal opportunity to amend section 1983 action should have been granted when error in pleading probably was result of *pro se* litigant's unfamiliarity with law); Balistreri v. Pacifica Police Dep't, 901 F.2d 696, 701 (9th Cir. 1990) (district court erred in failing to grant section 1983 plaintiff's request to amend made in plaintiff's response to motion to dismiss; if court can "conceive of facts" that would render plaintiff's claim viable, amendment shall be freely granted even if only informally requested).

[15] *See, e.g.,* authority cited *infra* notes 23-25. *See also supra* § 11.3b nn.12-15 and accompanying text (suggesting procedure under which habeas corpus petitioner (1) pleads claims that she reasonably believes to be supported by as yet undiscovered facts that can only be discovered through investigative and discovery procedures that become available after a federal petition is filed, then (2) either amends in new facts or amends out claims in light of the results of the post-filing investigation and discovery). New claims may become available because of retroactive changes in the law, newly surfaced legal or factual theories, or the expansion of state remedies. *See* Advisory Committee Note to Rule 5 of the Rules Governing § 2254 Cases (answer "'may reveal to the petitioner's attorney grounds for release that the petitioner did not know [about]'" (quoting *Developments in the Law, supra* note 1, at 1178)); Love v. Jones, 923 F.2d 816, 818 (11th Cir. 1991) (amended petition filed after magistrate appointed counsel to represent *pro se* petitioner); United States v. Weintraub, 871 F.2d 1257, 1259 (5th Cir. 1989) (amendment permitted after discovery revealed new information); other authority cited *infra* notes 23-25.

[16] Rule 2(c) of the Rules Governing § 2254 Cases.

[17] Rule 9(b) of the Rules Governing § 2254 Cases. *See generally infra* Chapter 28.

[18] 512 U.S. 849 (1994).

[19] *Id.* at 860 (O'Connor, J., concurring in the judgment in part). *Accord id.* at 856 (citing McCleskey v. Zant, 499 U.S. 467 (1991)). *See supra* § 11.2a n.5, 11.3a n.4, 11.3b nn.12-15 and accompanying text (discussing rule generated by *McCleskey* requiring inclusion in initial habeas corpus proceedings of all potentially colorable claims).

[20] 455 U.S. 509 (1982).

[21] *See supra* § 13.3c, 15.2d.

[22] *See supra* note 5 and accompanying text.

court's judgment (and even possibly thereafter, on appeal[23]) courts should allow amendment of any claim that was not "available to the petitioner" at the time he filed the petition and any claim about which the petitioner could not have had "knowledge at that time despite exercise of reasonable diligence."[24] Liberal

---

[23] *See, e.g.*, Ross v. Kemp, 785 F.2d 1467, 1478 (11th Cir. 1986) (record enlarged on appeal to avoid successive litigation); Petty v. McCotter, 779 F.2d 299, 302 (5th Cir. 1986), *cert. dismissed,* 480 U.S. 699 (1987) (*pro se* petitioner may supplement claim with facts alleged for first time on appeal); Stephens v. Zant, 631 F.2d 397, 406-07 (5th Cir. 1980), *modified on other grounds,* 648 F.2d 446 (5th Cir. 1981), *question certified on other grounds,* 456 U.S. 410 (1982), *rev'd on other grounds,* 462 U.S. 862 (1983) (petitioner on remand may amend in new claims raised for first time in appellate *amicus curiae* brief); other authority cited *infra* § 37.1b, 37.2. *Cf.* Pelmer v. White, 877 F.2d 1518, 1523 (11th Cir. 1989) (district court did not abuse discretion by denying postjudgment motion to amend made one year after district court rendered final judgment and during pendency of appeal); Hurd v. Mondragon, 851 F.2d 324, 329 (10th Cir. 1988) (district court has discretion to accept or reject petitioner's motion to withdraw petition in order to add new claim following magistrate's report but before district court has ruled). *But see* Ward v. Whitley, 21 F.3d 1355, 1360 (5th Cir. 1994), *cert. denied,* 513 U.S. 1192 (1995) (denying motion to remand case to district court for amendment of petition to add new claim because "[a] habeas petitioner may not add new constitutional claims to a petition after the district court has entered judgment"). Petitioners should seek leave to amend in a timely fashion, *e.g.,* Duff-Smith v. Collins, 973 F.2d 1175, 1179-80 (5th Cir. 1992), *cert. denied,* 507 U.S. 1056 (1993) (district court did not abuse discretion in denying leave to amend, notwithstanding change of counsel, because substitute counsel had worked on case for seven and one-half months before seeking leave to amend), and should include in the motion seeking leave to amend all known or discoverable claims, *e.g.,* Giarratano v. Procunier, 891 F.2d 483, 485-86 (4th Cir. 1989), *cert. denied,* 498 U.S. 881 (1990) (discussed *infra* note 24); Richardson v. Thigpen, 883 F.2d 895, 899 (11th Cir.) (*per curiam*), *cert. denied,* 492 U.S. 934 (1989) (failure to include new claim in motion to amend prior petition may later result in "abuse of writ" denial of successive petition presenting that claim); Thomas v. Dugger, 846 F.2d 669, 673 (11th Cir. 1988), *cert. denied,* 493 U.S. 921 (1989) (court of appeals refuses to permit petitioner to add newly exhausted claim given claim's omission from prior motion to amend); Wright, *supra* note 1, at 240.

[24] Rule 2(c) of the Rules Governing § 2254 Cases. *See, e.g.,* Willis v. Collins, 989 F.2d 187, 189 (5th Cir. 1993); Diaz v. United States, 930 F.2d 832, 835 (11th Cir. 1991) (because movant "proceeding *pro se* [] asserted a potentially meritorious claim which he said he did not know about and which arguably was unavailable when the original petition was filed" and "[g]iven the liberal rules governing amendment" of section 2255 motions, district court erred in denying motion to amend); Love v. Jones, 923 F.2d 816, 818 (11th Cir. 1991) (amended petition filed after magistrate appointed counsel to represent *pro se* petitioner); Mayo v. Lynaugh, 893 F.2d 683, 685 (5th Cir. 1990); *Giarratano v. Procunier, supra,* 891 F.2d at 485-86 (petitioner allowed to amend petition twice; court denied request to amend a third time); Lowery v. Young, 887 F.2d 1309, 1311 (7th Cir. 1989) (permitting amendment made via traverse asserting new claim); United States v. Weintraub, 871 F.2d 1257, 1259 (5th Cir. 1989) (amendment after new information revealed during discovery); Williams v. Lockhart, 849 F.2d 1134, 1139-40 (8th Cir. 1988) (ordering district court to grant leave to amend because petitioner may be foreclosed from raising new claim in subsequent petition, and justice requires amendment); Reddy v. Coombe, 846 F.2d 866, 870 (2d Cir.), *cert. denied,* 488 U.S. 929 (1988) (*pro se* petitioner permitted on remand to add new claim

leave to amend in new claims is particularly appropriate in capital cases.[25]

As is indicated above,[26] the Antiterrorism and Effective Death Penalty Act of 1996 changes the foregoing standards in capital cases in those States that have qualified for "opt-in" treatment. In these cases, the traditional rules permitting liberal amendment apply until the State files its answer. Thereafter, however, amendments are permissible only if they raise a "new claim" of the extremely narrow sort that AEDPA permits a habeas corpus petitioner to raise in a second

after appellate court vacated district court's grant of habeas corpus relief); Kiendra v. Hadden, 763 F.2d 69, 71-72 (2d Cir. 1985) (reaching merits of claim omitted from petition but raised in affidavit in opposition to state's response); Byrd v. Martin, 754 F.2d 963, 965 (11th Cir. 1985); Franklin v. Murphy, 745 F.2d 1221, 1228 & n.9 (9th Cir. 1984) (citing cases); Espey v. Wainwright, 734 F.2d 748, 750 (11th Cir. 1984) ("discretion of the district court is not broad enough to permit denial" of leave to amend in new claims when amendment would facilitate simultaneous resolution of all petitioner's claims, unless claim was available and known to petitioner at time petition was filed); Chenault v. Stynchcombe, 581 F.2d 444, 447-48 (5th Cir. 1978); authority cited *infra* note 25. *See also* Sanders v. United States, 373 U.S. 1, 19 (1963) (amendment to add new claims is "better course" to avoid successive litigation); Forman v. Davis, 371 U.S. 178, 182 (1962) (unexplained denial of amendment motion in civil action is abuse of discretion). *Compare* Moore v. Balkcom, 716 F.2d 1511, 1526 (11th Cir. 1983), *cert. denied,* 465 U.S. 1084 (1984) (leave to amend denied) *with* Moore v. Kemp, 824 F.2d 847 (11th Cir. 1987) (*en banc*) (partially successful successive litigation based on claims not amended into petition in *Moore v. Balkcom, supra*). *Cf.* Stafford v. Saffle, 34 F.3d 1557, 1560-62 (10th Cir. 1994), *cert. denied,* 514 U.S. 1099 (1995) (district court did not abuse its discretion in denying leave to amend petition to add two claims, both of which were obviously nonmeritorious and one of which was fully available to petitioner at time of filing of petition seven years earlier); Scott v. Dugger, 891 F.2d 800, 806 (11th Cir. 1989) (*per curiam*), *cert. denied,* 498 U.S. 881 (1990) (district court did not err in denying motion to amend because recent Supreme Court decision foreclosed petitioner's claim); *Espey v. Wainwright, supra* at 750 ("'undue delay, bad faith or dilatory motive on the part of the movant, repeated failure to cure deficiencies by amendments previously allowed, and undue prejudice to the opposing party'" may justify denial of motion to amend (quoting Dussouy v. Gulf Coast Invest. Corp., 660 F.2d 594, 598 (5th Cir. 1981))).

[25] *See, e.g.,* Collins v. Byrd, 510 U.S. 1185, 1185-88 (1994) (*mem.*) (Scalia, J., dissenting from denial of motion to vacate stay) (describing 6th Circuit order, which Supreme Court declined to vacate, directing district court, following filing of apparently incomplete capital federal habeas corpus petition, to grant stay of execution and give petitioner 120 days "'for further investigation and discovery of possible habeas claims'" and 60 days to amend new claims into petition); *Moore v. Balkcom, supra,* 716 F.2d at 1526 (*dicta*) ("Certainly in a capital case, the district court should be particularly favorably disposed toward a petitioner's motion to amend."); the *Ross, Stephens, Giarratano, Mayo,* and *Chenault* decisions cited *supra* notes 23, 24. As the *Moore* litigation in the 11th Circuit reveals, *see supra* note 24, petitioners denied leave to amend should consider appealing that denial, rather than simply resigning themselves to inclusion of the claim in a second or successive petition. *See* Moore v. Zant, 885 F.2d 1497, 1500-01 (11th Cir. 1989), *cert. denied,* 497 U.S. 1010 (1990) (*en banc*) (plurality opinion) (petitioner found to have defaulted new claim even though he unsuccessfully asked district court (but not court of appeals) to amend in the new claim).

[26] *See supra* notes 2-3 and accompanying text.

or successive petition.[27] (As Chapter 28 explains, AEDPA limits second or successive petitions to claims that are based on either (1) new legal rules that are retroactively applicable to the case or (2) facts that previously were unavailable and that, when viewed in light of the evidence as a whole, enable the petitioner to satisfy the statutory standard of "innocence."[28])

§ 17.3. Petitioner-initiated summary proceedings.

"The [Supreme] Court stated in *Walker v. Johnston* that there could be situations where 'on the facts admitted, it may appear that, as a matter of law, the prisoner is entitled to the writ and to a discharge,'" and the Supreme Court and federal courts thereafter "have acknowledged the power of a federal district court to discharge a habeas corpus petitioner from state custody without conducting an evidentiary hearing, when the facts are undisputed and established a denial of petitioner's constitutional rights."[1] "As in civil cases generally, there exists a procedure whose purpose is to test whether facially adequate [habeas corpus] allegations have sufficient basis in fact to warrant plenary presentation of evidence" or whether, in the absence of any factual dispute, they warrant relief as a matter of law. "That procedure is, of course, the motion for summary judgment."[2] Although, as discussed above,[3] summary judgment and the similar habeas-corpus-specific procedure of "summary dismissal" typically are used *against* petitioners, "in unusual cases, the court may *grant* [habeas corpus] relief ... without a hearing."[4]

---

[27] *See supra* § 3.3c nn.62-63.

[28] *See supra* § 3.3c n.64 and accompanying text; *infra* § 28.3, 28.4.

§ 17.3. [1] Browder v. Director, 434 U.S. 257, 266 n.10 (1978) (quoting Walker v. Johnston, 312 U.S. 275, 284 (1941), and citing authority). *Accord* authority cited *infra* note 4.

[2] Blackledge v. Allison, 431 U.S. 63, 80-81 (1977) (citing FED. R. CIV. P. 56). *Accord, e.g.,* Johnson v. Rogers, 917 F.2d 1283, 1284-85 (10th Cir. 1990) (granting mandamus requiring district court to rule on habeas corpus petitioner's summary judgment motion filed 14 months earlier); Valles v. Lynaugh, 835 F.2d 126, 127 (5th Cir. 1988) (summary judgment appropriate when there are no genuine issues of material fact and moving party entitled to judgment as matter of law (citing Fed. R. Civ. P. 56(c))).

[3] *See supra* § 15.2a, 16.1c.

[4] Advisory Committee Note to Rule 8 of the Rules Governing § 2254 Cases. *See, e.g.*, Liles v. Saffle, 945 F.2d 333 (10th Cir. 1991), *cert. denied*, 502 U.S. 1066 (1992) (district court properly granted petitioner's motion for summary judgment on basis of excerpts from state record and other affidavits showing that petitioner was denied psychiatric assistance at guilt and sentencing phases of trial in violation of Ake v. Oklahoma, 470 U.S. 68 (1985)); Marzano v. Kincheloe, 915 F.2d 549, 552 (9th Cir. 1990) (discussed *infra* note 11); Bailey v. Hamby, 744 F.2d 25, 26 (6th Cir. 1984) (summary judgment for petitioner based on facts in state court record); United States ex rel. Ross v. Franzen, 668 F.2d 933, 939 (7th Cir. 1982) (record flatly contradicts state factfindings; writ granted without hearing). *See also Browder v. Director, supra*, 434 U.S. at 266 & n.10. *Cf.* United States ex rel. McCall v. O'Grady, 908 F.2d 170, 175 (7th Cir. 1990) (summary judgment on behalf

Technically, the habeas corpus statute authorizes — indeed, it seems to require — the court to treat the petition itself as the equivalent of a petitioner-initiated summary judgment motion and "forthwith [to] award the writ ... unless it appears from the application that the applicant or person detained is not entitled thereto."[5] Especially, however, in the case of petitions with multiple claims, as to some of which evidentiary proceedings may be required but as to others of which "there is no genuine issue as to any material fact,"[6] it is appropriate for the petitioner to file a motion for summary judgment,[7] utilizing the procedures set out in Rule 56 of the Federal Rules of Civil Procedure.[8]

A petitioner-initiated summary judgment motion might be appropriate if, for example, state court factfindings create a right to relief under controlling federal law;[9] the answer admits petitioner's version of dispositive facts;[10] the facial constitutionality of a state statute, rule, written policy, or established practice is at stake and the provision's or practice's application in the particular case is not

---

of petitioner was inappropriate on ineffective assistance claim because of record's ambiguity on determinative factual issue).

[5] 28 U.S.C. § 2243 (1994). *See id.* ("The court shall ... dispose of the matter as law and justice require."); Rule 8(a) of the Rules Governing § 2254 Cases ("If it appears that an evidentiary hearing is not required, the judge shall make such disposition of the petition as justice shall require.").

[6] FED. R. CIV. P. 56(c). *See infra* note 8.

[7] *See, e.g., Browder v. Director, supra,* 434 U.S. at 260, 266. *See generally infra* § 35.1 (conflicting views on appealability of judgments affording relief on some claims without ruling on others).

[8] FED. R. CIV. P. 56. On the applicability of Civil Rule 56 in habeas corpus cases, *see* Hill v. Linahan, 697 F.2d 1032, 1034 (11th Cir. 1983); other authority cited *supra* § 16.1c n.20. *See also* Rule 11 of the Rules Governing § 2254 Cases (Civil Rules apply in habeas corpus cases if "appropriate" and not inconsistent with Habeas Rules); *supra* notes 1-5 and accompanying text (consistency of petitioner-initiated summary judgment with Habeas Rule 8 and appropriateness of the procedure in "unusual" circumstances). *See generally supra* § 15.2a, 16.2, 17.1. Counsel or the prisoner should carefully study Civil Rule 56's detailed procedural requirements, which are generally discussed *supra* § 16.1c n.20.

[9] *See, e.g., Browder v. Director, supra,* 434 U.S. at 260, 266 (summary judgment based on facts established by state court record). *See also* Burden v. Zant, 510 U.S. 132 (1994) (*per curiam*); Burden v. Zant, 498 U.S. 433 (1991) (*per curiam*). State-court factfindings favoring the petitioner are entitled to the same presumption of correctness due findings favoring the state. *See* Burden v. Zant, 498 U.S. 433 (1991) (*per curiam*); Bland v. California Dep't of Corrections, 20 F.3d 1469, 1474 (9th Cir.), *cert. denied,* 513 U.S. 947 (1994); Craker v. Procunier, 756 F.2d 1212, 1214 (5th Cir. 1985); Tinsley v. Purvis, 731 F.2d 791, 793 (11th Cir. 1984); *infra* § 20.2c n.47. Because the standards governing the presumption of correctness reserve for the *petitioner* most of the mechanisms for rendering the presumption of correctness of state court factfindings inapplicable or for rebutting the presumption, the state may have no basis for securing a hearing to overcome adverse state factfindings. *See infra* § 20.2, 20.3, 30.3.

[10] *See, e.g.,* Walker v. Johnston, 312 U.S. 275, 284 (1941).

in dispute;[11] a recent decision of a higher court or of the same district court or in a companion case controls the petitioner's claim and warrants relief; or, for any other reason, no facts are in dispute.

Summary judgment motions also may be premised on the factual record made by the parties in prior state-court proceedings (whether or not there are favorable state-court factfindings)[12] or on facts developed in the habeas corpus proceeding itself through discovery, expansion of the record, or the petitioner's investigation as reflected in affidavits appended to the motion.[13]

If the district court issues an order granting summary judgment in favor of the petitioner on some or all claims and in so doing affords her all the relief she seeks, the order is an appealable final order.[14] If, however, the court denies summary judgment and orders further proceedings, or grants summary judgment as

---

[11] See, e.g., Marzano v. Kincheloe, 915 F.2d 549, 552 (9th Cir. 1990) (petitioner-initiated summary judgment motion granted because, on its face, state statute could not constitutionally be read to permit sentence imposed on petitioner). Other examples are provided by the Supreme Court's affirmance and grant of habeas corpus relief in Estelle v. Smith, 451 U.S. 454 (1981), and Adams v. Texas, 448 U.S. 38 (1980), each of which ruled unconstitutional a capital-sentencing practice utilized in Texas and occasioned grants of a number of petitioner-initiated summary judgment motions in cases in which the record clearly established that the forbidden practice was followed. See 5th Circuit decisions collected supra § 11.2c (para. (11)(a)(i)).

[12] See, e.g., Liles v. Saffle, 945 F.2d 333 (10th Cir. 1991), cert. denied, 502 U.S. 1066 (1992) (discussed supra note 4); Bailey v. Hamby, 744 F.2d 25, 26 (6th Cir. 1984) (discussed supra note 4).

[13] See FED. R. CIV. P. 56(c) (summary judgment may be predicated on "pleadings, depositions, answers to interrogatories and admissions on file, together with affidavits, if any"); FED. R. CIV. P. 56(e) (form of affidavits). See infra § 19.4, 19.5 (discovery, expansion of record). See, e.g., Liles v. Saffle, supra, 945 F.2d at 335, 340-41. Premising summary judgment on affidavits presents unusual tactical risks in habeas corpus cases because of Habeas Rule 7, which allows the court to "expand the record" to include affidavits and, notwithstanding hearsay objections, to treat the affidavits as substantive evidence and decide the case based upon them. See id. Accordingly, the filing of a summary judgment motion based upon affidavits, which permits the state to file counter-affidavits (FED. R. CIV. P. 56(e); see also 28 U.S.C. § 2246 (1994); Rule 7(c) of the Rules Governing § 2254 Cases), gives the court four options, only the first two of which are available in other civil litigation: The court may conclude that the facts are not in dispute and enter summary judgment in favor of (1) the petitioner or (2) the state, FED. R. CIV. P. 56(d); or the court may conclude that the facts are in dispute but nonetheless treat the affidavits as evidence under Habeas Rule 7, resolve the factual dispute without a formal hearing based on the affidavits, and enter judgment for (3) the petitioner or (4) the state. But cf. Hill v. Linahan, 697 F.2d 1032, 1034 (11th Cir. 1983) (district court erred in granting summary judgment for state on basis of documents submitted by petitioner in response to answer because petitioner did not have adequate notice of summary judgment motion). Also, because a summary judgment motion limited to one of several claims in the petition may undermine the district court's willingness to grant a hearing on the petition as a whole, a decision to file a summary judgment motion in that situation must be weighed against the importance of a hearing on the other claims.

[14] See infra § 35.1.

to only a subset of claims that give the petitioner only *part* of the relief she seeks, the order generally is not treated as an appealable final order or as a nonfinal order appealable under the "collateral order" doctrine.[15]

---

[15] *See* Johnson v. Jones, 515 U.S. 304, 313-18 (1995) (section 1983 action); Swint v. Chambers County Comm'n, 514 U.S. 35, 41-42 (1995) (same). The "collateral order" rule is discussed *supra* § 12.1, 12.5, 13.6b, 14.2 nn.15-18 and accompanying text, 16.1c n.20; *infra* § 35.1.

PART V

MAGISTRATE JUDGE PRACTICE AND FACT-DEVELOPMENT PROCEDURES

Chapter 18

MAGISTRATE JUDGE PRACTICE

§ 18.1. Matters referable.[1]

a. *Nondispositive matters.* As in all federal cases, the Federal Magistrates Act authorizes the district judge in habeas corpus actions to designate a United States Magistrate Judge to "hear and determine" any nondispositive pretrial matter.[2] Typical of such nondispositive matters are motions for production of the state court record, discovery, a continuance, and the like.[3] Under the Magistrates Act, the district judge "may reconsider" the magistrate judge's determination of nondispositive pretrial matters "where it has been shown that the magistrate's

---

§ 18.1. [1] *See generally* LARRY W. YACKLE, POSTCONVICTION REMEDIES § 138 (1981 & Supp. 1998); Linda J. Silberman, *Masters and Magistrates Part II: The American Analogue,* 50 N.Y.U. L. REV. 1297 (1975); Charles Alan Wright, *Procedure for Habeas Corpus,* 77 F.R.D. 227, 246-47 (1978); *Developments in the Law — Federal Habeas Corpus,* 83 HARV. L. REV. 1038, 1188 (1970); Note, *Proposed Reformation of Federal Habeas Corpus Procedure: Use of Federal Magistrates,* 54 IOWA L. REV. 1147 (1969). Although the term "magistrate" appears occasionally in this chapter and elsewhere in the book (primarily in quotations from pre-1990 court decisions or legislation), the appropriate title as of 1990 is "magistrate judge." *See* The Judicial Improvements Act of 1990, Pub. L. No. 101-650, 104 Stat. 5089, 5117 (1990).

[2] 28 U.S.C. § 636(b)(1)(A) (1994) (district judge "may designate a magistrate to hear *and determine* any pretrial matter ... except a motion for injunctive relief, for judgment on the pleadings, for summary judgment, ... to dismiss or to permit maintenance of a class action, to dismiss for failure to state a claim upon which relief can be granted, and to involuntarily dismiss an action" (emphasis added)). *See* Rule 10 of the Rules Governing § 2254 Cases ("The duties imposed upon the judge of the district court by these rules may be performed by a United States magistrate pursuant to 28 U.S.C. § 636."); Gomez v. United States, 490 U.S. 858, 867-68 & n.16 (1989) (listing relatively routine types of "pretrial matter[s]" that judge may assign to magistrate judge to resolve); Thomas v. Arn, 474 U.S. 140, 151 n.10 (1985) (characterizing matters magistrate judges may hear *and determine* as "nondispositive"); United States v. Raddatz, 447 U.S. 667, 673 (1980). *See also* FED. R. CIV. P. 72(a) (procedure for disposition by magistrate judge of "pretrial matter not dispositive of a claim or defense of a party").

[3] *See* Ainsworth v. Vasquez, 759 F. Supp. 1467, 1474 (E.D. Cal. 1991) (routine pretrial hearings by magistrate judges to determine if capital habeas corpus petitioners are adequately represented and have raised all available claims are "well within the magistrate judges' discretion under existing authority and practice"). *See, e.g., infra* §§ 19.2, 19.4, 21.1b. *Cf.* Heinrichs v. Marshall & Stevens, Inc., 921 F.2d 418, 420 (2d Cir. 1990) (imposition of discovery sanctions is *dispositive* matter as to which *de novo* district court review is (and in this case was made) available, upon party's objection).

order is clearly erroneous or contrary to law."[4] Rule 72(a) of the Federal Rules of Civil Procedure requires magistrate judges "promptly [to] conduct such [nondispositive] proceedings as are required and to enter into the record a written order setting forth the disposition of the matter," and it affords the parties 10 days after the entry of the order to file objections with the "district judge to whom the case is assigned."[5] Upon concluding that the magistrate judge's order is clearly erroneous or contrary to law, the district court "shall modify or set aside" that portion of the order.[6]

b. *Dispositive matters.* Also as in other federal civil and criminal cases, the Magistrates Act[7] and Rule 8(b) of the Rules Governing § 2254 Cases[8] give the district court in habeas corpus cases — acting either as a body via the promulgation of local rules or through the rulings of individual judges in particular cases — the discretion to designate magistrate judges to hear, but *not* finally to

---

[4] 28 U.S.C. § 636(b)(1)(A) (1994). *Accord* FED. R. CIV. P. 72(a). *See Gomez v. United States, supra,* 490 U.S. at 867-68, 874 n.28 ("clearly erroneous"/"contrary to law" review standard appropriate for "less important," nondispositive matters; for dispositive matters, *de novo* review required); *id.* at 871 (Magistrates Act "specif[ies] two levels of review depending on the scope and significance of the magistrate's decision" — a higher level of review for dispositive matters, a lower level for nondispositive matters); *United States v. Raddatz, supra,* 447 U.S. at 673. *See also* McKeever v. Block, 932 F.2d 795, 799 (9th Cir. 1991) (because magistrate judge's resolution of nondispositive matter does not need district judge's review and approval to become effective, district judge's obligation to review is not triggered unless aggrieved party brings ruling and objections to district court's attention within 10 days; *pro se* litigant's communications to court should be liberally construed as objections, although court decides not to treat *pro se* letter as objection because document promised further filings that never materialized and did not request review of magistrate judge's action).

[5] FED. R. CIV. P. 72(a). *See* Rule 11 of the Rules Governing § 2254 Cases ("appropriate" Civil Rules that are not inconsistent with Habeas Rules apply in habeas corpus proceedings). *See also* Advisory Committee Note to FED. R. CIV. P. 72 (indicating by negative implication that Civil Rule 72(a), unlike Civil Rule 72(b), *see infra* note 15, applies in habeas corpus proceedings).

[6] FED. R. CIV. P. 72(a). A number of federal district courts have adopted or modified the requirements of Civil Rule 72(a) by local rule. *Cf.* 28 U.S.C. § 636(b)(1) (1994) (10-day rule for objections to magistrate judge's recommendations on "dispositive" matters); *Thomas v. Arn, supra* (discussed *infra* § 18.2a) (federal circuits may treat knowing failure to file objections to magistrate judge's recommendations regarding "dispositive" matters as waiver of right to appeal district court's adverse determination of those matters on basis of magistrate judge's recommendation).

[7] 28 U.S.C. § 636(b)(2) (1994). *See also* Rule 10 of the Rules Governing § 2254 Cases ("The duties imposed upon the judge of the district court by these rules may be performed by a United States magistrate pursuant to 28 U.S.C. § 636.").

[8] Rule 8(b) of the Rules Governing § 2254 Cases.

determine, *dispositive* matters,[9] as long as the magistrate judge's recommendations are subject to meaningful *de novo* review by the district judge.[10]

In one important respect, the Magistrates Act and Habeas Rule 8(b) give magistrate judges authority in habeas corpus cases that they do not have in other federal proceedings. In most federal civil proceedings, the Magistrates Act requires the consent of all parties to the litigation before the district judge may refer the ultimate trial on the merits to a magistrate judge (although, upon consent, the magistrate judge may enter a final judgment).[11] By contrast, in habeas

---

[9] Thomas v. Arn, 454 U.S. 140, 150 n.8 (1985); United States v. Raddatz, 447 U.S. 667, 673-74 (1980) (discussing 28 U.S.C. § 636(b)(1)(B)). *See* Gomez v. United States, 490 U.S. 858, 868-69 & n.16 (1989) (listing types of "pretrial matter[s]" that magistrate judge may be assigned); *id.* at 864-65 (rejecting opposing views that magistrate judges are "'supernotar[ies]'" relegated to "'irksome ministerial tasks'" and that they are "'para-judge[s]' with 'a wide range of substantive judicial duties and advisory functions,'" Court reiterates middle position that "limited, advisory review, subject to the district judge's ongoing supervision and final decision, [is] among the 'range of duties' that Congress intended magistrates to perform" and emphasizes that final decision rests with district judge); McLeod, Alexander, Powel & Apffel, P.C. v. Quarles, 925 F.2d 853, 856-57 & n.5 (5th Cir. 1991) (permitting assignment to magistrate judge of FED. R. CIV. P. 60(b) motion to vacate judgment, conditioned on safeguards that magistrate judge may only recommend disposition and that parties may secure *de novo* review by filing objections); Heinrichs v. Marshall & Stevens, Inc., 921 F.2d 418, 420 (2d Cir. 1990) (imposition of discovery sanctions is dispositive matter as to which *de novo* district court review is (and in this case was made) available, upon party's objection); United States v. Koenig, 912 F.2d 1190, 1191-92 (9th Cir. 1990) (decision to detain defendant before trial is dispositive matter subject to *de novo* district court review of magistrate judge's decision); Flournoy v. Marshall, 842 F.2d 875, 877 (6th Cir. 1988) (discussing 28 U.S.C. § 636(b)(1)).

[10] *See Gomez v. United States, supra,* 490 U.S. at 874-75 (district judge should not assign magistrate judges tasks that district court thereafter cannot "review ... meaningfully"; matters depending upon "not only spoken words but also gestures and attitude" may not be appropriate for referral if "transcript can[not] recapture the atmosphere"). *See also* United States v. Williams, 919 F.2d 266, 270-71 (5th Cir. 1990) (matters that require factfinding and turn on credibility judgments are not appropriate for referral to magistrate judges for final disposition).

[11] 28 U.S.C. § 636(c) (1994). *See generally* Pacemaker Diagnostic Clinic of Am., Inc. v. Instromedix, 725 F.2d 537 (9th Cir.) (*en banc*), *cert. denied,* 469 U.S. 824 (1984) (constitutionality of 28 U.S.C. § 636(c)). Section 636(c) encompasses habeas corpus proceedings among those that, upon consent of the parties, the district judge may delegate to a magistrate judge for trial and "entry of judgment." 28 U.S.C. § 636(c) (1994) ("any or all proceedings in a jury or nonjury civil matter"). *See* Orsini v. Wallace, 913 F.2d 474, 477-78 (8th Cir. 1990), *cert. denied,* 498 U.S. 1128 (1991) (consent jurisdiction allowing magistrate judges to enter final order in habeas corpus proceedings is constitutional and consistent with legislative intent); Andersen v. Thieret, 903 F.2d 526, 529 (7th Cir. 1990); Wilson v. O'Leary, 895 F.2d 378, 381-83 (7th Cir. 1990) (pursuant to 28 U.S.C. § 636(c), habeas corpus parties consented to full adjudication and entry of judgment by magistrate judge; pursuant to *id.* § 636(c)(4), parties consented to appeal to district court and discretionary review by court of appeals); Williams v. Lockhart, 873 F.2d 1129, 1132 (8th Cir.), *cert. denied,* 493 U.S. 942 (1989) (habeas corpus parties consented to magistrate judge's entry of final judgment); *supra* § 2.2 (habeas corpus as civil proceeding). *See also* Fuente Cigar, Ltd. v.

corpus and other federal postconviction proceedings, the Magistrates Act and Habeas Rule 8(b) grant the district court discretion, whether or not the parties agree, to refer the case as a whole, including final hearings on the merits, to United States magistrate judges with instructions to conduct whatever proceedings and to propose whatever dispositions are appropriate.[12]

Roadway Express, Inc., 925 F.2d 370, 372-74 (11th Cir. 1991) (comprehensive discussion of standards and procedure for residual discretionary review by court of appeals upon parties' agreement, under § 636(c), to try matter before magistrate judge and to pursue appeal as of right to district court). *But cf. Orsini v. Wallace, supra* at 483 (Bright, J., dissenting) (although issue was not raised by parties, court should exercise discretion to consider validity of petitioner's uncounseled consent, using nonexplanatory consent form, to final disposition of habeas corpus case by magistrate judge). The difference between habeas corpus and other civil proceedings is that in the former, but not the latter, the court can delegate the trial (subject to *de novo* review) to a magistrate judge *without* the consent of the parties. *See infra* notes 12-15 and accompanying text. In federal criminal cases, the Magistrates Act limits magistrate judges to conducting misdemeanor trials. 28 U.S.C. § 636(a)(3) (1994).

Normally, consent to entry of final judgment by a magistrate judge ends the district judge's participation in the case and requires appeals to be filed in the court of appeals, pursuant to 28 U.S.C. § 636(c)(3) (1994). *See, e.g., Andersen v. Thieret, supra* at 529; *Williams v. Lockhart, supra* at 1132. Pursuant to 28 U.S.C. § 636(c)(4) (1994), however, the parties may consent to substitute an appeal to the district court for the usual appeal to the court of appeals. *See also Wilson v. O'Leary, supra*, 895 F.2d at 381-82 (discussing but leaving open question whether consent to take habeas corpus appeal to district court supersedes certificate of probable cause requirement of 28 U.S. § 2253 (*see generally infra* § 35.4)). If agreement on the latter approach is reached, the court of appeals nonetheless retains jurisdiction and the discretion to grant a petitioning party "leave to appeal ... specific objections to the judgment," in which case the court of appeals uses a "clearly mistaken" standard of review. 28 U.S.C. § 636(c)(5) (1994); *Wilson v. O'Leary, supra* at 381-83. The appellate route chosen by the parties does not affect the availability of Supreme Court review. 28 U.S.C. §§ 636(c)(3), 636(c)(5) (1994).

[12] 28 U.S.C. § 636(b)(1)(B) (1994); Rule 8(b)(1) of the Rules Governing § 2254 Cases. *See* McCarthy v. Bronson, 500 U.S. 136, 140 (1991) ("Congress intended to include in their entirety" in category of matters that district court may refer to magistrate judge for recommended disposition on merits of underlying suit "the two primary categories of suits brought by prisoners — applications for habeas corpus relief pursuant to 28 U.S.C. §§ 2254 and 2255 and actions for monetary or injunctive relief under 42 U.S.C. § 1983"); *United States v. Raddatz, supra*, 447 U.S. at 674; Sullivan v. Cuyler, 723 F.2d 1077, 1085 (3d Cir. 1983); Hinman v. McCarthy, 676 F.2d 343, 346-47 (9th Cir.), *cert. denied*, 459 U.S. 1048 (1982); Hill v. Jenkins, 603 F.2d 1256, 1258 (7th Cir. 1979); *infra* § 41.6a (same rule for federal prisoner postconviction motions under 28 U.S.C. § 2255 (West 1994 & Supp. 1998)). Congress amended both the Magistrates Act and Habeas Rule 8(b) in 1976 in order to "'restat[e] and reclarif[y]' [its] intent to permit magistrates to hold evidentiary hearings and perform other judicial functions" in habeas corpus cases. *Thomas v. Arn, supra*, 474 U.S. at 152 n.12 (quoting S. Rep. No. 94-625, 94th Cong., 2d Sess. 3 (1976)). *See* Act of Oct. 21, 1976, §§ 1, 2(a)(1), 2(b)(1), Pub. L. No. 94-577, 90 Stat. 2729, *codified*, 28 U.S.C. § 636(b) (1994); Rule 8(b) of the Rules Governing § 2254 Cases (overruling Wingo v. Wedding, 418 U.S. 461 (1974)). Prior to the 1976 amendment, Supreme Court decisions forbade magistrate judges to hold habeas corpus hearings on the merits. *Wingo v. Wedding, supra* at 468-74 (citing United States v. Hayman, 342 U.S. 205, 213 n.16 (1952); Holiday v. Johnston, 313 U.S. 342, 353-

In situations involving pretrial and post-trial[13] adjudication by magistrate judges of dispositive matters, only the district judge has the power to enter a final judgment. The magistrate judge's role is limited "to submit[ting] to a judge of the court proposed findings of fact and recommendations for the disposition, *by a judge of the court.*"[14] Simply by objecting in a timely manner, any party aggrieved by the magistrate judge's findings and recommendations may secure a "de novo determination" of any aspect of the magistrate judge's report.[15]

c. *Distinguishing between dispositive and nondispositive matters.* Deciding which referable tasks fit into the category of "nondispositive" matters subject to magisterial determination and "clearly erroneous" review by the district judge[16] and which qualify as "dispositive matters subject to *de novo* review by the district judge as of right"[17] is somewhat more complicated than at first appears. Clearly, "motions for judgment on the pleadings and dismissal for failure to state a claim on which relief can be granted"[18] as well as adjudication of the merits of the petition fall into the latter, "dispositive," category. Similarly, the Magistrates Act exempts from "determin[ation]" by a magistrate judge "motion[s] for injunctive relief" — including, in particular, motions for a stay of execution — and "motions for summary judgment, ... to dismiss or to permit

---

54 (1941)). *See generally* Washington v. Estelle, 648 F.2d 276, 280-82 (5th Cir.), *cert. denied,* 454 U.S. 899 (1981) (survey of magistrate judges' powers in habeas corpus cases).

[13] *See, e.g., McLeod, Alexander, Powel & Apffel, P.C. v. Quarles, supra,* 925 F.2d at 856-57 & n.5 (pursuant to 28 U.S.C. § 636(b)(3), authorizing assignment to magistrate judges of "such additional duties as are not inconsistent with the Constitution and laws of the United States," district court may assign to magistrate judge a FED. R. CIV. P. 60(b) motion to vacate judgment for limited purpose of holding evidentiary hearing and preparing proposed findings of fact and recommendations for disposition, subject to *de novo* review).

[14] 28 U.S.C. § 636(b)(1)(B) (1994) (emphasis added). *See* Rule 8(b)(1) of the Rules Governing § 2254 Cases; *United States v. Raddatz, supra,* 447 U.S. at 673 ("as to 'dispositive' [matters], ... magistrate has no authority to make a final and binding disposition"); *McLeod, Alexander, Powel & Apffel, P.C. v. Quarles, supra,* 925 F.2d at 856 n.5.

[15] 28 U.S.C. § 636(b)(1) (1994). *See* Rule 8(b)(4) of the Rules Governing § 2254 Cases; *Thomas v. Arn, supra,* 474 U.S. at 154 ("Any party that desires plenary consideration by the Article III judge of any issue need only ask."); *McLeod, Alexander, Powel & Apffel, P.C. v. Quarles, supra,* 925 F.2d at 856 n.5. *See also* FED. R. CIV. P. 72(b) (similar provision governing magistrate judge's handling of dispositive matters in civil cases; although Advisory Committee Note to Civil Rule 72(b) states that Habeas Rule 8(b) superseded Civil Rule 72(b), two rules are similar, and local rules of number of district courts call for application of Civil Rule 72 in habeas corpus cases). *See infra* § 18.2a (reasons why party aggrieved by any aspect of magistrate judge's report should object to report in timely fashion).

[16] 28 U.S.C. § 636(b)(1)(A) (1994).

[17] Thomas v. Arn, 474 U.S. 140, 150 n.8 (1985).

[18] *Id.* (paraphrasing 28 U.S.C. § 636(b)(1)(A)).

maintenance of a class action, ... and to involuntarily dismiss an action."[19] Because denials of applications for *in forma pauperis* status and for appointment of counsel effectively may dispose of habeas corpus petitions,[20] they, too, seem appropriately treated as dispositive matters subject to *de novo* review by the district court as of right. Perhaps the simplest rule for distinguishing between nondispositive and dispositive matters, insofar as the latter are not expressly specified in section 636(b)(1) of the Magistrates Act, is that matters are "dispositive" if they are appealable as of right either as a final judgment or its equivalent[21] or as a grant or denial of an injunction.[22]

d. *Procedure for referral*. Neither the Magistrates Act nor Habeas Rule 8(b) specifies how the district judge should decide whether to refer a petition or a related matter to a magistrate judge. Instead, referrals depend on highly variable local rules and practices and on the workloads and preferences of individual district judges.

The rules of a number of district courts require district judges automatically to refer all or at least all noncapital postconviction petitions to magistrate judges, or to do so unless one or both parties formally oppose referral in their initial pleading.[23] In other districts, the district judge to whom the petition initially is assigned has the discretion to refer to a magistrate judge either all matters pertaining to the petition or such tasks (for example, discovery motions) as the district judge designates. In the latter districts, the parties may file motions asking the court to refer the petition or matters pertaining to it to a magistrate judge.

---

[19] 28 U.S.C. § 636(b)(1)(A) (1994). *See* Rilling v. Burlington Northern Ry. Co., 909 F.2d 399, 400 (9th Cir. 1990) (review of magistrate judge's grant of summary judgment is *de novo*). *Cf.* Lakes v. Ford, 779 F.2d 1578, 1579 (11th Cir. 1986) (apparently treating magistrate judge's order dismissing one of petitioner's claims on motion by *petitioner* as nondispositive).

[20] *See* Roberts v. United States Dist. Ct., 339 U.S. 844, 845 (1950) (denial of *in forma pauperis* status is appealable final judgment because of its capacity effectively to end the litigation); *supra* §§ 12.1 (same), 12.5 (potentially dispositive effect of applications for appointment of counsel).

[21] *See* 28 U.S.C. § 1291 (1994); Cohen v. Beneficial Indus. Loan Corp., 337 U.S. 541 (1949) (collateral order doctrine). *See supra* §§ 12.1, 12.5, 13.6b, 14.2 & *infra* § 35.1 (collateral order rule permits appeals from denial of applications for *in forma pauperis* status, appointment of counsel, stays of execution, and bail as well as in other habeas corpus contexts).

[22] *See* 28 U.S.C. § 1292(a) (1994).

[23] *See* Wingo v. Wedding, 418 U.S. 461 (1974) (discussing automatic referral rule), *overruled on other grounds*, Act of Oct. 21, 1976, Pub. L. No. 94-577, 90 Stat. 2730, *codified*, 28 U.S.C. § 636(b) (1994); Rule 8(b) of the Rules Governing § 2254 Cases.

§ 18.2. Objections and *de novo* determinations on dispositive matters.[1]

a. *Objections.* Once the magistrate judge issues a report and recommendation on a dispositive matter, any party aggrieved by the recommended disposition or *any* aspect of the report has 10 days from the date the report is served on that party to file objections with the district judge.[2] Because the decision not to object to unfavorable portions of a magistrate judge's report may have a decisive impact on a party's rights at both the trial and appellate levels, such a decision requires careful and timely consideration of its short- and long-term consequences.

In the first place, the failure to object to a factfinding, legal conclusion, recommendation, or other "portions of the [magistrate judge's] report" forgoes the petitioner's otherwise unqualified right to insist upon a "de novo determination" of that aspect of the report.[3] To illustrate, by objecting to an aspect of the magistrate judge's report, a party *obliges* the district judge (1) to review that aspect of the report *de novo* — whether or not it is a factual or legal matter;[4] (2) to substitute the district judge's judgment for that of the magistrate judge on the matter,[5] hence to "reject, or modify, in whole or in part" any finding, reasoning, or recommendation with which the district judge disagrees;[6] and (3) to consider the need to "receive further evidence or recommit the matter to the magistrate with instructions."[7] By contrast, if no objection is made, the district judge has

---

§ 18.2. [1] *See generally* authority cited *supra* § 18.1a n.1. Review of magistrate judges' actions on "nondispositive" pretrial matters is discussed *supra* § 18.1a, and the distinction between dispositive and nondispositive matters is discussed *supra* § 18.1c. The local rules of individual district courts modify many of the rules discussed in this section.

[2] 28 U.S.C. § 636(b)(1) (1994); Rule 8(b)(3) of the Rules Governing § 2254 Cases. *See* FED. R. CIV. P. 6(a) (method for counting days; if prescribed time period is less than 11 days, intermediate Saturdays, Sundays, and holidays do *not* count). The 10-day period runs from the date the objecting party is "served with a copy" of the magistrate judge's report, not necessarily from the date the report is filed. 28 U.S.C. § 636(b)(1) (1994). Mail service extends the 10-day period by three days. FED. R. CIV. P. 6(e). At least one circuit has held that the "mailbox rule" for notices of appeal filed by *pro se* prisoners — which deems a document to be filed upon delivery to prison authorities (*see infra* § 35.2a) — applies to a *pro se* prisoner's written objections to a magistrate judge's report and recommendation. *See* Lara v. Johnson, 141 F.3d 239, 241 n.2 (5th Cir. 1998); Thompson v. Raspberry, 993 F.2d 513, 515 (5th Cir. 1993) (*per curiam*).

[3] 28 U.S.C. § 636(b)(1) (1994); Rule 8(b)(4) of the Rules Governing § 2254 Cases.

[4] *See* Thomas v. Arn, 474 U.S. 140, 150 & n.8 (1985) (plain language of statute recognizes no distinction between legal and factual matters); McLeod, Alexander, Powel & Apffel, P.C. v. Quarles, 925 F.2d 853, 856 n.5 (5th Cir. 1991).

[5] *See Thomas v. Arn, supra,* 474 U.S. at 151 n.10 (distinguishing nondeferential review of dispositive matters as of right from less exacting standards).

[6] 28 U.S.C. § 636(b)(1) (1994). *See* Rule 8(b)(4) of the Rules Governing § 2254 Cases.

[7] 28 U.S.C. § 636(b)(1) (1994). *See* United States v. Koenig, 912 F.2d 1190, 1191-93 (9th Cir. 1990) (describing *de novo* review in context of pretrial detention determination); Rilling v. Burlington

the all but unreviewable discretion to enter the magistrate judge's recommendation as a final judgment — with or without reading it[8] — or to subject the report to review "under a de novo or any other standard" and take such action as the district judge chooses.[9]

Equally or more critical, a majority of the federal circuit courts, exercising their "supervisory powers" over appeals,[10] *entirely precludes* appellate review of legal conclusions or, at least, the factual findings that a district judge has adopted without objection from a magistrate judge's report, except upon grounds of plain error or manifest injustice or (in some circuits) if explicit notice of the preclusion rule was not given.[11] Although the Supreme Court has resisted reading

---

Northern Ry. Co., 909 F.2d 399, 400 (9th Cir. 1990) (describing *de novo* review of magistrate judge's grant of summary judgment).

[8] *See Thomas v. Arn, supra*, 474 U.S. at 151 (practice of Judge Metzner, then chairman of Judicial Conference Committee on administration of magistrate judge system, who informed congressional committee that he "'merely sign[s] the magistrate's order'" if no party objects to it).

[9] *Id.* at 154 ("while the statute does not require the judge to review an issue *de novo* if no objections are filed, it does not preclude further review by the district judge, *sua sponte* or at the request of a party, under a *de novo* or any other standard"). *See, e.g.*, United States v. Jaramillo, 891 F.2d 620, 624, 628 (7th Cir. 1989), *cert. denied*, 496 U.S. 939 (1990) (under Magistrates Act, district judge has "'widest discretion' possible" to review any part of magistrate judge's report; magistrate judge's decision to view argument as waived not binding on district judge).

[10] *Thomas v. Arn, supra*, 474 U.S. at 146.

[11] *See, e.g.*, Griffini v. Mitchell, 31 F.3d 690, 692 (8th Cir. 1994); Kelly v. Withrow, 25 F.3d 363, 365-66 (6th Cir.), *cert. denied*, 513 U.S. 1061 (1994) (failure to file objections to magistrate's report precludes appellate review; if objections are filed but are insufficiently specific, error is nonjurisdictional and may be excused in interests of justice); Roldan v. Racette, 984 F.2d 85, 89 (2d Cir. 1993); Wilson v. McMacken, 786 F.2d 216, 220 (6th Cir. 1986); Praylow v. Martin, 761 F.2d 179, 180 n.1 (4th Cir.), *cert. denied*, 474 U.S. 1009 (1985); McCarthy v. Manson, 714 F.2d 234, 237 (2d Cir. 1983); Deloney v. Estelle, 661 F.2d 1061, 1063 (5th Cir. 1981); Pendleton v. Rumsfeld, 628 F.2d 102, 106 (D.C. Cir. 1980); Park Motor Mart, Inc. v. Ford Motor Co., 616 F.2d 603, 605 (1st Cir. 1980). *But see* Whitmore v. Avery, 26 F.3d 1426, 1428 n.3 (8th Cir. 1994), *vac'd & remanded on other grounds*, 513 U.S. 1141 (1995) (8th Circuit has not adopted rule that failure to object to magistrate's report and recommendation constitutes waiver of appeal); Cavanaugh v. Kincheloe, 877 F.2d 1443, 1447-49 (9th Cir. 1989) (in absence of local rule of court treating failure to object to aspect of magistrate judge's report as waiver of appeal, court refuses to interpret FED. R. CIV. P. 72(b) or any other generally applicable provision to bar petitioner's appeal of claim that magistrate judge failed to address and petitioner failed to mention in objections to magistrate judge's report). The same rule applies when the state fails to make a timely objection. *See e.g.*, Martinez v. Ylst, 951 F.2d 1153, 1156 & n.2 (9th Cir. 1991); *Praylow v. Martin, supra* at 180 n.1; Weir v. Fletcher, 658 F.2d 1126, 1127 n.1 (6th Cir.), *rev'd on other grounds*, 455 U.S. 603 (1981).

The 5th, 9th, and 11th Circuits limit their waiver rules to unobjected-to *factual* determinations. *See* United States v. Carrillo-Morales, 27 F.3d 1054, 1061-62 (5th Cir. 1994), *cert. denied*, 513 U.S. 1178 (1995) (given 5th Circuit rule that appellate bar for failure to object to magistrate judge's report applies "only to a magistrate judge's findings of fact and not to his conclusions of law," state did not waive appellate argument by failing to object to portion of report that resolved relevant "question of law, although based upon factual findings"); Carter v. Collins, 918 F.2d

1198, 1203 (5th Cir. 1990); Britt v. Simi Valley Unified School Dist., 708 F.2d 452, 454 (9th Cir. 1983); Tijerina v. Estelle, 692 F.2d 3, 5 n.1 (5th Cir. 1982); Nettles v. Wainwright, 677 F.2d 404, 409 (5th Cir. 1982) (*en banc*); McCall v. Andrus, 628 F.2d 1185, 1187 (9th Cir. 1980), *cert. denied,* 450 U.S. 996 (1981). *See also* Brand v. Lewis, 784 F.2d 1515, 1517 (11th Cir. 1986). *See generally Thomas v. Arn, supra,* 474 U.S. at 146 n.4 (discussing cases). In the 5th and 11th Circuits, no waiver occurs unless the magistrate judge expressly informs the parties that they have 10 days to object to any adverse determinations and that failure to object will bar review of the matter on appeal. *See, e.g., United States v. Carrillo-Morales, supra* at 1061 n.14; Wiley v. Wainwright, 709 F.2d 1412, 1413 n.1 (11th Cir. 1983); Sockwell v. Maggio, 709 F.2d 341, 343 (5th Cir. 1983), *cert. denied,* 471 U.S. 1020 (1985). *See also Thomas v. Arn, supra* at 155 (similar practice of 6th Circuit). In the latter circuits, absent affirmative indicia in the record that the magistrate judge informed the parties of the consequences of a failure to object, there is no bar to raising an unobjected-to issue on appeal. *See* Ware v. King, 694 F.2d 89, 91 (5th Cir. 1982), *cert. denied,* 461 U.S. 930 (1983); *Tijerina v. Estelle, supra* at 5; Hardin v. Wainwright, 678 F.2d 589, 591 (5th Cir. 1982); *Deloney v. Estelle, supra* at 373. The 2d and 10th Circuits apply a similar "warning" rule when a habeas corpus petitioner acts *pro se. See, e.g.,* Frank v. Johnson, 968 F.2d 298, 300 (2d Cir.), *cert. denied,* 506 U.S. 1038 (1992) ("To alleviate the unreasonable burden placed on a *pro se* litigant by a waiver rule found only in case law, this Court requires the magistrate's report to warn the *pro se* litigant of the consequences of the failure to object."); Moore v. United States, 950 F.2d 656, 659 (10th Cir. 1991) (*pro se* petitioner's failure to object will not be deemed waiver unless petitioner was adequately advised of time period for filing objections and consequences of failure to object). The 8th Circuit vacillated for some years (*compare* Lorin Corp. v. Goto & Co., 700 F.2d 1202, 1205-07 (8th Cir. 1983) (failure to object to magistrate judge's report does not bar appeal) *with* Matter of Assarsson, 687 F.2d 1157, 1160 (8th Cir. 1982) (party that did not include issue in objections to magistrate judge's report may not appeal resolution of that issue)), but now appears to have settled on the rule that the petitioner does not waive "appeal by failing to object [to a magistrate judge's report] when the questions involved are questions of law or mixed questions of law and fact, or when neither the local district court rule nor the magistrate's notice has clearly informed the plaintiff that failure to object to the magistrate's report will result in waiver of the right to appeal." Thompson v. Nix, 897 F.2d 356, 357 (8th Cir. 1990) (*per curiam*).

On the "plain error"/"manifest injustice" exception, see, *e.g., Carter v. Collins, supra* at 1203 (because petitioner failed to object to magistrate judge's report, appellate court reviews magistrate judge's factual findings only for plain error or manifest injustice); Snyder v. Ridenour, 889 F.2d 1363, 1366 (4th Cir. 1989) (under 4th Circuit's "fundamental error doctrine," court of appeals will address issue not addressed in petitioner's objections to magistrate judge's report if alleged error is "plain," "'refusal to consider [the error] would result in the denial of fundamental justice,'" and error is "so serious and flagrant that it goes to the very integrity of the trial" (quoting Stewart v. Hall, 770 F.2d 1267, 1271 (4th Cir. 1985))); Henley v. Johnson, 885 F.2d 790, 794 (11th Cir. 1989) (*dicta*) ("plain error or manifest injustice" will excuse failure to object to magistrate judge's factfinding and permit appeal to 11th Circuit). If the magistrate judge's ruling is not brought to the district court's attention and is neither adopted nor rejected by the district court, there is no final order, and the court of appeals has no jurisdiction to review the matter. *See* United States v. Ecker, 923 F.2d 7, 8-9 (1st Cir. 1991) (discussed *infra* note 37).

this "waiver of appeal by nonobjection" rule into the Magistrates Act,[12] it has upheld the supervisory authority of courts of appeals to adopt and enforce a waiver rule as long as the magistrate judge informs the parties that a failure to object in a timely fashion waives the aggrieved party's right to appeal a subsequent district court order endorsing the magistrate judge's report.[13] Because, in a majority of the circuits, a knowing failure to object all but ends the litigation on the note struck by the magistrate judge,[14] a party should proceed with extreme caution before forgoing the opportunity to object to a magistrate judge's report or to any of its contents.

The brevity of the period in which a petitioner must act in order to prevent statutory waiver of district court review as of right (and, in most circuits, to prevent some kind of appellate waiver) makes magistrate judge practice a dangerous trap for the unwary.[15] This is especially so in "waiver of appeal" circuits because the right being waived has not even accrued at the time it is waived.[16] To ensure that parties are making meaningful decisions about objections and not simply waiving rights by failing to act quickly enough, the courts should liberally grant extensions of time upon appropriate request.[17]

The Magistrates Act and Habeas Rule 8(b) state that the district judge "shall make a de novo determination of those portions of the report *or* specified proposed findings or recommendations to which objection is made."[18] It is clear enough from this provision that, to avoid waiver, a party must object specifically to proposed magisterial *findings*.[19] Beyond findings, however, the "or" italicized

---

[12] *Thomas v. Arn, supra*, 474 U.S. at 148-49 ("we need not decide whether the Act mandates a waiver of appellate review absent objections"). *See id.* at 155 (waiver rule is "nonjurisdictional").

[13] *Id.* at 155.

[14] *But cf. supra* note 11 & *infra* notes 27-37 and accompanying text (exceptions to waiver rule).

[15] Because prisoner proceedings are the only ones in which the district judge may refer hearings on the merits to magistrate judges without the parties' consent, *see supra* § 18.1b, the waiver rules approved in *Thomas v. Arn, supra* (a habeas corpus case) have their greatest impact in such proceedings.

[16] *Cf. Thomas v. Arn, supra*, 474 U.S. at 156 (Brennan, J., dissenting) ("I fail to understand how petitioner could have waived her right to appeal a final order *before* that order was rendered" (emphasis in original)).

[17] *See id.* at 144 (majority opinion) (waiver recognized in case occurred only after magistrate judge informed petitioner that "[f]ailure to file objections within the specified time waives the right to appeal" and petitioner "sought and received [a month-long] extension of time to file objections"). The 1985 amendment to FED. R. CIV. P. 6(a) excluding weekends and legal holidays from the computation of the 10 days modestly ameliorates the problems identified here. *See supra* note 2.

[18] 28 U.S.C. § 636(b)(1) (1994) (emphasis added). *See* Rule 8(b)(4) of the Rules Governing § 2254 Cases.

[19] *See, e.g.,* Praylow v. Martin, 761 F.2d 179, 180 n.1 (4th Cir.), *cert. denied,* 474 U.S. 1009 (1985) (state's failure to object to magistrate judge's finding with regard to date of appointment of

above, in conjunction with the reference to "portions" of the report and "recommendations to which objection is made," leave in doubt whether the objecting party need specify only the disposition or outcome to which objection is made or whether, in addition, the objecting party must specify particular conclusions of law or even individual aspects of the magistrate judge's legal reasoning that are objectionable.[20] The Magistrates Act's and Habeas Rules' ambiguity and the severe consequences of a failure to object give parties little choice but to object in a comprehensive manner to any aspect of the magistrate judge's report that is by itself objectionable or that does or could contribute to an objectionable fact-finding, legal conclusion, or proposed disposition.[21]

Tricky timing and content questions also may arise when reference of the entire petition to the magistrate judge relegates both dispositive and non-dispositive matters to the magistrate judge. If, for example, a magistrate judge denies petitioner's motion for discovery, grants her a hearing, and rules adversely to her at the hearing on an evidentiary point, the question arises whether the petitioner may await the magistrate judge's final recommendation before objecting to the denial of discovery and the evidentiary ruling, or whether she must immediately (*i.e.*, within 10 days) object to the denial of discovery and the evidentiary ruling, notwithstanding that the recommendation may render objection unnecessary.[22]

---

trial counsel prevents state from arguing on appeal that appointment occurred earlier than magistrate judge found).

[20] *Cf. Thomas v. Arn, supra*, 474 U.S. at 152 ("Congress apparently assumed ... that any party who was dissatisfied *for any reason* with the magistrate's report would file objections and those objections would trigger district court review." (emphasis added)); Matter of Assarsson, 687 F.2d 1157, 1160 (8th Cir. 1982) (discussed *supra* note 11).

[21] Courts have shown some liberality in interpreting less-than-comprehensive objections filed by *pro se* petitioners. *See, e.g.*, Belk v. Purkett, 15 F.3d 803, 814-15 (8th Cir. 1994) (although *pro se* petitioner's objections were "not as ideally precise as a pleading from a trained lawyer," district court should have conducted *de novo* review, especially given relative brevity of record); McKeever v. Block, 932 F.2d 795, 799 (9th Cir. 1991) (*pro se* litigant's communications to court should be liberally construed as objections, although court decides not to treat *pro se* letter as objection because document promised further filings that never materialized and did not specifically request review of magistrate judge's action); Williams v. Lockhart, 849 F.2d 1134, 1138 (8th Cir. 1988) (although petitioner's *pro se* objections to magistrate judge's recommendations did not specifically address conflict of interest aspect of ineffective assistance claim, court liberally construes *pro se* petitioner's objections to include reference to factual matters relevant to that aspect of claim). *See also* Kelly v. Withrow, 25 F.3d 363, 365-66 (6th Cir.), *cert. denied*, 513 U.S. 1061 (1994) (applying "interests of justice" standard to excuse attorney's failure to make specific objections because counsel's reference to prior pleadings adequately informed district court of petitioner's position on disputed issues).

[22] FED. R. CIV. P. 72(a), discussed *supra* § 18.1a, seems to require parties to object to all nondispositive matters within 10 days of the challenged ruling. The Magistrates Act is silent on the matter.

Difficult questions also may arise if portions of the magistrate judge's report — for example, individual findings or the rejection of alternative legal arguments — are adverse to a party, although the bottom-line proposed disposition favors that party. In this situation, the winning litigant may find it advisable to object to unfavorable aspects of a favorable report in order to avoid waiving the right to have the district judge redetermine *de novo* or the appellate court reconsider on appeal the *unfavorable* aspect of the report in the event that the district judge rejects the magistrate judge's *favorable* determinations and rules against the party who prevailed before the magistrate judge.[23]

One solution to these problems is to ask the magistrate judge or the district judge to establish an orderly and efficient schedule for filing objections that permits the parties (1) to await the magistrate judge's final report before deciding whether to object to preliminary or procedural actions taken by the magistrate judge before producing the report;[24] (2) to respond to each other's objections and file counterobjections; and (3) to seek reconsideration in the district court and to appeal rulings of the district court if its bottom-line disposition differs from that recommended by the magistrate judge.[25] The policy of limiting judicial caseloads, which the Supreme Court has emphasized in interpreting the Magistrates Act and in approving the courts of appeals' "waiver of appeal" rules, should make magistrate judges particularly receptive to procedures designed to limit the occasions on which objections must be filed and the length, inclusivity, and contingent character of the objections.[26]

---

[23] The courts have *not* routinely found that objections were waived in the situations postulated in this and the preceding paragraph in text. *See, e.g.,* Turpin v. Kassulke, 26 F.3d 1392, 1399-400 (6th Cir. 1994), *cert. denied,* 513 U.S. 1118 (1995) (state did not waive right to contest magistrate judge's and district court's determination on appeal by failing to object to unfavorable finding in magistrate judge's report that ultimately recommended that state prevail on summary judgment motion; "[i]f we were to require a party in the Commonwealth's position to present objections to a magistrate judge's proposed adverse resolution of a secondary issue, we would force that party to articulate objections to a recommendation that it prevail. Such a requirement would only frustrate the judicial economy and litigant expense policies that underlie the ... rule [requiring objections to magistrate judge's report]."). *But cf. Praylow v. Martin, supra,* 761 F.2d at 180 n.1 (discussed *supra* note 19). Indeed, the judicial economy policies underlying the Magistrates Act, *see infra* note 26 and accompanying text, suggest that the courts would resist the hypertechnical outcomes imagined here. Rather than predicting how the courts would decide these issues, the discussion here is designed to prevent the issues from arising.

[24] In some situations, a party may need to object immediately to preliminary rulings to avoid irreparable injury. Grants of discovery of arguably privileged materials or denials of stays of execution are examples.

[25] The third proposal is supported by the notice requirements the courts have endorsed in adopting and upholding "waiver of appeal" rules. *See, e.g.,* Thomas v. Arn, 474 U.S. 140, 144, 145, 155 & n.15 (1985); *supra* note 11; *infra* notes 27-31 and accompanying text.

[26] *See Thomas v. Arn, supra,* 474 U.S. at 146-47, 150-51, 152-53; United States v. Raddatz, 447 U.S. 667, 677 (1980).

In upholding "waiver of appeal" rules, the Supreme Court has recognized the need for fair administration of such rules and for exceptions "in the interests of justice."[27] As a "waiver" provision[28] affecting the important right to appeal,[29] a rule attaching adverse consequences to nonobjection ought to require a knowing and intelligent default on the part of the waiving party.[30] At the least, the magistrate judge or district judge should (1) inform the litigants at the beginning and end of magisterial proceedings in "waiver of appeal" circuits that a failure to object in a timely manner to a magistrate judge's report or to any aspect of it waives the parties' right to appeal a judgment adopting the report or that aspect of it;[31] (2) liberally grant reasonable extensions of the 10-day filing period on request;[32] and (3) "excuse the default" when doing so is "in the interests of justice."[33] Although the Supreme Court has reserved deciding "what standards the courts of appeals must apply in considering exceptions to their waiver rules," it has suggested a "plain error" rule[34] and noted one circuit's practice of making exceptions for *pro se* petitioners who file late objections.[35]

---

[27] *Thomas v. Arn, supra*, 474 U.S. at 155.

[28] *Id.* at 152, 155.

[29] *See generally* Evitts v. Lucey, 469 U.S. 387 (1985); *supra* §§ 7.2e, 9.1 n.28.

[30] *See* Orsini v. Wallace, 913 F.2d 474, 483-84 (8th Cir. 1990) (Bright, J., dissenting), *cert. denied*, 498 U.S. 1128 (1991) (although issue not raised by parties, court should exercise discretion to consider validity of petitioner's uncounseled consent, using nonexplanatory consent form, to final disposition of habeas corpus case by magistrate judge). The traditional waiver standard is in Johnson v. Zerbst, 304 U.S. 458, 464 (1938). *Accord, e.g.*, Tague v. Louisiana, 444 U.S. 469, 470-71 (1980); Fay v. Noia, 372 U.S. 391, 439 (1963). *See Thomas v. Arn, supra*, 474 U.S. at 144-45, 155 (waiver apparently was knowing and intelligent); *infra* § 26.2d nn.24-43 and accompanying text.

[31] *See Thomas v. Arn, supra*, 474 U.S. at 144; 2d, 5th, 8th, 9th, 10th, and 11th Circuit decisions cited *supra* note 11. *Cf.* Snyder v. Ridenour, 889 F.2d 1363, 1366 (4th Cir. 1989) (in personal injury action, magistrate judge's notice using words "may result in waiver," instead of "waives," complies with notice requirement of *Thomas v. Arn*).

[32] *See supra* note 17 and accompanying text.

[33] *Thomas v. Arn, supra*, 474 U.S. at 155. *See* authority cited *supra* note 11. *See also* Collier v. Jones, 910 F.2d 770, 774 n.3 (11th Cir. 1990) ("Although normally we do not consider arguments on appeal that have not been presented to the magistrate or district court, the argument raised by [petitioner] ... is sufficiently similar to the argument [that petitioner] presented ... to the magistrate that we are confident that the magistrate's ruling implicitly encompassed such an argument.").

[34] *Thomas v. Arn, supra*, 474 U.S. at 155 n.15 (citing FED. R. CRIM. P. 52(b)). Lower court decisions applying the "plain error" and "miscarriage of justice" exceptions to the rule forbidding appeal of unobjected-to magistrate judges' determinations are cited *supra* note 11.

[35] *Thomas v. Arn, supra*, 474 U.S. at 146 (discussing Patterson v. Mintzes, 717 F.2d 284 (6th Cir. 1983)). *See* 2d and 10th Circuit decisions cited *supra* note 11. *See also* decisions cited *supra* note 21. Excuses might include the absence of a "knowing and intelligent" waiver, *see supra* note 11; *infra* § 26.2d nn.24-43 and accompanying text, and "cause" as defined in Wainwright v. Sykes, 433 U.S. 72 (1977), and its progeny, *see infra* §§ 26.3b, 28.3c. In one respect, *Thomas v. Arn*,

The rule of preclusion forbidding district courts and courts of appeals to consider objections to magistrate judges' proposed findings and conclusions if objections were not timely filed in the district court can be waived by the opposing party's or the district court's failure to invoke the rule.[36]

Alternatively, a party may seek to overcome the preclusive effect of a failure to object by filing either (1) a motion for reconsideration after the district court rules, asking that court to exercise its discretion to review the magistrate judge's determinations *de novo* or under a lesser standard, or (2) a "motion for permission to appeal," asking the court of appeals to exercise its discretion to hear the case.[37]

District court rules sometimes control the form and length of objections to magistrate judges' reports.[38] There are limits, however, on a district court's abil-

---

supra, suggests a broader range of excuses than is available under *Sykes'* procedural default rules. *Compare Thomas v. Arn, supra,* 474 U.S. at 155 n.15 (suggesting plain error excuse for default) *with* Smith v. Murray, 477 U.S. 527, 533-36, 537-38 (1986) (plain error provides no excuse for *Sykes*-type default). In another respect, however, *Thomas* suggests a narrower range of excuses. *Compare Thomas v. Arn, supra,* 474 U.S. at 155 *and id.* at 158 (Stevens, J., dissenting) (district court's reaching merits despite petitioner's failure to file objections does not require appeals court to reach merits) *with, e.g.,* Ulster County Ct. v. Allen, 442 U.S. 140, 154 (1979) (state court's reaching merits of unobjected-to claim bars *Sykes*-type default) *and infra* § 26.2e (same).

[36] *See, e.g.,* Nabors v. United States, 929 F.2d 354, 354-55 (8th Cir. 1990) (although section 2255 movant filed untimely objections to magistrate judge's report, government did not object to consideration of objections as untimely and district court addressed them; court of appeals accordingly treats filing deadline as having been extended implicitly). *Cf. infra* § 22.1 nn.38, 47 and accompanying text (procedural defenses waived by state's failure to invoke them in adequate and timely manner).

[37] There is some basis for these last-resort procedures in the inherent discretion of a court to waive nonjurisdictional procedural bars in the interests of justice. *See Thomas v. Arn, supra,* 474 U.S. at 154 (quoted *supra* note 9); Park Motor Mart, Inc. v. Ford Motor Co., 616 F.2d 603, 605 (1st Cir. 1980) (motion for reconsideration and appeal from denial of motion is possible remedy for failure to object in timely fashion to magistrate judge's order); *infra* Chapter 34 (reconsideration motions). *See also* Summers v. Utah, 927 F.2d 1165, 1168-69 (10th Cir. 1991) (upon district court's adoption of magistrate judge's recommendations because plaintiff did not file timely objections, and upon district court's summary denial of plaintiff's FED. R. CIV. P. 60(b) motion for reconsideration alleging that objections *were* timely filed but were erroneously omitted from docket sheet, court of appeals remands for express consideration of Rule 60(b) motion); United States v. Ecker, 923 F.2d 7, 8-9 (1st Cir. 1991) (after magistrate judge committed defendant to mental institution for evaluation of competency to stand trial, defendant erroneously failed to seek review by district court and instead appealed commitment order to court of appeals; court of appeals dismisses appeal for lack of jurisdiction, recommending that defendant ask district court to reconsider commitment order as basis either to obtain relief or to secure final judgment that court of appeals could review).

[38] *See* Smith v. Frank, 923 F.2d 139, 140-42 (9th Cir. 1991).

ity to treat such rules as "jurisdictional" by making their violation a basis for refusing to hear timely objections.[39]

b. De novo *determination.* Once objections to the magistrate judge's report with regard to dispositive matters have been filed, the district judge must determine those matters *de novo.*[40] *De novo* review as of right applies to all factual and legal matters to which objection is made.[41] "*De novo*" review requires the district judge to substitute her judgment for that of the magistrate judge on all objected-to matters[42] but does not require her to rehear the evidence or additional arguments,[43] although she *may* do so.[44] Procedurally, *de novo*

---

[39] *See id.* at 142 (remanding district court's order rejecting plaintiff's timely filed objections to magistrate judge's report that violated local rule on length of objections with instructions that "objections ... be deemed timely filed but thereafter subject to application of the local rules which are not to be regarded as limitations on jurisdiction").

[40] 28 U.S.C. § 636(b)(1) (1994); Rule 8(b)(4) of the Rules Governing § 2254 Cases. *See* Gomez v. United States, 490 U.S. 858, 864-69, 874 n.28 (1989) (discussed *supra* § 18.1b n.9); Hudson v. Gammon, 46 F.3d 785, 786 (8th Cir. 1995), *cert. denied,* 518 U.S. 1025 (1996) (district court's failure to conduct *de novo* review of objected-to portions of magistrate judge's report and recommendations required reversal and remand); Koetting v. Thompson, 995 F.2d 37, 40 (5th Cir. 1993) (*per curiam*); Ramirez v. Turner, 991 F.2d 351, 354 (7th Cir. 1993); Stokes v. Singletary, 952 F.2d 1567 (11th Cir. 1992); Andrews v. Deland, 943 F.2d 1162, 1170 (10th Cir. 1991), *cert. denied,* 502 U.S. 1110 (1992); McLeod, Alexander, Powel & Apffel, P.C. v. Quarles, 925 F.2d 853, 856 n.5 (5th Cir. 1991); Kelley v. McGinnis, 899 F.2d 612, 615 (7th Cir. 1990) (*per curiam*) (section 1983 case); Flournoy v. Marshall, 842 F.2d 875, 875-76 (6th Cir. 1988); Hernandez v. Estelle, 711 F.2d 619, 620 (5th Cir. 1983); Hinman v. McCarthy, 676 F.2d 343, 346-47 (9th Cir.), *cert. denied,* 459 U.S. 1048 (1982); Thompson v. Scurr, 668 F.2d 999, 1004 (8th Cir.), *cert. denied,* 459 U.S. 883 (1982); Washington v. Estelle, 648 F.2d 276, 282 (5th Cir.), *cert. denied,* 454 U.S. 899 (1981); *supra* § 18.1b.

[41] *See* Stokes v. Singletary, 952 F.2d 1567 (11th Cir. 1992) (*de novo* review of factual issues); LoConte v. Dugger, 847 F.2d 745, 750 (11th Cir.), *cert. denied,* 488 U.S. 958 (1988) (district court must consider factual issues *de novo* if any party files timely and specific objection to magistrate judge's factfinding); *supra* §§ 18.1b, 18.2a nn.4-9 and accompanying text.

[42] *See* United States v. Koenig, 912 F.2d 1190, 1191-93 (9th Cir. 1990) (describing *de novo* review in context of pretrial detention determination); Rilling v. Burlington Northern Ry. Co., 909 F.2d 399, 400 (9th Cir. 1990) (describing *de novo* review of magistrate judge's grant of summary judgment); *supra* § 18.2a notes 3-7 and accompanying text.

[43] *See, e.g.,* United States v. Raddatz, 447 U.S. 667, 673-84 (1980) (district court properly concurred with magistrate judge's resolution, following hearing, of credibility dispute between criminal defendant and law enforcement official without rehearing conflicting testimony itself; rejecting due process and Article III objections to denial of hearing); Johnson v. Rodgers, 756 F.2d 79, 81 (10th Cir. 1985) ("*de novo* determination does not, however, mean that a *de novo* hearing is required"); United States v. Miller, 609 F.2d 336, 340 (8th Cir. 1979); Campbell v. United States Dist. Ct., 501 F.2d 196, 206-07 (9th Cir. 1973), *cert. denied,* 419 U.S. 879 (1974).

[44] 28 U.S.C. § 636(b)(1) (1994) ("judge may receive further evidence"); Rule 8(b)(4) of the Rules Governing § 2254 Cases. *See United States v. Raddatz, supra,* 447 U.S. at 676, 680 ("'[i]f

determination simply requires the district judge to give careful consideration to the transcript of the proceedings before the magistrate judge and the objections and to reach an independent judgment.[45]

[the judge] finds there is a problem as to the credibility of a witness or witnesses or for other good reasons, *it may, in the exercise of its discretion,* call and hear the testimony of a witness or witnesses in an adversary proceeding'" (quoting *Campbell v. United States Dist. Ct., supra,* 501 F.2d at 206 (emphasis in original))); United States v. Lieberman, 608 F.2d 889, 900-01 (1st Cir. 1979), *cert. denied,* 444 U.S. 1019 (1980) (*de novo* review obligation met by oral argument on objections and review of record before magistrate judge).

[45] *See, e.g.,* Hudson v. Gammon, 46 F.3d 785, 786 (8th Cir. 1995), *cert. denied,* 518 U.S. 1025 (1996) (although objected-to portions of magistrate's report involved state court findings of fact subject to presumption of correctness, district court nonetheless was obliged "to make a de novo assessment, independent of the magistrate judge's conclusions" of whether factual findings were "'fairly supported by the record'"); Ramirez v. Turner, 991 F.2d 351, 354 (7th Cir. 1993) (district judge could not have conducted requisite *de novo* determination because transcript was not prepared until two months after judge's decision); United States v. Hamell, 931 F.2d 466, 468 (8th Cir.), *cert. denied,* 502 U.S. 98 (1991) (*dicta*) (*de novo* review cannot properly occur when district court reviews magistrate judge's factfindings without having access to transcript of magistrate judge's evidentiary hearing); Williams v. Armontrout, 855 F.2d 578, 579 (8th Cir. 1988) (district court obliged to consider objections to magistrate judge's report); *LoConte v. Dugger, supra,* 847 F.2d at 750 (when magistrate judge's finding is based upon oral testimony, district court is obliged to review transcript or listen to tape-recording of proceedings if party objects to magistrate judge's proposed finding); Thompson v. Scurr, 668 F.2d 999, 1004 (8th Cir.), *cert. denied,* 459 U.S. 883 (1982); Moran v. Morris, 665 F.2d 900, 901 (9th Cir. 1981); Washington v. Estelle, 648 F.2d 276, 282 (5th Cir.), *cert. denied,* 454 U.S. 899 (1981); Calderon v. Waco Lighthouse for the Blind, 630 F.2d 352, 355-56 (5th Cir. 1980); United States v. Lewis, 621 F.2d 1382, 1387 (5th Cir. 1980), *cert. denied,* 450 U.S. 935 (1981). *Compare* Nabors v. United States, 929 F.2d 354, 354-55 (8th Cir. 1990) (remanding district court's order adopting magistrate judge's findings because *de novo* consideration required review of tape or transcript of magistrate judge's evidentiary hearing and record contained no indication that review took place) *with* Sumlin v. United States, 46 F.3d 48, 49 (8th Cir. 1995) (*per curiam*) ("mere fact th[at] district court prematurely adopted the magistrate judge's report" prior to receipt of petitioner's objections does not make out "prima facie showing that the district court failed to conduct de novo review") *and* Andrews v. Deland, 943 F.2d 1162, 1170-71 (10th Cir. 1991), *cert. denied,* 502 U.S. 1110 (1992) (on appeal of district court's *de novo* review, court of appeals must examine record to ensure that district court "'consider[ed] the actual testimony ... and not merely ... the magistrate's report and recommendations'"; court of appeals, however, generally "will not look behind a district court's express statement that it engaged in a *de novo* review of the record") *and with* United States v. Hamell, 931 F.2d 466, 468 (8th Cir. 1991) (because transcript of magistrate judge's hearing was available to district court, court of appeals presumes that district court properly conducted *de novo* review of magistrate judge's factfindings, although district court did not affirmatively say it reviewed trial transcript; only upon *prima facie* showing that review was improper — *e.g.,* when district court could not have read transcript because transcript was not yet prepared at time of district court's ruling — does burden shift to district court to specify that *de novo* review occurred) *and* Diaz v. United States, 930 F.2d 832, 835-36 (11th Cir. 1991) (*de novo* review requirement satisfied, although district court adopted magistrate judge's report in entirety without explicitly addressing petitioner's objections to magistrate judge's report and without reiterating magistrate judge's findings and conclusions to

If the district judge *agrees* with the magistrate judge's report and recommendations or disagrees with them *on the law,* the district judge may enter an order saying so without further ado.[46] The district judge may "reject, or modify in whole or in part, the ... recommendations made by the magistrate" or "recommit the matter to the magistrate with instructions."[47] If, however, the district judge *disagrees* with the magistrate judge on a *matter of fact,* particularly a matter having to do with the credibility of a witness, the district judge generally must "recommit the matter to the magistrate with instructions" or conduct a new hearing and personally listen to the witnesses.[48]

---

which petitioner objected) *and* Longmire v. Guste, 921 F.2d 620, 623 (5th Cir. 1991) (district court need not specify that its review of magistrate judge's recommendations was *de novo,* and court of appeals will assume that it was, unless there is evidence to contrary). A "careful scrutiny" requirement is appropriate if the magistrate judge's report turns on credibility issues. Hernandez v. Estelle, 711 F.2d 619, 620 (5th Cir. 1983). *See LoConte v. Dugger, supra,* 847 F.2d at 750. *See generally United States v. Raddatz, supra,* 447 U.S. at 676 (discussed *supra* note 43).

[46] *See United States v. Raddatz, supra,* 447 U.S. at 673-76, 680-81; United States v. Fry, 622 F.2d 1218, 1221 (5th Cir. 1980); *United States v. Lewis, supra,* 621 F.2d at 1386-87.

[47] 28 U.S.C. § 636(b)(1) (1994); Rule 8(b)(4) of the Rules Governing § 2254 Cases. *See United States v. Raddatz, supra,* 447 U.S. at 673-76, 680-81.

[48] *See United States v. Raddatz, supra,* 447 U.S. at 681 n.7 (*dicta*) ("unlikely that a district judge would *reject* a magistrate's proposed findings on credibility when those findings are dispositive and substitute the judge's own appraisal; to do so without seeing and hearing the witness ... whose credibility is in question could well give rise to serious questions which we do not reach" (emphasis in original)); *id.* at 686 (Powell, J., concurring and dissenting in part); Jordan v. Hargett, 34 F.3d 310, 312-14 (5th Cir. 1994), *reh'g en banc granted,* 42 F.3d 1483(5th Cir.), *vac'd & remanded on other grounds,* 53 F.3d 94 (5th Cir. 1995) (*en banc*) (*per curiam*) (district court erred in "rejecting the magistrate's credibility-based fact findings without conducting its own evidentiary hearing"); Louis v. Blackburn, 630 F.2d 1105, 1109 (5th Cir. 1980) ("district judge should not enter an order inconsistent with the credibility choices made by the magistrate without personally hearing the live testimony of the witnesses whose testimony is determinative"); United States v. Bergera, 512 F.2d 391, 393 (9th Cir. 1975). *See also* Gomez v. United States, 490 U.S. 858, 874 (1989) (by implication) (district judge should not assign magistrate judges tasks that district court thereafter cannot "review ... meaningfully"; matters depending upon "not only spoken words but also gestures and attitudes" may not be appropriate for referral if "transcript can[not] recapture the atmosphere" of relevant statement). *But cf.* Proffitt v. Wainwright, 685 F.2d 1227, 1242-43 (11th Cir. 1982), *cert. denied,* 464 U.S. 1002 (1983) (hearing not needed if judge rejects magistrate judge's interpretation of meaning, not credibility, of witness).

Review by the court of appeals of a magistrate judge's findings of fact that the district judge adopted is only for plain error or manifest injustice, as is review of the district court's own findings following its review of the record made before, and of the findings made by, a magistrate judge. *See, e.g.,* Carter v. Collins, 918 F.2d 1198, 1203 (5th Cir. 1990); Harrison v. Ryan, 909 F.2d 84, 85 n.1 (3d Cir.), *cert. denied,* 498 U.S. 1003 (1990) (deferring to magistrate judge's factual finding that district court adopted); Thompson v. Nix, 897 F.2d 356, 357 (8th Cir. 1990) (*per curiam*); *LoConte v. Dugger, supra,* 847 F.2d at 750; *infra* § 37.3b. A less deferential standard of appellate review may apply to factual determinations that the magistrate judge based on documentary evidence, rather than live testimony, and to factual determinations as to which the district court and

Failure of the district judge to review dispositive matters *de novo* following objection, to review the record independently, or to conduct or to order new evidentiary proceedings before overturning a factual (and especially a credibility) finding by the magistrate judge favorable to a party may amount to a violation not only of the Magistrates Act and Habeas Rule 8(b),[49] but also of Article III and the Due Process Clause of the 5th Amendment to the United States Constitution.[50]

---

the magistrate judge disagreed. *See* Fuente Cigar, Ltd. v. Roadway Express, Inc., 925 F.2d 370, 373 (11th Cir. 1991) (if district court rejects magistrate judge's factfindings and substitutes its own, presumption in favor of lower court findings may be relaxed); Case v. Mondragon, 887 F.2d 1388, 1392 n.2 (10th Cir. 1989), *cert. denied,* 494 U.S. 1035 (1990) ("[b]ecause the magistrate did not receive any live testimony on the issue, but merely made findings based upon a review of the state record, the 'clearly erroneous' standard does 'not apply with full force' to the magistrate's findings," and "findings are not given the special deference normally accorded findings based upon a court's assessment of witnesses' credibility" (quoting Archuleta v. Kerby, 864 F.2d 709, 711 n.2 (10th Cir.), *cert. denied,* 490 U.S. 1084 (1989))); Jeffers v. Sargent, 842 F.2d 1008, 1009 (8th Cir. 1988) (because magistrate judge's decision dismissing petition "was based on documentary evidence," court of appeals, upon reviewing that evidence, could "render independent judgment on the proper disposition"). On the standards and procedures for discretionary court of appeals review of a consented-to final decision by the magistrate judge followed by an appeal as of right to the district court, see *supra* § 18.1b n.11.

[49] *See, e.g.,* Stokes v. Singletary, 952 F.2d 1567, 1576 (11th Cir. 1992) (district court violated Magistrates Act by "fail[ing] to accord a *de novo* review of the magistrate's factual findings to which Stokes objected"); Hernandez v. Estelle, 711 F.2d 619, 620 (5th Cir. 1983) (remand with directions to conduct *de novo* determination of question subject to conflicting testimony); other authority cited *supra* notes 40, 45. *Cf.* Williams v. Armontrout, 855 F.2d 578, 579-80 (8th Cir. 1988) (district court obliged to consider objections to magistrate judge's report; if district court improperly fails to consider objections, petitioner must appeal error; failure to appeal district court's error in this regard may result in loss of claim).

[50] *See Gomez v. United States, supra,* 490 U.S. at 864, 872 n.25 (possible Article III implications of cession to magistrate judge of dispositive matters that are not thereafter reviewed or reviewable by district judge); *Louis v. Blackburn, supra,* 630 F.2d at 1105-06 (5th Amendment's Due Process Clause requires judge to hear witnesses if judge's credibility determination is inconsistent with magistrate judge's). *See also United States v. Raddatz, supra,* 447 U.S. at 681 n.7 (quoted *supra* note 48); *id.* at 686 (Powell, J., concurring and dissenting in part). *Cf.* Thomas v. Arn, 474 U.S. 140, 153 (1985) (consistent with Article III, district court may refer dispositive motions to magistrate judge for recommendation if "'entire process takes place under the district court's total control and jurisdiction'" and if district "judge 'exercise[s] the ultimate authority to issue an appropriate order'" (quoting *United States v. Raddatz, supra,* 447 U.S. at 681)); *id.* at 154 (no Article III problem with "waiver of appeal" rules because "[a]ny party that desires *plenary consideration* by the Article III judge of any issue need only ask" (emphasis added)); Moran v. Morris, 665 F.2d 900, 901-02 (9th Cir. 1981) (pretermitting state's argument that "district court could not, consistently with Article III ... delegate an evidentiary hearing where the ultimate issue is the validity of a state court judgment").

Chapter 19

PREHEARING FACT-DEVELOPMENT PROCEDURES

§ 19.1. Counsel's responsibility.

Federal habeas corpus often is a prisoner's last opportunity to ensure that the process by which the state convicted and sentenced her accords with federal law; in capital cases, habeas corpus almost always is the last meaningful chance to do so and, indeed, to appeal to any judicial authority to spare the prisoner's life.[1] In all, and especially in capital, cases, therefore, counsel bears the responsibility of ensuring that all reasonably available avenues of legal redress are considered. This responsibility requires counsel not only to explore thoroughly the *legal* bases for the petitioner's claims,[2] but also to take full advantage of the capacity of federal proceedings to develop the *factual* bases for the claims.[3]

---

§ 19.1. [1] *See* McFarland v. Scott, 512 U.S. 849, 855 (1994) (Congress' adoption of provision of Anti-Drug Abuse Act of 1988, 21 U.S.C. § 848(q), creating right to counsel and support services in capital cases "reflects a determination that quality legal representation is necessary in capital habeas corpus proceedings in light of 'the seriousness of the death penalty and ... the unique and complex nature of the litigation'" and that the services of both counsel and "of investigators and other experts may be critical in the preapplication phase of a habeas corpus proceeding, when possible claims and their factual bases are researched and identified" (quoting *id.* § 848(q)(7))); Brown v. Vasquez, 952 F.2d 1164, 1167-68 (9th Cir.), *cert. denied,* 503 U.S. 1011 (1992) (heavy burden that current law places on habeas corpus prisoners to allege and litigate all possibly available constitutional claims in initial petition creates need for prepetition assistance of counsel and other procedural devices to enable petitioners to meet burden); *supra* §§ 7.1a, 7.2f, 12.3a. *See generally* authority cited *supra* §§ 7.1a n.2, 7.2 n.1.

[2] *See supra* §§ 6.2, 7.1a, 11.1-11.3; *supra* Chapter 9.

[3] *See supra* §§ 4.1, 4.2, 6.2, 7.1a, 11.2, 11.3. Justices O'Connor and Kennedy have suggested that the Court is, and should be, *more* willing to grant habeas corpus petitioners leave to utilize effective *fact*-development procedures than it is to recognize the cognizability of certain kinds of *legal* claims. *See* Keeney v. Tamayo-Reyes, 504 U.S. 1, 19-20 (1992) (O'Connor, J., dissenting) (Court's recent cases cutting back on habeas corpus "all concern the question whether the federal court will *consider* the merits of the claim, that is, whether the court has the *authority* to upset a judgment affirmed on direct appeal.... The question we are considering here [the petitioner's right to an evidentiary hearing] is quite different. Here, the Federal District Court has already determined that it will consider the claimed constitutional violation; the only question is how the court will go about it. When it comes to determining whether a hearing is to be held to resolve a claim that is already properly before a court, the federalism concerns underlying our procedural default cases are diminished somewhat. By this point, our concern is less with encroaching on the territory of the state courts than it is with managing the territory of the federal courts in a manner that will best implement our responsibility to consider habeas petitions.... Federalism, comity, and finality are all advanced by declining to permit relitigation of claims in federal court in certain circumstances; these interests are less significantly advanced once relitigation properly occurs...."); *id.* at 24 (Kennedy, J., dissenting) (Court's recent decisions limit habeas corpus to "actions which present questions federal courts are bound to decide in order to protect constitutional rights. *We ought not to take steps which diminish the likelihood that those courts will base their legal decision on an accurate assessment of the facts*" (emphasis added)). In this view, "once [the cognizability hurdles]

The Rules Governing § 2254 Cases make available several fact development procedures, discussed below, including (1) an order requiring the state to furnish the court with all relevant records of prior trial, appellate, postconviction, and other proceedings (section 19.2); (2) provision of funds to indigent petitioners for essential investigative and expert assistance, including, in some circumstances, before a petition is filed (section 19.3); (3) discovery (section 19.4); (4) "expansion of the record" through the filing of affidavits or other newly developed or discovered documentary or physical evidence (section 19.5); and (5) evidentiary hearings (Chapters 20, 21). Although recent legislation has limited the availability of evidentiary hearings in certain circumstances, that legislation does not amend the Rules Governing § 2254 Cases nor otherwise cut back on the other listed fact-development procedures, which are discussed in this Chapter.[4] The timing of requests for the procedures listed above is discussed in §§ 11.7d, 16.2, and 17.1 *supra* and below.

§ 19.2. The state record.[1]

In its answer, the state must "indicate what transcripts (of pretrial, trial, sentencing, and post-conviction proceedings) are available, when they can be furnished, and also what proceedings have been recorded and not transcribed."[2] Respondent also must append to the answer copies of (1) all the portions of the transcripts of prior (pretrial, trial, appellate, postconviction, and other) proceedings that the answering party deems relevant;[3] (2) petitioner's brief(s) on direct appeal from the judgment of conviction and sentence; (3) the state appellate

---

have been surmounted — once a claim is properly before the district court — a habeas petitioner [should be treated] ... like any civil litigant" for purposes of the "right to a hearing [or, presumably, any other less intrusive fact-development procedure] where [the procedure] is necessary to prove the facts supporting his claim." *Id.* at 14-15 (O'Connor, J., dissenting).

[4] *See* Antiterrorism and Effective Death Penalty Act of 1996, Pub. L. 104-132, 110 Stat. 1214 (1996), *codified in relevant part in* 28 U.S.C. § 2254(e)(2) (West 1994 & Supp. 1998) (discussed *infra* Chapter 20). *See also infra* §§ 19.3 n.26, 19.4a n.4, 19.4d n.27, 19.5 n.6 and accompanying text.

§ 19.2. [1] *See generally* RONALD P. SOKOL, FEDERAL HABEAS CORPUS 215-20 (2d ed. 1969); LARRY W. YACKLE, POSTCONVICTION REMEDIES § 120 (1981 & Supp. 1998).

[2] Rule 5 of the Rules Governing § 2254 Cases. *See* Sizemore v. District Ct., 735 F.2d 204, 207 (6th Cir. 1984); *supra* § 16.1.

[3] Bundy v. Wainwright, 808 F.2d 1410, 1414-15 (11th Cir. 1987) ("[p]etitioner is not required by statute or Rules to attach to his petition or to file a state court record in order to avoid a dismissal for facial insufficiency ..."; "[t]he obligation to come forward with the state court record is squarely upon the respondent"). *See also* Russell v. Jones, 886 F.2d 149, 152-53 (8th Cir. 1989) (state, not federal, courts must pay fees to transcribe state trial court record on behalf of indigent petitioner); Duttry v. Petstock, 878 F.2d 123, 124 (3d Cir. 1989) (state or district court must provide state records needed on exhaustion issue when *pro se* petitioner is unable to do so).

decision(s) on direct appeal of petitioner's conviction and sentence; (4) petitioner's brief(s) on appeal from the denial of her state postconviction petition(s); and (5) the state appellate decision(s) on appeal of the denial of the state postconviction petitions.[4]

On request of the petitioner or *sua sponte*, the district court may order the respondent to provide the court and the petitioner with copies of relevant portions of the transcripts and other parts of the record. Such an order may be entered: (1) before the petition is filed, upon a showing that the prisoner is indigent and that at least one claim she expects to include in the petition is not "frivolous"[5] (and, in a capital case, probably even without a showing of nonfrivolousness);[6] (2) at any time after the petition is filed, if the prisoner

---

[4] Rule 5 of the Rules Governing § 2254 Cases. In one circumstance, nonindigent *petitioners* have the responsibility to provide the court with portions of the record. *See* 28 U.S.C.A. § 2254(f) (West 1994 & Supp. 1998) ("If the applicant challenges the sufficiency of the evidence ... to support the State court's determination of a factual issue ..., the applicant, if able, shall produce that part of the record pertinent to a determination of the sufficiency of the evidence"; "if the applicant, because of indigency or other reason is unable to produce such part of the record," court must direct State to produce it). *Cf.* Hamilton v. Vasquez, 882 F.2d 1469, 1471 (9th Cir. 1989) ("district court is under no obligation to obtain and review the state court record when disposing of purely factual questions"; accordingly, "petitioner who raises only questions of fact has the burden of providing the district court with the relevant portions of the state court record, or of showing his inability to do so"); Austad v. Risley, 761 F.2d 1348, 1353-54 (9th Cir.), *cert. denied*, 474 U.S. 856 (1985) (court not required *sua sponte* to insist that state produce additional portions of record when petitioner did not produce them or show inability to do so). By adopting statutes of limitations that sometimes are triggered by the completion of particular state judicial proceedings and sometimes are tolled by the pendency of those proceedings, recent legislation enhances the importance of records documenting the timing of state proceedings. The new legislation and the cases to which it applies are discussed *supra* §§ 3.2, 3.3, and 3.4. The legislation's statutes of limitations are discussed in more detail *supra* § 5.1b.

[5] Under 28 U.S.C. § 753(f) (1994), indigent prisoners may secure a free copy of the record *before* filing a habeas corpus petition in order to enable them to file the petition. *See* Elmo B. Hunter, *Post Conviction Remedies*, 50 F.R.D. 153, 173-78 (1970). Section 753(f) requires the prospective petitioner to establish indigence under 28 U.S.C.A. § 1915 (West 1994 & Supp. 1998), which in turn requires the prisoner to demonstrate that the claims the petition would present are not "frivolous." *See* United States v. MacCollom, 426 U.S. 317, 322 & n.2 (1976) (discussing and upholding requirement of showing that at least one claim in projected petition is not frivolous); Sistrunk v. United States, 992 F.2d 258, 259 (10th Cir. 1993); Ruark v. Gunter, 958 F.2d 318, 319 (10th Cir. 1992); Henderson v. United States, 734 F.2d 483, 484 (9th Cir. 1984); *supra* § 12.1 & *infra* § 35.3 (indigence qualifications and nonfrivolousness standard under 28 U.S.C. § 1915). Presumedly, satisfying the nonfrivolousness prerequisite to securing a transcript under section 753(f) does not require much specificity as to matters reflected in the unavailable portion of the record. *See, e.g.,* Kitchens v. Alderman, 376 F.2d 262 (5th Cir. 1967) (because claim of exclusion of blacks from jury was not facially frivolous, district court erred in refusing to allow petitioner to proceed as indigent and receive free transcript).

[6] In capital federal postconviction cases, the Supreme Court's decision in McFarland v. Scott, 512 U.S. 849 (1994), suggests that, at least in some circumstances, indigent prisoners have a right

establishes the right to proceed *in forma pauperis* and if the state voluntarily files the records with the clerk's office or is ordered to do so by the court;[7] or (3)

to access to the record at state expense even before a petition is filed and even before any claims have been identified. The *McFarland* Court interpreted the statute giving indigent capital prisoners a mandatory right to counsel and necessary investigative and expert services, 21 U.S.C. § 848(q), to apply during the period when a federal petition is being investigated and prepared but has not yet been filed. *Id.* at 855-56. *See id.* at 858 ("the right to counsel necessarily includes a right for that counsel meaningfully to research and present a defendant's habeas claims"); *supra* § 12.3a. Reading the federal statute governing habeas corpus stays of execution, which limits stays to periods during which "a habeas corpus petition *is pending*," 28 U.S.C. § 2251 (1994) (emphasis added), *in pari materia* with 21 U.S.C. § 848(q), the *McFarland* Court also concluded that the prepetition filing of an application for appointment of counsel is sufficient to initiate the "habeas corpus proceeding." *McFarland v. Scott, supra* at 855-56. *See supra* §§ 13.1-13.2b. The Court gave McFarland the benefit of these rulings notwithstanding that he had filed no papers indicating the claims he expected to include in the petition. *See supra* § 13.2b nn.47-49 and accompanying text. These rulings, together with the Court's intent to give capital prisoners access to "services ... critical in the preapplication phase of a habeas corpus proceeding, when possible claims and their factual bases are researched and identified," *McFarland v. Scott, supra* at 855, would seem to encompass a right on the part of indigent capital prisoners to the entire record during the period when their court-appointed attorneys are investigating potential claims and preparing federal habeas corpus petitions. *See also id.* at 860 (O'Connor, J., concurring in the judgment in part) (goal of appointed counsel is to assure that, when filed, "first petition adequately sets forth all of a state prisoner's colorable claims for relief"); Brown v. Vasquez, 952 F.2d 1164, 1167-69 (9th Cir.), *cert. denied,* 503 U.S. 1011 (1992) (given burden imposed on incarcerated and ill-educated habeas corpus petitioners to include all possibly meritorious constitutional claims in their initial petitions, district court has jurisdiction, even prior to petitioners' filing of habeas corpus petition, to issue stay of execution and appoint counsel to assist capital petitioner in preparing petition).

Although there is no automatic right to counsel at the prepetition stage in *non*capital habeas corpus proceedings, the federal courts have discretion to appoint counsel at that or "*any* stage of the case if the interest of justice so requires." Rule 8(c) of the Rules Governing § 2254 Cases (emphasis added). *Accord* Rule 8(c) of the Rules Governing § 2255 Proceedings. *See McFarland v. Scott, supra* at 863 (O'Connor, J., concurring in the judgment in part); *supra* §§ 12.2, 12.3b. Arguably, if a court concluded that prepetition appointment of counsel was warranted in a noncapital case for purposes of investigating claims and preparing a petition, the court also, then, could order the state to produce the transcript to facilitate that process. At the least, the prepetition appointment of counsel would seem to establish that the "nonfrivolousness" threshold discussed *supra* note 5 has been crossed. *See supra* § 12.3b. In the event that prepetition access to the record is not available, counsel or petitioner should consult the discussion *supra* § 11.3b nn.12-15 and accompanying text, which lays out a procedure for including in the habeas corpus petition and specially pleading potentially available claims that are not yet factually developed in cases in which the lack of access to the record or other fact-development procedures prevents counsel from determining whether the claims actually exist. *See also infra* §§ 19.3 n.13, 19.4f n.34.

[7] *See* 28 U.S.C. § 2250 (1994) ("If on any application for a writ of habeas corpus an order has been made permitting the petitioner to prosecute the application in forma pauperis, the clerk of any court of the United States shall furnish to the petitioner without cost certified copies of such documents or parts of the record on file in his office as may be required by order of the judge before whom the application is pending."); Townsend v. Sain, 372 U.S. 293, 319 (1963); United

after the state's answer is filed, upon a showing that the record materials attached to the answer omit "relevant" portions of the record.[8] Certainly, if the

---

States v. Connors, 904 F.2d 535, 536 (9th Cir. 1990) (after filing petition, "prisoner proceeding in forma pauperis on a habeas corpus petition is entitled to receive at government expense copies of court documents" including trial transcript). Although the Habeas Rules only explicitly provide for a court order requiring the production of portions of the record *following* the state's compliance with a directive to answer the petition, *see* Rule 5 of the Rules Governing § 2254 Cases; *see also* Rule 4 of *id.* (answer not required except upon order of court), Habeas Rule 4 gives the court the power not only to choose between summarily dismissing the petition or ordering an answer but also "to take such other [intermediate] action as the judge deems appropriate." *Id. See supra* § 15.2a. This latter provision apparently authorizes actions focused, *inter alia*, on "the availability of transcripts." Advisory Committee Note to *id.* The rules thus give the court ample authority to require the state, even before answering (or in lieu of immediately answering), to produce all or portions of the record, which an indigent petitioner then could obtain free of charge under section 2250 if so ordered by the court.

[8] Rule 5 of the Rules Governing § 2254 Cases (court may order state to arrange for transcription of untranscribed portions of record). *See* Advisory Committee Note to *id.* (on its own or petitioner's motion, court may require respondent to furnish relevant records, apparently including: pretrial motions; requests for instructions; exhibits; appellate postconviction, and *certiorari* pleadings and briefs; etc.); Duttry v. Petstock, 878 F.2d 123, 124 (3d Cir. 1989) (discussed *supra* note 3); Ruff v. Kincheloe, 843 F.2d 1240, 1242-43 n.5 (9th Cir. 1988) (over dissent, court faults district court for failing to order production of record *sua sponte* prior to finding that improper burden of proof instruction was harmless, notwithstanding that petitioner had not produced record, demonstrated inability to do so, or drawn district court's attention to parts of record that district court failed to review); Bundy v. Wainwright, 808 F.2d 1410, 1415 (11th Cir. 1987); Dillard v. Blackburn, 780 F.2d 509, 513 (5th Cir. 1986) (state only required to furnish parts of record it deems relevant, but court may require state to supply, and may expand record to include, entire record; no error in not *sua sponte* requiring production of additional portions of record when petitioner did not request additional records); Thompson v. Housewright, 741 F.2d 213, 216 (8th Cir. 1984); Sizemore v. District Ct., 735 F.2d 204, 207 (6th Cir. 1984) (state ordered to produce guilty plea transcripts); Fendler v. Goldsmith, 728 F.2d 1181, 1190 (9th Cir. 1983); Williams v. Kullman, 722 F.2d 1048, 1051 (2d Cir. 1983); Harris v. Pulley, 692 F.2d 1189, 1199-200 (9th Cir. 1982), *rev'd on other grounds,* 465 U.S. 37 (1984) (records relating to venue change claim); Salkay v. Wainwright, 552 F.2d 151, 153 (5th Cir. 1977); United States ex rel. Irons v. Montanye, 520 F.2d 646, 649 (2d Cir. 1975) (probable cause affidavit). *See also* Dobbs v. Zant, 506 U.S. 357, 358-59 (1993) (*per curiam*) ("[w]e have emphasized before the importance of reviewing capital sentences on a complete record," so "'entire [trial] transcript should have been made available'" to habeas corpus petitioner; after state represented that transcript of closing argument at capital sentencing phase was unavailable, and after petitioner subsequently discovered copy of transcript and proffered it to Court of Appeals on motion "to supplement the record on appeal," "Court of Appeals erred when it refused to consider the full transcript," which "flatly contradicted the account [of the closing argument] given by [defense] counsel in key respects"); Yates v. Evatt, 500 U.S. 391, 405-06 & n.10, 409-10 (1991) (discussing situations in which reviewing court must have entire record before it); Footman v. Singletary, 978 F.2d 1207, 1211-12 (11th Cir. 1992) (district court erred in assigning petitioner burden of producing copy of postconviction motion lost by state courts; "[w]e will not require a habeas corpus petitioner, particularly one proceeding pro se in state court, to maintain copies of state court post-conviction motions in case the state court loses them").

petitioner determines at any time after the answer is filed that the court should have before it a portion of the record that is not appended to the answer, the petitioner expeditiously should move the court for an order requiring the state to furnish the missing materials. Failure to do so not only may result in the court's disposing of the petition on the basis of the incomplete portions of the record that the state submitted but also may deprive the petitioner of access to the missing record on appeal. The motion should be accompanied by a brief memorandum delineating the portions of the record desired and the reasons why those materials are relevant to the petitioner's claims.

Habeas Rule 5 states that if "a transcript is neither available nor procurable" for some reason not attributable to bad faith on the part of the state, a "narrative summary of the evidence may be submitted."[9] The courts have held that substitutes for actual copies of the record — for example, trial or appellate court summaries of the evidence presented at a hearing in lieu of the actual record — generally are not acceptable bases for a ruling on the merits,[10] unless the

---

Cf. Maynard v. Dixon, 943 F.2d 407, 411 (4th Cir. 1991), *cert. denied*, 502 U.S. 1110 (1992) (district court did not err in granting summary judgment prior to state's submission of transcripts and other state court records because portions of transcript appended to petition were sufficient to resolve claim); decisions cited *supra* note 4. *See generally* authority cited *supra* § 15.2c n.59.

Because Habeas Rule 5 states that "relevant" portions of the record "shall be attached to the answer," any order under Rules 4 and 5 of the Rules Governing § 2254 Cases requiring the state to answer the petition and to serve its answer on the petitioner, *see supra* § 16.1b, also presumedly requires the state to serve on the petitioner — whether or not indigent — the "attached" portions of the record.

[9] Rule 5 of the Rules Governing § 2254 Cases.

[10] *See, e.g,* United States ex rel. Jennings v. Ragen, 358 U.S. 276, 277 (1959) (appellate summary of evidence is insufficient); Footman v. Singletary, 978 F.2d 1207, 1211-12 (11th Cir. 1992) (magistrate judge and district court improperly relied on state trial court's order to establish what allegations of ineffectiveness were presented in petitioner's state postconviction motion, which was lost through no fault of petitioner); Carter v. Collins, 918 F.2d 1198, 1202 (5th Cir. 1990) (magistrate judge properly refused to rely on petitioner's unofficial reconstruction of quotations from record after official transcript was lost through no fault of state and petitioner's brother lost only existing copy of official transcript); United States v. Butt, 731 F.2d 75, 77 (1st Cir. 1984) (statements made by counsel for state are insufficient substitutes for relevant portions of record); Mitchell v. Wyrick, 698 F.2d 940, 944 (8th Cir.), *cert. denied,* 462 U.S. 1135 (1983) (failure to produce transcript of state hearing); Little Light v. Crist, 649 F.2d 682, 686 (9th Cir. 1981) (excerpts of proceedings are insufficient); Thacker v. Bordenkircher, 557 F.2d 98, 99 (6th Cir. 1977) (similar); White v. Estelle, 556 F.2d 1366, 1369 (5th Cir. 1977) (certificate of trial judge concerning hearing is insufficient); Hill v. Nelson, 466 F.2d 1346, 1348 (9th Cir. 1972) (similar); United States ex rel. Davis v. Yeager, 453 F.2d 1001 (3d Cir. 1971) (trial court summary of record is insufficient); United States ex rel. Rebenstorf v. Pate, 417 F.2d 1222, 1226 (7th Cir. 1969) (decision of state supreme court on direct appeal is inadequate substitute for record of state postconviction proceedings); United States ex rel. Worlow v. Pate, 411 F.2d 972, 974 (7th Cir. 1969), *cert. denied,* 403 U.S. 921 (1971) (similar); Haacks v. Wainwright, 387 F.2d 176, 179 (5th Cir. 1968) (*pro forma* minute entry insufficient); Elsperman v. Wainwright, 358 F.2d 259 (5th Cir.

petitioner makes no objection.[11] Upon objection by the petitioner to substituted records, the district court must hold an evidentiary hearing on the factual issues addressed in the missing parts of the record.[12]

By statute, rule, and Supreme Court decision,[13] any portion of the prior record of proceedings in the petitioner's case is admissible in evidence at an evidentiary hearing held during the course of habeas corpus proceedings. The district court may base conclusions on the state record even if no evidentiary hearing is held and even if the federal record has not been expanded formally to include the state court record.[14]

§ 19.3. Financial assistance.[1]

Preparing and litigating postconviction claims sometimes requires expensive factual investigation, statistical analyses, and expert assistance and testimony that are beyond the financial means of indigent state prisoners.[2] Moreover, in

---

1966) (minutes of trial or hearing, as opposed to verbatim transcript, is insufficient). *See also* Magouirk v. Phillips, 1998 WL 320934, at *15 (5th Cir. June 18, 1998) (reversing district court's dismissal of claim of insufficiency of evidence which was based "solely upon the rendition of the facts reported in the Louisiana Court of Appeal decision denying Magouirk's sufficiency claim on direct appeal"; "We are at a loss to understand how a federal habeas court can conduct a meaningful sufficiency review without a transcript of trial.").

[11] *See* Baker v. Estelle, 711 F.2d 44, 46 (5th Cir. 1983), *cert. denied,* 464 U.S. 1048 (1984).

[12] At such a hearing, the state bears the burden of proving any facts upon which it relies to dispute petitioner's claims and which the missing portion of the record addressed. *See* Townsend v. Sain, 372 U.S. 293, 318-19 (1963); Jones v. Parke, 734 F.2d 1142, 1148-49 (6th Cir. 1984); Jackson v. McKaskle, 729 F.2d 356, 359 (5th Cir. 1984); Rogers v. Maggio, 714 F.2d 35, 37 (5th Cir. 1983); Fortenberry v. Maggio, 664 F.2d 1288, 1291 (5th Cir. 1982); United States ex rel. Howard v. Rundle, 452 F.2d 904, 906 (3d Cir. 1971); Valdez v. California, 439 F.2d 1405 (9th Cir. 1971); Thornhill v. Peyton, 420 F.2d 477, 478 (4th Cir. 1969); Conner v. Wingo, 409 F.2d 21, 22 (6th Cir. 1969), *cert. denied,* 406 U.S. 921 (1972). *Cf.* 28 U.S.C.A. § 2254(f) (West 1994 & Supp. 1998) ("[i]f the State cannot provide [a] pertinent part of the record, then the court shall determine under the existing facts and circumstances what weight shall be given to the State court's factual determinations" premised on missing record).

[13] 28 U.S.C. § 2247 (1994); 28 U.S.C.A. § 2254(g) (West 1994 & Supp. 1998); Rules 5 and 8(a) of the Rules Governing § 2254 Cases; *Townsend v. Sain, supra,* 372 U.S. at 319.

[14] *See* Advisory Committee Note to Rule 8 of the Rules Governing § 2254 Cases. *See also* Coleman v. Zant, 708 F.2d 541, 547 n.9 (11th Cir. 1983) (relevant parts of record of trial of petitioner's codefendant are admissible in habeas corpus proceeding); *infra* §§ 19.5 (expansion of record), 21.2 (evidentiary rules).

§ 19.3. [1] *See generally* Joe Margulies, *Resource Deprivation and the Right to Counsel,* 80 J. CRIM. L. & CRIMINOLOGY 673 (1989); other sources cited *supra* §§ 7.1a n.2, 7.2 n.1.

[2] *See* McFarland v. Scott, 512 U.S. 849, 855 (1994) (decision's holding limited to capital cases) ("The services of investigators and other experts may be critical in ... a habeas corpus proceeding ...."); authority discussed *infra* notes 19-29 and accompanying text. For examples of the types of claims to which the statement in text applies, see *supra* § 11.2c paras. (1), (3)-(7), (11)(a)(i) & (iii),

many cases, adequate financial assistance is unavailable in the state courts or will have been denied in the particular case.[3] When that is so, or when for any other reason, an indigent federal petitioner can show that financial assistance for litigation support services is reasonably necessary for the full and fair discovery, development, and consideration of claims cognizable in habeas corpus proceedings, the petitioner may request assistance from the federal courts, and, if warranted thereafter, may request a federal evidentiary hearing or use the "expansion of the record" or other effective factfinding procedure to present the fact-based claims and evidence that the petitioner has developed.[4]

In noncapital cases, requests for financial assistance should be made under the Criminal Justice Act, which enables "[c]ounsel for [an indigent[5]] person" to

---

(13). *See generally supra* §§ 2.3, 2.4, 11.2, 11.3; *supra* Chapter 9 (all discussing claims cognizable in habeas proceedings and means of discovering them).

[3] In addition to creating a right in some circumstances to a federal hearing on claims requiring financial assistance for full adjudication, *see supra* § 7.1b nn.41-44 and accompanying text; *infra* § 20.3e nn.115-19, 133-34, 146 and accompanying text, the state courts' denial of financial assistance at trial, *see* Ake v. Oklahoma, 470 U.S. 68 (1985); cases listed *supra* § 11.2c (para. (4)), or in state postconviction proceedings, *see supra* § 7.1b; *but cf. supra* § 7.1b n.48, may establish an independent constitutional violation cognizable in habeas corpus. To preserve the right to financial assistance and a federal hearing at the federal habeas corpus stage, as well as the ability to pursue habeas corpus relief on a constitutional claim based on the denial of necessary support services, the defendant or petitioner should (1) seek the relevant assistance at the earliest point during state court proceedings that such assistance becomes necessary; (2) premise requests for assistance on the applicable federal constitutional and other principles, *see* Ake v. Oklahoma, *supra*; authority discussed *supra* §§ 7.1b, 7.2; and (3) appeal adverse rulings on federal grounds in all available state appellate forums. *See generally supra* §§ 7.1a, 7.1b nn.41-46 and accompanying text.

[4] *See infra* § 19.5 (expansion of the record); *infra* Chapter 20 (evidentiary hearings). Seeking but being denied necessary financial assistance in the state courts usually is a sufficient basis for receiving financial assistance in the federal courts. *See supra* § 7.1b nn.41-44 and accompanying text; *infra* notes 7, 16 and accompanying text; *infra* § 20.3e nn.115-19, 133-34, 146 and accompanying text. Being denied necessary services in the state courts does not, however, appear to be a *prerequisite* for federal financial assistance. The governing provisions of the Criminal Justice Act and the Anti-Drug Abuse Act of 1988, discussed below, mention no such prerequisite and, instead, premise the availability of financial assistance for support services on their "necess[ity]" for fair *federal* court litigation and, perhaps, on whether the petitioner has a right (or other access) to *federal* counsel (which must be provided to indigents in capital cases and, generally, is discretionary in noncapital cases). *See infra* notes 5-29 and accompanying text. *See generally supra* §§ 12.3, 12.4 (right to counsel in federal habeas corpus proceedings). The right to a federal evidentiary *hearing* is governed by a different set of statutes and judge-made rules, *see* 28 U.S.C.A. § 2254(e) (West 1994 & Supp. 1998); Rule 8 of the Rules Governing § 2254 Cases; Keeney v. Tamayo-Reyes, 504 U.S. 1 (1992); Townsend v. Sain, 372 U.S. 293 (1963); *infra* Chapter 20, which *do* make the denial of a request for a full and fair hearing in the state courts important to (although not always dispositive of) the right to a federal hearing. *See supra* § 20.2b; *infra* § 20.3e nn.90-113 and accompanying text. *See also infra* note 26.

[5] *See supra* § 12.1.

apply to the district court *ex parte*[6] for funds "to obtain investigative, expert, or other services necessary for adequate representation." Upon finding that such "services are necessary," "the [petitioner] is financially unable to obtain them," and "the interests of justice so require," the court must provide the requested funds.[7] The requisite timing of such requests is not clearly specified in the Criminal Justice Act. In the relatively uncommon event that counsel is appointed to represent an indigent prospective habeas corpus petitioner before a petition actually is filed,[8] the reference in the Criminal Justice Act to requests by "[c]ounsel" for necessary financial assistance clearly includes (but is not limited to[9]) counsel appointed under the Act, and thus would seem to authorize appointed counsel to apply for assistance even though a petition has not yet been filed. Moreover, the justification relied upon by a court for exercising its discretion to appoint counsel to assist the prisoner at the prepetition stage of a noncapital case[10] very likely will provide a strong justification for any support services needed to assist the attorney in identifying and adequately pleading

---

[6] 18 U.S.C. § 3006A(e)(1) (1994) ("Counsel ... may request [support services] in an ex parte application."). *See also* 18 U.S.C. §§ 3006A(e)(2), 3006A(e)(3) (1994) (partially quoted *infra* note 9) (circumstances in which appointed counsel may spend small amounts of money on experts and investigators without prior authorization); *infra* note 17 and accompanying text.

[7] 18 U.S.C. §§ 3006A(a), 3006A(e) (1994). *See* Lawson v. Dixon, 3 F.3d 743, 750 (4th Cir. 1993), *cert. denied*, 511 U.S. 1013 (1994) ("appointment of an expert for purposes of mounting a defense at trial is mandatory under Title 18 [§ 3006(A)(e)] if the defendant satisfies the statutory prerequisites of indigence and necessity."); Westbrook v. Zant, 704 F.2d 1487, 1497 n.12 (11th Cir. 1983) (before rejecting application for funds under this provision, trial judge must make "'appropriate inquiry' to determine whether the [petitioner] needs such assistance and whether he is financially unable to obtain it" (quoting Pedrero v. Wainwright, 590 F.2d 1383 (5th Cir.), *cert. denied*, 444 U.S. 943 (1979))). *See generally Ake v. Oklahoma, supra*, 470 U.S. at 79-80 (discussed *supra* § 7.2b). *Cf.* Manning v. Nix, 901 F.2d 671, 672 (8th Cir.), *cert. denied*, 498 U.S. 839 (1990) (district court's denial of funds to hire investigator is "not reversible error absent clear and convincing evidence of prejudice"; because petitioner's claim was procedurally defaulted, district court denied petitioner's request for investigator to determine if two jurors who were married to each other discussed case during trial).

[8] *See supra* §§ 12.3a nn.25-32 and accompanying text, 19.2 n.6.

[9] Section 3006A(e)(1) authorizes *any* "[c]ounsel for a person who is financially unable to obtain investigative, expert, or other services necessary for adequate representation ... [to] request them ...." By contrast, section 3006A(e)(2) authorizes only "[c]ounsel *appointed under this section* ... [to] obtain, subject to later review, investigative, expert, and other services *without prior authorization* if necessary for adequate representation" and if the unauthorized expense is limited (generally) to $300 plus reasonable expenses (emphasis added). Clearly, therefore, the Act contemplates an application for support services by volunteer or other counsel *not* "appointed under this section."

[10] *See supra* § 12.3a nn.11-17 & 25-32 and accompanying text.

claims in the petition.[11] Indeed, as Justice O'Connor has noted, "[f]or [investigative, expert, or related] services to be meaningful in the habeas context, they ... must be available prior to the filing of the first federal habeas petition."[12] Certainly, requests for necessary financial assistance that are filed by appointed or volunteer counsel simultaneously with the petition or following the state's answer will be entertained.[13] Whether an indigent petitioner acting *pro se* may request financial services under the Criminal Justice Act (either before or after the petition is filed) is less clear, given the Act's references to requests by "[c]ounsel."[14] If an indigent, *pro se* petitioner encounters this objection to necessary financial assistance, the appropriate response is that the reasons creating the need for financial assistance, together with the statute's implication that counsel is needed to administer funds provided by the court, requires appointment of counsel under the standards discussed in § 12.3 *supra*.

In capital cases, requests for necessary financial assistance should be made under section 848(q) of the Anti-Drug Abuse Act of 1988.[15] That provision authorizes federal habeas corpus courts to provide funds for all "reasonably necessary" investigative and expert services requested by indigent habeas corpus petitioners challenging the constitutionality of their convictions and death sentences.[16] In order to allow petitioners to establish need without providing

---

[11] *See infra* note 19 and accompanying text (importance of prefiling support services in capital cases). *See also supra* § 11.6 (need for habeas corpus petition to provide more factual specificity than other civil complaints).

[12] McFarland v. Scott, 512 U.S. 849, 860 (1994) (O'Connor, J., concurring in the judgment in part). *Accord id.* at 858 (majority opinion) (quoted *infra* text accompanying note 19) (decision's holding limited to capital context). Recently enacted statutes of limitations, the contents and applicability of which are discussed *supra* §§ 3.2, 3.3, 3.4, 5.1b, and doubts whether the filing of prepetition requests for counsel and financial assistance within the limitations period satisfies those statutes, *see supra* §§ 5.1b nn.80-91 and accompanying text, 11.1, add an important strategic consideration to the decision whether to make a prepetition request for financial assistance.

[13] On timing questions generally, see *supra* §§ 11.7, 12.3a. *See also supra* § 5.1b (recently enacted statutes of limitations). In the event that prepetition financial assistance is not available, counsel or petitioner should consider the discussion *supra* § 11.3b nn.12-15 and accompanying text, which lays out a procedure for including in the habeas corpus petition and specially pleading potentially available claims that are not yet factually developed in cases in which the lack of financial assistance or other fact-development procedures prevents counsel from determining whether the claims actually exist. *See also supra* § 19.2 n.6; *infra* § 19.4f n.34.

[14] *See supra* note 9.

[15] Pub. L. No. 100-690, 102 Stat. 4181, 4393-94 (1988), 21 U.S.C. §§ 848(q)-848(r) (West 1994 & Supp. 1998). *See id.* §§ 848(q)(4)(B), 848(q)(9), 848(q)(10).

[16] *Id.* § 848(q)(9) ("Upon a finding in ex parte proceedings that investigative, expert or other services are reasonably necessary for the representation of the defendant, whether in connection with issues relating to guilt or sentence, the court shall authorize the defendant's attorneys to obtain such services...."). *See id.* § 848(q)(4)(B) ("In any post-conviction proceeding under § 2254 ... of Title 28 seeking to vacate or set aside a death sentence, any defendant who is or becomes

unilateral discovery of their cases to the state or the government, the Anti-Drug Abuse Act, as amended in important respects in 1996, provides a mechanism for *ex parte* showings in support of applications for funds for investigative, expert, and other services.[17]

---

financially unable to obtain ... investigative, expert, or other reasonably necessary services shall be entitled to the ... furnishing of such ... services"); *McFarland v. Scott, supra,* 512 U.S. at 855 (quoted *infra* text accompanying note 19); *id.* at 860 (O'Connor, J., concurring in the judgment) ("statute entitles capital defendants not only to qualified counsel, but also to 'investigative, expert or other services ... reasonably necessary for the representation of the defendant'"); Lawson v. Dixon, 3 F.3d 743, 751 (4th Cir. 1993), *cert. denied,* 511 U.S. 1013 (1994) ("By the terms of the statute, Congress mandated the application of federal funds for legal representation of habeas corpus petitioners as well as investigative, expert, and other services, provided the prisoner can demonstrate that he is financially unable to secure the assistance on his own and that such assistance is 'reasonably necessary' for his representation."). *See also* Addendum to the Plan for the Representation of Defendants in the United States District Court for the Eastern District of North Carolina Pursuant to the Criminal Justice Act–18 U.S.C. § 3006A, ¶ 5(a) (E.D.N.C. 1990) ("With respect to services rendered in federal proceedings on or after November 18, 1988, the presiding judicial officer shall set compensation for investigative, expert and other services [pursuant to 21 U.S.C. §§ 848(q)(9) and (10)] in an amount reasonably necessary to obtain such services in capital cases without regard to CJA [Criminal Justice Act] limitations"); *id.* ¶ 5(b) ("Upon a finding in *ex parte* proceedings that investigative, expert or other services are reasonably necessary for the representation of the [petitioner] in a capital [habeas corpus] case, the presiding judicial officer shall authorize counsel to obtain such services on behalf of the [petitioner]. Upon a finding that timely procurement of necessary investigative, expert and other services could not await prior authorization, the presiding judicial officer may authorize such services *nunc pro tunc*.").

[17] In adopting section 848(q), Congress recognized that petitioners often cannot demonstrate the "reasonable necessity" of investigative and expert services without disclosing confidential work product, attorney theories and conclusions, and expert consultative advice, information that parties to litigation usually are permitted to withhold from their adversaries, at least until trial. As originally enacted, the Anti-Drug Abuse Act called for "*ex parte* proceedings" to assess the necessity in all cases of funds for investigation and expert assistance. In 1996, as part of the Antiterrorism and Effective Death Penalty Act (AEDPA), Pub. L. 104-132, 110 Stat. 1214 (1996), Congress amended the relevant section of the Anti-Drug Abuse Act to require that a petitioner seeking to proceed *ex parte* make a threshold "proper showing ... concerning the need for confidentiality" in order to justify *ex parte* proceedings. 21 U.S.C. § 848(q)(9) (West 1994 & Supp. 1998). Section 848(q)(9) apparently contemplates motions for leave to proceed *ex parte* by petitioners intending thereafter to apply for investigative or expert services. Exactly how petitioners can explain the need to proceed *ex parte* without disclosing the very information they claim a need to keep secret is unclear. Because of this problem, district judges seem to be following the practice of hearing the petitioner's presentation in support of the motion to proceed *ex parte* either orally *in camera* or via papers filed with the motion but under seal, subject in both cases to disclosure to the state if the court decides that *ex parte* proceedings are not justified and if the petitioner decides, nonetheless, to apply for support services. *See, e.g.,* Miller-El v. Johnson, Civ. No. 3:96-CV-1992-H (N.D. Tex. June 18, 1997) ("recogniz[ing] that there is some ambiguity in the [1996] statute as to whether the request for *ex parte* consideration itself can be made in an *ex parte* motion," court denied State's request to strike petitioner's *ex parte* sealed motions for investigative funds and

allowed petitioner to proceed *ex parte;* "[a]llowing the Respondent access to the confidential information contained in Petitioner's request to proceed *ex parte* directly conflicts with Congress' intent to authorize *ex parte* proceedings upon a proper showing"); Hawkins v. Calderon, CIV S-96-1155 LKK/PAN (E.D. Cal. May 6, 1997) (magistrate judge erred in permitting state to participate in proceedings to determine whether petitioner's funding request should be placed under seal and in requiring petitioner to serve state with copy of brief on need for confidentiality).

Also unclear is whether this amendment applies to federal habeas corpus proceedings initiated prior to AEDPA's enactment on April 24, 1996. *See generally supra* § 3.4. Although the section of AEDPA containing this amendment has no clause delineating the cases to which it applies, AEDPA's other provisions relating to counsel and support services in habeas corpus cases expressly apply only to cases "commenced" after the date of enactment. *Compare* Antiterrorism and Effective Death Penalty Act of 1996 § 108, Pub. L. 104-132, 110 Stat. 1214, 1226 (1996) *with id.* § 903, 110 Stat. at 1318. The latter provisions provide some basis for viewing the new statute governing *ex parte* showings as similarly limited. So does the Supreme Court's decision in Lindh v. Murphy, 117 S. Ct. 2059 (1997), which, without directly answering the question, suggests that the only habeas-corpus-related provisions of AEDPA that Congress intended to apply to pre-enactment cases are the capital opt-in procedures in § 107. *See id.* at 2063-68; *supra* §§ 3.3, 3.4. Additionally, applying the new provisions regarding *ex parte* showings to requests filed prior to AEDPA's effective date would evidently violate the Supreme Court's restrictions on "retroactive" application of new legislation. *See* Calderon v. United States Dist. Ct., 107 F.3d 756, 761 & n.11 (9th Cir.), *cert. denied,* 118 S. Ct. 265 (1997) (state has no standing to appeal district court's treatment of request for investigative and expert funds; in any event, retroactive application of AEDPA's amendment of *ex parte* provision of § 848(q)(9) to requests filed before statute's effective date would "create retroactively a new right of a State: standing to challenge federal fees awards to certain state prisoners; it would also impermissibly impair a right [petitioner] had when he 'acted,' making the fee request: to avoid state interference with or knowledge of the details of his request"); *see also* Morris v. Calderon, CIV-S-92-0483-EJG-GGH-P (E.D. Cal. April 30, 1997) (amendments to § 848(q)(9) "do not apply to fee requests filed prior to April 24, 1996").

In applying the new "need for confidentiality" standard in individual cases, the courts may appropriately consider the extensive caselaw — developed under the original version of the Anti-Drug Abuse Act as well as the Criminal Justice Act, the Constitution, and state statutes — documenting the need for and propriety of *ex parte* proceedings to guard against unwarranted unilateral provision of discovery to the government. *See, e.g.,* Addendum to the Plan for the Representation of Defendants in the United States District Court for the Eastern District of North Carolina Pursuant to the Criminal Justice Act–18 U.S.C. § 3006A, ¶ 5(b) (E.D.N.C. 1990) (quoted *supra* note 16); *id.* ¶ 5(c) ("*Ex parte* applications for services other than counsel shall be heard *in camera,* and shall not be revealed without the consent of the person represented. Such application shall be placed under seal until the final disposition of the case in the trial court, subject to further order of the judge or magistrate"); *Lawson v. Dixon, supra,* 3 F.3d at 751 ("[E]*x parte* proceedings are the only proper means of adjudicating appointment motions contemplated by the language of both the Title 18 and Title 21 statutes."). *See also* 18 U.S.C. § 3006A(e)(1) (1994) (discussed *supra* note 6); Fed. R. Crim. P. 17(b) (authorizing indigent defendants to make requests for subpoenas *ex parte*); Ake v. Oklahoma, 470 U.S. 68, 82-83 (1985) (threshold showing sufficient to invoke constitutional right to expert assistance at trial may be made *ex parte*); United States v. Greschner, 802 F.2d 373, 379-80 (10th Cir. 1986), *cert. denied,* 480 U.S. 908 (1987) (absent waiver by defendant, it is error for trial court to allow government attorneys to attend hearing on defendant's application for penologist, pathologist, blood tests, and subpoenas); United States v. Edwards, 488 F.2d 1154, 1162 (5th Cir. 1974) (government access to information critical to

In this capital setting, the right to financial assistance for necessary support services clearly attaches even before the petition is filed, from the moment counsel is appointed under section 848(q):[18]

21 U.S.C. § 848(q)(9) ... entitles capital [postconviction petitioners] to a variety of expert and investigative services upon a showing of necessity.... The services of investigators and other experts may be critical in the pre-application phase of a habeas corpus proceeding, when possible claims and their factual bases are researched and identified. Section 848(a)(9) clearly anticipates that capital defense counsel will have been appointed under

---

defense is "forbidden under our concept of criminal procedure"); United States v. Meriwether, 486 F.2d 498, 506 (5th Cir.), *cert. denied,* 417 U.S. 948 (1973) (purpose of *ex parte* provision is to "shield theory of ... defense from the prosecutor's scrutiny"); United States v. Sutton, 464 F.2d 552, 553 (5th Cir. 1972) (district court's failure to conduct hearing *ex parte* on defendant's motion for investigator requires reversal of conviction); Marshall v. United States, 423 F.2d 1315 (10th Cir. 1970) (defendant entitled to *ex parte* hearing). *See also* H.R. REP. No. 864, 88th Cong., 2d Sess. (1963) *reprinted in* 2 U.S. CODE CONG. & ADMIN. NEWS 2990 (1964) (Criminal Justice Act's *ex parte* procedure "prevents the possibility that an open hearing may cause a defendant to reveal his defense"); S. REP. No. 346, 88th Cong., 1st Sess. 3 (1963) (*ex parte* requirement was included in Criminal Justice Act "in order to protect the accused from premature disclosure of his case"). *Compare* Smith v. McCormick, 914 F.2d 1153, 1159-60 (9th Cir. 1990) (order conditioning expert assistance on criminal defendant's pretrial disclosure of expert's findings regardless of whether defendant elects to use expert violates due process, privilege against self-incrimination, and right to effective assistance of counsel) *and* United States v. Meriwether, *supra* at 506 ("serious equal protection question" raised by requiring indigent defendants to make pretrial disclosures of work product that wealthier defendants would not have to make) *and* Brooks v. State, 385 S.E.2d 81, 84 (Ga. 1989), *cert. denied,* 494 U.S. 1018 (1990) (indigent defendant's due process right to expert assistance at trial comprehends due process right to apply for assistance *ex parte*) *and* State v. Greene, 438 S.E. 2d 743, 744-45 (N.C. 1944) (similar) *and* McGregor v. State, 733 P.2d 416 (Okla. Crim. App. 1987) (*ex parte* procedures required to avoid self-incrimination, ineffective assistance, and other constitutional violations) *with* State v. Apelt, 861 P.2d 634, 650 (Ariz. 1993), *cert. denied,* 513 U.S. 834 (1994) (criminal defendant has no constitutional right to apply for expert services *ex parte*) *and* State v. Floody, 481 N.W.2d 242, 255-56 (S.D. 1992) (similar). *Cf.* In re Pruett, 133 F.3d 275, 281 (4th Cir. 1997) (unless statutes or rules authorize *ex parte* showings, habeas corpus petitioners' requests for discovery should include notice to opposition); Lawson v. Dixon, *supra* at 752 & n.6 (although *ex parte* proceedings generally are required, district court did not abuse discretion in denying request for *ex parte* proceedings on application for expert under specific circumstances of case, which included nonexhaustion of claim for which expert was being sought, state's prior voluntary waiver of exhaustion, and district court's desire to "avoid the waste of judicial resources" by inquiring of state whether it would demand exhaustion if expert were appointed). *But see* McKinney v. Paskett, 753 F. Supp. 861, 862-64 (D. Idaho 1990) (refusing to permit *ex parte* or *in camera* proceedings on capital prisoner's request for support services under Anti-Drug Abuse Act of 1988).

[18] *See supra* § 12.3a (discussing timing of appointment of counsel in capital habeas corpus cases).

§ 848(q)(4)(B) before the need for such technical assistance arises, since the statute requires "the defendant's attorneys to obtain such services."[19]

The Criminal Justice Act does not define the phrase "necessary for adequate representation." Nor does the Anti-Drug Abuse Act define the analogous phrase "reasonably necessary." Taken together with established habeas corpus jurisprudence, however, the language of both Acts suggests that Congress intended to provide prisoners, upon request, with all resources needed to discover, plead, develop, and present evidence determinative of their "colorable" constitutional claims.[20] Congress and the Court have both recognized that habeas corpus claims often turn on factual questions, and that "'the procedures by which the facts of a case are determined assume an importance fully as great as the validity of the substantive rule of law to be applied.'"[21] Both have insisted, therefore, that full development of determinative factual questions precede the final adjudication of habeas corpus claims,[22] and both have made a variety of fact-determining

---

[19] *McFarland v. Scott, supra*, 512 U.S. at 855. *Accord id.* at 860 (O'Connor, J., concurring in the judgment in part) (quoted *supra* text accompanying note 12; *supra* note 16).

[20] *See id.* at 860 (O'Connor, J., concurring in judgment in part) (goal of counsel appointed under Act is to assure that "first petition adequately set forth all of a state prisoner's colorable grounds for relief"). *Cf.* Burris v. Parke, 116 F.3d 256, 259 (7th Cir.), *cert. denied*, 118 S. Ct. 462 (1997) ("appointment [of expert psychologist] is authorized if the expert services 'are reasonably necessary for the representation of the defendant'"; standard requires that "defendant ... make a preliminary showing, which [petitioner] has not done," given that "[a]ll the record shows ... is that [petitioner] complains of headaches," had once suffered "'superficial'" gunshot wound to head, but had been found in two separate psychiatric evaluations available at time of alleged ineffective assistance of counsel to exhibit "'no indications of mental illness or deficiency'").

[21] Wingo v. Wedding, 418 U.S. 461, 474 (1974) (quoting Speiser v. Randall, 357 U.S. 513, 520 (1958)). *See, e.g., McFarland v. Scott, supra*, 512 U.S. at 855 (purpose of habeas corpus procedures is development of "possible claims and their factual bases"); *Wingo v. Wedding, supra* at 468 ("More often than not, claims of unconstitutional detention turn upon the resolution of contested issues of fact."); *id.* at 474 ("'To experienced lawyers it is commonplace that the outcome of a [habeas corpus case] — and hence the vindication of legal rights — depends more on how the factfinder appraises the facts than on a disputed construction of a statute or interpretation of a line of precedents'" (quoting *Speiser v. Randall, supra* at 520)); Townsend v. Sain, 372 U.S. 293, 312 (1963) ("it is the typical, not the rare, [habeas corpus] case in which constitutional claims turn upon the resolution of contested factual issues").

[22] *See, e.g.,* 28 U.S.C. § 2243 (1994); Rule 8 of the Rules Governing § 2254 Cases; Jackson v. Virginia, 443 U.S. 307, 318 (1979) ("A federal court has a duty to assess the historic facts when it is called upon to apply a constitutional standard to a conviction obtained in state court"); Blackledge v. Allison, 431 U.S. 63, 82-83 (1977) (habeas corpus petitioner is "entitled to careful consideration and plenary processing of [his claim], including full opportunity for presentation of the relevant facts" (quoting Harris v. Nelson, 394 U.S. 286, 298 (1969))); *Wingo v. Wedding, supra*, 418 U.S. at 468 ("since the Judiciary Act of February 5, 1967, ... Congress has expressly vested plenary power in the federal courts 'for taking testimony and trying the facts anew in a habeas hearing'" (quoting Fay v. Noia, 372 U.S. 391, 416 (1963))). By statute, rule, and precedent,

procedures available to habeas corpus petitioners, including evidentiary hearings,[23] discovery,[24] and (even if an evidentiary hearing is not available or required) expansion of the record to include documentary evidence.[25] Moreover, essentially the same standard governs the determination whether each of these fact-determining procedures is available to habeas corpus petitioners: Subject to the special set of rules governing evidentiary hearings that is discussed in Chapter 20 *infra*, federal courts have a "duty" to provide a particular fact-development procedure whenever (1) "specific allegations before the court show reason to believe that the petitioner may, if the facts are fully developed, be able to demonstrate that he is confined illegally and is therefore entitled to relief," and when (2) the fact-determining procedure in question is "'indispensable to a fair, rounded, development of the material facts.'"[26]

The policies favoring provision of financial services are even stronger in capital cases than in noncapital cases because the "finality" of death and its "qualitative[]

---

therefore, Congress and the Court have applied to federal habeas corpus proceedings the general principle that whenever "there is a reasonable likelihood that the production of evidence will make the answer to the [constitutional] questions clearer," Borden's Farm Products Co. v. Baldwin, 293 U.S. 194, 213 (1934) (Cardozo, J., concurring), "the essential facts should be determined before passing upon [the] constitutional questions," Polk v. Glover, 305 U.S. 5, 10 (1938). *See, e.g.,* Edwards v. Oklahoma, 577 F.2d 1119, 1121 (10th Cir. 1978) (habeas corpus courts are "disinclined to grapple with potentially close constitutional issues until [the issues] have a ... secure factual underpinning"); *infra* § 20.1b nn.10-17 and accompanying text.

[23] *See* 28 U.S.C. § 2243 (1994); Rule 8 of the Rules Governing § 2254 Cases; *Wingo v. Wedding, supra,* 418 U.S. at 468; *infra* Chapter 20.

[24] *See* Rule 6 of the Rules Governing § 2254 Cases; Harris v. Nelson, 394 U.S. 286 (1969); *infra* § 19.4.

[25] *See* Rule 7 of the Rules Governing § 2254 Cases; *infra* § 19.5.

[26] *Harris v. Nelson, supra,* 394 U.S. at 300; Coleman v. Zant, 708 F.2d 541, 547 (11th Cir. 1983) (quoting Townsend v. Sain, 372 U.S. 293, 322 (1963)). *See* Keeney v. Tamayo-Reyes, 504 U.S. 1, 14-15 (1992) (O'Connor, J., dissenting) ("once a claim is properly before the district court ... a habeas petitioner [should be treated] ... like any civil litigant" for purposes of "right to a hearing [or, presumably, any other fact-development procedure] where [the procedure] is necessary to prove the facts supporting his claim"); *supra* § 15.2c; *infra* §§ 19.4, 19.5, 20.1b. *See also* Ford v. Wainwright, 477 U.S. 399 (1986) (due process includes fact-development procedures capable of providing factfinder with all necessary neutral and professional expert assistance); Ake v. Oklahoma, 470 U.S. 68, 77 (1985) ("fundamental fairness entitles indigent defendants to an 'adequate opportunity,'" including through state-funded assistance of experts, "'to present their claims fairly within the adversary system'" (quoting Ross v. Moffitt, 417 U.S. 600 (1974))). Although recent legislation, discussed *infra* Chapter 20, *see generally supra* §§ 3.2, 3.3, 3.4, limits the availability of evidentiary hearings in certain circumstances, it does not appear to limit other fact-development techniques — mainly, expansion of the record, *see infra* § 19.5 — for proving factual allegations through evidence generated with the aid of financial assistance, discovery (*see infra* § 19.4), and other investigative measures. *See supra* § 19.1 n.4 and accompanying text; *infra* §§ 19.4d n.27, 19.5 n.6 and accompanying text.

differen[ce] from a sentence of imprisonment, however long," magnifies the "need for reliability"[27] and, accordingly, the need for reliable fact-determination procedures.[28] As Chief Judge Merritt of the 6th Circuit stated in a letter drawing the attention of district judges in the circuit to the support-services provisions of the Anti-Drug Abuse Act:

> The Act ... provides that "investigative, expert or other services [which] are reasonably necessary for the representation of a defendant, whether in connection with issues relating to guilt or sentence," 21 U.S.C. § 848(q)(9), shall be authorized by the court....
>
> These requirements for ... support services have been promulgated in federal legislation due to the peculiar, diverse and demanding characteristics of capital defense. Generally, see, *"ABA Guidelines for the Appointment and Performance of Counsel in Death Penalty Cases,"* adopted February 1989. The defense is confronted with a substantively and procedurally complex body of law in all capital litigation; the defense is also confronted ... with a different sentencing procedure, in which the client's life is at stake. Psychiatric and other mental health experts for evaluation, consultation and testimony, may be necessary for the defense in order to competently ... make an evaluation on collateral review.[29]

Both in noncapital and capital cases, the prisoner must accompany the *ex parte* requests for funds for investigative, expert, or other services with a supporting memorandum, an application to proceed *in forma pauperis,* an affidavit of indigence, and the other supporting documentation discussed in section 12.1 *supra.* The application also should include one or more relatively detailed affidavits by the prospective investigator or expert, or at the least by the prisoner or counsel, specifying the types of assistance and amount of funds required and the reasons why the requested assistance is necessary for the full and fair litigation of a substantial federal claim.[30] The petitioner also should file a motion and

---

[27] Woodson v. North Carolina, 428 U.S. 280, 305 (1976).

[28] *See supra* § 2.6. On the central role that evidentiary proceedings play in achieving reliable outcomes in capital habeas corpus proceedings, *see, e.g., Ford v. Wainwright, supra,* 477 U.S. at 410. *See also* McFarland v. Scott, 512 U.S. 849, 855 (1994) ("Congress' provision of a right to counsel under § 848(q)(4)(B) reflects a determination that quality legal representation is necessary in capital habeas corpus proceedings in light of '[t]he seriousness of the possible penalty and ... the unique and complex nature of the litigation.'" (quoting 21 U.S.C. § 848(q)(7))).

[29] Letter from Hon. Gilbert S. Merritt to Hon. Thomas A. Wiseman, dated Oct. 11, 1990.

[30] *Cf.* Caldwell v. Mississippi, 472 U.S. 320, 323 n.1 (1985) ("Given that [the defendant at trial] offered little more than undeveloped assertions that the requested assistance would be beneficial, we find no deprivation of due process in the trial judge's [denial]."); United States v. Samples, 897 F.2d 193, 195-96 (5th Cir. 1990) (*per curiam*) (magistrate judge did not err in issuing subpoenas at government expense for only those individuals whose testimony would be

supporting memorandum asking the court to direct the clerk to file the motion for financial assistance and supporting documents under seal, to protect the statutorily authorized *ex parte* nature of the proceeding.[31] Generally, it will suffice for the memorandum in support of the application for financial assistance to discuss the particular claims for relief at issue, the facts of the case, the affidavit explanations of the need for support services to develop those claims and facts, and the provisions of the Criminal Justice Act or Anti-Drug Abuse Act of 1988 that are addressed above.[32]

§ 19.4. Discovery.[1]

a. *In general.* Rule 6(a) of the Rules Governing § 2254 Cases entitles litigants "to invoke the processes of discovery available under the Federal Rules of Civil Procedure if, and to the extent that, the judge in the exercise of his discretion and for good cause shown grants leave to do so."[2] The discovery devices available

---

relevant). Criminal Justice Act and Anti-Drug Abuse Act funds come out of the federal courts', not the State's, budget. Counsel should take pains to justify not only the need for but also the amount of requested financial assistance. An affidavit from the prospective expert verifying the importance and cost of the requested services — and, when possible, agreeing to a reduced fee in view of the petitioner's indigence and the need to draw on public funds — are helpful.

[31] *See supra* notes 6, 17 and accompanying text.

[32] The memorandum may, but need not, discuss the constitutional bases for a right to necessary financial assistance. *See supra* § 7.2.

§ 19.4. [1] *See generally* 4 JAMES W. MOORE & JO DESHA LUCAS, MOORE'S FEDERAL PRACTICE § 26.05 (2d ed. 1994); LARRY W. YACKLE, POSTCONVICTION REMEDIES § 121 (1981 & Supp. 1998); David E. Bagwell, *Procedural Aspects of Prisoner § 1983 and § 2254 Cases in the Fifth and Eleventh Circuits*, 95 F.R.D. 435, 461 (1982); Elmo B. Hunter, *Post Conviction Remedies*, 50 F.R.D. 153, 164-65 (1971); Charles Alan Wright, *Procedure for Habeas Corpus*, 77 F.R.D. 227, 242-44 (1978); *Developments in the Law — Federal Habeas Corpus*, 83 HARV. L. REV. 1038, 1179-87 (1970). On civil discovery generally, see 4 MOORE'S FEDERAL PRACTICE, *supra* at §§ 26.01-28.10; 4A *id.* at §§ 29.01-37.09; 8 CHARLES ALAN WRIGHT, ARTHUR MILLER & RICHARD L. MARCUS, FEDERAL PRACTICE AND PROCEDURE §§ 2001-93 (2d ed. 1994 & Supp. 1998).

[2] *See* Bracy v. Gramley, 117 S. Ct. 1793, 1796-97 (1997) ("habeas petitioner, unlike the usual civil litigant in federal court, is not entitled to discovery as a matter of ordinary course," but "'discovery [is] available under the Federal Rules of Civil Procedure ... for good cause shown'" (quoting Rule 6(a) of the Rules Governing § 2254 Cases)); Lonchar v. Thomas, 517 U.S. 314, 326 (1996) (discussing Habeas Rule 6(a)); Herrera v. Collins, 506 U.S. 390, 444 (1993) (Blackmun, J., dissenting on other grounds) (although "prisoner ... in a federal habeas [proceeding] ... is not entitled to discovery as a matter of right ... district court retains discretion to order discovery ... when it would help the court make a reliable determination with respect to the prisoner's claim" (citing Harris v. Nelson, 394 U.S. 286, 299-300 (1969); Advisory Committee Note to Rule 6 of the Rules Governing § 2254 Cases)); Toney v. Gammon, 79 F.3d 693, 700 (8th Cir. 1996); Teague v. Scott, 60 F.3d 1167, 1172 (5th Cir. 1995); East v. Scott, 55 F.3d 996, 1001-02 (5th Cir. 1995); Christian v. Rhode, 41 F.3d 461, 470 & n.12 (9th Cir. 1994); Campbell v. Blodgett, 982 F.2d 1356, 1357 (9th Cir. 1993); Harris v. Pulley, 852 F.2d 1546, 1564 (9th Cir. 1988), *cert. denied,*

under Rule 26(a) of the Federal Rules of Civil Procedure include depositions, production of documents or other physical materials, physical and mental examinations, requests for admission, written interrogatories, and permission to enter upon land or other property for inspection or other purposes.[3] Habeas corpus

---

493 U.S. 1051 (1990). A prisoner may not be prevented on grounds of indigence from utilizing or defending against discovery. *See* Rule 6(a) of the Rules Governing § 2254 Cases (discussed *supra* § 12.3b) (court must appoint counsel for indigent prisoners if "necessary for effective utilization of discovery"); Advisory Committee Note to *id.* ("petitioner who qualifies for the appointment of counsel under 18 U.S.C. § 3006A(a)(2)(B) and is granted leave to take a deposition will be allowed witness [and recording and transcription] costs" pursuant to 28 U.S.C. § 1825); Advisory Committee Note to Rules 6 and 8 of the Rules Governing § 2254 Cases (Rule 6(c) authorizes court to require respondent to pay indigent petitioner's counsel fees when respondent deposes petitioner or other person). *See also* United States Dep't of Justice v. Landano, 508 U.S. 165, 168 (1993) (reflecting informal discovery mechanism, not requiring leave of court or even filing of habeas corpus petition, Court adjudicates issues growing out of state prisoner's search for evidence of prosecutorial misconduct via Freedom of Information Act "requests with the FBI for information that the Bureau had compiled in the course of its involvement in the investigation" of crime that prisoner was convicted of committing); *supra* § 19.3; *infra* § 41.6b (somewhat broader discovery under Rules Governing § 2255 Proceedings in federal prisoner cases).

[3] FED. R. CIV. P. 26(a). *See* FED. R. CIV. P. 27-32 (depositions), 33 (interrogatories), 34 (production of documents and physical materials and entry upon land for inspection), 35 (physical and mental examinations), 36 (requests for admission). Many of the discovery devices available under the Civil Rules have been used in federal postconviction litigation. *See, e.g., Bracy v. Gramley, supra,* 117 S. Ct. at 1796 & n.3, 1799 ("given the facts of this particular case, it [was] ... an abuse of discretion not to permit *any* discovery" (emphasis added), although "scope and extent of [required] discovery" short of blanket denial "is a matter confided to the discretion of the District Court"; petitioner's discovery motion, denial of which abused lower courts' discretion, requested production of "sealed transcript" of corruption trial of judge who presided at petitioner's trial and sentenced him to death, "reasonable access to prosecution's materials in [judge's prosecution]," depositions of judges' associates in corruption schemes, and production of prosecution's "'computer printouts'" analyzing verdicts obtained in corrupt judge's cases in particular types of cases); *Toney v. Gammon, supra,* 79 F.3d at 700 (district court abused discretion in denying petitioner's Rule 6(a) motion to "conduct DNA and other scientific testing of various exhibits introduced at Toney's state court trial ... [which] remain in the custody of St. Louis County authorities and are available for testing if ordered by the court"); Love v. Jones, 923 F.2d 816, 819 (11th Cir. 1991) (district court afforded petitioner discovery in support of claim that prosecutor's office routinely exercised peremptory challenges to exclude blacks from juries); Rice v. Clarke, 923 F.2d 117, 118-19 (8th Cir. 1991) (discovery of FBI records of audiotape analysis); McKenzie v. Risley, 915 F.2d 1396, 1398 (9th Cir. 1990) (remanded for discovery to ascertain substance of *ex parte* communications between prosecutor and trial judge prior to sentencing petitioner); Warden v. Gall, 865 F.2d 786, 787-88 (6th Cir. 1989) (deposition of juror; physical evidence sent to petitioner's out-of-state experts for examination); Ross v. Kemp, 785 F.2d 1467, 1469, 1478-79 (11th Cir. 1986) (depositions; production of documents); Coleman v. Zant, 708 F.2d 541, 547 (11th Cir. 1983) (depositions; production of documents by newspaper and media organizations in support of excessive pretrial publicity claim); Dickson v. Wainwright, 683 F.2d 348, 352 (11th Cir. 1982) (interrogatories); Barry v. United States, 528 F.2d 1094, 1101 (7th Cir.), *cert. denied,* 429 U.S. 826 (1976) (depositions and affidavits); Schiebelhut v. United States, 318 F.2d 785 (6th Cir.

1963) (interrogatories); Clemons v. Bowersox, No. 4:97CV2344 (E.D. Mo. Aug. 10, 1988) (depositions of prosecutors and police officers; production of documents including sealed settlement agreement); United States v. Debose, 496 F. Supp. 341 (W.D. Okla. 1980) (interrogatories); Knowles v. Gladden, 254 F. Supp. 643, 644 (D. Or. 1965) (depositions); Smith v. United States, 174 F. Supp. 828, 832 (S.D. Cal.), *appeal dismissed,* 272 F.2d 228 (9th Cir. 1959), *cert. denied,* 362 U.S. 954 (1960) (medical examination); Esposito v. Manson, 65 F.R.D. 658, 660-61 (D. Conn. 1975) (interrogatories followed by depositions). *See also* Keeney v. Tamayo-Reyes, 504 U.S. 1, 14-15 (1992) (O'Connor, J., dissenting) ("once a claim is properly before the district court ... a habeas petitioner [should be treated] ... like any civil litigant" for purposes of "right to a hearing [or, presumably, any other fact-development procedure] where [the procedure] is necessary to prove the facts supporting his claim"); *id.* at 14 (habeas corpus' characteristic "functions" include "taking of depositions and ... propounding of interrogatories" (citing 28 U.S.C. § 2246)). Potentially relevant decisions outside the habeas corpus context include: Castle v. Jallah, 142 F.R.D. 618 (E.D. Va. 1992) (permitting discovery of factual statements in prison records that related to plaintiff inmate's claim of prison officials' use of excessive force); Mueller v. Walker, 124 F.R.D. 654, 658 (D. Or. 1989) (permitting discovery of witness statements and other factual material relating to plaintiff's arrest and of documents reflecting defendant police officers' use of excessive force); Johnson v. McTigue, 122 F.R.D. 9, 10-11 (S.D.N.Y. 1986) (permitting discovery of police records to prove prior conduct consistent with challenged conduct); King v. Conde, 121 F.R.D. 180, 197-98 (E.D.N.Y. 1988) (permitting discovery of documents reflecting police officers' recollection of incidents in which their misconduct is alleged); Wood v. Brier, 54 F.R.D. 7, 12-13 (E.D. Wis. 1972) (permitting discovery of internal investigation). *See also* Montalvo v. Hutchinson, 837 F. Supp. 576, 579-80 (S.D.N.Y. 1993) (upon plaintiff's objections to magistrate judge's denial of discovery requests as overly broad, district court in police misconduct case suggests that plaintiff submit, either to magistrate judge or to district judge, narrower requests for *in camera* inspection and disclosure of relevant portions of grand jury minutes and police personnel files).

In 1993, the Supreme Court proposed and Congress (by taking no action) approved modifications in FED. R. CIV. P. 26 that significantly expand the procedures that, via Habeas Rule 6, a federal court might impose on parties to a habeas corpus action. For example, in situations in which "disputed facts" have been pleaded "with particularity" (a requirement in habeas corpus cases in any event, *see supra* § 11.6), the new rule requires civil litigants, "without awaiting a discovery request," to provide their adversaries with (1) "the name and, if known, the address and telephone number of each individual likely to have discoverable information relevant" to the particularly pleaded facts and (2) "a copy of, or a description by category and location of, all documents, data compilations, and tangible things in the possession, custody, or control of the party that are relevant" to the particularly pleaded facts. FED. R. CIV. P. 26(a)(1)(A), 26(a)(1)(B). Similarly, the 1993 amendment to FED. R. CIV. P. 26(a)(3) requires the parties, at a later point in the proceedings, again without awaiting a discovery request, to inform the opposing party of the witnesses the party intends to call and the documents and other exhibits the party intends to offer at trial. Because these obligations apply reciprocally, a habeas corpus party seeking to impose them on the opposing party via a Habeas Rule 6 motion would, if successful, impose the same obligations on itself.

The availability in habeas corpus proceedings of these new procedures is unclear. The determinative question seems to be whether the new procedures constitute "the processes of discovery available under the Federal Rules of Civil Procedure" within the meaning of Habeas Rule 6. Favoring the proposed rule's availability in habeas corpus proceedings are two considerations. First, the new Rule 26 uses the phrases "information otherwise discoverable" and "discovery" to refer to materials subject not only to traditional forms of discovery on demand, such

petitioners may use discovery to develop facts sufficient either to require an evidentiary hearing or — following "expansion of the record" to include the discovered materials — to justify relief without a hearing.[4] The subsections that

as depositions and interrogatories, but also to production absent demand pursuant to the rule's new mandatory disclosure duties. *See* FED. R. CIV. P. 26(c). *See also* Advisory Committee Note to 1993 amendment to FED. R. CIV. P. 26(b)(5) (Rule 26(b)(5)'s reference to "information otherwise discoverable" encompasses "materials otherwise subject to [mandatory] disclosure under the rule *or* pursuant to a discovery request." (emphasis added)). Second, the Advisory Committee Notes repeatedly describe the new disclosure duties as forms of discovery or as attempts to increase the effectiveness of the discovery mechanisms long included in Rule 26. *See, e.g.,* Advisory Committee Notes to 1993 amendment to FED. R. CIV. P. 26(a) ("A major purpose of the revision is to accelerate the exchange of basic information about the case and to eliminate the paper work involved in requesting such information ...."; revised Rule 26(a)(1) "[i]s the functional equivalent of court-ordered interrogatories" and "requires early disclosure, without need for any request, of four types of information that have been customarily secured early in litigation through formal discovery"; revised Rule 26(a)(1)(B) "is ... a substitute for the inquiries routinely made about the existence and location of documents and other tangible things"; revised Rule 26(a)(2)(b) is substitute for "information disclosed under the former rule in answering interrogatories about the 'substance' of expert testimony"); Advisory Committee Note to 1993 amendment to FED. R. CIV. P. 33(a), ("Revision of this subdivision limits interrogatory practice. Because Rule 26(a)(1)-(3) requires disclosure of much of the information previously obtained by this form of discovery, there should be less occasion to use it."). *See also* 113 S. Ct. at CCIX (Scalia, J., dissenting from Court's transmittal of Proposed Rule 26 to Congress) ("duty-to-disclose regime does not replace the current, much-criticized discovery process; rather, it *adds a further layer of discovery.* It will likely *increase* the discovery burdens on district judges ....." (emphasis in original)). Countervailing considerations suggesting that the disclosure obligations in revised Rule 26 do *not* constitute "discovery" for purposes of Habeas Rule 6 are that (1) the drafters gave the new procedures a new name, other than "discovery," namely, the "duty of disclosure," and (2) Justice Scalia, among others, has characterized the amendment as a sea change — something quite new and different — from prior discovery practice. *See id.* at CCCX ("The proposed new regime does not fit comfortably within the American judicial system, which relies on adversarial litigation to develop the facts before a neutral decisionmaker.").

    [4] *See infra* §§ 19.4c, 19.4d. Although recent legislation, discussed *infra* Chapter 20, *see generally supra* §§ 3.2, 3.3, 3.4, limits the availability of evidentiary hearings in certain circumstances, it does not appear to limit other fact-development techniques — mainly, expansion of the record, *see infra* § 19.5 — for proving factual allegations through evidence generated with the aid of financial assistance (*see supra* § 19.3), discovery, and other investigative measures. *See supra* § 19.4a n.4 and accompanying text; *infra* §§ 19.4d n.27, 19.5 n.6 and accompanying text. Discovery may be particularly useful in establishing out-of-court misconduct by law enforcement personnel, for example, prosecutorial suppression of exculpatory evidence or presentation of false inculpatory evidence, extraction of involuntary confessions, illegal searches and arrests, discriminatory jury selection procedures, and selective prosecution. *See* claims catalogued *supra* § 11.2c (paras. (1), (3)); authority cited *supra* note 3. Frequently, misconduct hidden by police officers or prosecutors, or both, can be uncovered by obtaining production of prosecutors' files or depositions of officers unwilling to talk to counsel. *See* Strickler v. Pruett, 1998 WL 340420 (4th Cir. June 17, 1998) (*per curiam*), *cert granted,* 119 S. Ct. 40 (1998) (discovery of police file reveals statements to police made by crucial prosecution witness that contradicts her trial testimony); United States v.

follow discuss the development of Habeas Rule 6, the bases for a federal court's exercise of discretion to order that procedure, and the timing and form of discovery requests.

b. *Pre-Rules discovery.* The Supreme Court's 1969 decision in *Harris v. Nelson*[5] led to the adoption several years later of Habeas Rule 6 and, indeed, of the Habeas Rules as a whole. In *Harris,* the Court addressed the question whether a federal habeas corpus petitioner could require the respondent to answer a set of written interrogatories propounded pursuant to Federal Rule of Civil Procedure 33.[6] Although *Harris* held that the 1938 Federal Rules of Civil Procedure did not apply as a matter of course in habeas corpus proceedings, it concluded that the fair and efficient conduct of such proceedings demands a range of flexible methods for securing information, including discovery in some cases.[7] Under authority of the All Writs Act, therefore, the Court authorized federal district courts to grant discovery procedures when "necessary ... in order that a fair and meaningful evidentiary hearing may be held."[8] "[W]here specific allegations

---

Weintraub, 871 F.2d 1257, 1259 (5th Cir. 1989) (discovery reveals prosecutorial suppression of evidence); Coleman v. Kemp, 778 F.2d 1487 (11th Cir. 1985), *cert. denied,* 476 U.S. 1164 (1986) (relief granted on prejudicial pretrial claim developed through extensive discovery ordered in Coleman v. Zant, 708 F.2d 541, 547 (11th Cir. 1983)). *Cf.* Amadeo v. Zant, 486 U.S. 214 (1988) (prosecutor's manipulation of jury selection process to underrepresent African-Americans and women uncovered by attorney in unrelated civil suit who found misfiled handwritten memorandum buried within master jury lists).

[5] 394 U.S. 286 (1969).

[6] *See* FED. R. CIV. P. 33 (party's service of interrogatories on opposing party obligates opposing party to answer or move court for order absolving it of duty to answer). Prior to *Harris,* the 9th Circuit had held the Civil Rules' discovery provisions wholly inapplicable to habeas corpus proceedings. Wilson v. Harris, 373 F.2d 141, 144 (9th Cir. 1967). Other courts had held the Civil Rules' discovery provisions wholly applicable because habeas corpus is a civil procedure. *See, e.g.,* Schiebelhut v. United States, 318 F.2d 785, 786 (6th Cir. 1963); United States ex rel. Seals v. Wiman, 304 F.2d 53, 64 (5th Cir. 1962), *cert. denied,* 372 U.S. 915, 924 (1963). Still other courts had held that the discovery provisions in the Civil Rules were applicable by "analogy" in some cases, *e.g.,* Wilson v. Weigel, 387 F.2d 632, 634 n.3 (9th Cir. 1967), *cert. denied,* 394 U.S. 961 (1969), or that the use of particular discovery provisions in the Civil Rules was necessary to effectuate statutory policy with respect to habeas corpus, *e.g.,* Knowles v. Gladden, 254 F. Supp. 643, 644-45 (D. Or. 1965). *See Harris, supra,* 394 U.S. at 289 n.1.

[7] *Harris, supra,* 394 U.S. at 290, 299. Although the Court noted that 28 U.S.C. § 2246 allows evidence to be taken in habeas corpus cases by "oral testimony, by deposition, or upon affidavit and written interrogatory," *id.* at 296, 299, it read section 2246 to create substitute hearing procedures, *see* Rule 7 of the Rules Governing § 2254 Cases; *infra* § 19.5 (expansion of record), not a right to discovery. *See also infra* § 19.5 n.20. *But cf.* Keeny v. Tamayo-Reyes, 504 U.S. 1, 14 (1992) (O'Connor, J., dissenting) (suggesting that section 2246 authorizes discovery).

[8] *Harris, supra,* 394 U.S. at 300 (citing 28 U.S.C. § 1651). *See* Bracy v. Gramley, 117 S. Ct. 1793, 1797 (1997) (*Harris* held that All Writs Act "gave federal courts the power to 'fashion

before the court show reason to believe that the petitioner may, if the facts are fully developed, be able to demonstrate that he is confined illegally and is therefore entitled to relief," the Court concluded, the discretion to grant discovery may rise to the level of a "duty."[9]

By way of example, if a district court concluded that a hearing must be held on a claim that law enforcement officers illegally arrested the petitioner, induced the petitioner to confess involuntarily, or withheld exculpatory evidence, *Harris* authorized the district court to grant the petitioner leave to depose those officers or to serve them with interrogatories "in order that a fair and meaningful hearing may be held."[10] Under *Harris*, these procedures would be appropriate if, for instance, the knowledgeable officers were unwilling to talk to counsel for the prisoner and discovery were necessary to avoid the inefficiency of, and perhaps the need for, an evidentiary hearing involving the direct testimony of witnesses with whom counsel never before has spoken.

In a footnote, the *Harris* Court proposed that general rules of procedure be formulated for federal habeas corpus proceedings analogous to the Federal Rules of Civil Procedure.[11] In 1976, acting upon this suggestion, the Court promulgated, and Congress adopted, the Rules Governing § 2254 Cases.[12] As noted

---

appropriate modes of procedure,' including discovery, to dispose of habeas petitions 'as law and justice require'" (citing *Harris, supra*, 394 U.S. at 299, 300)).

[9] *Id. Accord Bracy v. Gramley, supra*, 117 S. Ct. at 1799 ("In *Harris*, we stated that 'where specific allegations before the court show reason to believe that the petitioner may, if the facts are fully developed, be able to demonstrate that he is ... entitled to relief, it is the duty of the courts to provide the necessary facilities and procedures for an adequate inquiry.' Habeas Corpus Rule 6 is meant to be 'consistent' with *Harris*." (quoting *Harris, supra*, 394 U.S. at 299; Advisory Committee Note to Rule 6 of the Rules Governing § 2254 Cases)); *Coleman v. Zant, supra*, 708 F.2d at 547 (discovery required because facts petitioner sought to discover through depositions and production of documents were "'indispensable to a fair, rounded, development of the material facts'" (quoting Townsend v. Sain, 372 U.S. 293, 322 (1963))).

[10] *Harris, supra*, 394 U.S. at 300. *See, e.g.*, McKenzie v. Risley, 915 F.2d 1396, 1398 (9th Cir. 1990) (remanded for hearing after allowing discovery to ascertain substance of *ex parte* communications between prosecutor and trial judge prior to petitioner's sentencing).

[11] *Harris, supra*, 394 U.S. at 300 n.7. *See Bracy v. Gramley, supra*, 117 S. Ct. at 1797 (discussing genesis of Habeas Rules and particularly Rule 6(a)). In the period between the announcement of *Harris* and the adoption of Habeas Rule 6, federal courts relied upon *Harris* and the All Writs Act, 28 U.S.C. § 1651, as the bases for ordering discovery. *See, e.g.*, United States ex rel. Williams v. Walker, 535 F.2d 383, 386 (7th Cir. 1976); Barry v. United States, 528 F.2d 1094, 1101 (7th Cir.), *cert. denied*, 429 U.S. 826 (1976) (depositions and affidavits); Moorhead v. United States, 456 F.2d 992, 996 (3d Cir. 1972); Wagner v. United States, 418 F.2d 618 (9th Cir. 1969) (interrogatories followed by depositions); Esposito v. Manson, 65 F.R.D. 658, 659-61 (D. Conn. 1975).

[12] *See* Advisory Committee Note to Rule 11 of the Rules Governing § 2254 Cases. *See also* Rule 11 of the Rules Governing § 2254 Cases ("appropriate" Federal Rules of Civil Procedure apply in habeas corpus cases when not inconsistent with Habeas Rules).

in the next subsection, because *Harris* so directly led to the discovery rules that the Court and Congress adopted, the decision continues to be authoritative in habeas corpus discovery litigation.

c. *Habeas Rule 6.* Habeas Rule 6 affords district judges considerable discretion as to discovery.[13] The Advisory Committee Note to Rule 6 indicates that the Supreme Court's treatment of discovery in *Harris v. Nelson*[14] should inform the exercise of that discretion. In particular, the Advisory Committee Note reaffirms the district court's "duty" under *Harris* to order discovery when a petitioner's specific allegations suggest that full development of the facts may enable her to demonstrate a right to relief.[15] Habeas Rule 6(a) accordingly authorizes at least as much discovery as *Harris* permitted.

---

[13] *See* Bracy v. Gramley, 117 S. Ct. 1793, 1799 (1997) ("Although, given the facts of this particular case, it would be an abuse of discretion not to permit any discovery, Rule 6(a) makes it clear that the scope and extent of ... [habeas corpus] discovery is a matter confided to the discretion of the District Court").

[14] 394 U.S. 286 (1969) (discussed in Advisory Committee Note to Habeas Rule 6).

[15] Advisory Committee Note to Rule 6 of the Rules Governing § 2254 Cases (Rule 6 is "consistent" with *Harris'* discussion of the district courts' duty to order discovery in certain circumstances). *See Bracy v. Gramley, supra,* 117 S. Ct. at 1798-99 & n.10 (*Harris* "stated that 'where specific allegations before the court show reason to believe that the petition may, if the facts are fully developed, be able to demonstrate that he is ... entitled to relief, it is the duty of the courts to provide the necessary facilities and procedures for an adequate inquiry,'" and "Habeas Corpus Rule 6 is meant to be 'consistent' with *Harris*" (quoting *Harris, supra,* 394 U.S. at 299; Advisory Committee Note to Rule 6 of the Rules Governing § 2254 Cases); district court's blanket denial of petitioner's discovery request constituted abuse of discretion under standard quoted above where petitioner claimed that trial judge endeavored to produce harsh outcome in petitioner's case in order to camouflage judge's taking of bribes in return for leniency in other cases, and where petitioner established that (1) his "murder trial was sandwiched tightly between other murder trials that [judge] fixed," (2) petitioner's appointed attorney "announced that he was ready for trial just a few weeks" after being appointed to handle capital murder case requiring investigation of events in another State and only sought continuance, which was denied, in middle of trial when continuance was barred by state law, and (3) appointed lawyer was "a former associate of [judge's] in a law practice that was familiar and comfortable with corruption [and] may have agreed to take this capital case to trial quickly so that petitioner's conviction would deflect any suspicion that the [contemporaneous] rigged ... cases might attract"); Herrera v. Collins, 506 U.S. 390, 444 (1993) (Blackmun, J., dissenting on other grounds) (quoted *supra* § 19.4a n.2); Toney v. Gammon, 79 F.3d 693, 700 (8th Cir. 1996) ("Although it is generally within a district court's discretion to grant or deny discovery requests under Rule 6, a court's denial of discovery is an abuse of discretion if discovery is 'indispensable to a fair, rounded development of the material facts.'"); Perillo v. Johnson, 79 F.3d 441, 444-45 (5th Cir. 1996) (district court erred in denying discovery on "factual dispute which, if resolved in [petitioner's] favor, would entitle her to relief and [on which] there are no state factfindings ... that are entitled to the presumption of correctness"); Teague v. Scott, 60 F.3d 1167, 1172 (5th Cir. 1995) ("Denial of an opportunity for discovery is an abuse of discretion when the discovery is necessary to fully develop the facts of a claim."); East v. Scott, 55 F.3d 996, 1001-02 (5th Cir. 1995) (petitioner, whose factual allegations were "facially sufficient to establish

There are several ways in which Rule 6 authorizes *wider* discovery than *Harris*. Although language in *Harris* suggests that the petitioner might have to establish "a prima facie case for relief" as a prerequisite to discovery,[16] Rule 6(a)'s "good cause shown" standard permits the use of discovery to *establish* a *prima facie* case for relief.[17] Moreover, the Advisory Committee Note to Rule 6 approves the use of discovery in appropriate cases *before* an evidentiary hearing has been granted, a possibility not contemplated in *Harris*.[18] The Supreme Court's

---

a *prima facie* due process claim," was entitled to discovery "to fully develop the facts"; "[w]hile the district court generally has discretion to grant or deny discovery requests under Rule 6, a court's blanket denial of discovery is an abuse of discretion if discovery is 'indispensable to a fair, rounded, development of the material facts'"). *Cf.* Ward v. Whitley, 21 F.3d 1355, 1367 (5th Cir. 1994), *cert. denied*, 513 U.S. 1192 (1995) (petitioner's "[c]onclusionary" factual allegations were insufficiently "specific" to entitle him to discovery under Habeas Rule 6).

[16] *Harris, supra*, 394 U.S. at 290.

[17] *See, e.g., Bracy v. Gramley, supra*, 117 S. Ct. at 1798-99 & n.10 (district court abused discretion in denying discovery under circumstances discussed *supra* note 15); *Toney v. Gammon, supra*, 79 F.3d at 700 (district court abused discretion in denying petitioner's Rule 6(a) motion to conduct DNA testing of exhibits prosecution introduced at trial in order to show that trial counsel "was ineffective for failing to pursue ... claim of mistaken identity or to obtain state's evidence so as to conduct scientific examinations"). The Advisory Committee's discussion of *Harris* omits the "prima facie case" language the Court used in *Harris*. *See* Advisory Committee Note to Rule 6 of the Rules Governing § 2254 Cases; Coleman v. Zant, 708 F.2d 541, 547 n.9 (11th Cir. 1983) (applying "good cause" standard). The Supreme Court's decision in *Bracy v. Gramley, supra*, rather clearly rejects any requirement of a "*prima facie*" case for relief in advance of discovery. First, *Bracy* omits any reference to *Harris*'s "*prima facie*" language, relying instead on a considerably more forgiving formulation of the "good cause" rule taken from the same case, which only requires some "'*reason to believe* that the petitioner *may, if* the facts are fully developed, be able to demonstrate that he is ... entitled to relief.'" 117 S. Ct. at 1799 (emphasis added) (quoted in full *supra* note 15). In addition, the Court rejected the court of appeals' conclusion that discovery was properly denied "because petitioner had failed to uncover any evidence of actual bias without discovery," so that "'the probability is slight that a program of depositions aimed at crooks and their accomplices ... will yield such evidence.'" *Id.* at 1796. Finally and most importantly, *Bracy* held that denying discovery was an abuse of discretion even though the petitioner's factual allegation of unconstitutional, case-specific judicial bias was concededly "quite speculative," "only a theory at this point," "not supported by any solid evidence," and premised on facts that "might be equally likely" to support an inference contrary to the one the petitioner advanced. *Id.* at 1797, 1799.

[18] *See, e.g.,* Jones v. Wood, 114 F.3d 1002, 1008-09 (9th Cir. 1997) (rejecting state's contention that habeas corpus petitioners are entitled to discovery only "on issues that are to be considered in an already-scheduled evidentiary hearing" and explaining that "discovery is available to habeas petitioners at the discretion of the district court for good cause shown, regardless of whether there is to be an evidentiary hearing"); *see also Bracy v. Gramley, supra*, 117 S. Ct. at 1799 (holding that denial of discovery was abuse of discretion notwithstanding that no evidentiary hearing had been ordered or, as far as decision indicates, requested); Clemons v. Bowersox, No. 4:97CV2344 (E.D. Mo. Aug. 10, 1988) (granting discovery even though court defers ruling on petitioner's request for evidentiary hearing until respondent files response and record of state court

decision in *Blackledge v. Allison*,[19] handed down at approximately the same time Habeas Rule 6 was adopted, supports the Advisory Committee's interpretation. In *Blackledge,* the Court held that the district court should not have dismissed a petition summarily without further factual inquiry. The Court cited with approval the Advisory Committee's suggestion that federal judges utilize prehearing discovery as one means of determining, without resort to an evidentiary hearing, whether there is a factual basis for the petitioner's claims.[20] In general, *Blackledge* suggests that district judges consider ordering discovery before deciding whether an evidentiary hearing is appropriate whenever the claim on which discovery is sought is not so "'palpably incredible' [or] 'patently frivolous or false' as to warrant summary dismissal."[21] Finally, the Advisory Committee Note to Habeas Rule 9(a) points out that Habeas "Rule 6 can be used by the court to allow petitioner liberal discovery" to establish that her delay in filing the petition did not prejudice the state.[22] In addition to emphasizing the liberality of

---

proceedings). *Compare Harris, supra,* 394 U.S. at 300 (discovery permissible "in order that a fair and meaningful evidentiary hearing may be held") *with* Advisory Committee Note to Habeas Rule 6 ("While requests for discovery in habeas proceedings normally follow the granting of an evidentiary hearing, there may be instances in which discovery would be appropriate beforehand."). *See infra* § 19.4d.

[19] 431 U.S. 63 (1977).

[20] *Id.* at 81 (citing Advisory Committee Note to Rule 6 of the Rules Governing § 2254 Cases). *Accord, e.g., East v. Scott, supra,* 55 F.3d at 1002 (relying on *Blackledge v. Allison, supra,* court of appeals holds that district court should have ordered discovery and then, "[f]ollowing discovery, ... decide[d] whether East has raised a genuine question of material fact requiring an evidentiary hearing"; "[a]llegations that are facially sufficient to entitle a petitioner to discovery under Rule 6 might not entitle a petitioner to an evidentiary hearing if discovery reveals the absence of any genuine issues of disputed fact"); Jones v. Parke, 734 F.2d 1142, 1148 (6th Cir. 1984); Dickson v. Wainwright, 683 F.2d 348, 352 (11th Cir. 1982) (district court may use discovery or evidentiary hearing to "test substance of petitioner's allegations"); Stewart v. Estelle, 634 F.2d 998, 1000 (5th Cir. 1981). *See also Blackledge, supra,* 431 U.S. at 82 n.25 ("before dismissing facially adequate allegations short of an evidentiary hearing, ordinarily a district judge should seek as a minimum to obtain affidavits from all persons likely to have firsthand knowledge"); Williams v. Kullman, 722 F.2d 1048, 1051 (2d Cir. 1983) (*dicta*); *supra* § 15.2a. Cases decided before the adoption of Habeas Rule 6 endorse a similar use of prehearing discovery. *See, e.g.,* United States ex rel. Williams v. Walker, 535 F.2d 383, 386 (7th Cir. 1976); Wagner v. United States, 418 F.2d 618, 621 (9th Cir. 1969) (cited in Advisory Committee Note to Rule 6 of the Rules Governing § 2254 Cases); Wilson v. Weigel, 387 F.2d 632 (9th Cir. 1967).

[21] *Blackledge, supra,* 431 U.S. at 76, 82-83 (quoting Machibroda v. United States, 368 U.S. 487, 495 (1962); Pennsylvania ex rel. Herman v. Claudy, 350 U.S. 116, 119 (1956)). *See also* Keeney v. Tamayo-Reyes, 504 U.S. 1, 14-15 (1992) (O'Connor, J., dissenting) ("once a claim is properly before the district court ... a habeas petitioner [should be treated] ... like any civil litigant" for purposes of "right to a hearing [or, presumably, any other fact-development procedure] where [the procedure] is necessary to prove the facts supporting his claim").

[22] *See* Rule 9(a) of the Rules Governing § 2254 Cases (prefiling delay harming state's ability to defend is grounds for dismissing petition); *infra* Chapter 24.

the discovery right contemplated by the drafters of the Habeas Rules, this passage (1) confirms that discovery is available not only to explore the petitioner's factual allegations but also to refute factual defenses asserted by the state, another use of discovery not contemplated in *Harris,* and (2) emphasizes the availability of discovery to uncover factual information especially accessible to the state.[23] Overall, therefore, Rule 6 warrants discovery "when[ever] it would help the court make a reliable determination with respect to the petitioner's claim."[24]

d. *In lieu of a hearing.* As *Blackledge v. Allison*[25] makes clear, the drafters of Habeas Rule 6 envisioned that discovery would serve not only as an issue-clarifying preface to evidentiary hearings but also, in appropriate cases, as a substitute for such hearings.[26] In the latter role, discovery may generate information establishing either that the petitioner's claim is so clearly meritorious that relief must be granted without a hearing[27] or that the claim is so clearly without

---

[23] *See* Bracy v. Gramley, 117 S. Ct. 1793, 1796 & n.3, 1799 (1997) (denial of habeas corpus petitioner's request for discovery of nonpublic documents in state's possession was abuse of discretion under circumstances); Coleman v. Zant, 708 F.2d 541, 547-48 (11th Cir. 1983) (discovery permitted to assist petitioner in showing that state court factfindings were not adequate); *supra* § 19.4a n.4.

[24] Herrera v. Collins, 506 U.S. 390, 444 (1993) (Blackmun, J., dissenting on other grounds).

[25] 431 U.S. 63 (1977).

[26] *Id.* at 81.

[27] *See infra* § 19.5 (Habeas Rule 7 allows district courts to "expand the record" to include — and to rule on the basis of — documentary and other materials that otherwise would be inadmissible hearsay, such as affidavits, deposition transcripts, and prosecutor's file). The drafters expressly contemplated that Rule 6 discovery, in tandem with Rule 7 expansion of the record, would obviate the need for hearings in some meritorious cases. *See* Advisory Committee Notes to Rules 6 and 7 of the Rules Governing § 2254 Cases. *See also Blackledge, supra,* 431 U.S. at 81-82; Matta-Ballesteros v. Henman, 896 F.2d 255, 259 (7th Cir. 1990) (*dicta*); *supra* § 19.4a n.4 and accompanying text. *See generally supra* §§ 16.1c (respondent-initiated summary judgment proceedings), 17.3 (petitioner-initiated summary judgment). Although recent legislation, discussed *infra* Chapter 20, *see generally supra* §§ 3.2, 3.3, 3.4, limits the availability of evidentiary hearings in certain circumstances, it does not appear to limit other fact-development techniques — *e.g.,* expansion of the record, *see infra* § 19.5 — for proving factual allegations through evidence generated with the aid of financial assistance (*see supra* § 19.3), discovery, and other investigative measures. In appropriate cases, therefore, a habeas corpus petitioner who has been denied a federal evidentiary hearing may nonetheless establish a right to relief on a fact-based claim by demonstrating that (1) evidence developed during discovery (or using any other investigative technique) justifies relief even absent in-court evidentiary proceedings conducted by the petitioner, and (2) the evidence may appropriately be placed before the court via the "expansion of the record" device discussed *infra* § 19.5.

merit that it may be dismissed without further proceedings.[28] In either event, the illumination of factual issues through party-driven proceedings conducted without court supervision is a major virtue of the procedure, which parties and judges in habeas corpus cases ought to use more often.

Discovery may serve judicial economy in other ways as well. For example, the court may authorize discovery to: (1) determine whether it is necessary for out-of-state witnesses to appear at a hearing at court expense; (2) minimize the possibility of surprise at or inadequate preparation for hearings, thereby preventing delays and continuances; or (3) assist in resolving defenses asserted by the state, such as nonexhaustion of state remedies.[29]

e. *Capital cases.* When an individual's life hangs in the balance, the Supreme Court repeatedly has insisted that higher standards of reliability and fairness be observed.[30] Because habeas corpus discovery is designed to aid courts in determining the validity of the petitioners' claims, it often can add — and may in

---

[28] *See* Rice v. Clarke, 923 F.2d 117, 118-19 (8th Cir. 1991) (because discovery of FBI records failed to show that FBI gave analysis of audiotapes to local law enforcement officials, no further discovery or evidentiary hearing required on claim that local law enforcement officials withheld exculpatory evidence from petitioner); United States v. Wilson, 901 F.2d 378, 380 (4th Cir. 1990) (hearing and relief denied on basis of information provided after district court thrice expanded record to include additional documentary material); Matta-Ballestros v. Henman, 896 F.2d 255, 258-59 (7th Cir. 1990) (evidentiary hearing was unnecessary because discovery placed all facts essential to consideration of claim before court); Dickson v. Wainwright, 683 F.2d 348, 352 (11th Cir. 1982) (interrogatories to petitioner may establish that claims lack merit); *Developments in the Law, supra* § 19.4a n.1, at 1182. If the court relies on this rationale to deny a post-discovery hearing, the petitioner contemplating an appeal should ask that the fruits of discovery on which the court relied be made part of the record. *See* Ross v. Kemp, 785 F.2d 1467, 1470, 1478-79 (11th Cir. 1986) (products of court-ordered discovery are not automatically made part of record; incorporation in record requires motion to and order by court); *infra* § 19.5. *See also infra* § 19.4h n.41 and accompanying text (court generally may not resolve matters turning on credibility of affiants or deponents without viewing their testimony in court).

[29] *See* Moorhead v. United States, 456 F.2d 992 (3d Cir. 1972) (deposition of prisoner in Pennsylvania may be appropriate to determine necessity of transporting him to hearing in Virgin Islands); *Developments in the Law, supra* § 19.4a n.1, at 1181. *See generally* Hickman v. Taylor, 329 U.S. 495, 500-01 (1947) ("instruments of discovery [in Civil Rules 26-37] now serve (1) as a device ... to narrow and clarify the basic issues between the parties, and (2) as a device for ascertaining the facts, or information as to the existence or whereabouts of facts, relative to those issues. Thus civil trials in the federal courts no longer need to be carried on in the dark. The way is now clear ... for the parties to obtain the fullest possible knowledge of the issues and facts before trial").

[30] *See, e.g.,* Lockett v. Ohio, 438 U.S. 586, 604 (1978) (plurality opinion) ("'the penalty of death is qualitatively different' from any other sentence.... We are satisfied that this qualitative difference between death and other penalties calls for a greater degree of reliability when the death sentence is imposed." (quoting Woodson v. North Carolina, 428 U.S. 280, 305 (1976))); *supra* § 2.6.

fact be indispensable — to the reliability of habeas corpus proceedings in capital cases. For this reason, liberal use of discovery is appropriate in such cases.[31]

f. *Timing.* Earlier sections discuss the bases for obtaining fact-development procedures in habeas corpus proceedings, especially in capital cases, *before* a petition has been filed in order to enable the petitioner to include and "adequately set forth all of [the] ... colorable claims for relief" in the first habeas corpus petition.[32] Those bases may apply by analogy to permit the granting of prepetition requests for discovery.[33] When a prepetition request is not appropriate, the petitioner generally should file a motion for discovery before or at the same time as a motion for an evidentiary hearing — that is, simultaneously with the petition or within a reasonably short period of time after the state answers.[34] Early filing of discovery motions maximizes the chances that inform-

---

[31] *See* Bracy v. Gramley, 117 S. Ct. 1793, 1797-99 (1997) (discussed *supra* § 19.4c nn.15, 17) (denial of capital habeas corpus petitioner's discovery request abused district court's discretion); McFarland v. Scott, 512 U.S. 849, 859 (1994) (heavy burden that current law places on habeas corpus prisoners to allege and litigate all possibly available constitutional claims in initial petition creates need for prepetition appointment of counsel and other procedural devices to enable petitioners to meet burden); *id.* at 860 (O'Connor, J., concurring in the judgment in part) (similar); Brown v. Vasquez, 952 F.2d 1164, 1167 (9th Cir.), *cert. denied,* 503 U.S. 1011 (1992) (similar); McKenzie v. Risley, 915 F.2d 1396, 1398 (9th Cir. 1990); *Ross v. Kemp, supra,* 785 F.2d at 1478-79; Coleman v. Zant, 708 F.2d 541, 547 (11th Cir. 1983) (same).

[32] *McFarland v. Scott, supra,* 512 U.S. at 860 (O'Connor, J., concurring in the judgment in part). *Accord id.* at 855 (majority opinion). *See supra* §§ 12.3a, 19.2 nn.5-6 and accompanying text, 19.3 nn.8-14 & 18-19 and accompanying text.

[33] *See also* FED. R. CIV. P. 27(a) (permitting depositions to be taken before civil action is filed in order to perpetuate testimony of witness who may not be able or available to testify by time action is filed); MOORE'S FEDERAL PRACTICE, *supra* note 1, § 27-07[2] (Civil Rule 27 is appropriately invoked by state prisoner under sentence of death to preserve testimony in anticipation of future habeas corpus petition to be filed if alleged constitutional violations are not cured in state proceedings (citing In re Sims, 389 F.2d 148 (5th Cir. 1967))). *But cf.* United States ex rel. Nunes v. Nelson, 467 F.2d 1380, 1380-81 (9th Cir. 1972) (pre-Rule 6 decision disallowing prepetition discovery). *But see* In re Netherland, No. 97-8 (4th Cir. Apr. 10, 1997) (Luttig, J., Circuit Judge) (staying district court's *ex parte* grant of prepetition discovery to state habeas corpus prisoner); Calderon v. United States Dist. Ct., 98 F.3d 1102, 1104-07 (9th Cir. 1996), *cert. denied,* 117 S. Ct. 1830 (1997) (denying prepetition discovery). Recently enacted statutes of limitations, the contents and applicability of which are discussed *supra* §§ 3.2, 3.3, 3.4, 5.1b, and doubts whether the filing of prepetition requests for counsel and discovery within the limitations period satisfies those statutes, *see supra* §§ 5.1b nn.80-91 and accompanying text, 11.1, add an important strategic consideration to the decision whether to make a prepetition request for financial assistance.

[34] *See* Bracy v. Gramley, 117 S. Ct. 1793, 1796, 1799 (1997) (holding that, under circumstances of case, district court abused discretion in denying, in its entirety, discovery motion filed simultaneously with habeas corpus petition). *See generally supra* §§ 11.7c, 11.7d, 16.2, 17.1. In the event that prepetition discovery is not available, counsel or petitioner should consider the

ation gathered through discovery will dissuade the court from dismissing the petition summarily and encourage the court to grant a hearing or relief in lieu of a hearing.

g. *The discovery motion.* The reasons for each discovery request should be discussed in a memorandum or affidavits in support of a motion for discovery. The discussion should identify the claim on which the party is seeking discovery and explain why the full factual development of the claim requires the requested discovery.[35] The discovery applicant also should explain why prior state proceedings in the case did not adequately develop the information sought and why the applicant is not at fault for inadequacies in the state court record.[36] Typically, the courts insist upon a specific but not overly detailed explanation of the connection between the requested discovery and the claims at issue. For example, the 8th Circuit affirmed the denial of a section 2255 movant's request for discovery because the movant "alleged no facts showing good cause for discovery," "merely listed the records he sought to obtain, including those belonging to the 'city jail,' the 'central jail,' the police, the postal inspector and the

---

discussion *supra* § 11.3b nn.12-15 and accompanying text, which lays out a procedure for including in the habeas corpus petition and specially pleading potentially available claims that are not yet factually developed in cases in which the lack of discovery or other fact-development procedures prevents counsel from determining whether the claims actually exist. *See also supra* §§ 19.2 n.6, 19.3 n.13.

[35] *See* Lynott v. Story, 929 F.2d 228, 232-33 (6th Cir. 1991) (to justify discovery, petitioner must make specific allegations, not present here, that petitioner may be entitled to relief if facts are fully developed through discovery or other procedure); other authority cited *infra* note 37. *Cf.* Bracy v. Gramley, 117 S. Ct. 1793, 1797 (1997) (suggesting that discovery motion should "identify the 'essential elements'" of petitioner's constitutional claim).

[36] *See* Advisory Committee Note to Habeas Rule 6 (motion should "advise the judge of the necessity for discovery and enable him to make certain that the inquiry is relevant and appropriately narrow"); Maynard v. Dixon, 943 F.2d 407, 412 (4th Cir. 1991), *cert. denied,* 502 U.S. 1110 (1992) (district court did not abuse discretion in denying discovery motion because petitioner "had ample opportunity to seek the[] [requested] documents at the state post-conviction proceeding, but chose not to"); United States v. Wilson, 901 F.2d 378, 381-82 (4th Cir. 1990) (petitioner denied right to depose witness whom he had reason to interview, and could have interviewed, before trial); Byrd v. Armontrout, 880 F.2d 1, 7 (8th Cir. 1989), *cert. denied,* 494 U.S. 1019 (1990) (discovery properly denied because petitioner failed to explain his failure in state proceedings to try to discover and present evidence now sought in federal proceedings); Coleman v. Zant, 708 F.2d 541, 547 & n.9 (11th Cir. 1983) (discovery permitted to assist petitioner in showing that state court factfindings were not adequate). *See also* Hoffa v. United States, 471 F.2d 391 (6th Cir.), *cert. denied,* 414 U.S. 880 (1973) (denial of discovery upheld because witness whom movant sought to depose had been cross-examined for five days at trial, covering all issues raised in motion); Gilday v. Calahan, 99 F.R.D. 308 (D. Mass. 1983) (discovery denied because facts sought were disproved at state trial); *supra* §§ 19.3 n.3 and accompanying text, 19.3 n.4.

FBI," and "did not state what he hoped to find in these records or how they would help him prosecute his ... motion."[37]

---

[37] Smith v. United States, 618 F.2d 507, 509 (8th Cir. 1980). *Accord, e.g., Lynott v. Story, supra,* 929 F.2d at 232-33 (discussed *supra* note 35); Rice v. Clarke, 923 F.2d 117, 118-19 (8th Cir. 1991) (discussed *supra* § 19.4d n.28); United States v. Wilson, 901 F.2d 378, 382 (4th Cir. 1990) (discovery request was too broad and unspecific to suggest that requested materials existed or would reveal state's suppression of material evidence); Harris v. Pulley, 885 F.2d 1354, 1373, 1375 (9th Cir. 1988), *cert. denied,* 493 U.S. 1051 (1990) (discovery properly denied because statistical evidence petitioner sought would not prove individualized discrimination); Porcaro v. United States, 832 F.2d 208, 211-12 (1st Cir. 1987) (discovery properly denied because petitioner failed to explain or make apparent the basis of discovery request); Grubbs v. Delo, 734 F. Supp. 395, 397 (E.D. Mo. 1990), *aff'd,* 948 F.2d 1459 (8th Cir. 1991), *cert denied,* 506 U.S. 835 (1992); United States v. Rubio, 722 F. Supp. 77, 79-80 (D. Del. 1989), *aff'd,* 908 F.2d 965 (3d Cir.), *cert. denied,* 498 U.S. 986 (1990) (discovery denied because of lack of factually specific allegations of need). *See also* Evans v. Thompson, 881 F.2d 117, 119 (4th Cir. 1989), *cert. denied,* 497 U.S. 1010 (1990) (district court "conducted an *in camera* review of the [state's] files and, finding nothing relevant to petitioner's assertions, denied his [discovery] request"); Willis v. Newsome, 771 F.2d 1445, 1448 (11th Cir. 1985), *cert. denied,* 475 U.S. 1050 (1986) (not abuse of discretion to deny requested discovery — exhumation of body of victim — where discovered material could not establish, and petitioner did not proffer other evidence satisfying, one of two legal prerequisites to ineffective assistance claim; discovery also not available on issue of prisoner's guilt, which is not cognizable in habeas corpus); Willie v. Maggio, 737 F.2d 1372, 1395 (5th Cir.), *cert. denied,* 469 U.S. 1002 (1984); United States ex rel. Nunes v. Nelson, 467 F.2d 1380 (9th Cir. 1972) (discovery denied to assist petitioner in preparing future petition).

Examples of decisions finding that discovery requests revealed "good cause" for discovery are, *e.g., Rice v. Clarke, supra* at 118 n.3 (statement of local assistant police chief suggesting that FBI made analysis of audiotape provided good cause for discovery of FBI records to determine whether analysis had been made and, if so, whether FBI gave potentially exculpatory analysis to local law enforcement officials who never turned it over to defense); *Coleman v. Zant, supra,* 708 F.2d at 547 & n.9; Clemons v. Bowersox, No. 4:97CV2344 (E.D. Mo. Aug. 10, 1988) (petitioner adequately supported requests for depositions of prosecutors and police officers and production of documents by proffering "some evidence tending to support his allegations"); other decisions cited *supra* § 19.4a n.3.

Prior to 1970, FED. R. CIV. P. 34 included a "good cause" requirement for discovery, *see* Stark v. Photo Researchers, Inc., 77 F.R.D. 18, 20 (S.D.N.Y. 1977), suggesting that pre-1970 decisions under the provision might assist in interpreting the "good cause" requirement in Habeas Rule 6. *Compare* Crowe v. Chesapeake & Ohio Ry. Co., 29 F.R.D. 148, 148-51 (E.D. Mich. 1961) ("good cause" for discovery under Civil Rule 34 because adverse party possessed only contemporaneous records of critical events and witnesses accessible to movant could not remember critical events) *and* Loew's, Inc. v. Martin, 10 F.R.D. 143, 145-46 (N.D. Ohio 1949) ("good cause" for discovery under Rule 34 includes showing that information sought is relevant and that requested documents are principal source of information) *with* G & P Amusement Co. v. Regent Theater Co., 9 F.R.D. 721, 723-24 (N.D. Ohio 1949) (Civil Rule 34 "good cause" not shown when movant can obtain documents through other means).

The Supreme Court's decision in Bracy v. Gramley, 117 S. Ct. 1793 (1997), illustrates the importance of providing the district court with as much factual support for ordering discovery as possible. In *Bracy,* the Court held that the district court abused its discretion in denying discovery motions that made relatively specific discovery requests and attached several detailed documentary

Habeas Rule 6(b) requires the discovery applicant to submit with the motion any written interrogatories or requests for admission to be served on the opposing party. The motion also must list the documents the applicant seeks to obtain from a person subject to discovery.[38] Although Rule 6(b) imposes no similar requirements on parties seeking leave to conduct depositions (apart from requiring a list of the documents the applicant will ask the deponent to produce[39]), a request for depositions should indicate the subject matters on which the applicant seeks to question the deponent.

h. *Discovery by the state.* If the state is allowed to rely on affidavits in lieu of a hearing or otherwise to make affidavits a part of the record, the petitioner apparently has a statutory right to propound written interrogatories to the affiants.[40] In general, before relying on the fruits of the state's discovery to deny relief, the court should insist upon in-court testimony by the state's affiants or deponents if there is any substantial reason to doubt the witnesses' credibility.[41]

---

exhibits. *Id.* at 1796, 1798. Although "counsel admitted that he 'ha[d] not made th[e] exact same argument'" to the district court in support of his discovery request as he made in the Supreme Court, the latter Court nonetheless granted relief because petitioner's argument, as eventually refined on appeal, was "'supported by the record'" made in conjunction with the discovery motions. *Id.* at 1799 n.11.

[38] Rule 6(b) of the Rules Governing § 2254 Cases ("Requests for discovery shall be accompanied by a statement of the interrogatories or requests for admission and a list of the documents, if any, sought to be produced."). *See Coleman v. Zant, supra,* 708 F.2d at 547 (describing successful discovery motion in support of allegations of prejudicial pretrial publicity).

[39] Once a court orders a particular form of discovery under Rule 6(a) of the Rules Governing § 2254 Cases or Rule 6(a) of the Rules Governing § 2255 Proceedings, the parties must follow the procedures for conducting that form of discovery set forth in FED. R. CIV. P. 26-37, unless the court modifies those procedures. Most of these rules were substantially amended in 1993, *see, e.g., supra* § 19.4a n.3, and the revised version should be consulted.

[40] 28 U.S.C. § 2246 (1994). *See infra* § 19.5 (expansion of the record). *Cf. supra* § 19.4b n.7; *infra* § 19.5 n.20 and accompanying text.

[41] *See, e.g.,* Smith v. Zant, 887 F.2d 1407, 1433 n.15 (11th Cir. 1989) (*en banc*) (district court generally should not base habeas corpus credibility determinations on paper record); Case v. Mondragon, 887 F.2d 1388, 1392 n.2 (10th Cir. 1989), *cert. denied,* 494 U.S. 1035 (1990) (magistrate judge's credibility determination not given usual deference because based on paper record); Raines v. United States, 423 F.2d 526, 530 (4th Cir. 1970) (quoted in Advisory Committee Note to Habeas Rule 7) (if credibility is at stake, affidavits are "rarely conclusive"); authority cited *infra* § 19.5 n.13. *See also* United States v. Raddatz, 447 U.S. 667, 679 (1980) ("courts must always be sensitive to the problems of making credibility determinations on the cold record"); Wingo v. Wedding, 418 U.S. 461, 474 (1974) ("'appraisal of the truth of ... oral testimony' based on ... a recording of it" is not "'equivalent of the judge's own exercise of the function of the trier of the facts'" (quoting Holiday v. Johnston, 313 U.S. 342, 352 (1941))); Watts v. United States, 841 F.2d 275, 277 (9th Cir. 1988) (*per curiam*) (although resolution of credibility issues on basis of affidavits rarely can be conclusive, if prisoner failed to mention alleged secret agreement with prosecutor until 14 months after imposition of sentence, judge properly may dismiss motion based

§ 19.5. Expansion of the record.[1]

Either on a party's motion or *sua sponte*, a federal court "may direct that the record be expanded by the parties by the inclusion of additional materials relevant to the determination of the merits of the petition."[2] "The expanded record may include without limitation, letters predating the filing of the petition in the district court, documents, exhibits, and answers under oath, if so directed, to written interrogatories propounded by the judge. Affidavits may be submitted and considered as part of the record."[3] Although Habeas Rule 7, which embodies

on documents without hearing); Porcaro v. United States, 832 F.2d 208, 212-13 (1st Cir. 1987) (noting, but finding inapplicable, general rule that credibility issues cannot be resolved on basis of conflicting affidavits); *infra* § 20.3e n.147 (habeas corpus decisions requiring hearing and denying presumption of correctness to state factfindings because state courts made credibility judgments based on affidavits or similar evidence rather than live testimony). *Cf.* Bliss v. Lockhart, 891 F.2d 1335, 1338 (8th Cir. 1989) (affirming denial of state's request for evidentiary hearing at which live testimony would be heard because state failed to explain how live testimony would conflict with paper record already before court). *See generally* Advisory Committee Notes to Habeas Rules 7 and 8 (most petitions raising factual issues "require a hearing" before court may dispose of them); Townsend v. Sain, 372 U.S. 293, 313 (1963) (hearing mandatory, *inter alia,* when there is "substantial allegation of newly discovered evidence" or when facts were not adequately developed at state court hearing).

§ 19.5. [1] *See generally* WAYNE R. LaFAVE & JEROLD H. ISRAEL, CRIMINAL PROCEDURE § 28.1(a) (1992); LARRY W. YACKLE, POSTCONVICTION REMEDIES § 122 (1981 & Supp. 1998); David Bagwell, *Procedural Aspects of Prisoner § 1983 and § 2254 Cases in the Fifth and Eleventh Circuits,* 95 F.R.D. 435, 461 (1982); Charles Alan Wright, *Procedure for Habeas Corpus,* 77 F.R.D. 227, 244 (1978).

[2] Rule 7(a) of the Rules Governing § 2254 Cases. *See* Lonchar v. Thomas, 517 U.S. 314, 326 (1996) (discussed *infra* note 6).

[3] Rule 7(a) of the Rules Governing § 2254 Cases. *See, e.g.,* Advisory Committee Note to Rule 7 of the Rules Governing § 2254 Cases (statements by petitioner) (citing Machibroda v. United States, 368 U.S. 487, 495 (1962)); Schlup v. Delo, 513 U.S. 298, 308-10 & n.18 (1995) (approvingly discussing petitioner's request to "supplement the record" — and thereby "buttress his claims of innocence" in support of "manifest miscarriage of justice" exception to successive petition defense — by expanding record to include "affidavits from inmates [and others] who stated that they had witnessed the event and that [petitioner] had not been present"); Herrera v. Collins, 506 U.S. 390, 445 (1993) (Blackmun, J., dissenting on other grounds) ("It is common to rely on affidavits at the preliminary-consideration stage of a habeas proceeding."); Dobbs v. Zant, 506 U.S. 357, 358-59 (1993) (*per curiam*) (court of appeals erred in failing to supplement record to include previously missing transcript of closing argument at capital sentencing hearing); Keeney v. Tamayo-Reyes, 504 U.S. 1, 14 (1992) (O'Connor, J., dissenting) (habeas corpus' characteristic "functions" include "introduction" through nonhearing procedures "of documentary evidence" (citing 28 U.S.C. § 2247)); Mitchell v. Kemp, 483 U.S. 1026, 1026 (1987) (Marshall, J., dissenting from denial of *certiorari*) (ineffective assistance claim litigated on basis of 170 pages of affidavits made part of district court record); Murray v. Carrier, 477 U.S. 478, 487 (1986); Vasquez v. Hillery, 474 U.S. 254, 257-60 (1986) (approving district court's expansion of record to include computer-generated statistical analyses on jury discrimination claim); Weidner v. Thieret, 932 F.2d 626, 627-28 (7th Cir. 1991), *cert. denied,* 502 U.S. 1036 (1992) (affidavit of state trial judge);

this "expanded record" option, is discretionary, courts may abuse their discretion by failing to utilize the procedure in compelling circumstances.[4]

Habeas Rule 7 is a "simplifying procedure[]" designed to "minimize the burden to all concerned" of the fact development process.[5] Rule 7 pursues this goal in two ways. First, it permits the court to receive all or at least some of the evi-

---

Lesko v. Lehman, 925 F.2d 1527, 1538 (3d Cir.), *cert. denied,* 502 U.S. 898 (1991) (district court ordered petitioner to file affidavit of counsel in support of allegation that guilty plea was induced by promise later broken by state); Brown v. Dixon, 891 F.2d 490, 492-94 (4th Cir. 1989) (record expanded on appeal to include affidavits discussing interviews with newly discovered witness; court did not factor affidavits into decision because new "information remained largely undeveloped and unsubstantiated"); Shah v. United States, 878 F.2d 1156, 1162-63 (9th Cir.), *cert. denied,* 493 U.S. 869 (1989) (record expanded to include affidavit state submitted with its response); Ross v. Kemp, 785 F.2d 1467, 1472, 1478-80 (11th Cir. 1986); Porcaro v. United States, 784 F.2d 38, 41 (1st Cir.), *cert. denied,* 479 U.S. 916 (1986); Dillard v. Blackburn, 780 F.2d 509, 513 (5th Cir. 1986); Coleman v. Kemp, 778 F.2d 1487 (11th Cir. 1985), *cert. denied,* 476 U.S. 1164 (1986) (materials discovered via Habeas Rule 6 and made part of record via Habeas Rule 7 provide basis for relief on prejudicial pretrial publicity claim); Jones v. Parke, 734 F.2d 1142, 1143 (6th Cir. 1984); Isaacs v. Zant, 709 F.2d 634, 635 (11th Cir. 1983) (record expanded to include transcript of proceedings in codefendants' case); Coleman v. Zant, 708 F.2d 541, 547 (11th Cir. 1983); Harris v. Pulley, 692 F.2d 1189, 1199-200 (9th Cir. 1982), *rev'd on other grounds,* 465 U.S. 37 (1984); United States v. Carlino, 400 F.2d 56, 58 (2d Cir. 1968), *cert. denied,* 394 U.S. 1013 (1969) (affidavits); Accardi v. United States, 379 F.2d 312, 313 (2d Cir. 1967) (affidavits); other authority cited *infra* notes 5, 6, 10. *See also* 28 U.S.C. § 2246 (1994) (provision largely superseded by Habeas Rule 7, *see* 28 U.S.C. § 2072 (1994)) ("On application for a writ of habeas corpus, evidence may be taken ... by deposition, or, in the discretion of the judge, by affidavit. If affidavits are admitted, any party shall have the right to propound written interrogatories to the affiants, or to file answering affidavits."); Harris v. Nelson, 394 U.S. 286, 296, 299 (1969); Love v. Johnson, 57 F.3d 1305, 1316 (4th Cir. 1995) (remanding to district court to obtain, "either by voluntary production by the state or such processes of the court as are required," state agency records which petitioner subpoenaed prior to trial so that district court can examine records *in camera* to determine whether trial judge's quashing of subpoenas violated due process); *supra* §§ 19.4b, 19.4h; *infra* note 20 and accompanying text (discussing section 2246). *Cf.* Abdullah v. Norris, 18 F.3d 571, 573 n.3 (8th Cir.), *cert. denied,* 513 U.S. 857 (1994) (denying motion to supplement record with state crime lab report because report is irrelevant to petitioner's claims); McDougall v. Dixon, 921 F.2d 518, 532 (4th Cir. 1990), *cert. denied,* 501 U.S. 1223 (1991) (district court properly refused to expand record to include affidavit of experts regarding empirical study on comprehension of jury instruction because student participants' understanding of portion of instruction given at trial is irrelevant to how reasonable juror would have understood charge as a whole).

[4] *See Dobbs v. Zant, supra,* 506 U.S. at 358 (after state represented that transcript of closing argument at capital sentencing phase was unavailable, and after petitioner thereafter discovered copy of transcript and proffered it to Court of Appeals on motion "to supplement the record on appeal," "Court of Appeals erred when it refused to consider the full transcript," which "flatly contradicted the account [of the closing argument] given by [defense] counsel in key respects").

[5] *Murray v. Carrier, supra,* 477 U.S. at 487. *See* Advisory Committee Note to Rule 7 of the Rules Governing § 2254 Cases; United States ex rel. Simmons v. Gramley, 915 F.2d 1128, 1139 (7th Cir. 1990) (Habeas Rule 7 is designed to avoid evidentiary hearings).

in two ways. First, it permits the court to receive all or at least some of the evidence relevant to the disposition of the petition without a formal hearing — even, possibly, in situations in which a hearing would be inappropriate or impermissible.[6] Second, it relaxes the rules of evidence by giving the court

---

[6] *See* Advisory Committee Note to Rule 7 of the Rules Governing § 2254 Cases (Rule 7's "purpose is to enable the judge to dispose of some habeas petitions not dismissed on the pleadings without the time and expense required for an evidentiary hearing," hence to "eliminate ... unnecessary hearings"; "expanded record may also be helpful when an evidentiary hearing is ordered"); Lonchar v. Thomas, 517 U.S. 314, 326 (1996) ("The [Habeas] Rules afford the district court substantial discretion in the conduct of a case once an answer has been ordered ... [including to] decide to order expansion of the record to facilitate a disposition on the merits without the need for an evidentiary hearing."); Zettlemoyer v. Fulcomer, 923 F.2d 284, 314 (3d Cir.), *cert. denied,* 502 U.S. 902 (1991) (Sloviter, J., dissenting) ("expansion of the record" procedure might enable district court to limit burden of trying prejudice prong of ineffective assistance claims); *United States ex rel. Simmons v. Gramley, supra,* 915 F.2d at 1130-31, 1139 (district court properly expanded record in lieu of evidentiary hearing on ineffective assistance claim because expansion procedure developed all facts essential to consideration of petitioner's claim); Mathis v. Zant, 903 F.2d 1368, 1370 (11th Cir. 1990) (district court adjudicated prejudice prong of ineffective assistance claim entirely on basis of "substantial body of [documentary] evidence" with which court expanded record); Burden v. Zant, 903 F.2d 1353, 1358 (11th Cir. 1990), *rev'd on other grounds,* 498 U.S. 433 (1991) (*per curiam*) (facts developed in part through filing of supplementary documents); United States v. Wilson, 901 F.2d 378, 380 (4th Cir. 1990) (hearing and relief denied on basis of information provided after district court thrice expanded record to include additional documentary material); Matta-Ballesteros v. Henman, 896 F.2d 255, 259 (7th Cir. 1990); Porcaro v. United States, 832 F.2d 208, 210-12 (1st Cir. 1987) (when allegations in petition are barely sufficient to avoid summary dismissal, most expeditious course may be to require petitioner to file supporting affidavits and then, based on their content, determine whether evidentiary hearing is warranted); Bookish v. Cunningham, 787 F.2d 1, 5 (1st Cir. 1986) (court properly permitted petitioner to present in-court testimony of only some witnesses for whom subpoenas were sought while ordering submission of additional, largely duplicitous, testimony through affidavits); Mitchell v. Kemp, 762 F.2d 886, 890 (11th Cir. 1985), *cert. denied,* 483 U.S. 1026 (1987) (hearing held on "reasonableness of representation" prong of ineffective assistance claim, but prejudice prong handled through affidavits). *See also Murray v. Carrier, supra,* 477 U.S. at 487 (expansion of record with prior counsel's affidavit is means of refuting state's defense that attorney inexcusably defaulted federal claim by not objecting). Although recent legislation, discussed *infra* Chapter 20, *see generally supra* §§ 3.2, 3.3, 3.4, limits the availability of evidentiary hearings in certain circumstances, it does not appear to limit the availability of the expansion of the record device for proving factual allegations through evidence generated with the aid of financial assistance (*see supra* § 19.3), discovery (*see supra* § 19.4), or other investigative measures. In appropriate cases, therefore, a habeas corpus petitioner who has been denied a federal evidentiary hearing may nonetheless establish a right to relief on a fact-based claim by demonstrating that (1) evidence developed during discovery or through some other investigative technique justifies relief even absent in-court evidentiary proceedings conducted by the petitioner, and (2) the evidence may appropriately be placed before the court via the "expansion of the record" device. Another common use of the procedure of expanding the record is to determine whether there is enough of a factual basis or factual dispute to warrant a hearing. *See, e.g., Porcaro v. United States, supra,* 784 F.2d at 41 (remanding to district court to hold hearing or require petitioner to file affidavits showing that

discretion to admit virtually all evidence that (1) is "relevant to the determination of the ... petition";[7] (2) was in existence prior to the filing of the petition,[8] or is tangible or "real" evidence that was not created in anticipation of litigation,[9] or is comprised of or supported by a sworn statement;[10] and (3) is not already part of the record of prior proceedings in the case.[11] The hearsay, best evidence, authentication, and other evidentiary rules are abandoned, therefore, except to the extent that a violation of those rules either undermines the relevance of the proffered material or tends to establish that unsworn out-of-court testimony was recorded for purposes of the litigation and, therefore, is inadmissible.[12] Rule 7's relaxation of traditional rules of procedure is qualified, however, by the requirement that when resolution of the issues presented by the petition turns on the credibility of the proffered evidence and the court is presented with some reason to question the evidence's credibility, the court must conduct an evidentiary hearing at which the rules of evidence are observed.[13]

---

hearing is warranted); Mitchell v. Hopper, 564 F. Supp. 780, 781 n.1 (S.D. Ga. 1983), *aff'd sub nom.* Mitchell v. Kemp, 762 F.2d 886 (11th Cir. 1985), *cert. denied*, 483 U.S. 1026 (1987) (court orders hearing on ineffective assistance based upon affidavits showing factual basis).

[7] Rule 7(a) of the Rules Governing § 2254 Cases.

[8] Rule 7(b) of the Rules Governing § 2254 Cases.

[9] *Id.* ("expanded record may include ... documents [and] exhibits").

[10] *Id.* ("[t]he expanded record may include ... answers under oath ... to written interrogatories" and "[a]ffidavits"). *See* Schlup v. Delo, 513 U.S. 298, 308-10 & nn.18, 19 (1995) (discussed *supra* note 3); Herrera v. Collins, 506 U.S. 390, 445 (1993) (Blackmun, J., dissenting on other grounds) ("It is common to rely on affidavits at the preliminary-consideration stage of a habeas proceeding."); Ross v. Kemp, 785 F.2d 1467, 1472 (11th Cir. 1986) (depositions); Mulligan v. Kemp, 771 F.2d 1436, 1438 (11th Cir. 1985). This aspect of Habeas Rule 7 most frequently applies to the fruits of discovery ordered pursuant to Habeas Rule 6. *See supra* § 19.4 (discovery).

[11] *See* Rule 5 of the Rules Governing § 2254 Cases (discussed *supra* § 19.2) (court, on party's motion or *sua sponte*, may make any portion of the record of state court proceedings part of federal record).

[12] *See* Rule 7(a) of the Rules Governing § 2254 Cases ("court *may* require the authentication of any material" proffered for inclusion in the record (emphasis added)); Abdur'Rahman v. Bell, 1998 WL 168735, at *28 n.30 (M.D. Tenn. April 8, 1998) (Rule 7 of the Rules Governing § 2254 Cases "contemplates a relaxed application of the hearsay, best evidence, authentication, and other evidentiary rules under the Federal Rules of Evidence."). *Cf.* Advisory Committee Note to FED. R. EVID. 803(6); Palmer v. Hoffman, 318 U.S. 109 (1943) (evidentiary principles generally discouraging admission of documents prepared for litigation).

[13] *See* Advisory Committee Note to Rule 7 of the Rules Governing § 2254 Cases (if "'issue is one of credibility, resolution on the basis of affidavits can rarely be conclusive'" (quoting Raines v. United States, 423 F.2d 526, 530 (4th Cir. 1970))); other authority cited *supra* § 19.4h n.41. When credibility is or may be a controlling issue, affidavits still may be "helpful" in establishing that a hearing is necessary and in narrowing the scope of the hearing to disputed matters. *See Raines v. United States, supra* at 529-30. *See also* Advisory Committee Note to Rule 7 of the Rules Governing § 2254 Cases (expansion of record most likely to obviate need for hearing when further factual

The manner in which a party seeks to use an expanded record will determine the timing of a Habeas Rule 7 motion. Such motions are appropriate early in the proceedings, if an expanded record is sought in lieu of a hearing[14] or to demonstrate that the claims in the petition are sufficiently substantial to render summary dismissal inappropriate and to require the granting of a hearing.[15] When used to narrow the issues to be addressed at a hearing, a Rule 7 motion should accompany a request for a hearing or be filed after the court has granted a hearing. Courts also may entertain Rule 7 motions at the hearing itself, in conjunction with motions for reconsideration of the dismissal or denial of the petition,[16] and even on appeal.[17]

The materials that the party seeks to include in the record[18] should accompany the motion, as should a brief memorandum of law discussing Habeas Rule 7 (with which many judges are unfamiliar) and the authority supporting the motion. The memorandum and, when appropriate, supporting affidavits[19] also should establish the relevance of the proffered materials and the reasons why the circumstances of the case warrant the court's exercise of its discretion to expand the record. Habeas Rule 7(c) requires the party asking the court to expand the record to supply the opposing party with copies of the proffered materials. If the items submitted are in the form of affidavits, the pre-Rules habeas corpus statute gives the opposing party "the right to propound written interrogatories to the affiants,

---

development is "necessitated by slight omissions in the state record which [may be] cured by the use of an expanded record").

[14] *See also supra* §§ 16.1c (respondent-initiated summary judgment proceedings), 17.3 (petitioner-initiated summary judgment).

[15] *See* Lesko v. Lehman, 925 F.2d 1527, 1538 (3d Cir.), *cert. denied,* 502 U.S. 898 (1991) (district court ordered petitioner to file affidavit of counsel in support of allegation that petitioner pled guilty to prior crime based on promise, later broken, that state would not use prior conviction as aggravating circumstance in support of death penalty in subsequent trial; because affidavit supported petitioner's allegation, hearing was required); *supra* notes 6-13 and accompanying text. *See also supra* §§ 11.7d, 16.2, 17.1 (other means of establishing need for additional proceedings); *supra* § 15.2 (summary dismissal).

[16] *See generally infra* Chapter 34.

[17] *See, e.g.,* Ross v. Kemp, 785 F.2d 1467, 1472 (11th Cir. 1986). *See infra* § 37.1b (enlargement of the record on appeal). *See also* Brown v. Dixon, 891 F.2d 490, 492-94 (4th Cir. 1989) (discussed *supra* note 3); *supra* §§ 11.7d, 16.2, 17.1 (all discussing timing of analogous motions). *But cf.* United States v. Kennedy, 869 F.2d 1336, 1338 n.4 (9th Cir. 1989), *cert. denied,* 494 U.S. 1008 (1990) (court of appeals disregards documents obtained after hearing and included in reply brief because they were not part of district court or appellate record).

[18] *See* Rule 7(c) of the Rules Governing § 2254 Cases.

[19] A party may address authentication, "best evidence," and related concerns in affidavits accompanying the motion. *See supra* note 12 and accompanying text.

or to file answering affidavits,"[20] and Habeas Rule 7(c) requires the court to afford the opposing party "an opportunity to admit or deny the[] correctness" of any proffered evidence. When warranted by the opposing party's submission of a Rule 7 motion, a party may take steps to inform the court that resolution of the issues in the petition will require the court to ascertain the credibility of the proffered evidence or testimony and, accordingly, that an evidentiary hearing is required.[21]

---

[20] 28 U.S.C. § 2246 (1994) (quoted in part *supra* note 3). The post-Rules status of section 2246 is uncertain. *See* 28 U.S.C. § 2072 (1994) (Habeas Rules supersede prior inconsistent statutes); Rule 7(c) of the Rules Governing § 2254 Cases (quoted in text) (establishing procedure that might be viewed as inconsistent with section 2246). *See also supra* note 3; *supra* § 19.4b n.7 and accompanying text.

[21] *See supra* note 13 and accompanying text; *supra* § 19.4h n.41 and accompanying text.

Chapter 20

RIGHT TO A HEARING; EFFECT OF STATE FACTFINDINGS

§ 20.1. Introduction.[1]

To experienced [habeas corpus] lawyers it is commonplace that the outcome of a lawsuit — and hence the vindication of legal rights — depends more on how the factfinder appraises the facts than on a disputed construction of a statute or interpretation of a line of precedents. Thus the procedures by which the facts of the case are determined assume an importance fully as great as the validity of the substantive rule of law to be applied.[2]

a. *Importance of hearings.* Hearings are held in a very small proportion of all habeas corpus cases.[3] But they are held in a fairly large proportion of cases in which something more than summary review and dismissal takes place.[4] It stands

---

§ 20.1. [1] *See generally* WAYNE R. LaFAVE & JEROLD H. ISRAEL, CRIMINAL PROCEDURE § 28.7 (2d ed. 1992); RONALD P. SOKOL, FEDERAL HABEAS CORPUS 110-31 (2d ed. 1969); LARRY W. YACKLE, POSTCONVICTION REMEDIES §§ 124-36 (1981 & Supp. 1998); David A. Bagwell, *Procedural Aspects of Prisoner § 1983 and § 2254 Cases in the Fifth and Eleventh Circuits*, 95 F.R.D. 435, 461-62 (1982); Henry P. Monaghan, *Constitutional Fact Review*, 85 COLUM. L. REV. 229 (1986); Frank J. Remington, *Post-Conviction Review — What State Trial Courts Can Do to Reduce Problems*, JUDICATURE, June-July 1988, at 53; Charles D. Weisselberg, *Evidentiary Hearings in Federal Habeas Corpus Cases*, 1990 B.Y.U. L. REV. 131; Charles Alan Wright, *Procedure for Habeas Corpus*, 77 F.R.D. 227, 245-47 (1978); J. Skelly Wright & Abraham D. Sofaer, *Federal Habeas Corpus for State Prisoners: The Allocation of Fact-Finding Responsibility*, 75 YALE L.J. 895 (1966); Larry W. Yackle, *Federal Evidentiary Hearings Under the New Habeas Corpus Statute*, 6 B.U. PUB. INT. L.J. 135 (1996); *Developments in the Law — Habeas Corpus*, 83 HARV. L. REV. 1038, 1113-53 (1970); Comment, *Voluntariness of Confessions in Habeas Corpus Proceedings: The Proper Standard for Appellate Review*, 57 U. CHI. L. REV. 141 (1990); Note, *Federal Habeas Corpus for State Prisoners: The Isolation Principle*, 39 N.Y.U. L. REV. 78 (1964); Note, *Keeney v. Tamayo-Reyes and Federal Habeas Corpus Evidentiary Hearings: Has the Court Deliberately Bypassed Section 2254(d)?*, 1994 WIS. L. REV. 171; Note, *Supreme Court Review of State Findings of Fact in Fourteenth Amendment Cases*, 14 STAN. L. REV. 328 (1962).

[2] Wingo v. Wedding, 418 U.S. 461, 474 (1974) (quoting Speiser v. Randall, 357 U.S. 513, 520 (1958)).

[3] *See supra* § 2.4b n.29 (less than 2% of all habeas corpus filings result in evidentiary hearing). *See also* Keeney v. Tamayo-Reyes, 504 U.S. 1, 24 (1992) (Kennedy, J., dissenting) ("there is no clear evidence that [the right to hearings in habeas corpus proceedings has burdened the dockets of the federal courts").

[4] *See* Advisory Committee Note to Rule 7 of the Rules Governing § 2254 Cases ("by far the majority" of habeas corpus petitions that are not summarily dismissed "require an evidentiary hearing"; of 469 state prisoners' habeas corpus petitions adjudicated in 1970 that were not summarily dismissed, 403 (90%) required evidentiary hearing; total state prisoner habeas corpus filings were approximately 9000 (citing DIRECTOR OF THE ADMINISTRATIVE OFFICE OF THE UNITED STATES COURTS, ANNUAL REPORT 245a-c (table C4) (1970))).

to reason, therefore, that the likelihood of relief in a habeas corpus case is related to the federal court's decision whether or not to conduct an evidentiary hearing. Although federal courts have the power to grant habeas corpus relief without holding an evidentiary hearing,[5] even on fact-based claims,[6] they are disinclined to do so.[7] Taken together, the paucity of grants of the writ absent a hearing and the statutory requirement that federal courts defer to fairly derived state court factfindings[8] suggest that in most cases in which the state courts fail to vindicate the rights of the accused, they do so because of faulty fact-development procedures.[9] The apparently higher frequency of factual as opposed to strictly legal miscues at the state level suggests, in turn, that a federal hearing often is the unlawfully incarcerated petitioner's first (and probably last) meaningful opportunity to develop and present the facts necessary to reveal the illegality of confinement.

---

[5] See, e.g., Hitchcock v. Dugger, 481 U.S. 393, 395 (1987); Landano v. Rafferty, 897 F.2d 661, 683 (3d Cir.), cert. denied, 498 U.S. 811 (1990) (Rosenn, J., dissenting); Tague v. Puckett, 874 F.2d 1013, 1015 (5th Cir. 1989); authority cited supra §§ 17.3, 19.4d, 19.5.

[6] See supra §§ 19.4d n.27 and accompanying text, 19.5 n.6 and accompanying text.

[7] See Advisory Committee Note to Rule 8 of the Rules Governing § 2254 Cases; Wingo v. Wedding, 418 U.S. 461, 468 (1974) ("More often than not, claims of unconstitutional detention turn upon the resolution of contested issues of fact."); Townsend v. Sain, 372 U.S. 293, 312 (1963) ("it is the typical, not the rare, [habeas corpus] case in which constitutional claims turn upon the resolution of contested factual issues"); United States ex rel. McCall v. O'Grady, 908 F.2d 170, 174 (7th Cir. 1990) (before granting writ on basis of ineffective assistance of counsel, district court normally should hold hearing so that petitioner can make "specific, detailed showing as to the content of the evidence into which trial counsel should have investigated or which should have been presented to the jury, and, where necessary, a showing as to the reasons for trial counsel's failure to do so").

[8] See 28 U.S.C.A. § 2254(e)(1) (West 1994 & Supp. 1998); infra §§ 20.2, 20.3, 30.3.

[9] There is no readily available statistical data to confirm this conjecture. The supposition is premised on the rarity of pro-petitioner summary judgments, the authors' experience litigating and studying habeas corpus cases, the higher frequency of "ineffective assistance of counsel" determinations overturning state criminal judgments based on inadequacies in the factual as opposed to the legal representation afforded state defendants (even though legal errors should be more easily proved than inadequate factual preparation), the nearly blanket refusal of some state postconviction courts to grant evidentiary hearings, and the generally less sophisticated fact-development procedures available in state, as opposed to federal, postconviction proceedings. Noting and explaining the fact that federal courts are more likely than state courts to protect the federal rights of state prisoners, are, e.g., Gary L. Anderson, Post-Conviction Relief in Tennessee — Fourteen Years of Judicial Administration Under the Post-Conviction Procedure Act, 48 TENN. L. REV. 605, 650-53 (1981); Robert M. Cover & T. Alexander Aleinikoff, Dialectical Federalism, 86 YALE L.J. 1035, 1046 & n.62 (1977); Burt Neuborne, The Myth of Parity, 90 HARV. L. REV. 1105, 1115-30 (1977); Walter V. Shaefer, Federalism and State Criminal Procedure, 70 HARV. L. REV. 1, 6-7 (1956); David L. Shapiro, Federal Habeas Corpus: A Study in Massachusetts, 87 HARV. L. REV. 321, 342 (1973); Wright & Sofaer, supra note 1, at 898-99; supra §§ 2.4d nn.326-35 and accompanying text, 2.5, 2.6.

b. *Evolution of fact-development standards.* The habeas corpus statute, rules, and caselaw have long made ample provision for the holding of evidentiary hearings on fact-based claims. Ever since Congress passed the Federal Habeas Corpus Act of 1867, federal courts have had the authority and responsibility to "hear and determine the facts, and dispose of the matter as law and justice require."[10] In 1948 and 1966, Congress enacted statutes that codified the petitioner's right to receive, and the district court's even broader discretion to hold, a hearing.[11] Interpreting the statute that was enacted in 1948, the Supreme Court in *Townsend v. Sain*[12] held that the federal judiciary must resolve any factual dispute material to a claim appropriately raised by a habeas corpus petition and that resolution of factual disputes requires an evidentiary hearing in most cases.[13]

---

[10] Act of February 5, 1867, ch. 28, § 1, 14 Stat. 385-86, *currently codified,* 28 U.S.C. § 2243 (1994). *See Wingo v. Wedding, supra,* 418 U.S. at 468; *Townsend v. Sain, supra,* 372 U.S. at 311; Brown v. Allen, 344 U.S. 443, 462 (1953); Frank v. Mangum, 237 U.S. 309, 330 (1915); *supra* § 2.4d nn.131-50 and accompanying text.

[11] *See* 28 U.S.C. § 2243 (1994) (para. 4) (codified in 1948) ("When the [state answers the petition] a date shall be set for a hearing."); *id.* (para. 5) ("Unless the application for the writ and return present only issues of law the person to whom the writ is directed shall be required to produce at the hearing the body of the person detained."); *id.* (para. 8) ("The court shall summarily hear and determine the facts, and dispose of the matter as law and justice require."); 28 U.S.C. § 2254(d) (1994) (added in 1966) (authorizing "evidentiary hearing in the [habeas corpus] proceeding in the Federal court").

[12] 372 U.S. 293 (1963). Prior to *Townsend v. Sain,* the Court's decision in Brown v. Allen, 344 U.S. 443 (1953), governed the scope of the right to hearings. *See* Smith v. Yeager, 393 U.S. 122, 125 (1968) *(per curiam) (Townsend,* "which must be considered to supersede ... *Brown,* ... substantially increased the availability of evidentiary hearings in habeas corpus proceedings, and made mandatory much of what had previously been ... discretion[ary]").

[13] *Townsend, supra,* 372 U.S. at 313-19. *Accord, e.g.,* Keeney v. Tamayo-Reyes, 504 U.S. 1, 10 n.5 (1992); Ford v. Wainwright, 477 U.S. 399, 410-11 (1986); Cabana v. Bullock, 474 U.S. 376, 388 n.5 (1986); Vasquez v. Hillery, 474 U.S. 254, 266-67 (1986) (O'Connor, J., concurring); Marshall v. Lonberger, 459 U.S. 422, 430 (1983); Jackson v. Virginia, 443 U.S. 307, 318 (1979) ("A federal court has a duty to assess the historic facts when it is called upon to apply a constitutional standard to a conviction obtained in state court."); Wainwright v. Sykes, 433 U.S. 72, 87 (1977) (petitioner is "entitled to have the federal habeas corpus court make its own independent determination of his federal claim, without being bound by the determination on the merits of that claim reached in the state proceedings"); Blackledge v. Allison, 431 U.S. 63, 83-84 (1977) (state prisoner is "entitled to careful consideration and plenary processing of his claim, including full opportunity for presentation of the relevant facts"); *Wingo v. Wedding, supra,* 418 U.S. at 468 ("since the Judiciary Act of February 5, 1967, ... Congress has expressly vested plenary power in the federal courts 'for taking testimony and trying the facts anew in habeas hearing'" (quoting Fay v. Noia, 372 U.S. 391, 416 (1963))); Fontaine v. United States, 411 U.S. 213, 215 (1973) *(per curiam); Smith v. Yeager, supra,* 393 U.S. at 125; Machibroda v. United States, 368 U.S. 487, 495 (1962); Pennsylvania ex rel. Herman v. Claudy, 350 U.S. 116, 120-21 (1956);

In *Townsend*, the Supreme Court reversed the district court's dismissal of a habeas corpus petition because the lower court improperly had refused to hold an evidentiary hearing on the petition. Chief Justice Warren's opinion for the Court identified a strong federal policy favoring hearings, or at least equally sufficient fact-development and fact-resolution procedures, because "detention ... obtained [in violation of the Constitution] is intolerable" and because "the opportunity for redress, which presupposes the opportunity to be heard, to argue and present evidence, must never be totally foreclosed."[14] To protect this policy, the Court concluded, the "hearing power" must be broad and independent, for

> a narrow view of the hearing power would totally subvert Congress' specific aim in passing the Act of February 5, 1867, of affording state prisoners a forum in federal trial courts for the determination of claims of detention in violation of the Constitution. The language of Congress, the history of the writ, the decisions of this Court, all make clear that the power of inquiry on federal habeas corpus is plenary.[15]

United States ex rel. McCann v. Adams, 320 U.S. 220, 220-22 (1943) (*per curiam*); authority cited *supra* § 15.2c nn.57-60 & *infra* note 27.

[14] *Townsend, supra,* 372 U.S. at 312, 322 (citing *Frank v. Mangum, supra,* 237 U.S. at 345-50 (Holmes, J., dissenting)). The Court tied this policy to the constitutional proscription against suspending the writ of habeas corpus except in times of war or rebellion. *See Townsend, supra,* 372 U.S. at 311 (discussing U.S. CONST. art. I, § 9, cl. 2). *Townsend* also may be understood to follow another "salutary principle" — namely, that whenever "there is a reasonable likelihood that the production of evidence will make the answer to the [constitutional] questions clearer," Borden's Farm Products Co. v. Baldwin, 293 U.S. 194, 213 (1934) (Cardozo, J., concurring), the "essential facts should be determined before passing upon grave constitutional questions ...," Polk Co. v. Glover, 305 U.S. 5, 10 (1938). *Accord* Wilshire Oil Co. v. United States, 295 U.S. 100, 102-03 (1935) (adjudication of "important constitutional question on the pleadings is not favored," and court is obliged in first instance to "determin[e] ... the facts of the case."). "Judges make constitutional law as they make other kinds of law, on the basis of facts proved and assumed. They are likely to do a better job when their assumptions rest on information rather than hunch." Kenneth L. Karst, *Legislative Facts in Constitutional Litigation,* 1960 SUP. CT. REV. 75. *See* Henry W. Biklé, *Judicial Determination of Questions of Fact Affecting the Constitutional Validity of Legislative Action,* 38 HARV. L. REV. 6 (1924). *See also* Ake v. Oklahoma, 470 U.S. 68, 82, 84 (1985); Rose v. Lundy, 455 U.S. 509, 519 (1982) (need for "complete factual record to aid the federal courts in their review").

[15] *Townsend, supra,* 372 U.S. at 292. *See* Keeney v. Tamayo-Reyes, 504 U.S. 1, 15-16 (1992) (O'Connor, J., dissenting):

> Even before *Townsend,* federal courts deferred to state court findings of fact where the federal district judge was satisfied that the state court had fairly considered the issues and the evidence and had reached a satisfactory result.... But where such was not the case, the federal court examining the habeas petition would examine the facts anew. *See, e.g., Ex parte* Hawk, 321 U.S. 114, 116, 118 (1944).... In *Hawk,* for example, we stated that a state prisoner would be entitled to a hearing, 321 U.S. at 116, "where resort to state court remedies had failed to afford a full and fair adjudication of the federal contentions raised ... because in the

Then, in 1976 and 1977, respectively, the Court and Congress reaffirmed the importance and availability of evidentiary hearings on potentially meritorious federal habeas corpus claims when the former promulgated, and the latter adopted, Rule 8 of the Rules Governing § 2254 Cases.[16] The Advisory Committee notes to Rule 8 identify *Townsend* as authoritative on the question of when habeas corpus hearings are available and when they are required.[17]

In 1992 and 1996, however, the Court and then Congress tempered somewhat their emphatic endorsement of habeas corpus hearings. In its closely divided 1992 decision in *Keeney v. Tamayo-Reyes*,[18] the Court limited mandatory[19] (but not discretionary[20]) hearings to facts that were not previously the subject of a full and fair hearing in the state courts for reasons beyond the control of the habeas corpus petitioner or his attorney. In so ruling, *Tamayo-Reyes* overturned a passage in *Townsend* that had required federal hearings on all material facts not addressed in the state courts unless the prisoner himself had "deliberate[ly] bypass[ed]" (*i.e.*, personally, knowingly, and intelligently had waived) a state court hearing on the issue.[21] In place of the "deliberate bypass" rule, the Court substituted a "procedural default" rule that withheld mandatory hearings on material facts on which the petitioner (for whatever reason, including ignorance or mistake) failed to seek a state court hearing, unless the state did not object to a federal hearing, there was a good reason not attributable to the petitioner for the failure to seek a state hearing (including obstruction by the state or ineffective

---

particular case the remedy afforded by state law proves in practice unavailable or seriously inadequate." *Id.*, at 118. In *Brown* [*v. Allen, supra*, 344 U.S. at 463], we explained that a hearing may be dispensed with only "[w]here the record of the application affords an adequate opportunity to weigh the sufficiency of the allegations and the evidence, and no unusual circumstances calling for a hearing are presented."

See also Keeney v. Tamayo-Reyes, supra at 6 n.2 (majority opinion) (disagreeing with details, but accepting broad outlines, of Justice O'Connor's history of right to habeas corpus hearing); *id.* at 16-17 (O'Connor, J., dissenting) (*Townsend* "marked no significant departure from our understanding of the writ," but simply "clarified how the district court should measure the adequacy of the state court proceeding" and "elaborat[ed] ... prior cases regarding the holding of hearings in federal habeas cases....").

[16] *See* Rule 8(a) of the Rules Governing § 2254 Cases ("If the petition is not dismissed at a previous stage in the proceedings, the judge, after the answer and the transcript and record of state court proceedings are filed, shall, upon a review of those proceedings and of the expanded record, if any, determine whether an evidentiary hearing is required.").

[17] *See* Advisory Committee Notes to Habeas Rules 7 and 8 (discussing *Townsend*).

[18] 504 U.S. 1 (1992).

[19] *See generally infra* § 20.3.

[20] *See generally infra* § 20.4.

[21] *Townsend, supra*, 372 U.S. at 317.

assistance of counsel in violation of the 6th Amendment), or the petitioner could show that he is probably innocent.[22]

In 1996, Congress enacted the Antiterrorism and Effective Death Penalty Act (AEDPA).[23] AEDPA alters habeas corpus procedures in a number of important respects,[24] including by narrowing yet further the right to an evidentiary hearing in the situation the Court previously had addressed in *Tamayo-Reyes*. Under AEDPA (assuming it applies[25]), a petitioner who is to blame for failing to develop the facts in state court may not do so by evidentiary hearing in federal court unless the petitioner satisfies the statute's stringent "cause" and "innocence" standards.[26] In *other* respects, however, the preexisting standards remain in effect. Even after AEDPA, that is, *Townsend*'s mandatory-hearing standards — and its delegation to district courts of broad discretion to hold evidentiary hearings that are not mandated — continues to govern all situations save those in which the petitioner's procedural default accounts for the state courts' failure to develop the material facts.

Under the statutes, rules, and caselaw discussed above, federal habeas corpus hearings are required if three conditions are met — (1) the petition alleges facts that, if proved, entitle the petitioner to relief;[27] (2) the fact-based claims survive

---

[22] *Tamayo-Reyes, supra,* 504 U.S. at 5-8. The various prerequisites for and exceptions to the procedural default rule that the Court adopted in *Keeney* (as codified and revised by recent legislation) are discussed in the federal-hearing context *infra* § 20.3e (para. (2)), and in other contexts *infra* Chapters 26, 28.

[23] Pub. L. 104-132, 110 Stat. 1214 (1996).

[24] For an overview of AEDPA's provisions and the changes it makes in federal habeas corpus procedures, see *supra* §§ 3.2, 3.5b.

[25] As is explained in § 3.4 *supra*, AEDPA does not apply to "nonopt-in cases" filed on or before April 24, 1996, and may not apply (for "retroactivity" reasons) to "opt-in" cases filed before that date and to some "nonopt-in" and "opt-in" cases filed after that date. For an explanation of AEDPA's "opt-in" and "nonopt-in" categories of cases, see *supra* § 3.2.

[26] For further discussion of the standard AEDPA establishes, see *infra* § 20.2b nn.23-38 and accompanying text. As is discussed *supra* §§ 19.1, 19.3, 19.4d n.27 and accompanying text, 19.5 n.6 and accompanying text, 20.1a n.6 and accompanying text, the right to habeas corpus relief on fact-premised claims as to which an evidentiary hearing is not permissible may still sometimes be established using federal fact-development mechanisms (*e.g.*, discovery and expansion of the record) short of evidentiary hearings.

[27] *See, e.g.,* Hill v. Lockhart, 474 U.S. 52, 60 (1985); Blackledge v. Allison, 431 U.S. 63, 82-83 (1977); *Townsend, supra,* 372 U.S. at 312 ("where an applicant for a writ of habeas corpus alleges facts which, if proved, would entitle him to relief, the federal court to which the application is made has the power to receive evidence and to try the facts anew"); Pennsylvania ex rel. Herman v. Claudy, 350 U.S. 116, 120-21 (1956); Blackmon v. Scott, 22 F.3d 560, 565 (5th Cir. 1994) (hearing required to resolve "genuine issue of material fact" because affidavit of witness who testified for prosecution at trial stated that affiant was promised favorable treatment for testifying and because affiant's statement was supported by other evidence that prosecutor hid promises but witness himself denied promise at trial and state continued to deny making any such promises);

summary dismissal because their factual allegations are not "'palpably incredible' [or] 'patently frivolous or false'" — the standard for summary

---

Houston v. Lockhart, 982 F.2d 1246, 1250-53 (8th Cir. 1993) (*en banc*) (district court erred in denying hearing to petitioner who had alleged sufficient grounds for release and whose allegations were "not palpably incredible, and were never the subject of a hearing in state court"); Cave v. Singletary, 971 F.2d 1513, 1516 (11th Cir. 1992) ("A petitioner is entitled to an evidentiary hearing in federal court if he alleges facts which, if proven, would entitle him to relief."); Diaz v. United States, 930 F.2d 832, 835 (11th Cir. 1991); Lesko v. Lehman, 925 F.2d 1527, 1536 (3d Cir.), *cert. denied*, 502 U.S. 898 (1991); Dumond v. Lockhart, 911 F.2d 104, 108 (8th Cir. 1990); Stano v. Dugger, 901 F.2d 898, 902-05 (11th Cir. 1990) (*en banc*); Smith v. Freeman, 892 F.2d 331, 338 (3d Cir. 1989); Prejean v. Smith, 889 F.2d 1391, 1403 (5th Cir. 1989), *cert. denied*, 494 U.S. 1090 (1990) ("district court must hold an evidentiary hearing on factually disputed constitutional issues if adequate, relevant evidence does not appear in the state court record"); United States v. Birdwell, 887 F.2d 643, 645 (5th Cir. 1989) (evidentiary hearing warranted if petition contains "specific factual allegations not directly contradicted in the record"); Estes v. United States, 883 F.2d 645, 649 (8th Cir. 1989) (court remands case for evidentiary hearing "[b]ecause the record does not 'conclusively show that the prisoner is entitled to no relief'" (quoting 28 U.S.C. § 2255)); United States v. Popoola, 881 F.2d 811, 812 (9th Cir. 1989); Myatt v. United States, 875 F.2d 8, 10 (1st Cir. 1989); Adamson v. Ricketts, 865 F.2d 1011, 1018-20 (9th Cir. 1988) (*en banc*), *cert. denied*, 497 U.S. 1031 (1990); Harris v. Pulley, 852 F.2d 1546, 1565 (9th Cir. 1988), *cert. denied*, 493 U.S. 1051 (1990) (hearing required if petitioner alleges facts that, if proved, entitle him to relief and if evidentiary hearing required to establish truth of allegations); Harich v. Dugger, 844 F.2d 1464, 1469 (11th Cir. 1988), *cert. denied*, 489 U.S. 1071 (1989) ("Petitioner is entitled to an evidentiary hearing if his allegations, taken as true, might merit relief."); Agan v. Dugger, 835 F.2d 1337, 1338 (11th Cir. 1987), *cert. denied*, 487 U.S. 1205 (1988) ("[a]n evidentiary hearing is necessary whenever a habeas petitioner alleges facts that, if true, establish his or her right to relief" and state court did not hold hearing; in assessing need for hearing, district court must assume that facts alleged are true); Cooper v. Wainwright, 807 F.2d 881 (11th Cir.), *cert. denied*, 481 U.S. 1050 (1987); Porcaro v. United States, 784 F.2d 38, 40 (1st Cir.), *cert. denied*, 479 U.S. 916 (1986); Rogers v. Maggio, 714 F.2d 35, 37 (5th Cir. 1983); Harris v. Pulley, 692 F.2d 1189, 1197 (9th Cir. 1982), *rev'd on other grounds*, 465 U.S. 37 (1984) ("To be entitled to the [evidentiary] hearing, a habeas [corpus] petitioner must show that (1) he has alleged facts which, if proved, would entitle him to relief, and (2) an evidentiary hearing is required to establish the truth of his allegations."); authority cited *supra* note 13 & *supra* § 15.2c nn.57, 59. *Cf.* Dziurgot v. Luther, 897 F.2d 1222, 1225 (1st Cir. 1990) (no hearing necessary if allegations, accepted as true, do not entitle petitioner to relief or if allegations cannot be accepted as true because record contradicts them, they are inherently incredible, or they are conclusions rather than statements of fact); Matta-Ballesteros v. Henman, 896 F.2d 255, 258-59 (7th Cir. 1990) (evidentiary hearing not required when "facts essential to consideration of the constitutional issue are already before the [federal] court"); Harris v. Pulley, 885 F.2d 1354, 1378 (9th Cir. 1988), *cert. denied*, 493 U.S. 1051 (1990) (petitioner "not entitled to an evidentiary hearing to present a purely *legal* argument. An evidentiary hearing is to present disputed facts." (emphasis in original)); Wright v. Minnesota, 833 F.2d 746, 749 (8th Cir. 1987), *cert. denied*, 485 U.S. 1011 (1988) (no hearing required "if the allegations, even if true, fail to state a claim cognizable in a federal habeas corpus proceeding").

dismissal in habeas corpus proceedings;[28] and (3) for reasons beyond the control of the petitioner and her lawyer (assuming her lawyer rendered constitutionally satisfactory assistance), the factual claims were not previously the subject of a full and fair hearing in the state courts or, if a full and fair state court hearing was held, it did not result in state court factfindings that resolve all the controlling factual issues in the case.[29] Mandatory hearings are also available on factual issues raised by the state as bases for avoiding relief on meritorious constitutional claims, as is discussed in § 20.1c *infra*. Hearings are particularly important and appropriate in capital cases, as is discussed in § 20.1d *infra*.

The standards governing mandatory federal hearings are discussed in more detail in §§ 20.2 and 20.3 *infra*. Section 20.2 compares those standards to the overlapping but somewhat different standards determining when state court factfindings do not deserve a presumption of correctness. Section 20.3 describes deficiencies in state court fact-development procedures or factfindings that make federal evidentiary hearings mandatory and, conversely, state court procedures and factfindings that are sufficient to keep federal court hearings and findings from being mandatory. Section 20.4 then explores the extent to which a federal court has discretion to hold a hearing when one is not mandatory.

Given the importance of federal hearings as a prerequisite to relief in many cases and as the first (and probably last) opportunity aggrieved prisoners have to prove the facts showing unlawful incarceration, and given the range of jurisdictional, merits, and defensive[30] issues that may require a hearing, petitioners usually are well-advised to file — either with the petition itself or thereafter — a motion for an evidentiary hearing.[31] Exceptions arise when available alternative fact-development procedures obviate the need for a hearing[32] or when the state court record and findings require relief as a matter of federal law.[33]

c. *Hearings on defenses.* The need for evidentiary hearings extends not only to the factual issues presented by the petitioner's claims but also to those presented by the many prerequisites and exceptions to the state's procedural

---

[28] Blackledge v. Allison, 431 U.S. 63, 75-76 (1977) (quoting Machibroda v. United States, 368 U.S. 487, 495 (1962); Pennsylvania ex rel. Herman v. Claudy, 350 U.S. 116, 119 (1956)); *supra* § 15.2c nn.42-50 and accompanying text. Unless the factual allegations are patently unbelievable, the district court is obliged to assume they are true in determining both whether summary dismissal is appropriate and whether an evidentiary hearing is required. *See* authority cited *supra* § 15.2c n.57.

[29] *See infra* §§ 20.2, 20.3.

[30] *See infra* § 20.1b.

[31] *See supra* §§ 11.7d, 16.2, 17.1, 17.3 (all discussing timing considerations).

[32] *See supra* §§ 19.4d, 19.5; *supra* note 26.

[33] *See supra* § 17.3.

defenses,[34] including failure to exhaust state remedies,[35] prejudicial delay,[36] waiver and procedural default,[37] the preclusive effect of prior "full and fair"

[34] The same standards govern the state's and the petitioner's requests for an evidentiary hearing, *see* Camarillo v. Estelle, 670 F.2d 473, 474 (5th Cir. 1981); *see also infra* § 20.2c n.47 (presumption of correctness of state court factfindings applies to findings favoring petitioner as well as state), and either party may request a hearing on either its own or the opposing party's claims and defenses.

[35] *See, e.g.,* Purnell v. Missouri Dep't of Corrections, 753 F.2d 703, 708 (8th Cir. 1985). *See generally infra* Chapter 23.

[36] *See, e.g.,* Walters v. Scott, 21 F.3d 683, 687 (5th Cir. 1994) (state's claim of witness's memory loss was insufficient to satisfy prejudice prong of prejudicial delay defense without hearing to determine precise extent of witness's recollections); Campas v. Zimmerman, 876 F.2d 318, 326 (3d Cir. 1989); Davis v. Adult Parole Auth., 610 F.2d 410, 415-16 (6th Cir. 1979) (hearing required on whether delay in filing petition prejudiced state). *See generally infra* Chapter 24.

[37] *See, e.g.,* Schlup v. Delo, 513 U.S. 851, 308-12 & nn.18, 19, 25, 331 (1995) (question whether procedural default and successive petition bars are overcome by showing of "manifest miscarriage of justice" based on petitioner's innocence is "fact-intensive"; given "District Court's ability to take testimony from the few key witnesses [on the issue] if it deems that course advisable," case is remanded to district court for further proceedings on petitioner's "request for an evidentiary hearing"; in deciding whether to order evidentiary hearing on manifest miscarriage of justice, district court need not assume that proffered evidence is credible but, instead, "must assess the probative force of the newly presented evidence in connection with the evidence of guilt adduced at trial" and "may consider how the timing of the submission [of the new evidence of innocence] and the likely credibility of the affiants bear on the probable reliability of that evidence"; also discussing petitioner's request to "supplement the record" and thereby "buttress his claims of innocence" by expanding the record to include "affidavits from inmates [and others] who stated they had witnessed the event and that [petitioner] had not been present"); *id.* at 339, 341-42 (Rehnquist, C.J., dissenting) ("new evidence not presented at trial will almost always be involved in these claims of actual innocence," and court "may need to make credibility determinations as to witnesses who did not appear before the original jury"; "where the district court believes on the basis of written submissions that the necessary showing of 'actual innocence' may be made out, it should conduct a limited evidentiary hearing at which the affiants whose testimony the Court believes to be crucial to the showing of actual innocence are present and may be cross examined as to veracity, reliability, and all of the other elements which affect the weight to be given the testimony of a witness"); McCleskey v. Zant, 499 U.S. 466, 494 (1991) (petitioner may be entitled to evidentiary hearing to satisfy burden of proving cause and prejudice unless "district court determines as a matter of law that petitioner cannot satisfy the standard"); Jenkins v. Anderson, 447 U.S. 231, 234 n.1 (1980); Amrine v. Bowersox, 128 F.3d 1222, 1228-29 (8th Cir. 1997) (*en banc*), *cert. denied*, 118 S. Ct. 1807 (1998) (petitioner entitled to evidentiary hearing to determine whether new evidence obtained since district court's denial of relief satisfies "miscarriage of justice" exception established in *Schlup v. Delo, supra*); Williams v. Turpin, 87 F.3d 1204, 1208-09 (11th Cir. 1996) ("A habeas petitioner is entitled to an evidentiary hearing to show cause and prejudice if he proffers specific facts sufficient to support such a finding."); Porter v. Singletary, 49 F.3d 1483, 1489-90 & n.13 (11th Cir. 1995) (*per curiam*) (petitioner was entitled to evidentiary hearing to show "cause" for procedural default on ground that he did not know and could not reasonably have known factual predicate for claim at time of default); Watson v. New Mexico, 45 F.3d 385, 386-88

state court adjudication of legal issues in the 4th Amendment context governed by the *Stone v. Powell* doctrine and perhaps in other contexts,[38] abuse of the

---

(10th Cir. 1995) (because district court denied petition on merits without ever addressing procedural default, court of appeals reverses and remands for consideration of "cause," "prejudice," and "miscarriage of justice," including possible evidentiary hearing on validity of factual allegations underlying petitioner's argument of "cause"); United States v. Wright, 43 F.3d 491, 497-500 (10th Cir. 1994) (remanding for evidentiary hearing on existence of "cause" for failure to challenge guilty plea on direct appeal); Barnard v. Collins, 13 F.3d 871, 878 (5th Cir. 1994); Ratliff v. United States, 999 F.2d 1023, 1026 (6th Cir. 1993); Stano v. Dugger, 901 F.2d 898, 905 (11th Cir. 1990) (*en banc*) (granting hearing on question of cause and prejudice exception to procedural default doctrine); Rosenwald v. United States, 898 F.2d 585, 588 (7th Cir. 1990); Simmons v. Lockhart, 856 F.2d 1144, 1145-46 (8th Cir. 1988); Buffalo v. Sunn, 854 F.2d 1158, 1165-66 (9th Cir. 1988) (hearing mandatory, even if not requested, when affidavits conflict on issue of "cause" for procedural default); Clanton v. Muncy, 845 F.2d 1238, 1241 (4th Cir.), *cert. denied*, 485 U.S. 1000 (1988) (by implication); Walker v. Davis, 840 F.2d 834, 839-40 (11th Cir. 1988) (remanding for hearing on "cause" for procedural default); Smith v. Wainwright, 741 F.2d 1248, 1254 (11th Cir. 1984), *cert. denied*, 470 U.S. 1087 (1985); Jackson v. McKaskle, 729 F.2d 356, 359 (5th Cir. 1984); Carrier v. Hutto, 724 F.2d 396, 401 (4th Cir. 1983), *adhered to en banc*, 754 F.2d 520 (4th Cir. 1985), *rev'd on other grounds sub nom. Murray v. Carrier*, 477 U.S. 478 (1986); Dyas v. Lockhart, 705 F.2d 993, 996 (8th Cir.), *cert. denied*, 464 U.S. 982 (1983); Ashby v. Wyrick, 693 F.2d 789, 794 (8th Cir. 1982); United States ex rel. Caruso v. Zelinsky, 689 F.2d 435, 443 (3d Cir. 1982); Wade v. Franzen, 678 F.2d 56, 58 (7th Cir. 1982); Huffman v. Wainwright, 651 F.2d 347, 349 (5th Cir. 1981); In re Kravitz, 488 F. Supp. 38, 47 (M.D. Pa. 1979); *infra* § 26.3e (hearings on "cause and prejudice"); other decisions cited *infra* § 26.3e n.79. *See also* Herrera v. Collins, 506 U.S. 390, 443 (1993) (Blackmun, J., dissenting) ("In considering whether a prisoner is entitled to relief on an actual-innocence claim [that prisoner asserts in order to establish "manifest miscarriage of justice" exception to procedural default bar], a court should take all the evidence into account, giving due regard to its reliability" (citing, *e.g.*, Sawyer v. Whitley, 505 U.S. 333, 339 n.5 (1992)). *Cf.* Weeks v. Bowersox, 119 F.3d 1342, 1353 (8th Cir. 1997) (*en banc*), *cert. denied*, 118 S. Ct. 887 (1998) (district court did not err in denying petitioner's request for evidentiary hearing to establish "miscarriage of justice" exception, given that petitioner did not support request with affidavits other than his own or with other documentary evidence); Andrews v. Deland, 943 F.2d 1162, 1185 (10th Cir. 1991), *cert. denied*, 502 U.S. 1110 (1992) (district court did not err in denying hearing on cause and prejudice in writ abuse context because "record in this case, including affidavits from ... attorneys involved in the case, makes it clear as a matter of law that Andrews will be unable to satisfy the cause and prejudice standard"); Henderson v. Dugger, 925 F.2d 1309, 1314-15 (11th Cir. 1991), *cert. denied*, 506 U.S. 1007 (1992) (hearing on whether ineffective assistance of appellate counsel constituted cause for default was unnecessary because issue could be resolved by examining record); Smith v. Jones, 923 F.2d 588, 589-90 (8th Cir. 1991) (petitioner not entitled to hearing on cause and prejudice because he made only vague allegations of cause and no allegations of prejudice). *See generally infra* Chapter 26.

[38] *See, e.g.*, Singer v. Court of Common Pleas, 879 F.2d 1203, 1210 (3d Cir. 1989); Doleman v. Muncy, 579 F.2d 1258, 1266 n.17 (4th Cir. 1978). *See generally infra* Chapter 27. On the question whether full and fair state court adjudication (assuming the facts show such adjudication occurred) requires federal courts to defer to state court determinations of law outside the 4th Amendment context, see *infra* § 30.2.

writ,[39] harmless error,[40] and the like. Determining whether the petitioner's status places him within the federal courts' habeas corpus jurisdiction — whether, for example, the petitioner is "in custody" or whether a third-party applicant qualifies as a "next friend" authorized to petition on behalf of an incarcerated prisoner[41] — also may require a hearing. Indeed, sometimes the determination whether to hold a federal evidentiary hearing on the merits of the petition requires a preliminary hearing to assess whether the petitioner is entitled to a hearing on the merits.[42]

---

[39] *See, e.g., Schlup v. Delo, supra,* 513 U.S. at 308-12 & nn.18, 19, 25, 331 (discussed *supra* note 37); *id.* at 341, 342 (Rehnquist, C.J., dissenting) (same); *McCleskey v. Zant, supra,* 499 U.S. at 493 (discussed *supra* note 37); Price v. Johnston, 334 U.S. 266, 292 (1948); Howard v. Lewis, 905 F.2d 1318, 1324 (9th Cir. 1990); Demps v. Dugger, 874 F.2d 1385, 1391 (11th Cir. 1989), *cert. denied,* 494 U.S. 1090 (1990); Williams v. Lockhart, 862 F.2d 155, 160 (8th Cir. 1988); Simmons v. Lockhart, 856 F.2d 1144, 1146 (8th Cir. 1988); Andre v. Guste, 850 F.2d 259, 262 n.1 (5th Cir. 1988); Hamilton v. McCotter, 772 F.2d 171, 178 (5th Cir. 1985); Ford v. Strickland, 734 F.2d 538, 540 n.1 (11th Cir. 1984), *rev'd on other grounds sub nom. Ford v. Wainwright,* 477 U.S. 399 (1986) (court is unwilling to find abuse of writ "without the benefit of an evidentiary hearing to give [petitioner] and his counsel an opportunity to explain their actions"); Baker v. Estelle, 715 F.2d 1031, 1034-35 (5th Cir. 1983), *cert. denied,* 465 U.S. 1106 (1984); Baldwin v. Maggio, 704 F.2d 1325, 1328 n.6 (5th Cir. 1983), *cert. denied,* 467 U.S. 1220 (1984); Jones v. Estelle, 692 F.2d 380, 384-85 (5th Cir. 1982); McShane v. Estelle, 683 F.2d 867, 870 (5th Cir. 1982). *See generally infra* Chapter 28.

[40] *See* United States v. Olano, 507 U.S. 725, 740 (1993) *(dicta)* (evidentiary hearing may be available to assess prejudice, if any, caused by violation of rule forbidding alternate jurors to observe deliberations of regular jurors, but defendant "never requested a hearing and thus the record before us contains no direct evidence that the alternate jurors influenced the verdict"); other authority cited *infra* § 32.4f n.75. *Cf.* Sullivan v. Louisiana, 508 U.S. 275, 284 (1993) (Rehnquist, C.J., concurring) ("[T]he reviewing court is usually left only with the record developed at trial to determine whether it is possible to say ... that the error did not contribute to the jury's verdict."). *See generally infra* Chapter 32.

[41] *See, e.g.,* Groseclose ex rel. Harries v. Dutton, 589 F. Supp. 362 (M.D. Tenn. 1984); *supra* Chapter 8.

[42] *See* Townsend v. Sain, 372 U.S. 293, 312-18 (1963); *Price v. Johnston, supra,* 334 U.S. at 291; Wright v. Gramley, 125 F.3d 1038, 1043-45 (7th Cir. 1997) (remanding to district court to allow *pro se* petitioner to submit affidavit to explain failure to develop facts in state court and "convince the district court that his failure to present the facts in plenary fashion to the state court was not due to his own neglect"); Lahay v. Armontrout, 923 F.2d 578, 578-79 (8th Cir. 1991) (remanding for hearing to determine whether witness for state committed perjury at state postconviction hearing, thus removing presumption of correctness of state court factfindings based on that testimony); Myatt v. United States, 875 F.2d 8, 10-11 (1st Cir. 1989) (by implication from allocation to petitioner of burden of proving right to hearing); Ross v. Kemp, 785 F.2d 1467, 1471 (11th Cir. 1986); Birt v. Montgomery, 709 F.2d 690, 702 (11th Cir. 1983), *cert. denied,* 469 U.S. 874 (1984); Thomas v. Zant, 697 F.2d 977, 987 (11th Cir. 1983), *vac'd & remanded on other grounds sub nom. Kemp v. Thomas,* 478 U.S. 1016 (1986); In re Wainwright, 678 F.2d 951, 953 (11th Cir. 1982) ("section 2254(d) contemplates that in some cases the federal court will hold an evidentiary hearing for the purpose of determining whether to apply the presumption of

d. *Capital cases.* The Supreme Court repeatedly has said that the "qualitative difference" between death and imprisonment enhances the "need for reliability in the determination that death is the appropriate punishment in a specific case."[43] The Court has extended the requirement of enhanced reliability to many aspects of the proceedings leading to the execution of a prisoner, including the guilt or innocence phase of trial,[44] sentencing,[45] appeal,[46] and the postconviction process of determining whether a capital inmate is sufficiently *compos mentis* to be executed.[47] So, too, the Court has emphasized the special importance in capital cases — to society as well as to individuals facing execution — of maintaining the integrity of the processes by which the state takes life and assuring that those processes are *and appear to be* fair.[48] The Court, finally, has consistently recognized that evidentiary hearings play a central role in enabling capital[49] and noncapital[50] habeas corpus (as well as other[51]) proceedings to achieve their long-acknowledged goal of assuring both the reality and appearance of reliability and integrity in the processes leading to criminal judgments.[52] Together, these lines of decisions make clear that evidentiary hearings are critical in cases involving condemned prisoners whenever such hearings may shed light on the reliability or fairness of the procedures leading to the execution.[53]

---

correctness[ ]" of state findings); United States ex rel. Gorham v. Franzen, 675 F.2d 932, 937 n.1 (7th Cir. 1982); Maldonado v. Eyman, 377 F.2d 526 (9th Cir. 1967). *See also* Coleman v. Zant, 708 F.2d 541, 547 & n.9 (11th Cir. 1983) (discovery permitted to assist petitioner in showing that state court factfindings were not adequate).

[43] Woodson v. North Carolina, 428 U.S. 280, 305 (1976). *Accord* authority cited *supra* § 2.6.

[44] *See, e.g.,* Ake v. Oklahoma, 470 U.S. 68, 87 (1985) (Burger, C.J., concurring); Beck v. Alabama, 447 U.S. 625, 637-38 (1980).

[45] *See, e.g.,* Cabana v. Bullock, 474 U.S. 376, 387 (1986); Strickland v. Washington, 466 U.S. 668, 686-87 (1984); Lockett v. Ohio, 438 U.S. 586, 604 (1978).

[46] *See, e.g.,* Gardner v. Florida, 430 U.S. 349, 360-61 (1977).

[47] *See, e.g.,* Ford v. Wainwright, 477 U.S. 399, 411-12 (1986). *See also supra* § 7.2f (indications that Constitution may require counsel in capital state postconviction proceedings, even if not in noncapital proceedings).

[48] *See, e.g., Gardner v. Florida, supra,* 430 U.S. at 358.

[49] *See, e.g., Ford v. Wainwright, supra,* 477 U.S. at 411-12.

[50] *See, e.g.,* Jackson v. Virginia, 443 U.S. 307, 323 (1979); Townsend v. Sain, 372 U.S. 293, 312 (1963); authority cited *supra* § 20.1b nn.13-15 and accompanying text.

[51] *See* authority cited *supra* § 20.1b n.14.

[52] *See supra* §§ 2.6, 7.2f, 19.4e.

[53] *See, e.g.,* Siripongs v. Calderon, 35 F.3d 1308, 1310 (9th Cir. 1994), *cert. denied,* 513 U.S. 1183 (1995) ("In a capital case, a habeas petitioner who asserts a colorable claim to relief, and who has never been given the opportunity to develop a factual record on that claim, is entitled to an evidentiary hearing in federal court."); Cunningham v. Zant, 928 F.2d 1006, 1012 (11th Cir. 1991) (because "Supreme Court has stated that 'fact-finding procedures aspire to a higher standard of

§ 20.2. Overview of fact-development and fact-determination procedures in AEDPA and non-AEDPA cases.

a. *Introduction.* Sections 20.3 and 20.4 discuss circumstances in which the absence of, or deficiencies in, prior state court fact-development procedures and factfindings require — and circumstances in which the existence and adequacy of those procedures and findings preclude — federal court hearings and findings. That topic actually presents two discrete questions, one affecting the process of *hearing* the facts, the other affecting the process of *deciding* them. First, under what conditions are federal evidentiary hearings an available or even mandatory means of resolving dispositive factual questions presented by the petitioner's claims and the state's responses, notwithstanding that the state courts previously heard and made findings on some or all of those questions? Second, once the federal court is ready to decide the case, under what conditions may the court reach an independent judgment as to the dispositive facts, notwithstanding that the state courts previously reached their own judgments as to those facts? The purpose of this section is to distinguish the related but not identical standards that provide the answers to these two questions. The first two subsections clarify the standards that govern, respectively, fact-development and fact-determination, and discuss the effect of the Antiterrorism and Effective Death Penalty Act of 1996[1] (AEDPA) on each set of standards. The final subsection discusses the relationship between the two sets of standards.

b. *Right to a hearing in AEPDA and non-AEDPA cases.* In 1963 in *Townsend v. Sain*,[2] in the context of reversing a lower court's denial of a habeas corpus hearing, the Supreme Court ruled that district courts always have the discretion to hold evidentiary hearings on dispositive factual questions arising in habeas corpus litigation.[3] The Court further ruled that "the holding of a [federal] hearing is *mandatory*" in six situations,[4] including some circumstances in which the state

---

reliability' in capital cases," and because state courts did not explicitly and directly address critical factual issue, court refuses to infer state court finding on issue and makes its own factual determination); Autry v. Estelle, 719 F.2d 1251, 1252 (5th Cir. 1983) (stay granted and case remanded to lower federal courts for "a full and complete evidentiary hearing" in order to assure the death-sentenced petitioner every opportunity to present his constitutional claims).

§ 20.2. [1] Pub. L. 104-132, 110 Stat. 1214 (1996). For an overview of AEPDA and the changes it makes in habeas corpus procedures, see *supra* §§ 3.2, 3.5b. For an explanation of the cases to which AEDPA applies, see *supra* § 3.4.

[2] 372 U.S. 293 (1963).

[3] *Id.* at 318. *See infra* § 20.4.

[4] *Townsend, supra,* 372 U.S. at 313 (emphasis added). *See id.* at 313-19 (extensively discussing the six situations). Each of the six situations is discussed in detail in the portions of section 20.3

courts previously held a hearing[5] and made factfindings:[6]

> If (1) the merits of the factual dispute were not resolved in the state hearing;[7] (2) the state factual determination is not fairly supported by the record as a whole;[8] (3) the fact-finding procedure employed by the state court was not adequate to afford a full and fair hearing;[9] (4) there is a substantial allegation of newly discovered evidence;[10] (5) the material facts were not adequately developed at the state court hearing;[11] or (6) for any reason it appears that the state trier of fact did not afford the habeas applicant a full and fair fact hearing.[12]

Townsend governed *all* evidentiary hearing questions from 1963 until 1992. In the latter year, the Supreme Court decided *Keeney v. Tamayo-Reyes*, which replaced the *Townsend* hearing standard with a narrower standard in one — but only one — important context.[13] *Townsend* had required federal hearings on all material facts not addressed in the state courts unless the prisoner herself had "deliberate[ly] bypass[ed]" (*i.e.*, personally, knowingly, and intelligently waived) a state court hearing on the issue.[14] *Tamayo-Reyes* held that a failure to present evidence which is attributable to *either* the prisoner *or* her counsel[15] can constitute a "procedural default" that eliminates the right to a mandatory federal hearing unless (1) the state waives reliance on the default[16] or (2) the petitioner demonstrates that the default is "excusable" because there is "cause" for and "prejudice" from the failure to present the evidence in state court,[17] or (3) the

---

infra to which reference is made in the bracketed footnote. *See also supra* § 20.1b n.13 (other Supreme Court decisions discussing right to hearing).

[5] Under *Townsend*, federal hearings are mandatory if the state courts did not hold a hearing. *See infra* § 20.3e nn.90-94 and accompanying text.

[6] Under *Townsend*, a federal hearing is mandatory if the state courts did not issue written factfindings on dispositive factual questions. *See infra* § 20.3c.

[7] *See infra* § 20.3c (para. (4)), 20.3d (paras. (1)(c), (7)), 20.3e n.106 and accompanying text, 20.3e (para. (6)(n)).

[8] *See infra* § 20.3f.

[9] *See infra* § 20.3e (para. (6)).

[10] *See infra* § 20.3e (para. (1)).

[11] *See infra* § 20.3e (para. (2)).

[12] *See infra* § 20.3e. *See also infra* § 20.3d (paras. (5), (6)), 20.3e (paras. (5), (6)). The quoted passage, minus the bracketed footnotes, appears in *Townsend, supra*, 372 U.S. at 313.

[13] 504 U.S. 1 (1992). *See id.* at 18 (O'Connor, J., dissenting).

[14] *Townsend, supra*, 372 U.S. at 317, 320.

[15] *See Tamayo-Reyes, supra*, 504 U.S. at 5-9 (discussed *infra* § 20.3e n.104 and accompanying text).

[16] *See infra* § 20.3e n.106 and accompanying text.

[17] *Tamayo-Reyes, supra*, 504 U.S. at 11 (discussed *infra* § 20.3 n.107 and accompanying text).

petitioner shows that the denial of a hearing will result in a "fundamental miscarriage of justice" because there is a probability that the petitioner is innocent of the crime of which she has been convicted.[18]

Before the enactment of the Antiterrorism and Effective Death Penalty Act (AEDPA) in 1996, the law governing a habeas corpus petitioner's right to a federal evidentiary hearing was principally judge-made — consisting of the *Townsend* doctrine, as modified by *Tamayo-Reyes* and as elaborated by the lower federal courts.[19] In AEDPA, Congress amended 28 U.S.C. § 2254 by adding the following provision in section 2254(e)(2):

> (2) If the applicant has failed to develop the factual basis of a claim in State court proceedings, the court shall not hold an evidentiary hearing on the claim unless the applicant shows that —
>
>   (A) the claim relies on —
>
>   (i)   a new rule of constitutional law, made retroactive to cases on collateral review by the Supreme Court, that was previously unavailable; or
>
>   (ii) a factual predicate that could not have been previously discovered through the exercise of due diligence; and
>
>   (B) the facts underlying the claim would be sufficient to establish by clear and convincing evidence that but for constitutional error, no reasonable factfinder would have found the applicant guilty of the underlying offense.[20]

Section 2254(e)(2) substantially changes prior law in one — but only one — important context, the same context in which the Court previously had modified *Townsend* through its decision in *Tamayo-Reyes*, namely, in cases in which "the *applicant* has failed to develop the factual basis in State court proceedings" and now seeks to do so in federal court.[21] AEDPA thus supersedes *Tamayo-Reyes*

---

[18] *Id.* at 11-12 (discussed *infra* § 20.3e n.108 and accompanying text).

[19] AEDPA, Pub. L. 104-132, 110 Stat. 1214 (1996), actually supplements (1) an evidentiary hearing provision, 28 U.S.C. § 2243 (1994), that dates back to the Habeas Corpus Act of 1867, and (2) the more recently adopted Rule 8 of the Rules Governing § 2254 Cases. *See supra* § 20.1b nn.10-17 and accompanying text. During the last several decades, however, the meaning of both these provisions has been governed by *Townsend* and its progeny — which interpreted the former provision and have been understood to have been codified by the latter rule. *See id.*

[20] 28 U.S.C.A. § 2254(e)(2) (West 1994 & Supp. 1998).

[21] *Id.* (emphasis added). *See, e.g.,* Lawrie v. Snyder, 1998 WL 276252, at *8 & n.5 (D. Del. May 15, 1998) ("[I]n effect, the 1996 [AEDPA] amendment supersedes *Keeney,* which superseded a portion of *Townsend,* namely, the fifth circumstance in which an evidentiary hearing is mandatory. The remainder of *Townsend,* however, appears to have been left intact, including the other five factors under which an evidentiary hearing is mandatory, as well as the court's overriding

and the portion of *Townsend v. Sain* that *Tamayo-Reyes* itself had superseded — governing evidentiary hearings on facts that the petitioner is responsible for failing to develop (*i.e.*, for "procedurally defaulting") in state court. But AEDPA leaves entirely intact the portion of *Townsend* that *Tamayo-Reyes* also previously had left intact — governing evidentiary hearings on facts that the *state* or the *state courts* are responsible for not having developed in state court (*e.g.*, because the state suppressed evidence or the state court improperly denied a subpoena or hearing to develop facts that the petitioner conscientiously proffered).[22]

---

ability to hold a hearing in its discretion.... Also left untouched by these developments is the situation where someone other than petitioner or his attorney is responsible for the failure to develop an adequate factual record in the state court." (**citing FHCPP**)); Hunter v. Vasquez, 1996 WL 612484, at *5 (N.D. Cal. Oct. 3, 1996) (section 2254(e)(2) codifies preexisting law regarding right to evidentiary hearings except in cases in which petitioner "failed to develop" facts in state court).

[22] *See, e.g.*, Cardwell v. Greene, 152 F.3d 331, 337-38 (4th Cir. 1998) ("We join four of our sister circuits in holding that where an applicant has diligently sought to develop the factual basis of a claim for habeas relief, but has been denied the opportunity to do so by the state court, § 2254(e)(2) will not preclude an evidentiary hearing in federal court.... [A]n applicant 'fail[s]' to develop the evidence supporting a claim only if he or she relinquishes an opportunity to introduce evidence or neglects to seek such an opportunity.... Section 2254(e)(2) should not be interpreted to allow a state court to deny a petitioner meaningful review of a federal claim by refusing to permit development of the factual record at the state level."); McDonald v. Johnson, 139 F.3d 1056, 1059 (5th Cir. 1998) ("We join the Third and Seventh Circuits in concluding that, for purposes of 28 U.S.C. § 2254(e)(2), a petitioner cannot be said to have 'failed to develop' a factual basis for his claim unless the undeveloped record is a result of his own decision or omission."); Burris v. Parke, 116 F.3d 256, 258-59 (7th Cir.), *cert. denied*, 118 S. Ct. 462 (1997) ("Section 2254(e)(2) ... applies only when 'the applicant has failed to develop the factual basis of a claim in State court proceedings.' 'Failure' implies omission — a decision not to introduce evidence when there was an opportunity, or a decision not to seek an opportunity.... To be attributable to a 'failure' under federal law the deficiency in the record must reflect something the petitioner did or omitted. Like the Third Circuit [in *Love v. Morton, infra*], we think that the word 'fail' cannot bear a strict-liability reading, under which a federal court would disregard the reason for the shortcomings of the record. If it did, then a state could insulate its decisions from collateral attack in federal court by refusing to grant evidentiary hearings in its own courts. Nothing in § 2254(e) or the rest of the AEDPA implies that states may manipulate things in this manner." (citations omitted)); Love v. Morton, 112 F.3d 131, 136 (3d Cir. 1997) ("plain language of § 2254(e)(2)" renders provision inapplicable when "factors other than the defendant's action prevented a factual record from being developed"); Williams v. Netherland, 1998 WL 300570, at *2 (E.D. Va. June 3, 1998) ("plain meaning of section 2254(e)(2) prohibits a federal evidentiary hearing only in those cases where a petitioner has been afforded an opportunity to develop evidence in state habeas court, but has failed to do so"); Weeks v. Angelone, 1998 WL 171121, at *5-6 (E.D. Va. April 1, 1998) ("This court agrees with other courts that have ... held that § 2254(e)(2) does not apply when a petitioner attempted to, but was denied the opportunity to develop the facts by the state courts.... Thus, where the faulty record is attributable to the state, and not the defendant, § 2254(e)(2) will not apply."); Zuern v. Tate, 938 F. Supp. 468, 476 (S.D. Ohio 1996) (section 2254(e)(2) essentially codifies *Townsend* and *Tamayo-Reyes*); Cox v. Turner, No. C-2-95-356 (E.D. Ohio July 21, 1996)

(magistrate judge's report) ("habeas petitioner who has diligently pursued his claims in the state courts should neither be faulted nor penalized for the failure of the state courts" to conduct hearing); Silva v. Calderon, No. CV 90-3311 DT (C.D. Cal. June 26, 1996); Douglas v. Calderon, No. CV 91-3055 RSWL (C.D. Cal. June 11, 1996) ("The Act is silent as to the remaining factors of *Townsend*. This silence suggests that the Act was not intended to overrule *Townsend* ... [but only to] provide for one circumstance when a federal court may not hold an evidentiary hearing .... Therefore a federal petitioner would still be entitled to an evidentiary hearing if he did not receive a full and fair hearing in state court"); Wilkins v. Bowersox, 933 F.2d 1496, 1504 n.3 (W.D. Mo. 1996). *Cf.* Porter v. Gramley, 112 F.3d 1308, 1315 n.6, 1317 n.8 (7th Cir. 1997), *cert. denied*, 118 S. Ct. 886 (1998) (apparently superseded by *Burris v. Parke, supra*) (recognizing that "*Townsend*'s requirements are ... in force" but questioning in *dicta* whether section 2254(e)(2)'s provision for nondevelopment of facts in state court may apply even if petitioner was not at fault for nondevelopment); United States ex rel. Crivens v. Washington, 1997 WL 120017, at *5-6 (N.D. Ill. March 13, 1997) (also apparently superseded by *Burris v. Parke, supra*) (construing section 2254(e)(2) broadly to apply to any nondevelopment of facts in state court regardless of petitioner's responsibility but thereafter applying standard of discoverability of "factual predicate" that permits evidentiary hearing because state courts prevented petitioner from developing requisite factual record). *Compare, e.g.*, Breard v. Greene, 118 S. Ct. 1352, 1353-54 (1998) (*per curiam*) (section 2254(e)(2) applies to case and bars federal hearing because petitioner "fail[ed] to raise the claim in the state courts" and never sought state court hearing to establish facts essential for prevailing on claim) *and* Hines v. Lensing, 1998 WL 603397, at *1 (E.D. La. Sept. 9, 1998) (section 2254(e)(2) bars federal hearing on claim of ineffective assistance in failing to investigate because petitioner could have, but did not, support request for state court hearing with "[a]ffidavits, exhibits [or] other materials ... to make an initial showing of the circumstances he believes should have been investigated") *and* Royal v. Netherland, 1998 WL 234185, at *13 (E.D. Va. May 5, 1998) (section 2254(e)(2) bars hearing on claim that trial counsel was ineffective in failing to interview prosecution witnesses, because "petitioner did not take or seek the opportunity to develop ... the factual basis of the claim in ... state court") *and* United States ex rel. Smith v. Washington, 992 F. Supp. 964, 968 (N.D. Ill. 1998) ("[f]ailure to develop the factual basis implies that the deficiency in the record reflects something the petitioner did or omitted, such as deciding not to introduce evidence when there was an opportunity to do so"; court denies hearing because petitioner had opportunity to develop factual basis for claim in state postconviction review proceedings but did not present evidence) *with* Jones v. Wood, 114 F.3d 1002, 1012 (9th Cir. 1997) (petitioner entitled to hearing because he "did not 'fail[ ] to develop' the factual basis of his claims; rather, the state courts denied him the opportunity to develop the facts by failing to hold an evidentiary hearing") *and* Grosso v. Artuz, 1998 WL 108011, at *4 (S.D.N.Y. March 12, 1998) (magistrate judge's report) ("[p]etitioner put before the state court the pertinent facts through the affidavits of the relevant witnesses who were prepared to support his case, and thus he cannot fairly be taxed with having 'failed to develop the factual basis of his claim' in state court"; federal hearing is appropriate because claim requires factfinding and state court ruled on basis of affidavits without holding hearing) *and* Crane v. Director, No. 4:95CV049 (E.D. Tex. Oct. 3, 1996) ("petitioner is entitled to an evidentiary hearing" because it was "state court [that] failed" to develop facts) *and* Hunter v. Vasquez, *supra*, 1996 WL 612484, at *5-*6 ("Court cannot find that Petitioner failed adequately to develop the facts of his claim in state court" because he "requested discovery, requested investigation funds and requested a hearing" in state court and "state court denied each of Petitioner's requests"; petitioner accordingly is entitled to federal hearing) *and* Caro v. Vasquez, 1996 WL 478683, at *5 (N.D. Cal. Aug. 19, 1996) (section 2254(e)(2) does not bar evidentiary

In cases in which the omission of material facts from the state court record is attributable to the petitioner, AEDPA generally follows the approach the Court developed in *Tamayo-Reyes* but narrows the availability of hearings still further, in two respects. First, when the petitioner's default caused the failure to develop the material facts, section 2254(e)(2) deprives the federal court of the discretion it had under *Townsend*, and even under *Tamayo-Reyes*,[23] to hold a hearing and permits a hearing only if the petitioner can make a showing of exceptional circumstances.[24] Second, in contrast to the *Tamayo-Reyes* rule, which excused a default if the petitioner showed *either* "cause and prejudice" *or* a "miscarriage of justice" (requiring proof of "innocence" by a preponderance of the evidence), AEDPA requires a showing of *both* "cause" *and* "innocence," and defines both more narrowly than under prior law.[25] The following standards apply under AEDPA:

- "Cause" may be shown in either of two ways. The first is by demonstrating that the claim on which the petitioner failed to proffer the facts in state court relies on a new rule of constitutional law made retroactive to habeas corpus cases by the Supreme Court.[26] The "new rule of constitutional law" standard somewhat resembles the preexisting "novel law" basis for establishing "cause."[27] The standard also seems to refer to the narrow category of new rules of constitutional law that the Supreme Court's *Teague* doctrine makes retroactive to cases subject to federal habeas corpus review.[28] Although section 2254(e)(2)(A)(i)'s reference to new rules "made retroactive to cases on collateral review *by the Supreme Court*" might be intended to limit that category still further by requiring a Supreme Court (as opposed to a lower court) decision stating explicitly that a particular new rule applies retroactively to cases on collateral review under the *Teague* doctrine,[29] the

---

hearing on facts that petitioner proffered to state court in unsuccessful requests for discovery, funds, and evidentiary hearing, because it was not petitioner who "failed to develop" those facts).

[23] *Tamayo-Reyes* had limited *Townsend* only with respect to the circumstances under which a hearing is *mandatory*; it had left intact the portion of *Townsend* that recognized a federal court's discretion to hold a hearing even when such a hearing is not mandatory. *See infra* § 20.4 nn.10-11 and accompanying text.

[24] *Cf. infra* § 20.4 (discretionary hearings).

[25] For the preexisting definitions of "cause" and "manifest miscarriage of justice," which continue to govern the treatment of *legal* claims defaulted in the state courts, see *infra* §§ 26.3b, 26.4.

[26] 28 U.S.C.A. § 2254(e)(2)(A)(i) (West 1994 & Supp. 1998) ("new rule of constitutional law, made retroactive to cases on collateral review by the Supreme Court, that was previously unavailable").

[27] *See infra* §§ 26.3b n.27, 28.3c nn.68-76.

[28] *See infra* § 25.1 nn.2-9 and accompanying text. *See also infra* § 25.7.

[29] *Cf. infra* § 30.2c n.29 and accompanying text.

744

provision instead might be read as requiring only that the new rule be one that qualifies for retroactive treatment as a matter of the Supreme Court doctrine that controls retroactivity questions (*i.e.*, the *Teague* doctrine). This latter reading makes sense because AEDPA adopts a retroactivity provision of its own, which is narrower in several respects than the *Teague* retroactivity rule,[30] thus requiring that the statute indicate whether the applicable "retroactivity" standard in any given context is to be drawn from AEDPA itself or from preexisting Supreme Court doctrine.[31]

- The only other way to show "cause" is by demonstrating that the facts the petitioner failed to develop in state court were not discoverable at the time of the state hearing through the exercise of due diligence.[32]

- "Innocence" is established only if "the facts underlying the claim would be sufficient to establish by clear and convincing evidence that, but for constitutional error, no reasonable factfinder would have found the applicant guilty of the underlying offense."[33] This provision evidently codifies the definition

---

[30] *See* 28 U.S.C.A. § 2254(d)(1) (West 1994 & Supp. 1998) (discussed *infra* § 30.2 nn.25-30 and accompanying text).

[31] Because the "new rule of constitutional law" standard also appears in the Act's successive petition provisions, *see* 28 U.S.C.A. § 2244(b)(2)(A) (West 1994 & Supp. 1998) (albeit without any "innocence" requirement), the caselaw that arises under the analogous successive petition provision will assist courts in resolving this evidentiary hearing issue. *See infra* § 28.3e nn.128-33 and accompanying text.

[32] 28 U.S.C.A. § 2254(e)(A)(ii) (West 1994 & Supp. 1998) ("factual predicate that could not have been previously discovered through the exercise of due diligence"). *See, e.g.*, Tokar v. Bowersox, 1998 WL 125656, at *31 (E.D. Mo. March 19, 1998) (petitioner has not shown "cause" under section 2254(e)(A)(ii) because "record clearly indicates that the facts underlying this claim could have been previously discovered through the exercise of due diligence"; issue of mental incompetence, on which petitioner seeks hearing, "was raised and examinations of petitioner were conducted prior to petitioner's trial"). For discussion of the "due diligence" standard, see *supra* § 3.3c n.64. For caselaw developing a similar basis for "cause" under preexisting law, see *infra* § 26.3b n.28 and accompanying text.

[33] 28 U.S.C.A. § 2254(e)(2)(B) (West 1994 & Supp. 1998). *See* United States ex rel. Crivens v. Washington, 1997 WL 120017, at *7 (N.D. Ill. March 13, 1997) (granting evidentiary hearing because, "assuming petitioner can make the showing he offers to make, ... that showing could be found by the habeas court to prove clearly and convincingly that, but for the constitutional error petitioner could not have been found guilty beyond a reasonable doubt"; court rejects interpretation of statute as requiring that "before [petitioner] is entitled to a hearing, the petitioner must satisfy the habeas court that the evidence he proposes to offer will clearly and convincingly establish that no reasonable factfinder could have found him guilty .... Clearly, the statute cannot mean that petitioner must establish that he is entitled to relief before he can have a hearing to determine whether he is entitled to relief."). *Cf.* Williams v. Netherland, 1998 WL 300570, at *3 (E.D. Va. June 3, 1998) (petitioner cannot make requisite showing of "innocence" under section 2254(e)(2) because petitioner's "own testimony established that he shot [decedent] during the commission of a robbery and subsequent to the rape of [decedent's wife]" and because petitioner's claims "do not

of "innocence" or "manifest miscarriage of justice" that the Supreme Court adopted in *Sawyer v. Whitley*[34] and that it carefully explicated three years later — and a year before AEDPA's adoption — in *Schlup v. Delo*.[35] As *Schlup* makes clear, although the *Sawyer* standard is narrow, it is not *as* narrow as the standard of *Jackson v. Virginia* (which requires proof that no rational trier of fact could have found the defendant guilty).[36] What is not clear is whether section 2254(e)(2)(B)'s phrase "[not] guilty of the underlying offense" includes petitioner's "ineligibility" for the death penalty. Because the provision verbally replicates the Supreme Court's *Sawyer* standard, and because *Sawyer* established that standard in the process of defining the phrase "innocence of the death penalty,"[37] the provision arguably is meant to encompass ineligibility for the death penalty, as several courts have concluded.[38]

The restrictiveness of these provisions is revealed by an inexplicable anomaly in AEDPA. By contrast to the extremely narrow "cause *and* innocence" route to an evidentiary hearing on a *first* habeas corpus petition where the petitioner pre-

---

have any bearing on the evidence presented at trial of Williams' guilt in the shooting death of [decedent]").

[34] 505 U.S. 333 (1992).

[35] 513 U.S. 298, 326-28 (1995).

[36] 443 U.S. 307 (1979). For a detailed discussion of the *Sawyer* standard as explicated and distinguished from the *Jackson* standard by *Schlup*, see *infra* § 26.4.

[37] *Sawyer, supra*, 505 U.S. at 339-40.

[38] *See* Housel v. Thomas, 1997 WL 67823, at *4 (N.D. Ga. 1997); Burris v. Parke, 948 F. Supp. 1310, 1326 (N.D. Ind. 1996), *aff'd on other grounds*, 116 F.3d 256 (7th Cir.), *cert. denied*, 118 S. Ct. 462 (1997); Rich v. Calderon, No. CIV-S-89-0823 EJG GGH P (E.D. Cal. August 2, 1996); Silva v. Calderon, No. CV 90-3311 DT (C.D. Cal. June 26, 1996); Bean v. Calderon, No. CIV S-90-0648 WBS/GGH (E.D. Cal. May 15, 1996). *See also* O'Dell v. Netherland, 117 S. Ct. 1969, 1980 n.3 (1997) (Stevens, J., dissenting) (although some formulations of exception to *Teague* rule "focus[ ] on the accuracy of a guilt-innocence determination, ... [a]n unfair procedure that seriously diminishes the likelihood of an accurate determination that a convicted defendant should receive the death penalty ... — that the defendant is 'innocent of the death penalty' — is plainly encompassed by *Teague*'s exception" (citation omitted)). Both section 2254(e)(2)'s first definition of "cause" and its definition of "innocence" seem to require proof of "constitutional" (as opposed to other federal law) violations. *But cf. supra* § 9.1 nn.60-69 and accompanying text. *But see* Burris v. Parke, 116 F.3d 256, 258 (7th Cir.), *cert. denied*, 118 S. Ct. 462 (1997); cases cited *infra* § 28.3e n.140 (concluding that section 2254(e)(2)(B) and allied successive petition provision are limited to claims attacking guilt-innocence judgment and do not reach "innocence of the death penalty" claims).

Because section 2254(e)(2)(B)'s "innocence" standard also appears in the Act's successive petition provisions, *see* 28 U.S.C.A. § 2244(b)(2)(B)(ii) (West 1994 & Supp. 1998), the caselaw that arises under the analogous successive petition provision will assist courts in resolving this evidentiary hearing issue. *See* Burris v. Parke, *supra* at 258 (equating standards in sections 2244(b)(2)(B)(ii) and 2254(e)(2)(B)); *infra* § 28.3e nn.134-40 and accompanying text.

viously defaulted the facts in state court, AEDPA allows a showing of "cause" alone, of the "new rule" variety, to entitle a petitioner to file a *second or successive* habeas corpus petition on a claim previously defaulted in state *and* federal courts.[39] Why Congress would limit the right to develop the critical *facts* in *first*-petition contexts more stringently even than it limits the right to develop "new *legal* rule" claims in *successive* petition contexts is beyond comprehension.[40]

As § 3.4 *supra* explains, AEDPA does not apply to "nonopt-in cases"[41] that were filed on or before April 24, 1996. As to nonopt-in cases filed after that date, and "opt-in" cases[42] filed before *and* after it, AEDPA's modifications of the right to a hearing sometimes may not apply (for "retroactivity" reasons) if the relevant state proceedings occurred prior to that date.[43] If AEDPA does *not* apply to the case, the applicable standard is the one adopted by *Townsend* and modified by *Tamayo-Reyes.*

c. *Presumption of correctness in AEDPA and non-AEDPA cases.* In 1966, Congress amended the habeas corpus statute to answer a question different from the one previously resolved by the Supreme Court in *Townsend v. Sain* in 1963,[44] namely, how much weight a district court must accord, in assessing the evidence in *both* the state *and* federal records, to "a determination after a hearing on the merits of a factual issue, by a state court of competent jurisdiction."[45] In answering this question, Congress (1) accorded a presumption of correctness to certain types of explicit state court factual determinations except in eight situations enumerated in the statute,[46] and (2) created a procedure through which a

---

[39] *See* 28 U.S.C.A. § 2244(b)(2)(A) (West 1994 & Supp. 1998) (discussed *infra* § 28.3e).

[40] *Cf.* Lonchar v. Thomas, 517 U.S. 314, 320-21, 324-26, 328-29 (1996) (sharply distinguishing "first habeas petition[s]" — the dismissal of which "is a particularly serious matter, for that dismissal denies the petitioner the protections of the Great Writ entirely, risking injury to an important interest in human liberty" — and second petitions as to which the federal courts' discretion to dismiss on "abuse" grounds is wide); *Tamayo-Reyes, supra,* 504 U.S. at 19-20 (O'Connor, J., dissenting) (discussing caselaw sharply distinguishing the wide latitude federal courts have traditionally enjoyed to develop the facts on habeas corpus with the narrow role for new rules of constitutional law in habeas corpus adjudication).

[41] The category of "nonopt-in cases" encompasses all habeas corpus proceedings in States that have not qualified for AEDPA's "opt-in" provisions and also noncapital cases in those States that have qualified for "opt-in" status. *See supra* §§ 3.2, 3.3.

[42] *See supra* §§ 3.3a, 3.3b (discussing how States qualify for "opt-in" status).

[43] *See supra* § 3.4b nn.35-38, 44 and accompanying text.

[44] 372 U.S. 313. *See supra* § 20.1b nn.12-15 and accompanying text (discussing *Townsend*).

[45] 28 U.S.C. § 2254(d) (1994) (superseded).

[46] *Id.* § 2254(d)(1)-(8) (superseded).

party (whether the petitioner or the state[47]) could rebut the presumption when it arises "by establish[ing] by convincing evidence" at a federal hearing "that the factual determination by the State court was erroneous."[48] As adopted in 1966 and until its amendment in 1996, section 2254(d) read as follows:[49]

> In any proceeding instituted in a Federal court by an application for a writ of habeas corpus by a person in custody pursuant to the judgment of a State court, a determination after a hearing[[50]] on the merits of a factual

---

[47] The presumption of correctness is sometimes loosely referred to herein as a "defense" to habeas corpus relief. Although the presumption most often runs against habeas corpus petitioners — habeas corpus cases are only brought if the state courts denied the petitioner relief, thus making it more likely than not that the state court factfindings that are presumed to be correct run *against* the petitioner — the presumption actually applies equally to all state court factfindings, regardless of which party they support. Thus, endorsing the unanimous view of the circuit courts that previously had addressed the issue, the Supreme Court held in 1991 that section 2254(d)'s presumption of correctness applies to factfindings adverse to the state as well as those adverse to a habeas corpus petitioner. *See* Burden v. Zant, 498 U.S. 433, 436 (1991) (*per curiam*) (statement in state trial judge's summary of evidence that central prosecution witness testified pursuant to immunity agreement is factfinding to which federal habeas corpus courts must accord presumption of correctness, unless one of the exceptions in section 2254(d)(1)-(8) (since superseded) is present); Bland v. California Dep't of Corrections, 20 F.3d 1469, 1474 (9th Cir.), *cert. denied*, 513 U.S. 947 (1994); United States ex rel. Partee v. Lane, 926 F.2d 694, 700 (7th Cir. 1991), *cert. denied,* 502 U.S. 1116 (1992) (by implication); Pinkney v. Keene, 920 F.2d 1090, 1092 n.1 (2d Cir. 1990), *cert. denied,* 501 U.S. 1257 (1991) (by implication); Nelson v. Fulcomer, 911 F.2d 928, 932 (3d Cir. 1990) (state court finding that petitioner invoked right to silence during interrogation is due presumption of correctness because, although record did not affirmatively support finding, neither did record contradict it); Bliss v. Lockhart, 891 F.2d 1335, 1338 (8th Cir. 1989); Price v. Wainwright, 759 F.2d 1549, 1553 (11th Cir. 1985); Craker v. Procunier, 756 F.2d 1212, 1214 (5th Cir. 1986). *See also* Camarillo v. Estelle, 670 F.2d 473, 474 (5th Cir. 1981) (same *Townsend* standard that governs habeas corpus petitioners' requests for evidentiary hearings also governs hearing requests by state); *supra* § 20.1c n.34. To this extent, the presumption of correctness is more accurately denominated a decisionmaking rule or, more particularly, a standard of review that federal courts use in what amounts to appellate review of state court factfindings. *See* Monaghan, *supra* § 20.1 n.1, at 274 n.249 (section 2254(d)'s intent is to "require[ ] that deference be given to state court findings of fact so long as they find substantial support in a fairly constructed record"); *infra* § 30.3. *See generally supra* § 2.4 (appellate nature of habeas corpus review of state court determinations). As noted *supra* § 2.4b & *infra* §§ 20.3h, 31.3, the "presumption of correctness" and its rebuttal on the basis of "clear and convincing evidence" operate much like the "clearly erroneous" standard of review of facts that generally applies in other appellate settings.

[48] 28 U.S.C. § 2254(d) (1994) (superseded).

[49] The quotation, minus the bracketed footnotes, is from 28 U.S.C. § 2254(d) (1994) (superseded). Each of the specified prerequisites and exceptions to the presumption of correctness and the specified conditions for its rebuttal are discussed in detail in the portions of section 20.3 *infra* and the other sections of this book to which reference is made in the bracketed footnote.

[50] *See infra* § 20.3e nn.90-94 and accompanying text.

issue,[51] made by a State court of competent jurisdiction[52] in a proceeding to which the applicant for the writ and the State or an officer or agent thereof were parties,[53] evidenced by a written finding, written opinion, or other reliable and adequate written indicia,[54] shall be presumed to be correct, unless the applicant shall establish[55] or it shall otherwise appear, or the respondent shall admit —

(1)   that the merits of the factual dispute were not resolved in the State court hearing; [56]

(2)   that the factfinding procedure employed by the State court was not adequate to afford a full and fair hearing; [57]

(3)   that the material facts were not adequately developed at the State court hearing;[58]

(4)   that the State court lacked jurisdiction of the subject matter or over the person of the applicant in the State court proceeding;[59]

(5)   that the applicant was an indigent and the State court, in deprivation of his constitutional right, failed to appoint counsel to represent him in the State court proceeding;[60]

(6)   that the applicant did not receive a full, fair, and adequate hearing in the State court proceeding;[61] or

(7)   that the applicant was otherwise denied due process of law in the State court proceeding;[62]

(8)   or unless that part of the record of the State court proceeding in which the determination of such factual issue was made, pertinent to a determination of the sufficiency of the evidence to support such factual determination, is produced as provided for hereinafter,[63] and the Federal court on a consideration of such part of the record as a

---

51 *See infra* § 20.3d (para. (1)(a)).

52 *See infra* § 20.3d (para. (5)).

53 *See infra* § 20.3d (para. (6)).

54 *See infra* § 20.3c.

55 *See infra* § 31.3.

56 *See infra* §§ 20.3d (paras. (1)(c), (7)), 20.3e n.106 and accompanying text, 20.3e (para. (6)(n)).

57 *See infra* § 20.3e (para. (6)).

58 *See infra* § 20.3e (para. (2)).

59 *See infra* § 20.3d (para. (5)).

60 *See infra* § 20.3e (para. (4)).

61 *See infra* § 20.3e.

62 *See infra* § 20.3e (para. (5)).

63 *See supra* §§ 15.2c n.59 and accompanying text, 19.2; *infra* § 20.3b.

whole concludes that such factual determination is not fairly supported by the record.[64]

And in an evidentiary hearing in the proceeding in the Federal court,[65] when due proof of such factual determination has been made, unless the existence of one or more of the circumstances respectively set forth in paragraphs numbered (1) to (7), inclusive, is shown by the applicant, otherwise appears, or is admitted by the respondent, or unless the court concludes pursuant to the provisions of paragraph numbered (8) that the record in the State court proceeding, considered as a whole, does not fairly support such factual determination, the burden shall rest upon the applicant to establish by convincing evidence[66] that the factual determination by the State court was erroneous.

In cases in which the state invoked the protection of section 2254(d) in a timely fashion, the statute established a four-stage process for determining the effect of state court factfindings:

- A threshold issue was whether the record revealed that a state court with jurisdiction had made a qualifying factfinding, *i.e.*, generally, an explicit or at least clearly inferrable[67] determination of the merits of a question of historical fact.[68]
- If so, a second issue was whether the state procedure for finding the fact was "full, fair, and adequate" and whether "the material facts were adequately developed at the State court hearing."[69]
- If so, a third issue was whether the factfinding in question was "fairly supported by the state court record."[70]
- If so, the state factfinding was subject to a presumption of correctness that was rebuttable only "by convincing evidence."[71]

---

[64] *See infra* § 20.3f.

[65] *See infra* § 20.3h.

[66] *See infra* §§ 20.3h, 30.3, 31.3.

[67] On inferred or "reconstructed" factfindings, see *infra* § 20.3c.

[68] *See* superseded 28 U.S.C. § 2254(d) (1994) (preamble) (discussed *infra* §§ 20.3b-d). By longstanding interpretation, superseded section 2254(d) did not cover so-called "mixed questions" of law and fact. *See* Thompson v. Keohane, 516 U.S. 99, 110 (1995) (discussing cases); *infra* note 75; *infra* § 20.3d.

[69] Superseded 28 U.S.C. §§ 2254(d)(2), 2254(d)(3), 2254(d)(6) (1994) (discussed *infra* §§ 20.3d, 20.3e). *See id.* §§ 2254(d)(1), 2254(d)(4), 2254(d)(5), 2254(d)(7) (discussed *infra* §§ 20.3d, 20.3e).

[70] Superseded 28 U.S.C. § 2254(d)(8) (1994) (discussed *infra* § 20.3f).

[71] *See* superseded 28 U.S.C. § 2254(d) (1994) (discussed *infra* §§ 20.3h, 31.3).

The Antiterrorism and Effective Death Penalty Act of 1996 (AEDPA)[72] repealed the former section 2254(d) and replaced it with two new provisions dealing with state court factfindings and factfinding procedures, 28 U.S.C. §§ 2254(d)(2) and 2254(e)(1):

> (d) An application for a writ of habeas corpus on behalf of a person in custody pursuant to the judgment of a State court shall not be granted with respect to any claim that was adjudicated on the merits in State court proceedings unless the adjudication of the claim —
>
> . . .
>
> (2) resulted in a decision that was based on an unreasonable determination of the facts in light of the evidence presented in the State court proceeding.
>
> (e) (1) In a proceeding instituted by an application for a writ of habeas corpus by a person in custody pursuant to the judgment of a State court, a determination of a factual issue made by a State court shall be presumed to be correct. The applicant shall have the burden of rebutting the presumption of correctness by clear and convincing evidence.

On first reading, section 2254(d)(2)'s provision for habeas corpus *relief* when the state court's "determination of the facts" is "unreasonable ... in light of the evidence presented in the state court proceeding" appears to be contradicted by section 2254(e)(1)'s attachment of a strong, typically *relief-barring*, presumption of correctness to (apparently any) "determination of a factual issue made by a State court." The two provisions must be read *in pari materia*, however. Doing so leads to the conclusion that section 2254(d)(2) divides "determination[s] of the facts" into two categories — state court factfindings that are flawed because they are "unreasonable," hence are a basis for habeas corpus relief without more; and findings that are not flawed because they are "[ ]reasonable," hence are presumed to be correct unless the petitioner proves otherwise "by clear and convincing evidence." In other words, the "determination[s] of a factual issue made by a State court" that section 2254(e)(1) tells courts to "presume[ ] to be correct" are only those determinations that survive section 2254(d)(2)'s winnowing out of "*unreasonable* determination[s]."

When thus read *in pari materia*, new sections 2254(d)(1) and 2254(e)(1) dictate an analysis of the effect of state court factfindings that proceeds in four

---

[72] Pub. L. 104-132, 110 Stat. 1214 (April 24, 1996).

steps — assuming the state has invoked the new provisions in a timely fashion.[73] As is set forth below, the *new* four-step process under section 2254(d)(1) and 2254(e)(1) is similar,[74] but not identical, to the preexisting four-step process under superseded section 2254(d):

- The threshold issue is whether the record reveals an "adjudicat[ion of a factual issue] on the merits in State court proceedings" that "resulted in a decision" — meaning, apparently, an explicit or at least clearly inferrable finding of historical fact[75] that can be subjected to federal

---

[73] Under the new Act, the state apparently bears the burden of invoking new sections 2254(d) and (e) and waives the benefits of both provisions by failing to assert them in an adequate and timely manner. *See, e.g.*, Davis v. Executive Director, 100 F.3d 750, 755 n.1 (10th Cir. 1996), *cert. denied*, 117 S. Ct. 1903 (1997) (1996 amendments to section 2254 do not apply to case because state affirmatively waived their application); Farmer v. McDaniel, 98 F.3d 1548, 1549 n.1 (9th Cir. 1996), *cert. denied*, 117 S. Ct. 1474 (1997) (AEDPA does not apply because "no one has suggested that" it does); Mason v. Hanks, 97 F.3d 887, 892 n.1 (7th Cir. 1996) (habeas relief granted without consideration of impact of amendments to section 2254, which state waived by not asserting it); Huynh v. King, 95 F.3d 1052, 1055 n.2 (11th Cir. 1996) (refusing to apply section 2254 amendments to case in part because "neither party argues for such an application"); Watkins v. Meloy, 95 F.3d 4, 6 (7th Cir. 1996) (court accepts state's express waiver of application of AEDPA because "provisions of the new Act governing the scope of federal judicial review do not affect the subject-matter jurisdiction of the federal courts, and are therefore waivable"); Rehbein v. Clarke, 94 F.3d 478, 481 n.4 (8th Cir. 1996) (amendments to section 2254 not applied because both parties seem to agree that it should not apply to petitioner's appeal); Emerson v. Gramley, 91 F.3d 898, 900 (7th Cir. 1996), *cert. denied*, 117 S. Ct. 1260 (1997) (state bears burden of asserting applicability of new section 2254(d) and waives the provision's protection by failing to assert it in a timely fashion); Samuel v. Duncan, 1996 WL 413632, at *1 (9th Cir. July 8, 1996), *cert. denied*, 117 S. Ct. 1338 (1997); Rodriguez v. Coughlin, 1996 WL 631693, at *1 (S.D.N.Y. Oct. 31, 1996) (refusing to apply amendments to section 2254 in part because "neither party relied on [it]"); United States ex rel. Barksdale v. Williams, 1996 WL 596414, at *9 (N.D. Ill. Oct. 9, 1996) (similar). *Cf.* Lindh v. Murphy, 117 S. Ct. 2059, 2071 (1997) (Rehnquist, C.J., dissenting) ("There is a good argument that § 2254(d) [of the 1996 Act] is itself jurisdictional.... But even if it is not jurisdictional, it shares the most salient characteristic of jurisdictional statutes: its commands are addressed to courts rather than to individuals."). *But cf.* Diaz v. Moore, 1998 WL 112526, at *3 n.6 (4th Cir. March 16, 1998) ("application of the AEDPA's standards may be waived where neither party has raised the issue and where the statute's applicability is in question" but are not necessarily waiveable if AEDPA clearly applies to case).

[74] *See* Childress v. Johnson, 103 F.3d 1221, 1225 (5th Cir. 1997) (AEDPA's section 2254(e)(1) "appears to retain the traditional presumption of correctness afforded to state court factual determinations"); Flowers v. Hanks, 941 F. Supp. 765, 768-69 (N.D. Ind. 1996) (AEDPA's and preexisting presumption of correctness are similar).

[75] As recently affirmed in Thompson v. Keohane, 516 U.S. 99 (1995), the Court consistently has interpreted the "determination ... of a factual issue" language of superseded 28 U.S.C. § 2254(d) (1994) to refer to "'basic, primary, or historical facts'" but not to "'[s]o-called mixed questions of fact and law, which require the application of a legal standard to the historical-fact determinations.'" *Id.* at 110 (quoting Townsend v. Sain, 372 U.S. 293, 309 n.6 (1963)). The relevant language in new sections 2254(d)(2) and 2254(e)(1) — respectively, "determination of the

court review.[76] Although phrased somewhat differently, the threshold issue under prior law and this new threshold inquiry are substantially the same.

- If the record reflects a qualifying state court adjudication on the merits and decision of the factual issue, the second issue is whether the state court engaged in a procedurally "[ ]reasonable determination" of the facts "in light of the evidence presented in the State court proceeding."[77] For the most part, this inquiry is similar to the prior one. True, the new inquiry's all-purpose "reasonableness" standard is somewhat more general than the standards delineated in superseded section 2254(d)'s various subsections. But the difference appears to be of limited significance.[78] The one respect in which the

---

facts" and "determination of a factual issue" — is identical to the language of the superseded provision and, assumedly, will be interpreted identically so as to apply to questions of historical fact but not to "mixed questions." *See, e.g.*, State ex rel. Robinson v. Buchler, 936 F. Supp. 590, 595 (E.D. Wis. 1996) (Act's presumption of correctness, like prior version, does not apply to mixed questions of fact and law, which are subject to "independent" review); *See also* Evans v. United States, 504 U.S. 255, 260 & n.3 (1992) ("[A]s Justice Frankfurter advised, 'if a word is obviously transplanted from another legal source, whether the common law or other legislation, it brings the old soil with it.'" (quoting Felix Frankfurter, *Some Reflections on the Reading of Statutes*, 47 COLUM. L. REV. 527, 537 (1947))). For a compilation of questions the Court has deemed to be "mixed," not "historical," see *infra* § 20.3d. For discussion of whether a separate provision of AEDPA does, and constitutionally may, require federal courts to defer to some or all state court determinations of mixed questions, see *infra* § 30.2.

[76] 28 U.S.C.A. §§ 2254(d) (preamble), 2254(d)(2) (West 1994 & Supp. 1998). For caselaw interpreting the analogous pre-AEDPA provision, superseded 28 U.S.C. § 2254(d) (preamble) (1994), see *infra* §§ 20.3b-d. *See also infra* § 30.2b (further developing these requirements).

[77] 28 U.S.C.A. § 2254(d)(2) (West 1994 & Supp. 1998). For caselaw interpreting the analogous pre-AEDPA provisions, superseded 28 U.S.C. §§ 2254(d)(1), (2), (4)-(7) (1994), see *infra* § 20.3e. The word "determination" in section 2254(d)(2) has two meanings in common parlance — the *process* by which a decision is reached, and the *substance* of the decision that is reached. *See, e.g.*, WEBSTER'S NINTH NEW COLLEGIATE DICTIONARY 346 (1983) (determination defined as both "act of deciding definitely" and "decision settling and ending a controversy"). Section 2254(d) appears to use the word in both senses. The inquiry under discussion here asks whether the *process* of deciding was unreasonable. The next inquiry, *see infra* notes 82-83 and accompanying text, asks whether the decision *itself* was unreasonable. In both situations, the inquiry focuses on the reasonableness of the state court's handling of the facts "in light of the evidence presented in the State court proceeding." 28 U.S.C.A. § 2254(d)(2) (West 1994 & Supp. 1998). This phrase is critical *procedurally* because it limits the inquiry to the facts the petitioner endeavored to put before the state court and accordingly prevents the petitioner from relying (as was permitted under superseded section 2254(d)(3)) on "material facts [that] were *not* developed at the State court hearing" (often because of the petitioner's own default). *See infra* notes 80-81 and accompanying text. Similarly, the analysis of the determination's *substantive* reasonableness does not ask whether the state court "got it right" in a general or abstract sense that might call for additional hearings on the issue but, rather, whether the state court reached a reasonable conclusion based on the evidence actually before it.

[78] *See, e.g.*, Williamson v. Ward, 110 F.3d 1508, 1521 n.14 (10th Cir. 1997) (petitioner satisfied section 2254(d)(2) standard because state court's resolution of claim was based on

new inquiry *is* clearly different is its limitation of its reasonableness analysis to procedures the state court used to process evidence that actually was *put before* it, *i.e.*, to "the evidence *presented* in the State court proceeding."[79] In contrast, superseded section 2254(d) permitted the petitioner to avoid a presumption of correctness by showing that "the material facts were *not* adequately developed at the State court hearing" — including sometimes if the petitioner herself had failed to proffer the material facts to the state court.[80] Under the new inquiry, unlike the prior one, gaps in the material facts in the state court record that are attributable to the petitioner can never be a basis for avoiding a presumption of correctness.[81]

"'unreasonable determination of the facts in light of the evidence presented in the State court proceeding'"); United States ex rel. Gooch v. McVicar, 953 F. Supp. 1001, 1011-12 (N.D. Ill. 1997) (same); Burris v. Parke, 948 F. Supp. 1310, 1321 (N.D. Ind. 1996), *aff'd*, 116 F.3d 256 (7th Cir.), *cert. denied*, 118 S. Ct. 462 (1997) (state court's decision denying postconviction petition "cannot be considered a careful and well-reasoned opinion requiring deference under § 2254(d)" because state court incorrectly categorized postconviction petition as successive, misconstrued nature of substantive claim, and applied incorrect legal standard). *Cf.* Moore v. Johnson, 101 F.3d 1069, 1075 (5th Cir. 1996), *vac'd on other grounds*, 117 S. Ct. 2054 (1997) ("In applying [section 2254(d)], we must first determine whether Moore's claim regarding ineffective assistance of counsel was adjudicated on the merits during the state court proceedings.... Our review of the state post-conviction record indicates that there is no question that Moore's ineffective assistance of counsel claim received a full and fair adjudication on the merits by the state trial court. The state trial court conducted an evidentiary hearing, heard testimony and received evidence from both parties, and issued detailed findings of fact and conclusions of law in support of its judgment. Neither party claims that Moore's claim for ineffective assistance of counsel was not adjudicated on the merits by the state court."). Two of the superseded subsections referred to unconstitutional state court procedures, which almost certainly qualify as "unreasonable" under the 1996 Act. *See* superseded 28 U.S.C. § 2254(d)(5) (1994) (petitioner "depriv[ed] of his constitutional right ... to ... counsel"); *id.* § 2254(d)(7) ("applicant was ... denied due process of law"). Two other superseded subsections referred to the state court's failure to resolve the factual dispute on the merits or lack of jurisdiction, factors encompassed by the first of the new Act's four inquires, discussed above. *Compare* superseded 28 U.S.C. §§ 2254(d)(1) *and* 2254(d)(4) (1994) *with* 28 U.S.C. § 2254(d)(2) (preamble) (1994) (discussed *supra* notes 75-76 and accompanying text). And the inquiry required by two additional superseded subsections — into the "full[ness], fair[ness], and adequa[cy]" of the state court's "factfinding procedure," superseded 28 U.S.C. §§ 2254(d)(2), 2254(d)(6) (1994) — is not appreciably different from the new Act's "reasonableness" inquiry.

[79] 28 U.S.C.A. § 2254(d)(2) (West 1994 & Supp. 1998). *See, e.g.*, Duncan v. Calderon, 946 F. Supp. 805, 813 (C.D. Cal. 1996).

[80] Superseded 28 U.S.C. § 2254(d)(3) (1994) (emphasis added) (discussed *infra* § 20.3e nn.96-108 and accompanying text).

[81] This reading of the impact of 28 U.S.C.A. § 2254(d)(2) (West 1994 & Supp. 1998) on the presumption of correctness in *id.* § 2254(e)(1) brings both provisions into line with *id.* § 2254(e)(2), which also makes a strong distinction between gaps in the state court record for which the petitioner is, and those for which she is not, responsible. *See supra* § 20.2b nn.21-22 and accompanying text.

- If the state court's determination of the facts was procedurally reasonable, the third issue is whether its "determination of the facts" was *substantively* "[ ]reasonable ... in light of the evidence presented in the State court proceeding."[82] The question thus posed — whether a factfinding is "[ ]reasonable" in light of the record evidence — seems identical in substance to the question the superseded statute posed (whether the factfinding was "fairly supported by the State court record").[83]

- If (but only if) the state factfinding qualifies as a "determination of a factual issue made by a State court"[84] because it is not "*un*reasonable,"[85] it "shall be presumed to be correct" unless the "applicant ... [satisfies] the burden of rebutting the presumption of correctness by clear and convincing evidence."[86] The switch from the superseded statute's rebuttal "by convincing evidence" to the new Act's rebuttal by "clear and convincing" evidence is insubstantial. Both standards invoke the "clearly erroneous" test.[87]

As noted above,[88] AEDPA does not apply to "nonopt-in cases" filed on or before April 24, 1996. In those cases, the preexisting standard for assessing the effect of state court factfindings continues to apply. In nonopt-in cases filed after April 24, 1996 and "opt-in" cases filed before and after it, AEDPA's modifications of the presumption of correctness apply, unless such applications raise "retroactivity" concerns.[89]

---

[82] 28 U.S.C.A. § 2254(d)(2) (West 1994 & Supp. 1998). For caselaw interpreting the analogous pre-AEDPA provision, superseded 28 U.S.C. § 2254(d)(8) (1994), see *infra* § 20.3f. In regard to the dual (procedural and substantive) meaning of the word "determination" in section 2254(d)(2), and in regard to the implications of the provision's limitation of the inquiry to facts before the state court, see *supra* note 77.

[83] Superseded 28 U.S.C. § 2254(d)(8) (1994).

[84] 28 U.S.C.A. § 2254(e)(1) (West 1994 & Supp. 1998).

[85] *Id.* § 2254(d)(2) (emphasis added).

[86] *Id.* § 2254(e)(1). *See* Gosch v. Johnson, 118 S. Ct. 1072, 1072 (1998) *(mem.)* (statement of Souter, J, respecting denial of *certiorari*) (characterizing section 2254(e)(1) as subjecting review of "state court record," *i.e.*, the "state court evidence and findings," to rule of "conditional deference"). For caselaw interpreting the analogous pre-AEDPA provision requiring rebuttal of presumptively correct state factfindings "by convincing evidence," superseded 28 U.S.C. §§ 2254(d) (last para.) (1994), see *infra* §§ 20.3h, 31.3.

[87] *See infra* §§ 20.3h, 31.3. *But cf.* Jackson v. Anderson, 112 F.3d 823, 824-25 (5th Cir. 1997), *cert. denied*, 118 S. Ct. 1054 (1998) (observing that new statutory language "apparently places a more onerous burden on the petitioner in that the petitioner must now rebut the presumption of correctness by clear and convincing evidence").

[88] *See supra* § 20.2b n.41 and accompanying text.

[89] *See supra* § 3.4b n.44 and accompanying text.

d. *Relationship between* Townsend *and the presumption of correctness.* In habeas corpus cases involving state factfindings, reviewing federal courts have sometimes confused the *Townsend* standard for the "right to a hearing" (as partially modified by *Keeney v. Tamayo-Reyes* and AEDPA's section 2254(e)(2)) with the statutory standard for determining the effect of state factfindings (as modified by AEDPA's sections 2254(d)(2) and 2254(e)(1)).[90] The confusion likely stems from the fact that the eight situations in which the pre-AEDPA (now superseded) section 2254(d) forswore a presumption of correctness of state court factfindings to some extent paralleled the six situations *Townsend* enumerates in which a federal hearing must be held.[91]

In *Keeney v. Tamayo-Reyes*, the Court distinguished the discrete issues that *Townsend* and section 2254's presumption of correctness address:

> [I]t is evident that § 2254(d) does not codify *Townsend*'s specifications of when a hearing is required. *Townsend* described categories of cases in which evidentiary hearings would be required. Section 2254(d) ... does not purport to govern the question of when hearings are required; rather, it lists exceptions to the normal presumption of correctness of state-court findings and deals with the burden of proof when hearings are held. The two issues are distinct, and the statute indicates no assumption that the presence or absence of any of the statutory exceptions will determine whether a hearing is held.[92]

---

[90] On *Tamayo-Reyes'* and AEDPA's partial transformation of the *Townsend* standard, see *supra* §§ 20.1b, 20.2b. On AEDPA's partial transformation of the presumption of correctness, see *supra* § 20.2c.

[91] *Compare* superseded 28 U.S.C. § 2254(d)(1)-(8) (1994) (quoted *supra* § 20.2c nn.56-64 and accompanying text) *with Townsend, supra,* 372 U.S. at 313-19 (quoted *supra* § 20.2b nn.7-12 and accompanying text). *See generally* Keeney v. Tamayo-Reyes, 504 U.S. 1, 20 (1992) (O'Connor, J., dissenting) ("Most of these circumstances [in § 2254(d)] are taken word for word from *Townsend*...."); *id.* at 10 (majority opinion) (quoted *infra* text accompanying note 92); Tamayo-Reyes v. Keeney, 926 F.2d 1492, 1498 & n.13 (9th Cir. 1991), *rev'd on other grounds,* 504 U.S. 1 (1992) ("as a matter of form, it is still the case that the same basic criteria generally are employed in both the *Townsend* and section 2254(d) inquiries" and "in most cases, though not in all, the inquiries will merge"; "this case presents an example of how the tests in *Townsend* and section 2254(d) are not always coextensive").

[92] 504 U.S. 1, 10 n.5 (1992). *Accord id.* at 20 (O'Connor, J., dissenting) ("Section 2254(d) is not, in the strict sense, a codification of our holding in *Townsend.* The listed circumstances in *Townsend* are those in which a hearing must be held; the nearly identical listed circumstances in § 2254(d) are those in which facts found by a state court are not presumed correct."). Pre-*Tamayo-Reyes* attempts to distinguish the *Townsend* standards governing the right to a hearing from the section 2254(d) standards governing the presumption of correctness include, *e.g., Tamayo-Reyes v. Keeney, supra,* 926 F.2d at 1496-98 & n.13; Smith v. Freeman, 892 F.2d 331, 339 n.13 (3d Cir. 1989); Richmond v. Ricketts, 774 F.2d 957, 961-62 (9th Cir. 1985); In re Wainwright, 678 F.2d

Townsend (as modified) and the presumption of correctness thus address what may be viewed as sequential questions. The first issue, addressed by *Townsend* and section 2254(e)(2), is whether the district court may or must conduct an evidentiary hearing on some factual question presented by the habeas corpus petition. The second issue, addressed by sections 2254(d)(2) and 2254(e)(1), is whether the district court is bound by state court findings on any of the dispositive factual questions presented by the petition. A federal court reaches the latter issue only after hearing and considering all the relevant evidence, including evidence that may have been adduced at a federal hearing, on the questions whether the presumption of correctness of state court factfindings applies and, if so, whether that presumption is rebutted.

It is important to note, however, that although the two inquiries are distinct, they also overlap. As Justice O'Connor has pointed out, the sets of criteria governing the availability of an evidentiary hearing under *Townsend* and the statutory presumption of correctness

> are obviously intertwined. If a habeas petitioner fulfills one of the *Townsend* requirements he will be entitled to a hearing, and by virtue of fulfilling a *Townsend* requirement he will necessarily have also fulfilled one of the [exceptions to the presumption of correctness], so that at his hearing the presumption of correctness will not apply. On the other hand, if the petitioner has not fulfilled one of the *Townsend* requirements he will generally not have [established] the corresponding [exception to the presumption of correctness] either, so he will be entitled neither to a hearing nor to an exception from the presumption of correctness.[93]

The Advisory Committee Note to Rule 8 of the Rules Governing § 2254 Cases puts the same point even more directly: "[C]ircumstances under which a federal hearing is mandatory are now specified in [superseded] 28 U.S.C. § 2254(d)."[94]

951, 952-53 (11th Cir. 1982). *See* 1 JAMES S. LIEBMAN, FEDERAL HABEAS CORPUS PRACTICE AND PROCEDURE § 20.2 (1st ed. 1988).

[93] *Tamayo-Reyes, supra,* 504 U.S. at 20-21 (O'Connor, J., dissenting). *Accord* Thompson v. Keohane, 516 U.S. 99, 109 n.7 (1995) (**citing FHCPP**). Decisions acknowledging the overlap between the *Townsend* mandatory-hearing criteria and section 2254(d)'s list of situations in which a presumption of correctness is not appropriate are, *e.g.,* Ford v. Wainwright, 477 U.S. 399, 410-11 (1986) (hearing required if one of circumstances in 28 U.S.C. § 2254(d)(2),(3), or (6) (since superseded) is present); Miller v. Fenton, 474 U.S. 104, 111-12 (1985) (sections 2254(d)(1)-(8) (since superseded) codify *Townsend* mandatory-hearing criteria); Marshall v. Lonberger, 459 U.S. 422, 432 (1983) (28 U.S.C. § 2254(d)(8) (since superseded) defines one circumstance in which hearing is required); Loveday v. Davis, 697 F.2d 135, 137-38 (6th Cir. 1983); Fowler v. Jago, 683 F.2d 983, 988 (6th Cir. 1982), *cert. denied,* 460 U.S. 1098 (1983); Crosswhite v. Swenson, 444 F.2d 648, 650 (8th Cir. 1971), *cert. denied,* 405 U.S. 1042 (1972) (section 2254(d) expands *Townsend* mandatory-hearing criteria).

[94] Advisory Committee Note to Rule 8 of the Rules Governing § 2254 Cases.

The difficulty, then, is that the *Townsend* question of when a hearing may or must be held and the entirely statutory question of when state court factfindings are not due a presumption of correctness are neither entirely the same nor entirely different. The legal authority governing the answer to one of the questions often may bear on, but sometimes will not be dispositive of, the answer to the other question. There is, then, no substitute for a careful analysis in each case of whether the issue before the court falls within an area of overlap (in which event, precedents answering one question may be consulted in answering the other) or within an area of exclusivity (in which event, only the law governing the particular question before the court will be relevant).

§ 20.3. Mandatory hearings.[1]

a. *Introduction.* As is developed in § 20.1b *supra*, an evidentiary hearing is mandatory if three conditions are met: (1) A petitioner alleges facts that, if proved, entitle the party to relief; (2) the petitioner's factual allegations survive summary dismissal because they are not palpably incredible or patently frivolous or false; and (3) for reasons beyond the control of the petitioner and the petitioner's attorney (assuming the attorney rendered constitutionally satisfactory assistance), the factual issues were not previously the subject of a full and fair hearing in the state courts or, if a full and fair state court hearing was held, the hearing did not result in factfindings that resolve all the controlling factual issues.[2] Section 20.1b discusses conditions (1) and (2). This section focuses on condition (3).

In its 1963 decision in *Townsend v. Sain*,[3] the Supreme Court clarified condition (3) by identifying six situations in which a petitioner is entitled to a federal habeas corpus hearing because the state courts did not afford the petitioner a full and fair state court hearing on the factual issues. *Townsend*'s list of these six factors is quoted above.[4] (*Townsend* also *permits* hearings in cases in which a hearing is not mandatory — the subject of section 20.4 *infra*.)

As § 20.2d *supra* explains, *Townsend*'s six criteria for a mandatory hearing substantially overlapped the eight factors that Congress had enumerated in the 1966 (now superseded) version of 28 U.S.C. § 2254(d) as bases for withholding

---

§ 20.3. [1] *See generally* authority cited *supra* § 20.1 n.1.

[2] *See supra* § 20.1b nn.27-29 and accompanying text. For the reasons discussed *supra* §§ 20.1c n.34, 20.2c n.47, this same set of standards applies to requests for hearings by either the petitioner (the party more frequently seeking a hearing) or the state. Although we generally refer here to the petitioner as the party requesting a hearing, the same analysis applies in most cases to requests for hearings by the state.

[3] 372 U.S. 293 (1963).

[4] *See supra* § 20.2b nn.7-12 and accompanying text.

a presumption of correctness from a state court factfinding.[5] (Superseded section 2254(d)'s list of eight factors also is quoted earlier in this Chapter.[6]) Because of the considerable overlap that existed between the two standards, many of the precedents addressing the meaning of a factor in superseded section 2254(d) bore equally or at least analogously on the meaning of the equivalent factor in the *Townsend* context.[7] Notwithstanding section 2254(d)'s supersession, decisions construing the eight listed exceptions to its presumption of correctness continue to be relevant to the interpretation of *Townsend*'s six analogous mandatory-hearing criteria insofar as recent legislation has left the *Towsend* criteria intact. Likewise, decisions interpreting the "unreasonable[ness]" catch-all exception to the newly simplified presumption of correctness — now codified in sections 2254(d)(2) and 2254(e)(1) — are likely to be relevant to various of the *Townsend* criteria. (Conversely, prior and recent decisions interpreting the *Townsend* criteria are likely to be helpful in interpreting the "unreasonable[ness]" catch-all in the newly simplified presumption of correctness.) For this reason, although the focus of the following discussion is on the right to a hearing and not on the presumption of correctness, the section relies upon and cites precedents from the caselaw construing former section 2254(d), as well as precedents under current sections 2254(d)(2) and 2254(e)(1), whenever doing so sheds light on analogous aspects of *Townsend*'s criteria for a mandatory hearing.[8]

b. *Absence of state record.* Under the standards in *Townsend v. Sain*,[9] the court must grant an evidentiary hearing (or some alternative and equally fair and adequate fact development procedure[10]) to resolve controverted factual questions whenever the state has not produced all the portions of "the transcript of [the]

---

[5] *See supra* § 20.2d nn.90-91 and accompanying text.

[6] *See supra* § 20.2c nn.50-66 and accompanying text.

[7] *See supra* § 20.2d nn.93-94 and accompanying text. As § 20.2c *supra* explains, the current version of superseded section 2254(d) — codified in 28 U.S.C.A. §§ 2254(d)(2), 2254(e)(1) (West 1994 & Supp. 1998) — largely preserves the preexisting standard.

[8] For discussion of the continuing viability of the *Townsend* criteria in most, but not all circumstances, see *supra* §§ 20.1b, 20.2b. For discussion of the similarity between the presumption of correctness criteria under superseded section 2254(d) and the simplified but largely similar presumption of correctness that now is codified in sections 2254(d)(2) and 2254(e)(1), see *supra* § 20.2c. A rough means of determining whether the standards governing the mandatory-hearing and no-presumption issues are the same is by noting whether the relevant footnotes on a particular topic in this section include citations both of *Townsend v. Sain* and of superseded 28 U.S.C. § 2254(d).

[9] 372 U.S. 293 (1963).

[10] *See, e.g.,* Carter v. Collins, 918 F.2d 1198, 1202 (5th Cir. 1990); *supra* § 19.5 (expansion of the record).

759

testimony [in the state court], the pleadings, court opinions [or] other pertinent documents" that delineate the factfinding on which the state now relies, or that the state court relied upon in making the finding, or that demonstrate how the state court reached the factual determination.[11] Under *Townsend*, the lower court caselaw elaborating on it, the caselaw construing an analogous provision of the superseded section 2254(d), and the terms of the new presumption of correctness provision that supersedes the former section 2254(d),[12] a hearing is required if:

(1)   The state court record as a whole is not before the court.[13]

---

[11] *Townsend v. Sain, supra,* 372 U.S. at 293. *See id.* at 319. *Accord* Conner v. Wingo, 409 F.2d 21, 22 (6th Cir. 1969), *cert. denied,* 406 U.S. 921 (1972) ("how will the district judge know that the factfinding procedure employed by the state court was adequate for reaching reasonably correct results or that the applicant was afforded a full and fair hearing ... resulting in reliable findings if he doesn't have before him a transcript of the evidence upon which the state trial judge made his findings?"); *supra* §§ 16.1, 19.2 (procedure for supplying record).

[12] *See* 28 U.S.C. § 2254(d)(8) (1994) (superseded) (state court's factual determination not entitled to presumption of correctness unless "that part of the record of the State court proceeding in which the determination of such factual issues was made, pertinent to a determination of ... such factual determination, is produced ...."); 28 U.S.C.A. § 2254(d)(2) (West 1994 & Supp. 1998) (discussed *infra* § 30.2b) (state court's determination of factual issue deserves deference only if state court "adjudicated [issue] on the merits" and reflected its conclusion in "decision" that may be reviewed for "unreasonable[ness] ... in light of the evidence presented in the State court pro-ceeding" — all suggesting need, as under superseded section 2254(d), for record of state court's resolution of factual issue). *See also* Conner v. Wingo, *supra,* 409 F.2d at 22 (quoted *supra* note 11).

[13] *See, e.g.,* United States ex rel. Jennings v. Ragen, 358 U.S. 276, 277 (1959) (summary dismissal is inappropriate absent state record); Thames v. Dugger, 848 F.2d 149, 151 (11th Cir. 1988) (without record, district court ordinarily cannot conclude that state court hearing was full and fair, and federal hearing accordingly is required; because district court did not thoroughly review complete state court record, district court could not properly determine whether petitioner's counsel refused to request severance for tactical reasons); Williams v. Owens, 731 F.2d 391, 393 (7th Cir. 1983); Williams v. Estelle, 681 F.2d 946, 948 (5th Cir. 1982), *cert. denied,* 469 U.S. 1075 (1984) (in absence of transcript of plea hearing and given confused nature of subsequent postconviction proceedings, well-pleaded claim could not be dismissed summarily without further proceedings); Dickerson v. Alabama, 667 F.2d 1364, 1367 (11th Cir.), *cert. denied,* 459 U.S. 878 (1982) (hearing required because state trial transcript was not part of record; state *coram nobis* transcript in record did not reach several issues raised by petitioner); Fortenberry v. Maggio, 664 F.2d 1288, 1291 (5th Cir. 1982) (hearing required in absence of state record); Little Light v. Crist, 649 F.2d 682, 686 (9th Cir. 1981); Caver v. Alabama, 511 F.2d 124, 126 (5th Cir. 1975), *cert. denied,* 430 U.S. 910 (1977); United States ex rel. Lasky v. LaVallee, 472 F.2d 960, 964 (2d Cir. 1973); Valdez v. California, 439 F.2d 1405, 1406 (9th Cir. 1971); Thornhill v. Peyton, 420 F.2d 477, 478 (4th Cir. 1969); Maes v. Patterson, 401 F.2d 200, 201 (10th Cir. 1968); authority cited *supra* § 19.2 nn.5-8. *See also* Yates v. Evatt, 500 U.S. 391, 406 & n.10, 410 (1991) (discussing situations in which reviewing court must have entire record before it in order to assess whether error was harmless); *Carter v. Collins, supra,* 918 F.2d at 1202 ("magistrate ... properly refused to consider the purported quotations from the state trial court transcript ... because no part of the official transcript, nor any claimed copy thereof, was ever tendered in evidence"); authority cited

(2)   A relevant portion of the state court record is not before the court.[14]

(3)   The respondent relies on documents other than the state court record as substitutes for or to reconstruct that record.[15]

(4)   The respondent relies on portions of the state court record as to which there is a *bona fide* question of accuracy.[16]

---

supra § 15.2c n.59 (summary dismissal is inappropriate in advance of independent review of state court record, all of which must be available to court).

[14] *See, e.g.,* United States v. Woods, 870 F.2d 285, 287 (5th Cir. 1989) (although absence of state court transcript of plea hearing is not *per se* basis for habeas corpus relief, it allows petitioner to establish through hearing or otherwise that plea was involuntary); Williams v. Lockhart, 849 F.2d 1134, 1137-38 (8th Cir. 1988); *Thames v. Dugger, supra,* 848 F.2d at 151 (discussed *supra* note 13); Thomas v. Lockhart, 738 F.2d 304, 307 n.3 (8th Cir. 1984) (hearing required because of absence of record of plea proceedings); Rogers v. Maggio, 714 F.2d 35, 39 (5th Cir. 1983) (absence of sentencing hearing transcript); United States ex rel. Ballard v. Bengston, 702 F.2d 656, 663 (7th Cir. 1983); Harris v. Pulley, 692 F.2d 1189, 1199-1200 (9th Cir. 1982), *rev'd on other grounds,* 465 U.S. 37 (1984) (absence of articles, broadcasts and *voir dire* transcript regarding pretrial publicity); *Dickerson v. Alabama, supra,* 667 F.2d at 1367 (absence of state trial transcript; *coram nobis* transcript was insufficient); Salkay v. Wainwright, 552 F.2d 151, 153 (5th Cir. 1977) (absence of on-the-record disclosure of plea bargain); United States ex rel. Irons v. Montanye, 520 F.2d 646, 649 (2d Cir. 1975) (absence of probable cause affidavit); Flores v. Craven, 464 F.2d 1293, 1294 n.1 (9th Cir. 1972) (absence of allegedly invalid search warrant); United States ex rel. Howard v. Rundle, 452 F.2d 904, 906 (3d Cir. 1971) (absence of transcript of disputed closing argument). *See also* Madera v. Risley, 885 F.2d 646, 647-49 (9th Cir. 1989) (magistrate held hearing to reconstruct record of unrecorded portions of state trial that bore on petitioner's claim); other authority cited *supra* § 19.2 nn.9-12 (discussing hearings to reconstruct missing state court records). *Cf.* Henderson v. Lockhart, 864 F.2d 1447, 1449, 1452 (8th Cir. 1989) (writ granted based on due process violation because record established that trial judge entered jury room during deliberations but it was impossible to determine what transpired there because court reporter's notes were lost, trial judge was dead, and trial counsel was immune from process as sitting judge); Austad v. Risley, 761 F.2d 1348, 1353-54 (9th Cir.), *cert. denied,* 474 U.S. 856 (1985) (district court was not obliged to order state to produce pertinent parts of state court record because petitioner did not request production or allege inability to produce record portions himself).

[15] Generally, the state may not substitute reconstructions for missing portions of the record. *See, e.g., United States ex rel. Jennings v. Ragen, supra,* 358 U.S. at 277 (opinion of state appellate court is not sufficient record of factfindings made and procedures followed at trial level); *Williams v. Owens, supra,* 731 F.2d at 393; *Little Light v. Crist, supra,* 649 F.2d at 686; Thacker v. Bordenkircher, 557 F.2d 98, 99 (6th Cir. 1977); United States ex rel. Worlow v. Pate, 411 F.2d 972, 974 (7th Cir. 1969), *cert. denied,* 403 U.S. 921 (1971). Nor, generally, may the state rely on an affidavit of the trial judge, court reporter, or other witness to the procedures to reconstruct missing records. *See, e.g.,* Ricalday v. Procunier, 736 F.2d 203, 208 (5th Cir. 1984); United States ex rel. Sullivan v. Fairman, 731 F.2d 450, 456 (7th Cir. 1984); United States v. Butt, 731 F.2d 75, 77 (1st Cir. 1984); Johnson v. Estelle, 704 F.2d 232, 240 (5th Cir. 1983), *cert. denied,* 465 U.S. 1009 (1984). *See* authority cited *infra* note 16. *Cf. supra* § 19.2 nn.9-12 and accompanying text (procedure for holding hearing to reconstruct state court *record*); *infra* § 20.3c (circumstances in which *findings* may be "reconstructed" based on complete record of state proceedings).

[16] *See, e.g.,* White v. Estelle, 556 F.2d 1366, 1369 (5th Cir. 1977) (certificate signed by trial judge is not sufficient record of state court proceedings); United States ex rel. Davis v. Yeager, 453

761

(5) The state court record before the federal court is in any relevant manner incomplete or insufficient to reveal the facts necessary to a proper analysis of an issue in the petition.[17]

c. *Absence of state factfindings.* Under *Townsend v. Sain*,[18] the district court must grant a hearing or alternative procedure to resolve controverted factual questions whenever the state court made "no express [*i.e.*, written] findings of fact" and it is not "possible for the District Court to reconstruct the findings of the state trier of fact, ... because his view of the facts is [not] plain from his opinion or [from other written] indicia."[19] Superseded section 2254(d) withheld

---

F.2d 1001 (3d Cir. 1971) (summary prepared by trial judge is not adequate); United States ex rel. Rebenstorf v. Pate, 417 F.2d 1222, 1226 (7th Cir. 1969) (memorandum limited to factfindings is not sufficient record); Elsperman v. Wainwright, 358 F.2d 259 (5th Cir. 1966) (*pro forma* minute entry is not sufficient). *See also* Kimmelman v. Morrison, 477 U.S. 365, 390 (1986) (trial judge's statement as to role played by certain evidence at trial is not finding of fact that precludes need for hearing); United States ex rel. Smith v. Fairman, 769 F.2d 386, 394-95 (7th Cir. 1985).

[17] *See, e.g., Rogers v. Maggio, supra*, 714 F.2d at 37 (hearing required in absence of record of reasons for sentence); Speedy v. Wyrick, 702 F.2d 723, 726 (8th Cir. 1983), *cert. denied*, 471 U.S. 1019 (1985); Essex v. Elliott, 456 F.2d 1039 (5th Cir. 1972) (scanty state record requires hearing on whether petitioner bypassed state remedies); Anderson v. Page, 454 F.2d 432, 434-35 (10th Cir. 1972) (appearance docket was insufficient to resolve issues).

[18] 372 U.S. 293 (1963).

[19] *Townsend, supra,* 372 U.S. at 314, 320. *Accord, e.g.*, Purkett v. Elem, 514 U.S. 765, 769 (1995) (Stevens, J., dissenting) (no deference due to state court conclusion if state court failed to make finding on determinative issue); Ford v. Wainwright, 477 U.S. 399, 411 (1986); Cabana v. Bullock, 474 U.S. 376, 388 n.5 (1986); Goodwin v. Johnson, 132 F.3d 162, 182-84 (5th Cir. 1998) (petitioner entitled to evidentiary hearing because "neither the state district court nor the Court of Criminal Appeals made any [explicit or] implicit findings of fact on the issue of whether Goodwin requested to have an attorney present during custodial interrogation"; "when the state court did not resolve a fact issue that would entitle the petitioner to relief if resolved in his favor, the petitioner is entitled to an evidentiary hearing on the issue"); Johnson v. Trigg, 28 F.3d 639, 644 (7th Cir. 1994) ("so-called finding" by state court, which "was simply an observation offered in the course of a ruling on an objection to evidence," is not type of "finding[ ] to which deference is due under section 2254(d)"); Blackmon v. Scott, 22 F.3d 560, 566-67 & n.27 (5th Cir. 1994) (because "[n]o state court findings were made with respect to [one] aspect of [petitioner's] claim" that state's handling of evidence and secreting of witnesses unfairly surprised petitioner at trial, "[r]emand is necessary for an evidentiary hearing"; hearing also required on claim that state planted informer in petitioner's cell after attachment of right to counsel "[b]ecause no state court findings were entered relating to this claim"); Cave v. Singletary, 971 F.2d 1513, 1516-17 (11th Cir. 1992) (affirming district court's grant of hearing on ineffective assistance of counsel claim because state trial and appellate courts did not make express or implicit findings on central factual issue); Meeks v. Singletary, 963 F.2d 316, 319-20 (11th Cir. 1992), *cert. denied*, 507 U.S. 950 (1993) (petitioner entitled to hearing on ineffective assistance of counsel notwithstanding hearing in state post-conviction court because state courts made no express factfindings); United States ex rel. Partee v. Lane, 926 F.2d 694, 700 (7th Cir. 1991), *cert. denied*, 502 U.S. 1116 (1992) (applying "self-evident proposition that a state court must have made a finding on a particular issue before a

— and an analogous portion of the superseding statute appears to continue withholding — the presumption of correctness in analogous circumstances.[20] Under caselaw applying this *Townsend* factor or construing the analogous provision of superseded section 2254(d), the "reconstructed finding" exception[21]

federal court can defer to that finding"); Tukes v. Dugger, 911 F.2d 508, 514 & n.6 (11th Cir. 1990); Moore v. Jarvis, 885 F.2d 1565, 1570 n.9 (11th Cir. 1989) ("as the trial court apparently made no record of the findings of fact and conclusions of law," its legal "determination that [petitioner's] pleas were knowingly and voluntarily made is due no deference"); Dispensa v. Lynaugh, 847 F.2d 211, 218-20 (5th Cir. 1988) (because state appellate court merely concluded that out-of-court identification was not so unreliable as to be inadmissible, federal courts had no, even implicit, state factual findings on which to rely; federal courts accordingly must resolve facts themselves); United States ex rel. Cross v. DeRobertis, 811 F.2d 1008, 1011 (7th Cir. 1987); Cooper v. Wainwright, 807 F.2d 881, 889 (11th Cir. 1986), *cert. denied,* 481 U.S. 1050 (1987) (hearing required to assess impact on trial of error not recognized by state courts); Porter v. Wainwright, 805 F.2d 930, 933, 935, 940-41 (11th Cir. 1986), *cert. denied,* 482 U.S. 918 (1987); Beavers v. Lockhart, 755 F.2d 657, 663 (8th Cir. 1985); Green v. Zant, 715 F.2d 551, 557 (11th Cir. 1983), *cert. denied,* 469 U.S. 1098 (1984) (existence of state court findings is "threshold" question in considering right to a hearing); authority cited *infra* §§ 20.3d (para. (1)(e)), 20.3e (paras. (1), (2), (6)(n)). Cf. Carter v. Collins, 918 F.2d 1198, 1202 n.4 (5th Cir. 1990) (statement on trial court's docket sheet that petitioner was informed of sentencing consequences of plea constitutes written finding subject to presumption of correctness); Case v. Mondragon, 887 F.2d 1388, 1393 (10th Cir. 1989), *cert. denied,* 494 U.S. 1035 (1990) (presumption of correctness applies, and no hearing required, when claim is resolved by state court findings of "basic, primary, or historical facts and the inferences that can properly be drawn regarding them"). A transcript of oral remarks by a judge may qualify as "written" findings. *See, e.g.,* Wainwright v. Witt, 469 U.S. 412, 429-30 (1985) (judge's statements during *voir dire* of prospective jurors); Ball v. Ricketts, 779 F.2d 578, 580 (10th Cir. 1985) (oral findings delivered from bench). So may statements in a report trial judges are required by law to file with the state supreme court describing procedures occurring in each capital case handled by the trial judge. *See* Burden v. Zant, 498 U.S. 433, 435 & n.2, 436-37 (1991) (*per curiam*). *Cf.* Burden v. Zant, 510 U.S. 132, 133 (1994) (*per curiam*) (noting, but not agreeing or disagreeing with lower federal court's conclusion that statement in trial judge's capital punishment report did not deserve presumption of correctness because it "was not labeled a finding of fact or conclusion of law [and] amounted to the trial judge's mere personal 'impression' on an issue not subject to significant dispute" that was "contained in an administrative report").

[20] *See* 28 U.S.C. § 2254(d) (1994) (superseded) (no presumption of correctness if state determination was not "evidenced by a *written* finding, *written* opinion, or other reliable and adequate *written* indicia" (emphasis added)); 28 U.S.C.A. § 2254(d)(2) (West 1994 & Supp. 1998) (discussed *infra* § 30.2b) (state court's determination of factual issue deserves deference only if state court "adjudicated [issue] on the merits" and reflected its conclusion in "decision" that may be reviewed for "unreasonable[ness] ... in light of the evidence presented in the State court proceeding" — all suggesting need, as under superseded section 2254(d), for actual or at least implied state court factfinding).

[21] *See, e.g.,* Minnesota v. Dickerson, 508 U.S. 366, 377-79 (1993) (over dissent, Court on direct review of state conviction discerns and defers to appellate court's findings in regard to scope of and motivation behind police officer's pat-down search and seizure of drugs); Wainwright v. Witt, supra, 469 U.S. at 429-30; Marshall v. Lonberger, 459 U.S. 422, 433 (1983); LaVallee v. Delle Rose, 410 U.S. 690, 692-94 (1973); *Townsend, supra,* 372 U.S. at 314. *See also* Parke v.

does not apply unless the state court has denied the party's claim in a written form and in circumstances that, notwithstanding the absence of findings, allow the federal court conclusively to determine that the state courts rejected the party's factual allegations, not his legal theories.[22] Even if these requirements are met, reconstruction is not appropriate when:

Raley, 506 U.S. 20, 35 (1992) ("questions of historical fact, *including inferences properly drawn from such facts*, are in this [habeas corpus] context entitled to the presumption of correctness accorded state court factual findings" (emphasis added) (citing *Marshall v. Lonberger, supra* at 435)); Tinsley v. Borg, 895 F.2d 520, 525 (9th Cir. 1990), *cert. denied*, 498 U.S. 1091 (1991); Campaneria v. Reid, 891 F.2d 1014, 1019 (2d Cir. 1989); Hulsey v. Sargent, 865 F.2d 954, 956-57 (8th Cir.), *cert. denied*, 493 U.S. 923 (1989); Jones v. Newsome, 846 F.2d 62, 64 (11th Cir.), *cert. denied*, 488 U.S. 911 (1988).

[22] *See, e.g., Cave v. Singletary, supra*, 971 F.2d at 1516 ("state court findings of fact can be inferred from [state court's] opinion and the record" only when implicit finding is clearly apparent and "cannot be imagined from thin air"); Andersen v. Thieret, 903 F.2d 526, 529-30 (7th Cir. 1990); Wicker v. McCotter, 783 F.2d 487, 493 (5th Cir. 1986); Rault v. Louisiana, 772 F.2d 117, 131 (5th Cir. 1985), *cert. denied*, 476 U.S. 1178 (1986). *See also* Hurley v. Irish-American Gay Group, 515 U.S. 557, 567 (1995) (on direct review, Court must, "without deference," "'review the findings of fact by a State court ... where a conclusion of law as to a Federal right and a finding of fact are so intermingled as to make it necessary, in order to pass upon the Federal question, to analyze the facts'" (quoting Fiske v. Kansas, 274 U.S. 380, 385-86 (1927); citing other authorities)). To make clear that the state court ruled on the facts and not the law, the court's written decision (1) should demonstrate "what was considered by the [state] judge" in rejecting the claim, White v. Estelle, 556 F.2d 1366, 1369 (5th Cir. 1977), and (2) may contain no indication that an incorrect legal standard was applied. *Compare Wainwright v. Witt, supra*, 469 U.S. at 431 (absent indication that wrong legal standard was used, trial judge is presumed to have applied correct standard; transcription of *voir dire* of prospective jurors showing that prosecution challenged juror for cause based on conscientious scruples against death penalty and that judge, in midst of *voir dire* in which appropriate standard for excusing jurors on that basis was followed, said "step down," is sufficient to permit reconstructed finding that juror was not impartial and thus was properly excused) *and* Williams v. Johnson, 845 F.2d 906, 909 (11th Cir. 1988) (credibility determinations implied from state court's ruling on voluntariness of confession) *and* Lavernia v. Lynaugh, 845 F.2d 493, 500 (5th Cir. 1988) (similar) *with Townsend, supra,* 372 U.S. at 316 (reconstruction not permissible when record indicates that state court may have applied incorrect standard or when there is "any hypothesis" or it is "possibl[e]" that state trier of fact "believed facts which show a deprivation of constitutional rights and yet (erroneously) concluded that relief should be denied") *and* Weidner v. Thieret, 866 F.2d 958, 961-63 (7th Cir. 1989) (Posner, J.) (trial judge's oral ruling at suppression hearing was ambiguous and inexplicit with regard to critical credibility questions; district court erred in implying factfindings on basis of presumption that trial judge knew and properly applied the law). Note also the Supreme Court's treatment of "reconstructed facts" in the 1st Amendment libel/malice context in Harte-Hanks Communications, Inc. v. Connaughton, 491 U.S. 657, 687-91 (1989) (in determining whether facts supporting jury's libel verdict in favor of public figure and against newspaper satisfy constitutionally required "actual malice" standard, court may defer to reconstructed factfindings that the jury "must have" made; court, however, may not defer to findings jury "may have" made because doing so is "speculative"). *Cf. id.* at 694, 696-700 (White, J., concurring; Kennedy, J., concurring; Scalia, J.,

(1)   "[T]he 'so-called facts and their constitutional significance [are] ... so blended that they cannot be severed in consideration.'" [23]

(2)   "[T]he issue of law presents a difficult or novel problem for decision," so that the outcome reached by the state courts does not clearly imply an identifiable fact determination.[24]

(3)   The facts do not support the findings, or the factual issues are sufficiently complex that there is more than one possible factual basis for a decision.[25]

(4)   The state record does not rule out facts the party alleges.[26]

(5)   Any implicit finding is ambiguous because it was made by a jury based on instructions that allowed the jury to reach the verdict it did without adopting the factual theory to which deference is sought.[27]

---

concurring in the judgment) (all expressing support for reliance on reconstructed factfindings that jury reasonably *may* have made).

[23] *Townsend, supra,* 372 U.S. at 316 (quoting Rogers v. Richmond, 365 U.S. 534, 546 (1961)). *See infra* § 20.3d (para. (1)(a)) (mixed questions of law and fact).

[24] *Townsend, supra,* 372 U.S. at 315. *Accord, e.g.,* Green v. Zant, 715 F.2d 551, 558 (11th Cir. 1983), *cert. denied,* 469 U.S. 1098 (1984) (reconstruction inappropriate because there is "no clear settled standard governing the need for a hearing prior to dismissing an allegedly ill juror"); Pierce v. Cardwell, 572 F.2d 1339, 1342 (9th Cir. 1978) (*Miranda* issues are too complex to permit reconstruction); Heisler v. Cox, 431 F.2d 581, 583-84 (4th Cir. 1970). *Cf. Witt v. Wainwright, supra,* 469 U.S. at 431 (reconstruction permitted because legal standard was clear and clearly understood by state judge).

[25] *See, e.g.,* Parker v. Dugger, 498 U.S. 308, 316 (1991) ("To the extent there is ambiguity in the [state trial court's] sentencing order, we will not read [findings into] it [that are] against the weight of the evidence"); Jackson v. Denno, 378 U.S. 368, 391-92 (1964); Cunningham v. Zant, 928 F.2d 1006, 1012 (11th Cir. 1991) (refusing to infer state trial or appellate court finding that jurors, who were improperly instructed orally, ignored error because they read, understood, and followed written instructions, which properly stated law); Cole v. Lane, 830 F.2d 104, 105 n.1, 107 (7th Cir. 1987), *cert. denied,* 484 U.S. 1076 (1988); United States ex rel. Ballard v. Bengston, 702 F.2d 656, 663 (7th Cir. 1983); Fowler v. Jago, 683 F.2d 983, 990 (6th Cir. 1982), *cert. denied,* 460 U.S. 1098 (1983); Guice v. Fortenberry, 661 F.2d 496, 506 (5th Cir. 1981); White v. Finkbeiner, 570 F.2d 194, 201 (7th Cir. 1978).

[26] *See, e.g.,* Weidner v. Thieret, *supra,* 932 F.2d at 633 ("Where state trial judges fail to adequately develop the relevant facts[,] ... implicit findings" cannot "be gleaned from the record."); Dispensa v. Lynaugh, 847 F.2d 211, 219-20 (5th Cir. 1988); *Green v. Zant, supra,* 715 F.2d at 558; Dixon v. Caldwell, 471 F.2d 767, 770-71 (5th Cir. 1972). *See also* superseded 28 U.S.C. § 2254(d)(1) (1994) ("merits of the factual dispute were not resolved in the State court hearing"); *Parker v. Dugger, supra,* 498 U.S. at 316 (discussed *supra* note 25); *Townsend, supra,* 372 U.S. at 313 (hearing required because "merits of the factual dispute were not resolved in the state hearing"); *infra* §§ 20.3d (paras. (1)(c), (1)(e), (7)), 20.3e (para. (6)(n)).

[27] *See, e.g.,* Jackson v. Denno, *supra,* 378 U.S. at 386-88. *See also supra* note 22 (discussing *Harte-Hanks* decision).

(6) The state court may have applied the wrong legal standard.[28]

(7) The state court did not hold an evidentiary hearing, and the facts could not properly be found without a hearing.[29]

Occasionally, the federal courts encounter what amount to *unwritten* state trial court "factfindings" that state appellate courts have effectively reconstructed by concluding that a lower state court implicitly did make, or must have made, such findings in the course of rendering a decision. The Supreme Court has held that

---

[28] *See, e.g.,* Kyles v. Whitley, 514 U.S. 419, 440 (1995) (refusing to credit lower court's determination because "[t]here is room to debate whether" lower court applied correct legal standard requiring cumulative, not piecemeal, analysis of effect on trial of multiple items of evidence suppressed by prosecutor before trial); Dres v. Campoy, 784 F.2d 996, 998 (9th Cir. 1986) (unclear if state court applied federal standard for ascertaining unavailability of witness); Sullivan v. Cuyler, 723 F.2d 1077, 1084-85 (3d Cir. 1983) (legal error in state opinion); Griffin v. Winans, 684 F.2d 686, 689 (10th Cir. 1982); *Fowler v. Jago, supra,* 683 F.2d at 990-91 (lack of record support for conviction suggests that court applied wrong "constitutional sufficiency of evidence" standard); Wade v. Franzen, 678 F.2d 56, 58 (7th Cir. 1982); Clark v. Jago, 676 F.2d 1099, 1112 (6th Cir. 1982), *cert. denied,* 479 U.S. 833 (1986); Fortenberry v. Maggio, 664 F.2d 1288, 1291 (5th Cir. 1982); Harris v. Oliver, 645 F.2d 327, 330 (5th Cir.), *cert. denied,* 454 U.S. 1109 (1981); Jackson v. Fogg, 589 F.2d 108, 111 (2d Cir. 1978) (state court opinion indicated lack of familiarity with controlling law); Pierce v. Cardwell, 572 F.2d 1339 (9th Cir. 1978) (state court did not discuss facts relevant to proper legal standard); Todd v. Lockhart, 490 F.2d 626, 628 (8th Cir. 1974); United States ex rel. Williams v. LaVallee, 487 F.2d 1006, 1010-12 (2d Cir. 1973), *cert. denied,* 416 U.S. 916 (1974) (controlling law changed after state hearing); authority discussed *infra* § 20.3d (para. (2)). *See also* Minnesota v. Dickerson, 508 U.S. 366, 383 (1993) (Rehnquist, C.J., dissenting) (discussed *infra* § 20.3d (paras. (1)(c), (2))); Yates v. Evatt, 500 U.S. 391, 413 (1991) (Scalia, J., concurring in the judgment) (state postconviction case) (criticizing majority for its willingness to permit courts to infer harmlessness of improper jury instructions from evidence of guilt and jury's verdict and expressing "view [that it is] utterly impossible to say beyond a reasonable doubt, from an examination of the record, that the jury *in fact* found guilt on a proper basis ... [because] the jury would have been examining the evidence *with the wrong question in mind.*" (emphasis in original)). *Compare* Weidner v. Thieret, 866 F.2d 958, 961-63 (7th Cir. 1989) (Posner, J.) (trial judge's oral ruling at suppression hearing was ambiguous and inexplicit with regard to critical credibility questions; district court erred in implying factfindings on basis of presumption that trial judge knew and properly applied law) *with Wainwright v. Witt, supra,* 469 U.S. at 431 ("where the record does not indicate the standard applied by a state trial judge, he is presumed to have applied the correct one") *and* Tinsley v. Borg, 895 F.2d 520, 525 (9th Cir. 1990), *cert. denied,* 498 U.S. 1091 (1991) (state trial judge presumed to have used correct legal standard) *and* Campaneria v. Reid, 891 F.2d 1014, 1019 (2d Cir. 1989) (same).

[29] *See e.g.,* Greene v. Georgia, 117 S. Ct. 578 (1996) (*per curiam*) (direct review case) (discussed *infra* § 20.3d n.82); In re Heidnik, 112 F.3d 105, 108, 111, 112 n.7 (3d Cir. 1997) (discussed *infra* § 20.3d n.82); Zilich v. Reid, 36 F.3d 317, 322-23 (3d Cir. 1994) (district court should have granted evidentiary hearing because factual issues, which were never resolved by state court, turned upon credibility determinations that could only be made on basis of live testimony); Tiller v. Esposito, 911 F.2d 575, 578 n.6 (11th Cir. 1990) (in absence of evidentiary hearing by state trial court, federal court refuses to infer trial court finding that petitioner was competent to stand trial).

the state appellate court determinations that such "implicit" factfindings were made below are themselves factual determinations to which the federal courts should defer if those determinations were made on the basis of a full and fair examination of the lower court record.[30] A similar rule apparently applies to state appellate court determinations that lower state courts made or conducted other kinds of pertinent findings, conclusions, and proceedings.[31]

d. *Inadequate state factfindings.* Under *Townsend v. Sain*,[32] caselaw construing relevant provisions of superseded section 2254(d), and the terms of the new presumption of correctness provision that supersedes former section 2254(d),[33] the court must grant a hearing or alternative procedure to resolve

---

[30] *See, e.g.,* Parker v. Dugger, 498 U.S. 308, 320 (1991) ("we conclude that a determination [by a state appellate court] of what the trial judge found is an issue of historical fact.... Because it is a factual issue, the deference we owe is that designated by 28 U.S.C. § 2254"; state appellate court's determination that trial court found no mitigating circumstances is factfinding, albeit one that Court ultimately concludes was not fairly supported by record); Wainwright v. Goode, 464 U.S. 78, 83-85 (1983) (state appellate court's determination that state trial court did not rely upon improper aggravating circumstance in imposing death sentence is treated as factfinding entitled to deference). This rule is an instance of the broader rule that determinations of fact that were fully and fairly made by state appellate courts are entitled to the same respect as factfindings that were fully and fairly made by state trial courts. *See infra* §§ 20.3d (para. (4)), 20.3e n.94 and accompanying text, 20.3e (para. (6)(x)).

[31] *See, e.g.,* Lewis v. Jeffers, 497 U.S. 764, 782-84 (1990) (state appellate court determination that state trial court properly followed state law in making aggravating circumstance judgment is entitled to deference).

[32] 372 U.S. 293 (1963).

[33] Former section 2254(d)(1), which rendered the presumption of correctness inapplicable if "the merits of the factual dispute were not resolved in the State court hearing," paralleled the first *Townsend* factor, which requires a hearing if "the merits of the factual dispute were not resolved in the state hearing" (*Townsend, supra,* 372 U.S. at 313). Former section 2254(d)'s provisions eliminating the presumption if "the State court [that held the hearing or made the factfindings] lacked jurisdiction of the subject matter or over the person of the applicant in the State court proceeding" (28 U.S.C. § 2254(d)(4) (1994)) or if the hearing was not held in or the factfindings were not made "by a State court ... in a proceeding to which the applicant for the writ and the State or an officer or agent thereof were parties" (28 U.S.C. § 2254(d) (1994)) apply to situations that would fall within *Townsend*'s category of cases in which "for any reason it appears that the state trier of fact did not afford the habeas applicant a full and fair hearing" (*Townsend, supra,* 372 U.S. at 313). Former section 2254's reservation of the presumption of correctness for "determination[s] ... on the merits of a factual issue" (28 U.S.C. § 2254(d)) was, as its legislative history makes clear (*see supra* § 2.4d nn.269-74 and accompanying text), designed to parallel *Townsend*'s recognition that a federal court has a responsibility to conduct an independent inquiry when the issue is a mixed question of fact and law (*see Townsend, supra,* 372 U.S. at 315). Analogously, the provision that replaces former section 2254(d) grants deference to a state court's resolution of a factual issue only if the issue "was adjudicated on the merits in State court proceedings" — which assumedly requires that the court actions in question fall within the jurisdiction of the state court in question and that some minimal due process have been observed — and that the court's resolution be

factual disputes if the determinations of fact made by the state courts are for some reason inadequate. A state court fact determination is inadequate and a federal hearing is required if, for example:

(1) Although the state trier of fact purported to make findings of fact, those findings are insufficiently historical (as opposed to conclusional or legal), specific, considered, or comprehensive to relieve the federal court of the responsibility to make its own independent factual inquiry because:

    (a) The state court determination is not a finding of historical fact but instead a legal or "mixed factual-legal" conclusion.[34] As the Supreme

---

reflected in a "decision" capable of being reviewed for "unreasonable[ness] ... in light of the evidence presented in the State court proceeding." 28 U.S.C.A. § 2254(d)(2) (West 1994 & Supp. 1998) (discussed *infra* § 30.2b). On the interpretive and constitutional controversies surrounding the treatment of mixed questions of law and fact by the new 28 U.S.C.A. § 2254(d)(1) (West 1994 & Supp. 1998), see *infra* §§ 30.2c, 30.2d.

[34] *See, e.g.,* Thompson v. Keohane, 516 U.S. 99, 108 (1995); Schiro v. Farley, 510 U.S. 222, 232-33 (1994); Parke v. Raley, 506 U.S. 20, 35 (1992); Arizona v. Fulminante, 499 U.S. 279, 286 (1991) (direct appeal case); *id.* at 303 (Rehnquist, C.J., dissenting); Miller v. Fenton, 474 U.S. 104, 113-15 (1985); Strickland v. Washington, 466 U.S. 668, 698 (1984) (statements of law or of mixed law and fact are not "finding[s] of fact binding on the federal court to the extent stated by 28 U.S.C. § 2254(d)," hence do not obviate need for hearing on unresolved factual questions imbedded in those statements); Maggio v. Fulford, 462 U.S. 111, 118 (1983) (White, J., concurring); Marshall v. Lonberger, 459 U.S. 422, 432 (1983); Sumner v. Mata II, 455 U.S. 591, 597 (1982); Sumner v. Mata I, 449 U.S. 539, 543-44 (1981); Cuyler v. Sullivan, 446 U.S. 335, 341-42 & n.5 (1980) (state-court conclusions of law and mixed factual-legal conclusions cannot substitute for independent federal factfinding); *Townsend, supra,* 372 U.S. at 315 (state courts' legal and mixed factual-legal conclusions cannot be bases for denying federal hearing); Rogers v. Richmond, 365 U.S. 534, 546 (1961); Brown v. Allen, 344 U.S. 443, 506 (1953); Greer v. Parke, 1997 WL 73830, at *2 (7th Cir. Feb. 14, 1997), *cert. denied*, 117 S. Ct. 2524 (1997) (presumption of correctness does not apply because "trial court's statement that [petitioner] had 'distinct criminal states of mind' is not a recital of facts but a legal conclusion concerning the scope of the protection against double jeopardy in relation to [petitioner's] two convictions"); other authority cited *supra* §§ 2.4b n.9, 2.4d nn.198-205, 233-36, 249, 259, 274; authority discussed *infra* paras. (1)(a)(A)- (CC); *infra* § 30.2. *See also* Hurley v. Irish-American Gay Group, 515 U.S. 557, 567 (1995) (on direct review, Court must, "without deference," "'review the findings of fact by a State court ... where a conclusion of law as to a Federal right and a finding of fact are so intermingled as to make it necessary, in order to pass upon the Federal question, to analyze the facts'" (quoting Fiske v. Kansas, 274 U.S. 380, 385-86 (1927); citing other authorities)); Bose Corp. v. Consumer's Union of Am., Inc., 466 U.S. 485, 501 (1984) (Civil "Rule 52(a) does not inhibit an appellate court's power to correct errors [in] ... mixed finding[s] of law and fact"); *supra* § 2.4d nn.80-197 and accompanying text (discussing historically applicable rule of non-deferential habeas corpus review of legal questions); *supra* §§ 2.4b-2.4c, 2.4d nn.198-315 and accompanying text, 2.4e (all discussing rule of non-deferential habeas corpus review of mixed legal and factual questions, as well as purely legal questions, beginning in early part of 20th century). On the other hand, state findings of clearly historical fact, subsidiary to or made in order to resolve a "mixed question of law and fact," *are* accorded a presumption of correctness. *See, e.g., Miller v. Fenton, supra* at 113;

Court has observed in the section 2254 context, it "will not always be easy to separate questions of 'fact' from 'mixed questions of law and fact' for § 2254(d) purposes."[35] The difficulty arises from the slippery distinction between "law" and "fact" or, as the matter sometimes is put, between "ultimate" and "historical" fact.[36] "[A]ny distinction between 'law' and 'fact' does not imply the existence of static, polar opposites. Rather, law and fact have a nodal quality; they are points of rest and relative stability on a continuum of experience."[37] In an analysis adopted by the Supreme Court in a habeas corpus case, Professor Monaghan defined "mixed questions of law and fact" as often broad and variegated factual questions that (1) are critical to the courts' application of constitutional doctrine, and (2) present special circumstances that justify abandoning the usual rule that forbids *de novo* appellate review of facts[38] and granting appellate courts the discretion necessary "to protect the constitutional order" against lower court findings hostile to that order.[39] Professor Monaghan identified two principal special circumstances warranting *de novo* review — (1) the "need to guard against systemic bias brought about or threatened by other

---

Patton v. Yount, 467 U.S. 1025, 1036 (1984); Rushen v. Spain, 464 U.S. 114, 121-22 n.6 (1983) (reasonable inferences factfinder drew from evidence); *Sumner v. Mata II, supra* at 597; Haynes v. Washington, 373 U.S. 503, 515 (1963) (factfinder's resolution of conflicting evidence); Lyons v. Oklahoma, 322 U.S. 596, 602 (1944); Doyle v. Dugger, 922 F.2d 646, 650 (11th Cir.), *cert. denied*, 502 U.S. 926 (1991); authority collected *infra* notes 43, 45, 48, 51, 52, 55, 57, 58. On the treatment of determinations of fact made by state appellate courts, see *infra* para. (4). On the treatment of state appellate court conclusions in regard to whether a lower state court implicitly made certain factual findings or engaged in other procedures, see *supra* § 20.3c nn.30-31 and accompanying text; *infra* §§ 20.3e n.94, 20.3e (para. (6)(x)).

The treatment by federal habeas corpus courts of mixed questions of law and fact that a state court previously adjudicated on the merits is a matter of great controversy under new 28 U.S.C.A. § 2254(d)(1) (West 1994 & Supp. 1998), both as a matter of the provision's interpretation and constitutionality. For discussion of the relevant issues, see *infra* § 30.2.

[35] Wainwright v. Witt, 469 U.S. 412, 429 (1985).

[36] *See, e.g.,* Pullman-Standard v. Swint, 456 U.S. 273, 288 (1982).

[37] Monaghan, *supra* § 20.1 n.1, at 233-34 & n.16.

[38] FED. R. CIV. P. 52(a). *See, e.g.,* Anderson v. City of Bessemer, 470 U.S. 564 (1985).

[39] Monaghan, *supra* § 20.1 n.1, at 271 (analysis quoted and paraphrased in Miller v. Fenton, 474 U.S. 104, 113-14 (1985)). *See supra* §§ 2.4b n.9, 2.4d nn.198-205, 233-36, 249, 259, 274 (all citing cases and providing additional definitions of "mixed questions" and additional explanations for mixed question doctrine). *See also* Fields v. Murray, 49 F.3d 1024, 1029-32 (4th Cir.) (*en banc*), *cert. denied*, 516 U.S. 884 (1995) (discussing "methodology set forth in *Miller* [*v. Fenton, supra*] for distinguishing questions of fact from mixed questions of fact and law").

actors in the judicial system";[40] and (2) "the perceived need for case-by-case development of constitutional norms," given that "norm elaboration occurs best when the Court has power to consider fully a series of closely related situations involving a claim of constitutional privilege."[41] Examples of law-to-fact applications in the habeas corpus context that clearly do, or at least may, present

---

[40] *See* Monaghan, § 20.1 n.1, at 272-73 (it is "no accident that the most salient modern examples of constitutional fact review are found in the Supreme Court review of the state courts. Norris [v. Alabama, 294 U.S. 587 (1935)] and its progeny proceed on a premise of institutional distrust: constitutional fact review in the Supreme Court is necessary not because of the danger of occasional mistakes but because of the fear of systematic distortion of factfinding and law application. The coerced confession cases are illustrative.... [F]or nearly five decades the Court [in those cases] has, in substance, asserted a power to respond to perceived dangers of distorted factfindings and law application in the state courts." (footnotes omitted; citing, *e.g.,* Jackson v. Denno, 378 U.S. 308, 382-87 (1964))); *id.* at 272 n.237 ("death penalty cases might also be thought of in these terms. It has long been a matter of grave concern that blacks are far more frequently found to qualify for the death penalty than are whites under the applicable state statutes.... Constitutional fact review may lessen the chances of racially based miscarriages of justice.... It is arguable ... that eighth amendment due process requires that at least some state appellate courts engage in constitutional fact review."). *See also* Harte-Hanks Communications, Inc. v. Connaughton, 491 U.S. 657, 686 & n.33 (1989); *supra* §§ 2.4e, 2.5, 2.6 (all generally explaining habeas corpus as means of deterring and avoiding results of state court hostility to federal legal norms in situations in which hostility is likely to be most pronounced).

[41] Monaghan, *supra* § 20.1 n.1, at 274-75 (comparing Wainwright v. Witt, 469 U.S. 412 (1985) (legal standard for excluding partial jurors is sufficiently clear to be left to state trial judges) with Strickland v. Washington, 466 U.S. 668 (1984) (new ineffective assistance standard requires considerable elaboration of underlying constitutional norms for foreseeable future); "careful examination of the Supreme Court's recent habeas corpus cases also shows a marked tendency toward a discretionary concept of constitutional fact review ... where the norms are perceived to be in need of additional elaboration on a case-by-case basis.... This elaboration can best occur only when the Court has had experience on a case-by-case basis with the difficulties experienced by the lower courts in applying the Court's general norms."). *Accord* Thompson v. Keohane, 516 U.S. 99, 116 (1995) ("case-by-case elaboration when a constitutional right is implicated may more accurately be described as law declaration than as law application" (citing and paraphrasing Monaghan, *supra* § 20.1 n.1, at 273-76)). *See* Monaghan, *supra* § 20.1 n.1, at 272 n.239 (citing cases) (equating Supreme Court review of state court findings in *certiorari* proceedings and lower federal court review of state court findings in habeas corpus proceedings, given writ's function as means of expanding Supreme Court's ability to "respond to perceived dangers of distorted factfinding and law application in the state courts" through "us[e of] the factfinding capacities" of the lower courts); *id.* at 274 n.249 (when deciding which arguably mixed legal and factual determinations to subject to presumption of correctness of state findings under 28 U.S.C. § 2254, Supreme Court applies distinction between constitutional doctrine that does and does not need norm elaboration through application of law to fact). On the parity between the Supreme Court's treatment of mixed questions on direct review and the federal courts' treatment of such questions on habeas corpus review, see *supra* §§ 2.4b, 2.4d nn.198-238 and accompanying text, 2.4e.

special circumstances requiring substantial federal judicial supervision over state court fact determinations include: [42]

(A) Whether a confession or a guilty plea was voluntary.[43]

---

[42] *See generally infra* § 25.5 nn.101-122 and accompanying text. Professor Monaghan's thesis that so-called "mixed questions" of law and fact are in reality questions of fact, albeit ones that require especially close scrutiny by the "higher" court, suggests a wider role for federal evidentiary hearings as well as for federal review in the resolution of such questions.

[43] *See, e.g., Thompson v. Keohane, supra*, 516 U.S. at 109-13 (*dicta*); United States v. Gaudin, 515 U.S. 506, 525-26 (1995) (Rehnquist, C.J., concurring) ("voluntariness of confessions" is "mixed question[ ] of law and fact"); Withrow v. Williams, 507 U.S. 680, 693-94 (1993) (voluntariness of confession is subject to independent federal review); Parke v. Raley, 506 U.S. 20, 35 (1992) ("'governing standard as to whether a plea of guilty is voluntary for purposes of the Federal Constitution is a question of federal law,' [but] questions of historical fact, including inferences properly drawn from such facts, are in this context entitled to the presumption of correctness accorded state court factual findings" (citations omitted) (quoting Marshall v. Lonberger, 459 U.S. 422, 431-32 (1983))); Miller v. Fenton, 474 U.S. 104, 112-13 (1985); *Marshall v. Lonberger, supra* at 430; Stokes v. Singletary, 952 F.2d 1567, 1572 (11th Cir. 1992) (confession); Bae v. Peters, 950 F.2d 469, 474 (7th Cir. 1991) (confession); Evans v. Dowd, 932 F.2d 739, 741-42 (8th Cir.) (*per curiam*), *cert. denied,* 502 U.S. 944 (1991) (confession); Hill v. Lockhart, 927 F.2d 340, 346 (8th Cir.), *cert. denied,* 502 U.S. 927 (1991) (confession); Towne v. Dugger, 899 F.2d 1104, 1110 (11th Cir. 1990) (confession); Wilson v. O'Leary, 895 F.2d 378, 382-83 (7th Cir. 1990) (confession); Medeiros v. Shimoda, 889 F.2d 819, 822 (9th Cir. 1989), *cert. denied,* 496 U.S. 938 (1990) (confession); Moore v. Jarvis, 885 F.2d 1565, 1570 n.9 (11th Cir. 1989) (guilty plea); Oppel v. Meachum, 851 F.2d 34, 38 (2d Cir.), *cert. denied,* 488 U.S. 911 (1988) (guilty plea); Cooper v. Scroggy, 845 F.2d 1385, 1392 & n.1 (6th Cir. 1988) (confession); Hawkins v. Lynaugh, 844 F.2d 1132, 1137 (5th Cir.), *cert. denied,* 488 U.S. 900 (1988) (confession). *But see* Tran v. Lockhart, 849 F.2d 1064, 1067-69 (8th Cir. 1988), *cert. denied,* 489 U.S. 1091 (1989) (over dissent, court treats voluntariness of guilty plea as fact question; voluntariness finding of state postconviction judge who also served as trial judge presumed correct; hearing held to have been properly denied); Perri v. Director, 817 F.2d 448 (7th Cir.), *cert. denied,* 484 U.S. 843 (1987); Matusiak v. Kelly, 786 F.2d 536, 544 (2d Cir. 1986), *cert. denied,* 479 U.S. 805 (1986); Hayes v. Kincheloe, 784 F.2d 1434, 1436 (9th Cir. 1986); Wicker v. McCotter, 783 F.2d 487, 498 (5th Cir. 1986); Caudill v. Jago, 747 F.2d 1046, 1050 (6th Cir. 1984); Fowler v. Jago, 683 F.2d 983, 990 (6th Cir. 1982), *cert. denied,* 460 U.S. 1098 (1983); Gray v. Lucas, 677 F.2d 1086, 1107 (5th Cir. 1982), *cert. denied,* 461 U.S. 910 (1983). Direct review decisions in which the Supreme Court conducted independent fact review of involuntary confession claims include: Arizona v. Fulminante, 499 U.S. 279, 287 (1991) ("We normally give great deference to the factual findings of the state court.... Nevertheless, 'the ultimate issue of "voluntariness" [of a confession] is a legal question requiring independent federal determination'"; holding that confession was coerced (quoting habeas corpus decision in *Miller v. Fenton, supra* at 110)); *id.* at 303 (Rehnquist, C.J., dissenting) ("Without exception, the court's confession cases hold that the ultimate issue of 'voluntariness' is a legal question requiring independent federal determination"; concluding that confession was not coerced); Cassell v. Texas, 339 U.S. 282, 283 (1950); Pierre v. Louisiana, 306 U.S. 354, 358 (1939); Norris v. Alabama, 294 U.S. 587, 589-90, 593 n.1, 595-96 (1935). *See* Jurek v. Estelle, 623 F.2d 929, 931 (5th Cir. 1980) (*en banc*), *cert. denied,* 450 U.S. 1001 (1981) (collecting cases); Monaghan, *supra* § 20.1 n.1, at 260.

(B)   Whether the petitioner made a request for counsel during interrogation sufficient under *Edwards v. Arizona*[44] to require the interrogation to cease until counsel was provided.[45]

(C)   Whether the petitioner was in "custody"[46] and subject to "interrogation"[47] at the time he made inculpatory statements to police officers in the absence of *Miranda* rights, or whether the petitioner waived constitutional or *Miranda* rights.[48]

State court findings of historical fact that underlie the ultimate voluntariness determination are subject to a presumption of correctness and may obviate the need for an evidentiary hearing. *See, e.g., Parke v. Raley, supra* at 525; *Marshall v. Lonberger, supra* at 431-32; *Self v. Collins,* 973 F.2d 1198, 1204-05 (5th Cir. 1992), *cert. denied,* 507 U.S. 996 (1993); *Hill v. Lockhart, supra* at 346; Derrick v. Peterson, 924 F.2d 813, 817 (9th Cir. 1990), *cert. denied,* 502 U.S. 853 (1991); Mayo v. Lynaugh, 882 F.2d 134, 137-38 (5th Cir. 1989) (state court findings that petitioner initiated contact with police, that police did not promise leniency, and that prosecution witnesses were credible are subsidiary factual issues entitled to presumption of correctness); Ray v. Duckworth, 881 F.2d 512, 517 (7th Cir. 1989) (subsidiary questions, such as "familiarity with the *Miranda* warnings," entitled to presumption of correctness); Stevens v. Armontrout, 787 F.2d 1282, 1284-85 (8th Cir. 1986) (state finding as to whether petitioner was intoxicated at time of confession is question of fact "subsidiary" to ultimate voluntariness question and entitled to presumption of correctness).

[44] 451 U.S. 477 (1981).

[45] *See, e.g.,* Robinson v. Borg, 918 F.2d 1387, 1390 (9th Cir. 1990), *cert. denied,* 502 U.S. 868 (1991) ("Whether the suspect's words constitute a request for counsel [under *Edwards*] is a legal determination which we review *de novo.*"). *Cf.* Aiken v. Blodgett, 921 F.2d 214, 216-17 (9th Cir. 1990), *cert. denied,* 502 U.S. 839 (1991) (subsidiary question whether officers heard petitioner's request for counsel is one of fact subject to presumption of correctness).

[46] *See, e.g., Thompson v. Keohane, supra,* 516 U.S. at 106-07 (resolving lower court "division of authority" on question "whether state-court 'in custody' determinations are matters of fact entitled to a presumption of correctness under 28 U.S.C. § 2254(d), or mixed questions of law and fact warranting independent review" by "hold[ing] that the issue whether a suspect is 'in custody' and therefore entitled to Miranda warnings, presents a mixed question of law and fact qualifying for independent review"). For lower court decisions anticipating the holding in *Thompson v. Keohane, supra,* see, *e.g.,* Jacobs v. Singletary, 952 F.2d 1282, 1291 (11th Cir. 1992) (custody determination is mixed question); Cobb v. Perini, 832 F.2d 342, 346 (6th Cir. 1987), *cert. denied,* 486 U.S. 1024 (1988) ("Whether a person is in custody is a question of law....").

[47] *Cf.* Endress v. Dugger, 880 F.2d 1244, 1249 (11th Cir. 1989), *cert. denied,* 495 U.S. 904 (1990) ("whether the *functional equivalent* of interrogation has taken place is a mixed question of law and fact," but whether "*express* interrogation occurred" is a question of fact (emphasis added)); Bailey v. Hamby, 744 F.2d 24, 26 (6th Cir. 1984). *But cf.* Medeiros v. Shimoda, 889 F.2d 819, 822 (9th Cir. 1989), *cert. denied,* 496 U.S. 938 (1990) ("district court's conclusion that [petitioner] was subjected to custodial interrogation is essentially a factual determination").

[48] *See, e.g.,* Brewer v. Williams, 430 U.S. 387, 398 (1977); Strozier v. Newsome, 926 F.2d 1100, 1104 (11th Cir.), *cert. denied,* 502 U.S. 930 (1991) (in adjudicating challenge to petitioner's decision at trial to waive representation by counsel and proceed *pro se,* court's "assessment of whether the waiver of counsel was knowing and intelligent is a mixed question of law and fact that we review de novo"); Smith v. Zant, 887 F.2d 1407, 1431 (11th Cir. 1989) (*en banc*) (Kravitch, J.,

(D) Whether a particular search or arrest was justified by "reasonable suspicion" or "probable cause" to believe that a crime had been committed.[49]

(E) Whether a consent to search was voluntarily given.[50]

---

concurring in part and dissenting in part); United States ex rel. Tonaldi v. Elrod, 716 F.2d 431, 437 (7th Cir. 1983); Hance v. Zant, 696 F.2d 940, 947 (11th Cir.), *cert. denied,* 463 U.S. 1210 (1983). *See also* Miller v. Fenton, 474 U.S. 104, 108 n.3 (1985) (reserving decision on question whether presumption of correctness is due state findings on validity of waiver); Fike v. James, 833 F.2d 1503, 1506 (11th Cir. 1987). *Cf.* Jones v. Dugger, 928 F.2d 1020, 1027 (11th Cir.), *cert. denied,* 502 U.S. 875 (1991) (subsidiary state court finding that petitioner did not assert right to remain silent is entitled to presumption of correctness); Nelson v. Fulcomer, 911 F.2d 928, 931-32 (3d Cir. 1990) (similar); Winfrey v. Wyrick, 836 F.2d 406, 410 (8th Cir. 1987), *cert. denied,* 488 U.S. 833 (1988) ("subsidiary issue" whether petitioner understood rights is question of fact). *But cf.* Kelly v. Lynaugh, 862 F.2d 1126, 1131 n.7 (5th Cir. 1988), *cert. denied,* 492 U.S. 925 (1989) (presumption of correctness applied after federal court concludes, based on careful review of record, that record supports state court finding that waiver of right to silence was voluntary); Meeks v. Cabana, 845 F.2d 1319, 1323 (5th Cir. 1988) (waiver of right to appeal treated as question of fact). The 7th Circuit treats the question whether the petitioner properly waived constitutional rights as one of fact. *See, e.g.* Wilson v. O'Leary, 895 F.2d 378, 383 (7th Cir. 1990) (waiver of *Miranda* rights); Galowski v. Murphy, 891 F.2d 629, 636 (7th Cir. 1989), *cert. denied,* 495 U.S. 921 (1990) (waiver of right to testify at trial); Quadrini v. Clusen, 864 F.2d 577, 582 (7th Cir. 1989) (waiver of *Miranda* rights); Perri v. Director, 817 F.2d 448, 451 (7th Cir.), *cert. denied,* 484 U.S. 843 (1987) ("questions of whether a defendant understood his or her rights and knowingly and intelligently waived them" are due presumption of correctness). Panels of the 9th Circuit have split on the questions. *Compare* Derrick v. Peterson, 924 F.2d 813, 823 (9th Cir. 1990), *cert. denied,* 502 U.S. 853 (1991) ("state trial court's determination that a defendant knowingly and intelligently waived his *Miranda* rights is [a question of fact] entitled to a presumption of correctness") *with* Norman v. Ducharme, 871 F.2d 1483, 1486 (9th Cir. 1989), *cert. denied,* 494 U.S. 1031 (1990) *and* Terrovona v. Kincheloe, 852 F.2d 424, 428 (9th Cir. 1988) (both rejecting 7th Circuit precedent to contrary and holding that waiver of *Miranda* rights is mixed question subject to *de novo* review).

[49] *See, e.g.,* Ornelas v. United States, 517 U.S. 690, 696, 699 (1996) (direct review case) ("The principal components of a determination of reasonable suspicion or probable cause will be the events which occurred leading up to the stop or search, and then the decision whether these historical facts, viewed from the standpoint of an objectively reasonable police officer, amount to reasonable suspicion or to probable cause. The first part of the analysis involves only a determination of historical facts, but the second is a mixed question of law and fact.... [A]s a general matter determinations of reasonable suspicion and probable cause should be reviewed *de novo* on appeal.... A reviewing court should take care both to review findings of historical fact only for clear error and to give due weight to inferences drawn from those facts by resident judges and law enforcement officers."); United States v. Gaudin, 515 U.S. 506, 521 (1995) (*dicta*) ("question of probable cause to conduct a search" is "mixed question of law and fact"); *id.* at 525-26 (Rehnquist, J., concurring) ("legality of searches and seizures" is "mixed question[ ] of law and fact"); New Jersey v. T.L.O., 469 U.S. 325, 343 (1985) (direct review case) (reasonable suspicion); Florida v. Rodriguez, 469 U.S. 1, 6 (1984) (direct review case) ("articulable" suspicion); Monaghan, *supra* § 20.1 n.1, at 273-74.

[50] *See, e.g.,* Hoover v. Beto, 439 F.2d 913, 919 (5th Cir. 1971), *vac'd & remanded on other grounds,* 467 F.2d 516 (5th Cir.) (*en banc*), *cert. denied,* 409 U.S. 1086 (1972).

(F) Whether pretrial identification procedures were unduly suggestive, and, if so, whether the suggestiveness rendered the procedures impermissibly unreliable.[51]

(G) Whether counsel's representation was constitutionally ineffective, including both whether counsel's performance was "unreasonable" and, if so, whether counsel's failings "prejudiced" the petitioner.[52]

---

[51] *See, e.g.*, Sumner v. Mata, 455 U.S. 591, 597 (1982); Neil v. Biggers, 409 U.S. 188, 198-200 (1972); Tomlin v. Myers, 30 F.3d 1235, 1241 & n.12 (9th Cir. 1994) ("[w]hether [eyewitness's] ... identification was derived from an independent source is a mixed question of law and fact ... [subject to] de novo review"; based on review of factual record, court of appeals rejects district court's determination that there was "independent source" for eyewitness's in-court identification following lineup that was unconstitutionally conducted without defense counsel present); Montgomery v. Greer, 956 F.2d 677, 680 (7th Cir.), *cert. denied*, 506 U.S. 972 (1992); Peters v. Whitley, 942 F.2d 937, 939 (5th Cir. 1991), *cert. denied*, 502 U.S. 1113 (1992); Archuleta v. Kerby, 864 F.2d 709, 710-11 (10th Cir.), *cert. denied*, 490 U.S. 1084 (1989); Dispensa v. Lynaugh, 847 F.2d 211, 218-20 (5th Cir. 1988); Jones v. Newsome, 846 F.2d 62, 64 (11th Cir.), *cert. denied*, 488 U.S. 911 (1988); Lavernia v. Lynaugh, 845 F.2d 493, 500 (5th Cir. 1988); Dooley v. Duckworth, 832 F.2d 445, 447 (7th Cir. 1987), *cert. denied*, 485 U.S. 967 (1988); Ponce v. Cupp, 735 F.2d 333, 336 (9th Cir. 1984); Dickerson v. Fogg, 692 F.2d 238, 243 (2d Cir. 1982); Gullick v. Perrin, 669 F.2d 1, 4 n.8 (1st Cir. 1981). State court factual findings underlying the ultimate reliability issue are presumed correct and may obviate the need for a hearing. *See, e.g.*, Armstrong v. Young, 34 F.3d 421, 427-28 (7th Cir. 1994), *cert. denied*, 514 U.S. 1021 (1995); Dumond v. Lockhart, 885 F.2d 419, 421 (8th Cir. 1989); United States ex rel. Lee v. Flannigan, 884 F.2d 945, 948 (7th Cir. 1989), *cert. denied*, 497 U.S. 1027 (1990) (whether witness had opportunity to observe suspect).

[52] *See, e.g.*, Thompson v. Keohane, 516 U.S. 99, 109-13 (1995) (*dicta*); Kimmelman v. Morrison, 474 U.S. 365, 378-80 (1986); Strickland v. Washington, 466 U.S. 668, 698 (1984) ("[I]n a federal habeas challenge to a state criminal judgment, a state court conclusion that counsel rendered effective assistance is not a finding of fact binding on the federal court to the extent stated by 28 U.S.C. § 2254(d). Ineffectiveness is not a question of 'basic, primary, or historical fac[t],' Townsend v. Sain, 372 U.S. 293, 309 n.6 (1963). Rather, ... it is a mixed question of law and fact.... [B]oth the performance and prejudice components of the ineffectiveness inquiry are mixed questions of law and fact."); Cuyler v. Sullivan, 446 U.S. 335, 341-43 (1980); Chacon v. Wood, 36 F.3d 1459, 1465 (9th Cir. 1994) (district court erred in deferring to state court's ruling on ineffective assistance, which was mixed finding of fact and law that is not subject to deference); Bryant v. Scott, 28 F.3d 1411, 1414 (5th Cir. 1994) (because "'state court's ultimate conclusion that counsel rendered effective assistance is not a fact finding to which a federal court must grant a presumption of correctness under 28 U.S.C. § 2254(d), but instead is a mixed question of law and fact,' ... [w]e therefore independently decide whether counsel's conduct passes constitutional muster"); United States v. Faubion, 19 F.3d 226, 228 (8th Cir. 1994); Bolender v. Singletary, 16 F.3d 1547, 1558 n.12 (11th Cir.), *cert. denied*, 513 U.S. 1022 (1994) ("Ineffectiveness of representation is a mixed question of law and fact subject to de novo review."); Winkler v. Keane, 7 F.3d 304, 308 (2d Cir. 1993), *cert. denied*, 511 U.S. 1022 (1994) ("Whether a defendant's representation was constitutionally inadequate is a mixed question of law and fact and thus we exercise *de novo* review."); Hockett v. Duckworth, 999 F.2d 1160, 1165 (7th Cir. 1993); Nelson v. Nagle, 995 F.2d 1549, 1554 (11th Cir. 1993) ("Whether [petitioner] had ineffective assistance of

counsel is reviewed *de novo*."); Haislip v. Attorney General, 992 F.2d 1085, 1087 (10th Cir.), *cert. denied*, 510 U.S. 896 (1993); Lilly v. Gilmore, 988 F.2d 783, 785 (7th Cir.), *cert. denied*, 508 U.S. 911 (1993); Loyd v. Whitley, 977 F.2d 149 (5th Cir. 1992), *cert. denied*, 508 U.S. 911 (1993); Lahay v. Armontrout, 974 F.2d 979, 981 (8th Cir. 1992), *cert. denied*, 507 U.S. 987 (1993); McCann v. Armontrout, 973 F.2d 655, 659-60 (8th Cir. 1992), *cert. denied*, 507 U.S. 942 (1993); Reese v. Fulcomer, 946 F.2d 247, 254 (3d Cir. 1991), *cert. denied*, 503 U.S. 988 (1992); Atkins v. Attorney General, 932 F.2d 1430, 1432 (11th Cir. 1991) (reasonableness of counsel and existence of prejudice are mixed questions of law and fact subject to independent review); United States ex rel. Partee v. Lane, 926 F.2d 694, 700 (7th Cir. 1991), *cert. denied*, 502 U.S. 1116 (1992) ("presumption of correctness does not apply at all to the state courts' ultimate conclusion as to whether the petitioner's counsel rendered effective assistance, as that conclusion flows from the application of legal standards and constitutional principles to the facts"); Becton v. Barnett, 920 F.2d 1190, 1192 (4th Cir. 1990) (hearing required on ineffective assistance of counsel because state court determination on that ultimate issue is not question of fact but, rather, mixed question of law and fact subject to independent federal review); Hopkinson v. Shillinger, 866 F.2d 1185, 1217 (10th Cir. 1989), *cert. denied*, 497 U.S. 1010 (1990); Mannhalt v. Reed, 847 F.2d 576, 579-80 (9th Cir.), *cert. denied*, 488 U.S. 908 (1988); Robison v. Maynard, 829 F.2d 1501, 1513 (10th Cir. 1987); Hoots v. Allsbrook, 785 F.2d 1214, 1219 (4th Cir. 1986); Porcaro v. United States, 784 F.2d 38, 40 (1st Cir.), *cert. denied*, 479 U.S. 916 (1986) (petitioner entitled to hearing because factual allegations sufficient on both "unreasonableness" and "prejudice" prongs); Nealy v. Cabana, 764 F.2d 1173, 1176-77 (5th Cir. 1985); Butcher v. Marquez, 758 F.2d 373, 376 (9th Cir. 1985); Meeks v. Bergen, 749 F.2d 322, 327 (6th Cir. 1984); Ricalday v. Procunier, 736 F.2d 203, 207 (5th Cir. 1984); Adams v. Jago, 703 F.2d 978, 980 (6th Cir. 1983); Eldridge v. Atkins, 665 F.2d 228, 236-37 n.5 (8th Cir. 1981), *cert. denied*, 456 U.S. 910 (1982) (inadequate preparation and improper use of witnesses are questions of law to which no section 2254 presumption of correctness applies); Monaghan, *supra* § 20.1 n.1, at 274-75 (discussing *Strickland v. Washington*, *supra*). Cf. Hill v. Lockhart, 474 U.S. 52, 60 (1985) (hearing properly denied because petition did not allege facts sufficient to satisfy prejudice prong of *Strickland v. Washington* test).

State court findings of historical fact that underlie the ultimate determinations on the "unreasonableness" and "prejudice" issues *are*, however, subject to a presumption of correctness and may obviate the need for an evidentiary hearing. See, e.g., *Strickland v. Washington*, *supra* at 698 ("state court findings of fact made in the course of deciding an ineffective assistance claim are subject to the deference requirement of § 2254(d)"); Meyers v. Gillis, 142 F.3d 664, 667 (3d Cir. 1998) (district court correctly presumed that state court findings of fact underlying ruling on ineffective assistance were correct but also acted properly in rejecting findings as "clearly inconsistent with th[e] record"); Perillo v. Johnson, 79 F.3d 441, 446 (5th Cir. 1996) (although "state court background factfindings [underlying ruling on ineffective assistance claim] are subject to the deference requirement of § 2254(d)," state court's factfindings did not address relevant factual issue, so "there are no factfindings entitled to a presumption of correctness"); Jackson v. Herring, 42 F.3d 1350, 1367 (11th Cir.), *cert. denied*, 515 U.S. 1189 (1995) ("The question of whether an attorney's actions were a product of a tactical decision is an issue of fact, and a state court's decision as to this issue is therefore presumed correct, absent convincing evidence to the contrary.... Nonetheless, whether an attorney's tactical decision is a *reasonable* one, falling within the range of professional competence, is an issue of law reviewed de novo by this court."); *Bryant v. Scott*, *supra* at 1414 n.3; Sanders v. Ratelle, 21 F.3d 1446, 1451 (9th Cir. 1994) (underlying factfindings "are presumed to be correct unless they fall within one of the eight exceptions listed in 28 U.S.C.§ 2254(d)"); Battle v. Delo, 19 F.3d 1547, 1552 (8th Cir. 1994), *cert. denied*, 517 U.S. 1235 (1996); Deputy v. Taylor, 19 F.3d 1485, 1494-95 (3d Cir.), *cert. denied*, 512 U.S. 1230

(H)   Whether the trial court deprived the petitioner of the right to a speedy trial.[53]

(I)   Whether the petitioner was tried for or convicted of two identical or insufficiently distinct offenses, or was subjected to contradictory jury findings as to particular facts, in violation of the right not to be placed in jeopardy twice.[54]

(J)   Whether the petitioner was competent to stand trial.[55]

(1994); Kenley v. Armontrout, 937 F.2d 1298, 1305 (8th Cir. 1991) (state court factfindings on ineffective assistance not entitled to deference under 28 U.S.C. § 2254(d) because "fact findings are unfairly slanted against [petitioner], are incomplete and are only partially supported by the record"); Cunningham v. Zant, 928 F.2d 1006, 1016-19 (11th Cir. 1991) (although deferring to state postconviction court's finding of fact that counsel "made an informed tactical decision" to present only three "quality" character witnesses and not others who were available, court of appeals concludes that counsel's failure to prepare witnesses adequately for testifying and failure to present other noncumulative mitigating evidence amounted to ineffective assistance of counsel); Guinan v. Armontrout, 909 F.2d 1224, 1229-31 (8th Cir. 1990), *cert. denied,* 498 U.S. 1074 (1991) (although ultimate issue of effectiveness of counsel is legal question, subsidiary issues — in this case, trial counsel's reason for failing to call family members to testify in mitigation — are treated as questions of fact, requiring deference to state court determinations); Smith v. Jago, 888 F.2d 399, 407 (6th Cir. 1989), *cert. denied,* 495 U.S. 961 (1990) ("credibility findings made by the [state court] are findings of fact ... subject to the severely restricted review of 28 U.S.C. § 2254(d)"); Young v. Zant, 677 F.2d 792, 798 (11th Cir. 1982), *cert. denied,* 464 U.S. 1057 (1984) (although court of appeals must defer to district court's "findings on such primary facts as to what the attorney did or did not do during the course of the trial[,] ... we will apply our own judgment to the question of whether that conduct constituted ineffective assistance").

[53] *See, e.g.,* Haggins v. Warden, 715 F.2d 1050, 1055 (6th Cir. 1983), *cert. denied,* 464 U.S. 1071 (1984); Cain v. Smith, 686 F.2d 374, 380 (6th Cir. 1982).

[54] *See, e.g.,* Schiro v. Farley, 510 U.S. 222, 232 (1994) ("The preclusive effect of the jury's verdict" for collateral estoppel purposes "is a question of federal law which we must review *de novo*"); Freer v. Dugger, 935 F.2d 213, 222 (11th Cir. 1991) (in assessing whether trial judge's finding of evidentiary insufficiency on post-trial motion to set aside jury verdict was acquittal for double jeopardy purposes, federal habeas corpus court is resolving question of law and owes no deference to state appellate court's conclusion); Mars v. Mounts, 895 F.2d 1348, 1351-52 (11th Cir. 1990); Pryor v. Rose, 724 F.2d 525, 528 (6th Cir. 1984).

[55] The circuits are divided on the question whether competency to stand trial is a factual issue entitled to a presumption of correctness or a mixed question of law and fact. *Compare* Washington v. Johnson, 90 F.3d 945, 951 & n.4 (5th Cir. 1996), *cert. denied,* 117 S. Ct. 1259 (1997) ("The question of competency is treated in our circuit as a mixed question of law and fact.... Some earlier cases have treated a determination of competency as a finding of fact reviewable under a 'clearly arbitrary or unwarranted standard.'... More recent cases, however, have viewed competency as a mixed question of law and fact ....") *and* Levine v. Torvik, 986 F.2d 1506, 1514 (6th Cir.), *cert. denied,* 509 U.S. 907 (1993) ("A number of courts have held that the question of mental competency is a mixed question of law and fact.... We agree.") *and* Card v. Singletary, 981 F.2d 481, 484 & nn.5-6 (11th Cir. 1992) ("Whether one is competent to stand trial under the Fourteenth Amendment is a mixed question of law and fact ....") *and* James v. Singletary, 957 F.2d 1562, 1574 n.18 (11th Cir. 1992) ("[a]s competency to stand trial constitutes a mixed question of law and fact,"

state court findings of competence are not "entitled to a presumption of correctness") *with* In re Heidnik, 112 F.3d 105, 111, 112 n.7 (3d Cir. 1997) (treating state court and district court judgment that prisoner was competent to waive rights, give up appeals, and be executed as factfindings due a presumption of correctness, but concluding that no presumption arose under circumstances of case because prior courts had applied incorrect legal standard and committed "clear [factual] error" that rebutted presumption) and Medina v. Singletary, 59 F.3d 1095, 1106 (11th Cir. 1995), *cert. denied*, 517 U.S. 1247 (1996) ("A presumption of correctness attaches to a state court's finding of competence.") *and* In re Zettlemoyer, 53 F.3d 24 (3d Cir. 1995) (*per curiam*) (apparently treating question of competency to waive habeas corpus remedies as one of fact) *and* Moran v. Godinez, 40 F.3d 1567, 1573 (9th Cir. 1994), *modified*, 57 F.3d 690 (9th Cir. 1995) (state court determination that petitioner was mentally competent to waive counsel and plead guilty was entitled to presumption of correctness) *and* DeVille v. Whitley, 21 F.3d 654 (5th Cir.), *cert. denied*, 513 U.S. 918 (1994) ("A factual finding of competency by the state court is presumed to be correct.") *and* Barnard v. Collins, 13 F.3d 871, 877 (5th Cir. 1994) (concluding that competency to be executed is factual issue on which state court findings are entitled to deference and distinguishing contrary cases on ground that they "concern the issue of competency to stand trial and *not* the issue of competency to be executed") *and* Hamilton v. Collins, 905 F.2d 825, 827 (5th Cir.), *cert. denied*, 498 U.S. 895 (1990) (competence of petitioner to waive appeals and be executed is factual issue) *and with* Senna v. Patrissi, 5 F.3d 18, 20 (2d Cir. 1993) (*per curiam*) (state court's finding of competence to stand trial is entitled to presumption of correctness) *and* Brewer v. Lewis, 989 F.2d 1021, 1027 (9th Cir. 1993) (court has "obligation to accord a presumption of correctness to the state court's determination of [petitioner's] competence") *and* Spitzweiser-Wittgenstein v. Newton, 978 F.2d 1195, 1197 (10th Cir. 1992) ("Competency is a question of fact subject to the rebuttable presumption of correctness established in § 2254 ....") *and* Griffin v. Lockhart, 935 F.2d 926, 930 (8th Cir. 1991) ("In a habeas lawsuit, we generally presume that a state court's factual finding of competency is correct."). *Cf.* United States v. Gaudin, 515 U.S. 506, 525-26 (1995) (Rehnquist, C.J., concurring) ("competency of *witnesses*" to testify is "mixed question[ ] of law and fact" (emphasis added)).

The conflict among the circuits stems from a disagreement about the proper interpretation of two Supreme Court decisions. The first decision is Maggio v. Fulford, 462 U.S. 111 (1983) (*per curiam*), in which the Court reversed the court of appeals for overturning a state court's "factual conclusions" regarding the habeas corpus petitioner's competency to stand trial. *Id.* at 117. Emphasizing that "factual conclusions" are entitled to deference under 28 U.S.C. § 2254 unless they are not "'fairly supported by the record'" (*id.*), the Court deferred to the state court's factual findings after concluding that they were amply supported by the record. *See id.* at 117-18. Although one passage in the *Fulford* opinion might be read to characterize "conclusion[s] as to ... competency" as factual findings subject to a presumption of correctness, *see id.* at 117, a close examination of the decision reveals that the Court was referring exclusively to findings of historical fact *subsidiary* to an ultimate competency determination. *See id.* at 113, 117-18 ("Court of Appeals erroneously substituted its own judgment as to the credibility of witnesses for that of the Louisiana courts — a prerogative which 28 U.S.C. § 2254 does not allow it"). *Fulford* accordingly did not address, and certainly did not resolve, the issue of whether the ultimate competency determination is a purely factual question or a mixed question of law and fact. *See id.* at 118-19 (White, J., concurring).

The second Supreme Court decision about which the lower courts have disagreed is Demosthenes v. Baal, 495 U.S. 731 (1990) (*per curiam*), in which a bare majority of the Court, acting summarily, once again reversed a federal court for failing to accord sufficient deference to a state court's finding relating to competence. The *Demosthenes* majority opinion began its analysis by stating that the Court had previously "held" in *Maggio v. Fulford* "that a state court's conclusion regarding a defendant's competency is entitled to ... a presumption [of correctness]." *Id.* at 735. The weight due this statement is unclear, not only given the limited reach of *Fulford* but also given the fact that one of the five Justices who joined the statement was Justice White, who wrote separately in *Fulford* to make clear that the Court's *per curiam* opinion in *Fulford* should *not* be read as holding that state court conclusions of competency are factual findings entitled to a presumption of correctness. *See Fulford, supra* at 118-19 (White, J., concurring). The *Demosthenes* majority then proceeded to apply the *Fulford* "holding" to the facts of the case, concluding that the federal court improperly failed to accord a presumption of correctness to the state court's finding of competency. Again, however, as in *Fulford*, the state court "finding" at issue in *Demosthenes* was a finding of historical fact *subsidiary* to the ultimate competency determination. *See Demosthenes, supra* at 735-37 (federal court failed to accord adequate deference to state court's assessment of factual evidence regarding petitioner's competency, including "the reports of the three psychiatrists, the hospital report, and testimony regarding Baal's prior suicide attempts").

Some lower courts have viewed *Fulford* or *Demosthenes*, or both, as "holding" that competency is a question of fact entitled to a presumption of correctness. *See, e.g., Brewer v. Lewis, supra* at 1027 (citing *Fulford* and *Demosthenes*); Lafferty v. Cook, 949 F.2d 1546, 1549 (10th Cir. 1991), *cert. denied,* 504 U.S. 911 (1992) (citing *Demosthenes*); *Griffin v. Lockhart, supra* at 930 (citing *Fulford*). But, as other lower courts have recognized, *Fulford's* and *Demosthenes's* observations regarding the deference due state determinations of competence are merely *dicta*; the "holdings" of those cases are that a presumption of correctness attaches to state determinations of historical fact subsidiary to a determination of competence. *See, e.g., Card v. Singletary, supra* at 484 n.5 (*Demosthenes's* apparent pronouncement regarding the deference due state court findings of competence actually stands for unremarkable proposition that "state court *factual* findings regarding a petitioner's competency are entitled to a presumption of correctness under 28 U.S.C. § 2254 (emphasis added))." *See also Barnard v. Collins, supra* at 877.

The Court might have avoided this controversy by using greater precision in its language in *Fulford* and *Demosthenes*. Precision in thinking about the process of assessing "competency" (whether it is competency to stand trial or to waive available legal remedies) also is helpful. That assessment can be viewed as essentially a two-part inquiry. The reviewing court first must evaluate the factual evidence regarding "competence," including the credibility of the psychiatric and lay assessments of the individual's mental state. *See, e.g., Demosthenes, supra* at 732-33, 735-37 (factual record on issue of competency included testimony of psychiatrist who had examined Baal, reports of three other examining psychiatrists, affidavit of psychiatrist who had not examined Baal but had read prior reports, and testimony of state prison official who gave his lay opinion of Baal's competency). Thereafter, the reviewing court must determine whether the basic facts proven by the evidence satisfy the applicable legal standard of competence. *Cf.* Godinez v. Moran, 509 U.S. 389, 401-02 (1993) (when assessing waivers of right to trial and counsel by possibly incompetent defendant, judge must use facts regarding defendant's mental capacity to determine whether defendant is competent to stand trial and whether his waivers are voluntary, knowing, and intelligent). Once these two aspects of the competency assessment are distinguished, it becomes more clear that, although state court findings on the threshold factual issues generally are subject to a presumption of correctness, the subsequent determination (based on those facts) "[w]hether one is competent to stand trial under the Fourteenth Amendment [or competent to waive legal remedies] is a mixed question of law and fact" that is not subject to a presumption of correctness under section 2254. *Card v. Singletary, supra* at 484 n.6.

The Supreme Court recently stated in very clear terms, although again in *dicta*, that an assessment of competency to stand trial is a factual determination entitled to a presumption of correctness. *See Thompson v. Keohane, supra*, 516 U.S. at 109-13.

Characterizing competence as a purely factual question subject to a presumption of correctness would have untoward consequences for most cases in which a habeas corpus petitioner requests an evidentiary hearing on a claim that he was incompetent to stand trial or to waive available legal remedies. Because the reviewing court "must accept as true petitioner's alleged facts" for purposes of assessing the propriety of denying a hearing (*id.* at 484; *see supra* § 15.2c n.57 and accompanying text), habeas corpus courts arguably would have to treat the petitioner's allegation of his own incompetence as a presumptively true "fact" requiring a hearing in every case absent a controlling state court determination on the issue. *Cf. Card v. Singletary, supra* at 484 n.6 (rejecting petitioner's argument that his factual allegation of incompetence was "entitled to deference under the *Townsend v. Sain* standard" because court of appeals deems assessment of competence to be mixed question of fact and law).

Whether or not a determination of competency is deemed a legal, factual, or mixed question, a state court finding of competence is not entitled to deference if the state courts never held a hearing, *see, e.g., James v. Singletary, supra* at 1574, or if the state factfinding process was not full and fair, *see, e.g., Griffin v. Lockhart, supra* at 930; Bouchillon v. Collins, 907 F.2d 589, 592 & n.6 (5th Cir. 1990) (discussed *infra*, next paragraph); *cf. Lafferty v. Cook, supra* at 1551-56 (although treating competency as purely factual issue rather than mixed question of fact and law, court nonetheless accords no deference to state court finding of competency because "state trial court's evaluation ... was infected by a misperception of the legal requirements"). *See infra* § 20.3e.

In situations in which the district court determines that there was a *bona fide* doubt about the petitioner's competence to stand trial and that the state trial court unconstitutionally failed to hold an adequate hearing on the petitioner's competency to stand trial, the district court must determine (based, for example, on the length of time since trial, the availability of witnesses, and the availability of evidence of the petitioner's mental state at the time of trial) whether it reasonably can determine retrospectively the petitioner's mental state at the time of trial. Although retrospective competency hearings are not favored, they may be conducted in federal habeas corpus proceedings if the circumstances reasonably permit. The state bears the burden of proving competency at such a hearing, and if the state fails to meet its burden of proof, the writ must be granted. If, on the other hand, a retrospective competency hearing is *not* feasible, the court must grant the writ and order the state courts to retry the petitioner or release her. *See, e.g.,* Blazak v. Ricketts, 1 F.3d 891, 894 n.3 (9th Cir. 1993), *cert. denied*, 511 U.S. 1097 (1994) ("When a petitioner establishes that the evidence before the state trial court raised a bona fide doubt as to his competency, a further inquiry into his actual competency is not necessary due to the difficulties in making retrospective competency determinations."); *Lafferty v. Cook, supra* at 1556 (because "passage of time has rendered impractical a remand for an after-the-fact hearing on competency," court vacates conviction and sentence, specifying that "[t]he state is of course free to retry" petitioner); *Griffin v. Lockhart, supra* at 931 (granting habeas corpus relief because "due process was violated by the state court's failure to provide an adequate hearing" on petitioner's competency to stand trial and "it seems impossible to now conduct a meaningful nunc pro tunc hearing" on competency three years after the trial); McInerney v. Puckett, 919 F.2d 350, 351-52 (5th Cir. 1990); Tiller v. Esposito, 911 F.2d 575, 576-77 (11th Cir. 1990); United States ex rel. Bilyew v. Franzen, 842 F.2d 189, 192-93 (7th Cir. 1988); Estock v. Lane, 842 F.2d 184, 186-88 (7th Cir. 1988); Miller v. Dugger, 838 F.2d 1530, 1543-44 (11th Cir.), *cert. denied*, 486 U.S. 1061 (1988) (citing cases). *Cf.* Hull v. Freeman, 932 F.2d 159, 170 & n.9 (3d Cir. 1991) (when retrospective competency hearing is appropriate, federal court should conduct hearing rather than remanding to

(K) Whether the petit or grand jury was selected in a systematically unrepresentative or racially discriminatory manner[56] or whether a particular practice deprived the petitioner of an impartial jury.[57]

---

state courts to do so); *Bouchillon v. Collins, supra* at 592 & n.6 (although state court *did* hold competency hearing, hearing was not full and fair, and federal court must hold proper hearing and make its own competency judgment; adhering to prior circuit precedent giving habeas corpus *petitioners* in this situation the burden of proving incompetence to stand trial, but noting discrepancy between 5th Circuit and other circuits on burden of proof issue and questioning 5th Circuit rule).

[56] *See, e.g.*, Rose v. Mitchell, 443 U.S. 545, 561 (1979); Castaneda v. Partida, 430 U.S. 482, 496 (1977); Johnson v. Puckett, 929 F.2d 1067, 1072 (5th Cir.), *cert. denied*, 502 U.S. 898 (1991) (question whether underrepresentation of minorities among jurisdiction's grand jury forepersons lasted for "significant" period of time is mixed question of law and fact subject to independent review); Love v. Jones, 923 F.2d 816, 819 (11th Cir. 1991) (whether prosecutor has engaged in ongoing pattern of peremptorily challenging prospective jurors who are members of minority groups in violation of Swain v. Alabama, 380 U.S. 202 (1965), is mixed question of law and fact). When the racial or other bias alleged is not systemic, but specific to a particular prosecutor, judge, or juror, the courts tend to treat the question of "discriminatory intent" as one of fact. *See, e.g.*, Hernandez v. New York, 500 U.S. 352, 367 (1991) (plurality opinion) (direct appeal decision holding that question whether particular prosecutor's peremptory challenges were racially biased in violation of Batson v. Kentucky, 476 U.S. 79 (1986), is question of fact); *id.* at 372 (O'Connor, J., concurring); Johnson v. Maryland, 915 F.2d 892, 896-97 (4th Cir. 1990); Harrison v. Ryan, 909 F.2d 84, 85 n.1 (3d Cir.), *cert. denied*, 498 U.S. 1003 (1990) (similar to *Hernandez, supra*). *Compare* Purkett v. Elem, 514 U.S. 765, 769 (1995) (third prong of test for unconstitutionally discriminatory exercise of peremptory challenges under Batson v. Kentucky, 476 U.S. 79 (1986) — whether peremptory strike "was ... motivated by discriminatory intent" — is factual "finding which turn[s] primarily on an assessment of credibility" and deserves presumption of correctness) *with id.* at 777 (Stevens, J., dissenting) (in evaluating third prong of *Batson* test, court may determine that explanation for peremptory strike is "pretextual [and thus discriminatory] as a matter of law") *and id.* at 769 (majority opinion) (suggesting that second prong of *Batson* test — whether prosecutor's proffered explanation for strike is "race-neutral," *i.e.*, is "a reason that does not deny equal protection" — is question of law not subject to presumption of correctness) *and id.* at 776 (Stevens, J., dissenting) (as "Court's opinion today implicitly ratifies," second prong of *Batson* test "presents a pure legal question" which federal court of appeals must "evaluate on its own"). For a similar distinction between the collective impartiality of the jury (which the courts tend to treat as a legal question) and the individual impartiality of a single juror (which is treated as a question of fact), see *infra* note 57.

[57] *See, e.g.*, Irwin v. Dowd, 366 U.S. 717, 723 (1961) (effect of prejudicial pretrial publicity); Grancorvitz v. Franklin, 890 F.2d 34, 37 & n.4 (7th Cir. 1989), *cert. denied*, 495 U.S. 959 (1990); Harris v. Pulley, 885 F.2d 1354, 1360-61 (9th Cir. 1988), *cert. denied*, 493 U.S. 1051 (1990); Norris v. Risley, 878 F.2d 1178, 1181 (9th Cir. 1989) (impact of courtroom demonstration on jury); Cummings v. Dugger, 862 F.2d 1504, 1509 (11th Cir.), *cert. denied*, 490 U.S. 1111 (1989) (question whether facts required court to "presume[ ] prejudice" resulting from jury nonneutrality treated as mixed question of fact and law). *See also* Lockhart v. McCree, 476 U.S. 162, 168-69 n.3 (1986) (effect of jury selection practice on neutrality of juries is matter of "legislative fact" and reviewable *de novo*). *But cf.* Johnson v. Maryland, 915 F.2d 892, 896-97 (4th Cir. 1990) (treating

question whether jury deliberations were tainted by racial discrimination as one of fact). *But see* Aiken v. Blodgett, 921 F.2d 214, 217 (9th Cir. 1990), *cert. denied,* 502 U.S. 839 (1991) (state court determinations of effects of pretrial publicity on ability of jury to try petitioner fairly are factfindings due presumption of correctness); Swindler v. Lockhart, 885 F.2d 1342, 1347 (8th Cir. 1989), *cert. denied,* 495 U.S. 911 (1990) (state court's determination concerning prejudicial effect of pretrial publicity is "entitled to deference" (citing Patton v. Yount, 467 U.S. 1025 (1984) (discussed *infra*) and *Irwin v. Dowd, supra*)); Wicker v. McCotter, 783 F.2d 487, 495 (5th Cir. 1986) (state court's factual determination concerning prejudicial effect of pretrial publicity is finding of fact due presumption of correctness under 28 U.S.C. § 2254(d)).

Whether an individual juror is partial or impartial is a question of fact subject to the presumption of correctness. *See, e.g., Thompson v. Keohane, supra,* 516 U.S. at 109-13; Mu'Min v. Virginia, 500 U.S. 415, 428 (1991) (direct appeal case) ("A trial court's findings of juror impartiality may 'be overturned only for "manifest error."'"); *id.* at 432-34 (O'Connor, J., concurring); Wainwright v. Witt, 469 U.S. 412, 430 (1985); Patton v. Yount, 467 U.S. 1025, 1036 (1984); Lesko v. Lehman, 925 F.2d 1527, 1548 (3d Cir.), *cert. denied,* 502 U.S. 898 (1991); Sizemore v. Fletcher, 921 F.2d 667, 672-73 (6th Cir. 1990); Tinsley v. Borg, 895 F.2d 520, 525 (9th Cir. 1990), *cert. denied,* 498 U.S. 1091 (1991); Kordenbrock v. Scroggy, 889 F.2d 69, 84 (6th Cir. 1989); McCoy v. Lynaugh, 874 F.2d 954, 960 (5th Cir. 1989); *Harris v. Pulley, supra* at 1360-61; Cummings v. Dugger, 862 F.2d 1504, 1509 (11th Cir.), *cert. denied,* 490 U.S. 1111 (1989) (question of "actual prejudice" resulting from bias of individual juror treated as fact question); Monaghan, *supra* § 20.1 n.1, at 274 n.249. Justice Kennedy has explained why the Court in *Patton v. Yount, supra,* decided to treat as a question of fact "a state court's determination that a particular juror could be impartial" — namely, that "the determination has been made only after an extended *voir dire* proceeding designed specifically to identify biased veniremen" and because "the determination is essentially one of credibility, and therefore largely one of demeanor." *Mu'Min v. Virginia, supra* at 450-51 (direct appeal case) (Kennedy, J., dissenting). In Justice Kennedy's view, if those favorable conditions for assessing a juror's impartiality did not actually prevail at trial, the Court should independently review the impartiality question even as it applies to solely that juror. *Id.* at 451. *Accord* Johnson v. Armontrout, 961 F.2d 748, 753-54 (8th Cir. 1992) (discussed *infra* note 84). *See, e.g.,* Burton v. Johnson, 948 F.2d 1150, 1158 (10th Cir. 1991) ("Whether a juror's bias may be implied from the circumstances is a question of law for [federal] court."); Depree v. Thomas, 946 F.2d 784, 788-89 n.6 (11th Cir. 1991) (*dicta*) (trial court's assessment of venirepersons' impartiality would be deemed inadequate under (since superseded) section 2254(d)(7) (*see infra* § 20.3e) if "State denied due process during the jury selection phase of the trial" by, for example, limiting petitioner's ability "to interrogate fully the venirepersons and to challenge their empanelment"). Justice Kennedy's analysis helps explain why the Court traditionally has accorded different treatment to the question of a *particular* juror's impartiality as explored through direct questioning on *voir dire* and the very different question of the jury's *collective* ability to provide the defendant with a fair trial, which is *not* simply a credibility or demeanor question, nor is it one on which a focused factual proceeding has taken place — or can take place — at trial. *See also supra* note 56.

On all questions of jury and juror impartiality, subsidiary issues of historical fact, such as witness credibility, are subject to a presumption of correctness. *See, e.g.,* Case v. Mondragon, 887 F.2d 1388, 1393 (10th Cir. 1989), *cert. denied,* 494 U.S. 1035 (1990).

(L) Whether the state or state trial judge engaged in misconduct in violation of the Due Process Clause.[58]

(M) Whether evidence improperly suppressed or misrepresented by the prosecution was material.[59]

(N) Whether a judicial evidentiary or other ruling was an abuse of discretion or otherwise sufficient to deprive the petitioner of due process.[60]

---

[58] *See, e.g.,* Darden v. Wainwright, 477 U.S. 168, 178-83 (1985) (independently reviewing question whether prosecutor's argument at capital sentencing phase violated due process); Fero v. Kerby, 39 F.3d 1462, 1473 (10th Cir. 1994), *cert. denied,* 515 U.S. 1122 (1995) ("allegations of prosecutorial misconduct present mixed issues of law and fact, subject to *de novo* review"); Wiggerfall v. Jones, 918 F.2d 1544, 1550 & n.5 (11th Cir. 1990) (independently reviewing question whether evidence required lesser included offense instruction under rule of Beck v. Alabama, 447 U.S. 625 (1980)); Nichols v. Sullivan, 867 F.2d 1250, 1253 (10th Cir.), *cert. denied,* 490 U.S. 1112 (1989) (whether witness's unsolicited remarks about petitioner's prior convictions were prejudicial in violation of due process is mixed question subject to *de novo* review); Dickson v. Sullivan, 849 F.2d 403, 405-08 (9th Cir. 1988) (whether statement by deputy sheriff to jurors affected jury's deliberations or verdict is mixed question); United States ex rel. Shaw v. DeRobertis, 755 F.2d 1279, 1282 n.2 (7th Cir. 1985) (question whether unconstitutional prosecutorial misconduct occurred is mixed question). State court findings of historical fact that underlie the ultimate prejudice and due process questions are subject to a presumption of correctness and may obviate the need for a hearing. *See, e.g.,* Riddick v. Edmiston, 894 F.2d 586, 592 (3d Cir. 1990) (credibility of prosecutor's reason for peremptory challenge treated as question of fact); Evans v. Thompson, 881 F.2d 117, 122-23 (4th Cir. 1989), *cert. denied,* 497 U.S. 1010 (1990) (finding that prosecutors did not delay in bad faith when they waited until after new law took effect before confessing error treated as question of fact).

[59] *See, e.g.,* Kyles v. Whitley, 514 U.S. 419, 441-42 (1995) (reviewing "materiality" of suppressed evidence *de novo*); *id.* at 457 (Scalia, J., dissenting) (acknowledging by way of "Cf." citation of 28 U.S.C. § 2254(d), that "materiality" question under review is not question of fact); United States v. Buchanan, 891 F.2d 1436, 1440 (10th Cir. 1989), *cert. denied,* 494 U.S. 1088 (1990); Carter v. Rafferty, 826 F.2d 1299, 1306 (3d Cir. 1987), *cert. denied,* 484 U.S. 1011 (1988); United States ex rel. Smith v. Fairman, 769 F.2d 386, 391 (7th Cir. 1985); Chaney v. Brown, 730 F.2d 1334, 1345-46 (10th Cir.), *cert. denied,* 469 U.S. 1090 (1984); Davis v. Heyd, 479 F.2d 446, 451 (5th Cir. 1973). *See also* United States v. Gaudin, 515 U.S. 506, 511-14, 519-22 (1995) (question "'whether [a] statement was material to [a] decision'" is "a 'mixed question of law and fact'"; questions of "materiality," "pertinence," and "relevance" are mixed questions of law and fact); Kungys v. United States, 485 U.S. 759, 772 (1988) ("materiality" as used in denaturalization statute is question of law); Cooper v. Wainwright, 807 F.2d 881, 889 (11th Cir. 1986), *cert. denied,* 481 U.S. 1050 (1987) (hearing required to determine whether mitigating evidence unconstitutionally excluded from sentencing hearing "is probative and, if so, whether its omission may have affected the outcome of petitioner's sentencing proceeding").

[60] *See, e.g.,* Estelle v. McGuire, 502 U.S. 62, 70-72 (1991) (independently reviewing question whether introduction of evidence of prior bad acts violated due process); Jones v. Meyer, 899 F.2d 883, 884 (9th Cir. 1990); Case v. Mondragon, 887 F.2d 1388, 1393 (10th Cir. 1989), *cert. denied,* 494 U.S. 1035 (1990) (trial court's refusal to allow counsel to *voir dire* jury regarding alleged juror misconduct); Hamilton v. Vasquez, 882 F.2d 1469, 1471 (9th Cir. 1989) (trial court's decision to

(O)   Whether the petitioner was denied the 6th Amendment right to confront adverse witnesses, including the often subsidiary question whether an absent declarant was "unavailable."[61]

(P)   Whether counsel "in effect" made a waiver of or stipulated away the petitioner's rights.[62]

(Q)   Whether the evidence presented at trial was constitutionally sufficient to convict or to make the defendant eligible for the death penalty.[63]

---

shackle defendant during trial); Lesko v. Owens, 881 F.2d 44, 50 (3d Cir. 1989), *cert. denied,* 493 U.S. 1036 (1990) ("Whether an error reaches the magnitude of a constitutional violation is an issue of law, subject to plenary review" (citing Sullivan v. Cuyler, 723 F.2d 1077, 1082 (3d Cir. 1983))); Nichols v. Sullivan, 867 F.2d 1250, 1253 (10th Cir.), *cert. denied,* 490 U.S. 1112 (1989) (whether witness' unsolicited remarks about petitioner's prior convictions were prejudicial in violation of due process is mixed question subject to *de novo* review); Bundy v. Wainwright, 808 F.2d 1410, 1418 (11th Cir. 1987) (propriety of admitting hypnotically induced testimony of eyewitness to murder is mixed question of law and fact, hence not subject to presumption of correctness); Williams v. Maggio, 730 F.2d 1048, 1049-50 (5th Cir. 1984) (judge's ignorance of his own discretionary power); Hickerson v. Maggio, 691 F.2d 792, 795 (5th Cir. 1982) (*per curiam*); Dickerson v. Alabama, 667 F.2d 1364, 1368-69 (11th Cir.), *cert. denied,* 459 U.S. 878 (1982); *infra* subpara. (R).

[61] *See, e.g.,* Acosta-Huerta v. Estelle, 7 F.3d 139, 143 (9th Cir. 1992) ("A state trial court's decision that a witness is constitutionally 'unavailable' is an evidentiary question we review de novo."); Swan v. Peterson, 6 F.3d 1373, 1379 (9th Cir. 1993) ("Whether the hearsay statements were sufficiently reliable to be admitted without violating the Confrontation Clause is a mixed question ... [which] [w]e review de novo."); Myatt v. Hannigan, 910 F.2d 680, 685 (10th Cir. 1990) (question whether child's hearsay statements about sexual abuse were sufficiently "reliable" to satisfy confrontation clause is mixed question of law and fact); Martinez v. Sullivan, 881 F.2d 921, 926 n.2 (10th Cir. 1989), *cert. denied,* 493 U.S. 1029 (1990); United States ex rel. Ashford v. Director, 871 F.2d 680, 683 (7th Cir. 1989); Dres v. Campoy, 784 F.2d 996, 998 (9th Cir. 1986) ("unavailability" of absent witness reviewed *de novo*); United States ex rel. Scarpelli v. George, 687 F.2d 1012, 1015 (7th Cir. 1982), *cert. denied,* 459 U.S. 1171 (1983). *Cf.* Allen v. Morris, 845 F.2d 610, 614 (6th Cir. 1988), *cert. denied,* 488 U.S. 1011 (1989) (state court's finding of unavailability for purposes of state hearsay rule arises under state law, hence is due presumption of correctness).

[62] *See, e.g.,* Carter v. Sowders, 5 F.3d 975, 980-82 (6th Cir. 1993), *cert. denied,* 511 U.S. 1097 (1994) (rejecting state court's and district court's findings that counsel waived habeas corpus petitioner's 6th Amendment right to confrontation by leaving pretrial deposition of prosecution witness when petitioner failed to appear); United States ex rel. Ross v. Franzen, 668 F.2d 933, 938 (7th Cir. 1982).

[63] *See, e.g.,* Tison v. Arizona, 481 U.S. 137, 155-56 n.11 (1987) (question whether defendant was sufficiently culpable to warrant death penalty renewed *de novo*); Cabana v. Bullock, 474 U.S. 376, 385 n.3, 387, 390 (1986) (similar); Jackson v. Virginia, 443 U.S. 307, 323 (1979) (although "[a] judgment by a state appellate court rejecting a challenge to evidentiary sufficiency is of course entitled to deference by the federal courts, ... Congress ... has selected the federal district courts as precisely the forums that are responsible for determining whether state convictions have been secured in accord with federal constitutional law"); Kelly v. Roberts, 998 F.2d 802, 807 (10th Cir.

(R)   Whether the jurors understood a jury instruction given at trial to misallocate or misdescribe the burden of proving the petitioner's guilt or otherwise to misstate the law,[64] or to limit the evidence that the capital sentencer could consider in mitigation,[65] or whether jury instructions otherwise deprived the petitioner of due process or of some other constitutional right.[66]

(S)   Whether the state courts' definition of a facially vague capital aggravating circumstance, such as that the killing was "especially heinous, atrocious and cruel," provides "a sufficiently narrowing limiting construction" to pass muster under the 8th Amendment.[67]

1993); Cunningham v. Zant, 928 F.2d 1006, 1014 n.10, 1016 (11th Cir. 1991) ("The district court erroneously concluded that the state habeas court's finding that the evidence overwhelmingly proved intent to kill was a question of fact entitled to a presumption of correctness ...."); Case v. Mondragon, 887 F.2d 1388, 1392 (10th Cir. 1989), *cert. denied,* 494 U.S. 1035 (1990); O'Blasney v. Solem, 774 F.2d 925, 927 (8th Cir. 1985) (sufficiency of evidence to convict); Hawkins v. LeFevre, 758 F.2d 866, 871 n.7 (2d Cir. 1985) (same); Greider v. Duckworth, 701 F.2d 1228, 1233 n.8 (7th Cir. 1983) (federal court reviews historical facts to determine whether state met reasonable doubt burden for conviction). *Cf.* Hopkinson v. Shillinger, 866 F.2d 1185, 1216 (10th Cir. 1989), *cert. denied,* 497 U.S. 1010 (1990) (state appellate court's finding that evidence established sufficient culpability with regard to killing to render death sentence proportionate under 8th Amendment treated as fact question subject to presumption of correctness).

[64] *See, e.g.,* Francis v. Franklin, 471 U.S. 307, 314 (1985); Mullaney v. Wilbur, 421 U.S. 684 (1975).

[65] *See, e.g.,* Buchanan v. Angelone, 118 S. Ct. 757, 762-63 (1998) (whether "'there is ... a reasonable likelihood that the jurors in the case understood the challenged instructions to preclude consideration of relevant mitigating evidence offered by petitioner'"); Penry v. Lynaugh, 492 U.S. 302 (1989); Hitchcock v. Dugger, 481 U.S. 393 (1987). *See also* Mills v. Maryland, 486 U.S. 367, 377-78, 384 (1988) (question whether instruction unconstitutionally caused jury to refrain from considering mitigating circumstances found by less than all 12 jurors is matter of law subject to *de novo* review).

[66] *See, e.g.,* Estelle v. McGuire, 502 U.S. 62 (1991); Donnelly v. DeChristoforo, 416 U.S. 637 (1974); Cupp v. Naughton, 414 U.S. 141 (1973); McDougall v. Dixon, 921 F.2d 518, 532 (4th Cir. 1990), *cert. denied,* 501 U.S. 1223 (1991) (by implication from affirmance of district court's refusal to take evidence on issue); other decisions cited *supra* § 9.1 nn.20-22.

[67] *See* Creech v. Arave, 507 U.S. 463, 478 (1993) (by implication); Stringer v. Black, 503 U.S. 222, 232-37 (1992) (by implication); Lewis v. Jeffers, 497 U.S. 764, 780 (1990) ("federal habeas review of a state court's application of a constitutionally narrowed aggravating circumstance is limited, at most, to determining whether the state court's finding was so arbitrary or capricious as to constitute an independent due process or Eighth Amendment violation" under "'rational factfinder' standard established in Jackson v. Virginia, 443 U.S. 307 (1979)"); Maynard v. Cartwright, 486 U.S. 356 (1988); *supra* subpara. (Q) (discussing "mixed" factual and legal nature of standard established in *Jackson v. Virginia, supra*).

(T) Whether the state courts' novel interpretation of a state criminal statute was sufficiently foreseeable to permit retroactive application to the petitioner.[68]

(U) Whether the petitioner was indigent for purposes of the right to appointed counsel or to proceed *in forma pauperis*.[69]

(V) Whether under the circumstances "bail is available to a state prisoner granted conditional habeas corpus relief." [70]

(W) Whether a legal claim is "baseless" or "frivolous."[71]

(X) Whether a claim is subject to a procedural defense to federal habeas corpus review or relief (including, for example, whether state remedies have been adequately exhausted, whether petitioner committed a "procedural default," or whether a rule is "new" for purposes of the nonretroactivity doctrine).[72]

---

[68] *See, e.g.,* Hagan v. Caspari, 50 F.3d 542, 544-45 (8th Cir. 1995) (question whether state supreme court's overruling of decision of intermediate appellate court "was an unforeseeable change in state law," so as to come within due process rule prohibiting "retroactive application of an unforeseeable interpretation of a criminal statute, if detrimental to a defendant," is "question of federal law, which we review *de novo*"); Moore v. Wyrick, 766 F.2d 1253, 1255 (8th Cir. 1985), *cert. denied,* 475 U.S. 1032 (1986).

[69] *See, e.g.,* Barry v. Brower, 864 F.2d 294, 299 (3d Cir. 1988).

[70] Marino v. Vasquez, 812 F.2d 499, 507 (9th Cir. 1987).

[71] *See, e.g.,* Professional Real Est. Inves., Inc. v. Columbia Pictures Indus., Inc., 508 U.S. 49, 67 (1993) (Souter, J., concurring) (question "whether [the suit at issue here] was objectively baseless is purely one of law, which we are obliged to consider *de novo*").

[72] *See, e.g.,* Elder v. Holloway, 510 U.S. 510, 516 (1994) (in section 1983 context, question "[w]hether an asserted federal right was clearly established at a particular time ... presents a question of law, not one of 'legal facts.' ... That question of law, like the generality of such questions, must be resolved de novo on appeal."); Sloan v. Delo, 54 F.3d 1371, 1379 (8th Cir. 1995), *cert. denied,* 516 U.S. 1056 (1996) (in addressing procedural default argument, issue of "adequacy of a state procedure presents a question of federal law"); Cochran v. Herring, 43 F.3d 1404, 1408 (11th. Cir.), *modified,* 61 F.3d 20 (11th Cir. 1995), *cert. denied,* 516 U.S. 1073 (1996) ("The district court's holding that, under the facts of this case, the *Batson* claim is not procedurally barred is a mixed question of law and fact subject to de novo review by this court."); Johnson v. Cowley, 40 F.3d 341, 344 (10th Cir. 1994) ("Whether a petitioner has procedurally defaulted his federal claims is a question of federal law."); Turner v. Williams, 35 F.3d 872, 890-91 (4th Cir. 1994), *cert. denied,* 514 U.S. 1017 (1995) (notwithstanding state court's characterization of its ruling as resting upon "procedural default," court of appeals concludes that state court actually was applying "a collateral estoppel rule" and that petitioner did not commit procedural default within meaning of federal habeas corpus doctrine); Macklin v. Singletary, 24 F.3d 1307, 1313 (11th Cir. 1994), *cert. denied,* 513 U.S. 1160 (1995) ("abuse of the writ doctrine presents objective, threshold questions involving the application of law to facts," which court of appeals "review[s] ... *de novo*"); Givens v. Green, 12 F.3d 1041, 1043-44 (11th Cir. 1994) (*per curiam*) (reviewing *de novo* and reversing district court's determination that some claims in petition were unexhausted); Couch v. Jabe, 951 F.2d 94, 96 (9th Cir. 1991) (question "whether a state court rested its holding on

(Y) Whether a legal violation was "harmless."[73]

procedural default, thus barring federal habeas review, is a question of law to be reviewed *de novo*"); Harris v. Pulley, 885 F.2d 1354, 1370 (9th Cir. 1988), *cert. denied,* 493 U.S. 1051 (1990) (exhaustion); Kim v. Villalobos, 799 F.2d 1317, 1320 (2d Cir. 1986) (exhaustion question reviewed *de novo*). *See also* Johnson v. Jones, 515 U.S. 304, 313-14 (1995) (whether proposition of law was "clearly established" at particular time for purposes of qualified immunity law — which Court has held is somewhat analogous to "new rule" question under nonretroactivity doctrine, *see* Reynoldsville Casket Co. v. Hyde, 514 U.S. 749, 757-59 (1995) — "'is a question of law'" and "purely legal issue" subject to *de novo* review (quoting Mitchell v. Forsyth, 472 U.S. 511, 528 (1985)); *infra* §§ 25.5 n.2, 37.3a n.6 (various habeas corpus defenses including nonretroactivity, nonexhaustion, and procedural default). *Cf.* Rust v. Zent, 17 F.3d 155, 161 (6th Cir. 1994) ("We review the district court's findings of fact supporting its determination of cause and prejudice for clear error."). *But cf.* Wilton v. Seven Falls Co., 515 U.S. 277, 283, 289-90 (1995) (suggesting that district court's discretion whether to dismiss, stay, or proceed with case presenting issues raised in related state court litigation — discretion analogous to that granted by Granberry v. Greer, 481 U.S. 129 (1987), in regard to acceptance of state waivers of exhaustion requirement, *see infra* § 23.2a, and also analogous to district court's discretion to hold unexhausted petition in abeyance under stay of execution rather than dismissing, *see supra* § 13.3 — is reviewable for "abuse of discretion," not "*de novo*").

[73] *See, e.g.,* Brecht v. Abrahamson, 507 U.S. 619, 640, 642 (1993) (Stevens, J., concurring); *id.* at 655-56 (O'Connor, J., dissenting); Yates v. Evatt, 500 U.S. 391, 404-05 (1991) (in overturning state postconviction court's conclusion that improper instruction constituted harmless error, Court reviews question *de novo,* albeit without discussion of proper standard of review); *id.* at 412-13 (Scalia, J., concurring in the judgment); Arizona v. Fulminante, 499 U.S. 277, 295 (1991) (direct appeal case) ("The Court has the power to review the record *de novo* in order to determine an error's harmlessness."); Rushen v. Spain, 464 U.S. 114, 120 (1983) (*per curiam*) (whether *ex parte* contact between judge and juror was harmless); Bonner v. Holt, 26 F.3d 1081, 1083 (11th Cir. 1994), *cert. denied,* 514 U.S. 1010 (1995) ("Harmless error is a mixed question of law and fact subject to de novo review."); Deputy v. Taylor, 19 F.3d 1485, 1496 (3d Cir.), *cert. denied,* 512 U.S. 1230 (1994) ("A state court's conclusion that constitutional error was harmless does not constitute a factual finding entitled to the presumption of correctness. Rather, it is a mixed question of fact and law."); Orndorff v. Lockhart, 998 F.2d 1426, 1432 (8th Cir. 1993) (harmless error under *Brecht* standard is mixed question subject to *de novo* review); Suniga v. Bunnell, 998 F.2d 664, 667 (9th Cir. 1993); Lowery v. Collins, 988 F.2d 1364, 1372 & n.34 (5th Cir. 1993) (collecting authorities concluding that harmless error determination under *Chapman* standard is mixed question of fact and law subject to *de novo* review); Cunningham v. Zant, 928 F.2d 1006, 1014 n.10 (11th Cir. 1991) ("The district court erroneously concluded that the state habeas court's finding that the evidence overwhelmingly proved intent to kill was a question of fact entitled to a presumption of correctness ...."); Booker v. Dugger, 922 F.2d 633, 636 n.4 (11th Cir.), *cert. denied,* 502 U.S. 900 (1991) ("Federal courts are not ... bound by state court rulings on harmless error."); United States ex rel. Lee v. Flannigan, 884 F.2d 945, 950-51 (7th Cir. 1989), *cert. denied,* 497 U.S. 1027 (1990); Gunn v. Newsome, 881 F.2d 949, 964 (11th Cir.) (*en banc*), *cert. denied,* 493 U.S. 993 (1989); Dickey v. Lewis, 859 F.2d 1365, 1370 (9th Cir. 1988); Dickson v. Sullivan, 849 F.2d 403, 406 (9th Cir. 1988); McKenzie v. Risley, 842 F.2d 1525, 1531 & n.8, 1532 (9th Cir.), *cert. denied,* 488 U.S. 901 (1988); United States ex rel. Savory v. Lane, 832 F.2d 1011, 1018 (7th Cir. 1987); Hunt v. Oklahoma, 683 F.2d 1305, 1309 (10th Cir. 1982); Panzavecchia v. Wainwright, 658 F.2d 337, 339 (5th Cir. 1981); Annuziato v. Manson, 566 F.2d 410, 413 (2d Cir. 1977); authority discussed *infra* § 32.4f. *See also* Holland v. Attorney General, 777 F.2d 150, 153-

(Z)   Any "dispute [that] is not so much over the elemental facts as the constitutional significance to be attached to them."[74]

(AA) Any issue dependent on "legislative" or "social," as opposed to "historical" or case-specific facts.[75]

---

55 (3d Cir. 1985) (*de novo* review of question whether jury could disregard testimony). *But cf.* Johnson v. Maryland, 915 F.2d 892, 896-97 (4th Cir. 1990) (treating state court's harmless-error determination as factfinding subject to deference, although court of appeals apparently also addresses merits and concludes that no error occurred at all).

[74] Neil v. Biggers, 409 U.S. 188, 193 n.3 (1972). *See, e.g.,* Maggio v. Fulford, 462 U.S. 111, 118 (1983) (White, J., concurring); Sumner v. Mata, 449 U.S. 539, 543-44 (1981); Cuyler v. Sullivan, 446 U.S. 335, 342 (1980); Brown v. Allen, 344 U.S. 443, 507 (1952); Bruni v. Lewis, 847 F.2d 561, 563 (9th Cir.), *cert. denied,* 488 U.S. 960 (1988) (habeas corpus courts must exercise independent judgment as to "legal weight" due facts found by state court); Marino v. Vasquez, 812 F.2d 499, 504 (9th Cir. 1987) ("application of a legal standard to historical facts does not constitute a factual finding entitled to a presumption of correctness under Section 2254(d)"); Brantley v. McKaskle, 722 F.2d 187, 189 (5th Cir. 1984) ("If, however, the challenge goes to the inferences drawn from the facts, the reviewing court need not accept the conclusion and may independently examine and weigh the facts."). *See also* Bose Corp. v. Consumer's Union, 466 U.S. 485, 509-10 (1984). Although the formulation in text potentially turns "all issues relating to the application of law to facts" into "mixed questions," Monaghan, *supra* § 20.1 n.1, at 274 n.249, it also might be seen as emphasizing that federal review of factual issues is appropriate when the controlling rule is sufficiently new, vague, or unformed that its application to major factually defined classes of cases is uncertain, hence that additional rule-elaboration is required before the "constitutional significance" of paradigmatic cases is clear. *See supra* note 41 & *infra* note 77 and accompanying text.

[75] *See* Lockhart v. McCree, 476 U.S. 162, 168-69 n.3 (1986) ("[w]e are far from persuaded ... that the 'clearly erroneous' standard of Federal Rule of Civil Procedure 52(a)" and, by implication, analogous "presumption of correctness" standard of section 2254 "applies to the kind of legislative facts at issue here" (citing Dunagin v. City of Oxford, 718 F.2d 738, 748 n.8 (5th Cir. 1983) (*en banc*) (plurality opinion of Reaveley, J.))). *See also* Wisconsin v. Mitchell, 508 U.S. 476, 484 (1993) (question of statute's "operative" or "practical effect" on free speech interests is question on which reviewing court "may form [its] own judgment"). *Compare* Murray v. Giarratano, 492 U.S. 1, 10 (1989) (plurality opinion joined by four Justices) ("perceived difficulty of capital sentencing law and the general psychology of death-row inmates" are not "'factual findings,' presumably subject only to review under the 'clearly erroneous' standard," else "a different constitutional rule [would] apply in a different State if the district judge hearing that claim reached different conclusions") *with id.* at 27 & n.19 (Stevens, J., dissenting, joined by three Justices) (subjecting district court's findings on difficulty of capital sentencing law and psychology of capital inmates to "clearly erroneous" test and criticizing plurality for doing otherwise). "Legislative" or "social" facts are distinguished from "historical" facts by the former's capacity to be ascertained once for all cases and their dependence upon statistical as opposed to perceptual, experiential, or mechanical proof. *See generally* MICHAEL A. REBELL & ARTHUR R. BLOCK, EDUCATIONAL POLICY MAKING AND THE COURTS: AN EMPIRICAL STUDY OF JUDICIAL ACTIVISM 44-57, 447-50 (1982); Abram Chayes, *The Role of the Judge in Public Law Litigation,* 89 HARV. L. REV. 1281, 1297-301 (1976); Ronald Dworkin, *Social Sciences and Constitutional Rights: The Consequences of Uncertainty,* 6 J. L. & EDUC. 3, 5-7 (1977). *Lockhart* does not resolve — even its *dicta* does not directly address — the question of the proper standard of federal habeas corpus

(BB) Any other issue that presents a "need to guard against systemic bias" or "the ... systematic distortion of factfinding and law application" by state courts.[76]

(CC) Any other issue presenting a new or as yet not fully developed constitutional norm or rule that needs additional elaboration through federal judicial consideration of "a series of closely related situations involving a claim" under that constitutional rule.[77]

(b)   The state determination is conclusionary and does not indicate the factual basis for the conclusion reached.[78]

---

review of *state* court determinations of legislative fact. Nonetheless, the drift of the Court's thinking is clear: Because legislative facts define causal relationships that should link the same stimuli to the same effects no matter where and when the former are present, the determination whether such causal relationships exist does not simply affect but essentially controls the definition of the constitutional norm. Accordingly, to preserve its law-elaboration function, the reviewing court necessarily must control the fact-determination process. Legislative facts, therefore, are simply an extreme case falling within Professor Monaghan's second, "norm elaboration," special circumstance warranting *de novo* appellate and habeas corpus review. *See* Monaghan, *supra* § 20.1 n.1, at 276 (when "law application [to a given set of facts] necessitates an appreciable measure of further constitutional norm elaboration, the [reviewing] court's function is more accurately seen as law declaration, not law application" and *de novo* review is appropriate). Any other rule would enable courts in the 50 States to reach conflicting judgments about the controlling social fact, hence about the definition and scope of the underlying constitutional norm. *See Lockhart v. McCree*, *supra* at 168-69 n.3. Furthermore, legislative fact judgments may be less dependent than historical fact judgments upon credibility and demeanor determinations of the sort that trial, as opposed to reviewing, courts are especially competent to make.

[76] Monaghan, *supra* § 20.1 n.1, at 272 & n.237 (examples include coerced confession and death penalty cases, *supra* note 40, and "issues involving racial discrimination, especially by the state courts themselves or other state officials"). Systemic racial discrimination is implicated by claims attacking grand and petit jury selection procedures (*see, e.g.,* Rose v. Mitchell, 443 U.S. 545, 561 (1979); Castaneda v. Partida, 430 U.S. 482 (1977)); the prosecutorial exercise of peremptory challenges (*see, e.g.,* Batson v. Kentucky, 476 U.S. 79 (1986); Swain v. Alabama, 380 U.S. 202 (1965)); bias on the part of the trier of fact (*see, e.g.,* Turner v. Murray, 476 U.S. 28 (1986)); selective prosecution; and the like. *See* authority cited *supra* notes 56, 57. *See also supra* §§ 2.4e, 2.5, 2.6 (all discussing role of federal habeas corpus generally as means of protecting federal rights against systemic biases of state judges).

[77] Monaghan, *supra* § 20.1 n.1, at 273-75 (discussed, with examples, *supra* note 41). *See* Miller v. Fenton, 474 U.S. 104, 109-10 (1985). *See also* Container Corp. of Am. v. Franchise Tax Bd., 463 U.S. 159, 175-76 (1983).

[78] *See, e.g.,* Johnson v. Trigg, 28 F.3d 639, 644 (7th Cir. 1994) ("so-called finding" by state court, which "was simply an observation offered in the course of a ruling on an objection to evidence," is not type of "finding[ ] to which deference is due under section 2254(d)"; state appellate court's opinion also was not entitled to deference on relevant factual issue because opinion merely "endors[ed] ... the state's version of the facts" without "purport[ing] to make independent findings [of fact]"); Strozier v. Newsome, 871 F.2d 995, 998-1000 (11th Cir. 1989); Williams v. Lockhart, 849 F.2d 1134, 1137-38 (8th Cir. 1988); Beavers v. Lockhart, 755 F.2d 657,

(c)   The state determination did not address or resolve all of the controlling factual issues raised.[79]

---

663 (8th Cir. 1985); Peek v. Kemp, 746 F.2d 672, 676-79 (11th Cir. 1984), *cert. denied,* 479 U.S. 939 (1986); United States ex rel. Ballard v. Bengston, 702 F.2d 656, 663 (7th Cir. 1983) (hearing required because record does not show why trial judge concluded that pretrial motions were filed for dilatory purposes); Fowler v. Jago, 683 F.2d 983, 991 (6th Cir. 1982), *cert. denied,* 460 U.S. 1098 (1983); Thomas v. Estelle, 587 F.2d 695, 697 (5th Cir. 1979); Mason v. Balkcom, 531 F.2d 717, 722 (5th Cir. 1976) (hearing required because state court made no specific factual findings on ineffective assistance claim). *See also* Burden v. Zant, 510 U.S. 132 (1994) (*per curiam*) (noting but not agreeing or disagreeing with lower court's conclusion that statement in report that trial judge was required to file with state supreme court in every capital case did not deserve presumption of correctness because it "was not labeled a finding of fact or conclusion of law [and] amounted to the trial judge's mere personal 'impression' on an issue not subject to significant dispute" that was "contained in an administrative report").

[79] *See, e.g.,* Purkett v. Elem, 514 U.S. 765, 775-78 (1995) (Stevens, J., dissenting) (no deference due state court conclusion because governing rule requires three separate determinations and state courts only made first of three); Minnesota v. Dickerson, 508 U.S. 366, 383 (1993) (Rehnquist, C.J., dissenting) (direct review case) (because state court's findings were "imprecise and not directed expressly to the question" made dispositive by Court's new rule of law, Court should not defer to state court's findings); Wilkerson v. Texas, 493 U.S. 924, 925 (1989) (*mem.*) (Marshall, J., dissenting from denial of *certiorari*) (direct review case) (state court's factual findings do not discuss prosecutor's admission that race played part in peremptory challenges); Cabana v. Bullock, 474 U.S. 376, 388 n.5 (1986) (state courts did not make constitutionally necessary findings as to culpability of capitally sentenced defendant); *Townsend, supra,* 372 U.S. at 313 ("merits of the factual dispute were not resolved in the state hearing"); Perillo v. Johnson, 79 F.3d 441, 446 & n.6 (5th Cir. 1996) (state court factfindings on ineffective assistance did not address factual issue that was critical to assessment of counsel's possible conflict of interest); Armstead v. Scott, 37 F.3d 202, 208-09 (5th Cir. 1994), *cert. denied,* 514 U.S. 1071 (1995) (state court's factual findings did not address one of petitioner's central contentions); Chacon v. Wood, 36 F.3d 1459, 1465 (9th Cir. 1994) (state court's ruling on ineffective assistance of counsel did not include finding on central question of historical fact); Blackmon v. Scott, 22 F.3d 560, 566 (5th Cir. 1994) (evidentiary hearing ordered on petitioner's claim that state's "hiding" of witnesses before trial prejudiced him by preventing effective cross-examination at trial; state court finding "that it could not determine what ... counsel might have done differently had more time been given to prepare" not dispositive, given evidence that more preparation time would have enabled petitioner to produce transcripts of witnesses' prior inconsistent statements); Cumbie v. Singletary, 991 F.2d 715, 723-24 (11th Cir.), *cert. denied,* 510 U.S. 1031 (1993) (state court failed to identify precisely and to examine potential harm to child complainant in ruling that effects on child justified denial of petitioner's 6th Amendment right to face-to-face confrontation at trial); Hernandez v. Ylst, 930 F.2d 714, 720 (9th Cir. 1991); United States ex rel. Partee v. Lane, 926 F.2d 694, 700 (7th Cir. 1991), *cert. denied,* 502 U.S. 1116 (1992); Lesko v. Lehman, 925 F.2d 1527, 1539-40 (3d Cir.), *cert. denied,* 502 U.S. 898 (1991) (state court finding that plea agreement existed does not resolve issue whether plea was voluntary); McKenzie v. Risley, 915 F.2d 1396, 1398 (9th Cir. 1990) (findings concerning whether judge and prosecutor actually discussed petitioner's sentence during *ex parte* conversation about petitioner's case prior to sentencing do not resolve issue whether topics that were discussed might have influenced sentence imposed by trial court); Nelson v. Fulcomer, 911 F.2d 928, 938-39 (3d Cir. 1990) (remanding for hearing because state court

(d) The party would prevail if the federal court resolved in the party's favor factual questions not decided by the state court or if it made additional findings consistent with those made by the state court.[80]

(e) The state findings are capable of multiple interpretations, one of which entitles the party seeking a hearing to the outcome the party seeks.[81]

---

finding that petitioner asked incriminating question of jailhouse informant whom police planted in cell without being "prompted" does not resolve critical factual questions concerning what cellmate said to petitioner before petitioner asked incriminating question); Tukes v. Dugger, 911 F.2d 508, 514 & n.6 (11th Cir. 1990), *cert. denied,* 502 U.S. 898 (1991); Lawrence v. Armontrout, 900 F.2d 127, 130-31 (8th Cir. 1990) (no inexcusable neglect for failure to develop material facts in state court because state court decided against petitioner without reaching dispositive factual issue); Campaneria v. Reid, 891 F.2d 1014, 1019 (2d Cir. 1989) (state court did not resolve dispute); Weidner v. Thieret, 866 F.2d 958, 961-63 (7th Cir. 1989) (Posner, J.) (hearing required because state trial judge's oral ruling at suppression hearing was ambiguous and inexplicit with regard to critical credibility questions); Stockton v. Virginia, 852 F.2d 740, 743-45 (4th Cir. 1988), *cert. denied,* 489 U.S. 1071 (1989) (given absence of state court factfinding on critical question whether and how third party contacted juror during deliberations, state court finding of lack of prejudice not due deference and federal hearing required); Jones v. Davis, 835 F.2d 835, 838-40 (11th Cir.), *cert. denied,* 486 U.S. 1008 (1988) (state court hearing considered propriety of striking minority jurors under standard of Batson v. Kentucky, 476 U.S. 79 (1986), but not propriety under different standard of Swain v. Alabama, 380 U.S. 202 (1965); federal hearing required); Chaney v. Brown, 730 F.2d 1334, 1345 (10th Cir.), *cert. denied,* 469 U.S. 1090 (1984); Williams v. Maggio, 730 F.2d 1048, 1050 (5th Cir. 1984) (*per curiam*) ("state court did not address the sole issue presented to it by the habeas petitioner"); Sullivan v. Cuyler, 723 F.2d 1077, 1084-85 (3d Cir. 1983) (state court "never reached the heart of the conflict of interest inquiry"); Green v. Zant, 715 F.2d 551, 558-59 (11th Cir. 1983), *cert. denied,* 469 U.S. 1098 (1984); Speedy v. Wyrick, 702 F.2d 723, 726 (8th Cir. 1983), *cert. denied,* 471 U.S. 1019 (1985); Bishop v. Rose, 701 F.2d 1150, 1155 (6th Cir. 1983); Martin v. Texas, 694 F.2d 423, 425 (5th Cir. 1982); Fritz v. Spalding, 682 F.2d 782, 785 (9th Cir. 1982); Dickerson v. Alabama, 667 F.2d 1364, 1368 (11th Cir.), *cert. denied,* 459 U.S. 878 (1982) (state appellate court's omission of critical factual issues renders its decision "'not fairly supported by the record'"); Walker v. Solem, 648 F.2d 1188, 1191 (8th Cir. 1981), *cert. denied,* 460 U.S. 1091 (1983); Schmidt v. Hewitt, 573 F.2d 794, 801 (3d Cir. 1978) (facts suggesting that confessions secured by coercion were "simply ignored" by factfinders); *infra* para. (7); *infra* §§ 20.3e n.106 and accompanying text, 20.3e (para. (6)(n)).

[80] *See, e.g., Blackmon v. Scott, supra,* 22 F.3d at 566 (discussed *supra* note 79); Sandstrom v. Butterworth, 738 F.2d 1200, 1207 (11th Cir. 1984), *cert. denied,* 469 U.S. 1109 (1985); White v. Estelle, 685 F.2d 927, 928 (5th Cir. 1982) (district court findings that state concealed witness were consistent with state findings); Goodwin v. Balkcom, 684 F.2d 794, 804 (11th Cir. 1982), *cert. denied,* 460 U.S. 1098 (1983) (circuit court accepted "historical findings made by the state court concerning what [defendant's] trial counsel did to prepare for his trial" but went on to make factfindings as to "trial counsel's inactions and reasons therefor"); Fields v. Wyrick, 682 F.2d 154, 157 n.4 (8th Cir.), *rev'd on other grounds,* 459 U.S. 42 (1982) ("no part of the [state] court's version of the relevant events [was] inconsistent with [federal court's] conclusion that the confession was involuntary"). *See also supra* note 79 and sections referenced there.

[81] *See, e.g., Minnesota v. Dickerson, supra,* 508 U.S. at 383 (Rehnquist, C.J., dissenting) (discussed *supra* note 79); *Williams v. Maggio, supra,* 730 F.2d at 1050 ("The right to an

(2) Although the state court made express findings, it did so in the context of applying an erroneous legal standard.[82]

---

evidentiary hearing and to findings of fact intrinsically implies the right to a result not insulated from review by rails of garble."); Fowler v. Jago, 683 F.2d 983, 990 (6th Cir. 1982), *cert. denied,* 460 U.S. 1098 (1983) (citing Townsend v. Sain, 372 U.S. 293 (1963)); Leventhal v. Gavin, 396 F.2d 441 (1st Cir. 1968) *(per curiam), cert. denied,* 398 U.S. 941 (1970) (ambiguous wording of state court's denial left question whether finding was or was not made).

[82] *See, e.g.,* Kyles v. Whitley, 514 U.S. 419, 440 (1995) (discussed *supra* § 20.3c n.28); Stansbury v. California, 511 U.S. 318, 326-27 (1994) *(per curiam)* (direct review case) (state court's finding that defendant was not in "custody" when interrogation occurred is remanded because it was premised on improperly subjective legal definition of "custody"); *Minnesota v. Dickerson, supra,* 508 U.S. at 383 (Rehnquist, C.J., dissenting) (because state court made findings pursuant to "Fourth Amendment analysis which differs significantly from that now adopted by this Court," findings deserve no deference); Yates v. Evatt, 500 U.S. 391, 413-14 (1991) (state postconviction case) (Scalia, J., concurring in the judgment) (discussed *supra* § 20.3c n.28); *Townsend, supra* at 315; Rogers v. Richmond, 365 U.S. 534, 547 (1961) ("Historical facts found in the perspective framed by an erroneous legal standard cannot plausibly be expected to furnish the basis for correct conclusions if and merely because a correct standard is later applied to them."); In re Heidnik, 112 F.3d 105, 108, 111, 112 n.7 (3d Cir. 1997) (state court and district court judgments that prisoner was competent to waive rights, give up appeals, and be executed not due presumption of correctness because prior courts applied incorrect legal standard (state court assessed prisoner's sanity at time of execution, not his competence to waive rights; district court omitted "rationality" requirement in assessing competence)); Moran v. Godinez, 972 F.2d 263, 266 (9th Cir. 1992), *rev'd on other grounds,* 509 U.S. 389 (1993); Lafferty v. Cook, 949 F.2d 1546, 1551-56 (10th Cir. 1991), *cert. denied,* 504 U.S. 911 (1992) (factfindings accorded no deference because "state trial court's evaluation ... was infected by a misperception of the legal requirements"); Russell v. Lynaugh, 892 F.2d 1205, 1221 (5th Cir. 1989) (Johnson, J., dissenting) (hearing should have been held because state court findings may be based on incorrect legal standard); Smith v. Zant, 887 F.2d 1407, 1431-32, 1433 n.15 (11th Cir. 1989) *(en banc)* (Kravitch, J., concurring in part and dissenting in part) (same); Compton v. Butler, 887 F.2d 80, 81 (5th Cir. 1989) ("sentencing judge was unaware of discretionary sentencing alternatives"); Dunn v. Simmons, 877 F.2d 1275, 1279 (6th Cir. 1989), *cert. denied,* 494 U.S. 1061 (1990); Williams v. Lockhart, 849 F.2d 1134, 1137-38 (8th Cir. 1988); *Jones v. Davis, supra,* 835 F.2d at 838-40 (discussed *supra* note 79); Code v. Montgomery, 725 F.2d 1316, 1321 (11th Cir. 1984); Pryor v. Rose, 724 F.2d 525, 528 (6th Cir. 1984); *Sullivan v. Cuyler, supra,* 723 F.2d at 1084-85 (state courts' determination on attorney conflict-of-interest claim rendered prior to new Supreme Court standard); Spencer v. Zant, 715 F.2d 1562, 1582-83 (11th Cir. 1983) (state court misapplied legal standard for determining discrimination in capital sentencing); Fuller v. Luther, 575 F.2d 1098, 1101 (4th Cir. 1978); Lee v. Hopper, 499 F.2d 456, 461 (5th Cir.), *cert. denied,* 419 U.S. 1053 (1974); Seiling v. Eyman, 478 F.2d 211, 215 (9th Cir. 1973); *supra* § 20.3c (para. 6). *See also* Greene v. Georgia, 117 S. Ct. 578 (1996) *(per curiam)* (direct review case) (reversing conviction because state supreme court, misapplying Supreme Court's caselaw on federal courts' review of state factfindings in federal habeas corpus proceedings, improperly deferred to trial judge's factfindings); Schlup v. Delo, 513 U.S. 298, 333 (1995) (O'Connor, J., concurring) ("It is a paradigmatic abuse of discretion for a court to base its judgment on an erroneous view of the law." (citing Cooter & Gell v. Hartmarx Corp., 496 U.S. 384, 405 (1990)); Thornburg v. Gingles, 478 U.S. 30, 79 (1986) (Civil "Rule 52(a) does not inhibit an appellate court's power to correct ... a finding of fact ... predicated on a misunderstanding

(3)   Although a state trial court made findings, a state appellate court either did not rely on those findings or rejected them without making alternative findings.[83]

(4)   A state appellate court purported to make findings of fact (a) without evidentiary basis,[84] (b) without full and adequate argument on the factual issue, (c) without sufficient clarity,[85] or (d) by implicitly or explicitly

---

of the governing law"); United States Postal Service Bd. of Governors v. Aikens, 460 U.S. 711, 717 (1983) (remanding because "we cannot be certain that [lower court's] findings of fact ... were not influenced by its mistaken view of the law"); Hernandez v. Ylst, 930 F.2d 714, 720 (9th Cir. 1991) (no deference to state court factfindings required when findings were made in response to legal claim different from claim being addressed by federal court). *Cf.* Tinsley v. Borg, 895 F.2d 520, 525 (9th Cir. 1990), *cert. denied,* 498 U.S. 1091 (1991) (state trial judge presumed to have used correct legal standard); Campaneria v. Reid, 891 F.2d 1014, 1019 (2d Cir. 1989) (same).

[83] *See, e.g.,* Micheaux v. Collins, 944 F.2d 231, 232 & n.1 (5th Cir. 1991) (*en banc*) (*per curiam*), *cert. denied,* 502 U.S. 1115 (1992) (state trial court's finding of fact, which it denominated a "'proposed finding,'" entitled to no deference because it was never "adopted nor incorporated" by Texas Court of Criminal Appeals and was "directly inconsistent with that court's peremptory denial of relief"); Bailey v. MacDougall, 392 F.2d 155, 158-59 (4th Cir.), *cert. denied,* 393 U.S. 847 (1968) (*dicta*). *See also In re Heidnik, supra,* 112 F.3d at 112 n.7 (state trial court determination that prisoner was competent to be executed not due presumption of correctness because finding was still on appeal in state system at time federal court ruled on question whether petitioner was competent to waive appeals, so "presumption [of correctness] would not appear to be operative"). *But cf.* Pinkney v. Keene, 920 F.2d 1090, 1092 n.1 (2d Cir. 1990), *cert. denied,* 501 U.S. 1217 (1991) (because it was unclear whether state appellate court "rejected the facts as found by the [state] trial court, or simply concluded that those facts did not, as a matter of law, support" trial court's legal conclusion, federal court deferred to state trial court's factfindings).

[84] *See, e.g.,* Johnson v. Armontrout, 961 F.2d 748, 753-54 (8th Cir. 1992) (state appellate court's finding on direct appeal that jurors were impartial not entitled to deference because neither prosecutor nor ineffective trial counsel questioned jurors during *voir dire* to provide evidence to support finding); Smith v. Black, 904 F.2d 950, 975 (5th Cir. 1990), *vac'd & remanded on other grounds,* 503 U.S. 930 (1992); United States ex rel. Smith v. Fairman, 769 F.2d 386, 395 (7th Cir. 1985) (federal hearing required because state trial court did not hold hearing on controlling factual issues and state appellate court's factual determinations lacked evidentiary support). *See also* Parker v. Dugger, 498 U.S. 308, 316 (1991) ("To the extent there is ambiguity in the [state trial court's] order, we will not read [findings into] it [that are] against the weight of the evidence"); other authority discussed *supra* § 20.3(c) (para. (3)). *Cf.* Sumner v. Mata, 449 U.S. 539, 546 (1981) (state appellate court findings due presumption of correctness when based on "review of the trial court record," including transcript of trial court hearing).

[85] *See, e.g., Pinkney v. Keene, supra,* 920 F.2d at 1092 n.1 (given ambiguity of state appellate court's treatment of factual issue, suggestion in state appellate court's opinion that it disagreed with state trial court's factfindings is ignored and federal courts defer to state trial court's findings). *See also* Johnson v. Trigg, 28 F.3d 639, 644 (7th Cir. 1994) (state appellate court's opinion was not entitled to deference on relevant factual issue because opinion merely "endors[ed] ... the state's version of the facts" without "purport[ing] to make independent findings [of fact]").

making demeanor or credibility judgments of a type not within the competence of appellate judges.[86]

(5) The state factual determination was not made "by a state court of competent jurisdiction" over either "the subject matter or ... the person of the applicant."[87]

(6) The state factual determination was not made "in a proceeding to which

---

[86] *See* Cabana v. Bullock, 474 U.S. 376, 388 n.5 (1986) ("question whether the defendant killed, attempted to kill, or intended to kill, might in a given case turn on credibility determinations that could not be accurately made by an appellate court on the basis of a paper record"). In Sumner v. Mata I, 449 U.S. 539 (1981), the Supreme Court read section 2254(d) to require federal courts to accord state *appellate* court factfindings the same treatment due state trial court findings when (1) the appellate findings were based on "a review of the trial court record," (2) the petitioner "had an opportunity to be heard by the appellate court and his claim received plenary consideration," and (3) the petitioner, in lieu of a remand to the trial court, "requested" that the appellate court "determine the [factual] issue." *Id.* at 546. *Accord* Parke v. Raley, 506 U.S. 20, 36 (1992) (on habeas corpus, federal courts are bound to respect factual "conclusions of the state appellate court" (citing Marshall v. Lonberger, 459 U.S. 422, 435 (1983)); Parker v. Dugger, 498 U.S. 308, 320 (1991); *Cabana v. Bullock, supra* at 388 n.5; Sumner v. Mata II, 455 U.S. 591, 597 (1982); Andersen v. Thieret, 903 F.2d 526, 530-31 (7th Cir. 1990); Harriman v. Lynn, 901 F.2d 64, 65 n.1 (5th Cir. 1990); Towne v. Dugger, 899 F.2d 1104, 1110 (11th Cir. 1990); Tinsley v. Borg, 895 F.2d 520, 526 (9th Cir. 1990), *cert. denied,* 498 U.S. 1091 (1991); Smith v. Jago, 888 F.2d 399, 408 nn.5-6 (6th Cir. 1989), *cert. denied,* 495 U.S. 961 (1990) (credibility findings of state appellate court presumed correct, given that state trial court on postconviction review reiterated state appellate court findings made on direct review); Case v. Mondragon, 887 F.2d 1388, 1392 (10th Cir. 1989), *cert. denied,* 494 U.S. 1035 (1990); Dumond v. Lockhart, 885 F.2d 419, 422 (8th Cir. 1989) (state supreme court findings presumed correct); authority cited *supra* § 20.3c nn.30-31; *infra* § 20.3e n.94; *infra* § 20.3e (para. (6)(x)). *See also* Minnesota v. Dickerson, 508 U.S. 366, 378-79 (1993) (over dissent, Court on direct review of state conviction discerns and defers to appellate court's findings in regard to scope of and motivation behind police officer's pat-down search and seizure of drugs); Dispensa v. Lynaugh, 847 F.2d 211, 219-20 (5th Cir. 1988).

[87] 28 U.S.C. §§ 2254(d), 2254(d)(4) (1994) (superseded). *See* 28 U.S.C.A. § 2254(d) (West 1994 & Supp. 1998) (discussed *infra* § 30.2b); Ford v. Wainwright, 477 U.S. 399, 410 (1986); *id.* at 423 (Powell, J., concurring) (Florida Governor's finding that condemned prisoner was sane, hence eligible for execution, did not obviate need for federal hearing to adjudicate prisoner's constitutional right not to be executed if insane because finding not made by court of competent jurisdiction); Kimmelman v. Morrison, 477 U.S. 365, 390 (1986) (determinations at bail hearing not due presumption of correctness). *See also* Poyner v. Murray, 508 U.S. 931, 932 (1993) (Souter, J., respecting denial of *certiorari*) (court of appeals's dismissal "with prejudice" of action challenging constitutionality of electrocution as method of execution does not bar same parties from bringing same challenge in subsequent action because court of appeals acted on interlocutory appeal, as to which it clearly lacked jurisdiction). *See generally* Celotex Corp. v. Edwards, 514 U.S. 300, 306-07 (1995) (although generally forbidden, collateral attack on injunction is permissible if court issuing injunction had no subject-matter jurisdiction); *id.* at 331-32 (Stevens, J., dissenting) (same).

the [petitioner] and the State or an officer or agent thereof were parties."[88]

(7) The state court did not actually reach and determine issues of fact tendered by the party, either because it decided the party's claim "based upon a procedural issue" apart from the merits, or because it otherwise denied relief without "actually reach[ing] and decid[ing]" the merits.[89]

e. *Absence or inadequacy of state hearing.* Under *Townsend v. Sain*,[90] caselaw construing analogous provisions of superseded section 2254(d), and the terms of

---

[88] 28 U.S.C. § 2254(d) (1994) (superseded). *See* 28 U.S.C.A. § 2254(d) (West 1994 & Supp. 1998) (discussed *infra* § 30.2b). *See also* Burden v. Zant, 510 U.S. 132 (1994) (*per curiam*) (noting but not agreeing or disagreeing with lower court's conclusion that statement in report that trial judge was required to file with state supreme court in every capital case did not deserve presumption of correctness because it "was not labeled a finding of fact or conclusion of law [and] amounted to the trial judge's mere personal 'impression' on an issue not subject to significant dispute" that was "contained in an administrative report"); *Ford v. Wainwright, supra*, 477 U.S. at 416; *id.* at 425 (Powell, J., concurring); *id.* at 428 (O'Connor, J., concurring) (state administrative conclusion that condemned prisoner was sane, reached during proceedings in which prisoner could not present evidence or be heard, does not obviate need for federal hearing).

[89] *Townsend, supra*, 372 U.S. at 313-14. *See, e.g.*, 28 U.S.C. § 2254(d)(1) (1994) (superseded) ("merits of the factual dispute were not resolved in the State court hearing"); 28 U.S.C.A. § 2254(d)(2) (West 1994 & Supp. 1998) (discussed *infra* § 30.2b) (issue was not subject of "adjudicat[ion] on the merits" resulting in "decision" and "determination" of issue); Kelley v. Kaiser, 992 F.2d 1509, 1514-16 (10th Cir. 1993) (state court's summary rejection of claim of improper transfer from juvenile to adult court was based on petitioner's failure to satisfy burden of pleading, but federal law imposes burdens of pleading and proof on government, thus requiring evidentiary hearing); Smith v. Black, 904 F.2d 950, 975-76 (5th Cir. 1990), *vac'd & remanded on other grounds*, 503 U.S. 930 (1992) (because state supreme court rejected claim on procedural default grounds, it gave claim only "glancing ... scrutiny"); Williams v. Maggio, 730 F.2d 1048, 1050 (5th Cir. 1984); Sullivan v. Cuyler, 723 F.2d 1077, 1084-85 (3d Cir. 1983) (state court's decision on one issue prevented it from considering other issues); Dyas v. Lockhart, 705 F.2d 993, 996 (8th Cir.), *cert. denied*, 464 U.S. 982 (1983); Ashby v. Wyrick, 693 F.2d 789, 794 (8th Cir. 1982) (state courts refused on procedural grounds to render findings on issues surrounding dismissal of petitioner's direct appeal); Riley v. Gray, 674 F.2d 522, 527 (6th Cir.), *cert. denied*, 459 U.S. 958 (1982); Ford v. Parratt, 673 F.2d 232, 233 (8th Cir.), *cert. denied*, 459 U.S. 878 (1982); Wiley v. Sowders, 647 F.2d 642 (6th Cir.), *cert. denied*, 454 U.S. 1091 (1981) (state appellate court declined to rule on ineffective assistance claim for procedural reasons); Boyd v. Mintz, 631 F.2d 247, 249-51 (3d Cir. 1980); Dixon v. Caldwell, 471 F.2d 767, 769-70 (5th Cir. 1972) (state courts "rejected petitioner's claims solely because he did not support them by corroborative testimony"); *supra* para. (1)(c); *infra* § 20.3e (para. (6)(n)). In the circumstances discussed *infra* § 26.3b, this *Townsend* mandatory hearing category may require a federal hearing, even though the absence of a state hearing is due to the petitioner's failure to ask for one or otherwise to raise the claim properly in the state courts. *See, e.g.*, Hall v. Wainwright, 733 F.2d 766, 777-78 (11th Cir. 1984), *cert. denied*, 471 U.S. 1111 (1985).

[90] 372 U.S. 293 (1963).

the new presumption of correctness provision that supersedes former section 2254(d),[91] "a district court must hold an evidentiary hearing and determine the relevant facts when the state court has failed to [hold] a hearing" on dispositive factual issues presented by the petition.[92] To serve as the basis for denying a

---

[91] Former section 2254(d)'s reservation of the presumption of correctness for situations in which "the factfinding procedure employed by the State court was ... adequate to afford a full and fair hearing" (28 U.S.C. § 2254(d)(2) (1994)) and in which "the applicant ... receive[d] a full, fair and adequate hearing in the State court proceeding" (id., § 2254(d)(6)) paralleled *Townsend*'s declaration of a right to hearing when "the fact-finding procedure employed by the state court was not adequate to afford a full and fair fact hearing" (*Townsend, supra*, 372 U.S. at 313). *See also* 28 U.S.C. §§ 2254(d)(4), 2254(d)(5), 2254(d)(7) (all superseded) (rendering presumption inapplicable if "State court lacked jurisdiction of the subject matter or over the person of the applicant," "applicant was an indigent and the State court, in deprivation of his constitutional right, failed to appoint counsel to represent him in the State court proceeding, or "applicant was otherwise denied due process of law in the State court proceeding"). These same requirements are subsumed in whole or in part by the language of the new presumption of correctness provision, which withholds deference from any state court determination of a factual issue that was not "adjudicated on the merits in a State court proceeding," 28 U.S.C.A. § 2254(d) (West 1994 & Supp. 1998), or any state court factfinding "that was based on an unreasonable determination of the facts." *Id.* § 2254(d)(2). *See supra* §§ 20.2c, 20.3d n.33 and accompanying text; *infra* § 30.2b.

[92] Jackson v. Estelle, 570 F.2d 546, 547 (5th Cir. 1978) (*per curiam*). *See, e.g.,* Ford v. Wainwright, 477 U.S. 399, 410 (1986) (plurality opinion) (hearing required unless state trier of fact reasonably found relevant facts after full hearing); *Townsend, supra,* 372 U.S. at 312-13; Glock v. Singletary, 84 F.3d 385, 386 (11th Cir.), *cert. denied,* 117 S. Ct. 616 (1996) (petitioner entitled to evidentiary hearing because claim of ineffective assistance is "not meritless on its face" and "has heretofore been resolved on the record, without an evidentiary hearing" in either state or federal court); Toney v. Gammon, 79 F.3d 693, 696-97 (8th Cir. 1996) (petitioner entitled to evidentiary hearing on substantial claims of ineffective assistance on which state court failed to hold hearing); Perillo v. Johnson, 79 F.3d 441, 444-45 (5th Cir. 1996) (petitioner entitled to federal evidentiary hearing because state court proceedings did not include hearing on factual questions that could be dispositive in resolving claim of conflict of interest by trial counsel); Houston v. Lockhart, 982 F.2d 1246, 1250-53 (8th Cir. 1993) (*en banc*) (district court erred in denying hearing to petitioner who had alleged sufficient grounds for release and whose allegations were "not admitted by the State, ... not palpably incredible, and ... never the subject of a hearing in state court"); Tate v. Wood, 963 F.2d 20, 24 (2d Cir. 1992) (remanding for hearing on claims of prosecutorial suppression of evidence and state curtailment of accused's ability to conduct own defense because state courts did not hold hearing on claims); James v. Singletary, 957 F.2d 1562, 1575 (11th Cir. 1992) (district court should have held hearing on petitioner's claim of incompetency to stand trial because state courts erroneously rejected claim "without a hearing on the basis that it failed to allege facts sufficient to warrant relief"); Heiser v. Ryan, 951 F.2d 559 (3d Cir. 1991) (district court should have held hearing on voluntariness of plea because state courts never conducted evidentiary hearing on issue); Lesko v. Lehman, 925 F.2d 1527, 1539 (3d Cir.), *cert. denied,* 502 U.S. 898 (1991) (remanded for hearing on voluntariness of plea, as to which no state court hearing had been held); Capps v. Sullivan, 921 F.2d 260, 261-62 (10th Cir. 1990) (state findings not given deference and evidentiary hearing ordered because state court held no evidentiary hearing and refused to hear evidence proffered by petitioner); Becton v. Barnett, 920 F.2d 1190, 1192 (4th Cir. 1990) (evidentiary hearing on ineffective assistance claim required because state courts summarily

federal hearing, a prior state hearing must have been (1) "on the merits" of all the dispositive factual issues, (2) a formal, judicial hearing, and (3) "full and fair."[93] Administrative procedures, oral argument, and other nonjudicial or nonevidentiary hearings do not obviate the need for a federal hearing.[94]

---

denied claim without hearing); Tiller v. Esposito, 911 F.2d 575, 578 n.6 (11th Cir. 1990) (district court improperly deferred to implied state court factfinding of competence to stand trial, even though state court never held hearing on issue; remanded for hearing on competence question); Bouchillon v. Collins, 907 F.2d 589 (5th Cir. 1990) (because state trial court did not hold hearing on competence to stand trial, relying instead on statements of trial counsel and trial judge's own observations, federal hearing required); Stano v. Dugger, 901 F.2d 898, 899 (11th Cir. 1990) (*en banc*) ("If there has been no evidentiary hearing in state court on an issue raised on habeas corpus, one is required if petitioner alleges facts which, if true, would entitle him to relief "); Lawrence v. Armontrout, 900 F.2d 127, 129-31 (8th Cir. 1990) (petitioner who was unable to prove prejudice prong of ineffective assistance of counsel in state courts because no state forum was available is entitled to federal hearing on issue); Dick v. Scroggy, 882 F.2d 192, 196-97 (6th Cir. 1989); Keller v. Petsock, 853 F.2d 1122, 1129-30 (3d Cir. 1988); Estock v. Lane, 842 F.2d 184, 186-88 (7th Cir. 1988) (state court failed to hold hearing on competency to stand trial); Harich v. Wainwright, 813 F.2d 1082, 1090 (11th Cir. 1987) ("In cases where a petitioner raises a colorable claim of ineffective assistance, and where there has not been a state or federal hearing on this claim, we must remand to the district court for an evidentiary hearing."); United States ex. rel. Smith v. Fairman, 769 F.2d 386, 395 (7th Cir. 1985); Wade v. Lockhart, 763 F.2d 999, 1001 (8th Cir. 1985) (state court's failure to hold hearing after defendant claimed financial inability to retain counsel may violate 14th Amendment and necessitates federal hearing); Young v. Duckworth, 733 F.2d 482, 484 (7th Cir. 1984); Narcisse v. Maggio, 725 F.2d 969 (5th Cir. 1984) (*per curiam*); Hilliard v. Spalding, 719 F.2d 1443, 1447 (9th Cir. 1983), *cert. denied,* 479 U.S. 1055 (1987); Doescher v. Estelle, 666 F.2d 285, 287 (5th Cir. 1982) (petitioner denied evidentiary hearing on 4th Amendment claims in state court); Martinez v. Romero, 661 F.2d 143, 145 (10th Cir. 1981) (*per curiam*); Walker v. Wilmot, 603 F.2d 1038, 1042 (2d Cir. 1979), *cert. denied,* 449 U.S. 885 (1980); Schram v. Cupp, 425 F.2d 612, 615 (9th Cir. 1970).

[93] *Townsend, supra,* 372 U.S. at 313. *See* Herrera v. Collins, 506 U.S. 390, 441 (1993) (Blackmun, J., dissenting on other grounds) ("If, as is the case here, the petition raises factual questions and the State has failed to provide a full and fair hearing, the district court is required to hold an evidentiary hearing."). *Cf.* Smith v. Jago, 888 F.2d 399, 407 n.4 (6th Cir. 1989), *cert. denied,* 495 U.S. 961 (1990) ("review by a state appellate court of the trial record constitutes a 'hearing' as is contemplated by [superseded] 28 U.S.C. § 2254(d)"); *infra* para. (6).

[94] *See, e.g., Ford v. Wainwright, supra,* 477 U.S. at 416 (because of informality and lack of essential elements of full and fair hearing, state administrative determination of sanity is insufficient to absolve federal court of duty to ascertain condemned prisoner's sanity, given that sanity is constitutionally mandated prerequisite to execution); Denton v. Ricketts, 728 F.2d 489, 492 (10th Cir. 1984) (federal magistrate judge's investigation does not qualify as hearing; judicial hearing required); Jensen v. Satran, 651 F.2d 605, 608 (8th Cir. 1981), *cert. denied,* 460 U.S. 1007 (1983) (hearing before prison disciplinary board is insufficient); Scott v. Estelle, 567 F.2d 632, 633-34 (5th Cir. 1978) (*per curiam*). *See also* Burden v. Zant, 510 U.S. 132 (1994) (*per curiam*) (noting but not agreeing or disagreeing with lower court's conclusion that statement in report that trial judge was required to file with state supreme court in every capital case did not deserve presumption of correctness because it "was not labeled a finding of fact or conclusion of law [and] amounted to the trial judge's mere personal 'impression' on an issue not subject to significant

Even if the state court purported to conduct a hearing, that hearing will not suffice to avoid a federal hearing unless it was "full and fair." The state court proceeding is inadequate if:

(1) Although a state court conducted a hearing, the party relies upon "substantial newly discovered evidence" that "bear[s] upon the constitutionality of the applicant's detention" and that "could not reasonably have been presented to the state trier of facts." [95]

(2) Whether or not the state court conducted a hearing, "the material facts were not adequately developed" in state court for a reason "not attributable to the inexcusable neglect of petitioner."[96] In order to obtain

---

dispute" that was "contained in an administrative report"). On the question of the sufficiency of evidentiary proceedings in which affidavits substitute for in-court testimony, *see infra* para. (6)(x). As discussed *supra* § 20.3d (para. (4)), the holding in Sumner v. Mata I, 449 U.S. 539 (1981), that appellate findings sometimes are due a presumption of correctness does not overrule the line of cases dating back to *Townsend v. Sain* (*e.g.*, Harris v. Oliver, 645 F.2d 327, 329-30 (5th Cir.), *cert. denied*, 454 U.S. 1109 (1981)) that requires a federal hearing whenever the state trial court denied the petitioner a full and fair evidentiary hearing. Rather, *Sumner I* requires state appellate findings to have a proper evidentiary basis before they may obviate the need for federal reconsideration. *See* Cabana v. Bullock, 474 U.S. 376, 388 n.5 (1986); United States ex. rel. Smith v. Fairman, 769 F.2d 386, 395 (7th Cir. 1985). *But cf.* Camarillo v. Estelle, 670 F.2d 473, 475 (5th Cir. 1981).

[95] *Townsend, supra,* 372 U.S. at 313, 317 (quoted and reaffirmed in *Herrera v. Collins, supra,* 506 U.S. at 400 (majority opinion)). *See, e.g., Ford v. Wainwright, supra,* 477 U.S. at 411-12, 416-18 (federal hearing required on petitioner's present mental condition which, he claims, deteriorated since trial); Price v. Johnston, 334 U.S. 266, 291 (1948); Chacon v. Wood, 36 F.3d 1459, 1465-66 (9th Cir. 1994) (district court should have granted evidentiary hearing because petitioner's claim was predicated on "newly discovered evidence" and therefore fell within *Townsend*'s fourth factor; cases falling within fourth factor are not subject to analysis of cause and prejudice under Keeney v. Tamayo-Reyes, 504 U.S. 1 (1992), which applies exclusively to *Townsend*'s fifth factor); Allen v. Montgomery, 728 F.2d 1409, 1412 n.2 (11th Cir. 1984) (*dicta*); Walker v. Lockhart, 726 F.2d 1238, 1265 (8th Cir.), *cert. denied,* 468 U.S. 1222 (1984) (Arnold, J., concurring) (discovery of exculpatory diary entry); Thomas v. Zant, 697 F.2d 977, 987-88 (11th Cir. 1983), *vac'd & remanded on other grounds,* 478 U.S. 1016 (1986) (trial counsel's newly introduced affidavit admitting lack of strategy creates need for hearing on ineffective assistance); Guice v. Fortenberry, 661 F.2d 496, 500 (5th Cir. 1981) (*en banc*); Quigg v. Crist, 616 F.2d 1107, 1112 (9th Cir.), *cert. denied,* 449 U.S. 992 (1980); Austin v. Swenson, 522 F.2d 168, 169-70 (8th Cir. 1975); McDonald v. Arkansas, 501 F.2d 385, 387 (8th Cir.), *cert. denied,* 419 U.S. 1004 (1974) (newly discovered evidence undermining veracity of complaining witness's testimony); Selz v. California, 423 F.2d 702, 703 (9th Cir. 1970) (*per curiam*); *infra* para. (3). *See also infra* para (2). *Cf.* United States v. Barboa, 777 F.2d 1420, 1423 (10th Cir. 1985) (hearing required to determine veracity of new evidence adduced to show that coconspirator was government agent); Harper v. Grammer, 654 F. Supp. 515 (D. Neb. 1987).

[96] *Townsend, supra,* 372 U.S. at 313, 317. *See, e.g., Ford v. Wainwright, supra,* 477 U.S. at 411-13; Boyd v. Dutton, 405 U.S. 1, 3 (1972) (*per curiam*). *Cf.* 28 U.S.C. § 2254(d)(3) (1994) (superseded) (using same language as *Townsend* but subject to different interpretation for reasons discussed *supra* § 20.2c).

a hearing on the ground that material facts were not adequately developed in the state courts, the party (usually, but not always, the petitioner[97]) must show that material facts pertaining to a federal claim or defense were not developed adequately in state court [98] and that the failure to develop the facts was not "inexcusable."[99] *Townsend* originally defined "inexcusable neglect" very narrowly as the petitioner's knowing and intelligent waiver of the right — as opposed to merely her attorney's inadvertent failure — to present the evidence she now proffers.[100] As a

---

[97] *Cf.* Craker v. Procunier, 756 F.2d 1212, 1214 (5th Cir. 1985) ("both logic and equity require imposition on the state of the same inexcusable neglect ... standard imposed on petitioners as a prerequisite to a federal hearing"; federal hearing denied because state did not prove that failure to develop material facts at state hearing was excusable); *supra* §§ 20.1c n.34, 20.2c n.47.

[98] The category of "material facts that were not adequately developed in the state courts" is broader than the "conventional notion of newly discovered evidence." *Townsend, supra,* 372 U.S. at 317, 321-22 (hearing required because prosecution witness at state hearing did not volunteer full facts regarding truth serum used to obtain confession). *See supra* note 95 ("newly discovered evidence" cases). Examples of previously omitted material evidence include: Tamayo-Reyes v. Keeney, 926 F.2d 1492, 1500 (9th Cir.), *rev'd on other grounds,* 504 U.S. 1 (1992) (material evidence omitted from state hearing included "critical questions bearing on petitioner's claim that his ... plea to manslaughter was involuntary because the interpreter failed to translate essential information about petitioner's rights and the nature of the offense to which he was pleading"); Moore v. Kemp, 809 F.2d 702, 718-30 (11th Cir.) *(en banc), cert. denied,* 481 U.S. 1054 (1987) (federal hearing required because state court denied petitioner access to probation file of critical prosecution witness after reviewing it *in camera,* thereby preventing petitioner from adducing evidence relevant to claim that prosecutor at trial unconstitutionally withheld information about promises made to witness to secure his testimony); Williams v. Griswald, 743 F.2d 1533, 1544 (11th Cir. 1984), *cert. denied,* 470 U.S. 1088 (1985) (material facts concerning state's knowledge of false testimony were not developed at state hearing); Folsten v. Allsbrook, 691 F.2d 184, 186 (4th Cir. 1982), *cert. denied,* 461 U.S. 939 (1983); Marble v. Edwards, 457 F.2d 759, 760 (5th Cir. 1972) *(per curiam)* (results of important ballistics test were not before state trier of fact); Hunter v. Swenson, 442 F.2d 625, 631 (8th Cir.), *cert. denied,* 404 U.S. 863 (1971) (witness to plea bargain did not testify during state hearing); United States ex rel. Maselli v. Reincke, 383 F.2d 129, 131 (2d Cir. 1967) ("glaring absence" from state court record of "crucial testimony ... which was then available," warranted federal hearing). The incomplete development, as well as the absence, of material evidence at the state court hearing may qualify under this basis for an evidentiary hearing and for avoiding the presumption of correctness. *See, e.g.,* Strozier v. Newsome, 871 F.2d 995, 998-1000 (11th Cir. 1989) (evidence on waiver of right to counsel "ambiguous," "contradictory," incomplete, and inaccurate); Code v. Montgomery, 725 F.2d 1316, 1322 (11th Cir. 1984) (vital testimony at state hearing was "sketchy"); King v. Ponte, 717 F.2d 635, 639 (1st Cir. 1983) (state hearing left "too many open questions"); Lufkins v. Solem, 716 F.2d 532, 540 (8th Cir. 1983), *cert. denied,* 467 U.S. 1219 (1984) (counsel performed poorly at state hearing, hence facts not fully developed).

[99] *Townsend, supra,* 372 U.S. at 317.

[100] *Id.* (discussed *supra* § 20.1b n.21 and accompanying text) ("deliberate bypass" (citing Fay v. Noia, 372 U.S. 391, 435-38 (1963))); Price v. Johnston, 334 U.S. 266, 291 (1948). *See, e.g.,* Streetman v. Lynaugh, 812 F.2d 950, 958 (5th Cir. 1987); Rogers v. Israel, 746 F.2d 1288, 1295-

result of the Supreme Court's broadening of the definition of inexcusable neglect in *Keeney v. Tamayo-Reyes*,[101] and Congress' codification and further broadening of the *Tamayo-Reyes* definition in the Antiterrorism and Effective Death Penalty Act of 1996 (AEDPA),[102] the following standards now govern the right to a hearing in cases in which the omission of material facts from the state record is attributable to the petitioner:

(a) In cases that are *not* governed by AEDPA,[103] the relevant standard continues to be the one adopted by the Court in *Tamayo-Reyes*, which (i) expands the *Townsend* category of "inexcusable neglect" to encompass all failures to produce evidence in the state courts that can be attributed to the party *or to her attorney*,[104] (ii) treats

---

96 (7th Cir. 1984); Jones v. Parke, 734 F.2d 1142, 1148 (6th Cir. 1984); Chaney v. Brown, 730 F.2d 1334, 1345 (10th Cir.), *cert. denied*, 469 U.S. 1090 (1984); Bishop v. Rose, 701 F.2d 1150, 1155 (6th Cir. 1983); Thomas v. Zant, 697 F.2d 977, 981-89 (11th Cir. 1983), *vac'd & remanded on other grounds*, 478 U.S. 1016 (1986); Guice v. Fortenberry, 661 F.2d 496, 507 n.25 (5th Cir. 1981) (*en banc*); Walker v. Wilmot, 603 F.2d 1038, 1042 (2d Cir. 1979), *cert. denied*, 449 U.S. 885 (1980) (trial judge's statement to defense counsel concerning defendant's right to testify was not sufficient, "in the case of a young defendant with no previous criminal experience," to render defendant's failure to testify inexcusably neglectful); Hawkins v. Bennett, 423 F.2d 948, 950 (8th Cir. 1970) (hearing required because petitioner of limited education was without counsel in state habeas corpus proceedings and was unable to develop material facts).

101 504 U.S. 1 (1992) (discussed *supra* §§ 20.1b nn.18-22 and accompanying text, 20.2c).

102 Pub. L. 104-132, 110 Stat. 1214 (1996).

103 For an explanation of the categories of cases to which AEDPA does and does not apply, see *supra* § 3.4.

104 *See Keeney v. Tamayo-Reyes*, *supra*, 504 U.S. at 5-9 (in Wainwright v. Sykes, 433 U.S. 72 (1977), and its progeny, Court rejected "deliberate bypass" test for handling petitioners' and counsel's defaults of *legal* claims in state court, and "it is ... irrational to distinguish between failing to properly assert a federal [legal] claim in state court and failing in state court to properly develop [the evidence supporting] such a claim, and to apply to the latter a remnant of a decision that is no longer upheld with regard to the former"; "concerns that motivated the rejection of the deliberate bypass standard in *Wainwright* ... and other cases are equally applicable to this case"). *See* Mathis v. Zant, 975 F.2d 1493, 1497 (11th Cir. 1992); Rosenwald v. United States, 898 F.2d 585, 588 (7th Cir. 1990); Byrd v. Armontrout, 880 F.2d 1, 7 (8th Cir. 1989), *cert. denied*, 494 U.S. 1019 (1990). *But see Keeney v. Tamayo-Reyes*, *supra*, 504 U.S. at 19-20 (O'Connor, J., dissenting) ("The[ ] cases [the majority cites in favor of its decisions to limit *Townsend*] all concern the question whether the federal court will *consider* the merits of the claim, that is, whether the court has the *authority* to upset a judgment affirmed on direct appeal.... The question we are considering here is quite different. Here, the Federal District Court has already determined that it will consider the claimed constitutional violation; the only question is how the court will go about it. When it comes to determining whether a hearing is to be held to resolve a claim that is already properly before a court, the federalism concerns underlying our procedural default cases are diminished somewhat. By this point, our concern is less with encroaching on the territory of the state courts than it is with managing the territory of the federal courts in a manner that will best implement our

those failures as procedural defaults[105] generally barring a federal hearing, and (iii) allows a petitioner who committed such a default to obtain a hearing only by demonstrating *one* of the following circumstances: (A) No default of state procedural requirements occurred, *e.g.*, because the state has waived any reliance on the default, because state court forums remain open to hear the evidence (in which case, the appropriate procedure is to dismiss the petition without prejudice or hold it in abeyance pending exhaustion of the remaining state remedy), or because the state courts decided the claim on the law, not the facts;[106] (B) the failure

---

responsibility to consider habeas petitions.... Federalism, comity, and finality are ... less significantly advanced [by restrictions on habeas corpus proceedings that come into play] once relitigation properly occurs...."); *id.* at 24 (Kennedy, J., dissenting).

[105] *See generally infra* § 26.1 (discussing procedural default doctrine developed in Wainwright v. Sykes, 433 U.S. 72 (1977)).

[106] As is developed at length *infra* § 26.2, under the *Sykes* or "adequate and independent state grounds" doctrine, a default of state court procedural rules is required before a federal court can deny relief on an otherwise determinative legal or factual question in habeas corpus proceedings on the basis of the party's failure to present the question in the state courts. A default exists only if five prerequisites are satisfied — (1) the state timely asserted the default as a basis for denying federal review, *see infra* § 26.2a; (2) a state procedural rule was applicable under the circumstances, *see infra* § 26.2b; (3) the party violated the applicable state procedural rule, *see infra* § 26.2c; (4) the state procedural rule was "adequate" and its application was not dependent on the resolution of a federal question of law, *see infra* § 26.2d; and (5) the state courts unambiguously relied on the default as a basis for denying relief, *see infra* § 26.2e. Prerequisite (1) is likely to apply in the hearing context in the same manner as in other procedural default contexts. *See, e.g.*, Miller v. Lockhart, 65 F.3d 676, 680 (8th Cir. 1995) (state waived *Tamayo-Reyes* procedural bar to petitioner's introduction of new evidence at federal evidentiary hearing by raising defense for first time in post-hearing briefing). *See infra* §§ 23.2a, 26.2a, 28.3c. Prerequisites (2) and (3) often will be satisfied in the hearing context, given the rule in most States that litigants must present the state courts with any evidence on the basis of which the litigant seeks relief — assuming that the party exhausted *all* available forums for presenting the material evidence and inexcusably failed to offer it. In the event, however, that a state remedy (say, a state postconviction procedure) remains available notwithstanding the litigant's failure to adduce the evidence in a prior proceeding (say, at trial), then no default has yet occurred. *See, e.g., infra* § 26.2b (para. (5)). Instead, the petitioner can be faulted only for having failed to exhaust state remedies. *See infra* § 23.3c (discussing, *inter alia*, requirement of exhaustion of factual, as well as legal, claims). In that event, the proper procedure is either to dismiss the case without prejudice pending exhaustion of state remedies, *see supra* §§ 11.1, 15.2d n.74; *infra* § 23.1 nn.14-16 and accompanying text, or, in a capital case in which maintenance of a federal court stay of execution is important, to hold the case in abeyance in federal court while exhaustion occurs in state court, *see supra* §§ 11.1, 13.3. *See also infra* § 23.2a (possibility that state and district court will waive exhaustion requirement in this situation). As in the procedural default context (*see infra* § 26.2c), a petitioner self-evidently cannot be deemed to have defaulted if she did everything she could to comply with the applicable state rule. *See, e.g.*, Correll v. Stewart, 137 F.3d 1404, 1413 (9th Cir. 1998) ("Simply put, the state cannot successfully oppose a petitioner's request for a state court evidentiary hearing, then argue in federal habeas

to present the evidence in state court is "excusable" because there is "cause" for and "prejudice" from that failure;[107] or (C) the

---

proceedings that the petitioner should be faulted for not succeeding."); Jones v. Wood, 114 F.3d 1002, 1012 (9th Cir. 1997) (petitioner entitled to federal hearing because state court deprived him of opportunity to adduce relevant facts by dismissing personal restraint petition without hearing). *See also* Wright v. Gramley, 125 F.3d 1038, 1043-45 (7th Cir. 1997) (remanding to district court to allow *pro se* petitioner to submit affidavit to explain failure to develop facts in state court). Prerequisite (4) is not satisfied, and a federal hearing is required, if the procedure available for the presentation of evidence in the state courts was unduly restricted or otherwise unfair or inadequate. *See* authority cited *infra* note 107; *infra* §§ 23.4, 26.2d, 27.3, 28.3c. Prerequisite (5) is not satisfied, and a federal hearing is required, if the state courts decided the claim against the party, not on the insufficiency of the party's evidence to make out the claim, but instead on a legal ground unaffected by the absence of the material evidence on which the party now seeks to rely. *See, e.g.,* Lawrence v. Armontrout, 900 F.2d 127, 130-31 (8th Cir. 1990) (no inexcusable neglect bar to hearing on new material facts because state court decided against petitioner without reaching dispositive factual issue); Sullivan v. Cuyler, 723 F.2d 1077, 1084-85 (3d Cir. 1983) (federal hearing on new evidence required because, in resolving matter, state court "never reached the heart of the conflict of interest inquiry"); other authority discussed *supra* §§ 20.3c (para. (4)), 20.3d (para. (1)(c)); *infra* § 20.3e (6)(n)).

[107] *Tamayo-Reyes, supra,* 504 U.S. at 11 ("Respondent Tamayo-Reyes is entitled to an evidentiary hearing if he can show cause for his failure to develop the facts in state-court proceedings and actual prejudice resulting from that failure."). *Accord* McCleskey v. Zant, 499 U.S. 467, 490, 494 (1991) (avoiding finding of "inexcusable neglect" "demands more from a petitioner than [satisfying] the standard of deliberate abandonment"; petitioner must "show cause for failing [to develop the material facts] and prejudice therefrom as those concepts have been defined in our procedural default decisions"). Extended discussions of the "cause and prejudice" standard in the procedural default and successive petition contexts — discussions that are incorporated by reference here — are presented *infra* §§ 26.3, 28.3c. Among the bases for "cause" that *Tamayo-Reyes* itself recognizes — and that are discussed at greater length in the referenced sections — are: constitutionally ineffective assistance of counsel at those trial and appellate proceedings, and the small number of state postconviction proceedings, in which the 6th Amendment right to counsel applies; "objective factors external to the defense [that] ... impede counsel's efforts" to present evidence in the state courts; "a showing that the factual or legal basis for a claim was not reasonably available to counsel"; and proof that "'"some interference by officials,'" Brown v. Allen, 344 U.S. 443, 486 (1953), made [the presentation of evidence] impracticable," including interference through "the denial by a court of a full and fair hearing" or "where facts were inadequately developed because of interference from [law enforcement or prosecutorial] officials." *Tamayo-Reyes, supra,* 504 U.S. at 10-11 n.5. *See, e.g., id.* at 12-13 (O'Connor, J., dissenting) (under Court's holding, hearings are still required when "material facts ... were unknown at the time [of the state hearing] or ... the state denied a full and fair opportunity to develop them" or when, for some other reason not attributable to petitioner, the absence of evidence renders state court's factfindings "dubious"); *Townsend, supra,* 372 U.S. at 317, 321-22 (hearing required because prosecution witness at state hearing withheld full facts regarding truth serum used to obtain confession); Rhoden v. Rowland, 10 F.3d 1457, 1460 (9th Cir. 1993) (failure to develop facts regarding claim of unconstitutional shackling not "inexcusable" because petitioner "took all steps possible to make a timely record of prejudice" during and after trial and because state trial and appellate courts limited scope of inquiry; contrary to state's claim, petitioner could not

"reasonably" be expected to prejudice client by questioning jurors during trial and thereby focusing greater attention on shackles); Spitzweiser-Wittgenstein v. Newton, 978 F.2d 1195 (10th Cir. 1992) (inadequate development of material facts requires remand for hearing because state courts refused to hear evidence despite petitioner's reasonable efforts to present it); Johnson v. Armontrout, 961 F.2d 748, 753-54 (8th Cir. 1992) (state appellate court's finding on direct appeal that jurors were impartial was not entitled to deference because ineffective trial counsel did not adequately question jurors during *voir dire*); Williams v. Whitley, 940 F.2d 132, 133-34 (5th Cir. 1991) (district court erred in denying evidentiary hearing on prosecutorial suppression of evidence claim concerning "recently disclosed police report [that] has never been the subject of an evidentiary hearing"); Smith v. Freeman, 892 F.2d 331, 339-40 (3d Cir. 1989) (no inexcusable neglect because "[a]ll attempts by counsel to probe the issue ... were blocked by the court" at trial and because state postconviction court "summarily dismissed" petition as previously litigated at trial; when petitioner's or counsel's ignorance of facts or law is due to counsel's insufficient preparation or other neglect, court will not find inexcusable neglect); Ross v. Kemp, 785 F.2d 1467, 1476-77 (11th Cir. 1986) (neglect "excusable" if failure to discover jury records during state postconviction proceedings was due to misrepresentations of state official); Smith v. Wainwright, 741 F.2d 1248, 1256 (11th Cir. 1984), *cert. denied,* 470 U.S. 1088 (1985) (prosecutorial suppression of evidence forestalled development of facts at state hearing); Bibby v. Tard, 741 F.2d 26, 31 (3d Cir. 1984) (judge excluded information); Williams v. Maggio, 730 F.2d 1048, 1050 (5th Cir. 1984) (petitioner did not receive sufficient notice of state hearing, hence evidence not developed); Owen v. Duckworth, 727 F.2d 643, 645 (7th Cir. 1984) (state court terminated hearing before petitioner presented all his evidence); Jones v. Wainwright, 490 F.2d 1222, 1224-25 (5th Cir. 1974) (absence of eyewitness to crime never explained by prosecution; because her knowledge was so vital and her absence so unusual, court orders hearing); Cooper v. Picard, 428 F.2d 1351, 1353-54 (1st Cir. 1970) (police confrontation with defendant in absence of counsel shifts burden to state to prove that "in-court identification was independent of the tainted line-up"; hearing required because state did not meet burden of proof in state proceedings); the *Ford, Walker,* and *McDonald* decisions discussed *supra* note 95; other decisions cited *infra* paras. (3)-(6). *See also* Dobbs v. Zant, 506 U.S. 357, 359 (1993) (*per curiam*) ("delay in discovery" of transcript is excused, and court of appeals's refusal to consider evidence is reversed, because "delay resulted substantially from the State's own erroneous assertions that closing arguments had not been transcribed"; petitioner's "position that he legitimately relied on the State's representation is well taken"); Vasquez v. Hillery, 474 U.S. 254, 260 (1986) (exhaustion of remedies decision) (district court properly supplemented record with sophisticated computer-generated analyses of jury discrimination to which petitioner, acting *pro se*, did not have access at state hearing); Birt v. Montgomery, 709 F.2d 690, 696 (11th Cir. 1983), *cert. denied,* 469 U.S. 874 (1984) (if petitioner was not inexcusably negligent for failing to present evidence to state trial court, he also was not inexcusably negligent for failing to challenge adequacy of state hearing on direct appeal). *Cf.* Griffin v. Wainwright, 760 F.2d 1505, 1516 (11th Cir. 1985), *vac'd & remanded on other grounds,* 476 U.S. 1112 (1986) (petitioner did not establish that his failure to develop the material facts was excusable because he "ha[d] not shown that he utilized any means more stringent than a mere 'request' to obtain the records"); Craker v. Procunier, 756 F.2d 1212, 1214 (5th Cir. 1985) (discussed *supra* note 97); Neron v. Tierney, 841 F.2d 1197, 1199-200 (1st Cir.), *cert. denied,* 488 U.S. 832 (1988) (upon post-trial discovery that juror had been romantically involved with defendant's son, state trial court conducted hearing and, without summoning juror, found no bias present; federal hearing not appropriate because state court held "fair" hearing and information that did not come to light "was not because of roadblocks unfairly erected by the prosecution, the trial court, or the circumstances ... [but] because of a series of deliberate tactical choices on petitioner's part"). As the *Williams v.*

denial of a hearing will result in a "fundamental miscarriage of justice."[108]

(b)   In cases that *are* governed by AEDPA,[109] a failure by the petitioner or counsel "to develop the factual basis of a claim in State court proceedings"[110] constitutes a default that bars a federal evidentiary hearing unless the petitioner (i) demonstrates that no default of state procedural requirements in fact occurred, *e.g.*, because the state has waived any reliance on the default, because state court forums remain open to hear the evidence (in which case, the appropriate procedure is to dismiss the petition without prejudice or hold it in abeyance pending exhaustion of the remaining state remedy), or because the state courts decided the claim on the law,

---

Whitley, Smith v. Wainwright, Jones v. Wainwright, and *Cooper v. Picard* decisions above make clear, a party's failure to adduce evidence at a state court hearing is more likely to be treated as excusable if the *other* party bore the burden of producing that evidence at the hearing.

[108] *Tamayo-Reyes, supra,* 504 U.S. at 11-12 ("We ... adopt the narrow exception to the cause-and-prejudice requirement: A habeas petitioner's failure to develop a claim in state-court proceedings will be excused and a hearing mandated if he can show that a fundamental miscarriage of justice would result from failure to hold a federal evidentiary hearing." (citing *McCleskey v. Zant, supra,* 499 U.S. at 494)). *See* Hadley v. Groose, 1994 WL 14855, at *1, *5 n.1 (W.D. Mo. Jan. 19, 1994), *rev'd on other grounds sub nom. Hadley v. Caspari,* 36 F.3d 51 (8th Cir. 1994) (*per curiam*) ("*Keeney* hearing is 'mandated' ... for a petitioner who 'can show that a fundamental miscarriage of justice would result from failure to hold a federal evidentiary hearing,'" which requires "adequate showing of actual innocence" or, alternatively, "constitutional violation undermining 'the structural integrity of the criminal tribunal itself'" (quoting *Tamayo-Reyes, supra,* 504 U.S. at 12; *Vasquez v. Hillery, supra,* 474 U.S. at 263)). Extended discussions of the relatively narrow "miscarriage of justice" standard in the procedural default and successive petition contexts — discussions that are incorporated by reference here — are presented *supra* § 2.5; *infra* §§ 26.4, 28.3c.

Even if the failure to present material evidence was inexcusable, so that a hearing is not mandatory under the above standards, some federal courts have concluded that the importance of deciding important constitutional questions accurately on the basis of all the relevant evidence, *see supra* § 20.1b nn.14-15 and accompanying text, warrants exercise of their discretion to hold a hearing. *See, e.g.,* Burden v. Zant, 975 F.2d 771, 775-76 n.13 (11th Cir. 1992) ("*Keeney* did not affect a federal court's discretion to hold an evidentiary hearing on material facts not adequately developed in state court, even if the hearing is not mandatory."); Osborn v. Shillinger, 861 F.2d 612, 622 & n.10 (10th Cir. 1988) (although petitioner failed to request hearing on issue in state court, federal court properly ordered hearing on same issue because *Townsend* gives federal courts discretion to grant hearing whenever the merits of a constitutional claim are properly before court); other authority cited *infra* § 20.4 (para. (4)).

[109] For an explanation of the categories of cases to which AEDPA does and does not apply, see *supra* § 3.4.

[110] 28 U.S.C.A. § 2254(e)(2) (West 1994 & Supp. 1998) (discussed *supra* § 20.2b nn.21-22 and accompanying text).

not the facts,[110.01] or (ii) demonstrates *both* of circumstances (i) and (ii) below:

  (i) The claim relies on either (A) "a new rule of constitutional law, made retroactive to cases on collateral review by the Supreme Court, that was previously unavailable"[111] or (B) "a factual predicate that could not have been previously discovered through the exercise of due diligence";[112] and

  (ii) "[T]he facts underlying the claim would be sufficient to establish by clear and convincing evidence that but for constitutional error, no reasonable factfinder would have found the applicant guilty of the underlying offense."[113]

(3) Although a state court conducted a hearing, the party is relying on facts necessarily outside the state record.[114]

[110.01] If (i) the state acknowledges that the petitioner was not to blame for the state courts' failure to develop the facts, (ii) state law provides multiple opportunities to develop the facts, some of which remain available, or (iii) the state courts assumed the validity of the facts the petitioner alleged and denied relief based on the law, then it is not the case that "the applicant has failed to develop the factual basis of [the] claim in State court proceedings" (*id.*), and section 2254(e)(2)'s predicate for denying a hearing is not present. *See supra* § 20.2c n.73 and accompanying text (caselaw suggesting that state bears burden of invoking new section 2254(e) and waives benefits of provision by failing to assert it in adequate and timely manner); *supra* note 106.

[111] 28 U.S.C.A. § 2254(e)(2)(A)(i) (West 1994 & Supp. 1998) (discussed *supra* § 20.2b nn.26-31 and accompanying text).

[112] *Id.* § 2254(e)(2)(A)(ii) (discussed *supra* § 20.2b n.32 and accompanying text.).

[113] *Id.* § 2254(e)(2)(B) (discussed *supra* § 20.2b nn.33-38 and accompanying text).

[114] *See, e.g.,* Ford v. Wainwright, 477 U.S. 399, 402-03 (1986) (hearing required on allegation that petitioner's mental condition deteriorated after he was adjudged competent at trial and that, due to insanity, he could not constitutionally be executed); Blackledge v. Allison, 431 U.S. 63, 72-73 (1977) (guilty plea induced by clandestine prosecutorial promises); Fontaine v. United States, 411 U.S. 213 (1972); Machibroda v. United States, 368 U.S. 487, 494-95 (1962); Waley v. Johnston, 316 U.S. 101, 104 (1942) (*per curiam*) (coerced guilty plea allegation "stand[s] undenied on the record"); Beaulieu v. United States, 930 F.2d 805, 808 (10th Cir. 1991) (hearing required to assess federal prisoner's ineffective assistance of counsel claim, which alleged that counsel failed to prepare properly, and which accordingly relied on facts necessarily outside trial record and record of post-trial proceeding in trial court); United States v. Rodriguez-Rodriguez, 929 F.2d 747, 750 (1st Cir. 1991) (hearing on counsel's conflict of interest required because issue depends on matters outside record); Card v. Dugger, 911 F.2d 1494, 1519-20 (11th Cir. 1990) (trial court's determination that petitioner was competent to stand trial does not obviate need for hearing on petitioner's allegations that psychiatric evaluations on which trial court relied were inadequate); Bouchillon v. Collins, 907 F.2d 589 (5th Cir. 1990) (because state trial court did not hold hearing on competence to stand trial, relying instead on statements of trial counsel and trial judge's own observations, evidentiary hearing on issue is required); United States v. Bigman, 906 F.2d 392, 394-95 (9th Cir. 1990) (evidentiary hearing required because transcript of plea hearing, although reflecting that counsel "discussed" plea with petitioner, did not establish that counsel properly advised petitioner about *mens rea* element of offense); Hill v. Lockhart, 894 F.2d 1009, 1010 (8th

(4) Although a state court conducted a hearing, the petitioner is an indigent and the state court, in deprivation of the petitioner's constitutional rights, failed to appoint constitutionally effective counsel to represent him.[115] This mandatory-hearing criterion clearly applies whenever the state court hearing on which the respondent relies and at which the petitioner was unrepresented — or at which the petitioner received the ineffective assistance of counsel — took place at trial or at any other "critical" pretrial or post-trial proceeding to which the Supreme Court has extended a 6th or 14th Amendment right to counsel.[116] With one or two

---

Cir.) (*en banc*), *cert. denied*, 497 U.S. 1011 (1990) (petitioner's allegation that he pled guilty based on erroneous parole eligibility advice requires federal hearing); United States v. Espinoza, 866 F.2d 1067, 1069-70 (9th Cir. 1988) (petitioner's allegation that he pled guilty based on attorney's representations about sentencing arrangement not thereafter carried out requires federal hearing (citing cases)); Thames v. Dugger, 848 F.2d 149, 151 n.2 (11th Cir. 1988) (suggesting need for hearing because state trial court made findings of fact that trial counsel strategically chose to eschew severance motion based on court's recollection of proceedings and court's surmise about trial counsel's awareness of rules governing severance); Hyman v. Aiken, 824 F.2d 1405, 1411-12 (4th Cir. 1987) (federal court not bound by state finding premised on credibility of witness whose testimony state factfinder did not actually hear); Dutton v. Brown, 788 F.2d 669, 672-74 (10th Cir. 1986) (evidence that trial counsel was not adequately prepared); Damiano v. Florida Parole and Probation Comm'n, 785 F.2d 929, 932 (11th Cir. 1986) (*per curiam*) (equal protection attack on differential treatment of similarly situated prisoners); United States v. Barboa, 777 F.2d 1420, 1423 (10th Cir. 1985) (claim that co-conspirator was government agent); Thompson v. Blackburn, 776 F.2d 118, 121-22 (5th Cir. 1985) (*ex post facto* claim requires hearing to determine precise date of offense); Edgemon v. Lockhart, 768 F.2d 252, 255 (8th Cir. 1985), *cert. denied,* 475 U.S. 1085 (1986) (allegation that trial counsel also represented sheriff and chief prosecution witness); McAffee v. Procunier, 761 F.2d 1124, 1128 (5th Cir.), *cert. denied,* 474 U.S. 907 (1985) (state sentencing court allegedly relied upon petitioner's past criminal record that was not properly before court and record does not make clear that petitioner had opportunity to rebut past record); Diagre v. Maggio, 705 F.2d 786, 788 (5th Cir. 1983) (alleged denials of counsel at line-up and effective assistance at trial); Spivey v. Zant, 661 F.2d 464, 476 (5th Cir. 1981), *cert. denied,* 458 U.S. 1111 (1982) (claim that counsel did not begin active representation of petitioner on date shown in record); Friedman v. United States, 588 F.2d 1010, 1016 (5th Cir. 1979) (trial court's effective assistance finding based on in-court viewing of attorney does not avoid hearing on inadequate-preparation claim); *infra* para. (6)(g).

[115] *See* 28 U.S.C. § 2254(d)(5) (1994) (superseded) (no presumption of correctness of state court factfindings in these circumstances); Carter v. Montgomery, 769 F.2d 1537, 1543 (11th Cir. 1985) (*dicta*) (discussed *infra* note 119). *See also* Wade v. Lockhart, 763 F.2d 999, 999-1001 (8th Cir. 1985) (state's failure to hold hearing after defendant claimed he was financially unable to retain counsel may have been violation of right to counsel; hearing required on that question); Lane v. Henderson, 480 F.2d 544, 545 (5th Cir. 1973) (*per curiam*) (indigent petitioner claims he did not "knowingly and intelligently" waive right to counsel and "state court hearing was not enough to resolve the issue"); Roach v. Bennett, 392 F.2d 743, 748 (8th Cir. 1968).

[116] *See, e.g.,* Johnson v. Armontrout, 961 F.2d 748, 753-54 (8th Cir. 1992) (state appellate court's finding on direct appeal that jurors were impartial was not entitled to deference because ineffective trial counsel did not adequately question jurors during *voir dire*). *See generally*

exceptions,[117] the courts generally have not been sympathetic to claims that the denial of counsel to indigent state postconviction petitioners violates the Constitution and always requires a federal hearing[118] or even that such a denial requires a federal hearing if the petitioner demonstrates that the denial rendered the state postconviction proceeding fundamentally unfair.[119]

(5)   Although a state court conducted a hearing, the party was "denied due process of law in the state court proceeding."[120]

Coleman v. Alabama, 399 U.S. 1 (1970) (right to counsel at preliminary hearing); Mempa v. Rhay, 389 U.S. 128 (1967) (sentencing proceedings); United States v. Wade, 388 U.S. 218 (1967) (certain pretrial eyewitness identification procedures); Douglas v. California, 372 U.S. 353 (1963) (on appeal); Gideon v. Wainwright, 372 U.S. 335 (1963) (at felony trial); Hamilton v. Alabama, 368 U.S. 52 (1961) (arraignment); authority cited *supra* §§ 7.2, 26.3b n.35.

[117] Five Justices, in concurring and dissenting opinions in Murray v. Giarratano, 492 U.S. 1 (1989), appeared to accept the proposition that there is a right to counsel in *capital* state postconviction proceedings. See *supra* §§ 7.2a, 7.2f. Supreme Court *dicta* also suggests that there is a constitutional right to the effective assistance of counsel at an initial state postconviction hearing that, as a matter of law or of practical fact, was the prisoner's first opportunity to present a particular claim in the state courts. See *supra* §§ 7.1b nn.77-83 and accompanying text, 7.2e, 9.1 nn.21, 26, 28, 33, 34; *infra* § 25.4 nn.40-45 and accompanying text; *infra* § 26.3b nn.30, 32, 41; *infra* §§ 33.3 n.11, 33.4 n.2, 41.4a n.7 (all citing authority, providing examples). See *also* Evans v. Clarke, 868 F.2d 267, 270 (8th Cir. 1989) (state postconviction consideration of certain issues presented by *pro se* petitioner was not sufficient to overcome unconstitutional denial of right to direct appeal on those issues).

[118] *Compare supra* § 7.2 (bases for constitutional right to counsel in state postconviction proceedings) *with* Murray v. Giarratano, 492 U.S. 1 (1989) (discussed *supra* §§ 7.2a, 7.2f) (divided Court fails to resolve question of what kind of legal representation is constitutionally required in capital postconviction proceedings but finds that representation actually provided under circumstances was sufficient) *and* Pennsylvania v. Finley, 481 U.S. 551 (1987) (discussed *supra* §§ 7.1b, 7.2a) (*dictum* that there is no right to counsel in state postconviction proceedings; holding merely forswears certain procedural protections when state law requires counsel for indigents).

[119] *But cf.* Carter v. Montgomery, 769 F.2d 1537, 1543 (11th Cir. 1985) (*dicta*) (petitioner might have been entitled to hearing based on denial of counsel at state habeas corpus hearing if he had presented any "specific facts from which one could have concluded that his state hearing lacked fundamental fairness"). *But see* Hawkins v. Bennett, 423 F.2d 948, 950 (8th Cir. 1970) (hearing required because petitioner of limited education was without counsel in state habeas corpus proceedings, and was unable to develop material facts). The absence of a "full and fair" state postconviction hearing due to the ineffective assistance of counsel or other circumstances may provide a separate basis for a mandatory hearing under *Townsend*. See *infra* paras. (6)(k), (6)(l).

[120] 28 U.S.C. § 2254(d)(7) (1994) (superseded). *Accord Townsend, supra,* 372 U.S. at 313. See *infra* para. (6)(a). See generally *infra* para. (6). Examples of situations falling within this mandatory-hearing category are: Ford v. Wainwright, 477 U.S. 399, 409-17 (1986); *id.* at 423-26 (Powell, J., concurring); *id.* at 428 (O'Connor, J., concurring) (all concluding that *ex parte* determination of sanity by governor violated due process because petitioner was not afforded opportunity to be heard); Depree v. Thomas, 946 F.2d 784, 788-89 n.6 (11th Cir. 1991) (*dicta*) (on claim that trial court improperly rejected challenges for cause to two venirepersons and that trial

(6) Although a state court conducted a hearing, "the factfinding procedure employed by the state court was not adequate to afford [the party] a full and fair hearing" or was an "unreasonable" method for "determin[ing] the facts."[121] This mandatory-hearing category "is intentionally open-ended," and its definition is "the province of the district judges."[122]

---

judge's factual findings of venirepersons' impartiality were not entitled to deference, section 2254(d)(7) (since superseded) would apply if petitioner "allege[d] that the State denied him due process during the jury selection phase of the trial" by, for example, limiting his ability "to interrogate fully the venirepersons and to challenge their empanelment"); McAffee v. Procunier, 761 F.2d 1124, 1128 (5th Cir.), *cert. denied,* 474 U.S. 907 (1985) (possible due process violation exists and hearing required because state sentencing court apparently relied on criminal record not properly before court and petitioner was not given opportunity to rebut record).

[121] *Townsend, supra,* 372 U.S. at 313 (hearing required if "for any reason it appears that the state trier of fact did not afford the habeas applicant a full and fair fact hearing"). *See, e.g.,* 28 U.S.C.A. § 2254(d)(2) (West 1994 & Supp. 1998) (no presumption of correctness, hence by implication hearing must be held, if state court "decision" of factual issue "was based on an unreasonable determination of the facts in light of the evidence presented in the State court proceeding"); 28 U.S.C. §§ 2254(d)(2), 2254(d)(6) (1994) (superseded) (no presumption of correctness, hence by implication hearing must be held, if state court did not afford petitioner "full and fair hearing" or "full, fair and adequate hearing"); Keeney v. Tamayo-Reyes, 504 U.S. 1, 10 (1992) (to avoid federal court hearing, "State must afford the petitioner a full and fair hearing on his federal claim"); Mu'Min v. Virginia, 500 U.S. 415, 450-52 (1991) (Kennedy, J., dissenting) (direct review case) (state court conclusion that juror was impartial is not due deference if trial court did not conduct sufficient *voir dire* to determine credibility of juror professing to be impartial; *voir dire* must be sufficient to evaluate prospective jurors' credibility); Weidner v. Thieret, 932 F.2d 626, 633 (7th Cir. 1991), *cert. denied,* 502 U.S. 1036 (1992) (*dicta*) ("Where state trial judges fail to adequately develop the relevant facts so that not even implicit findings ... can be gleaned from the record, the habeas procedure is better served by a de novo hearing than by allowing state judges to [file affidavits explaining their rulings and thereby] cast their minds back to the state trial."); Lahay v. Armontrout, 923 F.2d 578, 578-79 (8th Cir. 1991) (if there is reason to doubt reliability of state court findings of fact, petitioner is entitled to evidentiary hearing); Manocchio v. Moran, 919 F.2d 770, 771 n.1 (1st Cir. 1990), *cert. denied,* 500 U.S. 910 (1991) (affirming district court's determination that state court factfindings were not entitled to presumption of correctness because state court's factfinding procedure was inadequate to afford full and fair hearing); Smith v. Black, 904 F.2d 950, 975-76 (5th Cir. 1990), *vac'd & remanded on other grounds,* 503 U.S. 930 (1992) (because state court rejected claim on procedural default grounds, it gave merits of claim only "glancing ... scrutiny"); Neron v. Tierney, 841 F.2d 1197, 1199-200 (1st Cir.), *cert. denied,* 488 U.S. 832 (1988) (federal hearing required in absence of "'opportunity for full and fair litigation'" in state courts (quoting Stone v. Powell, 428 U.S. 465, 482 (1976))).

[122] *Townsend, supra,* 372 U.S. at 317. *See id.* at 319 ("[o]rdinarily," review of entire state record "is indispensable to determining whether the habeas applicant received a full and fair state court evidentiary hearing resulting in reliable findings"); *supra* §§ 15.2c n.59 and accompanying text, 20.3b.

Exercising their broad authority under this *Townsend* category, the federal courts have ordered hearings, for example, because:[123]

(a) The state factfinding procedure violates the Constitution and is inadequate for the ascertainment of truth.[124]

(b) The state procedure, even if it "does not violate the Constitution ... appears to be seriously inadequate for the ascertainment of truth."[125]

(c) The state court procedure was not capable of "reliably" finding "the relevant facts."[126]

(d) The state court hearing was "not a meaningful one."[127]

---

[123] *See also infra* §§ 23.4, 26.2d, 27.3 (analogous exceptions to procedural defenses that arise when state procedures were inadequate).

[124] *See, e.g., Ford v. Wainwright, supra,* 477 U.S. at 430 (O'Connor, J., concurring) (discussed *supra* note 120); *Neron v. Tierney, supra,* 841 F.2d at 1199-1200.

[125] *Townsend, supra,* 372 U.S. at 316. *See, e.g.,* Rose v. Mitchell, 443 U.S. 545, 563 (1979) (state court determination was not dispositive because "judge whose conduct [the petitioner] challenged decided the validity of that challenge"); Dickerson v. Alabama, 667 F.2d 1364, 1367 (11th Cir.), *cert. denied,* 459 U.S. 878 (1982) (state *coram nobis* proceeding did not include independent review of issues); Guice v. Fortenberry, 661 F.2d 496, 507 (5th Cir. 1981) (*en banc*); Johnson v. Prast, 548 F.2d 699, 701 (7th Cir. 1977) (state judge's statement that he "strongly suspect[ed]" he had considered petitioner's presentence custody was not enough to establish that petitioner was accorded equal protection right to sentence adjustment due to inability to present bail); Gibson v. Blair, 467 F.2d 842, 844 (5th Cir. 1972) (trial court ruling prevented full development of jury discrimination issue); Jenkins v. Kropp, 424 F.2d 665, 666 (6th Cir. 1970) (*per curiam*); Conner v. Wingo, 409 F.2d 21, 22 (6th Cir. 1969), *cert. denied,* 406 U.S. 921 (1972); Roach v. Bennett, 392 F.2d 743, 748 (8th Cir. 1968) (under circumstances, denial of counsel prevented fair ascertainment of truth).

[126] *Townsend, supra,* 372 U.S. at 313, 318. *See* Mu'Min v. Virginia, 500 U.S. 415, 450-52 (1991) (Kennedy, J., dissenting) (discussed *supra* note 121); Weidner v. Thieret, 932 F.2d 626 (7th Cir. 1991), *cert. denied,* 502 U.S. 1036 (1992) (discussed *supra* note 121); Lahay v. Armontrout, 923 F.2d 578, 578-79 (8th Cir. 1991) (discussed *supra* note 121); *infra* subpara. (u). This mandatory-hearing category is particularly important in capital cases because of the especially high degree of reliability that the 8th and 14th Amendments require of factfinding procedures — at whatever stage of a case — that result in or leave standing a sentence of death. *E.g., Ford v. Wainwright, supra,* 477 U.S. at 413 (plurality opinion) (need for reliability in post-trial determination that capital prisoner is sufficiently sane to be executed); Eddings v. Oklahoma, 455 U.S. 104, 117-18 (1982) (O'Connor, J., concurring) (need for reliability in capital sentencing procedures); Beck v. Alabama, 447 U.S. 625, 638 (1980) (need for reliability in guilt-determining procedures in capital cases); Gardner v. Florida, 430 U.S. 349, 358 (1977) (need for reliability in sentencing and appellate procedures in capital cases); authority cited *supra* § 2.6.

[127] O'Neal v. Smith, 413 F.2d 269, 270 (5th Cir. 1969) (petitioner "entitled to a meaningful hearing with findings that are based on evidence, not assumptions"). *See, e.g.,* Demosthenes v. Baal, 495 U.S. 731, 734 (1990) (Brennan, J., dissenting) ("Because the proceedings in this case have been so hurried, it is not at all clear that the state hearing was 'full and fair'"); Denton v. Ricketts, 728 F.2d 489, 492 (10th Cir. 1984) (hearing consisting of taped interviews was not an "evidentiary hearing" conducted in sufficiently "adversarial manner").

(e)   "[T]he state trial judge ... made serious procedural errors ... in such things as the burden of proof."[128]

(f)   "[P]rocedural errors" at the state proceedings, while not "so grave as to require" habeas corpus relief themselves, "are nevertheless grave enough to deprive the state evidentiary hearing of its adequacy as a means of finally determining facts upon which constitutional rights depend."[129]

(g)   The state trier of fact relied on events observed in the courtroom as the basis for its finding, but the party's claim is based on events occurring outside the courtroom.[130]

(h)   The state judge who conducted the state hearing and found the facts was not an impartial decisionmaker, either because the judge's own conduct was at issue or for some other reason.[131]

---

[128] *Townsend, supra,* 372 U.S. at 316. *See, e.g.,* McAffee v. Procunier, 761 F.2d 1124, 1128 (5th Cir.), *cert. denied,* 474 U.S. 907 (1987) (hearing required because sentencing court relied on criminal record not properly before court); Schnepp v. Hocker, 429 F.2d 1096, 1099 n.5 (9th Cir. 1970) (*dicta*) (misallocation of burden of proof in state proceeding requires federal hearing); Jenkins v. Kropp, 424 F.2d 665, 666 (6th Cir. 1970); Des Bouillons v. Burke, 418 F.2d 297, 300 (7th Cir. 1969) (*dicta*) (burden of proof error); *Conner v. Wingo, supra,* 409 F.2d at 22; United States ex rel. Jefferson v. Follette, 396 F.2d 862, 865 (2d Cir. 1968) (trial court denied petitioner opportunity to develop case adequately through testimony of witness).

[129] *Townsend, supra,* 372 U.S. at 316.

[130] *See, e.g.,* Blackledge v. Allison, 431 U.S. 63, 78 (1977) (plea bargain outside presence of judge); Bouchillon v. Collins, 907 F.2d 589 (5th Cir. 1990) (because state trial court did not hold hearing on competence to stand trial, relying instead on statements of trial counsel and trial judge's own observations, evidentiary hearing on issue was required); United States v. Espinoza, 866 F.2d 1067, 1069-70 (9th Cir. 1988) (petitioner's allegation that he pled guilty based on attorney's representations about sentencing arrangement not thereafter carried out requires federal hearing notwithstanding state trial court's finding that guilty plea was knowingly made (citing cases)); Estock v. Lane, 842 F.2d 184, 186-88 (7th Cir. 1988) (postconviction court's determination of petitioner's competency to stand trial based on familiarity with trial counsel and surmises about trial counsel's behavior in event that client was incompetent is insufficient basis to obviate need for federal determination of issue); Friedman v. United States, 588 F.2d 1010, 1016 (5th Cir. 1979) (finding of effective assistance of counsel based on trial judge's observations in court were insufficient because petitioner alleged inadequate preparation); Lee v. Beto, 429 F.2d 524, 525 (5th Cir. 1970) (out-of-court intimidation of witnesses and racial prejudice); *supra* para. (3).

[131] *See, e.g.,* Rose v. Mitchell, 443 U.S. 545, 563 (1979). *See also* Murchu v. United States, 926 F.2d 50, 57, 58 n.12 (1st Cir.), *cert. denied,* 502 U.S. 828 (1991) (district judge erred in summarily dismissing prisoner's section 2255 motion challenging judge's own conduct as improper attempt to coerce guilty plea and vindictive imposition of higher sentence because movant refused to plead; "to avoid any appearance of impropriety, the matter should be ... assigned to a different judge" for hearing); McKenzie v. Risley, 915 F.2d 1396, 1397-98 (9th Cir. 1990) (by implication; rejecting state trial judge's determination, federal court orders hearing to assess whether state judge's *ex parte* meeting with prosecutor prior to sentencing prejudiced petitioner); Anderson v. Jones, 743 F.2d 306, 308 (5th Cir. 1984) (because genuine issue was raised as to

(i)   The judge who made the state factfindings did not preside at the hearing or hear the evidence.[132]

(j)   The petitioner was not afforded any or adequately funded counsel at the state court hearing in violation of his constitutional right to counsel.[133]

(k)   The petitioner was not afforded any or adequately funded counsel at the state court hearing and that deprivation, under the circum-

---

sentencing judge's understanding of range of discretion, that judge's explanation during state postconviction of meaning of his own remarks at sentencing does not obviate need for federal hearing); Williams v. Maggio, 730 F.2d 1048, 1050 (5th Cir. 1984); Guice v. Fortenberry, 661 F.2d 496, 507 (5th Cir. 1981) (*en banc*); Tyler v. Swenson, 427 F.2d 412, 415 (8th Cir. 1970) (state judge relied on memory of prior proceedings and did not allow himself to be cross-examined). *Cf.* Liteky v. United States, 510 U.S. 540, 562-65 (1994) (Kennedy, J., concurring in the judgment) (although it sometimes is "prudent to permit judges to preside over successive causes involving the same parties or issues" (citing Rule 4(a) of Rules Governing § 2255 Proceedings), judges should be cognizant of "'motivation to vindicate a prior conclusion' when confronted with a question for the second or third time" and that a "judge may find it difficult to put aside views formed during some earlier proceeding," in which event disqualification might be appropriate (quoting David L. Ratner, *Disqualification of Judges for Prior Judicial Actions*, 3 HOW. L.J. 228, 229-30 (1957))); Weidner v. Thieret, 932 F.2d 626, 633 (7th Cir. 1991), *cert. denied*, 502 U.S. 1036 (1992) (*dicta*) ("Where state trial judges fail to adequately develop the relevant facts so that not even implicit findings ... can be gleaned from the record, the habeas procedure is better served by a de novo hearing than by allowing state judges to [file affidavits explaining their rulings and thereby] cast their minds back to the state trial."); *infra* § 21.2 n.13 and accompanying text (discussing question whether federal district courts may rely upon "evidence" in form of affidavits from trial judges discussing historical facts or explaining their mental processes). *But cf.* Polizzi v. United States, 926 F.2d 1311, 1320 (2d Cir. 1991); Panzardi-Alvarez v. United States, 879 F.2d 975, 985 n.8 (1st Cir. 1989), *cert. denied*, 493 U.S. 1082 (1990) (in section 2255 proceeding, "if the claim is based upon facts with which the [federal] trial court, through ... observation at trial, is familiar, the court may make findings without an additional hearing" (quoting United States v. DiCarlo, 575 F.2d 952, 954-55 (1st Cir.), *cert. denied*, 439 U.S. 834 (1978))); Buxton v. Lynaugh, 879 F.2d 140, 144 (5th Cir. 1989), *cert. denied*, 497 U.S. 1032 (1990) (over dissent, court gives special deference to findings of state habeas corpus judge because he also conducted state trial); Aleman v. United States, 878 F.2d 1009, 1012 (7th Cir. 1989) (similar to *DiCarlo, supra*). *See generally Liteky v. United States, supra* (extensive discussion, in various opinions, of circumstances requiring recusal of judge, including judge's prior participation in case); Robert P. Davidow, *Federal Habeas Corpus: The Effect of Holding State Capital Collateral Proceedings Before a Judge Running for Re-Election*, 8 NOTRE DAME J. L., ETH. & PUB. POL. 317 (1994).

[132] *See, e.g.*, Estock v. Lane, 842 F.2d 184, 186-88 (7th Cir. 1988); United States ex rel. Ackerman v. Russell, 388 F.2d 21, 24 (3d Cir. 1968); *infra* subpara. (x). *But cf.* authority cited *supra* § 20.3d (para. (4)) (in proper circumstances, state appellate findings based upon plenary appellate consideration of disputed issue and trial court record may obviate need for federal hearing).

[133] *See supra* para. (4).

stances, rendered the state proceeding fundamentally unfair.[134]

(l) The performance of petitioner's counsel at the state court hearing was so egregiously inadequate or ineffective that counsel's presence actually hindered the petitioner's exercise of rights.[135]

(m) The party was not given adequate time to prepare for the state court hearing.[136]

(n) The state court hearing did not consider the full scope of the party's factual claims.[137]

---

[134] *See, e.g.,* Boyd v. Dutton, 405 U.S. 1, 3 (1972) (Blackmun, J., concurring) (absence of counsel at state proceeding rendered it unfair because petitioner did not know how to compel attendance of witnesses); Hopkinson v. Shillinger, 866 F.2d 1185, 1199-2000 (10th Cir. 1989) (depending on circumstances, denial of state postconviction counsel to death sentenced inmate may form basis for withholding presumption of correctness from state postconviction factfindings and for requiring federal hearing); Carter v. Montgomery, 769 F.2d 1537, 1543 (11th Cir. 1985) (*dicta*) (lack of counsel is grounds for federal hearing if it rendered state proceeding fundamentally unfair); Wade v. Lockhart, 763 F.2d 999, 1001 (8th Cir. 1985) (hearing required to determine whether state court's failure to hold hearing after defendant claimed he was financially unable to retain counsel was violation of 14th Amendment); Walters v. Jago, 642 F.2d 194 (6th Cir. 1981); Lane v. Henderson, 480 F.2d 544, 545 (5th Cir. 1973) (state habeas corpus hearing at which petitioner was unrepresented by counsel is not so "full and fair" that federal habeas corpus court could safely accept state findings); Hawkins v. Bennett, 423 F.2d 948, 951 (8th Cir. 1970) (*dicta*) ("in certain circumstances the absence of counsel at the [state] habeas corpus proceedings may infect the fairness of the hearing afforded the petitioner"); Harris v. Wainwright, 399 F.2d 142, 143 (5th Cir. 1968); Roach v. Bennett, 392 F.2d 743, 748 (8th Cir. 1968) (state hearing in absence of counsel not full and fair, given complexity of issues and petitioner's below-average intelligence). *See also* Evans v. Clarke, 868 F.2d 267, 270 (8th Cir. 1989) (state postconviction consideration of certain issues presented by *pro se* petitioner was insufficient to overcome unconstitutional denial of right to direct appeal on those issues). *Cf.* Meeks v. Cabana, 845 F.2d 1319, 1322 (5th Cir. 1988) (absence of counsel did not render state postconviction factfindings inadequate under circumstances, because issue resolved in state court was narrow and important witnesses appeared and testified). *But cf. supra* § 7.2a; *supra* notes 117-19 and accompanying text (discussing courts' resistance to notion that there is right to counsel, at least in noncapital state postconviction proceedings, unless postconviction proceedings served as substitute for first appeal as of right).

[135] *See, e.g.,* Johnson v. Armontrout, 961 F.2d 748, 753-54 (8th Cir. 1992) (state appellate court's finding on direct appeal that jurors were impartial was not entitled to deference because neither prosecutor nor ineffective trial counsel adequately questioned jurors during *voir dire*); Smith v. Freeman, 892 F.2d 331, 339 n.13 (3d Cir. 1989) (trial counsel made misrepresentations); Wesley v. Alabama, 488 F.2d 30, 31-32 (5th Cir. 1974) (although record of state proceedings indicate that two court-appointed attorneys were present, there was no indication they took part in proceedings). *But cf.* Coleman v. Thompson, 501 U.S. 722 (1991) (discussed *supra* §§ 7.2a, 7.2e; *supra* note 117; *infra* § 26.3b nn.31, 34-41 (unless, possibly, when initial postconviction proceeding serves as substitute for first direct appeal as of right, there generally is no 6th Amendment right to effective assistance of counsel in state postconviction proceedings).

[136] *See, e.g.,* Williams v. Maggio, 730 F.2d 1048, 1050 (5th Cir. 1984).

[137] *See, e.g.,* 28 U.S.C. § 2254(d)(1) (1994) (superseded) ("merits of the factual dispute were not resolved in the State court hearing"); *Townsend, supra,* 372 U.S. at 313 ("merits of the factual

811

(o)   The state trier of fact limited the proceeding to its own or its agent's (for example, a magistrate judge's) investigation of the facts or for any other reason prevented the party from making an evidentiary presentation.[138]

---

dispute were not resolved in the state hearing"); McKenzie v. Risley, 915 F.2d 1396, 1397-98 (9th Cir. 1990) (state court's resolution of question whether prosecutor and judge discussed petitioner's sentencing during improper *ex parte* meeting did not resolve question whether other matters were discussed that could have prejudicially influenced sentencing decision); United States v. Bigman, 906 F.2d 392, 394-95 (9th Cir. 1990) (evidentiary hearing required in section 2255 proceeding because transcript of plea hearing, although reflecting that counsel "discussed" plea with petitioner, did not establish that counsel properly advised petitioner about *mens rea* element of offense); Smith v. Black, 904 F.2d 950, 975-76 (5th Cir. 1990), *vac'd & remanded on other grounds,* 503 U.S. 930 (1992); Stano v. Dugger, 901 F.2d 898, 899 (11th Cir. 1990) (*en banc*) (state court hearing on claim of ineffective assistance of counsel did not provide full and fair forum for petitioner's evidence concerning suppression of evidence and police use of jailhouse informer); Magwood v. Smith, 791 F.2d 1438, 1448-50 (11th Cir. 1986); Damiano v. Florida Parole & Probation Comm'n, 785 F.2d 929 (11th Cir. 1986); Thompson v. Blackburn, 776 F.2d 118, 122-24 (5th Cir. 1985); Edgemon v. Lockhart, 768 F.2d 252, 255-57 (8th Cir. 1985), *cert. denied,* 475 U.S. 1085 (1986); Chaney v. Brown, 730 F.2d 1334, 1345-46 (10th Cir.), *cert. denied,* 469 U.S. 1090 (1984) (state court failed to explore whether withheld evidence may have affected imposition of death sentence); Sullivan v. Cuyler, 723 F.2d 1077, 1084-85 (3d Cir. 1983) (state court failed to explore how conflict of interest influenced counsel); Dyas v. Lockhart, 705 F.2d 993, 996 (8th Cir.), *cert. denied,* 464 U.S. 982 (1983) (state court failed to explore whether defendant knew judge's relationship to prosecutor when defendant waived recusal); Valenzuela v. Griffin, 654 F.2d 707, 709-11 (10th Cir. 1981) (failure to consider whether prosecution made good-faith efforts to obtain absent witness); Fuller v. Luther, 575 F.2d 1098, 1101 (4th Cir. 1978); Stidham v. Swenson, 506 F.2d 478, 488-89 (8th Cir. 1974) (*en banc*), *cert. denied,* 429 U.S. 941 (1976); Goodspeed v. Beto, 460 F.2d 398, 400 (5th Cir. 1972) (failure to explore waiver issue); Brown v. Lash, 432 F.2d 1129, 1135 (7th Cir. 1970), *cert. denied,* 401 U.S. 948 (1971); United States ex rel. McCloud v. Rundle, 402 F.2d 853, 857 (3d Cir. 1968), *cert. denied,* 398 U.S. 929 (1970) ("In the absence of an adequate record indicating that the [state] court has properly ascertained whether a guilty plea was knowingly and voluntarily entered, it is incumbent upon the federal habeas corpus court to make this determination on the basis of all the relevant facts and circumstances."); *supra* note 106; *supra* §§ 20.3c (para. (4)), 20.3d (paras. (1)(c), (7)).

[138] *See, e.g.,* Ford v. Wainwright, 477 U.S. 399, 409-19 (1986) (federal hearing on petitioner's sanity required because only finding of sanity in record was made by governor, *ex parte,* on basis of report made by psychiatrists whom governor picked to examine petitioner and in absence of opportunity for petitioner to present evidence); Rhoden v. Rowland, 10 F.3d 1457, 1460 (9th Cir. 1993) (petitioner "took all steps possible to make a timely record of prejudice" during and after trial but state trial and appellate courts limited scope of inquiry); Smith v. Freeman, 892 F.2d 331, 339-40 (3d Cir. 1989) ("[a]ll attempts by counsel to probe the issue ... were blocked by the court" at trial and state postconviction court thereafter "summarily dismissed" petition as previously litigated at trial; when petitioner's or counsel's ignorance of facts or law is due to counsel's insufficient preparation or other neglect, court will not find inexcusable neglect); Bulger v. McClay, 575 F.2d 407, 410-11 (2d Cir.), *cert. denied,* 439 U.S. 915 (1978) (hearing required because state judge made only "cursory" examination and disallowed cross-examination of juror whose deliberations allegedly were tainted by prejudicial extra-record information); Woodcock v.

(p)   The party was not permitted to introduce material evidence proffered at the state court hearing.[139]

(q)   The petitioner was not permitted or was not able to subpoena or present witnesses at the state hearing.[140]

(r)   The petitioner was not permitted or was not able to testify at the state court hearing.[141]

McCauley, 563 F.2d 806, 807-09 (7th Cir. 1977) (state court's decision based on public defender's report was insufficient); Wesley v. Alabama, 488 F.2d 30, 31-32 (5th Cir. 1974) (federal hearing required because state *coram nobis* hearing consisted of only a few questions by judge addressed to petitioner and no written reasons were given for dismissal); Macon v. Graven, 457 F.2d 342, 343 (9th Cir. 1972); Pope v. Turner, 426 F.2d 783, 785 (10th Cir. 1970) (state court relied on investigation by attorney); authority cited *infra* note 139. *See also* Thames v. Dugger, 848 F.2d 149, 151 (11th Cir. 1988) (factfindings based on trial judge's surmises, rather than evidence, cannot forestall federal factfinding); Estock v. Lane, 842 F.2d 184, 186-88 (7th Cir. 1988) (similar); Hyman v. Aiken, 824 F.2d 1405, 1411-12 (4th Cir. 1987) (federal court was not bound by state finding premised on credibility of witness whose testimony state factfinder did not actually hear).

[139] *See, e.g.,* In re Heidnik, 112 F.3d 105, 112 n.7 (3d Cir. 1997) (state court judgment that prisoner was competent to waive rights, give up appeals, and be executed not due presumption of correctness because state trial judge refused to let prisoner's next-friend present testimony of psychologist documenting prisoner's incompetence); Spitzweiser-Wittgenstein v. Newton, 978 F.2d 1195 (10th Cir. 1992) (inadequate development of material facts requires remand for hearing because state courts refused to hear evidence despite petitioner's reasonable efforts to present it); Capps v. Sullivan, 921 F.2d 260, 261-62 (10th Cir. 1990) (state findings not given deference and evidentiary hearing ordered because state court held no evidentiary hearing and refused to hear evidence proffered by petitioner); Spencer v. Kemp, 781 F.2d 1458 (11th Cir. 1986) *(en banc)*; Bibby v. Tard, 741 F.2d 26, 31 (3d Cir. 1984) (judge excluded information); Owen v. Duckworth, 727 F.2d 643, 645 (7th Cir. 1984) (state court terminated hearing on petitioner's motion before he had presented all his evidence); Guice v. Fortenberry, 661 F.2d 496, 507 (5th Cir. 1981) *(en banc)*. *Cf.* Praylow v. Martin, 761 F.2d 179, 183 (4th Cir. 1985) (federal district court did not err in refusing to conduct hearing because state court afforded petitioner adequate opportunity to present evidence and he failed to do so); *supra* note 138. *But cf.* McCoy v. Lynaugh, 874 F.2d 954, 966 (5th Cir. 1989) (hearing not mandatory even though state habeas corpus court failed to consider evidence).

[140] *See, e.g.,* Birt v. Montgomery, 709 F.2d 690, 695-96 (11th Cir. 1983), *cert. denied,* 469 U.S. 874 (1984) (hearing required because state statute restricting enforceability of subpoenas to 150 miles from courthouse prevented petitioner from compelling attendance of major witness); Coleman v. Zant, 708 F.2d 541, 548 (11th Cir. 1983). *Cf. Praylow v. Martin, supra,* 761 F.2d at 183 (district court did not err in refusing to hear testimony of witnesses whom petitioner had failed to subpoena when state court gave him opportunity to do so).

[141] *See, e.g., Ford v. Wainwright, supra,* 477 U.S. at 413-14 (plurality opinion) (state executive clemency procedure did not allow petitioner to testify or present evidence); *id.* at 423-25 (Powell, J., concurring); McAffee v. Procunier, 761 F.2d 1124, 1128 (5th Cir.), *cert. denied,* 474 U.S. 907 (1985) (unclear from record whether state court afforded petitioner opportunity to rebut information used against him); Walker v. Wilmot, 603 F.2d 1038, 1042 (2d Cir. 1979), *cert. denied,* 449 U.S. 885 (1980) (unclear whether young defendant who had no previous experience

    (s)   The petitioner was not present at the state hearing.[142]

    (t)   The prosecutor withheld or misrepresented, or the trial judge excluded, critical facts at the state court hearing.[143]

    (u)   The state presented false, misleading, or incomplete testimony at the state court hearing.[144]

    (v)   The state's conduct at the state court hearing was otherwise improper or unfair.[145]

---

with criminal justice matters understood he had right to offer proof and testify at suppression hearing); United States ex rel. Ackerman v. Russell, 388 F.2d 21, 24-25 (3d Cir. 1968).

[142] *See, e.g., Ford v. Wainwright, supra,* 477 U.S. at 413 (administrative inquiry at which petitioner was not present); United States ex rel. Davis v. Yeager, 453 F.2d 1001, 1003 (3d Cir. 1971) (testimony in petitioner's absence on material issue within his personal knowledge). *But cf.* Cook v. Florida Parole & Probation Comm'n, 749 F.2d 678, 680 (11th Cir. 1985) (*dicta*) (consensual absence of petitioner might not render state proceedings insufficient).

[143] *See, e.g.,* Dobbs v. Zant, 506 U.S. 357, 359 (1993) (*per curiam*) ("delay in discovery" of transcript is excused, and court of appeals's refusal to consider evidence is reversed, because "delay resulted substantially from the State's own erroneous assertions that closing arguments had not been transcribed"; petitioner's "position that he legitimately relied on the State's representation is well taken"; fact that transcript "flatly contradicted the account [of the closing argument] given by counsel" in prior postconviction testimony supports requirement that federal court consider evidence); Williams v. Whitley, 940 F.2d 132, 133-34 (5th Cir. 1991) (district court erred in denying evidentiary hearing on claim of prosecutorial suppression of evidence, which concerned "recently disclosed police report [that] has never been the subject of an evidentiary hearing"); Smith v. Wainwright, 741 F.2d 1248, 1256 (11th Cir. 1984) (prosecution withheld evidence); Bibby v. Tard, 741 F.2d 26, 31 (3d Cir. 1984) (judge excluded information); Lockett v. Blackburn, 571 F.2d 309, 313 (5th Cir.), *cert. denied,* 439 U.S. 873 (1978) (state hearing unfair because state concealed witness); Caputo v. Henderson, 541 F.2d 979, 982 (2d Cir. 1976) (state court misinformed petitioner about sentencing alternatives).

[144] *See, e.g.,* Dobbs v. Zant, *supra,* 506 U.S. at 359 (discussed *supra* note 143); *Townsend, supra,* 372 U.S. at 317, 321-22 (hearing required because prosecution witness at state hearing withheld full facts regarding truth serum used to obtain confession); Lahay v. Armontrout, 923 F.2d 578, 578-79 (8th Cir. 1991) (state postconviction court's findings that trial counsel had valid tactical reasons for questionable conduct at trial did not obviate need for hearing, given evidence that trial counsel perjured himself at petitioner's and other similar state postconviction hearings and had license removed on that basis); Ross v. Kemp, 785 F.2d 1467, 1476-77 (11th Cir. 1986) (hearing warranted if state official misrepresented existence of jury records during state postconviction proceedings); Code v. Montgomery, 725 F.2d 1316, 1321-22 (11th Cir. 1984) (deposition testimony "too sketchy"); Edwards v. Oklahoma, 577 F.2d 1119, 1121 (10th Cir. 1978) (alleged destruction of breathalyzer test sample); Selz v. California, 423 F.2d 702, 703 (9th Cir. 1970) (substantial allegation of perjury at state hearing).

[145] *See, e.g.,* Manning v. Jarnigan, 501 F.2d 408, 412-13 (6th Cir. 1974) (improper questions by prosecution); Bruce v. Estelle, 483 F.2d 1031, 1040 (5th Cir. 1973) (improper argument by prosecution); authority cited *supra* notes 143, 144.

(w)   The petitioner requested but was not afforded the financial resources necessary to make an adequate evidentiary presentation in the state courts.[146]

(x)   The petitioner was not permitted or able adequately, or at all, to cross-examine adverse witnesses or otherwise to challenge the credibility of adverse evidence, *inter alia,* because of the state's reliance on depositions or affidavits of adverse witnesses.[147]

---

[146] *See, e.g.,* Coleman v. Zant, 708 F.2d 541, 548 (11th Cir. 1983) (state court declined to provide funds for indigent petitioner, thereby effectively precluding him from deposing critical witnesses).

[147] *See, e.g.,* Lewis v. Jeffers, 497 U.S. 764, 801 (1990) (Blackmun, J., dissenting) (findings of state supreme court not due deference because state court "did not see the witnesses and was forced to rely upon a paper record"); Ford v. Wainwright, 477 U.S. 399, 415 (1986) (plurality opinion) (state administrative findings based on report of state-appointed psychiatrists in proceeding in which petitioner was not able to be heard); Walker v. Johnston, 312 U.S. 275, 285 (1941) (*ex parte* affidavits); Salazar v. Johnson, 96 F.3d 789, 791-92 (5th Cir. 1996) (district court erred in according presumption of correctness to state court findings of fact which were based entirely on paper record and which included credibility assessments of conflicting affidavits); Perillo v. Johnson, 79 F.3d 441, 446-47 (5th Cir. 1996) (state habeas corpus judge's reliance on transcripts and affidavits to resolve ineffective assistance claim presented unacceptable "danger of 'trial by affidavit,'" especially given that judge did not preside at trial and "could not supplement the affidavits with his own recollection of the trial and [defense counsel's] performance in it"); Shillinger v. Haworth, 70 F.3d 1132, 1136-37 (10th Cir. 1995) (state supreme court's factfindings were not subject to presumption of correctness, and federal evidentiary hearing was required, because factfindings were entirely based on transcript of in-chambers conferences between judge and lawyers, and petitioner was never afforded opportunity to cross-examine relevant witnesses); Lawson v. Borg, 60 F.3d 608, 611 (9th Cir. 1995) (state court hearing was not "full and fair" because court "refused to hold an evidentiary hearing and resolved the factual issue of alleged juror misconduct solely on the contradictory declarations submitted by the prosecution and defense"); Blackmon v. Scott, 22 F.3d 560, 566-67 (5th Cir. 1994) (federal evidentiary hearing was required because resolution of claim required assessments of witnesses' credibility and state court relied solely on affidavits and paper record); Nethery v. Collins, 993 F.2d 1154, 1157 & n.8 (5th Cir. 1993) (state court findings not entitled to presumption of correctness because they were based solely on paper record and claim required "assess[ment] [of] the credibility of the conflicting affiants"); Smith v. Zant, 887 F.2d 1407, 1433-34 n.15 (11th Cir. 1989) (*en banc*) (Kravitch, J., concurring in part and dissenting in part) (credibility determination made on paper record not due deference); Hyman v. Aiken, 824 F.2d 1405, 1411-12 (4th Cir. 1987) (federal court was not bound by state finding premised on credibility of witness whose testimony state factfinder did not actually hear); Bulger v. McClay, 575 F.2d 407, 410 (2d Cir.), *cert. denied,* 439 U.S. 915 (1978) (petitioner denied right to cross-examine juror); United States ex rel. Fisher v. Driber, 546 F.2d 18, 21-22 (3d Cir. 1976) (deposition did not allow fair determination of credibility); Lee v. Hopper, 499 F.2d 456, 461 (5th Cir.), *cert. denied,* 419 U.S. 1053 (1974) (affidavits); Campbell v. Minnesota, 487 F.2d 1, 4 (8th Cir. 1973); Tyler v. Swenson, 427 F.2d 412, 415 (8th Cir. 1970) (state judge relied on memory of prior proceedings and did not allow himself to be cross-examined); Kerrigan v. Scafati, 348 F.2d 187, 188 (1st Cir. 1965) (state court chose between conflicting affidavits); Doyle v. United States, 336 F.2d 640, 641 (9th Cir. 1964); Grosso v. Artuz, 1998 WL 108011, at *4-*5 (S.D.N.Y. March 12, 1998) (magistrate judge's report) (hearing appropriate under 28 U.S.C.

f. *Unsupported state factfindings.* Under *Townsend v. Sain*,[148] caselaw construing analogous provisions of superseded section 2254(d), and the terms of the new presumption of correctness provision that supersedes former section 2254(d),[149] the district court must grant a hearing to resolve controverted factual questions whenever the state factual determination is not fairly supported by (or, put another way, is unreasonable in light of) the record as a whole.[150] Because a

---

§ 2254, as amended by AEDPA, because petitioner's due process claim that conviction based on materially false testimony requires factfinding on reliability of witness's recantation and state court based ruling entirely on affidavits). *See also supra* §§ 19.4h n.41, 19.5 n.13 and accompanying text. *Cf.* Armstead v. Scott, 37 F.3d 202, 207-08 (5th Cir. 1994), *cert. denied,* 514 U.S. 1071 (1995) (state court "paper hearing" was adequate because postconviction judge was also trial judge and had opportunity to assess credibility of affiants); May v. Collins, 955 F.2d 299, 310-15 (5th Cir.), *cert. denied,* 504 U.S. 901 (1992) (state judge's factfinding procedure adequate, even though based on affidavits, because judge also presided over trial and had opportunity to observe and gauge credibility of witnesses who prepared affidavits). *But see* Carter v. Collins, 918 F.2d 1198, 1202 (5th Cir. 1990) ("Rather than conduct a formal hearing, a state court may evaluate an ineffective assistance of counsel claim by making credibility determinations based on affidavits submitted by the petitioner and the attorney"); Buxton v. Lynaugh, 879 F.2d 140, 144 (5th Cir. 1989), *cert. denied,* 497 U.S. 1032 (1990) (over dissent, court concludes that, under circumstances, state court made fair "credibility choice between ... [conflicting] affidavits"); Ellis v. Lynaugh, 873 F.2d 830, 840 (5th Cir.), *cert. denied,* 493 U.S. 970 (1989) (citing Evans v. McCotter, 805 F.2d 1210, 1214 (5th Cir. 1986)) (under circumstances, "denial of a state writ application on the basis of pleadings and affidavits constitutes an adequate 'hearing'"). On the question whether federal district courts may rely upon "evidence" in the form of affidavits from trial judges discussing the historical facts or explaining their mental processes, see *supra* § 19.5 n.13 and accompanying text; *supra* note 114; *infra* § 21.2 n.13 and accompanying text.

[148] 372 U.S. 293 (1963).

[149] Former section 2254(d)(8)'s provision rendering the presumption of correctness inapplicable if "a consideration of [the "pertinent"] part of the record as a whole" showed that the "factual determination is not fairly supported by the record" paralleled *Townsend*'s recognition of the right to a hearing if the "factual determination is not fairly supported by the record as a whole" (*Townsend, supra,* 372 U.S. at 313). To like effect is the language of 28 U.S.C.A. § 2254(d)(2) (West 1994 & Supp. 1998), which withholds deference from a state court "decision" of a factual question that "was based on an unreasonable determination of the facts in light of the evidence presented in the State court proceeding."

[150] *See, e.g.,* 28 U.S.C. § 2254(d)(8) (1994) (superseded) (no presumption of correctness in these circumstances; quoted *supra* note 149); 28 U.S.C.A. § 2254(d)(2) (West 1994 & Supp. 1998) (similar; quoted *supra* note 149); Purkett v. Elem, 514 U.S. 765, 769 (1995) (*per curiam*) (state court factfindings "may be set aside ... if they are 'not fairly supported by the record'" (quoting superseded 28 U.S.C. § 2254(d)(8))); Parker v. Dugger, 498 U.S. 308, 316-17, 320, 323-24 (1991) ("Florida Supreme Court's conclusion that the trial judge found no mitigating circumstances is not fairly supported by the record in this case."); *Townsend, supra,* 372 U.S. at 316 ("This Court has consistently held that state factual determinations not fairly supported by the record cannot be conclusive of federal rights. Fiske v. Kansas, 274 U.S. 380, 385; Blackburn v. Alabama, 361 U.S. 199, 208-209. Where the fundamental liberties of the person are claimed to have been infringed, we carefully scrutinize the state court record. The duty of the federal district court on habeas is no

federal hearing is required unless the state court record *as a whole* (or, put another way, unless the whole of the evidence presented in the state court proceeding) fairly supports the state findings, the federal court must "carefully scrutinize" the entire state record,[151] which accordingly must be before the federal court and must be made a part of the federal record.[152] Among the

---

less exacting." (some citations omitted)); Carriger v. Stewart, 132 F.3d 463, 473-75 (9th Cir. 1997) (*en banc*), *cert. denied*, 118 S. Ct. 1827 (1998) (presumption of correctness did not apply because state courts' assessment of credibility of state's star witness was "not fairly supported by the record" under superseded 28 U.S.C. § 2254(d)(8)); Jackson v. Herring, 42 F.3d 1350, 1366 (11th Cir.), *cert. denied*, 515 U.S. 1189 (1995) (district court properly held evidentiary hearing because "crucial finding of the state coram nobis court was not fairly supported by the record"); Campaneria v. Reid, 891 F.2d 1014, 1019 (2d Cir. 1989); Dunn v. Simmons, 877 F.2d 1275, 1279 (6th Cir. 1989), *cert. denied*, 494 U.S. 1061 (1990); Stone v. Cardwell, 575 F.2d 724, 726 (9th Cir. 1978); United States ex rel. Irons v. Montanye, 520 F.2d 646, 649 n.8 (2d Cir. 1975); decisions discussed *supra* § 2.4d nn.198-238 and accompanying text & *infra* notes 153-56 and accompanying text. *See also* Parke v. Raley, 506 U.S. 20, 36 (1992) (petitioner's burden of proving that state court findings are not "fairly supported by the record" is "different" from and lower than burden of proving constitutional "[in]sufficiency of the evidence under *Jackson v. Virginia*, 443 U.S. 307 (1979)," which requires proof that no rational factfinder could find defendant guilty). *Cf. id.* at 36 (Court defers to "Kentucky courts' factual determinations," which Court finds to be "'fairly supported by the record' within the meaning of [superseded] 28 U.S.C. § 2254(d)(8)"). *Compare* Rushen v. Spain, 464 U.S. 114, 120 (1983) (*per curiam*) (appearing to equate "not fairly supported" standard in superseded 28 U.S.C. § 2254(d)(8) and "convincing evidence" standard in presumption-rebuttal portion of *id.* § 2254(d) (superseded)) *with infra* § 31.3 (only logical interpretation of superseded section 2254(d) is that it treats "not fairly supported" burden as lower than "convincing evidence" burden). (As is discussed *supra* § 20.2c nn.82-83 and accompanying text, the "not fairly supported" standard in superseded section 2254(d)(8) seems to have been subsumed without significant change by the "unreasonable determination in light of the evidence presented in the State court proceeding" standard in current section 2254(d)(2). Likewise, the rebuttal standard ("by convincing evidence") in superseded section 2254(d) seems to have been subsumed without significant change by the rebuttal standard ("by clear and convincing evidence") in current 28 U.S.C.A. § 2254(e)(1) (West 1994 & Supp. 1998). *See supra* § 20.2c nn.84-86 and accompanying text; *infra* § 20.3h.)

[151] *Townsend, supra,* 372 U.S. at 316. *See* 28 U.S.C. § 2254(d)(8) (1994) (superseded) (review of all "pertinent" parts of record is required); Cabana v. Bullock, 474 U.S. 376, 387 (1986) (district court erred in limiting its inquiry to examination of instructions rather than considering entire record); Mincey v. Arizona, 437 U.S. 385, 398 (1978) (direct appeal case) ("this Court is under a duty to make an independent evaluation of the [state] record"); Harris v. Pulley, 885 F.2d 1354, 1360 (9th Cir. 1988), *cert. denied*, 493 U.S. 1051 (1990); Price v. Wainwright, 759 F.2d 1549, 1552 (11th Cir. 1985) ("federal court should make an independent review of the record to determine whether the historical facts found by the state court support its ultimate finding of competency"); Jurek v. Estelle, 623 F.2d 929, 931 (5th Cir. 1980) (*en banc*), *cert. denied*, 450 U.S. 1014 (1981) ("Supreme Court has frequently stated that it is [a federal court's] affirmative duty 'to examine the entire record and make an independent determination'" of state findings); *supra* §§ 15.2c n.59 and accompanying text, 20.3b.

[152] *See* Dobbs v. Zant, 506 U.S. 358, 358-59 (1993) (*per curiam*) ("[w]e have emphasized before the importance of reviewing capital sentences on a complete record," so "'entire [trial]

recurring circumstances in which the federal courts have concluded that (i) the record did not fairly support state factual determinations (or, put another way, that the fact determination was unreasonable in light of the evidence in the record) and (ii) that a federal hearing accordingly was required, are the following:

(1) The state bore the burden of proof in the state hearing and did not satisfy its burden.[153]

(2) The evidence in the state court record supporting the state finding is ambiguous, inconclusive, or irrelevant.[154]

---

transcript should have been made available'" to habeas corpus petitioner; after state represented that transcript of closing argument at capital sentencing phase was unavailable, and after petitioner subsequently discovered copy of transcript and proffered it to Court of Appeals on motion "to supplement the record on appeal," "Court of Appeals erred when it refused to consider the full transcript," which "flatly contradicted the account [of the closing argument] given by [defense] counsel in key respects"); Thames v. Dugger, 848 F.2d 149, 151 & n.2 (11th Cir. 1988); *supra* §§ 15.2c, 19.2, 20.3b.

[153] *See, e.g.,* Williams v. Nix, 700 F.2d 1164, 1170 (8th Cir. 1983), *rev'd on other grounds,* 467 U.S. 431 (1984); Annunziato v. Manson, 566 F.2d 410, 413-14 (2d Cir. 1977) (hearing necessary on harmless error, on which state bears burden); Prince v. Alabama, 507 F.2d 693, 706 (5th Cir.), *cert. denied,* 423 U.S. 876 (1975) (state failed to carry burden of showing that petitioner frustrated extradition); Cooper v. Picard, 428 F.2d 1351, 1353-54 (1st Cir. 1970) (state failed to carry burden of demonstrating that in-court identification was independent of tainted lineup). *Cf.* Nelson v. Fulcomer, 911 F.2d 928, 931-32 (3d Cir. 1991) (trial court's finding that petitioner did not waive right to silence was fairly supported by record because counsel for state, which bore burden of proving waiver of rights, conceded during pretrial hearing that "'pre-interrogation warning form ... indicates that the defendant ... did not want to talk to the police'" and state did not present any other evidence bearing on issue).

[154] *See, e.g.,* Keeney v. Tamayo-Reyes, 504 U.S. 1, 13 (1992) (O'Connor, J., dissenting) (hearing required when gaps in evidence available to state courts render their findings "dubious"); *Parker v. Dugger, supra,* 498 U.S. at 316, 324 (findings "against the weight of the evidence" will not be inferred and are not due deference; although state court tried to apply law to facts "faithfully and responsibly," Court overturns factfinding for lack of "fair support" in record); Blackmon v. Scott, 22 F.3d 560, 566 n.20 (5th Cir. 1994) (state court finding that "'record is devoid of any evidence that there were undisclosed agreements on the part of the State to provide lenient treatment for any of the State's witnesses in exchange for their testimony' ... is clearly unsupported by the record which contains conflicting evidence" on point, and thus issue "must be resolved" by means of federal hearing); Cumbie v. Singletary, 991 F.2d 715, 723-24 (11th Cir.), *cert. denied,* 510 U.S. 1031 (1993) ("scant record" on claim of denial of face-to-face confrontation did not fairly support state trial court's finding that child complainant would suffer emotional or mental harm by testifying in defendant's presence); Hakeem v. Beyer, 990 F.2d 750, 770-71 (3d Cir. 1993) (record relating to speedy trial claim too ambiguous to support state court's finding that petitioner was solely responsible for pretrial delays); Lahay v. Armontrout, 923 F.2d 578 (8th Cir. 1991) (rejecting state court factfindings and ordering federal hearing because findings apparently were based on perjured testimony at state postconviction hearing); Bouchillon v. Collins, 907 F.2d 589, 594 n.12 (5th Cir. 1990); Prejean v. Smith, 889 F.2d 1391, 1403 (5th Cir. 1989), *cert. denied,* 494 U.S. 1090 (1990) ("adequate, relevant evidence does not appear in the state court record"); Strozier

(3) The record evidence contradicting the state court findings of fact is too strong to justify relying on those findings without conducting a federal hearing.[155]

---

v. Newsome, 871 F.2d 995, 998-1000 (11th Cir. 1989) (evidence on waiver of right to counsel "ambiguous," "contradictory," incomplete, and inaccurate); Burden v. Zant, 871 F.2d 956, 957 (11th Cir. 1989) (hearing required because record on counsel's conflict of interest was incomplete); Escalera v. Coombe, 826 F.2d 185, 192-93 (2d Cir. 1987) ("crucial facts" missing); Cola v. Reardon, 787 F.2d 681, 699 (1st Cir.), cert. denied, 479 U.S. 930 (1986) (state findings supported only by "arguable and incidental references"); Hayes v. Kincheloe, 784 F.2d 1434, 1437-39 (9th Cir. 1986) (evidence that defendant understood elements of charge was scant and conflicting); Peek v. Kemp, 746 F.2d 672, 676-79 (11th Cir. 1984), cert. denied, 479 U.S. 939 (1986); Byrd v. Wainwright, 722 F.2d 716, 719 (11th Cir.), cert. denied, 469 U.S. 869 (1984) (no evidence on key issue); King v. Ponte, 717 F.2d 635, 639 (1st Cir. 1983) ("too many open questions"); Lufkins v. Solem, 716 F.2d 532, 540 (8th Cir. 1983), cert. denied, 467 U.S. 1219 (1984) (state record on counsel's effectiveness was not adequately developed); Plunkett v. Estelle, 709 F.2d 1004, 1010 (5th Cir. 1983), cert. denied, 465 U.S. 1007 (1984) (nothing in record supported reasonable contention that petitioner was aware he could be convicted of uncharged offense; additionally, state court failed to consider crucial part of trial record); Thomas v. Estelle, 582 F.2d 939, 942 (5th Cir. 1978) (no clear testimony on controlling issue); Suggs v. LaVallee, 570 F.2d 1092, 1114 (2d Cir.), cert. denied, 439 U.S. 915 (1978) ("several material facts were not adequately developed at the state hearing"); Todd v. Lockhart, 490 F.2d 626, 628 (8th Cir. 1974); Lofton v. Procunier, 487 F.2d 434, 436 (9th Cir. 1973) (state record was "barren of proof" on disputed matter); Knight v. Minnesota, 484 F.2d 104, 107 (8th Cir. 1973) (state record raises "serious doubts" as to correctness of state factual finding); United States ex rel. Johnson v. Johnson, 471 F.2d 264, 267 (3d Cir. 1973) ("[state] record, far from supporting the findings relied on ... is at best equivocal"); Hunter v. Swenson, 442 F.2d 625, 631 (8th Cir.), cert. denied, 404 U.S. 863 (1971); Shepard v. Wainwright, 424 F.2d 535, 536 (5th Cir. 1970); Oswald v. Crouse, 420 F.2d 373, 374 (10th Cir. 1969) (record was "indefinite and inconclusive"); Bryan v. Pope, 416 F.2d 21, 21-22 (9th Cir. 1969) (record "confusing, and upon it, a certain conclusion cannot be reached"); Myers v. Frye, 401 F.2d 18, 22 (7th Cir. 1968); Collins v. Maroney, 382 F.2d 547, 548 (3d Cir. 1967) (key factual questions unanswered). Cf. Parker v. Dugger, supra at 737 (state trial court findings accepted by multiple state and federal reviewing judges are more likely to deserve deference than findings as to which some state or federal judge has dissented (citing Wainwright v. Goode, 464 U.S. 78, 85 (1983) (per curiam))); Wainwright v. Goode, supra at 85 (possibly ambiguous state court record does not undermine deference due state court factfindings when interpretation of facts adopted by state court "find[s] fair support in the record"; federal court may not "substitut[e] its view of the facts" for view of state court); Henderson v. Smith, 903 F.2d 534, 538 (8th Cir.), cert. denied, 498 U.S. 989 (1990) (state court finding that petitioner received adequate warnings from counsel before waiving conflict-free representation is fairly supported by record, which showed repeated, albeit not well-explained, warnings about potential conflicts; "[u]nder [section 2254(d)(8) (since superseded)] we cannot reject the state court's factual findings merely because we would have come to the opposite conclusion ... [but] only ... if they are not fairly supported by the record").

[155] See, e.g., Shillinger v. Haworth, 70 F.3d 1132, 1136-38 (10th Cir. 1995) (based on review of relevant portions of transcript, court of appeals concludes that state supreme court's factfinding "is not 'fairly supported by the record'"); Jackson v. Herring, 42 F.3d 1350, 1366 (11th Cir.), cert. denied, 515 U.S. 1189 (1995) (although state court found that trial counsel made "informed tactical decision" to forgo presenting mitigation witnesses at capital sentencing hearing, state court's

(4)   The evidence supporting petitioner's claim is compelling.[156]

g. *Nexus to mandatory hearing issues.* The district court also should grant an evidentiary hearing on any claim that is closely related to, or intertwined with, another issue on which a hearing must be held.[157]

---

analysis was based on erroneous understanding of "fact[s] which counsel knew or should have known"); Hart v. Marion Correctional Inst., 927 F.2d 256, 259 (6th Cir.), *cert. denied,* 502 U.S. 816 (1991) (state court factfinding that petitioner was aware of actual sentencing possibilities when he pled guilty was not due presumption of correctness, given inaccuracies in information provided to petitioner, on record, both before and after plea was entered); *Bouchillon v. Collins, supra,* 907 F.2d at 594 n.12; *Cola v. Reardon, supra,* 787 F.2d at 698 ("independent review of the record" reveals "significant evidence" refuting state court findings); *Hayes v. Kincheloe, supra,* 784 F.2d at 1438; Thomas v. Lockhart, 738 F.2d 304, 307 (8th Cir. 1984); Velez v. Schmer, 724 F.2d 249, 252 (1st Cir. 1984); Dickerson v. Fogg, 692 F.2d 238, 243 (2d Cir. 1982) (state factfindings were logically inconsistent); United States ex rel. Gorham v. Franzen, 675 F.2d 932, 936-37 (7th Cir. 1982); Moore v. Ballone, 658 F.2d 218, 222 (4th Cir. 1981) (no evidence of *Miranda* warnings in tape of interrogation and no documents executed by petitioner to show that he had been informed of rights). *See also* Burden v. Zant, 510 U.S. 132, 133 (1994) (*per curiam*) (overturning district court's and court of appeals's finding that petitioner's counsel did not negotiate immunity agreement for codefendant in return for codefendant's testimony against petitioner (and thus did not have conflict of interest in representing petitioner) because of "evidence strongly supporting Burden's contention that some sort of immunity deal had, in fact, been struck" and because lower courts' finding accordingly "was grounded on manifest mistake").

[156] *See, e.g.,* Howell v. Barker, 904 F.2d 889, 894-95 & n.7 (4th Cir.), *cert. denied,* 498 U.S. 1016 (1990) (presumption in favor of state court factfindings overcome by state's concession in brief and oral argument that petitioner accurately alleged facts contrary to facts found by state court); Magwood v. Smith, 791 F.2d 1438, 1448, 1450 (11th Cir. 1986) ("evidence of the existence of the mitigating factors ... is so overwhelming as to make the trial court's rejection of their existence clearly erroneous"; "evidence is more than sufficient to overcome the presumption of correctness"); *Cola v. Reardon, supra,* 787 F.2d at 698; Bailey v. Hamby, 744 F.2d 25, 26 (6th Cir. 1984); United States ex rel. Ross v. Franzen, 668 F.2d 933, 939 (7th Cir. 1982) (record flatly contradicts state factfindings); Fitch v. Estelle, 587 F.2d 773, 777 (5th Cir.), *cert. denied,* 444 U.S. 881 (1979) (finding of "competence to stand trial" belied by petitioner's bizarre actions at trial and robbery of sheriff); DuRain v. Wingo, 412 F.2d 852, 853 (6th Cir. 1969) (alleged robbery victim signed affidavit stating he had not been robbed). *See also* Burden v. Zant, *supra,* 510 U.S. 132, 133 (discussed *supra* note 155). In the situation described here, summary judgment based on the state-court record may be appropriate. *See Bailey v. Hamby, supra; United States ex rel. Ross v. Franzen, supra; supra* § 17.3.

[157] *See, e.g.,* Salkay v. Wainwright, 552 F.2d 151, 153 (5th Cir. 1977) (because hearing was required on claim that *nolo contendere* plea was not knowing and voluntary, court also should hold hearing on related claim of ineffective assistance of counsel). *See also* Coleman v. Zant, 708 F.2d 541, 548 (11th Cir. 1983) (although petitioner's entitlement to hearing was clear only with respect to one of his three issues, parties would be permitted, if they desire, to present evidence at hearing on other two issues as well); authority cited *infra* § 20.4 (para (2)).

h. *Rebuttal of state factfindings.* Even if the district court rules that state court factfindings on controlling issues are subject to a presumption of correctness, section 2254(e)(1) permits the petitioner to rebut that presumption.[158] Until the enactment of the Antiterrorism and Effective Death Penalty Act of 1996 (AEDPA),[159] the applicable statutory provision required that the petitioner rebut the presumption by presenting "convincing evidence."[160] Although AEDPA replaced that statutory language with the phrase "clear and convincing evidence"[161] (a change that applies to those federal habeas corpus proceedings that are governed by AEDPA[162]), the verbal modification does not appear to alter the preexisting substantive standard in any appreciable way.[163] AEDPA also does not alter the well-established rule that a petitioner is entitled to a federal court evidentiary hearing to present the rebuttal evidence.[164]

---

[158] 28 U.S.C.A. § 2254(e)(1) (West 1994 & Supp. 1998) (superseding 28 U.S.C. § 2254(d)). The superseded § 2254(d) continues to apply to those federal habeas corpus proceedings that are not governed by AEDPA. *See infra* notes 161-62 and accompanying text. *See generally supra* § 3.4.

[159] Pub. L. 104-132, 110 Stat. 1214 (1996).

[160] 28 U.S.C. § 2254(d) (1994) (superseded).

[161] 28 U.S.C.A. § 2254(e)(1) (West 1994 & Supp. 1998).

[162] For an explanation of which cases are governed by AEDPA, see *supra* § 3.4.

[163] *See supra* § 20.2c n.87 and accompanying text; *infra* § 31.3.

[164] *See, e.g.,* Demosthenes v. Baal, 495 U.S. 731, 735 (1990) (*per curiam*) (petitioner may rebut presumption of correctness of state factfindings by establishing that state courts' factfindings "are not 'fairly supported by the record'" (quoting superseded 28 U.S.C. § 2254(d)(8))); Patton v. Yount, 467 U.S. 1025, 1028 (1984) (at hearing, petitioner fails to rebut presumption of correctness); Sumner v. Mata, 449 U.S. 539, 550 (1981) (similar); In re Heidnik, 112 F.3d 105, 112 n.7 (3d Cir. 1997) ("evidence presented in the district court demonstrates [that] petitioner has rebutted this presumption [of correctness of state court factfinding] here by clear and convincing evidence"); Lahay v. Armontrout, 923 F.2d 578 (8th Cir. 1991) (presumption in favor of state court factfindings overcome by proof that state court factfindings are based on perjured testimony at state postconviction hearing); Howell v. Barker, 904 F.2d 889, 894-95 & n.7 (4th Cir.), *cert. denied,* 498 U.S. 1016 (1990) (presumption in favor of state court factfindings overcome by state's concession in brief and oral argument that petitioner accurately alleged facts contrary to those found by state court); Estock v. Lane, 842 F.2d 184 (7th Cir. 1988) (presumption of correctness overcome); Richmond v. Ricketts, 774 F.2d 957, 962 (9th Cir. 1985) (hearing required despite findings due presumption of correctness because "section 2254(d) presumes that state court findings are correct, 'unless the applicant shall establish *or it shall otherwise appear*' that this presumption should be abandoned" (emphasis in original)); Price v. Wainwright, 759 F.2d 1549, 1553 (11th Cir. 1985) ("petitioner becomes entitled to an evidentiary hearing by proffering clear and convincing evidence that raises a substantial, threshold doubt" about state court finding); Birt v. Montgomery, 709 F.2d 690, 694 (11th Cir. 1983), *cert. denied,* 469 U.S. 874 (1984). *See infra* §§ 30.3, 31.3. Justice O'Connor's incidental comment in Keeney v. Tamayo-Reyes, 504 U.S. 1 (1992), that "if the petitioner has not fulfilled one of the *Townsend* requirements [for establishing a right to a mandatory hearing,] he will *generally* not ... be entitled ... to a hearing ...," *id.* at 20-22 (O'Connor, J., dissenting) (emphasis added), does not consider — and thus should not be understood to

§ 20.4. Discretionary hearings.[1]

In *Townsend v. Sain*,[2] the Supreme Court held that "where an applicant for writ of habeas corpus alleges facts which, if proved, would entitle him to relief, the federal court ... has the power to receive evidence and try the facts anew."[3] Going beyond the delineation of situations in which the district court *must* conduct an evidentiary hearing,[4] this passage in *Townsend* recognized the district court's *"discretion"* to hold a hearing "[i]n *every* case" in which a factual dispute exists.[5] The only limit the Court placed on the "sound discretion" of the district courts in this regard was that hearings should not be held on claims that are "frivolous," [6] which the statute and Habeas Rules require the court to dismiss summarily.[7]

---

question — the availability of hearings to enable the petitioner, as is expressly contemplated in section 2254(d), to rebut the presumption of correctness "by [presenting] convincing *evidence*." 28 U.S.C. § 2254(d) (emphasis added). A similar analysis is appropriate in interpreting Justice O'Connor's statement that: "[w]here a petitioner has a right to a hearing he must prove facts by a preponderance of the evidence, but where he has no right to a hearing he must prove facts by the higher standard of convincing evidence. Without the opportunity for a hearing, it is safe to assume that this higher standard will be unattainable for most petitioners." *Keeney v. Tamayo-Reyes, supra* at 21. In this passage, Justice O'Connor was considering only the petitioner's right to a hearing under the *Townsend* criteria and not under superseded section 2254(d).

§ 20.4.   [1] *See generally* authority cited *supra* § 20.1 n.1.

[2] 372 U.S. 293 (1963).

[3] *Id.* at 312.

[4] *See supra* § 20.3.

[5] *Townsend, supra,* 372 U.S. at 318 (emphasis added). *Accord* Jackson v. Virginia, 443 U.S. 307, 318 (1979); Brewer v. Williams, 430 U.S. 387, 396-97 (1977); Blackledge v. Allison, 431 U.S. 63, 76 (1977) (discretion to conduct factfinding procedures whenever claim raised is not "'palpably incredible'" or "'patently frivolous or false'" (quoting Pennsylvania ex rel. Herman v. Claudy, 350 U.S. 116, 119 (1956))). *See, e.g.,* Craker v. Procunier, 756 F.2d 1212, 1214 (5th Cir. 1985); Chaney v. Brown, 730 F.2d 1334, 1357 n.30 (10th Cir.), *cert. denied,* 469 U.S. 1090 (1984) (*dicta*); United States ex rel. Shank v. Commonwealth of Pennsylvania, 461 F.2d 61, 62 (3d Cir. 1972), *cert. denied,* 409 U.S. 1110 (1973); Muniz v. Beto, 434 F.2d 697, 714 (5th Cir. 1970); Parker v. Sigler, 413 F.2d 459, 461 (8th Cir. 1969), *vac'd & remanded on other grounds,* 396 U.S. 482 (1970); Silver v. Dunbar, 407 F.2d 1182, 1184 (9th Cir.), *cert. denied,* 395 U.S. 914 (1969); authority cited *infra* notes 7, 15-22.

[6] *Townsend, supra,* 372 U.S. at 318.

[7] *See* 28 U.S.C. § 2243 (1994); Rule 4 of the Rules Governing § 2254 Cases; Sims v. Livesay, 970 F.2d 1575, 1579 (6th Cir. 1992) ("'In every case, [the district court] has the power, constrained only by his sound discretion, to receive evidence bearing upon the applicant's constitutional claim.'" (quoting *Townsend, supra,* 372 U.S. at 318)); Landano v. Rafferty, 897 F.2d 661, 683 (3d Cir.) (Rosenn, J., dissenting), *cert. denied,* 498 U.S. 811 (1990) ("*Townsend* leaves it to the discretion of the trial court to determine if an evidentiary hearing is necessary"); Crosswhite v. Swenson, 444 F.2d 648, 650 (8th Cir. 1971), *cert. denied,* 405 U.S. 1042 (1972) ("In every case

As is discussed above, Congress's 1966 enactment of section 2254(d) of the Judicial Code largely endorsed *Townsend*'s requirement of hearings in certain situations without in any way restricting the district courts' discretionary power to order hearings.[8] Even more clearly, the enactment in 1976 of the Rules Governing § 2254 Cases placed Congress's imprimatur on *Townsend*'s delineation both of the situations in which hearings are "mandatory" and of other situations in which the decision whether to hold a hearing is committed to the "discretion of the district judge."[9] Although the Court thereafter placed limits on *mandatory* hearings in its 1992 decision in *Keeney v. Tamayo-Reyes*,[10] it did not limit in any way the federal courts' discretion to hold hearings on any nonfrivolous factual allegation in a habeas corpus petition or response.[11]

The first and only limitation on a district court's discretionary power to hold an evidentiary hearing was recently imposed by Congress in the Antiterrorism

---

[the district judge] has the power, constrained only by his sound discretion, to receive evidence bearing upon the applicant's constitutional claim."); Fisher v. Scafati, 439 F.2d 307, 309 (1st Cir.), *vac'd & remanded on other grounds*, 408 U.S. 913 (1971) (hearing is permissible unless appellate court finds abuse of discretion); authority cited *supra* note 5 & *infra* notes 15-22. *See also supra* § 15.2c (legal standards for summary dismissal). *But cf.* Mathis v. Zant, 975 F.2d 1493, 1497 (11th Cir. 1992) (by remanding for district court to justify its *sua sponte* decision to hear evidence of ineffective assistance of counsel, court suggests that district court must explain bases on which it exercised discretion to hold hearing).

[8] *See supra* §§ 20.2a, 20.3h. *See, e.g.*, Lawrie v. Snyder, 1998 WL 276252, at *8 & n.5 (D. Del. May 15, 1998) ("[I]n effect, the 1996 [AEDPA] amendment supersedes *Keeney*, which superseded a portion of *Townsend*, namely, the fifth circumstance in which an evidentiary hearing is mandatory. The remainder of *Townsend*, however, appears to have been left intact, including the other five factors under which an evidentiary hearing is mandatory, as well as the court's overriding ability to hold a hearing in its discretion.").

[9] Advisory Committee Note to Rule 8 of the Rules Governing § 2254 Cases. *See* Rule 8 of the Rules Governing § 2254 Cases; Advisory Committee Note to Rule 7 of the Rules Governing § 2254 Cases. The degree of scrutiny Congress gave to the Habeas Rules and their commentary before enacting them, *see, e.g., supra* §§ 11.5, 15.1; *infra* § 28.2b, demonstrates the authoritativeness of the Advisory Committee Notes cited above.

[10] 504 U.S. 1 (1992) (discussed *supra* §§ 20.1a, 20.3e (para. (2)).

[11] *See, e.g.*, Lonchar v. Thomas, 517 U.S. 314, 326 (1996) ("district court is afforded a degree of discretion in determining whether to hold an evidentiary hearing" (citing Rule 8(a) of the Rules Governing § 2254 Cases; *Tamayo-Reyes, supra*, 504 U.S. at 11-12; *Townsend, supra*, 372 U.S. at 318)); Pagan v. Keane, 984 F.2d 61, 64 (2d Cir. 1993) (standard adopted in *Tamayo-Reyes* for mandatory hearings does not limit district court's discretion under *Townsend* "to hold a hearing even though one [is] not required"; factors relevant to exercise of discretion include "the existence of a factual dispute, the strength of the proffered evidence, the thoroughness of prior proceedings, and the nature of the state court determination"); Jamison v. Lockhart, 975 F.2d 1377, 1381 (8th Cir. 1992) ("We do not read *Tamayo-Reyes* as altering our discretionary power to order ... [a] hearing."); Burden v. Zant, 975 F.2d 771, 775-76 n.13 (11th Cir. 1992) (*Tamayo-Reyes* does "not affect a federal court's discretion to hold an evidentiary hearing on material facts not adequately developed in state court, even if the hearing is not mandatory.").

and Effective Death Penalty Act of 1996 (AEDPA).[12] In those cases that are governed by AEDPA,[13] the statute categorically forbids a hearing if the petitioner's default was responsible for the state courts' failure to develop the material facts and if the petitioner fails to satisfy the statutory requirements for excusing the default.[14] In all other situations in AEDPA-governed cases — and in all cases that are not governed by AEDPA — the federal courts retain the discretionary powers that the Court recognized in *Townsend* and that Congress subsequently endorsed in the Rules Governing § 2254 Cases.

Recurring situations in which district courts have exercised their discretion to conduct evidentiary hearings include the following:

(1) Although ultimately resolved against the petitioner, the question whether a hearing is mandatory was close,[15] *e.g.*, because the evidence before the court leaves the "factual disputes seemingly unresolved in essential totality," [16] or because the factual disputes are substantial and complex.[17]

---

[12] Pub. L. 104-132, 110 Stat. 1214 (1996). For an overview of the changes AEDPA makes in federal habeas corpus standards and procedures, see *supra* § 3.2.

[13] For an explanation of the cases to which AEDPA applies, see *supra* § 3.4.

[14] *See* 28 U.S.C.A. § 2254(e)(2) (West 1994 & Supp. 1998) (discussed *supra* §§ 20.2b nn.20-40 and accompanying text, 20.3e nn.109-13 and accompanying text).

[15] *See, e.g., Pagan v. Keane, supra*, 984 F.2d at 64; Hillery v. Pulley, 533 F. Supp. 1189, 1204 (E.D. Cal. 1982), *aff'd*, 733 F.2d 644 (9th Cir. 1984), *aff'd sub nom. Vasquez v. Hillery*, 474 U.S. 254 (1986); United States ex rel. Mangiaracina v. Case, 439 F. Supp. 913 (E.D. Pa. 1977), *aff'd*, 577 F.2d 730 (3d Cir. 1978); United States ex rel. Clayton v. Mancusi, 326 F. Supp. 1366 (E.D.N.Y. 1971), *aff'd*, 454 F.2d 454 (2d Cir.), *cert. denied*, 406 U.S. 977 (1972).

[16] United States ex rel. Griffin v. Vincent, 359 F. Supp. 1072, 1073 (S.D.N.Y. 1973). *See* Landano v. Rafferty, No. 85-4777 (D.N.J. Sept. 29, 1987); Rice v. Wolff, 388 F. Supp. 185, 195 (D. Neb. 1974), *aff'd*, 513 F.2d 1280 (8th Cir. 1975) (hearing ordered to make state record "more complete" on two unresolved issues).

[17] *See, e.g.*, Blodgett v. Campbell, 508 U.S. 1301 (1993) (O'Connor, Circuit Justice, in chambers) (noting lower court's decision in habeas corpus case to remand to district court for evidentiary hearing "because [court of appeals] had 'chosen to address whether hanging is cruel and unusual punishment'" and because "it would be helpful to have 'the benefit of an evidentiary hearing, with findings and conclusions by the district court'"); Fowler v. Jago, 683 F.2d 983, 991 (6th Cir. 1982), *cert. denied*, 460 U.S. 1098 (1983) (hearing "compelled by the failure of the state trial judge to articulate the legal standard applied or the factual findings upon which it was based in light of the complex facts of the case"); Edwards v. Oklahoma, 577 F.2d 1119, 1121 (10th Cir. 1978) (record contains "too many unanswered questions"); United States ex rel. Oliver v. Vincent, 498 F.2d 340, 344 (2d Cir. 1974) (hearing needed to determine merit of petitioner's claims presenting "substantial issue of fact").

(2) A hearing is mandatory on one issue raised by the petitioner and it is accordingly convenient to address the other claims at that hearing,[18] or a hearing is for some other reason likely to save judicial resources.[19]

(3) The state finding in question is based on a state judge's memory, conclusions about his own conduct, or other matters not clearly reflected in the record,[20] or the petition in some other way questions the fairness of the factfinder.[21]

(4) The petitioner is under sentence of death and this habeas corpus proceeding is his last opportunity before being executed to produce evidence demonstrating the unconstitutionality of the procedure that resulted in his death sentence.[22]

---

[18] *See, e.g.,* Stano v. Dugger, 901 F.2d 898, 905 (11th Cir. 1990) (*en banc*) (because hearing is required on question whether state officials suppressed evidence, district court also should hear evidence on petitioner's separate claim alleging that state improperly used jailhouse informant); Smith v. Wainwright, 741 F.2d 1248, 1256 (11th Cir. 1984), *cert. denied,* 470 U.S. 1088 (1985); Coleman v. Zant, 708 F.2d 541, 548 (11th Cir. 1983) (because hearing required on one issue, parties would be allowed, if they desire, to present evidence on two other issues as well); Salkay v. Wainwright, 552 F.2d 151, 153 (5th Cir. 1977); United States ex rel. Pugach v. Mancusi, 411 F.2d 177, 181 (2d Cir.), *cert. denied,* 396 U.S. 889 (1969); Rhinehart v. Rhay, 409 F.2d 208 (9th Cir. 1969), *cert. denied,* 404 U.S. 825 (1971); *supra* § 20.3g.

[19] *See, e.g.,* Ross v. Kemp, 785 F.2d 1467, 1477-78 (11th Cir. 1986) (remand for further hearings was in interest of justice and was efficient in that it avoided later filing of successive petitions); Mitchell v. Scully, 746 F.2d 951, 953 n.2 (2d Cir. 1984), *cert. denied,* 470 U.S. 1056 (1985) ("we must nevertheless remark on the number of occasions on which ... much time could have been saved by [conducting a] hearing").

[20] *See, e.g.,* Thames v. Dugger, 848 F.2d 149, 151 (11th Cir. 1988) (discussed *supra* § 20.3e n.114); United States ex rel. Gorham v. Franzen, 675 F.2d 932, 937 (7th Cir. 1982) (state court's conclusion on admissibility of petitioner's confession was based on record that was "somewhat ambiguous and inconclusive"); Friedman v. United States, 588 F.2d 1010, 1015 (5th Cir. 1979); Tannahill v. Arizona, 440 F.2d 555, 556 (9th Cir. 1971) (*per curiam*) (district court had discretion to order hearing to receive additional evidence concerning circumstances surrounding petitioner's confession); Tyler v. Swenson, 427 F.2d 412, 415 (8th Cir. 1970) (state trial judge improperly served as material witness as well as trier of fact); other authority discussed *supra* § 20.3e (para. (3)).

[21] *See, e.g., Tyler v. Swenson, supra,* 427 F.2d at 415 (state judge was both material witness and factfinder). *Cf.* Rose v. Mitchell, 443 U.S. 545, 561, 563 (1979) (federal review necessary when state judge whose fairness petitioner challenges on 14th Amendment grounds is same judge who decided merits of jury discrimination claim). *See also supra* § 20.3e.

[22] *See, e.g.,* Blodgett v. Campbell, 508 U.S. 1301 (1993) (O'Connor, Circuit Justice, in chambers) (noting lower court's decision in habeas corpus case to remand to district court for evidentiary hearing "because [court of appeals] had 'chosen to address whether hanging is cruel and unusual punishment'" and because "it would be helpful to have 'the benefit of an evidentiary hearing, with findings and conclusions by the district court'"); Ford v. Wainwright, 477 U.S. 399, 418 (1986) (plurality opinion) (hearing required, given need for trustworthiness of factfindings that permit execution to take place); Autry v. Estelle, 719 F.2d 1251, 1252 (5th Cir. 1983); Bass v.

Estelle, 696 F.2d 1154, 1161 (5th Cir.), *cert. denied,* 464 U.S. 865 (1983) (Goldberg, J., concurring); *supra* § 20.1c. *See generally supra* § 2.6.

Chapter 21

CONDUCT OF THE HEARING

§ 21.1. Preparing for the hearing.[1]

a. *Preparation.* Preparation for a habeas corpus hearing deserves as much attention as preparation for any other trial of fact. To be sure, prior state proceedings, together with such mechanisms as "expansion of the record" and summary judgment based on state factfindings,[2] have the capacity to narrow the triable issues in habeas corpus cases in ways not available in other kinds of trial-level litigation. But habeas corpus issues that *are* on for trial are likely, for a number of reasons, to require intensive and time-consuming preparation.

First, the habeas corpus statute and rules tend to reserve hearings for cases in which the state factfinding process was inadequate or unfair.[3] Despite its technically "collateral" or appellate nature, therefore, any federal hearing that is ordered is likely to be "the main event"[4] insofar as the petitioner's constitutional rights are concerned. Counsel's responsibilities in preparing for a hearing accordingly may be as weighty as those imposed on criminal trial and state postconviction attorneys.[5]

Second, because the events that are the focus of the hearing usually occurred at or before the original criminal trial, hence also before appellate and state postconviction proceedings, the critical events are unlikely to be fresh in the witnesses' minds as the hearing approaches. So, too, many of the key witnesses are likely to be either difficult to contact (as often is true of codefendants and alleged coperpetrators who were not convicted or never even charged, as well as clients' friends and families) or reluctant to cooperate (as typically is true of the victims of the offense; law enforcement, prosecutorial, and state court personnel; prison officials; and, in some situations, prior counsel).[6] Rarely, therefore, are critical habeas corpus witnesses easy to find, interview, or prepare for testifying. Because habeas corpus clients typically are incarcerated, and because habeas corpus proceedings generally focus on investigatory and judicial conduct rather

---

§ 21.1. [1] *See generally* RONALD P. SOKOL, FEDERAL HABEAS CORPUS 116-32 (2d ed. 1969); LARRY W. YACKLE, POSTCONVICTION REMEDIES §§ 124, 137 (1981 & Supp. 1998); Charles Alan Wright, *Procedure for Habeas Corpus*, 77 F.R.D. 227, 245-47 (1978); *Developments in the Law — Federal Habeas Corpus*, 83 Harv. L. REV. 1038, 1140-42, 1188-92 (1970).

[2] *See supra* §§ 15.2, 17.3, 19.5.

[3] *See supra* Chapter 20.

[4] Granberry v. Greer, 481 U.S. 129, 132 (1987) (quoting Wainwright v. Sykes, 433 U.S. 72, 89-90 (1977)).

[5] *See generally* AMERICAN BAR ASSOCIATION, STANDARDS FOR CRIMINAL JUSTICE (2d ed. 1980 & 3d ed. 1993). *See also* Rule 8(c) of the Rules Governing § 2254 Cases and Advisory Committee Note to *id.* (importance of prehearing "investigation and preparation"); *supra* §§ 7.1a, 19.1.

[6] *See supra* § 11.2b (sources of information relevant to habeas corpus claims).

than on things the clients themselves did or witnessed, even the client is unlikely to provide as much help in preparing for the hearing as clients provide in other settings.

Finally, and most critically, the issues to be tried in habeas corpus cases often are more complex than they at first seem.[7] Consider, for example, the process of establishing that the representation the petitioner received at trial was ineffective, in violation of the 6th and 14th Amendments. Although at first blush it might seem possible to support this claim simply by pointing to relevant passages of the trial transcript (perhaps supplemented by live testimony of the trial attorney and petitioner), the standards applied by the Supreme Court require much more, *i.e.,* that the petitioner conduct for the federal judge what amounts to two criminal trials: (1) a reprise of the petitioner's trial as it *did* occur, including a description of its pretrial investigatory phase, in order to reveal — perhaps with the assistance of an expert witness — that prior counsel's representation was not reasonably competent; and (2) the trial as it *would* have occurred but for prior counsel's unreasonable conduct, in order to show that a reasonably competent defense could have led to a more favorable outcome than did the actual trial.[8]

Other claims requiring similar showings of "prejudice" — *e.g.,* improper denial of a continuance, of funds necessary for an adequate defense, or of the ability to present defensive evidence; or prosecutorial suppression of exculpatory evidence[9] — place similarly complex demands on counsel in preparing for a

---

[7] *See supra* §§ 9.1, 11.2c (discussing potential habeas corpus claims).

[8] *See* Strickland v. Washington, 466 U.S. 668, 687, 691, 694 (1984) (petitioner must show that trial counsel's performance "was not 'within the range of competence demanded of attorneys in criminal cases'" and "that there is a reasonable probability that, but for counsel's unprofessional errors, the result of the proceeding would have been different" (quoting McMann v. Richardson, 397 U.S. 759, 770-71 (1970))); United States ex rel. Cross v. DeRobertis, 811 F.2d 1008, 1016 (7th Cir. 1987) (petitioner alleging ineffective assistance based on failure to investigate must make "comprehensive showing" of "what information would have been obtained from an investigation and whether such information, assuming its admissibility in court, would have produced a different result"; "[u]nder usual circumstances, we would expect that such information would be presented to the habeas court through the testimony of potential witnesses"). *See generally* Vivian O. Berger, *The Supreme Court and Defense Counsel: Old Roads, New Paths — A Dead End?,* 86 COLUM. L. REV. 9 (1986); Gary Goodpaster, *The Trial for Life: Effective Assistance of Counsel in Death Penalty Cases,* 58 N.Y.U. L. REV. 299 (1983); William W. Schwarzer, *Dealing with Incompetent Counsel — The Trial Judge's Role,* 93 HARV. L. REV. 633 (1980).

[9] *See, e.g.,* United States v. Bagley, 473 U.S. 667, 677 (1985) (prejudice or "materiality" element of claim of prosecutorial suppression of evidence). *See also infra* § 21.2 n.12 and accompanying text (evidentiary consequences of expanding prejudice requirements in habeas corpus litigation); *infra* §§ 26.3c, 28.3c (discussing "prejudice" prong of "cause and prejudice exception" to procedural default and a related defense to habeas corpus relief); *infra* § 32.4d (distinguishing harmless error and "prejudice" analyses).

hearing. So, too, claims based on the unconstitutional admission of inculpatory statements, unlawfully seized evidence, unduly suggestive eyewitness identification testimony, and other tainted evidence may require counsel to conduct what amounts to one or more full-fledged suppression hearings in federal court of the sort that typically precede criminal trials, as also may claims based on an improper denial of a venue change or on racially discriminatory jury selection techniques. And virtually any habeas corpus claim may oblige the petitioner to present evidence not only on the constitutional merits but also in rebuttal to the state's defenses, such as nonexhaustion, procedural default, or delay.[10] For these and other reasons, preparation for a habeas corpus hearing often requires counsel to review, retrace, or for the first time undertake most or all of the investigatory and preparatory steps that typically must precede both the criminal trial itself and then, later, the filing of the habeas corpus petition.[11] A good bit of legal preparation often is required as well, both to assure that the evidence satisfies the prerequisites for each of the claims on which a hearing is ordered and to anticipate the legal and factual responses the petitioner may marshal against the state's procedural defenses.[12]

If the district court orders a hearing, counsel should consider whether the ruling provides a basis for applying for (or seeking reconsideration of previous denials of) appointment of counsel or experts, provision of other financial assistance, production of the state record, discovery, or expansion of the record.[13] Although some of these procedures (*e.g.,* expansion of the record) may come into play in determining whether a hearing is appropriate, others (*e.g.,* appointment of counsel) are especially appropriate once a hearing has been

---

[10] Cases discussing the need for hearings on issues presented by defenses to habeas corpus relief are collected *supra* § 20.1b; *infra* §§ 26.3e, 32.4f. *See generally supra* Chapter 20 (issues on which evidentiary hearings are required or appropriate); *infra* Chapters 22-28, 32 (habeas corpus defenses).

[11] *See supra* §§ 6.2, 7.1a, 11.2, 19.1.

[12] *See supra* Chapter 9 (cognizable claims); *supra* § 11.2c (same); *supra* Chapter 20 & *infra* Chapters 22-28, 32 (defenses). *Compare, e.g.,* Mathis v. Zant, 975 F.2d 1493, 1497 (11th Cir. 1992) (reversing district court's posthearing grant of writ and remanding for further findings on applicability of presumption of correctness to state court factfindings on ineffective assistance of counsel and determination whether petitioner's introduction of "additional evidence to bolster his claim of ineffective assistance of counsel at sentencing by developing and submitting evidence never presented to the state court that first addressed this claim" was barred by defenses of nonexhaustion or procedural default) *with, e.g.,* Meeks v. Singletary, 963 F.2d 316, 320 n.5 (11th Cir. 1992), *cert. denied,* 507 U.S. 950 (1993) (remanding for evidentiary hearing on ineffective assistance of counsel and instructing district court that state has already implicitly waived any defenses it might have invoked to bar petitioner from "present[ing] to the district court any instances of alleged ineffectiveness not raised in state court").

[13] *See supra* Chapters 12, 19.

ordered,[14] and all the procedures (*e.g.*, discovery directed at crucial but un-cooperative witnesses) have the capacity in some circumstances to aid counsel in preparing for a hearing. As counsel may wish to point out in a memorandum supporting a request for one or more of these pretrial procedures, they also often have the capacity to benefit the court by streamlining the hearing.

b. *Continuances; speedy hearing.* Rule 8(c) of the Rules Governing § 2254 Cases provides that an evidentiary "hearing shall be conducted as promptly as practicable, having regard for the need of counsel for both parties for adequate time for investigation and preparation." This rule provides for the granting of continuances upon motion of counsel when necessary to allow adequate preparation and fair proceedings. The Advisory Committee Note to Habeas Rule 8 explains that the court, in scheduling and rescheduling the hearing, should consider "the complexity of the case, the availability of important materials, the workload of the attorney general, and the time required by appointed counsel to prepare."[15]

Rule 8(c) also imposes an analogue to the constitutional and statutory speedy-trial requirements in criminal proceedings.[16] As the rule states, the "hearing shall be conducted as promptly as practicable." This mandatory language may appear at first to be inconsistent with one of the purposes of Habeas Rule 8(c), namely, to *soften* the preexisting statutory requirement that a hearing date be set "not more than five days after the [state's answer] unless for good cause additional

---

[14] *See* Rule 8(c) of the Rules Governing § 2254 Cases; Bashor v. Risley, 730 F.2d 1228, 1234 (9th Cir.), *cert. denied,* 469 U.S. 838 (1984) ("appointment of counsel [for impoverished petitioner] becomes mandatory when an evidentiary hearing is required"); *supra* § 12.3.

[15] *See also* FED. R. CIV. P. 6(b) ("When by these rules or by a notice given thereunder *or by order of court* an act is required or allowed to be done at or within a specified time, the court for cause shown may at any time in its discretion" extend the time within which the act is to occur, including "upon motion made after the expiration of the specified period ... where the failure to act was the result of excusable neglect ..." (emphasis added)); Rule 11 of the Rules Governing § 2254 Cases (Civil Rules applicable in habeas corpus proceeding to extent those rules are consistent with Habeas Rules and statute); Pioneer Invest. Serv. Co. v. Brunswick Assoc. Ltd. Partnership, 507 U.S. 380, 391-92 (1993) ("in applying Rule 6(b), the courts of appeals have generally recognized that 'excusable neglect' may extend to inadvertent delays"; "'excusable neglect' under Rule 6(b) is a somewhat 'elastic concept' and is not limited to omissions caused by circumstances beyond the control of the movant." (quoting 4A CHARLES A. WRIGHT & ARTHUR MILLER, FEDERAL PRACTICE AND PROCEDURE § 1165, at 479 (2d ed. 1987)) (footnotes omitted)). For discussion of the severe limitations on continuances that are imposed by recently adopted legislation in so-called capital "opt-in" habeas corpus cases, see *infra* note 21.

[16] *Cf.* U.S. CONST., amend. VI (right to speedy trial); Speedy Trial Act, 18 U.S.C. §§ 3161-74 (1994); United States v. Samples, 897 F.2d 193, 195 (5th Cir. 1990) (*per curiam*) (no statutory or constitutional right to disposition of section 2255 motion within specific time; "28 U.S.C. § 1657 requires that courts expedite such actions [but] requirement is relative, not specific").

time is allowed."[17] It is clear however, that the precise purpose of this procedural change was to assure that *counsel* has "the time required to prepare adequately for an evidentiary hearing" and not to absolve federal courts of their duty to review the constitutionality of a prisoner's incarceration in an expeditious manner.[18] Taken together, therefore, the mandatory language of Rule 8(c)'s prompt-hearing requirement, the longstanding preference for promptly remedying unlawful incarceration,[19] and the partial analogy to the constitutional right to a speedy criminal trial[20] afford incarcerated petitioners a basis for seeking to expedite habeas corpus proceedings lest their right to prompt release from unlawful custody be mooted by unnecessary delay.[21]

---

[17] 28 U.S.C. § 2243 (1994). *See* Advisory Committee Note to Rule 8(c) of the Rules Governing § 2254 Cases (Habeas Rule 8(c) was added to provide "more flexibility" than section 2243 allowed). *See also* 28 U.S.C. § 2072 (1994) (Habeas Rules supersede conflicting statutes).

[18] Advisory Committee Note to Rule 8 of the Rules Governing § 2254 Cases.

[19] *See, e.g.,* Granberry v. Greer, 481 U.S. 129, 135 (1987) (policy in favor of "avoid[ing] unnecessary delay in granting [habeas corpus] relief that is plainly warranted"); Wingo v. Wedding, 418 U.S. 461, 468 (1974) ("Under our constitutional framework, the 'great constitutional privilege' of habeas corpus ... has historically provided 'a *prompt* and efficacious remedy for whatever society deems to be intolerable restraints.'" (quoting Ex parte Bollman, 8 U.S. (4 Cranch) 75, 95 (1807) and Fay v. Noia, 372 U.S. 391, 401 (1963)) (emphasis added)); Johnson v. Rogers, 917 F.2d 1283, 1284-85 (10th Cir. 1990) (discussed *infra* note 21). *See also infra* § 23.4a n.22 and accompanying text (petitioners excused from exhausting inordinately delayed state remedies); *supra* § 2.4b n.31 (increased importance of speedy resolution following advent and codification of exhaustion doctrine). *See also* 28 U.S.C.A. § 2266(b)(1)((C)(i) (acknowledging "best interests of ... the [habeas corpus] applicant in a speedy disposition of the application").

[20] One goal of the constitutional speedy-trial provision applicable to criminal trials is to limit the state's coercive power to hold citizens in custody or otherwise to unsettle their lives in advance of a full and fair determination that unlawful behavior by the citizens warrants such treatment. *See generally* Advisory Committee Note to FED. R. CRIM. P. 50; 2 ANTHONY G. AMSTERDAM, TRIAL MANUAL FOR THE DEFENSE OF CRIMINAL CASES § 306 (5th ed. 1989); WAYNE R. LaFAVE & JEROLD H. ISRAEL, CRIMINAL PROCEDURE § 18.1 (2d ed. 1992). Because habeas corpus helps assure that the determination of a prisoner's guilt was "full and fair," *see supra* § 20.3, delays in processing petitions that are not justified by a need for adequate investigation or preparation interfere with the policy underlying the constitutional guarantee of a speedy trial.

[21] *See* O'Connor v. United States, 133 F.3d 548 (7th Cir. 1998) ("Congress expressed in the AEDPA a strong preference for swift and conclusive resolution of collateral attacks. A petition should be granted at once if it is clearly meritorious; keeping a person in prison just because an existing yet unsuccessful challenge is still in the works would be a perversion of justice. A petition should be denied at once if the issues it raises clearly have been forfeited or lack merit under established law. Only the more difficult petitions, whose evaluation requires an evidentiary hearing or a substantial investment of judicial time, should be deferred."); *Johnson v. Rogers, supra,* 917 F.2d at 1284-85 (granting writ of mandamus that directed district court to rule on habeas corpus petitioner's motion for summary judgment, which had been pending for 14 months; explaining that delays of this length do not automatically warrant mandamus and that relief might be inappropriate if petitioner or preparation of transcript caused delay, but if delays of this length due to court backlogs "were routinely permitted, the function of the Great Writ would be eviscerated"); Prantil

c. *Subpoenas.* The Advisory Committee Note to Habeas Rule 8 recognizes that subpoenas are available to compel the appearance and testimony of wit-

---

v. California, 843 F.2d 314, 319 (9th Cir.) (*per curiam*), *cert. denied*, 488 U.S. 861 (1988) (although petitioner did not raise claim in district court that district judge violated due process by delaying seven months before dismissing habeas corpus petition, court of appeals considered claim because it questioned federal judicial system's integrity); Aziz v. Leferve, 830 F.2d 184, 187 (11th Cir. 1987) (when state fails to respond to petition in timely fashion, court should decide merits without further delay). *See also* Spencer v. Kemna, 118 S. Ct. 978, 988 (1998) ("We are confident that, as a general matter, district courts will prevent dilatory tactics by the litigants and will not unduly delay their own rulings; and that, where appropriate, corrective mandamus will issue from the court of appeals."). *But cf. id.* (delays caused by state attorney general's office and district court, even if they caused or contributed to mootness of case by delaying habeas corpus proceeding until petitioner was released from custody, did not provide basis for Court to overlook or remedy mootness problem); Hale v. Lockhart, 903 F.2d 545, 547-48 & n.2 (8th Cir. 1990) (district court's three-year delay in ruling on petition provides no basis for relief from underlying state conviction; in any event, three years does not constitute unreasonable delay, under circumstances, because district court's thorough treatment of petition exemplified careful review that habeas corpus warrants); United States v. Samples, 897 F.2d 193, 195 (5th Cir. 1990) (*per curiam*) (discussed *supra* note 16). In rare instances involving lengthy delays and egregious constitutional violations, appellate courts should enforce Rule 8(c)'s speedy-trial policy by means of mandamus under the All Writs Act, 28 U.S.C. § 1651 (1994). *See also supra* § 16.1b n.18 and accompanying text & *infra* § 22.1 n.47 (both discussing sanctions short of dismissal, such as withdrawal of defenses, that are available if state delays responding to habeas corpus petition); *supra* § 13.2b & *infra* Chapter 24 (discussing sanctions available if petitioner delays filing or prosecuting habeas corpus petition).

A provision of the Antiterrorism and Effective Death Penalty Act of 1996, Pub. L. 104-132, 110 Stat. 1214 (1996), 28 U.S.C.A. § 2266 (West Supp. 1998), requires that district judges adjudicating habeas corpus petitions in capital cases that (1) are governed by the Act, *see supra* § 3.4, and (2) qualify for "opt-in" treatment as defined in the Act, *see supra* §§ 3.2, 3.3, must "give[] priority" to the case, 28 U.S.C.A. § 2266(a) (West Supp. 1998), "shall render a final determination and enter a final judgment on any application for a writ of habeas corpus ... not later than 180 days after the date on which the application is filed," *id.* § 2266(b)(1)(A), and "shall afford the parties at least 120 days in which to complete all actions, including the preparation of all pleadings and briefs, and if necessary, a hearing, prior to the submission of the case for decision," *id.* § 2266(b)(1)(B). "A district court may delay for not more than one additional 30-day period beyond the [180-day] period ... the rendering of a determination of an application for a writ of habeas corpus if the court issues a written order making a finding, and stating the reasons for the finding, that the ends of justice that would be served by allowing the delay outweigh the best interests of the public and the applicant in a speedy disposition of the application." *Id.* § 2266(b)(1)(C)(i). *See also id.* §§ 2266(b)(1)(C)(ii) (specifying "factors, among others, that a court shall consider in determining whether a delay in the disposition of an application is warranted"); *id.* § 2266(c) (time limits on determination of habeas corpus appeals to circuit court). *But cf. id.* § 2266(b)(4)(A) ("failure of a court to meet or comply with a time limitation under this section shall not be a ground for granting relief from a judgment of conviction or sentence," although apparently such failure may be ground for overturning district court decision in appropriate circumstances). For discussion of the onerous and often unfair burdens these provisions place on capital habeas corpus petitioners in "opt-in" cases, see *supra* §§ 3.3c nn.40-54 and accompanying text, 5.1b nn.109-23 and accompanying text, 11.1 nn.20-28 and accompanying text.

nesses and that the statutory provisions and local rules that permit the payment of witness fees and expenses apply to habeas corpus cases.[22] Subpoena procedures generally are governed by section 1825 of the Judicial Code,[23] Rule 45 of the Federal Rules of Civil Procedure,[24] the local rules of the individual district courts, and the practices of local United States Marshal's offices. Because habeas corpus proceedings often take place in the district of incarceration rather than the district of conviction,[25] and because many of the witnesses are likely to reside in the latter district, habeas corpus hearings frequently require time-consuming interdistrict filing and service of subpoenas.[26] The courts should consider the time necessary for filing and serving subpoenas, and the difficulties such procedures often present to indigent, incarcerated, and *pro se* litigants, in setting hearing dates, ruling on continuance requests, and determining the responsibility that the clerk's and marshal's office should bear in preparing and serving subpoenas.[27]

Unlike the rules governing federal criminal proceedings, which permit nationwide service of subpoenas,[28] the Civil Rules, which apply to habeas corpus

---

[22] Advisory Committee Note to Rule 8 of the Rules Governing § 2254 Cases (Rule 8 relies upon "local practice" with regard to obtaining and processing subpoenas and upon 28 U.S.C. § 1825 (1994) (as explained by the Comptroller General's Feb. 28, 1974 opinion) with regard to payment of witness fees). Section 1825 of the Judicial Code authorizes payment of witness fees for parties previously granted *in forma pauperis* status. See Dorthy v. Bailey, 431 F. Supp. 247, 248 (M.D. Fla. 1977) ("The 1965 amendment to [28 U.S.C.] § 1825 provides that in all habeas corpus proceedings and postjudgment proceedings under 28 U.S.C. § 2255, where the petitioner has been granted leave to proceed in forma pauperis, the United States Marshal shall pay the petitioner's witness fees if the district judge so certifies."); Xanthull v. Beto, 296 F. Supp. 129, 130 (S.D. Tex. 1969) ("financial assistance [*i.e.,* witness fees] sought by petitioner was authorized in 1965 by an amendment to 28 U.S.C. § 1825"); *supra* § 12.1.

[23] 28 U.S.C. § 1825 (1994) (discussed *supra* note 22).

[24] FED. R. CIV. P. 45.

[25] *See supra* § 10.2 (personal jurisdiction, venue, convenient forum).

[26] Typically, subpoenas are filed with the United States Marshal in the district in which the proceeding is taking place and referred for service to the United States Marshal's office in the district in which the witness resides.

[27] *See generally* Puett v. Blandford, 912 F.2d 270, 275 (9th Cir. 1990) (*Bivens* action) ("incarcerated pro se plaintiff is entitled to rely on the U.S. Marshal for service of the summons and complaint, and, having provided the necessary information to help effectuate service, plaintiff should not be penalized by having his or her action dismissed for failure to effect service where the U.S. Marshal or the court clerk has failed to perform the duties required of each of them under 28 U.S.C. § 1915(c) and Rule 4 of the Federal Rules of Civil Procedure."); Fowler v. Jones, 899 F.2d 1088, 1094-95 (11th Cir. 1990) (in section 1983 case, 11th Circuit agrees with 2d, 5th, and 9th Circuit holdings that incarcerated *in forma pauperis* litigants are entitled to rely on court officers to effect proper service of subpoenas and other documents and should not be penalized for failure to effect service when such failure is not prisoner's fault).

[28] FED. R. CRIM. P. 17(e)(1).

proceedings in this instance, limit the subpoena power to the district in which the habeas corpus petition is filed plus areas located within 100 miles of the courthouse in which the proceeding is to be heard.[29] Should this limitation prevent any party from compelling the important testimony of a recalcitrant witness or prevent an indigent petitioner from securing the presence of willing witnesses because their costs are not reimbursable absent a subpoena, the options are: (1) to seek leave to transfer the case to some other appropriate and more convenient judicial district or division within the judicial district; (2) to seek leave to conduct a deposition of the witness in her home district, with court reimbursement of expenses in the case of an indigent prisoner; or (3) to secure and present the witness's testimony in some other form (by affidavit, audio- or videotaping, letter, or the like) and then to seek leave to expand the record to include that evidence.[30]

To secure the testimony of an incarcerated witness, the appropriate procedure is to apply to the court for a writ of habeas corpus *ad testificandum* directing the officials of the incarcerating institution to produce the witness at a specified place and time.[31] Unlike subpoenas, which usually are self-executing and place on the witness the burden of complying or moving to quash, the writ of habeas corpus *ad testificandum* requires judicial action in order to become effective and places on the party seeking the writ the burden of establishing (typically by

---

[29] FED. R. CIV. P. 45(e)(1) (applicable via Rule 11 of the Rules Governing § 2254 Cases). *See* Chessman v. Teets, 239 F.2d 205, 211 (9th Cir. 1956), *rev'd on other grounds,* 354 U.S. 156 (1957) (applying Civil Rule 45 in habeas corpus case); ROBERT POPPER, POST-CONVICTION REMEDIES IN A NUTSHELL 90 (1978) (advocating application in habeas corpus cases of nationwide service rule).

[30] *See supra* §§ 10.2d, 19.4, 19.5. For discussion of the constitutionality of denying necessary procedures that are beyond the means of an indigent petitioner, *see supra* §§ 7.1b, 7.2.

[31] 28 U.S.C. § 2241(c)(5) (1994) (authorizing writ of habeas corpus *ad testificandum* when "necessary to bring [a prisoner] into court to testify"). *See supra* § 10.2 (personal jurisdiction and venue over *ad testificandum* and other habeas corpus actions); *infra* § 21.3 (petitioner's right to attend, hence to testify at, evidentiary proceedings in her case without writ of habeas corpus *ad testificandum*). *See also* Demarest v. Manspeaker, 498 U.S. 184, 191 (1991) ("28 U.S.C. § 1821 requires payment of witness fees to a convicted state prisoner who testifies at a federal trial pursuant to a writ of habeas corpus *ad testificandum,*" notwithstanding that "[t]here may be good reasons not to compensate prisoners for testifying at federal trials"); Miller v. Hambrick, 905 F.2d 259, 262 (9th Cir. 1990) (writ of habeas corpus *ad testificandum* "authorizes a trip not a change of custodians," hence prisoner moved to another prison pursuant to writ remains in custody, for purposes of filing her own habeas corpus action, in prison in which she was confined prior to execution of writ (citing cases)); Sales v. Marshall, 873 F.2d 115, 118-19 (6th Cir. 1989) (section 1983 case) (absent exceptional circumstances, 28 U.S.C. §§ 2241 and 2243, not All Writs Act, 28 U.S.C. § 1651, authorize courts to issue writs of habeas corpus *ad testificandum;* court may not tax losing prisoner-litigant for custodian's costs incurred in transporting prisoner to court pursuant to writ of habeas corpus *ad testificandum* (citing Pennsylvania Bur. of Corrections v. United States Marshals, 474 U.S. 34, 43 (1985))).

means of a brief memorandum and appropriate affidavits) that the testimony sought is necessary to the party's case.[32] "'When the issue [to be resolved at the hearing] is one of [an incarcerated witness's] credibility, resolution on the basis of affidavits'" or other alternatives to in-court testimony "can rarely be conclusive."[33]

d. *Prehearing conference.* Habeas Rule 8 "does not make specific provision for a prehearing conference" of the sort permitted in other civil cases under Civil Rule 16, but "the omission is not intended to cast doubt on the value of such a conference" as a means of "'limit[ing] the questions to be resolved, identify[ing] areas of agreement and dispute, and explor[ing] evidentiary problems that may be expected to arise.'"[34] Habeas Rule 8 thus permits and its commentary favors, but neither the rule nor the commentary requires, the use of prehearing conferences, and the rules of most federal districts exempt such proceedings entirely from Civil Rule 16 or at least from the scheduling conference requirements of Civil Rule 16(b). A greater responsibility accordingly falls to the parties to

---

[32] *See, e.g.,* United States v. Smith, 924 F.2d 889, 896-97 (9th Cir. 1991) (direct review case) ("unsupported and conclusory claims" are insufficient to warrant issuance of writ of habeas corpus *ad testificandum;* standards for granting such writs discussed; district court's decision reviewed for abuse of discretion); United States v. Butler, 885 F.2d 195, 199-200 (4th Cir. 1989) (trial court did not abuse discretion in denying petitioner writ of habeas corpus *ad testificandum* to obtain testimony of incarcerated witness because petitioner did not request writ until two weeks after hearing began); Cookish v. Cunningham, 787 F.2d 1, 4-5 (1st Cir. 1986) (writ of habeas corpus *ad testificandum* denied because testimony of incarcerated witness was duplicative and petitioner was allowed to present proffered testimony through affidavits); Malinauskas v. United States, 505 F.2d 649, 655-56 (5th Cir. 1974); Bistram v. United States, 248 F.2d 343, 347 (8th Cir. 1957).

[33] Advisory Committee Note to Rule 7 of the Rules Governing § 2254 Cases (quoting Raines v. United States, 423 F.2d 526, 529-30 (4th Cir. 1970)). *See, e.g.,* United States v. Cruz-Jiminez, 977 F.2d 95, 99, 103-05 (3d Cir. 1992) (reversing denial of writ of habeas corpus *ad testificandum* and remanding "with instructions to determine what [the witness's] testimony is likely to be by holding a hearing or otherwise arranging to secure the substance of his testimony under oath"). *See also* Wingo v. Wedding, 418 U.S. 461, 474 (1974) (quoting Holiday v. Johnson, 313 U.S. 342, 352 (1941)); *supra* §§ 19.4h n.41, 19.5 n.13 and accompanying text, 20.3e n.147 and accompanying text.

[34] Advisory Committee Note to Rule 8 of the Rules Governing § 2254 Cases (discussing FED. R. CIV. P. 16 and quoting AMERICAN BAR ASSOCIATION, STANDARDS RELATING TO POST-CONVICTION REMEDIES § 4-6, commentary, at 74-75 (Approved Draft 1968)). *See* Rule 11 of the Rules Governing § 2254 Cases ("appropriate" Civil Rules apply in habeas corpus cases if they are not inconsistent with Habeas Rules). *See also* Ainsworth v. Vasquez, 759 F. Supp. 1467, 1474-76 & n.11 (E.D. Cal. 1991) (*en banc*) (although declining to conclude that FED. R. CIV. P. 16 "directly applies to habeas corpus cases," court relies on Civil Rule 16, by analogy, as well as All Writs Act, 28 U.S.C. § 1651 (1994), as authority for magistrate judges to conduct routine hearings upon filing of capital habeas corpus cases to ascertain that petitioner is adequately represented and has raised all available claims in petition).

advise the court of circumstances warranting exercise of its discretion to hold pretrial conferences in order, for example, to facilitate the reasonable scheduling or orderly and expeditious conduct of the hearing, to narrow the issues to be addressed or enable the court to understand those issues better, or to permit the resolution of motions *in limine*.[35]

§ 21.2. Rules of evidence.[1]

With the notable exception of the previously discussed procedure for expanding the record, which allows habeas corpus courts in some circumstances to receive affidavits and other hearsay documentary evidence in lieu of in-court testimony of the sort generally required in federal trials,[2] the habeas corpus hearing should proceed much like federal bench trials and other evidentiary proceedings tried to a judge alone.[3] Counsel unfamiliar with the Federal Rules of Civil Procedure and the Federal Rules of Evidence should review all pertinent rules before the hearing.

Counsel should be aware that the Federal Rules of Evidence generally give the court discretion to admit a wider range of evidence than many States' pre-Rules evidentiary statutes, codes, and practices.[4] The Federal Evidence Rules take a relatively inclusive view, for example, of relevance,[5] potentially admissible expert and other opinion testimony,[6] matters subject to judicial notice,[7] and admissible out-of-court statements (some of which are excluded from the definition of hearsay; others of which fall within either liberalized specific

---

[35] *See infra* § 21.2 n.11 and accompanying text (motions *in limine*).

§ 21.2. [1] *See generally* LARRY W. YACKLE, POSTCONVICTION REMEDIES §§ 124, 137 (1981 & Supp. 1998); JACK B. WEINSTEIN & MARGARET A. BERGER, WEINSTEIN'S EVIDENCE MANUAL (1993); Note, *Jailhouse Informants and the Need for Judicial Use Immunity in Habeas Corpus Proceedings*, 78 CALIF. L. REV. 755 (1990).

[2] *See supra* § 19.5.

[3] The same is true of evidentiary proceedings assigned to a United States Magistrate Judge. *See* 28 U.S.C. §§ 636(a), 636(b)(1), 636(d), 636(e) (1994); *supra* Chapter 18. *See generally* Rule 11 of the Rules Governing § 2254 Cases ("appropriate" Federal Rules of Civil Procedure apply in habeas corpus proceedings if they are not inconsistent with the Habeas Rules).

[4] *See generally* Richard S. Walinski & Howard Abramoff, *The Proposed Ohio Rules of Evidence — The Case Against*, 28 CASE W. RES. L. REV. 344 (1978) (critical review of ways in which Federal Rules of Evidence give courts more discretion to admit evidence than comparable state rules).

[5] FED. R. EVID. 401-11.

[6] FED. R. EVID. 701-06. *See generally* Daubert v. Merrell Dow Pharmaceuticals, Inc., 509 U.S. 579 (1993); Samuel R. Gross, *Expert Evidence*, 1991 WIS. L. REV. 1113.

[7] FED. R. EVID. 201.

exceptions or broad catch-all exceptions to the hearsay rule).[8] As a result, skillful counsel often can find some more-than-colorable means of arguing that the Evidence Rules require the court, or at least give the court the discretion, to admit any evidence that is relevant to the issues at hand.[9] The discretion generally afforded judges in making evidentiary rulings is widened in habeas corpus cases both by the nonjury nature of the proceeding and by Rule 7 of the Rules Governing § 2254 Cases, which allows introduction into the record of materials that would be excludable on hearsay and other evidentiary grounds in most federal trial contexts.[10]

When an evidentiary ruling will have an important impact on the conduct of a habeas corpus hearing, and a ruling in advance of the hearing will assist a party in preparing for or planning its presentation, the party should raise the issue in a written motion *in limine* seeking a pretrial ruling. The Advisory Committee Note to Habeas Rule 8 seems to contemplate this procedure.[11]

---

[8] FED. R. EVID. 801-05. For a helpful evidence manual organized around the Federal Rules of Evidence, see WEINSTEIN & BERGER, *supra* note 1. For a similarly organized but more comprehensive treatise, see JACK B. WEINSTEIN & MARGARET M. BERGER, WEINSTEIN'S EVIDENCE (1993). *See also* Dutton v. Brown, 788 F.2d 669, 670 (10th Cir. 1986) (example of wide-ranging types of evidence received in habeas corpus proceedings); Advisory Committee Notes to the Federal Rules of Evidence; JOHN W. STRONG, ET AL., MCCORMICK ON EVIDENCE (4th ed. 1992). The Evidence Rules do not codify a set of privilege rules, relying instead on "the principles of the common law as they may be interpreted ... in light of reason and experience." FED. R. EVID. 501.

[9] *See* Walinski & Abramoff, *supra* note 4.

[10] *See supra* § 19.5. *See also* Amadeo v. Zant, 486 U.S. 214, 227 n.5 (1988) ("[t]o be sure, the testimony" relied upon by district court "was hearsay, and ... was prompted by a leading question on redirect examination. Nonetheless, [district court's finding credited because] no objection ... was made at the hearing and the State does not argue that the District Court's admission of the statements was 'plain error' under Fed. Rule Evid. 103(d)"). Although a petitioner cannot be compelled to provide testimony at a habeas corpus hearing that might incriminate her in subsequent criminal proceedings, some courts have ruled that the petitioner may not refuse on 5th Amendment grounds to testify on nonincriminating matters such as the reason why she failed to raise a claim in an earlier petition, *e.g.,* Neuschafer v. Whitley, 860 F.2d 1470, 1473-74 (9th Cir. 1988), *cert. denied,* 493 U.S. 906 (1989), and that a petitioner's invocation of the 5th Amendment privilege as a basis for refusing to testify on such matters permits the habeas corpus trier of fact to draw appropriate inferences against the petitioner, *e.g.,* Machado v. Commanding Officer, 860 F.2d 542, 544-45 (2d Cir. 1988). *Cf.* State v. Taylor, 393 S.E.2d 801 (N.C. 1990) (by raising ineffective assistance claim, postconviction petitioner waives attorney-client and work-product privileges with regard to portions of defense counsel's records found, upon *in camera* inspection, to be specifically relevant to ineffective assistance claim).

[11] Advisory Committee Note to Habeas Rule 8 (prehearing conference is appropriate way "'to explore evidentiary problems that may be expected to arise'" at hearing (quoting AMERICAN BAR ASSOCIATION, STANDARDS RELATING TO POST-CONVICTION REMEDIES § 4.6, commentary, at 74-75 (Approved Draft 1968))).

Federal judicial decisions and recent revisions to the habeas corpus statute have relied with increasing frequency on the requirement that petitioners prove not only that the procedures the state used to convict or sentence them violated federal law but also that (and how) any such errors prejudiced the petitioner.[12] The modern preoccupation with prejudice has increased the importance of a set of evidentiary issues surrounding the testimony by the decisionmaker at the state criminal trial or appeal on the question whether the constitutional error affected the outcome of the proceeding. The emerging rule seems to be that, except in rare circumstances, the testimony of trial *judges* who presided at criminal trials (and assumedly those who adjudicated the petitioners' state appeals and post-conviction proceedings) is not admissible on the question whether constitutional errors affected either their own deliberations or those of jurors.[13] As for *jurors*,

---

[12] Expanding prejudice requirements may affect (1) the definition of the federal right (consider, *e.g.*, the materiality component of a claim of prosecutorial suppression of evidence, *see* United States v. Bagley, 473 U.S. 667, 677 (1985), and the prejudice component of a claim of ineffective assistance of counsel, *see* Strickland v. Washington, 466 U.S. 668, 694 (1984) (discussed *supra* § 21.1a n.8 and accompanying text)); (2) the circumstances in which a proven violation of a constitutional right nonetheless is not a basis for relief because the violation is deemed to be "harmless" — a category the Supreme Court broadened considerably in habeas corpus litigation, *compare* Brecht v. Abrahamson, 507 U.S. 619 (1993) (adopting rule of Kotteakos v. United States, 328 U.S. 750 (1946) (discussed *supra* §§ 2.4b nn.32-35 and accompanying text, 2.4d nn.309-10 & 313-15 and accompanying text; *infra* Chapter 32)) *with* Chapman v. California, 386 U.S. 18 (1967) (narrower harmless error standard that applies in direct review proceedings and perhaps in some habeas corpus contexts (discussed *infra* § 32.1 & n.18)) *with infra* § 32.3 (certain kinds of constitutional violations to which harmless error analysis does not apply and that always are reversible); or (3) the petitioner's ability to establish an exception to a procedural defense available to the state (for example, the cause and *prejudice* exception to the procedural default rule, *see infra* §§ 26.3c, 28.3c; *see also supra* § 2.5). For general discussion of various new prejudice requirements in the Antiterrorism and Effective Death Penalty Act of 1996, Pub. L. 104-132, 110 Stat. 1214 (1996), with cross-references to more detailed discussions, *see supra* §§ 3.2, 3.3c. Prejudice definitions range from (1) presumed or automatic prejudice, *see infra* § 32.3; to requirements of (2) a violation that cannot be shown by the state (a) to be harmless beyond a reasonable doubt, *see Chapman v. California, supra; infra* § 32.1, or (b) to be harmless under the lower standard of *Kotteakos v. United States, supra,* which examines whether an error "'had substantial and injurious effect or influence in determining the jury's verdict,'" *Brecht v. Abrahamson, supra* at 623 (quoting *Kotteakos, supra*); *infra* § 32.4; to requirements of (3) a violation that the petitioner proves (a) had a substantial effect on the outcome, *cf. infra* § 26.3c, or (b) probably changed the outcome, *see United States v. Bagley, supra,* or (c) probably or certainly caused an innocent individual to be convicted, *see, e.g., supra* § 2.5; *infra* §§ 26.4, 28.3c.

[13] *See, e.g.,* Fayerweather v. Ritch, 195 U.S. 276, 306-07 (1904) ("no [judge's] testimony should be received [explaining a judgment] except of open and tangible facts — matters which are susceptible of evidence on both sides"; "judgment is a solemn record" that "should not lightly be disturbed, and ought never to be overthrown or limited by the oral testimony of a judge or juror of what he had in mind at the time of the decision"); Perkins v. LeCureux, 58 F.3d 214, 220-21 (6th Cir.), *cert. denied*, 516 U.S. 992 (1995) (district court erred in considering "statement made by the sentencing judge ten years after the fact, regarding his thought processes at the time of sen-

in keeping with the policies behind Evidence Rule 606(b), the courts generally permit their testimony only on the question whether they were subject to prejudicial external influences (*e.g.,* bribery, intimidation, lobbying by court officers, unauthorized visits to the scene of the crime, and the like), and have refused to allow jurors to testify about (1) either the fact or effect of intrinsic influences on the jury (*e.g.,* the effect of proceedings in court, and the fact and effect of, for instance, racially charged comments made or actions taken during deliberations); (2) their mental processes based upon information properly brought before them; and even (3) the effect on their mental processes — as opposed to the existence — of extrinsic information improperly brought before the jury.[14]

---

tencing"); Washington v. Strickland, 693 F.2d 1243, 1263 (5th Cir. 1982) (*en banc*), *rev'd on other grounds,* 466 U.S. 668 (1984); Proffitt v. Wainwright, 685 F.2d 1227, 1255 (11th Cir. 1982), *cert. denied,* 464 U.S. 1002 (1983). *See also* FED. R. EVID. 606(b) (discussed *infra* note 14) (drawing similar distinction between juror testimony on matters intrinsic to their deliberations, which is inadmissible, and extrinsic to their deliberations, which is admissible); King v. Champion, 55 F.3d 522, 524-25 (10th Cir. 1995) (analogizing to rule barring trial testimony by trial judges, court of appeals upholds district court's denial of petitioner's request to call appeals court judge to explain appellate delay by "testify[ing] about that court's decisional process"); *supra* § 20.3e nn.114, 138 (collecting cases requiring federal hearing or withholding presumption of correctness of state factfindings, *inter alia,* because findings were based on state judges' recollections or surmises about events occurring in court rather than on independent evidence about what occurred). *Cf.* Hamilton v. Vasquez, 17 F.3d 1149, 1155 (9th Cir.), *cert. denied,* 512 U.S. 1220 (1994) (district court did not err in permitting state to call trial judge as witness on historical facts underlying petitioner's claim of unconstitutional shackling at trial); Weidner v. Thieret, 932 F.2d 626, 632-33 (7th Cir. 1991), *cert. denied,* 502 U.S. 1036 (1992) (court's prior decision in same case directing district judge to request affidavit from state trial judge explaining "'cryptic and ambiguous ruling'" on voluntariness of petitioner's confession was not so "clearly erroneous" as to warrant deviation from "law of the case doctrine" binding court to follow prior decision; given that some courts have extended 28 U.S.C. § 2245 (which permits trial judges to certify facts to habeas corpus court) to include affidavit "inquiries into the mental process of state trial judges," and that facts of "this case" did not "implicate" usual concerns about accuracy, time lapse, finality of state judgments, and state-federal tension, court rules that request for trial court's affidavit was permissible; acknowledging rule of other circuits limiting trial judges' affidavits to questions of historical fact and forbidding them as to trial judges' mental processes and agreeing that latter affidavits are dangerous because "essentially irrebuttable," court cautions that "recourse to the testimony of a state trial judge concerning the mental processes that underlay his ruling should be had only in the unfortunate circumstance when the reasons supporting the ruling are wholly unavailable from the record," that "affidavits [discussing judges' mental processes] must be carefully evaluated to determine if they are consistent with the relevant record evidence," and that "[w]here state trial judges fail to adequately develop the relevant facts so that not even implicit findings ... can be gleaned from the record, the habeas procedure is better served by a de novo hearing than by allowing state judges to cast their minds back to the state trial").

[14] *See* FED. R. EVID. 606(b) (jurors in particular case may "testify" in that case only "on the question whether extraneous prejudicial testimony was improperly brought to the jury's attention or whether any outside influence was improperly brought to bear upon any juror"); United States v.

Olano, 507 U.S. 725, 738, 740 (1993) (although Court characterizes error — alternate jurors' presence during regular jurors' deliberations — as an "outside intrusion[] upon the jury," no hearing on prejudice was requested, and Court accordingly reserves question "whether testimony on [prejudice] ... by the alternate jurors or the regular jurors through affidavits or at a *Remmer*-like hearing would violate Rule 606(b) of the Federal Rules of Evidence, or whether the Courts of Appeals have authority to remand for *Remmer*-like hearings on plain error review" (citing Remmer v. United States, 347 U.S. 227, 229-30 (1954) (remanding for evidentiary hearing on question whether FBI investigation of juror during trial prejudiced defendant))); Tanner v. United States, 483 U.S. 107 (1987) (under Fed. R. Evid. 606(b), federal courts only may inquire into external influences on jury deliberations; alleged alcohol and drug ingestion by jurors is internal influence not subject to inquiry); Bonner v. Holt, 26 F.3d 1081, 1082 (11th Cir. 1994), *cert. denied*, 514 U.S. 1010 (1995) (jurors testified at evidentiary hearing that they heard prosecutor's statement to judge that petitioner was habitual offender); Bibbins v. Dalsheim, 21 F.3d 13, 16-18 (2d Cir.), *cert. denied*, 513 U.S. 901 (1994) (pursuant to Fed. R. Evid. 606(b), court of appeals considers posttrial affidavits of jurors only to extent they demonstrate jury's receipt of extra-record information, excluding portions of affidavits that describe effects of information on individual jurors' thinking and group deliberations); Williams v. Collins, 16 F.3d 626, 636 (5th Cir. 1994) (district court did not abuse discretion by excluding testimony from state trial jurors "as to whether their deliberations would have been different if they had been presented with the mitigating evidence that was allegedly available, but not presented at trial"); Capps v. Sullivan, 921 F.2d 260, 263 (10th Cir. 1990) (in assessing whether trial counsel's unreasonable failure to seek entrapment instruction prejudiced petitioner, district court erred in allowing two of petitioner's trial jurors to testify that they would have voted differently had trial judge given entrapment instruction; Evidence Rule 606(b) prohibits habeas corpus testimony about jurors' mental processes; considering evidence apart from jurors' testimony *de novo,* court affirms lower court's finding of prejudice); Silagy v. Peters, 905 F.2d 986, 1008-09 (7th Cir. 1990), *cert. denied,* 498 U.S. 1110 (1991) (habeas corpus petitioner may not rely on trial jurors' after-the-fact statements evidencing mistaken understanding of capital sentencing procedures "to impeach the jury's sentencing determination" (citing Shillcutt v. Gagnon, 827 F.2d 1155 (7th Cir. 1987))); Stockton v. Virginia, 852 F.2d 740, 743-45 (4th Cir. 1988), *cert. denied,* 489 U.S. 1071 (1989) (if petitioner proves improper outsider contact with jury, rebuttable presumption of bias arises, and state must demonstrate absence of prejudicial effect using circumstantial evidence alone; juror testimony on prejudicial effect is inadmissible); Dickson v. Sullivan, 849 F.2d 403, 405-08 (9th Cir. 1988) (question whether extrinsic evidence contributed to verdict is mixed question of law and fact, which is reviewable *de novo*); Brogdon v. Butler, 838 F.2d 776, 778 n.1 (5th Cir. 1988) (jury conduct cannot be challenged on basis of juror's affidavit if such evidence is not permitted under state law); United States ex rel. Buckhana v. Lane, 787 F.2d 230, 238 (7th Cir. 1986) (jurors' testimony properly admitted on question whether improper remarks to jury by sheriff affected jurors' deliberations); Adamson v. Ricketts, 758 F.2d 441, 447 (9th Cir. 1985), *rev'd on other grounds,* 483 U.S. 1 (1987) (in habeas corpus action, "jury's deliberative process may not be inquired into"); Owen v. Duckworth, 727 F.2d 643, 646 (7th Cir. 1984) (court must determine "nature, content, and extent of the extra-judicial contact" with jurors, then determine on its own "whether the contact likely affected the juror's impartiality"); United States ex rel. Tobe v. Bensinger, 492 F.2d 232, 237 (7th Cir. 1974) ("In an attempt to make a showing of prejudice based on the affidavits of jury members, actual evidence of the nature of outside influence exerted on the jury during deliberations will be considered, but evidence relating to the effect of such influences on the mental processes of jury members is inadmissible"). *Cf.* J.E.B. v. Alabama, 511 U.S. 127, 153 (1994) (Kennedy, J., concurring in judgment) ("The wise limitation on the authority of courts to inquire into the reasons underlying a jury's verdict does not

§ 21.3. The petitioner's presence.[1]

"Unless the application for the writ and the return present only issues of law the person to whom the writ is directed shall be required to produce at the hearing the body of the person detained."[2] Production of the prisoner at evidentiary or other factually oriented proceedings is "[a] basic consideration in *habeas corpus* practice" and "the crux of the statutory scheme established by Congress; indeed, it is inherent in the very term *'habeas corpus.'*"[3] Accordingly, "if an issue of fact is presented, the practice [has] been to issue the writ, have the prisoner produced, and hold a hearing at which evidence is received."[4] Of course, the filing of a habeas corpus petition does not guarantee a prisoner an excursion to the courthouse.[5] If the petition is summarily dismissed, if the court is able to resolve the petition on the papers (whether or not summarily), or if the court reserves in-court proceedings at which counsel are present to "only issues of law," the petitioner need not be present.[6]

It is the rare on-the-record proceeding in a habeas corpus case that assuredly will consider only matters of law. This is so because of (1) the informality with which the Habeas Rules now permit evidence to be taken in habeas corpus cases,[7] (2) the longstanding treatment of the record of prior state court proceedings as evidence,[8] (3) the importance of evidentiary proffers as bases for

---

mean that a jury ought to disregard the court's instructions. A juror who allows racial or gender bias to influence assessment of the case breaches the compact and renounces his or her oath."). *But see* Pilchak v. Camper, 935 F.2d 145, 148 (8th Cir. 1991) (relying in part on jury foreman's testimony about jury's reasons for conviction and sentence to find that counsel's ineffective assistance prejudiced petitioner). *See generally* State ex rel. Butler v. Howard, 1994 WL 4300 (Mo. Ct. App. Jan. 11, 1994) (extensive treatment of question of postconviction interviews of jurors; postconviction interviews of actual or prospective jurors may be necessary in some cases; trial judge may decide to conduct such interviews in court to assure reliability).

§ 21.3.   [1] *See generally* RONALD P. SOKOL, FEDERAL HABEAS CORPUS 127-29 (2d ed. 1969); LARRY W. YACKLE, POSTCONVICTION REMEDIES § 136 (1981 & Supp. 1998); *Developments in the Law — Federal Habeas Corpus,* 83 HARV. L. REV. 1038, 1189 (1970).

[2] 28 U.S.C. § 2243 (1994). Section 2243, which governs state-prisoner proceedings, differs substantially from the statute governing federal-prisoner proceedings. *See* 28 U.S.C.A. § 2255 (West 1994 & Supp. 1998); *infra* § 41.6d.

[3] Johnson v. Eisentrager, 339 U.S. 763, 778 (1950).

[4] Walker v. Johnston, 312 U.S. 275, 285 (1941). *Accord* Ahrens v. Clark, 335 U.S. 188, 190-91 (1948).

[5] *See Walker v. Johnston, supra,* 312 U.S. at 284. *See also* Sanders v. United States, 373 U.S. 1, 20 (1963).

[6] 28 U.S.C. § 2243. *See* Wingo v. Wedding, 418 U.S. 461, 473 n.20 (1974); *supra* §§ 15.2, 16.2, 17.3, 20.1.

[7] *See, e.g.,* Rule 7 of the Rules Governing § 2254 Cases; *supra* §§ 19.5, 21.2 n.10 and accompanying text.

[8] *See supra* § 19.2.

determining the propriety of dismissal on the one hand or the granting of discovery, a hearing, or other procedures on the other hand,[9] and (4) the possibility that disposition of the state's defenses will require resolution of evidentiary matters (including ones — waiver, for example — on which the petitioner may be the best or only source of the critical facts).[10] Thus, to avoid the delays and false starts engendered by commencing a proceeding in the absence of the petitioner and only thereafter finding that she has a right to attend (a right that is virtually unwaivable, except in person), the better practice is to produce the prisoner at all but routine proceedings, including ones intended to discuss important procedural and substantive motions.[11]

Even if counsel could waive the petitioner's right to presence at evidentiary hearings, that course generally would be inadvisable. Given the significance of such proceedings to the client and the client's possible familiarity with and ability to advise counsel concerning factual issues, the prisoner's presence is important. For this same reason, counsel generally should insist that the petitioner be present whenever there is any likelihood that an in-court proceeding will result in the taking or discussion of evidence. The prisoner's presence also may be useful in reminding the judge that the case does not involve the application of technical rules to disembodied facts, but instead will determine whether a human being will continue to be incarcerated or, in some cases, will live or die. Counsel accordingly should take steps to ensure not only that the client is present, but also to make clear that, to counsel at least, the client is a human being who deserves to be treated with fairness and dignity.[12] Counsel should insist that the client sit at counsel table throughout the proceeding and that any physical restraints be reasonable and not impede counsel's ability to consult freely and regularly with the client.

The statute places the burden on the state to produce the prisoner and imposes no requirement that the petitioner ask to be present at the hearing. Counsel should remind the representatives of the state of their obligation under section 2243 and, that failing, should raise the matter with the court whenever (1) the state may not acknowledge the evidentiary character of the proceeding, (2) there is reason to suspect a lack of, or breakdown in, communications between the state's attorney and prison officials, or (3) time is of the essence.

Although the burden of producing the client is the state's, counsel for the petitioner should take care that the client is transported, housed, and fed under safe and humane conditions. Not infrequently, the authorities transporting a

---

[9] *See, e.g., supra* §§ 11.7d, 15.2b, 16.1c, 16.2e, 19.4, 20.1.

[10] *See generally supra* § 20.1b.

[11] *See* SOKOL, *supra* note 1, at 128. *See generally* United States v. Gordon, 829 F.2d 119 (D.C. Cir. 1987) (accused's constitutional right to presence at trial cannot be waived by counsel).

[12] *See generally supra* § 4.1.

prisoner from state prison to a federal courthouse and back make no arrangements for feeding the client until she is returned to the incarcerating facility, with the result that the client may be deprived of food for as long as 36 hours. Conditions in local jails in which prisoners may be held overnight can be both uncomfortable and physically dangerous for the client. Counsel should inquire into such circumstances and bring shortcomings to the attention of the United States Marshal and, if necessary, the court.